Psychology

Science, Behavior, and Life

Psychology

Science, Behavior, and Life

Third Edition

R. H. Ettinger
Eastern Oregon State College

Robert L. Crooks
Portland Community College

Jean Stein

Harcourt Brace College Publishers

Fort Worth   Philadelphia   San Diego   New York   Orlando   Austin   San Antonio
Toronto   Montreal   London   Sydney   Tokyo

For my family

BOB CROOKS

In memory of my father, Norman H. Ishler

JEAN STEIN

Publisher	Ted Buchholz
Senior Acquisitions Editor	Eve Howard
Developmental Editor	John Haley
Senior Project Editor	Katherine Vardy Lincoln
Project Editor	Nancy Lombardi
Senior Production Manager	Ken Dunaway
Senior Art Director	Diana Jean Parks
Photo Editor	Sue C. Howard
Permissions Editor	Sheila Shutter
Text Design	Brian Salisbury
Copyediting	Charles Naylor
Proofreading	Ivy Doak
Page Makeup	Artspan Graphics
Composition	Progressive Typographers
Cover photo	Olivia Parker © 1987

ISBN 0-15-500998-2

Library of Congress Catalog Number 92-75742

Address for Editorial Correspondence
Harcourt Brace College Publishers, 301 Commerce Street, Suite 3700, Fort Worth, TX 76102

Address for Orders
Harcourt Brace & Company, 6277 Sea Harbor Drive, Orlando, FL 32887
1-800-782-4479, or 1-800-433-0001 (in Florida)

Photo and Figure Credits appear on pages C-1–C-2 and constitute a continuation of the copyright page.

Printed in the United States of America

3 4 5 6 7 8 9 0 2 1   0 3 2   9 8 7 6 5 4 3 2 1

We live in an age in which science and technology have revolutionized the way we view the world, yet many students fail to realize that scientific methods can also be applied to the study of human behavior. While many students have no difficulty mastering numerous facts and theories, their behavior appears to be little changed by this experience. That is, there is little evidence that a first course in psychology has changed the way they interpret behavioral events. Perhaps this is because it is so difficult to remain objective about behavior—and perhaps it is due, in part, to the ways in which texts present and support principles of psychology.

If psychology is a science, then it should be presented as a science. Throughout this text we have attempted to involve students actively in the discovery process by inviting them to question assumptions and to participate in the scientific process of supporting or refuting ideas. Although the text is rich with content, it endeavors to bring students, and their own behavior, closer to the scientific process of observation and control.

The text was originally conceived with the aim of presenting psychology as an active scientific discipline. We offered students a unique array of features not found in the numerous other texts available to them. It is our belief that earlier editions of this text were successful in these attempts. The enthusiastic response by both students and instructors to the first two editions served as encouragement for this revised edition. We hope that you find the book as stimulating to read as we did to write.

Throughout this new edition we have attempted to keep the features that were successful in previous editions, while at the same time incorporating new research in areas where significant developments have occurred. As a result, we have a text that is both up-to-date and continues to present the diverse discipline of psychology in an engaging and challenging manner.

The major goals for this revision were essentially the same as those of the previous editions: First, we wanted to demonstrate to students how the science of psychology has evolved and continues to develop. Second, we wanted to make the content of the text both accurate and academically challenging to students of varying levels of academic ability while at the same time keeping it interesting and relevant to their lives. Third, we wanted to create a textbook that engaged students in the scientific process by asking stimulating questions and demonstrating how scientific research proceeds to answer them. And, finally, we wanted to introduce students to several contemporary and influential psychologists in order to show them how researchers think about important issues as well as to illustrate how controversy still surrounds much of this important discipline. We believe that it is important to show students how we know what we know by discussing facts of psychology in terms of the scientific context in which they are demonstrated. More importantly we discuss the methods of research throughout the text as we display hundreds of classic and contemporary experiments in detail. There are more than 2500 references to published research, much of it published since 1990.

Special Features

What makes this text different from others that are also well grounded in current research is the way in which research is presented. We attempt to demonstrate how research evolves from simple questions about behavior. We then show how research answers these questions and how theories of psychology develop from research. In many cases we discuss how both the questions and the research are influenced by individual personalities and the political climate of the time. Psychology, like any other science, is a dynamic, social process within which our knowledge continually changes.

CRITICAL QUESTIONS   Throughout each chapter there are numerous questions that students are asked to consider and attempt to answer. Immediately following many of these questions are descriptions of research designed to answer them. Students are thus led through the research process so that they become accustomed to how questions lead to research and research provides answers. In many cases research does not lead to clear answers and we discuss how to evaluate both sides of an issue critically.

HEALTH PSYCHOLOGY AND LIFE SEGMENTS   At the end of selected chapters we discuss important topics related to health psychology. In these segments we attempt to show how current psychological research can lead to ways to improve our health and well-being. In addition, these segments demonstrate to students how basic research, often with animals, can lead to important human applications.

PERSPECTIVES ON RESEARCH   Dispersed throughout the text are several discussions with psychologists who are currently engaged in research. In each case we have selected two psychologists to discuss the same topic from different perspectives. Students will quickly see that there are few black-and-white positions in psychology. Rather, there is currently considerable disagreement among researchers about important issues. These discussions also serve to familiarize students with several important psychologists by allowing students to "hear" these discussions as they occurred.

Supplements

FOR THE STUDENT   *Study Guide*   Each chapter consists of learning objectives, a chapter summary, matching exercises, true/false statements, multiple choice questions, and review diagrams and charts. Additionally, the study guide contains application exercises which challenge students to apply chapter content to "real life" situations and/or problems, and critical thinking exercises that encourage students to analyze and evaluate psychological research and concepts.

ExamTutor This computerized study guide allows the student to review a chapter by answering questions grouped around learning objectives or by selecting randomly from whole chapters. The student can create reviews covering one or more chapters.

Psychlearn This computer simulation software allows students to review important concepts and participate in and manipulate psychological experiments. Topics include: Reaction Time Laboratory, Schedules of Reinforcement, Short-Term Memory, and the Self-Consciousness Scale.

Instructor's Resource Kit Prepared by Josephine Wilson of Wittenberg University, this contains learning objectives coordinated with the student study guide, lecture suggestions, discussions, activities, Whole Psychology Catalog handouts, 122 overhead transparencies, and audiovisual resources, including a coordination guide for the Dynamic Concepts in Psychology videodisc. Each chapter also features suggestions for fostering critical thinking about research and bringing biological and physiological material into the presentation of psychology. Also included is a built-in Video Instructor's Manual for users of the Harcourt Brace Teaching Modules.

Test Bank Prepared by Lisa Valentino of Seminole Community College, this contains approximately 150 multiple-choice questions for each chapter of the text. Each question is linked to a learning objective and a page in the text on which the answer can be found and is also identified as one of three cognitive types: definition, knowledge and application. Each chapter contains 10–15 test items that appear in the student Study Guide as well.

Computerized Test Bank Available in IBM, Macintosh, and Apple II formats, Harcourt Brace's new testing software, **ExaMaster**™, allows you to create tests using fewer keystrokes, with all steps defined in easy-to-follow screen prompts. ExaMaster offers the following three easy-to-use options for test creation.

- **EasyTest** lets you create a test from a single screen, in just a few easy steps. You can select questions from the data base or let EasyTest randomly select the questions for you, given your parameters.

- **FullTest** lets you use the whole range of options available:

  select questions as you preview them on the screen,

  edit existing questions or add your own questions,

  add or edit graphics in the MS-DOS version,

  link related questions, instructions and graphics,

  have FullTest randomly select questions from a wider range of criteria,

  create your own criteria on two open keys,

  block specific questions from random selection, and

  print up to 99 different versions of the same test and answer sheet.

- **RequesTest** is there for you when you do not have access to a computer. When that happens, just call 1 (800) 447-9457. We will compile the questions according to your criteria and either mail or fax the test master to you within 48 hours!

Included with the IBM and Macintosh versions of ExaMaster is **ExamRecord,** our gradebook program that allows you to record, curve, graph and print out grades. ExamRecord takes raw scores and converts them into grades by criteria you set. You can set the curve you want, and see the distribution of the grades in a bar graph or a plotted graph.

If questions arise, our Software Support Hotline is available Monday through Friday, 9 AM–4 PM Central Time at 1 (800) 447-9457.

Dynamic Concepts in Psychology   Developed by John Mitterer of Brock University exclusively for Harcourt Brace, this innovative video disc program covers every major concept in introductory psychology. Numerous computer animated sequences, film and video footage, still images, and demonstrations vividly illustrate each topic, bringing psychology to life in the classroom. Easy-to-use features and modular format allow instructors to customize the program to their course. *Lecture Builder,* a Level III software package available for IBM® or Macintosh®, allows instructors to pre-program classroom presentations and to import material from other video discs.

A detailed Instructor's Manual, fully keyed to concepts and to *Psychology: Science, Behavior, and Life*, Third Edition, offers complete instructions for using the video disc and Lecture Builder software.

The Harcourt Brace Video Library   Five different video sources are available as supplemental teaching aids: The Discovering Psychology Telecourse, the Harcourt Brace Teaching Video Modules from the Discovering Psychology Telecourse, PBS' "The Brain" Series teaching modules, CBS' "60 Minutes" segments, and PBS' "Nova" series.

Discovering Psychology Telecourse Faculty Guide   This supplement was created for use with the Telecourse and provides the link between the text and the Telecourse Units. Included are page references to the text and synopses of the Telecourse Units, along with readings, activities, and test questions related to each Unit.

ACKNOWLEDGMENTS

As we complete this third edition, we again acknowledge our debt to many people who participated by critically reading our revised chapters. Without their thoughtful suggestions this revision would not have been possible. We particularly acknowledge:

Catalina Arata, University of South Alabama

Carolyn Biediger, Southwest Texas Jr. College

Victor Broderick, Ferris State University

Daryl Butler, Ball State University

Karen Cianci, Franklin & Marshall College

Richard Deyo, Winona State University

Dan Fawaz, Dekalb Community College

Herman Feldman, Indiana University, NW

Gary Greenberg, Wichita State University

Tim Hubbard, Eastern Oregon State College

Dorothy Johnson, Calhoun Community College

Wesley Jordan, St. Mary's College of MD

Melvin King, SUNY, Cortland

Thomas Lombardo, University of Mississippi

Jacqueline Ludel, Guilford College

Al Maisto, University of North Carolina, Charlotte

T. James Matthews, New York University

John Mavromatis, St. John Fisher College

James Mitchell, Kansas State University

Thomas Rowe, University of Wisconsin– Stevens Point

Tim Smock, University of Colorado

James Todd, Eastern Michigan University

Richard Troelstrup, Tennessee Technical University

Barbara Turpin, SW Missouri State University

Lisa Valentino, Seminole Community College

William Wallace, University of Nevada–Las Vegas

Paul Wellman, Texas A & M University

We also acknowledge the participants in our Research Perspectives discussions. Their willingness to share their insights and opinions about important issues greatly enhances this edition. We are greatly indebted to the following:

A. Charles Catania, University of Maryland– Baltimore County

Beatrix Gardner, University of Nevada–Reno

Howard Gardner, Harvard University

R. Allen Gardner, University of Nevada–Reno

Irving Gottesman, University of Virginia

Stephen M. Kosslyn, Harvard University

Kurt Salzinger, Hofstra University

Robert Sternberg, Yale University

Herbert Terrace, Columbia University

Finally, we express our sincere thanks to the people at Harcourt Brace College Publishers for their competent efforts in making this revision possible. We give special thanks to John Haley who patiently supervised and guided every step of this revision.

176   *Part 2*   **BIOLOGICAL FOUNDATIONS, PERCEPTION AND SLEEP**

neurotransmitter acetylcholine is believed to be directly involved in dreaming and REM sleep. Injections of acetylcholine into the pons of animals can cause REM sleep leading to the remark that "Acetylcholine is the stuff of which dreams are made" (Palca, 1989).

THE FUNCTION OF SLEEP

IS SLEEP NECESSARY?   In a widely reported personal experiment in 1959, New York disc jockey Peter Tripp staged a wakeathon, remaining awake for 200 hours. It was not easy. Halfway through his wakeathon, he began to hallucinate. His ability to think and reason deteriorated dramatically, and by the end of his ordeal he was unable to distinguish between fact and fantasy. He also became increasingly paranoid. At one point, Tripp was convinced that a physician who had arrived to examine him was planning to haul him off to jail (Luce, 1965).

SLEEP DEPRIVATION STUDIES   Peter Tripp's experience, though fascinating, is of limited scientific value because it took place in an uncontrolled environment. Several subsequent studies have been carefully controlled, and they provide more reliable findings. In one experiment, for instance, six volunteers were deprived of sleep for 205 consecutive hours (Kales et al., 1970). By the end of the third day, subjects were hallucinating and experiencing delusions (false or distorted beliefs). They also developed hand tremors, double vision, and reduced pain thresholds. Their reflexes were largely unimpaired, however, and physiological functions such as heart rate, respiration, blood pressure, and body temperature showed little change from normal throughout the course of the experiment. After the experiment was over, no long-term effects were evident. Subjects slept a few days, then awoke feeling fine.

In another experiment conducted by famed sleep researcher William Dement (1972), a 17-year-old subject stayed awake for 268 consecutive hours, after which he needed only 14 hours of sleep to recover to a normal state. In contrast to Peter Tripp, this young man remained lucid and coherent throughout his vigil.

Findings such as these caused some researchers to question the importance of sleeping in our lives. A few even speculated that people might learn to get by without any sleep, particularly if scientists could isolate the factor that makes us sleepy and find a way to counter it. With this idea in mind, a team of researchers at the University of Chicago Sleep Research Laboratory devised an ingenious device to study the effects of total sleep deprivation in rats.

Rats were studied in pairs: One was deprived of sleep, and the other acted as a control. Both rats were placed on a plastic disk located above a water pan, as shown in Figure 5.7. If the disk rotated, the rats had to walk to avoid falling into the water. The rats were connected to an EEG that monitored their brain waves. Whenever the sleep-deprived rat fell asleep, the EEG registered the changes and opened a circuit, causing the disk to rotate. Both rats would have to walk to avoid falling into the water. The control rat could sleep when his counterpart was awake, but the sleep-deprived rat was jarred awake at each lapse of consciousness. The sleep-deprived rats lasted as long as 33 days, but they all eventually died. In contrast, all the control animals survived, apparently no worse for the experience (Rechtschaffen et al., 1983). A more recent experiment by researchers in the same laboratory, using the same research design and apparatus, reported similar results. All 10 of the totally sleep-deprived rats in this study died within 11 to 32 days, whereas all paired controls survived (Everson et al., 1989).

In both of these experiments, the University of Chicago scientists were unable to determine the precise cause of death. A variety of sleep deprivation effects were observed prior to death, including a progressively scrawny appearance, skin ulcers, increased food intake, weight loss, an increase in energy expenditure, a

This scene from the film They Shoot Horses, Don't They? *depicts a dance marathon popular in the 1930s and 1940s, where contestants who danced the longest won prizes. Prolonged periods of sleep deprivation can produce hallucinations and delusions.*

EXPLANATIONS OF RESEARCH

Research presented in a unique manner tells the stories of psychological researchers: the questions they asked, the studies they conducted to answer the questions, and the theories they developed as a result of those studies.

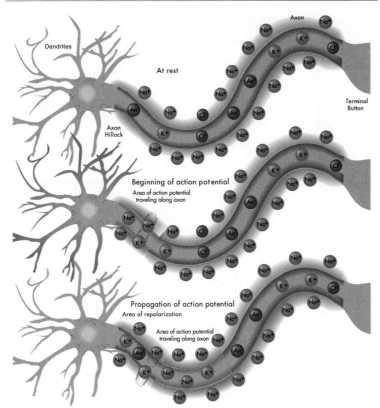

transmitter substances from the terminal buttons, thus making them 'talk' to the receiving cells (Carlson, 1981, p. 47).

THE ALL-OR-NONE LAW Unlike the graded potential, the strength of an action potential does not vary according to the degree of stimulation. Once a nerve impulse is triggered within an axon, it is transmitted the entire length of the axon with no loss of intensity. Partial action potentials or nerve impulses do not occur; thus an axon is said to conduct without decrement. Because of this, the nerve impulse in the axon is said to follow the **all-or-none law:** If the sum of the graded potentials reaches a threshold, there will be an action potential; if the threshold is not reached, however, no action potential will occur.

FIGURE 3.4

A. Neuron at rest. Resting membrane potential is maintained by distribution of charged ions on either side of cell membrane. B. Initiation of action potential. Action potential is initiated at axon hillock by movement of sodium (Na+) ions to inside of cell. C. Movement of action potential. Action potential moves (propagates) along axon as Na+ ions enter cell. After an action potential occurs, membrane potential is restored by movement of both potassium (K+) and sodium (Na+) ions from the cell.

ANATOMICAL ART

Original art enhances student understanding of biologically-oriented material.

Stephen M. Kosslyn is professor of psychology at Harvard University. He received his graduate education at Stanford University, where he was involved in research using ideas and concepts from artificial intelligence. His current work involves using techniques such as PET and MRI to map brain activity during various tasks including mental imagery and higher-level perception. He hopes to gather information that can help psychologists understand how the mind arises from activity of the brain. He is also working to apply results of this work to understanding migraines, obsessive-compulsive disorder, and the mechanisms that underlie placebo effects.

PERSPECTIVE #2

Dr. Stephen M. Kosslyn

One of the central ideas in the work of B. F. Skinner has all kinds of implications for this question. Skinner wrote a paper in 1945 in which he was concerned about the philosophy of science, how people come to know things, and he asked how we could learn the words for our private feelings, our private emotions. How could a group of people agree on the vocabulary for that sort of thing? Skinner suggested some ways in which that could happen. Suppose you wanted to teach a word for a certain kind of pain, like a sharp pain or a dull pain. This is supposed to be a private sensation and psychologists are interested in the nature of these private things like sensations. Skinner proposed that the only way in which a verbal community could come up with a consistent language for private things was for the verbal community to base it on public behavior. Therefore, we only can learn about the ways of talking about private things through the public terms for them. So, for example, if you're hurting, that's a private thing. Nobody else can feel your pain. How can we teach people when it's appropriate to say "I'm hurt"? We do it by learning words for public things like parts of the body. When a child falls down, scrapes an elbow, or the child is crying, these are public kinds of things and the parents can teach the children the public words. So all of our language begins with what's public. We learn words like "I'm angry, I'm happy, I'm afraid" in large part on the basis of seeing how people act and seeing what kind of situations they're in. In my courses I occasionally arrange an experiment in the classroom. For example, I unexpectedly come in the classroom with

---

PERSPECTIVE #1

Dr. A. Charles Catania

A. Charles
University of
ior analyst w
and function
his Ph.D. in
University, w
low, he ran B
fellow and fo
more than 10
analysis of b
verbal behavi

PERSPECTIVE #1

Q: Dr. Cata
and behavioral
A: In cogni
things that the
gists are study
sponds in som
theoretical eve
those kinds of
quences of beh
chology is that
that was worth
else. The idea is that we're not interested in behavior because behavior is important, but because it's going to tell us something about some kind of inner stuff. And it's hard to imagine what we would say or do about that inner stuff if we didn't also include in it the way in which it makes contact with our activities in the world.

An interview forum in which two psychologists offer different perspectives on a single topic. Shows students how researchers think about important issues and illustrates how controversy still surrounds much of this discipline.

CLASSICAL CONDITIONING OF THE IMMUNE SYSTEM

A few years ago, researchers Robert Ader and Nathan Cohen (1982) observed a curious effect as they were studying classically conditioned taste aversion. In their experiment, rats were given drinks of a saccharin-flavored water (the CS) followed immediately by injections of a drug that made them nauseous (the UCS). As you might predict, the animals immediately aquired a taste aversion that caused them to avoid or reduce their consumption of the sweet solution. The rats were then exposed to several extinction trials in which they were presented with the sweet solution but no toxic drug. (Extinction is a process designed to reduce the strength of the association between the CS and UCS through repeated presentations of the CS alone without the UCS.)

During this stage of the study, something unexpected happened. For no apparent reason, some of the rats died. Ader and Cohen considered a variety of possibilities to explain what had happened. One of their primary clues was that the drug they used to induce nausea, cyclophosphamide, is also known to suppress the body's immune system.

Ader and Cohen reasoned that perhaps the saccharin water had become a conditioned signal that suppressed the rats' immune systems in the same way as the drug with which it had been paired. If this were the case, the repeated exposures to the sweetened water alone during the extinction trials may have suppressed their immune systems so much that they fell victim to disease-bearing microorganisms in the laboratory.

To test this possibility, they conditioned other rats, using the original design with one modification. Before the extinction trials in which rats received only the CS of sweet water, they were injected with red blood cells from sheep foreign bodies that would normally trigger the rats' immune systems to produce high levels of defensive antibodies. The researchers' hypothesis was supported: The conditioned animals produced significantly fewer antibodies than control animals for whom the sweet water was not a CS.

Ader and Cohen also tested the immune-system responses of mice who had been classically conditioned to respond to the sweet water. They found that if these conditioned mice received only half the usual dosage of cyclophosphamide, together with exposure to the CS, their immune systems were suppressed as completely as if they had been given a full dosage of the toxic drug.

Other researchers have confirmed and extended Ader and Cohen's findings. For instance, Grochowicz et al., (1991) demonstrated that conditioned immunosuppression effectively prolonged the survival of transplanted heart tissue in rats. Immunosuppression in tissue transplant procedures is neccessary to prevent the immune system from attacking the newly transplanted tissue.

HEALTH IMPLICATIONS

Certainly, these findings extend our knowledge of how the mind and body interact to reduce or increase our vulnerability to disease. But beyond this, they may lead to a practical medical application in the future. Consider, for instance, that a major problem associated with many drugs used to combat disease is that they often produce serious side effects. For example, although cyclophosphamide is toxic enough to have been selected as the nausea-inducing UCS in Ader and Cohen's experiment, it has a legitimate and very valuable medical use as treatment for lupus, an immune-system disorder in which the body turns against itself. If classical conditioning could be used to condition the body of a lupus victim into responding to a significantly lowered dosage of the drug, a diseased person might be able to benefit from cyclophosphamide without having to experience its debilitating side effects. Experiments are currently being conducted with lupus patients to determine whether conditioned immunosuppression can effectively augment drug therapy.

The same kinds of benefits might also obtained with drugs used to treat cancer and AIDS. Hopefully, in the years to come these conditioning principles can be applied to alleviate suffering and improve the treatment of many victims of disease.

HEALTH PSYCHOLOGY AND LIFE DISCUSSIONS

Shows the practicality and relevance of the science of psychology, frequently providing the tips, techniques, and suggestions for applying psychology to deal with concerns in students' own lives.

CONTENTS IN BRIEF

Part 1
Nature, Origins, and Methods of Psychology
Chapter 1 The Origins of Psychology 2
Chapter 2 The Methods of Psychology` 32

Part 2
Biological Foundations, Perception, and Sleep
Chapter 3 The Biology of Behavior 60
Chapter 4 Sensation and Perception 110
Chapter 5 Consciousness: Sleep, Dreaming, and Hypnosis....................166

Part 3
Learning, Memory, Cognition, Motivation and Emotion
Chapter 6 Learning and Behavior...196
Chapter 7 Memory 232
Chapter 8 Motivation 272
Chapter 9 Emotion and Stress..314
Chapter 10 Cognition: Thinking and Language 348

Part 4
Developmental Processes and Individual Differences
Chapter 11 Development 1: Conception through Childhood....................402
Chapter 12 Development 2: Adolescence to the End of Life 452
Chapter 13 Intelligence...484
Chapter 14 Personality: Theories and Assessment................................522

Part 5
The Nature and Treatment of Behavioral Disorders
Chapter 15 Behavioral Disorders 562
Chapter 16 Treatment of Behavioral Disorders....................................620

Part 6
Social Psychology
Chapter 17 Social Psychology 660

TABLE OF CONTENTS

Part 1
Nature, Origins, and Methods of Psychology 1

1 *The Origins of Psychology* 2
THE STUDY OF PSYCHOLOGY 3
DEFINITION OF PSYCHOLOGY 4
  Psychology as a Science 4
  The Study of Behavior 5
  Studying Humans and Other Animals 6
    Learning about Psychology from Nonhuman Animals 6
PSYCHOLOGY'S HISTORY 8
  Structuralism 9
    William Wundt (1832–1920) 9
    Problems with Structuralism 9
  Functionalism 10
    William James (1842–1910) 10
  Psychoanalysis 10
    Sigmund Freud (1856–1939) 10
  Behaviorism 11
    John Watson (1878–1958) 11
  Gestalt Psychology 12
    Wolfgang Köhler (1887–1967) 12
  Humanistic Psychology 13
    Abraham Maslow (1908–1970) 13
CONTEMPORARY PSYCHOLOGY 14
  Fields of Specialization in Psychology 14
    Cognitive Psychology 14
    Developmental Psychology 14
    Social Psychology 14
    Personality Psychology 15
    Experimental Psychology 15
    Biological Psychology 15
    Clinical and Counseling Psychology 16
    Educational and School Psychology 16
    Industrial/Organizational Psychology 17
    Engineering Psychology 17
    Health Psychology 17
    Forensic Psychology 18
    Artificial Intelligence and Connectionism 18
    The American Psychological Association 19
THE GOALS OF PSYCHOLOGY 20

RESEARCH PERSPECTIVES: PSYCHOLOGICAL EXPLANATION
  DR. A. CHARLES CATANIA AND DR. STEPHEN M. KOSSLYN *24*

2   *The Methods of Psychology* *32*
  THE SCIENTIFIC METHOD AND BEHAVIOR...*33*
    The Purpose of Psychological Research *34*
      Basic Research: Research to Test a Hypothesis.............................*34*
      Applied Research: Research to Solve a Problem *34*
      Replication Research: Research to Confirm Previous Findings..............*35*
  RESEARCH METHODS..*36*
    Non-Experimental Research Methods...*38*
      Research on the Effects of Alcohol on Sexual Behavior....................*38*
      Case Studies...*38*
        Limitations of the Case Study...*38*
      Surveys and Questionnaires...*39*
      How Samples Are Selected for Surveys.....................................*40*
        Representative Samples *40*
        Random Samples *40*
      Limits of the Survey Method *41*
        Survey Methods: Alcohol and Sexual Behavior *42*
      The Observational Method *42*
        Limitations of the Observational Method...............................*43*
      Correlational Method *44*
        Interpreting a Negative Correlation Between Variables *44*
        Limitations of Correlational Studies..................................*45*
    Experimental Research Methods...*45*
      The Experimental Method *45*
        Independent and Dependent Variables *46*
      Experimental and Control Groups *46*
        Examples of the Experimental Method...................................*46*
        How Samples are Selected for Experiments *47*
        Limitations of the Experimental Method *47*
    Ethics in Psychological Experiments *48*
      The Milgram Obedience to Authority Study.................................*48*
      The Stanford University Prisoner Study *48*
      Replication of the Stanford Prisoner Study *49*
      Stroke Simulation in Monkeys...*49*
    Ethical Guidelines for Research *49*
  STATISTICAL CONCEPTS FOR RESEARCH *50*
    Descriptive Statistics..*51*
      Using Graphs to Describe Data *51*
        Normal Distributions..*51*
        Measures of Central Tendency..*52*
        Measures of Variability...*52*
        Applying Standard Deviation...*53*
    Inferential Statistics *53*
    Evaluating Opinions, Beliefs, and Scientific Evidence *54*

Part 2
Biological Foundations, Perception, and Sleep *58*

3 *The Biology of Behavior* *60*

OVERVIEW OF THE NERVOUS SYSTEM: ORGANIZATION
   AND FUNCTION *62*

NEURONS: BASIC UNITS OF THE NERVOUS SYSTEM *62*

   Neuron Structure *64*

   The Cell Body or Soma *64*

   The Dendrites *64*

   The Axon *65*

   The Terminal Buttons *65*

   Neural Transmission *65*

   Neuron Electrical Activity *65*

   Resting Potentials *66*

   Graded Potentials *66*

   Action Potentials *66*

   The All-or-None Law *67*

   Neurotransmitters and the Synapse *68*

   Steps in Neural Transmission *69*

   Excitatory and Inhibitory Effects *70*

   Neurotransmitter Breakdown and Reuptake *70*

   Identifying Neurotransmitter Substances *70*

   Neurotransmitter Substances *71*

         Acetylcholine *(ACh)* *71*

         Norepinephrine *72*

         Dopamine *72*

         Seratonin *72*

         Gamma-amino-butyric Acid *(GABA)* *72*

         Endorphins *72*

         Glutamate *72*

   Neurotransmitters and Behavior *73*

   Schizophrenia *73*

   Depression *73*

THE PERIPHERAL NERVOUS SYSTEM *73*

   The Somatic Nervous System *74*

   The Autonomic Nervous System *74*

THE CENTRAL NERVOUS SYSTEM *76*

   The Spinal Cord *76*

   The Medulla *78*

   The Pons *78*

   The Cerebellum *78*

   The Reticular Formation *78*

THE LIMBIC SYSTEM..*79*

The Amygdala..*80*

The Hippocampus...*80*

The Septum *80*

The Hypothalamus..*81*

The Thalamus...*81*

THE BASAL GANGLIA..*82*

THE CEREBRAL CORTEX *82*

Localization of Cortical Functioning *84*

The Frontal Lobe *84*

The Parietal Lobe *85*

The Occipital Lobe *86*

The Temporal Lobe *86*

Sex Differences in the Brain *86*

Lateralization of Function *86*

Split-Brain Research *87*

Testing the Effects of Split-Brain Surgery *89*

How the Brain Is Studied *90*

Surgical Lesions *90*

Brain Stimulation *91*

Electrical Recording *91*

Radioactive Labeling *91*

Electroencephalography (EEG) *92*

Computerized Axial Tomography (CAT) *92*

Positron Emission Tomography (PET) *93*

Magnetic Resonance Imaging (MRI) *93*

THE ENDOCRINE SYSTEM *94*

The Pituitary Gland..*94*

The Thyroid Gland *95*

The Adrenal Glands..*96*

The Gonads *97*

DRUGS AND BEHAVIOR...*97*

Depressants: Sedatives, Opiates, and Alcohol.............................*98*

Sedatives...*98*

Opiates *98*

Alcohol..*99*

Stimulants: Caffeine, Nicotine, Amphetamines, and Cocaine............*100*

Caffeine *100*

Nicotine *101*

Amphetamines...*101*

Cocaine *102*

Hallucinogens: LSD, PCP, and Marijuana *103*

LSD *104*

PCP...*105*

Marijuana *105*

HEALTH PSYCHOLOGY AND LIFE: MAGNESIUM TREATMENT AFTER

BRAIN INJURY *106*

4 **Sensation and Perception** 110
PRINCIPLES OF SENSATION AND PERCEPTION 111
Transduction..111
Distinguishing Types of Sensory Impulses...112
What Do We Perceive?...112
Psychophysics 112
Sensory Thresholds..112
Absolute and Difference Thresholds 113
Absolute Thresholds..113
Difference Thresholds..114
Weber's Law and the Just Noticeable Difference 114
Attention..115
Sensory Adaptation 116
Signal Detection Theory 116
Response Criterion and Signal Detection..117
VISION..118
Light: The Stimulus for Vision 119
Properties of Light 120
Structure and Function of the Eye...121
The Retina 122
Rods and Cones 122
Dark and Light Adaptation 123
Neural Processing of Vision 124
Lateral Inhibition 126
Artificial Vision 126
Color Vision 127
Additive and Subtractive Color Mixing...127
Theories of Color Vision 128
The Trichromatic Theory of Color Vision 128
The Opponent-Process Theory of Color Vision.............................129
AUDITION 131
Sound: The Stimulus for Audition...131
Properties of Sound Waves 132
Distinguishing Different Sounds of the Same Pitch 133
Structure and Function of the Ear..134
The Outer Ear 134
The Middle Ear..134
The Inner Ear 134
Auditory Receptors 136
Theories of Audition 137
The Place Theory 137
Frequency Theory 137
Perceiving Pitch in the 1,000 to 4,000 Hz. Range..............................137
Auditory Localization 138
Hearing Loss 138
Sensorineural Hearing Loss 138
Conduction Hearing Loss 139

GUSTATION AND OLFACTION *139*

   Gustation *140*

   Olfaction *141*

     Chemical Communication: Pheromones *142*

THE SKIN SENSES *142*

   Pressure *143*

   Temperature *143*

     Theories of Temperature Sensation *144*

   Pain *144*

     Theories of Pain *144*

       Gate Control Theory of Pain *145*

       Neurotransmitters and Pain *145*

KINESTHESIS AND EQUILIBRIUM *146*

PERCEIVING THE WORLD *147*

   Perceptual Organization *147*

     Figure and Ground *148*

     Perceptual Grouping *148*

     Closure *148*

     Attention and Perception *149*

       Complex Stimuli *150*

       Sudden Change *150*

       Contrast and Novelty *150*

       Stimulus Intensity *150*

       Repetition *150*

       Key Stimuli *150*

   Spatial Perception *150*

     The Perception of Depth *151*

       Binocular Cues *151*

       Monocular Cues *152*

     Gibson's Theory of Direct Perception *153*

     Perceiving Depth: The Visual Cliff Experiment *154*

     Size, Color, and Shape Constancies *155*

       Size Constancy *155*

       Brightness and Color Constancy *156*

       Shape Constancy *156*

   Visual Illusions *157*

     The Ames Illusion *157*

     The Müller-Lyer Illusion *158*

     The Moon Illusion *159*

     The Ponzo Illusion *160*

     The Poggendorff Illusion *160*

   Perceptual Sets *161*

5   ***Consciousness: Sleep, Dreaming, and Hypnosis*** *166*

BIOLOGICAL RHYTHMS *168*

   Circadian Rhythms *168*

THE SCIENCE OF SLEEP AND DREAMING..169

  Stages of Sleep..169

    REM and NREM Sleep...169

    Measuring Stages of Sleep..171

    Characteristics of Waking and Sleeping States..171

      Stage 1..172

      Stage 2..173

      Stage 3..173

      Stage 4..173

  The Sleep Cycle...173

  Changes in Sleep Patterns with Age...174

  Brain Mechanisms of Sleep..174

    Neurotransmitters and Sleep..175

  The Function of Sleep..176

    Is Sleep Necessary?...176

    Sleep Deprivation Studies..176

  Theories of Sleep Function...177

    Sleeping to Conserve Energy...177

    Sleeping to Avoid Predation..178

    Sleeping to Restore Depleted Resources..178

    Sleeping to Clear the Mind..178

    Sleeping to Consolidate Memory..178

    Sleeping to Dream..178

  Dreaming...179

    REM Deprivation Studies..179

    Do Animals Dream?..180

  Theories of Dreaming...180

    Dreaming as the Brain's Explanation for Stimuli...180

    Dreaming as Mental Reprogramming..181

    Dreaming for Problem Resolution..182

    Dreams as Expressions of the Unconscious...182

DISORDERS OF SLEEP...183

  Insomnia...183

  Sleep Apnea..183

  Narcolepsy..184

  Nightmares and Sleep Terrors...184

  Sleepwalking...185

  Sleeptalking...185

    Problems Related to the Sleep–Wake Schedule..186

HYPNOSIS...186

  Phenomena Associated with Hypnosis...187

    Hypnosis and Athletic Ability..187

    Hypnosis and Relief of Physical Ailments...187

    Hypnosis and Pain Relief...188

    Hypnosis and Memory Enhancement in Criminal Investigations....................188

    Hypnosis and Age Regression...188

    Posthypnotic Suggestion...189

Explaining Hypnosis *189*

HEALTH PSYCHOLOGY AND LIFE: SUGGESTED REMEDIES FOR INSOMNIA...................*191*

Part 3
Learning, Memory, Cognition, Motivation and Emotion *194*

6   *Learning and Behavior* *196*
    DEFINING LEARNING...*198*
      How Learning Takes Place *198*
    CLASSICAL CONDITIONING...*199*
      Classical Conditioning of Fear..*199*
      Pavlov's Discovery *200*
        Differentiating Between the UCR and the CR..............................*201*
      Acquisition of Classical Conditioning *202*
      Stimulus Contingency and Conditioning *202*
      CS-UCS Timing and Conditioning *204*
        Conditioned Taste Aversions *204*
          Preparedness and Selective Associations *204*
      Extinction and Spontaneous Recovery *205*
      Stimulus Generalization and Discrimination *205*
      Second-Order Conditioning...*206*
    OPERANT CONDITIONING *207*
      Operant Conditioning in a Skinner Box......................................*208*
        Response Strength or Response Selection? *208*
        Measuring Operant Behavior *208*
        Discriminative Stimuli *209*
      Reinforcement *209*
        Positive and Negative Reinforcement..*210*
        Escape and Avoidance Procedures..*210*
        Primary and Conditioned Reinforcers *211*
        Continuous versus Partial Reinforcement....................................*212*
        Partial Reinforcement Schedules...*212*
          Fixed Ratio Schedule *213*
          Variable Ratio Schedule *213*
          Fixed Interval Schedule...*214*
          Variable Interval Schedule...*214*
        Applying Reinforcement Schedules...*215*
          An Application of Reinforcement Schedules *215*
      Reinforcing the Initial Operant Response *215*
        Verbal Instruction *216*
        Shaping...*216*
        Modeling *216*
        Physical Guidance..*217*
      Punishment and Operant Behavior..*217*

Limitations of Punishment 217

Temporary Suppression Instead of Elimination 217

Emotional Side Effects of Punishment 218

Physical Punishment and Modeling 218

Advantages of Punishment 218

Immediate Application of Punishment 218

Consistent Application of Punishment 219

Intensity of Punishment 219

Conditioned Punishment 219

COMPARING CLASSICAL AND OPERANT CONDITIONING 219

Two-Factor Theory of Avoidance Learning 221

COGNITIVE INFLUENCES ON LEARNING 221

Latent Learning 222

Cognitive Processes in Learning 223

Observational Learning 224

Evaluating the Effect of Inconsistent Modeling 225

BIOLOGICAL BASES OF LEARNING 225

Classical Conditioning of the Aplysia 225

HEALTH PSYCHOLOGY AND LIFE: CLASSICAL CONDITIONING OF
THE IMMUNE SYSTEM 228

7   **Memory** 232

WHAT IS MEMORY? 234

Information Processing and Memory 234

Memory Processes 234

Encoding 234

Storage 235

Retrieval 235

A MODEL OF MEMORY 235

Three Memory Systems 235

Sensory Memory 235

Short-Term Memory 236

Long-Term Memory 236

Sensory Memory 236

Iconic (Visual) Memory 237

Echoic (Auditory) Memory 238

The Modality Effect 239

Short-Term Memory 239

Chunking 240

Coding in Short-Term Memory 240

Acoustic Coding 240

Visual and Semantic Coding 241

Long-Term Memory 242

Types of Long-Term Memory 243

Procedural Memory 243

Declarative Memory 243

Semantic Memory 244

Encoding Long-Term Memory 245

Clustering 245

Method of Loci 245

Narrative Story 245

The Peg-Word System 246

Acrostics 246

Acronyms 246

Retrieval from Long-Term Memory 247

Retrieval Cues 247

Association Networks 247

Testing Long-Term Memory 249

Recall 249

Recognition 249

Relearning 250

MEMORY AS A DYNAMIC PROCESS 251

Constructive Memory 251

Schemas 252

Eyewitness Testimony 253

Context 256

State Dependency 256

Extreme Emotions 256

FORGETTING 257

Decay of the Memory Trace 257

Interference 258

Retroactive Interference 258

Proactive Interference 258

The Serial Position Effect 258

Retrieval Failure 259

Motivated Forgetting 259

Organic Causes of Forgetting 260

Amnesia Caused by Disease 260

Retrograde Amnesia 260

Anterograde Amnesia 260

THE BIOLOGY OF MEMORY 260

Hebb's Theory of Neural Connections 260

Neural Plasticity 261

Distributed Memory 262

Where Are Long-Term Memories Processed? 263

The Case of H.M. 263

The Case of N.A. 263

Korsakoff's Syndrome 264

Electroconvulsive Shock 264

Where Are Short-Term Memories Processed? 265

IMPROVING ACADEMIC MEMORY 266

Reducing the Material to a Manageable Amount 266

Learning the Whole versus Piecemeal Learning *266*

Using Recitation to Check Recall *267*

Overlearning *267*

Making Use of Study Breaks and Rewards *267*

Spacing Study Sessions *268*

Avoiding Interference *268*

Managing Your Time *268*

8 *Motivation* *272*

THE NATURE OF MOTIVATION *273*

Defining Motivation *274*

MOTIVATIONAL EXPLANATIONS OF BEHAVIOR *274*

Instinct Theory *275*

Drive-Reduction Theory *276*

Maslow's Hierarchy of Needs *277*

Cognitive Theories of Motivation *278*

   Cognitive Expectancies *278*

   Achievement Motivation *278*

   Hope of Success versus Fear of Failure *279*

   Fear of Success *280*

   Influencing Achievement Motivation *281*

   Cognitive Dissonance *281*

Biological Bases of Motivation *282*

   Biological Bases of Hunger and Eating *282*

      The Stomach *283*

   The Hypothalamic Control Theory of Hunger *284*

   The Glucostatic Theory of Hunger *285*

      Long-Term Weight Regulation *286*

   The Lipostatic Theory of Hunger *286*

   Other Mechanisms in Long-Term Weight Regulation *287*

Obesity *287*

   Theories of Obesity *289*

      Genetic Causes of Obesity *289*

      Early Childhood Experience *289*

      Metabolic Factors *289*

      Reactions to Emotional Stress *290*

   Dieting to Control Weight *290*

Eating Disorders *291*

   Anorexia Nervosa *291*

   Bulimia *292*

SENSATION-SEEKING MOTIVATION *292*

Optimum Level of Arousal *293*

   The Yerkes-Dodson Law *294*

   Arousal and Emotions *294*

Explaining Variation in Arousal Preferences *295*

   Minimizing Arousal: Sensory Deprivation Experiments *295*

SEXUAL MOTIVATION AND BEHAVIOR *297*

Biological Bases of Sexual Behavior 298
    Hormones and Sexuality 298
        Hormone Levels and Male Sexual Behavior 298
        Hormone Levels and Female Sexual Behavior 299
    Psychosocial Factors in Sexual Behavior 300
    Societal Influences on Sexual Behavior 300
        Mangaia 302
        Inis Beag 302
        The Dani of New Guinea 303
Sexual Orientation: Homosexuality 303
    The Incidence of Homosexuality 303
    Attitudes Toward Homosexuality 304
    Theories of Homosexuality 304
        Psychosocial Theories 305
        Biological Theories of Homosexuality 305
The Effect of AIDS on Sexual Behavior 307

HEALTH PSYCHOLOGY AND LIFE: SOME SUGGESTIONS FOR
OVERCOMING OBESITY 309

9   *Emotion and Stress* 314
THE COMPONENTS OF EMOTION 315
    Cognitive Processes 315
    Affect 315
    Physiological Arousal 316
    Behavioral Responses 316
THE RANGE OF HUMAN EMOTION 316
    Plutchik's Emotion Wheel 316
THEORIES OF EMOTION 317
    Historical Perspectives 317
        The James-Lange Theory 317
        The Cannon-Bard Theory 320
    Contemporary Theories 321
        The Schachter-Singer Theory 321
        Tomkins' Facial Feedback Theory 323
        Solomon and Corbit's Opponent-Process Theory 326
STRESS 328
    The Nature of Stress 328
    Physiological Responses to Stress 329
        Alarm, Resistance, and Exhaustion 330
    Psychological Responses to Stress 332
        Cognitive Responses to Stress 332
        Emotional Responses to Stress 333
        Behavioral Responses to Stress 333
    Stressors 335
        Factors That Contribute to Stress 335
        Lack of Control 335
        Suddenness 335

Ambiguity *335*

Life Changes and Stress *336*

Measuring Stress by Life Change Units *336*

Stress and Disease *338*

Coronary Heart Disease *338*

Hypertension *340*

Cancer *341*

Stress and the Immune System *342*

HEALTH PSYCHOLOGY AND LIFE: MANAGING STRESS *344*

10 *Cognition: Thinking and Language* *348*

THINKING *350*

Components of Thinking *350*

Thinking as Behavior *350*

Mental Images *351*

Concepts *351*

Concept Formation *354*

Association Theory *354*

Hypothesis-Testing Theory *354*

Exemplar Theory *354*

PROBLEM SOLVING *356*

Stages of Problem Solving *356*

Representing the Problem *356*

Generating Possible Solutions *358*

Evaluating the Solution *359*

Strategies for Problem Solving *359*

Trial and Error *359*

Testing Hypotheses *359*

Algorithms *359*

Heuristics *360*

Characteristics of Difficult Problems *361*

Defining Problems *361*

Complex Problems *362*

Cognitive Influences on Problem Solving *362*

Mental Set *362*

Functional Fixedness *363*

Confirmation Bias *364*

REASONING AND DECISION MAKING *365*

Logical Reasoning for Decisions *365*

Syllogisms *366*

Some Common Causes of Reasoning Errors *366*

Faulty Premises *367*

Belief-Bias Effect *367*

Subjective Probability and Reasoning for Decisions *368*

Representativeness Heuristic *368*

Availability Heuristic *369*

Framing *370*

ARTIFICIAL INTELLIGENCE 371

   Expert Systems 372

   General Problem Solvers 372

LANGUAGE 373

   Psycholinguistics 373

     The Structure and Rules of Language 373

       Phonemes 374

       Morphemes 374

       Syntax 374

       Semantics 374

   Theories of Language Acquisition 374

     The Learning Perspective 375

     The Nativistic Perspective 375

     Interactionist Perspective 377

     Newborn Language Competency 377

     Early Vocalizations 377

       Crying 377

       Cooing and Babbling 378

     First Words 378

     Condensed Speech 378

     Expanded Language 379

     Pragmatics of Language 380

   Brain Mechanisms for Language 380

     Broca's Area 380

     Wernicke's Area 380

   Is Language Unique to Humans? 382

THINKING AND LANGUAGE 385

   Does Language Structure Thought? 386

   Does Thought Structure Language? 387

   RESEARCH PERSPECTIVES: LANGUAGE COMPETENCE OF APES

   DR. HERBERT S. TERRACE AND ALLEN AND BEATRIX GARDNER 392

Part 4

Developmental Processes and Individual Differences

......................................400

11 *Development 1: Conception through Childhood*

............402

DEVELOPMENTAL ISSUES 403

   Heredity and Environment 403

     The Nature–Nurture Argument 403

       Nurture Argument 403

       Nature Argument 403

       Interaction Argument 404

   Continuous versus Stage Development 404

   Critical Periods in Development 405

DEVELOPMENTAL RESEARCH *407*

The Cross-Sectional Design *407*

The Longitudinal Design...*407*

The Cross-Sequential Design *408*

THE BEGINNING OF LIFE *408*

Mechanisms of Heredity *410*

Genes and Chromosomes *410*

Genotypes and Phenotypes *410*

Dominance and Recessiveness *410*

Sex-Linked Inheritance..*411*

Problems in Inheritance *412*

Huntington's Disease *412*

Phenylketonuria *414*

Down Syndrome *414*

Genetic Counseling *414*

Genetic Engineering *416*

PRENATAL DEVELOPMENT *417*

Germinal Stage *417*

Embryonic Stage *417*

Fetal Stage *417*

PHYSICAL DEVELOPMENT *418*

Development of the Brain *418*

Effects of Experiences on Brain Development *418*

Physical Growth *420*

Motor Development...*421*

COGNITIVE DEVELOPMENT *423*

Piaget's Theory of Cognitive Development *423*

Schemas *423*

Assimilation and Accommodation *423*

Four Stages of Cognitive Development *424*

Sensorimotor Stage (Birth to About 24 Months)...............................*424*

Preoperational Stage (Ages Two to Seven)..*425*

Concrete Operations Stage (Ages Seven to 12) *426*

Formal Operations Stage (Age 12 and Older) *428*

Evaluation of Piaget's Theory..*428*

Gender Differences in Cognitive Abilities *429*

Verbal Skills *429*

Spatial Abilities *429*

Mathematical Skills...*430*

Trends in Gender Differences *431*

PSYCHOSOCIAL DEVELOPMENT *431*

Attachment *431*

How Attachment Develops *432*

Effects of Attachment Deprivation..*433*

Secure and Insecure Attachments *434*

Father–Child Attachment *436*

Parenting Styles and Social-Emotional Development.....................................*436*

Permissive Parents *436*

Authoritarian Parents...*436*

Authoritative Parents *436*

Erikson's Theory of Psychosocial Development...............................*437*

Stage 1: Trust versus Mistrust..*438*

Stage 2: Autonomy versus Shame and Doubt *438*

Stage 3: Initiative versus Guilt...*438*

Stage 4: Industry versus Inferiority...*438*

Stage 5: Identity versus Role Confusion *438*

Stage 6: Intimacy versus Isolation *438*

Stage 7: Generativity versus Stagnation *439*

Stage 8: Ego Integrity versus Despair *439*

GENDER IDENTITY...*439*

Biological Influences on Gender Identity *439*

Normal Prenatal Differentiation..*439*

Chromosomal Sex..*439*

Gonadal Sex *440*

Hormonal Sex *440*

Sex Differentiation of the Brain *440*

Abnormal Prenatal Differentiation *441*

Fetally Androgenized Females *441*

Androgen Insensitivity Syndrome *442*

DHT-Deficient Males...*442*

Differentiation Errors and Gender Identity: A Critique *443*

Social Learning Influences on Gender Identity................................*444*

The Interaction of Biological and Social Influences on
Gender Identity...*445*

The Socialization of Gender Roles *446*

The Influence of Parents on Gender Roles..*446*

The Influence of Peer Groups..*446*

The Influence of Schools on Gender Roles...*447*

The Influence of Television and Film on Gender Roles.........................*447*

12 ***Development 2: Adolescence to the End
of Life***...*452*

ADOLESCENCE *453*

Physical Development during Adolescence *454*

Physical Changes during Puberty..*454*

Effects of Early and Late Maturation *454*

Cognitive Development during Adolescence *455*

Piaget's Formal Operations Stage *456*

Critique of Formal Operations Stage... ....*456*

Moral Development during Adolescence *456*

Kohlberg's Theory of Moral Development *457*

Evaluating Kohlberg's Theory...*459*

Psychosocial Development during Adolescence..................................*460*

Identity Formation *460*

The Role of Parents and the Peer Group *461*

Sexual Development *462*

The Double Standard during Adolescence *462*

Peer Pressure and Sexual Liberation *463*

The Effect of AIDS on Premarital Sex *463*

ADULTHOOD *464*

Physical Development in Early and Middle Adulthood *465*

Physical Capacities *465*

Hormonal Changes and the Climacteric *466*

The Double Standard of Aging *466*

Cognitive Development in Early and Middle Adulthood *466*

Intelligence *466*

Crystallized versus Fluid Intelligence *467*

A Fifth Stage of Cognitive Development *467*

Psychosocial Development in Early and Middle Adulthood *468*

Single and Married Life-styles *468*

Single Living *468*

Cohabitation *469*

Does Cohabitation Lead to Better Marriages? *469*

Marriage *470*

Commitments to Parenting and Work *471*

Having Children *471*

The World of Work *472*

Job Satisfaction and Age *473*

THE OLDER YEARS *474*

The Graying of America *474*

Physical Development in the Older Years *475*

Neuronal Changes during Aging *476*

Theories of Aging *476*

Cognitive Development in the Older Years *477*

Intelligence and Aging *477*

Senile Dementia *477*

Psychosocial Development in the Older Years *479*

Successful Aging *479*

13 *Intelligence* *484*

DEFINING INTELLIGENCE *485*

MEASURING INTELLIGENCE *487*

Binet and Intelligence Testing *487*

The Intelligent Quotient *488*

The Stanford-Binet Intelligence Scale *489*

The Wechsler Adult Intelligence Scale *489*

Group versus Individual Intelligence Tests *490*

EVALUATING INTELLIGENCE TESTS *491*

How Intelligence Tests Are Developed *491*

Developing a Pool of Test Items *491*

Evaluating the Test Items *492*

Standardizing the Test 492

Establishing Norms 492

Test Reliability and Validity 493

Determining Test Reliability 493

Assessing Test Validity 494

Measuring Test Validity 494

Achievement and Aptitude Tests 494

THEORIES OF INTELLIGENCE 495

Factorial Theories 495

Spearman's Two-Factor Theory 495

Thurstone's Primary Mental Abilities 496

Guilford's Structure of Intellect 496

Process Theories 496

Sternberg's Information-Processing Approach 496

Gardner's Theory of Multiple Intelligences 498

BIAS IN INTELLIGENCE TESTING 499

HEREDITARY AND ENVIRONMENTAL INFLUENCES

ON INTELLIGENCE 501

Isolating Contributions to Intelligence 502

Twin Studies 502

Adoption Studies 504

Orphanage and Environmental Enrichment Studies 504

Enrichment Programs 505

Birth-Order Studies 506

Animal Research 507

Evaluating the Hereditary and Environmental Evidence 507

Within- and Between-Group Differences and Intelligence 508

RACIAL DIFFERENCES IN INTELLIGENCE 509

RESEARCH PERSPECTIVES: ARE INTELLIGENCE TESTS
INTELLIGENT? DR. ROBERT STERNBERG AND DR. HOWARD GARDNER *514*

14 ***Personality: Theories and Assessment*** 522

DEFINING PERSONALITY 523

THEORIES OF PERSONALITY 524

Trait Theories 524

Allport's Cardinal, Central, and Secondary Traits 524

Cattell's Sixteen Personality Factors 526

Evaluating the Trait Theories 527

Descriptions versus Explanations of Behavior 527

PSYCHOANALYTIC THEORY 528

The Historical Context of Freud's Theory 528

Personality and the Unconscious 529

The Structure of Personality 530

The Id 530

The Ego 530

The Superego 531

Personality Dynamics 532

Anxiety and the Defense Mechanisms *532*
    Repression *532*
    Rationalization *533*
    Projection *533*
    Displacement *533*
    Regression *535*
    Reaction Formation *535*
Freud's View of Personality Development........................*535*
    Psychosexual Development.......................................*535*
    Fixation *536*
    Fixation at the Oral Stage *536*
Evaluating Freud's Psychoanalytic Theory.....................*536*
Other Psychodynamic Theorists: The Neo-Freudians.......*538*
    Carl Jung *538*
    Alfred Adler *538*
    Karen Horney *539*
HUMANISTIC THEORIES OF PERSONALITY *540*
Rogers: The Concept of Self....................................*540*
Maslow: Self-Actualization......................................*541*
Evaluating Humanistic Theories *542*
BEHAVIORAL, SOCIAL-LEARNING, AND BIOLOGICAL
THEORIES OF PERSONALITY *543*
The Behavioral Perspective......................................*543*
The Social-Learning Perspective..............................*544*
    Bandura's Social-Cognitive Perspective....................*545*
Evaluating Behavioral and Social-Learning Theories.......*546*
Biological Determinants of Personality *547*
    Heritability Studies with Twins..............................*547*
    Criticism of Heritability Studies *547*
THE ASSESSMENT OF PERSONALITY *548*
Behavioral Observation *548*
Interviews...*549*
Questionnaires..*550*
    Minnesota Multiphasic Personality Inventory *550*
    California Psychological Inventory...........................*552*
Projective Tests *552*
    The Rorschach Inkblot Test *553*
    The Thematic Apperception Test..............................*554*

Part 5
The Nature and Treatment of Behavioral Disorders *560*

15 *Behavioral Disorders* *562*
    DEFINING ABNORMAL BEHAVIOR *565*

CLASSIFYING BEHAVIORAL DISORDERS..*566*

ANXIETY DISORDERS *567*

   Panic Disorders *567*

   Social Phobias *568*

   Specific Phobias *569*

   Obsessive-Compulsive Disorder..*569*

   Posttraumatic Stress Disorder *570*

   Generalized Anxiety Disorder *571*

   Theoretical Perspectives on Anxiety Disorders................................*571*

      The Psychoanalytic Perspective *571*

      The Behavioral Perspective *572*

      The Biological Perspective *574*

SOMATOFORM DISORDERS..*577*

   Somatization Disorders..*577*

   Hypochondriasis *578*

   Conversion Disorder *578*

   Theoretical Perspectives on Somatoform Disorders.........................*580*

DISSOCIATIVE DISORDERS..*580*

   Dissociative Amnesia *580*

   Dissociative Fugue..*581*

   Dissociative Identity Disorder *581*

   Theoretical Perspectives on Dissociative Disorders *582*

MOOD DISORDERS *582*

   Major Depressive Disorder *584*

   Bipolar (Manic-Depressive) Disorder..*584*

   Seasonal Affective Disorder *587*

   Theoretical Perspectives on Mood Disorders *588*

      The Psychoanalytic Perspective *588*

      The Behavioral Perspective *588*

      The Biological Perspective *590*

         Genetics *590*

         Brain Biochemistry...*592*

      Sex Differences and Depression *595*

SCHIZOPHRENIA *595*

   Primary Symptoms of Schizophrenia *596*

      Delusions and Disturbances of Thought *597*

      Hallucinations and Disturbance of Perception........................*598*

      Disturbance in Emotional Expression *598*

      Disturbances in Speech *599*

      Disorganized or Catatonic Behavior *599*

      The Development of Schizophrenia *599*

      Prodromal Stage *599*

      Active Stage *599*

      Residual Stage..*599*

   Subtypes of Schizophrenia *599*

      Disorganized Schizophrenia *600*

      Catatonic Schizophrenia *600*

Paranoid Schizophrenia *601*

Undifferentiated and Residual Schizophrenia *601*

Theoretical Perspectives on Schizophrenia *601*

The Psychoanalytic Perspective *601*

The Behavioral Perspective *601*

The Biological Perspective *602*

Genetics *602*

Brain Biochemistry...*603*

Brain Structural Abnormalities *604*

PERSONALITY DISORDERS *604*

Antisocial Personality Disorder *606*

Theoretical Perspectives on Antisocial Personality Disorder........*607*

RESEARCH PERSPECTIVES: VIEWS ON THE BIOLOGICAL BASES OF
BEHAVIORAL DISORDERS
DR. IRVING GOTTESMAN AND DR. KURT SALZINGER.......................*612*

16 ***Treatment of Behavioral Disorders***..............................*620*

PSYCHOLOGICAL THERAPIES *621*

Psychoanalysis..*621*

Techniques of Psychoanalysis...*621*

Free Association...*622*

Dream Analysis *622*

Resistance...*622*

Transference *623*

Interpretation...*623*

The Present Status of Psychoanalysis *624*

Humanistic Therapies *624*

Person-Centered Therapy...*624*

Genuineness *625*

Unconditional Positive Regard *625*

Empathic Understanding *625*

Gestalt Therapy..*626*

Evaluating Humanistic Therapies *627*

Cognitive Therapies *628*

Rational-Emotive Therapy..*628*

Cognitive Restructuring Therapy *631*

Evaluating Cognitive Therapies *632*

Behavioral Therapies..*632*

Classical Conditioning Therapies *632*

Systematic Desensitization *633*

Aversive Conditioning *634*

Operant Conditioning Therapies *635*

Positive Reinforcement..*635*

Extinction Technique...*636*

Punishment...*636*

Modeling *637*
Token Economies *637*
Evaluating Behavioral Therapies *638*
Group Therapies *638*
Family Therapy *639*
Couple Therapy *640*
EVALUATING PSYCHOTHERAPY *641*
Is Psychotherapy More Beneficial Than No Therapy? *642*
Is One Type of Psychotherapy More Effective Than Another? *643*
Common Features of Psychotherapeutic Approaches *644*
Combating the Clients Demoralization *644*
Providing a Rationale for Symptoms and Treatment *644*
Providing a Warm, Supportive Relationship *644*
Providing a Professional Setting *644*
BIOLOGICALLY-BASED THERAPIES *645*
Psychosurgery *645*
Electroconvulsive Therapy *647*
Psychoactive Drugs *649*
Antipsychotics *651*
Antidepressants *651*
Antimanics *652*
Antianxiety Drugs *652*

HEALTH PSYCHOLOGY AND LIFE: GUIDELINES FOR SEEKING
PROFESSIONAL HELP *653*

Part 6
Social Psychology

Social Psychology *658*

17 *Social Psychology* *660*
SOCIAL PERCEPTION *662*
First Impressions *663*
Person Schemas *663*
Implicit Personality Theories *664*
ATTRIBUTION THEORIES *665*
The Correspondent Inference Theory *665*
Attributions and Socially Undesirable Behavior *666*
Covariation Principle *667*
Attribution Errors *668*
Fundamental Attribution Error *668*
False Consensus *670*
Illusion of Control *670*
ATTITUDES *671*
Acquiring Attitudes *672*
Behavioral Observation *672*
Observing Ourselves *672*
Learning Attitudes *672*

Classical Conditioning 672
Operant Conditioning 672
Direct Experience 673
The Function of Attitudes 673
Do Attitudes Predict Behavior? 674
Social Expectations and Behavior...675
Attitude Specificity..676
Attitude Recognition 676
Does Our Behavior Affect Our Attitudes? 676
Changing Attitudes..677
Balance Theory..677
Cognitive Dissonance Theory...677
Persuasion 678
The Communicator...678
The Message 679
The Audience 680
PREJUDICE..681
Outgroups, Ingroups, and the Causes of Prejudice..682
Competition Between Groups 682
Frustration, Scapegoating, and Prejudice 683
Social Learning and Prejudice 683
A "Prejudiced Personality"..684
SOCIAL INFLUENCE ON BEHAVIOR 685
Conformity 685
The Asch Experiments 686
When Are We Most Likely to Conform? 687
Compliance 687
Foot-in-the-Door Technique 688
Door-in-the-Face Technique 688
Obedience 688
Milgram's Experiments on Obedience to Authority 688
INTERPERSONAL BEHAVIOR: ATTRACTION AND
AGGRESSION 690
Attraction 690
Factors That Contribute to Interpersonal Attraction...690
Proximity...690
Similarity..691
Reciprocity 691
Physical Attractiveness 692
Aggression 693
Biological Bases of Aggression 693
Psychological Bases of Aggression 695
The Frustration-Aggression Hypothesis 695
Social-Learning Perspectives on Aggression..696
The Effects of Violence in the Media and on Film..697
HEALTH PSYCHOLOGY AND LIFE: REDUCING THE RISK OF
ACQUAINTANCE RAPE 698

Appendix *A-1*

Glossary *G-1*

Bibliography *B-1*

Copyright Acknowledgments *C-1*

Name Index *I-1*

Subject Index *I-11*

Health Psychology and Life

Magnesium Treatment After Brain Injury *106*
Suggested Remedies for Insomnia *191*
Classical Conditioning of the Immune System *228*
Some Suggestions for Overcoming Obesity *309*
Managing Stress..*343*
Guidelines for Seeking Professional Help *653*
Reducing the Risk of Acquaintance Rape *698*

Research Perspectives

Psychological Explanation *24*
Language Competence of Apes...*392*
Are Intelligence Tests Intelligent? *514*
Views on the Biological Bases of Behavioral Disorders *612*

Psychology

Science, Behavior, and Life

CHAPTER 1
The Origins of Psychology

CHAPTER 2
The Methods of Psychology

PART 1

Nature, Origins, and Methods of Psychology

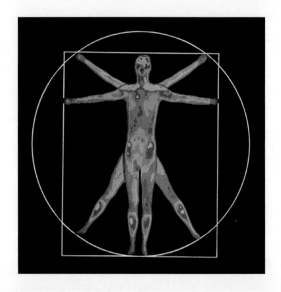

CHAPTER 1

The Origins of Psychology

THE STUDY OF PSYCHOLOGY

DEFINTION OF PSYCHOLOGY

Psychology as a Science
The Study of Behavior
The Study of Humans and Other Animals

PSYCHOLOGY'S HISTORY

Structuralism
Functionalism

Psychoanalysis
Behaviorism
Gestalt Psychology
Humanistic Psychology

CONTEMPORARY PSYCHOLOGY

Fields of Specialization in Psychology

THE GOALS OF PSYCHOLOGY

Are the things you see, feel, and hear every day only in your mind or do they exist in the external world? How can you know for sure? How can you know anything for sure? As John Locke, a seventeenth century philosopher, put it,

The knowledge of the existence of any other thing we can have only by sensation . . . For the having the idea of anything in our mind no more proves the existence of that thing than a picture of a man evidences his being in the world.

Questions about the mind were of great interest to philosophers of the seventeenth and eighteen centuries and can actually be traced back to the Greek philosophers Aristotle and Plato. Although the philosophers' answers contribute relatively little to our current understanding of psychology, their methods of inquiry did. During the nineteenth century philosophers became less reliant on theological and nonempirical explanations of mind and behavior and more and more dependent on direct observation. However, as the following quote points out,

mental philosophy (the term used before psychology became a discipline of its own) was making very little progress in understanding the mind.

There is no department of knowledge in which so little progress has been made as in that of mental philosophy . . . No attempt indeed has been made to examine its phenomena by the light of experiment and observation. (Brewster 1854)

However, by the middle of the nineteenth century, psychological phenomena like perception, thought, and learning would be studied scientifically. Rapid advances in the physical sciences using scientific methods suggested that the study of mind, which had made relatively little progress, might also benefit from a new methodology. This dramatic shift in the way the mind was studied led the way for modern psychology.

We will trace these beginnings of psychology in this first chapter. An appreciation of where psychology has been will help you to see where it is going.

THE STUDY OF PSYCHOLOGY

For many of you, this text may be your first formal exposure to a science that is central to ourselves. Perhaps you have wondered as you were taking some other courses, What has this to do with my life? Psychology has everything to do with your life.

Although we admit to some bias, we do believe that a knowledge of psychology is helpful even to people who do not plan to pursue it as a career. Studying psychology provides insights into why people behave as they do. It also helps us to better understand our own thoughts, feelings, behaviors, and attitudes—and hopefully, it can strengthen our appreciation of and tolerance for the wide differences that exist among people.

Psychology investigates a wide variety of questions and attempts to answer them using scientific methods. Among the questions that will be explored in this book are these:

Can something as complex as human behavior be studied scientifically?

Is there a relationship between brain processes and mental life?

How does something we learn get represented in the brain?

Are mental disorders caused by abnormalities in the brain?

What causes some people to overeat and become obese?

Are dreams necessary? What happens if people are prevented from dreaming?

What do intelligence tests really measure?

Why are you less likely to be assisted in an emergency when there are many bystanders than when in the presence of only a few?

Can one person possess two or more distinct personalities at the same time?

How does psychological stress contribute to illnesses such as heart disease, hypertension, and the flu?

Does psychotherapy help people overcome psychological problems such as depression and anxiety?

Is punishment a more effective method for controlling behavior than the use of reinforcement?

Psychology also helps us evaluate the many so-called psychological facts we encounter every day in the popular media. When was the last time you read a newspaper or magazine article or heard a talk-show host present the latest findings on the meaning of dreams, how to become more successful, or why men behave differently from women? Many people accept such "scientifically based facts" without questioning whether they are founded on reliable evidence. We hope that an understanding of psychology will help you think critically and carefully evaluate such claims. You will see that many of your unquestioned assumptions about human behavior have no scientific basis.

DEFINITION OF PSYCHOLOGY

Formally defined, **psychology** is *the scientific study of the behavior of humans and other animals.* This definition can be broken down into three parts. Psychology is a scientific study; it studies behavior; and it includes the study of other animals as well as humans.

PSYCHOLOGY AS A SCIENCE

The first part of our definition states that psychology is a scientific study. Indeed, the theories and facts of psychology emerge from the careful application of scientific methods. This aspect of our definition may contradict many people's views of psychology, for it is often assumed that psychology is just a matter of common sense. After all, are we not applying psychology when we mix enough praise with criticism to make a child feel good about changing bad habits, or when we carefully discuss relationship problems with our partners rather than keeping those concerns within us? If syndicated columnists in the daily paper can provide advice for dealing with people, what sets psychology apart as a science?

Psychology certainly involves knowing how to deal with people effectively, but it involves a great deal more than this. In fact dealing with people effectively is only a small part of the science of behavior. And, as you will soon see, it involves much more than common sense explanations. For example, take a minute to consider the following question:

Would you expect that the number of people present in an emergency can determine whether or not one of them responds with help?

Most people when asked this question immediately reply that the more people present, the more likely someone will help. After all, some individual in the crowd is bound to see the emergency and assist. However, numerous case studies and experiments conducted by psychologists tend to confirm the opposite: Assistance is more likely to be given if very few bystanders are present.

According to research conducted by Latané and Darley (1970), the presence of other people affects our perception of an emergency situation and we tend to diffuse our responsibility to act in an emergency to others who are present. In a now classic experiment subjects were asked to participate in an interview about urban life. While waiting to be called to the interview they were instructed to wait in a specific room and fill out some forms. Some of the subjects waited alone and others waited with two others. After working on the forms for several minutes smoke began to infiltrate the room through a vent. Observations of the subjects revealed that 63 percent of the subjects working alone noticed the smoke within five seconds while only 26 percent of the subjects working with others noticed it. Subjects working alone also were more likely to report the smoke than subjects working with others.

This research along with numerous other experiments have helped to explain bystander apathy. It is only through carefully designed experiments such as these that our common sense assumptions can be validated or refuted.

Psychological research using scientific methods often provides enlightening and reliable information about behavior that we might not otherwise learn. In contrast, relying on common sense produces subjective opinions that may have little basis in fact. One only has to look at the history of other sciences to see that psychology is not alone here. It was not all that long ago that stars were known as windows to the heavens, diseases thought to be caused by spirits invading the body. As science progresses subjective opinions and folklore are either confirmed or left behind.

Psychology uses scientific methods to investigate its subject. Many of these methods are discussed in detail in Chapter 2. Despite its careful methodology, however, many questions about behavior remain unanswered by the science of psychology, and much of our understanding of people and behavior is subject to constant review and revision. You will learn that very few psychological principles are carved in stone; new theories as well as technological developments are constantly providing fresh directions and methods for expanding knowledge.

THE STUDY OF BEHAVIOR

The second part of our definition states that psychology is the study of behavior. There have been times in the history of psychology, as you will see later in this chapter, when psychology focused almost entirely on unobservable mental processes. At other times, psychologists have been concerned only with behavior that could be observed directly, strictly avoiding any reference to mental processes.

At present psychologists are interested in studying both behavioral processes and mental processes. It is hoped by many that theories about mental processes can be based on direct observations of behavior. To illustrate how behavior and mental processes can both be the subject matter of psychology, imagine participating in a psychological experiment where a psychologist displays a moving object on a computer screen. After the object has moved up (or down) the screen for several seconds it disappears. Your task is to locate the exact spot on the screen where the object disappeared. The psychologist here is interested in both direct measurements (your reported estimate of position) and discovering something about how movement and velocity are represented internally (by developing a theory based on numerous observations). For example, psychologists have found that if the object is moving downward people tend to exaggerate its velocity by overestimating how far it travelled before disappearing. When the object is moving upward the velocity estimate is often too low (Hubbard, 1990). Interestingly, these observations are consistent with how "real" moving objects are affected by gravity. That is, as an object goes up it slows down and when an object is going down it accelerates due to gravity. Thus it appears as though our mental representations of moving objects have some of the same characteristics as real moving objects. In this example a theory about a mental process (our representation of movement) is developed through direct observation of observable behavior (placement of the cursor on the computer screen).

Thus, psychology does not solely study behaviors that can be observed directly by onlookers or research scientists (although those observations are an important part of psychology). Nor—contrary to some people's assumptions that all psychologists are interested in analyzing dreams and probing for repressed memories—does psychology confine itself only to the inner workings of the mind. Instead, contemporary psychologists are often interested in both observable behavior and mental processes.

THE STUDY OF HUMANS AND OTHER ANIMALS

The third part of our definition states that psychology is the study of humans and other animals. Psychologists study rats, dogs, cats, and pigeons, among other animals; even insects have provided useful information about behavior.

The study of psychology includes using nonhuman animals and even computers to discover the mysteries of behavior.

LEARNING ABOUT PSYCHOLOGY FROM NONHUMAN ANIMALS Students are often surprised to discover that the subject matter of psychology includes the behavior of all animals, not just humans. How can psychologists generalize from rats to people? Why study nonhuman animals when there are so many pressing problems threatening the quality of human lives? Try to formulate at least a few answers to this question before reading on.

There are at least five major reasons why psychology includes the study of animal behavior as well as human behavior. One is the need to find a simpler model. Scientists in all fields generally attempt to understand a particular phenomenon by first studying the simplest examples available in nature. For instance, to understand respiration, metabolism, and other cellular processes, a biologist might first examine them in a simple, one-celled amoeba, as opposed to a more complex multicelled organism. Similarly, scientists seeking to understand the neurological processes that underlie behavior can benefit from examining the nervous system of a relatively simple organism like a sea slug, which may have about 20,000 nerve cells, rather than by beginning their investigations with humans, who have about 100 billion nerve cells.

A second reason to study animal behavior is the greater control that it provides. In a typical experiment, a number of different factors or variables may influence behavior. The more control the experimenter has over these variables, the more precise the conclusions can be. To illustrate, suppose you wanted to study the relationship between environmental noise levels and problem-solving behavior. You might anticipate that a number of variables (such as how rested, hungry, or relaxed a subject is) could also influence problem solving. If you were to use human subjects, it would be hard to control precisely the events occurring in their lives in the 24-hour period before they arrived at your laboratory for testing. In contrast, the life of an experimental animal, such as a monkey, can be controlled 24 hours a day. Thus, by using animal subjects, you could carefully monitor important conditions such as levels of hunger, rest, and stress.

Ethical considerations are a third reason for studying animals. Psychologists often ask questions that for ethical reasons cannot be addressed initially in research with humans. For example, over the last four decades psychologists involved in brain research have conducted experiments in which they have placed electrodes into the brain to stimulate or record brain activity. You can imagine the ethical questions that would surface if we were limited to human subjects in these pioneer efforts. Just as medical researchers must test experimental drugs extensively with nonhumans before they can begin clinical testing on people, research psychologists cannot apply new laboratory procedures to human subjects until they have ruled out the possibility of harmful effects.

The fact that psychologists conduct experiments on nonhuman animals that may be unethical to conduct on humans does not mean that ethical guidelines are not followed in animal research. Quite the contrary, virtually everywhere that research is conducted in the United States, ethics committees review all proposed studies to ensure that the welfare of subjects (human or otherwise) is safeguarded. The vast majority of scientists conducting animal research are aware of their responsibilities regarding humane treatment of their subjects and work within the confines of these limitations (Pincus et al., 1986, p. 1586).

Another reason for using nonhuman subjects is a practical one. Animals are readily available for experimentation, often at minimal cost. White rats, for instance, are generally in plentiful supply at a price well within most researchers' budgets. In addition, some experiments require frequent testing of subjects, often over an extended period. Few humans would commit to any kind of research that required more than a few hours conveniently taken from their daily routines. Laboratory animals, on the other hand, are available night and day for as long as is necessary.

Finally, psychologists study the behavior of animals simply to learn more about animal behavior. For example, psychologists and other scientists who study animal behavior have provided important information about feeding, social, and reproductive behaviors of countless species. This information is critical when developing policy that may affect animal environments. In the Northwest United States there is currently much heated discussion about the habitat of the Spotted Owl. What effects will extensive logging have on this population of endangered birds? Only research on the behavior of this species can answer this question.

Even if you acknowledge that animal research has some advantages, you may still be unconvinced that such research is worthwhile. If so, the findings of research psychologist James Olds (1973) may persuade you to modify this view somewhat, for they illustrate how animal studies can have direct value for humans. Olds identified an area within a rat's brain that produces intense pleasure when stimulated electrically (see Chapter 3). His pioneering work encouraged researchers to look for similar pleasure centers in human brains. Their discovery in humans has had many important applications, including pleasure center stimulation to provide relief for severely disturbed psychiatric patients and to counteract debilitating pain in terminally ill patients (Heath, 1972; Olds & Forbes, 1981). Now that the rewarding effects of electrical stimulation of various brain sites have been established, researchers are attempting to discover what mechanisms underlie these effects (Gallistel, 1986; Mora & Ferrer, 1986; Velley, 1986). We expect that this exciting area of research will continue to yield important clues about the intricate workings of our brains.

We have defined psychology as the scientific study of behavior, yet this definition represents only a contemporary view of psychology. In its short history (the discipline had its formal beginnings only a little over a century ago), the answer to the question, What is psychology? has varied considerably, depending on the era in which it was asked. The following section presents a brief overview of the history of psychology.

PSYCHOLOGY'S HISTORY

Although psychology is a very young science, its roots go back to antiquity. Since the earliest recorded civilizations, people have been concerned about issues still considered central to present-day psychology. This focus was particularly true for philosophers such as Plato, Aristotle, Descartes, and Locke, who raised provocative questions about human thoughts, feelings, and behaviors.

These philosophers speculated about the mind. Where was it located? How did ideas within the mind gain expression in physical actions? By what processes did events in our external environment become part of our awareness? Such questions all reflected a fundamental interest in the relationship between mind and body. The early philosophers endeavored to understand this relationship by formulating assumptions, then applying logical thought processes as they reasoned their way to conclusions. While based on logic, this approach had an important limitation because it relied on subjective assumptions about how the world seemed to be, rather than scientific assessments about how the world really is. As a result, logical reasoning of early philosophers sometimes led to inaccurate conclusions.

For instance the influential seventeenth-century philosopher René Descartes, proposed that mind and body are distinct entities that interact at a point represented by the brain's tiny pineal gland. Descartes' position was known as *dualism*. He believed that the physical body was mechanical and obeyed known laws of physics. The mind or soul, however, was not physical but interacted in some way through the pineal gland to produce intentional behavior. Descartes' dualistic view is summarized in the following statement:

> I here remark, in the first place, that there is a vast difference between mind and body, in respect that body, from its nature, is always divisible, and that mind is entirely indivisible . . . This would be sufficient to teach me that the mind or soul of man is entirely different from the body. (Descartes)

As you might have guessed, Descartes' ideas have greatly influenced the way we commonly think of mind and body. For example, the concept of *free will* is central to our everyday assumption that our behavior is influenced by our wants, desires, and intentions. This is contrary to the position that behavior is caused or determined by *physical* events either within or outside of our body. This position, referred to as *determinism*, is central to the science of psychology. Determinism assumes that all physical events (including behavior and mental processes) are caused or determined by other physical events. These other physical events include the activity of our nervous system.

Psychology also has roots in *physiology*, a division of biology concerned with the systematic study of bodily processes. An interest in how the bodies of humans and other animals function led a number of influential nineteenth-century physiologists to begin exploring some of the same psychological issues as their philosopher counterparts. However, unlike the philosophers who relied on reasoning and speculation, the physiologists adhered to the concept of *empiricism*, the idea that knowledge is best acquired through observation. These early physiologists were well schooled in the **scientific method**, which involves careful observation of events in the world, the formation of predictions based on these observations, and then the testing of these predictions by further systematic observations.

The physiologists of the mid-nineteenth century provided important new insights into how the brain and the rest of the nervous system influence behavior. For example, in the mid-1800s a group of German scientists led by Hermann von Helmholtz pioneered a series of experiments in which they measured the

René Descartes

John Locke

speed of conduction of a nerve impulse and assessed the nature of neural communication within the nervous system. By 1870, researchers at the University of Berlin had begun to study the exposed brains of laboratory animals and found that electrical stimulation of certain locations caused specific bodily movements. Studies such as these marked the way for later laboratory research that has helped reveal the relationship between brain processes and behavior.

Thus, while psychology has roots in philosophical questions about the relationship of mind and body, the empirical nature of contemporary psychology and its adherence to the scientific method also reflects the science of physiology, which provided the tools for careful examination of these questions. The next logical step in the evolution of psychology was to take the questions about behavior and mental process posed by philosophy into the laboratory.

STRUCTURALISM

WILHELM WUNDT (1832–1920) Entering the laboratory is exactly what Wilhelm Wundt, a German scientist trained in physiology, did in the late 1800s. The establishment of Wundt's small laboratory at the University of Leipzig in 1879 marked the formal beginning of psychology as a scientific discipline.

Wundt defined the task of psychology as the systematic study of the structure of the conscious adult mind. He believed that the conscious mental processes involved in such things as perceiving colors, reacting to stimuli, and experiencing emotions could be understood best by breaking them down into their basic elements and then analyzing how the elements were connected with one another. In this sense, he hoped to pattern psychology after the physical sciences of chemistry, physics, and physiology.

Wundt borrowed a tool of philosophy, *introspection* (looking inward), for studying mental processes. For example, subjects listening to music might be asked to break their perceptual experience down into its basic elements of pitch, volume, timbre, and so forth. Subjects were trained in introspection so that they could provide clear reports of their sensations. Wundt also believed that introspection needed to be supplemented by experiments. Therefore, he would systematically vary some physical dimension of a stimulus, such as the volume of a particular sound, to see how sensations changed. This approach came to be known as *experimental self-observation*. Throughout Wundt's career, he continued to emphasize gaining information about the mind from observable, measurable events.

Many of the pioneers of American psychology received their training in Wundt's laboratory in Germany. One of these students, Edward Titchener, brought his mentor's particular brand of psychology to America when he established a psychology laboratory at Cornell University in 1892. Like Wundt, Titchener thought the proper goal of psychology was to describe mental structures. This approach to psychology was called **structuralism.**

Structuralism attempted to develop a kind of mental chemistry by breaking experience down into its basic elements or structures in the same way that a substance such as water could be broken down into molecules of hydrogen and oxygen. This approach seemed reasonable at the time because it was proving successful for the sciences of chemistry and physics.

PROBLEMS WITH STRUCTURALISM Can you see any problems associated with trying to break an experience into its basic elements? Will an experience retain its essential character when subjected to this reductionist approach? Think about this question for a few moments before reading on.

Structuralism enjoyed only short-lived popularity. Psychologists soon discovered that introspection, the major research tool of structuralism, often altered

Wilhelm Wundt

the nature of the conscious mental processes they wished to analyze. The next time you find yourself entranced by an exquisite sunset or a haunting melody, stop and pay attention to your sensations, thoughts, and feelings. You will probably find, as did many of the early introspectionists, that analyzing what you are experiencing changes the experience. An even more damaging flaw became apparent when a number of researchers who were using introspection independently of one another discovered that their results were often different. Finally, many American psychologists criticized structuralism as impractical; they thought psychology should offer solutions to the problems of everyday life. This movement toward a more pragmatic psychology culminated in the functionalist school.

FUNCTIONALISM

William James

WILLIAM JAMES (1842–1910)   Perhaps one of the greatest of all American psychologists was William James. James distinguished himself as a writer of psychology, as a reactionist against the introspective method, and by his new approach to investigating the mind. He agreed with the structuralists that psychology should study mental processes. However, he felt that the science would be better served by attempting to understand the fluid, functional, continually changing, personal nature of conscious experience. He was particularly interested in trying to understand mental processes that helped humans and other animals adapt to their environments. Because of his emphasis on the functional, practical nature of the mind, his conception of psychology's proper task became known as **functionalism.** One of the most important events in psychology's history was the publication in 1890 of James' landmark text, *Principles of Psychology.* This two-volume book, which detailed his view of the nature of psychology, is still considered to be one of the most important psychological texts of all time.

James was greatly influenced by Charles Darwin's theory of evolution by *natural selection.* According to Darwin, characteristics of a species change or evolve over time as environmental conditions change. Those characteristics that aid in the survival and reproduction of the species are maintained while others are eliminated. For instance, the protective coloration of some types of moths or the opposable thumbs of humans are traits that were preserved because they helped these species adapt to their environments. Similarly, functionalists concluded that psychological states or processes such as consciousness also evolved because they served particular functions, such as guiding the activities of the individual. Functionalists wanted to learn how various mental processes, such as perceiving, learning, and thinking, helped people adapt. To accomplish this purpose, they continued to use introspection in their research. However, they also introduced another research method: collecting data from observations of human and animal behavior.

Both structuralism and functionalism played important roles in the development of psychology as a science. Structuralism brought psychology into the laboratory by demonstrating that mental processes were a legitimate focus for scientific research. Functionalism broadened psychology to include the study of nonhuman animals and it expanded the data of psychology to include observations of behavior. James' contributions have had enduring effects on both psychology and education.

PSYCHOANALYSIS

SIGMUND FREUD (1856–1939)   During the time when Wundt's structuralism was both active and vital in America, an Austrian physician named Sigmund Freud was developing a new psychological theory. Freud's theory, psychoanalysis, was named after the procedure employed in interviewing patients with neurotic symptoms. One such patient, named Anna O., was particularly significant in the development of psychoanalysis. Anna O. was an attractive woman in her early twenties with severe neurotic symptoms of paralysis, nausea, memory loss, and mental deterioration. Through psychoanalysis, conducted by Freud's mentor Dr. Breuer, Anna O.'s problems appeared to be related to early childhood experiences. Once these experiences were told, usually during hypnosis, some of her symptoms would disappear. This talking cure became known as catharsis and continues to be an important part of psychoanalysis. Early on, it became apparent to Freud that most of his patients' symptoms had a sexual basis. Many of Freud's views, particularly his belief that sexual urges were powerful energizers of human behavior, shocked both professionals and laypeople. His emphasis on the *unconscious mind*, with its irrational urges and drives beyond the control of conscious rational processes, upset many people; it was a blow to human pride to be told that we are often not the masters of our own lives.

Freud's theories are more widely recognized among nonpsychologists than is any other school of psychological thought. This is not to say that Freud's analytic approach has been at the forefront of scientific psychology since it was first introduced to America in the early 1900s. Quite the contrary, much of the impact of psychoanalysis lies in the critical reactions it has generated, not on the contributions it has made to modern psychology. Psychoanalysis has been widely criticized, in part because its assertions cannot be tested in the laboratory.

Despite these criticisms, Freud's impact on psychology was profound. He provided important insights into understanding the emotional lives of people. He encouraged psychologists to consider the impact on behavior of processes not immediately available to conscious inspection. He also helped to legitimize the study of human sexuality. Though psychoanalysis is not a major force in contemporary psychology, the practice of psychoanalysis by psychiatrists treating emotionally disturbed patients continues. We discuss Freud's views in several places throughout the book, particularly in Chapters 14 and 16.

Sigmund Freud

BEHAVIORISM

The change in psychology from structuralism to functionalism in the United States was both gradual and incomplete. Certainly functionalism did not completely replace the methods of structuralism and both schools agreed that mental processes were the subject of psychology. However, in 1913 a revolution against both of these schools occurred. This revolution, initiated by John Watson, was both sudden and quite dramatic. The new and revolutionary approach to psychology was called **behaviorism.**

JOHN WATSON (1878–1958)   Behaviorism was founded in the first few decades of this century by John B. Watson. Although trained as a functionalist, Watson ultimately came to believe it was impossible to study the mind objectively. He especially opposed the use of introspection, which he considered unscientific, and he chastised the functionalists for not going far enough in their rebellion against structuralism. Watson proclaimed a new psychology, free of introspection, whose task was simply to observe the relationship between environmental events (stimuli) and an organism's responses to them. This stimulus-response (S-R) approach to psychology was a radical departure from Watson's predecessors' focus on mental processes.

The goal of behaviorism was (and still is) to identify the processes by which stimuli and responses become connected or associated. In other words, how we learn. Watson believed that complex human behavior could be analyzed in terms of simple learned associations. The early goal of behaviorism was to discover the rules of association and how combinations of simple associations lead to complex behavior. Watson's work was greatly influenced by the Russian physiologist Ivan Pavlov (1849–1936) and another American psychologist Edward Thorndike

John Watson

Wolfgang Köhler

(1874–1949) who both provided Watson and later behaviorists with new ways of investigating behavior and clues to the rules of association. We will have much more to say about Pavlov and Thorndike in Chapter 6.

Behaviorism quickly caught on and soon most younger American psychologists were calling themselves behaviorists. Behaviorism continues to exert a profound influence on contemporary American psychology due mainly to the monumental contributions of Harvard's B. F. Skinner (1904–1990). Skinner's major contributions to psychology include his important work in operant conditioning where he systematically investigated the effects of reinforcement on behavior. In addition, Skinner's contributions include his extensive writings on language learning, programmed instruction, philosophy of science, and politics.

Behaviorism is characterized by its insistence upon an empirical, objective science of behavior which has no need for theories of mind or personal freedom. The behaviorist position on the free will–determinism controversy is well summarized in Skinner's statement:

> . . . the issue of personal freedom must not be allowed to interfere with a science of behavior. . . . We cannot expect to profit from applying the methods of science to human behavior if for some extraneous reason we refuse to admit that our subject matter cannot be controlled. (Skinner, 1953, p. 322)

Skinner and behavioral psychology will be discussed in more detail in Chapter 6. In fact, behaviorism and modern behaviorists will be discussed throughout this book.

GESTALT PSYCHOLOGY

WOLFGANG KÖHLER (1887–1967)   At about the same time as behaviorism was catching hold in America, a group of German psychologists were mounting their own opposition to Wundtian structuralism and the new behaviorism of American psychologists. These scientists, most notably Max Wertheimer, Wolfgang Köhler, and Kurt Koffka, disagreed with the principles and methods of both structuralism and behaviorism. They argued that it was a mistake to try to break psychological processes into basic components like elementary sensations or simple associations. Structuralists claimed that the perception of objects results from the accumulation of elements into groups or collections. These German psychologists argued that when sensory elements are brought together something new is formed. This something new is our perception of the stimulus. Put another way, the whole (our perception) is more than the sum of its parts (sensory elements). For example, put together a number of simple musical notes and a melody emerges. The melody you hear did not exist in any of the individual notes. This new approach to the investigation of perception was called **Gestalt psychology.**

Consider a typical experiment in perception which demonstrates the Gestalt approach (Figure 1.1). In a small darkened laboratory room you are seated in front of a viewing screen where images can be projected through a shutter that controls how long they appear on the screen. This device is called a *tachistiscope*. The psychologist presents images so quickly you can't really recognize them. The first image projected by the tachistiscope is a small red circle on the left of the screen. Then, almost immediately after the red circle, a larger yellow circle is presented on the right side of the screen. Before reading on, think about what you might report seeing. Remember both images were presented so quickly that you really don't recognize them individually.

What subjects typically report seeing in such an experiment is much more than was actually presented. Most likely you would have seen a small reddish orange circle moving across the screen from left to right. As it moved, it appeared to get larger or move towards you getting less red and more yellowish orange.

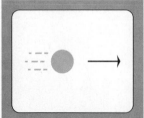

FIGURE 1.1

Gestalt experiment illustrating perception as more than stimulus elements. The top screen shows the stimuli that were actually presented. The bottom screen illustrates what subjects typically report seeing.

Both the movement and the change in color were constructed by perception and not characteristics of the stimuli themselves.

Because many of our experiences as humans cannot be broken down into separate pieces, Gestalt psychology remains an active force in our present-day investigation of perceptual processes. For example, much of what we now know about producing the illusion of movement through film or through the successive illumination of lights was discovered by Gestalt psychologists. These and many other perceptual phenomena will be discussed in more detail in Chapter 4.

HUMANISTIC PSYCHOLOGY

ABRAHAM MASLOW (1908–1970) Although humanistic psychology is still too new to be viewed as a part of psychology's history, we consider it here because it developed out of strong criticism to behaviorism and psychoanalysis.

Humanistic psychology differs from both the psychoanalytic approach and behaviorism in that it does not view humans as being controlled either by events in the environment or by internal, unconscious forces. Humanistic psychologists, most notably Abraham Maslow and Carl Rogers, deemphasize the influence of both environmental events and unconscious processes in determining human behavior. They argue that the images of man provided by both behavioral and psychoanalytic approaches are incomplete and inaccurate because they do not emphasize what is unique about being human. Instead, humanistic psychologists emphasize the role of *free will* and our ability to make conscious rational choices about how we live our lives. Humanistic psychologists also believe that people have a natural inclination to fulfill their human potential, a process called *self-actualization*. A person's striving towards self-actualization is seen as the motivating force of behavior.

Although many of humanistic psychology's major tenets are just as difficult to test objectively as the concepts of psychoanalysis, many psychologists respond favorably to this movement's optimism. This is in sharp contrast to Freud's psychology which viewed the outlook for personal fulfillment very pessimistically. Humanistic psychology has increased psychologists' awareness of the importance of such things as love, feeling needed, personal fulfillment, and self-esteem, and in this sense its contributions are of value. While humanistic psychology has been criticized sharply for its reliance on a nonscientific approach to understanding human behavior, its proponents have steadily maintained that human behavior is not a subject to be investigated scientifically. As

Carl Rogers

Abraham Maslow

Maslow phrased it, "We are offered beautifully executed, precise, elegant experiments which, in at least half the cases, have nothing to do with enduring human problems" (Maslow, 1965).

CONTEMPORARY PSYCHOLOGY

The previous section briefly introduced the major historical contributions to modern psychology. Many of those approaches have endured and even thrived into the present. For example, modern behaviorism and gestalt psychology are still quite influential. The methods of psychoanalysis are still taught and practiced widely throughout the United States. And the functional approach of William James is emphasized in contemporary education. Modern psychology, however, is not dominated by any single theoretical approach. Rather, there are many specialties within the field of psychology and each emphasizes a particular theoretical approach. The following section describes several major areas of specialization which, together with the enduring historical perspectives, define modern psychology.

FIELDS OF SPECIALIZATION IN PSYCHOLOGY

COGNITIVE PSYCHOLOGY   Although internal mental processes were considered important in the days of structuralism and functionalism, these processes received little attention while psychology was dominated by behaviorism. Now cognitive psychology is refocusing our attention on processes such as thinking, memory, language, problem solving, and creativity. Although some of these are problems currently studied by behaviorists, cognitive psychologists are more interested in internal mental processes, as opposed to behavioral processes. For example, a cognitive psychologist might describe your ability to navigate through campus in terms of internal representations or *cognitive maps* of your environment. They are interested in how these "maps" are constructed and the characteristics of the representations. A behavioral psychologist, on the other hand, might explain this same ability to navigate in terms of stimulus control and learning. The major difference would be the cognitive psychologists' reference to internal, mental processes, as opposed to observable stimulus events and learned behavior. You will recognize that both of these approaches are discussed throughout this text.

DEVELOPMENTAL PSYCHOLOGY   Another important field is **developmental psychology.** Psychologists in this field are interested in factors that influence development and shape behavior throughout the life cycle, from conception through old age. These specialists typically focus on a particular phase of the growth process, such as adolescence or old age, and examine how a particular ability or trait unfolds during that phase of development. For example, a developmental psychologist might investigate how the viewing of television violence influences the development of aggressive behavior in children. Chapters 11 and 12 are devoted to the study of human development.

SOCIAL PSYCHOLOGY   **Social psychology** is concerned with understanding the impact of social environments on the individual. Social psychologists are interested in attitude formation and change, social perception, conformity, social roles, prejudice, interpersonal attraction, and aggression. These topics will be discussed in detail in Chapter 17.

PERSONALITY PSYCHOLOGY   **Personality psychology** explores the uniqueness of the individual and describes the key elements that provide the foundation for human personalities. There is considerable diversity of opinion among personality theorists as to what constitute the major components of personality. For example, do our personalities consist of three interacting and sometimes conflicting forces (the id, ego, and superego) described by Sigmund Freud, or are we better characterized as a composite of 16 primary traits, as suggested by Raymond Cattell? Perhaps as you read Chapter 14, you will form your own opinion on this matter. Many personality psychologists devote their professional careers to investigating how personality develops, evolves, and influences people's activities.

EXPERIMENTAL PSYCHOLOGY   Psychologists in every area of specialization usually conduct experiments at some point in their careers. Thus it may be a bit misleading to call **experimental psychology** a separate field. Nevertheless, approximately 4 percent of the profession classify themselves as experimental psychologists whose primary activity involves conducting research.

In Chapter 2 we discover that psychologists use a number of research methods in their efforts to understand the nature and causes of behavior. Most experimental psychologists prefer to conduct research in a laboratory setting where they have precise control over the varied factors that influence behavior. For example, an experimental psychologist might investigate the relationship between sexual response and alcohol consumption by precisely measuring sexual arousal to erotic stimuli at different levels of alcohol consumption. (The results of these experiments are discussed in Chapter 2.)

BIOLOGICAL PSYCHOLOGY   Still another field, **biological psychology** (also called physiological psychology), studies the relationship between physiological processes and behavior. Biological psychologists investigate such things as the association between behavior and drugs, hormones, genes, and brain processes.

Biological psychologists attempt to explain behavior in terms of physiological or biological processes.

Biological psychology often captures the attention of the public. Over the years there have been countless cases in which irrational and sometimes violent behavior have been linked to abnormal biological processes. For instance, in one widely discussed event in 1966, Charles Whitman, a student at the University of Texas, climbed a tower and opened fire on the campus with a high-powered hunting rifle. Before he was killed by police, Whitman had murdered 14 people and wounded 24. While a number of explanations were suggested to account for Whitman's behavior, a postmortem exam revealed a large, malignant tumor in a region of the brain that psychologists have shown to be involved in aggressive behavior. Biological psychology is the topic of Chapter 3.

CLINICAL AND COUNSELING PSYCHOLOGY   More than half of the psychologists in America are engaged in either of two closely related fields: **clinical psychology** and **counseling psychology.** Both of these groups of psychologists are involved in the diagnosis and treatment of psychological problems, including such things as developmental disorders, substance abuse, relationship difficulties, vocational and educational problems, and behavior disorders.

While a great deal of overlap exists between counseling and clinical psychology, it is generally accurate to state that individuals specializing in counseling psychology tend to focus on less serious problems of adjustment than their counterparts in clinical psychology. Thus a counseling psychologist in a high school, college, or university setting might assist students with problems of social or academic adjustment or provide guidance in the area of career decisions. In contrast, clinical psychologists are more likely to work in mental health clinics, mental hospitals, juvenile and adult courts, medical schools, and prisons. Specialists in both areas often see clients in private practice.

Clinical psychology and *psychiatry* are often confused, since professionals within these respective fields often perform comparable functions, such as providing psychotherapy. However, these occupations differ in several important ways.

Most clinical psychologists obtain a doctor of philosophy degree (Ph.D.) in training that is likely to consist of three to five years of university graduate school instruction in psychological theory, research methods, techniques of clinical diagnosis, and psychotherapy strategies, followed by a one-year internship in an institutional setting. In contrast, a psychiatrist is a medical doctor who undergoes several years of specialized training in psychiatry after earning an M.D. degree. Of the two, only psychiatrists can prescribe medical treatments, such as drugs, in treating psychological disorders. However, clinical psychologists generally obtain a more intensive education on the psychological determinants of behavior problems and the methods of conducting research.

Clinical psychologists and psychiatrists may also differ somewhat in their perspectives about the causes of psychological problems and appropriate treatment for such difficulties (Kingsbury, 1987). For example, psychiatrists are more inclined to look for physical causes, such as abnormal brain chemistry or hormonal imbalances, and to use medical or biological therapies as remedies for disorders. In contrast, clinical psychologists tend to emphasize psychosocial causes, such as inappropriate learning, faulty attitudes, and disturbed interpersonal relationships, and to focus on psychotherapy as the best road to improvement. Exceptions to these generalizations are not uncommon, however, and clinical psychologists and psychiatrists sometimes meld their respective skills as they collaborate in the design and implementation of treatment strategies.

EDUCATIONAL AND SCHOOL PSYCHOLOGY   Many important discoveries of psychology have direct application to the educational process. **Educational psy-**

chology involves the study and application of learning and teaching methods. Psychologists in this field conduct research on ways to improve educational curricula, and they often help train teachers. They may work in primary or secondary schools, but more often they are found in a university's school of education.

School psychology encompasses work in elementary or secondary schools, dealing primarily with individual children, teachers, and parents in an effort to evaluate and resolve learning and emotional problems. They often administer and interpret personality, interest, and ability tests. School psychologists are a valuable resource both for troubled students and for concerned teachers trying to cope with the stresses of classroom problems.

INDUSTRIAL/ORGANIZATIONAL PSYCHOLOGY The field of **industrial/organizational (I/O) psychology** uses psychological concepts to make the workplace a more satisfying environment for both employees and management. I/O psychologists may work with businesses either as company employees or as consultants, designing programs to improve morale, increase job satisfaction, foster better communication within the corporation, enhance productivity, and increase workers' involvement in decision making. They are also frequently involved in designing job training programs and in selecting the most suitable people for a particular job.

ENGINEERING PSYCHOLOGY **Engineering psychology** (sometimes called human factors psychology) focuses on the creation of optimal relationships among people, the machines they operate, and the environments in which they work. For example, engineering psychologists have helped design the lighting and instrumentation within the cockpits of sophisticated aircraft to maximize pilot efficiency. These professionals have also been involved in America's space program, helping to develop optimal functional efficiency within the severely limited confines of spacecraft.

HEALTH PSYCHOLOGY In recent years there has been a mounting interest in achieving and maintaining good health, both physical and psychological. Psychologists have known for many years that emotional conditions such as stress or depression often play a major role in the development of physical ailments such as ulcers, skin diseases, stomach disorders, infectious diseases, and probably even cancer. Increasing evidence also indicates that psychological factors have a great deal to do with prevention of and recovery from illness. This growing body of data on the interaction between physical and psychological health factors has led to the emergence of a dynamic new area of specialization known as **health psychology.** In recognition of the importance of this new field of study, the National Institutes of Health (NIH) recently designated health psychology as a priority training area and allocated funds for developing training programs within psychology departments throughout the country.

Health psychologists are currently active in such diverse areas as assessing the psychological and physical effects of stress, developing programs to help people reduce stress in their lives, studying coping strategies for dealing with serious or catastrophic illness, evaluating the impact of psychological factors on diseases such as cancer and cardiovascular illness, devising ways to test people for susceptibility to disease, and seeking to identify the factors that motivate people to engage in health-threatening activities such as smoking, overeating, and

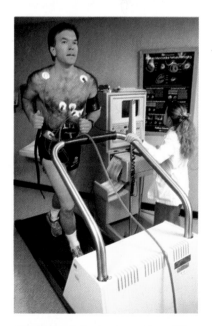

Health psychologists investigate how our behaviors such as smoking, lack of exercise, social isolation, and stress contribute to disease.

Jeffrey Dahmer, convicted of multiple murder in 1992. Dahmer mutilated and even ate selected parts of his victims.

undereating (Taylor, 1986, 1990). Throughout this text we will comment on the relationship between current research and theory and our health.

FORENSIC PSYCHOLOGY   **Forensic psychology** is another emerging specialty, and it works hand in hand with the legal, court, and correctional systems. Forensic psychologists assist police in a variety of ways, from developing personality profiles of criminal offenders to helping law-enforcement personnel understand problems like family conflict and substance abuse. They may also assist judges and parole officers in making decisions about the disposition of convicted offenders. The recent case of Jeffrey Dahmer who murdered, dismembered, and apparently ate selected body parts from numerous victims has attracted the attention of both the public and forensic psychologists. Before reading on consider how you might decide whether Dahmer was competent to stand trial or whether he was insane and didn't understand the nature of his crimes.

ARTIFICIAL INTELLIGENCE AND CONNECTIONISM   An emerging field that is fast capturing the interest of many psychologists is the specialty known as **artificial intelligence (AI)**. AI researchers attempt to develop models that simulate such complex human cognitive processes as perceiving stimuli, solving problems, learning, and making decisions (Churchland & Churchland, 1990; Searle, 1990; Waldrop, 1988). Encouraged by recent developments in this fast-growing subfield, AI theorists are hopeful that as they become more proficient in designing sophisticated computer models of cognitive processes they will achieve a better understanding of how we think, learn, and how we perceive our surroundings. AI has a practical side as well, evidenced by its successful application to such varied pursuits as the diagnosis of illness and the location of deposits of valuable resources such as oil (Waldrop, 1984; Winston & Prendergast, 1984).

Connectionism is a relatively new approach to studying complex human abilities like learning, problem solving, and perception. Like artificial intelligence, it too employs computer models to help solve these problems. However, connectionist researchers are attempting to design computer hardware that simulates the kinds of connections among neurons in the brain. These connectionist machines have proven to be much more powerful than their predecessors for certain kinds of tasks.

Computers are powerful tools for examining a variety of psychological phenomena. They have some limitations, however, particularly in some types of information-processing tasks. For instance, even a young child has no trouble identifying a tree in a picture of a farm scene, yet this same task presents a serious challenge to powerful computers. One reason for this is that the task of recognizing a tree requires knowledge of essentially every conceivable variation of what a tree can be, including myriad shapes and sizes as well as variations in leaves or needles, bark, color, seasonal phases, and so forth. For a typical computer to solve such a pattern-recognition task, it would need to have stored (memorized) a set of all possible solutions, and then be able to compare input data with this stored memory and quickly select the best possible solution. In this type of information processing, even the most sophisticated programs running on powerful computers cannot match the memorization and recollection capability of the human brain, which regularly and effortlessly conquers pattern recognition problems. (Abu-Mostafa & Psaltis, 1987, p. 88). Connectionist computers, however, have no difficulty with these kinds of perceptual and learning tasks where the set of all possible solutions is quite large or even undefined. They can be designed to learn about the necessary features of trees so they can identify them under many different situations.

Gary Kasparov, a world champion chess player, plays chess against the chess-playing computer program, Deep Thought. Sophisticated chess-playing computers can now beat the very best human players.

THE AMERICAN PSYCHOLOGICAL ASSOCIATION   During its brief history, psychology has grown by leaps and bounds. **The American Psychological Association (APA),** the major professional organization of psychologists in the United States, was founded in 1892 by 31 charter members. The APA now has almost 70,000 members, and there are countless numbers of professional psychologists who are not listed in its membership (American Psychological Association, 1988). As the APA's ranks have increased, so have the numbers of fields within the profession. There are some generalists, just as there are general practitioners in medicine. However, most psychologists find that as their careers evolve they become increasingly specialized in both their interests and professional activities.

A recent report by a committee commissioned by the APA expressed some concerns about the changing face of American psychology (Howard et al., 1986). The authors of this report noted that in recent years there has been a marked increase in the number of psychologists who obtain doctorates in applied areas such as clinical, counseling, and school psychology, coupled with a pronounced decline in doctorates in such research-oriented subfields as experimental, social, and personality psychology as well as biological psychology. Commensurate with this shift in interest toward more human service provider specializations, there has been a significant decline in the number of psychologists employed full-time in academic settings.

What is the impact of these changes? On the one hand, the greater number of psychologists working as clinicians has had the positive effect of helping meet growing demands for mental health services. However, there is also a somewhat unsettling side to these recent trends. The decline in both the number of psychologists trained in research-oriented specialties and in those who work in academic settings, where most research is conducted, coupled with evidence that individuals trained in clinical, counseling, and school psychology tend to spend little time conducting research (Gottfredson, 1987), suggests the possibility of a reduction in future research efforts. Though these changes may be cause for concern, it is unlikely that psychology will forsake its commitment to quality research in the rush to meet escalating demands for health care.

During the mid-1980s, serious consideration was given to a major reorganization of the structure and methods of operation of the APA in an effort to counteract a perceived shift in the emphasis of the APA toward the interests of independent health care practitioners and away from the interests of academic and scientifically oriented psychologists (Howard et al., 1987). This push to reemphasize psychology's scientific/research focus within the APA was ultimately defeated. However, the story did not end there, for the movement was influential in instigating a major splintering of the APA in 1988. Several thousand academic and research psychologists founded the American Psychological Society (APS), with the stated purpose of better representing the academic and research interests of psychology. This event reflects the tensions between the empirically based discipline of psychology and the applied aspects of psychology as a profession.

THE GOALS OF PSYCHOLOGY

Essentially all scientists, psychologists included, share the common goals of *understanding*, *predicting*, and *controlling* or influencing the phenomena that constitute the subject matter of their respective disciplines (Kimble, 1989). A biologist, for example, after first acquiring an understanding of how the AIDS virus invades a healthy body, might then seek to predict conditions under which infection is likely to occur, followed by efforts to control or influence the infectious process in a manner that minimizes transmission of the virus. Similarly, a psychologist might seek to understand the mechanisms whereby our psychological and physiological responses to stress increase our susceptibility to disease, in order to predict which of us are likely to develop coronary heart disease, hypertension, or other stress-related diseases. The psychologist might also try to apply this knowledge to influence or modify certain behaviors that make people susceptible to the ravages of stress.

While many of us accept the goals of using psychological knowledge to understand and predict behavior, the idea of applying psychology to control people's behavior is more controversial. What do you think of this goal? Is it a legitimate aim of psychology? Always? Sometimes? Never? Give some thought to this complex issue before reading on.

People often react with concern or skepticism to the notion that behavioral control is a legitimate goal of psychology, and indeed, it would be misleading to imply that all the knowledge acquired through psychological research leads directly to behavioral control. Nevertheless, psychologists have been able to influence behavior under a wide variety of situations. For example, understanding the processes and predicting the circumstances under which prejudices are formed has resulted in the development of educational programs which have reduced the formation and expression of prejudicial behavior in some schoolchildren (see Chapter 17). Similarly, knowledge about the psychobiological causes of certain severe psychological disorders has provided the impetus of developing various therapies effective in controlling some disruptive symptoms, as we see in Chapter 15.

People seldom object to such examples of legitimate and helpful behavioral control. However, there are many gray areas where the wielding of psychological influence over various behaviors is more controversial, raising important questions. For instance, is it appropriate for industrial psychologists to manipulate work conditions in a manner known to increase worker productivity, or for forensic/clinical psychologists to subject imprisoned sexual offenders to extremely aversive or negative stimuli in order reduce inappropriate sexual arousal patterns? Such questions suggest that the pursuit of the goal of controlling behavior is often modified or tempered by complex ethical issues.

Although psychology in its relatively short history has managed to accumulate in-depth knowledge about many important areas of human behavior, a vast array of questions remains to be answered. Actually, all science never really finishes its pursuit of the previously outlined goals. However, most disciplines are much further along in their journey toward understanding, prediction, and control than the infant science of psychology. Nevertheless, this incompleteness of knowledge is in many ways parent to much of the excitement, anticipation, and vitality of contemporary psychology.

Most of our present understanding of behavior and mental processes must be evaluated cautiously, with a healthy realization that little in this developing discipline should be considered absolute. Thus, for the most part, our understanding of varied behavioral phenomena is couched in the language of theories. Theories are tentative attempts to organize and fit into a logical explanatory framework all of the relevant data or facts scientists have observed regarding certain phenomena. For example, psychologists who study sleep and dreaming often formulate theories about why we need sleep or why we dream. Some dream researchers have noted that people spend more time dreaming when they are experiencing relationship conflicts, problems at work, or other emotionally stressful situations. These and similar observations have generated a theory of dreaming that views dreams as a relatively safe, low-stress way to deal with problems that occur during working hours.

Good psychological **theories** generate predictions, or *hypotheses*, which are assumptions about how people should respond under certain conditions assuming the overall theory is correct. Hypotheses can be subjected to **empirical tests** in which scientists manipulate conditions or behaviors and observe the results. Thus a psychologist who adheres to the theory that dreaming allows people to deal with emotional problems might set up an experiment to test the hypothesis that people who are presented with waking state problems and then deprived of nighttime dreaming will be less likely to suggest reasonable solutions the following morning than are other subjects who are allowed a normal night's rest. (See Chapter 5 for a discussion of research supporting this hypothesis.) We say more about hypothesis testing in Chapter 2.

We have considered in some detail the history, scope, and goals of the science of psychology. In Chapter 2, we look more closely at some of the methods psychologists have developed for exploring the many questions posed by the richly varied behaviors of humans and other animals. An appreciation of the methods used by psychologists will help you to evaluate critically the numerous facts and opinions presented throughout this book.

SUMMARY

DEFINITION OF PSYCHOLOGY

1. Formally defined, psychology is the scientific study of the behavior of humans and other animals.
2. The theories and facts of psychology emerge from the careful application of scientific methods.
3. Psychology includes the study of animal behavior as well as human behavior. Nonhuman animal research offers several advantages, including providing a simpler model, the benefits associated with greater control afforded by nonhuman subjects, ethical considerations, time and cost factors, and the advantages of short life spans in assessing genetic contributions to behavior.

PSYCHOLOGY'S HISTORY

4. Psychology has roots in both philosophy, which posed many of the important questions, and physiology, which provided the tools for careful, scientific examination of these questions.

5. The establishment of Wilhelm Wundt's laboratory at the University of Leipzig in 1879 marks the formal beginnings of psychology as a scientific discipline.

6. Wundt employed the methods of introspection and experimental self-observation to pursue what he considered to be the task of psychology—the systematic study of the structure of the conscious adult mind.

7. Edward Titchener, who brought Wundt's brand of psychology to America, introduced the label structuralism to describe his attempt to develop a kind of mental chemistry by breaking experience down into its basic elements or structures.

8. Structuralism soon gave way to the more practical psychology of William James, who emphasized the functional, practical nature of the mind. His conception of psychology's proper task became known as functionalism.

9. During the period when psychology was struggling to become more scientific and objective, Sigmund Freud traveled a different road as he developed his highly subjective psychoanalytic approach with its emphasis on the unconscious mind and repressed irrational urges and drives.

10. In the first few decades of this century a new force in psychology emerged called behaviorism. This approach, championed by John B. Watson, defined the task of psychology as one of simply observing the relationship between environmental events (stimuli) and an organism's response to them. Modern behav-

iorism continues to be a powerful force within psychology today.

11. At the time behaviorism was catching hold in America, a group of German psychologists decried the principles of both structuralism and behaviorism. They argued that it was a mistake to try to break psychological processes into basic components like elementary sensations or stimuli and responses because the whole of an experience is different than the sum of its parts. This approach became known as Gestalt psychology.

12. Humanistic psychology de-emphasizes the impact of both stimulus-response events and unconscious processes in determining human behavior. Instead, it focuses on the role of free choice and our ability to make conscious rational choices about how we live our lives.

CONTEMPORARY PSYCHOLOGY

13. In recent years the emergence of cognitive psychology as an important force in psychology has led to a refocusing of attention on processes such as thinking, language, problem solving, and creativity.

14. Two other important areas in psychology that are achieving increasing prominence in the field are connectionism, which uses computers to help develop models of cognitive processes and learning, and biological psychology, the study of the relationship between behavior and physiological events that occur within the brain and the rest of the nervous system.

15. Both clinical and counseling psychologists are involved in the diagnosis and treatment of psychological problems. Individuals specializing in counseling psychology tend to focus on less serious problems of ad-

justment than their counterparts in clinical psychology.

16. While psychologists in every area of specialization usually conduct experiments at some point in their careers, individuals who classify themselves as experimental psychologists devote their primary efforts to conducting research.

17. Biological psychologists study the relationship between physiological processes and behavior.

18. Educational psychologists focus their efforts on the study and application of learning and teaching methods.

19. School psychologists work in elementary or secondary schools where they seek to evaluate and resolve learning and emotional problems of students.

20. Industrial/organizational psychology is concerned with using psychological concepts to make the workplace a more satisfying environment for both employees and management.

21. Engineering psychologists focus on creating optimal relationships among people, the machines they operate, and the environments in which they work.

22. Developmental psychologists investigate the factors that influence development and shape behavior throughout the life cycle.

23. Social psychologists seek to understand the impact of social environments and social processes on the individual.

24. Personality psychologists focus on exploring the uniqueness of the individual and describing the key elements that provide the foundation for human personalities.

25. Health psychologists are interested in behavioral contributions to disease like smoking, drinking, lack of exercise, social isolation, and stress.

26. Forensic psychology is the study of criminal behavior and the law.

THE GOALS OF PSYCHOLOGY

27. The goals of psychology include understanding, predicting, and controlling behavior.

28. For the most part, our understanding of behavioral phenomena is expressed in the language of theories. Theories are tentative attempts to organize and fit into a logical framework all relevant data or facts regarding certain phenomena.

29. Good psychological theories generate hypotheses, which are assumptions about how people should respond under certain conditions assuming the overall theory is correct.

TERMS & CONCEPTS

psychology
scientific method
structuralism
functionalism
behaviorism
Gestalt psychology
humanistic psychology
cognitive psychology
connectionism
biological psychology
American Psychological Association (APA)
counseling psychology
clinical psychology

experimental psychology
educational psychology
school psychology
industrial/organizational (I/O) psychology
engineering psychology
developmental psychology
social psychology
personality psychology
forensic psychology
health psychology
artificial intelligence (AI)
American Psychological Society (APS)

PERSPECTIVE #1

Dr. A. Charles Catania

A. Charles Catania, professor of psychology at the University of Maryland, Baltimore County, is a behavior analyst whose major concern is with the origins and function of verbal behavior. In 1961, he received his Ph.D. in Experimental Psychology from Harvard University, where he was an NSF fellow. As a postdoctoral research fellow, he ran B.F. Skinner's pigeon laboratory until 1962. Dr. Catania is a fellow and former president of Division 25 of the APA. He has written more than 100 articles and book chapters on topics in the experimental analysis of behavior, including learning, reinforcement schedules, and verbal behavior. His text *Learning* (1992) is now in its fifth edition.

PERSPECTIVE #1 ----------------------------------- PSYCHOLOGICAL EXPLANATION

Dr. A. Charles Catania

Q: Dr. Catania, what do you see as the main differences between the cognitive and behavioral explanations of behavior?

A: In cognitive science, as I see it, a lot of the treatment is concerned with things that the cognitive psychologist calls processing. Some cognitive psychologists are studying how processing works. They stimulate an organism and it responds in some way, but some of their work is also very concerned with inner theoretical events that occur between the stimulus and response. I worry about those kinds of approaches leaving out the role of the environment or the consequences of behavior. One of the other problems that I have with cognitive psychology is that behavior is often presented as if it was really not a subject matter that was worthy of studying for its own sake, but it was an index of something else. The idea is that we're not interested in behavior because behavior is important, but because it's going to tell us something about some kind of inner stuff. And it's hard to imagine what we would say or do about that inner stuff if we didn't also include in it the way in which it makes contact with our activities in the world.

24

PERSPECTIVE #2

Dr. Stephen M. Kosslyn

Stephen M. Kosslyn is professor of psychology at Harvard University. He received his graduate education at Stanford University, where he was involved in research using ideas and concepts from artificial intelligence. His current work involves using techniques such as PET and MRI to map brain activity during various tasks including mental imagery and higher-level perception. He hopes to gather information that can help psychologists understand how the mind arises from activity of the brain. He is also working to apply results of this work to understanding migraines, obsessive-compulsive disorder, and the mechanisms that underlie placebo effects.

One of the central ideas in the work of B. F. Skinner has all kinds of implications for this question. Skinner wrote a paper in 1945 in which he was concerned about the philosophy of science, how people come to know things, and he asked how we could learn the words for our private feelings, our private emotions. How could a group of people agree on the vocabulary for that sort of thing? Skinner suggested some ways in which that could happen. Suppose you wanted to teach a word for a certain kind of pain, like a sharp pain or a dull pain. This is supposed to be a private sensation and psychologists are interested in the nature of these private things like sensations. Skinner proposed that the only way in which a verbal community could come up with a consistent language for private things was for the verbal community to base it on public behavior. Therefore, we only can learn about the ways of talking about private things through the public terms for them. So, for example, if you're hurting, that's a private thing. Nobody else can feel your pain. How can we teach people when it's appropriate to say "I'm hurt"? We do it by learning words for public things like parts of the body. When a child falls down, scrapes an elbow, or the child is crying, these are public kinds of things and the parents can teach the children the public words. So all of our language begins with what's public. We learn words like "I'm angry, I'm happy, I'm afraid" in large part on the basis of seeing how people act and seeing what kind of situations they're in. In my courses I occasionally arrange an experiment in the classroom. For example, I unexpectedly come in the classroom with

PERSPECTIVE #1

a bunch of exam books and start handing them out. The students are wondering whether I got the dates mixed up and I'm giving them an exam. Then I tell them to write down their feelings when they saw me hand out these books. What they almost invariably write down is not anything that's going on inside their skin. They'll begin telling me what they thought. For example, "I saw you walking in the room and I thought that you were about to give an exam, and I wasn't expecting an exam on this day"; I knew I wasn't prepared," and so forth. You ask people to describe feelings and it turns out most answers are descriptions of the situation. So if you actually ask what people do when they describe their feelings, you discover that they start with the public stuff. And so that's the starting place—the public—for the way I think about a whole bunch of things. The thing about cognitive psychology is many of the terms that are involved in thinking about what goes on with people's behavior are words that have their origins in that language of private stuff, feeling and so forth. Therefore, if you say those are the starting places, those are the central parts of our science, what it means is you're starting from something that's very derivative. I would say start from the behavior and then we'll get to that stuff. The central difference, between behavior analysts—it's so easy to overgeneralize—and some cognitive psychologists is that they see the fundamental elements of their science as being in those kinds of mechanisms while behavior analysts start with everything in the public and then look for ways to deal with it, instead of starting from the inside and trying to work out.

Q: Do you believe that concepts such as "mind" can be explained by psychologists, or should references to mind be avoided in explanations of behavior?

A: At one time, psychologists used to talk about the contrast between the mind and behavior. It goes all the way back to the old introspection in psychology. When people talked about the mind, they often argued as if the mind existed in a different kind of physical dimension. It had special properties, and behavior reflected the mind. What got left out of those ways of thinking was the notion that a word like "mind" is a word that's in everyday vocabulary and it used to be a verb. If we look back in the evolution of the word "mind," people used to think of children who were supposed to mind their parents. And we say things like, "Do you mind?" And one of the things that's happened in psychology is that when we look at the evolution of the words that we use for these things we call cognitive processes, we tend to forget that they originated in the everyday language in the sort of casual ways in which people talked about things. Somehow, these terms that started out as casual—everyday—interaction kinds of words got elevated to the position where they had this special status. And the part of cognitive psychology that I guess troubled some behavioral folks is the part that has taken everyday words and elevated them to being explanatory without worrying enough about how these words originated in the everyday vocabulary. An analogy can be found in physics. Words like "force" and "work" were everyday words, and people still use these words. But a physicist uses the word "work" in a technical sense, which is very different from the way a lay person uses the word. Therefore, there may be some problems if we take these words from the everyday vocabulary and try to use them in a technical vocabulary without really worrying about what the differences are.

PERSPECTIVE #1

Q: Can psychology give us any clearer insights into the relationship between the brain and what many people refer to as "the mind"?

A: Clear ones? I'd be surprised. I find it interesting that more and more students seem to use the words "mind" and "brain" almost interchangeably. That's really a curious thing that's happening in our culture. I also think that most cognitive psychologists do not think of the cognitive stuff as being non-physical, as a different dimension of things, and that all of these processes are parts of things that work in the physical world. They are not identifiable with physical structures, in the same way that a computer program is not identifiable with any particular structure. Computer programs could be the printed lines of the program, or they could be the memory in a computer memory core, or they could be the magnetic charges on a hard disk. So a computer program has a real existence, but you can't identify it with particular physical structures. But it's still part of the physical world; it's a structure in the physical world. The structure, though, can manifest itself in a lot of different ways. So I don't see a problem with identifying structures. So the mind/brain thing doesn't necessarily imply two different levels of reality or something like that. Even with respect to words like "soul," "mind," and so forth, those words also come from people observing themselves, having certain kinds of experiences. And therefore, the same kinds of arguments I made about the origins of the verbal communities setting up the language for private events holds with respect to words like that. How did people learn to talk about their souls and things of this sort? I think it's important to ask those kinds of questions. Now you could say, well, somehow this was given to us independently of any physical things in the world, as an unnatural phenomenon. Or you could say that these are all parts of our interacting with things in the world and with a special kind of social environment in which we teach each other things, and that one way to deal with those kinds of concepts is to ask where they came from. We don't have all the answers to those kinds of things and I'm willing to say there's a lot we don't know. But I think we've always been most successful by assuming that, by studying natural phenomena, we can find out more about them. If they are non-physical phenomena, and have properties that you can never touch or feel or identify in any other way, then how could you ever study them?

Q: Many cognitive psychologists are involved in research which involves computer simulations of these internal processes. How useful do you feel such simulations are for understanding behavior?

A: Sometimes they're fascinating. Sometimes they can show you the way things work. Computer simulation isn't necessarily the only thing that goes on in cognitive science; it's one of many methods, and computer simulations can often tell you about how things work. But, on the other hand, it somebody has come up with a computer model of human memory and has done a few experiments and shows there are a few things in some limited areas of human memory that look a little bit like some things that happen inside computers, that doesn't necessarily mean that we've now explained what goes on in human memory. It's a very elaborate metaphor. The computer, you know, is a metaphor for the way in which the brain works. And the trouble with that sort of thing is—it's not that you want to discourage people from having good ideas and having hunches; very

PERSPECTIVE #1

"The concern is that sometimes cognitive approaches worry too much about things that have no easy connection to behavior."

often good things follow from that—if you start taking those things too seriously, you end up forgetting that what you're dealing with is real processes. You get carried away with the metaphorical things and begin studying artificial systems instead of real ones and failing to make the connection to the things that happen in the real world. The best cognitive psychologists don't do that—they're pretty careful about always grounding things in their data—but the concern is that sometimes cognitive approaches worry too much about things that have no easy connection to behavior.

Q: Do you think we will eventually be able to simulate human intelligence in a computer, or do you see inherent limitations in that?

A: If you did a computer simulation of chess playing—and computers do that pretty damn well nowadays—the problem is that you could end up with computer simulations that do a very, very good job of playing chess, so much so that they challenge and maybe soon will always be able to beat even the strongest grand masters. But we know that the way chess programs work is different from the way human chess players do. So simulations don't necessarily tell us all we need to know. They can give us good ideas, and there are ways in which simulations can produce something that resembles human behavior. But just producing something that behaves in what superficially seems the same way doesn't mean that it works the same way in general. The real processes may even be fundamentally different. So the problems are more than just finding that, for example, some mathematical model produces the same data that one gets in several different kinds of experiments. And in psychology we're nowhere near producing models that have the breadth of generality that models in physics do. But behavioral systems usually have much simpler kinds of constraints, and the degrees of freedom they have are much, much larger. So the message that comes out of computer simulations of things like chess playing and other cognitive processes is that, in spite of the tremendous power of the computer, everything about the ways those programs work suggests that they don't work in the same way the human chess player does when playing that game. So we really have to be very careful about the limitations of models that simply behave in a way that seem to correspond with behavior. They certainly don't tell us that human behavior is produced in the same way.

PERSPECTIVE #2

PSYCHOLOGICAL EXPLANATION

Dr. Stephen M. Kosslyn

Q: Dr. Kosslyn, do you believe concepts such as "mind" can be explained by psychologists, or should references to mind be avoided in explanations of behavior?

A: I think the notion of the mind is a bit ambiguous. There are two senses in which the term "mind" is used in psychology. One sense refers to mental activity such as remembering or perceiving or imagining or using language—things that can be understood in terms of information processing. The other sense of word "mind" is phenomenology, the life of the mind, experience. I think those sorts of explanations that rely on that notion of mind are to be avoided. If we are talking about the first sense of mind, psychologists can and should address such questions. If we are talking about the second sense, I think we are better off not evoking such fuzzy ideas at this point.

Q: Does anything in psychology prepare us to see if there is a relationship between the brain and what many people refer to as "the mind"?

A: The first sense of the term "mind," as mental function or mental activity, is just what the brain does. In that sense, the mind is what the brain does. Just like hands stroke and grasp, what minds do is process information. So what we're doing is talking about the brain, but in a slightly different way. If you're talking about a building, you can talk about the architecture or you can talk about the bricks and boards. Well, that's parallel to talking about what goes on in the head. You can talk about the function of the physical substrate—that is, not the arches and doorways but, in this case, processing information—or about the physical substrates themselves. So there is a direct relationship between brain activity and mental activity. The connection between phenomenology—that is, the subjective experience of how things feel—and brain activity is really murky. I don't think anyone has anything very clear to say about that at this point.

Q: Some behaviorists feel there is an imprecision in language in the cognitive explanations of behavior which limit the usefulness of what other researchers can draw from the research projects being conducted. Do you see this as a problem?

A: My suspicion is that they are echoing some of Skinner's complaints of the cognitive psychology of 20 years ago, prior to serious computer modeling. If you tie your theorizing to computer modeling, you get extremely precise language that is quite mathematical. I would question whether people who say this are really up on what's happening now, or whether they are just carrying prejudice along from previous days, which is my suspicion.

Q: How useful are computer simulations in explaining or allowing us to posit human behavior? Are they sophisticated enough to allow us to draw from them inferences on internal processes?

A: One must make a distinction between a theory and a model. The thing that's on a computer is a model and it's only useful insofar as it incorporates principles that are part of a theory. The theory should be doing all the work. In a way, the model is like a notepad when you're doing arithmetic that's too complicated to keep in your head. To the extent that you have a good theory, the model makes good predictions. There are plenty of examples of such uses of computer models. You can go back and look at the McClelland and Rumelhart's work on reading and word perception. They make subtle and elegant predictions based on their simulation models. There are many examples of that kind of work these days. So to the extent that there's a set of principles behind the model, and there's a well-defined domain for the model—a clear idea of what it is you're trying to explain—then sure, there is already much evidence that you can use such models to explain some aspects of thinking.

Q: Do you think we will eventually be able to simulate human intelligence in a computer or do you see inherent limitations in that?

PERSPECTIVE #2

"If you think that the brain is a machine, then why shouldn't we be able to build a machine that can eventually act like the brain?"

A: There's been a lot of discussion about this. The answer will only be obvious once it's done. If it's never done, we won't know whether it was just attempted the wrong way or whether it simply can't be done. But if such efforts are successful, then we'll know the answer for sure. In terms of my own intuition, I see absolutely no reason we can't build machines that are intelligent. I've never encountered a counterargument that I thought held any water at all. If you think that the brain is a machine, then why shouldn't we be able to build a machine that can eventually act like the brain? That doesn't mean you wire it all in advance. You may have it learn, as most all neural network models to today but, essentially, it's a mechanism. So I don't see any reason why one couldn't build intelligent machines.

Q: Have you done such work yourself?

A: Yes. If you look at the book *Wet Mind*, which I wrote with Oliver Koenig, it summarizes a lot of it in there. We've done various kinds of simulation work. The behaviorists probably shudder at the thought that one can discover enough about mental imagery that one could program a computer to mimic what people do when they use mental imagery, but we've done so. And, moreover, one can do brain scans of people while they engage in different sorts of mental activity and identify specific types of processes with specific brain areas.

Q: Can you tell us about some of your findings of your research into mental imagery?

A: Some of my work, like that of many other researchers, shows that objects in mental images behave in ways that are similar to objects in the real world. For example, if you close your eyes and scan across a mental image of an object, the further you have to scan, the longer it takes. If you imagine that you're seeing an object far in the distance, it will take you longer to answer questions about it; you have to mentally "squint" or "zoom in" on it. There's also a lot of work studying how images are formed. That is, when I ask you a question like, "Does a German shepherd dog have pointed ears?" you visualize the dog's head. You may not be aware of it, but you're probably building up the image of the dog's head a part at a time. It takes more time—very small amounts, but more time nonetheless—for each additional part that you have to place on the image. We've studied the process of putting of the parts, showing that the left and right cerebral hemispheres have different strategies for putting together parts to form an image. The left more effectively uses categories of spatial relations prototypes of objects. The right is better at using specific sorts of spatial relationships and specific examples of shapes.

Q: Can you describe some of your current research that might have implications in this area?

A: We are doing a lot of work using various brain scanning techniques where we're showing that parts of your brain that are involved in vision are, in fact, active when your eyes are closed, forming mental images. As we vary the way you visualize an object, we can actually see the way that the activation in your brain is moved around.

Q: Is there still a large difference between the ways the cognitive and behavioral schools of thought would describe behavior, or do you see them coming together?

PERSPECTIVE #2

A: I do see them coming together, but I still think there's a critical difference between them: the cognitive explanations rely upon characterizations of internal processes whereas the behavioral ones do not. The big difference is the cognitive psychologist tries to infer computations that are going on between the stimulus and response. The behavioral explanations skip that step. They try to relate the stimulus situation directly to the kind of behaviors that are evoked. The point of contact is that behavioral explanations have gotten much more sophisticated. So they've developed principles—for example, the Matching Law that my colleague Richard Herrnstein developed—that describe systematic relationships between input and output. And the principles are of a form that lend themselves to computational analysis. So we can start thinking about how those principles describe the inner workings of the head. They're not just principles like the original work on reinforcement schedules, which are simple descriptions of relations between input, and response, and reinforcement relations. So there is a big difference in that cognitivist, as the word implies, focus on what goes on in the head, and behaviorists, as the word implies, don't. But they are coming together because the behaviorists are really more sophisticated in the way they think about behavior and describe it, and the kind of principles they are formulating are making direct contact with events that are being posited in the head.

Q: Do you see the coming together of cognitive psychology and behaviorism as portending a new revolution in psychology, a synthesis of those views?

A: Yes. It's already happening in the context of something called cognitive neuroscience, where people are studying animals like the aplysia, a kind of sea slug, and working out in detail the synapses and the particular neurons that are involved in learning. They look at behaviorist phenomena, conditioning phenomena, and they're working out the neural circuits that are responsible for them. I see that as sort of the ultimate synthesis of cognitive and behavioral work. Some of the behaviorists aren't going to like that because they've always said they want a special science focused on behavior, and they don't like the idea of being reduced to physiology. But I think it's a mistake to think of it as being reduced to physiology because what the research is really doing is describing how these neurons function, which is not the same thing as describing neurons.

Q: Do you have any closing comments you'd like to share with our readers?

A: Well, one thing. Because of the new technologies, like those used in brain scanning, the ability to record from individual neurons in simple systems like sea slugs, and so forth, there are huge breakthroughs just right around the corner. It's an extremely exciting time to get involved in psychology. If you really want to know answers to questions philosophers and other thinkers have worried about for centuries, we may be able to provide them shortly. Anybody who is really fascinated by these kinds of questions has a golden opportunity to get involved in helping to discover the answers.

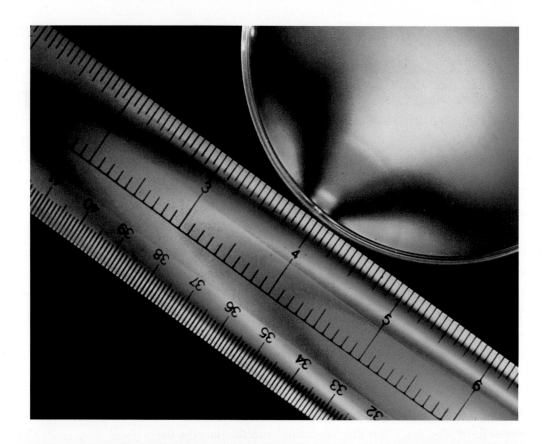

CHAPTER 2

The Methods of Psychology

THE SCIENTIFIC METHOD AND BEHAVIOR

The Purpose of Psychological Research

RESEARCH METHODS

Nonexperimental Research Methods
Experimental Research Methods
Ethics in Psychological Experiments
Ethical Guidelines for Research

STATISTICAL CONCEPTS FOR RESEARCH

Descriptive Statistics
Inferential Statistics
Evaluating Opinions, Beliefs, and
Scientific Evidence

*E*xamine the following statements and decide whether they are typically true or false. Base your conclusions on both your personal experiences and your assumptions about human behavior. If you want to examine any of these questions more fully later, chapter references are provided for each.

- Sleepwalking most often occurs during a dreaming phase of sleep (Chapter 5).
- Under hypnosis, people can perform feats of physical strength or mental prowess that they could not otherwise perform (Chapter 5).
- Punishment is not as effective as reinforcement in bringing about change in behavior (Chapter 6).
- Humans are the only organisms that use symbolic language to communicate (Chapter 10).
- Couples who cohabit (live together) before marriage generally experience happier and more stable marriages than couples who do not live together before getting married (Chapter 12).
- Evidence suggests that the wide variation in human intelligence is due more to environmental factors than to heredity (Chapter 13).
- You are more likely to be assisted in an emergency if there are numerous bystanders than if there are only one or two (Chapter 17).
- The most beneficial way to treat severe mental disorders is to have people relive traumatic childhood experiences through psychoanalysis (Chapter 16).

Most students evaluate all or most of the preceding statements incorrectly when they first begin studying psychology; you may also be surprised to find that they are all false. Indeed, many of the things people presume to be true about behavior are fallacies. To safeguard against the fallibility of common sense, psychologists have developed a number of tools or methods for systematically collecting data about behavior. These scientific methods have disproven many widely held beliefs about human behavior; they have also verified some other common assumptions. In this chapter we discuss the reasons for psychological research and outline the methods that psychologists use.

THE SCIENTIFIC METHOD AND BEHAVIOR

Chapter 1 discussed an important research finding of the 1950s, but it did not tell you the story of how that finding was made. James Olds and a fellow researcher at McGill University, Peter Milner, were investigating the ways in which electrical stimulation of the brain affected exploratory behavior in rats. As they implanted electrodes in the rats' brains, one electrode was placed incorrectly, and Olds and Milner stumbled onto an important finding (Olds, 1956). When electrodes were placed in sites within the hypothalamus and the septal areas (discussed in Chapter 3), the rats seemingly could not get enough stimulation. They preferred stimulation of these brain areas even to food when they were hungry. This unexpected finding led to a series of experiments with animals and humans that clearly indicated that there are pleasure centers within the brain.

THE PURPOSE OF PSYCHOLOGICAL RESEARCH

Although some psychological studies have their origins in serendipity, or a lucky discovery such as this one, Olds and Milner's situation is hardly typical. Most psychological research is carefully planned and conducted with a specific end in mind. In this section we look at three of the most common reasons why psychologists conduct research: to test a hypothesis, to solve a problem, and to confirm findings of previous research.

BASIC RESEARCH: RESEARCH TO TEST A HYPOTHESIS

A **hypothesis** is a statement proposing the existence of a relationship between variables. Hypotheses are typically offered as tentative explanations for relationships or events, and they are often designed to be tested by research. For example, a clinical psychologist who notes an unusual number of obese individuals among clients she has treated for depression and anxiety disorders might hypothesize that excess weight increases people's susceptibility to certain emotional disturbances.

Hypotheses frequently emerge from psychologists' observations of behavior or from the results of previous investigations. For example, psychologists Robert Hicks and Eliot Garcia (1987) noted that people often complain about not sleeping well when they are under stress, an observation consistent with previous research reports linking insomnia to the stressful effects of anxiety and worry (Kales et al., 1984). This information prompted Hicks and Garcia to hypothesize that during periods of high stress people sleep less than normal, while during periods of low stress they increase their sleep time. To test this hypothesis they asked a group of college students to keep diaries of sleep and stress levels for a four-month period. All subjects maintained a daily record of overall level of stress and total sleep duration (including naps). Consistent with their hypothesis, Hicks and Garcia found that sleep was reduced significantly during periods of high stress, and increased during intervals of low stress.

APPLIED RESEARCH: RESEARCH TO SOLVE A PROBLEM

A second reason to conduct research is to find a solution to a problem. While some applied research is initiated to address specific human problems, not all applied research starts out with this goal. For example, results from basic research often lead to solutions to problems even though this was not the original intent. Quite often basic research helps us understand "normal" behavior and function and leads to procedures that allow for the assessment of abnormal or impaired behavior. This is exactly how Smith and Langolf (1981) discovered that exposure to low levels of mercury in certain chemical industries was neurotoxic to workers.

Although exposure to certain chemicals has long been suspected to cause certain diseases and possibly impairments in behavior, the identification of subtle behavioral deficits following chemical exposure has been difficult. This is either because the behavioral measures used to assess performance are too insensitive to detect behavioral deficits or, quite possibly, because people exposed to toxic chemicals gradually adjust to these deficits, making them even more difficult to find. The assessment of behavioral changes produced by drugs and environmental toxins is of utmost importance to human welfare, and procedures used in basic research have proven valuable in identifying them. By using a well understood memory-scanning procedure, Smith and Langolf found clear signs of memory impairment in workers exposed to mercury. In addition, this impairment increased corresponding to increased levels of mercury in workers' urine. These impairments were not previously identified by the workers' job performance or by other methods of psychological testing. In this case basic research in human memory provided psychologists with sensitive methods to detect subtle changes in performance caused by toxic chemical exposure.

In other cases applied research sets out to solve a particular problem. In the last several years increasing attention has been given to the relationship between stress in our lives and our ability to ward off disease. While stress has long been suspected to play a role in diseases such as heart disease, little evidence supported its role in infectious diseases (colds and flus) and cancer. Recently, however, studies have shown that stress can directly suppress the immune response making us more susceptible to disease as well as making it more difficult to fight existing diseases such as cancer (Kiecolt-Glaser & Glaser, 1988). Applied research conducted by psychologists and other scientists is now helping us to understand how stress affects our immune system and how we can learn to manage stress to reduce these debilitating effects. We will have more to say about this research in Chapter 9.

REPLICATION RESEARCH: RESEARCH TO CONFIRM PREVIOUS FINDINGS

Another reason for conducting research is to verify previous findings. When psychologists publish new research findings, they typically publish details about their work so that others may repeat the experiment to verify their results. This replication of prior research is the backbone of good science. Sometimes an especially controversial experiment is repeated in laboratories all over the world. This repetition occurred many years ago when researcher James McConnell (1962) published a study suggesting that memory could be transferred from one organism to another by cannibalism (that is, one organism eating the other)! This amazing experiment generated countless replication efforts, some successful and others not (Gaito, 1974). Because the results of these follow-up investigations were inconsistent, and most laboratories failed to find a transfer effect, psychologists have abandoned this line of research.

In many cases, the results of replication studies are less ambiguous. For example, a number of studies conducted over 30 years ago revealed that *identical twins* (siblings with identical genes) raised in different environments are more similar in intelligence as measured by IQ scores than are *fraternal twins* (siblings born at the same time whose genes are not identical) who are raised in the same environment (Erlenmeyer-Kimling & Jarvik, 1963). These early findings met with considerable criticism from a number of psychologists, particularly those who believed that environment is more important then heredity in shaping human intelligence. As a result, numerous replication studies were conducted. A sizable number of these more recent studies have confirmed the early findings (Henderson, 1982; Plomin & Defries, 1980), and because of these successful replications, most psychologists consider the IQ data obtained from twin studies to be reliable. However, not all psychologists interpret the data in the same way. (See Chapter 13 for a discussion of the relative impact of heredity and environment on tested intelligence.)

Replication is an important part of all scientific research, not just psychological research. This is well illustrated in a highly publicized report in March of 1989 by two physicists (Fleischmann and Pons) who claimed to have discovered a process for cold fusion. This report excited the scientific world with both suspicion and hope. An inexpensive cold fusion procedure could theoretically solve worldwide energy problems with a clean unlimited energy source. On the other hand, since previous attempts to demonstrate fusion required more energy than they produced many scientists were quite skeptical of these reports. As you may recall, replication efforts were initiated by scientists all over the world and within a few months most agreed that the process observed by Fleischmann and Pons was not cold fusion but rather some other chemical reaction.

Replication is important because the results of a study can vary considerably depending on experimental conditions and the research method used. As we see in the following section, psychologists use a number of techniques to collect data, and a specific research method may not always be appropriate for a specific problem.

RESEARCH METHODS

As we learned in Chapter 1, the goals of psychological research are to understand behavior (explain its causes) and, hopefully, to predict and possibly control the circumstances under which certain behaviors are likely to occur. Although a researcher may ultimately be interested in accomplishing all of these goals, they often require different research methods. For example, a researcher interested in understanding the role of aggression in children's play might begin by carefully observing children at play in a variety of natural settings. Later, the investigator might test some hypotheses arising from those observations by modifying the setting or circumstances in specific ways. For instance, does denying children access to favored toys increase their tendency to become more aggressive? This kind of research might reveal a certain cause-and-effect relationship between a specific condition (toy removal) and aggression, allowing the researcher to predict circumstances under which aggression is likely to occur.

Psychologists use a number of methods to study behavior, ranging from measuring behavior in highly controlled laboratory environments to producing detailed case studies of specific individuals. Other research methods include conducting surveys based on questionnaires or interviews, observing behavior in a natural setting, and assessing statistical relationships between two traits, events, or behaviors. For example, is there a relationship between the amount or intensity of exercise and stress levels?

Table 2.1 summarizes the major research methods used by psychologists. Each of these strategies has advantages or disadvantages for investigating different types of questions about behavior. We begin by discussing methods which involve the least control over circumstances surrounding behavior and progress through more highly controlled methods. We will also show how some of these methods have been used to understand the relationship between alcohol consumption and sexual behavior.

TABLE 2.1 *A Summary of Research Methods*

METHOD	BRIEF DESCRIPTION	ADVANTAGES	LIMITATIONS
Experimental Method	Subjects are confronted with specific stimuli under precisely controlled conditions. Researchers using this method directly manipulate a particular set of conditions (independent variable), then observe the effect on behavior (dependent variable).	Design of laboratory experiments provides control over relevant variables and opportunities to draw conclusions about cause-and-effect relationships.	Artificial nature of the laboratory setting, which may influence subjects' behaviors, and the fact that some questions posed by psychologists do not lend themselves to experimental investigation.
Surveys	A representative group of people are questioned,	Allow researchers to obtain information from more people than it is practical	Demographic and sex bias, improperly worded questions that bias responses,

TABLE 2.1   *A Summary of Research Methods (Continued)*

METHOD	BRIEF DESCRIPTION	ADVANTAGES	LIMITATIONS
Surveys *(continued)*	views or written questionnaires, about their behaviors and attitudes	to study in the laboratory. Also may require less investment of time and financial resources than laboratory research.	and a tendency to provide only limited insights about factors that contribute to behaviors and attitudes of specific individuals.
Observational Method	Researchers observe their subjects as they go about their usual activities, which often take place in a natural setting.	Often provides a wealth of information which may generate hypotheses for further research in a more controlled environment. Also, there are some clear advantages to seeing and recording behavior firsthand instead of relying either on subjective reports of past experiences (surveys) or on the possibly biased behaviors occurring in artificial laboratory settings.	Subjects' behavior may be altered by the presence of an observer. Furthermore, the reliability of recorded observations may sometimes be compromised by preexisting observer biases.
Case Studies	Involve in-depth explorations of either a single case or a small group of subjects who are examined individually.	Many different methods can be used to gather data (direct observation, testing, etc.), and this flexibility provides researchers excellent opportunities for acquiring insight into specific behaviors. Furthermore, because of the clinical nature of case studies, and because they may continue for long periods of time, the researcher is able to explore important variables and possible relationships among them, in some detail.	Lack of investigative control of important variables, potential for subjective observer bias, poor sampling techniques that often limit generalization of findings to other people in the clinical category being investigated, and tendency for subjects to report earlier experiences inaccurately.
Correlational Method	Statistical methods are used to assess and describe the amount and type of relationship between two variables of interest.	Can be used to answer questions about some kinds of relationships that cannot be clarified by other research methods. Findings expressed in mathematical values provide a strong basis for making predictions about behavior.	This technique, by itself, does not allow researchers to conclude that a demonstrated relationship between two variables means that one is causing the other.

NONEXPERIMENTAL RESEARCH METHODS

RESEARCH ON THE EFFECTS OF ALCOHOL ON SEXUAL BEHAVIOR Many people believe that a few drinks get them in the mood and enhance sexual pleasure. If you were a psychologist trying to determine whether alcohol really does have a positive effect on sexual response, what method would you use to test this relationship? See what you can come up with before reading on.

CASE STUDIES Our first approach might be to conduct case studies of people who drink considerable amounts of alcohol. A **case study** is an in-depth exploration of either a single subject or a small group of subjects who are examined individually. Many case studies of chronic alcoholics have revealed that these people often report reduced sexual interest and arousability. But here again, the evidence is difficult to interpret. It is unclear whether this reduced sexual interest is a direct result of drinking or a generalized side effect of the physical deterioration often associated with chronic alcoholism.

A related approach would be to have people keep personal diaries in which they record their daily alcohol intake along with some measure of sexual interest, such as frequency of orgasm or occurrence of sexual fantasies. We might then determine if a relationship exists between these two measures.

Assume that an analysis of people's personal diaries did indicate an apparent relationship between sexual interest and alcohol consumption. Could this finding be interpreted as clear evidence that alcohol has a positive or stimulating effect on sexual response? Can you think of any factors that might call this conclusion into question? Give this some thought before reading on.

As tempting as it might be to jump to conclusions, the results of such an analysis might be clouded by a number of factors. One potential problem is inconsistent record keeping, since different individuals might take different approaches to making diary entries. In addition, some people might alter their normal behavior patterns simply because they are keeping records. And again, even if alcohol intake was found to be related to sexual response, could we be certain that it represented a cause-and-effect relationship? For example, if sexual activity and drinking both increase during the summer, is the increased drinking the cause of the sexual activity? It might be but it is also possible that the summer heat is the cause of both of these phenomena. People are more thirsty in hot weather; they may also sleep less on hot nights, so there are additional opportunities for sexual activity.

A number of methods can be used to gather data in a case study, including direct observation, testing and experimentation, and interviews or questionnaires. Because of this flexibility, case studies often provide opportunities to acquire insight into specific behaviors. Highly personal, subjective information about how individuals actually feel regarding their behavior represents an important step beyond simply recording activities. And case studies have another advantage. Because of their clinical nature and because they may continue for long periods of time (months or even years), the researcher is able to explore important variables, and possible relationships among them, in some detail.

Limitations of the Case Study There are some important limitations to the case study method, however. One of these is lack of investigative control. A set of circumstances typically gives rise to the research investigation, rather than the other way around. Thus the researcher's role is to gather as much information as possible from a given situation, but the variables are beyond his or her control. For instance, people often become subjects for case studies because they have some physical or emotional disorder or because they have manifested a specific atypical behavior. Much of our current information about criminal behavior, incest victims, disorders such as multiple personality, and other unusual conditions has been obtained using this approach. Case studies have provided valuable insights into such conditions and have led to other methods to study them.

A second limitation is the potential for subjective bias on the researcher's part. Since the case study usually arises out of a rare case, it is often impossible to obtain objective verification such as is provided when experiments are replicated. For instance, it is often difficult to verify someone's recollections of a particularly traumatic event during childhood. As you will see in later chapters, our memory of events can be greatly influenced by subsequent events.

Because an individual's past usually does not become a target of research interest until that person develops some sort of problem much later in life, the researcher must often reconstruct the subject's earlier history in order to gather data (Bradburn et al., 1987). For example, suppose we want to evaluate Sigmund Freud's theory that agoraphobia (an intense fear of being in open, public places) is related to separation anxiety, which is an underlying fear of being separated from parents. According to this view, certain individuals are predisposed to develop agoraphobia as a result of incidents of traumatic separation from their parents during early childhood. The case study method would be a logical way to evaluate this hypothesis: People with agoraphobia might be asked to recall events from early childhood in which they were separated from their parents; then the frequency of these experiences could be compared to a control sample of nonagoraphobic people matched with the agoraphobic group on other variables. Unfortunately, however, many subjects might have trouble remembering these early experiences accurately, especially if they are inclined to repress or block them from conscious memory. Thus the recall of past events in the case study method is subject to errors in memory and sometimes to intentional efforts to distort or repress facts.

A third limitation of case studies is that, because they tend to focus on small samples of particularly interesting or unusual cases, the findings are often difficult to generalize to other people. This potential source of error is illustrated in the writings of investigators in the 1960s and 1970s who explored and reported on motivations for committing rape. Most of these earlier studies used small clinical samples of imprisoned rapists as their primary subjects, and their findings suggested that rape represents an act of domination, power, and violence that has little to do with sexual urges. More recent data, obtained from multiple large-scale surveys, contradicts this notion. Instead, these findings have revealed that a substantial majority of rapes are committed by someone who knows the victim (acquaintance rapes) and whose motivation for committing this criminal act is largely sexual gratification (Crooks & Baur, 1990).

SURVEYS AND QUESTIONNAIRES A second important research method is the **survey,** in which a representative group of people are questioned about their behaviors or attitudes. Psychologists use this method when they are interested in obtaining information from more people than it is practical to study in the laboratory, for instance, to find out how college students feel about men and women sharing domestic chores at home or to determine whether publicity about AIDS (acquired immune deficiency syndrome) has changed people's sexual practices in recent years.

Since such questions cannot be put to everybody in a population, psychologists may elect to survey a representative sample group. A carefully constructed questionnaire may reveal trends that exist in the general population even though only a relatively small percentage of that population is surveyed.

HOW SAMPLES ARE SELECTED FOR SURVEYS   Most research questions relate to a population much too large to be studied in its entirety. For example, if you wished to find out how the use of marijuana affects adolescent problem-solving ability and scholastic achievement, your relevant population would include teenagers from all over the world. Even if you decided to limit your observations to American adolescents, your target group would still be prohibitively large: You could never evaluate all its members.

Psychologists get around this difficulty by gathering data from a relatively small **sample** or selected segment of the entire population that interests them. Our ability to draw inferences or conclusions confidently about a much larger population rests chiefly on the techniques we use for selecting subjects for the sample study group. We will review two important types of samples.

Representative Samples   The ideal sample is called a **representative sample,** where the sample of subjects accurately represents the larger population about which we wish to draw conclusions. A representative sample closely matches the characteristics of the population of interest. If it does not, it is considered a biased sample.

How would you go about selecting a representative sample to investigate the effects of alcohol on sexual arousal? In order to draw broad conclusions about college students, your sample would need to be representative of that group. How could you ensure this? Take a few moments to consider what procedures you might use before reading on.

You might begin selecting your representative sample by obtaining the registration lists of college students in a variety of geographic areas throughout the United States. You would need to select these regions very carefully to reflect the actual distribution of the population you are studying. For instance, you wouldn't want to select either all private colleges or colleges and universities from a particular state. Provided that your final sample was sufficiently large, you could be reasonably confident in generalizing your findings to all American college students.

Random Samples   Another kind of sample, called a **random sample,** is not necessarily the same as a representative sample. A random sample is selected by randomization procedures, which assure that every member of the population of interest has an equal chance of being selected. For example, suppose you have an opportunity to buy into a café on campus. The café has been only marginally profitable, and you think that converting to a health food–oriented menu may help to increase profitability. You decide to survey students' attitudes about patronizing a health food restaurant on campus. Since summer provides you the most free time, you decide to conduct your poll during this period. A friend who works in the registrar's office supplies you with the roster of summer session enrollees, and you select your survey sample from this group.

Assuming that your question about patronizing a health food restaurant is clearly stated, and that a large percentage of the sample respond to your poll, can you be confident that your findings reflect the views of the entire student body at your school? Consider this question before reading on.

The answer to the question just posed is no, for two reasons that you may already have guessed. First, students enrolled in summer classes are not necessarily representative of all students at your college or university. For example, if more graduate students enroll in the summer program, the average age will be higher than that of students in the fall and winter sessions. And second, your sample was not random because all students did not have an equal chance of being selected. Remember, your list was only for summer session students and you wish to generalize your results to all students.

Once an unbiased random sample is selected, survey data may be obtained in two major ways: either orally, through a face-to-face interview or by telephone, or in written form, using a paper-and-pencil questionnaire. Questionnaire design can vary tremendously; questionnaires may range from a few questions to over a thousand; they may be multiple-choice, true-false, or discussion questions; respondents may fill out the questionnaire either alone or in the presence of a researcher.

Each of the two major survey methods has both advantages and shortcomings. Because questionnaires are more anonymous, some people may be less likely to distort information about their lives by boasting, omitting facts, and so forth. (The presence of an interviewer sometimes encourages such false responses.) Questionnaires have another advantage in that they are usually cheaper and quicker than interview surveys. However, interviews have the advantage of flexibility. The interviewer may clarify confusing questions and vary their sequence in order to meet the needs of the participant. A competent interviewer can establish a sense of rapport that may encourage more candor than that produced by an impersonal questionnaire.

LIMITS OF THE SURVEY METHOD The survey is effective for gathering a large amount of data, but, like any method, it has limitations. An important caution has to do with sample selection; researchers need to be wary of demographic bias. In a famous example illustrating the danger of demographic bias, a 1936 survey poll of more than 2 million people led to a prediction that Republican presidential candidate Alf Landon would defeat Democratic incumbent Franklin Roosevelt by a landslide. In fact, the reverse happened.

The poll was dead wrong because the survey sample was selected by picking names from telephone directories. In those Depression years, few but the well-to-do had telephones, and the wealthy favored Landon. Political survey techniques have been refined so that such errors rarely happen nowadays.

Consider the political polls prior to the 1992 presidential election that indicated during the final week before the election that Bill Clinton would win by 4 to 6 percentage points. Clinton's actual margin of victory was indeed 5 percent! These polls were representative polls in that they only included registered voters who were likely to vote. Therefore, when polls and surveys use representative sampling techniques, accurate predictions about the underlying population can be made. On the other hand, when samples are not representative or predictions go beyond the represented population, survey results can be very misleading.

For instance, much of what we know about human behavior is gathered from college students. This population is hardly representative of the general population in terms of age, socioeconomic status, and education—all variables which might well influence a subject's responses. Although the segment of the population from which subjects are drawn may have little impact on some types of research (for instance, the study of how receptors in the eye respond to different colors), it may have an important influence on other types of research. Thus we need to be very careful in generalizing from a sample of college students to a broader population. This caution applies to experiments and some other research methods as well as to surveys.

Another potential bias in sample selection is sex bias. Males are used as subjects for psychological investigation far more commonly than are females (Holmes & Jorgensen, 1971; McHugh et al., 1986; Rohrbaugh, 1979; Rothblum, 1988). Females are not widely represented in medical research, either. This bias has led some people to suggest that our data reflect a psychology (or medicine) of men more than of people in general. Preference for male or female subjects can have a serious biasing effect on research. For example, a substantial majority of investigations of human aggressive behavior have studied only male subjects, suggesting that psychologists may have been influenced by our society's tendency to view males as more active and aggressive than females. This assumption would have little chance of being proven false by research that systematically ignored women.

Fortunately, research psychologists are becoming more aware of the implications of sex bias in research (Denmark et al., 1988). Recent investigations of aggressive behavior, using subjects of both sexes, have revealed that under some circumstances women may behave just as aggressively as men. Unbiased sampling procedures will allow us to make accurate conclusions about both the similarities and differences between males and females.

Still another caution in using the survey method concerns the design of the questions themselves. Psychologists have learned, often to their dismay, that even very minor changes in the wording of a question can alter people's responses. For example, Elizabeth Loftus (1975) found that subjects who were asked, Do you get headaches occasionally and if so how often?, reported an average of 0.7 headaches a week; a comparable group of subjects who were asked, Do you get headaches frequently and if so how often?, reported a weekly average of 2.2 headaches. Clearly, a considerable amount of thought and careful attention must be applied in constructing survey questions.

Finally, surveys are not appropriate for every research project. A survey can provide a broad profile of attitudes and behaviors of a large group, but it cannot look closely at specific individuals to understand their behaviors or attitudes. Psychologists must use other methods to provide that kind of information.

Survey Methods: Alcohol and Sexual Behavior   Let us return to our question on the relationship between alcohol and sexual arousal and see how this kind of research question might incorporate the survey method. In fact, this method was used in the early 1970s. In a survey of 20,000 middle-class and upper-middle-class Americans, 60 percent of respondents reported that drinking increased their sexual pleasure (Athanasiou et al., 1970). There was a pronounced sex difference, with significantly greater numbers of women reporting this effect. However, this research might be questioned because it relies on subjective reports: What people believe to be true may not always be the case. There is sometimes considerable discrepancy between actual behavior and the way people report it.

THE OBSERVATIONAL METHOD   A third research method is the **observational method** wherein researchers observe their subjects as they go about their usual activities. This research method often takes place in a natural setting, and when it does it is called **naturalistic observation.**

Like the survey method, the observational method provides descriptive information. For instance, in the study of children's aggressive behavior discussed earlier in this chapter, researchers might observe that when children become aggressive, adults pay more attention to them. This observation might lead to the hypothesis that aggressive behaviors in children are likely to increase commensurate with the amount of adult attention they produce. This hypothesis could not be tested using the observational method, since it does not provide any way of controlling variables. Nevertheless, such observations could serve as an excellent starting point for further research in a more controlled environment.

Another example of the observational method is a study by Daniel Stern of the Cornell Medical School and his associates (1986). Interested in discovering how the interaction between parents and infants affects personality development, researchers in this study periodically videotaped normal everyday interactions between mothers and infants over a span of about two years. They found that the numerous small interactions that take place, for instance, when an infant makes a squealing sound and the mother echoes it back, or when the infant seeks eye contact and the mother rewards it with a smile, appear to influence how the infant will interact with other people.

Limitations of the Observational Method Like the case studies and the survey, direct observation is not appropriate for every research question. Take a minute or two and try to anticipate some potential drawbacks of the observational method. See if you can list one or two limitations before reading on.

One potential problem of the observational method is the risk of subjectivity, or **observer bias:** An observer may read more into a situation than is actually there. For instance, a psychologist observing children's play may be tempted to record that a child is frustrated upon finding a favored merry-go-round temporarily out of order, when in reality all that is observed is a period of suspended activity. Far from sulking in frustration, the child might simply be considering alternative things to do.

Observer bias may also take the form of investigators seeing what they expect to see. In one study, for instance, teachers were asked to observe and rate children who had been labeled normal, emotionally disturbed, or intellectually impaired (Foster & Ysseldyke, 1976). As you might guess, the labels were assigned arbitrarily in an effort to induce observer bias artificially. That was indeed the effect: The researchers found that the teachers rated the children in markedly different ways that were clearly influenced by the labels applied to each child. This finding is rather sobering, considering the widespread tendency of American educators to evaluate students as disruptive, cooperative, and so forth, and to enter these evaluations into permanent records that future teachers rely on. Psychologists conducting observational research generally try to avoid making biased interpretations by keeping very careful records of their observations. Sometimes audiovisual records that can be evaluated by independent observers are also used in the effort to minimize observer bias.

Another potential problem is that the presence of a human observer may affect the behavior being observed. For example, children on a playground may behave less aggressively simply because they are being watched by a strange adult. This problem of **observer effect** may require special attention when researchers take the observational method into the laboratory. For instance, when William Masters and Virginia Johnson (1966) used direct observation to document male and female sexual response patterns in the laboratory, many people questioned the validity of their findings.

Actually, in much of Masters and Johnson's work no one directly observed the volunteer subjects. When investigators did use direct observation, they were as unobtrusive as possible, observing from a peripheral location or from behind one-way glass, or using videotapes to be viewed later, and so forth. According to a subsequent report, the vast majority of volunteers found it surprisingly easy to respond sexually in the laboratory in much the same way as they responded at home in private (Brecher & Brecher, 1966, p. 56). Although there may be some merit to the concern about the artificial nature of Masters and Johnson's laboratory observations, time has demonstrated that their research findings are accurate enough to be applied beneficially to such areas as sex therapy, infertility counseling, birth control, and general sex education.

Thus, despite its potential disadvantages, direct observation often produces valuable information when it is carefully conducted. In addition, there are some clear advantages to seeing and measuring behavior firsthand instead of relying on subjective reports of past experiences. Firsthand direct observation virtually eliminates the possibility of data falsification, either through a subject's inaccurate recollections or through deceptive reporting. In addition, direct observation can provide some important insights into relationships that may exist in a particular behavioral area.

Naturalistic observations can lead to misleading conclusions.

Jane Goodall studies the behavior of chimps in their natural environment.

SUBJECT	SAT SCORE	GPA
1	595	2.15
2	621	2.67
3	650	3.45
4	652	3.20
5	712	3.85

CORRELATIONAL METHOD   Some types of questions cannot be answered by surveys, direct observation, or case studies. For instance, suppose that you wanted to determine how high school seniors' Scholastic Aptitude Test (SAT) scores related to their grade point averages (GPAs) during the first year of college. The best approach would be simply to collect the SAT scores and first-year GPAs of a large sample of college freshmen and use a statistical technique to determine the relationship between these two variables. This research technique is called the **correlational method,** and the statistic used to describe the amount and type of relationship is a **coefficient of correlation.**

A coefficient of correlation always falls somewhere between +1.00 and -1.00. A minus sign is used to signify negative correlations. A correlation of around zero indicates a weak or nonexistent relationship between the two variables in question. A positive correlation indicates that the variables vary together in the same direction, so that increases in one measure are accompanied by increases in the other. For instance, it is known that SAT scores are positively correlated with college GPAs, because students who obtain high SAT scores tend to achieve high GPAs and those with low SAT scores tend to have lower grades. This relationship is far from a perfect 1.00, however. In the real world, correlations between variables are virtually never perfect.

It is important to note that a high positive correlation between two variables does not mean that the matched scores are nearly identical in value. It simply means that a generally consistent proportional relationship exists. For example, suppose we find a strong positive correlation of .90 between student's scores on SATs and their freshman GPAs at a particular college. In the top left example, it is clear that the two scores are far from identical as SAT scores range from about 200 to 800 while GPAs range from 0 to 4.0. For example, suppose we obtained the scores on the left from 5 freshman at our college.

This is what we meant by a generally consistent proportional relationship. As SAT scores increase, we see a corresponding increase in GPA. This is best illustrated in Figure 2.1. Had all the points fallen directly on the straight line the correlation would have been 1.00. As the points get further from the line the correlation gets closer to 0.

Interpreting a Negative Correlation Between Variables   Based on what you have just learned about positive correlation, take a moment to consider what kind of relationship must exist between variables to yield a negative correlation.

A negative correlation indicates that increases in one measure are associated with decreases in the other. If you have ever followed the stock market, you may have noted that as interest rates go up, market averages tend to come down. This relationship is by no means a perfect -1.00, but it indicates a definite trend. Another example of a negative correlation is the well-known relationship between outdoor temperature and the incidence of colds. The following data represent what we might find on a typical college campus during several weeks of the winter.

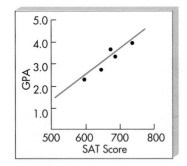

FIGURE 2.1

Positive Correlation Between SAT Scores and Freshman GPA for Five Students

WEEK #	AVERAGE DAILY TEMPERATURE	STUDENTS WITH COLDS
1	63	9
2	57	26
3	46	32
4	42	40
5	38	55

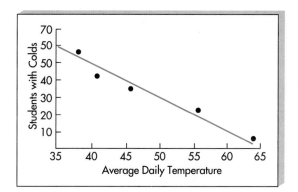

FIGURE 2.2
Negative Correlation Between Average Daily Temperature over a Five-week Period and the Incidence of Colds During the Same Five-week Period

These data are graphically presented in Figure 2.2. As you can see, the straight line through these points is negatively sloped indicating a negative correlation. That is, as temperature goes down, the incidence of colds goes up. The correlation in this case is -0.94. Again, because the points don't always fall on the line the correlation is not exactly -1.00.

Knowing the type and degree of relationship that exists between variables may be especially helpful to psychologists and others who wish to make predictions about behavior. For example, if you know that a high school senior scored high on the SAT, you can predict with some confidence that she or he is likely to earn good grades in college. Using Figure 2.1, can you predict the GPA of a student with an SAT score of 700?

Limitations of Correlational Studies   Correlational studies help us discover relationships between variables, but it is important not to read more into them than is there. One of the most common mistakes people make in interpreting correlational studies is to conclude that because two factors are related, one causes the other. Certainly, this is sometimes the case. Observations of drivers negotiating obstacle courses under the influence of alcohol, for instance, reveal a positive correlation between error scores and blood alcohol levels (the higher the level, the greater the number of errors). This correlational relationship is a causal one, since alcohol is known to impair the brain's ability to perceive, interpret, and respond to stimuli.

On the other hand, a consistent relationship between two factors is not always causal. In some cases a third factor, related to each of the other two, may account for the apparent causal relationship. For example, upon examining our data on the relationship between outside temperature and the incidence of colds, one might be tempted to make the conclusion that getting a cold is caused by being cold. The fact is, getting a cold is probably more related to being indoors among many others during cold weather than *being* cold. This increases your exposure to the virus and therefore your likelihood of getting a cold. In sum, it is dangerous to read causal effects into correlational studies. There is a more in-depth discussion of statistical correlation in the Appendix.

The problem with the research methods just discussed is that they do not allow for precise control over the various factors that may influence the behavior being studied. One research technique that does allow this control is the experimental method. All things considered, this is often the research approach preferred by psychologists. Also, as we shall see, it is the method that provides us with a clear answer to the question: Does alcohol affect sexual behavior?

THE EXPERIMENTAL METHOD   In **experimental research,** subjects are confronted with specific stimuli under precisely controlled conditions that allow their reactions to be reliably measured. The major advantage of the experimental method is that it allows the researcher to control conditions, ruling out all

EXPERIMENTAL RESEARCH METHODS

possible influences on subjects' behaviors other than the factors that are being investigated. A research psychologist using this method directly manipulates a particular set of conditions, then observes the effect on behavior. The purpose of the experimental method is to discover causal relations between variables, whether, for example, the consumption of alcohol causes a change in sexual behavior.

Independent and Dependent Variables   There are two kinds of variables in scientific experiments: independent and dependent. An **independent variable** is a condition or factor that the experimenter manipulates; the resulting behavior that is measured and recorded is called the **dependent variable.** In our alcohol study the independent variable would be the amount of alcohol consumed while our dependent variable would be any measurable change in sexual behavior.

EXPERIMENTAL AND CONTROL GROUPS   To determine the effects of alcohol on sexual behavior a researcher might compare sexual responsiveness in several groups of subjects each receiving different amounts of alcohol (including no alcohol) before measurements of arousal are taken. In this case the groups of subjects receiving alcohol are called **experimental groups** and the group of subjects receiving no alcohol would be the control group. Differences in sexual responsiveness (the dependent variable) between the experiment groups and the control group could then be attributed to the effects of alcohol (the independent variable).

Not all experiments involve comparisons between experimental and control groups, however. In some cases it is more desirable to compare an individual subject with himself or herself under different conditions. For example, a psychologist might compare a subject's sexual arousal after receiving alcohol to a level of arousal without alcohol. In this case the same subject serves in both the experimental and control conditions, but at different times.

Examples of the Experimental Method   Now that we have some understanding of the experimental method, let us examine how alcohol affects sexual behavior. Recall that in an earlier survey, a majority of respondents had reported that alcohol enhanced their sexual pleasure. However, a survey is limited to asking people what they think happens when they drink, and these subjective assessments may not match up with what actually happens. Two subsequent experimental studies revealed that there was good cause to be wary of the survey's findings. Both investigations were conducted at Rutgers University's Alcohol Behavior Research Laboratory.

The first experiment involved 48 male college students between the ages of 18 and 22 (Briddell & Wilson, 1976). During an initial session the researchers obtained baseline data on flaccid (nonerect) penis diameter for all subjects. The participants were then shown a 10-minute erotic film of explicit sexual interaction between male and female partners. Penile tumescence, (engorgement) was measured continuously during the film, using a flexible rubber band–like device. This measurement provided information about these men's level of sexual arousal when they were not under the influence of alcohol. That is, in this phase of the experiment subjects served as their own controls.

A second session was held a week later. Here, subjects drank measured amounts of alcohol prior to viewing a somewhat longer version of the erotic film. The 48 men were assigned to four experimental groups, with 12 subjects in each group. Depending on his group assignment, each subject consumed 0.6, 3, 6, or 9 ounces of alcohol. After a 40-minute rest period, the subjects viewed the film during which sexual arousal was again precisely measured.

The results of the experiment indicated that alcohol significantly reduced sexual arousal in subjects, compared to their control levels. In addition, the arousal-reducing effects of alcohol were greater at higher intake levels.

A second investigation of alcohol effects was conducted with 16 college women between the ages of 18 and 22 (Wilson & Lawson, 1976). Here, a group of 16 women participated in weekly experimental sessions under varying conditions. Each received four different doses of alcohol (0.3, 1.4, 2.9, and 4.3 ounces) on different occasions, and then watched either a control film or an erotic film. The control film was a boring 12-minute review of the computer facilities at Rutgers University; the erotic film portrayed explicit heterosexual interaction. Sexual arousal was measured continuously during the film by use of a vaginal photoplethysmograph, a device designed to measure increased vaginal blood volume in a sexually aroused female. As expected, subjects showed significantly more arousal in response to the erotic than the nonerotic film. More importantly, there was clear evidence that alcohol reduced sexual arousal, especially in higher dosages.

Both of these experiments tend to refute the belief that alcohol enhances erotic experiences; they also reveal the advantages of controlled laboratory conditions for measuring behavior. Clearly, the experimental method provided a more accurate indication of how alcohol affects sexual arousal than did the survey.

Laboratory experiments offer researchers a number of advantages, including the ability to control variables and, frequently, the ability to draw direct conclusions about cause-and-effect relationships between variables. None of the previously described methods allow for conclusions about cause-and-effect.

How Samples Are Selected for Experiments   Sample selection is not just important for survey research. Because the results from experiments are often generalized to larger populations, the appropriate sampling considerations discussed under survey research apply to experimental research as well. That is, for the results of the experiment on the effects of alcohol on sexual arousal to be generalized to all college students the sample selected for the experiment must be representative of all college students. If a representative sample cannot be obtained, the results of experiments are greatly limited.

Likewise, researchers attempt to obtain random samples from a population to avoid restricting the experiment to a select group of subjects. Also, subjects (once selected) are often randomly assigned to different treatment conditions to avoid further bias. For example, in the alcohol study conducted on 48 males the subjects were randomly assigned to groups receiving different amounts of alcohol. Consider for a moment how the results might have differed had the experimenter allowed the subjects to choose which group they were assigned to, or if group selection was determined by the amount of prior alcohol experience subjects had.

Limitations of the Experimental Method   We have discussed some of the positive aspects of experimental laboratory research. Before reading on, take a couple of minutes to look at the other side of the coin. Can you think of any potential drawbacks associated with this research method?

The experimental method also has some limitations. First, the somewhat artificial nature of the laboratory setting may influence subjects' behaviors. The very fact that people know they are in an experiment can cause them to respond differently from the way they might normally behave. For instance, the artificial nature of the laboratory might limit our interpretations of the research previously discussed on the effects of alcohol on sexual arousal. Although both experiments measured differences in sexual arousal that could be attributed to alcohol, it may be that in a more natural setting with a sexual partner these differences wouldn't show up. Further research in a variety of settings would be necessary to confirm this.

A second limitation of the experimental method is simply that not all questions posed by psychologists lend themselves to experimental investigation. For

Animal research is often conducted in a laboratory setting.

Large enclosures can be used to study the social behavior of primates.

instance, you might be interested in finding out whether children of divorced parents are as emotionally secure as children from two-parent families. Similarly, we might be interested in the effects of severe malnutrition on learning and memory. These kinds of data could not be gathered by manipulating variables in a laboratory setting. Instead, you would need to take your investigation to real families or natural settings.

The appropriateness of the experimental method has sometimes been questioned for another reason besides its artificial nature; a number of experimental studies have been criticized on ethical grounds.

ETHICS IN PSYCHOLOGICAL EXPERIMENTS

In past years, several controversial studies have prompted serious questions about the ethics of some psychological experiments. Consider the following four examples and decide whether you think any ethical principles were violated.

THE MILGRAM OBEDIENCE TO AUTHORITY STUDY

In the 1960s, social psychologist Stanley Milgram (1963) used deception in a widely discussed study of obedience to authority. Milgram's goal was to determine whether subjects would administer painful electric shocks to others merely because an authority figure instructed them to do so. Milgram's subjects, all male, thought they were participating in a study of how punishment affects learning. They were told to use an intercom system to present problems to a learner who was strapped in a chair in another room, out of sight, and to administer a shock each time the learner gave a wrong answer to a problem. Labeled switches on the shock apparatus ranged from a low of 15 volts to a high of 450 volts; subjects were instructed to increase the voltage with each successive error the learner made.

In spite of protests and cries from the other room, most of the subjects delivered what they believed was a full range of these painful shocks. Although they followed the experimenter's instructions, the task was not easy for them. Virtually all of the subjects exhibited high levels of stress and discomfort as they administered the shocks. Later, these subjects were told that the experiment was merely a contrived situation in which they had been deceived, and that no shocks had actually been given. How would you feel about yourself if you had been one of Milgram's subjects? Do you think Milgram violated ethical principles by placing people in a position where they might feel compelled to engage in hurtful behavior? Was deception appropriate in this experiment, or, for that matter, is it acceptable in any psychological research with human subjects?

THE STANFORD UNIVERSITY PRISONER STUDY

A second controversial study, the now famous Stanford University prisoner study, was conducted some years ago by social psychologist Philip Zimbardo and his colleagues (Haney & Zimbardo, 1977; Zimbardo, 1975). These investigators created a simulated prison environment to study how incarceration influenced the behavior of healthy, well adjusted people. Student recruits played the roles of either guards or inmates.

No one anticipated the profoundly disturbing impact of this experience on students cast in either of the roles. The guards soon became so cruel that several of the prisoners suffered emotional reactions ranging from depression to anxiety and even extreme rage (not unlike the responses of many inmates in genuine penal institutions). As soon as Zimbardo and his associates became aware of the severe impact their study was having on their subjects, they terminated the experiment, even before it had run its course. Should this experiment have been conducted? Was it unethical to place humans in a situation the researchers might have anticipated could lead to hostile confrontations?

REPLICATION OF THE STANFORD PRISONER STUDY In 1983 the press widely reported a repeat of the Zimbardo research conducted by a high school teacher who used volunteer students. This researcher obtained permission from both parents and school officials to conduct this investigation. The results were similar to those obtained by the Stanford group a decade earlier, and many of the students were severely upset by their participation in this follow-up study. Needless to say, parents were irate, school officials were chagrined, and the press had a field day. Were ethical principles violated in this repeat of Zimbardo's earlier research?

STROKE SIMULATION IN MONKEYS A fourth controversial study was conducted a few years ago by a prominent researcher. In an effort to find ways of helping stroke victims regain use of their limbs, this investigator experimented with monkeys. Nerves in one of each monkey's arms were cut to simulate the loss of feeling that might result from a stroke. The undamaged arms were then bound to the monkeys' bodies to force them to use their nerve-dead limbs. Unfortunately, the surgically altered arms were susceptible to injury because they lacked feeling; some monkeys even treated their damaged arms as foreign objects and inflicted further damage by chewing on their fingers.

Some time after the initial surgery was conducted, the researcher went on vacation. While he was away, an animal welfare activist who had volunteered to work in that laboratory became concerned about the monkeys' deteriorating physical condition. He contacted local authorities, and the research scientist was ultimately charged with a variety of criminal acts, including cruelty to animals. The researcher maintained that his investigation was appropriate and that the physical condition of the monkeys was the fault of workers who had not properly cared for the animals during his absence. Do you believe that he was guilty of violating ethical principles in his research?

ETHICAL GUIDELINES FOR RESEARCH

The four examples we have described present complex ethical issues. Perhaps the most controversial was Milgram's research, which generated a great deal of criticism. Many psychologists questioned the ethics of exposing unsuspecting people to a situation that might cause them considerable stress and might even have lasting harmful effects. Psychologist Diana Baumrind (1964), for example, argued that subjects' feelings and rights had been abused. She suggested that many would have trouble justifying their willingness to administer high levels of shock, and that their self-respect would be damaged. Milgram pointed out, however, that all subjects had gone through extensive debriefing after the study, in which they were told that they had not actually shocked anyone and were reassured that many other subjects had responded in the same way. He documented the success of these debriefing sessions, citing results from a follow-up questionnaire returned by 92 percent of the original subjects. A large majority, 84 percent, said they were glad to have participated in the study. Fifteen percent indicated neutral feelings, and only 1 percent of the subjects reported being sorry they had participated in the experiment (Milgram, 1964).

Some researchers seemed relatively satisfied by Milgram's response to his critics. One psychologist recently commented that Milgram seems to have employed little more deception in his work than is used regularly on TV programs such as "Candid Camera" (McConnell, 1983, p. 629). Nevertheless, such studies generated a debate about ethics in research that ultimately culminated in the American Psychological Association's (APA) adopting in 1973 (subsequent revisions were published in 1979, 1981, and 1990) a list of ethical guidelines requiring, among other things, that researchers avoid procedures that might cause serious physical or mental harm to human subjects. If an experiment involves even the slightest risk of harm or discomfort, investigators are required to obtain informed consent from their subjects. Researchers must also respect a subject's right to refuse to participate at any time during the course of a study, and special steps must be taken to protect the confidentiality of the data and maintain participants' anonymity unless they agree to be identified.

The issue of deception in research remains controversial. Some studies would lose their effectiveness if participating subjects knew in advance exactly what the experimenter was studying. The APA's guideline provides that if deception must be used, a postexperiment debriefing must thoroughly explain to participants why it was necessary. At such time, subjects must be allowed to request that their data be removed from the study and destroyed.

Were ethical principles violated in the prison studies and the stroke simulation study? Keeping the APA's ethical guidelines in mind, how would you now evaluate the other three research examples in the preceding discussion? Take a few moments to think critically about the ethics of these studies before reading on.

Most psychologists believe that Zimbardo's simulated prison study did not violate ethical principles. The researchers were as shocked as anyone by their experiment's effects, and they terminated the study as soon as it became clear that some subjects were experiencing severe emotional reactions. Also, all subjects had voluntarily participated in the study after being carefully informed of its nature.

The second prisoner study is a different case entirely. Unlike Zimbardo's group, the high school teacher who replicated the prisoner study had access to previous research findings which strongly indicated the possibility of psychological harm to subjects. These findings were ignored, however, and the experiment was recreated in clear violation of research ethics.

The final research example presents very complex ethical issues. A considerable amount of important medical and behavioral research, some with potentially great benefits for humans, could not be conducted without animal experimentation. The mere fact that nonhumans are used, however, does not justify an any-treatment-goes attitude, and researchers must ensure that animals be treated humanely. Despite the monkey researcher's claim that others were responsible for laboratory conditions during his vacation, the court determined that his role as primary investigator made him ultimately responsible for the animals' welfare. He was found guilty of cruelty to animals and fined (Holden, 1981).

Sometimes it is hard for researchers to weigh objectively the potential benefits of a study against the possibility of harming its subjects. Recognizing the difficulty of this task, virtually every institution conducting research in the United States has established ethics committees that review all proposed studies. If they perceive that subjects' welfare (humans or other animals) is insufficiently safeguarded, the proposal must be modified or the research cannot be conducted.

The APA's list of ethical principles, together with the activities of institutional ethics committees, makes it very unlikely that research along the lines of Stanley Milgram's study could be conducted today. Researchers who do not adhere to this strict code of ethics risk serious professional and legal consequences.

STATISTICAL CONCEPTS FOR RESEARCH

Regardless of the research method used, psychologists generally end up with data that must be described and interpreted. Usually the data are in the form of numbers that can be analyzed by **statistics,** mathematical methods for describing and interpreting data. There are essentially two kinds of statistics: descriptive

and inferential. The Statistics Appendix provides detailed information about using statistics to make sense out of research findings; therefore, our discussion in this section provides only a brief overview.

- -

DESCRIPTIVE STATISTICS

Suppose that you are enrolled in a psychology class attended by 130 students, the size of class actually taught by one of the authors. On the first exam, you receive 51 points out of a possible 60. Naturally, you want to know how your score compares with the class as a whole. For example, were you among the top 10 percent or the bottom 25 percent of your class? Your instructor announces that the top score is 58 points. This information still does not provide sufficient data for you to evaluate your score. Your score of 51 may be well above average, but it is also possible that most of the class scored higher than you. What you need is a statistical description of overall class performance that will allow you to make sense out of your score. This is what **descriptive statistics** is about: summarizing large amounts of data into a form that is easily interpreted. There are three major ways of describing data such as the class scores on a psychology exam: graphs, measures of central tendency, and measures of variation.

USING GRAPHS TO DESCRIBE DATA A graph is particularly useful to present data because the way scores are distributed can be interpreted at a glance. Figure 2.3 shows a graph of actual scores from 130 students taking General Psychology. The highest score possible was 60 points. This particular type of graph is called a histogram, or bar graph. Each bar on the graph represents an interval width of 5 points on the test. The vertical axis (frequency) represents the number of students that received scores within each interval. If your score was 51 points it is included in the interval 50 to 54 points.

Normal Distributions This distribution of scores represents an approximation of a normal distribution. A normal distribution is a bell-shaped distribution of scores that is symmetrical in shape. The dashed line in Figure 2.3 represents the shape of a normal distribution. As you can see, the scores from your test approximate this shape with your score of 51 points falling among those of the top half of the class.

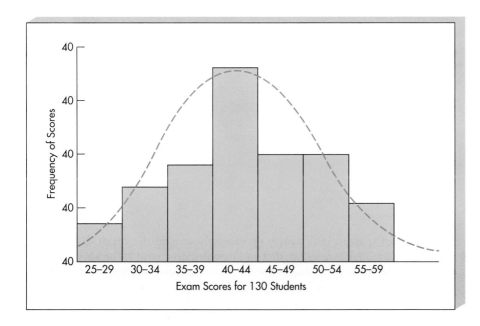

FIGURE 2.3

Bar Graph (Histogram) for 130 Scores from One of Authors' General Psychology Classes

The numbers above each bar indicate how many scores fell within each interval. The dashed line represents the shape of a normal distribution of scores.

Measures of Central Tendency   A **measure of central tendency** is a value that reflects the middle or central point of a distribution of scores. There are three measures of central tendency: the **mean,** the **median,** and the **mode.** The mean is an arithmetic average obtained by adding all of the scores and dividing by the number of scores (130). For our test scores the mean was 43 points.

The median is the score that falls in the middle of a distribution of numbers that are arranged from the lowest to the highest. If we were to arrange our test scores from the lowest (27 points) to the highest (58 points), the middle value (the 65th score) of these 130 scores would have been 44 points. The median is especially useful as a descriptor of data when there are extreme values at either end of the distribution. For this reason the median is often used to represent annual incomes, as it isn't inflated by a few excessive values like the mean would be.

The mode is the score in the distribution that occurs most frequently. In this case the most frequent score on our psychology exam was 42 points. In some cases distributions can have several modes. When this occurs, the distribution is said to be multimodal.

Had the distribution of test scores been exactly normal, all three measures of central tendency (the mean, median, and mode) would have been the same value. In our distribution of test scores these values were quite similar, suggesting that our distribution approximates a **normal distribution.** When these values are very different the distribution is considered to be **skewed** or unbalanced. This might have occurred if our test had been either too easy or too difficult. For instance, if the test was too difficult the distribution would have been skewed to the left, towards lower scores. In such situations, a person needs to decide which measure most accurately reflects central tendency. All things considered, the mean is generally the most commonly used measure of central tendency.

Returning to our previous example, suppose you find out that 43 is the mean score on the psychology exam. You now know that your 51 is at least above average. With only this information, however, you still do not have a sense of how your score ranks. That average of 43 could result from the fact that, aside from your 51, half of the class scored 58s and the other half scored 35s (all *A*s and *F*s), or it could result from most of the class scoring in the 40-to-47 range. Your class position would be very different in these two situations. What you need to know in addition to the mean is how variable the scores were.

Measures of Variability   The histogram in Figure 2.3 shows you that scores were quite variable, ranging from the upper 20s to the upper 50s. One measure of variability is the range, which is the difference between the highest and lowest score. The range is the easiest measure of variability to calculate. However, it may provide a misleading indication of how dispersed scores are. For example, suppose that all but one student in your psychology class received a test score somewhere between 36 and 58. Excluding this one exception, the range would be 22 (58 to 36). However, the one score outside the spread, a 14, had the effect of doubling the range to 44 (58 to 14). As you can see, whenever there are extreme scores at either end of a distribution, the range will provide a biased, inflated estimate of variation.

A much better measure of variability is provided by the **standard deviation.** This measure is an indication of the extent to which the scores in a distribution vary from the mean. The standard deviation is much more accurate than the range because it takes into account all the scores in a data set, not just the extreme values at either end. The standard deviation effectively describes whether a distribution of scores varies widely or narrowly around the mean. If the standard deviation is small, we know that individual scores tend to be very close to the mean. If it is large, we know that the mean is less representative because the scores are much more widely dispersed around it. For our distribution of test scores the standard deviation was 8. This means that the average amount scores deviated from the mean was 8 points.

Knowing the mean and standard deviation allows us to make relatively precise judgments about how a particular score relates to other scores. Since the standard deviation on your psychology test was 8, this would place you exactly one standard deviation unit above the mean, which was 43. Because your class's test scores were fairly normally distributed, you would know that roughly 85 percent of your classmates (110 out of 130) scored below your score of 51. This conclusion is derived from known properties of the normal distribution that are described in the Statistics Appendix.

Applying Standard Deviation   Assume that two classes with an equal number of students take the psychology exam. The mean is 46 in both classes, and the distributions of scores are approximately normal. However, the standard deviations are different: In class *A* the standard deviation is 8; in class *B* it is 4. Assuming that your score is 4 points above the mean and that your instructor grades on a curve (i.e., assigns grades based on relative standing in the overall distribution of scores), in which class would you prefer to be enrolled? Think about your answer before reading on.

If you selected class *B*, you are correct. In this class a standard deviation of 4 indicates scores are clustered much more closely around the average than in class *A*, where the variation is much greater. This greater dispersion of scores would place more people above you in class *A*, thereby lowering your relative rank.

Graphs, central tendency, and variability are just three kinds of statistics that psychologists use to summarize and characterize data. The coefficient of correlation, discussed earlier, is another important descriptive statistic. Other descriptive statistics include percentiles and standard scores. The **percentile** represents the percentages of scores that lie below a particular score. For example, your percentile score was 85 because 85 percent of the class had a score lower than yours. A **standard score** measures how far a score deviates from the average in standard deviation units. Your standard score for the psychology test would have been 1 because 51 was 1 standard deviation (8 points) above the mean. These and other descriptive measures are discussed in more detail in the Statistics Appendix.

INFERENTIAL STATISTICS

Using descriptive statistics is often just the first step in analyzing and interpreting research results. Once data have been described, psychologists often wish to draw inferences or conclusions about their findings. The process of using statistical procedures to draw conclusions about the meaning of data is called **inferential statistics.**

As we have seen in this chapter, research often begins with some type of hypothesis about how things are related. For example, you may believe that people who use special relaxation techniques are likely to have lower anxiety levels than those who do not use such techniques. To test this hypothesis, you might begin by selecting a group of subjects, none of whom have been trained in relaxation techniques, who are matched on a number of important variables that might influence anxiety (things such as age, socioeconomic status, profession, health factors, etc.). Subjects might then be randomly assigned to one of two groups (the independent variable), one group trained in relaxation techniques and the other receiving no training. You would then collect data on the subjects' anxiety levels for a number of weeks or months.

Anxiety, the dependent variable, could be measured in a number of ways, depending on how you define it for the purpose of your study. Many of the variables studied by psychologists (such as anxiety, hunger, intelligence, or aggression) cannot be investigated until we specify precisely what we mean by the term. This is accomplished by providing an **operational definition** that specifies the operations we use to measure or observe the variable in question. For instance, you might use physical measures such as blood pressure or muscle tension to measure anxiety, or you could use a score on a psychological test that measures anxiety levels.

At the completion of your experiment you would have lots of data to analyze. Suppose you find that after eight weeks the relaxation training group scores markedly lower on your measure of anxiety than does the control group. This difference seems meaningful. However, whenever you evaluate the performance or characteristics of two or more groups of subjects, it is likely there will be some differences based on chance alone. The problem for the researcher is to determine whether differences between research groups are due to the experimental condition (your independent variable) or whether the difference is simply a chance result.

How can you assess whether the difference in anxiety levels (your dependent variable) of the two groups is genuine rather than a chance result? A variety of tests have been devised to answer this question. Such procedures are called tests of **statistical significance.** When scientists conclude that a research finding is statistically significant, they are merely stating, at a high level of confidence, that the difference is attributable to the experimental condition being manipulated by the researcher. This topic will be discussed in greater detail in the Statistics Appendix.

EVALUATING OPINIONS, BELIEFS, AND SCIENTIFIC EVIDENCE

We have seen in this chapter that psychological research can be hindered by a number of factors, including difficulties in obtaining representative samples, ethical considerations, experimenter bias, subject bias, and a variety of other problems. We have also seen that research psychologists have shown remarkable versatility in their efforts, collecting data in many different ways. Thus a major strength of psychological research is its reliance on a wide assortment of methodological techniques.

It is important that any serious student of psychology learn to differentiate between nonscientific polls and opinions and the results of scientific research conducted by serious investigators. A major goal of this text is to teach you to think critically and to ask questions about how we have come to conclusions about behavior. Even research conducted by reputable scientists must be critically evaluated according to the following criteria:

Are the researchers considered to be unbiased regarding the outcome or do they have special interests in supporting a particular conclusion?

Were the results of the research published in scientific journals where peer review occurs prior to publication or were the results published in popular magazines or newspapers?

What type of methodology was used? Were sufficient scientific principles adhered to?

Is there any reason to suspect bias in the selection of subjects?

Can the results be applied to individuals other than those in the sample group? How broad can these generalizations be and still remain legitimate?

Is it possible that the method used to obtain information may have biased the findings? For instance, did the questionnaire promote false replies? Is it likely that the artificial nature of the laboratory setting influenced subjects' responses?

Have there been any other published reports that confirm or contradict the particular study in question?

Keeping questions like these in mind is helpful in finding a middle ground between absolute trust and offhand dismissal of a given research study.

Throughout this text we will be discussing research findings related to a wide variety of topics. It will be useful for you to remember some of the advantages and limitations of different research methods as we discuss this research. In addition, this brief review of statistical methods will provide you with a better understanding of how research is interpreted to be either supportive of, or contradictory to, a particular perspective or theory.

SUMMARY

THE SCIENTIFIC METHOD AND BEHAVIOR

1. Three of the most common reasons why psychologists conduct research are to test a hypothesis, to solve a problem, and to confirm findings of previous research.

2. A hypothesis is a statement proposing the existence of a relationship between variables. Hypotheses are typically offered as tentative explanations for relationships or events, and they are often designed to be tested by research.

3. When psychologists publish new research findings they include details so that others may repeat the experiment to verify the results. The replication of prior research is the backbone of good science.

RESEARCH METHODS

4. Psychologists use a number of methods to study behavior. These techniques include surveys, the observational method, case studies, the correlational method, and the experimental method.

5. An important research method is the survey, in which a representative group of people are questioned, in face-to-face interviews or using written questionnaires, about their behaviors or attitudes.

6. Surveys are often conducted with a representative sample. That is, a sample in which critical subgroups are represented according to their incidence in the larger population about which one wishes to draw conclusions.

7. Another kind of sample, called a random sample, is selected by randomization procedures, which alone do not ensure a representative sample.

8. Potential limitations of the survey method include demographic and sex bias, improperly worded questions that bias responses, and a tendency to provide only limited insights about factors that contribute to behaviors and attitudes of specific individuals.

9. Researchers employing the observational method observe their subjects as they go about their usual activities. When this research takes place in a natural setting it is called naturalistic observation.

10. A potential problem with the observational method is the risk that an observer may read more into a situation than is actually there, a phenomenon called observer bias.

11. Another possible limitation of the observational method is the problem of observer effect, in which the presence of a human observer may affect the behavior being observed.

12. The case study is an in-depth exploration of either a single subject or a small group of subjects who are examined individually.

13. Shortcomings of the case study method include lack of investigative control of important variables, a potential for subjective observer bias, a lack of proper sampling techniques that limits generalization of findings to other people in the clinical category being investigated, and a tendency for subjects to report earlier experiences inaccurately.

14. The correlational method utilizes statistical methods to assess and describe the amount and type of relationship between two variables of interest, such as the SAT scores of high school seniors and their GPAs during the first year of college.

15. One major limitation of the correlational method is that this technique, considered alone, does not provide sufficient evidence to determine if a demonstrated correlational relationship between two variables is reflective of a causal relationship or merely indicative of another factor (or factors) related to each of the variables.

16. In experimental research, subjects are confronted with specific stimuli under precisely controlled conditions that allow their reactions to be reliably measured. The purpose of the experimental method is to discover causal relationships among independent and dependent variables.

17. An independent variable is a condition or factor that the experimenter manipulates; the resulting behavior that is measured and recorded is called the dependent variable.

18. Many experiments utilize both experimental groups, which consist of various groups of subjects exposed to different varieties of independent variables, and a control group composed of subjects who experience all the same conditions as subjects in the experimental group except for the key factor the researcher is evaluating.

19. Special advantages of the experimental method include control over relevant variables and opportunities to draw conclusions about cause-and-effect relationships.

20. Limitations of the experimental method include the artificial nature of the laboratory setting, which may influence subjects' behaviors, and the fact that some questions posed by psychologists do not lend themselves to experimental investigation.

21. The APA has adopted ethical guidelines for research that require, among other things, that researchers avoid procedures that might cause serious physical or mental harm to human subjects, that they protect confidentiality of the data, and that they respect a subject's right to refuse to participate at any time during the course of a study.

STATISTICAL CONCEPTS FOR RESEARCH

22. There are two kinds of statistics: descriptive and inferential. Descriptive statistics provide succinct descriptions by reducing a quantity of data to a form that is more understandable. Inferential statistics include a variety of mathematical procedures to draw conclusions about the meaning of data.

23. Measures of central tendency (descriptive statistics that reflect the middle or central point of a distribution) include the mean, median, and mode. The mean is the arithmetic average; the median is the score that falls in the middle of a distribution; and the mode is the most frequent score.

24. Measures of variability (descriptive statistics that indicate the spread of a distribution of scores) include the range and the standard deviation. The range is the difference between the highest and lowest score, and the standard deviation is an approximate

indication of the average extent to which all scores in a distribution vary from the mean.

25. Inferential statistics allows researchers to make judgments about whether their research findings are statistically significant. When scientists conclude that a research finding is statistically significant, they are merely stating, at a high level of confidence, that obtained differences in the performances of different groups of subjects are attributable to the experimental condition being manipulated by the researcher.

hypothesis
replication
experimental research
independent variable
dependent variable
experimental groups
control group
survey
sample
representative sample
random sample
observational method
naturalistic observation
observer bias
observer effect
case study
correlational method

coefficient of correlation
statistics
descriptive statistics
measure of central tendency
mean
median
mode
normal distribution
skewed
measure of variability
range
standard deviation
percentile
standard score
inferential statistics
operational definition
statistical significance

CHAPTER 3
The Biology of Behavior

CHAPTER 4
Sensation and Perception

CHAPTER 5
*Consciousness: Sleep,
Dreaming,
and Hypnosis*

Biological Foundations, Perception and Sleep

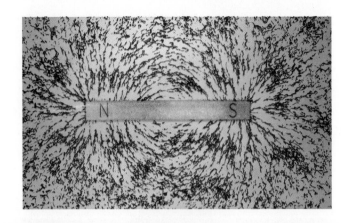

CHAPTER 3

The Biology of Behavior

OVERVIEW OF THE NERVOUS SYSTEM: ORGANIZATION AND FUNCTION

NEURONS: BASIC UNITS OF THE NERVOUS SYSTEM

Neuron Structure
Neural Transmission
Neuron Electrical Activity
Neurotransmitters and the Synapse
Neurotransmitters and Behavior

THE PERIPHERAL NERVOUS SYSTEM

The Somatic Nervous System
The Autonomic Nervous System

THE CENTRAL NERVOUS SYSTEM

The Spinal Cord
The Medulla
The Pons
The Cerebellum
The Reticular Formation

THE LIMBIC SYSTEM

The Amygdala
The Hippocampus

The Septum
The Hypothalamus
The Thalamus

THE BASAL GANGLIA

THE CEREBRAL CORTEX

Sex Differences in the Brain
Lateralization of Function
How the Brain is Studied

THE ENDOCRINE SYSTEM

The Pituitary Gland
The Thyroid Gland
The Adrenal Glands
The Gonads

DRUGS AND BEHAVIOR

Depressants: Sedatives, Opiates, and Alcohol
Stimulants: Caffeine, Nicotine, Amphetamines, and Cocaine
Hallucinogens: LSD, PCP, and Marijuana

The series of photographs shown in Figure 3.1 are PET (positron emission tomography) scans of a live human brain. PET scans are sensitive to different levels of neuronal activity by measuring the accumulation of radioactive chemicals in active brain cells. These are views of the left side of the head, with the front of the head at the left of the picture and the back of the head at the right. The photographs show a subject performing a variety of intellectual tasks related to language. The PET scan reveals that blood flow in the brain shifts to different locations depending on which intellectual task is being performed.

The different patterns in the photographs are related to activities within the brain. In the PET scan, a bright red or orange glow indicates a high activity area. When we hear a word, as in the left photograph, the neurons in a special area of our brains called the auditory cortex region of the temporal lobes become active; they are busy processing information about the sound. The visual cortex of the brain is more active while looking at words, and the frontal cortex becomes active when we speak. The PET scan lets us see such functions as thinking, seeing, or listening by revealing areas of high activity in the brain. It is one of several new techniques that biological psychologists use to learn about the relationship between behavior and biological functions. (The method by which these photographs were produced is discussed later in the chapter, along with other techniques for studying the brain.)

The PET scan provides a good starting point for this chapter because it illustrates the basic concept of biological psychology: that human behaviors, thoughts, memories, emotions, and even qualities of the mind such as intelligence and creativity are based on biological processes that take place within and between cells. We still do not have a clear picture of where or how each of these functions happens. New techniques and new discoveries are being made every year, however, and many scientists believe that it is only a matter of time before even complex behaviors and emotions can be understood at the cellular level.

Until recently, both laypersons and many brain scientists viewed behaviors like thinking, feeling, and remembering as something more than complex interactions between cells in the brain. For example, the mind was thought to consist of nonphysical entities such as a spirit or soul. However, many researchers are becoming increasingly convinced that the mind consists of a collection of mental processes that will eventually be explained in terms of molecular changes in the brain (Fischbach, 1992).

This chapter provides a very broad overview of what we know about the biology of behavior. Biological structures including individual neurons, the central and peripheral nervous systems, and the endocrine systems are examined to see how they influence or regulate behaviors. We begin with a look at the nervous system.

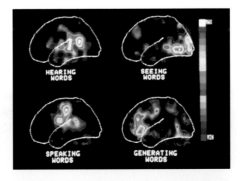

FIGURE 3.1

PET Scans from a Human Brain

These PET scans were taken while a person was performing a variety of tasks related to language. Notice that different areas of the brain become active during different tasks.

OVERVIEW OF THE NERVOUS SYSTEM: ORGANIZATION AND FUNCTION

All of our activities—sensing, perceiving, moving, feeling, thinking, or remembering—depend on the functioning of our nervous systems. Although the brain is the hub of the nervous system, it is by no means the sole component. The nervous system of humans and all other vertebrates (organisms with a spinal cord encased in bone) consists of two major parts: the central nervous system (CNS) and the peripheral nervous system (PNS). (The PNS has two subdivisions: the somatic and autonomic nervous systems.) These components are all shown in Figure 3.2. We shall examine each of these parts in depth after a preliminary overview.

The **central nervous system (CNS)** consists of the brain and the spinal cord, which are the most protected organs of the body. Both are encased in bones and surrounded by protective membranes called meninges. The CNS plays a central role in coordinating and integrating all bodily functions. It acts as an intermediary between stimuli we receive and our responses. For example, if your bare foot comes in contact with something hairy and wiggly when you put on a shoe, this alarming message will travel through nerves in your legs, enter your spinal cord, reach your brain, and trigger a rapid response.

In the situation just described, the CNS acts as a processor of incoming and outgoing messages. But the brain also sends commands directly to various parts of our bodies without first receiving an incoming stimulus. For instance, the decision to put on your shoes in the first place may have been the result of a decision to go outdoors that was unrelated to any immediate stimulus.

Our brains can also send commands to glands or organs. If you are dressed too warmly in an overheated classroom, for example, you will probably begin to perspire. This response is mediated by the hypothalamus, a small structure in the brain that serves many critical functions including temperature regulation. When our bodies become too hot, the hypothalamus signals our sweat glands to perspire, a process that helps to regulate body temperature.

Although the CNS occupies the commanding position in the nervous system, it could neither receive stimuli nor carry out its own directives without the **peripheral nervous system (PNS),** which transmits messages to and from the central nervous system. The peripheral nervous system is subdivided in two functional parts, the somatic nervous system and the autonomic nervous system, both of which are discussed later in this chapter. Before looking further at both the central and peripheral nervous systems, it is helpful to have an understanding of the building blocks that are the basis of the entire nervous system. The individual cells that make up the nervous system are called neurons.

NEURONS: BASIC UNITS OF THE NERVOUS SYSTEM

Our bodies are made up of trillions of living cells including blood, skin, muscle, and bone cells. The cells of particular interest in this chapter are the cells of the nervous system called **neurons.** Neurons are the basic units of the brain and the rest of the nervous system. They vary in shape, size, and other characteristics according to their location and function in the nervous system. The brain, for instance, contains the most concentrated mass of neurons. It is impossible to say how many neurons it contains, but estimates range around 100 billion

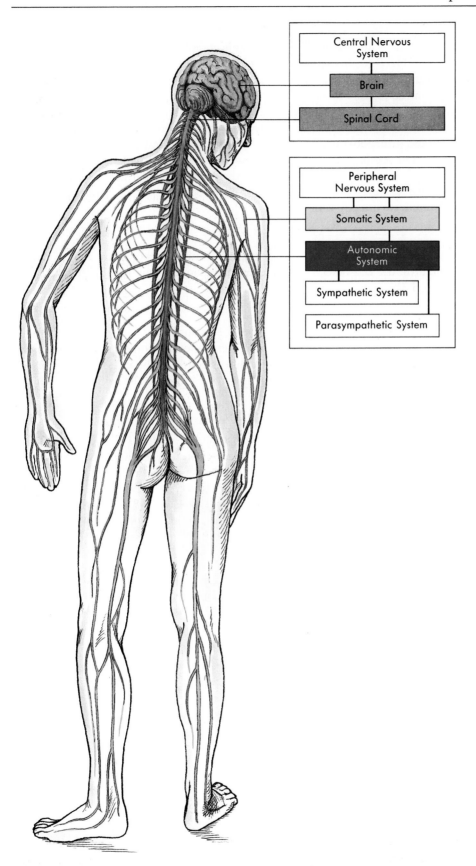

FIGURE 3.2
Divisions of the Nervous System

(Fischbach, 1992). Although this is an extraordinarily large number, sheer number alone does not account for the extreme complexity of the brain.

There are three major classes of neurons. One class, called **sensory** or **afferent neurons,** carries messages to the CNS from receptors in the skin, ears, nose, eyes, and so forth. The brain and sometimes the spinal cord interpret these messages and send appropriate responses through a second type of neuron called **motor** or **efferent neurons** that lead to muscles and glands. A third class of neurons, **interneurons,** reside only within the central nervous system. Since motor and sensory neurons rarely communicate directly, interneurons play the critical role of intermediary. Without these connecting neurons, sensory messages would never result in the appropriate bodily responses. Interneurons also communicate directly with each other.

NEURON STRUCTURE

Although neurons vary in size, shape, and function, they share four common structures: the cell body, the dendrites, the axon, and the terminal buttons (see Figure 3.3).

THE CELL BODY OR SOMA The **cell body** or soma is the largest part of the neuron. It contains structures that handle metabolic functions; it also contains the nucleus, which holds genetic information encoded in the cells' DNA. The cell body can receive impulses from other neurons, although the cell body is not the primary receptor.

THE DENDRITES Neurons typically receive neural messages at one end and pass them on at the other end. The part of the neuron that receives most transmitted signals is a collection of fibers called **dendrites** that extend out from the cell body like branches of a tree. (The word *dendrite* comes from the Greek word for tree.) Dendrites may receive information from a few to thousands of surrounding neurons. The more extensive the neuron's network of dendrites, the more connections can be made with other neurons. (Interneurons in the brain typi-

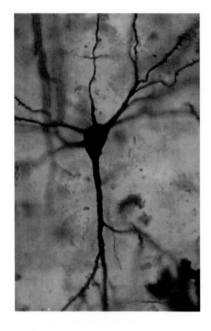

FIGURE 3.3
A. Photograph of an isolated neuron. B. Neural messages from surrounding neurons are received by the dendrites and then passed down to the cell body, the portion of the neuron where metabolic functions take place. The neural signal then moves along the axon, the transmitting fiber of the neuron. Terminal buttons at the end of the axon release a chemical called a neurotransmitter that activates adjacent neurons.

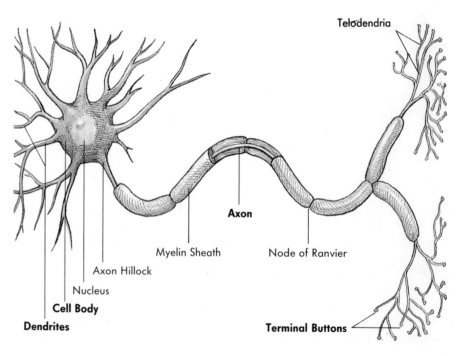

Telodendria

Axon

Myelin Sheath

Node of Ranvier

Axon Hillock

Nucleus

Cell Body

Dendrites

Terminal Buttons

cally contain far more dendritic fibers than neurons in the spinal cord or the peripheral nervous system.) Signals received by the dendrites are passed on to the cell body, which in turn passes them through the axon.

THE AXON   The **axon** is a slender, extended fiber that takes a signal from the cell body at a point called the axon hillock and transmits it along its entire length, which may range from two or more feet in spinal cord and PNS neurons to a tiny fraction of an inch in brain neurons. The axon may divide into two or more major branches called collaterals, thereby increasing its capacity to communicate with other neurons. Axons may be myelinated or unmyelinated. Myelin is a type of cell that wraps around the axon providing it with insulation. Most peripheral axons are myelinated and most (but not all) of the axons in the brain are unmyelinated. Myelin serves both to insulate the axon, much like insulation on a wire, and to increase the speed of conduction along the axon.

THE TERMINAL BUTTONS   The transmitting end of the axon consists of small bulblike structures known as **terminal buttons.** The terminal buttons store and release chemical substances (called neurotransmitters) that enable nerve impulses to cross from one neuron to adjacent neurons. In the next section we look at this complex process.

NEURAL TRANSMISSION

People often think of the nervous system as a vast, complex network of interconnected wirelike structures. However, the multitude of neural circuits or pathways within the central nervous system are not at all like electric wires. Instead of a continuous filament, these circuits are made up of perhaps hundreds of thousands of individual neurons. In order for a message to travel from neuron to neuron, it must move from the terminal buttons at the end of one neuron's axon to the dendrites or cell body of an adjacent neuron. The process by which impulses are transmitted in the CNS is not just electrical, as it is in the wiring system of a house. It also involves chemical substances called neurotransmitters; the process is called neural transmission.

Within the peripheral nervous system, messages are transmitted along the extended axonal fibers of both motor and sensory neurons that are contained within bundles of neural fibers called *nerves.* These fibers extend as continuous structures from sensory receptors or muscles to the CNS. For example, a sensory message from a pain receptor in the skin of your finger is transmitted along a single axonal fiber that extends the length of your arm to a point where it enters the spinal cord and transfers its message to an interneuron.

NEURON ELECTRICAL ACTIVITY

Like all cells, neurons are surrounded by a membrane. This membrane acts as a kind of skin that permits the cell to maintain an internal environment different from the fluid outside the membrane. On both sides of the cell membrane are many particles called ions which carry either a positive or a negative electrical charge. Ions that are particularly important in electrical conduction are negatively charged organic ions (An−) and chlorine ions (Cl−) and positively charged sodium ions (Na+) and potassium ions (K+). If the cell membrane did not act as a barrier, these ions would be equally distributed both inside and outside of the neuron. However, some charged particles, such as the negative organic ions, do not pass through the cell membrane to the surrounding fluid. The membrane is semipermeable to other ions. For instance, sodium and potassium ions pass through only when "gates" are open for them.

RESTING POTENTIALS Thus the negative and positive charges are unequal on either side of the membrane, and its interior has a negative electrical potential with respect to its exterior. This phenomenon is due primarily to a high concentration of positively charged sodium ions outside the membrane and more negatively charged organic ions on the inside. A neuron at rest (that is, not transmitting a nerve impulse) contains a net negative charge of about -70 millivolts (70/1,000 of a volt) relative to the outside environment. The membrane is said to be in a polarized state when the neuron is at rest.

This differential charge gives the resting neuron a state of potential energy known as the **resting potential.** In other words, it is in a constant state of readiness to be activated by an impulse from an adjacent neuron. Maintaining this resting potential allows the neuron to store the energy that it utilizes when it transmits an impulse (Kolb & Whishaw, 1985). The resting potential is maintained because the membrane is impermeable to the positively charged sodium (Na +) ions concentrated on the outside of the neuron (see Figure 3.4).

GRADED POTENTIALS The resting potential is disturbed when an impulse is received from another neuron. This disturbance is referred to as a **graded potential** and its strength varies with the intensity of stimulation. If we were to measure the charge on the axon during a graded potential we would observe a change from -70 millivolts to perhaps -60 millivolts depending on the amount of stimulation the cell receives. A graded potential by itself is of little consequence. However, when several graded potentials occur simultaneously or in rapid succession they may be sufficient to depolarize the neuron to a threshold value (the minimum voltage change sufficient to activate a response) of about -55 millivolts.

The determination of whether or not a graded potential is sufficient to bring the axon to its threshold level is made at the axon hillock, a specialized region of the cell body near the base of the axon (refer back to Figure 3.3). Like a tiny computer, the axon hillock combines and totals all the graded potentials that reach it. If the sum of these graded potentials reaches a sufficient magnitude or threshold the axon hillock triggers a sudden depolarization of the axon membrane. This is referred to as an action potential.

ACTION POTENTIALS An **action potential** is initiated when the axon is depolarized to its threshold level (approximately -55 millivolts). When the membrane reaches this threshold level a sudden complete depolarization results. That is, the axon goes from about -55 millivolts to approximately $+55$ millivolts. This rapid depolarization is the result of the membrane changing its permeability to sodium (Na+) and potassium (K+ ions. When the membrane is no longer impermeable to Na+ it enters the cell bringing the charge on the inside of the membrane to a positive value (about $+50$ millivolts). Some potassium ions begin to leave the axon at this time because the electrical gradient inside the axon becomes weakened as sodium ions enter. However, the number of potassium ions that leave the inside of the axon is far outweighed by the number of sodium ions that enter.

The change in permeability to Na+ is extremely brief and quickly the resting potential is restored by the closing of the Na+ gates and the rapid expulsion of K+ from within the axon. Potassium ions are repelled because of the positive charge now inside the membrane. As potassium ions leave, the charge across the membrane returns to its resting state. In fact, an excess of potassium outflow briefly hyperpolarizes the membrane. This complete process for an action potential takes about 1 millisecond (1/1,000 of a second).

The action potential is an electrical signal that flows (or propagates) along the entire surface of the axon to the terminal buttons (Wang & Freeman, 1987). Action potentials have been defined as the event that initiates the release of

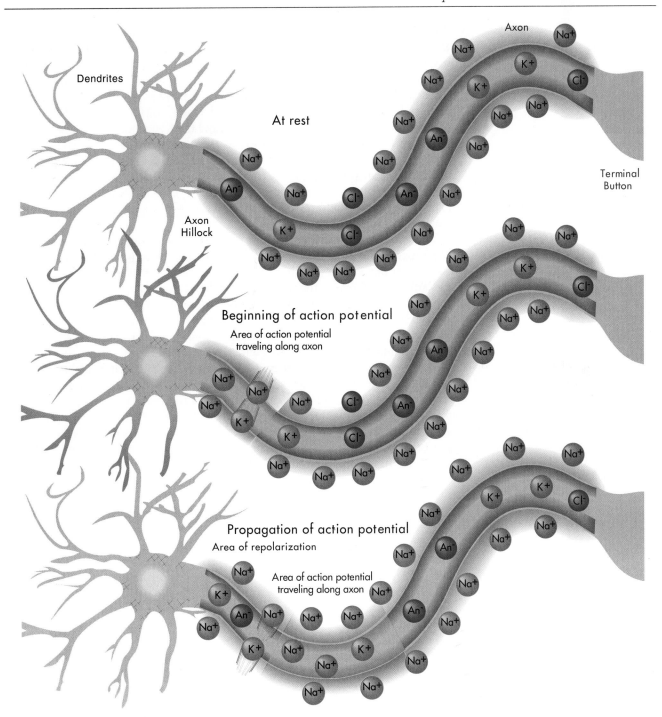

FIGURE 3.4

A. Neuron at rest. Resting membrane potential is maintained by distribution of charged ions on either side of cell membrane. B. Initiation of action potential. Action potential is initiated at axon hillock by movement of sodium (Na+) ions to inside of cell. C. Movement of action potential. Action potential moves (propagates) along axon as Na+ ions enter cell. After an action potential occurs, membrane potential is restored by movement of both potassium (K+) and sodium (Na+) ions from the cell.

transmitter substances from the terminal buttons, thus making them 'talk' to the receiving cells (Carlson, 1981, p. 47).

THE ALL-OR-NONE LAW   Unlike the graded potential, the strength of an action potential does not vary according to the degree of stimulation. Once a nerve impulse is triggered within an axon, it is transmitted the entire length of the axon with no loss of intensity. Partial action potentials or nerve impulses do not occur; thus an axon is said to conduct without decrement. Because of this, the nerve impulse in the axon is said to follow the **all-or-none law:** If the sum of the graded potentials reaches a threshold, there will be an action potential; if the threshold is not reached, however, no action potential will occur.

According to the all-or-none law, a neuron fires at only one level of intensity. How, then, is it possible to distinguish between different levels of stimulus intensity (for instance, a loud noise and a soft sound, or a light or heavy touch)? Consider this question before reading on.

The answer to our question lies in the fact that, even though a single neuron's impulse level is always the same, two important variables may still change: the number of neurons affected by an impulse and the frequency with which neurons fire. Very weak stimuli may trigger impulses in only a few neurons, whereas very strong stimuli may cause thousands of neurons to fire. The frequency in which neurons fire can also vary greatly, from fewer than 100 times per second for weak stimuli to as often as 1,000 times per second. Thus the combination of how many neurons fire and how often they fire allows us to distinguish different intensities of stimuli.

The speed with which an impulse travels through a neuron varies with the properties of the axon, ranging from less than one meter per second to as fast as 100 meters per second (roughly 224 miles per hour). At least two important factors affect speed: One is the resistance to current along the axon—there is an inverse relationship between resistance and impulse speed, so that speed is reduced as resistance increases. Resistance is most effectively decreased by an increase in axon size, which helps explain why large axons such as those in PNS neurons tend to conduct impulses at a faster rate than do small axons.

However, if the nervous system had to depend only on axon size to transmit impulses quickly, there would not be enough room in our bodies for all the large axons we would need. Fortunately, a second property also helps to speed the transmission of nerve impulses. Specialized cells, called **glia cells,** wrap around some axons, forming an insulating cover called a **myelin sheath.** (One type of glia cell, the oligodendrocytes, forms the myelin within the CNS. In the PNS the insulating sheaths are built from another type of glia cell known as Schwann cells.) Between each glia cell the axon membrane is exposed by a small gap called a **node of Ranvier,** as shown in Figure 3.3.

In these myelinated neurons, nerve impulses do not travel smoothly down the axon. Instead, they jump from node to node, in a process called *saltatory conduction* (from the Latin *saltare,* meaning to leap). Saltatory conduction is so efficient that a small myelinated axon can conduct a nerve impulse just as quickly as an unmyelinated axon 30 times larger. Given the critical importance of myelin in the nervous system, you can better understand the devastating effects of certain diseases, such as *multiple sclerosis (MS),* that involve progressive breakdown in these insulating sheaths. In MS the loss of myelination may short-circuit or delay the transmission of signals from the brain to the muscles of the arms and legs. As a consequence, a person with MS often experiences a weakness or loss of control over the limbs.

NEUROTRANSMITTERS AND THE SYNAPSE

The transmission of an electrical impulse from one end of a neuron to the other provides only a partial explanation of how messages are transmitted. When an electrical nerve impulse reaches the end of an axon, it cannot flow directly into other neurons. That is because there is a space between neurons known as the synaptic gap. The space is minuscule, generally no more than five-millionths of an inch across, but the electrical impulse does not bridge it alone. A chemical process is necessary in bridging the synaptic gap. Figure 3.5 illustrates a **synapse** which includes the membrane on the terminal button (the presynaptic membrane), the synaptic gap, and the membrane on the dendrite or receiving neuron (the postsynaptic membrane).

Many years ago some scientists speculated that impulses were transmitted from neuron to neuron when something like an electric spark jumped the synaptic gap. We now know that this explanation is incomplete. Neurons communicate primarily through the release of chemicals. These chemical messengers, called **neurotransmitters,** are contained within tiny sacs in the axon terminal buttons called synaptic vesicles. Far less common is the electrical synapse where an electrical potential "jumps" across the synaptic gap. These rare electrical synapses will not be discussed here.

STEPS IN NEURAL TRANSMISSION When the axon fires, the action potential travels along the axon to the terminal button. When it arrives at the terminal button, the membrane there changes its permeability to another ion, calcium (Ca++). Calcium then enters the terminal button and allows the synaptic vesicles to migrate to the presynaptic membrane, where they release their contents into the synapse (Cooper et al., 1986; Wang & Freeman, 1987). The total amount of neurotransmitter released depends on how much Ca++ enters the terminal button. More intense stimulation produces a greater frequency of action potentials, which in turn allows more Ca++ to enter, thus increasing the amount of neurotransmitter released.

FIGURE 3.5
A. An electron micrograph of neural tissue showing a synapse. B. Illustration of an active synapse with neurotransmitter being released into the synaptic gap.

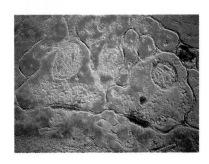

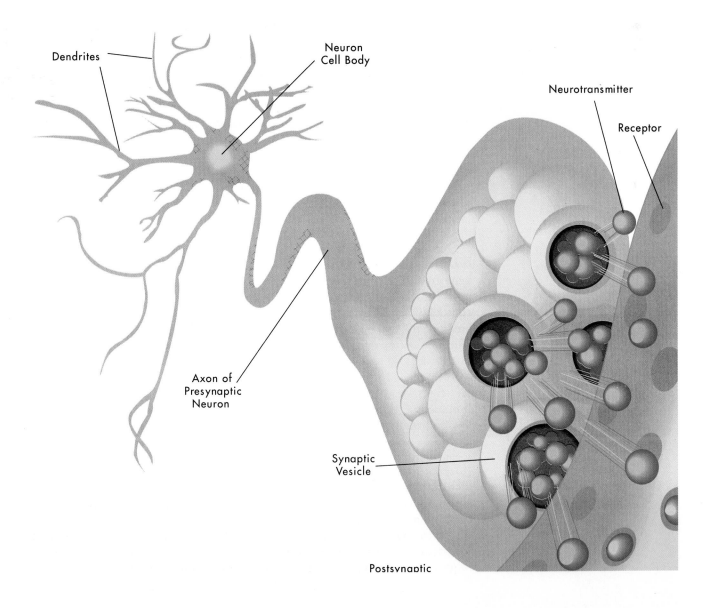

Dendrites

Neuron Cell Body

Neurotransmitter

Receptor

Axon of Presynaptic Neuron

Synaptic Vesicle

Postsynaptic

EXCITATORY AND INHIBITORY EFFECTS   The postsynaptic membrane of the receiving neuron contains specialized receptor sites that respond to a variety of neurotransmitters. Neurotransmitters act on these receptor sites to produce a rapid change in the permeability of the postsynaptic membrane. Depending on the receptor site and the type of neurotransmitter, this change in permeability can either excite or inhibit action potentials in the receiving neuron.

In simplified terms, neurotransmitters exert their effects by opening gates or channels in the postsynaptic membrane, letting ions of one kind or another pass through. If positively charged sodium ions enter, the membrane is excited or depolarized and graded potentials are caused. Neurotransmitters that cause these changes are called excitatory neurotransmitters, and their effects are referred to as **excitatory postsynaptic potentials,** or **EPSPs.** Conversely, if positively charged potassium ions pass to the outside of the postsynaptic membrane or negatively charged chloride ions enter, the membrane is inhibited and the graded potential results in making the membrane more negative (a process called hyperpolarization). Neurotransmitters that act in this way are called inhibitory neurotransmitters, and their effects are called **inhibitory postsynaptic potentials,** or **IPSPs.**

Since hundreds or even thousands of axon terminals may form synapses with any one neuron, EPSPs and IPSPs may be present at the same time. The combination of all these excitatory and inhibitory signals determines whether or not the receiving neuron will fire. For an action potential to occur, EPSPs must not only predominate; they must do so to the extent of reaching the neuron's threshold. To prevent this from happening, there needs to be a sufficient number of IPSPs present to prevent the algebraic sum of EPSPs and IPSPs from reaching the threshold of depolarization.

Some neurotransmitters seem to be exclusively excitatory or inhibitory; others seem capable of producing either effect under different circumstances. When transmitters have both capabilities, the postsynaptic receptor site determines what the effect will be, so that these neurotransmitters may have an inhibitory effect at one synapse and an excitatory effect at another.

Neurotransmitters interact with receptors on the postsynaptic cell membrane to change its electrical potential. If the change is sufficient to depolarize the cell membrane, a graded potential is initiated, thus beginning the cycle outlined earlier in Figure 3.3.

NEUROTRANSMITTER BREAKDOWN AND REUPTAKE   What keeps the supply of neurotransmitters from being exhausted? There are several answers to this question. First, the raw materials used in the manufacture of neurotransmitters are constantly being replenished by the cell body. Second, some neurotransmitters are broken down by enzyme action once they have accomplished their function. Their breakdown products then reenter the terminal buttons to be recycled for further use. Third, in many cases the transmitter substance is retrieved intact, in a process called reuptake. The breakdown and reuptake processes, which are essential for normal neuronal functioning, can be influenced by a number of drugs. For example, drugs like amphetamine and cocaine inhibit the reuptake of several neurotransmitters resulting in heightened alertness and activity. Finally, neurons contain regulatory mechanisms which prevent depletion as well as regulate their sensitivity to neurotransmitters.

IDENTIFYING NEUROTRANSMITTER SUBSTANCES   As much as scientists know about the electrochemical process of transmitting nerve impulses, the neurotransmitters themselves have been hard to identify because they often occur in very small quantities. Table 3.1 presents a list of several important substances known to be neurotransmitters, as well as the functions they are thought to perform. For a substance to be considered a neurotransmitter it must meet the following criteria: (a) It must be contained in the axon terminal buttons, (b) it must be released into the synapse when the neuron fires, and (c) it must cause a post-synaptic effect after it interacts with the receptor.

NEUROTRANSMITTER SUBSTANCES What are some of the chemicals that are known to serve as neurotransmitters? Although the list of substances so far identified as neurotransmitters is quite large, we will discuss a few that are well understood and play important roles in behavior to be discussed in later chapters.

Acetylcholine (ACh) Acetylcholine was the first neurotransmitter to be discovered. It plays an important role in motor movement as it is the neurotransmitter released from motor neurons onto muscle fibers to make them contract. In addition, acetylcholine appears to be involved in both learning and memory. Several toxins such as botulism, nerve gas, and black widow spider venom interfere with acetylcholine transmission producing paralysis in their victims. A common disorder that involves acetylcholine is Alzheimer's disease which appears to involve a

TABLE 3.1 *Chemicals Known to Be Major Neurotransmitters*

Neurotransmitter Effects	Location	Functions
Acetylcholine (ACh) Excitatory	Cortex, spinal cord, target organs activated by parasympathetic nervous system	Excitation in brain. Either excitation or inhibition in target organs of PNS. Involved in learning, movement, memory.
Norepinephrine (NE) Excitatory	Spinal cord, limbic system, cortex, target organs of sympathetic nervous system	Arousal of reticular system. Involved in eating, emotional behavior, learning, memory.
Dopamine (DA) Inhibitory	Limbic system, basal ganglia, cerebellum	Involved in movement, emotional behavior, attention, learning, memory.
Serotonin (SE) Inhibitory	Brain stem, most of brain	Involved in emotional behavior, arousal sleep.
Gama-amino-butyric acid (GABA) Inhibitory	Most of brain and spinal cord	Involved in regulating arousal, major inhibitory neurotransmitter in brain.
Endorphins Inhibitory	Spinal cord, most of brain	Functions as a natural analgesic for pain reduction, involved in emotional behavior, eating, learning.
Glutamate Excitatory	Brain and spinal cord	Major excitatory neurotransmitter, in brain. Involved in learning.

degeneration of acetylcholine neurons in the brain. The causes of Alzheimer's disease are not well understood.

Norepinephrine   Norepinephrine is distributed throughout the central and peripheral nervous systems. It is important in emotional arousal, stress, and perhaps learning and memory. Norepinephrine is a major excitatory neurotransmitter in the brain. Deficiencies in norepinephrine are linked to depression and some eating disorders.

Dopamine   Dopamine is located primarily in the brain and involved with the initiation of motor movement, attention, and learning and memory. Deficiencies in dopamine result in Parkinson's disease which is a severe motor disorder. Parkinson's disease is treated with a drug that is converted into dopamine in the brain. The major psychotic disorder, schizophrenia, appears to be associated with an excess of dopamine in certain regions of the brain.

Serotonin   Serotonin is distributed throughout the brain and spinal cord and is involved in the control of your sleep/wake cycle, mood, and appetite. Deficiencies in serotonin are associated with sleep disorders and depression.

Gamma-amino-butyric Acid (GABA)   GABA is the major inhibitory neurotransmitter in the brain and spinal cord. It plays an important role in regulating arousal and anxiety. Drugs like Valium increase the activity of GABA producing a calming effect and even sleep.

Endorphins   Endorphins are a family of neurotransmitters chemically similar to opiates like morphine. They are widely distributed throughout most of the brain. Extensive research has linked the endorphins to an array of behavioral and mental processes, including inducing a sense of well-being and euphoria, counteracting the influence of stress, modulating food and liquid intake, facilitating learning and memory, and reducing pain (Cesselin et al., 1989; Martinez et al., 1988; Nakamura et al., 1989; Olson et al., 1986; Panksepp, 1986). Medical science is particularly interested in the pain-reducing properties of endorphins, some of which may be as much as 100 times stronger than morphine. Researchers are hopeful that one day a synthetic version of these powerful brain chemicals will be developed for use in pain control programs.

Glutamate   Glutamate or glutamic acid is an amino acid derived from glucose. Glutamate is one of the most important excitatory neurotransmitters in the brain. It is believed to play an important role in a process called long-term potentiation which is a change in neuronal functioning that mediates some forms of learning (Cotman, Monaghan, and Ganong, 1988). The food additive monosodium glutamate (MSG) contains glutamate and may produce symptoms of dizziness and numbness after eating foods containing large amounts of it.

This is only a brief review of several of the most important neurotransmitter substances. New neurotransmitters and other neuroactive chemicals are still being discovered and investigated, a trend that has been central to the development of the science of molecular neurobiology, a field devoted in part to a study of the molecular bases of behavior. At present the number of substances identified and believed to be neurotransmitters exceeds 50.

You may have noticed in Table 3.1 that different neurotransmitter substances seem to have different effects. Instead of transmission of a signal from one neuron to another, the function of some neurotransmitters is listed as inhibition (that is, they restrain or suppress the transmission of neural impulses). This label may seem contrary to logic, especially since we have just seen that neurotransmitters are essential for the transmission of neural impulses. Sometimes, however, neurotransmitters have just the opposite effect.

Although the information about cell structures that we have discussed so far may seem like a collection of dry facts, it relates directly to our behavior. The most striking examples are associated with schizophrenia, depression, and the use of certain drugs.

SCHIZOPHRENIA Schizophrenia is a severe psychological disorder characterized by disturbed thought processes, delusions, hallucinations, and exaggerated inappropriate emotions. In many cases, the most bizarre symptoms of schizophrenia can be controlled by drugs such as chlorpromazine and haloperidol, both of which have similar effects: They inhibit the effects of dopamine, a neurotransmitter found in the brain (Davison & Neale, 1990; Kimble, 1988; Lipper, 1985; Wolkin et al., 1989). This finding has led some psychologists to hypothesize that the disorder may be linked to excessive levels of dopamine or above-normal reactivity to this neurotransmitter (Carlsson, 1977, 1990; Cortes et al., 1989; Grey et al., 1991; Langer et al., 1981). This argument has been supported by studies that have found an abnormal number of dopamine receptors in the brains of some schizophrenics (Wong et al., 1986).

Neurotransmitter systems are complex, and conclusions about the relationship between schizophrenia and dopamine are not yet possible. Nevertheless, it seems possible that at least some symptoms of this disorder may be related to the neurotransmitter dopamine.

DEPRESSION Other studies have linked another disorder, depression, to two neurotransmitters: norepinephrine and serotonin (Kimble, 1988). A group of drugs called tricyclics, among the most successful in relieving depression, are believed to increase the availability of both these neurotransmitters in certain areas of the brain (Colasanti, 1982a). Research suggests that the antidepressant effects of these drugs may be related to increased sensitivity of the receptors for these two neurotransmitters rather than a mere change in the actual levels of these brain chemicals (Charney et al., 1984; Heninger et al., 1983).

Another drug which has been quite successful in alleviating depression is Prozac. Prozac appears to specifically increase levels of serotonin in the brain. Since studies (Carlson, 1981) have linked norepinephrine and serotonin to people's positive feelings, it seems possible that either insufficient brain levels of these chemicals or decreased responsivity to these neurotransmitters may be related to depression. Recent research has also implicated dopamine in depression, but the mode of action remains to be clarified (Depue & Iacono, 1989; Maj et al., 1989). As with theories about dopamine and schizophrenia, however, the evidence is not yet conclusive. Chapter 16 explores the evidence linking neurotransmitter abnormalities to depression, schizophrenia, and some other psychological disorders.

As stated at the outset of the chapter the nervous system is divided into two major divisions: the peripheral nervous system and the central nervous system. We will now examine these systems in some detail.

THE PERIPHERAL NERVOUS SYSTEM

The peripheral nervous system (PNS) consists of all the nervous system structures located outside the central nervous system (CNS). Its primary purpose is to serve the CNS by transmitting information to and from the spinal cord and brain. The PNS has two divisions, the somatic and autonomic. (See Figure 3.6.)

THE SOMATIC NERVOUS SYSTEM

The **somatic nervous system** contains nerves that serve the major skeletal muscles, such as the arm and leg muscles. These muscles, often called striated because they appear striped or striated when seen under a microscope, carry out intentional movements directed by messages from higher brain centers. The somatic nervous system also contains nerves that transmit sensory information from the skin, muscles, and various sensory organs of the body to the spinal cord and brain.

THE AUTONOMIC NERVOUS SYSTEM

The other division of the PNS, the **autonomic nervous system (ANS),** controls the glands and the smooth muscles of the heart, lungs, stomach, intestines, blood vessels, and various other internal organs. The ANS is named for the fact that the muscles and glands it serves operate reflexively without intentional or voluntary control. Thus they are autonomous or self-regulating.

The autonomic nervous system is itself subdivided into two branches, the **sympathetic** and the **parasympathetic.** In most cases, each internal organ serviced by the autonomic nervous system has a separate set of connections with the sympathetic and the parasympathetic branches. These two distinct sets of connections operate quite differently, often having opposing effects on the organs they control, as shown in Figure 3.6. For example, the sympathetic system increases heart rate, dilates the pupils, and inhibits digestive activity; the parasympathetic system has the opposite effect in each case.

The sympathetic and parasympathetic systems do not operate in a counterproductive fashion, however. Instead, they work together to allow our bodies to function well when either relaxed or highly aroused. Our normal state, somewhere between extreme excitement and complete relaxation, is maintained by the balance between these two systems. However, there are times when we need an emergency source of energy as when we are stressed or feeling strong emotion and at these times our sympathetic nervous systems come into play.

For instance, imagine that you are hiking in the wilderness when you are suddenly confronted by a bear. The result will probably be the classic response that prepares you (and probably the bear, too) for fight or flight. Your pupils dilate, your heart pumps like mad, and epinephrine (commonly called adrenalin) pours into your blood vessels. These effects produce distinct sensations in your body, but they also serve a critical function. Under the influence of the sympathetic nervous system, organs such as the heart operate at their upper limits.

This response serves us well in emergencies, whether we need to escape from a bear in the woods or to rescue a child from a burning house, but our bodies cannot continue at this pace for very long. If they did, we would soon be exhausted. It is at this point that the parasympathetic nervous system comes into play, providing a braking mechanism for each of the organs activated by the sympathetic nervous system. This countersystem helps us conserve energy and resources and is active in restoring our bodies to normal.

Sympathetic and parasympathetic responses take place in different ways. The parasympathetic nervous system tends to affect specific glands and organs independently of one another, often one at a time. In an emergency, however, there is no time to waste. As a result, the sympathetic nervous system acts as a unit, simultaneously mobilizing most or all of the various sympathetic effects outlined in Figure 3.6.

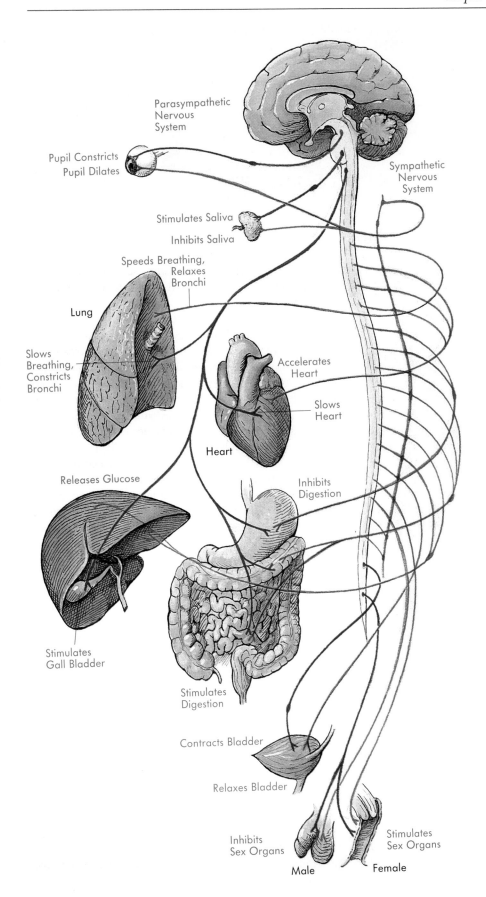

Parasympathetic
Nervous
System

Pupil Constricts
Pupil Dilates

Sympathetic
Nervous
System

Stimulates Saliva

Inhibits Saliva

Speeds Breathing,
Relaxes
Bronchi

Lung

Slows
Breathing,
Constricts
Bronchi

Accelerates
Heart

Slows
Heart

Heart

Releases Glucose

Inhibits
Digestion

Stimulates
Gall Bladder

Stimulates
Digestion

Contracts Bladder

Relaxes Bladder

Inhibits
Sex Organs

Stimulates
Sex Organs

Male   Female

FIGURE 3.6
*Functions of the Sympathetic and
Parasympathetic Nervous System*

These two systems work together to allow our
bodies to react quickly to our environments and to
relax.

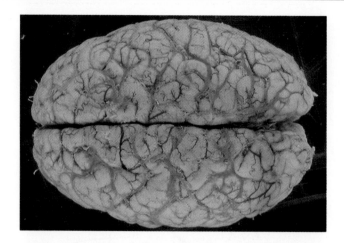

FIGURE 3.7

Top View of the Human Brain Showing the Cerebral Cortex

THE CENTRAL NERVOUS SYSTEM

The average human brain weighs approximately 1390 grams (or roughly three pounds). Yet it can store more information than many great libraries combined, and its communication network has more potential interconnections between cells than the number of atoms in our solar system. How does the brain work? How do electrical impulses and chemical transmissions translate to memories, creating insights, intelligence, and feelings? The answers to these questions are still far from complete, but we are piecing together more and more clues. Much of what we know has to do with the brain's physical structure.

If the top of a person's skull were removed so that you could look straight down on the brain, you would see something like Figure 3.7. In its natural state, the human brain looks much like a soft, wrinkled walnut, its outer surface filled with crevices and folds. The left and right sides appear to be separated by a long, deep cleft (called the longitudinal sulcus) that runs from the front to the back. The area of the brain visible from the top is known as the cortex. The cortex is divided into two sides or **cerebral hemispheres** which, while not precisely identical, are almost mirror images of each other.

Under the cortex are many other structures, as shown in Figure 3.8. Starting from the spinal cord and working roughly upward through the base of the brain, these include the medulla, the pons, the cerebellum, the reticular formation, the structures of the limbic system, the hypothalamus, and the thalamus.

THE SPINAL CORD

Housed within a hollow tubelike structure composed of a series of bones called vertebrae, the spinal cord looks something like a long, white, smooth rope extending from the neck to the small of the back. Along the length of the spinal cord are spinal nerves that branch out between pairs of vertebrae. These nerves connect with various sensory organs, muscles, and glands served by the peripheral nervous system. The spinal nerves occur in 31 matched pairs, with one nerve of each pair connected to the right side of the spinal cord and its counterpart connected to the left side. Thus the spinal cord can help coordinate the two sides of the body.

The spinal cord is often overlooked in discussions of the biological bases of behavior, since the brain occupies the commanding position in the CNS. However, the spinal cord fills the very important function of conveying messages to and from the brain. In addition, the spinal cord controls reflexes which are simple circuits of sensory and motor neurons that initiate responses to specific stimuli.

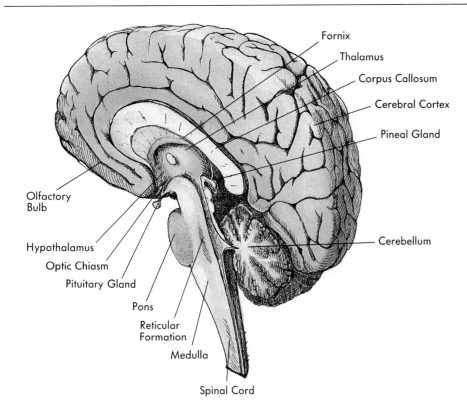

Fornix
Thalamus
Corpus Callosum
Cerebral Cortex
Pineal Gland

Olfactory
Bulb

Hypothalamus
Optic Chiasm
Pituitary Gland
Pons
Reticular
Formation
Medulla
Spinal Cord

Cerebellum

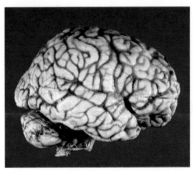

FIGURE 3.8
*Bisected Views of the Human Brain
Showing the Locations of Major
Structures and Areas*

All complex behaviors require integration and coordination at the level of the brain. However, certain basic reflexive behaviors (such as a leg jerk in response to a tap on the kneecap or the quick withdrawal of a hand from a hot stove) do not require brain processing. Different parts of the spinal cord control different reflexes: Hand withdrawal is controlled by the upper spinal cord, whereas the knee jerk response is controlled by an area in the lower cord. The brain is not directly involved in controlling these simple reflexive responses, but it is clearly aware of what action has transpired (see Figure 3.9).

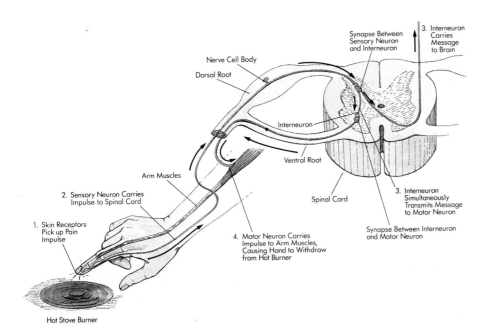

FIGURE 3.9
Neural Control of Simple Reflexes

A simple reflexive response involves the interaction of a sensory neuron, an interneuron, and a motor neuron. Interneurons function to both convey sensory information to the brain and to stimulate motor neurons to activate the withdrawal reflex.

THE MEDULLA

The **medulla** is the lowest part of the brain, located just above the spinal cord. This structure is in a well-protected location, deep and low within the brain which is fortunate, since it contains centers that control many vital life-support functions such as breathing, heart rate, and blood pressure. Even the slightest damage in a critical region of the medulla can cause death. The medulla also plays an important role in regulating other reflexive, automatic physiological functions such as sneezing, coughing, and vomiting.

THE PONS

The **pons** is a large bulge in the lower brain core, just above the medulla. The pons plays an important role in fine-tuning motor messages as they travel from the motor area of the cerebral cortex down through the pons to the cerebellum. Species-typical behaviors (such as the feeding patterns of a particular species of animals) have been shown to be strongly influenced by the pons, which appears to program the patterns of muscle movement that produce these behaviors.

The pons also plays a role in processing some sensory information, particularly visual information. In addition, the pons contains specialized nuclei that help control respiration and influence facial expression.

THE CEREBELLUM

The **cerebellum** is a distinctive structure about the size of a fist, tucked beneath the back part of the cerebral hemispheres. It consists of two wrinkled hemispheres covered by an outer cortex. The cerebellum's primary function is to coordinate and regulate motor movements (Stein, 1986) that are broadly controlled by higher brain centers. The cerebellum fine-tunes and smooths out movements, particularly those required for rapid changes in direction. For example, when you reach out to catch a moving ball your cerebellum is involved in the timing of your movements. This kind of timed movement clearly involves learning. Experiments with animals have shown that the activity of specific cells in the cerebellum change during the course of learning (Thompson, 1989).

Damage to the cerebellum results in awkward, jerky, uncoordinated movements and may even affect speech. Professional boxers are especially susceptible to slight damage to the cerebellum which results in a condition called punch-drunk syndrome. Motor impairment following alcohol intoxication may also be related to cellular changes in the cerebellum. Researchers have recently demonstrated that alcohol facilitates inhibition in the cerebellum by activating GABA receptors (Luddens, et al., 1990; Urrutia et al., 1992).

THE RETICULAR FORMATION

The **reticular formation** consists of a set of neural circuits that extend from the lower brain, where the spinal cord enters, up to the thalamus (refer back to Figure 3.8). Research has demonstrated that the reticular formation plays a critical role in controlling arousal or alertness. For this reason, it has become common to refer to this weblike collection of nerve cells and fibers as the **reticular activating system,** or **RAS.** These neurons are primarily noradrenergic, that is, they use the neurotransmitter norepinephrine. Drugs such as amphetamine facilitate norepinephrine and increase alertness.

Some of the neural circuits that carry sensory messages from the lower regions of the brain to the higher brain areas have ancillary or detouring fibers that connect with the reticular system. Impulses from these fibers prompt the reticular formation to send signals upward, making us more responsive and alert to our environment. Experiments have shown that mild electrical stimulation of certain areas within this network causes sleeping animals to awaken slowly, whereas stronger stimulation causes animals to awaken rapidly, with greater alertness.

The reticular formation also seems to be linked to sleep cycles. When we fall asleep, our reticular systems cease to send alerting messages to our brains. While sleeping, we may screen out our extraneous stimuli, with the possible exception of critical messages like the sounds of thunder or a baby's cough. The role of the reticular formation in sleep is still not fully understood. We do know, however, that serious damage to this structure may cause a person to be extremely lethargic or to enter into a prolonged comalike sleep (Kalat, 1981). Research also suggests that the reticular formation may play an important role in dreaming (Hobson & McCarley, 1977). The impact of the RAS on sleep and dreaming patterns is considered further in Chapter 5.

THE LIMBIC SYSTEM

The **limbic system** is the portion of the brain most closely associated with emotional expression; it also plays a role in motivation, learning, and memory. The limbic system is a collection of structures located around the central core of the brain, along the innermost edge of the cerebral hemispheres. Figure 3.10 shows some key structures of the limbic system, including the amygdala, the hippocampus, the septal area, and parts of the hypothalamus. Damage to or stimulation of sites within this system may profoundly affect emotional expression, either by causing excessive reactions to situations or by greatly reducing emotional responses.

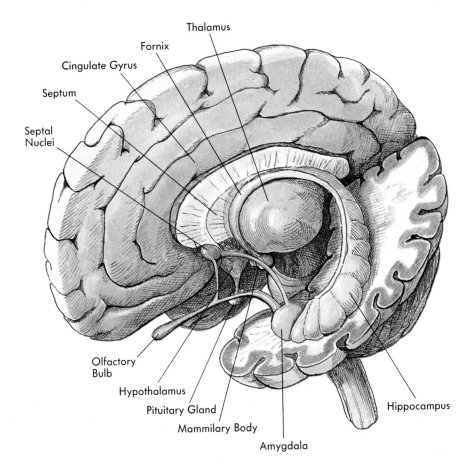

Thalamus
Fornix
Cingulate Gyrus
Septum
Septal Nuclei
Olfactory Bulb
Hypothalamus
Pituitary Gland
Mammilary Body
Amygdala
Hippocampus

FIGURE 3.10

The Limbic System

Major limbic structures include the amygdala, the septum and septal nuclei, the fornix, the hypothalamus, and the cingulate gyrus.

THE AMYGDALA

The **amygdala,** a small structure next to the hippocampus, plays an important role in the expression of anger, rage, and aggressive and fear-motivated behavior (Chozick, 1986; Everitt et al., 1989). Electrical stimulation or surgical damage to some areas of the amygdala may cause an animal to go into a blind rage, attacking everything in sight, whereas on other parts of the amygdala the same procedures may produce extreme passivity, even in threatening situations. In one study, experimenters were easily able to handle normally aggressive wild rats after surgically altering their amygdalas (Galef, 1970). Humans with tumors located in the amygdala have been known to undergo dramatic changes in their ability to suppress aggressive responses. Surgical removal of the tumor returned them to normal.

Findings such as these have prompted some law-and-order activists to suggest that criminals with histories of repeated violent crimes should undergo surgery on their amygdalas. Indeed, voluntary amygdala surgery has occasionally been performed to alleviate uncontrollable rage in some psychiatric patients. Understandably, the ethical implications of such a radical treatment prevent it from being used except in voluntary cases.

THE HIPPOCAMPUS

Another limbic system structure, the **hippocampus,** seems to be important for learning and memory (Bridgman et al., 1989; Bures et al., 1987; Lynch, 1986; Mattson & Kater, 1989). Individuals who experience damage to this structure have difficulty storing new information in memory. In one sad case, a man whose hippocampus was completely removed from both sides of his brain was unable to retain any new information in memory. He remembered skills and information learned prior to the surgery but was unable to store memories of anything that happened after the surgery. We discuss the implications of this finding in Chapter 7. Recent evidence suggests that the hippocampus may also be involved in the regulation of some reproductive characteristics like female sexual behavior, the onset of puberty, and the release of pituitary hormones (Schumacher et al., 1989, p. 178).

THE SEPTUM

Still another area of the limbic system, the **septal area,** is associated with the experience of pleasure. This was demonstrated in the 1950s by James Olds in a series of experiments on brain stimulation in rats, which were mentioned in Chapters 1 and 2. Olds implanted electrodes in various regions of rats' limbic systems and wired the electrodes in a way that allowed the rats to stimulate their own brains by pressing a lever. When the electrodes were placed in sites within the hypothalamus and the septal area, the rats seemingly could not get enough stimulation. They would press the lever several thousand times per hour, often to the point of exhaustion. Because the animals labored so incessantly to produce this experience, such behavior was interpreted as meaning they liked the feeling. In fact, it seemed as though they were experiencing something akin to intense pleasure, which led to the label "pleasure center" (Olds, 1956).

Researchers have been more reluctant to study the effects of stimulating human limbic systems, although a similar procedure has been used in a few instances to achieve therapeutic effects. Robert Heath (1972), a Tulane University researcher, is one of the pioneers in this area. In the early 1970s he experimented with limbic system stimulation on two subjects, a female epileptic and a man troubled with emotional problems. Heath hypothesized that the pleasure associated with such stimulation would be of therapeutic value to these patients. When stimulation was delivered to the septal area, both individuals reported intense pleasure. The male patient, in fact, used a self-stimulating transistorized device to stimulate himself incessantly (up to 1,500 times per hour). According to

Heath, "He protested each time the unit was taken from him, pleading to self-stimulate just a few more time" (p. 6).

In other kinds of motivated behavior, such as eating, drinking, and sexual behavior, organisms typically cease when they are satiated, but this did not happen in experiments like those just described. Why? This question and related questions have led to the development of a separate area of study called *intracranial self-stimulation* (Olds & Forbes, 1981). Researchers are now actively involved in seeking to understand the mechanisms that underlie the reinforcing effects of electrical stimulation of various brain sites (Gallistel, 1986; Mora & Ferrer, 1986; Velley, 1986). Recent research suggests that endogenous opioids and dopamine may play an important role in the mediation of reinforcement associated with intracranial self-stimulation. When laboratory animals are administered drugs that temporarily block opioid or dopamine receptors in the brain, self-stimulation behavior is suppressed (Trujillo et al., 1989).

It is also possible to produce aversive rather than pleasurable responses by stimulating certain areas of the limbic system (Sem-Jacobsen, 1968). Earlier we mentioned that rage could be induced by electrode stimulation in the amygdala. Stimulation of areas in the middle and back of the hypothalamus produces unpleasant emotions such as fear, often disturbing the subject's overall tranquility. In some cases, surgical destruction of these sites has produced a calming, sedative effect in anxious, overagitated psychiatric patients (Sano, 1962).

THE HYPOTHALAMUS

As its name **hypothalamus** indicates (*hypo* means *below* in Greek), this grape-sized structure lies below the thalamus. Although it is small, the hypothalamus has an important impact on several bodily functions and behaviors; it has thus been a major focus of many investigations (some of which are discussed in later chapters). The hypothalamus contains control mechanisms that detect changes in body systems and correct imbalances to restore *homeostasis*, the maintenance of a relatively constant internal environment. Shivering when we are cold and perspiring when we are hot are both homeostatic processes that act to restore normal body temperature, and both are controlled by the hypothalamus. The hypothalamus is also critical to motivation. It contains nuclei (densely packed concentrations of specialized cell bodies) that govern eating, drinking, and sexual behavior. An area in the front and along the sides of the hypothalamus has also been shown to contain pleasure/reward sites as demonstrated by intracranial self-stimulation in laboratory animals (Blander & Wise, 1989; Carden & Coons, 1989).

The hypothalamus is also the hub of the neuroendocrine system, which is discussed later in this chapter. This system, composed of the hypothalamus, pituitary gland, and various other hormone-secreting endocrine glands, is essential to a variety of behaviors, including sexual expression, reproduction, aggression, and reactions to stress. You may have heard the brain's pituitary gland described as the master gland, since it secretes substances that control the activity of other glands throughout the body. However, the term *master* is somewhat a misnomer, since the pituitary gland itself takes direction from the hypothalamus. The hypothalamus plays an integrative role in the expression of emotions, partly through interacting with the endocrine system and partly as a key member of the limbic system.

THE THALAMUS

Located above the hypothalamus are two egg-shaped structures that lie side by side, one in each hemisphere. These are the left and right halves of the **thalamus,** a structure that has often been referred to as the brain's relay station because of the role it plays in routing incoming sensory information to appropriate areas within the cerebral cortex. Many of the cell nuclei in the thalamus also perform initial data processing before relaying information to the cortex.

Distinct regions in the thalamus are specialized for certain kinds of sensory information. For example, when you hear a sound, the message transmitted from your ears passes through specialized neurons in an auditory area of the thalamus and is then relayed to the auditory cortex, an area in the cerebral cortex specialized for processing sound impulses. With the sole exception of the sense of smell, all sensory information is routed through specialized regions of the thalamus. In addition to this function, the thalamus also appears to work in conjunction with the reticular formation to help regulate sleep cycles.

THE BASAL GANGLIA

The **basal ganglia** consist of several subcortical brain structures including the **caudate nucleus,** the **putamen,** and the **substantia nigra.** (See Figure 3.11 below.) These structures receive messages from the cortex and the thalamus. The primary function of the basal ganglia is in the control and initiation of motor movement. People with damage to the basal ganglia have great difficulty in initiating movement. In addition, movement is often weak and poorly coordinated. One of the most common disorders of the basal ganglia is a condition referred to as Parkinson's disease. Parkinson's disease results from the destruction of the dopamine-containing neurons of the substantia nigra. This disease occurs most often in the elderly, however, it may occur in individuals in their late forties or fifties. Parkinson's disease is characterized by difficulty in initiating movement, rigidity, and tremors often in the hands.

THE CEREBRAL CORTEX

A major structure of the human brain is the **cerebral cortex,** the thin outer layer of the brain. The Latin *cortex* means bark, and the cortex covers the brain in much the same way as bark covers a tree trunk. This portion of the brain is also called the neocortex, or new cortex, since it was the last part of the brain to develop during evolution. (See Figure 3.12.)

You may wonder why the cortex is wrinkled and convoluted. The answer has to do with the economics of space. The cortex's folds and wrinkles are nature's solution to the problem of cramming the huge neocortical area into a relatively small space within the skull. In the same way that crumpling a piece of paper allows it to fit into a smaller container than will a flat sheet, the cortex's folds permit it to fit into the fixed space of the skull.

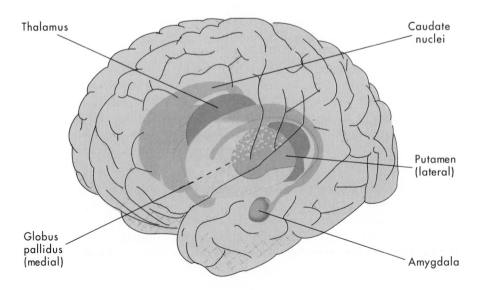

FIGURE 3.11

The Basal Ganglia

Major structures of the basal ganglia include the caudate nucleus, the putamen, and the substantia nigra.

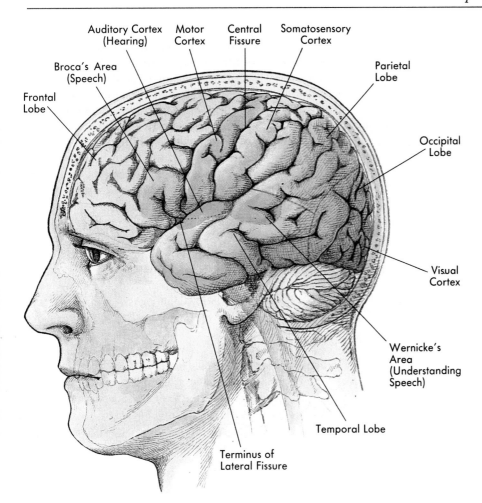

Frontal Lobe

Broca's Area (Speech)

Auditory Cortex (Hearing)

Motor Cortex

Central Fissure

Somatosensory Cortex

Parietal Lobe

Occipital Lobe

Visual Cortex

Wernicke's Area (Understanding Speech)

Temporal Lobe

Terminus of Lateral Fissure

FIGURE 3.12A

Localization of Cortical Functions in the Four Lobes of the Left Cerebral Cortex

FIGURE 3.12B

Primary Areas of the Motor Cortex and the Somatosensory Cortex

The body is represented in an upside-down fashion along the motor cortex and the somatosensory cortex. Larger cortical areas represent the hands and face as these areas require more motor control and sensation.

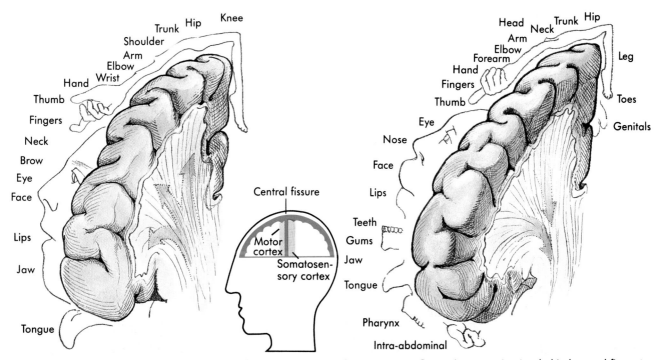

Knee

Hip

Trunk

Shoulder

Arm

Elbow

Wrist

Hand

Thumb

Fingers

Neck

Brow

Eye

Face

Lips

Jaw

Tongue

Central fissure

Motor cortex

Somatosensory cortex

Head

Neck

Trunk

Hip

Arm

Elbow

Forearm

Hand

Fingers

Thumb

Leg

Toes

Genitals

Eye

Nose

Face

Lips

Teeth

Gums

Jaw

Tongue

Pharynx

Intra-abdominal

Motor Cortex (cross section just in front of central fissure)

Somatosensory Cortex (cross section just behind central fissure)

The cortex is gray in color, which is why it is often referred to as the gray matter of the brain. The gray color comes from the lack of the whitish myelinated coating that insulates the neural fibers of the inner part of the brain. The inner core of the brain is often called the white matter because it contains three kinds of myelinated neural fibers: *commissural fibers*, which pass from one hemisphere to another; *projection fibers*, which convey impulses to and from the cortex; and *association fibers*, which connect various parts of the cortex within one hemisphere. The cortex is mainly composed of the unmyelinated fibers and cell bodies of billions of neurons, and it is the part of the brain responsible for higher processes such as perceiving, thinking, and remembering.

The cortex is where our memories are stored, where we make decisions, where we see a sunset or recognize and appreciate a melody, and where we organize our worlds and plan for the future. Without a cortex, we would cease to exist as unique, functioning individuals. This is not to say that the cortex acts alone in running our lives. Instead, it functions like an executive, interpreting incoming information and making decisions about how to respond. As we go about our daily lives, our cerebral cortexes constantly analyze a vast array of incoming messages, evaluating them against stored information about past experiences and then making decisions that are translated into messages that are sent to the appropriate muscles and glands.

Although we know the cortex functions in this manner, we are far from understanding precisely how it controls our lives. For example, while we know that memory is largely a cortical function, science has yet to explain exactly how the brain initiates a command to search and retrieve a specific recollection. Nor are we even sure where specific memories are stored, or how the cortex can spontaneously generate new ideas and insights. Investigations of the higher mental processes of the cortex are likely to remain at the frontier of psychology for many years to come, and only time will tell if the cortex is capable of unraveling and understanding all the complex mechanisms that govern its operation. Let us examine, however, what we do know about how the cortex functions.

LOCALIZATION OF CORTICAL FUNCTIONING As mentioned earlier, the two hemispheres of the brain are approximately symmetrical, with areas on the left side roughly matched by areas on the right. To some degree, researchers have been able to localize a variety of functions within various regions of the two cortical hemispheres. Approximately 25 percent of its total area is involved in receiving sensory messages or transmitting movement messages to our muscles. These regions are called the **sensory cortex** and the **motor cortex,** respectively. The remaining 75 percent of the cerebral cortex, called the **association cortex,** is involved in integrating sensory and motor messages, and in processing such higher functions as thinking, language, perception, memory, and planning.

To facilitate studying and describing the brain, researchers have found it convenient to divide each of the cortical hemispheres into four separate regions called lobes. These four regions, the frontal, parietal, occipital, and temporal lobes, are shown in Figure 3.12a. Two long valleys, called sulci, within the surface of the cortex separate these four lobes, and they also serve as landmarks. The frontal lobe includes everything in front of the *center sulcus* except the forward tip of the temporal lobe. The parietal lobe lies behind the central sulcus and above the *lateral sulcus.* The temporal lobe lies under the lateral sulcus, and the occipital lobe lies at the back of the brain.

The Frontal Lobe The **frontal lobe** is the largest of the four lobes in each hemisphere and is an important center for both the motor and association cortex. The motor cortex, a narrow strip just in front of the central sulcus along the back of the frontal lobe, contains neurons that contribute to the control, planning, and execution of motor movement. Virtually all body movement, from throwing a ball to wiggling a small toe, involves the motor cortex.

The body is represented in an upside-down fashion along the motor cortex, in that neurons which control facial muscles are at the bottom of the motor cortex, and those that control movement of the toes are at the top part. (Refer back to Figure 3.12b.) Larger areas of the motor cortex are devoted to the muscles involved in talking and moving the fingers, reflecting the critical role of speech and tool use in human behavior.

Nerve fibers that descend from the motor cortex on one side of the brain activate muscles on the opposite side of the body. That is, the right motor cortex controls movements of the opposite, or contralateral, side of the body.

In the nineteenth century a French neurosurgeon, Pierre Paul Broca, reported that damage to another area of the left frontal lobe caused difficulty in speaking. Subsequent research has confirmed that this frontal lobe region, called **Broca's area** after its discoverer, is the primary brain center for controlling speech. (Refer back to Figure 3.12a.) People who have been injured in this critical area typically have trouble articulating the right words to describe things, even though their comprehension of what they hear or read is unaffected (Mori et al., 1989). This condition is called *motor* or *expressive aphasia*.

The association areas of the frontal lobes seem to be important in making decisions, solving problems, planning and setting goals, memory, and adapting to new situations. If the association areas were damaged, we would probably have trouble understanding complex ideas and planning and carrying out purposeful behavior. A considerable amount of our emotional lives is probably influenced by our frontal lobes as well. Extensive, reciprocal connections exist between the association areas in the frontal lobes and certain lower brain structures (such as those in the limbic system) known to be involved in emotional expression.

Well into the 1960s, a fairly common surgical procedure was used to separate the most forward part (prefrontal) of the frontal lobe from the rest of the cortex. This procedure, known as a prefrontal lobotomy, was carried out on thousands of mental patients as a desperate attempt to minimize their dysfunction and calm their moods. This procedure, wrought with severe criticism, met with little success (Valenstein, 1973, 1980).

The Parietal Lobe   The **parietal lobe** lies just behind the central fissure and above the lateral fissure. At the front of the parietal lobe, directly across from the motor cortex in the frontal lobe, is an area called the **somatosensory cortex.** This portion of the parietal lobe receives sensory information about touch, pressure, pain, temperature, and body position. Like the motor cortex, the somatosensory areas in each hemisphere receive sensory input from the opposite sides of the body. Thus when you stub your left toe, the message is sent to your right somatosensory cortex. As in the motor cortex, the body is represented in an upside-down fashion, with the largest portions receiving input from the face and hands, as shown in Figure 13.12b. Each of the primary somatosensory areas in the parietal lobes lies directly across the central fissure from the corresponding area in the frontal lobe's motor cortex.

The parietal lobe is involved in relating visual and spatial information. For example, it allows you to know that an object is still the same even though you view it from a different angle. It also enables you to identify objects by touch. People with damage to their parietal lobe suffer a peculiar deficit referred to as sensory neglect. Sensory neglect occurs to the contralateral side of the body (opposite to the side of the brain that was damaged). That is, a person with damage to the left parietal lobe may neglect the right side of the body by failing to dress it as neatly as his left side, or he may draw a self-portrait with the right side either missing or drawn with a marked lack of detail. While reading, a person with sensory neglect may read only the left side of a page. Such persons also have difficulty following directions, either from instructions or from a map.

The Occipital Lobe At the rear of each hemisphere lies the **occipital lobe.** This lobe consists primarily of the **visual cortex,** a complex network of neurons devoted to vision. Most people think they see with their eyes, but although the eyes receive sensory information, it is the visual cortex that integrates this information into vision. The visual cortex of each hemisphere receives sensory messages from both eyes. Nerve fibers from the right visual field of each eye go to the right hemisphere; fibers from the left visual field send impulses to the left hemisphere. Damage to the occipital lobe results in varying degrees of visual impairment, ranging from partial to complete blindness (Aldrich et al., 1987).

The Temporal Lobe A primary function of the **temporal lobe** is hearing. The **auditory cortex,** located on the inner surface of the temporal lobe in a region below the lateral sulcus, receives information directly from the auditory system. These auditory signals are then transmitted to an adjacent structure, known as **Wernicke's area,** which is involved in interpreting sounds, particularly the sound of human speech (refer back to Figure 3.12a). This area was named after Germany's Carl Wernicke who reported that patients who were injured in the rear portion of the left temporal lobe, just below the lateral sulcus, often had trouble understanding the speech of others. This condition is known as sensory or receptive aphasia. Subsequent research has confirmed that this temporal lobe region is the brain's primary area for understanding speech (Naeser et al., 1987).

The temporal lobe also appears to contribute to visual perception. For example, the perception of faces and other complex patterns is dependent on the temporal lobe. Some kinds of temporal lobe damage even result in elaborate visual hallucinations.

SEX DIFFERENCES IN THE BRAIN

As you might expect, the brains of males and females are not identical. The differences are largely due to both the quantities and the distribution of sex hormones during early development. Females, on average, tend to be more proficient at language skills, arithemetic calculation, and in recalling landmarks along a route. Males, on the other hand, outperform females on certain spatial tasks, mathematical reasoning, and orientation skills (Kimura, 1992). These differences are partially explained by the differences in the thickness of the cerebral cortex. Females generally have thicker left hemispheres while males have thicker right hemispheres. The sex hormone estradiol influences the development of the cerebral cortex by increasing the rate of cell loss in areas where estradiol is present. Females have more estradiol in their right hemispheres, thus a greater cell loss, and males have more in their left hemispheres during development (Sandhu, Cook, and Diamond, 1986).

Another brain structure that differs in males and females is the hypothalamus, which was described earlier. Several structures within the hypothalamus are larger in males than in females. Again, these differences appear to result from different levels of sex hormones during early development. These anatomical differences appear to contribute to differences in sexual behavior and aggression.

LATERALIZATION OF FUNCTION

You may have noticed in a preceding discussion that both Broca's area and Wernicke's area were identified in the left hemisphere. Indeed, in most people (approximately 96 percent of right-handed people and 70 percent of left-handers), verbal abilities such as the expression and understanding of speech are governed more by the left hemisphere than the right hemisphere, and there are other differences as well (Ogden, 1989). Furthermore, the right side of the brain seems to be more specialized for spatial orientation, including the ability to recognize objects and shapes and to perceive relationships among them (Gordon, 1986; Patterson et al., 1989).

The term **lateralization of function** is used to describe the degree to which a particular function is controlled by one rather than both hemispheres. If, for example, a person's ability to deal with spatial tasks is controlled exclusively by the right hemisphere, we could say that this ability in this person is highly lateralized. In contrast, if both hemispheres contribute equally to this function, the person would be considered bilateral for spatial ability.

Studies have shown that the two hemispheres are asymmetrical, differing in anatomical, electrical, and chemical properties (Woods, 1986). For example, autopsies reveal that one hemisphere, usually the left, is larger than the other in about 95 percent of cases (Geshwind & Levitsky, 1976).

Although each hemisphere is specialized to handle different functions, they are not entirely separate systems. Rather, our brains function mostly as an integrated whole. The two hemispheres constantly communicate with each other through a broad band of millions of connecting nerve fibers called the **corpus callosum** (Cook, 1986; Gazzaniga, 1987; Gazzaniga et al., 1989), shown earlier in Figure 3.8. And while in most people a complex function such as language is controlled primarily by regions in the left hemisphere, interaction and communication with the right hemisphere also play a role. Furthermore, if a hemisphere that is primarily responsible for a particular function is damaged, the remaining intact hemisphere may take over the function. For example, if a person were to experience an injury to the language-processing area of the left hemisphere, the right hemisphere might develop a greater capacity to handle verbal functions (Ogden, 1989; Rudel et al., 1974). This is particularly true if the damage occurs early in life.

A vivid example of this phenomenon was provided in a recent report of an adolescent female who underwent surgical removal of her left hemisphere due to severe, progressive brain disease. Prior to the onset of her illness she was a normal, right-handed girl with above average language and reading capabilities. After surgery her verbal skills were markedly diminished, a finding consistent with loss of the hemisphere that had governed most of her verbal skills prior to the hemispherectomy. However, her right hemisphere clearly was able to assume the direction and organization of at least some verbal abilities, as evidenced by her demonstrated ability to recognize and comprehend words and to engage in oral reading of familiar material (Patterson et al., 1989). This capacity to switch cortical control from one hemisphere to another tends to diminish as we grow older.

SPLIT-BRAIN RESEARCH Many important discoveries about how each hemisphere influences behavior have come from split-brain research, which began in the 1950s with Roger Sperry's investigations of cats whose brains had been bisected. Initially, Sperry and his colleagues made the startling discovery that the left hemisphere of a split-brain cat could learn something while the right hemisphere remained ignorant of what had been learned, and vice versa (Sperry, 1968). In the decades since this landmark study, additional experiments with split-brain subjects have added greatly to our knowledge about hemispheric lateralization of function.

Some of these studies have involved split-brain research with human subjects. This radical surgery is not performed for experimental purposes but is occasionally performed to control very severe cases of epilepsy that have become incapacitating and even life threatening (Clark & Geffen, 1989; Gazzaniga & LeDoux, 1978). During an epileptic seizure, neurons in the site of a damaged area begin to fire wildly, and the abnormal activity can spread from one hemisphere to the other through the corpus callosum. Although drugs are often successful in localizing the abnormal brain activity, the medication is not always effective, and in these cases the only recourse may be to sever the corpus callosum. This procedure is usually very effective in controlling the seizures, and the patients appear to be essentially unchanged in intelligence, personality characteristics, and behavior. However, their brains do not function in entirely the same manner after the surgery. After being disconnected, the two hemispheres operate independently: Their motor mechanisms, sensory systems, and association areas can no longer exchange information.

This difference makes itself felt in a variety of ways. For instance, the right hand might arrange some flowers in a vase, only to have the left hand tear it apart. Occasionally, people with split brains may be embarrassed by the left hand making inappropriate gestures, or perhaps doing some bizarre thing like zipping down the fly on a pair of trousers after the right hand zipped it up. With time, such symptoms usually subside as the person learns to compensate for and adjust to the independent functioning of the two hemispheres.

Scientists have developed a number of procedures for detecting the effects of split-brain surgery. For instance, in one study a woman recently recovered from split-brain surgery sat in front of a screen with a small black dot at its center (see Figure 3.13). She was asked to stare continuously at the dot while pictures were flashed to either the left or the right of her visual field. Information presented to her left visual field was transmitted only to her right hemisphere, and vice versa. Each stimulus appeared on the screen for only about one-tenth of a second, so that the subject did not have time to shift her eyes to get a better look. Her task was to identify verbally what she was shown, and then to reach under the screen and select the object solely by touch from a collection of objects (LeDoux et al., 1977).

Images in the right visual field fall on the left side of each retina (the image-recording part of the eye), and images in the left visual field fall on the right side on each retina. Half of each retina sends information to the occipital cortex on the same side of the brain, while information from the other half of each retina crosses over to the cortex on the opposite side of the brain. Thus if a person stares straight ahead, information from the entire left visual field will reach the right hemisphere and vice versa.

FIGURE 3.13

Studying the Effects of Split-Brain Surgery

The subject focuses on images that are projected through the screen to the left or right of a central black dot.

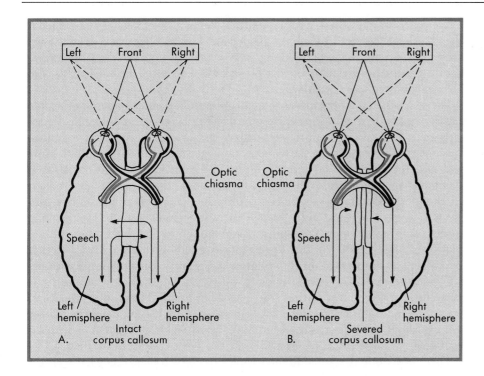

FIGURE 3.14

Passage of Visual Information in Brains with an Intact and a Severed Corpus Callosum

A. When the corpus callosum is intact visual information in the right visual field is focused on the left half of each retina; it then passes through the optic nerve to the left hemisphere of the brain. Information from either hemisphere can pass through the corpus callosum to the opposite side.
B. When the corpus callosum is severed information from the eyes is transmitted to the brain in the same way as described above. However, information from the left visual field (in the right hemisphere) cannot be processed by the left hemisphere (where language areas are located).

Normally, this information is transferred between the two hemispheres through the corpus callosum, so that both hemispheres have information about both the left and right visual fields. In split-brain people, however, this is no longer possible (see Figure 3.14); and in this particular experiment researchers made sure, by flashing the image for such a short period of time that each hemisphere received only the information in the opposite visual field. (In one-tenth of a second the subject would not have time to shift her eyes, an action which would have enabled her to perceive the image in both hemispheres.)

TESTING THE EFFECTS OF SPLIT-BRAIN SURGERY In the experiment just described, do you think that the woman was able to identify correctly, both verbally and by touch, objects projected in the left and right visual fields? If yes, why? If no, why not? What differences, if any, do you think were noted between her responses to left, versus right, visual field images? Take some time to reason out the probable results of this experiment.

The results of the experiment showed a difference in the subject's responses to images presented in her left and right visual fields. When a picture of a cup was projected to the right of the dot (and thus projected to her left hemisphere), the subject was able quickly to name the object, and she had no trouble locating the cup by touch. (She could locate the object with her left hand, since naming the object out loud conveyed information about its nature to her right hemisphere via auditory input from her ears.) Additional objects presented to her right visual field presented no problems.

When a picture of a spoon was flashed to the left side of the dot, however, the results were quite different. The subject reported seeing nothing. Despite this reply, the researchers pressed her into trying to pick out the object from the articles on the table. After feeling the various objects with her left hand, she held up the spoon, a result she dismissed as a lucky guess. When asked to identify it verbally, she called it a pencil. Time after time her sense of touch allowed her to identify objects presented to her right hemisphere, even though she insisted that she saw nothing each time a new image was flashed.

In a variation of this test, a sexually suggestive picture of a nude was flashed to the left side of the dot. The subject giggled and blushed, but when she was asked what she saw, she replied, "Nothing, just a flash of light." When the experimenter pressed further and asked why she was laughing, she exclaimed, "Oh, Doctor, you have some machine!"

These results reveal that in this individual (as well as in the majority of people) the left hemisphere is primarily responsible for language and speech. People with intact brains have no problem with tasks such as the one just described, since the two hemispheres work together in perceiving and naming things. However, after a split-brain operation each side of the bisected brain is cut off from the other side. Therefore, even though the subject of this study was able to identify the spoon with her hand, she could not name it. Her right hemisphere, with its undeveloped language and speech areas, was essentially mute. Her response to the picture of the nude was similar. Even though her left hemisphere did not know what had happened, her blushing and giggling revealed that her right hemisphere had processed the information and produced an emotional response.

Would she have been able to identify the spoon with her right hand after its image had been projected to the right side of her brain? The answer is no. Since her right hand is governed by the left hemisphere, and her left hemisphere knew nothing about the object, she would have been unable to identify it with her right hand.

The information presented in this chapter has only touched on what scientists know about the brain. Although there are still many unanswered questions, new methods developed in recent years have added greatly to our knowledge. In the next section we look at some techniques used to study the brain.

HOW THE BRAIN IS STUDIED

SURGICAL LESIONS Some of the earliest clues about how the brain functions came form observations of people with head injuries, as investigators attempted to link specific behavioral deficits with specific locations of brain damage. For example, if a person's vision was impaired by a blow to the back of the head, the natural conclusion was that the injured region of the brain was responsible for vision. This way of learning about the brain has provided some valuable insights, but it has some serious limitations. One is the impracticality of waiting for the right kind of injury to occur so that the role of a specific brain site can be assessed. In addition, it is often difficult to determine the precise location and amount of damage inflicted by a given injury. Because of such limitations, researchers concluded that it might be more efficient to create the injuries with surgical techniques. The areas of brain damage created by such procedures are called *lesions*, and the technique is called **lesion production.** The Health Psychology and Life discussion at the end of the chapter, Magnesium Treatment after Brain Injury, describes how lesion production research is helping scientists develop possible therapeutic techniques for treating brain injuries.

For obvious ethical reasons, lesion production is used with nonhuman subjects (although in some cases, lesions have been produced in human brains for therapeutic purposes, for example, to destroy an area in the amygdala that is responsible for abnormal cellular activity associated with uncontrollable rage). Typically, an animal is anesthetized, a small hole is drilled in its skull, and a specific part of the brain is destroyed. A special device called a *stereotaxic apparatus* allows researchers to insert a fine wire into a specific brain area. (See Figure 3.15.) Sufficient electric current is then passed through the wire to destroy a small amount of brain tissue at its tip. This refined lesioning technique has allowed researchers to identify the relationship of specific behaviors to precise locations in the brain.

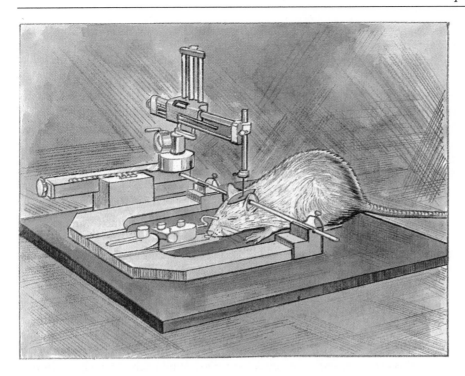

FIGURE 3.15
Stereotaxic apparatus
Brain researchers used to insert fine wires into precise regions of the brain.

BRAIN STIMULATION   A second technique, **brain stimulation,** involves stimulating precise regions with a weak electric current or specific chemicals that activate neurons. During electrical stimulation a stereotaxic device is used to implant tiny wires called microelectrodes at specific brain sites. Stimulation of the targeted area often results in some kind of behavioral response (for instance, the pleasure response that results from stimulating the septal area).

During chemical stimulation a small syringe needle called a *microcanula* is inserted into a specific region of the brain. Once the canula is inserted small amounts of chemical can be injected into surrounding cells which can either stimulate or inhibit specific receptors. Such results provide researchers with valuable information about where certain behavioral functions are localized within the brain. Because brain stimulation is generally painless, and because measures can be taken to minimize tissue damage, this method may be used with human as well as nonhuman subjects. For example, chemical stimulation of dopamine neurons in the septum with drugs like cocaine may help us understand the process of addiction.

ELECTRICAL RECORDING   Another technique used for studying the brain is **electrical recording:** Tiny wires implanted in the brain are used to record the electrical activity of neurons. Scientists using this technique have been able to record the responses of a single brain neuron to a stimulus such as a beam of light. In some studies, electrical activity is transmitted through several implanted electrodes while the subject engages in various behaviors. The electrical messages are then fed into a computer, which analyzes the complex relationships between the behaviors and patterns of neuron activity.

RADIOACTIVE LABELING   At any given time some areas of the brain are more active than others. While you are reading this text your occipital lobes are more active than your frontal lobes. Likewise, when you smell perfume your olfactory

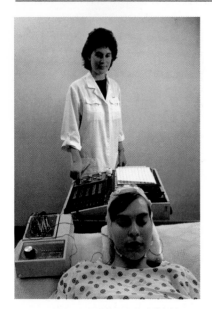

Electrodes are placed on the surface of the scalp and the electrical activity of the cortex is recorded. The electroencephalograph (EEG) is used as a diagnostic procedure as well as for research.

bulbs become more active. When cells, in this case neurons, become more active they require more energy in the form of glucose which is carried to cells via the blood supply. Researchers can take advantage of this fact and administer small amounts of radioactive chemical into the blood supply. One such chemical called 2-deoxy-D-glucose (abbreviated as 2-DG) is taken into active cells just like glucose. Several hours later the brain can be sliced into thin sections and placed on photographic plates. The sections of the brain that were most active following the administration of 2-DG are enhanced on the film. This technique, which is obviously restricted to laboratory animals, has been very valuable in identifying areas of the brain that are involved in different sensory, motor, and cognitive tasks.

ELECTROENCEPHALOGRAPHY (EEG)   Lesion production, stimulation, electrical recording, and 2-DG studies are all *invasive* in that they require surgery. Fortunately, technology has made possible a variety of brain study methods that do not require surgery and are noninvasive. One technique, **electroencephalography (EEG),** has been around for quite some time. Because the brain constantly generates electrical activity, electrodes placed on the scalp can be used to record the electrical activity of the cortex. The electroencephalograph amplifies these very small electrical potentials thousands of times and records them on paper in patterns called brain waves. Brain waves vary according to a person's state: whether they are alert and mentally active, relaxed and calm, sleeping, or dreaming. The EEG has been used to diagnose such conditions as epilepsy, brain tumors, and a variety of other neurological disorders that generate abnormal brain wave patterns.

Although the EEG provides general information about a person's brain state, it can tell us little about responses to specific stimuli. Typically, there is so much background noise (in the form of ongoing spontaneous brain waves) that it is difficult to identify what brain wave changes result from a specific stimulus. A relatively new variation of the EEG uses computers to extract the background noise so that brain wave responses can be identified. These wave patterns associated with specific stimuli are called *evoked potentials*.

Some years ago research psychologist Emanuel Donchin (1975) reported an interesting application of evoked potentials. Donchin recorded EEG activity in his subjects as they were exposed to various familiar or expected stimuli and an occasional unexpected or rare event. Enhanced computer analysis of the resulting evoked potentials revealed that the perception of an unexpected event was consistently associated with a particular brain wave component called P300. For example, a subject might be exposed to a series of visual stimuli, some familiar and others not. In this case the unfamiliar stimuli are unexpected and result in the recording of a P300 wave or evoked potential (P300 because it is a positive wave occurring 300 milliseconds after the unexpected stimulus). This kind of research contributes to our understanding of the relationship between mental processes, such as attention, and brain activity.

COMPUTERIZED AXIAL TOMOGRAPHY (CAT)   Neuroscientists have recently developed some effective techniques for observing living brains. The first of these, **computerized axial tomography (CAT),** was developed in the early 1970s. It is a refined X-ray technique that provides an accurate image of the brain. An X-ray scanner is rotated in a circular path around the skull, sending a thin beam of X-rays through the brain. A detector measures the amount of radiation that reaches the other side. Because different brain tissues absorb different amounts of radiation, the CAT scanners produce excellent pictures that can be used to locate tumors, lesions, and a variety of neurologic abnormalities. In the past this information could only be obtained by autopsy.

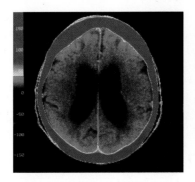

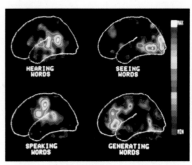

Computerized Axial Tomography (CAT) produces an x-ray–like image of the brain. CAT scans are very useful as diagnostic procedures to locate tumors and diseases of the brain.

POSITRON EMISSION TOMOGRAPHY (PET) A third noninvasive technique, the **PET** scan **(positron emission tomography),** was introduced at the beginning of this chapter. The PET scan also takes advantage of the fact that glucose is utilized at higher rates in active cells. Each time a neuron fires, it expends tremendous energy; thus active brain cells metabolize a great deal of glucose. The scientists who developed the PET scan reasoned that if they could find a way to measure glucose utilization, they could tell what parts of the brain are active at different times in response to different stimuli. The use of radioactive isotopes paved the way.

The technique works as follows: A patient receives an intravenous injection of a glucose-like sugar that has been tagged with a radioactive fluoride isotope. Active brain cells metabolize the sugar, but they cannot metabolize the radioactive component. Thus the isotope accumulates within the cells in direct proportion to their activity level. As it decays, it emits charged particles called positrons. Instruments scanning the brain detect the radioactivity and record its location, and a computer converts this information into colored biochemical maps of the brain, such as those shown at the beginning of the chapter.

The PET scan has proved to be a useful tool in mapping the brain, pinpointing locations involved in movement, sensation, thinking, and even memory (Altman, 1986; Depue & Iacono, 1989; Fox et al., 1986). There is also some evidence suggesting that PET scans may be helpful in both the diagnosis and treatment of various behavioral disorders. Some researchers report that the brains of schizophrenics and severely depressed people reveal different patterns from those of healthy people (Buchsbaum et al., 1987).

MAGNETIC RESONANCE IMAGING (MRI) A fourth noninvasive technique is **magnetic resonance imaging (MRI).** This procedure uses harmless radio waves to excite hydrogen protons in the brain tissue, creating a magnetic field change that is detected by a huge magnet that surrounds the patient. The information is fed into a computer, which compiles it into a highly detailed three-dimensional colored picture of the brain. The images created are much sharper and more detailed than those provided by the CAT scan. The MRI can pinpoint tumors and locate even the slightest reduction in blood flow in an artery or vein. It can also provide biochemical information, distinguishing between cancerous and noncancerous cells. In addition, MRI has been shown to be particularly helpful in diagnosing various diseases associated with brain abnormalities, such as multiple sclerosis (a degenerative disease of the CNS characterized by tremors and impaired speech, spinal cord abnormalities in children (Bale et al., 1986), and brain lesions associated with epilepsy (Jabbari et al., 1986).

Researchers are hopeful that MRI will ultimately pinpoint the precise location of neurotransmitters and other important brain chemicals. It is also possible that this powerful tool will help clarify differences in physiological processes between people with healthy brains and those who have physical and emotional disorders.

Positron Emission Tomography (PET) identifies areas of the brain that are most active in response to a variety of tasks. These images were shown at the beginning of the chapter and identify different areas of the brain that become active during different tasks related to language.

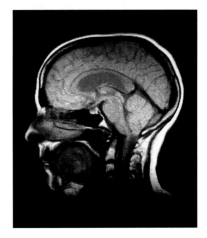

Magnetic Resonance Imaging (MRI) provides much clearer and more detailed images than a CAT scan. This imaging procedure is useful in locating small tumors, restrictions in blood flow, and distinguishing cancerous from noncancerous cell types.

THE ENDOCRINE SYSTEM

Up to this point in this chapter we have covered only the nervous system. However, the nervous system is not the only biological system that governs behavior. To be complete, a discussion of biological foundations of behavior should also consider the role of the endocrine system which is illustrated in Figure 3.16.

The **endocrine system** consists of several glands located throughout the body. Glands in the endocrine system are *ductless;* that is, they have no external excretory ducts but rather secrete internally directly into the bloodstream or lymph fluid (the lymph system is a system of vessels and organs which makes up your immune system). The major endocrine glands include the pituitary, the thyroid, the parathyroids, the adrenals, the pancreas, and the gonads. The location of the various endocrine glands is shown in Figure 3.16. Each of these glands produces **hormones,** which are secreted directly into the bloodstream. A single gland may produce several different hormones, however.

Like neurotransmitters, hormones act as chemical messengers. In fact, some important chemicals within the body can function as both neurotransmitters and **hormones.** Norepinephrine, for example, acts as a hormone when released by the adrenal glands and as a neurotransmitter when released by a neuron. There is, however, a key difference in the way these two classes of chemicals act. Because neurotransmitters need to travel only across a synaptic gap (a fraction of the distance that most hormones travel through the bloodstream), they have a much more immediate effect on behavior than the endocrine system.

The endocrine system often works in tandem with the nervous system. For example, when a person is suddenly exposed to a fearful stimulus, such as the bear in the earlier example, heart rate increases instantly in response to sympathetic nervous system input. At the same time, the adrenal glands secrete epinephrine, which has a similar effect on heart rate. In this fashion, the two major regulating systems of the body often work together.

The hypothalamus is a key interface between the nervous system and the endocrine system. As noted earlier, this region of the brain controls the activity of the pituitary gland through production of a group of chemicals known as *hypothalamic-releasing factors.* These chemicals in turn simulate the pituitary to produce hormones that stimulate other glands.

Once an endocrine gland releases a hormone into the bloodstream, the substance travels throughout the body. However, each hormone exerts its primary influence only on certain specific organs and cells, often referred to as *target organs.* Some hormones, called trophic hormones, affect only the activity of another endocrine gland. For example, hormones called gonadotropins stimulate only the gonads.

Endocrine glands do not produce a steady stream of hormones. Instead, target organs signal the secreting glands either to increase or decrease secretions. Hormones are secreted until the target organ is stimulated; at this point, the target organ releases another substance that circulates back through the system to regulate hormonal activity in the initiating gland. This *negative-feedback mechanism* provides an internal control that limits extremes of hormone production.

Through these general mechanisms, the endocrine system influences many important physiological functions including metabolism, emotional responses, and motivation. A number of these effects are of particular interest to psychologists.

THE PITUITARY GLAND

Located in the brain below the hypothalamus, the **pituitary gland** produces the largest number of different hormones, some of which trigger other glands to release hormones. For this reason, the pituitary gland is sometimes called the master gland, but, as we have seen, it is itself controlled by the hypothalamus.

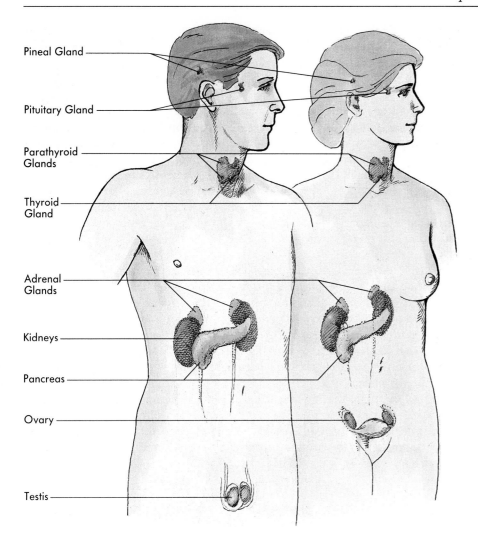

Pineal Gland

Pituitary Gland

Parathyroid
Glands

Thyroid
Gland

Adrenal
Glands

Kidneys

Pancreas

Ovary

Testis

FIGURE 3.16
*The Major Glands of the Endocrine
System*

The pituitary also produces a number of huge protein molecules called neuropeptides, mentioned in our earlier discussion of endogenous opioids. Each neuropeptide consists of a long chain of amino acids that are broken down by enzyme action into various lengths of small chains. These substances act as neurotransmitters, and they influence a number of functions such as eating and drinking, sexual behavior, sleep, temperature regulation, pain reduction, and responses to stress.

The **thyroid gland,** located within the neck, responds to pituitary stimulation by releasing the hormone **thyroxine.** This substance affects a number of biological functions, the most important of which is the regulation of metabolism (the transformation of food into energy). Because metabolism is in turn closely linked to motivational and mood states, the thyroid has an important impact on behavior. For example, if too little thyroxine is produced (a condition known as *hypothyroidism*), a person behaves in a lethargic manner, demonstrates little motivation to accomplish tasks, and often manifests symptoms of depression (Denicoff et al., 1990). Excessive thyroxine output *(hyperthyroidism)* may have just the opposite effect, causing hyperactivity, weight loss, anxiety, and excessive tension (Houston & Hay, 1990). An undersecretion of thyroxine early in life

THE THYROID GLAND

produces *cretinism*, a condition characterized by low intelligence and various body defects such as dwarfed stature and dry, wrinkled skin. Fortunately, all of these conditions can be prevented or remedied by medical treatments.

THE ADRENAL GLANDS

The **adrenals** are a pair of glands, located just above each kidney, that influence our emotional state, level of energy, and ability to cope with stress. They consist of two distinct parts: an inner core called the *adrenal medulla* and an outer layer called the *adrenal cortex*. The medulla produces epinephrine and norepinephrine, both of which prepare the body to respond to emergencies by making the heart beat faster, diverting blood from the stomach and intestines to the voluntary muscles (so a person can run faster or fight better), and enhancing energy resources by increasing blood sugar levels. The adrenal medulla is able to act quickly in threatening situations because it is stimulated directly by neural impulses.

As suggested earlier in the discussion of the peripheral nervous system, epinephrine and norepinephrine act in a way that is similar to the sympathetic nervous system. In fact, these hormones and the nervous system perform basically the same work. The sympathetic nervous system works more quickly, producing its effects almost instantly. Yet the effects of the adrenal hormones can persist much longer. It is the lingering effects of hormones that explain why it often takes time for strong emotional arousal to subside after the cause for anxiety has been removed.

At times of stress, the hypothalamus causes the pituitary to release ACTH, *adrenocorticotropic hormone*, which in turn stimulates the adrenal cortex to increase its secretion of a number of hormones that influence metabolism. The higher metabolic rate makes the stressed person more active, and therefore more able to cope with an emergency. Prolonged stress, however, can have a debilitating effect on mind and body. A chronic state of tension, nervousness, fear, or even panic can take a terrible toll on one's emotional and physical well-being. Furthermore, abnormally high metabolic rates deplete vital body resources, and

When you are caught in an emergency situation you experience the sympathetic activation of various organs in your body leading to an increase in heart rate, pupil dilation, and decreased salivation.

over time this can lead to exhaustion and increased susceptibility to illness. Stress-related problems and stress-management techniques are discussed in Chapter 9.

THE GONADS

The **gonads**—ovaries in the female and testes in the male—produce several varieties of sex hormones. The ovaries produce two classes of hormones: the estrogens (the most important of which is estradiol), which influence development of female physical sex characteristics and regulation of the menstrual cycle, and the *progestational compounds* (the most important is progesterone), which help to regulate the menstrual cycle and prepare the uterus for pregnancy. As we mentioned earlier, estradiol also contributes to sex differences in the cerebral cortex and the hypothalamus.

The primary output of the testes are the *androgens*. The most important of these hormones is testosterone, whose function is to influence the development of both male physical sex characteristics and sexual motivation. In both sexes, the adrenal glands also secrete sex hormones, including small amounts of estrogen and greater quantities of androgen.

Around the onset of puberty, the sex hormones play a critical role in initiating changes in the primary sexual systems (the growth of the uterus, vagina, penis, and so forth) and the secondary sex characteristics, including body hair, breast development, and voice changes. They also exert strong influences on the fertility cycle in women, and they seem to contribute to sexual motivation. Chapter 9 discusses the relationship of sex hormones to sexual motivation in more detail.

DRUGS AND BEHAVIOR

A wide variety of commonly used drugs have the effect of changing thought processes, emotional states, or behavior (Carboni et al., 1989; Snyder, 1986). Solomon Snyder, an expert on neurotransmitters, stated that "Virtually every drug that alters mental function does so by interacting with a neurotransmitter system in the brain" (1984), p. 23). This interaction may happen in a variety of ways. Some drugs increase neural activity by releasing neurotransmitters from the presynaptic vesicles; some actually mimic certain excitatory transmitters. Others drugs may prevent transmission of neural impulses by binding or attaching themselves to receptors on the postsynaptic membrane, thus preventing the kind of contact between excitatory transmitters and postsynaptic receptors that is necessary to trigger EPSPs. Still other drugs interfere with the reuptake of intact chemicals or the recycling of their breakdown products. In this section we examine some of the more common drugs used to alter behavior.

It is not uncommon for people in our society to have a few glasses of wine at a party, then follow through the next morning with a few cups of coffee or tea to help clear the cobwebs. Most of us regularly consume a variety of chemicals (such as alcohol and caffeine) that alter our perceptions and behavior. Such substances, as well as nicotine, marijuana, sleeping pills, cocaine, and narcotics, are called psychoactive drugs.

Continued use of many of the psychoactive drugs tends to lessen their effects, so that the user develops a tolerance for the drug. For example, repeated injections of opiates such as heroin cause the body to produce natural antiopiates (Snyder, 1984). The slow buildup of these antiopiates causes tolerance to develop, so that a person must increase intake of the drug in order to achieve the same effects. Eventually this increased tolerance may lead to a physiological dependence on the drug. The person becomes *addicted* so that withdrawal symptoms such as cramps, nausea, tremors, headaches, and sweating occur in the drug's absence. Physiological dependence seems to be related to the fact that excessive, chronic levels of the drug in the body deplete certain vital body substances such as neurotransmitters. One of the most ironic things about drug addiction is that the original reason for taking the substance (for example, to go to sleep more easily at night) may be replaced by a desperate need to maintain adequate levels of the drug just to avoid withdrawal symptoms.

Not all psychoactive drugs produce physiological dependence. Sometimes a person merely finds that a drug is so pleasurable or helpful in coping with life that a kind of psychological dependence develops. In this sense, a person can become either dependent on or addicted to a wide range of drugs. The addiction often involves both physiological and psychological components. It is important to note that drugs which induce psychological dependence may be just as harmful and addictive as those which produce physiological dependence.

The three major groups of drugs, classified by their effects, are depressants, stimulants, and hallucinogens. The remainder of this chapter looks at these types of drugs and their effects on people.

DEPRESSANTS: SEDATIVES, OPIATES, AND ALCOHOL

Drugs that tend to slow or depress activity in the central nervous system are classified as **depressants.** Substances in this category include sedatives, opiates, and alcohol.

SEDATIVES **Sedatives** are drugs that induce relaxation, calmness, and sleep. This group of drugs include *tranquilizers,* such as Librium and Valium, *barbiturates* such as Nembutal and Seconal, and the *nonbarbiturates* Miltown and Quaalude. Many of these drugs are widely prescribed by physicians as remedies for emotional and physical complaints such as anxiety, insomnia, gastrointestinal disorders, and respiratory problems. Tranquilizers are some of the most widely prescribed drugs in the world. Chapter 16 discusses some of their therapeutic uses for treating psychological disorders.

All the sedative drugs, particularly barbiturates (also known as barbs or downers) are prime candidates for drug abuse. Tolerance for barbiturates develops quite rapidly, and abusers of these drugs often increase their consumption to the point where respiratory function, memory, judgment, and other mental and physical processes are seriously impaired. Barbiturate abusers soon develop a physiological addiction that makes withdrawal an arduous, traumatizing experience. Recent statistics reveal that roughly one out of every three reported cases of drug-caused death is due to barbiturate overdose. The effects of depressant drugs taken in combination can be volatile: Combining a nonlethal dose of alcohol with a nonlethal dose of barbiturates can cause death (Carlson, 1988).

Virtually every drug that alters behavior does so by interacting with a neurotransmitter system in the brain. The sedative drugs are no exception. The mechanisms whereby they accomplish their effects are not fully understood, but it is known that sedative drugs increase the sensitivity of postsynaptic receptors for *gamma-amino-butyric acid (GABA),* an important neurotransmitter which acts to inhibit neural transmission. By increasing the inhibition generated by GABA, the sedative drugs reduce neural activity in the brain circuits involved with emotional arousal (Carlson, 1988; Kimble, 1989).

OPIATES **Opiates** or **narcotics** are another category of depressant drugs. *Opium* is derived from a sticky resin secreted by the opium poppy. Two of its natural ingredients, *morphine* and *codeine,* have been widely used as painkillers. A third derivative, *heroin,* is obtained by chemically treating morphine. It is the strongest of all known narcotics.

Heroin is snorted (inhaled through the nostrils) or injected directly into the veins. When it is injected, the almost immediate effect is a rush, which users describe as an overwhelming sensation of pleasure akin to sexual orgasm. This rush may be the closest many heroin addicts come to this experience, however, as regular use of opiates often significantly decreases sexual interest and activity (Abel, 1984). Shortly after it is injected, heroin decomposes into morphine, which produces other effects commonly associated with opiate usage: a sense of well-being, contentment, insulation from dangers or challenges, and drowsiness.

Increasingly larger doses of heroin are needed to produce these effects, however, and the user quickly acquires a physiological and psychological dependence. The long-term effects of this addiction can be devastating. People addicted to heroin do almost anything to ensure their supply of the drug—cheat, steal, or prostitute themselves. William Burroughs, a writer and former addict, called heroin the ultimate merchandise. The client will crawl through a sewer and beg to buy it (White, 1985, p. 149).

What happens when an addict tries to break the habit? After a few hours without heroin, the user begins to experience symptoms such as vomiting, running nose, aching muscles, and abdominal pain. These symptoms are very uncomfortable, but they are probably less painful than withdrawal from some other drugs, including alcohol and barbiturates.

Opiates themselves produce little physical damage to the user. Chronic opiate use may damage the body's immune system, thus increasing the addict's susceptibility to disease (McDonough et al., 1980). Recent research indicates that the mortality rate among narcotics addicts is approximately seven times greater than that of the general population (Joe & Simpson, 1987). There are a variety of reasons for this statistic. Addicts often cause harm to themselves through drug-related habits, such as using nonsterile needles, obtaining contaminated heroin, or not eating properly. Carelessness about using sterile drug paraphernalia increases the risk of potentially life-threatening infectious diseases such as hepatitis (a liver infection) and endocarditis (inflammation of a membrane in the heart). Recently, AIDS has taken an alarming toll on drug users, perhaps because heroin, cocaine, and other psychoactive drugs impair the immune system, leaving drug users susceptible to AIDS diseases.

ALCOHOL Like other depressants, alcohol retards the activity of neurons in the central nervous system, particularly in the cerebral cortex and the cerebellum, by increasing the sensitivity of postsynaptic GABA receptors (Carlson, 1988; Urrutia et al., 1992). It is an extremely potent drug that affects behavior in a highly variable manner. Some people become more communicative and expressive under its influence, perhaps even boisterous and silly. Others become aggressive, abusive, and sometimes violent. People under the influence of alcohol may engage in behaviors they normally keep in check, probably because alcohol suppresses the inhibitory mechanisms of the cerebral cortex.

These behavioral effects may be evident at relatively low levels of alcohol consumption. As intake increases, it is accompanied by more pronounced impairments of coordination, reaction time, thinking, and judgment (Ward & Lewis, 1987). When blood alcohol content reaches 0.10 percent (the equivalent of four to six beers or three to four 1.5–ounce shots of 80 proof alcohol), a person's chance of having a severe accident behind the wheel of a car or otherwise may be as much as five or six times greater than normal.

Alcohol is the nation's number one drug problem and, after heart disease and cancer, the third largest health problem. More than 200,000 alcohol-connected deaths occur each year. Alcohol is also linked to two-thirds of all incidents of domestic violence and one-third of all child abuse cases (Ziegler, 1984). The recently conducted National Adolescent Student Health Survey (NASHS), which queried a representative national sample of 11,419 eighth- and tenth-grade students drawn from 217 schools in 20 states, revealed that 26 percent of eighth graders and 38 percent of tenth graders reported having five or more drinks on one occasion during the past two weeks (Centers for Disease Control, 1989). Another recent study of substance abuse in a sample of 424 college students found the prevalence of alcohol abuse to be 8.2 percent (Deykin et al., 1987).

Like the other depressants, alcohol is physiologically addictive. Withdrawal is often accompanied by severe symptoms, including nausea, vomiting, fever, and shakes, and sometimes the d.t.s (*delirium tremens*, bizarre visual hallucinations). Occasionally, withdrawal from alcohol produces such a profound shock to the body that death may result. The symptoms of alcohol withdrawal are the result of the nervous system's oversensitivity to stimuli in the absence of the depressive effects of alcohol. Withdrawal symptoms are often treated with the administration of mild tranquilizers such as Valium.

Prolonged and excessive use of alcohol can have disastrous physical effects. Liver and heart disease are commonly associated with alcohol abuse (Cunningham, 1986; Davidson, 1986; Novick et al., 1986; Van Thiel et al., 1989). Malnutrition is also a problem: Alcoholics typically eat poorly, since their daily consumption of liquor provides hundreds of calories. In addition, alcohol interferes with the proper absorption of B vitamins, so vitamin B deficiency is common. A prolonged deficiency of these essential vitamins can lead to brain damage, a complication that occurs in about 10 percent of alcoholics (Johnson et al, 1986). Alcoholic brain damage, which can include cerebral and cortical atrophy and reduced brain weight, has been associated with a variety of cognitive and behavioral impairments (Carlen et al., 1986; Ellis & Oscar-Berman, 1989; Johnson et al., 1986; Kramer et al., 1989). Alcohol abusers have also been shown to be at increased risk for having a stroke (cerebral hemorrhage) (Gorelick et al., 1989). Alcoholics also tend to develop various kinds of infections at a rate higher than normal, due in part to a suppressed immune system (Dehne et al., 1989).

Heavy drinking during pregnancy causes further complications. Because alcohol passes from the mother's body to the fetus, the infant may be born with an alcohol addiction. Drug withdrawal in a baby can be fatal. Offspring of mothers who drink heavily while they are pregnant may suffer from *fetal alcohol syndrome*, which is characterized by retarded physical growth, intellectual development, and motor coordination as well as abnormalities in brain metabolic processes and liver functioning (Bonthius & West, 1990; Coles et al., 1987; Golden et al., 1982; Merikangas, 1990; Redei et al., 1989; Singh et al., 1986; Vinigan et al., 1986; Wright et al., 1983).

STIMULANTS: CAFFEINE, NICOTINE, AMPHETAMINES, AND COCAINE

Drugs that stimulate the central nervous system by increasing the transmission of nerve impulses are called **stimulants.** The most widely consumed of these drugs are caffeine and nicotine, both of which are mild stimulants. Amphetamines and cocaine are the most frequently used of the stronger stimulants.

CAFFEINE Found in a variety of products including chocolate, coffee, tea, and many carbonated soft drinks such as colas, caffeine has long provided people with a quick lift. Caffeine acts quickly. Within a few minutes after it is consumed, heart and respiration rates and blood pressure increase.

People experience these physical effects in a variety of ways. Most feel mentally stimulated; some experience a brief burst of energy. People who consume a large amount of caffeine (for example, six or more cups of coffee) may feel more pronounced effects: irritability, headaches, the jitters, difficulty concentrating, nausea, and sleep disturbances. A recent study revealed that adult subjects who received moderate doses of caffeine demonstrated increased scores on scales measuring anxiety, depression, and hostility, unlike control subjects who were administered placebos (Veleber & Templer, 1984). Caffeine has been implicated in anxiety disorders and learning difficulties in children (Dusek & Girdano, 1980). People who become physically dependent on caffeine, as evidenced by the countless numbers of people who just cannot function without their daily quota of coffee, tea, or cola.

Caffeine exerts its effects on the nervous system by blocking adenosine receptors. Adenosine is an inhibitory neurotransmitter that produces behavioral sedation and regulates the dilation of blood vessels (Julien, 1992).

NICOTINE Nicotine is second only to caffeine on the list of widely used stimulants. Found in tobacco, nicotine increases heart rate, blood pressure, and stomach activity, and constricts blood vessels. Paradoxically, it may have either a relaxing or a stimulating effect on the user, depending on the circumstances and the user's expectations. Nicotine is physiologically addictive, and people who stop smoking may experience a variety of withdrawal symptoms including craving for tobacco, increased appetite, stomach cramps, headaches, restlessness, irritability, insomnia, anxiety, and depression (Hughes et al., 1987).

The long-term effects of smoking have been well publicized: Nearly 500 thousand people die every year from coronary heart disease, cancer, respiratory diseases, and other diseases caused by smoking. Smoking also increases a person's risk for experiencing a stroke (Colditz et al., 1988; Gorelick et al., 1989). It has been estimated that as many as one-third of heavy smokers will die before age 85 from various diseases caused by smoking (Mattson et al., 1987). There is also evidence that women who smoke while pregnant have a higher incidence of miscarriages, stillbirths, and low birth-weight babies than women who do not smoke (Fox et al., 1987; Schwartz-Bickenbach et al., 1987).

Recent research indicates that the impaired health experienced by many smokers may be due to more than the impact of nicotine, per se. A disturbing report by Felipe Castro and his associates (1989) revealed that, compared to nonsmokers, smokers seem to be both less aware of and concerned about their health and more inclined to engage in unhealthy behaviors (such as excessive consumption of alcohol and coffee and avoiding aerobic exercise) that put them at risk for severe health problems such as coronary heart disease.

AMPHETAMINES **Amphetamines** are much more powerful stimulants, sold under the trade names Benzedrine, Dexedrine, and Methedrine and known on the street as uppers or speed. These drugs tend dramatically to increase alertness, counteract fatigue, and promote feelings of euphoria and well-being.

These effects are due to the way in which the neurotransmitter dopamine reacts to amphetamines (Carboni et al., 1989; Carlson, 1988). Dopamine is linked to feelings of emotional well-being, and amphetamines seem to increase its level in the brain. Amphetamines also enhance the activity of the neurotransmitter norepinephrine—exactly the opposite of the effect that sedatives have on this chemical. Thus, some students who take amphetamines to get through an all-night study session find it difficult to relax when they are ready to rest.

People use amphetamines for a variety of reasons: to stay awake, to feel good, to improve energy levels, to increase confidence, and to lose weight (amphetamines are short-term appetite suppressants). Most users take the drug orally, but some inject it directly into a vein. When amphetamines are used in excess, they can cause muscle and joint aches, tremors, and feelings of paranoia. In extreme cases amphetamines produce both punding, which is a repetitive motor response, and *psychosis*, which combines paranoia with hallucinations and difficulty recognizing people.

Users seem to develop a tolerance for the euphoric effects of amphetamines, but not for its antisleep effects (Blum, 1984). In addition, they often develop a profound psychological dependence on the drug. Until recently, it was believed that no physiological dependence developed among users. However, by the mid-1980s, researchers had accumulated enough evidence to suggest that the amphetamine hangover (characterized by depression, extreme fatigue, prolonged sleep, irritability, disorientation, and agitated motor activity) is a strong indicator of physical dependence (Blum, 1984).

COCAINE Cocaine is a powerful central nervous system stimulant that is extracted from leaves of the coca shrub. It is often sniffed (snorted) through a straw into the mucous membranes of the nasal passages. A solution of the drug may also be injected into the vein. In a somewhat different form, cocaine may also be smoked in a process called freebasing. Smoking freebase results in the most rapid delivery of the drug to the brain (its effect can be felt in 5 to 10 seconds), followed by snorting (30 to 120 seconds), and then intravenous injection (1 to 3 minutes) (Miller et al., 1989).

In 1985 a new form of freebase cocaine entered American drug culture. Crack is the street name given to cocaine that has been processed from cocaine hydrochloride (the crystalline derivative of the coca leaf that is sold on the street as coke) into freebase by using ammonia or baking soda and water and heating

When Coca-Cola first appeared on the market in 1885 it contained cocaine. Cocaine was removed from soft drinks in 1903.

the mixture. (It is believed that the baking soda causes a crackling sound when the base is heated, thus giving rise to the street name.) It is difficult to estimate the extent of crack use in America. However, since individual packages of crack may be purchased for a few dollars and since its effects are produced more rapidly than through snorting, it is likely that crack has, or will soon have, become the most common form of cocaine abuse.

No matter which form is used, many of cocaine's effects are similar to those of amphetamines. They include increased alertness and abundance of energy, feelings of euphoria, and a sense of well-being. Cocaine increases heart and respiration rates, constricts blood vessels, and dilates the pupils. It is metabolized very quickly, so its effects often last only 20 to 30 minutes. Thus to maintain a high, the user must take the drug frequently—one reason why a cocaine habit can become very costly.

Like other drugs, cocaine seems to derive its effects by altering normal patterns of neurotransmitter activity. There is good evidence that cocaine blocks the reuptake of dopamine and norepinephrine, increasing the time these chemicals actively stimulate emotional arousal (Carboni et al., 1989; Carlson, 1988; Choy-Kwong & Lipton, 1989).

Cocaine abuse can lead to severe problems, both physical and mental. It has been linked to heart and lung damage, anemia, damage to the nasal tissues, immune system impairment, and, in rare cases, sudden death (McCarthy, 1985; Smith, 1986; Wetli & Wright, 1979). In large doses, cocaine can impair judgment, create anxiety attacks, induce paranoid reactions, cause cerebral hemorrhage, and bring about seizures (Choy-Kwong & Lipton, 1989; Miller et al., 1989; Rowley et al., 1989); it can also depress centers in the brain's medulla that control breathing and heartbeat. The result may be sudden death due to cardiac or respiratory arrest (Blum, 1984; Miller et al., 1989; Wetli & Wright, 1979). This tragic consequence of cocaine abuse caused the death of superstar basketball player Len Bias in 1986. There is evidence that cocaine used during pregnancy may have an adverse effect on prenatal development and a negative impact on reproductive functions in both sexes (Bingol et al., 1987; Chasnoff et al., 1989; King et al., 1990; Mendelson et al., 1988; Zuckerman et al., 1989).

Cocaine users do not typically develop a tolerance to the euphoric effects of the drug. Drug authorities have generally assumed that although chronic cocaine use produces profound psychological dependence, it does not result in physiological dependence in the sense that alcohol or heroin does (Blum, 1984; Gawin & Kleber, 1984). However, a number of drug researchers maintain that it is not possible to distinguish clearly between physiological and psychological dependence on cocaine. These authorities point out that after crashing (coming down off the drug), the user often experiences a variety of withdrawal symptoms including fatigue, depression, irritability, aches, pains, and a restless protracted sleep (Miller et al., 1989).

Despite these facts, cocaine use is growing rapidly in America. A federal agency reported that the amount of high quality cocaine in this country is at an all-time high. With increased supplies, the price of the drug is going down—a trend with important implications, for many people who previously might not have been able to afford it are now experimenting with cocaine. Lower costs have also brought cocaine into the schools. The National Adolescent Student Health Survey recently revealed that 4 percent of eighth graders and 8 percent of tenth graders reported having used cocaine (Centers for Disease Control, 1989).

Drugs in a third group, **hallucinogens**, produce changes in sensory perceptions, thinking processes, and emotions. Under their influence, a person's sense of time and space may be altered. Other effects include delusions, impaired judgment,

HALLUCINOGENS: LSD, PCP, MARIJUANA

and visual, auditory, and tactile hallucinations. Some hallucinogenic drugs, such as LSD (lysergic acid diethylamide) and psilocybin (derived from a mushroom) appear to produce their hallucinogenic effects by interfering with the actions of the neurotransmitter serotonin.

Brain researchers are not sure how hallucinogenic drugs affect the nervous system but they theorize that hallucinations result from disinhibition of the neural circuits responsible for dreaming. During wakefulness serotonin inhibits the neurons in these circuits, preventing them from actively generating dreamlike activity. However, when drugs like LSD and psilocybin suppress the activity of serotonin, dream mechanisms become active and waking dreams (hallucinations) result (Carlson, 1988). Other hallucinogens, including mescaline (derived from the peyote cactus) and possibly marijuana, affect the way the brain reacts to norepinephrine.

LSD Derived from the ergot fungus that grows on rye grass, **LSD** became recognized for its psychoactive properties in the 1940s. Throughout the 1950s and early 1960s, researchers experimented with it as a tool for treating behavioral and emotional disorders, as a pain reliever for people suffering from terminal disease, and as a drug that might have possible military applications (Neill, 1987). Eventually, LSD fell into disrepute, largely because of its unpredictable effects. However, this official disfavor did not curtail its growing popularity as a street drug used to alter and expand consciousness. In recent years, LSD's popularity has declined as other drugs such as cocaine and marijuana have become more common.

LSD is one of the most powerful known hallucinogens. A tiny amount can produce profound distortions of sensations, feelings, time, and thought. Some users describe an LSD trip as spiritual, mind expanding, and a source of ecstasy. Some claim that the drug adds to their creativity, but this assertion is not supported by research (Dusek & Girdano, 1980; Janiger & DeRios, 1989). Others have painful, frightening experiences in which they may feel that they have lost control, that their body is disintegrating, or that they have died. Having a good

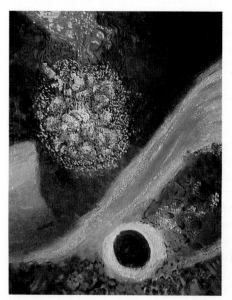

Examples of art produced by individuals under the influence of LSD. Some people believe that LSD increases their creativity. Science does not support these claims.

trip one time is no guarantee that the next LSD experience will not turn into a nightmare.

PCP   Phencyclidine hydrochloride, PCP or angel dust, has become more popular in recent years. We have placed PCP in the category of hallucinogens since one of its more pronounced effects is sensory distortions and hallucinations. However, it also has stimulant, depressant, and painkilling properties. PCP was originally used as an anesthetic, but its legal use was barred in medical practice when its side effects became known.

People take PCP because it sometimes produces euphoria, relaxation, and a sense of numbness. However, it also produces many dangerous effects, including loss of contact with reality (lack of responsiveness to external stimuli), memory distortions, depression, anxiety and paranoia, and the unpredictable unleashing of aggressive, violent behavior. Disrupted thought processes, mood disturbances, and aggression may persist for weeks after a single dose of the drug, and convulsions and coma may also result. In rare cases, people experience convulsions or respiratory failure that can cause death. PCP is not physiologically addictive, but there is evidence that users may become psychologically dependent on it (Bolter et al., 1976).

MARIJUANA   As a recreational drug, marijuana, the most widely used of the illegal psychoactive drugs, is second in popularity only to alcohol. It is derived from the flowering top of the Cannabis sativa, a hemp plant once known primarily as an excellent material for making ropes.

The mind-altering component of marijuana is the chemical THC (delta 9-tetrahydrocannabinol). Marijuana is classified as a hallucinogen because relatively high doses of THC can produce hallucinations. Sometimes marijuana is classified as a depressant because in low doses it often has a sedative effect. However, in higher doses it acts as a stimulant, which further complicates any efforts to categorize it.

Until recently researchers did not know how marijuana altered the activity of the brain to produce its euphoric effects. However, NIMH researcher William Devine and his coworkers have recently identified receptors for THC in the brain as well as a natural substance that binds with these THC receptors. The brain's natural THC has been named *anandamide* meaning bliss (Devine et al., 1992; Fackelmann, 1993). It is now believed that anandamide plays an important role in regulating mood, pain, movement, and appetite.

Two physiological effects of marijuana use are increased heart rate and enhanced appetite. Small doses often produce euphoria and enhance some sensory experiences, such as listening to music. Marijuana impairs reaction time and the ability to concentrate on complex tasks, and some people become confused, agitated, or extremely anxious under its influence (Relman, 1982; Yesavage et al., 1985). Marijuana impairs a person's perceptual skills and motor coordination, thus significantly increasing his or her risk of having an accident while operating an automobile (Fortenberry et al., 1986; Gieringer, 1988; Williams et al., 1985). Recall may also be impaired due to use of marijuana (Miller & Branconier, 1983). Large doses of marijuana may even induce hallucinations, paranoia, and dizziness.

Medical practitioners have discovered that marijuana can be therapeutic in some situations. For example, it can be helpful in epilepsy, glaucoma (a disease that can cause blindness). It has been shown to reduce the nausea that often accompanies chemotherapy treatment for cancer patients, and it may now be used to prevent some of the weight loss associated with AIDS diseases (Fackelman, 1993).

MAGNESIUM TREATMENT AFTER BRAIN INJURY ------------

Brain research has clearly demonstrated that magnesium ions (MG^{2+}) are essential for a number of important brain cell functions including protein synthesis, cellular respiration, neurotransmitter function, and maintenance of cellular membranes (Aikawa, 1981; Altura et al., 1984). Recent research has demonstrated that total magnesium levels in brain cells decline markedly after experimentally induced brain injury in rats. Furthermore, the more severe the brain injury, the greater the reduction of magnesium levels (Vink et al., 1988). This finding prompted the research team of Tracy McIntosh and colleagues (1989) to conduct an experiment designed to evaluate the therapeutic benefits of administering magnesium after brain injury.

Anesthetized rats were subjected to a procedure designed to produce brain trauma. Thirty minutes after the injury was induced the animals received injections of low-dose magnesium, high-dose magnesium, or inactive saline solution, depending on the group to which they were assigned. The rats treated with magnesium demonstrated a "significant dose-dependent improvement in neurological function when compared to saline-treated controls" (p. 252), with rats that received the highest dose of magnesium demonstrating the greatest improvement.

These findings indicate that postinjury treatment with magnesium may help to restore the ability of brain cells to perform essential cellular functions such as those mentioned earlier, thereby minimizing neurological deficits after brain injury. Such results suggest a potentially valuable therapeutic intervention with humans who are victims of traumatic brain injury. Hopefully, future research will clarify the applicability and potential benefits of such a treatment strategy with brain-injured humans.

HEALTH
PSYCHOLOGY
LIFE

SUMMARY ------------

OVERVIEW OF THE NERVOUS SYSTEM: ORGANIZATION AND FUNCTION

1. The nervous system of humans and other vertebrates consists of two major parts: the central nervous system (CNS) and the peripheral nervous system (PNS).

2. The CNS consists of the brain and the spinal cord. It occupies the commanding position in the nervous system, as it coordinates and integrates all bodily functions.

3. The PNS transmits messages to and from the CNS. It is subdivided into the somatic nervous system and the autonomic nervous system.

NEURONS: BASIC UNITS OF THE NERVOUS SYSTEM

4. There are three major classes of neurons: sensory neurons that carry messages to the CNS; motor neurons that transmit mes-

sages from the CNS to muscles and glands; and interneurons that act as intermediaries between sensory and motor neurons.

5. Neurons have four common structures: the cell body, which handles metabolic functions; the dendrites, which receive neural messages; the axon, which conducts a message to the end of the neuron; and the terminal buttons at the end of the axon, which release transmitter substances.

6. The transmission of a neural message involves both electrical and chemical aspects. Electrical processes are activated when the dendrites (or cell body) of a neuron respond to an impulse from neighboring neurons by undergoing a change in permeability of the cell membrane. Voltage changes then occur, due to an influx of positive sodium ions through the more permeable membrane. These voltage

changes are called graded potentials. When the sum of graded potentials reaches a sufficient magnitude, an electrical signal or action potential is generated that flows along the length of the neuron.

7. Neural impulses are transmitted from one neuron to another, across the synaptic gap, via chemical messengers called neurotransmitters. These transmitter substances may act either to excite or inhibit action potentials in the receiving neuron.

8. Variations in neurotransmitter levels or in responsivity to these chemical messengers have been linked with various psychological disorders and the action of numerous drugs.

9. Endogenous opioids, which are part of a family of neurotransmitters known as neuropeptides, have been linked to a range of behavioral and mental processes, including inducing euphoria, counteracting stress, modulating food and liquid intake, facilitating learning and memory, and reducing pain.

THE PERIPHERAL NERVOUS SYSTEM

10. The PNS, which transfers information to and from the CNS, has two divisions: somatic and autonomic.

11. The somatic nervous system serves the major skeletal muscles that carry out intentional movements. It also contains nerves that transmit sensory information from the skin, muscles, and sensory organs of the body.

12. The autonomic nervous system controls the glands and smooth muscles of internal organs. The two subdivisions of the autonomic nervous system, the sympathetic and parasympathetic systems, operate in an integrative fashion to allow the body to function optimally when either relaxed or highly aroused. The sympathetic system is particularly active during emotional emergencies. The parasympathetic system, which provides a braking mechanism for organs activated by the sympathetic system, is more involved during relaxation and body restoration.

THE CENTRAL NERVOUS SYSTEM

13. The spinal cord conveys messages to and from the brain, helps coordinate the two sides of the body, and mediates certain basic reflexive behaviors (such as the quick withdrawal of a hand from a hot stove.

14. The medulla, the lowest part of the brain, contains centers that control many vital life-support functions such as breathing, heartbeat, and blood pressure.

15. The pons, a large bulge in the lower brain core, plays a role in fine-tuning motor messages and in processing some sensory information.

16. The cerebellum, tucked beneath the back part of the cerebral hemispheres, coordinates and regulates motor movements.

17. The reticular formation or reticular activating system, a set of neural circuits extending from the lower brain up to the thalamus, plays a role in controlling levels of arousal and alertness.

18. The limbic system, a collection of structures located around the central core of the brain, is closely associated with emotional expression. It also is active in motivation, learning, and memory.

19. The hypothalamus, located beneath the thalamus, helps to maintain homeostasis within the body's internal environment. In addition, it plays a key role in controlling emotional expression and serves as the hub of the neuroendocrine system.

20. The thalamus, located beneath the cerebral cortex, plays a role in routing incoming sensory information to appropriate areas within the cerebral cortex.

21. The basal ganglia consists of several structures involved in motor

movement including the caudate nucleus, putamen, and substantia nigra.

THE CEREBRAL CORTEX

22. The cerebral cortex, the thin outer layer of the cerebral cortex, is the part of the brain responsible for higher mental processes such as perceiving, thinking, and remembering.

23. To some degree, researchers have been able to localize a variety of functions within various regions or lobes of the cortex of the two hemispheres. The frontal lobe contains the motor cortex, a narrow strip of brain tissue that controls a wide range of intentional body movements. The primary brain center for controlling speech is also in the frontal lobe. The parietal lobe contains the somatosensory cortex, which receives sensory information about touch, pressure, pain, temperature, and body position from various areas of the body. The occipital lobe consists primarily of the visual cortex, devoted to the business of seeing. A primary function of the temporal lobe, hearing, is localized in the auditory cortex.

24. Split-brain research, in which the primary connection between the two hemispheres (the corpus callosum) is severed, has revealed important information about the degree to which a particular function is controlled by one rather than both hemispheres (lateralization of function). This research has supported the interpretation that in most people the left hemisphere is primarily responsible for language and speech, logic, and mathematics. In contrast, the right hemisphere appears to be more important in perceiving spatial relationships, manipulating objects, synthesizing (generalizing the whole from segments), and artistic functions.

25. A number of techniques are employed to study the brain, including lesion production, brain stimulation and electrical recording via implanted wires, electroencephalography (EEG), computerized axial tomography (CAT), positron emission tomography (PET), and magnetic resonance imaging (MRI).

THE ENDOCRINE SYSTEM

26. The endocrine system is composed of several ductless glands that secrete hormones directly into the bloodstream. The endocrine system often works in tandem with the nervous system to regulate a variety of bodily responses. The hypothalamus functions as a key interface between the nervous system and the endocrine system.

27. The endocrine system influences many important physiological functions, mental processes, and behavior patterns, including disease regulation, metabolism, emotional responses, and motivation.

28. The pituitary gland produces hormones which trigger other glands to action. Among other important products of the pituitary are growth hormone, which controls a number of metabolic functions including the rate of growth, and neuropeptides, which act as neurotransmitters that influence such things as eating and drinking, sexual behavior, sleep, pain reduction, and responses to stress.

29. The thyroid gland produces thyroxine, which helps to regulate metabolism. Lethargy and hyperactivity are related to too little or too much thyroxine, respectively.

30. The paired adrenal glands produce a variety of hormones, including epinephrine and norepinephrine, that prepare the body to respond to emergencies and cope with stress.

31. The gonads secrete several varieties of sex hormones which influence development of physical sex characteristics, sexual reproduction, and sexual motivation.

DRUGS AND BEHAVIOR

32. Sedative drugs such as Librium, Valium, barbituates, and Seconal induce relaxation and sleep. They are often prescribed for anxiety and sleep disorders.

33. Opiates or narcotics like morphine and heroin induce a state or euphoria and are highly addictive. Opiates are prescribed to control pain.

34. Alcohol acts as a central nervous system depressant in the cerebral cortex and cerebellum. Alcohol is the nation's number one drug problem.

35. The major stimulants include caffeine, nicotine, amphetamine, and cocaine.

36. Amphetamine and cocaine are powerful stimulants that can be addictive.

37. The hallucinogens such as LSD and marijuana produce changes in perception and emotions.

TERMS & CONCEPTS

central nervous system (CNS)
peripheral nervous system (PNS)
neuron
sensory (afferent) neuron
motor (efferent) neuron
interneuron
cell body
dendrites
axon
terminal buttons
resting potential
graded potential
action potential
all-or-none law
glia cells
myelin sheath
node of Ranvier
synapse
neurotransmitters
excitatory postsynaptic potential (EPSPs)
inhibitory postsynaptic potentials (IPSPs)
cerebral cortex
cerebral hemispheres
medulla
pons
cerebellum
reticular formation (reticular activating system or RAS)
limbic system
amygdala
hippocampus
septal area
hypothalamus
thalamus
basal ganglia
caudate nucleus
putamen
substantia nigra
cerebral cortex
sensory cortex
motor cortex
association cortex
frontal lobe
Broca's area
parietal lobe
somatosensory cortex
occipital lobe
visual cortex
temporal lobe
auditory cortex
Wernicke's area
lateralization of function
corpus callosum
lesion production
brain stimulation
electrical recording
electroencephalography (EEG)
computerized axial tomography (CAT)
positron emission tomography (PET)
magnetic resonance imaging (MRI)
somatic nervous system
autonomic nervous system
sympathetic nervous system
parasympathetic nervous system
endocrine system
hormones
pituitary gland
thyroid gland
adrenal glands
gonads
stimulants
hallucinogens
sedatives
opiates
depressants

C H A P T E R 4

Sensation and Perception

PRINCIPLES OF SENSATION AND PERCEPTION

Transduction
What Do We Perceive?
Psychophysics

VISION

Light: The Stimulus for Vision
Structure and Function of the Eye
Color Vision

AUDITION

Sound: The Stimulus for Audition
Structure and Function of the Ear
Theories of Audition
Auditory Localization
Hearing Loss

GUSTATION AND OLFACTION

Gustation
Olfaction

THE SKIN SENSES

Pressure
Temperature
Pain

KINESTHESIS AND EQUILIBRIUM

PERCEIVING THE WORLD

Perceptual Organization
Spatial Perception
Visual Illusions
Perceptual Sets

*D*id you ever wonder whether other animals perceive the world as we do? What is the world like from a bird, a bat, or an insect's point of view? Psychologists have known for a long time that the sensory worlds of different animals are very unlike our own. The world to an insect is defined in terms of odors and tastes that tell it what foods to eat and how to find a mate. The world of the bat is a complex multidimensional acoustical space that allows for precise navigation and the perception of prey. Neither of these species perceive the world as we do. And, even though a bird's dominant sense is vision, like our own, their world is also quite different.

Consider the prairie falcon in Figure 4.1. The structure of its eye allows for high-resolution vision of the ground while in flight. In fact, it can keep its prey in sharp focus during a 150-mph. dive. At this speed our world becomes a blur. The prairie falcon's eye is not as well adapted to vision while perched, however. The reason this bird has its head tilted to one side is to allow an image to fall on the top part of its inner eye (the retina) where it can bring it into sharp focus. While the falcon is in flight this is not a problem because images from the ground normally fall on the top part of the retina (Waldvogel, 1990).

This chapter is concerned with both the sensory processes that bring us information about our environments and the neural activity that gives this information meaning. Although many of the processes described in this chapter may seem to be physiological, not psychological, it is important to remember that our sensations and perceptions form the raw material on which much of our behavior is based. As our prairie falcon demonstrates, behavior is both limited by and defines an organism's perceptual abilities.

PRINCIPLES OF SENSATION AND PERCEPTION

All perceptions begin with a *stimulus*, some type of physical energy such as a sound or a flash of light, to which we can respond. The stimulus produces a physiological change in specific sensory receptor cells, and this information is then transmitted to the brain, where it is organized and interpreted. The direct effect of stimulation of receptor cells by a stimulus is referred to as **sensation**. Our organization and interpretation of sensory experience is referred to as **perception**.

Five major senses provide us with important information about the outside world. These senses are vision, hearing, smell, taste, and the skin senses (pressure, temperature, and pain). In addition, the so-called body senses (kinesthesis) allow us to detect movement and the position of our bodies. Although the messages differ, the process by which sensory information reaches our brains is the same. This process is called transduction.

FIGURE 4.1

To focus on an object while perched, the Prairie Falcon must tip its head to the side.

TRANSDUCTION

In order for us to sense and perceive the surrounding world, information about external events must reach our brains. This information comes in many forms: mechanical energy for hearing and the skin senses; chemical energy for smelling and tasting; and light energy for seeing. However, as you recall from Chapter 3, the brain is able to respond only to the electrochemical events that are generated by neurons firing. Therefore, before we can perceive our environment, all sensory input must be transformed into neural activity that can be processed by the brain. The process by which sensory organs transform mechanical, chemical, or light energy into neural activity is called **transduction.**

Each sense receptor has specialized cells designed to respond to a particular kind of energy. For example, our eyes contain chemicals called photopigments that change their shape when they are hit by light. These shape changes initiate a series of events that ultimately culminate in the transmission of neuronal activity to the brain. Likewise, other kinds of receptors transduce other kinds of energy into electrical impulses.

DISTINGUISHING TYPES OF SENSORY IMPULSES   We know that the brain cannot respond directly to physical energy such as pressure or light: This information must first be transduced into neuronal signals. If all sensory messages are converted to neuronal signals, how does the brain distinguish among them? How can it differentiate among the impulses that represent sight, sound, taste, and smell? Take a moment to consider this question before reading on.

Perhaps a useful clue to this question comes from some discoveries made in brain surgery, when various sites on the surface of an alert patient's cortex have been electrically stimulated. Such stimulation may produce vivid sensations. For example, stimulation of the occipital cortex at the back of the brain can create sensations of flashing lights, and stimulating the auditory region on the side of the brain can cause the patient to hear tones (Penfield & Perrot, 1963).

As this evidence reveals, the ability to distinguish sensations does not depend on differences between the sense organs, but rather on that part of the brain which is activated by the sensory messages (Goldstein, 1989). Chapter 3 pointed out that sensory nerves carry impulses to particular target sites within the brain. It is now widely believed that the distinctiveness of sights, sounds, smells, and so forth is related to unique properties of tissue in various parts of the brain (Sekuler & Blake, 1985).

WHAT DO WE PERCEIVE?

The fact that sensations result from the transduction of physical energy in the environment into neural impulses raises an interesting question: Since we are surrounded by noises, smells, sights, and sounds, why are we not equally aware of all these sensations? For instance, as you are reading this your nervous system is being bombarded with stimuli from numerous different sources. Besides the visual stimuli this book provides there are other sounds, sights, smells, and tactile sensations. Your world is full of different kinds of physical energy.

Although many of these physical events are transformed into sensations and ultimately perceptions, many also go unheeded. What factors determine whether or not we perceive the things happening around us? There are several factors; the most important are sensory thresholds, attention, and adaptation. The investigation of these factors can be traced from the very beginnings of psychology to the present in a field of psychology called psychophysics. **Psychophysics** is that part of psychology which focuses on the relationship between physical aspects of external stimuli and our perceptions of them.

PSYCHOPHYSICS

SENSORY THRESHOLDS   The psychological world constructed by our brain is much simpler than the physical complexity of the world around us because our sense organs do not inform our brains about all of the events that take place. Our perception of various sensory inputs can occur only when the strength of a stimulus reaches a minimal or **threshold** level of intensity sufficient to activate a sensory process. For example, our sense of smell is activated only when an adequate number of chemical molecules are present in the air.

One of the most important reasons why we do not respond to many stimuli, therefore, is simply the biological limitations of our senses. If our senses responded to all the sights, sounds, smells, and other stimuli around us, we would be overwhelmed by too much stimulation. Two kinds of sensory thresholds operate to limit our perception of sensation: absolute thresholds and difference thresholds.

ABSOLUTE AND DIFFERENCE THRESHOLDS Imagine yourself waiting at a restaurant for a special person with whom you will dine. When the person arrives and takes a seat at your table you perceive a subtle scent of perfume or cologne but you're not quite sure. For several minutes you wonder whether you are imagining the scent or if you really do smell it. As you begin talking you move closer and suddenly you recognize the scent. It is not strong, but detectable enough to distinguish it clearly. How intense did the scent need to be just to notice it and how much more was necessary to recognize clearly its identity? Both of these questions are about sensory thresholds. The first question pertains to what psychologists call an absolute threshold and the second question refers to a difference threshold.

Absolute Thresholds When you first noticed the perfume or cologne but couldn't be sure what it was, its intensity was at your absolute threshold. An **absolute threshold** is defined as the minimum physical intensity of a stimulus that can be perceived by an observer 50 percent of the time. Figure 4.2 demonstrates some absolute thresholds for the five major senses. These values are average and your sensory organs may be more or less efficient than those of the sample. Absolute thresholds for various sensory modalities differ from person to person (Satow, 1987). In addition, these averages represent ideal conditions in a laboratory. Clearly, you could not hear a watch ticking 20 feet away under normal circumstances.

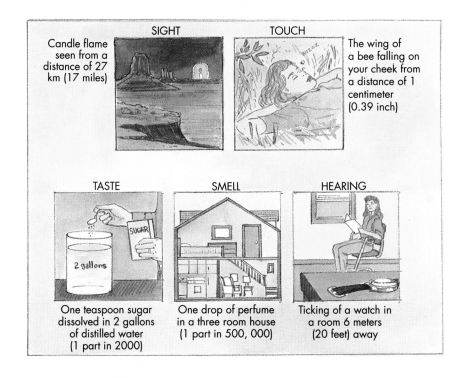

FIGURE 4.2
Absolute Sensory Thresholds

Difference Thresholds   As your friend moved closer and you could now distinguish the scent, this change in intensity was sufficient to reach your difference threshold. A **difference threshold** is the minimum increase in the intensity of a stimulus necessary to just notice a change 50 percent of the time. This increase in intensity is also referred to as a **just noticeable difference** or **jnd.**

You may wonder why thresholds are defined as stimulus intensities perceived 50 percent of the time. As you can see in Figure 4.3, our perception of a stimulus changes as stimulus intensity increases.

In an experiment to test your threshold for a particular stimulus the experimenter might present you with a series of stimuli at different intensities and you would report whether you perceived a stimulus or not after each trial. All of the stimuli would be presented several times to you in random order. A graph like Figure 4.3 could then be constructed with your responses, either yes or no, if you perceived a stimulus or not on each trial. The percent of correct responses at each stimulus intensity is then plotted on the figure. For example, if the stimulus intensity was very low you might report perceiving it only 25 percent of the time when it was actually presented. Responding yes 50 percent or more of the time to a particular stimulus intensity indicates better than chance. Below 50 percent is poorer than chance performance.

Weber's Law and the Just Noticeable Difference   Our perception of a particular stimulus is always relative to its background level or its context. Thus the degree of increase or decrease in intensity that is necessary to produce a jnd (just noticeable difference) depends on the original strength of the stimulus. In 1834 a German scientist, E.H. Weber (the *W* is pronounced as a *V*), conducted a classic experiment that revealed one of the first major principles of sensation. He discovered that the difference threshold for various stimulus intensities tends to be a constant fraction of the original stimulus intensity. Thus as the strength of the original stimulus increases, the magnitude of the change must also increase in order for a jnd to be perceived. This relationship is known as **Weber's law.**

In mathematical form, Weber's law is expressed as the following equation:

$$\Delta I = kI$$

where ΔI is the change in stimulus intensity necessary for a jnd, I is the initial stimulus intensity, and k is a value known as Weber's constant.

Although this sounds complicated, it is really quite simple to apply. In a psychophysics experiment you might be asked to judge the difference between two weights; say one 10 lb. weight and another 10.10 lb. weight. The difference of

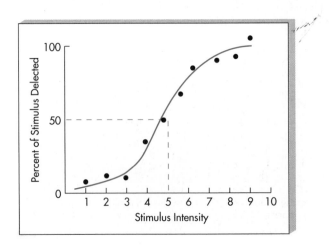

FIGURE 4.3
Measuring Stimulus Thresholds

.10 lbs. is not enough to tell the difference (.10 lbs. is less than 1 jnd for 10 lbs.).
However, if the second weight were increased to 10.20 lbs., you could now detect a noticeable difference. The ratio of stimulus intensity for a jnd of weight is
1/50 or .20 lbs. (Schiffman, 1990). Using this ratio and Weber's Law, how many
pounds would have to be added to a 100 lb. weight for you to just notice a difference? If you answered 2 lbs. (not 0.2 lbs.) this would be correct because $\Delta I = kI$,
or $2 = 0.02 \times 100$. The fraction, 0.02 or 1/50, is called a Weber's constant.
Weber discovered that this constant remains the same for each dimension of sensation, but changes for different stimulus dimensions. For instance, Weber's constant for brightness of light is 1/60 and for the taste of salt, 1/3.

ATTENTION   Another factor influencing how much of the outside world we perceive is attention. In most situations, it is impossible to be aware of all the stimuli
around us, even if we are biologically capable of responding to them. Instead, we
pay attention to some but not to others (Johnston & Dark, 1986). For example,
returning to your dinner date, you may not have been aware of the music in the
background because you were listening to your friend. After it stops, however,
your attention might shift so that you hear the next song.

    Attention is a selective psychological process in that we are aware of certain
stimuli and not others at any moment. Attention does not block the physical and
biological response of our sense organs to these stimuli; it simply increases or
decreases our psychological perception of these events. Of course, some stimuli
are difficult to overlook, for example, someone mentioning your name in a conversation at the next table. At other times attention to one stimulus interferes
with our perception of another. The *Stroop effect*, portrayed in Figure 4.4, illustrates this kind of interference. Later in this chapter we consider several characteristics of stimuli that are particularly effective in capturing our attention.

FIGURE 4.4
The Stroop Effect

This figure illustrates how difficult it is to ignore
some kinds of stimuli. Try naming the colors of
the boxes in A. Next, read the words in B. Now,
name the colors of the words in box C. Most
people find this last task much more difficult than
the previous two.

SOURCE: Adapted from Stroop, 1935.

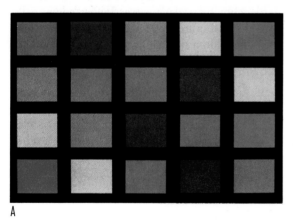

A

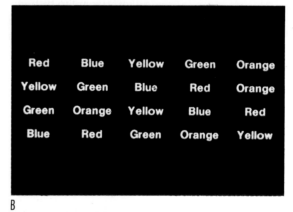

B

C

SENSORY ADAPTATION Sensory **adaptation** describes the decrease in the response of sensory receptors when they are exposed to continual, unchanging stimulation. Sensory adaptation occurs in all of the sensory organs, but some adapt more quickly than others. In fact, perception is actually dependent on stimulus change. If stimuli remain constant we adapt to them and they are no longer perceivable.

Take a few moments to think about how your various senses adapt to continual, unchanging stimulation. Which of the senses seems to adapt the most quickly? Which sense modality is the slowest to adapt?

Our receptors for smell are the quickest to adapt, which is fortunate for people who live near industrial plants or have jobs requiring them to work in foul-smelling environments. Most of our other senses adapt fairly quickly to constant stimulation. For example, you are probably not aware of background noises in your room until they actually change. You may only notice that your refrigerator is quite noisy when it shuts off.

Sensory adaptation in the visual system also occurs when a stimulus remains constant. Visual adaptation is much more difficult to detect because our eyes continually move, rapidly changing the location of the stimulus within the eye. These rapid scanning movements of the eye are called saccadic movements. Experiments with special contact lenses can fix an image on the surface of the eye allowing for visual adaptation. In such experiments subjects report seeing an image quickly fade and disappear.

You can conduct a simple experiment to demonstrate sensory adaptation to yourself. Place ice-cold water in one container, lukewarm water in another, and water so hot you can barely stand it in a third. Put your right hand in the ice water and your left hand in the very hot water. After a couple of minutes, put both hands into the container of lukewarm water. Since your right hand was previously adapted to ice water, the lukewarm water feels very hot. Conversely, your left hand feels cold, because it has adapted to the high temperature.

Unfortunately, the one sense modality that adapts very slowly (and usually only to a slight degree) is pain. People who are faced with chronic pain may learn to live with their discomfort, but seldom do they experience anything resembling acceptable adaptation. Research has demonstrated that although we often adapt somewhat to mild pain, we may not adapt to extremely painful stimuli (Coren & Ward, 1989). In one experiment, subjects rated the pain they felt from immersing their hands in hot water over a period of time. Figure 4.5 shows the results. Adaptation was complete for lower temperatures, but it diminished with increasing pain to the point where there was no adaptation to the most painful stimulus level (Hardy et al., 1968).

SIGNAL DETECTION THEORY Other important variables that influence what we do or do not perceive are addressed by **signal detection theory**. According to this perspective, our ability to detect a sensory stimulus (signal) depends not only on the intensity of the signal but also on other variables such as distracting factors and our own internal psychological state (expectations, motivation, fatigue, and so forth) (Egan, 1975; Green & Swets, 1974; Swets et al. 1961).

The origins of signal detection theory may be traced to early efforts to understand how people are able to distinguish certain target stimuli against a background of random noise. *Noise* is the term employed by psychologists to describe any kind of distracting and irrelevant stimuli. Noise is analogous to the background static you hear on the radio while cruising down the freeway and trying to tune in your favorite station. The stronger the static, the harder it is to detect the music. This example refers to *external noise*, or distracting factors in the outside environment.

Our signal detection performance may also be influenced by *internal noise* in our sensory systems caused by an ongoing, variable, random firing of neurons

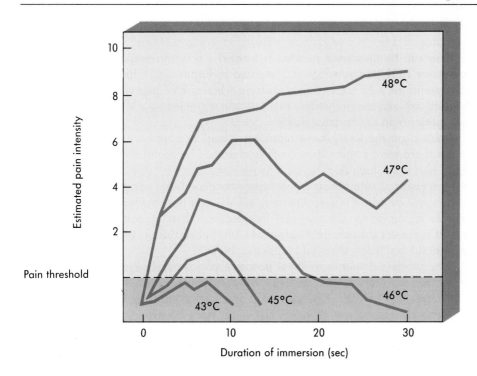

FIGURE 4.5
Pain Adaptation

Average estimates of intensity of pain from different durations of hand immersions in hot water of different temperatures.

SOURCE: Adapted from Hardy et al., 1968.

(the nervous system is never completely inactive). Thus sensory inputs occur against a variable background of external and internal noise, the level of which affects our ability to detect signals.

Background noise is not the only variable taken into account by signal detection theory. Other factors also play an important role, as is illustrated in the following example. Suppose that during a drive to a vacation destination you decide to pass the time by playing a game with your younger sibling. The game consists of seeing who can rack up the most spottings (detections) of a specific make of car—say a Volkswagen bug. How well you play the game will depend on a variety of factors including such things as distracting noise (radio playing, conversations, etc.), your *expectations* about when or where these particular stimuli are likely to occur, and the particular *criterion* you set for how sure you must be before reporting a signal has been detected, in this case the spotting of a VW bug. Do you wait until all features of the car are clear before announcing a spot, or do you react to the first buglike body style you see off in the distance? As we will see, response criterion plays a significant role in perception.

RESPONSE CRITERION AND SIGNAL DETECTION The setting of a response criterion involves going beyond the dimension of sensation. In our example, let's assume that there are no consequences for a *false alarm* (i.e., reporting a VW bug when none is present) and that winning the game is important to you. That is, you need all the correct spottings or "hits" (reporting a VW bug when it is present) you can get. Under these conditions, you would probably be inclined to report spottings for any distant vehicle that bore any resemblance, however vague, to a VW bug. Under these conditions your perception of bugs is going to be quite good. That is, every occurrence of a VW bug is spotted early. On the other hand, what happens to signal detection performance when the game plan is modified? For instance, suppose you agree with your opponent that the loser of this contest has to give the winner a dollar, and to make things more interesting, every false alarm (reporting a VW when none was present) results in a minus point. With this rule change, and the introduction of the added incentive of a dollar for the winner, you will probably try harder to avoid false alarms and thus

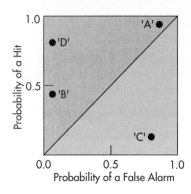

FIGURE 4.6

Receiver Operating Characteristic (ROC) Curve

Points falling above the diagonal line represent stimulus intensities above threshold. Points below the diagonal line represent stimulus intensities that are below threshold.

raise your response criterion by requiring a stronger stimulus before reporting a sighting.

This can be illustrated in what is termed a receiver operating characteristic curve, or ROC curve, which is presented in Figure 4.6. This figure shows the probability of a *hit* (reporting a spotting when a VW bug was present) on the vertical axis and the probability of a *false alarm* (reporting a VW bug when none was present) on the horizontal axis.

Point *A* on the ROC curve represents "bug" perception in our first example when there were no penalties for false alarms. The probability of both hits and false alarms are high because there is no cost to saying "bug" often. When false alarms result in subtracting a point from your total hits our perception changes and is reflected by Point *B*. We miss a few bugs, but we avoid costly mistakes. Points falling below the diagonal line indicate that the probability of a false alarm is greater than the probability of a hit. When this occurs (Point C) objects are considered below threshold (undetectable).

Our example demonstrates that potential positive and negative consequences associated with hits, misses, and false alarms create a response bias—an inclination or tendency to respond in a certain way. Let's consider a more serious example where response bias is quite important. Imagine your task is to monitor a radar screen for SCUD missiles. The detection of SCUDs on the monitor is difficult because of the background noise on the monitor and other friendly air traffic. In this case launching defensive missiles could result in destroying target SCUDs (a hit) or destroying friendly air cover (a false alarm). On the other hand, a miss (failing to detect a SCUD) could be fatal. Both of these considerations bias your perception of whether a blip on the radar screen represents a SCUD missile. Where on the ROC curve would you like to be in this case? If you answered position *D* you are correct. Special training under simulated conditions can alter one's response bias in this case towards position *D*.

According to signal detection theory, there is no such thing as an absolute threshold for a given stimulus modality because detecting a signal depends not only on stimulus strength but also on background noise and such psychological variables as expectation and response bias.

Signal detection theory has helped us to understand that detecting and responding to stimuli in our worlds is often much more complex than a simple relationship between physical energy and sensory processes. Furthermore, signal detection theory has provided the impetus for developing techniques to improve people's vigilance in important signal detection tasks such as monitoring radar screens (air traffic controllers, military radar technicians), reviewing X-ray screens at airport security checkpoints, or evaluating data readouts from medical monitoring equipment in hospital intensive care units. Some of the recommendations for improving performance include frequent breaks to counteract boredom and fatigue, mild physical exercise, providing occasional "real targets" to detect, and providing information about signal detection performance in the form of feedback about the number of hits, misses, and false alarms (Warm, 1984; Warm & Dember, 1986; Wickens, 1984).

The principles we have just discussed relate to all sensations, but each sense also has distinct properties that we respond to in unique ways. The following sections explore the major senses: vision, hearing, taste, smell, and the senses of touch and of body position.

VISION

In many ways, vision is our most important sense. It contributes enormously to our awareness of the surrounding environment, and it provides extremely valuable information that we can use to change our location or actions. Much of what we do depends on an adequately functioning visual system. When a person is deprived of his or her vision, as in an accident, the adjustment is often long and arduous. Vision's primary importance is reflected in the fact that a greater portion of our brains is devoted to vision than to any of the other senses.

Our visual systems are composed of three major parts: the eyes, which capture and respond to light energy; the neural circuits that transmit signals from the eye to the brain; and the visual centers within the brain that interpret these messages.

We see things because they reflect light. Light is a form of electromagnetic radiation. Virtually all matter consists of oscillating, electrically charged particles that discharge many forms of electromagnetic radiation, only one of which is light. Other varieties include cosmic rays, gamma rays, X rays, ultraviolet rays, infrared rays, microwaves, and TV and radio waves. Electromagnetic radiation travels in waves, and different forms of this energy have different wavelengths. A wavelength is precisely defined by how far the radiation travels between oscillations. Wavelength is measured in nanometers, abbreviated nm. A nanometer is equal to a billionth of a meter.

Figure 4.7 shows the full range of the electromagnetic spectrum. Note that light which is visible to humans ranges from roughly 400 to 750 nm., only a small portion of the electromagnetic spectrum. Our own blindness to other segments of the full spectrum is not shared by all living things. For example, some

LIGHT: THE STIMULUS FOR VISION

FIGURE 4.7

The Electromagnetic Spectrum

This figure shows the full range of the electromagnetic spectrum. Visible light represents only a small part of the complete spectrum. The visible spectrum can be obtained by passing white light (such as sunlight) through a prism. Visible light ranges from about 400 nm. to 750 nm.

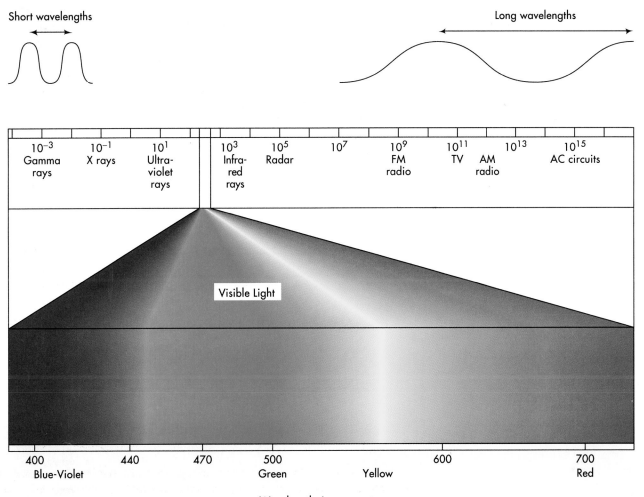

Short wavelengths

Long wavelengths

| 10^{-3} Gamma rays | 10^{-1} X rays | 10^1 Ultra-violet rays | 10^3 Infra-red rays | 10^5 Radar | 10^7 | 10^9 FM radio | 10^{11} TV | 10^{13} AM radio | 10^{15} AC circuits |

Visible Light

| 400 Blue-Violet | 440 | 470 | 500 Green | Yellow | 600 | 700 Red |

Wavelength in nanometers

insects can discern ultraviolet light, and some avian predators use infrared radiation to detect prey.

PROPERTIES OF LIGHT   Brightness, hue, and saturation are three properties of light that are particularly important in the psychological study of vision.

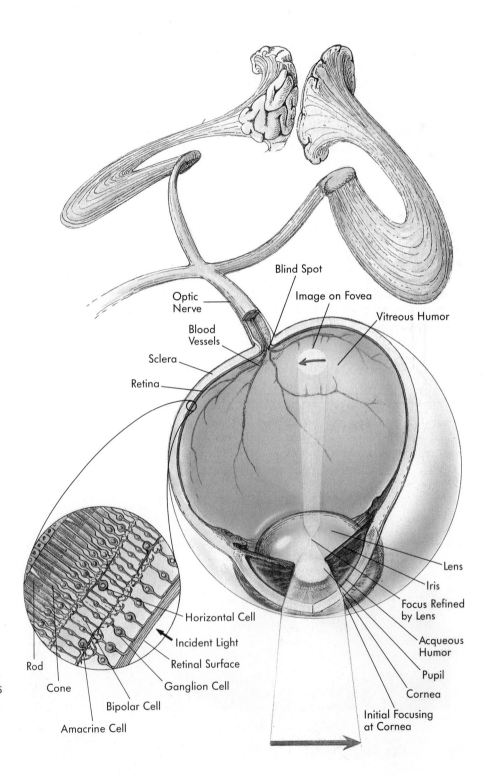

FIGURE 4.8

Structure of the Eye

A cross-sectional drawing of the eye illustrating several key structures, including the image-focusing structures — the cornea, lens, iris, and pupil — and the image-recording structure, the retina. The retina consists of several layers of cells as shown in the magnified inset. Visual information leaves the retina through the optic nerve which travels to several brain structures for vision.

Brightness, or the intensity of light, is measured by the number of *photons* (particles of electromagnetic radiation that we see as light). In general, the more intense the light source, the more photons are emitted, the brighter a light appears, and the higher the amplitude of the light wave.

Hue, or the color we perceive, is determined partly by the wavelength of light. In normal eyes, wavelengths of 400 nm. are perceived as violet, 500 nm. appear blue-green, 600 nm. appear yellow-orange, and 700 nm. look red. The perception of color is not just a matter of wavelength, however. Several colors, such as purple and white, are not even in the spectrum of visible light. Such colors are produced by a complex process in which the visual system mixes various wavelengths to produce a broad variety of colors.

A third dimension of light, **saturation,** determines how colorful light appears. White corresponds to a completely colorless state; the more white is present in color, the less saturated it is. If you were to add white paint slowly to red paint, the color red would undergo a gradual transition from a saturated deep red to a shade of pink, which is unsaturated red. Saturation may therefore be viewed as the proportion of colored *(chromatic)* light to noncolored *(achromatic)* light.

- -

Brightness, hue, and intensity describe the stimulus of light, but our primary concern is how we receive that stimulus. For that, we must have some understanding of how our eyes work.

Figure 4.8 illustrates several key structures of the human eye. Two components of the eye are most relevant to our discussion. One is the image-focusing part, roughly comparable to a camera. Major structures within this unit are the cornea, lens, iris, and pupil. The other primary component of the eye's visual system is the image-recording part, called the retina. The film in a camera is roughly analogous to the retina.

Visual sensations result when patterns of light that enter the eye are focused on the light-sensitive retina. (Images focused on the retina are inverted, as shown in Figure 4.9.) When a light beam first enters the eye, it passes through the *cornea,* a thin, transparent membrane that bends or refracts light waves to bring them into sharper focus on the retina. Light then passes through the *aqueous humor,* a watery fluid that helps nourish the cornea.

Light next passes through a small opening in the *iris* called the *pupil.* The iris is a pigmented set of muscles that constrict or expand to control the amount of

**STRUCTURE AND
FUNCTION OF
THE EYE**

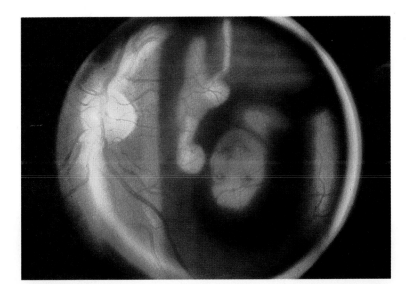

FIGURE 4.9

Inverted Retinal Image

A special camera photographs a person's retina while the person looks at a women talking on the telephone. Notice that the image is inverted on the retina. The round yellow structure on the left is the optic disk, or blind spot, where the optic nerve exits the eye.

light that can enter. The pupil dilates (opens wide) to let more light in when illumination is low, and it constricts (becomes smaller) in response to a bright light. Eye color is determined by the amount of pigmentation in the iris. Heavy pigmentation produces brown eyes; little pigmentation results in blue eyes.

After light passes through the pupil, it enters the *lens*, an oblong elastic structure that further refracts and focuses the light beam into an image that is projected through the *vitreous humor* (a clear fluid that supplies nutrients to the interior of the eye) onto the retina. The focusing power of the lens resides in its ability to adjust its shape from flat to more rounded, depending on the distance between the object viewed and the eye. This focusing process is called **accommodation.** If the lens is functioning properly, a clear image is projected onto the retina. However, abnormalities in eye shape often make it impossible for the lens to accommodate correctly. When this happens, a person may be either nearsighted or farsighted. (A nearsighted person is able to see distinctly for only a short distance; someone who is farsighted can see distant objects clearly but cannot see near objects in proper focus.)

THE RETINA   Most of the structures of the eye function to focus light onto the retina, a thin layer of tissue at the back of the eye that records images. The insert in Figure 4.8 shows the key parts of the retina: rods, cones, bipolar cells, and ganglion cells. Light focused on the retina passes through several layers of neurons en route to the primary *photoreceptor cells*, the **rods** and **cones.** Once light passes through the retina, excess light not absorbed by the receptor cells is absorbed by the backmost part of the eye called the pigment epithelium. In people the pigment epithelium is quite dark, allowing it to absorb most of the light not absorbed by photoreceptors. If this light were to be reflected back into the retina and not absorbed, vision would be distorted because of the scatter of light inside the retina.

Not all animals have dark-colored pigment epithelium, however. Animals that forage at night rely more on sensitivity (the ability to detect light) than on acuity (the ability to finely focus light) and their eyes reflect light off of the pigment epithelium rather than absorb it. This reflected light is absorbed by the photoreceptors on its second pass through the retina. Light reflected off of the pigment epithelium is what you see when your car headlights catch an animal at night. This kind of reflection occurs in human eyes when more light than can be absorbed enters the eye. For example, the "red eye" in flash photography is caused by red light being reflected off your pigment epithelium.

Rods and Cones   There are approximately 120 million rods and 6 million cones in each of our eyes (Goldstein, 1989). The rods and cones are distributed in an orderly fashion across the inner layer of the retina. The most dense concentration of cones occurs in a region of the retina called the *fovea* (see Figure 4.8). Because our vision is sharpest when images are focused on the fovea, we move our eyes around until the image is projected to the fovea when we wish to focus clearly on an object. The prairie falcon discussed in the opening to this chapter does this by tipping its head as shown in Figure 4.1.

Our perception of color depends largely on the cones (Nathans, 1987). Different cones respond to different wavelengths of light. However, the cones are relatively poor light sensors as compared to the rods. A considerable amount of light must be projected on a cone before it responds by converting this energy to neural signals. Thus the cones are not much good at night, which is why your friend's colorful sweater is hard to see in a dark theater and why that new paint job on your car is hardly noticeable at night.

Rods are extremely sensitive photoreceptors, allowing us to see in dim light. Our peripheral vision (vision away from the center of focus) depends primarily on the rods, which are concentrated around the edges of the fovea and elsewhere on the surface of the retina. (No rods are in the fovea and only a relatively few cones are located outside the fovea.)

You can demonstrate for yourself some of the distinguishing features between the rods and cones next time you are outside on a clear night. Pick out a distant object that is barely discernible, such as a faint star. If you look slightly to the side of the object, it is easier to detect because you have moved the image away from your fovea to the outer part of your retina, which is filled with light-sensitive rods.

Both the rods and the cones contain *photopigments* that respond to light. Their chemical response transduces light energy into neural signals (Pugh, 1987; Pugh & Miller, 1987). Neural signals are passed on from the rods and cones to the *bipolar cells*, which in turn pass information to the *ganglion cells*. The axons of the ganglion cells travel across the inner surface of the retina and converge to form the *optic nerve*, which carries visual messages to the brain.

The part of the retina where the optic nerve exits the eye is known as the *optic disk*. There are no photoreceptor cells at this point. Consequently, the optic disk region is a blind spot: An image that is projected there will not be recorded. We are usually unaware of our blind spot, for a number of reasons. For one, our eyes are constantly moving, allowing us to pick up the image in another part of the retina. Furthermore, an image that hits the blind spot in one eye is focused somewhere else in the other eye, thus compensating for the momentary blindness. To see your blind spot in action, try the exercise in Figure 4.10. When the image in the figure falls on your blind spot it will disappear.

In summary, visual information is passed through a three-cell chain, from rods and cones to bipolar cells to ganglion cells. Two other kinds of retinal cells, *horizontal cells* and *amacrine cells*, do not transmit visual signals toward the brain. Instead, they transmit signals laterally across the retina, allowing interaction between adjacent photoreceptor, bipolar, and ganglion cells (Coren & Ward, 1989; Tomita, 1986). This interaction, termed **lateral inhibition,** functions to enhance our perception of images by "turning off" neighboring photoreceptors.

DARK AND LIGHT ADAPTATION   You have probably had the experience of walking out of the light of your home or apartment into the dark of night. At first, you may not be able to see anything. In a short time, however, dim outlines of objects begin to appear, and soon you can find your way about fairly easily. This process is called **dark adaptation,** and it is due to a slow chemical change within

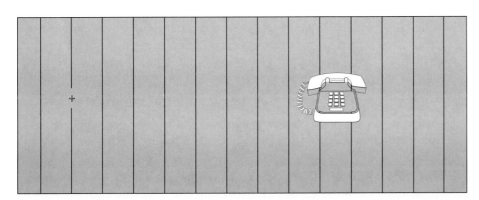

FIGURE 4.10
Finding Your Blind Spot

Because there are no photoreceptors where the optic nerve exits the eye, this leaves a blind spot on your retina. To find your blind spot close your left eye and focus your right eye on the black cross. Then, move the book to about 12 inches directly in front of your face. The figure should disappear, but not the vertical lines.

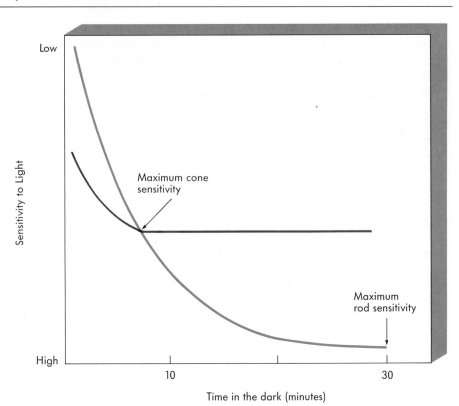

FIGURE 4.11

Dark Adaptation

The amount of light necessary for detection is related to the amount of time spent in the dark. Dark adaptation mainly occurs within the rods which reach their full sensitivity in about 30 minutes. The cones also adapt to the dark and reach their full sensitivity in about 10 minutes.

the cones and the rods as they gradually become more sensitive to minimal levels of light. As Figure 4.11 shows, the rods reach full sensitivity about 30 minutes after you enter darkness, compared to 10 minutes for the cones.

During World War II American pilots in Europe applied this knowledge to their advantage by wearing goggles with red lenses when they were on alert for air raids. The red lenses prevented their rods from adapting to the indoor light. When a night raid occurred these pilots were completely dark-adapted and ready for night flight.

When you return from the dark to your well-lit home, just the opposite process takes place. **Light adaptation** is a much faster process than dark adaptation. However, after your eyes have become completely dark-adapted, a brief exposure to bright light does not entirely reverse the process. For example, if you look into the bright lights of an approaching car for a few seconds, your dark adaptation is only slightly lessened for a brief moment or two.

A few specialized techniques can help you maintain your night vision if you must use a light for a short period of time. One suggestion is to avoid exposure to white light. If you must read a road map while driving at night, for example, use a flashlight with a red filter. In the absence of a colored light device, cover one eye with the palm of your hand while reading the map. This way, you can maintain night vision in one eye even though you lose it in the other. (Simply closing one eye is not sufficient, since a considerable amount of light can penetrate our rather thin eyelids.)

In poor lighting, our eyes are most responsive to light in the 550-to-655 nm. range, which corresponds to yellow-green. This is why many emergency vehicles such as fire engines are now often painted a lime or yellow-green color.

NEURAL PROCESSING OF VISION   Visual signals from the retina are projected to the brain along the optic nerve. Before reaching the visual cortex at the back of the brain, visual information from the two eyes converges in a region of the thalamus called the *lateral geniculate nucleus.* As discussed in Chapter 3, the thalamus acts as a relay station, directing incoming sensory information to appropriate areas within the cortex. The two lateral geniculate nuclei, located in the left and right hemispheres of the thalamus, combine information from both eyes before sending it on to the cortex. From the lateral geniculate nuclei, this information is then sent to the visual cortex in the right and left hemispheres of the occipital lobe.

Research has yet to determine exactly how these neural signals are translated into visions of the things that we see. Perhaps the most revealing research to date has been conducted by David Hubel and Thorsten Wiesel (1979), who received the Nobel Prize in 1981 in recognition of their work. Hubel and Wiesel inserted electrodes into the visual cortexes of cats in order to study the responses of single cells to a variety of visual stimuli. They discovered that many cortical cells respond only to specific stimuli, such as movement in one direction, or lines, or contours in particular orientations. From the responses of single cells, the visual cortex seems to be able to extract information about size, shape, and movement. But how do all these individual signals yield the solid images that we see?

If you used a powerful magnifying glass to examine a photograph in this book, you would discover that the image is composed of dots, as Figure 4.12 illustrates.

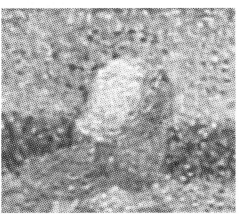

FIGURE 4.12

Pictures Composed of Dots

Colored pictures such as this one are often composed of small colored dots. The dots are not distinguishable unless a section of the picture is magnified. Visual information appears to enter the visual system as dots, edges, contours, movement, and shape. This information may then be analyzed by a pattern, or "dot-detection" system in the brain.

FIGURE 4.13

Mach Bands

The bands in this figure are uniformly shaded, but they appear to either lighten or darken at the borders. This illustrates the contour-enhancing effects of lateral inhibition.

The dots are closely packed in dark areas and farther apart in light areas. When we look at only a small area of the dots, highly magnified, it is difficult or impossible to decipher the overall image. However, when we back off, the individual dots become indistinguishable.

Lateral Inhibition   Our perception of particular patterns and shapes results from the inhibitory interaction between neighboring areas of the retina by a process called lateral inhibition. The effect of lateral inhibition is to enhance contours and edges by heightening the contrast between light and dark borders. An interesting demonstration of how lateral inhibition enhances contrast at borders is presented in Figure 4.13. This figure shows a series of uniformly shaded bands (called Mach bands) which appear to darken on their border with a lighter band. To prove to yourself that each band is indeed a uniform shade, cover the bands on each side of a selected band.

ARTIFICIAL VISION   As marvelous as they are for detecting light energy, our eyes are merely devices for gathering and sending visual messages. Visual perception occurs in the brain. We see only when our brains allow us to interpret incoming signals. If the visual cortex were destroyed, we could no longer see even though our eyes would continue to gather and transmit visual signals. Consequently, brain damage is the one type of sight-destroying injury which medical intervention cannot yet overcome. In contrast, many abnormalities of the eyes can often be treated by surgery or corrective devices.

The idea of a person seeing without functioning eyes might strike you as absurd. Until recently, most vision researchers would have agreed that the eyes are indispensable to the experience of vision. However, in the mid-1970s, a fascinating new line of research began to provide evidence that contradicts this assumption.

Many totally blind people cannot see because defects in the retina or optic nerve prevent neural signals from reaching the visual cortex. A team of researchers headed by William Dobelle (1977) reasoned that if they could bypass the affected area by sending signals to electrodes on the surface of the visual cortex, such patients might be able to have some kind of visual experience. After all, what is vision other than an intricate interrelationship of neurons within the visual cortex?

Applying this rationale, Dobelle and his coworkers implanted 64 electrodes in the visual cortex areas of totally blind volunteers' brains (see Figure 4.14). Stimulation of the cortex by a single electrode created some primitive visual experiences, causing a subject to "see" a *phosphene*, a tiny spot of glowing light that seemed to be located several feet in front of the viewer's face. Dobelle's team discovered that if a number of electrodes were activated at the same time, subjects could discern meaningful patterns among simultaneously occurring phosphenes. For example, one subject who had been blinded accidentally several years earlier was able to see various patterns and shapes, and even to differentiate letters of the alphabet.

Researchers are currently working to develop a more sophisticated visual prosthesis, such as the apparatus shown in Figure 4.14. A blind person might be provided with an artificial eye that consisted of a highly miniaturized TV camera mounted in a glass enclosure. The camera would convert light images from the environment into a pattern of electrical signals that would be relayed to a tiny computer, which in turn would process the information and transfer it to the visual cortex through implanted electrodes.

Many problems must be solved before an effective working model of this system is developed. For example, since an array of only 64 electrodes is not adequate to process complicated visual information, researchers are trying to

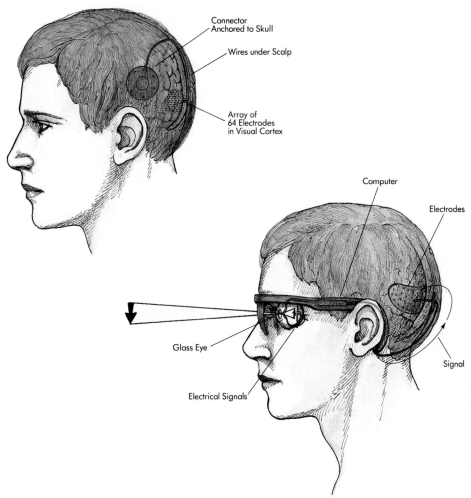

Connector
Anchored to Skull

Wires under Scalp

Array of
64 Electrodes
in Visual Cortex

Computer

Electrodes

Glass Eye

Signal

Electrical Signals

FIGURE 4.14
*Artificial Vision: Electrical
Stimulation of the Cortex*

Procedure used by Dobell to create primitive visual experience in the blind. An array of electrodes are implanted on the surface of the visual cortex. The electrodes can be activated by a small camera mounted behind a pair of glasses. Stimulation of the cortex causes the subject to "see" a phosphene. When several electrodes are activated subjects can distinguish shapes and patterns. Researchers are working on more sophisticated devices that will allow the blind to see.

develop a 512-electrode system that would let people respond more naturally to their changing environments (Goldstein, 1989). Perhaps you are familiar with Star Trek's Lt. LaForge who portrays the use of a similar device.

COLOR VISION

Among mammals, only primates (humans, apes, and monkeys) are able to perceive a full range of colors. Cattle have no color vision (the colorful cape of the matador is merely a prop for human observers). Most color vision experts think that dogs do not see color either, although some evidence suggests that they may have some limited capacity to discern colors (Jacobs, 1983). Surprisingly, simpler organisms such as fish, birds, reptiles, and insects have excellent color vision (Nathans, 1987). Before examining what is known about how we perceive colors, let us briefly consider how colors are mixed to produce all the various hues.

ADDITIVE AND SUBTRACTIVE COLOR MIXING   Color is a psychological phenomenon in that it is determined by our brains as they perceive light reflected from objects. The potential for color perception is not inherent in the objects themselves; instead, it is determined by the reflected beams of light. Most light, including light from incandescent lamps and from sunlight, is called *white light*. We do not perceive it as being colored, yet it contains all the wavelengths for the various colors within the visible spectrum. The grass growing outside your front door appears green because it absorbs most of the wavelengths in the white light falling on it but reflects green light. Thus the perception of different colors depends on different sets of wavelengths being absorbed and reflected.

From working with pigment agents, such as paints or crayons, you probably know that all the hues are produced by different mixtures of the primary colors: red, blue, and yellow. Interestingly, when colored lights rather than pigments are mixed, the primary colors are red, green, and blue. Physicists who have experimented with mixing different colors of light report that all the various hues can be obtained by mixing red, green, and blue lights. Combining this information about primary pigments and light colors leads us to conclude that humans with normal color vision are able to distinguish a vast array of colors formed from various combinations of four basic hues: red, blue, yellow, and green, and two hueless colors, white and black (Hurvich, 1981).

You probably know that if you mix yellow and blue paints, the result is green. However, when yellow and blue light are combined, the result is almost white. Why is this so? Take a moment to formulate an answer before reading on.

Explaining the difference between subtractive and additive color mixing provides an answer to our question. Most if not all of your experience mixing colors has probably been of the subtractive variety. **Subtractive color mixing** occurs when paint or other pigments are mixed. When light falls on a colored object, some wavelengths are absorbed (subtracted) and others are reflected. The wavelength of the reflected light determines the hue we perceive. For example, when yellow and blue paint are mixed, these two pigments subtract or absorb nonyellow and nonblue wavelengths. The result is a pigment that reflects only those wavelengths that are between yellow and blue, which is green.

Additive color mixing occurs when lights with different wavelengths simultaneously stimulate the retina. Our resulting color perception is based on the adding or combining of these respective wavelengths. Unlike subtractive color mixing, which takes place in the object we are viewing, additive mixing is done by our visual systems. The colors you perceive on your television screen are products of additive color mixing. If you were able to magnify this picture manyfold, you would see that images are composed of tiny red, green, and blue dots (that's why color monitors are called RGB monitors). A close examination of a yellow object would reveal that it consists of red and green dots.

THEORIES OF COLOR VISION   Two major theories have been proposed to explain how we see colors: the trichromatic theory and the opponent-process theory.

The Trichromatic Theory of Color Vision   In 1802 Thomas Young, an English physicist and physician, demonstrated that various combinations of red, green, and blue can produce all the other colors in the spectrum. He suggested that the human eye contains three types of color receptors corresponding to these three distinct hues, and that the brain somehow creates our perception of color by combining the information transmitted by each type of receptor. Half a century later, Young's theory was modified and expanded by the German physiologist Hermann von Helmholtz. Their combined theory became known as the **Young-Helmholtz theory,** or the **trichromatic theory of color vision.**

Neither Young nor Helmholtz was aware that the retina contained distinct photoreceptor cells. Over a century later, their theory was supported, however, when research revealed that there are three distinct kinds of cones in the human retina, each containing a different photopigment. These cones are maximally sensitive to light of three wavelengths: 435, 540, and 565 nm. (Nathans, 1987; Nathans et al., 1989). Figure 4.6 reveals that these wavelengths correspond to blue, green, and yellow-green. However, to be consistent with earlier convention, researchers continue to refer to these receptors as blue, green, and red cones. Although the photopigments in each of these types of cones respond most effectively to light in the wavelengths we have listed, light of a particular wavelength stimulates more than one type of receptor (Ohtsuka, 1985). Evidence supporting the notion that the human eye contains three types of color receptors was recently provided by genetic researchers who isolated specific genes that direct three kinds of cones to produce photopigments which are sensitive to light in the three wavelength categories listed (Nathans, 1989; Nathans et al., 1986).

The trichromatic theory explains the effects of mixing colors of different wavelengths. However, it does not explain some other phenomena, such as negative afterimages (discussed in the following section) and the fact that color-blind people almost always fail to distinguish pairs of colors rather than just one color. A second theory, the opponent-process theory, helps to explain these phenomena.

The Opponent-Process Theory of Color Vision   In the 1870s a German physiologist, Ewald Hering, proposed a theory of color vision asserting that yellow is as basic a color as red, blue, and green; that is, that yellow is not a mixture of other colors. Hering believed we see six primary colors (red, green, blue, yellow, black, and white) rather than the three proposed by Young and Helmholtz. He further theorized that these six colors are grouped into three pairs, which form three types of receptors. One receptor, the black-white pair, contributes to our perception of brightness and saturation; the other two receptors, a red-green and a blue-yellow pair, are responsible for our perception of color.

Hering believed that the two members of each pair tend to work in opposition to each other, one inhibiting the other (hence the name **opponent-process theory of color vision**). According to this viewpoint, if our eyes are struck by light containing more red wavelengths than green, the red inhibits the green and we perceive red. The blue-yellow system works similarly, which is why we never perceive such shades as greenish red or bluish yellow.

Hering's opponent-process theory is consistent with what we know about color blindness. Approximately 8 percent of males and .05 percent of females exhibit some form of color blindness (Nathans, 1987), but only rarely are individuals totally blind to color. Most people with color-vision problems have difficulty detecting pairs of colors. Red-green color blindness is the most common (see Figure 4.15 below and 4.16 on page 130). People with red-green color

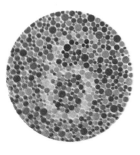

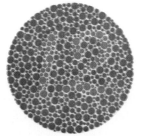

FIGURE 4.15

A Test for Color Blindness

A person with red-green color blindness cannot see the number 6 in the top illustration, and the number 12 in the bottom illustration is not visible to a person with yellow-blue color blindness. (These reproduced plates cannot be used to screen for color blindness.)

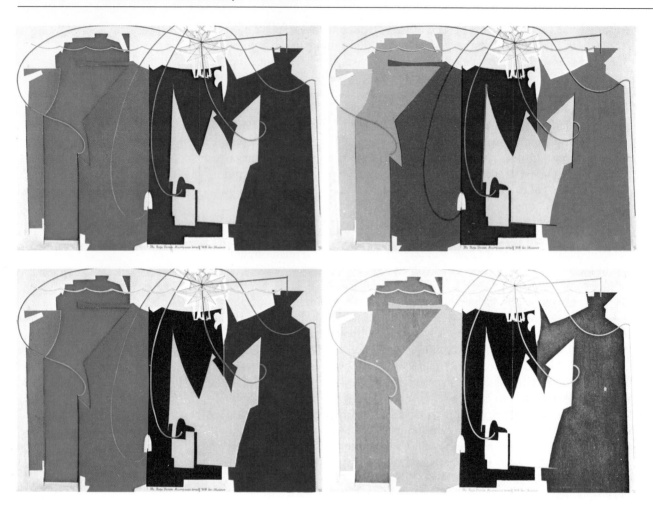

FIGURE 4.16

Color Blindness

The painting in the upper left panel — Rope Dancer Accompanies Herself with Her Shadows, by Man Ray — appears as it would to a person with normal color vision. The upper right panel shows how it would appear to a person with red-green color blindness, the lower left panel shows how it would appear to a person with yellow-blue color blindness, and the lower right panel shows how it would look to a person with total color blindness.

SOURCE: Painting by Man Ray, Museum of Modern Art, New York. Gift of G. David Thompson

blindness cannot see either red or green, but they can see other colors. Yellow-blue color blindness is much less common.

Hering was also intrigued with the phenomenon of *negative afterimages.* Figure 4.17 provides a demonstration. If you stare for about a minute at the center of the oddly colored American flag, then shift your gaze to any white surface, you will see the flag appear in the form of a negative afterimage in the familiar red, white, and blue of Old Glory.

This phenomenon fits in nicely with the opponent-process theory. When you stare at the green stripes, the green component of the red-green receptor becomes fatigued. However, the red component does not tire, since it is not being stimulated. When you shift your eyes to the white surface, the light it reflects stimulates the red and green components equally. Since the overloaded green component is fatigued, it responds only minimally. This imbalance in the opponent pair produces the faint red afterimage. A similar rationale explains why blue appears in the place of yellow, and white in the place of black.

Most contemporary vision experts believe that both the trichromatic theory and the opponent-process theory may be at least partly correct. In fact, our color perception may be a product of both mechanisms. The trichromatic system may operate at the level of the photoreceptors, with three kinds of light-sensitive pigments in the cones. At the same time, the on and off type of process described by Hering and later verified by Hurvich and Jameson (1957) has been identified in

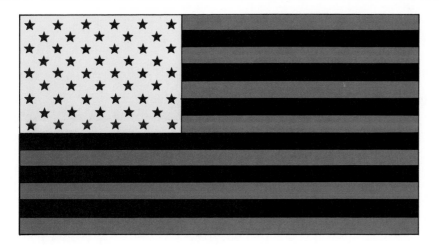

FIGURE 4.17
Negative Afterimages

Stare at the center of the flag for about 1 minute. Then, shift your focus to a white sheet of paper. You should notice a faint image of the American flag in its familiar colors. This is a negative afterimage.

ganglion cells of the retina and in the lateral geniculate nuclei (DeValois & DeValois, 1975, 1980; DeValois & Jacobs, 1984). These findings suggest that the opponent-process mechanism operates not at the level of the cones but rather along the neural path from the photoreceptor cells to the visual cortex. Thus color vision may result from an interplay between a trichromatic system operating at the level of the photoreceptor cells and an opponent-process mechanism working at later stages (Hurvich, 1978).

In the last few years, researchers have begun to explore the possibility that the trichromatic cone system might even interact in an opponent-process manner. This speculation was supported by a recent discovery that red and green cones are directly connected to each other in the retinas of turtles (Norman et al., 1984). Clearly, our understanding of how we see color is far from complete. New discoveries continue to be made, and many researchers are hopeful that science soon will provide a complete picture of how this complex process works.

AUDITION

People who become deaf after years of normal hearing often report feeling a great deal of stress and a profound sense of isolation (Sekuler & Blake, 1985). Audition allows us to enjoy perhaps the richest form of communication. A deaf person cannot easily engage in conversation with others, whereas a blind person can converse with people either person-to-person or over the phone. Thus while our ears may bring us less information than our eyes, they convey a special type of social communication that is exceedingly important to our appreciation of life.

Most of the sounds we hear consist of physical energy in the form of rhythmic pressure changes in the air. When an object vibrates to produce sound, it sets air molecules in motion. The vibrating motion of the sound source alternately pushes air molecules together and pulls them apart. The forward thrust of the vibrating object as it moves toward you *compresses* the air, making it denser; as the vibrating object moves away from you, it pulls the molecules farther apart, thus *rarefying* the air, making it thinner. These changes in air pressure constitute sound waves, and they travel at a speed of approximately 1,100 feet per second.

When the compressed-air portion of the sound wave arrives at your ear, it bends the tympanic membrane (your eardrum) inward. The negative pressure of

SOUND: THE STIMULUS FOR AUDITION

FIGURE 4.18

The Stimulus of Sound

Sound waves consist of changes in air pressure as air molecules are alternately compressed and pulled apart.

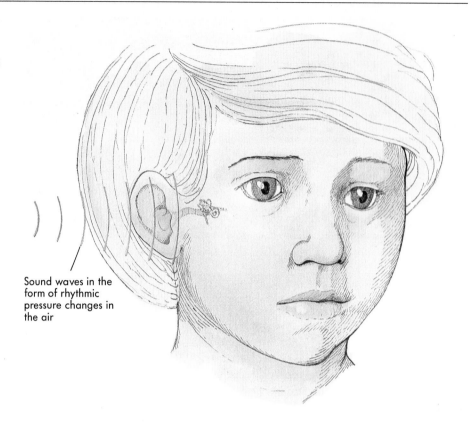

Sound waves in the form of rhythmic pressure changes in the air

the following rarefied portion of the sound wave causes your eardrum to bend out (see Figure 4.18). These movements or vibrations of the eardrum begin the complex process of transducing the energy of sound waves into the neural signals that carry auditory messages to the brain.

Sound waves most commonly travel through the medium of air. However, other media such as the ground, water, wood, or metal also convey sound waves. Perhaps you have listened to a conversation in the next room with your ear against the wall, have heard an approaching train by pressing your ear against a metal rail, or have heard sounds while swimming under water.

PROPERTIES OF SOUND WAVES   Two properties of sound waves influence our perception of sound: amplitude and frequency. The amplitude or intensity of a sound wave determines the **loudness** of a sound. Loudness is measured in *decibels* (db.). A decibel is not a linear unit like a pound or an inch; rather, it is a point on a sharply rising curve of intensity. For example, 10 db. is 10 times greater than 1 db., but 30 db. is 1,000 times greater than 1 db., and 100 db. is approximately 10 billion times greater than 1 db. To most people, a sound at 10 db. is quite soft, whereas one as loud as 130 db. is painful. Figure 4.19 shows the decibel levels of a number of common sounds.

A second important property of a sound wave is its frequency, which determines the **pitch** that we perceive. Sound wave frequency is measured in *Hertz* (Hz.), or cycles per second. The higher the pitch, the shriller we perceive a sound to be. The average human ear can perceive sound waves within the range of 20 to 20,000 Hz. We are most sensitive to sound waves in the 100 to 3,500 Hz. range, which is, conveniently, the range within which most human speech

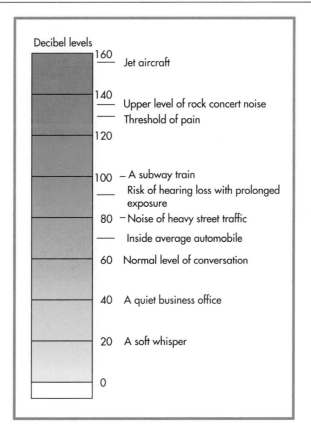

FIGURE 4.19

Decible Levels of Several Common Sounds

falls. The lowest-pitched note on a piano, at 27.5 Hz., is barely audible to us. The highest sound a piano can make has been recorded at 4,180 Hz.

Nonhuman animals can perceive sound wave frequencies well above the upper limits for humans. For example, dogs can hear up to about 80,000 Hz., which is why you can use a special whistle to call your dog in the middle of the night without waking your entire household. The upper limits of the audible pitch range are even higher for dolphins, extending well beyond 100,000 Hz. Pigeons and other birds apparently rely on very low frequency sounds to aid in long distance navigation.

DISTINGUISHING DIFFERENT SOUNDS OF THE SAME PITCH   You may have noticed that the same notes sound different when produced by different instruments. Middle C played on the piano sounds quite different from the same note played on the violin, in spite of the fact that both instruments produce sound waves with exactly the same frequency. What explains this distinction? Try to formulate an answer before reading on.

Neither the violin nor the piano produces a pure note of a single frequency. In fact, very few of the sounds we hear are pure tones. Most are a combination of a *fundamental frequency* and a unique set of additional frequency components called *overtones*. Combined with the fundamental frequency, these overtones add a characteristic quality called **timbre** to complex sounds. Our ability to distinguish between the sounds of various musical instruments depends on differences in timbre. If sound filters were used to screen out all overtones, it would be impossible for a person to identify various instruments just by hearing them play.

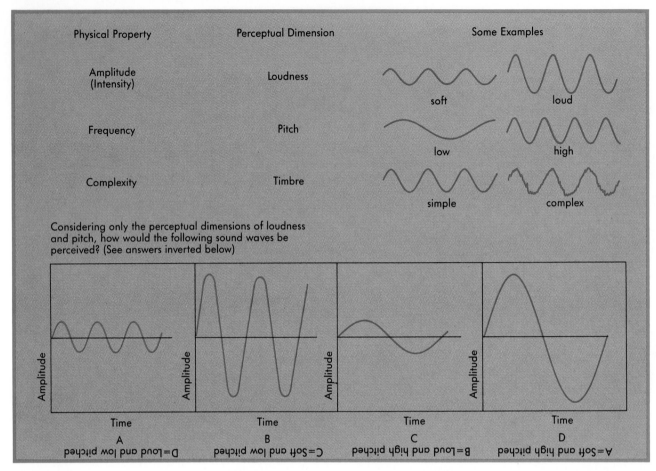

FIGURE 4.20
Physical Properties and Perceptual Dimensions of Sound Waves

Figure 4.20 summarizes the three properties of sound waves. Before reading on, see if you can tell how samples *A*, *B*, *C*, and *D* would be perceived.

STRUCTURE AND FUNCTION OF THE EAR

THE OUTER EAR   The ear has three major parts: the outer ear, the middle ear, and the inner ear (see Figure 4.21). What most of us call our ears are merely the pinnas, the odd-shaped, flesh-covered cartilage that protrudes from the sides of our heads. The function of the pinna is to collect and funnel sound waves down the *auditory canal*, which, along with the pinna, forms the outer ear.

THE MIDDLE EAR   At the end of the auditory canal, sound waves strike the eardrum, or **tympanic membrane,** causing it to start vibrating. The eardrum, which serves as the opening to the middle ear, is connected to a set of three tiny linked bones called **ossicles.** The ossicles act like a system of levers that transfer and amplify (or dampen) the intensity of a sound stimulus. When the eardrum vibrates, it nudges the first bone in the series, the *malleus* (hammer), which in turn moves the *incus* (anvil), which moves the *stapes* (stirrup).

THE INNER EAR   When the ossicles vibrate in response to sound waves, the last bone in the series, the stapes, pounds against an opening to the inner ear called the oval window. The inner ear consists of a snail-shaped, coiled chamber called the cochlea, which is filled with fluid. The **cochlea** consists of three wedge-

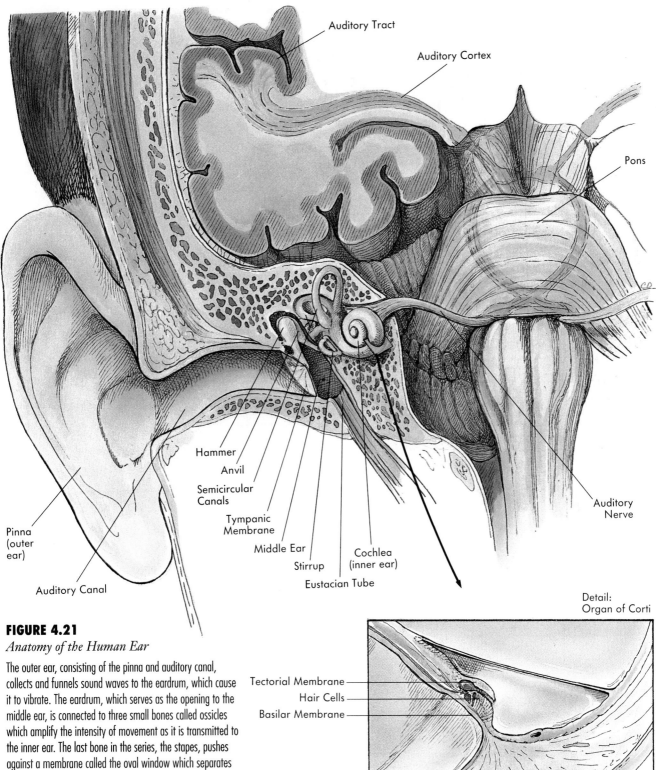

Auditory Tract

Auditory Cortex

Pons

Hammer

Anvil

Semicircular
Canals

Tympanic
Membrane

Middle Ear

Stirrup

Cochlea
(inner ear)

Eustacian Tube

Pinna
(outer
ear)

Auditory Canal

Auditory
Nerve

Detail:
Organ of Corti

Tectorial Membrane

Hair Cells

Basilar Membrane

FIGURE 4.21

Anatomy of the Human Ear

The outer ear, consisting of the pinna and auditory canal, collects and funnels sound waves to the eardrum, which cause it to vibrate. The eardrum, which serves as the opening to the middle ear, is connected to three small bones called ossicles which amplify the intensity of movement as it is transmitted to the inner ear. The last bone in the series, the stapes, pushes against a membrane called the oval window which separates the middle ear from the inner ear. The movement of the oval window generates pressure waves within the fluid-filled cochlea causing the flexible basilar membrane to bend. The bending of hair cells in the organ or corti causes neural messages to be transmitted along the auditory nerve to the brain.

FIGURE 4.22
The Cochlea of the Inner Ear

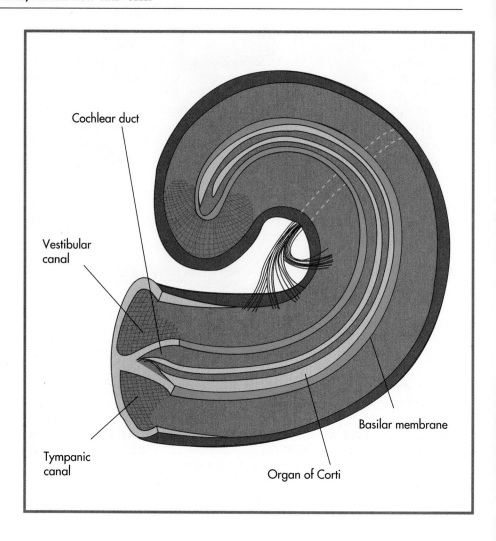

Cochlear duct

Vestibular
canal

Tympanic
canal

Basilar membrane

Organ of Corti

shaped chambers: the *vestibular canal*, the *cochlear duct*, and the *tympanic canal* (see Figure 4.22). The tympanic canal and cochlear duct are separated by the **basilar membrane.**

Except for two locations, where it is covered by flexible, elastic material, the cochlear wall consists of hard bone. The two flexible spots are the *oval window* and the *round window* at the base of the tympanic canal. These two flexible surfaces allow pressure waves to be generated within the fluid that fills the vestibular and tympanic canals.

AUDITORY RECEPTORS   When the oval window is pushed inward by the action of the stapes, the round window compensates by bulging outward. These mechanical displacements are translated into pressure waves that flow through the vestibular and tympanic canals, causing ripples in the flexible basilar membrane. Another structure, the **organ of Corti**, sits on top of the basilar membrane. It consists of a layer of supporting cells resting on the basilar membrane, rows of specialized neurons known as auditory hair cells that project upward, and a *tectoral membrane* that hangs over the basilar membrane like an awning. The hair cells terminate in tiny hairlike protrusions called *cilia*. When the basilar membrane ripples in response to pressure waves, the cilia are moved against the relatively stationary tectoral membrane, bending like tiny clumps of seaweed swept back and forth by invisible underwater currents (Sekuler & Blake, 1985, p. 311). This bending of the cilia causes the hair cells to release neurotransmitters that activate adjacent neurons of the *auditory nerve*, which carries messages to the auditory cortex in the brain.

In summary, sound waves are converted into mechanical movements of the ossicles in the middle ear, which in turn act on the inner ear to produce pressure waves that travel through the fluid of the cochlea, flexing the basilar membrane and activating hair cells of the organ of Corti, which in turn activate neurons of the auditory nerve. In this complex manner, the physical energy of sound waves is converted into neural impulses that our brains translate into sounds.

How can we distinguish between high- and low-pitched sounds, so that we can automatically tell a child's voice from an adult's or hear the differences between notes of a musical scale? There are two major theories explaining how we discriminate pitch: the place theory and the frequency theory.

THEORIES OF AUDITION

THE PLACE THEORY The **place theory of pitch discrimination** was developed primarily by Georg von Békésy, who was awarded the Nobel Prize in recognition of his monumental contributions to the science of hearing. Békésy theorized that sound waves of different frequency displace different regions on the basilar membrane, allowing us to perceive varying pitches. He conducted experiments with guinea pigs to test this theory, using a microscope to observe the basilar membrane through tiny holes cut in various locations along the cochlea. When the guinea pigs were exposed to tones of varying frequencies, different regions of the basilar membrane showed the greatest response.

For example, Békésy noted that high-pitched tones caused the most displacement in the portion of the basilar membrane close to the oval window, whereas intermediate-range tones caused the greatest response farther along the basilar membrane. Unfortunately, Békésy's theory did not hold up as well for low-frequency tones, below 4,000 Hz. The manner in which tones below this level displace the basilar membrane is largely indistinguishable (von Békésy, 1960). Subsequent research confirms that the place theory holds up well for all but tones in the lower frequency range (Lewis et al., 1982).

Another problem with the place theory is that it does not explain how we can make very fine discriminations between tones that differ only slightly. The displacement in the basilar membrane is virtually identical for two tones whose frequencies differ by as little as 1 or 2 Hz. and yet many people can discriminate tonal differences this small.

FREQUENCY THEORY The **frequency theory of pitch discrimination** helps account for our ability to distinguish tones in the 20 to 4,000 Hz. range. According to this interpretation, first advanced by Ernest Rutherford in the nineteenth century, our perception of low tones depends on the frequency with which the hair cells trigger firing of fibers in the auditory nerve. Thus our perception of pitch in the lower frequency range is determined by the frequency of impulses traveling up the auditory nerve. Research has demonstrated that fibers in the auditory nerve actually do fire in rhythm with tones in the low-frequency range (Rose et al., 1967). Thus if we listen to middle C on a piano (262 Hz.), our auditory nerve fibers fire at a rate of 262 times per second.

PERCEIVING PITCH IN THE 1,000 TO 4,000 HZ. RANGE Single auditory neurons are capable of firing up to 1,000 times per second. How, then, can we account for pitch perception in the 1,000 to 4,000 Hz. range? (Remember, place theory does not adequately explain our perception of tones below 4,000 Hz.) See if you can come up with a possible explanation before reading on.

Since one hair cell can fire no more than 1,000 times per second, researchers have theorized that groups of interrelated neurons fire in a staggered fashion to convey frequencies above 1,000 Hz. This conception of a group of neurons working together is a version of the frequency theory appropriately named **volley theory** (Wever, 1949). For example, three neurons working in concert, each firing at 1,000 impulses per second, could produce a perception of a 3,000 Hz. tone if their respective messages were appropriately integrated.

The best available evidence suggests that pitch is determined by both the *place* of maximal excitation of the basilar membrane and the *frequency* with which auditory nerve fibers fire (Coren & Ward, 1989). Place theory seems to explain how we discriminate among higher pitched tones above 4,000 Hz., whereas the frequency theory, with the volley principle, seems to offer the best explanation of pitch discrimination in the lower frequencies.

AUDITORY LOCALIZATION

People are usually able to locate the origins of sounds rather well. Infants can identify which side a sound comes from very early, and within a few months learn to localize sounds in their environments (Castillo & Butterworth, 1981). This ability, called **auditory localization,** is the result of the difference in the sounds that arrive in each of our two ears (Goldstein, 1989). One key difference is in the intensity of loudness of the sounds. If someone sitting to the left of you blows a whistle, the sound wave reaching your left ear is more intense than the sound striking your right ear. This occurs because a large object like the human head does not transmit high-frequency sounds very well; your right ear is in a sound shadow. By the time the sound wave circumnavigates your head to reach your right ear, its intensity diminishes somewhat. Our brains use this information about differing intensities to determine the origin of a sound (Semple & Kitzes, 1987).

In addition to intensity difference, another important auditory localization cue has to do with the time a sound arrives. As we learned earlier, sound waves travel through the air at the relatively slow rate of approximately 1,100 feet per second. Thus a sound originating from the left strikes the left eardrum fractions of a second before it completes the somewhat longer journey to our right ear. Here again, our brains utilize information about these minuscule time differences to help us localize sounds.

HEARING LOSS

Roughly 20 million people in the United States suffer some hearing loss, making it the most common of all physical disabilities. Hearing loss can have a number of causes, including prolonged exposure to loud noises, infection, head injuries, prolonged use of certain drugs, and excessive wax buildup. Regardless of the cause, all hearing difficulties can be divided into two classes: sensorineural hearing loss and conduction hearing loss.

SENSORINEURAL HEARING LOSS
Damage to either the hair cells of the inner ear or the auditory nerve can cause **sensorineural hearing loss.** The most common example of this type of impairment is the gradual loss of sensitivity to high frequencies that occurs with aging, a condition called *presbycusis.*

Research has shown that high-frequency deafness begins at a surprisingly early age: Most 30-year-olds are unable to hear tones above 15,000 Hz., and by ages 50 and 70 the upper limit of the average person's hearing range drops to 12,000 Hz. and 6,000 Hz., respectively (Davis & Silverman, 1960). Some medical researchers believe that presbycusis is due, at least in part, to a lessening of blood flow to the inner ear, which destroys some of the critical neural elements in this structure.

Exposure to excessively loud noises can also cause permanent damage to the sensitive structures of the inner ear (Goldstein, 1989). This type of hearing loss is often accompanied by an annoying condition called *tinnitus,* a continuous ringing in the ears. The effects of exposure to loud noises may accumulate over a person's life, thereby contributing to a steady loss of hearing with advancing age. Hearing loss is not just age related, however. Brief exposure to extremely loud noises can produce similar damage. In one study, extremely high decibel noises tore the cilia off the hair cells of experimental animals (Smith, 1947).

Most people do not willingly stand next to a jet as it takes off or expose themselves to some other equally intense sound that can cause permanent damage. However, many people go to rock concerts and discos where noise levels are often measured in the 100 to 300 db. range. Ear specialists warn that a person risks hearing loss with more than a two-hour exposure to 95 to 100 db. (Murray, 1985). The ringing in your ears you may have experienced after attending a rock concert may indicate damage to the hair cells of your inner ear. You may not notice any change in your hearing after one concert because the damage is often quite minimal. However, the effects are cumulative: In a few years you may notice that you no longer hear the phone ringing in the back bedroom, or that people complain that the volume on your TV is too loud.

Young people who spend a great deal of time listening to loud music can suffer permanent damage to the hair cells. Hearing tests conducted among college students have shown that as many as 60 percent have some form of hearing impairment (Sekuler & Blake, 1985). Rock guitarist Pete Townshend suffers a significant hearing loss believed to be caused by loud music.

CONDUCTION HEARING LOSS The role of the outer and middle ear is to conduct sound energy to the receptors of the inner ear. When they fail to function properly, the result is called **conduction hearing loss.** This loss may simply be due to a buildup of ear wax in the auditory canal, a condition that is usually easy to remedy. Sometimes an ear infection can cause so much pressure in the middle ear that the eardrum ruptures, resulting in impaired hearing. In young children ear infections frequently cause an increase in pressure because the eustacian tube may not be fully developed. This pressure can be relieved by inserting small tubes through the tympanic membrane.

A fairly common cause of conduction deafness is a disease called *otosclerosis,* in which a spongy substance around the base of the stapes hardens, cementing the bone in a locked position. This disease, which tends to occur in young adults, can be surgically repaired by replacing the stapes with a plastic substitute.

Conduction hearing loss does not produce total deafness, as is often the case with severe forms of sensorineural impairment. One reason is that sounds can be transmitted directly through the bones of the skull to the inner ear. (This is why a tape recording of your voice probably sounds odd to you. When you talk, the sound of your voice is normally transmitted not only through the air to your outer ear receptacles, but also directly through your skull to your inner ear. Since you are accustomed to hearing this blending, the tape-recorded sound of your voice sounds different.) Many hearing aids, designed to amplify sound transmission via bone conduction, can markedly reduce the effects of conduction hearing loss.

GUSTATION AND OLFACTION

The senses of taste, or **gustation,** and smell **(olfaction)** are classified as chemical senses because both are activated by chemical substances in the environment. Taste and smell are often called minor senses because, relatively speaking, humans utilize vision and audition more than these other senses. We may not rely as much on the senses of smell and taste as do many other animals. However, these minor senses contribute greatly to our experience. The smell of the air after a spring rain, meat sizzling on the barbecue, the sensuous smell of perfume — all contribute immeasurably to our zest for life. Sometimes smells and flavors provide crucial information. Odors like the smell of gas or smoke signal danger, for instance, and taste may have evolved as a signal for both bad and particularly nutritious foods.

GUSTATION

The sense of taste is somewhat limited in humans. Our taste receptors can distinguish only four different sensations: sweetness, saltiness, sourness, and bitterness. These four qualities may seem too simple to explain how we can distinguish between the flavors of spicy and mild mustards or vanilla, chocolate, and strawberry milk shakes and, indeed, they are. The sense of smell also contributes greatly to our ability to perceive differences in flavors. In fact, without the sense of smell, you could not distinguish many of the flavors you recognize. You have probably noticed that things taste flat when you have a bad head cold that plugs up your nose.

The receptors for taste are located in the little bumps on the tongue called *papillae*. Each papilla contains as many as 200 *taste buds*, which in turn contain a number of receptor cells called *microvilli*. The microvilli are hairlike projections that extend into the saliva that coats the tongue. When we take ingestible material into our mouths, chemicals that are dissolved by saliva stimulate the receptor cells, which transduce this chemical energy into neural signals that are transmitted to the brain (Travers et al., 1987).

As Figure 4.23 shows, different parts of the tongue are most sensitive to different taste qualities. The tip of the tongue is most responsive to sweet flavors; the tip and forward portion of each side respond to salty substances; the sides to sour substances; and the back or base to bitter flavors. These regional differences only reflect zones of greatest sensitivity. Actually, all areas that have taste buds can

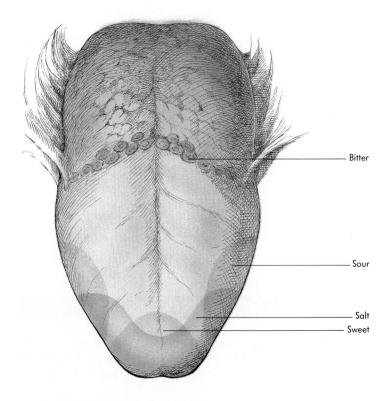

Bitter

Sour

Salt
Sweet

FIGURE 4.23

Distribution of Taste Buds on the Tongue

sense all four of the primary taste qualities. (The middle of the tongue is devoid of taste receptors.)

There is evidence that taste sensitivity undergoes considerable change over the course of our lives, which may account, in part, for changes in taste preferences (Cowart, 1981). For example, most children prefer sweetness to other flavors, but this preference often does not hold up in the adult years. Unfortunately, as we grow older, our taste buds become less sensitive, which is why many older people often complain that food does not taste as good as it once did.

OLFACTION

Unlike many other animals, humans do not depend on the sense of smell to identify friends, repel enemies, and attract mates. Nevertheless, odors do enhance our enjoyment of life, particularly those smells connected with the food we eat. Odors enter the nasal cavity as airborne molecules, either through the nostrils or through the back of the oral cavity. The receptor cells for odors lie in the *olfactory mucosa* or mucous membrane that lines the nasal cavity (see Figure 4.24). Tiny hairlike projections (cilia) extend outward from the receptor cells, catching the airborne molecules (Getchell, 1986; Lancet, 1986).

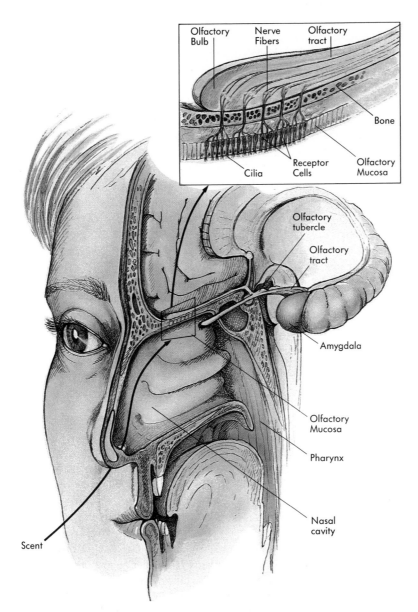

FIGURE 4.24

The Olfactory System

When we smell something, molecules of its fragrance enter the nasal passage from the nose and/or throat. Receptor cells in the olfactory mucosa transduce these stimuli into neural messages that are transmitted along the olfactory tracts to the brain.

We do not know exactly how the chemical energy of various odors is converted to neural signals that carry differing smell messages to the brain (Jones & Reed, 1989; Lancet, 1986). However, one widely held theory is that the cilia on the olfactory receptor cells are specialized to accommodate odor molecules with particular shapes. This viewpoint suggests that substances have different odors because they have different molecular shapes. There is not yet enough evidence to substantiate this theory fully, but research demonstrates that a relationship exists between the shape of a molecule and its odor (Amoore, 1970, 1982; Cain, 1988). Presumably, odor molecules and the receptor cells interact in some fashion that causes the receptor cells to fire, transmitting neural messages to the olfactory tract and on to the brain.

Although people can typically name only a few basic odors, such as floral, peppermint, musk, or putrid, most of us are able to differentiate among as many as 80 different odors (Cain, 1981). Researchers have exerted considerable effort to identify primary odors that would serve the same role as primary hues in color vision. Although it would be convenient to be able to explain the multiplicity of odors we perceive as mixtures of primary scents, efforts to distinguish primary odors have not yet succeeded (Lancet, 1986).

Odors have a powerful ability to stimulate recall of old memories and to elicit feelings connected with experiences well removed in time. Because of this effect, odors are often used to sell products. It is difficult to pass by the delectable odors emanating from the chocolate chip cookie franchise in a local shopping mall. Car dealerships often spray a new car scent into used vehicles. The outsides of bread wrappers may be infused with a fresh-baked smell, and inexpensive vinyl-covered furniture is sometimes moistened with a leather scent.

CHEMICAL COMMUNICATION: PHEROMONES   Some perfume manufacturers have implied, sometimes not so subtly, that their product contains an aphrodisiac-like product that will attract a potential mate. Other perfumes contain animal pheromones, presumably because if pheromones work for animals they must work for people. These odors that attract sexual interest, called *pheromones*, do exist among a variety of animals and the females of many species secrete pheromones during their fertile periods. Pheromones serve many other functions in animals besides identifying receptive mates. They may also function to define territories, identify dominance, signal alarm, aid in the location of food sources, and aid in the aggregation of social animals. Evidence supporting the existence of pheromones in people is not as conclusive. However, some research suggests that pheromones may be involved in the synchronization of menstrual cycles in women living in close proximity, such as in dormitories.

THE SKIN SENSES

The fourth type of sensation is the sense of touch. As Figure 4.25 shows, our entire skin surface is embedded with receptors for the various skin sensations. All of these various receptors are the dendrites of neurons: Unlike vision, hearing, and taste, our skin senses use no specialized receptor cells other than neurons. These neurons do have specialized dendrite endings, however, that modify the manner in which they transduce physical energy into a neural firing.

Receptors for different kinds of skin senses are distributed unevenly over the body. For example, our faces are much more sensitive to touch than our backs because the receptors are more densely packed in the skin of the face than that of the back. Researchers have attempted to link particular kinds of skin receptors to specific sensory experiences, with only limited success.

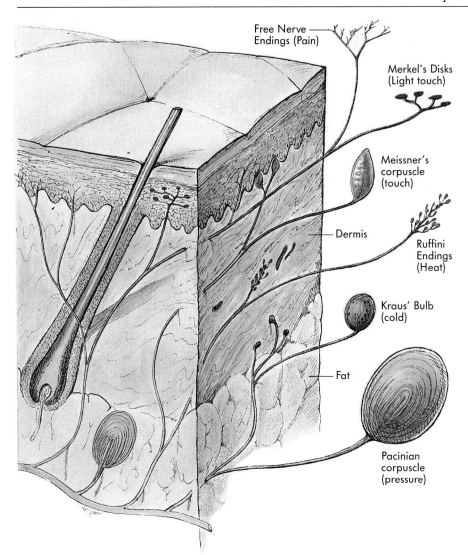

Free Nerve Endings (Pain)

Merkel's Disks (Light touch)

Meissner's corpuscle (touch)

Dermis

Ruffini Endings (Heat)

Kraus' Bulb (cold)

Fat

Pacinian corpuscle (pressure)

FIGURE 4.25
A Cross-Sectional Drawing of the Skin

Different receptors in the skin are sensitive to specific kinds of stimuli.

The sense of touch is actually a composite of three different senses: pressure, temperature, and pain. More complex sensory experiences such as tingling, itching, tickling, or wetness are produced from combinations of these three basic sensations.

PRESSURE

We experience the sensation of pressure when a mechanical force causes a displacement of the skin. Sensory adaptation occurs very quickly, which is why we are soon unaware of the pressure of tight-fitting pants or snug shoes. (If you continue to be aware of your tight shoes, it is probably because you are feeling the sensation of pain rather than pressure.) Some parts of our bodies are much more sensitive to pressure than others. The most sensitive regions are the face and fingers; the least sensitive are the back and the legs.

TEMPERATURE

The detection of changes in body temperature is of great importance because most animals cannot survive when body temperature either falls below or exceeds certain values. As body temperature decreases, organisms can adapt behaviorally by seeking warmth or insulation. As it rises, organisms may, for example, seek a cooler environment or water immersion.

Certain very localized areas of the skin seem to be sensitive to cold but not warmth; other spots show just the opposite sensitivity. This observation is consistent with general agreement among researchers that different specialized dendrite endings, called *thermoreceptors*, respond to cold and heat (Spray, 1986). Detectors for cold appear to be located closer to the skin's surface than are heat detectors. This may explain why you experience a brief sensation of cold when you place your hand in a stream of hot water to check the temperature of your morning shower. Under other conditions spots sensitive to cold can be stimulated with a hot stimulus. The perception of cold in this case is called paradoxical cold.

THEORIES OF TEMPERATURE SENSATION   There are two main theories of temperature sensation: specific-receptor theory and vascular theory. According to specific-receptor theory there are two receptor types; one for cold and the other for heat. The receptors for cold are called *Krause end bulbs* and those for heat are called *Ruffini cylinders*.

Although it is likely that these specific receptor types are sensitive to temperature changes we also experience the sensations of heat and cold in regions of the skin where these receptors either don't occur or are only sparsely located (Schiffman, 1990). A second explanation, vascular theory, holds that there are not specific receptor types for heat and cold sensations. Rather, temperature sensations are mediated by the neurovascular system. When the skin is cooled, smooth muscles of the vascular system contract; when heated, these smooth muscles relax. These muscle changes excite sensory nerve endings connected to the muscle walls.

At present it appears that both specific-receptor theory and vascular theory are necessary to account for all thermal sensation. For instance, vascular theory alone cannot account for the relative distributions of warm and cold sensitive spots throughout the skin.

PAIN

As much as we dislike pain, it is essential. Pain acts as a warning that something is harming us, and it drives us to seek necessary medical attention. Despite its importance (and regardless of the fact that nearly one-third of the American adult population experience persistent or recurrent chronic pain), very little is known about what causes pain and how to relieve it. One survey of 17 standard textbooks on surgery, medicine, and cancer found that only 54 out of 22,000 pages provided information about pain (Wallis, 1984).

THEORIES OF PAIN   Theories about the mechanisms involved in pain sensation and perception are highly controversial (Besson & Chaouch, 1987). One fact that makes understanding pain so difficult is that no specific physical stimulus exists for pain as it does for the other sensory processes we have been discussing. A sound that is too loud, a light too bright, or a temperature too hot or cold can all produce pain sensations. Some pain researchers maintain that pain results from overstimulation of any sensory receptors; others believe that pain results when damaged tissue releases chemicals that stimulate specialized nerve endings in the skin, which then transduce the chemical energy to neural signals that carry pain messages to our brains. Chemicals believed to be involved in this process include *prostaglandins, bradykinins*, and *substance P* (P for pain protein).

Researchers have identified nerve fibers that transmit pain signals from the point of injury to the spinal cord and then on to the brain (Besson & Chaouch, 1987). One set of rapidly transmitting, myelinated fibers convey a message of localized, sharp, pricking pain, probably the only sensation we feel when the pain begins and ends quickly (as when our skin is pierced by a needle). However, if the pain stimulus is more severe, as might result from a burn or a damaging body blow, we perceive a second sensation within a second or two. This message, which is conveyed by unmyelinated slow nerve fibers, induces an awareness of a burning, searing, throbbing, or aching pain that is usually more diffuse.

Gate Control Theory of Pain   One widely discussed attempt to explain some of the phenomena associated with pain perception is called the **gate-control theory** (Melzack, 1973, 1980; Melzack & Wall, 1965, 1983). It suggests that when nerve fibers conveying pain messages are activated, neural gates in the spinal cord are opened to allow passage of pain signals on their way to the brain. However, these pain gates can be closed by the firing of other nonpain nerve fibers if they are activated simultaneously with the pain fibers. Thus this theory suggests that competition from other sensations may block our perception of pain.

Research support for the gate-control theory has been inconsistent, and not all of its propositions have fared equally well under close scrutiny. Nevertheless, some of its major tenets, particularly its emphasis on pain as a perceptual as well as sensory phenomenon, have been widely supported by experimental evidence (Turk & Rudy, 1986; Warga, 1987). A number of phenomena make this interpretation seem particularly plausible. For example, we know that pain relief can be induced in both humans and other animals by electrical stimulation of certain areas within the spinal cord (Besson & Chaouch, 1987; Devulder et al., 1990; Meilman et al., 1989). Presumably, such stimulation inhibits the spinal transmission of pain messages, perhaps by closing pain gates.

The gate-control theory also suggests an explanation for why people are often unaware of pain when they are injured under conditions of high stress and intense emotions (Amit & Galina, 1986). For instance, a woman who cuts herself while rescuing a child from a broken window may not notice her own injury until the crisis has passed. It seems plausible that intense emotions can create competing stimuli that overload the neural circuits, thereby blocking the pain pathways.

Neurotransmitters and Pain   In Chapter 3 we discussed several neuropeptides that served as neurotransmitters. Two neuropeptides play important roles in the transmission of pain signals from sensory neurons to the brain. The first, **substance P**, is found throughout the midbrain, pons, and the medulla as well as in the spinal cord. In the spinal cord substance P appears to be the neurotransmitter released by incoming sensory neurons that signal pain. Another group of neuropeptides, called endorphins, possess painkilling (analgesic) properties similar to opiate drugs. The term **endorphin** means internal morphine (Groves and Rebec, 1992). The part of the brain where the endorphins are believed to inhibit pain is an area of the brainstem called the **periaqueductal grey area (PAG)**, which is believed to be the center of the pain circuit.

As sensory neurons transmit pain signals to the spinal cord they excite afferent neurons which ascend to the brainstem and the thalamus of the brain (see Figure 4.26). In the brainstem periaqueductal grey region these afferent neurons cause the release of endorphins which (through the involvement of several other neurons) results in the excitation of descending neurons. These descending neurons release serotonin at the original sensory neuron synapse in the spinal cord inhibiting the afferent neurons signalling pain. Therefore, **serotonin** appears to be involved in the inhibition of pain signals to the brain. Evidence for the role of serotonin in the inhibition of pain comes from studies where serotonin neurons in the brain stem are blocked or destroyed, rendering morphine analgesia ineffective (Morhland and Gebhart, 1980). In contrast, increasing levels of serotonin in the brain may help to alleviate some kinds of pain.

FIGURE 4.26

The Periaqueductal Gray Region of the Brainstem

Pain messages are transmitted through the spinal cord to the periaqueductal grey (PAG) region of the brain stem. Serotonin- and GABA-containing neurons interact to cause the release of endorphins in the spinal cord inhibiting pain transmission. Pain messages are also transmitted to the thalamus and other brain areas where pain is perceived.

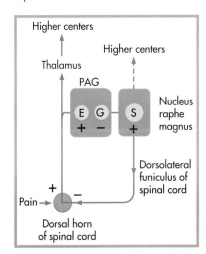

KINESTHESIS AND EQUILIBRIUM

Try closing your eyes and moving your hand to various positions. You will have no trouble keeping track of where your hand is. With your eyes still closed, try touching your nose. Again, you will have no problem. Finally, eyes closed, try standing on one foot. This task is a little tougher, but you will probably find you can maintain your balance reasonably well.

All of these simple exercises are accomplished without the aid of the senses discussed so far in this chapter. Rather, these tasks are aided by two interrelated sensory systems called kinesthesis and equilibrium. These two **body senses,** working in concert, tell us the orientation of our bodies in space, the relative position of the various body parts, and the movement of any parts of the body.

The sense of **kinesthesis** is diffuse throughout the entire body. It consists of specialized nerve endings embedded in the muscles, tendons, and joints that tell the brain whether muscles and tendons are being stretched, contracted, or relaxed. The cortex translates this sensory information into perceptions about locations of various parts of the body in relation to other parts. Kinesthesis allows us to throw a ball without watching what our arms are doing, and it helps us take appropriate corrective action when we stumble or slip.

The sense of **equilibrium,** or balance, is localized within the inner ear. It comprises two sets of sensory receptors: the semicircular canals and the vestibular sacs. The **semicircular canals** are three ring-shaped structures, oriented at right angles to each other so that they lie roughly in each of the three dimensions of space (see Figure 4.27). Each is filled with a fluid (endolymph) that moves when the head is rotated. The lining of the semicircular canals contains hair cells that bend in the direction of the fluid flow. When you move your head, the fluid flows in the canal along the plane in which your head is moving. This movement is transduced to neural messages which tell your brain that your head is either accelerating or decelerating. If velocity is kept at a constant rate (in an airplane or a subway, for example) motion is not usually detectable. The viscosity of endolymph fluid is apparently changed by alcohol consumption, which contributes to the "spins" when you've consumed too much.

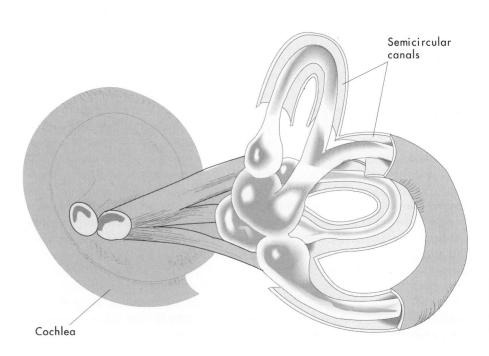

Semicircular canals

Cochlea

FIGURE 4.27

The Semicircular Canals

These fluid-filled canals contain specialized receptors cells that are stimulated by head movement.

Greg Lougainis has developed an exceptional ability to use kinesthetic information to perfect his dive.

Another source of information are the **vestibular sacs,** located at the junction of the semicircular canals and the cochlea. These sacs contain hair cells weighted with crystals of calcium carbonate. When the head is tilted, gravitational forces cause the weighted cilia to shift, and this action in turn triggers neural activity in adjacent nerve fibers. This information, in conjunction with information received from the semicircular canals (as occurs in a swaying car or a boat on a rough sea) sometimes produces motion sickness. Motion sickness is the result of unusual vestibular stimulation where motion information signalled by the visual system is mismatched with vestibular information.

PERCEIVING THE WORLD

To this point we have been looking at the processes by which we receive sensations about the physical world through our various sense organs. How we interpret or perceive these sensations depends on other processes. Our perceptions are much more than that which we see, hear, smell, taste, or sense with our skin and body senses. Our brains organize and give meaning to the constant input of sensory messages through an active process of selecting, ordering, synthesizing, and interpreting. In the rest of this chapter we consider some of the basic principles that govern our perceptions.

Look at the illustration in Figure 4.28 on page 148. Rather than meaningless dots, lines, and colors, you no doubt perceive a familiar animal. Virtually every-

PERCEPTUAL ORGANIZATION

FIGURE 4.28
Perceptual Organization

Perceptual organization is the process whereby we organize structural elements into objects.

FIGURE 4.29
The Rubin Vase

Used to illustrate the figure-ground principle of perceptual organization. The illustration is ambiguous because either green or blue can serve as figure or ground.

thing we perceive with our eyes is made up of elementary sensations in the form of points, lines, edges, brightness, and varied hues. The process by which we structure these elementary sensations into the objects we perceive is called **perceptual organization.**

The major principles of perceptual organization were identified in the first half of this century by Gestalt psychologists. This group of influential German psychologists included Max Wertheimer, Kurt Koffka, and Wolfgang Köhler. As mentioned in Chapter 1, they theorized that we perceive figures and forms as whole patterns that are different from the simple sum of individual sensations. They outlined several principles that influence how people organize sensations into whole patterns called *Gestalts*. These include figure and ground, perceptual grouping, and closure.

FIGURE AND GROUND   One feature of perceptual organization identified by the Gestalt psychologists is our tendency to differentiate between **figure** (the part of an image on which we focus our attention) and **ground** (the background against which the figure stands). For example, the black words on this page stand out as figure against the white background.

Figure 4.29 illustrates an ambiguous figure-ground relationship. At first glance, you may see either two blue face profiles as a figure against a green ground, or a green vase as the figure against a blue ground. This figure further demonstrates the distinction between sensation and perception. The pattern of sensory receptors activated in our retinas remains constant while our perceptions shift between the two figure-ground patterns. The manner in which our brains organize these constant sensory stimuli allows us to perceive either the faces or the vase, but not both at the same time.

The figure and ground organization principle also applies to senses other than vision. For example, when you listen to music, the melody may stand out as the figure against a background of chords that serve as ground. However, a sudden change in tempo, rhythm, or volume may suddenly bring a chord to the forefront, where it becomes the central figure. Perhaps you are listening to a friend describe some important political event when a voice on the TV set behind you mentions your favorite athletic team. Suddenly the TV announcement becomes the focal point of your attention, and your friend's voice becomes background noise. You cannot focus on your friend's voice and the TV announcer at the same time: One must be figure, and one must be ground.

PERCEPTUAL GROUPING   Gestalt psychologists also demonstrated the role of **perceptual grouping** to explain how we organize sensory input into meaningful wholes. Patterns of stimuli are grouped into larger units in three major ways: by **proximity, similarity,** and **good continuation.**

Figure 4.30 illustrates these three perceptual grouping principles. The principle of proximity suggests that, all else being equal, we tend to organize our perceptions by grouping elements that are the nearest to each other. The principle of similarity suggests that we group elements that are similar to one another. A final grouping principle, good continuation, suggests that we are more likely to perceive stimuli as a whole or single group if they flow smoothly into one another as opposed to being discontinuous.

CLOSURE   Another powerful organizing principle is our inclination to perceive incomplete figures as complete. A careful examination of Figure 4.31 reveals that what appear to be two overlapping triangles are actually incomplete figures. Furthermore, the solid white triangle does not exist; it is merely an illusion. The perceptual process that allows us to see these as complete figures is referred to as **closure.**

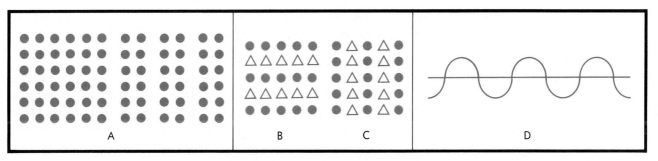

A   B   C   D

FIGURE 4.30
Perceptual Grouping Principles

Part A illustrates the principle of proximity: The pattern on the left can be seen as either columns or rows because the dots are spaced equally. The patterns to the right are seen as columns because of the horizontal spacing. Parts B and C demonstrate the grouping principle of similarity (in B we see rows and in C we see columns). Pattern D illustrates the principle of continuity in which stimuli that flow smoothly into one another form a group.

ATTENTION AND PERCEPTION   Another basic principle of perceptual processing is **selective attention,** the process of focusing on one or a few stimuli of particular significance while ignoring others. As was shown earlier in this chapter in the discussion of your dinner date, we never attend equally to all the stimuli we receive at any given point in time. If we did, our nervous systems would become hopelessly overloaded. Instead, certain stimuli are focused on, and the other events fade into the background (Johnston & Dark, 1986). Through this process of selective attention our perceptual ability is enhanced (Moran & Desimone, 1985).

To some extent, we control our attention. For example, at this moment your attention is focused on the printed words of this book. Hopefully, your desire to understand the principles discussed here is sufficient inducement to allow you to screen out a variety of background stimuli. Psychologists have discovered that

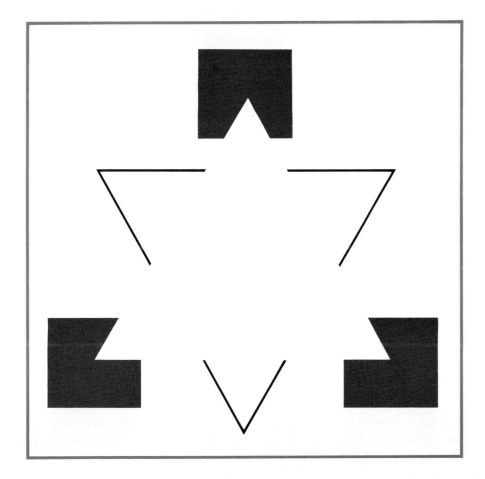

FIGURE 4.31
The Principle of Closure

We can see two overlapping triangles in this illustration because of our tendency to fill in missing perceptual information. The solid white triangle is merely an illusion induced by closure.

certain characteristics of stimuli tend to capture attention almost automatically. We next examine several important principles that effect our attention to stimuli.

Complex Stimuli   There is evidence that stimuli which are difficult to process may command additional attention. For example, some of the complex illustrations in this chapter require a fair amount of effort to comprehend. Psychologists believe that the more we focus on one category of stimuli, the less we can respond to others (Norman & Bobrow, 1975). This also relates to the concept of selective attention. The more complex the stimulus the less attention we can focus on any particular aspect of it.

Sudden Change   A sudden change in either the quality or quantity of a background stimulus generally causes a shift in attention. For example, you may notice the quiet as a fan or motor that you haven't noticed shuts off. Or, a sudden movement to your side can catch your attention while driving. As we mentioned earlier, a main characteristic of our sensory systems is to respond to stimulus change.

Contrast and Novelty   Contrast and novelty also tend to capture our attention. For example, a brightly lit neon sign along a dark stretch of highway often diverts our attention because it contrasts with its surroundings. The same sign among many neon signs downtown might not get our attention. Things that are novel or unusual also tend to attract our attention. For instance, wearing an unusual hairstyle or clothing is a good way to get noticed.

Stimulus Intensity   Another way to get attention is to vary the intensity of a stimulus. This is why TV commercials may increase their volume slightly above the sound of normal TV programming, and why they often use very bright and colorful images. Sudden reduction of stimulus intensity can also command attention. If your friends talking on the other side of the room suddenly begin whispering, you may prick up your ears in an effort to hear what they are saying.

Some professors may use this perceptual concept in their lectures. To cause their students to pay attention to a point, they may lower their voices to a level that is barely audible. As a result, students often lean forward in their seats while they concentrate on the ensuing words of wisdom.

Repetition   Repetition is another way to attract attention. This is one reason why TV and radio ads often use jingles that are repeated again and again. Many popular tunes draw our attention because they have a catchy beat that repeats over and over again.

Key Stimuli   Finally, some stimuli appear to attract our attention by activating motivational mechanisms such as fear, hunger, or sexual arousal. When certain stimuli or features of a stimulus activate motivation they are referred to as *key stimuli*. These stimulus features are believed to have played important roles in guiding and directing behavior throughout our evolution (Eibl-Eibesfeldt, 1991). While key stimuli are probably more important in guiding the behavior of lower animals, they are also important in motivating and directing human behavior. The all too familiar use of an attractive, exposed body to catch our attention for advertising is an example of how key stimuli attract our attention.

SPATIAL PERCEPTION

The major function of vision is to represent the spatial arrangement of objects in our environment. Objects are seen at varying distances and from different perspectives, yet we recognize their form and size quite accurately. This poses two related problems for perception. First, how do we perceive depth or distance? And second, how do we recognize objects from different perspectives?

THE PERCEPTION OF DEPTH   Earlier in this chapter, we learned that visual images are focused on the retina, which is essentially an image-recording layer of neural tissue that lines the back of the eye. Since retinal images are two-dimensional, how can we perceive that objects in our environment are three-dimensional, and how do we determine how close or far away they are? Clearly, these types of discrimination are essential for normal functioning. Can you imagine what it would be like to walk through a busy city if you could not accurately estimate how far away approaching cars happened to be? A variety of perceptual cues allows us to judge accurately the distance of objects. Some of these cues, called **binocular cues,** depend on both eyes working together; others, called **monocular cues,** can be used with just one eye.

Binocular Cues   Seeing with both our eyes provides important binocular cues for distance perception (Foley, 1985). Perhaps the most accurate of these is **binocular** or **retinal disparity.** Binocular disparity is based on the fact that since the eyes are a couple of inches apart, each has a slightly different view of the world. To demonstrate this phenomenon, stare at this page and alternately close one eye at a time. Note that the page appears to shift its position slightly. Normally our brains fuse these two images into a single three-dimensional image (O'Shea, 1987). At the same time, the brain analyzes the differences in the two images to obtain information about distance.

There is greater binocular disparity when objects are close to our eyes than when they are far away. Hold the index finger of one hand very close to your face and align it with the same finger of the other hand as far away as possible. Now alternately close each eye. Your closest finger seems to leap back and forth, while the far one shifts only slightly. Figure 4.32a shows why close objects create more

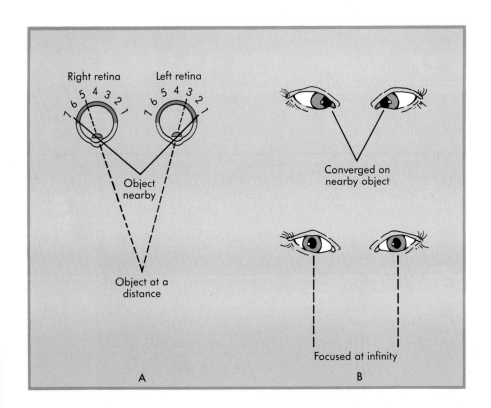

FIGURE 4.32

Binocular (Retinal) Disparity and Convergence

Part A illustrates that the closer an object is the greater the retinal disparity. Part B illustrates the convergence of the eyes that is necessary to view nearby objects. Both binocular (retinal) disparity and convergence are important depth cues for perception.

significant disparity whereas those that are far away create only minor disparity: The difference in the angle of the two eyes to the far object is much slighter than the difference for the close object. The ability of the visual system to utilize binocular disparity is quite impressive. The minimum disparity required to detect a depth difference is 1 micron (1 millionth of a meter). This is less than the diameter of a photoreceptor!

Another important binocular distance cue is called **convergence.** When we look at an object that is no more than 25 feet away, our two eyes must converge (rotate to the inside) in order to perceive it as a single, clearly focused image. This rotation of the eyes is necessary to allow them to focus on the same object, but it creates tension in the eye muscles. As Figure 4.32b shows, the closer the object, the greater the tension. Objects far away require no convergence for sharp focusing. Consequently, muscular feedback from converging eyes becomes an important cue for judging the distance of objects within roughly 25 feet of our eyes.

Monocular Cues   If objects that are far away create little retinal disparity and no convergence, how can we judge their distance? A number of one-eye, or monocular, cues provide that information.

Figure 4.33 illustrates several important monocular cues for distance perception. One of these is elevation, or **height on a plane.** Note that the objects in the photo that appear to be farther away are higher on your plane of view. This cue is always present. If you look around your room or gaze out the window, you will see that the farther away an object is, the higher it will be on your plane of view and the more you have to lift your gaze to perceive it.

Another distance cue, called **overlap** or interposition, describes the phenomenon in which objects close to us tend to block out parts of objects that are farther away from us. If you look around your room again, you will notice that

FIGURE 4.33

Monocular Cues for Depth Perception

Many monocular cues also contribute to depth perception. Objects far away tend to be higher on our plane of view A, objects closer to us block objects that are further away B, when you look at this stretch of road the sides (lines) of the road converge C, and objects that are closer tend to be larger than similar objects at a distance D.

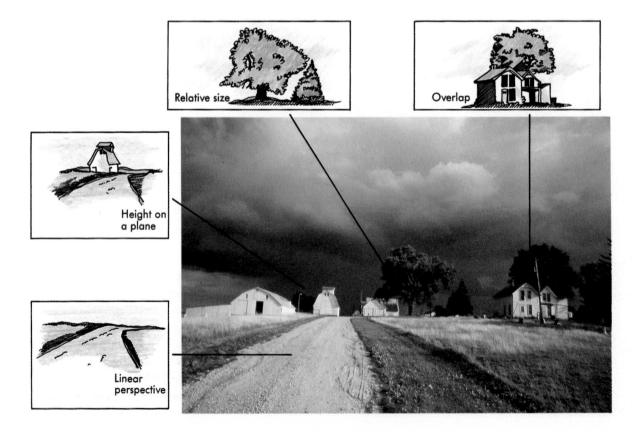

Relative size

Overlap

Height on a plane

Linear perspective

your textbook blocks your view of the desk under it, that the desk in turn blocks your view of the floor, and so forth.

A third distance cue, called **linear perspective,** is based on the fact that parallel lines converge when stretched into the distance. For example, when you look at a long stretch of road or railroad tracks, it appears that the sides of the road or the parallel tracks converge on the horizon.

If we know how large objects are, we can judge their distance by their apparent size in relation to each other. If you look out your window and see two people, one 50 yards away and the other 200 yards away, you notice a great difference in their **relative size.** Instead of concluding that one person is a pygmy and the other a giant, you take this cue as evidence that the smaller person is a greater distance from you.

Another monocular cue, **texture gradient,** involves perceived change in the texture of surfaces as they extend farther from our eyes. For example, if you look at a textured surface such as an expanse of grassy lawn or a rock-strewn field, the elements close to you seem to be farther apart or less dense than those that are farther away. The close elements are also clearer. A striking illustration of this phenomenon is provided in Figure 4.34.

Objects that are far away appear fuzzier than those close by because as distance increases, smog, dust, and haze reduce the clarity of the projected image. This depth cue, called **aerial** or **atmospheric perspective,** can sometimes cause us to judge distance inaccurately, especially if we are accustomed to the smoggy atmosphere of urban areas.

A final monocular cue for distance may be demonstrated if you gaze at the scene outside your window and move your head from side to side. You will notice that objects nearby seem to move a much greater distance than objects farther away. This cue, called **relative motion** or **motion parallax,** is particularly noticeable when you look out the window of a moving car and observe nearby objects moving much more rapidly than distant ones.

GIBSON'S THEORY OF DIRECT PERCEPTION   Our preceeding discussion of spatial perception assumes that perceptual processing is necessary. That is, the spatial

FIGURE 4.34
Texture Gradients

The fine texture in the foreground of this picture fades away in the distance.

cues we described draw upon both past experience (memory) and cognitive processing for spatial representation such as depth. An intriguing and quite different perspective has been proposed by Gibson (1979) who argues that all of the visual information necessary for spatial representation is available from the environment. That is, spatial representation is a process of **direct perception,** not a process of cognition. **Gibson's theory of direct perception** holds that certain information from the environment is invariant. These **invariants** are sufficient to represent depth or distance without additional cognitive processing. For instance, consider texture gradients as a cue for depth. Texture is invarient in that it always appears finer or denser as distance increases and coarser as objects move closer. Similarly, the apparent movement differences between near and far away objects (motion parallax) remain invariant and directly reveal distance information (Schiffman, 1990).

Not all psychologists agree with Gibson, however. Considerable evidence suggests that we do not just "pick up" spatial information, but rather we construct it out of perceptual data. Further research on perceptual invariances and direct perception will either support or weaken Gibson's theory.

PERCEIVING DEPTH: THE VISUAL CLIFF EXPERIMENT   There can be little doubt that many distance cues are enhanced by experience. In fact, before a classic experiment over 30 years ago, many psychologists believed that distance or depth perception depended on learning. However, Eleanor Gibson and Richard Walk (1960) provided convincing evidence that some aspects of depth perception are inborn or innate, at least in some species.

The device created by Gibson and Walk is called the visual cliff, and it is illustrated in Figure 4.35. The **visual cliff** is an elevated glass surface. A checkerboard-patterned plane lies just under half of the glass surface; there is nothing under the other half except for the checkerboard painted on the floor, roughly three and one-half feet below. This design produces the illusion of a deep side and a shallow side.

Infants of many species that can walk immediately after birth were tested on the apparatus. All of these newborn animals, including kittens, puppies, lambs,

FIGURE 4.35

The Visual Cliff

The pattern of squares on the floor can produce an illusion of greater depth. In this case a kitten hesitates to move across the glass surface.

chickens, piglets, and kids, refused to cross over to the deep side, suggesting that depth perception is innate in these species. Even chicks whose initial visual experience occurred on the visual cliff would not step over the deep side. Evidence also suggests that depth perception in this case is based on the monocular cue motion parallax which is the dominant cue for depth perception in most animals.

Since human babies could not be tested until they were able to crawl (usually around the age of six months), their depth perception was more difficult to interpret. Obviously, a lot of learning can take place in the first six months of life. Most of the infants tested would not spontaneously crawl onto the deep side, something that infants of other species would never do. Yet some infants, especially those who began crawling at a very young age, could be enticed to crawl over the cliff (Rader et al., 1981).

Some researchers argue that by the time human infants can be tested on the visual cliff, they may have already learned to avoid drop-offs (Campos et al., 1978). Others have argued that the kind of depth perception required for the cliff is an innate capacity in humans that emerges at about six months after birth, the age at which most infants begin to need this capability (Rader et al., 1981; Richards & Rader, 1981). Which explanation is correct? At this point, we can say with confidence that depth perception is an innate ability in many species of animals. In humans it is either innate, or it is learned very early in life. Human infants are clearly not living in a visual world which is "one great blooming, buzzing confusion" as stated by William James in 1890. Rather, their world appears to be perceived much like our own.

SIZE, COLOR AND SHAPE CONSTANCIES *Size Constancy* When you bid farewell to friends at the dock and see them sail off into the distance, you do not assume that their boat is shrinking. Instead, you realize that the boat remains the same size even though the image projected onto your retinas gets smaller and smaller. Your perception of the boat adjusts automatically, taking into consideration changes in the distance between you and it. This perceptual phenomenon, known as **size constancy,** is but one of several forms of **perceptual constancy** that allow us to adjust for varying conditions and changing patterns as we perceive the world (Rock & DiVita, 1987). Size constancy is illustrated in Figure 4.36. In this illustration the man walking is the same size in both pictures. However, as he approaches the foreground, he appears to shrink.

FIGURE 4.36
Size Constancy
The man who is walking in these pictures is the same size in each shot. As he moves closer he appears to shrink.

In a classic study of size constancy, A. H. Holway and Edwin Boring (1941) found that subjects were able to make extremely accurate judgments of the size of a circle located at varying distances from their eyes, under conditions that were rich with distance cues. As distance cues were progressively eliminated, however, subjects' judgments of circle size became increasingly dependent on the size of the retinal image. Thus the subjects' perception of the size of the circle increased when it was moved closer and decreased as it was moved away, a complete breakdown in size constancy. Therefore an important cue for size constancy is apparent retinal size.

Brightness and Color Constancy   **Brightness constancy** and **color constancy** also help us perceive our world as constant. When you look out your window at night, the trees, grass, and bushes do not appear to be the same color or brightness as they are during the daytime. Since you already know that the leaves of the bushes are a dark green and the grass and trees are brighter green, however, you perceive these qualities to be constant even under conditions of different illumination.

Shape Constancy   Another element of perceptual constancy is **shape constancy.** When we look at objects from different angles, the shape of the image projected to our retinas is different in each instance. Nevertheless, we perceive the object as unchanged (see Figure 4.37). When we view a door from straight on, it appears rectangular in shape. When the door is opened, we still perceive it as rectangular despite the fact that the image projected on our retinas is trapezoidal.

In summary, we perceive our dynamic environment as essentially stable and containing constant stimulus properties. This occurs even though our visual system receives a varied array of stimulus properties including changes in size, brightness, color, and shape. These constancies are the result of several factors. One critical factor appears to be object familiarity. Experience may influence our perception of an object as its visual properties change, for example as with relative size. However, as we noted for depth perception, perceptual constancies have been demonstrated very early on in human development and early on in the development of other animals suggesting that some perceptual constancies may be innate.

Throughout this chapter we have emphasized that our perceptions of physical stimuli are not exactly the same as the properties of the physical stimulus. Some of this discrepancy is produced by our nervous system during the process of transducing the physical sensation. Other discrepancies are more related to the perceptual organization of stimuli. In the next section we will examine stimuli that produce considerable perceptual ambiguity because of these discrepancies.

FIGURE 4.37

Shape Constancy

We perceive the opening door as being rectangular despite the image projected on our retinas.

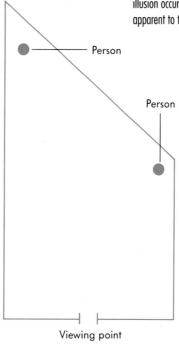

FIGURE 4.38
The Ames Room

In the Ames room people appear to change sizes as they move about. As you can see from the diagram the person on the left in both pictures is twice as far away as the person on the right. The illusion occurs because the depth cues are not apparent to the viewer.

Person

Person

Viewing point

VISUAL ILLUSIONS

Visual **illusions** are of interest to psychologists because they provide insights into normal perception, not because they are errors in perception. The illusions discussed here are important because of their relation to spatial perception.

THE AMES ILLUSION Perhaps one of the most vivid illusions is provided by the *Ames room*, shown in Figure 4.38. A person standing on one side of the room appears to be a giant; someone on the other side appears to be a dwarf. It is even more amazing that when people cross the Ames room, they steadily appear to grow or shrink, depending on the direction in which they are walking. This illusion is produced by conflicting environmental cues.

The Ames room was designed to fool the observer into thinking it is shaped like a normal rectangular room. However, as you can see from the diagram in the figure, the room is definitely not rectangular. Both windows are trapezoidal, and one is much larger than the other. In addition, the floor is uneven so that one end of the Ames room is higher on the plane than the other. The relationships between the various objects in the room were altered in this manner to change relationships that we are accustomed to perceiving between people and their environments. Since we have not experienced this kind of arrangement before, however, our perceptual constancy processes cause us to perceive the room as rectangular and the windows as equal in size and rectangular in shape. Recent research has shown that the Ames room illusion persists (although in somewhat diminished form) even when subjects are allowed to leave the viewing point indicated in the figure and move about the room (Gehringer & Engel, 1986).

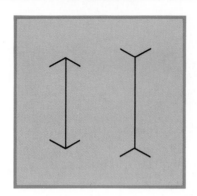

FIGURE 4.39

The Müller-Lyer Illusion

The two vertical lines are equal in length.

THE MÜLLER-LYER ILLUSION One of the most widely analyzed visual illusions is the *Müller-Lyer illusion*, illustrated in Figure 4.39. Ignoring the angled lines (arrowheads) at the ends of each vertical line, decide which line is longer. Most people see the line on the right as longer, but actually the two are of equal length. How can the Müller-Lyer illusion be explained? Think back to what you have learned about perceptual constancy in this chapter, and try to formulate an answer before reading on.

Actually, psychologists do not all agree about why the Müller-Lyer illusion fools us. According to one interpretation that enjoyed popularity for a period of time, the illusion is created by the fact that the outward-turned angles draw the viewer's eyes farther out into space; the inward-turning angles draw the eyes back toward the center.

One study cast serious doubt on this interpretation, however. In this experiment an apparatus was designed to hold a subject's eyes and head very still while the lines of the Müller-Lyer illusion were flashed into one eye and the arrowheads into the other. When these sensations were combined in the subject's brain, the same illusion resulted (Gillam, 1980). This finding indicates that the illusion is created by something more than the movement of the eyes.

A British psychologist, R. L. Gregory (1978), has proposed a more likely interpretation—that the Müller-Lyer illusion is the result of size constancy. According to Gregory, the angled lines provide linear perspective cues. As Figure 4.40 shows, the vertical line on the left, enclosed by the inward-turning angled lines, is perceived as being closer than the line with the outward-turning angled lines. We have already learned that if two objects appear to be the same size, and we think one is closer, then size constancy causes us to assume that the farther one is bigger.

Gregory's theory is supported by research demonstrating that the Müller-Lyer illusion is either very weak or absent in cultures in which people have little expo-

FIGURE 4.40

What Causes the Müller-Lyer Illusion?

This illustration suggests that the Müller-Lyer illusion results from depth cues and size constancy.

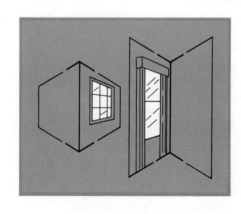

FIGURE 4.41
The Zulu Culture

The Zulus of southeast Africa live in an environment where there are few straight lines or corners. Because they have not learned to judge depth from these cues they are less susceptible to the Müller-Lyer illusion than people from Western cultures where straight lines and corners are common.

sure to angles (Seagall et al., 1966). For example, the Zulus of southeast Africa, who live in circular huts with few straight lines and corners (see Figure 4.41), do not judge distance from such linear cues as effectively as we do. These people respond only minimally to the Müller-Lyer illusion.

THE MOON ILLUSION An illusion you are probably familiar with is the *moon illusion* (see Figure 4.42). Most people have had the experience of looking at a full moon on the horizon and thinking how huge it looks. When the moon is low on the horizon, it appears larger than when it is overhead, yet the actual size of the moon's image on the retina is the same regardless of its position in the sky. Why does this illusion occur?

The moon illusion also seems to result from size constancy. When the moon is low, it appears to be farther away than when it is overhead. This effect results

FIGURE 4.42
The Moon Illusion

The greater number of visual cues for depth on the horizon create the illusion that the moon is larger (because it is perceived as further away) than when it is higher in the sky on a cloudless night.

FIGURE 4.43

The Ponzo Illusion

The two horizontal lines are of equal length.

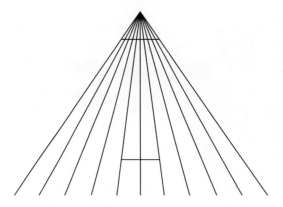

from the presence of visual cues for distance, such as overlapping structures and relative size. Compared to the trees or buildings on the horizon, we perceive the moon to be very far away. In contrast, when we look at the moon overhead, we have no visual cues for distance. Consequently, we tend to underestimate its distance. As in the Müller-Lyer illusion, we assume that the moon on the horizon is larger because distance cues tell us it is farther from us than the identically sized moon overhead.

THE PONZO ILLUSION   The *Ponzo illusion* is illustrated in Figure 4.43. The two horizontal lines are equal in length although we perceive the "distant" line as longer. The Ponzo illusion is an illusion of perspective. The converging lines at the top of the figure are associated with distance, falsely suggesting that the top horizontal line is farther away. An object that is farther away and yet occupies the same visual angle as an object that is closer to us must then be longer.

THE POGGENDORFF ILLUSION   One last illusion is the *Poggendorff illusion*, shown in Figure 4.44a. It appears that if the diagonal lines were continued toward each other, the one on the right would pass above the left line. In reality, they would join, as you can determine by laying a straight edge along their projected paths. Many psychologists believe this illusion results from our inclination to maintain shape constancy. Figure 4.44b illustrates one possible example of something we have experienced that influences our perception of the Poggendorff illusion. Clearly, if lines *A* and *B* were the leg and back support, respectively, of an overturned chair, they could never meet.

FIGURE 4.44

The Poggendorff Illusion

The illusion created in part a of this figure gives us the impression that if line A were extended it would pass below line B, when in fact they would meet. This illusion may result from our inclination to maintain shape constancy. For example, if lines A and B in part b were the back and leg support, respectively, of an overturned chair, they could never meet.

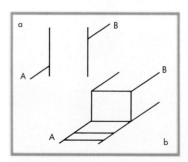

PERCEPTUAL SETS

In addition to the cues we have been discussing, our perceptions are also influenced by many subjective factors. Such factors include our tendency to see (or hear, smell, feel, or taste) what we expect or what is consistent with our preconceived notions of what makes sense.

This phenomenon is known as **perceptual set,** and it is illustrated in Figure 4.45. You can try this demonstration out on two friends. Show one friend picture *A* (keep *B* and *C* covered), and ask what is seen. The response will probably be an old woman. Then show picture *C* while covering *A* and *B*. Again, an old woman is likely to be seen. Next, repeat the procedure with a different friend, but this time start with picture *B* followed by *C*. In this situation, your friend is likely to report seeing a young woman in both pictures. The difference is explained by the fact that the particular image seen in picture *C* depends on the viewer's previous experience. Since the first friend was initially exposed to the picture of the old lady, he or she developed a perceptual set to see an old lady in picture *C*. In contrast, the second friend's perceptual set was geared toward seeing the youthful image in picture *B*.

Motivational state can also have a strong impact on how we perceive our environments, presumably by the mechanism of establishing perceptual sets. For example, if you drive down a main thoroughfare while feeling hunger pangs, you probably notice almost every sign advertising food. You may even misread signs so that an ad in the window of the local garden store seems to say steaks instead of stakes.

Another form of perceptual set is the tendency to perceive stimuli that are consistent with our expectations, and to ignore those that are inconsistent. This phenomenon is frequently referred to as **selective perception.** For example, if you believe that all neatly dressed elderly women are honest, you might not even think twice about the elderly woman at the next table when your wallet disappears in a restaurant, even if she is the most obvious suspect. Likewise, people who distrust groups of people because of their appearance, religion, or ethnic background are unlikely to recognize the good qualities of an individual who is a member of one of those groups. We're sure if you think about it for a while you can recognize instances where your behavior was influenced by a perceptual set of this sort.

In this chapter we examined the process of sensation where some aspect of the physical environment is transduced into neural activity. This neural activity is interpreted by the nervous system as either vision, audition, olfaction, gustation, or

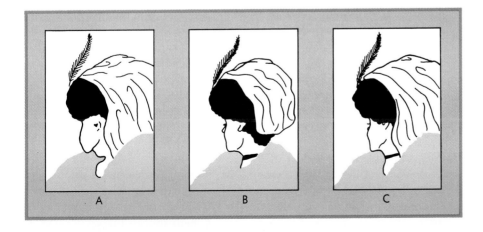

FIGURE 4.45
A Demonstration of Perceptual Set

one of the skin senses. The way we organize this information into useful representations of our environment was described as perceptual organization. We discussed a number of these organizational processes and showed how conflicting processing cues can lead to illusions. Although experience can clearly influence these organization processes, much of perceptual organization appears to be either innate or defined very early in development.

SUMMARY

PRINCIPLES OF SENSATION AND PERCEPTION

1. Sensations are basic, immediate experiences that a stimulus elicits in a sense organ. Perception refers to the process of interpreting, organizing, and elaborating on the raw materials of sensation.

2. The process by which sensory organs transform mechanical, chemical, or light energy into neural firing is called transduction.

3. The ability to distinguish sensations does not depend on differences between the sense organs, but rather on what part of the brain is activated by the sensory messages.

4. Many of the physical events surrounding us go unheeded. The most important variables determining whether or not we perceive things happening around us are sensory thresholds, attention, and adaptation.

5. Our perception of various sensory inputs can occur only when the strength of a stimulus reaches a minimal or threshold level of intensity sufficient to activate a sensory process. Weber's law describes the relationship between stimulus intensity and our perception of stimulus change.

6. Attention refers to the control of our behavior by specific stimuli or stimulus situations.

7. Adaptation refers to the decrease in the response of sensory receptors when they are exposed to continual, unchanging stimulation.

8. Signal detection theory maintains that our ability to detect a sensory stimulus (signal) depends not only on the intensity of the signal but also on other variables such as distracting factors like noise, expectations, motivation, and fatigue.

VISION

9. Our visual systems consist of three major parts: the eyes, which capture and respond to light energy; the neural circuits that transmit signals from the eye to the brain; and visual centers within the brain that interpret these messages.

10. Visible light, the stimulus for vision, has three particularly important properties: brightness, or the intensity of light; hue, or the color we perceive; and saturation, which is the proportion of colored light to noncolored light.

11. Two key components of the eye are the image-focusing part, consisting of the cornea, lens, iris, and pupil; and the image-recording part, called the retina.

12. The primary photoreceptor cells in the retina, the rods and cones, contain photopigments that respond to light. Our perception of color is largely dependent on the cones; the rods are extremely sensitive photoreceptors that allow us to see in dim light.

13. Two major theories of color vision have been proposed: the trichromatic theory and the opponent-process theory. Most vi-

sion experts believe that color vision may result from an interplay between a trichromatic system operating at the level of photoreceptor cells and an opponent-process mechanism working at later stages.

AUDITION

14. Most of the sounds we hear consist of physical energy in the form of rhythmic pressure changes in the air.
15. Three characteristics of sound waves that influence our perception of sound are loudness (amplitude), pitch (frequency), and timbre (a combination of a fundamental frequency and additional frequency components called overtones).
16. Auditory perception results when sound waves are converted into mechanical movement of the ossicles in the middle ear, which in turn act to produce pressure waves within the fluid of the inner ear that stimulate hair cells which transduce the physical energy of sound waves into neural impulses that our brains translate into sounds.
17. The best available evidence suggests that our perception of pitch is determined by both the place of maximal excitation on the basilar membrane and the frequency with which auditory nerve fibers fire.
18. Auditory localization is the result of differences in both the loudness and the time of arrival of sounds reaching each of our ears.
19. Hearing loss may result from either damage to the neural structures that transmit auditory messages to the brain (sensorineural hearing loss) or inability of the outer and middle ear to conduct sound energy to the receptors in the inner ear (conduction hearing loss).

GUSTATION AND OLFACTION

20. Our taste receptors, located on little bumps on the tongue called papillae, can distinguish only four different sensations: sweetness, saltiness, sourness, and bitterness.
21. The receptors for odors lie in the mucous membrane that lines the nasal cavity.

THE SKIN SENSES

22. The sense of touch is a composite of three different senses: pressure, temperature, and pain.
23. The sensation of pressure occurs when a mechanical force causes a displacement of the skin.
24. Different specialized dendrite endings respond to cold and heat.
25. Some pain researchers maintain that pain results from overstimulation of any sensory receptor; others believe that pain occurs when damaged tissue releases chemicals that stimulate specialized nerve endings in the skin.

KINESTHESIS AND EQUILIBRIUM

26. The two body senses of kinesthesis and equilibrium, working in concert, tell us the orientation of our bodies in space, the relative position of the various body parts, and the movement of any parts of the body.

PERCEIVING THE WORLD

27. The process by which we structure elementary sensations into the objects we perceive is called perceptual organization.
28. Three important principles that influence how people organize sensations into whole patterns, called Gestalts, are figure and ground, perceptual grouping, and closure.
29. Figure and ground refers to our tendency to differentiate between the part of an image we focus on (figure) and the background

against which the figure stands (ground).

30. According to the principle of perceptual grouping, we tend to group patterns of stimuli into larger units in three major ways: by proximity, similarity, and good continuation.

31. Another organizing principle is our inclination to perceive incomplete figures as complete, a process known as closure.

32. Selective attention refers to the process of focusing on one or a few stimuli of particular significance while ignoring others.

33. Characteristics of stimuli that tend to capture attention almost automatically include sudden change, contrast and novelty, intensity, repetition, and stimulus difficulty.

34. Key stimuli capture attention by activating motivational systems.

35. Binocular cues for perceiving distance include retinal disparity and convergence.

36. Important monocular cues for distance perception include height on a plane, interposition, linear perspective, relative size, texture gradients, aerial perspective, and relative motion.

37. According to Gibson's theory of direct perception, all of the information necessary for spatial representation is available to us from the environment in the form of environmental invariances. Other theories of perception argue that spacial representation requires complex cognitive processing of available stimuli.

38. Research has revealed that depth perception is clearly an innate ability in many species of animals, and that in humans it is either innate or is learned very early in life.

39. Perceptual constancy allows us to adjust for varying conditions and changing patterns as we perceive the world. When we look at objects at different distances and angles and under different levels of illumination, we are able to make the necessary adjustments to maintain a degree of constancy in our perception of size, shape, brightness, and color.

40. A perceptual illusion is a false perception in that it differs from the actual physical state of the perceived object.

41. A tendency to perceive what we expect or are inclined to see, a phenomenon known as perceptual set, may have a strong impact on how we perceive our environments.

TERMS & CONCEPTS

sensation
perception
transduction
psychophysics
threshold
absolute threshold
difference threshold
just noticeable difference (jnd)
Weber's law
attention
adaptation
signal detection theory
brightness
hue
saturation
accommodation
retina
rods

cones
lateral inhibition
dark adaptation
light adaptation
subtractive color mixing
additive color mixing
Young-Helmholtz theory
trichromatic theory of color vision
opponent-process theory of color vision
loudness
pitch
timbre
tympanic membrane
ossicles
cochlea
basilar membrane
organ of Corti

place theory of pitch discrimination
frequency theory of pitch
    discrimination
volley theory
auditory localization
sensorineural hearing loss
conduction hearing loss
gustation
olfaction
gate-control theory
substance P
endorphins
periaqueductal grey area
serotonin
body senses
kinesthesis
equilibrium
semicircular canals
vestibular sacs
perceptual organization
figure
ground
perceptual grouping
proximity
similarity
good continuation

closure
selective attention
key stimuli
binocular cues
monocular cues
binocular (retinal) disparity
convergence
height on a plane
overlap
linear perspective
relative size
texture gradients
aerial (atmospheric) perspective
relative motion (motion parallax)
Gibson's theory of direct perception
invariants
visual cliff
size constancy
perceptual constancy
brightness constancy
color constancy
shape constancy
illusion
perceptual set
selective perception

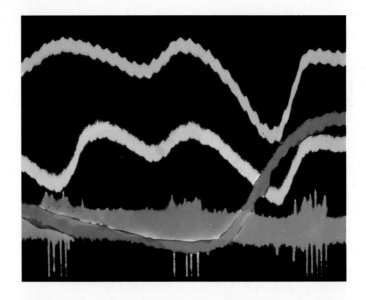

CHAPTER 5

Consciousness: Sleep, Dreaming, and Hypnosis

BIOLOGICAL RHYTHMS

Circadian Rhythms

THE SCIENCE OF SLEEP AND DREAMING

Stages of Sleep
The Sleep Cycle
Changes in Sleep Patterns with Age
Brain Mechanisms of Sleep
The Funciton of Sleep
Theories of Sleep Function
Dreaming
Theories of Dreaming

DISORDERS OF SLEEP

Insomnia
Sleep Apnea
Narcolepsy
Nightmares and Sleep Terrors
Sleepwalking
Sleeptalking

HYPNOSIS

Phenomena Associated with Hypnosis
Explaining Hypnosis

You are sitting in the library trying to concentrate on your studies, but just not attending to the words before you. Instead, your attention wanders to that gorgeous person in psychology class, and you begin to fantasize a situation in which you both feel drawn to each other. Then you are stopped short by the realization that that gorgeous person likes someone else, anyway. Speaking of psychology, you are behind in your homework. You again focus on your studies but it is only a moment before your attention wanders once more, this time to consider whether you should have something to eat. . . .

Sound familiar? If you are like most people, you spend a great deal of time making up fantasies and mulling over issues of similarly grandiose proportions. Such *daydreams* are mild shifts from a state of alertness, in which your thoughts move from external focal points to internal stimuli. When you day-dream, you create pictures in the "mind's eye" that are akin to waking dreams. Most of us spend a significant portion of our waking hours daydreaming (Singer, 1975, 1978), according to one study, about one-third of our time (Bartusiak, 1980). The viv-idness of daydreams waxes and wanes over a 90-minute cycle, with peak vividness occurring roughly every 90 minutes (Kripke & Sonnenschein, 1978).

Interestingly, this cycle is remarkably similar to the cycle of dreaming in our sleep. It is a natural variation in alertness that occurs without our attempting to regulate it and often without our even being aware that we are drifting in and out of daydreams. This chapter looks at variations in alertness, both in natural states, such as sleeping and dreaming, and states that are induced by hypnosis. Before we examine these states we will first examine their cyclic nature.

Most of us drift in and out of daydreams without being aware we are doing so. Studies indicate that we may spend up to one-third of our waking hours daydreaming.

BIOLOGICAL RHYTHMS

All biological systems (plants and animals) are influenced by cycles or **biological rhythms** of physiological activity. For instance, many plants are on annual rhythms of growth that are influenced by variations in the level of illumination. Behavior, body temperature, and other physiological processes of most animals vary on a 24-hour cycle that is also influenced by available illumination. When a cycle is approximately annual, like growth cycles in some plants, it is called a *circumannual cycle* (*circa* meaning about, *annual* year). Cycles that vary around a 24-hour period are referred to as circadian rhythms (*dia* meaning day).

CIRCADIAN RHYTHMS

Circadian rhythms are typically examined under conditions where illumination can be varied. For example, the activity of rats is on a circadian rhythm occurring primarily during the night. When maintained on a 12-hour light-on, 12-hour light-off cycle the activity of rats nicely conforms to a circadian pattern. If the 12-hour light on/off periods are shifted, activity also shifts to conform to the new day-night schedule. This can be seen on the activity chart in Figure 5.1a and 5.1b. On this chart each square across represent 30 minutes and each square down represents another 24-hour day.

When there is no day-night schedule and light is continually on, the activity of rats (and people) becomes free-running. That is, the activity cycles are no longer under the control of the light schedule but on the animal's own biological clock. Interestingly most biological clocks are not adjusted to 24-hours. As you can see

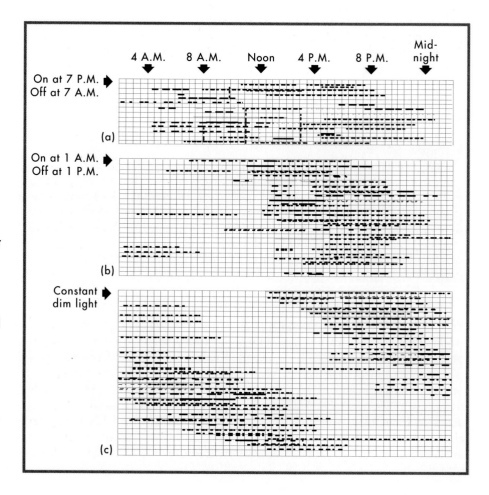

FIGURE 5.1

Records of Wheel-Running Activity of a Rat

In this figure each square across represents 30 minutes and each square down represents another 24-hour day. The dark marks represent activity. Note that most of the wheel-running activity occurs during the dark phase of a 12-hour light/dark cycle. In part a the dark phase is from 7 PM to 7 AM. In part b the dark phase was shifted from 1 AM to 1 PM. Note that the activity adjusts quickly to this new schedule. Under constant illumination in part c you can see that the activity becomes free-running. In rats, and people, the free-running clock runs about 1 hour slow each day (that is, the free-running clock is set for a 25-hour day). This is illustrated by the advancement of wheel running by about 1 hour (2 30-minute squares) each 24 hours.

in Figure 5.1c the animal's clock runs about 1 hour slow each day (it moves forward about 2 squares each 24-hours). Regular variations in daily illumination normally keep biological clocks adjusted to 24-hours much like a slow-running watch that is reset each day.

People exhibit circadian rhythms of activity as well. We normally begin to feel less active several hours after the onset of the dark part of our day/night cycle and most alert several hours after light onset. As with other animals without a light-dark schedule we also adjust to a 25-hour free-running clock. The implications of biological clocks for shift work and jet lag will be discussed later in this chapter.

Researchers have identified the **suprachiasmatic nucleus (SCN)** of the hypothalamus as the location of the biological clock (Moore and Eichler, 1972). The SCN is located on the floor of the hypothalamus just above the optic chiasm (the point where the optic tracts from each eye intersect). This location easily allows the SCN to "monitor" the activity of the visual system. During periods of illumination the optic tracts will be more active than during dark periods. Lesions of the SCN have been shown to disrupt circadian rhythms of activity and other physiological processes. These lesions also disrupt normal sleep/wake cycles but not the total amount of sleep during a 24-hour period.

THE SCIENCE OF SLEEP AND DREAMING

At least once every day, we experience a dramatic shift in consciousness when we go to sleep; we experience still another state of consciousness if we dream while sleeping. We spend roughly one-third of our lives sleeping, and the question of what happens when we sleep and dream has fascinated people for ages. As far back as 4,000 years ago Egyptians were interpreting dream symbols (a distant crowd, for example, was seen as a warning of death), and dream diaries existed long before the emergence of psychology as a science. Systematic sleep and dream research was not possible, however, until the technological breakthroughs of the past half century.

Sleep is a natural, periodically recurring state of rest characterized by reduced activity, lessened responsiveness to stimuli, and distinctive brain wave patterns. In 1937 Loomis, Harvey, and Hobart used the recently invented *electroencephalogram (EEG)* to demonstrate that brain waves change in form when a person shifts from a waking to a sleeping state. These researchers also observed further systematic changes in brain waves throughout the sleep period, a discovery which ultimately provided the basis for distinguishing between different stages of sleep.

REM AND NREM SLEEP   In the early 1950s, Eugene Aserinsky, a graduate student working with sleep researcher Nathaniel Kleitman at the University of Chicago, observed systematic changes in the eye movements of sleeping infants. He noted periods of sleep when the eyes moved very rapidly, followed by intervals of little or no eye movements. This observation provided the distinction between **REM** (rapid eye movement) and **NREM** (nonrapid eye movement) sleep. These researchers found that when adult subjects were awakened during REM sleep, they almost invariably reported dreaming, but that they rarely reported dreams when awakened after NREM sleep (Aserinsky & Kleitman, 1953; Dement & Kleitman, 1957).

STAGES OF SLEEP

Research since the 1950s has confirmed the connection between REM sleep and dreaming. However, we have also learned that dreaming is not limited to REM sleep and that REM is not synonymous with dreaming (Williamson et al., 1986). People awakened during REM sleep do not always report dreams. Likewise, people awakened from NREM sleep sometimes report having some kind of mental activity (such as a vague recall of some event), although they do not consistently label such activity dreaming (Herman et al., 1978; Webb, 1975). For this reason, it is difficult to estimate the exact proportion of NREM dreaming to REM dreaming. However, there is widespread agreement among sleep researchers that NREM sleep is considerably more dream-free than REM sleep and that dreams reported during REM sleep are usually much more vivid, tend to last longer, and are more visual than the thought-like processes that occur during NREM sleep (Foulkes & Schmidt, 1983).

Rapid eye movements have little if anything to do with dream content. For example, people who have been blind for over 50 years and cats raised in the dark who have never seen anything still show normal rapid eye movements during sleep (Webb & Bonnet, 1979). Some researchers believe that the rapid eye movements may be comparable to the occasional muscle twitches that occur during dreaming, in that both of these processes reflect a kind of overflow from a nervous system activated by dream activity. During REM sleep skeletal muscle activity is greatly suppressed leaving us relatively paralyzed.

Of course, our eyes are not the only part of our bodies to show activity as we sleep. During a night's sleep, body activity may vary from lying very still to thrashing and twisting in bed. In extreme cases, some people may talk in their sleep, sleepwalk, or have sleep terrors.

At what stage of sleep would you expect people to sleepwalk, talk, or have sleep terrors? You now know that dreams generally take place during REM sleep. Based on this information can you predict during which phase of the sleep cycle the greatest amount of body movements occur? Do you think sleepwalking is most likely to occur during REM sleep, or during one of the stages of NREM sleep?

It seems logical that sleepwalking and sleep terrors would take place when people dream, during REM sleep. When we are dreaming, our sympathetic nervous system causes an increase in breathing and heart rate as well as an elevation of blood pressure. Certain hormones associated with emergency situations may be released, and genital tissues may become engorged with blood, resulting in penile erection or vaginal lubrication. All of these signs of activation and arousal, together with brain waves similar to those of the waking state, suggest that the greatest amount of body movement should take place during REM sleep.

However, the true state of affairs is just the reverse. Typically, the only part of the body to move vigorously during dreams is the eyes. Muscular movement is inhibited during REM sleep by activity in a network of cells called the *pontine reticular formation*, located in the pons of the brain. When these cells become active, the body experiences a profound loss of muscle tone, making it almost impossible for a dreaming person to move. Thus sleepwalking and sleep terrors almost invariably occur during NREM sleep. One study of cats demonstrated the link between the pons and the loss of muscle tone during dreaming. When researchers destroyed a small portion of the region of the pons that produces *atonia* (loss of muscle tone), cats became very active during REM sleep (Morrison, 1983). Sometimes the inhibitory processes of REM sleep lessen for a moment. When this occurs, the nerve fibers in our muscles fire sporadically, resulting in jerks and twitches (Chase & Morales, 1983, 1990).

It seems puzzling that body movement is inhibited during periods of sleep when the eyes and brain are the most active. However, it is probably a good thing that our movements are inhibited when we dream. Can you imagine how battered and bruised we might be if we physically acted out all our dreams?

Recently, however, sleep researchers have discovered that some humans, when they enter REM sleep, thrash violently about, leap out of bed, and may even attack their bedpartners; they are not paralyzed during REM as most people are (Chase & Morales, 1990, p. 558). This recently recognized abnormality is called *REM Behavior Disorder* (Mahowald & Schenck, 1989). In an interesting court case a husband awoke to find that he had attacked and killed his wife while they both slept. His only (but successful) defense was that he recalled dreaming that he was being attacked and he fought back. Clearly more research on the relationship between dreaming, REM, and motor movement is needed.

MEASURING STAGES OF SLEEP   Further distinctions between various stages of sleep have been made possible by sophisticated measuring devices such as the EEG, the *electroculogram (EOG)*, which measures movements of the eye, and the *electromyograph (EMG)*, which measures electrical activity in the muscles. Figure 5.2 shows the left and right eye movements of a person during REM sleep, as measured by an EOG. Research using these and other devices has revealed systematic changes in brain wave patterns, muscular activity, levels of breathing, and heart rate during the course of a night's sleep. These measures have not only clarified the differences between REM and NREM sleep; they have also allowed researchers to identify four distinct stages of sleep in addition to REM sleep. Figure 5.3 (on page 172) demonstrates characteristic brain wave patterns of each of these stages as well as REM sleep and wakefulness.

CHARACTERISTICS OF WAKING AND SLEEPING STATES   When we are awake and alert, the EEG reveals low-amplitude, high-frequency waves called *beta waves*. (The two key characteristics of brain waves are their *amplitude*, or height, and

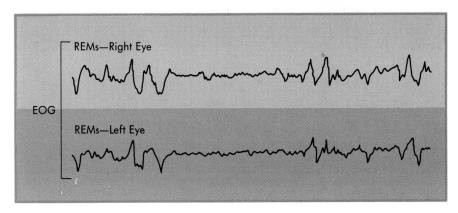

FIGURE 5.2
Electroculogram Recordings of Eye Movements During Sleep

This illustration shows the left and right eye movements of a person during REM sleep.

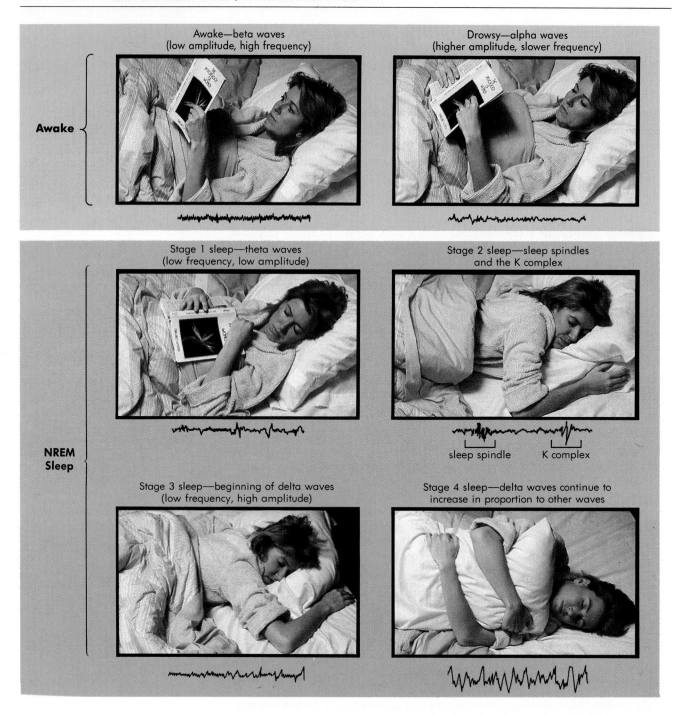

FIGURE 5.3
Different Stages of Sleep and Characteristic Brain Patterns

their *frequency*, measured in cycles per second.) When we are relaxed and drowsy, just before falling asleep, our brain waves show an *alpha* rhythm of higher amplitude and slower frequency (8 to 12 cycles per second). In this drowsy state, breathing and heart rate also slow down, body temperature drops, and muscles relax. The different brain waves associated with different states of arousal are shown in Figure 5.3.

Stage 1 The light sleep that occurs just after dozing off is known as **Stage 1 sleep.** It is characterized by low-frequency (3 to 7 cycles per second), low-amplitude brain waves called *theta waves.* Stage 1 sleep may be accompanied by some

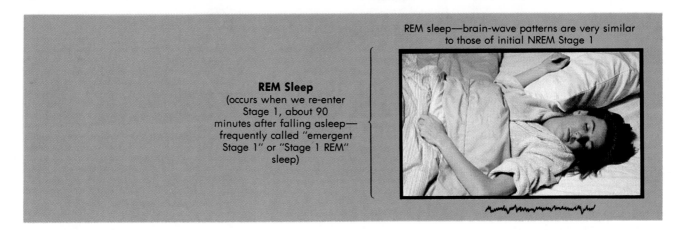

REM sleep—brain-wave patterns are very similar to those of initial NREM Stage 1

REM Sleep
(occurs when we re-enter Stage 1, about 90 minutes after falling asleep—frequently called "emergent Stage 1" or "Stage 1 REM" sleep)

slow eye movements, irregular breathing, and muscle relaxation. People are easily awakened during Stage 1 sleep and often they do not realize they have been sleeping. This stage typically lasts from about one to ten minutes.

Stage 2 After a period of Stage 1 sleep we gradually drift into the deeper **Stage 2 sleep,** characterized by brief bursts of brain activity called *sleep spindles* (12 to 14 cycles per second) as well as another brain wave pattern called the *K complex,* a low-frequency, high-amplitude wave that occurs in response to either an external stimulus, such as the sound of a voice, or an internal stimulus such as stomach cramps. Eye movements are minimal during Stage 2 sleep, and muscular activity often decreases to an even lower level.

Stage 3 About 30 to 45 minutes after falling asleep the cycle progresses into an even deeper level of sleep, there is a gradual increase in the incidence of low-frequency (0.5 to 2 cycles per second), high-amplitude *delta waves.* When these waves account for 20 percent to 50 percent of the EEG tracing, a person is in **Stage 3 sleep.**

Stage 4 As sleep continues, delta waves continue to increase in proportion to other brain waves. When they exceed 50 percent, a person is said to be in **Stage 4 sleep,** the deepest level of sleep. It is difficult to arouse a person from Stage 4 sleep. If your alarm clock rings at this point, you will probably be disoriented and confused when you awaken. During Stages 3 and 4 there are virtually no eye movements and the EEG patterns become much more synchronized.

FIGURE 5.3 (continued)
Different Stages of Sleep and Characteristic Brain Patterns

THE SLEEP CYCLE

It takes roughly 45 minutes to reach Stage 4 sleep after first dozing off. People typically remain in Stage 4 for about 30 to 40 minutes, then return gradually through Stages 3 and 2 to Stage 1 again. The first period of REM sleep occurs when we reenter Stage 1, about 90 minutes after falling asleep. During this period, which is frequently called emergent Stage 1 or Stage 1 REM sleep, brain wave patterns are very similar to those of the initial NREM Stage 1, with the exception that "sawtooth"-like waves are present.

In a night's sleep, we move through successive cycles, drifting up and down between the various phases of REM and NREM sleep. These cycles last about 90 minutes, and we generally complete about five of them during the course of a night. The first episode of REM sleep may last only 5 to 10 minutes. However, with each subsequent cycle, the REM periods become progressively longer and deep sleep stages become shorter (Lavie, 1987). In later cycles, we may go only

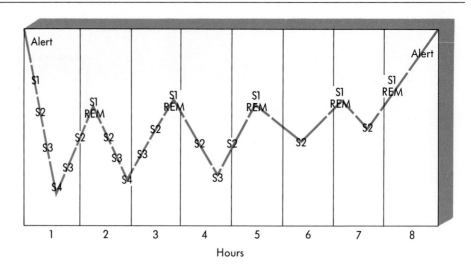

FIGURE 5.4

Typical Sequence of Sleep Stages

Sleep grows progressively less deep throughout the sleep cycle and REM periods tend to lengthen throughout the night. S1 refers to Stage 1.

to Stage 2 and then back to REM. The final episodes of REM sleep before awakening may last 45 minutes or more. Figure 5.4 demonstrates the typical sequence of sleep stages.

CHANGE IN SLEEP PATTERNS WITH AGE

Sleep patterns are not stable throughout our lives. The percentage of the night's sleep that is spent in an REM state decreases throughout the life cycle. Newborn babies may sleep an average of 16 hours per day, with roughly 50 percent of that time spent in REM sleep. Adults in their twenties sleep about eight hours, of which about 20 percent is REM sleep. Throughout middle age, there is further decline in both the time spent sleeping and the proportion of sleep spent in the REM phase, until at the age of 60 to 70, a person is likely to sleep only about six hours and be in an REM phase only 15 percent (approximately 1 hour) of this time.

The amount of time spent in Stage 4 sleep also changes with age, so that by the time we are in our sixties, deep sleep (Stage 4) is likely to disappear altogether. As a consequence, older people are more easily awakened. It is not uncommon for people who were sound sleepers throughout most of their lives to find that in old age they awaken five or six times during a typical night.

Different animals also appear to require different amounts of sleep. Figure 5.5 compares the duration of sleep for several species of animals.

BRAIN MECHANISMS OF SLEEP

Figure 5.6 shows the major brain areas involved in sleep and wakefulness. The **reticular activating system (RAS)** is a pathway of neurons which originate in the medulla and extend to the cortex. This system is primarily responsible for our awakened state. The RAS is activated by any sensory input but it also generates its own activity. When the RAS is activated it increases our alertness and level of arousal. Damage to the RAS can lead to a marked lack of activity and an increase in sleep. On the other hand, electrical stimulation of the RAS increases arousal and will awaken a sleeping animal.

Another brain area involved in sleep is the **raphe system.** This pathway originates below the RAS in the brainstem and ascends through the pons and the medulla to the midbrain. The raphe system becomes most active at the time of sleep onset. This increase in raphe system activity acts to inhibit the RAS, thus decreasing arousal and promoting sleep onset. In experimental animals electrical stimulation of the raphe system can induce sleep while damage to this system greatly reduces sleep.

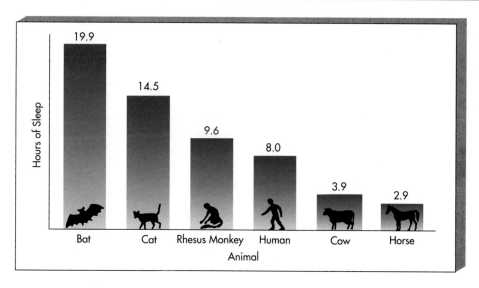

FIGURE 5.5

Comparison of Sleep Duration for Different Animals

NEUROTRANSMITTERS AND SLEEP The primary neurotransmitter of the RAS is norepinephrine. And, as you might expect, drugs that increase the activity of these norepinephrine neurons, such as amphetamine, increase alertness and activity. Drugs, or our diet, can also act to promote sleep by increasing levels of the neurotransmitter serotonin which is the major neurotransmitter in the raphe system. In fact, meals rich in carbohydrate lead to increases in serotonin levels by indirectly increasing blood levels of tryptophan, which is necessary for serotonin production (Wurtman, 1983). This partially explains why people often get sleepy after meals.

Although serotonin is believed to be involved in sleep onset, its role in maintaining sleep and dreaming is less certain. Other hormones and neurotransmitters are probably involved to a greater extent once sleep is initiated. In fact, the

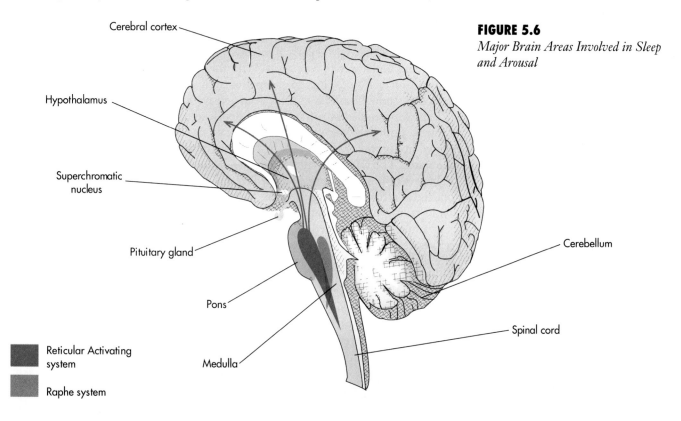

FIGURE 5.6

Major Brain Areas Involved in Sleep and Arousal

neurotransmitter acetylcholine is believed to be directly involved in dreaming and REM sleep. Injections of acetylcholine into the pons of animals can cause REM sleep leading to the remark that "Acetylcholine is the stuff of which dreams are made" (Palca, 1989).

THE FUNCTION OF SLEEP

IS SLEEP NECESSARY? In a widely reported personal experiment in 1959, New York disc jockey Peter Tripp staged a wakeathon, remaining awake for 200 hours. It was not easy. Halfway through his wakeathon, he began to hallucinate. His ability to think and reason deteriorated dramatically, and by the end of his ordeal he was unable to distinguish between fact and fantasy. He also became increasingly paranoid. At one point, Tripp was convinced that a physician who had arrived to examine him was planning to haul him off to jail (Luce, 1965).

SLEEP DEPRIVATION STUDIES Peter Tripp's experience, though fascinating, is of limited scientific value because it took place in an uncontrolled environment. Several subsequent studies have been carefully controlled, and they provide more reliable findings. In one experiment, for instance, six volunteers were deprived of sleep for 205 consecutive hours (Kales et al., 1970). By the end of the third day, subjects were hallucinating and experiencing delusions (false or distorted beliefs). They also developed hand tremors, double vision, and reduced pain thresholds. Their reflexes were largely unimpaired, however, and physiological functions such as heart rate, respiration, blood pressure, and body temperature showed little change from normal throughout the course of the experiment. After the experiment was over, no long-term effects were evident. Subjects slept a few days, then awoke feeling fine.

In another experiment conducted by famed sleep researcher William Dement (1972), a 17-year-old subject stayed awake for 268 consecutive hours, after which he needed only 14 hours of sleep to recover to a normal state. In contrast to Peter Tripp, this young man remained lucid and coherent throughout his vigil.

Findings such as these caused some researchers to question the importance of sleeping in our lives. A few even speculated that people might learn to get by without any sleep, particularly if scientists could isolate the factor that makes us sleepy and find a way to counter it. With this idea in mind, a team of researchers at the University of Chicago Sleep Research Laboratory devised an ingenious device to study the effects of total sleep deprivation in rats.

Rats were studied in pairs: One was deprived of sleep, and the other acted as a control. Both rats were placed on a plastic disk located above a water pan, as shown in Figure 5.7. If the disk rotated, the rats had to walk to avoid falling into the water. The rats were connected to an EEG that monitored their brain waves. Whenever the sleep-deprived rat fell asleep, the EEG registered the changes and opened a circuit, causing the disk to rotate. Both rats would have to walk to avoid falling into the water. The control rat could sleep when his counterpart was awake, but the sleep-deprived rat was jarred awake at each lapse of consciousness. The sleep-deprived rats lasted as long as 33 days, but they all eventually died. In contrast, all the control animals survived, apparently no worse for the experience (Rechtschaffen et al., 1983). A more recent experiment by researchers in the same laboratory, using the same research design and apparatus, reported similar results. All 10 of the totally sleep-deprived rats in this study died within 11 to 32 days, whereas all paired controls survived (Everson et al., 1989).

In both of these experiments, the University of Chicago scientists were unable to determine the precise cause of death. A variety of sleep deprivation effects were observed prior to death, including a progressively scrawny appearance, skin ulcers, increased food intake, weight loss, an increase in energy expenditure, a

This scene from the film They Shoot Horses, Don't They? *depicts a dance marathon popular in the 1930s and 1940s, where contestants who danced the longest won prizes. Prolonged periods of sleep deprivation can produce hallucinations and delusions.*

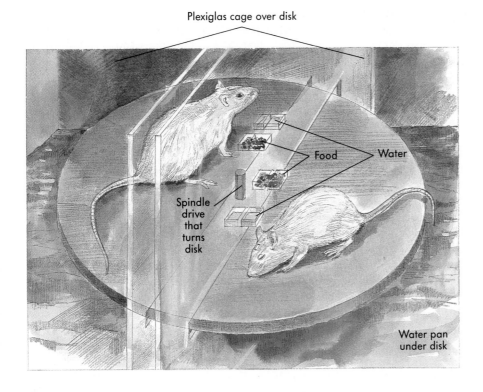

Plexiglas cage over disk

Food   Water

Spindle drive that turns disk

Water pan under disk

FIGURE 5.7

Experimental Apparatus for Producing Sleep Deprivation in Animals

Rats are placed on the disk located above a tub of water. As the disk rotates, the animals must keep moving to avoid being pushed into the water by the plastic divider. Brain waves of the animals are constantly recorded by an EEG. Whenever the sleep-deprived rat falls asleep the monitor activates a motor to rotate the disk. The control animal is allowed to sleep while the experimental animal is awake. The sleep-deprived animal can never sleep.

decrease in body temperature, and shifts in levels of the hormones nor-epinephrine (increase) and thyroxine (decrease). These physiological correlates of prolonged total sleep deprivation constitute a reliable syndrome indicative of the importance of sleep, at least for rats. However, the University of Chicago researchers recently observed that "The significance of this syndrome for the function of sleep is not entirely clear, but several changes suggested that sleep may be necessary for effective thermoregulation" [heat regulation] (Rechtschaffen et al., 1989, p. 68). Hopefully, further research will clarify the nature of the factor(s) underlying sleep deprivation effects in rats.

The few studies of sleep-deprived humans have not revealed the syndrome of severe physiological effects, including death, observed in studies of total sleep deprivation in rats. However, Allan Rechtschaffen and his colleagues maintain that humans have not been subjected to total sleep deprivation anywhere near long enough to show the severe physiological effects observed in rats (1989, p. 80). Understandably, researchers might be quite reluctant to subject humans to significantly lengthened periods of total sleep deprivation.

From the studies just described, it seems evident that sleep is necessary, but why it is necessary is not clear. A number of theories have been suggested to explain why we need sleep. However, none of them have become widely accepted by psychologists.

**THEORIES OF
SLEEP FUNCTION**

SLEEPING TO CONSERVE ENERGY   One explanation for why we sleep roughly one-third of every 24-hour period is that sleep conserves energy, thus preventing exhaustion. We burn more calories while awake than asleep. Perhaps in our evolutionary history, when food resources were limited, sleeping eight hours a day may have been a helpful mechanism for limiting the use of scarce energy resources.

SLEEPING TO AVOID PREDATION A related theory argues that sleeping enhances survival by prohibiting animals from interacting with their environment during times when they are not physiologically suited to function adaptively. For example, prehistoric man adapted to sleeping at night because night vision was poor relative to his predators, like the saber-toothed tiger. Grazing animals sleep only two to four hours per day presumably because they need to spend considerably more time foraging.

SLEEPING TO RESTORE DEPLETED RESOURCES According to this theory, sleep restores resources that we deplete in our daily activities. This explanation is supported by studies showing that people often sleep longer after particularly tiring events. In one study, for example, human subjects' sleep was monitored after they ran a 57-mile race. Not only did they sleep longer than normal, but their sleep also contained an unusual amount of deep, Stage 4 sleep (Shapiro et al., 1981).

We still do not know exactly what restorative processes occur during sleep, or what (if any) kinds of physiological processes or energy sources are depleted when we are awake. There is tentative evidence that certain kinds of tissue restoration, such as cell repair, may occur during sleep (Adams & Oswald, 1977). Growth hormone, which promotes tissue growth, is secreted at higher levels in Stage 4 sleep. Some researchers also believe that certain brain chemicals such as neurotransmitters are restored during sleep and that the amount of sleep we need is related to the levels of these chemicals that are present when we fall asleep. This condition may be genetically influenced (Hartmann, 1973; Webb & Campbell, 1983).

SLEEPING TO CLEAR THE MIND Another explanation, proposed by Francis Crick and Graeme Mitchison (1983), suggests that people sleep to clear their minds. According to this theory, our brains accumulate a great deal of extraneous, largely useless information during the course of each day. If these varied memories and associations were allowed to remain, they would clutter our brains, interfering with the learning and recall of new information. Crick and Mitchison suggest that the heightened electrical activity typical of REM sleep acts as an eraser, wiping away this extraneous information and leaving the brain more receptive to new learning.

SLEEPING TO CONSOLIDATE MEMORY An alternative to this idea is the suggestion that sleep aids in memory consolidation. It is well-known that information learned prior to sleep is better remembered than if sleep did not occur. For example, animals demonstrate better retention of a learned task if REM sleep is allowed to occur and poor retention when REM sleep is prevented (Bloch, Hennivan, & Leconte, 1977). In a more recent study Avi Karni (1992) trained people to recognize patterns portrayed on a computer screen before going to sleep. Karni found that people's performance on a pattern recognition task was poorer if they were awakened during REM sleep than if they were awakened during non-REM sleep. These studies suggest that sleep (at least REM) may promote the storage of newly learned information. Perhaps you could use this to your advantage by studying psychology just before you sleep as opposed to just after waking!

SLEEPING TO DREAM Finally, it has been proposed that people sleep so that they can dream. Although a few people claim they never dream, virtually every subject ever studied has reported dreams when awakened during REM sleep. The fact that we all dream suggests that dreaming serves some important function in life. Perhaps we need to dream during the course of a night's sleep. In the next section we will examine dreaming.

In conclusion, there is no definite answer to the question of why we sleep. In the end the answer may turn out to be quite simple as some of these theories suggest, or it may be of tremendous significance that we will only appreciate once we are closer to a complete answer.

What is the function of dreaming? How many times per night do we dream? Is the content of a dream significant? Do animals dream? What happens when people are permitted to sleep but not to dream? Answers to some of these questions have been sought by depriving people of REM sleep and observing changes in their well-being and behavior.

DREAMING

REM DEPRIVATION STUDIES Experiments designed by William Dement have attempted to answer these questions. In a study conducted in 1960 Dement used both an EEG and an EOG to register the beginning of REM sleep. For seven consecutive nights, human subjects were permitted to sleep during other stages but were awakened as soon as they entered REM sleep. The total amount of REM sleep they could experience was reduced by about 75 percent. In contrast, a control group was awakened the same number of times as the REM-deprived subjects, but only during NREM sleep. Both groups were monitored throughout the course of the experiment.

REM-deprived subjects demonstrated a number of effects not shown by the control group. They became increasingly irritable, anxious, hostile, and aggressive as the experiment progressed; they also had trouble concentrating on tasks. In addition, they showed signs of being REM-starved, entering REM sleep almost as soon as they dozed off, so that over the course of the one-week experiment, Dement found it more and more difficult to prevent REM sleep. On the first night, subjects had to be awakened an average of 12 times. By the seventh night, this figure had more than doubled to an average of 26 awakenings. When Dement's subjects were allowed to sleep without interruption on the eighth night, most (but not all) showed an REM rebound effect, spending about 50 percent more time in REM than they had prior to the onset of the experiment. This REM rebound effect has recently been shown to occur immediately after a period of forced wakefulness during a night's sleep. Subjects who were awakened and asked to sit quietly in an illuminated room for varying periods of time demonstrated a marked increase in the length of their first and second REM episodes after returning to sleep (Campbell, 1987).

Such results have been interpreted as supporting the theory that we sleep to dream, and Dement's findings have been cited by some psychologists as evidence that REM deprivation can produce severe emotional consequences. To investigate this possibility further, researchers turned to animal studies, with mixed results.

In one study, rats were placed on tiny platforms over water where the only possible way to sleep was standing up (Morden et al., 1967). The rats were able to experience NREM sleep because their muscle tone allowed them to sleep standing up. Recall, however, that muscle tone is lost when REM begins. Thus whenever REM sleep began, the rat's legs would collapse, toppling it into the water. What happened to these rats? Contrary to what we might expect based on Dement's earlier findings, the REM-deprived rats did not show any significant behavioral or emotional difficulties.

Other research has reported quite different results. In one recent study at the University of Chicago Sleep Laboratory, 12 rats were deprived of REM sleep using a disk apparatus similar to that shown in Figure 5.7. Whenever one of these rats entered the forbidden REM stage of sleep, the disk rotated, thus forcing the animal to walk to avoid falling into the water. In contrast, a paired control group of rats was permitted to sleep during any of the four stages. While the rats in the control group survived with no sign of debilitation, all 12 rats assigned to the REM deprivation condition died (or were sacrificed when death seemed imminent) within 16 to 54 days. An exact cause of death could not be pinpointed, but it was noted that all of the REM-deprived rats exhibited the same syndrome of physiological effects outlined in our earlier discussion of total sleep deprivation in rats (Kushida et al., 1989).

Not surprisingly, this research model has not been used on humans. However, some studies have been able to test the effects of REM deprivation by using drugs that prevent REM sleep. Two extensive reviews of the literature (Vogel, 1975; Webb, 1975) revealed no serious emotional or behavioral consequences associated with lack of REM sleep, although some evidence suggests that REM-deprived subjects may have difficulty learning complex things (Greenberg & Pearlman, 1974; Webb & Bonnet, 1979). Other than consistent evidence for the REM rebound effect, researchers have not found support for the claim that REM deprivation might threaten a person's emotional or physical health. However, sleep researcher Allan Rechtschaffen and his colleagues (1989) note that 16 nights, which was the longest period of REM deprivation studied in people, would be unlikely to produce signs of physiological deterioration based on the length of deprivation used in rat studies.

DO ANIMALS DREAM?   Perhaps you've wondered whether your pet dog or cat was actually dreaming as it jerked about during its sleep. The fact is, REM sleep has been recorded in all mammals studied as well as several species of birds (cf., Anch, Browman, Mitler, & Walsh, 1988). In fact, there is good evidence that REM sleep in animals corresponds with dreaming. Recall the cats with lesions in the pons which prevented the normal motor inhibition which occurs during REM sleep? These cats were observed to stalk and attack nonexistent objects during REM sleep. Perhaps we will never know for sure whether animals dream during REM sleep, but these and other observations make it seem quite possible. Keep these observations in mind as you consider the following theories of dreaming.

THEORIES OF DREAMING

Regardless of whether dreaming is necessary or not, the fact still remains that we spend roughly one and one-half hours dreaming each night.

A number of theories attempt to explain dreaming. However, it is possible that dreaming has more than one cause; thus several of the following viewpoints may be necessary to explain it. Note, however, that to date none of these theoretical explanations of why we dream has been conclusively confirmed or disconfirmed by research.

DREAMING AS THE BRAIN'S EXPLANATION FOR STIMULI   One theory, proposed by Allan Hobson and Robert McCarley, suggests that dreams are the brain's attempt to make sense out of random bursts of neuronal activity. Studies of REM sleep in cats indicate that certain cells in the brain stem region of the reticular formation produce random spikes of electrical activity during REM sleep, and that this activity arouses adjacent neurons that influence eye movements, balance, and actions such as walking and running (Hobson, 1989; Hobson & McCarley, 1977). Although most of these body movements are blocked during REM sleep, these cells still send signals to higher cortical centers. The brain has to reconcile the inconsistency between signals that indicate movement and the fact that the body is still. To accomplish this task, it searches through its existing file of memories and manufactures a dream. Dreams are thus the brain's solution to an absence of logical connections in the stimuli reaching the cortex.

This theory is known as the *activation-synthesis hypothesis*, and it seems to fit many common dreaming experiences. Thus dreams of falling, flying, or floating might be the brain's interpretation of messages from cells involved in balance; sexual dreams might reflect an effort to fit a logical explanation to physiological arousal of the genital tissues. Table 5.1 lists the most common dream experiences of college students. You might see how many of these can be explained by the activation-synthesis hypothesis.

DREAMING AS MENTAL REPROGRAMMING   Another theory explains dreams as a form of mental reprogramming in which the brain reorganizes its memory systems to accommodate new information. From this perspective, the REM sleep of humans and other animals should increase following activities requiring unusual mental efforts.

A number of studies have supported this theory. In one experiment awake subjects wore special lenses so that they saw things upside down, a situation that demands great mental adjustments. When they slept following this experience, they spent more time in REM sleep (Zimmerman et al., 1970). Subjects in other experiments who have worn lenses that severely distort the visual field have also shown increased REM sleep (Herman & Roffwarg, 1983). And in still other experiments, subjects asked to perform particularly complex or frustrating tasks have been shown to spend more time in REM sleep (Lewin & Gambosh, 1973;

TABLE 5.1 *A Sample of the 20 Most Common Dreams of College Students*

TYPE OF DREAM	PERCENTAGE OF STUDENTS
Falling	83
Being attacked or pursued	77
Trying repeatedly to do something	71
School, teachers, studying	71
Sexual experiences	66
Arriving too late	64
Eating	62
Being frozen with fright	58
A loved person is dead	57
Being locked up	56
Finding money	56
Swimming	52
Snakes	49
Being dressed inappropriately	46
Being smothered	44
Being nude in public	43
Fire	41
Failing an examination	39
Flying	34
Seeing self as dead	33

SOURCE: From Griffith, Miyago, & Tago, 1958.

McGrath & Cohen, 1978). Even rats exposed to new learning show increased REM sleep (Leconte et al., 1972), and kittens and rats placed in stimulating environments spend more time in REM sleep than control animals in sterile environments (McGinty, 1969).

The fact that older people spend less time in REM sleep seems to fit in nicely with this mental reprogramming viewpoint. Presumably, as people grow older, they assimilate less new information. This theory also seems consistent with the experience of many college students who report that they dream more after a marathon study session.

DREAMING FOR PROBLEM RESOLUTION   A third explanation sees dreams as a relatively safe, low-stress way to deal with problems that occur during waking hours. To test this theory, dream researcher Rosalind Cartwright (1978) presented student subjects with stories about common problems faced by young adults, none of which included a solution. The subjects then spent the night in a laboratory where their sleep was monitored; some were allowed to dream and others were not. In the morning, subjects who had dreamed were able to suggest more realistic solutions to the problems than those who had not been permitted to dream. This finding suggests that dreams may well help people resolve problems that occur when they are awake, an explanation that is supported further by evidence that people spend more time in REM sleep when they are experiencing relationship conflicts, problems at work, or other emotionally stressful events (Hartmann, 1973; Monroe, 1967).

DREAMS AS EXPRESSIONS OF THE UNCONSCIOUS   A final theory of why we dream was proposed almost a century ago by Sigmund Freud. In his classic book *Interpretation of Dreams* (1900), Freud called dreams the royal road to the unconscious and dream content and interpretation played a major role in the development of his theories. According to Freud, the content of a dream is coded by symbolic processes which represent wishes or desires that become fulfilled by the dream. That is, dreams are disguised expressions of wishes that have been repressed. For example, a person who is sexually frustrated might dream repeatedly about sexual themes. Freud noted that these dreams might not seem to be sexual to the untrained observer, however. The reason for this discrepancy is that we recall only the manifest content of our dreams. The **manifest content** is a disguised version of the **latent** (hidden) **content,** which is the true meaning of our dreams. Thus a train passing through a tunnel in a dream might be the manifest representation of a penis entering a vagina. If the person having this dream also reported other dreams in which umbrellas, rifles, or swords (all representing the male organ) and boxes, chests, and ovens (female representations) appeared, Freud would be convinced that the dreams expressed a sexual conflict.

Why do we dream about manifest representations instead of the real thing? Freud believed that if people expressed their true desires directly in dreams, the result would be such startling, upsetting dreams that they would awaken immediately. Thus our unconscious mind expresses our deep-seated wishes symbolically to ensure a good night's sleep.

Freud saw dreams as a mechanism to discharge libidinous energy stored in the *id*. The *id*, according to Freud, was the biological component of personality consisting of life and death instincts. During wakefulness the expression of the id's wishes are constrained by the *superego*, an individual's conscience. However, during dreaming the wishes of the id are left unrestrained and may be expressed symbolically. People often either forget their dreams or they are remembered only incompletely because they are selectively forgotten as a protective cover-up by the ego. The ego functions as a protective intermediary between the wishes of the id and the reality of the real world.

DISORDERS OF SLEEP

It's now 2:00 A.M. and you haven't been able to fall asleep even though you're exhausted. By 3:00 A.M. you still haven't slept and all you seem to be able to think about is your midterm exam in psychology at nine o'clock. At four o'clock you realize that you dozed off briefly but now you're pondering your decision to trade in your old car for a newer one. Can you really afford the higher payments?

This occasional pattern of sleeplessness is quite common. However, a sizable minority (perhaps one in five adults) find little comfort in the night. These children and adults suffer from a variety of **sleep disorders** including insomnia, sleep apnea, sleep terrors and nightmares, and sleepwalking.

INSOMNIA

People with **insomnia** have difficulty going to sleep. Less commonly, they may experience frequent awakenings. Figures released in the early 1980s by the U.S. Department of Health and Human Services suggest that approximately 25 million Americans are insomniacs; approximately twice as many women as men seem to be affected (Cirignotta et al., 1985; Kripke & Simons, 1976).

Insomnia may have a variety of causes, including stressful events, health problems, emotional disturbances, and drug use. The most common form of insomnia, *temporary* or *situational insomnia*, is related to stress associated with a particular situation—loss of a job, death or illness of a loved one, a relationship that falls apart, and so on. Such events cause stress or worry that may produce heightened physical arousal, which inhibits sleep. Stress may be the most common cause of sleep loss among college students, who have been found to experience marked reductions in sleep during periods of high stress (Hicks & Garcia, 1987).

People who suffer from long-lasting sleep loss, or *chronic insomnia*, are more likely to report a serious erosion of the quality of their lives. Although we are not sure exactly what causes chronic insomnia, this condition seems to be associated with anxiety or depression (Kales et al., 1976; Nicassio et al., 1985). Some chronic insomniacs have been found to have irregular sleep patterns (Monroe, 1967).

Sleeping potions (benzodiazapines or barbiturates) may be prescribed to relieve insomnia (Declerck et al., 1992). These drugs may be helpful in small doses for a brief period. However, they often have an effect that is just the opposite of that desired. Sleeping potions erode the quality of sleep by reducing the amount of REM sleep and Stage 4 sleep. In addition, people quickly develop a tolerance to these drugs, requiring ever-increasing dosages to produce a sedative effect. The result is a kind of drug dependence insomnia. Nonprescription, over-the-counter drugs are not the answer either, for they have little or no sleep-inducing capability. People who find these substances helpful are probably demonstrating a placebo effect, experiencing relief simply because they believe the drugs work (Webb & Bonnet, 1979).

Because drugs tend to be ineffective at best and potentially dangerous, psychologists have emphasized stress reduction techniques as alternatives for the management of insomnia. Stress reduction techniques probably work because they refocus attention away from stressful events or problems allowing one to fall asleep, as opposed to inducing sleep, as do medications (Gustafson, 1992). Refer to the *Health, Psychology and Life* segment at the end of this chapter for additional suggestions for overcoming insomnia.

SLEEP APNEA

A second sleep disorder is a disturbing condition known as **sleep apnea.** People with this disorder do not breathe regularly during sleep. In fact, their breathing actually stops for as long as a few seconds to a minute or two (Brouilette et al., 1982; Guilleminault & Dement, 1978; Hall, 1986). As the need for oxygen becomes acute, the person briefly awakens, gulps in air, and then settles back to sleep, only to repeat the cycle when breathing stops again. A person with this disorder is unlikely to be aware that he or she wakes up to breathe as often as several hundred times a night. In one extreme case, a man monitored in the sleep laboratory could not sleep and breathe at the same time. Fortunately, most cases are not so severe. It has been estimated that about 5 percent of the general population and as many as one out of 10 men over age 40 have this disorder (Raymond, 1986). Sleep apnea in old age may be even more common, perhaps occurring in as many as one-third of elderly people (Berry & Philips, 1988).

Sleep apnea seems to occur when the brain stops sending signals that trigger the breathing response. It may also be caused by a blockage in the upper air passage. (Some apnea victims are older, obese men whose airways may become blocked by their overly thick necks.) Some researchers believe that sleep apnea may be one cause of *sudden infant death syndrome (SIDS)*, commonly called crib death. There is speculation that immature breathing centers in the brain stem malfunction, causing susceptible infants to stop breathing (Hales, 1980).

Extreme cases of apnea may be relieved by a *tracheostomy*, an operation in which a valve is surgically inserted into the throat. In recent years, medical researchers have developed a nonsurgical approach to treating severe sleep apnea in which a continuous flow of air is applied to the nostrils through a nose mask. This technique, called *nasal continuous positive airway pressure (nCPAP)*, is now often the treatment of choice for this disorder (Aubert-Tulkens et al., 1989; Miller, 1986).

NARCOLEPSY

A peculiar sleep disorder called narcolepsy manifests itself as uncontrollable sleep attacks in which a person falls asleep suddenly, perhaps while talking, standing, or driving. The attack may last only a few minutes, or it may last half an hour or more. EEG monitoring reveals that these sleep attacks involve the immediate onset of REM sleep. Since REM sleep produces a loss of muscle tone, most victims collapse the moment they lapse into sleep. For this reason, narcoleptic attacks can endanger a person's life, particularly if they occur while driving or operating dangerous machinery.

One of the authors knew a student who displayed narcoleptic attacks prior to or during examinations. This student would suddenly slump off to sleep while sitting, only to awaken after he hit the floor. Although we still don't know why narcolepsy occurs, the fact that many narcoleptics seem most likely to have sleep attacks during periods of high anxiety or tension suggests that narcolepsy may be some kind of reaction to stress. However, many researchers link narcolepsy to an inherited abnormality in the brain mechanisms that control sleep and waking (Douglass et al., 1989). This deficiency may involve inadequate production of the neurotransmitter dopamine, which is believed to play a role in arousal (Mefford et al., 1983). Recent research has also linked structural brain abnormalities with this condition (Erlich & Itabashi, 1986). Although physicians sometimes prescribe stimulant drugs to reduce the frequency of sleep attacks, there is no effective treatment yet (Burton, 1989).

NIGHTMARES AND SLEEP TERRORS

A **nightmare** is a bad dream that occurs during REM sleep (Kellerman, 1987; Pagel, 1989). Nightmares typically leave a strong impression on the dreamer; people often awaken after a nightmare with vivid recall of the dream. Sometimes nightmares are repetitive. Many dream theorists believe that repetitive nightmares may reflect areas of conflict or sources of emotional turmoil in a person's waking life. Some research suggests that people who have frequent nightmares tend to be sensitive and open persons with creative interests and greater than normal tendencies to exhibit symptoms of psychological disorder (Belicki & Belicki, 1982; Hartmann et al., 1981, 1987; Pagel, 1989). However, recent research conducted by University of Arizona psychologists James Wood and Richard Bootzin (1990) calls this interpretation into question. These researchers had 220 college undergraduate students fill out questionnaires assessing their anxiety and artistic creativity. The subjects were then instructed to keep dream logs for two-week periods in which they recorded nightmares, if any, upon awakening each morning. Almost half (47 percent) of these students reported at least one nightmare during the course of the study. Of particular interest was the finding that neither anxiety nor creativity was found to be associated with increased frequency of nightmares.

People often confuse sleep terrors with nightmares. **Sleep terrors,** like nightmares, are frightening experiences associated with sleep, but sleep terrors occur during Stages 3 and 4 of NREM sleep, not during REM sleep. Sleep terrors are characterized by a piercing scream or cry for help. Typically, he or she sits up, stares unseeingly, and perhaps gasps or hyperventilates. Occasionally the sleeper jumps out of bed. Full awakening doesn't always occur following a sleep terror. In fact, it is more common for the individual to lie down and continue sleeping. People awakened by a sleep terror usually recall a sense of intense fear but do not recall the content of a dream. They go back to sleep easily and do not recall the experience when they awaken the next morning.

Sleep terrors seem to be related to daytime stress and fatigue. For example, a child who moves to another city or school may be more prone to sleep terrors. Although sleep terrors may be associated with some personality disorders, they are not themselves evidence of an underlying disorder or considered abnormal.

SLEEPWALKING

For many years it was believed that people who sleepwalk (called somnambulism) are acting out dream events. We now know that **sleepwalking** occurs during Stage 3 or 4 of NREM sleep, when the body is capable of movement. The duration of sleepwalking can vary from a few minutes to over half an hour. During this time it is virtually impossible to awaken the person. If awakening occurs the individual is typically disoriented but does not recall the episode. Contrary to popular belief there is no danger involved in awakening a sleepwalker; it is just difficult. After awakening, the person typically returns to sleep. Approximately 20 percent of the population has experienced sleepwalking with the majority of episodes occurring between 6 and 12 years of age (Anch et al., 1988).

Sleepwalkers can negotiate obstacles, although they move quite clumsily and often fall down or bump into things. Occasionally sleepwalking may subject a person to extreme danger. In one case reported in a news account, a man sleepwalked out the door of a travel trailer as it was being pulled along a highway. Parents can reduce the possibility of their child being injured during sleepwalking by adjusting the environment. For instance, by putting gates across windows and at the tops of stairs. Frequent sleepwalking in adults is considered serious and can reflect fatigue, drug use, or serious stress.

SLEEPTALKING

Practically everyone talks during sleep on occasion but it is much more prevalent in children than adults. Unlike sleepwalking, **sleeptalking** (somniloquy) appears to occur equally across periods in the sleep cycle. Some people talk during NREM sleep while others talk exclusively during REM sleep. In some individuals, however, sleeptalking can occur during both NREM and REM sleep. When sleeptalking occurs during REM sleep it may reflect dream content. Contrary to myth, sleeptalkers rarely reveal secrets.

In contrast to sleepwalking, talking while asleep is usually purposeless and unrelated to stress or other events that occur during the waking state. The typical duration of sleeptalking is just a few seconds but it may last several minutes. The talking may be either unintelligible or fully articulated speech. There is usually no recollection of sleeptalking if the person is awakened during talking or when they awaken the following morning. Sleeptalking is not considered a symptom of any underlying disorder nor is it of any clinical significance.

PROBLEMS RELATED TO THE SLEEP–WAKE SCHEDULE People who continually change their sleep–wake schedule because of rotating shifts, frequent travel, or other interruptions from a consistent schedule often have difficulty with sleep and alertness later during the day. No matter what the cause of the disturbance in the schedule, the severity of the sleep problem is proportional to the size of the disturbance. For example, we have no difficulty adjusting to a one-hour shift that occurs during changes from standard time to daylight savings time. However, an eight-hour shift that results from a changing work schedule or a long flight can cause difficulty.

Because the normal sleep–wake cycle is slightly longer than 24 hours (approximately 25 hours) it is generally less disruptive to travel from east to west than west to east; that is, it is easier to delay than to advance sleep–wake behavior. This explains why it is easier to adjust to forward rotations in shift work. For example, it is easier to adjust to schedules rotating clockwise (from an 8:00 A.M. to 4:00 P.M. schedule to a 4:00 P.M. to 12:00 P.M. schedule) than the reverse. Can you figure out how many days one should stay on a shift before rotating, given that our internal clocks governing sleep–wake cycles are on a 25-hour schedule as opposed to a 24-hour schedule?

The last section of this chapter will discuss the topic of hypnosis which, like sleep and dreaming, is associated with a particular physiological state of arousal.

HYPNOSIS

Hypnosis is a fascinating phenomenon that has aroused considerable controversy within the discipline of psychology. It is also an area that some psychologists consider worthy of research. Much of its credibility stems from the thoughtful research and writings of renowned psychologist Ernest Hilgard (see Hilgard & Hilgard, 1983). According to Hilgard hypnosis represents a state of dissociated experience as opposed to a passive experience controlled by the hypnotist. A dissociated experience involves a deliberate cognitive effort to conform to the demands of the hypnotist. In addition, an amnesia-like process separates or dissociates this cognitive effort from awareness. For instance, in using hypnosis to treat pain a subject dissociates pain and the cognitive effort to reduce it from immediate experience, perhaps by amnesia.

It has been suggested that hypnotized people are experiencing an altered level of arousal similar to a dreaming state. In fact, the word hypnosis was derived from Hypnos, the Greek god of sleep. Hypnosis is not a state of sleep, however. Hypnotized people are very relaxed and calm, but EEG recordings demonstrate that they are not asleep. Efforts to differentiate between the brain waves, heart rates, and respiration of hypnotized and nonhypnotized people have been largely unsuccessful (cf., Wallace & Fisher, 1991).

If hypnotized subjects are not in a different state of physiological arousal in what way is a hypnotic state unique? Observations of countless hypnotized people indicate that hypnosis is characterized by total relaxation and a strong sense of detachment. Hypnotized people are alert and particularly attentive to the hypnotist's words, appearing to have few or no independent thoughts. Under hypnosis a person may become largely oblivious to stimuli other than the hypnotist's voice.

Although psychologists have not agreed on a precise definition of hypnosis, a functional working definition is that hypnosis is a state of heightened suggestibility in which a person is unusually willing to comply with the hypnotist's directives, including those that alter perceptions of self and the environment.

Hypnosis has been linked to a number of phenomena, sometimes accurately and sometimes with a fair amount of hyperbole. Its reputed effects include improved athletic performance, symptomatic relief of physical ailments, pain reduction, enhanced memory, age regression, imaginary sensory experiences, and posthypnotic suggestions subjects carry out as if they were their own ideas. The evidence for these effects is evaluated in the following paragraphs.

PHENOMENA ASSOCIATED WITH HYPNOSIS

HYPNOSIS AND ATHLETIC ABILITY You may have heard reports about people demonstrating amazing feats of strength or other outstanding athletic performances, allegedly as a direct result of hypnotic suggestion. Although many of the reports of performance are true, a caveat must be kept in mind: There is no evidence that hypnosis can increase a person's capacity to perform beyond natural limits. It may act as a powerful motivator, providing the extra impetus to close the gap between potential and actual performance. In this sense, its effects may be similar to the emergency response that enables a 150-pound man to lift a 500-pound steel pipe off an injured child.

HYPNOSIS AND RELIEF OF PHYSICAL AILMENTS Well documented evidence shows that suggestions given to hypnotized people can help relieve the symptoms of a variety of stress-related illnesses, including asthma, ulcers, and colitis.

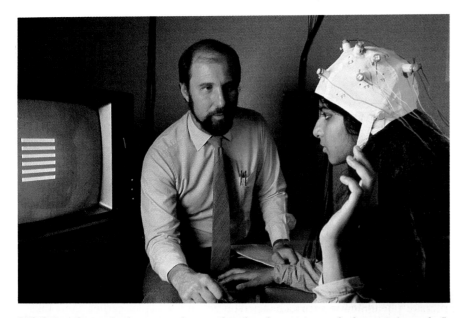

While in a hypnotized state people are relaxed and attentive to the hypnotist's words. In a deep hypnotized state people may be oblivious to everything but the hypnotist's voice. Here, Dr. David Spiegel of Stanford University monitors a hypnotized subject.

Hypnotism has also been used to help clear up warts, psoriasis, and a variety of other skin ailments (Smith, 1985; Spanos et al., 1990). Hypnosis has not been so effective in treating self-initiated addictive disorders such as alcoholism, smoking, and overeating (Wadden & Anderton, 1982).

HYPNOSIS AND PAIN RELIEF　In the nineteenth century, before anesthesia was discovered, a few surgeons used hypnosis to block surgical pain. However, most of the medical community looked on this practice with suspicion, and it was even suggested that hypnotized patients were faking pain relief. Today, most medical practitioners acknowledge that hypnosis can be very effective in reducing the pain associated with childbirth, back problems, arthritis, dental procedures, burns, and even major surgery (Evans, 1988, 1989; James et al., 1989; Spanos et al., 1989). One study found that hypnosis was more effective than aspirin, acupuncture, or morphine in reducing pain (Stern et al., 1977). One particularly noteworthy recent development in pain control has been the use of hypnotic suggestion to augment the effectiveness of chemical painkillers (Davidson, 1984).

HYPNOSIS AND MEMORY ENHANCEMENT IN CRIMINAL INVESTIGATIONS　For a time, claims about the memory enhancement capabilities of hypnosis led to its widespread use by police departments, often to help witnesses recall criminal acts. Certainly, some limited benefits are associated with its use in law enforcement—for example, as a way to calm a frightened, traumatized victim of an assault so that he or she can concentrate on the events surrounding the crime. However, there is little substance to claims that it can enhance a person's recall of a criminal act. Furthermore, there may actually be danger to relying too heavily on hypnosis. Recent findings have shown that when hypnotized subjects are pressed to recall specific events, they report many things that are not true (Dywan & Bowers, 1983). For these reasons, there is now a strong trend to bar testimony from hypnotized witnesses (Stark, 1984).

HYPNOSIS AND AGE REGRESSION　One of the most widely reported phenomena associated with hypnosis is **age regression,** in which a hypnotized subject is instructed to move back in time to an earlier age. In one demonstration of age regression, a young woman was systematically moved backward through the years of her youth, in an effort to trace her dislike of eggs. At each suggested age, she described her experiences on the farm where she was raised. As he regressed his subject backward in increments of two years, the hypnotist asked the same question, Do you like eggs? At each level, she responded no until it was suggested that she was six. At this point, she indicated that she did eat eggs. The hypnotist then moved her forward to age seven, and she described her daily task of collecting eggs from the chicken house. She reported that she was appalled at how dirty the eggs were, apparently the cause of her dislike for eggs. The hypnotist then explained to her, as he would to a child, that nature put a shell around the egg so that the inside would remain pure; he suggested that she would no longer dislike eggs when she awoke from the trance. In the weeks that followed, people who knew this woman reported that she was eating eggs.

What really happened in the situation we just described? Is age regression a legitimate phenomenon in which a person actually visits an earlier age? Take a moment to try to answer these questions before reading on.

The best available evidence suggests that age-regressed subjects behave in a manner consistent with their *present* conception of past behavior. In other words, such subjects are playing a role rather than actually reliving events that occurred many years ago. Many observations of logical incongruities in what age-regressed subjects say have led psychologists to draw this conclusion (Orne, 1972).

POSTHYPNOTIC SUGGESTION   **Posthypnotic suggestions** motivate people to perform a variety of actions after they return to a normal state of consciousness. Subjects typically carry out these suggestions without any recall of the instructions they received, and they often attempt to justify or rationalize the behavior in other ways. For example, in one classroom demonstration, a hypnotized student volunteer was given a posthypnotic suggestion to open a window when she observed her instructor loosen his tie. Right on cue, she raised her hand and asked if it would be OK to open a window, since the room seemed stuffy.

Can hypnosis be used to make you do something you would not ordinarily do? Could it be used to get you to commit a crime, disrobe in front of strangers, or engage in some type of act that you would normally consider unacceptable? Take a moment to evaluate this question based on what you have already learned about hypnosis before reading on.

A common misconception is that hypnosis cannot be used to motivate behavior in which a person would not ordinarily engage. It is true that most hypnotized people would not comply with direct suggestions to behave in an antisocial or inappropriate way. However, a hypnotist can alter the perceptions or awareness of a susceptible subject in such a way that such behaviors seem necessary or appropriate.

For example, a software designer might be induced to give away corporate secrets when hypnotized by a friend operating in the guise of an amateur hypnotist trying to liven up a party. The unsuspecting victim, who might go along with the stunt just to be a good sport, could be told that he was appearing before the board of directors to explain his latest design innovations. As we have learned, hypnotic suggestions can sometimes alter a subject's sensory and perceptual experiences. Consequently, the software designer might actually reveal secrets in the mistaken belief that the other partygoers were board members. There are numerous accounts in the literature of unscrupulous hypnotists using such strategies to induce subjects to engage in inappropriate or unacceptable behavior. This potential negative application of hypnotic suggestion, together with other possible deleterious effects, suggests that this consciousness-altering technique is not without risks when it is employed by someone other than a clinician who is well versed in the proper use of hypnosis (Echterling & Emmerling, 1987; Kleinhauz & Eli, 1987).

EXPLAINING HYPNOSIS

A number of theories have been offered to explain hypnosis. One explanation that was briefly mentioned at the beginning of this section is Ernest Hilgard's (1977) **dissociation theory.** According to Hilgard, a hypnotized person operates on more than one level of awareness, which allows some behaviors to become divorced or dissociated from our experience by an amnesialike process. According to this theory a part of a hypnotized person's awareness (which Hilgard calls the hidden observer) is observing and remembering all that goes on, even though the person is not consciously aware of this process.

Hilgard formulated this hidden observer concept during a classroom demonstration in which he suggested that his subject would be unable to hear anything until Hilgard touched his shoulder. The suggestion worked, and the subject ceased responding to any verbal stimuli. A student then asked if the subject really could not hear. Hilgard asked his subject if some part of him could hear, and if so, he was to signal by raising a finger. The finger rose. Everybody in the room was surprised, including Hilgard (and the subject, who asked why he had raised his finger).

Hilgard touched the subject's shoulder (so that he could hear again), then asked him what he had experienced. The subject said that the room had suddenly grown very quiet and that he had let his mind wander when suddenly he felt his finger move. Hilgard asked the part of the subject that had made his finger rise to explain what had happened. This second part of the subject's "mind," the so-called hidden observer, accurately reported everything that had transpired (Hilgard, 1977).

This account suggests that two separate states of awareness may occur concurrently which, incidentally, is how Hilgard defines the hypnotic state. There is nothing mystical about this: All of us have had experiences in which our awareness seems divided or dissociated. An example of this phenomenon is driving your car while thinking about a complex problem and then suddenly realizing that you have arrived at your destination without remembering your drive. The route you drove was dissociated from your awareness by amnesia.

A modified version of Hilgard's dissociation theory proposes that there are several levels of behavioral control: Conscious, executive control (similar to Hilgard's cognitive effort) and lower levels of control that can be directly activated by hypnosis. For instance, when a subject undergoes hypnosis for pain analgesia the hypnotic suggestions directly activate lower levels of control for pain reduction. That is, pain analgesia resulting from hypnosis is not mediated through a cognitive effort (consciously thinking about a reduction in pain). Thus there is no need for amnesia to dissociate this cognitive effort from our experience as hypothesized by Hilgard.

As a test of this version of dissociation theory researchers had subjects engage in cognitively demanding tasks while they underwent hypnosis for pain reduction. According to Hilgard's dissociation theory the cognitively demanding tasks should compete with the cognitive resources for analgesia resulting in little reduction in pain. On the other hand, if cognitive processing is not necessary for analgesia subjects under hypnosis should experience a reduction in pain. This is, in fact, what the researchers found (Miller and Bowers, 1993).

Not all psychologists agree that hypnosis involves dissociation of our awareness. As an alternative they argue that hypnosis is an example of compliance to the hypnotist's suggestions and does not involve an altered state of arousal. According to Barber (1975), all of the phenomena associated with hypnosis can be demonstrated in people who are not hypnotized: Hypnosis works because the subject is willing to go along with the hypnotist's suggestions uncritically. Barber compares being hypnotized to becoming a vicarious participant in the story line of a good novel or movie. To support this viewpoint, Barber and others have demonstrated that many hypnotic phenomena can be shown by nonhypnotized subjects who are instructed to think along with the hypnotist or merely to pretend they are hypnotized.

In one experiment, 66 nurses were divided into three matched groups. Subjects in one group were hypnotized using traditional techniques. Subjects in a second group were encouraged to focus their imaginations uncritically on whatever suggestions were provided. The third group, acting as a control, received no special instructions. All subjects were then asked to perform the same tasks, such as watching an imaginary TV program, drinking imaginary water, and hearing nonexistent music, and their performance on these tasks was rated using a scoring system.

If Barber's ideas about hypnosis are correct how should these groups compare in their hypnosis scores? Think about this before reading on.

Comparisons of the scores obtained by subjects in the different groups revealed that those in the pretend hypnosis group actually obtained somewhat higher scores, on the average, than those in the hypnotized group which is what Barber's theory predicted (Barber & Wilson, 1977). That is, hypnosis may not represent a different state of alertness, but a predisposition to attend to the hypnotist's suggestions.

At present there is no universally accepted theory of hypnosis. This is in part because of our inability to describe adequately and objectively a hypnotic state. Until we can define hypnosis in objective terms—such as a particular physiological state—different investigators will not know whether they are indeed studying the same phenomenon. As a result, several conflicting theories are bound to exist. On the positive side, there is evidence that there is an increasing interest in hypnosis research from several related disciplines including medicine, dentistry, and psychology.

SUGGESTED REMEDIES FOR INSOMNIA

HEALTH PSYCHOLOGY & LIFE

Psychologists have developed a number of behaviorally based remedies for insomnia. Perhaps one or more of the following suggestions may be helpful to you or someone you know.

1. Adopt a regular schedule. Go to sleep and get up at about the same time every day, even on weekends. Many insomnia sufferers have erratic sleep patterns. A regular schedule can establish a predictable rhythm that will greatly improve sleep. Avoid spending excessive time in bed, since this behavior can perpetuate insomnia (Spielman et al., 1987).
2. Try to engage in a relaxing, calming activity before going to bed. Some people find that a warm bath is helpful; others prefer reading or listening to soothing music. Avoid high-stress activities such as discussing money with your partner or trying to debug a computer program.
3. A number of procedures are designed to relax your body; these may be helpful before retiring. You can learn about relaxation techniques from several books that are easily found in bookstores. In a recent study, 18 of 22 insomnia sufferers found relaxation training improved sleep even after a one-year follow-up (Gustafson, 1992).
4. A daily exercise routine can also help promote a good night's sleep. It is probably not a good idea to engage in this activity just before going to sleep, however, since exercise can be very energizing.
5. Avoid drinking large quantities of beer, wine, or distilled spirits before retiring. These substances may help you fall asleep, but they are likely to interfere with your ability to stay asleep once their sedative effect wears off. In addition, avoid all stimulants after midday. One of the most commonly consumed stimulants, caffeine, is found in chocolate, coffee, tea, and many carbonated soft drinks. Caffeine-free forms of these products are available.
6. Avoid eating a large meal just before retiring to bed. If you need a snack, choose something high in carbohydrates.
7. Make your bedroom environment as sleep-compatible as possible. Use curtains or shades that shut out external light. If you must sleep in a noisy area, try using earplugs or turning on a fan or air conditioner to mask the noise.
8. Finally, try not to get upset about not sleeping. This suggestion is often easier said than done. However, remember that anger will only energize you more, thus adding to your problem. It would probably be much better to get up and read a book or engage in some form of relaxation until you feel sleepy enough to doze off.
9. Finally, if these suggestions are not working, a physician may be able to prescribe a mild hypnotic (benzodiazepine). Such a drug, over the course of a short time, may be quite effective in alleviating insomnia (Declerck et al., 1992).

SUMMARY ------------------------------

BIOLOGICAL RHYTHMS

1. All biological systems are influenced by rhythms of physiological activity. When these rhythms are on a 24-hour cycle they are called circadian rhythms.
2. Circadian rhythms appear to be controlled by the suprachiasmatic nucleus of the hypothalamus.

THE SCIENCE OF SLEEP AND DREAMING

3. Sleep is a natural, periodically recurring state of rest, which is characterized by reduced activity, lessened responsiveness to stimuli, and distinctive brain wave patterns.
4. Researchers distinguish between REM (rapid eye movement) and NREM (nonrapid eye movement) sleep. Dreaming is more likely to occur in REM than in NREM sleep. However, dreaming is not limited to REM sleep, and REM is not synonymous with dreaming.
5. During a normal night's sleep we pass through four stages of sleep in naturally recurring, successive cycles. These stages range from very light sleep, characteristic of Stage 1, through Stage 4, the deepest level of sleep. Dreaming occurs most commonly during Stage 1 sleep.
6. During dreaming, muscular activity is inhibited. Sleepwalking almost invariably occurs during NREM sleep, Stage 3 or 4.
7. As people grow older there is a decline in both the time spent sleeping and the proportion of sleep spent in the REM phase.
8. Different species of animals seem to require different amounts of sleep.
9. The major brain areas involved in sleep and waking are the ascending reticular activation system (RAS) and the raphe system.
10. Research suggests that sleep is necessary, but it is not clear why.

A number of theories have been suggested: Sleeping conserves energy, it restores depleted resources, it helps to clear the mind of useless information, it facilitates memory, or it allows us the opportunity to dream.

11. People deprived of dreaming tend to increase their time spent dreaming in subsequent uninterrupted sleep periods, a phenomenon known as REM rebound.
12. To date, research has not provided a definitive answer to why we dream. Some explanatory theories are that dreams are the brain's attempt to explain random bursts of neuronal activity, that dreams are a form of mental reprogramming in which the brain is reorganized to accommodate new information, that dreaming provides a low-stress solution to dealing with problems, and that dreams are disguised expressions of unconscious wishes.

DISORDERS OF SLEEP

13. Sleep disorders include insomnia, sleep apnea, narcolepsy, sleep terrors and nightmares, and sleepwalking.

HYPNOSIS

14. Hypnosis is a state of heightened suggestibility in which a person is unusually willing to comply with the hypnotist's directives.
15. Hypnosis can act as a powerful motivator, but it cannot increase a person's capacity to perform beyond natural limits.
16. Evidence suggests that hypnosis can help to alleviate pain and relieve the symptoms of a variety of stress-related illnesses. However, it has been shown to be only marginally beneficial when used in criminal investigations.
17. Explanations of hypnosis include dissociative theories.

biological rhythms
circadian rhythms
suprachiasmatic nucleus (SCN)
reticular activating system (RAS)
raphe system
sleep
REM
NREM
Stage 1 sleep
Stage 2 sleep
Stage 3 sleep
Stage 4 sleep
manifest content

latent content
sleep disorders
insomnia
sleep apnea
narcolepsy
nightmare
sleep terrors
sleepwalking
sleeptalking
hypnosis
age regression
posthypnotic suggestion
dissociation theory

CHAPTER **6**
Learning and Behavior

CHAPTER **7**
Memory

CHAPTER **8**
Motivation

CHAPTER **9**
Emotion and Stress

CHAPTER **10**
*Cognition: Thinking
and Language*

PART 3

Learning, Memory, Cognition, Motivation and Emotion

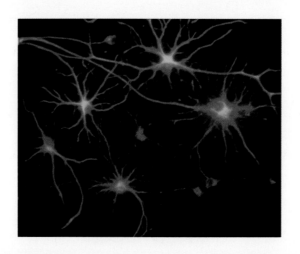

C H A P T E R 6

Learning and Behavior

DEFINING LEARNING

How Learning Takes Place

CLASSICAL CONDITIONING

Pavlov's Discovery
Acquisition of Classical Conditioning
Stimulus Contingency and Conditioning
CS-UCS Timing and Conditioning
Extinction and Spontaneous Recovery
Stimulus Generalization and
    Discrimination
Second-Order Conditioning

OPERANT CONDITIONING

Operant Conditioning in a Skinner Box
Reinforcement
Reinforcing the Initial Operant Response
Punishment and Operant Behavior
Advantages of Punishment

COMPARING CLASSICAL AND OPERANT CONDITIONING

Two-Factor Theory of Avoidance
    Learning

COGNITIVE INFLUENCES ON LEARNING

Latent Learning
Cognitive Processes in Learning
Observational Learning

BIOLOGICAL BASES OF LEARNING

Classical Conditioning of the Aplysia

*I*n recent years there has been mounting concern that grizzly bears may become extinct. Trying to protect a species that many people consider just plain ornery, however, has presented some special problems for conservationists.

These problems are paticularly evident in the Yellowstone and Glacier National Parks regions of Montana. After years of living close to civilization (and foraging through civilization's garbage dumps), the bears in these areas behave as if they have lost their fear of humans. In the past, before these regions were as heavily populated, the bears avoided human contact whenever they could. But bears that have become accustomed to humans react differently with the result that in recent years a number of people have been injured. Bears that injure humans must be destroyed; thus rangers have been put in the position of bringing this endangered species even closer to extinction.

Most efforts to protect the grizzlies have been remarkable for their lack of success (Chadwick, 1986). For instance, when grizzlies are trapped and transported deep into the wild, they often return to human habitats, where the living is easy. Recently, however, wildlife officials have begun a new program that looks far more promising. The goal of this program is to reestablish fear of humans in these animals. The bears are trapped and caged; then a human delivers electric shocks to the animals. (The shocks produce pain for a brief time, but there is no lasting injury.) The bears appear to associate humans with painful shocks because later, when they are released in the wilderness, they are more likely to stay away from people (Peacock, 1983). We will have much more to say about this kind of avoidance learning later in this chapter.

Protecting endangered species may seem to be far from the topic at hand, but it illustrates some of the principles that are basic to learning processes, not just in grizzly bears, but in humans and other animals. As we will see, much of our learning takes place by associating events, just as the bears learned to associate painful shocks with the presence of humans.

An understanding of learning is relevant to many other fields that seem to have little to do with psychology, from designing employee incentive programs in industry to raising children to be responsible adults. The pages that follow present at least a portion of what psychologists have learned about learning, and they help to explain how we can apply this knowledge to our lives. Before we discuss the applications of learning, we begin by defining what we mean by learning.

How can scientists reinstate the fear of humans grizzly bears have lost after living in close proximity with humans?

DEFINING LEARNING ----------------------------------

Learning may be defined as a relatively permanent change in potential behavior that results from experience. This definition contains three important elements. The first element is change. Most learning tends to produce lasting changes in the behavior of the learner. We hope that the grizzly bears in the opening example of this chapter will continue to associate humans with the discomfort they experienced in captivity.

Second, this definition excludes changes in behavior that result from anything other than experience. For example, behavior can be modified by nonexperiential events like diseases, injury, or maturation. A broken leg will result in numerous changes in your behavior; few of which are learned.

The third element of this definition speaks of *potential* behavior. Although learning causes changes in behavior, it is not always reflected directly in performance. The absence of observable behavior change does not necessarily mean that no learning has taken place. However, a change in behavior under the appropriate conditions must be observable at some time to claim that learning has occurred.

For example, suppose a young boy often sees his father strike his mother during arguments. For the time being, the father's actions may have no apparent effect on the boy's behavior. When the boy becomes an adult, however, he strikes his wife during an argument. During the boy's childhood, we would have had no reason to believe that he had learned to be physically violent when frustrated. However, the potential for this behavior clearly was acquired; it simply required the necessary circumstances for it to occur.

Another example of learning that cannot be observed immediately is demonstrated by rats in a maze. If there is no reinforcement (such as food) at the end of the maze, rats explore the alleys with no indication that learning is taking place. When food is placed at the end of the maze, however, they quickly negotiate the twists and turns to reach it. Learning had taken place during the exploration, but it required a proper incentive to be reflected in actual performance.

HOW LEARNING TAKES PLACE

You should now have an understanding of what learning is. But how does it take place? For instance, you go to a familiar restaurant and order something unique that you've never eaten before. Throughout the meal you comment on how distinctive and flavorful your dish is. Later in the evening you become quite ill and nauseous. This illness may be completely unrelated to the meal you had eaten earlier. Perhaps it's a touch of the flu. However, the association of illness with the meal leads to an aversion to this unique dish that you found flavorful earlier. This aversion may last for years. Most of us can think of examples of food aversions we've acquired such as this. For patients undergoing radiation or chemotherapy food aversions can be quite common and they are acquired in the same fashion. A meal that is followed by treatment which makes the patient ill will be less desirable than before. This is an example of a conditioned taste aversion, a subject to which we will return later.

This kind of learning is called associative learning. It describes the process by which we make a connection or an association between two events, such as the flavor of a particular food and illness. Or how the bears in the opening example come to associate pain with humans. Associative learning may take place in two primary ways: through classical conditioning and through operant conditioning. Both of these processes contribute continually to your ongoing behavior.

Classical conditioning involves learning a connection between two stimuli and results in a change in behavior. For example, the flavor of our unique dish at the restaurant becomes associated with illness or a small child learns to associate the sight of a physician's syringe with the discomfort of an injection. In **operant conditioning,** people or other animals learn to associate their own behavior with its consequences which results in a change in behavior. Thus a child learns that pressing a button brings an elevator, a college student learns that answering questions in a certain class produces praise, a porpoise learns that jumping through a hoop results in a tasty morsel of fish and you learn that driving through a stop sign produces a ticket.

Psychologists believe that most kinds of learning can be described in terms of classical and operant conditioning. However, certain kinds of learning may involve more complex processes, such as thinking and reasoning. This kind of learning is labeled **cognitive learning.** In this chapter we also examine cognitive learning in some detail. First, however, we turn our attention to the classical and operant conditioning processes.

CLASSICAL CONDITIONING

Some years ago, one of the authors' psychology students came to him with a problem. She was enrolled in a biology class in which students spent much of their time in a laboratory. When she entered the lab early in the term she suddenly felt an overwhelming state of anxiety bordering on terror. She was unable to remain in the laboratory; consequently, she could not complete her assignments. Perplexed and concerned, she tried a number of times to return to the lab, but she could not shake her feeling of terror.

Here are some of the facts in the case just described: The student had completed two previous terms of biology without experiencing any discomfort in the laboratory segments. Between her previous biology class and the present term was a one-year absence from college, during which she gave birth to her first child. Her problem in the biology laboratory commenced immediately after returning to resume her studies. Take a moment to consider the facts and try to explain the woman's fear response before reading on.

If you guessed that the student had some terrible experience during her year's absence from college that somehow became associated with the environment of the biology laboratory, you are correct. Because of complications during the delivery of her baby, her physician decided to perform a caesarean section (surgical removal of the baby through an incision in the abdomen and uterus). There was not time for her to be psychologically prepared, and she panicked. She found herself unable to breathe when she received an injection of anesthesia (a rare response during this type of medical procedure, probably related to stress). For a few terrible moments she was convinced she would die. Fortunately, the feeling subsided quickly and the operation proceeded smoothly.

Let's see how classical conditioning may have contributed to her present anxiety in the biology laboratory. The trigger for this woman's original fear response was her experience on the operating table. Because this experience took place in an environment with medical smells, the woman associated these smells with her awful experience at the hospital. The odors of antiseptic and anesthetic agents in the biology laboratory were similar enough to the medical smells of the operating room to trigger the same fear response that the woman had developed while receiving anesthesia for her operation.

The connection was not a conscious one. In fact, learning rarely occurs at a conscious level. In this case the woman was not aware that she had been conditioned. Yet it followed a classical model that was first recognized around the turn of the century by the Russian physiologist Ivan Pavlov (1849–1936).

FIGURE 6.1

Pavlov's Conditioning Apparatus

During a typical conditioning session an assistant, sitting behind the mirror, rang a bell (the CS) and then presented food (the UCS) to the hungry dog. Salivation was measured by collecting it via a tube attached to the dog's salivary gland. A revolving drum recorded the amount of saliva collected. Initially salivation occurred only after food was presented (the UCR). After several conditioning trials salivation occurred (the CR) after the presentation of the CS.

PAVLOV'S DISCOVERY

Ivan Pavlov's real interest was the physiological mechanisms involved in digestion. (In fact, he never associated his own research with psychology, insisting that he was dealing only with physiological mechanisms.) Toward this end, Pavlov was investigating the salivation responses of dogs by placing the animals in the harnesslike apparatus shown in Figure 6.1. A surgical procedure exposed each dog's salivary glands, which were connected directly to a device that measured the flow of saliva. Pavlov then presented a stimulus, meat powder. When food entered the dog's mouth, the immediate result was the natural, reflexive response of salivation.

However, Pavlov soon noted an unexpected occurrence. His dogs began to salivate to stimuli other than food in their mouths. For example, an animal might start salivating at the mere sight of the experimenter. The sound of Pavlov's footsteps or the sight of the food dish also caused salivation.

This discovery changed the course of Pavlov's study, for Pavlov now began to investigate how other stimuli could cause dogs to salivate. His experiments are generally recognized as the first systematic study of learning, and the processes that he outlined came to be called classical (as in "the first") conditioning. (Today classical conditioning is frequently called Pavlovian conditioning.) A basic outline of this model of learning follows.

A hungry dog, secured in Pavlov's apparatus, hears a bell. A moment later, the dog is given meat powder; copious salivation results. This procedure is repeated several times, with one stimulus (the sound of the bell) followed consistently by another stimulus (food). Eventually, the dog salivates when it hears the bell, even when no food follows. The dog has associated the bell with food. However, what is learned is more than a mere association between two stimuli. Rather, classical conditioning may be best described as the learning of relations among events so as to allow the organism to represent its environment (Rescorla, 1988a, p. 151). Or, put another way, Pavlov's dog learned something about important relationships existing in its environment, namely that the sounding of a bell signaled the availability of food. Consequently, when the bell rang the dog salivated *in anticipation of* eating food. Many conditioned responses function to prepare the learner for a change in events.

Ivan Pavlov

The fact that a previously neutral stimulus (a stimulus, such as the sound of the bell, that does not elicit the to-be-learned response) eventually produces a response (salivation) ordinarily associated with another stimulus (food) is clear evidence that learning has taken place. Pavlov identified four key events or elements for classical conditioning.

1. *The unconditioned stimulus (UCS)*. Meat causes dogs to salivate. This response occurs automatically, without learning or conditioning. A stimulus that elicits an unlearned response or reflex is called an **unconditioned stimulus (UCS)**. Therefore, meat is a UCS.
2. *The unconditioned response (UCR)*. Salivating at the presentation of meat is an automatic response that does not require learning. An unlearned response is called an **unconditioned response (UCR)**. Thus salivation in response to meat is a UCR.
3. *The conditioned stimulus (CS)*. The bell initially is a neutral stimulus in that it does not elicit the to-be-learned response by itself. It causes salivation only when the dogs learn the association between the bell and the unconditioned stimulus, the food. A stimulus to which an organism learns to respond is called a learned or **conditioned stimulus (CS)**. Therefore, the bell is a CS.
4. *The conditioned response (CR)*. Pavlov's dogs were conditioned to salivate when a bell sounded. Such a learned response is called a **conditioned response (CR)**. Thus salivation in response to the bell is a CR.

Figure 6.2 summarizes the steps by which conditioning took place in Pavlov's model.

The conditioning in Pavlov's dogs was measured by collecting saliva secreted following the presentation of the CS. Other conditioned responses may take place and be measured at a physiological level. For instance, in the Health, Psychology and Life segment at the end of this chapter we discuss classical conditioning of the immune system which could have far-reaching medical implications.

DIFFERENTIATING BETWEEN THE UCR AND THE CR At first glance, the unconditioned response and conditioned response often appear to be identical. The UCR in Pavlov's experiments occurred when the dogs salivated in response to meat and the CR was also salivation. However, the UCR and the CR may be quite different depending on both the nature of the CS and the UCS. In our opening example of conditioned taste aversions, illness was the UCR and an aversion to food was the CR.

FIGURE 6.2
Pavlov's Conditioning Procedure

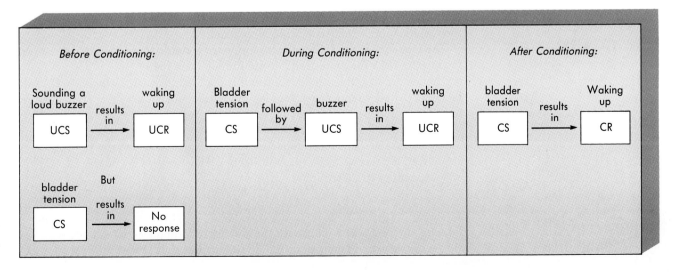

Although they may be similar, the unconditioned response and the conditioned response are rarely identical. An unconditioned response is generally more intense than is a response that has been conditioned. For example, dogs salivate more copiously when meat is actually placed in their mouths than they do when they either hear a bell or see the person who feeds them.

What do dogs salivating to a sound have to do with our lives as humans? We can best put this question in perspective by returning to the case of the biology student. The same elements that Pavlov traced in his dogs can be found in this conditioning experience. The unconditioned response is fear, a natural response to the frightening event in the hospital room (the UCS). Fear or anxiety is the learned or conditioned response. Just as Pavlov's dogs learned to associate the bell with food, the young woman may have learned to associate medical smells (the CS) with the hospital event.

In this case the woman needed to be exposed to only one conditioning event. One profoundly frightening event can establish a conditioned fear that may last a lifetime (Merckelbach et al., 1990). In other cases several conditioning trials or events may be necessary for learning. Fortunately, classically conditioned phobias (persistent, irrational fears) may be eliminated or extinguished using therapy techniques that are also based on classical conditioning principles (see Chapter 16). A few therapy sessions with the author's student were sufficient to extinguish her fear of the biology laboratory successfully.

The difference between the repeated pairing that Pavlov used on his dogs and the single experience of the young woman illustrates one way in which classical conditioning experiences may vary. The following discussions deal with other variations on the same theme, exploring both the ways in which learning is acquired and the ways in which it can be extinguished.

ACQUISITION OF CLASSICAL CONDITIONING

The period during which an organism learns to associate the conditioned stimulus with the unconditioned stimulus is known as the **acquisition** stage of conditioning. Each paired presentation of the two stimuli is called a *trial*. In cases such as Pavlov's conditioning experiments, these repeated trials strengthen, or reinforce, the association between the CS and the UCS.

Several factors influence how easily a classically conditioned response is acquired. For example, conditioning takes place more easily when the neutral or conditioned stimulus is clearly different from other stimuli. Had Pavlov signaled the arrival of food by quietly humming a Russian ballad, his dogs might never have perceived the connection since such sounds are commonplace and might not have been noticed. In contrast, Pavlov's dogs could hardly overlook a ringing bell. This property of the CS is referred to as *stimulus salience*. The more salient the CS, the more readily conditioning is acquired.

The intensity of the UCS will also influence conditioning. Typically, the more intense the UCS the more readily conditioning takes place.

Another factor influencing acquisition is the frequency with which the CS and UCS are paired. Frequent pairings generally facilitate conditioning. If bells were only occasionally accompanied by feeding, Pavlov's dogs would have been less likely to be conditioned.

Finally, and perhaps most important, is the degree to which the CS and UCS are related. By this we mean the contingency between the CS and the UCS. This issue demands extra attention.

STIMULUS CONTINGENCY AND CONDITIONING

Perhaps the best way to illustrate the concept of stimulus contingency is to review a classic experiment conducted by Robert Rescorla (1968). In Rescorla's ex-

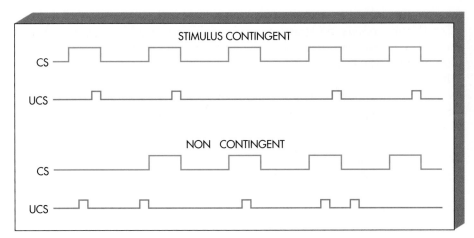

FIGURE 6.3
Stimulus Contingency in Classical Conditioning

Stimulus contingency and temporal contiguity occur in the top figure. That is, the occurrence of a UCS is always preceded by the occurrence of a CS. In the bottom figure there is no contingency. UCS presentations are occasionally paired with CS presentations but they are not contingent on the occurrence of a CS.

periment rats were exposed to one of two conditioning procedures: either a stimulus contingent procedure or a non-contingent procedure. In the stimulus contingent procedure a series of CSs and UCSs (tones and shocks) were presented, but a UCS (shock) never occurred unless a CS (tone) preceded it. That is, the presentation of the UCS was contingent upon a CS preceding it. Occasionally, however, CSs were presented without being followed by a UCS. This procedure is illustrated in the top part of Figure 6.3.

In the non-contingent procedure the same number of CS and UCS presentations occurred, however, the presentations of the CS and the UCS were independent. That is, the presentation of a UCS (shock) was not contingent upon the occurrence of a CS (tone). Occasionally in this procedure there were close pairings of the CS and the UCS, but these were random occurrences. This procedure is illustrated in the bottom part of Figure 6.3. When Rescorla tested both groups for conditioning he found that conditioning only occurred for the rats in the stimulus contingent procedure. No learning occurred with the non-contingent procedure. Rescorla's experiment is important because it demonstrates that more than occasional CS UCS pairings are necessary for conditioning as Pavlov and his followers had believed. For example, Pavlov believed that occasional pairings of the CS and UCS were sufficient for conditioning and therefore some conditioning should have taken place during the non-contingent procedure. In summary, what is necessary for classical conditioning is that the UCS be contingent (depend) on the occurrence of the CS.

The idea of stimulus contingency can perhaps be simplified by considering an example from weather forecasting. Imagine two forecasters, one proficient, the other not. Both predict rain on numerous occasions, but rain never occurs without a rain forecast from the proficient weatherman. On the other hand, rain is just as likely with as without a rain forecast from the unproficient weatherman. The proficient weatherman demonstrates a stimulus contingency because rain is contingent upon a forecast for rain. That is, rain doesn't occur unless it is forecast, even though rain doesn't occur after *every* rain forecast. Thus, upon hearing a forecast for rain, you prepare for it. The non-proficient weatherman demonstrates the lack of stimulus contingency because rain is just as likely whether or not it is forecast. As you can guess, you can't depend on the forecast so you don't prepare for rain.

There are several ways in which stimulus contingency can be presented and the ease of conditioning also depends upon them. We next consider several important examples of conditioning trials where the timing of CS and UCS presentations vary.

CS-UCS TIMING AND CONDITIONING

Conditioning occurs most easily when the CS is presented just moments before the UCS appears, and it is continued until after the presentation of the UCS. For example, the bell rings before food is presented to Pavlov's dog, and it continues until the animal begins to salivate as food enters its mouth. This timing sequence is called **delayed conditioning.** The ideal CS-UCS interval in delayed conditioning depends somewhat on the associations to be learned. Typically CS-UCS delays between 0.5 and 2 seconds are optimal.

Conditioning may still take place when timing is varied. For instance, **simultaneous conditioning** takes place when the conditioned stimulus is presented at the same time as the unconditioned stimulus. Another variation in timing is known as **trace conditioning.** Here, the conditioned stimulus begins and ends before the unconditioned stimulus is presented. Finally, in **backward conditioning** the UCS is presented prior to the CS. Figure 6.4 illustrates all four variations in timing.

Delayed conditioning with short CS-UCS intervals generally yields the most rapid rate of learning (Hulse et al., 1980). In contrast, the least effective sequence, backward conditioning, usually results in little or no learning (Hall, 1989). An exception to the rule that the delay between CS and UCS onset must be short is conditioned taste aversions which were introduced earlier.

CONDITIONED TASTE AVERSIONS   Conditioned taste aversions (sometimes called the Garcia Effect) were first studied by John Garcia (1961). In his experiments rats were first exposed to a novel taste; in this case saccharine. Several hours later the rats were exposed to moderate doses of radiation which made the rats ill. To test for conditioning the rats were given access to two drinking spouts, one containing plain water, the other, saccharine solution. Normally rats would prefer the saccharine solution over water, but these conditioned rats do not. The lack of a saccharine preference is called a **conditioned taste aversion.** Conditioned taste aversions reliably occur with long CS-UCS intervals. In numerous experiments the interval between the CS (the taste of saccharine) and the UCS (illness) has been as long as 24 hours.

Preparedness and Selective Associations   Not all associations are as readily learned as the association between a novel taste and illness. In fact, most learned associations require numerous trials containing CS-UCS presentations. When associations are learned quickly, like conditioned taste aversions, they are considered to be prepared. That is, animals may be prepared biologically to learn certain associations more quickly than others. The survival advantage for animals to learn quickly to avoid foods that have made them ill is fairly clear.

In addition, not all CSs are as easily associated with a UCS as others. For instance, in a similar experiment Garcia and Koelling (1966) used two types of CSs (taste and an audiovisual stimulus) and two types of UCSs (illness and mild shock) to test for selective associations. Before reading on consider which associations were easily learned in this experiment.

The results of the experiment clearly support the notion of selective associations. Rats easily learned the taste-illness and the audiovisual stimulus-shock associations, but they did not learn either the taste-shock or the audiovisual stimulus-illness associations. Other experiments have also demonstrated that certain CS-UCS associations are more easily learned than others. These learned associations are referred to as *selective associations* because certain CS-UCS combinations seem to belong together. Some psychologists have speculated that the concepts of preparedness and selective association may account for the relative ease with which people learn certain phobias (exaggerated fears—of heights or insects, for example).

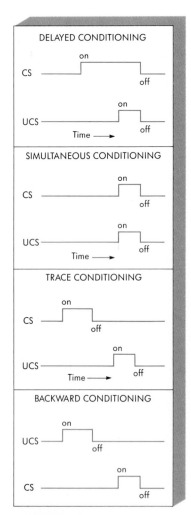

FIGURE 6.4

Variations in CS / UCS Presentations and Classical Conditioning

Delayed conditioning generally yields the most rapid conditioning. Backwards conditioning rarely results in conditioning.

Would Pavlov's dogs have continued to salivate at the sound of the bell if it were no longer accompanied by food? The answer, of course, is no. They would salivate less and less at the sound until, without any additional presentations of the UCS, they eventually would cease salivating altogether.

This process is called **extinction.** Extinction occurs in classical conditioning when the CS is repeatedly presented alone, without the UCS. Extinction does not mean that a response is totally stamped out, however. Once extinguished, a conditioned response can be reactivated in much less time than it took to acquire it in the first place. For instance, the classically conditioned response of salivating to a bell may have been established only after several pairings or trials. But after extinction, the conditioned response might be reestablished after only one or two pairings of the bell and the food.

In fact, a conditioned response will sometimes reappear at the beginning of a session after extinction. For example, we might thoroughly extinguish the salivation response and then, after keeping the dog away from the experimental procedures for a day or two, again present the bell. Even without food to help reestablish the old connection, the dog might salivate to the bell alone. This phenomenon is called **spontaneous recovery.**

As Figure 6.5 demonstrates, spontaneous recovery is not a complete recovery. A response does not come back to its previous level; it also extinguishes more rapidly if the CS is once more repeatedly presented alone.

EXTINCTION AND SPONTANEOUS RECOVERY

FIGURE 6.5
Acquisition, Extinction and Spontaneous Recovery

This figure, based on data from Pavlov (1927), demonstrates rapid acquisition of the CR (salivation to the bell) after several trials in which the bell (CS) was paired with food (UCS). During extinction the CS is no longer followed by the UCS and the CR decreases. Later, some salivation (CR) occurs following the presentation of the CS. This is referred to as spontaneous recovery.

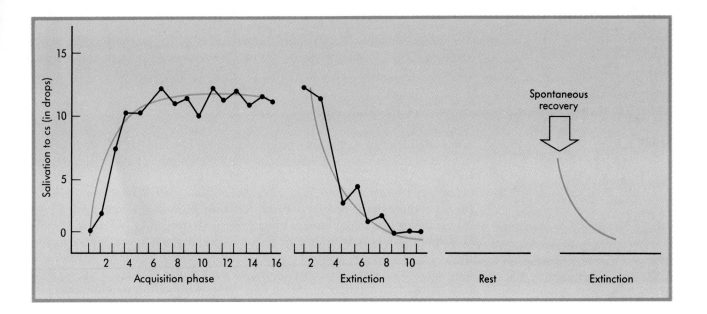

STIMULUS GENERALIZATION AND DISCRIMINATION

When a response has been conditioned to a particular stimulus, other stimuli may also produce the same response. For example, a war veteran who has been conditioned to dive for cover at the sound of gunfire may show the same response at the sound of a car backfiring. The more similar a new stimulus is to the original CS, the more likely it is to elicit the CR.

When people and other animals respond to similar stimuli without undergoing training for each specific stimulus, it is referred to as stimulus **generalization.** For example, Pavlov's dogs may have salivated to a variety of similar bell sounds or our biology student may experience anxiety when confronted with

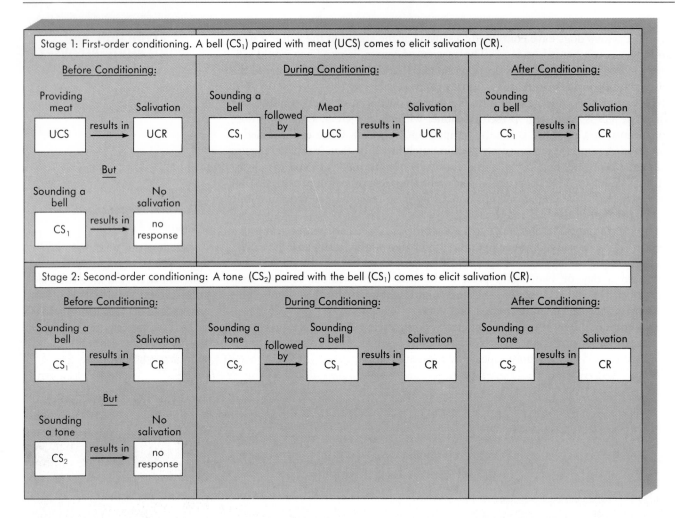

FIGURE 6.6
Second-Order Conditioning

In Stage 1, before conditioning sounding the bell (CS) does not elicit salivation (the CR). During conditioning the CS1 (bell) is paired with the UCS (food) which leads to conditioned salivation (the CR). In Stage 2, before conditioning a tone (CS2) does not elicit a response. During conditioning a tone (CS2) is paired with the bell (CS1). After conditioning the tone (CS2) will elicit a conditioned response.

other smells similar to the anesthetic used during her surgery, and we hope the bears associate pain with all humans, not just the rangers who administered the shocks.

Just as a learned response may generalize to similar situations, it may also be restricted through the process of **discrimination.** Early in the conditioning process, stimulus generalization may cause a learner to respond to a variety of similar stimuli. However, with time he or she learns that only one of these stimuli, the CS, is consistently associated with the UCS. Once the learner discriminates between stimuli, he or she responds only to the CS. For example, if the war veteran experienced a variety of jarring loud noises without the accompaniment of bullets whizzing through the air, he would soon learn to discriminate between noises like a car backfiring and a gunshot.

SECOND-ORDER CONDITIONING

We have seen that through classical conditioning, an organism learns to respond to a previously neutral stimulus, the CS, in a similar way as to the UCS. You might wonder whether the process can be carried one step further. With its newly acquired level, can the CS now be used to condition a response to other stimuli?

The answer is yes. For example, if a salient tone (CS1) is repeatedly paired with a mild shock (UCS) the tone will come to elicit fear (the CR). Now if a light (CS2) is paired with the tone (CS1) for several trials, it will elicit a fear response when presented alone. This process is called **second-order conditioning** (see Figure 6.6). In second-order conditioning a conditioned stimulus (CS) serves as an unconditioned stimulus (UCS) for the conditioning of a second association.

Second-order conditioning can greatly extend the impact of classical conditioning on our lives. We have a virtually unlimited capacity to make associations between events. This ability is one reason why therapists treating such things as classically conditioned phobias often trace convoluted processes by which everyday stimuli come to produce an unreasonable fear in a person.

We have seen that classical conditioning is a form of associative learning that accounts for certain types of behaviors. However, classical conditioning does not explain all forms of learning. It is clearly involved in the learning of emotional and motivational states but it does not by itself account for why you are diligently (we hope) reading this textbook? What is the UCS that automatically causes you to study? Obviously, there is none. To learn why you study and why you engage in a host of other voluntary behaviors, we must examine the second kind of associative learning, operant conditioning.

OPERANT CONDITIONING

Operant conditioning takes place when behavior is influenced by its consequences. We can trace the identification of operant conditioning to the American psychologist Edward Thorndike (1911). At about the same time that Pavlov was investigating involuntary, reflexive responses, Thorndike was analyzing the effects of stimuli on voluntary, operant behavior.

Thorndike believed that animals learn to make voluntary responses that help them adapt to their environments. To test his theory, he designed a device called a puzzle box. He placed hungry cats in wooden boxes latched from the inside. Outside he dangled a piece of fish in full view. The cats howled, meowed, clawed, and frantically explored in their attempts to get out of the box. Eventually, they accidentally tripped the latch and gained access to the food. The next time the cats found themselves inside the box, they repeated some of the same trial-and-error behavior as before, but they generally took less time to escape from the box. With each additional trial, the cats' actions became less variable until they learned to trip the latch immediately.

Thorndike explained his results by suggesting that behavior will be strengthened if it is followed by a positive consequence. Alternatively, behavior that does not lead to a satisfying consequence will be eliminated. Thus some of the cats' behaviors, such as clawing at the walls and howling, ceased to occur because they did not produce food. On the other hand, the latch-tripping behavior was strengthened because it produced fish. On the basis of these observations, Thorndike formulated the **Law of Effect,** which held that behavior followed by a satisfying consequence (effect) will be strengthened. This law, although considerably modified over the years, is the underlying foundation of operant conditioning.

Thorndike's puzzle box illustrates why the term *operant* has been applied to this type of learning. His cats learned to *operate* on their environment in a manner that resulted in satisfaction. Another way of saying the same thing is that their behaviors were instrumental in achieving a positive outcome. Thus, this conditioning model is sometimes called *instrumental conditioning.*

Thorndike's pioneering efforts were followed by the monumental contributions of Harvard psychologist B. F. Skinner. Skinner's research spanned several decades, and it provided much of what we know about operant conditioning. Perhaps the best way to become acquainted with the principles governing operant conditioning is to take a close look at one of Skinner's basic demonstrations.

E. Thorndike

B. F. Skinner

OPERANT CONDITIONING IN A SKINNER BOX

A hungry rat is placed in a box similar to that shown in Figure 6.7. This chamber, called a *Skinner box*, is empty except for a bar protruding from one wall with a small food dish directly beneath it.

After a short time in a Skinner box, the rat begins to examine its surroundings. As it explores, it eventually approaches the bar. When the rat is near the bar a food pellet is released into the dish. The next bar approach followed immediately by food delivery occurs after some additional exploration. Soon the rat spends most of its time around the bar. Next the rat must contact and exert some force on the bar before food is delivered. As with approaching the bar this activity soon comes to predominate. The operant response of bar pressing is "selected" by the food it produces, and the rate of pressing steadily increases.

RESPONSE STRENGTH OR RESPONSE SELECTION? The concept of selection here needs more elaboration because it is a part of Thorndike's original Law of Effect that has been changed considerably. Thorndike thought that reinforcement strengthened bonds or associations between behavior and the reinforcer. Thus the term reinforcement. Currently psychologists view the reinforcement process as one of selection. That is, reinforcement acts to select or guide behavior (Skinner, 1981). The rat in Skinner's box spends most of its time pressing the lever not because the association between lever pressing and food was strengthened but because it is the effective response and the other noneffective responses have dropped out. A statement made by Michelangelo when asked how he produced such marvelous statues illustrates this idea: He stated that he simply removed that part of the stone which was not the statue.

MEASURING OPERANT BEHAVIOR Perhaps the most common measure of operant behavior is its rate of occurrence. Skinner designed a device called a cumulative recorder (see Figure 6.8) that is used to measure operant behavior in a laboratory environment. A recording pen rests on paper that moves slowly at

FIGURE 6.7

A Skinner Box Used for Operant Conditioning

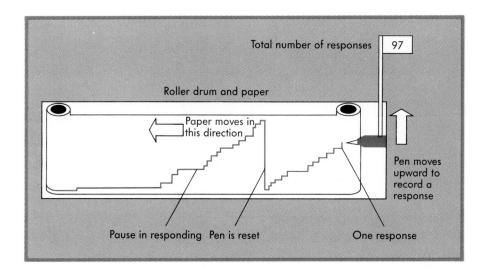

FIGURE 6.8
A Cumulative Recorder

A pen rests on paper that moves slowly as the drum turns. Each time a response occurs the pen moves upward a small amount. The more frequently the animal responds, the more rapidly the pen moves upward. Pauses in responding result in a flat section on the record. When the pen reaches the top of the chart it automatically resets at the bottom.

a fixed rate. Each time an animal makes an operant response, such as pressing a bar, the pen moves up a fixed distance and then continues on its horizontal path. The more frequently an animal responds, the more rapidly the pen climbs up the chart. The result, called a **cumulative record,** is a reliable measure of operant behavior.

DISCRIMINATIVE STIMULI You may have wondered about the light above the bar. Skinner used it to introduce a new variable, setting the dispenser to deliver food only when both the bar is pressed and the light is on. When the light is off, no food is delivered. Under these conditions of *differential reinforcement* (that is, reinforcement which takes place only under certain circumstances), the rat soon learns to make the appropriate discrimination: It presses the bar only when the light is on. In this circumstance, the light serves as a **discriminative stimulus,** that is, a stimulus that controls the response by signaling the availability of reinforcement.

Skinner's experiments illustrate the primary features of operant conditioning. An animal's behavior is selected or controlled by the immediate consequences of that behavior. For Skinner's rats, bar pressing was controlled by the delivery of food. Unlike classical conditioning, in which the learner passively responds to a stimulus, operant conditioning occurs when the learner acts on the environment as a result of the consequences for that act. Sometimes response consequences are quite apparent as with Skinner's example. However, consequences may be much more subtle such as an approving nod by a parent for acting politely or a change in facial expression by a friend for a compliment.

Operant conditioning stresses the effects of consequences on behavior. These consequences are described as reinforcement (or a reinforcer) and punishment (or a punisher). **Reinforcement** is defined as a stimulus whose delivery following a response leads to an increase in either the frequency or probability of that response. Punishment, on the other hand, is defined as a stimulus whose delivery following a response results in a decrease in the frequence or probability of that response (Domjan, 1993). We shall first examine procedures used to study the effects of reinforcement, then we will discuss punishment.

In studying operant conditioning, researchers have experimented with different types of reinforcers and different schedules for delivering reinforcement. Their findings help to explain how and why operant conditioning takes place.

REINFORCEMENT

POSITIVE AND NEGATIVE REINFORCEMENT   **Positive reinforcement** is any stimulus presented following a response that increases the probability of the response. **Negative reinforcement** is a stimulus that increases the probability of a response through its removal when the desired response is made. Introductory psychology students frequently misunderstand negative reinforcement, often confusing it with punishment assuming that it is used to stop a behavior (Deater & Tauber, 1987). In fact, quite the opposite is true: Negative reinforcement, like positive reinforcement, increases the occurrence of a desired behavior. Since the previous examples in this chapter have illustrated positive reinforcement, we look here at some examples of negative reinforcement and the procedures used to study them.

ESCAPE AND AVOIDANCE PROCEDURES   A rat is placed in a Skinner box, the floor of which consists of a metal grid that can be electrified. A mild current is activated and, as the rat tries to escape, it bumps into a bar and the shocking current immediately ceases. The pattern is repeated several times until the rat remains poised by the bar, ready to press it at the first jolt. This form of learning, called **escape conditioning** clearly involves negative reinforcement. The shock, an unpleasant stimulus, may be terminated only by the appropriate operant response. The removal of, or the escape from, the shock thus acts as the reinforcer for the bar press response. Taking aspirin to alleviate headache pain is essentially escape behavior maintained by the termination of the headache.

The escape conditioning procedure can be modified slightly by introducing a warning signal which allows the rat to avoid the shock altogether. If the light goes on a few seconds prior to each shock, the rat soon learns to respond to this discriminative stimulus by pressing the bar in time to avoid the shock. This type of learning is called **avoidance conditioning.**

These examples bring to mind many parallels in our own lives. For instance, if you live in a dormitory or an apartment building you may find that you pound on the wall of an adjoining room to get your noisy neighbor to quiet down. Your pounding behavior is thus maintained by negative reinforcement, the removal of the noise. People who live in western Oregon are accustomed to carrying umbrellas. Out-of-staters or optimistic natives have had to experience getting drenched while running back to fetch an umbrella (escape conditioning) before learning to have one always on hand on a cloudy day (avoidance conditioning). Much of human behavior is maintained by avoidance conditioning. In fact, our

After being caught in a rainstorm without a coat or an umbrella you may be more likely to carry one the next time rain is forecasted.

punitive legal system is a set of aversive consequences established to keep us in line. As long as we behave lawfully we avoid these aversive consequences. You may attend your classes not because of positive reinforcement but to avoid the aversive consequences of failing exams. We pay taxes promptly to avoid the punitive consequences of not paying them on time.

Two terms that are frequently confused are **punishment** and negative reinforcement. Again, the two are not the same. Negative reinforcement, by removing an unpleasant stimulus (the term negative here refers to removal), increases the rate or probability of a response. Thus a rat learns to press a bar to escape a shock. On the other hand, punishment decreases the probability of a response by presenting an unpleasant stimulus. For instance, if a rat trained to press a bar for food began to be shocked after each bar press, the response rate would decrease. Punishment will be discussed in more detail later in this chapter.

PRIMARY AND CONDITIONED REINFORCERS **Primary reinforcers** usually satisfy a biologically based need, such as hunger, thirst, sex, or sleep. However, some social events like parental contact may be primary reinforcers. It is obvious why food, water, sex, or sleep reinforce. But why do things like money reinforce? The answer lies in the concept of conditioned reinforcement. A variety of neutral stimuli associated with primary reinforcement can also become conditioned reinforcers. Much of our behavior is influenced more by conditioned reinforcement than by biologically significant primary reinforcement. Words of praise, pats on the back, good grades, and money are some of the conditioned reinforcers that influence our lives.

Humans are not the only animals who are influenced by **conditioned reinforcers** such as money. In a classic experiment conducted in the 1930s, chimpanzees learned that putting a coin (actually a token) into a chimp-o-mat vending machine produced goodies like grapes or raisins (see Figure 6.9). Through their association with food, the coins became conditioned reinforcers. The chimps were then trained to perform a variety of tasks just to get a coin. The coins soon acquired considerable reinforcing properties: The chimps worked hard to get the coins, often hoarded them, and sometimes even tried to steal them from each other (Wolfe, 1936).

FIGURE 6.9

A Chimp-O-Mat

In a classic experiment chimpanzees learned to perform a variety of tasks to earn tokens (conditioned reinforcers) that could be inserted into a vending machine to obtain primary reinforcers like raisins.

We have seen that conditioned reinforcers acquire their reinforcing properties through association with a primary reinforcer, but what is the critical element that determines this association? For many years, psychologists believed that the strength of conditioned reinforcement depended simply on the frequency with which it had been paired with primary reinforcement.

Research suggests otherwise. Instead of the frequency of pairings, the crucial factor seems to be the reliability with which the conditioned reinforcer predicts the availability of the primary reinforcer (Fantino, 1977; Rose & Fantino, 1978). For example, a coin that always produces raisins when inserted in a chimp-o-mat quickly becomes a strong conditioned reinforcer; coins that have less predictable results may be much weaker conditioned reinforcers, no matter how often they have been paired with raisins. Thus, conditioned reinforcers acquire their reinforcing properties just like Pavlovian conditioned stimuli: through stimulus associations.

CONTINUOUS VERSUS PARTIAL REINFORCEMENT   In addition to the type of reinforcer used, another factor that influences the effectiveness of reinforcement is the consistency with which a behavior is reinforced.

In laboratory demonstrations of operant conditioning, a behavior may be reinforced every time it occurs. This method is called a **continuous reinforcement schedule.** For instance, a rat receives a food pellet each time it presses a bar. Outside the laboratory, particularly in the everyday lives of humans, continuous reinforcement is unusual. For example, smiling at the food server in your college cafeteria does not always produce an extra large helping of food, nor does getting out of the house 20 minutes early always ensure your favorite parking space on campus. But these behaviors persist because they are sometimes reinforced. A **partial reinforcement schedule** exists when behavior is reinforced only part of the time. There are striking differences between the effects of continuous and partial reinforcement schedules on behavior.

Continuous reinforcement schedules almost always produce the highest rate of acquisition of a new behavior. For example, a rat learns to bar-press most rapidly when it receives food each time it makes the appropriate response. However, what happens when reinforcement is withdrawn? Extinction begins, and the rat quickly ceases its bar-pressing behavior.

Behaviors that are acquired on partial instead of continuous schedules of reinforcement are slower to be established. However, these behaviors are remarkably more persistent when no reinforcement is provided. For example, a rat accustomed to only intermittent reinforcement for bar pressing continues to press long after the food dispenser has run dry. This is particularly true when the partial reinforcement is delivered in an unpredictable fashion. This phenomenon is known as the **partial reinforcement effect.**

PARTIAL REINFORCEMENT SCHEDULES   Partial reinforcement is typically delivered in either of two basic ways, known as ratio or interval schedules. On a *ratio schedule*, a certain percentage of responses receive reinforcement. For instance, a slot machine in a casino might be programmed to provide some kind of payoff on 10 percent of all plays. An *interval schedule*, in contrast, is time-based: Subjects are reinforced for their first response after a certain amount of time has passed, regardless of how many responses might occur during that period. An example of an interval schedule is finally getting to speak to your friend after repeated dialings of her phone number resulted in busy signals or cruising in a parking lot for a vacant space.

Both ratio and interval schedules may be either variable or fixed. *Variable schedule* reinforcement is delivered unpredictably, with the amount of time or number of responses required varying randomly around an average. In contrast, *fixed schedule* reinforcement is always delivered after a constant number of re-

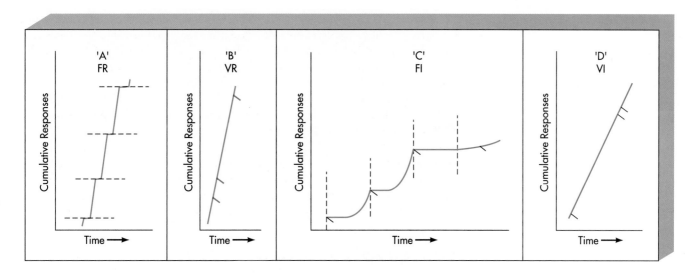

FIGURE 6.10

Schedules of Reinforcement

Stylized cumulative records from several common schedules of reinforcement. Panel *A* shows a fixed ratio schedule with characteristic pauses in responding, panel *B* illustrates a variable ratio schedule with typical high response rates, panel *C* illustrates the scalloped pattern of responding observed on fixed interval schedules, and panel *D* shows the stable pattern of responding found on variable interval schedules.

sponses or a fixed interval of time. These categories combine to form four basic partial reinforcement schedules: fixed ratio, variable ratio, fixed interval, and variable interval (see Figure 6.10).

Fixed Ratio Schedule On a **fixed ratio (FR) schedule,** reinforcement occurs after a fixed number of responses. For example, a rat receives a food pellet after 12 bar presses and a strawberry picker receives $1 after filling 12 small boxes with berries. Both are on an FR-12 schedule. This schedule tends to produce rather high rates of responding: The faster the rat bar-presses, the more pellets it gets, and the quicker the strawberry picker works, the more money she or he earns. Fixed ratio schedules are also used in programmed instruction where students proceed at their own pace and receive feedback after each section of work is completed. Programmed instruction is often quite successful in generating high rates of academic work. The fixed ratio schedule is illustrated in panel A of Figure 6.10.

This fact explains why some factories and businesses pay workers (like the strawberry picker) on a piecework basis. However, there are some limitations to this practice. For example, if workers in an automobile assembly plant were paid only according to the number of cars they ran through the assembly line, the quality of their work might suffer. Another potential limitation of the fixed ratio schedule is that people and other animals often pause briefly after reinforcement is delivered, probably because they have learned that their next few responses will not be reinforced. The pause following reinforcement on a fixed ratio schedule is termed *post-reinforcement pause*. Post-reinforcement pause may be one reason why payday typically occurs on Friday.

Variable Ratio Schedule **A variable ratio (VR) schedule** of reinforcement also requires the occurrence of a certain number of responses before reinforcement is delivered. Unlike a fixed ratio schedule, however, the number of responses required for each reinforcer varies. For example, a rat on a VR-6 schedule receives a food pellet on the average of every six bar presses, but any given reinforcer may require fewer or more than six responses. The pattern of behavior maintained by a VR schedule is illustrated in panel B of Figure 6.10.

Variable ratio schedules produce high response rates. Furthermore, because of the unpredictable nature of reinforcement, there is typically no post-reinforcement pause, for it is possible that reinforcement will occur on the very next response. Behavior that is maintained on this schedule is often very slow to extinguish.

These gamblers do not know when the slot machines will pay off. Their gambling behavior is maintained by a variable ratio schedule of reinforcement.

Gamblers are very familiar with variable ratio schedules. For example, a person who always bets on 13 at the roulette wheel is on a VR-38 schedule (the wheel has 36 numbers plus 0 and 00). On the average, 13 comes up every 38 spins. However, during a hot streak 13 might occur three times in 20 spins (of course, it also might not occur at all). Similarly, a slot machine may be rigged to pay off once every 20 times a coin is deposited, on the average (a VR-20 schedule). The gambler does not know when it will return a few of the coins it has swallowed. It is the unpredictable, highly variable nature of these payoffs that makes gambling so compelling to some people. In fact, gamblers often put in much more than they get back, a result that doesn't occur on interval schedules. Experimental animals also show the tendency to respond at very high rates on VR schedules, sometimes at the cost of forgoing the food they've earned on previous ratios.

Fixed Interval Schedule   On a **fixed interval (FI) schedule,** reinforcement is provided for the first response after a specified period of time has elapsed. For example, a rat on an FI-30 schedule, whose bar press has just produced a food pellet, will receive its next reinforcer the first time it bar-presses after 30 seconds have elapsed.

The response rates of animals on FI schedules quickly adjust to this contingency. Because no reinforcements occur for a period of time, no matter how often an animal responds, it typically stops working after reinforcement is delivered and then begins to respond toward the end of the interval. Thus this pattern of reinforcement tends to produce regular, recurring episodes of inactivity followed by short bursts of responding. This is illustrated in panel C of Figure 6.10.

Variable Interval Schedule   Finally, a **variable interval (VI) schedule** involves variable time intervals between opportunities for reinforcement. Thus an animal on a VI-45 schedule might receive reinforcement for a response after 30 seconds have elapsed, then after 60 seconds, and then after 45 seconds. This schedule averages out to reinforcement every 45 seconds. See panel D of Figure 6.10.

As you might guess, the random, unpredictable occurrence of reinforcement on this schedule tends to produce more steady rates of responding than fixed interval schedules. The steady persistent pattern of behavior maintained by VI schedules makes them quite useful to researchers studying the effects of other variables on behavior. For example, a researcher interested in examining the effects of certain drugs on behavior might examine the pattern of responding on a VI schedule both before and after drug administration.

APPLYING REINFORCEMENT SCHEDULES   We have seen that partial reinforcement affects behavior differently from continuous reinforcement, and that reinforcement schedules may further influence performance. What are the practical implications of these findings?

An Application of Reinforcement Schedules   Assume that you are the parent of a young boy who has not yet learned to clean his room each day. What type of reinforcement schedule(s) would be most effective in establishing room-cleaning behaviors? Would you use the same schedule throughout training? Think about these questions before reading on.

The best way to establish a daily room-cleaning routine would be to use a continuous reinforcement schedule. During the initial stages of training you would reinforce your son each time he completed his task, perhaps with points that could either be turned in for little payoffs (like reading a story) or accumulated for more sizable prizes like a trip to the zoo. It would also be important to praise the boy for each good job and perhaps display a chart of the child's performance. Associating the chart and praise with other reinforcers allows them to become conditioned reinforcers.

You cannot monitor and reinforce this behavior indefinitely, however. Once the room-cleaning behavior is established, you could begin shifting to a partial reinforcement schedule, reinforcing the behavior only some of the time. A variable ratio schedule would be the logical choice since it is very resistant to extinction and it is response, not time, dependent. Gradually, you would make the schedule more demanding until just a few words of praise delivered now and then would be sufficient.

Partial reinforcement can be a good way to maintain a child's room cleaning, but it may contribute to less desirable behavior in some circumstances. Consider the case in which a father tells his young daughter that she cannot leave their yard unless accompanied by an adult. Since children typically test the limits, the little girl sneaks over to her friend's house at the first opportunity, a lapse which the father overlooks because he is too busy. In this manner, a pattern of inconsistency is established, with the child discovering she can get away with inappropriate behavior at least some of the time. These unpredictable victories over the system can be powerfully reinforcing. In essence, parents who inconsistently enforce rules are training their children to be gamblers. Like Atlantic City slot machine players, these children are conditioned to keep pushing the button until the inevitable payoff is provided.

The reinforcement schedules we have been discussing share a common assumption: The learner will produce the desired behavior so that it can be reinforced. In operant conditioning, however, it is sometimes difficult to get an animal (humans included) to make the initial correct response so that it can be reinforced. The next section discusses methods for increasing the probability that a desired response will occur.

In operant conditioning, many responses occur spontaneously. For example, rats placed in Skinner boxes invariably get around to pressing the bar during the course of their explorations. In other circumstances, however, the behavior may

REINFORCING THE INITIAL OPERANT RESPONSE

not occur without some additional help. For instance, no matter how many times you say "roll over" to your untrained dog, the odds are remote that it will perform the trick so that you can reinforce it. Some special techniques can be used to encourage the desired response, however.

VERBAL INSTRUCTION   Sometimes desired behavior can be established by simply describing the appropriate response. Parents and educators often use this method. When you learned to drive, most of your instruction was probably verbal: Someone sat next to you and told you when to turn, brake, and accelerate. Verbal instruction is also provided in writing. Perhaps you first learned to operate a computer from a set of instruction manuals.

SHAPING   You may have wondered how researchers trained rats to press levers in several of the experiments already discussed in this chapter. The procedure used is referred to as shaping. **Shaping** involves a systematic process whereby responses that are increasingly similar to the desired behavior are reinforced step by step until finally the desired behavior occurs. For example, hungry rats are first reinforced for being near the lever. Later they must touch it, and finally they are required to exert sufficient force on the lever to operate it.

Shaping is especially effective for establishing novel behaviors. For instance, the learning of speech by a young child is shaped from nonsensical babbling to closer and closer approximations of the appropriate sounds of words. The reinforcement during this process may be as subtle as a change in facial expression of the parent. Later, reinforcement may be the appropriate response of the listener to a command.

Many therapists use shaping to obtain desirable behavior in emotionally disturbed children and adults. An example of this is the case of a nine-year-old boy with *autism*, a profound emotional disability that blocks normal patterns of social interaction. His parents consulted a behavior therapist, who used shaping to establish social behavior. At first the boy learned to obtain candy from a machine that was activated remotely. (Since no social pressures were imposed, this procedure was nonthreatening.) The next step was more complex. The boy was placed in a room that contained a variety of toys, the candy machine, and another boy about his age, a confederate of the therapist. The ensuing behavior was viewed through a one-way glass.

The disturbed youth made no overtures to the other boy. However, each time he looked at him, the therapist activated the candy dispenser. Once this behavior was established, the next step was to reinforce the boy when he took a step toward the other boy. In this fashion the autistic boy gradually learned to stand next to his would-be playmate, then to interact with him. (Even a normally undesirable act like grabbing a toy from him was acceptable at first, for it represented an interaction.) Gradually, over a period of weeks, a number of social behaviors were shaped, and eventually the candy machine became a less important reinforcer than the other boy.

MODELING   Another technique for producing a new operant response is modeling. **Modeling** involves demonstrating the desired behavior to the learner. Many athletic skills, such as diving, hitting a tennis ball, or riding a skateboard, are learned by watching someone else. In cases like these, reinforcement is the feedback from performance during acquisition of the skill.

Modeling teaches a wide range of behaviors, undesirable as well as desirable. For instance, a young child who admires an older youth who hates school may himself begin grumbling that he wants to quit school. Modeling is discussed in more detail later in this chapter under the heading "Observational Learning."

PHYSICAL GUIDANCE   The best strategy for training a dog to roll over is to guide compliance to the command by gently manipulating the animal. As the dog scrambles back on its feet, you can then provide a reinforcer such as a piece of meat or a pat on the head. After several sequences of command, manipulation, and reinforcement, the animal should begin to roll over on command without any manipulation.

This same technique might be used to train a child to drink from a cup. A parent's hand over a child's hand holding a cup can guide the child through the appropriate sequence of lifting the cup to the mouth. Each response is then reinforced by both the parent's praise and the act of drinking (it is a good idea to offer an especially tasty liquid in this initial training).

So far we've discussed the application of reinforcement to shape and increase rates of behavior; now we turn our attention to the use of punishment. From the very earliest experimental studies, its use and effectiveness have been controversial; however, because punishment is so frequently applied as a learning procedure, it deserves our careful consideration here.

PUNISHMENT AND OPERANT BEHAVIOR

Certainly punishment is widespread, from spanking misbehaving children to keeping students after school, meting out traffic fines, and incarcerating people in prisons. However, the fact that many people and institutions rely on punishment to control behavior does not necessarily mean that it is more effective than reinforcement. People have long debated the relative advantages and disadvantages of reinforcing desirable behavior versus punishing undesirable acts. There is no simple answer. Nevertheless, research has provided ample data that can help us make better informed choices as we confront this issue in our own lives. We begin by defining punishment.

Punishment (or a *punisher*) is defined as a stimulus whose delivery following a response results in a decrease in the frequency or probability of that response. We often think of punishment as an unpleasant or aversive stimulus, such as a spanking. However, punishment may also involve the withdrawal of positive reinforcers such as playtime, watching TV, money, or the use of the family car. Students sometimes confuse this second form of punishment with the process of extinction discussed earlier. The two are quite different. For example, if we wished to stop a child's temper tantrums through extinction, we would simply withhold our attention (which presumably is the reinforcer of this behavior). In contrast, modifying this behavior through punishment might be accomplished by withdrawing TV-watching privileges each time a temper tantrum occurred.

LIMITATIONS OF PUNISHMENT   Punishment, by definition, brings about a change in behavior, at least temporarily (Fantino, 1973). However, its effectiveness can be reduced by a number of limitations and negative side effects (Newsom et al., 1983). We'll next examine several of these.

TEMPORARY SUPPRESSION INSTEAD OF ELIMINATION   One limitation is in the long-term effectiveness of punishment. In most cases, punishment suppresses the unwanted behavior for a short time, but does not eliminate it (Clarizio & Yelon, 1974). In fact, there is ample evidence that suppressed behavior may reemerge when the prospect of punishment is gone or sharply curtailed. To eliminate a response, the contingency between the response and punishment must be maintained. When punishment is discontinued the response emerges. This is also true for reinforcement. When either reinforcement or punishment are discontinued responding returns to its pre-reinforcement or pre-punishment level. This is referred to as *extinction*.

For example, a child who is punished by a parent each time she raids the cookie jar will probably learn to suppress this behavior. However, if punishment hasn't occurred for some time she is likely to raid again.

EMOTIONAL SIDE EFFECTS OF PUNISHMENT Another potential problem is that punishment may produce undesirable emotional side effects such as fear and aggression. This outcome is particularly true when punishment is severe. For example, a child who receives constant, severe punishment from a parent may learn to fear that parent. The process by which this fear response is learned is classical conditioning. In this case a parent who consistently punishes may become a conditioned stimulus for fear. The subject will learn to withhold the punished behavior but also learns to fear the punishing situation. This could lead to problems interacting with the parent that may generalize to other relationships. In fact, punishment may induce aggression against the punisher.

The negative emotional effects of punishment are often generalized to related behaviors. Thus a child who is singled out for harsh punishment in one class may begin to react negatively to school in general. In contrast, people who are reinforced for desirable behavior generally feel good about themselves, are motivated to perform well, and are optimistic about future endeavors that they anticipate will lead to additional positive consequences. Similarly, the child who is punished by being sent to his or her room, write repeatedly on the chalkboard, or run extra laps on the track may actually be learning to associate these events and places with punishment and react negatively to them on later occasions.

PHYSICAL PUNISHMENT AND MODELING Children are often punished by physical means, such as slapping or spanking. Considerable evidence suggests that youngsters who are punished physically learn to model or imitate these aggressive acts and often become more aggressive in their interactions with others (Bandura & Walters, 1959; George & Main, 1979). Thus parents who spank or hit misbehaving children may be teaching them more than is intended, namely, that physical aggression is acceptable.

ADVANTAGES OF PUNISHMENT

While it is important to be aware of the limitations of punishment, most psychologists do not advocate total abolition of all punishment for controlling or modifying behavior. Although reinforcement is preferable in most cases, punishment is sometimes essential as a way to suppress undesirable actions so that a desirable alternative behavior may occur.

For instance, assume you are the parent of a young child who constantly strays out of your yard. To avoid establishing a pattern of partial reinforcement caused by inconsistent punishment, you might decide to wait until the day occurs when she stays home, so you can reinforce her. Theoretically, this idea is a good one. However, the behavior might not occur spontaneously, and in the meantime your child might get lost or hit by a car.

In other instances punishment is desirable because reinforcement of an alternative behavior is impractical. For example, punishment may be the only practical method to train your dog to refrain from barking at night. The immediate and consistent application of punishment can be very effective here.

In such cases, it is necessary to apply sufficient punishment to suppress an unwanted behavior. At the same time, you would also reinforce the desired behavior with appropriate reinforcement.

IMMEDIATE APPLICATION OF PUNISHMENT Punishment, like reinforcement, works best when it immediately follows behavior (Hall, 1989; Parke, 1969; Schwartz, 1984). Perhaps one of the more common violators of this rule is the parent who says to a misbehaving child, "Wait until Dad (or Mom) comes home." This long delay dramatically reduces the effectiveness of punishment.

Sometimes, however, punishment cannot be delivered immediately. For instance, punishing a child who intentionally emits distracting noises during a church service would disrupt the service for everyone. In cases like this, it is desirable to restate the past indiscretion before administering punishment, perhaps after returning to the scene of the crime.

CONSISTENT APPLICATION OF PUNISHMENT A second point that should be remembered in applying punishment is that it loses effectiveness if it is inconsistent (Schwartz, 1984). Inconsistencies may occur over time or from one person to another. In the first case, inappropriate behavior may be punished in one instance and ignored the next. As we noted earlier, such inconsistencies place the learner on a variable ratio schedule of reinforcement (not punishment), a practice that can produce remarkable persistence of undesirable behavior. The dog owner who only occasionally punishes his barking dog may be doing just this.

Inconsistencies from person to person are quite common. Two parents often have differing concepts of discipline. Children in this type of home environment frequently learn to play one parent against the other, a situation that can teach the child to manipulate others for personal gain.

INTENSITY OF PUNISHMENT Punishment needs to be strong enough to accomplish the desired goal of suppressing undesirable behavior, but it should not be too severe. You probably know some people who believe that if a little bit of punishment works, a lot will work even better. Unfortunately, this philosophy often results in negative side effects such as fear and aggression. Moderate punishment, especially when it is designed to be informative, can redirect behavior so that new responses can be reinforced. When punishment is severe, however, the intent is more likely to be retribution than a redirection of behavior.

In most circumstances, physical punishment should be avoided. Instead of getting a spanking, a misbehaving child could be sent to a time-out room for 5 minutes. (A time-out room is a boring but safe place, such as a laundry room with nothing but a stool for the child to sit on.) Note that even this type of punishment can be overdone, however. Whereas 5 minutes is usually ample time for a young child to be alone in a time-out room, one or two hours is probably unreasonable.

CONDITIONED PUNISHMENT As with reinforcement, stimuli associated with punishment can become powerful conditioned punishers when they reliably predict punishment. If the command *NO* reliably predicts a slap on the rear of your barking dog, the command alone on later occasions may be sufficient to suppress barking. However, the effects of a conditioned punisher, like a conditioned reinforcer, will extinguish if they are no longer occasionally paired with a primary punisher.

In all, it seems that punishment can be useful for modifying behavior under certain circumstances. When punishment is used, however, it should be applied in moderation, in combination with incentives for desirable behavior.

COMPARING CLASSICAL AND OPERANT CONDITIONING

As we have seen, both classical and operant conditioning involve learning relationships or associations between two events. Classical conditioning involves learning associations between a conditioned stimulus (CS) and an unconditioned stimulus (UCS). Operant conditioning involves learning associations between behavior and its consequences, reinforcement or punishment. Each learning process produces a change in response, whether it be the conditioned response of anxiety to medicinal smells or an operant response such as playing a video game. However, classical and operant conditioning involve very different procedures and result in different kinds of responses. These two differences will be examined more closely.

First, the procedures for classical and operant conditioning differ. In classical conditioning experiments the researcher typically presents two stimuli: a novel CS immediately preceding the UCS which naturally elicits some response. After several paired presentations of these stimuli the researcher can test for a conditioned response by presenting the CS alone. If learning occurred, the CS will now elicit a conditioned response. In operant conditioning experiments the researcher shapes a particular response by closely following approximations to that response with reinforcement. Learning has occurred when the new response is demonstrated.

Second, and perhaps more important, the kinds of responses for operant and classical conditioning are different. Classically conditioned responses are typically reflexive responses or changes in emotional or motivational states, not voluntary behavior. Salivation is not a voluntary response by dogs, but a reflexive response which occurs during and prior to the ingestion of food. The anxiety you may experience while waiting at your dentist's office is also a change in behavior, but it is emotional behavior, not a voluntary response. Operant responses on the other hand are typically voluntary responses such as lever pressing, riding a bicycle, verbal behavior, and covert behavior like thinking.

Although it is possible to dissociate classical and operant conditioning in the laboratory, rarely in nature is there so clean a distinction between the two processes. In fact, both are typically involved in the adaptive behavior of most animals, including people. Consider a squirrel foraging for nuts among several species of deciduous trees, some dropping nuts, others not. At first the behavior

The behavior of this squirrel foraging for food is determined by both classical and operant conditioning.

of the squirrel might appear somewhat random as it scrambles among the leaves under the different trees. When a nut is located under a leaf of a certain color and size this increases the likelihood that similar color and shaped leaves will be turned. Finally the squirrel attends primarily to the leaves with nuts among them and no longer forages near the others. In this example both classical and operant conditioning lead to the adaptive behavior of the squirrel. Classical conditioning was involved in learning the association between leaves of a certain color and shape and the nuts found under them. Operant behavior was involved in learning the association between approaching and turning these particular leaves and finding nuts. This is referred to as **two-factor learning.** Without both types of learning, the squirrel's foraging behavior would be far less successful.

Many learning situations like the example above involve both classical and operant conditioning. Let us return to the case of avoidance learning demonstrated by the biology student, discussed earlier in this chapter. This example was originally presented to illustrate classical conditioning, and classical conditioning was most likely the first learning process that took place: Through pairing with the frightening experience at the hospital, the medicinal odors became the CS that triggered a fear response.

Operant conditioning also occurred, however. Since fear is unpleasant, any responses that reduce or eliminate fear are strengthened through negative reinforcement. When the young woman avoided the biology lab, she was operating on her environment to alleviate her fear. The student's avoidance behavior kept her far from the biology lab. And since she was never exposed to the laboratory long enough to find out that the UCS would not occur, her conditioned fear was maintained. Thus her avoidance behavior involved two factors, the first being the acquisition of conditioned fear to the medicinal odors (classical conditioning), the second being the operant avoidance response which was maintained by negative reinforcement.

Many human phobias are products of two-factor learning. An understanding of the principles underlying this kind of conditioning provides a clue for treating such fear responses. In order to extinguish conditioned phobias, a person must be exposed to the CS in the absence of the UCS. To do this, the operant avoidance behavior must be prevented. One possible way to accomplish this would be initially to expose a relaxed subject to a very mild version of the feared stimulus (for example, a mildly medicinal odor in a nonthreatening situation). Gradually, more intense versions of the conditioned fear stimulus would be introduced. This technique, called systematic desensitization, is discussed in Chapter 16. Conditioned fear responses and anxiety are discussed in more detail in Chapter 15.

TWO-FACTOR THEORY OF AVOIDANCE LEARNING

COGNITIVE INFLUENCES ON LEARNING

To this point, we have focused on associative learning through either classical or operant conditioning. Many contemporary psychologists (including learning theorists) have argued that associative learning may provide too mechanistic an interpretation for all forms of learning. As conditioning was originally proposed by Pavlov, Thorndike, Skinner, and others, it did not take into account cognitive processes that cannot be observed. Another theoretical perspective, cognitive learning theory, attempts to identify the role that cognitive processes play in learning. Not all learning theorists agree that internal cognitive processes are necessary to account for learned behavior however. As you read this final section, keep in mind that the examples discussed can also be explained without reference to cognitive processes.

As you might guess, cognitive theorists stress the individual's active participation in the learning process. They suggest that we learn by forming a cognitive structure in memory that preserves and organizes information pertaining to the key elements in a situation. Thus, in addition to forming conditioned associations between stimuli (classical conditioning) and behavior and reinforcement (operant conditioning), we form mental representations of our environments. These representations, along with external stimuli, guide behavior. Although learning is involved in the formation of these representations, the roles of classical and operant conditioning are not clear.

Cognitive learning theories did not become an important force in psychology until the late 1960s, but their roots go back many years. One important early influence was Edward Tolman's research on latent learning in rats.

LATENT LEARNING

A fundamental principle of operant conditioning is that reinforcement is essential for learning new behavior. However, over 50 years ago psychologist Edward Tolman and his associates demonstrated that rats will learn a maze even when they are not reinforced. Tolman called this phenomenon **latent** (or hidden) **learning** because it is not demonstrated by an immediately observable change in behavior at the time of learning. Such learning typically occurs in the absence of a reinforcer, and it is not demonstrated until an appropriate reinforcement appears.

In a classic latent-learning experiment, three groups of rats were run for 16 consecutive days in the complex maze shown in Figure 6.11. An error was recorded each time a rat entered a blind alley in the maze. Rats in one group, the reinforcement group, received food when they reached the goal box at the end of the maze on each of the 16 days. A second group, the nonreinforcement group, also explored the maze each day, but they did not receive food when they reached the end. Rats in a third group, the latent-learning group, received no reinforcement for the first 10 days and then were reinforced for the remaining six days.

Over the first 10 days, rats in the reinforcement group showed considerably more improvement than animals in either of the other groups. In fact, the animals in the nonreinforcement group showed very little improvement in performance over the entire 16 days. However, after food was introduced on day 11 for rats in the latent-learning group, they immediately began to perform as well as animals in the reinforcement group. This occurrence clearly demonstrated that Tolman's rats were learning something about the maze even with no reinforcement (Tolman & Honzik, 1930).

This latent-learning experiment demonstrates the distinction between learning and performance, for learning can take place even when it is not demonstrated by performance. The experiment also poses a question: If no responses can be observed, what is being learned? Tolman answered this question by claiming that his rats were developing a **cognitive map,** or mental representation, of the maze in the absence of reinforcement. Later, when reinforcement was introduced, the map allowed the animals to reach a high level of performance quickly.

Tolman and his associates conducted a number of additional experiments that demonstrated how cognitive maps work in problem solving. For example, once rats had learned how to get through a complex maze to reach food, obstructions were placed in their way and new routes introduced. Tolman suggested that these complications were quickly mastered because the rats were able to resort and rearrange the mental picture of the maze, and thereby find the new route with ease (Tolman et al., 1946).

The performance of rats in a radial maze suggests that animals form an internal representation of their environment that aids in navigation.

Cognitive maps have become a very important concept in contemporary learning theory. Research suggests that a variety of organisms, including rats, chimpanzees, birds, and bees, use cognitive maps in adapting to their environments (Gould & Marler, 1987; Olton, 1979; Shettleworth, 1983; Whitam, 1977). Humans also appear to create mental representations of their environments that allow them to function more effectively (Evans, 1980).

We have presented cognitive learning as separate from the associative types of learning, which is the traditional way of viewing learning. Pavlov, for instance, stressed that *temporal contiguity* (that is, closeness in time) of the CS and the UCS is essential for classical conditioning, and most learning theorists after Pavlov continued to view classical conditioning as a relatively automatic form of learning that is strengthened through repeated pairings of the CS and the UCS.

Recent evidence has caused some psychologists to question this view, however. According to their interpretation, cognitive processes are involved even in classical conditioning (Rescorla, 1988a, 1988b; Turkkan, 1989).

According to this cognitive perspective, the learner during classical conditioning first observes that the CS and UCS typically occur together, and stores this information in memory. Later, when the CS appears by itself, the learner retrieves the information from memory and makes the conditioned response in anticipation that the UCS will occur. In other words, it appears that the CS and UCS become associated not simply because they occur contiguously in time, but rather because the CS provides information about the UCS (Rescorla, 1987, p. 121). Indeed this view is supported by Rescorla's experiment described earlier where he demonstrated that mere contiguity between a CS and UCS is not sufficient. Rather, it was stimulus contingency that was essential. Recent interpretations of Rescorla's experiments stress the importance of how much information the CS conveys about the UCS. That is, the more informative or predictive the CS is, the better conditioning will be.

Studies of a phenomenon known as *blocking* also support this interpretation. In such experiments, subjects are exposed to repeated CS-UCS pairings (for example, a light with a shock). Later, after conditioning is established, a second stimulus (such as a tone) is added to the original CS so that both stimuli now occur prior to the UCS. According to Pavlov, the second stimulus should quickly become conditioned since it is regularly paired with the UCS. However, this outcome does not occur (Halas & Eberhardt, 1987; Kamin, 1969). Apparently, the previous conditioning of the response to the light somehow interferes with or blocks the tone from becoming an effective CS.

Cognitive theorists refer to the information concept to explain these results. They argue that since the original stimulus already predicts the occurrence of the UCS, the new stimulus is irrelevant because it provides no new information about the occurrence of the UCS. If the UCS is now changed in some way, for example its intensity is increased, learning will occur to the second CS (the tone) because now tone predicts larger shocks than did the light alone.

Increasing numbers of learning theorists believe that the predictability of the relationship between the CS and UCS is probably more important than either the timing or the frequency of pairings (Fantino & Logan, 1979; Fuhrer & Baer, 1965). We now know that CS-UCS pairings, while necessary for classical conditioning, are not sufficient by themselves to ensure that learning will occur.

Cognitive factors may be important in operant as well as classical conditioning. Although the operant conditioning emphasizes the consequences of behavior, those consequences do not automatically strengthen or weaken responses. Rather, they provide the learner with important information about the probable consequences of a given behavior under certain circumstances (Colwill & Rescorla, 1986; Rescorla, 1987; Williams et al., 1990). Cognitive theorists view

COGNITIVE PROCESSES IN LEARNING

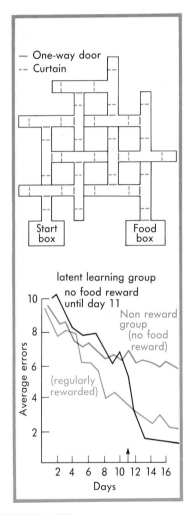

FIGURE 6.11

Classic Latent Learning Experiment

In Tolman's experiment three groups of rats were run for 16 consecutive days in the maze shown in the top part of the figure. Results for the three groups are shown at figure bottom. Notice that the rats in the latent learning group (black line) which received reward beginning on day 11 performed as well as rats that received reward beginning on day one (blue line).

SOURCE: Adapted from Tolman & Honzik, 1930.

individuals as information-processing systems that store this relevant information about consequences. Later, when confronted by similar circumstances, the learner retrieves this information from memory and acts accordingly. Thus, from the cognitive perspective, operant behavior is guided by expectations of probable outcomes (Bolles, 1979; Greeno, 1980).

The cognitive theorists stress the argument that the events occurring in classical and operant conditioning do not automatically stamp in behavior. Instead, they provide relevant information that helps to establish expectancies and it is these expectancies that form the basis for subsequent behavior.

OBSERVATIONAL LEARNING

Much of human as well as other animal learning occurs by watching or listening to others. This is referred to as **observational learning** and it involves both the classical and operant processes already discussed.

One of the major findings of observational-learning research is that children tend to behave in a manner similar to their parents, both during their childhood and later on in life. Thus child abuse and other maladaptive behaviors are often passed on from one generation to the next just as are warm, nurturant behaviors.

There are strong cognitive components in learning by observation. People observe the behaviors of others, then store cognitive representations of these acts in memory, where they remain until the right influence triggers the individual to enact that behavior.

The role of observation and imitation in learning is explained in **social learning theory,** and Albert Bandura (1977, 1986) of Stanford University is probably its leading proponent. Bandura and his colleagues have performed a number of studies that demonstrate the importance of observational learning in our lives. In one widely cited experiment, children observed adults beating on a five-foot inflated BoBo doll and were then placed in a similar situation. The researchers found that children who had observed this aggressive behavior were more likely to act aggressively when placed in the same situation than did children in control conditions who had observed a quiet model (Bandura et al., 1963).

Social learning theorists use the term *models* to describe the people whose behaviors we observe and often imitate. These models can range from parents (usually the most influential models in our lives) to people we see on television or in movies. Humans have a great capacity to store mental representations. In this fashion we learn from the examples of others.

Some of the behaviors we observe become part of our own behavioral repertoire, but we also observe many responses that we never imitate. (Watching another diner chew gum at an elegant restaurant, for instance, may cause you to resolve never to do such a thing.) Our brains process all these stored memories of previously observed behaviors, selecting out those that seem appropriate in a given situation. Once an observed behavior becomes part of our own response system, it becomes subject to the rules of reinforcement discussed earlier. In this fashion, imitative behaviors become either strengthened or weakened.

Bandura (1977) has identified four key steps in observational learning. The first is simply having our attention drawn to a modeled behavior. (As you recall modeling was already discussed as a procedure to produce an initial operant response.) Second, we store a mental representation of the behavior in our memories. Third, a specific type of situation triggers us to convert the remembered observation into actions. Finally, if our actions are reinforced, we add the behavior to our repertoire of responses.

Learning by observation, or modeling, can exert a powerful influence on our lives. Being able to learn by watching, listening, and even reading, is extremely useful. Can you imagine how tedious it would be to acquire all our behaviors by trial and error? Modeling allows us to profit from the experiences of others. For example, in one study researchers tried a variety of strategies to increase the sociability of nursery school children who normally kept to themselves. The most effective strategy turned out to be to have these youngsters watch a film showing sociable children. The film was even a faster agent of social change than a shaping procedure that involved praising and paying attention to children when they behaved sociably (O'Connor, 1972).

EVALUATING THE EFFECT OF INCONSISTENT MODELING The fact that children learn by observing, and that parents are particularly influential role models, raises the question of how behavioral inconsistencies in parental actions might affect children. We have all heard the familiar adage, "Do what I say, not what I do," and many of us have been told by our parents to act in certain ways when we knew, either as children or adults, that they themselves did not practice what they preached. What are the possible consequences of such inconsistencies, and how are children likely to respond to them? Consider this question for a moment before reading on.

At the present time, we know very little about how people are affected by inconsistencies in the actions of strong role models such as parents. However, common sense suggests that observing incongruence in the behaviors of important role models is likely to confuse and trouble the observer, and a recent study by Canadian researcher Michel Alain (1989) supports this interpretation. In a survey of 210 high school students, Alain found that children of incongruent parents were well aware of inconsistencies and were significantly more troubled and upset with their parents than were children of congruent parents.

In summary, cognitive psychologists attribute much of learning to the formation of cognitive maps or structures, to the establishment of expectancies in classical conditioning or to observation. Behaviorists maintain that reference to intervening cognitive process is not necessary and that by postulating such processes we deflect our attention away from important environmental variables. As you will see, this issue will resurface throughout the remainder of this book.

BIOLOGICAL BASES OF LEARNING

You now appreciate that learning involves relatively permanent changes in the behavior of the learner. You may wonder what kinds of changes actually occur to represent this learning. Searching for these changes has been a long and exciting endeavor. We end this chapter with a brief review of one of the most important research findings on the biology of learning and memory. (Other neurobiological approaches will be discussed in Chapter 7.) As you will see, even though these findings have important implications for human learning, we are a long way from observing the neuronal changes that represent learning in people.

Investigating the biological mechanisms of learning in humans, or even rats, is not practical at present because of the extremely large number of neurons involved. As you recall from Chapter 3 the human brain contains more than one hundred billion neurons. Thus researchers interested in the cellular changes that represent learning have focused on another species with a relatively simple nervous system. The species that has proven to be most valuable for this research is the Aplysia, a shell-less marine snail. The aplysia has about 20,000 neurons and many of their connections (synapses) have been well studied.

Investigations by Eric Kandell (1983) of classical conditioning in Aplysia have focused on a protective reflex of the gill which is the respiratory organ of the Aplysia. For instance, when the Aplysia is touched strongly on the tail or the

CLASSICAL CONDITIONING OF THE APLYSIA

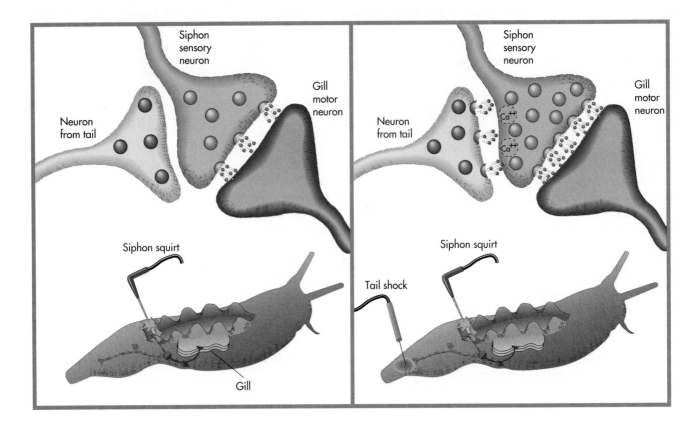

FIGURE 6.12

Marine Animal Aplysia Used to Study the Biology of Learning

Notice the changes in membrane permeability to Ca++ after conditioning. See text for details.

siphon the gill withdraws into the mantle. Refer to Figure 6.12 for a diagram of the Aplysia. Because this protective response is easily observed and occurs reliably, it is an ideal response for classical conditioning. To condition a gill withdrawal response, a mild touch (squirt of water) is applied to the siphon. This mild touch (the CS) by itself does not cause a gill withdrawal response. Immediately following the CS, a shock is applied to the tail (the UCS) which does cause the gill to withdraw. After a number of paired CS-UCS (touch-shock) trials, the siphon squirt (CS) results in a conditioned gill withdrawal response (the CR).

What kinds of changes in the nervous system of the Aplysia mediate this conditioning? Kandell and others have recently identified several cellular changes that occur. The neurons involved are illustrated in Figures 6.12 and 6.13. When stimulated, the UCS neuron (the sensory neuron receiving shock) transmits a strong signal to the modulatory neuron which in turn activates the motor neuron to cause the gill to withdraw.

In Figure 6.13 you can see that the modulatory neuron also has contact with the CS neuron (the sensory neuron receiving touch). Notice, however, that this synapse is at the end of the axon before its synapse with the motor neuron. If the CS neuron was recently active (because the CS was presented before the UCS) chemical events involving the neurotransmitter serotonin occur on the presynaptic membrane of the CS neuron. After several conditioning trials this chemical activity leaves the CS neuron facilitated. That is, the CS nerve terminal is now more permeable to calcium ions (Ca^{++}) than before conditioning. As you recall from Chapter 3, calcium is involved in the release of the neurotransmitter into the synapse. When more calcium flows into the nerve terminal, more neurotransmitter is released. Therefore, the next time the CS occurs (without the UCS) the activity of the CS neuron results in more neurotransmitter being released at the motor neuron synapse. If sufficient neurotransmitter is released

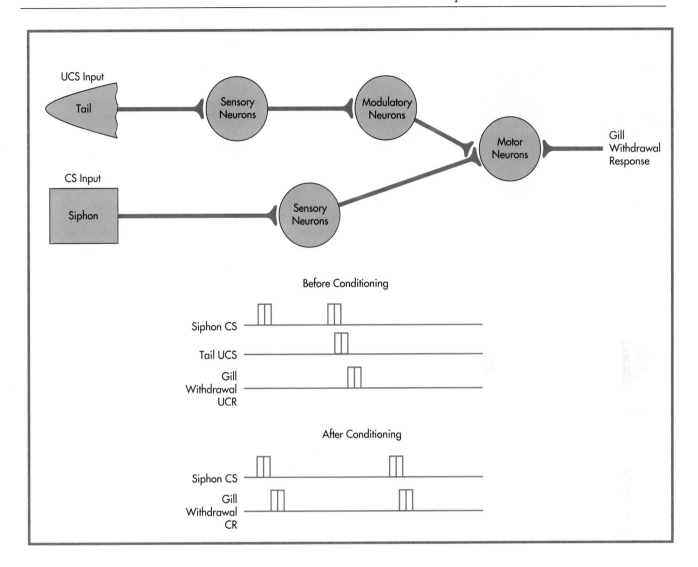

from the CS neuron the motor neuron will now fire causing the gill withdrawal response. The withdrawal response to the mild siphon touch is now a conditioned response.

In summary, paired presentations of the CS and the UCS leave the CS neuron facilitated. The **synaptic facilitation** allows the CS to activate the motor neuron for the gill response because it releases more neurotransmitter than before conditioning. This facilitation will not occur if the delay between the CS and the UCS is much longer than 0.5 seconds. Likewise, it will not occur if the CS follows the UCS as in backwards conditioning (Kandell and Hawkins, 1992).

Chemical changes like this are believed to underlie the learning processes discussed in this chapter. In fact, as you read this text or perfect your tennis serve, similar changes are occurring throughout your brain. Over the next few years scientists will be learning much more about the kinds of changes that occur in your nervous system that allow you to learn.

Without additional memory processes, however, learning would clearly be of little value. In the next chapter we discuss the processes of memory that allow our experiences, as represented, to influence our behavior. We conclude the next chapter with more discussion of the biological processes involved in learning and memory.

FIGURE 6.13
Model of Neuronal Connections in Aplysia

HEALTH
PSYCHOLOGY
LIFE

CLASSICAL CONDITIONING OF THE IMMUNE SYSTEM

A few years ago, researchers Robert Ader and Nathan Cohen (1982) observed a curious effect as they were studying classically conditioned taste aversion. In their experiment, rats were given drinks of a saccharin-flavored water (the CS) followed immediately by injections of a drug that made them nauseous (the UCS). As you might predict, the animals immediately aquired a taste aversion that caused them to avoid or reduce their consumption of the sweet solution. The rats were then exposed to several extinction trials in which they were presented with the sweet solution but no toxic drug. (Extinction is a process designed to reduce the strength of the association between the CS and UCS through repeated presentations of the CS alone without the UCS.)

During this stage of the study, something unexpected happened. For no apparent reason, some of the rats died. Ader and Cohen considered a variety of possibilities to explain what had happened. One of their primary clues was that the drug they used to induce nausea, cyclophosphamide, is also known to suppress the body's immune system.

Ader and Cohen reasoned that perhaps the saccharin water had become a conditioned signal that suppressed the rats' immune systems in the same way as the drug with which it had been paired. If this were the case, the repeated exposures to the sweetened water alone during the extinction trials may have suppressed their immune systems so much that they fell victim to disease-bearing microorganisms in the laboratory.

To test this possibility, they conditioned other rats, using the original design with one modification. Before the extinction trials in which rats received only the CS of sweet water, they were injected with red blood cells from sheep foreign bodies that would normally trigger the rats' immune systems to produce high levels of defensive antibodies. The researchers' hypothesis was supported: The conditioned animals produced significantly fewer antibodies than control animals for whom the sweet water was not a CS.

Ader and Cohen also tested the immune-system responses of mice who had been classically conditioned to respond to the sweet water. They found that if these conditioned mice received only half the usual dosage of cyclophosphamide, together with exposure to the CS, their immune systems were suppressed as completely as if they had been given a full dosage of the toxic drug.

Other researchers have confirmed and extended Ader and Cohen's findings. For instance, Grochowicz et al., (1991) demonstrated that conditioned immunosuppression effectively prolonged the survival of transplanted heart tissue in rats. Immunosuppression in tissue transplant procedures is neccessary to prevent the immune system from attacking the newly transplanted tissue.

HEALTH IMPLICATIONS

Certainly, these findings extend our knowledge of how the mind and body interact to reduce or increase our vulnerability to disease. But beyond this, they may lead to a practical medical application in the future. Consider, for instance, that a major problem associated with many drugs used to combat disease is that they often produce serious side effects. For example, although cyclophosphamide is toxic enough to have been selected as the nausea-inducing UCS in Ader and Cohen's experiment, it has a legitimate and very valuable medical use as treatment for lupus, an immune-system disorder in which the body turns against itself. If classical conditioning could be used to condition the body of a lupus victim into responding to a significantly lowered dosage of the drug, a diseased person might be able to benefit from cyclophosphamide without having to experience its debilitating side effects. Experiments are currently being conducted with lupus patients to determine whether conditioned immunosuppression can effectively augment drug therapy.

The same kinds of benefits might also obtained with drugs used to treat cancer and AIDS. Hopefully, in the years to come these conditioning principles can be applied to alleviate suffering and improve the treatment of many victims of disease.

SUMMARY

DEFINING LEARNING

1. Learning may be defined as a relatively permanent change in potential behavior that results from experience.

2. Associative learning, the process by which connections or associations are made between two events, may take place in two primary ways: through classical conditioning and through operant conditioning. Classical conditioning involves learned associations between two stimuli. In operant conditioning, people or other animals learn to associate their own behavior with its consequences.

CLASSICAL CONDITIONING

3. The four key elements in classical conditioning are the unconditioned stimulus (UCS), the unconditioned response (UCR), the conditioned stimulus (CS), and the conditioned response (CR). After pairing a previously neutral stimulus (CS) with a stimulus (UCS) that automatically elicits an unlearned response (UCR) the CS will cause a response on its own.

4. Factors which facilitate the acquisition of a classically conditioned response include a CS that is clearly different from other stimuli, frequent pairings of the CS and the UCS, and the order and timing with which the CS is paired with the UCS.

5. The acquisition of classical conditioning depends on a predictive relation between the CS and the UCS called stimulus contingency.

6. When certain associations are acquired very quickly they are called selective associations. Conditioned taste aversions are examples of selective associations.

7. Extinction, or cessation of the CR, occurs in classical conditioning when the CS is repeatedly presented alone, without the UCS.

8. A CR sometimes reappears spontaneously after extinction, a phenomenon called spontaneous recovery.

9. When a response has been conditioned to a particular stimulus, other stimuli may also produce the same response. This principle is called generalization.

10. Early in the conditioning process, a learner may respond to a variety of similar stimuli (generalization). However, with time he or she learns that only one of these stimuli, the CS, is consistently associated with the UCS. This process of learning to make distinctions between the CS and similar but not identical stimuli is called discrimination.

11. A classical conditioning variation in which a neutral stimulus becomes a CS through association with an already established CS is referred to as second order conditioning.

OPERANT CONDITIONING

12. In operant conditioning humans and other animals learn to associate their behavior with either reinforcing or punishing consequences.

13. Reinforcement is defined as a procedure which increases the probability that a response will occur.

14. A positive reinforcer is any stimulus presented following a response that increases the probability of the response. A negative reinforcer is a stimulus that increases the probability of a response through its removal when the desired response is made.

15. In escape conditioning, an organism learns to produce a response that will allow termination or escape from an aversive stimulus (negative reinforcer). In avoidance conditioning the individual learns to emit an appropriate avoidance response, thereby averting any exposure to the aversive stimulus.

16. A primary reinforcer is a stimulus that satisfies a biologically based drive or need. Secondary reinforcers are stimuli that acquire reinforcing properties through association with primary reinforcers.

17. A continuous reinforcement schedule exists when behavior is reinforced every time it occurs. A partial reinforcement schedule exists when behavior is reinforced only part of the time.

18. Behaviors that are acquired on partial instead of continuous schedules of reinforcement are slower to be established, but they are remarkably more persistent when no reinforcement is provided.

19. Four varieties of partial reinforcement schedules include those based on a percentage of responses that are reinforced (fixed ratio and variable ratio) or passage of a certain amount of time before a response is reinforced (fixed interval and variable interval).

20. Methods used to encourage the occurrence of an initial desired operant response include physical guidance, shaping, modeling, verbal instruction, and increasing motivation.

21. Punishment can be defined as a procedure which decreases the probability that a given behavior will occur.

22. The effectiveness of a punisher in producing a desired change in behavior depends upon its intensity, consistency, and the delay between a response and punishment.

23. Principles which may improve the effectiveness of punishment include immediacy, consistency, moderation, and combining it with positive reinforcement (always reinforcing acceptable alternatives to the punished behavior).

COMPARING CLASSICAL AND OPERANT CONDITIONING

24. Classical conditioning involves learning associations between a CS and a UCS. Operant conditioning involves learning associations between behavior and its consequence.

25. Most learning situations combine both classical and operant conditioning in what is called two-factor learning.

26. Many human phobias are a result of two-factor learning. First an individual acquires a fear of a neutral stimulus (classical conditioning), and then acts to reduce or eliminate this fear by learning to avoid the frightening stimulus (operant avoidance conditioning).

COGNITIVE INFLUENCES ON LEARNING

27. Cognitive learning theory attempts to clarify the role that perception, thinking, and memory play in learning.

28. Cognitive theorists suggest that we learn by forming a cognitive structure, or representation, in memory that preserves and organizes information relevant to a given situation.

29. The roots of cognitive learning theories go back many years to studies of insight in chimpanzees and latent learning in rats.

30. Insight is a sudden recognition of relationships that leads to the solution of a complex problem. Latent learning refers to learning that is not demonstrated by an immediately observable

change in behavior at the time of learning.

31. Cognitive theorists suggest that what is learned in classical conditioning is not a mere contiguity between the CS and UCS, but rather an expectancy that the UCS will follow the CS.

32. From the cognitive perspective, operant behavior is also viewed as being guided by expectations of probable outcomes.

33. Cognitive theorists believe that there are strong cognitive components in learning by watching and imitating others, a process called observational learning.

34. The role of observation and imitation in learning is explained

in social learning theory. In some circumstances, learning by observation, or modeling, may be even more effective than operant conditioning in shaping our behavior.

BIOLOGICAL BASES OF LEARNING

35. Learning involves structural and chemical changes at synapses within the brain.

36. Researchers have identified these changes in the marine snail, Aplysia.

37. In the Aplysia learning involves the long-term synaptic facilitation of motor neuron synapses.

TERMS AND CONCEPTS

learning
associative learning
classical conditioning
operant conditioning
cognitive learning
unconditioned stimulus (UCS)
unconditioned response (UCR)
conditioned stimulus (CS)
conditioned response (CR)
acquisition
delayed conditioning
simultaneous conditioning
trace conditioning
backward conditioning
conditioned taste aversion
extinction
spontaneous recovery
generalization
discrimination
second-order conditioning
Law of Effect
cumulative record
discriminative stimulus
reinforcement

positive reinforcement
negative reinforcement
escape conditioning
avoidance conditioning
punishment
primary reinforcement
conditioned reinforcement
continuous reinforcement schedule
partial reinforcement schedule
partial reinforcement effect
fixed ratio (FR) schedule
variable ratio (VR) schedule
fixed interval (FI) schedule
variable interval (VI) schedule
shaping
modeling
two-factor learning
latent learning
cognitive map
observational learning
social learning theory
synaptic facilitation

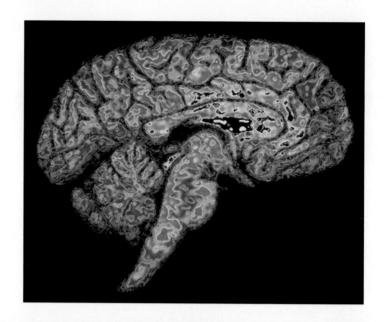

C H A P T E R 7

Memory

WHAT IS MEMORY?

Information Processing and Memory
Memory Processes

A MODEL OF MEMORY

Three Memory Systems
Sensory Memory
Short-Term Memory
Long-Term Memory

MEMORY AS A DYNAMIC PROCESS

Constructive Memory
Schemas
Eyewitness Testimony
Context
State Dependency
Extreme Emotion

FORGETTING

Decay of the Memory Trace
Interference
Retrieval Failure
Motivated Forgetting
Organic Causes of Forgetting

THE BIOLOGY OF MEMORY

Hebb's Theory of Neural Connections
Neural Plasticity
Distributed Memory
Where are Long-Term Memories
   Processed?
Where are Short-Term Memories
   Processed?

IMPROVING ACADEMIC MEMORY

The female digger wasp begins each day with an inspection tour of up to fifteen separate nesting sites where her larvae are kept in underground burrows. After this initial inspection tour the female wasp begins hunting for caterpillars to replenish her nests. Quite remarkably she returns to each burrow in turn with just enough food to replenish each nest. The female digger wasp not only remembers the condition of each nest as it was during her morning checkout visit, she must also remember where each burrow is located with respect to various landmarks. Her memory of nest condition and location serves to guide her behavior on return visits later in the day (Tinbergen, 1958).

John Kingsley came to our attention in a shocking news story about an 83-year-old Alzheimer's patient who was found unattended in his wheelchair at a dog race track outside of Spokane, Washington. Attached to his chair was a note misidentifying him. John did not know who he was or how he got to the races. He couldn't help authorities find his family or his previous caregivers. John Kingsley, like many other patients during advanced stages of Alzheimer's disease, is alive, but without life. Without a memory of his past, or the ability to remember anything new, John's life is nothing but the existing moment.

It has been said that memory is the most important function of our brains. Can you imagine what life might be like if you could not remember your experiences? Without memory, you, like John, would have no history and thus no identity. You would have no skills, for all knowledge is based on memory. All but the most primitive responses require memory. Perceiving, thinking, learning, feeling—they all depend on our ability to store and use information that we process each day. In lower animals, like the digger wasp, primitive memories can lead to extremely complex patterns of intelligent behavior that would otherwise not be possible.

Psychologists have studied memory for years, but in many ways it is still a mystery. What changes take place in our brains that allow us to store memories, sometimes for a lifetime? By what process do we retrieve these memories from a brain cluttered with information? We explore such questions in this chapter. Although we do not have all the answers, we will see that there is much that we do understand about what we remember, how we remember, why we forget—and even what we can do to improve memory. We begin by defining memory.

In the photograph above: A female digger wasp remembers the condition of numerous nest sites during a morning check-out visit. Later she returns to each nest with just enough food to replace what has been eaten.

John Kingsley, suffering from advanced Alzheimer's disease, caught the attention of the media after he was abandoned at a race track near Spokane, Washington.

WHAT IS MEMORY?

Memory, like the term *learning* from the previous chapter, is not something we can observe. Rather, we infer that you have memory from your behavior. That is, if your performance on exams is better after studying the material than before studying, we infer that memory has occurred. We assume that memories reside inside of you as structural changes within your brain. As we will see, these structural changes occur passively without your attention but they can be facilitated by actively participating in memory processes. We begin with a formal definition of memory that was offered by Estes (1975):

> Memory is some property or state of the organism which is assumed to have resulted from some experience and which has the consequence of altering the organism's potentialities for a response. . . .

INFORMATION PROCESSING AND MEMORY

Psychologists once viewed humans and other animals as organisms that merely experience and respond to stimuli. They did not concern themselves with the internal events that govern complex processes such as learning and memory.

This outlook has changed in the last two decades. Most psychologists have come to view the human brain as an information-processing system. That is, information is not simply stored in the brain and then later retrieved; instead, it is shaped or modified in ways that allow organisms to adapt to their environments efficiently. In other words, people and other animals actively participate in the assimilation of their experiences. Learning and memory are not static or fixed processes but dynamic processes that continue to change over the course of time.

The information-processing model is particularly helpful in conceptualizing memory processes. In the following pages we examine the various stages that appear to be part of the memory process.

MEMORY PROCESSES

You are sitting quietly at your desk, studying for an exam. From somewhere in your apartment complex you hear a muffled scream. This is not particularly unusual; you live in a big housing unit and you often hear strange noises, including an occasional scream or loud shouting. Nevertheless, your attention is diverted. A few moments later, you hear an engine start in the parking lot below. You hear the sound of an engine being revved, then of a car speeding through the parking lot. You rush to the window, and catch a fleeting glimpse of a low-slung red sports car. Could there be a connection between the scream and this vehicle? Maybe you will end up as a key witness in a murder trial. Your imagination runs rampant for a minute or two; then you return to your books.

Will you accurately remember what you have just seen and heard if a violent incident did occur on this day? The chances are very good that you will remember something. The accuracy of your recall will depend on three separate processes (Crick, 1989; Murdock, 1974). First, you encode or translate incoming information into a neural code that your brain can process. Second, the encoded information becomes stored so that it can be retained over time. Finally, you must be able to find and recover this stored information when you need it later on, through the process of retrieval.

ENCODING **Encoding** involves first perceiving some particular stimulus event, such as the sound of a scream or a revving engine, and then translating or coding the information so that it can be more easily stored. This process involves categorizing or organizing information in some meaningful way as described in Chapter 4. Is the information a sight, a sound, a smell, some tactile sensation? The scream is processed as a sound and we further categorize it as a signal of distress. When we encode material, it becomes associated or linked to what we already know. For instance, you encode the fact that the car has a manual transmission because you already know that glitches in the sound of acceleration indicate shift points. Memories that are connected to or associated with previous information are much easier to retain.

STORAGE **Storage** is the process by which encoded material is retained over time in memory. Exactly how memories are stored is the topic of some of the most important current research in psychology. We know that memories do not just float around in our brains waiting to be retrieved: Some changes must take place in the brain to allow memories to be stored for later use. We investigate this topic in some detail later in the chapter.

The efficiency of the storage process is greatly influenced by the effort we put into encoding or organizing new memories. Suppose your roommate asks you to order a pizza by calling 234-4454. This number is easy to remember because it is organized in two clusters; after one or two rehearsals, you have it memorized at least for a few moments. If your roommate asks you to call and check on the order ten minutes later, however, you will probably need to ask her to repeat the number.

Now, assume that you meet someone interesting at a party. That person gives you a telephone number, 245-5565, and says, Call me sometime. Of course, nobody seems to have a pen at critical moments like this. Chances are you will choose a much more effective method for encoding and storing this number than the one for the local pizzeria. Perhaps you note the logical progression of 10 units in the sequence 45, 55, 65, and use this method as a meaningful way to encode and store this information. You are likely to remember this number for a longer period after actively rehearsing and organizing it.

RETRIEVAL The final step in the process of remembering is **retrieval.** If you properly encoded and stored your new friend's telephone number, or information about the getaway car in the earlier example, you will be able to retrieve this information from memory at a later time. Generally speaking, the more effort we put into preparing information for storage, the more efficiently we can retrieve it.

A MODEL OF MEMORY

Psychologists distinguish between memories that stay with us, such as an important phone number, and those that are quickly lost. In fact, most psychologists today believe that there are three distinct memory systems that allow us to process, store, and recall information. This perspective has been articulated by Richard Atkinson and Richard Shiffrin (1968, 1971). We first introduce these three systems and then go into much more detail describing research which supports each system's role in memory.

Sensory Memory Research suggests that information which first comes to us through our senses is stored for a fleeting moment within **sensory memory.** Because of the highly transitory nature of this memory system, we usually are not consciously aware of sensory memory, nor do we actively organize or encode this information. The function of this memory system seems to be to hold or preserve impressions of sensory stimuli just long enough for important aspects of this information to be transferred to the next system, short-term memory.

THREE MEMORY SYSTEMS

FIGURE 7.1
A Theoretical Model of Memory

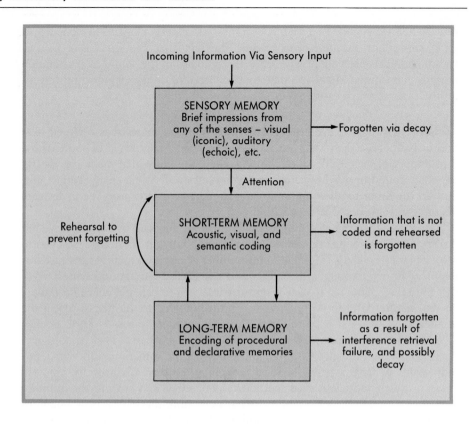

Short-Term Memory **Short-term memory (STM)** comprises our immediate recollection of stimuli that we have just perceived. The amount of information this memory system can store is much more limited than that of sensory memory. Unless we repeatedly reinstate the information transferred to short-term memory, it will probably be retained only momentarily, perhaps for no more than about 20 seconds (Brown, 1958; Muter, 1980; Peterson & Peterson, 1959). For example, you have probably forgotten the number of the local pizzeria by now. Unless you repeatedly rehearse a phone number, it is likely to fade from memory very quickly.

Long-Term Memory Information that is transferred from short-term memory into **long-term memory (LTM)** may remain for minutes, hours, days, or perhaps even a lifetime. When we retrieve information from long-term memory, it passes through short-term memory. Figure 7.1 presents a theoretical model of how information flows into and among these three memory systems.

Long-term memory is what most of us mean when we talk about memory. For some people, the concept of short-term memory does not correspond to their preconceived notion of what memory is. Information that is immediately put to use, such as a phone number or instructions given in exercise class, is not in memory, they say. Instead, such information is simply in one's "mind." Psychologists would disagree with this contention. What else are thoughts in your mind but memories? Any time we can recall information, no matter how recently it passed through our sensory/perceptual systems, we are tapping memory. Let us look more closely at how these three memory systems work.

SENSORY MEMORY

Sensory memories, sometimes called sensory registers, are brief impressions from any of our senses. We are surrounded by sights, sounds, smells, tactile sensations, and countless other stimuli. When we first receive a particular stimulus, it is held momentarily in sensory memory. These fleeting impressions appear to be largely accurate reproductions of the original sensory inputs. For example, when you glance out the window, for a fraction of a second your brain absorbs the entire visual panorama of varied colors, shapes, and patterns. A similar process occurs when you walk into a cafeteria: Your nose captures a variety of odors and you hear a different set of noises from those you heard on the street.

Unless they are successfully transferred to short-term memory, these sensory impressions disappear within a second or two. That is because the only coding that takes place in sensory memory appears to be the physiological processes of our sensory systems, for instance, the transduction of sound and light waves to messages that are transmitted to our brains (see Chapter 4).

ICONIC (VISUAL) MEMORY   Visual sensory memory is called **iconic memory** (*icon* means "image") (Neisser, 1967). It includes images of what we see. For many years, researchers thought that visual memory held only limited information. They based this assumption on evidence from research that had measured the storage capacity of visual sensory memory. Such studies would flash a grid of letters or numbers such as those shown here on a screen for a fraction of a second:

H   C   N   M
P   O   X   U
S   J   T   B

Subjects would then be asked to recall as many of the items as possible. When this *whole report procedure* was used, most people could remember only four or five items, no matter how many were shown in the grid.

One researcher, George Sperling (1960), was convinced that subjects in these studies actually registered more than just four or five items; the problem was simply that they forgot the rest while they were reporting the first few items. To test his theory, he designed a new research strategy called the *partial report procedure*. Subjects were told that they would view a grid for 1/20 of a second, then hear a tone. They would only have to report part of what they had seen. If they heard a high-pitched tone, they were to report only on the top row of four letters. A medium-pitched tone meant they were to report on the middle row, and a low tone meant the bottom row. The point at which a subject heard the tone varied from immediately after the letters disappeared to a maximum delay of one second. Figure 7.2 illustrates this partial report procedure.

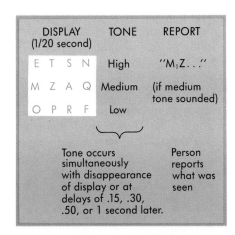

FIGURE 7.2

Sperling's Partial Report Procedure

Subjects viewed a grid of 12 letters for 1/20 of a second, then they heard a brief tone after a delay. If they heard a high tone they were to recall the top row of letters, if they heard a medium tone they were to recall the middle row, and a low tone meant they were to recall the bottom row.

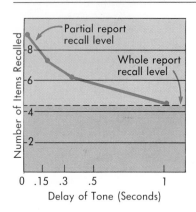

FIGURE 7.3

Result of Sperling's Partial Report Procedure

The solid line represents the average number of letters recalled after different delays between stimulus presentation and tone presentation. Longer delays resulted in poorer performance. The dashed line represents performance when subjects were to recall all 12 of the letters.

SOURCE: Adapted from Sperling, 1960

As Figure 7.3 shows, subjects' recall was best when the tone sounded immediately after the image disappeared—an average of 3.3 letters out of 4. Because subjects did not know what row they would be reporting until the image had disappeared, Sperling reasoned that they must have had 9 or 10 items available for immediate recall (3 rows times 3.3 per row)—roughly twice the earlier estimates of what we can register in iconic memory. The later the tone sounded, the less subjects remembered.

Sperling concluded that his subjects were actually reading the letters from a brief afterimage, or iconic reproduction, of the original stimulus pattern. This image fades quite rapidly. From Sperling's research as well as other evidence, we know that an image stored in iconic memory generally fades within approximately 0.3 seconds as new information replaces it (Irwin & Yeomans, 1986; Yeomans & Irwin, 1985).

ECHOIC (AUDITORY) MEMORY   You may have noticed an auditory image or echo when you have turned off the radio and the voice of a commentator seems to linger momentarily. This auditory sensory memory is called **echoic memory:** After the physical sound stimulus ceases, an auditory image or echo persists for a second or two (Neisser, 1967). Like iconic memory, echoic memories are held only briefly as they are replaced by new auditory stimuli.

We are constantly bombarded by sounds. Most of these go in one ear and out the other, which is to say that only a few selected sounds of importance are passed to our short- and long-term memory systems. It appears that echoic memory serves to filter incoming sounds quickly and to determine which (if any) are important enough to be transferred to short-term memory. For example, suppose you are sitting alone in a crowded airport. Every sound that is loud enough to be heard—talking voices, laughter, loudspeaker announcements, shuffling feet, background music—is temporarily stored in echoic memory. These unimportant auditory messages register fleetingly in your sensory memory system, but they are unlikely to be transferred into short-term memory. However, at some level you are aware of these sounds and they are being processed. If you find something important among these inputs, for example, if you hear your name in a loudspeaker message, your attention is captured and you transfer this information into short-term memory.

Are the auditory messages to which we do not attend actually lost, or is there an auditory image similar to the iconic image that remains for a moment? To find out, a number of researchers, most notably Anne Treisman (1960, 1964), have used a technique called *shadowing*. In this procedure, a subject wears headphones and is exposed simultaneously to two different recordings, one presented to each ear. To ensure that the subject pay attention to only one of the two messages, he or she is asked to shadow or repeat the message presented to one ear. This task is extremely demanding, so much so that subjects typically repeat the words in a dull monotone. Figure 7.4 demonstrates the experimental procedure. When questioned at the end of a shadowing task, subjects are unable to provide any information about the message they did not repeat.

Do you think that subjects' inability to repeat material presented to the other ear means that this channel of sensory input is blocked by the shadowing process? Or do words that enter through the unattended ear register momentarily in echoic memory? If you were conducting an experiment that used shadowing, how would you answer these questions? See if you can devise a procedure before reading on.

To see if the information that subjects did not repeat was really lost, Treisman added one additional task to her experiment. Although subjects had been instructed to concentrate all their attention on the shadowing task, they were also

College students often experience . . .

Right ear

Left ear

the car with the

Um, college students often . . .

FIGURE 7.4

The Shadowing Task

The subject is presented with two messages, a different one in each ear. The message in the right ear is to be repeated after presentation. As a result, the message in the left ear is ignored. What happens to it?

told that when the recordings stopped and they heard a signal, they were to try to recall anything they could of the unattended messages. This additional task provided interesting results: If the subjects' attention was switched soon enough, it was possible for them to rehear some of the last words of the other message in the form of an echo.

Research indicates that auditory sensory memory for language stimuli can last up to two seconds. This is considerably longer than the estimated 0.3-second capacity of iconic memory. This difference makes sense, however, when we consider the nature of the sensory messages received by our eyes and ears. When we look around us, we can almost always look back if we fail to process something important through our iconic memories. In contrast, if we miss something in an auditory message, we cannot listen back. Therefore, there seems to be a good functional reason why auditory images should last longer than visual images.

THE MODALITY EFFECT   We also seem to recall information better if we hear it rather than see it (Crowder, 1970, 1976). This phenomenon, known as the modality effect, probably reflects the fact that an echo lasts longer than a visual image in sensory memory. Have you ever noticed that you can remember a telephone number or items on a grocery list better if you read them aloud? Auditory afterimages give us more time to transfer this important information over into short-term memory for further organizing and processing.

Short-term memory, also called working memory, is an intermediate memory process sandwiched between sensory memory and long-term memory. STM is often referred to as our working memory, because it is the memory system within which we actively process information, both as we transfer it from sensory memory and as we retrieve it from long-term storage.

As its name suggests, short-term memory has a short duration. If you look up a term in this book's index and see that it is used on pages 342 and 563, you will probably find that after searching page 342, you must check again for the second

SHORT-TERM MEMORY

page reference. Unless we make an active effort to remember information, it fades from STM in about 20 seconds or less. However, we can retain information in our working memories for as long as we wish by active *rehearsal*—for example, by repeating the index references over and over.

Short-term memory has a limited capacity. You can test your STM capacity by reading the following list of numbers once, covering them, and writing down as many as you can in the order in which they appear.

$$9\ 2\ 5\ 7\ 6\ 1\ 3\ 7\ 8\ 4\ 5\ 6$$

If your short-term memory is like most people's, you probably recalled about seven of these numbers. The capacity of STM is about seven items or chunks of unrelated information if the information has been encoded on the basis of how it sounds (acoustic coding), and about three chunks when items are encoded based on what they look like or what they mean (visual and semantic coding) (Miller, 1956; Yu et al., 1985; Zhang & Simon, 1985). Note that this STM capacity does not necessarily refer to seven numbers or letters. It refers to seven pieces of information which can be letters, words, or even meaningful sentences. The term chunk describes a meaningful unit of short-term memory. One important way that we can increase the limited capacity of our STM systems is through chunking.

CHUNKING **Chunking** is the process of grouping items into longer, meaningful units to make them easier to remember (Frankish, 1985; Miller, 1956). For example, the sequence 1, 9, 4, 1 consists of four numbers which could be treated as four chunks. This would leave room for about three more chunks in STM. However, we could combine these four digits into one meaningful chunk 1941, the year America went to war with Japan. This method would leave space for at least five or six more chunks of information in STM.

You were probably unable to recall all 12 of the numbers in the previous short-term memory test. However, you might find it relatively easy to recall all 12 numbers by grouping or chunking them into four groups, a process that yields four individual numbers (925, 761, 378, 456). Many of us routinely chunk telephone numbers by grouping the first three digits together, and then treating the final four as separate chunks, thereby reducing the original seven numbers into five chunks. We may further improve our retention of the last four digits by chunking them by twos for example, remembering 39 and 15 instead of 3-9-1-5.

We can also organize or chunk information held in STM according to its personal meaning, or we can match it with codes already stored in long-term memory. For instance, try reading once through the following list of letters and then recalling as many as possible from memory.

$$C\ P\ A\ N\ O\ W\ M\ A\ D\ D\ N\ B\ A$$

If you tried to recall these items as 13 separate letters, you probably remembered no more than seven. However, if you coded them into four well-known chunks (CPA, NOW, MADD, NBA), you would have no trouble recalling them in proper sequence.

CODING IN SHORT-TERM MEMORY *Acoustic Coding* Most of the information placed in STM is held there in acoustic form, according to how it sounds. This seems to be true even when the information comes through our visual rather than our auditory sense. For example, suppose you are walking along the edge of a wheatfield with a friend, and suddenly a pheasant explodes out of the grass nearby. Your immediate recall of the name of the species of bird you just saw would probably be coded in your STM by the sound of the word pheasant, not by a visual image of the bird in flight.

We know that acoustic coding is important from a number of studies. In one (Conrad, 1964), subjects were asked to recall lists of letters immediately after they saw them. When errors occurred, they were likely to involve confusions of letters that sounded alike (for example, confusing T for B or D for E) rather than those that looked alike, such as F and E or D and O.

Visual and Semantic Coding   Not all of the encoding we do in STM is acoustic, however. If it were, deaf people would be unable to store information in short-term memory. It appears that people with this handicap rely heavily on visual coding, in which information is identified and stored as visual images of letters, words, shapes, and so on. For instance, the pheasant that flew out of the field a minute ago would be coded by its image or perhaps by the way its name appears in writing. Hearing-impaired people also use semantic coding, in which objects they see are categorized by class. For example, the pheasant is a bird, its size is about the same as a chicken's, and so forth. Research shows that the STM-recall errors of hearing-impaired people tend to result from confusing items that are similar in appearance or meaning rather than items that sound similar (Frumkin & Anisfeld, 1977). People who are not hearing-impaired also use visual or semantic encoding at times (Conrad, 1972).

In some cases auditory or semantic coding is not possible. For instance, briefly examine the two figures in Figure 7.5 and decide whether they are the same (but rotated) or different before reading on.

If you guessed that they were the same, but rotated, you were correct. The "mental" rotation to accomplish this was performed in short-term or working memory and the processing was clearly visual, not auditory. Experiments conducted by Shepard and Metzler (1971) have studied the processing of complex visual stimuli in short-term memory. In these experiments subjects examined pairs of visual stimuli such as those in Figure 7.5 and were asked if they were the same or different. The dependent variable here was the amount of time it took subjects to decide. In some cases the stimuli were mirror images and therefore different and in other cases they were the same, but rotated. The degree of rotation could range from 0 to 180 degrees. Interestingly subjects' response times were directly related to the amount of rotation difference between the two figures; that is, the larger the rotation difference, the longer it took subjects to

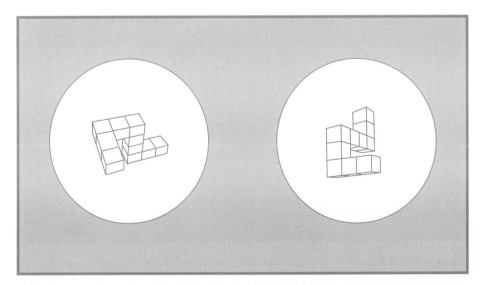

FIGURE 7.5

Typical Visual Stimuli Used by Shepard and Metzler

The objects are identical in this case, but rotated 90°. In other cases they may be mirror images of each other.

identify the figures as the same. This not only confirms that visual processing in short-term memory occurs, but that it is an orderly process determined by the amount of processing required.

LONG-TERM MEMORY

The third memory system, long-term or reference memory, is like a limitless storehouse that never quite fills up with the facts, feelings, images, skills, and attitudes that we keep accumulating. Long-term memory allows us to do more than simply store information from past experiences. Faced with new problems and situations, information in LTM is made available to our working (short-term) memory thereby allowing us to deal with and process new information. We may "live" in our short-term memory, but it is our long-term memory that allows us to understand and use the constant flow of new information we experience.

For example, suppose you are walking down the street and see a person lying prone next to a downed power line. In an instant, you would search your LTM to determine the significance of the scene. You have heard enough about the effects of high-voltage shock to guess that the person may be in cardiac arrest. Suppose this conjecture is confirmed by a pulse check. What next? If the person is lucky, your LTM also contains a knowledge of cardiopulmonary resuscitation (CPR). You transfer this information into short-term memory and administer CPR. Then you search long-term memory for information you can use to keep the victim from going into post-trauma shock. This new information would displace the CPR information in short-term memory, which you no longer need. It is this constant, ongoing interaction between short- and long-term memory that

Riding a bicycle depends on procedural memory and skills acquired through operant conditioning.

allows us to reason, solve problems, follow schedules, see relationships between events, ride a bike, and so forth.

TYPES OF LONG-TERM MEMORY The abilities just mentioned are diverse, including not only what we can do but what we know. Most psychologists categorize long-term memories along these lines, as either procedural or declarative memories.

Procedural Memory **Procedural memories** are memories for how to perform skills. These memories can be highly complex. Suppose you enter a local golf competition. Before teeing off, a friend provides you with some specific information about course conditions. As you play your round, you draw upon a storehouse of knowledge about how to adjust your strokes to accommodate all these factors: the proper follow-through on a sand shot, how much muscle to put behind a stroke on wet turf, how to adjust for wind at the third hole, and so forth. All of these actions are specific skills acquired through practice and reinforcement, and they constitute procedural memory.

Declarative Memory Not all memory, of course, is based on recalling how to execute specific skills or procedures. For instance, your memory of what you have learned so far in your psychology class is based primarily on lecture notes and your readings in this book. Recall of specific facts such as these is made possible by **declarative memory.**

Procedural memories are often hard to acquire. It may have taken months to perfect your golf swing. Once established, however, these skill memories can be remarkably persistent. Facts stored in declarative memory are often established more quickly, but they are much more susceptible to forgetting.

Another difference between procedural and declarative memory seems to be the location of their storage areas in the brain. One especially interesting source of information comes from an unfortunate accident in which a fencing foil (narrow sword) was thrust through a young man's nostril into the left side of his thalamus. Since his injury, this person, known in the literature as N.A., appears to be unable to store virtually any new declarative knowledge in LTM. It is impossible for him to read a textbook and remember information on a previous page that the author might refer back to. Even watching TV or carrying on a conversation are hopelessly confusing, since words and plots don't appear to be registered in LTM. Interestingly, however, N.A. is still able to store procedural knowledge. He can learn how to do things like ride a horse, swing a golf club, or swim (Kaushall et al., 1981). These observations seem to suggest that fact knowledge and skill knowledge might be stored in different parts of the brain. However, alternative explanations are plausible. For example, it may be that N.A. stores declarative memories but just cannot access them. Certainly more research will be needed here before we can be certain. We return to N.A. later in this chapter.

Procedural and declarative memories seem to develop at different rates. Infants from a variety of species, including humans, develop the ability to remember skills well before they are able to remember facts. For example, in one study three-month-old monkeys were just as proficient in a skill task as mature adult monkeys. In contrast, tasks requiring memory for facts could not be totally mastered until the monkeys were two years old (Mishkin, 1982).

Until recently, many psychologists divided declarative memory into two distinct categories, episodic memory and semantic memory—a categorization that was proposed by Endel Tulving (1972, 1983). Episodic memory represented essentially autobiographical facts about a person's experiences, stored in roughly chronological order. This type of memory included your memories of your first kiss, the day you graduated from high school, what you had for breakfast this

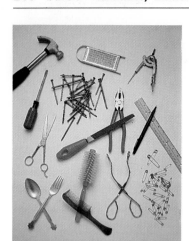

FIGURE 7.6
A Test of Visual Memory

morning, and the sequence in which you consumed these food items. **Semantic memory** contained general, nonpersonal knowledge about the *meaning* of facts and concepts without reference to specific experiences. Knowledge about the principles of grammar, mathematical formulas, different kinds of food, and the distinction between afferent and efferent neurons are all examples of facts believed to be stored in semantic memory. Because we often learn facts (semantic memories) within episodes (episodic memories) of our lives it is very difficult to distinguish between these two memory types.

Several efforts to test the hypothesis that episodic and semantic memory represent distinct memory subsystems have, for the most part, failed to support this distinction (Dosher, 1984; Neely & Durgunoglu, 1985). This failure has led to criticisms of the semantic-episodic distinction (McKoon et al., 1986; Ratcliffe & McKoon, 1986), which prompted Tulving to modify his theoretical framework. Tulving now conceptualizes episodic memory as a subsystem of semantic memory (1986).

Semantic Memory   Semantic memory is equivalent to an encyclopedic collection of facts about our world. In what form is this information stored in long-term memory? One widely discussed theory, the **dual-code model of memory** (Paivio, 1971; Paivio & Lambert, 1981), argues that memories may be stored either in *sensory codes* (for example, as visual images or sounds) or *verbal codes* (as words).

Study the photo in Figure 7.6 for 20 or 30 seconds and then look away and see how many items you can recall and write down. How did you remember the objects? Did you name them while studying the figure, or did you categorize them according to the use you would put them to? If the objects were stored as words, you employed a verbal code. However, perhaps you were able to retain a visual image of the picture and to use this sensory code to aid your recall of specific items.

Some people appear to be able to use visual codes so efficiently that they can retain a vivid image of large amounts of visual material for several minutes. Research subjects with this ability, called **eidetic imagery** (photographic memory), claim they can close their eyes and see an entire picture or printed page from a book as if they were looking directly at it rather than scanning their memory. Eidetic imagery is a very rare talent (some question whether it even exists [Lieblich, 1979]) that is more common among children than adults (Gray & Gummerman, 1975; Haber, 1969; Richardson, 1986). This difference may reflect the fact that children's memories are less cluttered with extraneous facts, thus allowing for clearer, less encumbered images.

Which type of coding, verbal or sensory, is most common? Do we even use two codes to store declarative memories? These questions have been the subject of much debate in psychology. To complicate matters further, it appears that we store some memories in the form of abstract codes that are neither strictly verbal nor sensory. For example, if you describe a movie you have just seen to a friend, you will not repeat word for word what you heard the actors say. Instead, you will have abstracted your impressions of the movie into a commentary that is your own creation, including your views on the cinematography, the acting, the plot, and the mood.

Since most of us do not use eidetic imagery to remember everything we see, we often have trouble extracting information from long-term memory. Some bits of information can be maddeningly elusive. Our ability to access information depends largely on how it was encoded for storage. That is, the kinds of associations that were formed. Although encoding is largely a passive associative process outside of our attention, there are several strategies that seem to facilitate efficient encoding, which we examine in the following section.

ENCODING LONG-TERM MEMORY Many memory experts draw an analogy between long-term memory and a set of file cabinets or the card catalog in a library. Encoding information for storage is like numbering books or files and using index cards to provide cues or access codes. The better we organize our file systems, the more quickly we can access information and the longer we can remember it. Therefore, a key to efficient long-term memory is in the organization of material. A number of memory aids or **mnemonic devices** can help us to do this (Bower, 1970; Nield, 1987). The appropriateness or effectiveness of the various mnemonic devices outlined here vary from task to task. You may want to experiment with more than one approach for a given memory task.

Clustering **Clustering** is a mnemonic device that involves grouping items into categories (Bousfield, 1953; Buschke, 1977; Forrester & King, 1971; Thompson et al., 1972). For example, suppose you want to memorize the following shopping list:

toilet paper	green beans	matches
hamburger	bacon	milk
asparagus	chicken	sour cream
corn	broom	cheese

These 12 items, if treated separately, include about five too many chunks for your short-term memory. Thus you can probably forget trying to hold them in STM by repeatedly rehearsing the list all the way to the grocery store. If you treat the items as separate, without trying to organize the list in some meaningful way, your LTM recall is also likely to prove inadequate for the task. A far easier method is to cluster or group the items under four subcategories: dairy items, meat, vegetables, and household products. Remembering four categories, each with three items, is a much more manageable task.

Method of Loci The method of loci, developed by the early Greeks, involves forming pictorial associations between items you wish to recall and specific locations along a designated route you might travel (*loci* means locations or places in Latin).

The first step is to develop a route you are familiar with. Imagine, for example, that you are walking from the campus library to your apartment. Pick out specific locations along the way that are easy to remember, such as a bus stop bench, a flagpole, a large oak tree, a broken-down van parked on the street, the sidewalk leading to your apartment house, and so forth. Then create a series of images that associates each item on your list with a specific location along your route.

For example, to use the loci method to remember the grocery list in the clustering discussion, you might imagine toilet paper strewn on the bus stop bench, cornstalks leaning against the flagpole, a chicken sitting in the oak tree, and so forth. Picture these associations as vividly as possible. Later, when you need to remember the list, take a mental walk along your route.

Narrative Story Another way to remember information is to organize it into a narrative (Wall & Routowicz, 1987). The story does not need to be particularly logical or plausible; it simply has to place items within a meaningful framework. For example, suppose you want to remember the five explanations for why we forget: interference, organic amnesia, decay of the memory trace, retrieval failure, and motivated forgetting. (These explanations are discussed later in this chapter.) The following narrative provides one possible way to encode this information (the key words describing explanations for forgetting are italicized).

The rotten odor emanating from his duffle bag was sufficient to run *interference* as Sam weaved his way through the crowded corridors. "Phew!" exclaimed his buddy Bill. "It smells like something *organic* is *decaying* in your duffle bag." "Oh, that is just the remnants of a crummy brown-bag lunch that my Mom *failed to retrieve* from my bag because she wants me to overcome my *motivation to forget* about the little details in my life," responded Sam.

An experiment by Gordon Bower and Michael Clark (1969) demonstrated how powerful a mnemonic device the narrative story can be. Subjects inexperienced in this technique were asked to try to memorize 12 lists, each containing 10 nouns. Half the subjects were instructed to make up 12 brief stories, each containing one of the groups of nouns. The other half of the subjects merely spent an equivalent amount of time attempting to memorize the lists with whatever technique they chose. When tested later, subjects who had used the narrative story technique recalled an average of 94 percent of the words; those who had not, remembered only an average of 14 percent.

The Peg-Word System The peg-word memory system involves first learning a series of words that correspond to a sequence of numbers (Miller et al., 1960). Each word and corresponding number represents a peg in the system. The following 10 rhyming pairs is a popular example of this approach:

One is a bun	Six is sticks
Two is a shoe	Seven is heaven
Three is a tree	Eight is a gate
Four is a door	Nine is wine
Five is a hive	Ten is a hen

Once you have memorized these associations, you can use them to recall a list of 1 to 10 items. Create a series of visual images that allows you to hang the item you wish to remember on the appropriate pad. For instance, to remember the following list of building supplies—nails, masking tape, saw, electric sander, electric drill, wire, hammer, tape measure, pliers, and vise grips—you would imagine each item on your list interacting with one peg-word. Thus you might imagine a hamburger bun stuffed with nails, two shoes taped together with masking tape, a large saw embedded in your mother's favorite fruit tree, and so forth.

Acrostics **Acrostics** are sentences in which the first letter of each word serves as a cue for recalling specific information. For example, suppose you need to remember the last eight presidents of the United States, starting with the Clinton administration and moving sequentially back in time. Here is a sentence that would help you accomplish this task: "Cereal Bowls of Rotten Canned Fruit Never Justify Killing." The names are Clinton, Bush, Reagan, Carter, Ford, Nixon, Johnson, and Kennedy. If you took piano lessons at some point in your life it is a good bet that you used another acrostic, the sentence "Every Good Boy Does Fine" to help you memorize the notes on the lines of the treble staff.

Acronyms Still another memory system is **acronyms,** or meaningful arrangements of letters that provide cues for the recall of material. For example, many people have learned the colors on a color wheel in their order of appearance by remembering Roy G. Biv (red, orange, yellow, green, blue, indigo, and violet). Another acronym, FACE, is often used by piano teachers to help students remember the notes in the spaces of the treble staff.

Do memory systems really work? One experiment demonstrates not only that they do, but also that we seem to learn memory systems at a fairly young age. Sixth grade children were shown to be much better at remembering lists than

tivated a specific node in a network of associations, and this activation spread to related concepts. Consequently, when a related word appeared, subjects recognized it more quickly (Schvaneveldt & Meyer, 1973).

In another study (Collins & Quillian, 1969), subjects were presented with simple sentences and asked to judge their accuracy by responding "yes" or "no". For example, referring to the network in Figure 7.8, a subject might be given a sentence like "Tranquilizers reduce anxiety," or "Amphetamines alter physiological processes." The researchers theorized that the length of time required to judge the accuracy of sentences is influenced by how far apart the concepts are stored in an association network in memory. Presented with our two sample sentences, a subject would respond most rapidly to the first since the concepts of "tranquilizers" and "reduce anxiety" are directly linked. The response to the second would be slower because "amphetamines" and "alter physiological processes" are two steps apart in the hierarchy. Indeed, the researchers found that a sentence containing facts stored together requires less time to judge than one in which facts are stored one or more steps apart in the network.

Associative network models of memory are receiving considerable attention currently as they have proven useful in the development of representational memory in computers. As well, recent work in the neurobiology of memory has provided additional support for associative networks, as we will see later in this chapter.

TESTING LONG-TERM MEMORY A number of methods have been used to measure our ability to store new material in long-term memory. The three most common techniques are recall tasks, recognition tasks, and relearning.

Recall In a **recall** task, the subject is asked to reproduce information to which he or she was previously exposed. For example, a recall question designed to test your knowledge of the material in this chapter might ask you to name the three memory processes. Fill-in-the-blank or essay questions are other examples of recall tasks.

Recognition A **recognition** task presents possible answers from which the subject must pick the correct one. Instead of having to pull information from memory, a recognition test simply involves realizing whether you have been previously exposed to a particular bit of information. In a recognition test format, the previous question regarding three memory processes might read, "What are the three primary memory processes? (1) encoding, networking, activation; (2) elaboration, storage, retrieval; (3) encoding, storage, retrieval; (4) association, networking, retrieval." This example is the familiar multiple-choice format often used in classrooms. However, not all multiple-choice questions are recognition tasks. Some cleverly worded questions may require respondants to synthesize information before an answer can be identified. True-false questions can be another example of recognition tasks.

Given the choice, most students prefer recognition tasks such as multiple-choice tests over recall tasks. This preference is not without justification, for research demonstrates that we can usually recognize much more than we can recall (Craik & McDowd, 1987). Can you explain why recognition tests yield better performances than recall tasks? Try to answer this question by yourself before reading on.

A recognition test simply requires you to perform one memory task: You search through your memory to see if stored information matches the new information. The test stimulus is typically rich with retrieval cues that help you gain access to stored information. In contrast, a recall test requires you to perform two tasks, both of which are more difficult than the recognition task. First you

Herman Ebbinghaus

must search through your memory and reconstruct possible answers from information that is not presented to you in the test. Then you must identify the correct answer from the varied possibilities and describe it well enough to demonstrate that you truly recall it.

Relearning   A third method of measuring memory, **relearning,** is perhaps the most sensitive measure of memory. Relearning is infrequently used today, however, primarily because it is so time consuming. Relearning involves measuring how much more quickly a person can relearn material that was learned at a previous time. For example, you might be asked to memorize a list of *nonsense syllables* (meaningless combinations of two consonants and a vowel, such as *ZUD* or *XUT*). The number of trials it took you to master the list would be recorded to measure your initial performance. The list would then be put aside for a period of time, and at a later point you would be asked to relearn it. If there is no memory trace of the nonsense syllables previously learned, it should take as much effort to relearn the list the second time as it did the first—that is, there would be no *savings* due to memory. However, if at least some recall for the nonsense syllables is prompted by your LTM, relearning should be faster than the original learning. For instance, if it takes 10 trials for you to master the original list but only five to relearn it, there will be a savings of five trials due to memory. This would yield a savings score of 50 percent (5 trials saved ÷ 10 original trials, or 50 percent).

The relearning method was used by Herman Ebbinghaus (1885) in the first systematic studies of human memory. He used the most reliable subject he could find, himself. He memorized countless lists of nonsense syllables, set them aside for varied periods of time, and then relearned the lists using savings scores as a measure of retention. Ebbinghaus invented the concept of nonsense syllables because he felt that people vary in their ability to make associations with real words like *dog, gun,* or *pit.*

Ebbinghaus' systematic studies of memory had a great impact on the then infant discipline of psychology. He is perhaps best remembered for *curves of forgetting,* which were derived from his accumulated data on savings scores. As Figure 7.9 shows, forgetting is strongly influenced by the passage of time. It occurs very rapidly at first: Within 20 minutes after mastering a list of nonsense syllables, Ebbinghaus had forgotten about 40 percent of it. However, after this initial rapid loss, the rate of forgetting declines significantly. Note that the savings score after 20 days was almost the same as the 10-day score. We will have more to say about this curve in the section on forgetting later in this chapter.

Ebbinghaus discovered that he could greatly improve his savings scores by rehearsing a list after he had already mastered it. This technique, called **overlearning,** is an extremely valuable approach to memorizing material that you wish to retain.

FIGURE 7.9

A Forgetting Curve

This curve illustrates the effects of time on retention.

SOURCE: Adapted from Ebbinghaus, 1913

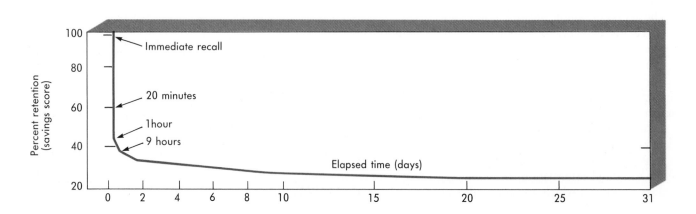

MEMORY AS A DYNAMIC PROCESS

We have seen that our ability to remember an event can be influenced by how that event was encoded or associated with earlier memories. What happens to those memories once stored? In this section we will see that memory is a dynamic process where our memories of events can change over time. For example, you may remember many details about the moment when you first heard about Challenger's explosion, but a good friend who was in the same room with you may have a different memory. Indeed, our memories often vary significantly from the actual facts. Why does this occur?

CONSTRUCTIVE MEMORY

Some psychologists suggest that vivid, photolike memories may actually represent our tendency to go back and fill in the details of an event after the fact (Neisser, 1982). This theory makes sense if we view memory as a constructive process in which information we have already stored affects the way we remember an event. From this perspective, our information processing is not limited to efforts to store facts as accurately as possible. Rather, we frequently add or delete details to make new information more consistent with the way we already conceive our world. Thus, remembering is often a process of reconstructing an event rather than simply searching long-term memory for a perfect copy of it. As a result, many of our memories are not necessarily accurate representations of what actually occurred. Instead, they may be accounts of what we think happened, or perhaps what we believe should have happened.

Serious investigations of constructive processes in memory did not catch on in psychology until the last couple of decades. However, this research was pioneered over 55 years ago by an English psychologist, Sir Frederick Bartlett (1932), who tested college students' memories of simple stories set in unfamiliar cultures. One story read by his subjects was an American Indian folktale titled "The War of the Ghosts." This story, along with a student's reproduction of the story from memory, is shown in Figure 7.10.

FIGURE 7.10

The Original Version of "The War of the Ghosts" and a Subject's Reproduction of It

SOURCE: From Bartlett, 1932

The War of the Ghosts

One night two young men from Egulac went down to the river to hunt seals, and while they were there it became foggy and calm. Then they heard war-cries, and they thought: "Maybe this is a war party." They escaped to the shore, and hid behind a log. Now canoes came up, and they heard the noise of paddles, and saw one canoe coming up to them. There were five men in the canoe, and they said:

"What do you think? We wish to take you along. We are going up the river to make war on the people."

One of the young men said: "I have no arrows."

"Arrows are in the canoe," they said.

"I will not go along. I might be killed. My relatives do not know where I have gone. But you," he said, turning to the other "may go with them."

So one of the young men went, but the other returned home.

And the warriors went on up the river to a town on the other side of Kalama. The people came down to the water, and they began to fight, and many were killed. But presently the young man heard one of the warriors say: "Quick, let us go home: that Indian has been hit." Now he thought "Oh, they are ghosts." He did not feel sick, but they said he had been shot.

So the canoes went back to Egulac, and the young man went ashore to his house, and made a fire. And he told everybody and said: "Behold I accompanied the ghosts, and we went to fight. Many of our fellows were killed, and many of those who attacked us were killed. They said I was hit, and I did not feel sick."

He told it all, and then he became quiet. When the sun rose he fell down. Something black came out of his mouth. His face became contorted. The people jumped up and cried.

He was dead. (p. 65)

Sample Reproduction

Two youths were standing by a river about to start seal-catching, when a boat appeared with five men in it. They were all armed for war.

The youths were at first frightened, but they were asked by the men to come and help them fight some enemies on the other bank. One youth said he could not come as his relations would be anxious about him; the other said he would go, and entered the boat.

In the evening he returned to his hut, and told his friends that he had been in a battle. A great many had been slain, and he had been wounded by an arrow; he had not felt any pain, he said. They told him that he must have been fighting in a battle of ghosts. Then he remembered that it had been queer and he became very excited.

In the morning, however, he became ill, and his friends gathered round; he fell down and his face became very pale. Then he writhed and shrieked and his friends were filled with terror. At last he became calm. Something hard and black came out of his mouth, and he lay contorted and dead. (p. 72)

Bartlett found that his subjects never recalled the material exactly as it had been presented. Rather, they stored a few primary facts and organized the rest of the story around these central themes. Bartlett's subjects tended to modify their memories of the original stories in any of three ways: by shortening and simplifying the story (a process called *leveling*); by focusing on and overemphasizing certain details *(sharpening)*; and by altering certain details to make the story fit their own views more closely *(assimilation)*. For example, in the student's rendition of "The War of the Ghosts," certain words have been changed and the supernatural theme has been minimized.

SCHEMAS

The tendency to change details to fit our own cultural perspectives is consistent with recent findings on the impact of schemas on reconstructive memory processes. Schemas are conceptual frameworks we use to make sense out of our world. Because schemas provide us with preconceived expectations, they help make the world seem more predictable. However, they can also lead to significant distortions in our memory processes in that they often exert a strong impact on the manner in which memory for a particular event is encoded (Brewer & Nakamura, 1984; Johnson & Hasher, 1987; Thorndyke, 1984). Many memory distortions are consistent with our established schemas.

This idea was demonstrated in a classic study conducted over 40 years ago, in which subjects were shown a picture of two men engaged in an argument, similar to that shown in Figure 7.11. One man was black and the other was white; the white man held a razor in his hand. After briefly viewing the picture, subjects were asked to describe the scene to someone who had not viewed the picture, who in turn passed the information on to someone else, and so on. As the information was passed from person to person, some of its features were altered. Most notably, the razor ended up in the hand of the black man (Allport & Postman, 1947). These findings suggest that the subjects' schemas (that is, their assumption that blacks were more prone to violence than whites) influenced the way they constructed and stored this information.

Some more recent studies have demonstrated another interesting point: When people remember information that is not consistent with their schemas, they are likely to distort the facts to make them fit better with their conceptual frameworks. For instance, in one study (Spiro, 1976) subjects read one of two different

FIGURE 7.11

Schemas Can Alter What We Remember

In a classic experiment subjects were shown a picture of two men apparently engaged in an argument. The picture contained a well-dressed black man and a white man holding a razor. After viewing the picture subjects were instructed to describe it to others. The descriptions became distorted. Most notably, the razor ended up in the black man's hand. These experiments suggest a subject's schema (that blacks are more violent than whites) caused them to distort the way they remembered the picture.

SOURCE: Adapted from Allport and Postman, 1947

versions of a story about an engaged couple. In both versions, the male partner did not want to have children. The difference between the stories was that in one version the woman did not want children either, whereas in the other version she was upset because she wanted children. Subjects were asked to read the story; when they were finished they performed some tasks involving paperwork. Then a postscript was added to the story: Some of the subjects were told that the couple married and lived together happily; others were told that they broke up and never saw each other again. Subjects were then asked to recall the story at a later date.

Can you predict the outcome of this experiment? Do you think that the relationship between the story version and the postscript influenced the way subjects remembered the story later on? Apply what you have learned about schemas and constructive memory processes to formulate a prediction before reading on.

If you predicted that subjects modified the story to fit their own views about men's and women's roles in the family, you were right. Subjects who heard a postscripted ending that did not seem to fit the rest of the story tended to "remember" information that resolved that contradiction. For example, those who read a version in which the couple disagreed about having children did not expect the couple to live together happily. When they remembered the story, they were likely to recall other facts that would make the ending fit the story, such as a compromise in which the couple had agreed to adopt a child instead of having one of their own.

Similarly, subjects who were told that the couple who agreed not to have children had broken up were likely to "remember" that this pair had other difficulties, such as parents who opposed the relationship. In contrast, subjects who read stories that matched the postscripted endings did not add new facts to the story. They had no reason to, for the stories were consistent with their schemas.

Although schemas can lead to memory distortions, they also provide important association cues that can aid recall. Consider an experiment in which subjects were asked to study a list of behaviors of a hypothetical person. Some participants were told that they were subjects in a memory experiment and that they should attempt to remember as many of the behaviors as possible; others were told they were in an experiment designed to evaluate how people form impressions of others, and they were asked to try to form an impression (a schema) of the person. A later recall test revealed that subjects who attempted to fit the information into a schema demonstrated better recall than those who had merely attempted to memorize a list of behaviors (Hamilton et al., 1980).

We have seen that our memories may sometimes involve fiction as well as facts, a result of our tendency to fill gaps in our knowledge of previous events or to modify memories to match existing schemas. Such active constructive processes, which may occur in both the storage and retrieval stages of memory, may have a profound impact on a number of areas of human experience: for example, eyewitness testimony.

EYEWITNESS TESTIMONY

The legal system places great value on the testimony of eyewitnesses. Police officers who file automobile accident reports, criminal investigators, and juries all tend to give considerable credence to the accounts of people who were on the scene. In recent years, however, several findings have raised questions about the reliability of eyewitness testimony.

Psychologist Elizabeth Loftus has been the leading investigator in this area of research. The accumulating evidence of memory as a constructive process prompted Loftus to wonder to what degree eyewitness testimony might be influenced by people's tendency to reconstruct their memory of events to fit their schemas. She also wondered whether information received after the fact might be integrated into witnesses' memories of what they had seen. Is it possible that subtle differences in the way questions are worded might cause a witness to remember the event in a different light? Can witnesses be misled into "remembering" things that did not actually occur?

A number of studies by Loftus and other researchers have investigated such questions. In one, subjects watched a film of a two-car accident and then filled out a questionnaire about what they had seen. There were four versions of the wording of one critical question. Some subjects were asked, "About how fast were the two cars going when they *contacted* each other?" In the three other versions, the words *hit*, *bumped*, or *smashed* were substituted for *contacted*. The word *contacted* yielded an average speed estimate of 32 mph, whereas the words *hit*, *bumped*, and *smashed* produced estimates of 34, 38, and 41 mph, respectively (Loftus & Palmer, 1974). The words used to describe the collision clearly influenced the way these subjects reconstructed their memories of the accident (see Figure 7.12). It seems clear that the way witnesses remember an event can be influenced by the kinds of questions they are asked about the event.

After-the-fact information may do more than merely change our recollections. In some cases, it may cause people to incorporate completely false information into their memories. This idea was suggested in another study in which subjects watched a videotape of an automobile accident, then were asked questions designed to introduce false information (Loftus, 1975). Half the subjects were asked, "How fast was the white sports car going when it passed the barn while traveling along the country road?" The remaining subjects were asked the same question, but without the words "when it passed the barn."

In point of fact, there was no barn in the videotape. When subjects were questioned again about the accident a week later, however, 17 percent of those who heard "when it passed the barn" reported seeing a barn in the videotape. In contrast, only 3 percent of the subjects who had heard nothing about a barn remembered seeing the barn.

In another study, Loftus and her colleagues showed subjects a series of color slides depicting the sequence of events in an automobile accident. Each subject saw one of two possible versions of a critical slide in the series. In one version, a car was stopped at an intersection posted with a stop sign. In the other, a yield sign was substituted for the stop sign. Immediately after viewing the slide series, subjects were asked follow-up questions that presumed the existence of either a stop or yield sign. (Sometimes this information was consistent with what they

FIGURE 7.12

Descriptive Language Can Influence What We Recall

Subjects viewed a film of an automobile accident. Later they were asked to judge the speed of the cars after hearing a description of the accident. If the words "smashed into each other" were used in the description the estimates of speed were greater than if the words "contacted each other" were used.

had seen; in other cases it was not.) Then, 20 minutes after completing the questionnaire, they were shown several pairs of slides and asked to pick which one out of each pair they had seen before.

When the follow-up questions presumed that subjects had seen the same sign as they had actually seen, subjects identified the correct slide in the retest 75 percent of the time. In contrast, when the questions had mentioned a sign not present in the original scene, the misled subjects identified the correct slide only 41 percent of the time (Loftus et al., 1978). This same research team also demonstrated that the longer the time interval between observing an event and later exposure to inaccurate information, the less accurate recall is likely to be.

Such findings are alarming when we consider what often happens to eyewitnesses. First a witness may be questioned repeatedly by police officers, some of whom may introduce erroneous information by asking leading questions. Friends and family members also ask questions and introduce new information. Later (probably much later), an attorney may question a witness on or off the stand. If intelligent college students can be misled into "remembering" erroneous information in controlled experiments such as those just described, how reliable are eyewitness accounts of real-world crimes and accidents?

Although such questions are valid, some researchers have disputed the findings of Loftus and her colleagues. Most notably, Maria Zaragoza and Michael McCloskey have suggested that flawed research techniques may have biased the Loftus team's findings, creating a high probability that misled subjects would exhibit poorer recall than control subjects even when the misleading information had no effect on memory for the original event (McCloskey & Zaragoza, 1985a, 1985b; Zaragoza et al., 1987). However, a recent study conducted by Barbara Tversky and Michael Tuchin (1989), which employed a slightly modified version of the original eyewitness research design, has corroborated the findings of Loftus and her colleagues. This study's results provided substantial support for the claim that misleading information affects memory for the original information.

Some controversy remains regarding the impact of misleading postevent information on memory. Researchers Zaragoza and McCloskey (1989) maintain that the misleading information to which eyewitnesses are often exposed may not actually impair memory for an earlier event. However, regardless of whether or not misleading postevent information actually alters memory for the original event, there is extensive evidence for a "misinformation effect"—that is, that misleading information presented after an event can lead people to erroneous reports of that misinformation (Ceci et al., 1988; Chandler, 1989; Geiselman, 1988; Gibling & Davies, 1988; Kroll & Ogawa, 1988; Register & Kihlstrom, 1988; Sheehan, 1988; Zaragoza & Koshmider, 1989).

A number of studies indicate that people exposed to violent events are especially likely to incorporate misinformation into their memory. Shocking events may interfere with our ability to store details accurately, even though we have vivid flashbulb memories of what we were doing or feeling at the time. Since an eyewitness's recall of a violent event may lack many details, he or she may be inclined to fill in the gaps with subsequent misinformation (Loftus & Burns, 1982).

An example of this tendency was a series of armed robberies committed in Delaware several years ago. The local media circulated a composite sketch of the robber that resembled a priest, Father Bernard Pagano. As unlikely as it might seem that a priest could be an armed robber, investigators suspected the father since many victims had said the robber was very polite and neatly dressed. Eventually, seven eyewitnesses identified Father Pagano, and he was taken to trial. Fortunately, court proceedings were halted when another man, Robert Clouser, confessed.

From the photographs of Pagano and Clouser, shown in Figure 7.13, you might wonder how seven witnesses could confuse two men who look so different. Why did the mistake occur? Apparently, criminal investigators working on

FIGURE 7.13

Would You Be Likely to Confuse These Men?

Father Bernard Pagano *(top)* would probably have been convicted for a series of armed robberies, based upon the eyewitness testimony of seven witnesses, if Robert Clouser *(bottom)* had not confessed to the crimes.

the case had mentioned to witnesses that the robber might be a priest. In the pictures of suspects that the witnesses examined, Father Pagano was the only suspect photographed wearing a clerical collar. In mentioning the possibility that the robber was a priest, the investigators seem to have influenced the eyewitnesses' memories. Had Pagano been dressed in lay clothes in the photo, it is unlikely that he would ever have been singled out.

It is clear from these cases that memory is a constructive process, involving much more than merely placing bits of data in storage and then retrieving them later on. In the next section we look at several additional factors that may effect the way we remember an event.

CONTEXT

Another factor that influences memory is context. Research reveals that it is easier to recall a particular event or experience if we are in the same location or context in which the information was first encoded (Estes, 1972; Watkins et al., 1976). Thus a return to the classrooms of our elementary school might help us remember the names of some of our classmates in the first and second grades. Sometimes memory is influenced by other sensations, such as an auditory or an olfactory experience. For instance, have you ever experienced the recall of past memories after smelling a particular perfume or upon hearing a special song?

STATE DEPENDENCY

Some research suggests that our internal state (for instance, emotions or physiological conditions) also forms a kind of context that influences recall. For example, research has demonstrated that recall of information learned while under the influence of a drug (such as alcohol or marijuana) occurs more easily in the same drug state than in a nondrug state (Deutsch & Folle, 1973; Goodwin et al., 1969; Horton & Mills, 1984; Swanson & Kinsbourne, 1976).

This phenomenon, known as **state-dependent memory**, also appears to hold true for emotional states. People seem to remember things better when they are in the same mood or emotional state as they were when the information first entered their memories (Blaney, 1986; Bower, 1981; Clark & Teasdale, 1982; Eich & Metcalfe, 1989; Johnson & Magaro, 1987; Rholes et al., 1987; Riskind, 1983; Riskind et al., 1982). However, the evidence for state-dependent memory associated with mood state is less convincing and certainly more controversial than the data demonstrating a drug-induced state-dependent memory effect. Some studies indicate that emotion-based state-dependency effects are small (Gage & Safer, 1985; Schare et al., 1984) or nonexistent (Bower & Mayer, 1985; Wetzler, 1985). Further research is needed to clarify the degree to which mood state influences state-dependent memory.

EXTREME EMOTION

If you ask virtually any American who was an adolescent or older in 1963 what they were doing when they heard about John F. Kennedy's assassination, the odds are very good that they will be able to tell you an amazing number of details about where they were, what the weather was like, perhaps even what they were wearing. You may have a similar recall of what you were doing the moment you heard of the explosion of the space shuttle Challenger in January of 1986 or when the bombing was initiated in Iraq in January 1991.

This kind of vivid recall for earlier events associated with extreme emotion, surprise, or uniqueness has been called **flashbulb memory** (Brown & Kulik, 1977; Pillemer, 1990; Winograd & Killinger, 1983). Such memories are so vivid that it is as if our brains had recorded them like a scene caught in the sudden glare of a camera's flashbulb. Our recall for such occurrences is not so precise for factual details surrounding the event itself, but rather for the specific setting and manner in which we first heard about the event. For example, you may have trouble remembering the exact date of Challenger's explosion, even though you may never forget the image of the explosion on the TV news broadcasts.

Are flashbulb memories more permanent than our memories for ordinary events? While it appears that flashbulb memories are more vivid and accurate than normal memories there is little evidence to support this perception. Flashbulb memories are prone to distortion and forgetting, just like normal memories. What appears to be different about flashbulb memories is not that they are more accurate, but that we are much more confident in their accuracy (Weaver, 1993).

Flashbulb memories may be triggered by any sudden shocking event that has great personal significance to an individual. Researchers Roger Brown and James Kulik (1977) surveyed 80 people, aged 20 to 40 (40 blacks and 40 whites), asking them to recall the circumstances in which they first heard about nine major events that had occurred during the previous 15 years. Included in these events were the successful or attempted assassinations of seven prominent Americans, including John Kennedy, Martin Luther King, and Robert Kennedy. In addition, subjects were asked if they had flashbulb memories for any shocking event of a personal nature, such as the death of a relative or friend or the diagnosis of a life-threatening disease.

Of the 80 subjects, 73 reported flashbulb memories associated with a personal shock, most commonly the sudden death of a relative. Many of the accounts were rendered in stunning detail, including specifics about the color of the sky, what they were wearing, and vivid anecdotes such as, "I was carrying a carton of Viceroy cigarettes, which I dropped." All but one subject had flashbulb memories for John Kennedy's assassination. However, while 75 percent of the blacks reported flashbulb memories for the death of Martin Luther King, only 33 percent of the white respondents recorded such vivid memories associated with this event. Brown and Kulik interpreted this racial difference as evidence that a link exists between the personal importance of an event and flashbulb memories.

Challenger explosion

FORGETTING

There is no single answer to the question "Why do we forget?" Forgetting seems to occur for many reasons. Among the explanations that psychologists have put forward to explain forgetting are the decay of the memory trace, problems with interfering material, a breakdown in the retrieval process, emotional and motivational conditions, and organic factors.

DECAY OF THE MEMORY TRACE

One explanation of why we forget is that the memory trace (the neurochemical and/or anatomical changes in the brain which encode memories) for some information simply deteriorates, fading away with the passage of time. For example, Ebbinghaus may have forgotten many of his nonsense syllables because the memory trace grew gradually dimmer until they faded altogether. Figure 7.9 showing Ebbinghaus' data may actually be interpreted as a forgetting curve with the most rapid decay occurring soon after initial learning. This suggests that decay is not a linear process and that a portion of Ebbinghaus' original list of nonsense syllables may be retained for a long time.

A number of psychologists believe that decay is at least partially responsible for forgetting. Some suggest that decay may cause us to lose material in short-term memory, but that any information in long-term memory is stored permanently and failure to recall it is due to a retrieval difficulty (Shiffrin & Atkinson, 1969; Tulving, 1977). Other psychologists do not agree that long-term information storage is forever. They maintain that some memories may decay over time and become lost (Loftus & Loftus, 1980). Since long-term memories must be stored through some type of physical change in the brain, it seems possible that these physical codes can sometimes break down with the passage of time.

The difficulty with proving that decay is ever the cause of forgetting lies in the need to rule out other possible explanations. We would have to ensure that no kind of activity occurs between initial learning and later recall that could interfere with establishing the memory trace. This task is not possible for both short- and long-term memory, since people's experiences cannot be held constant during such intervals. Consequently, it is virtually impossible either to prove or disprove the decay theory of forgetting.

INTERFERENCE

There is evidence that forgetting is probably influenced more by what we do before or after learning than by the passage of time. According to the interference interpretation of forgetting, experiences that occur either before or after we learn something new interfere with our memory. There may be two types of interference: retroactive and proactive.

RETROACTIVE INTERFERENCE   **Retroactive** (or backward) **interference** occurs when a later event interferes with recall of earlier information. Suppose, for instance, you look up a telephone number, and as you pick up the phone and prepare to dial, your roommate distracts you by asking what time it is. When you return to making the call, you discover that the number has slipped from your memory. This situation is an example of retroactive inhibition of memory.

PROACTIVE INTERFERENCE   In **proactive** (forward acting) **interference,** earlier learning disrupts memory for later learning. For example, if you learn a list of new vocabulary terms in your English class this afternoon, you may find that it is difficult to remember the psychology terms you review tonight. Figure 7.14 illustrates how psychologists study both types of interference effects.

You can put your knowledge of interference to practical use. For example, if you must study more than one subject in the same time period, you should choose subjects that are as dissimilar as possible since similarity of information increases interference (Chandler, 1989; Dempster, 1985; Underwood, 1983). Sleeping after you study material is the best way to reduce the possibility of retroactive interference. Even relatively brief naps (an hour or so after a study session) can help you remember new material.

THE SERIAL POSITION EFFECT   Have you ever noticed that when you memorize a list of formulas, terms, or grocery items, you are more likely to remember those items at the beginning and end of the list than those in the middle? This phenomenon is called the **serial position effect.**

Why is it easier to remember items at the beginning and end of a long list? One possible explanation draws upon our knowledge of short- and long-term

FIGURE 7.14

Studying the Effects of Retroactive and Proactive Interference

When retroactive interference occurs, later learning (learning task *B*) interferes with the recall of information learned earlier (recall of task *A*). In proactive interference, earlier information (learning task *A*) disrupts memory for later learning (task *B*). If the control groups outperform the experimental groups in Step 3 interference has occurred.

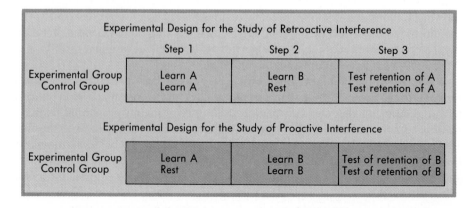

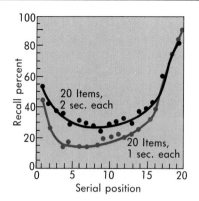

FIGURE 7.15
The Serial Position Effect
Subjects were shown a list of 20 words, one at a time for either 1 or 2 seconds, and asked to remember as many as they could. Subjects in both conditions were more likely to remember words at the beginning and end of the list.

memory. Presumably, items at the beginning of a list move successfully into long-term memory because there is no competing information, that is, little proactive interference. As additional items move into memory, however, they may displace previously processed items because short-term memory can hold only a limited number of chunks. Items at the end of the list are remembered better than those in the middle because they have not been bumped or replaced by any additional material. In other words, retroactive interference is minimal at the end. In contrast, items in the middle of a list encounter interference from both preceding (proactive) and subsequent (retroactive) items. A typical serial position effect curve is shown in Figure 7.15.

The serial position effect shows up in a variety of situations. For example, when children learn the alphabet, letters in the middle are most difficult to remember. Similarly, students are more likely to miss test questions drawn from material in the middle of a lecture than information at the beginning or end (Holen & Oaster, 1976).

RETRIEVAL FAILURE

Suppose you are having trouble recalling the title of an old love song you heard last week. A friend drops by and announces that it is a splendid day today. Suddenly you remember the title, "Love Is a Many Splendored Thing." It is clear that your memory for the song title was intact, but it was just out of reach, waiting for the right retrieval cue.

Failure to recall information does not necessarily mean it is not there. It may simply be inaccessible because it was poorly encoded in the first place or because we have inadequate retrieval cues. Forgetting of long-term memories often reflects a failure of retrieval cues rather than decay or interference. Even memories that seem impossible to retrieve may pop into mind when the right cues are used.

MOTIVATED FORGETTING

Sometimes we forget long-term memories because we do not want to remember them. Psychologists call this motivated forgetting: People often push certain kinds of memories out of conscious awareness because they are too embarrassing, frightening, painful, or degrading to recall.

Sigmund Freud's concept of repression is an example of motivated forgetting. Freud believed that we *repress* or forget certain ideas, feelings, and experiences because they are too painful to deal with on a conscious level. Repression thus lets us maintain a sense of self-esteem and avoid the anxiety that would result if this information were to surface in our awareness. As discussed in Chapter 14, there is some disagreement over the viability of Freud's concepts of repression and the unconscious mind as explanations of human behavior. However, psychologists agree that motivated forgetting does play a role in blocking at least some material stored in long-term memory (Davis & Schwartz, 1987).

ORGANIC CAUSES OF FORGETTING

Forgetting is not usually caused by organic pathology. However, certain physical illnesses or accidents can alter the physiology of the brain. Memory deficits caused by this condition are referred to as **organic amnesia.** There are many types of organic amnesia; in this section, we look at three main types: amnesia caused by disease, retrograde amnesia, and anterograde amnesia.

AMNESIA CAUSED BY DISEASE OR TRAUMA   Some diseases produce actual physical deterioration of brain cells, impairing memory as well as a variety of other functions. For instance, cardiovascular disease is characterized by decreased blood circulation, which sometimes limits the oxygen supply to the brain to the point that some brain cells die. Strokes are another common physical cause of memory impairment. Here, a vessel in the brain ruptures, with resulting damage to cells. Alzheimer's disease is another illness that produces progressive widespread degeneration of brain cells. This devastating disease produces severe memory deficits and other impairments of functioning. Alzheimer's disease is discussed in some detail in Chapter 12.

RETROGRADE AMNESIA   Sometimes a blow to the head may cause loss of memory for certain details or events that occurred prior to the accident. This condition is called **retrograde amnesia.** In many of these cases, lost memories return gradually, with older memories tending to come back first. In almost all cases investigated, memories for recent events have been shown to be more susceptible to disruption than older memories (Gold, 1987; Milner, 1989). This finding suggests that the amnesia reflects a temporary loss of access to information rather than an actual destruction of the memory trace.

Retrograde amnesia is more likely to impair declarative memory, particularly the episodic type, than to interfere with procedural memory. For example, accident victims may not remember who they are or what they were doing prior to the accident, but they can remember old skills such as playing a musical instrument or speaking a foreign language.

ANTEROGRADE AMNESIA   Amnesia can also work in the opposite direction. Some victims of brain damage may be able to recall old memories established before the damage, but cannot remember information processed after the damage occurred. This condition is called **anterograde amnesia.** It may be caused by injury to a specific area of the brain; it may also be associated with certain surgical procedures and chronic alcoholism. Unlike retrograde amnesia, anterograde amnesia is often irreversible. The following section provides some clues about how and why injuries may be associated with memory loss.

THE BIOLOGY OF MEMORY

We know that memories are not transitory mental events that float freely within our brains. When you learn the name of your psychology professor, your sweetheart's address, or how to play golf, some lasting changes must take place within your brain. For decades, researchers have tried to understand the nature of these changes and to identify where they take place. A number of recent discoveries suggest that they are closing in on the answer.

HEBB'S THEORY OF NEURAL CONNECTIONS

Years ago, physiological psychologist Donald Hebb (1949) suggested that short- and long-term memory have different physical bases. Short-term memory, he proposed, is maintained by the firing of a collection of neurons arranged in a specific circuit labeled a cell assembly. Our recall of a telephone number when we put down a phone book and begin to dial is thus kept alive by neurons firing in a repeated pattern that forms a briefly held memory trace. Hebb maintained that this brief electrical activity does not bring about changes in the physical structure of the brain; that is why short-term memory is transitory.

Long-term memory is a different matter, however. Hebb suggested that information is transferred to LTM when physical changes take place, in the form of new connections between neurons. These changes are thought to involve structural changes in the synapses between neurons which occur as a cell assembly is repeatedly activated.

Hebb's conception of short- and long-term memory as distinct phenomena has been recently supported by research. So has the idea that memory is transferred from short-term electrical activation of neuronal circuits to a more lasting long-term memory coded by physical changes in cells. This process is called **consolidation,** and it has been the subject of a great deal of research. Three questions that have been investigated are how long-term memory is stored, where it is stored, and where long-term memories are processed.

Hebb's idea that experiences are recorded and memories stored via changes in brain neurons remained novel and even controversial for many years. However, most neuroscientists today support this hypothesis. Of particular interest is evidence from several sources indicating that structural changes take place in the synapses between neurons when long-term memories are coded (Nelson et al., 1989; Morris & Willshaw, 1989; Schwartz & Greenberg, 1987; Stanton & Sejnowski, 1989). Repeated firings of nerve circuits **(Hebb's cell assemblies)** appear to induce structural changes in some synaptic connections. Recall from Chapter 3 that the synapse is the region where neural messages, in the form of chemical neurotransmitters, are passed from the axons of neurons to the dendrites of other neurons. The dendrites contain projections called dendritic spines that respond to transmitter substances.

NEURAL PLASTICITY

Several investigators have conducted postmortem examinations, comparing the brains of animals reared in enriched environments (for instance, rats raised in cages with many toys) with those of animals raised in environments with few learning opportunities. The brains of the animals from enriched environments have been found to contain far more dendritic spines, as well as more synapses with larger areas of contact (Crick, 1982; Hubbard, 1975; Rosenzweig, 1984; Rosenzweig et al., 1972; Sokolov, 1977). Changes in dendritic branching, called **neural plasticity,** of certain groups of neurons have also been shown to result from specific kinds of training (Greenough, 1984).

How do dendritic spines change as a result of experience? To find out, researcher Gary Lynch administered high-frequency electrical stimulation to neurons in a specific region of rats' brains. When these same neurons were later stimulated with low-frequency currents, they responded more extensively than they had before the high-frequency bursts (Lynch & Baudry, 1984). Lynch explains these results as follows: Stimulation causes neurotransmitters to flow across the synaptic gap to the dendrites, where they cause calcium ions to enter the dendritic spines. This activity triggers the release of an enzyme called *calpain,* which in turn stimulates the growth of additional spines that act like catchers' mitts, enabling neurons to receive messages more efficiently (Lynch, 1984).

Additional substantiation for Hebb's theory of how LTM is stored has emerged from the laboratories of Daniel Alkon (1989) and his colleagues at the National Institutes of Health. Alkon and his research associates have spent years investigating memory storage and the molecular nature of associative-memory formation in a species of marine snail *(Hermissenda crassicornis)* and in rabbits.

Using a classical conditioning paradigm (see Chapter 6), snails are taught to associate a flash of light (CS) with rotation that mimics ocean turbulence (UCS). Snails respond in nature to ocean turbulence by flexing their muscular feet to secure themselves to a hard surface. Similarly, rabbits are taught to associate an auditory tone (CS) with a puff of air (UCS) to the surface of the eye. The air puff causes the *nictitating* (eye-blinking) *membrane* to extend, thus causing the rabbit to blink. After a few trials the conditioned rabbits blink in response to the tone alone, and the snails flex their muscular feet in response to flashes of light.

Alkon and his associates have found that when a snail or a rabbit is conditioned, memory for the newly acquired association is stored in the form of alterations in particular synaptic interactions between neurons responsible for the behavioral changes. In both snails and rabbits, the repeated association of CS with UCS in the course of classical conditioning was shown to cause a persistent change in the involved neurons: The flow of potassium ions through channels in the membranes of postsynaptic dendritic membranes is reduced, an event which increases the ease with which neural impulses can be generated. This change, which increases the excitability of neurons involved in learning the described tasks, is mediated by the migration to the cell membrane of a key enzyme, protein Kinase C.

In summary, Alkon's research has demonstrated that memory is mediated by structural changes in neurons. These changes result in the reduction of potassium flow across the cell membrane making the neuron more excitable.

Thus we see that the pioneering research of Hebb followed by the more contemporary studies of such researchers as Lynch and Alkon have provided some insights into how long-term memory is stored. The next question is, where are these memory traces for specific experiences stored?

DISTRIBUTED MEMORY

Physiological psychologist Karl Lashley (1929, 1950) spent most of his research career searching for the **engram,** the place where memories are stored. His technique was to train rats in a variety of tasks, then surgically destroy selective regions of the cortex, and later test the rats' memories for the tasks. Lashley found that his rats could still perform learned tasks even after much of their brain was removed. He never did succeed in pinpointing specific brain sites of memory, a fact which led him to report humorously, "I sometimes feel in reviewing the evidence on the localization of the memory trace, that the necessary conclusion is that learning is just not possible" (1950, p. 477).

In a more serious vein, Lashley concluded that memories do not reside in precise locations in the brain, but rather involve large areas of cortical tissue. This conclusion has been supported by extensive evidence collected over the last several decades, suggesting that memories are represented by large networks of neurons distributed over broad portions of the brain (Black et al., 1987; Squire & Butters, 1984; Woody, 1982, 1984, 1986). However, some memory researchers continue to believe that at least some simple memories may be localized within precisely defined brain regions.

For instance, recent research by Richard Thompson (1985) has isolated the location of a memory trace for a specific experience. Rabbits were classically conditioned to blink one eye in response to a tone in the manner described earlier. After establishing this conditioned response, Thompson was able to obliterate it entirely by creating a lesion in the cerebellum. His finding: "Destruction of as little as one cubic millimeter of neuronal tissue in a region of the cerebellar deep nuclei on the left side permanently abolishes the learned eyelid response, and it can never be relearned" (Thompson, 1985, p. 300). While Thompson's research is noteworthy in its demonstration of a localized brain site for a specific memory, it should not be interpreted as evidence that the cerebellum is an important center for memory storage. Researchers continue to focus on the cortex as the primary structure where memories are stored.

We know more about where long-term memories are processed than about the brain site where they are stored. Much of this information comes from studies of people who have experienced memory impairment through brain damage or through electroconvulsive shock therapy. We examine some of this evidence here.

WHERE ARE LONG-TERM MEMORIES PROCESSED?

THE CASE OF H.M.   In one famous case in the mid-1950s, a young man identified as H.M. suffered from a severely debilitating epileptic condition. To ease his violent seizures, a neurosurgeon removed bilaterally (from both hemispheres) most of two limbic system structures, the hippocampus and amygdala (see Chapter 3). While the operation was successful in reducing the seizures, it had the unfortunate side effect of virtually eliminating the patient's ability to store newly acquired facts in long-term memory. H.M. remembers events that occurred up to three years before his surgery. Since he can learn new skills, it is also clear that his procedural memory is still intact. However, his declarative memory is virtually destroyed, so that he is unable to consolidate new factual information (Milner, 1966, 1989).

If you were introduced to H.M. and spent a few minutes with him, he would seem quite normal to you. However, if you left the room and returned a bit later, you would again be a total stranger to him. It is difficult to imagine what it would be like to have no sense of a past other than very old memories. H.M. expressed his frustration and confusion in an interview some years ago:

> Right now, I'm wondering. Have I done or said anything amiss? You see, at this moment everything looks clear to me, but what happened just before? That's what worries me. It's like waking from a dream. I just don't remember. (Thompson, 1985, p. 305)

Since H.M. was able to recall his earlier life after his hippocampus and amygdala were removed, we can deduce that long-term memory is not stored in either of these two structures. It does appear, however, that these structures are involved in transferring information from short-term to long-term memory. H.M.'s experience also suggests that the process of consolidation may continue for several years. Since he lost much of his memory for events within the three years preceding his surgery, these memories were probably not completely consolidated when portions of his brain were removed. Finally, the fact that H.M. could acquire new skills, such as playing tennis, suggests that procedural memory and declarative memory are distinct memory systems that involve processing by different portions of the brain.

THE CASE OF N.A.   Another famous case, mentioned earlier in this chapter, is that of N.A., the young man whose thalamus was damaged by a fencing foil. N.A.'s memory impairment was similar to that of H.M., although his retrograde amnesia affected only recent events dating back about one year. Like H.M., his ability to consolidate new information acquired after his injury is markedly impaired. The part of his thalamus affected was the left portion, and his impairment is most obvious when the material to be learned is verbal. (Recall from Chapter 3 that the left side of the brain is typically more involved in verbal tasks than the right side.) For example, he quickly forgets items on lists of words, but he is better at nonverbal tasks, such as remembering faces or learning how to negotiate mazes (Bloom et al., 1985). From the evidence presented by this case, it seems likely that the thalamus plays an important role in consolidation.

KORSAKOFF'S SYNDROME In the late 1800s a Russian physician, S. S. Korsakoff, called attention to a condition that often accompanies chronic, long-term alcoholism. The most pronounced characteristic of **Korsakoff's syndrome** is severe anterograde and retrograde amnesia. Not only are alcoholics with this condition unable to form new memories; their memories of events earlier in their lives are also impaired (Kolb & Whishaw, 1985). There is evidence of widespread brain damage associated with this disease. Perhaps most noteworthy is damage to the thalamic nucleus—the same damage that N.A. experienced in his fencing accident (Bloom et al., 1985).

ELECTROCONVULSIVE SHOCK In the late 1930s, psychiatrists began using **electroconvulsive shock** therapy (ECT) to treat severe depression. (The origins and rationale for this treatment method are discussed in Chapter 16.) In ECT, electrodes are placed against each temporal lobe and a current is sent through the brain, causing an epileptic-like seizure.

Research psychologists became interested in ECT when it was noted that patients experienced retrograde amnesia for events immediately preceding the shock. For example, Subin and Barrera (1941) asked psychiatric patients to learn lists of words before receiving ECT. Their subjects could not remember words they had learned immediately before the treatment, but they could remember words memorized some minutes earlier.

Similar findings have been reported in animal studies. In one experiment, rats learned that when they stepped off a platform onto a floor consisting of a metal grid, they would receive a foot shock. Animals trained in this fashion typically remain on the platform when they are placed there the following day. This behavior did not happen when rats received ECT within a few seconds after experiencing the foot shock. When tested on the platform the following day, they stepped right off as if they never had received a foot shock (Chorover & Schiller, 1965).

Such findings indicate that ECT produces retrograde amnesia only for events immediately preceding the treatment. Presumably, the electrical activity induced by the treatment disrupts the specific patterns of neural firing that provide the code for short-term memory. Researchers are not certain which areas of the brain are involved in this disruption of short-term memory. However, the hippocampus and amygdala are the brain structures most sensitive to seizures, and it is likely that the insult to these structures is involved in the memory loss associated with ECT (Kolb & Whishaw, 1985).

These various causes of amnesia provide a number of clues about the physical bases of memory. The case of H.M., together with ECT research, strongly suggests that the hippocampus and amygdala are necessary for memory consolidation, particularly when it involves the transfer of declarative information from short- to long-term memory. The thalamus is also involved in memory consolidation, as revealed by the case of N.A. and studies of alcoholics with Korsakoff's syndrome. The thalamus may play a primary role in the initial coding of verbal material.

Other studies have provided further clues. Mortimer Mishkin and his associates demonstrated two distinct memory circuits in limbic system structures. In one circuit, which seems to be involved in processing memories for things we see, visual messages are relayed from the occipital cortex to the hippocampus, which in turn directs the thalamus to begin the encoding necessary for long-term memory. Emotional events or experiences seem to be processed by a second circuit, this one mediated by the amygdala (Mishkin et al., 1984).

The research evidence just outlined together with other studies that are beyond the scope of this chapter suggest that memory processing involves a complex interplay between the cerebral cortex and certain key limbic system structures. This relationship is not surprising, since there are extensive reciprocal neural connections between the cerebral cortex and several limbic system structures (Milner, 1989). Recently, Peter Milner (1989) suggested that memories are initially sustained by "soft," easily produced but unenduring synaptic changes "to which are later added 'hard' changes that are more durable but require repeated synaptic activity over a long period to become established" (p. 23). Milner theorized that "soft" synapses are concentrated in the limbic system, whereas "hard" synapses occur in the cerebral cortex. This theoretical formulation is essentially a more modern version of Hebb's cell assemblies, with the important additional assumption that cell assemblies are not confined to the cerebral cortex, as implied by Hebb, but encompass neural circuits in the limbic system as well.

In sum, memory researchers are beginning to identify specific areas of the brain that play a role in placing new memories in storage. What is the final resting place of memories for things more complex than a simple conditioned eyeblink? Although we still cannot answer this question, it seems likely that complex memories are distributed in the cerebral cortex in the form of networks of interrelated neurons.

WHERE ARE SHORT-TERM MEMORIES PROCESSED?

We concluded from the previous section that long-term memories don't appear to be localized but rather are distributed in the cerebral cortex as vast networks of neurons. What about short-term or working memory, where is it processed?

The neurons which function to retain a visual or auditory image in working memory do appear to be localized in a relatively specific area of the frontal cortex called the prefrontal cortex. Figure 7.16 shows the prefrontal cortex and some of its connections to other brain regions. This area of the brain appears to play an intermediary role between memory and action. For example, in monkeys the neural activity of the prefrontal cortex corresponds to the working memory of a stimulus after the stimulus has been removed from view. In addition, damage to the prefrontal cortex does not effect long-term memory, but it does disrupt an

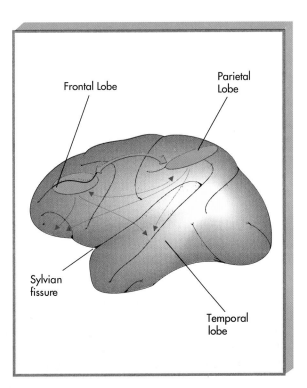

FIGURE 7.16
The Prefrontal Cortex

The prefrontal cortex along with connections to other brain areas is important for working memory.

organism's ability to bring this stored information to use (Goldman-Rakic, 1992). As we have seen, a major function of short-term memory is to bring long-term memories into action.

Further investigations of the prefrontal cortex have identified *dopamime* as the major neurotransmitter involved in short-term memory. Perhaps the decline in memory ability as we age is related to a decrease in the amount of dopamine in prefrontal cortex neurons. Evidence to support this idea has come from aged monkeys who perform poorly on tasks requiring short-term memory. Not only do these monkeys have depleted levels of dopamine, but injections of dopamine appear to restore their memory to levels of healthy young monkeys (Goldman-Rakic, 1992).

IMPROVING ACADEMIC MEMORY

Although we cannot recommend dopamine injections for students with memory problems, there are some things we can recommend. This next section identifies several strategies that may help to improve academic memory.

Professors are accustomed to hearing a sad refrain from students dismayed by poor test scores. It goes something like this: "I can't believe I did so poorly on the exam. I spent a lot of time studying, but I just couldn't remember the facts when it came to test time." In such cases, chances are that the problem was more a function of inefficient study methods than a bad memory. Research on learning and memory suggests a number of practical strategies that you may apply to improve your efficiency and therefore your performance as you study material assigned in your courses.

Reducing the Material to a Manageable Amount   Imagine that you have been assigned a few chapters to read for an exam. It is highly unlikely that you will be able to remember every single point made on every page of those chapters; it is also unlikely that every point is *important* to remember. Thus part of the science of effective studying is to pick out and underline the important points and to focus on learning these key items.

The logic of this approach is evident if you ask yourself the following question: Who will do better on an exam, the person who tries to review everything in the assigned chapters once, or someone who reviews a fifth of that amount of material five times? Common sense suggests that most of us with normal memory capacities do better if we start by reducing a chapter to its key points which might represent 20 percent of its total length and then review this manageable amount of material a number of times.

Of course, there is some risk that in reducing material to its salient points you might overlook something that will later appear on the test. However, here again logic prevails. Whereas you might miss a few questions because of an error in judgment about what is important, you are likely to miss far more questions—and perhaps more important questions—if you attempt to remember everything in the assigned chapters.

Learning the Whole Versus Piecemeal Learning   In most cases, your recall of material will usually be better if you review it as a whole rather than breaking it into smaller parts. For example, assume you are reading this chapter for the first time, presumably underlining key points as you go along. When you review this information later on, you will be better off spending a couple of hours going over the entire chapter rather than reviewing a few pages at a time.

Reviewing material from the beginning to the end is particularly effective when the information is well organized and not unusually long. If you must learn extremely long, complicated material, it would probably be more effective to break it into segments containing the largest meaningful amount of information that you can effectively process at any one time.

Using Recitation to Check Recall Recitation means repeating to yourself, either silently, in writing, or out loud, what you have just reviewed. When you take a test you have to retrieve information; recitation while studying allows you to determine if you are effectively encoding material for easy retrieval.

Many students are content to read and reread material passively, without ever stopping to check their recall. This approach virtually guarantees that an exam is the first retrieval test they encounter, and the results are often disappointing. Information is not going to be processed and stored in an efficient manner when all we do is silently and passively read through it. It is far more effective to organize, meaningfully encode, and review and recite material actively.

Recitation accomplishes more than simply providing a check on how well we are remembering material. Rehearsing by actively retrieving information from memory is a powerful tool for firmly implanting memory for that information. Don't assume that everything you've underlined is firmly committed to memory.

As you review your underlining, stop frequently and try to recall what you have just read by reciting it in summary form. Reciting can be done either verbally or in writing. This technique is called reciting after the fact. If your recall is accurate, move on to the next section. If not, review the same material again and recite it once more. Do not continue until your recall is complete. As you become more familiar with the material, try reciting it at the beginning of a section, before you review your underlining (a process known as "reciting before the fact"). For example, when you get to the section in this chapter titled "Forgetting," try reciting all that you can recall about the five suggested causes of forgetting *before* checking the points you have highlighted. You will find that with each subsequent review of the material, accurate recitation before the fact gradually replaces recitation after the fact.

A number of studies have demonstrated that active recitation pays high dividends in aiding recall. For example, in one experiment students were assigned to a variety of conditions for learning new material, ranging from spending all their time reading, with no time spent in recitation, to spending most of their time reciting. The best recall was exhibited by subjects assigned to a condition in which only 20 percent of their time was spent actually reading the material, with the other 80 percent allocated to active recitation (Gates, 1917).

Overlearning Many students have a tendency to stop reviewing material when they are finally able to recite it successfully. This tactic is a mistake. Recall that Ebbinghaus was able to improve his retention of nonsense syllables significantly by repeatedly reviewing them after he had reached 100 percent mastery. We encourage students to review material at least once or twice after they feel they have mastered it. The extra time spent in overlearning will pay handsome returns on test day.

Making Use of Study Breaks and Rewards People are often able to function at peak efficiency only so long before their concentration begins to break down. Such attention lapses interfere with learning, but they can be minimized with a routine of frequent but short study breaks. We suggest working 50 minutes, then taking a 10-minute break. Although some individuals may be able to work at peak efficiency for longer than 50 minutes, a 50 minute on and 10 minute off strategy seems to work well for many people.

To make the most of your 10-minute break, do something relaxing and enjoyable that provides a reward for 50 minutes of good effort: Call a friend, listen to a favorite piece of music, ask your roommate to give you a neck rub, take a walk, play with your dog. The key is to do something rewarding while avoiding heavy "mental" work, so that you can return to your studies refreshed.

Spacing Study Sessions   Spreading your study sessions out over time is usually more effective than trying to learn a great deal of material all at once; that is, distributed practice is typically better than massed practice. For example, assume that you plan to spend six hours reviewing the material in this chapter after your initial reading. Your recall will probably be much better if you distribute your reviews over three two-hour sessions as opposed to cramming it all into one massed six-hour session. Considerable experimental evidence supports this advice.

Avoiding Interference   Try to eliminate as much interference from competing material as possible. Earlier in this chapter we discussed the value of avoiding studying similar material on the same day (the more similar the material, the greater the interference with recall). If you must work on two or more subjects in the same time frame, make them as dissimilar as possible to reduce the impact of proactive and retroactive interference.

By all means, do not study for more than one test on the same day. You may think this suggestion is impossible, particularly during final exam season. However, if you plan in advance, and space your study sessions over time, you can probably avoid the need to double up your exam preparations on the same day. If you get in a bind and find that you must study for two tests on the same day, use the morning to study for one, followed by a nap, and then review the other subject before going to bed for your night's sleep. As we have seen, sleep helps us avoid interference while information is being consolidated into long-term memory.

Managing Your Time   Many of us tend to put tasks off until suddenly we find ourselves with too little time to do the job well. This human shortcoming is widely exhibited on college campuses.

One way to avoid the pitfalls of procrastination, while at the same time maintaining strong motivation in your college career, is to develop a formal schedule to manage your time. Although a schedule can be created in a number of ways, one method that we have found effective is to make multiple copies of a chart that lists all the hours of each day of the week. For a given week, first fill in all the slots of time that are already committed—time spent in class, at meals, sleeping, at your part-time job, and so forth. Next, designate several of the available slots as study time, keeping in mind the principles of spacing your study sessions as well as the value of sleep after study. For example, scheduling two to three hours of study followed by a nap is a good idea. If you have a good sense of how much study time each of your classes will demand, you may prefer to assign your study time slots to specific classes, leaving some flexibility in your schedule for day-to-day variations. The remaining empty slots on your chart may be designated as open or free time.

Time management works only when you treat your designated study times as serious commitments. Similarly, you should treat your free time as something you deserve, a time for renewal, and an opportunity to reward yourself for good effort. Sticking to a formal schedule can break the binds of procrastination while allowing you to enjoy your free time without worrying about your studies.

SUMMARY

INFORMATION PROCESSING AND MEMORY

1. The term memory describes both the storage and retrieval of information.

2. The information-processing perspective on memory suggests that people actively participate in the assimilation of their experiences.

3. Memory consists of three separate processes: encoding or translating incoming information into a neural code that the brain can process; storage of information over time; and, finally, the process of retrieval whereby stored information is located and recovered.

A MODEL OF MEMORY

4. One widely held perspective suggests that there are three distinct memory systems that allow us to process, store, and recall information: sensory memory, short-term memory (STM), and long-term memory (LTM).

5. Sensory memories are brief impressions from any of our senses. Visual sensory memory and auditory sensory memory are referred to as iconic memory and echoic memory, respectively.

6. STM, frequently referred to as our working memory, is an intermediate memory process, sandwiched between sensory memory and LTM, within which we actively process information.

7. STM has both a short duration and a limited capacity. Chunking, the process of grouping items into longer meaningful units, is an effective way to increase the limited capacity of STM.

8. Most of the information placed in STM is held there in an acoustic form, according to how it sounds. Information is also sorted in STM based on what it looks like or what it means (visual and semantic coding).

9. Long-term memories are composed of both procedural memories and declarative memories. Procedural memories are memories for how to perform skills. Recall of specific facts is made possible by declarative memory.

10. It has been suggested that declarative memory may be further subdivided into episodic memory (autobiographical facts about a person's experiences stored in roughly chronological order) and semantic memory (general, non-personal knowledge about the meaning of facts and concepts without reference to specific experiences). It has recently been suggested that episodic memory may be best conceptualized as a subsystem of semantic memory.

11. A number of memory systems or mnemonic devices can improve encoding of information in LTM. These include clustering, the method of loci, using narrative stories, the peg-word system, acrostics, and acronyms.

12. The more retrieval cues that can be linked with information stored in LTM, the more likely we are to recall that information later on.

13. Many psychologists believe that much of the information in our declarative memories is stored in the form of networks of association between concepts or fragments of knowledge we have about things in our worlds.

14. The three most common techniques for testing LTM are recall tasks, recognition tasks, and relearning.

15. Research by Herman Ebbinghaus revealed that forgetting tends to occur very rapidly during the initial period after learning and that the rate of forgetting declines significantly thereafter.

MEMORY AS A DYNAMIC PROCESS

16. When we memorize a list of items, we are most likely to remember those items at the beginning and end of the list, a phenomenon known as the serial position effect.

17. It is often easier to recall a particular event or experience if we are in the same context in which the information was first encoded. Context includes external environment and internal state (physiological conditions, emotions, etc.). This phenomenon is referred to as state-dependent memory.

18. Flashbulb memory refers to an apparent vivid recall for earlier events associated with extreme emotion.

19. Remembering is often a process of mentally reconstructing an event rather than simply searching LTM for a perfect copy of it.

20. People may change details to reconstruct memories and make them consistent with their schemas, which are conceptual frameworks that they use to make sense out of their worlds.

21. Research has called into question the reliability of eyewitness testimony. Considerable evidence suggests that eyewitness testimony may be flawed by people's tendency to reconstruct their memory of events to fit their schemas.

22. A number of studies indicate that people exposed to violent events are especially likely to incorporate misinformation into their memory.

FORGETTING

23. Among the explanations put forth by psychologists to explain forgetting are the decay of the memory trace, interference, retrieval failure, motivated forgetting, and organic causes of forgetting.

24. Psychologists are not in agreement as to whether some memories may decay over time and become lost.

25. According to the interference interpretation of forgetting, experiences that occur either before or after we learn something new interfere with our memory. Retroactive interference occurs when a later event interferes with recall of earlier information. Proactive interference occurs when earlier learning disrupts memory for later learning.

26. Failure to retrieve memory may occur because it was poorly encoded in the first place or because we have inadequate retrieval cues.

27. Sometimes we forget long-term memories because we do not want to remember them, a process called motivated forgetting.

28. Memory deficits caused by organic factors may be of three kinds: amnesia caused by disease (impaired brain circulation, Alzheimer's disease, etc.); retrograde amnesia (loss of recall for events occurring just before a brain trauma); and anterograde amnesia (inability to recall information processed after brain damage).

THE BIOLOGY OF MEMORY

29. Evidence from several sources indicates that structural changes take place in the synapses between neurons when long-term memories are coded. These synapses are referred to as Hebbian synapses.

30. Changes in dendritic branching of certain groups of neurons have been shown to result from specific kinds of learning.

31. Extensive evidence suggests that memories may be represented by large networks of neurons distributed over broad portions of the cortex.

32. Evidence from a variety of sources strongly suggests that the hippocampus and amygdala are necessary for memory consolidation, particularly when it involves the transfer of declarative information from STM to LTM. The thalamus also appears to be involved in memory consolidation.

33. The prefrontal cortex and its connections to the parietal lobe are necessary for spatial working memory.

IMPROVING ACADEMIC MEMORY

34. We can apply what we know about memory to improving study skills. Some of the most effective applications of the memory principles discussed in this

chapter include reducing material to a manageable amount of important points, encoding material in a meaningful fashion, avoiding piecemeal studying, using active recitation in studying, overlearning by continuing to study material after mastery, taking study breaks, spacing study sessions over time, planning study sessions to minimize proactive and retroactive interference, and using time management techniques to balance study time with free time and other commitments in the most effective way.

TERMS AND CONCEPTS

memory
encoding
storage
retrieval
sensory memory
short-term memory (STM)
long-term memory (LTM)
iconic memory
echoic memory
chunking
procedural memory
declarative memory
episodic memory
semantic memory
dual-code model of memory
eidetic imagery
mnemonic devices
clustering
acrostics
acronyms
maintenance rehearsal

elaborative rehearsal
recall
recognition
relearning
overlearning
schema
state-dependent memory
flashbulb memory
retroactive interference
proactive interference
serial position effect
organic amnesia
retrograde amnesia
anterograde amnesia
consolidation
Hebb's cell assemblies
neural placticity
engram
distributed memory
Korsakoff's syndrome
electroconvulsive shock

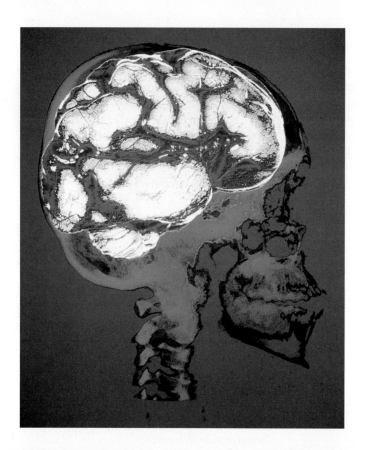

CHAPTER 8

Motivation

THE NATURE OF MOTIVATION

Defining Motivation

MOTIVATIONAL EXPLANATIONS OF BEHAVIOR

Instinct Theory
Drive-Reduction Theory
Maslow's Hierarchy of Needs
Cognitive Theories of Motivation
Biological Bases of Motivation
Obesity
Eating Disorders

SENSATION-SEEKING MOTIVATION

Optimum Level of Arousal
Explaining Variation in Arousal
Preferences

SEXUAL MOTIVATION AND BEHAVIOR

Biological Bases of Sexual Behavior
Sexual Orientation: Homosexuality
The Effect of AIDS on Sexual Behavior

I was smitten by love for the first time at the young age of 16. A few dates and a couple of exciting interludes in my father's Buick and I was in love. At least what I interpreted as love. Then disaster struck. An automobile accident, which was my fault, prompted my father to declare that his Buick was no longer available for my use. I was shattered. My girlfriend attended a different school and we lived five miles apart. I had to see her, so I walked the 10 miles round-trip to her house.

*T*his example of highly motivated behavior reveals something about the role of motivation and emotion in determining our behavior. These two concepts are very closely related. *Motivation* is a general term for the forces that prod us to do something, whereas *emotion* refers to our arousal feelings and moods. As we see in this chapter and the next, both of these processes are considerably more complex than these brief descriptions imply, and our behavior is often influenced by a combination of the two. For example, emotions often act as primary motivating forces for our actions. Indeed, without emotions, our motivated behavior would reflect an air of indifference. Can you imagine how boring dating would be if it were not colored by feelings of excitement, happiness, and possibly love? Similarly, think how hard it might be to become motivated to study for a test if you never experienced fear of failure or the anticipation of success.

In this chapter and Chapter 9 we examine the nature, sources, and manifestations of human motivation and emotion. We begin here by exploring motivation, some theories that try to explain motivation, and a few specific motivational forces that influence our behavior. In the following chapter we discuss what emotions are, how they are aroused, and how they impact on our lives.

THE NATURE OF MOTIVATION

A Vietnam veteran attracts national media attention by housing himself inside a cage and refusing to eat. A college graduate with great promise for an academic career gives up everything to work as a missionary under extremely impoverished conditions in a poor, undeveloped country. An athlete commits several hours a day to training even under adverse weather conditions. A distraught employee bursts into his employer's office firing a gun. You might ask the same question about each of these accounts: Why would someone do such a thing?

This question raises the issue of motivation, the *why* of behavior. In a sense, the entire study of psychology is concerned with the underlying causes of behavior. Thus far in this text, we have explored the biological foundations of behavior and the role that such processes as sensation, perception, and learning play in influencing our activities. However, these explanations still leave questions unanswered about our behavior.

One such question concerns inconsistencies or variations in behavior. Why do you dress to the hilt one day and go to class in a baggy sweatshirt the next? Why, when two people of comparable ability and training compete athletically, does one excel while the other fails? Motivation helps to explain both inconsistencies in a person's behavior over time and also variations between people's performance in the same situation, when these discrepancies cannot be attributed to differences in basic ability, training, or environmental conditions.

Besides explaining such inconsistencies, motivational concepts help to explain the distinction between learning and performance. Learning does not always lead directly to behavior. Recall the latent-learning experiment discussed in

Chapter 6, in which rats learned how to move through a complex maze but did not demonstrate this behavior until they were motivated by food. In a similar vein, if you learn to imitate the voice of Robin Williams, you probably will not use this voice to communicate with your dog, your professors, or your parents. You are likely to express this behavior only when you have an appreciative audience. Motivation is what often translates learning into overt behavior.

DEFINING MOTIVATION

Motivation can include physiological factors, such as the body signals that tell us we are hungry or tired, but there is more to motivation than the simple translation of body needs into action. Motivation may also include cognitive conditions such as a desire to achieve or an urge to be with friends. In fact, **motivation** can be defined as any condition that energizes and directs our actions.

To illustrate, suppose you are reading this chapter late at night and are becoming increasingly aware of a familiar urge. Finally, you close your book and decide to do something about your mounting need: It is time to get something to eat. But will any old food satisfy your need? Not when the best 24-hour doughnut shop in town is only a few blocks away. So off you go into the night in mouth-watering anticipation of lemon-filled doughnuts and chocolate éclairs.

This example of one of the most familiar motives, hunger, illustrates that motivation not only energizes or *activates* us to behave in a certain way but also *directs* or defines the direction of the resulting behavior. Motivation also has a direct impact on how *vigorous* or intense our behaviors are. If you had skipped dinner earlier in the evening, your trip to the doughnut shop might be characterized by brisk walking rather than a leisurely stroll, and you might consume all of the goodies you purchased rather than saving one or two for the morning.

In all, we might say it is motivation that makes our behavior more than the sum of parts such as physiology, learning, sensation, and perception. However, what explains motivation? As we see in the following discussion, this question has not been an easy one to answer and a complete answer will necessarily include several motivational influences.

MOTIVATIONAL EXPLANATIONS OF BEHAVIOR

Since its beginnings, psychology has attempted to conceptualize and explain behavior in terms of motivation. These explanations have not all been equally successful. Yet each of the approaches we consider here—instinct theory, drive-reduction theory, Maslow's need hierarchy, cognitive motivation, biological motives, and sensation-seeking motivation—help contribute to our understanding of human and animal behavior.

Whether we attribute behavior to inherited behavior patterns, to the need to reduce drives, to a humanistic striving toward self-fulfillment, to learned expectations, or to biological states, it seems clear that no one theory explains all aspects of motivation—probably because the range of human motivation is so broad. Certain behaviors, such as drinking a glass of water after exercising, might be explained predominantly by the reduction of a biological need. Yet other behaviors, such as continuing the habit of smoking despite the fact that it makes you cough, or devoting four years to earning a college degree, have more complex explanations. It seems, then, that to understand behavior we must first determine what types of motivation are in question. In general, it is useful to classify motivation under several categories: innate, or genetically determined motives, the reduction of drives, cognitive motives, biologically based motives, and sensation-seeking motives.

These bike racers, in the Tour de France, must be highly motivated to endure three weeks of racing in the mountains of France. Riders race between 100 and 200 miles each day.

INSTINCT THEORY

One of the earliest attempts to account for motivation was based on the notion of **instincts,** innate patterns of behavior that occur in every normally functioning member of a species under certain set conditions. For example, a salmon may swim thousands of miles through ocean waters and up a river system to reach the exact spot in a gravel bed where it was spawned several years earlier. Likewise, an arctic tern, hatched in the northland, will depart for the southernmost portion of South America when the arctic days grow shorter. Such behaviors occur in virtually identical fashion among all members of a species, generation after generation.

The attempt to explain human behavior in terms of instincts was the dominant force in psychology in the late 1800s and the early 1900s, due in large part to Charles Darwin's emphasis on the similarity between humans and other animals. William James (1890), a highly influential early psychologist, argued that humans are even more influenced by instincts than are lower animals because they are motivated not only by biological instincts but also by a variety of psychosocial instincts such as jealousy, sympathy, and sociability. James proposed a list of 15 instincts, which he suggested account for much of human behavior (Table 8.1).

TABLE 8.1 *Fifteen Instincts Proposed by William James That Account for Much of Human Behavior*

Cleanliness	Playfulness
Constructiveness	Pugnacity
Curiosity	Rivalry
Fearfulness	Secretiveness
Hunting	Shyness
Jealousy	Sociability
Modesty	Sympathy
Parental love	

These salmon swim thousands of miles to reach the same gravel beds where they were spawned several years earlier.

Other psychologists suggested their own lists. Predictably, by the early 1920s, almost 15,000 instincts had been proposed to account for virtually every kind of human behavior imaginable (Houston, 1985).

Psychologists realized that there was a basic flaw to instinct theory. Instincts did not explain behavior; they simply provided another way of labeling it. Today, psychologists do not totally discount the idea that there are inborn or inherited factors in human behavior. In fact, the concept that genetic factors influence our behaviors is very much alive. Behaviors considered by some to be under the influence of genetics include your selection of a potential mate, personality traits, intelligence, and even your susceptibility to addiction and severe behavioral disorders. However, since our behaviors are so profoundly influenced by learning, it is essentially impossible to find one example of human behavior that fits the literal definition of instincts as proposed by the early psychologists. At present psychologists are interested in determining the extent to which our genes influence certain aspects of our behavior.

DRIVE-REDUCTION THEORY

Just as instinct theory reflected the late nineteenth-century interest in Darwin's evolutionary theory, a second explanation of motivation fit well with early behavior theory. According to the *drive-reduction theory*, motivation originates with a need or drive (such as hunger or thirst) that is experienced as an unpleasant, aversive condition. This internal need motivates us to act in a way that will reduce the aversive condition. For instance, if we feel thirsty, we find something to drink; if we feel hungry, we seek food.

The drive-reduction theory explains motivation in these terms. According to this viewpoint, proposed by Clark Hull (1943), drives are any unpleasant internal conditions that motivate an organism to engage in behaviors that reduce this unpleasant state of tension. Hull postulated that there are two kinds of drives. *Primary drives* are induced by internal biological needs, such as water or food deprivation, and they do not depend on learning. In contrast, *secondary* or *acquired drives* are derived from experience.

The concept of acquired drives is directly linked with the idea of secondary reinforcement, discussed in Chapter 6. Any neutral stimulus associated with one or more primary reinforcers can acquire the power to motivate behavior. For instance, the motive of *affiliation*, the desire to be with others, would be explained as a secondary drive acquired through the process of associating primary need gratification (eating, being warm, and so forth) with a secondary reinforcer, the presence of other people.

While the drive-reduction theory seems to explain some motivation, it does not explain all motivation. A major problem with this approach is that a large number of events can serve as reinforcers. If we presume that these events are reinforcing because they reduce a drive, then we are left with the question, "What drive does this behavior reduce?" For example, many people enjoy working out. Does this statement mean there is an exercise drive that is reduced by running or cycling?

Another difficulty with the drive-reduction theory is that sometimes stimuli in our environments can energize or motivate us to behave in a certain way in the absence of an internal drive state. For instance, have you ever found yourself sampling home-baked cookies because they smell so good, even though you are not at all hungry? A number of studies have demonstrated that external stimuli, which psychologists call **incentives,** can motivate behavior even when no internal drive state exists. In one experiment, for instance, it was shown that a substance such as saccharine, which has no food value and does not satisfy hunger, reinforces behavior and motivates subsequent performance of animals just because it tastes good (Sheffield, 1966). In a related experiment Sheffield demonstrated that rats could learn a response that led to the initiation of copulatory be-havior, even when copulation was interrupted before completion (Sheffield, Wulff, and Backer, 1951). These results suggest that behavior can be maintained by conditions that increase drive or arousal.

Still another problem with the drive-reduction theory has to do with the fact that many motivated behaviors do not decrease as they are expressed. According to the drive-reduction hypothesis, an internal need directs us to a goal, and reaching that goal reduces the tension of the drive. It follows, then, that when the drive is reduced, the motivated behavior should cease. However, sometimes a motivated behavior seems to be self-perpetuating. An example is the desire to ex-plore our environments. When humans and other animals have the opportunity to explore their surroundings, these reinforcing experiences often motivate fur-ther exploration rather than less. Similarly, other motives, such as the need to achieve and the need for power, typically continue to grow and expand as they are expressed rather than diminish, as drive theory would predict.

For these and other reasons, the drive-reduction theory by itself is inadequate to deal with the entire range of human motivation, particularly more complex motives involving psychological and social factors. A number of other theoretical perspectives offer different explanations for motivation. One of these models is Abraham Maslow's hierarchy of human needs.

Humanistic psychologists have looked toward the role of motives such as love, personal fulfillment, the need to belong, and self-esteem in arousing and direct-ing human behavior. The most influential of these humanistic perspectives was provided by a theory of human motivation developed by Abraham Maslow (1970). Maslow proposed that human needs exist on a multilevel hierarchy con-sisting of five stages, ranging from the "lowest," most basic biological needs to the "highest" need—to fulfill one's own unique potential (see Figure 8.1).

According to Maslow, we all start our lives at the lowest level of the motiva-tional hierarchy. As infants we are dominated by basic *biological needs* for food, water, sleep, and so forth. (Drive-reduction theory operates at this level.) Rela-tively soon, however, we become concerned with our need to feel physically and psychologically safe, and so we are motivated by *safety needs* to secure some con-trol over our environment. As we continue to develop, we move into the next two stages or levels on the hierarchy, where more complex psychosocial motives become more important. We need to love, to be loved, and to feel a sense of be-longing. These socially based *love and belongingness needs* are satisfied both by our family involvements and by the relationships we form with others outside the family. As we express our social affiliation with others, we are also likely to be-come motivated by *esteem needs*. These include the need to achieve and see our-selves as competent, and the desire to be recognized, appreciated, and held in esteem by others.

Finally, if we are successful in satisfying all of these needs, some of us may progress to the highest level in Maslow's hierarchy, where the need for *self-actu-alization* may become a dominant motivating force in our lives. Self-actualization is a complex concept, perhaps best described as the need to reach our own high-est potential and to do the things we do best in our own unique way. Maslow characterized the self-actualized person as someone who is self-aware and self-accepting, striving to help others reach their goals, open to new experiences and challenges, and engaging in activities that are commensurate with that individ-ual's highest potential (for example, a musician making music or a poet writing). Figure 8.1 illustrates each of Maslow's need levels.

Maslow's conception that we must fulfill our basic needs before we can pursue needs at higher levels makes some sense. For example, if you are lost in the hills for days without food and then stumble upon a small mountain community, your

MASLOW'S HIERARCHY OF NEEDS

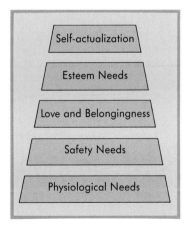

FIGURE 8.1

Maslow's Hierarchy of Needs

Maslow proposed a hierarchy of human needs ranging from the lowest, most basic biological needs to the highest need to become self-actualized.

desire to find food is likely to be much more powerful and immediate than your need to establish a sense of belonging. However, once your lower needs are satisfied, you are likely to be more concerned with higher needs such as those for belonging.

Yet Maslow's theory has also been criticized, especially his view that people's needs are precisely ordered in a five-level hierarchy with successive needs being satisfied only after those on a lower level have been met. This theoretical assumption is difficult to demonstrate by empirical research. Beyond the lowest level of the hierarchy, there is little evidence that human motives or needs are ordered in the exact sequence that Maslow proposed (Wahba & Bridwell, 1976).

Research-oriented psychologists have also criticized Maslow's theory because many of his major precepts, particularly the concept of self-actualization, are so vague that it is virtually impossible to define them operationally. Without operational definitions, Maslow's theory cannot be experimentally tested. Consequently, the need hierarchy theory has remained largely an unproven conceptualization of the various forces that motivate human behavior.

COGNITIVE THEORIES OF MOTIVATION

An additional explanation of motivation is offered by the cognitive perspective. According to this view, our cognitions, expectancies, beliefs, and other mental processes play an important role in motivating our actions (Bandura, 1982; Deci, 1980; Festinger, 1957; McClelland, 1961; Tolman, 1967). In this section we will review some of the more influential cognitive theories of motivation.

COGNITIVE EXPECTANCIES   This view is exemplified by the role of expectations in both classical and operant conditioning. Recall from Chapter 6 that the cognitive viewpoint sees expectations as important in both classically conditioned responses and operant behavior. For example, when we study for an exam (an operant behavior), a consequence occurs (hopefully a good grade) that serves as a reinforcer. We form an association between the behavior and the reinforcement that follows. This association then generates an *expectation* that if the behavior is repeated, it will again produce positive consequences (Bandura, 1982). These cognitive expectancies can also be learned by observation. For instance, if a child watches another behave aggressively with satisfactory consequences the child may come to expect positive consequences from aggressive behavior.

The idea that expectations are important motivators was championed in the 1930s and 1940s by Edward Tolman and later in the 1950s and 1960s by Julian Rotter (1954, 1966). Both Tolman and Rotter maintained that our likelihood of engaging in a given behavior depends on two factors: our expectations that a certain behavior will lead to a desired goal, and the value and location of that goal. According to Tolman, animals don't learn specific stimulus-response associations, they learn which behaviors lead to which goals. Thus the likelihood that you will gather your courage and ask that alluring person you just met for a date is determined to some degree by your past experiences in asking people out. If your last several overtures have all resulted in rejection, you are less likely to try again because your cognitive expectation is rejection. However, you may overcome your expectations of failure if you try another approach.

ACHIEVEMENT MOTIVATION   If you are the kind of person who is not content unless you make top grades, and who is committed to being highly successful in your chosen career, psychologists would say that you have a high **need for achievement (nAch).** The concept of achievement motivation was first defined in 1938 by Henry Murray as the need to ". . . accomplish something difficult. To overcome obstacles and attain a high standard. To rival and surpass others. To increase self regard by the successful exercise of talent" (p. 164). Murray developed the *Thematic Apperception Test (TAT)* to measure the need for achievement and other human motives. Not until the 1950s, however, was the TAT sufficiently refined (McClelland, 1953) to be an effective tool for assessing the need for achievement. The TAT asks people to make up stories about a series of ambiguous pictures. The idea is that people will project into the stories their own motives, interests, and values. We have more to say about the TAT in Chapter 14.

A number of studies show that people who score high in need for achievement differ notably from those with moderate or low nAch scores. Table 8.2 summarizes some of the traits that characterize people who have a high need for achievement.

HOPE OF SUCCESS VERSUS FEAR OF FAILURE   What determines whether we avoid a difficult task or try our best to achieve it? A number of researchers have theorized that the achievement motive is the result of a complex interaction between our *hope of success* and *fear of failure* (Atkinson, 1957; Atkinson & Litwin, 1960; Atkinson & Raynor, 1974). According to this interpretation, we may want to become involved in a task because we would like to succeed, but at the same time we may be repelled by a fear of failure. Overall, our net achievement motivation is seen as the combination of these two interacting forces.

The conceptualization that two opposite processes are involved in achievement motivation leads to a number of predictions. For example, when people are more interested in avoiding failure than in striving for success, they pursue goals that are either very easy or very difficult. Can you think of a commonsense basis for this prediction? Give this question some thought before reading on.

Logically, we might predict that people who are driven primarily by fear of failure will be equally comfortable tackling a very easy or a very difficult task. The reasoning here is as follows: Such individuals probably expect to succeed at the simple job, but are not overly worried about failing the difficult task because most people fail such assignments. Thus it is the tasks of moderate difficulty that are most likely to be avoided by people motivated by fear of failure. In contrast, people who are motivated by the hope or expectation of success are likely to set

TABLE 8.2   *Characteristics of High nAch Individuals*

1. Optimistic about personal prospects for success; feel personally in control of their destinies, and willing to delay gratification for the sake of achieving long-term goals (for example, willingness to extend education into postgraduate studies rather than going for the immediate economic rewards of a lesser job) (Kulka, 1972).
2. Tend to seek higher levels of socioeconomic success than parents, and are more often successful in achieving this than people with low nAch scores (McClelland et al., 1976).
3. Inclined to set realistic career goals that are neither too easy nor too difficult for their skills, whereas low nAch scorers tend to select career goals that are either too easy or unrealistic in light of their abilities (Mahone, 1960; Morris, 1969).
4. Attain higher grades in academic courses related to career goals than do low need achievers (Raynor, 1970).
5. Tend to be relatively independent and more concerned with succeeding on tasks than with how they affect other people (McClelland, et al., 1976).

more realistic goals and to become involved in tasks of intermediate difficulty that offer a moderate degree of challenge. Available research data provide strong support for the first of these predictions and moderate but not totally consistent support for the second (Geen et al., 1984; Houston, 1985).

FEAR OF SUCCESS   Do women fear success? Early in the study of achievement motivation, researchers noticed unexplainable differences between men and women in their motivation to achieve. For example, when men were placed in achievement-oriented situations, their thoughts and imagery about achievement increased significantly. In contrast, women subjected to the same conditions either demonstrated no increase or an actual decrease in achievement imagery. Why did men respond one way and women another? How would you explain these results?

Matina Horner (1969) was particularly perplexed about why nAch scores often do not predict academic and career performance of women and why some women seem to back away from success when it is within their grasp. To explain these disheartening observations, Horner hypothesized that some women may be motivated by **fear of success.** This assumption was based on the idea that in a society oriented toward rigid gender-role stereotyping, a strong, independent, and successful woman is likely to find herself bucking too many traditions with a consequent loss of friends and popularity. Thus, according to this view, a woman might avoid achievement, not because she fears failure, but rather because she fears the potential negative consequences of success.

Horner conducted an experiment that seemed to provide evidence supporting her hypothesized fear of success. She had women college students complete a story prompted by the sentence: "After first-term finals, Anne finds herself at the top of her medical school class." Male college students were provided the same sentence with one change—the name John was substituted for Anne. The stories were scored for various themes indicative of fear of success, such as responding to the academic achievement with guilt or denial, or stories in which success led to alienation from others. Horner found that 62 percent of the female-written stories demonstrated fear of success imagery, whereas only 9 percent of the stories written by males reflected similar themes.

Horner's apparent demonstration that women do indeed fear success captured the attention of many psychologists, as well as the popular media, and several additional studies were instigated by her findings. The results of these follow-up investigations were somewhat mixed; however a majority did not obtain evidence that women display more fear of success than their male counterparts (Bremer & Wittig, 1980; Condry & Dyer, 1976; Karabenick, 1977; Tresemer, 1976). In retrospect, it appears that Horner made a methodological error by having female and male subjects respond only to a cue sentence attributed to a person of the same sex as them. This shortcoming was corrected in a later study in which male and female college students from Australia and America responded to either the John or Anne cues (Feather & Raphelson, 1974). Australian women and males from both countries wrote stories in response to the Anne cue that reflected the fear of success theme to a much greater extent than when the cue was John. American women, however, were much less likely to be influenced by the sex of the fictitious character.

Perhaps the difference in the responses of Australian and American women reflected the increased inclination of American women to reject rigid gender-role stereotyping in the early 1970s, a time when the feminist movement was strong in the United States but only a weak voice in Australia. Of greater interest is Feather and Raphelson's finding that men were inclined to express fear of success themes in response to the Anne cue. This result suggests that the experimental procedure was measuring not so much a *motive* but rather an accurate perception of what is likely to happen to women who achieve unusual career success in a society dominated by traditional gender assumptions.

These results, supported by similar findings of other studies, have prompted psychologists to modify Horner's original conclusions. It now seems likely that the subjects in Horner's study were probably not projecting a fear of success that they felt personally, but rather were simply describing predictable consequences for a person who significantly deviated from the traditional gender-role stereotypes pervasive in American culture at the time of her research.

INFLUENCING ACHIEVEMENT MOTIVATION Since the achievement need is a cognitive motivation, it is highly influenced by learning and experience. Indeed, ample evidence demonstrates that the way in which we raise our children may significantly influence their need to achieve (McClelland, 1985; McClelland & Pilon, 1983). One way to help instill a desire to achieve is to encourage children to set reasonable goals and to provide ample reinforcements for their successes. Being realistic about goals is especially important because reasonable goals are likely to be achieved, thus allowing children to experience success and develop cognitive expectancies for success in other situations.

Of equal importance is fostering independence. In one study, Marion Winterbottom (1958) found that children who demonstrated high achievement motivation usually had parents who expected them to master their own environments and to show independent behavior (by doing things such as earning their own spending money) well before their teenage years. Little things like expecting a child to pick out what he or she is going to wear to school or letting children have a vote in certain family decisions may encourage a sense of independence and motivate them to achieve success.

What happens when our **cognitive expectancies** of a situation differ from the actual outcome? For example, what if we study hard for an exam expecting to earn an *A* and we actually receive a *C*? Does the discrepancy between expectancies and outcomes influence our behavior? In the next section we look at a theory of motivation that is based on these discrepancies.

COGNITIVE DISSONANCE **Cognitive dissonance** theory emphasizes the idea that we behave in ways to minimize inconsistencies in our beliefs, attitudes, opinions, and our behavior (Festinger, 1957). According to this theory, cognitions about ourselves and the world around us can be either consistent or inconsistent. When cognitions are inconsistent a negative motivational state results which activates us to resolve the inconsistency. For example, suppose that you know you should continue studying this chapter for an exam tomorrow but you also promised a friend you would go to the game. Because these two thoughts are inconsistent (because you can't do both) cognitive dissonance is generated. Cognitive dissonance motivates other thoughts or behaviors to resolve this inconsistency. For instance, you may resolve this either by generating a new belief that you already know the material well enough to pass the exam (so you might as well go to the game); or, dissonance could be resolved by changing your belief about the importance of keeping your promise (and calling off plans to go to the game). How could the dissonance that was created by getting a *C* on that exam be resolved? A common resolution would be to generate the belief that the exam wasn't a fair test of your knowledge.

Cognitive dissonance may also occur as a result of inconsistencies between your behavior and your beliefs, particularly when your behavior can be justified. Suppose someone holds the belief that cheating on exams is wrong but finds himself cheating on several occasions. This inconsistency will generate considerable dissonance unless the cheating can be justified by a new belief that the professor's exams aren't really fair anyway.

Dissonance theory has generated considerable research over the years. To test dissonance theory Aronson and Mills (1959) asked for female volunteers to participate in a series of discussions about sex. Before participation, however, the subjects had to pass a "test" to determine whether they were indeed capable of handling the discussion material. At this point the subjects were divided into two groups. For the first group the "test" consisted of reading aloud sex-related words and descriptions of sexual behavior in the presence of a male experimenter. The "test" for the second group consisted of reading aloud only mildly descriptive sexual material. After completing the "test" the subjects from both groups were allowed to listen to a boring tape recording of discussions of sexual behavior in animals. As a test for cognitive dissonance the subjects were then asked to rate the discussion and their willingness to participate again. Before reading on, consider which group of females had the greatest cognitive dissonance and how this might have influenced their rating of the discussion and their willingness to participate again.

Dissonance theory predicts that the subjects in the first group should have the greatest dissonance because of the discrepancy between their "test" (reading aloud sexually explicit material) and the boring nature of the discussions. To resolve this inconsistency these subjects should rate the discussions as more interesting as well as be more willing to participate in future discussions than the second group. The results of this experiment confirmed these predictions.

As we have seen, our behaviors may be energized and directed by a variety of complex cognitive motives that seem to demonstrate little or no relationship to biological needs. These motives are determined by learning, and they are aroused and satisfied by cognitive and social events rather than body tissue needs. Unlike the biological drives we discuss next, these motives do not need to be satisfied to ensure survival. However, much of human happiness and misery is associated with the satisfaction or thwarting of these important motives.

BIOLOGICAL BASES OF MOTIVATION

Biologically based motives are rooted primarily in body tissue needs, such as those for food, water, air, sex, sleep, temperature regulation, and the avoidance of pain. Psychologists generally use the term **drive** to refer to motives that are based on tissue needs: In both humans and other animals, such basic biological drives as hunger and thirst must be satisfied in order to ensure survival. (Recall that Clark Hull made a distinction between primary or biological drives and secondary or learned drives. Today most psychologists apply the term drive only to motives induced by internal biological needs.)

While the underlying needs behind biological drives are inborn, the expression of these drives is often learned. For example, a hungry person is motivated by a state of physiological food deprivation. Consequently, that person learns how to search the environment effectively for food that will satisfy this basic need.

BIOLOGICAL BASES OF HUNGER AND EATING

What processes let us know we are hungry, and how do we know when we have eaten enough? Researchers have tried to answer these seemingly basic questions since the beginning of this century. In spite of extensive research, however, we are still a long way from a complete understanding of this extremely complicated biological drive. The following discussion examines what we have learned about many of the factors that influence hunger and eating; it also considers two related topics: obesity and eating disorders.

Hunger performs a critical biological function: It tells us when our bodies require more nutrition. What are the mechanisms that tell us we are hungry? Although the obvious answer to this question is that our empty stomachs tell us, the picture is actually more complicated. Attempts to explain the possible biological bases of hunger have focused on a number of areas, including the stomach, monitoring mechanisms in the brain, and other body organs such as the liver and intestines. We consider the evidence in each of these areas of investigation.

The Stomach   We have all experienced hunger pangs and growling stomachs when we have not eaten for some time. We are also familiar with the feeling of a full stomach when we have completed a meal. From our own experience, then, it seems logical that the contractions of an empty stomach are what makes us hungry and that the pressure of food against the stomach walls tells us to stop eating. Do you believe that stomach contractions motivate you to eat? Think about this for a moment before reading on.

A classic study conducted by Cannon and Washburn (1912) tested this hypothesis. One of the investigators, Washburn, trained himself to swallow a small balloon. Once in the stomach, the balloon was inflated by air introduced through an attached tube. Each stomach contraction forced air out of the balloon, activating a recording device. Washburn also pressed a key whenever he felt a hunger pang. (Figure 8.2 demonstrates the apparatus used in this experiment.) These investigators found a close relationship between stomach contractions and reports of hunger, seemingly confirming their hypothesis that the hunger motive is caused by stomach contractions.

However, later investigations raised some serious questions. For instance, one line of research investigated what happens when the nerves that carry messages from the stomach to the brain are severed so that stomach sensations can no longer be felt. If the messages from our stomachs cannot reach our brains, we should be unaware that we are hungry, yet these experiments did not eliminate hunger either in rats (Morgan & Morgan, 1940) or in humans (Grossman & Stein, 1948). Even more serious questions were raised by the discovery that people whose cancerous stomachs have been entirely removed continue to experience normal hunger drives (Janowitz & Grossman, 1950; Wangensteen & Carlson, 1931).

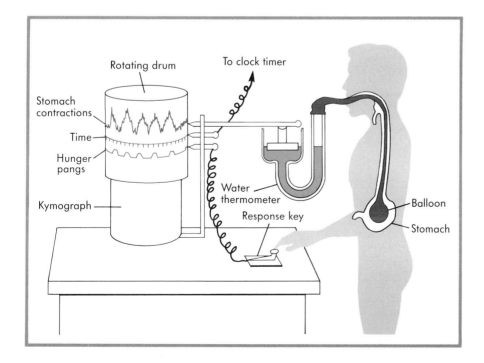

FIGURE 8.2

Cannon and Washburn's Apparatus

The subject swallowed a balloon, which was then inflated. Each contraction of the stomach forced air out of the balloon, which activated a recording device. The response key was pressed each time hunger pangs were felt.

Despite this evidence, however, most hunger researchers believe that stomach sensations do contribute to our overall feelings of hunger and satiety (fullness). For example, strong evidence suggests that the stomach contains pressure detectors that are activated when the stomach is distended with food and/or fluids. These sensors seem to play a role in signaling satiety and thus inhibiting further eating. Nevertheless, research has made it clear that stomach contractions are not necessary for hunger, and that we must look elsewhere for a complete explanation. One primary line of research has focused on the hypothalamus.

THE HYPOTHALAMIC CONTROL THEORY OF HUNGER   It has long been suspected that the hypothalamus is somehow involved in hunger motivation. A number of different studies have identified two specific regions within the hypothalamus that may possibly serve as control centers for eating. One is the **ventromedial hypothalamus (VMH),** located in the front center portion of this brain structure (see Figure 8.3). When the VMH is electrically or chemically stimulated, feeding behavior in animals is inhibited (Hess, 1957; Wyrwicka, 1976). Conversely, when the VMH is destroyed, the result in many species is extreme overeating and obesity, a condition called *hyperphagia* (Cox et al., 1968; Duggan & Booth, 1986; Hetherington & Ranson, 1940; Tokunago et al., 1986). These findings suggest that the VMH serves as a satiety center that inhibits eating by somehow signaling an organism when it has had enough to eat.

Just as the VMH seems to act as an "off switch" to inhibit eating, another structure in the hypothalamus seems to act as an "on switch" or feeding center. Damage to the **lateral hypothalamus (LH),** an area on the sides of the hypothalamus, produces just the opposite effect of lesioning the VMH. When the LH is destroyed, animals dramatically reduce food consumption or stop eating altogether, a condition known as *aphagia.* Conversely, electrical or chemical stimulation of the LH feeding center causes animals to eat even if they are already satiated (Anand & Brobeck, 1951; Bloom et al., 1985; Fukuda et al., 1986).

These findings lend support to the **hypothalamic control theory** (Stellar, 1954). This theory suggests that these structures in the hypothalamus operate together to maintain a relatively constant state of satiety, much as a thermostat maintains a constant temperature in a house. The VMH satiety center monitors the status of our bodies' energy resources. Most of the time, when we are not

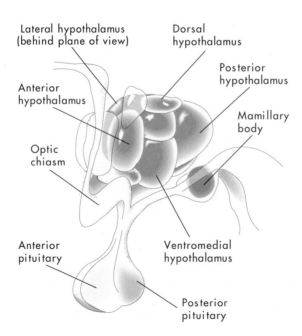

FIGURE 8.3

A Drawing of the Hypothalamus Showing the Locations of the Ventromedial and Lateral Areas

eating, the satiety center suppresses activity of the LH feeding center. When our fuel reserves are low, however, the VMH activates the LH, releasing it from its inhibited state. The result is a feeling of hunger.

This last interpretation is appealing but, like the stomach contraction theory, it still leaves questions unanswered. What internal bodily changes stimulate the feeding and satiety centers to trigger hunger and to regulate how much we eat? To answer this question, we need to know what internal biological conditions the VMH monitors. The search for this information has led to the formulation of the glucostatic theory.

THE GLUCOSTATIC THEORY OF HUNGER   The glucostatic theory, originally proposed by Jean Mayer (1955), tries to pinpoint what body conditions are monitored by the feeding and satiety centers. Because one of the most important body fuels is glucose, this theory sees glucose levels as the key. It seems logical that hunger might occur as time passes since our last meal and levels of glucose in the blood become lower.

The **glucostatic theory** suggests that levels of glucose are monitored by *glucoreceptors* (cells sensitive to glucose in the bloodstream). Another substance, *insulin* (a hormone secreted by the pancreas), is also monitored, for insulin must be present in order for glucose to be used by cells. (That is why people with untreated *diabetes mellitus*, or sugar diabetes, are chronically hungry despite high blood sugar levels.) Thus hunger results whenever the glucoreceptors detect that glucose is unavailable, either because of low blood sugar levels or because there is not enough insulin present to enable cells to use the glucose in the bloodstream. Support for this theory was provided by evidence that insulin injections and other treatments that lower blood sugar levels have the effect of stimulating hunger and eating (Epstein & Teitelbaum, 1967; Thompson & Campbell, 1977).

Where are the glucoreceptors located? For a time it was thought that they were in the VMH satiety center, an idea that has been supported by some research. It has been found, for instance, that when glucose is injected into the VHM, the firing rate of cells in this area is increased (Oomura, 1976). However, there has also been contradictory evidence. For example, direct injections of glucose into the VMH do not inhibit eating (Epstein, 1960) as one would expect according to the glucostatic theory. Perhaps one of the biggest shortcomings of this theory is related to the fact that unless mealtime is spread over an unusually long period, most of us stop eating before blood glucose levels have risen appreciably as a result of food intake (Geen et al., 1984).

During the 1970s researchers began to consider the possibility that glucoreceptors were located in another part of the body than the hypothalamus. Mauricio Russek (1971) demonstrated that although injections of glucose directly into a dog's bloodstream do not seem to influence a dog's eating behavior, comparable injections directly into the abdominal cavity cause it to stop eating quickly.

Russek concluded that the glucoreceptors must be somewhere in the abdomen rather than the brain. The liver seemed a likely candidate, since the bloodstream carries nutrients directly from the intestines to the liver. To test his hypothesis, Russek surgically implanted a small tube in the major blood vessel that carries nutrients from the intestines to the liver, then deprived the dog of food long enough to induce hunger. Just before presenting food, Russek injected a small amount of glucose into the blood vessel that supplies intestinal nutrients to the liver. The result was a sudden and dramatic loss of hunger: The dog was not interested in eating. To control for the possibility that any kind of fluid injections might produce the same effect, Russek repeated the procedure several times, substituting a variety of nonnutritive solutions. In all cases the hungry animal continued to eat. These findings led Russek to conclude that glucoreceptors in the liver are important in regulating hunger and eating behavior. Other studies

Hyperphagia resulting from a lesion in the ventromedial hypothalamus.

have confirmed Russek's findings (Niijima, 1982; Novin et al., 1983; Schmitt, 1973; Vanderweele & Sanderson, 1976).

The picture that emerges, then, is that the liver glucoreceptors detect changes in blood glucose levels, then send this information to the hypothalamus along the *vagus nerve* (the nerve that conveys sensory information to the brain from various organs in the abdomen, including the liver, spleen, kidneys, and stomach). This view has been supported by findings that when the vagus nerve is severed, injections of glucose into the liver's blood supply do not inhibit eating.

There is evidence that the liver can initiate as well as suppress eating behavior. In one study a substance that prevents cells from absorbing glucose was injected into the vein that carries nutrients to the liver. The result was a sudden stimulation of eating behavior. Apparently, the liver's temporary inability to utilize glucose caused it to react as though glucose levels were low. The authors of this experiment theorized that this message was then communicated along the vagus nerve to the feeding center in the lateral hypothalamus, which in turn triggered the feeding behavior (Novin, 1976; Novin et al., 1973).

Research also suggests that there may be glucoreceptors at another site, in the *duodenum*, the upper portion of the intestinal tract. When glucose solutions are injected directly into this structure, rats stop their feeding behavior (Campbell & Davis, 1974). The duodenum also secretes a variety of hormones that may influence eating. There is especially strong evidence linking the hormone *cholecystokinin* (CCK) to appetite suppression (Cox, 1986; Dourish et al., 1989; Garlicki et al., 1990; Maddison, 1977). CCK is released when food enters the duodenum; it then seems to travel through the bloodstream to the brain where it acts to inhibit eating behavior. In one study, investigators found that brain levels of this hormone were significantly lower in obese rats than in normal rats, suggesting that the overweight rats consumed excessive food because their CCK levels were not sufficient to suppress their eating behavior (Straus & Yalow, 1979). A number of other investigations have shown that injections of CCK inhibit motivation to eat either by promoting satiety (such as Gibbs, Young, and Smith, 1973) or by making food less palatable (Ettinger, Thompson, and Staddon, 1984).

All of this research, as well as much more that we have not discussed, suggests that several processes are involved in regulating hunger and eating. We have seen that specialized cells in the liver, and probably the duodenum, respond to the presence of nutrients, particularly glucose. These sensors appear to send messages through the nervous system to specialized control centers within the hypothalamus. It also appears that chemical messages, in the form of hormones secreted by the duodenum, help to regulate eating. As research continues, other receptor sites and specialized messages may also be implicated.

So far, we have been exploring only the hour-to-hour control of hunger and eating. In addition, there must also be some long-term control mechanism that allows most of us to maintain our weight at a relatively constant level over time.

Long-Term Weight Regulation   Although some people seem to be perpetually losing and regaining the same 10 or 20 pounds, most animals including people maintain a relatively constant weight that may fluctuate by only a few pounds over the long term. How do we manage to maintain a stable weight?

THE LIPOSTATIC THEORY OF HUNGER   The **lipostatic theory** helps explain why our weight usually remains constant. Just as blood glucose levels are the key to the glucostatic theory, stored fats, or *lipids*, are the key to the lipostatic theory. Fat acts as a long-term storage mechanism that is not subject to the rapid changes characteristic of glucose levels. The average adult consumes somewhere between 2,000 and 2,500 calories each day, much of which is immediately metabolized and used. Excess energy is stored as fat, or lipids.

According to the lipostatic theory of long-term eating control, our bodies monitor the amount of fat they contain and use this as a barometer to regulate food intake, so that fat levels are held relatively constant. This constant level, of course, varies from person to person. Many researchers now believe that our bodies may be preprogrammed in some fashion to maintain a specific body weight (Gurin, 1989; Keesey & Powley, 1986; Keesey et al., 1976). This physiologically preferred level of body weight for each individual is known as the **set point.**

Perhaps the most widely supported explanation of how we maintain a certain body weight is the theory that regions within our brains, most likely regulatory centers within the hypothalamus, respond to some kind of signal indicating the level of fat in our bodies at any given time (Houston, 1985). The question is, what might this signal be? Some researchers have theorized that it might be some blood component, such as glycerol (a component of triglycerides, the major form of stored fat). A positive correlation exists between glycerol levels in the blood and the size of a person's fat cells (Geen et al., 1984). Thus it seems possible that increased body weight might lead to increased blood glycerol, which in turn would trigger the hypothalamus to send signals that would reduce food consumption until the set point weight is reestablished.

This interpretation has received some support from research findings that daily injections of glycerol reduce food intake and body weight in rats (Davis & Wirtshafter, 1978; Wirtshafter & Davis, 1977). The excess glycerol in the rats' bloodstreams seems to have triggered some mechanism in the rats' brains, causing them to eat less.

OTHER MECHANISMS IN LONG-TERM WEIGHT REGULATION Earlier in this chapter we examined the hypothalmic control theory, which postulated that the LH feeding center triggers eating behavior when not restrained by the VMH satiety center. We saw that rats with VMH or LH lesions demonstrate dramatic shifts in food intake in the period following surgery. The story does not end there, however.

Several studies have shown that lesions in the satiety and feeding centers do not necessarily destroy a rat's capacity to regulate eating and body weight over the long term, although that may be the immediate effect. Rather, when VMH-lesioned or LH-lesioned rats are provided with free access to food after surgery, they eventually establish new set points in which they maintain a new constant higher-than-normal or lower-than-normal body weight (Geen et al., 1984; Hoebel & Teitelbaum, 1966; Powley & Keesey, 1970). These findings suggest that the VMH and LH are not absolutely essential for regulating hunger and eating. However, the fact that lesions in these two structures do appear to adjust the set point of body weight up or down certainly implicates both of these structures in long-term weight control.

Some researchers believe that the hunger-regulating processes attributed to the LH and VMH may actually be mediated, at least in part, by nerve tracts that pass through the hypothalamus (Almli, 1978). In fact, one study demonstrated that obesity resulted not from destruction of cells within the VMH, but rather from damage to axonal fibers passing through this region (Gold et al., 1977).

OBESITY

We are a nation that seems obsessed both by food and losing weight. Television commercials besiege us with images of beautiful bodies and athletic-looking people engaging in energetic aerobic exercises. At the same time we see ads for ice cream, doughnuts, "Big Macs," and "Whoppers." How many people do you know who are on a diet? Perhaps you are one. According to recent estimates, approximately 34 million Americans are **obese,** weighing 20 percent or more

TABLE 8.3 *Weights and Heights for Men and Women*

	MEN				WOMEN		
HEIGHT **FEET INCHES**	**SMALL FRAME**	**MEDIUM FRAME**	**LARGE FRAME**	**HEIGHT** **FEET INCHES**	**SMALL FRAME**	**MEDIUM FRAME**	**LARGE FRAME**
5 2	128–134	131–141	138–150	4 10	102–111	109–121	118–131
5 3	130–136	133–143	140–153	4 11	103–113	111–123	120–134
5 4	132–138	135–145	142–156	5 0	104–115	113–126	122–137
5 5	134–140	137–148	144–160	5 1	106–118	115–129	125–140
5 6	136–142	139–151	146–164	5 2	108–121	118–132	128–143
5 7	138–145	142–154	149–168	5 3	111–124	121–135	131–147
5 8	140–148	145–157	152–172	5 4	114–127	124–138	134–151
5 9	142–151	148–160	155–176	5 5	117–130	127–141	137–155
5 10	144–154	151–163	158–180	5 6	120–133	130–144	140–159
5 11	146–157	154–166	161–184	5 7	123–136	133–147	143–163
6 0	149–160	157–170	164–188	5 8	126–139	136–150	146–167
6 1	152–164	160–174	168–192	5 9	129–142	139–153	149–170
6 2	155–168	164–178	172–197	5 10	132–145	142–156	152–173
6 3	158–172	167–182	176–202	5 11	135–148	145–159	155–176
6 4	162–176	171–187	181–207	6 0	138–151	148–162	158–179

SOURCE OF BASIC DATA: 1979 Build Study Society of Actuaries and Association of Life Insurance Medical Directors of America, 1980. Copyright 1983 Metropolitan Life Insurance Company.

above the desirable weight for their height, as shown in Table 8.3. By midlife, more than half of Americans are overweight, (Brody, 1985; NOVA, 1983).

Most health professionals agree that obesity places a person at greater risk of developing one or more health problems. Obesity greatly increases the risk of high blood pressure, high blood cholesterol, diabetes, several types of cancer, heart disease, gall bladder disease, menstrual abnormalities, respiratory problems, and arthritis (Brody, 1985; Manson et al., 1987; Wolff, 1987). Still another frequent consequence is the psychological burden of obesity, which may be its most severe side effect. A number of studies have linked obesity with such negative psychological states as poor body image, low self-esteem, and depression (Davis et al., 1987; Leon & Roth, 1977; Mayer, 1968).

People try to get rid of excess weight by starving or sweating it off, but the grim fact is that in most cases fat wins. This is not to say that people cannot lose weight. Quite the contrary, many people lose and regain the same 10 or 20 pounds over and over again. Studies demonstrate that of those people who go on fad diets, approximately 95 percent regain all of their lost weight within one year. Furthermore, as many as 75 percent of individuals placed on medically supervised diets regain most if not all of their lost weight (Haney, 1983; NOVA, 1983). This seemingly never-ending struggle against obesity has been labeled "the rhythm method of girth control" by nutritionist Jean Mayer.

The following account is one woman's description of her experiences with this distressing yo-yo cycle of weight:

Since age 12, I have easily lost 1,200 to 1,400 pounds and gained them all back. There probably has not been a week of my life that I wasn't dieting or gaining weight back. I always thought I was a very good dieter. I lost weight time and time and time again. Every time that I really set my mind to it, I lost weight. And then, I gained it back, even though I did not want to. I tried not to. I never understood the concept of maintenance. I just always gained it back. I felt out of control. (NOVA, 1983, pp. 8–9)

Such extraordinary rates of failure have prompted researchers to study why people are obese, what the effects of obesity are, what happens when we lose weight, and how we can manage weight problems more effectively.

THEORIES OF OBESITY   There are many theories about why people become overweight. Blame has been placed on genes, conditions of early development, metabolic factors, and learned responses to emotional stress. We briefly consider the evidence for each of these viewpoints.

Many factors besides hunger influence when and how much we eat.

Genetic Causes of Obesity   Several studies have demonstrated that a child whose parents are both of normal weight has less than one chance in 10 of becoming obese. When one or both parents are overweight, however, the odds jump to approximately two out of five and four out of five, respectively (Haney, 1983). Of course, just because obesity runs in families is no proof that a genetic predisposition is involved. An equally logical explanation is that obese parents overfeed their children as well as themselves, thereby establishing a habit of excessive eating.

To control for these environmental factors, researchers have compared the concordance rate of obesity in identical twins who have the same genes with that of fraternal twins who do not share the same genes. (*Concordance* refers to the degree of agreement in the expression of a given trait in both members of a twin pair. Concordance is usually expressed as a correlation coefficient.) Investigators have also compared the weight correlations between adopted individuals and their biological parents with correlations between the weights of adopted individuals and their nonbiological, adopting parents. Data from both of these kinds of studies have led obesity researchers to conclude that genetic influences have an important role in determining human obesity (Grilo & Pogue-Geile, 1991; Stunkard et al., 1986). However, genetics is not the only factor contributing to obesity.

Early Childhood Experience   It has been found that the fat cells of obese people are as much as 50 to 100 percent larger than those of lean people. In addition, overweight people may have as many as five to 10 times the normal number of fat cells (Hirsch, 1983; Hirsch & Knittle, 1970). Many researchers believe that eating patterns during childhood and adolescence strongly influence the number and size of fat cells in the body of an adult, and this theory has been supported by some studies. For instance, rats placed on a fattening diet during early development have been found to produce a significantly increased number of fat cells (Knittle & Hirsch, 1968). In a similar way, it seems likely that obesity during a child's early development may cause an increase in fat cells that will make it difficult to maintain an ideal weight during adulthood.

There is ample research evidence that obesity is a common problem among children and that childhood obesity is associated with an increased risk of adult obesity (Dietz, 1986; Epstein & Wing, 1987; Epstein et al., 1987). An obvious implication of these findings is that adults are not doing children a service when they urge them to "have another helping of Grandma's good cooking."

Metabolic Factors   Metabolic disturbances have often been blamed for obesity. Some people do seem to convert food into body tissue, primarily fat, at a faster rate than others, and they are likely to have trouble maintaining a desirable weight. Several studies have demonstrated that at least some obese people do not eat more than people of average weight (Ries, 1973; Rodin, 1978; Stunkard, 1980). In fact, it has been shown that when pairs of subjects are matched for weight, height, age, and activity, one of the pair may consume on the average as much as twice the intake of his or her counterpart (Rose & Williams, 1961).

Reactions to Emotional Stress   Many of us have a tendency to overeat when we are under stress. Campus cafeterias and local pizzerias seem to do a lot of business just before and during finals week. Some people who are chronically stressed, depressed, or anxiety-ridden tend to overeat as a matter of course (Bruch, 1961; Mayer, 1968; Rodin, 1978). This tendency may be due to a number of factors.

One possible cause is experience. Unfortunately, some parents reinforce their children's good behavior with high-calorie goodies such as cookies or cake. This kind of experience helps a child learn to associate eating with feeling good, and food may also take on the symbolic meaning of love and acceptance. Again, parents often praise their children for eating lots of food—another experience that strengthens the association between food and feeling good. Later in life, these early experiences may show up as craving for food whenever a person feels rejected, depressed, disappointed, or unhappy.

Another factor that may contribute to the tendency to eat during emotional stress or depression is that certain foods, particularly those high in carbohydrates, produce a calming or sedative effect by altering levels of neurotransmitters. As we mentioned in Chapter 3, foods high in carbohydrates indirectly increase levels of serotonin in the brain which may alleviate symptoms of depression (Wurtman, 1982). Thus, eating may be maintained by reducing unpleasant emotional states.

Obesity is clearly a significant problem for a large number of individuals. Each year in the United States alone millions of dollars are spent annually trying to lose weight through diet and exercise programs and even more is spent on health problems related to obesity. While the review of causes of obesity presented here is fairly complete, there is no simple explanation for why an individual becomes obese and how to treat it.

DIETING TO CONTROL WEIGHT   Regardless of the cause, it is often very difficult for overweight people to take weight off and keep it off. Many dieters have had the experience of losing a great deal of weight and then discovering, much to their chagrin, that they regain the weight while eating much less than before they started their diet. Why does this happen?

When people go on a diet, especially a starvation diet, there is a pronounced reduction in their resting metabolic rate, the energy the body uses when in the resting state (Keys, 1983). This change in metabolic rate occurs because the body actually resists the weight loss. Ironically, the dieter and his or her body are working toward opposite goals. Although the dieter wants to take off extra pounds and inches, the body reacts to the sharp reduction in food intake as if it were protecting itself from starvation. It slows down its metabolic rate to conserve energy, thus ensuring that the brain, heart, and other vital organs will have sufficient fuel.

This change in metabolic rate produces highly inconvenient results for the dieter. For instance, assume that you normally consume 3,000 calories per day and you suddenly begin an 800-calorie diet. At first, you may experience a dramatic weight loss. Then your body will eventually lower its resting metabolic rate to conserve its fat stores with the result that you will likely hit a plateau. If you tough it out, however, you will be able to reach your weight goal.

At this point, you will want to begin eating a more reasonable diet again but beware. Your body is now likely to play one of its cruelest tricks. Used to conserving energy, your metabolism will continue running in low gear. Thus even a modest increase in calorie consumption (often well below your pre-diet level) may result in gaining the pounds back. It may take weeks or months for your metabolism to readjust to a normal level, and by then you may have given up in disgust.

This scenario sounds discouraging, but, as with everything else, there are right ways and wrong ways of dieting. The Health, Psychology and Life discussion at the end of this chapter provides additional information to keep in mind if you are trying to lose weight. Remember, however, that no safe method will work quickly and easily. All weight loss programs require considerable persistence.

EATING DISORDERS

Two types of eating disorders are quite common among certain segments of our society, particularly young women. The first of these disorders is anorexia nervosa, a form of self-starvation; the second is bulimia, in which a person may eat a full meal and then purge the stomach and intestines of food by inducing vomiting or using a laxative.

The incidence of both of these conditions seems to have increased in recent years. Why? Many health professionals and psychologists think that our society's emphasis on thinness and perfect bodies is at least partly to blame (Hesse-Biber, 1989; Moses et al., 1989). Young women seem particularly susceptible to the media-induced equation of "thin is beautiful." There are also indications that both conditions may be linked to psychological and physiological disturbances, as we see later.

ANOREXIA NERVOSA **Anorexia nervosa** may affect as many as one in every 100 teenage women (Wooley, 1983). In recent years, there has been increasing recognition that this disorder often demonstrates early onset, occurring in pre-pubertal children age 14 or younger (Fosson et al., 1987). This eating disorder is characterized by a prolonged refusal to eat adequate amounts of food. The result may be emaciation and even death in extreme cases (Sohlberg et al., 1989). Most recorded cases of anorexia occur among women in their teens or early twenties, although males, children, and middle-aged adults may also be afflicted.

The causes of anorexia are still being investigated. Social influence, via the media, probably plays a significant role in many cases (Bemis, 1978; Spillman & Everington, 1989; Wooley, 1983). People with anorexia nervosa often have an

Avoid crash diets which only allow several hundred calories per day. You will be more successful at losing weight if you cut back to a moderate caloric intake and increase the amount that you exercise.

extremely disturbed body image in which they perceive themselves as attractive only when pathetically thin (Striegel-Moore et al., 1986). In addition, it has been suggested that this disease may be linked to a variety of physical abnormalities including a malfunctioning hypothalamus, an endocrine disorder, and abnormalities in brain neurotransmitters, notably norepinephrine and serotonin (Fava et al., 1989, 1990; Geracioti & Liddle, 1988; Gwirtsman & Gerner, 1981; Muuss, 1985).

BULIMIA **Bulimia** is a disorder in which a person, most commonly a young woman in her teens or twenties, engages in periodic episodes of binge eating, then uses either vomiting or a laxative to purge the body (Fairburn et al., 1990). Some bulimics maintain normal weight, and others are also anorexic. In one study, approximately half of the patients hospitalized for anorexia indicated that they periodically resorted to bulimic purges (Casper et al., 1980). Bulimia is especially common among college women (Thelen et al., 1990); its incidence has been estimated to be as high as 20 percent (Wooley, 1983).

Many people with bulimia frequently manifest depression, anxiety, sleep disturbance, poor body image, inadequate communication with family members, guilt, alcohol abuse, and various biological anomalies, including metabolic abnormalities and disturbances in brain neurotransmitter systems (Attie & Brooks-Gunn, 1989; Krueger & Bornstein, 1987; Devlin et al., 1990; Kaye et al., 1990; Levy et al., 1989; Shisslak et al., 1990; McSherry & Ashman, 1990; Schlesier-Carter et al., 1989; Timmerman et al., 1990). In addition to these psychological problems, they may have a variety of physical complications including gastrointestinal difficulties, extensive tooth decay and enamel deterioration from vomiting, and hair loss.

Both anorexia and bulimia are serious disorders that are occurring with increasing frequency in our society. As a result, many campus health or counseling centers, and a growing number of urban hospital centers, have added specialists to their staff who are experienced in treating eating disorders. If allowed to continue unchecked, both of these conditions can seriously erode psychological and physical health. A variety of therapeutic strategies have been shown to be effective in treating anorexia and bulimia (Channon et al., 1990; Cox & Merkel, 1989; Dare et al., 1990; Schmidt & Marks, 1989; Sohlberg et al., 1989; Steiger, 1990; Yates, 1990).

SENSATION-SEEKING MOTIVATION

In addition to tissue needs, humans and other animals seem also to have an innate need for certain levels of stimulation. These **sensation-seeking motives** are perhaps most evident in the way people attempt to create their own sensations when they are placed in sensory isolation. As we see later in this chapter, some people even begin to hallucinate, apparently to compensate for a lack of external stimulation.

Humans and other animals seem to require a certain amount of stimulation in order to feel good and function effectively. The need to manipulate and explore the environment and the need for sensory stimulation both fall under the category of *sensation-seeking motives*. These motives seem to be natural to a broad range of mammals. Observation of infants of many species, including humans, reveals a strong inclination to explore and manipulate the environment as soon as they are able. Animals have been shown to expose themselves willingly to various kinds of stimulation in the apparent effort to raise their level of physiological

Anorexia Nervosa is most common in young women.

FIGURE 8.4
Young Monkeys Manipulating Objects in a Problem-Solving Situation
SOURCE: H.F. Harlow, University of Wisconsin Primate Laboratory

arousal. For example, young monkeys provided with mechanical puzzles, such as metal clasps used to seal a door, will tirelessly manipulate this object with no apparent reward beyond the opportunity to manipulate something (Harlow et al., 1950; see Figure 8.4).

We can observe this same drive in ourselves. Very few of us, if any, are content with constant, never-changing environments. Sometimes we seek quiet and solitude, but after a time we are likely to seek the sounds and sights of people and activity. We turn on the television, jog, play tennis, talk on the phone, and so forth. We may thrive on challenging games, complex puzzles, or the opportunity to explore new things.

Some psychologists believe that the motivation to seek stimulation evolved in many species because of its survival value: Organisms that explore and manipulate their environment become more aware of its parameters of safety and danger. Beyond these evolutionary implications for species survival, sensation-seeking motives also seem to be related to how we feel. This notion is central to the optimum level of arousal theory.

OPTIMUM LEVEL OF AROUSAL

Arousal is a general concept referring to a behavioral state; we experience arousal as the ability to process information effectively and to engage in motivated behavior. A certain minimum level of arousal is essential in order to express goal-directed behavior. Conversely, too much arousal may leave us overstimulated, overloaded, and temporarily incapable of effective action. A number of researchers, most notably Donald Hebb (1955), have theorized that people have an **optimum level of arousal,** which is the level where their performance will be most efficient.

According to Hebb's optimum level of arousal theory, our performance on a task will improve as arousal increases up to an optimal level. Further increases will begin to interfere with our efficiency. This theory has been generally supported by research, but with some exceptions (Houston, 1985). For example, low levels of arousal have frequently been shown to hinder performance, but not under all experimental conditions (Orne & Scheibe, 1964).

THE YERKES-DODSON LAW   The optimum level of arousal seems to vary according to the type of task a person is performing. For instance, the high arousal level you need to compete successfully in a 100-meter race would be inappropriate and even counterproductive for some other tasks, such as writing a book review.

According to the **Yerkes-Dodson law,** the optimum level of arousal for peak performance varies somewhat depending on the nature of the task (Yerkes & Dodson, 1908). If you are involved in a simple task, you probably perform best if your arousal level is relatively high. Conversely, you are likely to do better on a difficult task if your arousal level is somewhat lower. Figure 8.5 demonstrates the relationship between arousal and performance as predicted by the Yerkes-Dodson law. It is now generally recognized that the Yerkes-Dodson law somewhat oversimplifies the complex relationship between arousal and performance. Nevertheless, data from diverse studies have generally supported Yerkes and Dodson's formulation (Houston, 1985).

AROUSAL AND EMOTIONS   Just as arousal affects performance, it also affects how we feel. A number of researchers have suggested that extremes of arousal, either very low or high, produce unpleasant feelings in most people; intermediate levels of arousal are preferable (Berlyne, 1970, 1971). One experiment evaluated people's feelings as they reacted to a variety of stimuli, ranging from very simple and familiar to extremely complex and novel. Most of the people in this study indicated a preference for stimuli of moderate complexity and newness (Berlyne, 1970). Our own experience usually bears this out. Most of us prefer to be moderately aroused during the better part of our waking hours. We may enjoy attending a campus political rally or watching an athletic contest (both moderately arousing), but we probably prefer not to be leading the rally or providing a solo rendition of the national anthem at the start of the game (too arousing). Similarly, most people probably start to feel rather depressed if illness forces them to be bedridden alone in their rooms for several days (too little arousal). On the other hand, a visit from friends (moderate arousal) is likely to provide a lift.

On an intuitive level, then, it does seem that we usually prefer moderate levels of arousal. But there are exceptions. For instance, many people enjoy high arousal while riding a roller coaster or zooming down a ski slope. There are also times when we seek no arousal at all, when we want nothing more than to relax. To explain these exceptions, Walters, Apter, and Sveback (1982) have proposed two curves to reflect the relationship between arousal and emotions (see Figure 8.6). According to these theorists, there are two preferred levels of arousal, one low and one high, and we switch back and forth between these two states. When

FIGURE 8.5

The Yerkes-Dodson Law Applied to the Concept of an Optimal Level of Arousal

The optimal level of arousal varies depending on task difficulty.

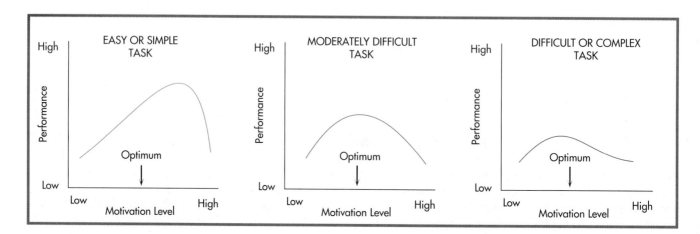

FIGURE 8.6
Two Kinds of Arousal Curves

According to Walters, Apter, and Sveback (1982), there are two preferred levels of arousal, one low and one high. When we want to be excited we find low levels of arousal to be boring and unpleasant. On the other hand, when we want to be relaxed we find low levels of arousal to be pleasant.

we want to be excited, we are likely to be bored or frustrated if we are unable to find something arousing to do. Similarly, when we want to relax, even a visit from talkative friends is likely to be experienced as aversive. What causes us to switch from one to the other of these states? Arousal theory has provided a theoretical basis for exploring this question.

EXPLAINING VARIATION IN AROUSAL PREFERENCES

According to the optimum level of arousal theory, we seek out stimulating experiences in order to maintain our arousal level within an optimal range. When we are overstimulated, negative feelings and/or lowered performance efficiency motivate us to seek out a more quiet environment; just the opposite happens when we are understimulated.

A variety of physical and cognitive consequences of arousal may cause us to switch from one preferred arousal level to the other. For example, we might be motivated to switch from high arousal to low arousal because we have become overloaded, physically fatigued, or fully satiated. Conversely, we may be motivated to switch from low to high arousal preference because we are feeling unproductive, uninspired, or physically sluggish.

Different people seem to prefer a different mix between these two states (Farley, 1986; Weiss, 1987). Some prefer to work alone or live alone: Their idea of a good time might be to curl up with a book. Other people seem motivated to seek out the high levels of stimulation provided by crowded, vibrant work environments and adventurous activities. Psychologist Marvin Zuckerman (1979) has coined the term *sensation-seeker* to describe this latter type of individual who prefers a very high level of arousal. Most of us probably fall somewhere between these two extremes.

MINIMIZING AROUSAL: SENSORY DEPRIVATION EXPERIMENTS
Perhaps the best examples of how arousal needs motivate sensation-seeking behavior have been provided by **sensory deprivation studies.** The classic experiment in this area was conducted by a group of Canadian psychologists at McGill University who paid male student volunteers to stay as long as possible in an isolation room. Subjects were asked to lie motionless when not eating, drinking, or using the

Extreme skiing must produce a high level of arousal.

bathroom; gloves and cardboard cuffs over their hands and lower arms prevented tactile sensations. Translucent coverings over their eyes reduced vision to a dim haze, and the hum of a fan drowned out all other sounds. Based on what you have learned about sensation-seeking motives and optimum levels of arousal, how do you think these subjects responded? Do you think this experiment was an easy way to make money for the volunteer subjects? Make your predictions before reading on.

Many of the subjects quit the experiment within the first few days. Of those who did not find the experience intolerable, nearly all said that it was unpleasant. Why did they respond in this way? Perhaps part of the answer is related to the stress of social isolation, but it also seems likely that experiencing a level of sensory stimulation dramatically below their optimal arousal level played an important role. The subjects seemed to develop such a strong need for sensory stimulation that they resorted to almost any kind of stimulation to raise their level of arousal. For example, when given a chance to listen to boring taped lectures, such as a report on the evils of alcohol written at a six-year-old level, they would repeatedly press a button that activated the tape. Furthermore, some subjects began to hallucinate after two or three days of sensory deprivation. Perhaps they were trying to generate their own sensory experiences to cope with the absence of external stimulation (Bexton et al., 1954).

Prolonged sensory deprivation often reduces a person's performance on a variety of tasks (Goldberger, 1982). This information has been applied by engineering psychologists and other design professionals to provide enriched sensory experiences to individuals forced to work in monotonous environments for long periods of time, from astronauts in space to workers on assembly lines.

However, not all research has demonstrated negative effects of sensory deprivation (Suedfeld & Kristeller, 1982). Several studies conducted in the 1970s and 1980s suggest that individuals who are exposed to reduced sensory input may experience some positive outcomes. For instance, depressed or anxious subjects who spend several days in a program of solitude and sensory restriction often experience a lessening in the severity of their negative symptoms (Reynolds, 1982, 1986). Other studies have shown that people who undergo 24 hours of voluntary sensory restriction often report increased ability to gain control over negative habits like smoking and overeating (Suedfeld, 1975, 1980). For example, in one study conducted by Allan Best and Peter Suedfeld (1982), smokers first attended stop-smoking instructional classes after which some of them spent 24 hours lying on beds in quiet, dark rooms where they listened to antismoking messages, drank a liquid diet through tubes, and rose from bed only to use bedside toilets. Two-thirds of the subjects exposed to this sensory restriction treatment, labeled *Restricted Environmental Stimulation Therapy (REST)*, were still not smoking one year later. These results were sharply contrasted to a much poorer nicotine-abstinence rate of only one-third among a matched sample of subjects who received instruction only without the accompanying day of REST.

It is important to note, however, that these later results do not necessarily contradict the earlier findings of the Canadian researchers. In the experiment at McGill University the severity of stimulus deprivation was much greater than in the subsequent studies of Best, Suedfeld, and others where subjects did not wear translucent goggles, cardboard cuffs, and so on. Milder forms of sensory *restriction*, typified by the REST regimen, may both reduce stress through peaceful relaxation and increase subjects' susceptibility to being influenced in positive ways. In contrast, more severe forms of sensory deprivation are more likely to induce the unpleasant effects previously outlined.

In recent years sensory restriction has entered the commercial market in the form of so-called flotation chambers that are billed as a way to obtain an enjoyably altered state of consciousness (see Figure 8.7). Customers pay a fee to spend

FIGURE 8.7
Subject in a Sensory Deprivation Study

Most subjects find sensory deprivation for extended periods of time to be boring and unpleasant. However, several hours of sensory restriction in a flotation tank may be quite relaxing.

an hour or more in a sound-deadened chamber filled with enough salty water to permit gentle floating. These flotation chambers minimize various sensations including the sense of gravity. Anecdotal evidence suggests that the experience of being in a flotation chamber leads people to report achieving what they often describe as a state of blissful relaxation. Recent research by Donald Forgays and Maureen Belinson (1986) found that most subjects exposed to 1.5 hours of flotation reported feeling more relaxed, a subjective impression consistent with measured reductions in heart rates.

SEXUAL MOTIVATION AND BEHAVIOR

Another important source of motivation is sexual motivation. Our sexuality is a richly varied, highly individualized, and potentially enriching aspect of our lives. We express our sexuality in many ways, and the feelings, thoughts, and attitudes we bring to this area of human experience also vary widely. In the remainder of this chapter we present a brief overview of selected topics which provide an introduction to certain behavioral, biological, psychosocial, and cultural aspects of sexuality. We will see how human sexual behavior can be motivated by all of these factors.

We begin by exploring the question of how biology and psychosocial factors influence human sexual behavior. Sexual behavior was once thought to be motivated primarily by a physiological drive, mostly because of the dominant role of physiology in animal sexual behavior. In nonprimate mammals such as rats, for instance, hormones appear to be essential to sexual arousal and function. However, there is now general agreement that learning, emotions, and social norms become more important as the complexity of the organism increases. In humans, sexual interest and expression are controlled both by hormones and more by the cerebral cortex, reflecting a combination of biological, psychological, and cultural factors.

All this is not to say that biology is irrelevant to human sexual motivation. In the following sections we compare the effects of biological and psychosocial factors to see how they contribute to sexual motivation and arousal.

BIOLOGICAL BASES OF SEXUAL BEHAVIOR

It is extremely difficult to distinguish between the effects of strictly physiological processes such as hormone production and those of psychosocial processes such as early socialization, peer group learning, and emotional needs. In recent years, however, a number of well-designed, carefully implemented studies have yielded information about the complex relationship between hormones and sexual activity. As we will see, the evidence linking hormones to sexuality is considerably more substantial for males than females.

HORMONES AND SEXUALITY   Which hormones are important in human sexuality? Have different hormones been linked with male versus female sexual functions? Take a few moments to consider these questions before reading on.

Hormone Levels and Male Sexual Behavior   The primary male sex hormones are **androgens.** About 95 percent of these androgens are secreted by the testes in the form of testosterone; the remaining 5 percent are produced by the adrenal glands. A number of lines of research have linked androgens with sexual activity. One source of information has been studies of men who have undergone castration (an operation involving removal of the testes, which is sometimes performed as medical treatment for such diseases as genital tuberculosis and prostate cancer). In one major investigation of a large group of castrated Norwegian males, most subjects reported significantly reduced sexual interest and activity within the first year after the operation (Bremer, 1959). A more recent study of 39 sex offenders in West Germany, who voluntarily agreed to surgical castration while in prison, obtained similar results (Heim, 1981). However, other research suggests that castration has a highly variable effect on sexual desire and functioning. In one case a 43-year-old man, castrated 18 years previously, reported having intercourse one to four times weekly (Hamilton, 1943). Other writers have recorded incidences of continued sexual desire and function as much as 30 years following castration, without hormone treatment (Ford & Beach, 1951).

Such findings, together with numerous other investigations, suggest that while sexual interest and activity generally diminish after castration, the amount of reduction is highly variable. The fact that this diminution occurs so frequently indicates that hormones are important in instigating sexual interest. However, we cannot rule out the possible impact of psychological factors. Emotional and cognitive reactions — including embarrassment due to a sense of physical mutilation, or a self-fulfilling belief in the myth that castration abolishes erectile response — may also inhibit sexual functioning after castration.

A second line of research investigating hormones and sexual functioning involves androgen-blocking drugs. In recent years a class of drugs known as *antiandrogens* has been used experimentally in Europe and America to treat sexual offenders. Antiandrogens drastically reduce the amount of testosterone circulating in the bloodstream (Pugeat et al., 1987; Rousseau et al., 1988). One of these drugs, *medroxyprogesterone acetate* (*MPA*, also known by its trade name, *Depo-Provera*), has received a great deal of media attention in the United States in the last few years. A number of studies have found that Depo-Provera and other antiandrogens may be effective in reducing both sexual interest and activity in human males (Crooks & Baur, 1990). However, altering sex hormone levels is far from a surefire treatment for sex offenders, especially in cases where sexual assaults have stemmed from nonsexual motives such as the need to express anger or to exert control over another person.

A third source of evidence linking androgens to sexual motivation is studies of hypogonadism, a state of androgen deprivation that results from certain diseases of the endocrine system. If this condition occurs before puberty, maturation of the primary and secondary sex characteristics is retarded, and the individual may never develop an active sexual interest. The results are far more variable if androgen deficiency occurs in adulthood. However, extensive studies conducted by a number of researchers provide strong evidence that androgens play an important role in male sexual motivation (Bancroft, 1984; Davidson, 1984). For example, it has been shown that when hypogonadal men receive hormone treatments to replace androgens in the bloodstream, they often experience a return of normal sexual interest and activity. If the treatments are temporarily suspended, sexual motivation and activity decline within two or three weeks (Carey et al., 1988; Cunningham et al., 1989; Findlay et al., 1989; Gooren, 1988).

Recent research further supports a link between male sexual functioning and androgens. In one study researchers assessed the relationship between androgen levels and sexual behavior in a group of young men with an average age of 25. The researchers found a strong positive correlation between blood androgen levels and the strength of sexual motivation as reflected by orgasm frequency (Knussmann et al., 1986). Another study provided very strong evidence of a relationship between blood androgen levels and sexual motivation and behavior in adolescent males (Udry et al., 1985). This research found that the higher the level of circulating androgens in the bloodstream, the more time their teenage subjects spent thinking about sex and the more likely they were to have engaged in coitus, noncoital sex play, and masturbation.

Finally there is evidence that males who take *anabolic steroids* (testosterone) for building muscle mass may experience increased levels of sexual motivation. It is important to note, however, that because the use of these drugs is illegal and potentially quite harmful scientific studies are limited. Reports from steroid users are difficult to interpret because dosages and methods of administration vary considerably.

Hormone Levels and Female Sexual Behavior   Many people assume that the female sex hormones, **estrogens,** play a major role in female sexual motivation and behavior. We do know that these hormones help maintain the elasticity of the vaginal lining and contribute to vaginal lubrication (Walling et al., 1990). However, the role of estrogens in female sexual motivation is far from clear.

A number of writers have maintained that estrogens play an insignificant role in female sexual activity. In support of this viewpoint, they quote studies of postmenopausal women (Masters & Johnson, 1966) and women who have had their ovaries removed for medical reasons (Kinsey et al., 1953). Neither change seems to have significant adverse effects on sexual arousal.

More recent studies of postmenopausal women or women whose ovaries have been removed suggest a more complicated picture, however. Some researchers have reported that when these subjects receive estrogen-replacement treatment, they experience not only heightened vaginal lubrication, but also increased sexual motivation, pleasure, and orgasmic capacity (Dennerstein et al., 1980; Dow et al., 1983). At the same time, other investigators have found estrogen therapy to have no discernible impact on the motivational aspects of sexual behavior (Campbell, 1976; Campbell & Whitehead, 1977; Coope, 1976; Furuhjelm et al., 1984). In view of these contradictory findings, the role of estrogen in female sexual motivation and functioning remains unclear.

Estrogens are not the only sex hormones present in females, however. Both the ovaries and the adrenal glands produce androgens in females, and the connection between androgens and female sexual motivation seems somewhat more substantial. Some of this evidence is anecdotal. For instance, the clinical literature on gynecology cites many cases in which women undergoing androgen therapy experience increased sexual interest and activity (Carter et al., 1947; Dorfman & Shipley, 1956; Kupperman & Studdiford, 1953).

Other evidence from better-controlled experimental evaluations of the effects of androgens on female sexuality have yielded strong evidence of a positive correlation between frequency of sexual activity and levels of circulating androgens (Morris et al., 1987; Persky et al., 1978; Walling et al., 1990). For instance, two investigations revealed that women who received an androgen-containing preparation after removal of their ovaries reported markedly greater levels of sexual desire, sexual arousal, and sexual fantasies than subjects who received estrogen alone or a *placebo* (a pharmacologically inert substance, such as a sugar pill) (Sherwin & Gelfand, 1987; Sherwin et al., 1985). Although women who receive androgen supplements are usually pleased with their increased sexual interest, some subjects (particularly those without a sexual partner) have found their heightened sex drive to be somewhat unsettling (Gallagher, 1988).

While the evidence linking androgens with female sexuality is certainly more substantial than for estrogen, the findings are somewhat contradictory. In three systematic investigations comparing the effects of androgens on female sexuality with those of a placebo, for instance, androgens proved no more effective than placebos (Mathews, 1981).

Future research may clarify the relationship between sex hormones and female sexual interest and behavior. At present, the picture is much less clear for women than for men, and the relationship between hormone levels and female sexuality is exceedingly difficult to decipher. Even in the case of male sexuality, it is important to remember that human sexual motivation varies tremendously from one person to another, so that it is difficult to generalize about the effects of hormones.

PSYCHOSOCIAL FACTORS IN SEXUAL BEHAVIOR   Although hormones can, and do, influence human sexual motivation, our sexual behaviors are not strongly correlated with reproductive cycles and related biological events. Other animals stand in sharp contrast. Female sexual receptivity in other animals is governed by the reproductive cycle; biological cues (such as odors) are often necessary to instigate sexual activity; and hormone levels are closely tied to the ability to respond sexually.

In contrast, hormones are far from the only important factor influencing human sexuality. Indeed, it is likely that psychological and cultural conditions play a greater role in human sexual arousal and expression. Some evidence of the influence of psychosocial factors comes from our own experiences and observations. Ask yourself, for instance, what motivates your own sexual behavior, and what are the most important restrictions on your sexual behavior?

Most of us continue to express our sexuality throughout much of our lives because sexual activity is reinforcing. This reinforcement takes many forms, including a sense of self-esteem that comes from being loved, erotic pleasure and gratification, reduction of feelings of anxiety, and a sense of closeness to another person. Sexual expression can even serve the function of providing a way of relieving boredom and raising arousal levels. This diversity of reinforcers suggests that our incentives for sexual expression are largely psychosocial. It also underscores the basically social nature of humans, a propensity that greatly influences the manner in which we express our sexuality.

SOCIETAL INFLUENCES ON SEXUAL BEHAVIOR   Social scientists have recorded in detail the tremendous variation that occurs in human sexual behavior in different societies (Crooks & Baur, 1990; Ford & Beach, 1951). Societies exist in which individuals in their sixties are more active sexually than the typical 30-year-old American. In many societies, the marked gender differences in adolescent sexual behaviors that typify our own society are totally lacking. Such widespread fluctu-ations in sexual norms and behavior cannot be attributed to the influence of hor-mones.

Nor can they be attributed to geographical factors. No other animal species have different sexual behaviors in different parts of the world. Rats in Ethiopia copulate the same way and are triggered by the same stimuli as rats in Oregon. The sexual patterns of dogs, cows, fowl, and higher primates are all highly simi-lar, regardless of where they live. Thus humans are unique in creating highly lo-calized patterns of sexual behavior. This is perhaps the strongest evidence for the preeminence of psychosocial factors in human sexual motivation and expression.

Many of us have our own ideas about what is "normal" sexual behavior and what is not, but often the meaning of a given act (sexual or otherwise) cannot be fully understood without also understanding its cultural context. For example, in our own North American society, we may attribute sexual overtones to the act of two men embracing each other. In Italy, however (and in many other societies), it is completely normal (and nonsexual) for men to hug one another.

Such diversity exists among the cultures of the world that the very definition of what is sexually arousing may vary greatly. In one society, exposed female breasts may trigger sexual interest in men, whereas in a different society this sight may induce little or no erotic interest. Furthermore, the acceptability of certain sexual activities varies widely from culture to culture. In some societies, such as the Mangaians of Polynesia, sex is highly valued and almost all manifes-tations of it are considered beautiful and natural. Other societies, such as the Manus of New Guinea, view any sexual act as undesirable and shameful (Crooks & Baur, 1990). Almost any sexual behavior is viewed in widely different ways in different societies. Masturbation by children may be overtly condemned in one society, covertly supported in another, openly encouraged in still another, and even occasionally initiated by parental example.

The diversity of sexual expression tends to mask a fundamental generalization that can be applied without exception to all social orders: Within the **cultural mores** (established customs and beliefs) of all societies, the conduct of sexual be-havior is regulated in some way. The rules vary from one society to the next, but in no social order is sexuality completely unregulated.

Gender roles are culturally defined. This public display of affection between men is quite common in Italy.

The best way to understand the diversity of sexual expression is through examples. We look briefly at three societies with very different views of sexuality: the Polynesian society of the island Mangaia, the inhabitants of an island off the coast of Ireland known as Inis Beag, and the Dani of New Guinea. (These social groups have all been studied at some time during the last few decades. However, they may have undergone cultural change since they were observed.)

Mangaia Mangaia is the southernmost of the Polynesian Cook Island chain. Its inhabitants were studied in the 1950s by anthropologist Donald Marshall (1971), whose accounts of Mangaian sexual practices have been widely quoted. When Marshall visited Mangaia, he observed a society in which sexual pleasure and activity is a principal concern, starting in childhood (Marshall, 1971). Children have extensive exposure to sexuality: They hear folktales containing detailed descriptions of sex acts and sexual anatomy, and they watch provocative ritual dances. At the onset of puberty, both sexes receive detailed instruction about sex. Once their instruction is completed, boys begin to seek out girls. Sex occurs in public privacy. Young males engage in a practice called *night-crawling*, in which boys enter their chosen lover's house at night and have sexual relations while other family members sleep nearby. (In the 1950s, when Marshall conducted his research, most Mangaian houses had only a single sleeping area.) If awakened, the other 5 to 15 family members politely pretend to sleep. Parents approve of this practice and listen for sounds of laughter as a sign that their daughter is pleased with her partner. They also encourage their daughters to have a variety of lovers so that they may find a sexually compatible marriage partner. Young men gain social prestige through their ability to please their partners. These patterns persist on a daily basis throughout the adolescent years for unmarried men and women.

Sexual relations continue to occur frequently after marriage. A wide range of sexual activity is approved, including oral-genital sex and a considerable amount of touching before and during intercourse. Among the Mangaians, then, sexual activity is not only condoned but is actively encouraged.

Inis Beag A sharp contrast to Mangaian practices is provided by the community of the Irish island known as Inis Beag (a pseudonym). Anthropologist John Messenger (1971) studied this society between 1958 and 1966. He observed that sexual expression is discouraged from infancy on: Mothers avoid breast-feeding their children, and after infancy parents seldom kiss or fondle them. Children learn to abhor nudity. They learn that elimination is dirty and that bathing must be done only in absolute privacy. Any kind of childhood sexual expression is punished.

As they grow older, children usually receive no information about sex from their parents. Young girls are often shocked by their first menstruation, and they are never given an adequate explanation of what has happened. Priests and other religious authorities teach that it is sinful to discuss premarital sexual activity, masturbation, or sex play. Religious leaders on the island have denounced even *Time* and *Life* magazines as pornographic.

Marriage partners generally know little or nothing about precoital sex play, such as oral or manual stimulation of the breasts and genitals. Beyond intercourse, sexual activity is usually limited to mouth kissing and rough fondling of the woman's lower body by the man. Men invariably initiate sex, using the man-on-top coital position, and both partners usually wear nightclothes during coitus. Female orgasm is unknown or considered a deviant response.

Sexual misconceptions continue through adulthood. For example, many women believe that menopause causes insanity, and some women confine themselves to bed from menopause to their death. During menstruation and also during the months following childbirth, men consider intercourse to be harmful to them. Many men also believe coitus to be debilitating, avoiding sex the night before a strenuous job. In general, sexual expression in Inis Beag is marked by anxiety-laden attitudes and rigid restrictions.

The Dani of New Guinea   In both Mangaia and Inis Beag, sexuality receives a great amount of attention, albeit in different ways. In contrast, the Dani people of West New Guinea seem to be largely indifferent to sexuality (Heider, 1976). Sexual activity is infrequent among adults. Although courtship covers an extended period (marriages are held only during a certain feast that occurs every four to six years), there is almost no premarital sex. After marriage, a couple abstains from sex for at least two years and then has infrequent coitus. Following the birth of a child, husband and wife do not have sex for four to six years. During this time there is no reported masturbation, and extramarital sex is rare.

According to Karl Heider, who studied this society in the 1960s, the Dani culture does not overtly enforce these behavior patterns. Heider also observed no indications of hormonal or physiological deficiencies that could result in low sexual interest. In general, the Dani are relaxed, physically healthy people who live in a moderate climate and have an adequate food supply. They appear to be very calm, only rarely expressing anger. Heider believes that the apparent infrequency of sexual activity reflects the Dani's relaxed life-style and their low level of emotional intensity.

SEXUAL ORIENTATION: HOMOSEXUALITY

We have seen that the norms of sexual expression may vary considerably from society to society. But even within a single society, individuals express their sexuality in different ways. In this section we explore one variation in sexual behavior, homosexuality. We also look at the impact of AIDS (acquired immunodeficiency syndrome) on sexual behavior patterns in recent years.

Different people have different views of what is sexually exciting, and sexuality can be expressed in a variety of ways. One way in which sexual expression varies from person to person is in **sexual orientation**—that is, the sex to which an individual is attracted. Attraction to partners of the same sex is called homosexual orientation, and attraction to partners of the other sex is called heterosexual orientation. Bisexuality refers to attraction to partners of both sexes.

Most people think of homosexuality as sexual contact between individuals of the same sex. However, this definition is limited in that it does not encompass all of the meanings of the term homosexual, which can refer to (1) sexual behavior, (2) emotional affiliation, and (3) one's own self-definition. The following definition incorporates a broader spectrum of elements: A **homosexual** person is an individual "whose primary erotic, psychological, emotional, and social interest is in a member of the same sex, even though that interest may not be overtly expressed" (Martin & Lyon, 1972, p. 1). A homosexual person's gender identity agrees with his or her biological sex. That is, homosexual individuals perceive themselves as male or female, respectively, and are attracted to people of the same sex.

In our society, we tend to make clear-cut distinctions between homosexuality and heterosexuality. The delineation is not so clear-cut, however. At one end of a broad spectrum, a relatively small percentage of people consider themselves exclusively homosexual; at the other end, a greater number think of themselves as exclusively heterosexual. Between the two groups exist varying degrees of preference and experience.

THE INCIDENCE OF HOMOSEXUALITY   According to Alfred Kinsey et al. (1948), the proportion of exclusively homosexual individuals in our society is approximately 2 percent of women and 4 percent of men (or roughly 3 percent of the total U.S. population). Some writers have speculated that the actual number of predominantly homosexual people is closer to 10 percent of the population. This higher estimate is based partly on the assumption that social pressures cause many homosexual people to conceal their orientation.

Between the extremes on the continuum are many individuals who have experienced sexual contact with or been attracted to people of the same sex. Kinsey's estimate of this group's number was quite high. Some 37 percent of males and 13 percent of females in his research populations reported having had overt homosexual experiences at some point in their lives, and even more had been erotically attracted to members of the same sex.

ATTITUDES TOWARD HOMOSEXUALITY A monumental survey of 190 societies throughout the world, conducted by an anthropologist and a psychologist (Ford & Beach, 1951), found that homosexuality was accepted in approximately two-thirds of these societies. Homosexuality was also widely accepted in many earlier cultures. For example, over half of 225 Native American tribes accepted male homosexuality, and 17 percent accepted female homosexuality (Pomeroy, 1965).

Our own Judeo-Christian tradition has had a far more negative view of homosexuality. Many religious scholars believe that the condemnation of homosexuality stems from a reformation movement beginning in the seventh century B.C., through which Jewish religious leaders wanted to develop a closed community distinct from others of the time. Homosexual activities had been a part of the religious services of many population groups, and one way of establishing the uniqueness of the Jewish religion was to reject religious rituals involving homosexual activities. Thus homosexual behaviors were condemned as a form of pagan worship (Kosnik et al., 1977). Strong prohibitive biblical scriptures were written, for example, "You shall not lie with man as one lies with a female, it is an abomination" (Leviticus 18:22).

In recent years there has been a shift in attitudes toward homosexuality. The view that homosexuality is immoral has been replaced to some degree by a common belief that homosexuality is a sickness. Most current research, however, contradicts this notion. Studies comparing nonpatient heterosexual and homosexual individuals have found no significant differences in adjustment between the two groups (Mannion, 1981; Wilson, 1984). Two noted researchers in this area, Alan Bell and Martin Weinberg, state that ". . . homosexual adults who have come to terms with their homosexuality, who do not regret their sexual orientation and who can function effectively sexually and socially, are no more distressed psychologically than are heterosexual men and women" (1978, p. 216).

Although attitudes towards homosexuality have changed towards more acceptance in recent years, there are some signs that the trend may be reversing somewhat. In 1992 a number of states had ballot measures on the general election restricting rights of homosexuals. In Colorado the measure passed, and in Oregon it came very close to passing. Whether this reflects a more general trend in attitude change remains to be seen.

THEORIES OF HOMOSEXUALITY Several theories have attempted to explain the development of homosexuality. There is still no single clear answer, but recent research conducted by Alan Bell, Martin Weinberg, and Sue Hammersmith (1981) helps shed some light on the question. Bell and his colleagues used a sample of 979 homosexual people matched to a control group of 477 heterosexual people. All subjects were questioned about their childhood, adolescence, and sexual practices, and their responses were analyzed using sophisticated statistical techniques. Much of the information presented in this discussion is based on this study's findings, to which we refer in evaluating both psychosocial and biological explanations of homosexuality.

Psychosocial Theories   Some theories seek to explain homosexuality as the result of learning, personal experiences, parenting patterns, or the individual's own psychological attributes. For instance, one explanation for homosexuality is that it may be the result of unhappy heterosexual experiences or the inability to attract partners of the other sex.

Is homosexuality a learned response? Does homosexuality result from unhappy heterosexual experiences? This view is commonly voiced in the effort to explain lesbianism, which people often assume is based in resentment, dislike, fear, or distrust of men rather than an attraction toward women.

Perhaps the best way to evaluate this explanation of homosexuality is to turn the argument around: Is female heterosexuality caused by dislike and fear of women? The answer is no—just as lesbianism is not caused by unhappy experiences with men. In fact, research indicates that up to 70 percent of lesbian women have had sexual experiences with men, and many report having enjoyed them. However, they prefer to be sexual with women (Klaich, 1974).

Bell and his colleagues report that lesbianism is not related either to unpleasant heterosexual experiences or to a lack of such experience (1981, p. 176). Their research found that homosexual and heterosexual people had dated about equally in high school, a finding that contradicts the notion that homosexuality results from a lack of heterosexual opportunity. Both male and female homosexual subjects did tend, however, to feel differently about dating than did heterosexual subjects, for few of them reported enjoying it. These feelings probably indicate that these subjects were less interested in heterosexual relationships. For example, although the homosexual males dated as much as the heterosexual males in the study, they tended to have fewer sexual encounters with females. The researchers concluded that "unless heterosexual encounters appeal to one's deepest sexual feeling, there is likely to be little about them that one would experience as positive reinforcement for sexual relationships with members of the opposite sex" (p. 108).

Another myth dispelled by the Bell research team is that young men and women become homosexual because they have been seduced by older homosexuals. In reality, not only did most subjects (both male and female) report that their first homosexual encounter had involved someone of about their own age, but homosexual subjects were less likely than heterosexual subjects to have had initial sexual encounters with a stranger or an adult.

Some people may believe that homosexuality can be "caught" from someone else—for instance, that a homosexual teacher, especially one who is well liked and respected, will become a role model for students. However, homosexual orientation appears to be established even before school age, and modeling is not a relevant factor (Marmor, 1980).

Another theory links homosexuality to certain patterns in family background. Sigmund Freud (1905) maintained that children's relationships with their fathers and mothers was a crucial factor. Although Freud viewed men and women as innately bisexual, he thought that individuals normally passed through a "homoerotic" phase in the course of heterosexual development. Certain people could become "fixated" at the homosexual phase if some kinds of life experiences occurred, especially if a boy had a poor relationship with his father and an overly close relationship with his mother. Although Freud's theory is frequently cited, it has received little support from research. In fact, Bell and his colleagues found that no particular phenomenon of family life could be singled out as especially consequential in the development of either heterosexual or homosexual orientations.

Biological Theories of Homosexuality   If psychosocial causes cannot explain homosexuality, does biology provide any more reliable answers? In the effort to answer this question, researchers have investigated a number of possible biological factors. The two most promising lines of research have explored genetic and hormonal factors.

According to one argument, a person's homosexuality may be determined by his or her genetic makeup. One study conducted by Franz Kallman (1952a, 1952b) tested this theory by comparing the sexual orientations of both fraternal and identical twins. In all cases, the twins had been reared together, so their prenatal (before birth) and postnatal environments were virtually identical. The primary difference between the two groups lay in their genetic makeup, which was identical for the identical twins but not for the fraternal twins.

Kallman reported an approximately 95 percent *concordance rate* for homosexuality among the identical twins. In contrast, the concordance rate for fraternal twins was only 12 percent. A more recent investigation reported concordance rates for homosexuality of approximately 75 percent and 19 percent, respectively, among identical and fraternal twins (Whitman & Diamond, 1986). However, other research has failed to find evidence of hereditary factors in homosexuality (Heston & Shields, 1968). Additional research is needed before we can conclude that genetic makeup determines sexual orientation.

Some researchers speculate that prenatal hormone imbalances can alter the masculine and feminine development of the fetal brain. There is a critical period during which the fetus is particularly sensitive to levels of testosterone. How could brain levels of testosterone be altered during gestation? Research suggests that maternal stress during a critical period (perhaps between the second and the sixth months of pregnancy) results in decreased levels of fetal testosterone. The stress, which causes large amounts of adrenal hormones to enter the fetal bloodstream, inhibits the masculinization of the hypothalamus by testosterone. According to this theory, prenatal hormone imbalances during this period could contribute to homosexuality (Ellis & Ames, 1987; Zuger, 1989). Laboratory research with animals has demonstrated that prenatal stress, which resulted in decreased levels of testosterone, also alters male sexual behavior. Prenatally stressed male rats responded to injections of testosterone with an increase in female sexual behavior (McLeod and Brown, 1988).

It is also possible for both prenatal masculination and feminization to coexist to some degree, with a consequent bisexual orientation. Nutritional changes, medicine and drugs, and maternal stress can alter maternal hormones in animals (Money, 1988). However, any conclusions about humans from animal studies are uncertain, and it is scientifically unethical to experiment on fetal humans.

Hormone levels may be a factor during adulthood as well as in prenatal development. Some researchers have compared hormone levels in adult homosexual men and women with those in heterosexual adults, with contradictory results. Some studies report that homosexual males have less androgen than heterosexual males; others indicate just the opposite; and still others reveal no difference (Meyer-Bahlburg, 1977; Tourney, 1980). Eminent sex researcher John Money (1988) has recently reviewed the literature and concluded that the data indicate no difference in the levels of circulating sex hormones in adult heterosexual and homosexual males. Only a few studies have explored hormone levels in lesbians, and as in male homosexual studies, their findings have been inconsistent (Gaitwell et al., 1977; Griffiths et al., 1974).

Although Bell and his coworkers did not measure hormone levels in their study, they suggest that biology may be a factor in the development of homosexuality. They believe that individuals are predisposed to be either heterosexual or homosexual, and they see homosexuality as "a pattern of feelings and reactions within the child that cannot be traced back to a single social or psychological root" (p. 192).

In conclusion, research seems to suggest that some people may be biologically predisposed toward homosexuality either genetically or as a result of stress hormones during prenatal development. At this point, however, it seems most appropriate to think of sexual orientation as influenced by a variety of psychosocial and biological factors that are unique for each person, rather than trying to find a single cause.

Many sexually active individuals today are concerned about the threat of **acquired immunodeficiency syndrome (AIDS).** No disease in modern times has received more attention or produced such hysteria, and with good reason. The AIDS epidemic constitutes a worldwide public health threat whose magnitude is growing rapidly; among some groups of people it is the number one cause of premature death.

Evidence suggests that AIDS results from infection with a virus called *human immunodeficiency virus (HIV).* In many people HIV specifically targets and destroys a type of lymphocyte which normally stimulates the immune system to fight disease. The resulting impairment of the immune system leaves the body vulnerable to a variety of cancers and opportunistic infections. The virus can also invade the brain, causing neurological damage.

HIV has been isolated from the semen, blood, vaginal secretions, saliva, tears, urine, and breast milk of infected individuals. Most commonly, the virus enters the body through intravenous needles, blood transfusions, and sexual contact. In sexual contact, the virus can enter the bloodstream if the mucous membranes which line the penile urethra, vagina, and mouth are torn and bleed during sex, or if these moist tissues contain open sores. In drug abuse, HIV can enter the body when blood-contaminated needles are shared by intravenous drug abusers (Chitwood & Comerford, 1990; McCoy et al., 1990). It can also be transmitted from an infected mother to her child, either in the late stages of pregnancy or shortly after birth (Falloon et al., 1989; Kennedy et al., 1989; Landesman et al., 1989). HIV has also been transmitted through transfusions of infected blood or blood products. However, transmission by this mode has become extremely rare since early 1985, when screening for HIV-tainted blood became routine. It is believed that the risk of transmitting the virus via semen, saliva, tears, urine, or vaginal secretions is extremely low, and there is no evidence that HIV can be transmitted through casual contact such as hugging, shaking hands, cooking, living in the same household, or other forms of nonsexual contact with an infected person (Hearst & Hulley, 1988; Lifson et al., 1988; Peterman et al., 1988).

In America certain groups of individuals have been identified as being at particularly high risk for developing AIDS. These high-risk groups include homosexual and bisexual men (men who are attracted to both male and female partners), intravenous drug abusers, and people with blood disorders who require blood transfusions or blood products. (Although the risk of contracting AIDS through transfusion is today very low, some individuals who were infected by tainted blood products before 1985 may not yet be symptomatic, due to the long incubation period of the virus.) Any person who has had a regular sexual partner who is a member of any of these groups must also be viewed as a high-risk individual.

Although within the United States homosexual transmission of HIV is far more common than heterosexual transmission, it is not always the rule. The reverse is true in Africa, where heterosexual contact is the primary mode of transmission of HIV (Belec et al., 1989; European Study Group, 1989). Heterosexual individuals are cautioned against a false sense of immunity to HIV. Anyone who engages in high-risk behaviors (drug abuse and unprotected sex) puts him- or herself at risk of AIDS.

At present there is no cure for AIDS, nor does a vaccine exist that can prevent infection. Consequently, the best hope for curtailing the epidemic spread of

THE EFFECT OF AIDS ON SEXUAL BEHAVIOR

AIDS is through education and behavioral change. Because the virus is transmitted almost exclusively by behavior that individuals can modify, health and education officials are hopeful that educational programs aimed at encouraging people to eliminate high-risk behavior will be effective in curtailing the spread of AIDS. A number of studies of high-risk populations of homosexual males have shown that fear of contracting AIDS has resulted in significant changes in sexual behavior (Centers for Disease Control, 1987; Lawrence et al., 1989; Lourea et al., 1986). Many of these men have reduced the number of their sexual partners or entered into monogamous relationships. Furthermore, large numbers of homosexual males have responded to AIDS education campaigns by making a commitment to avoid drug and sexual activities that place them at risk for contracting AIDS. Hopefully, educational efforts aimed at the broader population will accomplish similar shifts away from high-risk behavior.

Perhaps the single most important preventive step people can take is to spend several months getting to know prospective sexual partners before engaging in genital sex (Hearst & Hulley, 1988; Peterman et al., 1988). What do we look for in assessing the risk status of a potential sexual partner? Certainly this evaluation involves determining whether the individual belongs to a high-risk group. We should ask potential partners about their present and past behaviors in the areas of sex, drugs, receiving blood transfusions, and so forth. Remember, even if a person is not a member of a high-risk group, he or she may have been recently involved sexually with someone in those categories. Self-disclosure can be a marvelous strategy for getting a partner to open up. Thus you might begin your dialogue about these matters by providing information about your own sexual history and discussing why you think that such an information exchange is vitally important in the AIDS era.

Getting to know someone well enough to trust his or her answers to these important questions means taking the time to assess a person's honesty and integrity in a variety of situations. If you observe your prospective partner lying to friends, family members, or to you about other matters, you may rightfully question his or her honesty in responding to your risk-assessment queries.

Recent research by Susan Cochran (1988) suggests that we cannot always assume that potential sexual partners will accurately disclose their risk for AIDS. Cochran found that a sizable percentage of both male and female subjects said they would not be fully honest when questioned about their past sexual and drug use histories. Of over 400 sexually experienced southern California college students, 35 percent of the men and 10 percent of the women said they had lied about such things as pregnancy risk and other sexual involvements in order to have sex. In addition, 47 percent of the men and 42 percent of the women said they would report fewer previous sexual partners than they really had. Finally, 20 percent of the men and 4 percent of the women indicated they would falsely claim they had tested negative for HIV.

The preceding discussion makes it clear that it is difficult to determine whether a person is at risk for AIDS. It is also becoming clear that researchers do not agree on the cause or causes of AIDS diseases. For instance, there is a growing number of AIDS researchers who now believe that either HIV does not cause AIDS or that important cofactors along with HIV infection are necessary. Until these important issues are resolved by further research couples who wish to commence sexual relations should exercise caution.

Throughout this chapter we have discussed the major factors contributing to motivated behavior. We conclude that human motivation is often the complex product of several factors including biological, cognitive, and psychosocial influences. In the next chapter we will examine the role of emotion in energizing and directing behavior.

SOME SUGGESTIONS FOR OVERCOMING OBESITY

Countless solutions have, been proposed to deal with weight problems. Nevertheless, the great majority of obese people who try to reduce and maintain a lower weight ultimately fail. This discussion presents a few suggestions based on the clinical experiences and experimental findings of weight loss specialists. Note that it is a good idea to consult a physician before embarking on a weight loss program.

1. *Determine your calorie intake.* Many people are convinced they are overweight not because they eat too much, but rather because they have metabolic problems. Most adults of normal weight consume about 2,000 to 2,500 calories each 24-hour period, depending on their size, sex, and activity level. If you are overweight and convinced that you eat no more than your skinny friends, try keeping a record of everything you eat and drink for a period of a week or so. You can buy a convenient calorie counter to help you convert items consumed into average calories per day. Some people are shocked at the number of calories they consume without thinking about what they are doing.

2. *Reduce food intake, if necessary.* We add the disclaimer "if necessary" because for some obese people whose food consumption is in fact moderate, exercise without dieting may be more effective than eating less. However, if you are consuming more than a normal allotment of calories, it is helpful to reduce the amount you eat, particularly food high in fat and sugar content. "Calories consumed as fat are converted into fat on the body more readily than the same number of calories consumed as carbohydrate or protein" (Gurin, 1989, p. 33). Consult a physician, dietician, or authoritative textbook to be sure your reduced food intake provides a healthy, balanced diet.

Avoid crash diets that may reduce calories to only a few hundred a day. Your odds for success are much better if you cut back only moderately on daily calorie consumption. Research clearly demonstrates that a slow, steady weight loss, of perhaps only a pound or two per week, increases your chances of keeping excess pounds off once you reach your desired weight.

Several tips may help you lower food consumption moderately. First, try stocking up on nutritious food that does not inspire lust in your taste buds. Get rid of cookies, candies, ice cream, porterhouse steaks well marbled with fat, potato chips, cream cheese, soft drinks, or anything else you love to consume. It is a good idea to allow for some interesting variety in your diet so that you will not end up feeling so deprived that you lose all control and binge.

Second, commit yourself to eating only at mealtime, and always in the same place. This helps eliminate the urge to snack that often results from learned associations between certain activities and food (for example, raiding the refrigerator during TV commercials). It can also be helpful to reduce access to foods that require no preparation. It is all too easy to nibble from an open box of crackers or cookies without even thinking about what you are doing.

3. *Exercise.* When used in conjunction with reduced food intake, regular, moderate exercise is probably the best strategy for losing weight (Belko et al., 1987; Craighead, 1990; Gurin, 1989; Keesey & Powley, 1986; Thompson et al., 1982). Unfortunately, however, some people make the mistake of thinking they will drop all their excess weight in a herculean exercise program. Like crash diets, this strategy often fails, due to physical burnout, injury, or boredom.

Moderation is the key for most people. If you can burn off 200 to 300 calories each time you exercise, you will obtain noticeable results in a reasonable amount of time (assuming, of course, that your food intake is held to a moderate level). Most specialists recommend exercise sessions that last a minimum of 20 to 30 minutes and occur at least three times a week. The activities you choose should be strenuous enough to raise your heart rate appreciably and to allow you to burn 200 to 300 calories per session. All kinds of exercise possibilities exist. Choosing one that is relatively enjoyable, or at least not unpleasant, will pay dividends in greater perseverance. Studies indicate that 30 minutes of brisk walking burns off about 150 calories, 30 minutes of bicycling on normal terrain burns off 200 calories, swimming, 275 calories, and jogging, 370. For many people, exercise actually seems to decrease the appetite (Stunkard, 1983).

Recent research demonstrates that people who exercise either very intensively or for very long periods may experience an increase in their metabolic rate that can last for two or three days after cessation of exercise (Kolata, 1987a). In addition, the more muscle tissue a person has relative to fat, the greater his or her metabolic rate: Muscle tissue consumes more calorie energy than fat (Kolata, 1987a). Such findings suggest that an exercise regimen that combines muscle building with extended periods of cardiovascular exercise (such as jogging, bicycling, or swimming for a couple of hours several times a week) may be the optimal strategy for weight control. However, such a rigorous exercise program poses the risk of burnout or perhaps injury for individuals who do not build slowly into a program in accordance with the rate of improvement in their physical fitness.

4. *Keep records and reward yourself.* Research indicates that people who keep records of how much they eat, when they eat, and what they were doing before and during eating are more likely to benefit from a weight loss program than those who do not record this information. These records may reveal certain patterns of which you were unaware, such as a tendency to eat more in the company of a certain friend or to raid the refrigerator when you are feeling depressed.

It may be helpful to include others in your efforts to lose weight. Sometimes the first five or 10 pounds are the toughest because nobody seems to notice. However, having someone around to praise you for the pound or two you have lost can be very reinforcing. Setting up little rewards along the way can also be helpful. Perhaps you can treat yourself to a professional massage after you drop the first five pounds. Maybe after 10 or 15 pounds you can take yourself to a beach resort where you can show off your gorgeous new body.

SUMMARY

THE NATURE OF MOTIVATION

1. Motivation can be defined as any condition that energizes and directs behavior.
2. Motivation not only energizes or activates us to behave in a certain way; it also defines the direction of the resulting behavior. Motivation also has a direct impact on how vigorous or intense our behaviors are.

MOTIVATIONAL EXPLANATIONS OF BEHAVIOR

3. One of the earliest attempts to explain motivation was based on the notion of instincts, innate patterns of behavior that occur in every normally functioning member of a species under certain set conditions.
4. Our behaviors are so profoundly influenced by learning that it is essentially impossible to find one example of human behavior that fits the literal definition of instincts.
5. According to the drive-reduction theory, motivation originates with a need or drive, experienced as an unpleasant aversive condition, that motivates us to act in a way that will reduce the aversive condition. This theory, while limited in scope, does explain some aspects of motivation.
6. Maslow proposed that human needs exist on a multilevel hierarchy consisting of five stages ranging from the lowest, most basic biological needs to the highest need for self-actualization.
7. Criticisms of Maslow's theory include the fact that there is little evidence that human motives or needs are ordered in the sequence that Maslow proposed

and that many of his major precepts are so vague that it is virtually impossible to define them operationally.

8. According to the cognitive perspective, our beliefs and expectations play an important role in motivating our actions.

9. Researchers have theorized that our achievement motive is the result of a complex interaction between our hope of success and fear of failure.

10. Early research suggested that some women may be motivated by fear of success. However, follow-up studies found that this so-called fear of success was not so much a motive but rather an accurate perception of what is likely to happen to women who achieve career success in a society dominated by traditional gender assumptions.

11. One way to help instill a desire to achieve is to encourage children to set reasonable goals and to provide ample reinforcers for their successes.

12. It is useful to classify human motives under four categories: biologically based motives rooted primarily in body tissue needs; sensation-seeking motives expressed as a need for certain levels of stimulation; complex psychosocial motives that seem to demonstrate little or no relationship to biological needs; and multifactorial motives that are based on a combination of biological, psychological, and cultural factors.

13. Research has ruled out the hypothesis that the hunger motive is primarily caused by stomach contractions.

14. According to the hypothalamic control theory, two regions within the hypothalamus may possibly serve as control centers for eating. One region, the ventromedial hypothalamus, seems to act as a satiety center that sig-

nals when an organism has had enough to eat. In contrast, the lateral hypothalamus seems to act as an "on switch" that instigates eating. New research suggests that although these areas of the hypothalamus are important they do not act as mere switches for eating.

15. The glucostatic theory proposes that levels of glucose are monitored by glucoreceptors (cells sensitive to glucose in the bloodstream). Hunger results whenever the glucoreceptors detect that glucose is unavailable.

16. The lipostatic theory of long-term control of hunger and eating suggests that our bodies monitor the amount of fat they contain and use the result as a barometer to regulate food intake so that fat levels are held relatively constant.

17. Many researchers believe that our bodies may be programmed in some fashion to maintain a preferred level of body weight for each individual, a phenomenon known as set point.

18. Obesity places a person at risk for developing one or more serious health problems, such as high blood pressure, heart disease, and depression.

19. Genetic factors, conditions of early development, emotional stress, and metabolic factors have all been suggested as possible causes of obesity.

20. Two eating disorders particularly common among young women are anorexia nervosa, a form of self-starvation, and bulimia, in which a person may eat a full meal and then purge the stomach and intestines of food by inducing vomiting or using a laxative.

21. Suggested causes for anorexia nervosa and bulimia include a disturbed body image, depression, anxiety, and possibly physical abnormalities involving neurotransmitters, the

hypothalamus and/or the endocrine system.

22. The need to manipulate and explore the environment and the need for sensory stimulation both fall under the category of sensation-seeking motives.

23. Psychologists have theorized that people have an optimum level of arousal which is the level where their performance will be most efficient. According to the Yerkes-Dodson law, the optimum level of arousal for peak performance varies, depending on the difficulty of the task.

24. Subjects exposed to prolonged sensory deprivation appear to develop a strong need for sensory stimulation. Prolonged sensory deprivation frequently reduces a person's performance on a variety of mental tasks.

25. Milder forms of sensory restriction may both reduce stress through peaceful relaxation and increase people's susceptibility to being influenced in positive ways.

26. In humans, sexual interest and expression are controlled less by hormones and more by the cerebral cortex, reflecting a complex combination of biological, psychological, and cultural factors.

27. While it is difficult to distinguish the effects of sex hormones and learning experiences on sexual arousal, research does indicate that androgens appear to facilitate sexual interest in males. The relationship between female sexuality and hormones, if one exists, is very difficult to pinpoint.

28. Psychological and cultural conditions probably play a greater role than hormones in human sexual motivation. This tendency is reflected in the role of reinforcement and psychosocial conditioning, which maintain and constrain sexual expression, respectively.

29. Ideas about what is sexually arousing vary greatly across the cultures of the world. Sexual conduct is regulated in some way in all societies, but the rules vary from one society to the next.

30. A high rate of sexual activity and extensive sexual instruction of youths is the norm on the Polynesian island of Mangaia.

31. On the Irish island of Inis Beag, sexual expression is discouraged from infancy through old age. Sexual misinformation is common, and female orgasm is practically unknown.

32. The Dani people of New Guinea demonstrate little interest in sexual activity and abstain from sex for years at a time.

33. There are a number of psychosocial and biological theories that attempt to explain the development of homosexuality. Some of the psychosocial theories relate to parenting patterns, life experiences, or the psychological attributes of the person.

34. Theories of biological causation of homosexuality look to genetic and prenatal influences on hormone levels and sexual differentiation of the brain.

TERMS AND CONCEPTS

motivation
instincts
incentives
need for achievement (nAch)
fear of success
cognitive expectancies
cognitive dissonance

biologically based motives
drive
ventromedial hypothalamus (VMH)
lateral hypothalamus (LH)
hypothalamic control theory
glucostatic theory
lipostatic theory

set point
obese
anorexia nervosa
bulimia
sensation-seeking motives
arousal
optimum level of arousal
Yerkes-Dodson law

sensory deprivation studies
androgens
estrogens
cultural mores
sexual orientation
homosexual
acquired immunodeficiency
 syndrome (AIDS)

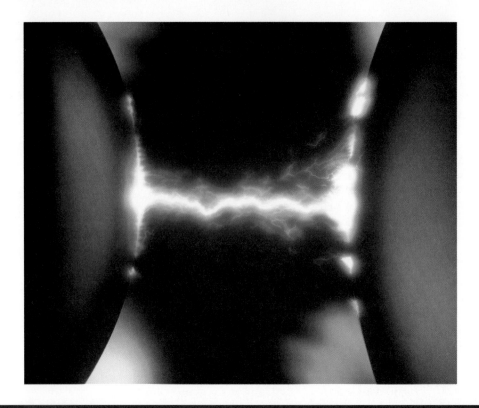

CHAPTER 9

Emotion and Stress

THE COMPONENTS OF EMOTION

Cognitive Processes
Affect
Physiological Arousal
Behavioral Responses

THE RANGE OF HUMAN EMOTION

Plutchik's Emotion Wheel

THEORIES OF EMOTION

Historical Perspectives
Contemporary Theories

STRESS

The Nature of Stress
Physiological Responses to Stress
Psychological Responses to Stress
Stressors
Stress and Disease

As we saw in Chapter 8, motivation and **emotion** are closely connected. Emotions often motivate actions, as when a child's anger leads to kicking a bedroom wall or when fear of failure motivates a student to withdraw from a class. The expectation of pleasant emotions also serves as an incentive, in that many of our purposeful, motivated behaviors induce feelings of happiness, joy, excitement, and pride.

Emotions do more than motivate behavior. They provide zing and zest to our existence. They can be confusing and difficult to identify, but can you imagine what life would be like without them? In this chapter we explore emotions in an effort to find out more about what they are, how they come about, and how they influence our lives. We also explore a closely related topic: stress, the effect of stress on our lives, and the ways in which we can moderate some of the negative effects of stress.

THE COMPONENTS OF EMOTION

Although the terms *emotion* and *feelings* are often used interchangeably, a careful analysis reveals that feelings are only one element of emotion. In fact, human emotions include four integral components: cognitive processes, affect or subjective feelings, physiological arousal, and behavioral reactions. Take a moment to read the following account. It illustrates all of the components just listed.

> My 10-year-old daughter has been testing me to the limit lately, to see what she can get away with. She went too far the other day. While she was at school, I went into her room to leave some clean laundry on her bed, and I could hardly believe what I saw. My new white sweater, which she had admired greatly, was crumpled up under the bed, partly visible from where I stood. When I pulled it out to make sure it was what I thought it was, I could see a large stain where nail polish had been spilled on it. She had borrowed my sweater without asking, carelessly ruined it, and then had hidden the evidence!
>
> My initial reaction was fury. It is lucky she wasn't there, since I am not sure how I might have responded in those first few moments — the juices were flowing and I was ready to become a child abuser! I threw the sweater down, muttering something very unmotherly about my child, and started rummaging madly through her drawers, looking for a favorite item of hers that I could ruin. Then I began to think more clearly. Rather than stooping to the level of a 10-year-old, I thought I stood a better chance of teaching her a lesson by dealing rationally with the incident. I neatly folded the sweater with the stain showing, wrote a brief note requesting that my daughter meet me in my room at 5 o'clock for a talk, and left the note on top of the sweater in the middle of her bed.

COGNITIVE PROCESSES

One component of emotion is cognitive processes. Although psychologists differ in the extent to which they emphasize the role of cognition in emotional arousal and expression, there is a general consensus that perception, thinking, and memory are very much involved in emotional expression. In the preceding account, the mother would not have experienced anger had she been unable to perceive and understand the implications of what she found in her daughter's room.

AFFECT

All emotions also include an *affective* component involving both a general positive or negative state such as joy, anger, fear, or disgust. The emotions recorded in the preceding account reflect both a general negative affect and the specific feeling of intense anger. When psychologists attempt to ascertain a person's emotional state, they typically ask the individual to describe the emotions he or she is experiencing. Most people respond by describing their feelings "I am depressed"; "I am extremely happy"; "I feel nervous and apprehensive." Thus, for most individuals, these *subjective feelings* constitute emotion.

PHYSIOLOGICAL AROUSAL

A third component of emotions is *physiological arousal.* When the mother described her anger by saying "the juices were flowing," her account was close to the mark. The "juices," in the form of epinephrine and other hormones associated with the arousal of anger, probably were flowing. As a result of this increased endocrine activity, we might guess that for a few moments at least her heart rate increased dramatically, her blood pressure probably increased significantly, and her breathing may have become rapid and uneven.

Indeed, emotions are associated with mild to extreme changes in the physiological processes occurring within our bodies. In addition to the changes we just listed, these processes may include metabolic changes, altered muscle tension, changes in activity of the salivary and sweat glands, modified digestive processes, and changes in the levels of certain neurotransmitters in the brain. (Recall from Chapter 3 that the autonomic nervous system is involved in most of the physiological changes associated with emotional arousal.)

BEHAVIORAL RESPONSES

Finally, emotion also includes *behavioral response.* Emotions often motivate us to act out or express our feelings. These expressions may range from crying, screaming, or verbal outbursts ("muttering something unmotherly") to smiling or laughing. Facial expressions, tone of voice, posture, and other kinds of body language are all common signals of emotion. In addition to being expressive, behavioral reactions to emotions may also serve to either promote or reduce the emotion. For example, avoiding a situation that produces fear or going out of your way to meet a special person are examples of behavior maintained by a change in emotion (recall two-factor theory in Chapter 6).

THE RANGE OF HUMAN EMOTION

Adoration, amazement, amusement, anger, anxiety, contempt, disgust, distress, ecstasy, embarrassment, envy, fear, guilt, humiliation, interest, jealousy, joy, loathing, rage, reverence, sadness, shame, sorrow, surprise, terror—these are just a few of the emotions we recognize. Some of these emotions overlap: Ecstasy and joy, for instance, clearly share certain elements. Thus differences between emotions are often more a matter of degree than of kind. Furthermore, many emotional experiences may represent a blending of more basic emotions. The mother in the previous account may have felt a combination of anger and anxiety about her daughter's behavior.

Some psychologists have attempted to identify a number of primary emotions, combinations of which provide the building blocks for more complex emotions. One of the best-known schemes was developed by Robert Plutchik.

PLUTCHIK'S EMOTION WHEEL

According to Plutchik (1980), there are eight primary or basic human emotions, which consist of four pairs of opposites: acceptance and disgust, fear and anger, surprise and anticipation, and sadness and joy. Plutchik adopted the unique ap-

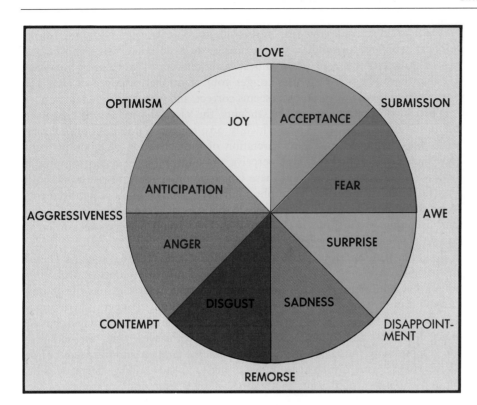

FIGURE 9.1
Plutchik's Emotion Wheel

According to Robert Plutchik, there are eight primary human emotions consisting of four opposite pairs. Adjacent emotions (such as joy and acceptance) blend to form more complex emotions (like love).

proach of arranging these eight primary emotions on an emotion wheel (see Figure 9.1). He maintains that all human emotions are variations or derivations of these eight. The closer to one another that emotions are located on the wheel, the more they have in common. For example, anticipation and joy both share an element of expectation, whereas fear and surprise share the quality of the unknown. Plutchik maintains that adjacent emotions blend to form the more complex feelings listed on the outer rim of the emotion wheel. Many of us would probably agree that love involves at least some elements of joy and acceptance, and that contempt certainly involves components of both anger and disgust.

THEORIES OF EMOTION

We have learned that emotional expression is a complex process involving cognitions, subjective feelings, physiological arousal, and behavioral reactions. How do these processes interact to produce an emotional response? What is the usual sequence of events? Is it necessary to think before we feel, or do we feel an emotion and then later interpret it as fear, happiness, and so forth? Psychologists have proposed contradictory answers to these questions, in a controversy that sometimes resembles the well-known debate about whether the chicken or the egg came first. We examine the evidence here as we review several historical perspectives as well as several contemporary theories of emotion.

THE JAMES-LANGE THEORY   Imagine that after having trouble sleeping, you decide to take a midnight walk. It is dark and still; no one else is in sight. Suddenly, you hear a rustling in the bushes behind you, followed by rapidly approaching footsteps. Your response will probably be one of terror: You are likely to run for your life.

HISTORICAL PERSPECTIVES

What would activate your fear in this situation? Is it triggered by the sounds you hear, which in turn induce you to run? Or is it more likely that your awareness of danger causes your heart to beat faster and your legs to carry you away, and that these physical responses trigger your emotional response of fear? Decide which of these interpretations seems correct, and why, before reading on.

When such questions are put to students, the vast majority answer that hearing noises in the dark causes fear, which in turn triggers a flood of physical reactions. This "commonsense" interpretation of the activation of emotion seems quite logical (see Figure 9.2). We perceive and interpret a particular stimulus, in this case threatening noises, and these cognitive processes give rise to an emotion (fear), which triggers certain physiological responses and body movements. Along these lines, we would also conclude that we cry because we feel sad, rather than becoming sad because we cry, and that we laugh because we are happy, rather than being happy because we laugh.

However, the American psychologist William James (1884), and the Danish physiologist Carl Lange (1885), writing independently of each other, both questioned this commonsense view. Their interpretation, referred to as the **James-Lange theory,** suggests that environmental stimuli trigger physiological responses from viscera (the internal organs such as the heart and lungs). For instance, heart rate and respiration both increase. At the same time, the body may also respond with muscle movements, as when we jump at an unexpected noise. These visceral and muscular responses then activate emotional states. Thus James and Lange would argue that your fear stems from your awareness of specific bodily responses that you associate with fear—a pounding heart, rapid breathing, running legs, and so forth—rather than from your cognitions about noises in the dark.

Although it might seem to contradict common sense, the James-Lange theory makes sense at some level. We have all encountered unexpected situations in which we seemed to respond automatically, before we had a chance to experience emotion. For example, if a car suddenly veered onto the sidewalk and threatened to run you down, you would no doubt leap out of the way. You might not label your heightened arousal and reactive state as one of "fear" until a moment later, when the danger had passed and you suddenly became aware that your knees were shaking and your heart was pounding. In such situations, the emotions seem to follow the bodily changes and behavioral reactions. James and Lange argued that we often encounter situations in which behavioral and physiological reactions occur too quickly to be triggered by emotions.

Some intriguing evidence collected from human subjects with spinal cord injuries provides some support for the James-Lange theory. If feedback from the internal organs through the autonomic nervous system is important, we might expect that individuals with damage high on the spinal cord (quadriplegics) would experience emotional feelings of lower intensity than those with low injury (paraplegics), because a high injury would cut off feedback from a greater portion of the body. This conclusion is exactly what research has revealed. The higher the injury to the spinal cord, and consequently the less sensory feedback received, the less intense are the emotional feelings reported by an individual (Hohmann, 1966). One quadriplegic with high injury describes these altered feelings, comparing them to the intensity of emotions he used to feel before his injury.

The sight of a bear may elicit a strong emotional response. Figure 9.2 describes several theoretical approaches to emotion.

Now, I don't get a feeling of physical animation. It's sort of cold anger. Sometimes I act angry when I see some injustice. I yell and cuss and raise hell, because if you don't do it sometimes, I've learned people will take advantage of you, but it just doesn't have the heat to it that it used to. It's a mental kind of anger. (Hohmann, 1966, p. 151)

The "Common Sense" View of Emotion. We perceive and interpret a particular stimulus and these cognitive processes give rise to an emotion which triggers certain physiological reactions and body movements. "I see a bear, feel fear, experience a flood of physiological reactions, and run because I am afraid."

FIGURE 9.2
Theories of Emotion

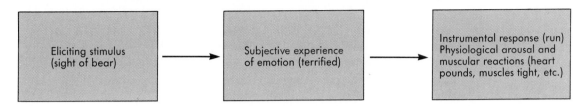

The James-Lange Theory. Environmental stimuli triggers physiological responses and bodily movements, and emotion occurs when the individual interprets his or her visceral and muscular responses. "I must be afraid because my heart is pounding and I am running like crazy."

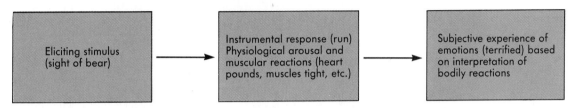

The Cannon-Bard Theory. Emotion is a cognitive event that is enhanced by bodily reactions. Bodily reactions do not cause emotion but rather occur simultaneously with the experience of emotion. "I am afraid because I know bears are dangerous."

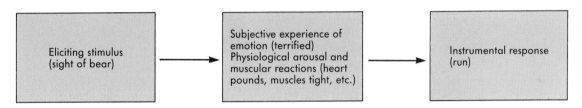

The Schachter-Singer Theory. Emotions depend upon a kind of double cognitive interpretation: we appraise the emotion-causing event while also evaluating what is happening with our bodies. "I am afraid because I know bears are dangerous and because my heart is pounding."

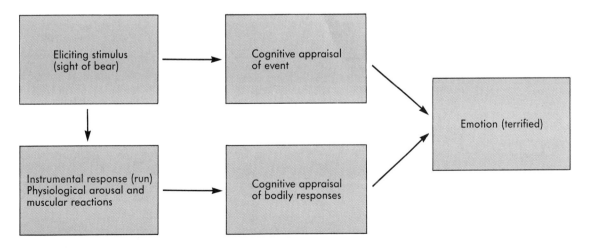

While such evidence seems to support the James-Lange theory, this interpretation has also been challenged. Prominent American physiologist Walter Cannon (1927) and his student, Philip Bard, objected to the idea that different emotions have distinct patterns of visceral and muscular responses that we recognize and then interpret as emotions. Cannon and Bard collected laboratory evidence indicating that physiological changes associated with happiness, sadness, and anger were quite similar. All of these emotions are typically accompanied by increased breathing and heart rate, secretion of epinephrine, and pupil dilation. How can people distinguish between different emotions that are accompanied by very similar physiological responses?

Psychologists today hesitate to reject the notion that people are able to discriminate between subtle differences in visceral and muscular patterns associated with specific emotions. Recent research has demonstrated that although different emotions are associated with similar physiological changes, these changes are not identical. For example, subtle distinctions have been demonstrated between emotions such as anger, fear, happiness, and sadness. These include variations in heart rate, resistance of the skin to the passage of a weak electrical current (galvanic skin response), temperature of the hands, patterns of activity in facial muscles, and neural activity in the frontal lobes of the brain (Davidson, 1984; Ekman et al., 1983; Schwartz, 1982).

Certainly, these more recent findings do not prove the James-Lange theory. There is little concrete evidence that people are able to discriminate accurately between varied, often highly similar patterns of physiological and muscular responses to determine what emotions they are experiencing. However, it is possible that we are sensitive to a wide variety of these responses, and that enough of these changes occur sufficiently quickly to serve as the basis for feelings of emotion.

THE CANNON-BARD THEORY   Walter Cannon not only criticized the James-Lange theory, he proposed an alternate theory of emotion. Cannon argued that physiological and muscular changes are not the cause of emotion. Instead, emotional experiences and physical changes occur simultaneously. This viewpoint, as modified by Philip Bard (1934), is known as the **Cannon-Bard theory.**

Cannon and Bard theorized that the thalamus (see Chapter 3) plays a key role in our emotional responses. It not only channels sensory input to the cerebral cortex, where it is interpreted, but at the same time it sends activation messages through the peripheral nervous system to the viscera and skeletal muscles. These activation messages trigger the physiological and behavioral responses that typically accompany emotions (refer back to Figure 9.2 on page 319).

Cannon and Bard would explain your emotional response to being approached in the dark in the following manner. The sensory input of the sounds you heard in the dark were relayed simultaneously to your cerebral cortex and your internal organs and muscles. This activity allowed you to perceive fear at the same time that your internal organs and muscles were reacting to the stimulus. Cannon and Bard would contend that your fear was enhanced by your pounding heart, rapid breathing, and flight from the source of the noise, rather than resulting from these physical changes, as James and Lange would suggest.

Subsequent research has revealed that the hypothalamus and certain other structures in the limbic system (see Chapter 3) are the brain centers most directly involved in integrating emotional responses—not the thalamus. However, the Cannon-Bard theory points out the important role of the brain in our emotional responses.

A major shortcoming of both the Cannon-Bard theory and the James-Lange theory is that neither adequately recognizes that emotions are more than automatic reactions to stimuli, and that they are often influenced by how we interpret feedback from our bodies. A more recent theory, known as the Schachter-Singer theory, presents an interesting assessment of the role of appraisal or judgment (cognitions) in the activation of emotion.

THE SCHACHTER-SINGER THEORY   In the early 1960s, Stanley Schachter and Jerome Singer (1962) developed the **Schachter-Singer theory** of emotions, which combined elements from both the James-Lange and the Cannon-Bard theories. Schachter and Singer believed that emotion follows behavioral and physiological reactions, as suggested by James and Lange, but they also agreed with Cannon and Bard that cognitive processes are central to emotional experience.

Instead of viewing emotion as a joint effect of both physical reactions and cognitive appraisal, Schachter and Singer maintained that emotions depend on a kind of double cognitive interpretation: We appraise the emotion-causing event while also evaluating what is happening with our bodies. The key process in emotional arousal is how we interpret feedback from our bodies in light of our present situation.

For example, suppose you have just run several blocks across campus to avoid being late to a class. You probably note that you are panting and sweating and that your heart is pounding, but you are unlikely to experience an emotional response to these heightened physical reactions. If you experience these same physical responses under different circumstances, however—for example, while running across a farmer's field to escape an enraged bull—you would probably interpret your arousal as fear.

The James-Lange view proposed that a given state of bodily reaction and arousal produces a specific emotion. Schachter and Singer suggested that a given physiological state could produce a variety of emotions, depending on the context within which it occurs. From this point of view, we might interpret highly similar patterns of arousal as reflecting distinctly different emotions in different contexts.

Schachter and Singer (1962) designed an ingenious experiment to test this theory. Male college student volunteers were told they would be participating in an experiment dealing with vision. All were given an injection of a substance the experimenters called Suproxin, which was described as a vitamin compound that would temporarily affect vision. In reality, some subjects were injected with the hormone epinephrine, which is known to increase heart and respiration rates and blood pressure, produce muscle tremors, and generally cause a jittery feeling. Other subjects, the control group, were merely injected with a placebo that produced no physical effects. The experimenters manipulated their subjects' cognitions about the cause of their arousal by providing accurate or inaccurate information about the connection between their symptoms and the earlier injection. Some of these subjects (the *informed group*) were told that some people react to Suproxin with the side effects just described. A second group of subjects (the *uninformed group*) received no information about side effects, and a third group (the *misinformed group*) received false information, for example that the drug might cause itching or facial numbness.

Next, all subjects experienced certain staged social cues during a 20-minute "waiting period" before the vision test (which never actually took place). Subjects were placed, one at a time, in the waiting room with another person who was introduced as a fellow subject, but who was actually a confederate of the experimenters. Half of the waiting subjects were exposed to a euphoria condition in which the accomplice behaved in a happy manner, engaging in such playful activity as shooting baskets by throwing paper wads into a trash can. These subjects were repeatedly asked to join in the good fun. In contrast, the other half of

CONTEMPORARY THEORIES

the subjects were assigned to an anger condition. They and the accomplice were asked to fill out a questionnaire, to which the accomplice reacted by grumbling loudly, tearing up the questionnaire, and eventually storming out of the room in a state of high anger. During these staged waiting periods, the subjects' behavior was observed through a one-way mirror; each subject was also questioned about his emotional state.

Assuming that Schachter and Singer's view of emotional arousal is correct, what pattern of results would you predict in this experiment? Were the subjects' assessments of their physiological state influenced by the confederate's antics? Were there differences between the informed, uninformed, and misinformed group? Before reading on, take some time and attempt to predict the probable outcome of this experiment.

Schachter and Singer predicted that subjects in the informed group, who knew that the injected drug was the cause of their physical arousal, would not experience any strong emotion. It was assumed they would observe their trembling hands and pounding heart and conclude that the drug was really doing its stuff. In contrast, subjects in the uninformed and misinformed groups would be aware of their arousal but have no obvious explanation for it. Therefore, it was assumed that they would cognitively appraise their environments for a logical explanation and a suitable label for the arousal they were experiencing (see Figure 9.3).

The researchers' hypothesis is essentially what occurred. The subjects who had been uninformed or misinformed tended to use the confederate's behavior as a relevant cue for identifying and labeling their own unexplained arousal as either anger or euphoria. In contrast, subjects in the informed group or the control group, who either were not aroused or who had an appropriate explanation for their arousal, tended not to share the confederate's emotional state.

The Schachter-Singer theory has directed the attention of psychologists to the important role of cognitive interpretation in emotional experience. However, Schachter and Singer's theory and supporting research are not without their critics. Several researchers have criticized the design of the classic 1962 experiment, and some attempts to replicate its findings have produced somewhat inconsistent

FIGURE 9.3

Result from the Schacter and Singer Experiment

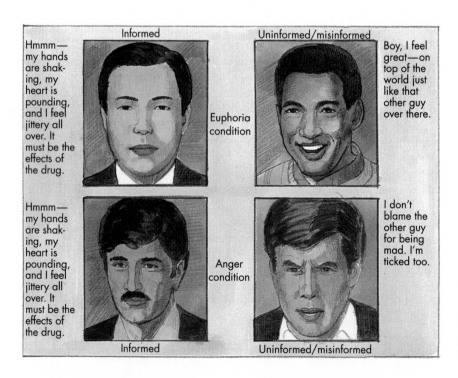

results (Leventhal & Tomarken, 1986; Marshall & Zimbardo, 1979; Maslach, 1979). Furthermore, our own everyday experiences suggest that many emotions, particularly those that are triggered spontaneously and instantly by sudden stimuli, do not appear to result from interpreting and labeling unexplained arousal. For example, if you heard screeching tires as you were walking across a street, you would probably experience fear long before you had cognitively assessed why your heart was in your throat.

TOMKINS' FACIAL FEEDBACK THEORY Still another explanation of emotions relates directly to some studies conducted by Charles Darwin in the late nineteenth century (1872). According to Darwin, each emotional "state of mind" was associated with a stereotyped set of reactions that were common within each species. In addition, emotional states that were essentially opposite were associated with an opposite set of reactions. For instance, in greeting its master a dog displays a submissive posture like that shown in Figure 9.4a. This set of reactions is opposite to those displayed in the aggressive posture shown in Figure 9.4b.

Can you think of reasons why opposite emotional states are displayed with essentially opposite postures? What selective advantage might this have? Darwin believed that the advantage of opposite postures for opposite emotional states was that this minimized the possibility of emotional states being confused. Because there are few, if any, postural similarities between aggressive and submissive postures, they are unlikely to be treated similarly.

Darwin also believed that many human emotional expressions, particularly patterns of facial display, result from inherited traits that are universal in the human species. Enlisting the aid of missionaries and other people from all over the world, he conducted the first recorded study of facial expression of emotions. Darwin asked his recruits to observe and record the facial expressions of the local population in a variety of emotional contexts. Comparing their observations, he found a remarkable consistency in the facial expressions associated with such emotions as anger, fear, disgust, and sadness.

Darwin's findings were borne out a century later in studies by Paul Ekman and his associates (Ekman, 1982; Ekman & Friesen, 1984). These researchers demonstrated that people in various parts of the world not only show emotion with similar facial expressions, they also interpret these expressions in the same way. Ekman and his colleagues took photographs of American faces depicting

FIGURE 9.4

Emotional Expression in Dogs

Note that opposite postures represent opposing emotions.

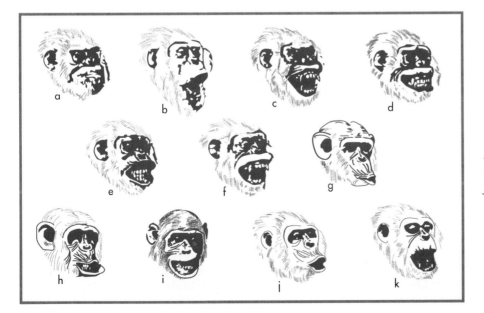

Animals can show a wide range of emotions. These illustrations show the facial expressions of chimpanzees:

(a) glaring anger;   *(g) frustration;*
(b) barking anger;   *(h) sadness;*
(c) fear;   *(i) crying;*
(d) submission;   *(j) excitement;*
(e) fear-affection;   *(k) playfulness*
(f) affection

FIGURE 9.5

Facial Expressions Used by Paul Ekman

The faces, from left to right, were intended to represent happiness, anger, sadness, surprise, disgust, and fear.

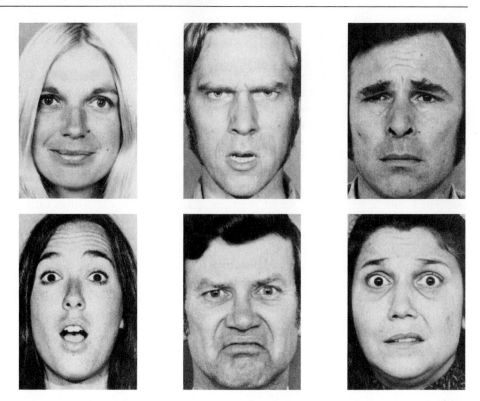

happiness, anger, sadness, surprise, disgust, and fear. (Figure 9.5 shows photographs of these six emotions.) They then asked people from several different cultures (including the United States, Japan, Brazil, Chile, Argentina, and the Fore and Dani tribes in remote regions of New Guinea) to identify the emotions shown in the photographs. People from all of these cultures were able to identify the emotion from the facial expression with better than 80 percent accuracy. Furthermore, American college students who viewed videotapes of emotions expressed facially by members of the Fore society were also able to identify these basic emotions, although they sometimes confused fear and surprise.

A number of researchers have argued that facial muscles respond very rapidly and with sufficient differentiation to account for a wide range of emotional experience; some have theorized that feedback from our own facial expressions determines our emotional experiences. Perhaps the most influential proponent of this **facial feedback theory** is Sylvan Tomkins (1962, 1963). Like James and Lange, Tomkins argues that different kinds of physical actions precede different emotional experiences, with genetically determined brain mechanisms linked to the emotions of fear, anger, happiness, sadness, surprise, interest, disgust, and shame. Tomkins also argues that a specific facial display is universally associated with each of these neural programs.

Tomkins' notion of universal facial expressions was supported by the cross-cultural research just discussed, and further support was provided by an intriguing two-part experiment conducted by Paul Ekman and his associates (1983). Here, professional actors were employed as subjects. In the first part of the experiment, each subject was coached, with the aid of a mirror, to assume a specific facial expression corresponding to each of the six emotions in Figure 9.5. They were told exactly which muscles to contract, but they were not asked to feel or express a particular emotion. As a control measure, some actors were coached to move muscles not involved in a particular emotional expression. As the subjects molded their facial expressions, several physiological responses were measured, including heart rate, galvanic skin response, temperature of the hands, and muscle tension in the arms. In the second phase of this experiment, subjects were simply asked to think of emotional experiences in their lives that produced each of the six emotions. For example, subjects might recall a recent encounter that made them angry.

Two major findings emerged from this study. First, the researchers noted that each of the four negative emotions of anger, fear, disgust, and sadness, whether induced by facial modeling or thinking of an emotional experience, was accompanied by a distinct physiological "fingerprint" or pattern of physical responses. For example, heart rate was much greater in anger than in disgust and the hands were colder in fear than in anger. Figure 9.6 shows the increases or decreases in heart rate and skin temperature for each of the six acted emotions. Ekman's findings seem to support James and Lange's assertion that different emotions are associated with distinct patterns of physiological response.

The second and perhaps the most intriguing finding in this experiment is that when the subjects simply followed instructions to move their facial muscles to mirror a given emotion, they also experienced patterns of physiological arousal that were comparable to those recorded when they relived an actual emotional experience. In some instances, the physiological signs of emotion were more pronounced when the subjects merely moved their facial muscles than when they thought of an emotional experience.

Can you think of a possible application of the research findings of Paul Ekman and his colleagues? Might this information be applied to enhance our emotional lives? Think about this question for a moment or two before reading on.

Ekman's findings do have some practical implications. We have all heard the sage advice to "keep our chins up" or to "put on a happy face" when we are feeling sad or depressed, and this research suggests that there may be some validity to this advice. Subjects felt happy just by contracting the facial muscles associated with happiness. Perhaps if we make the effort to act cheerful, smile, and laugh when we feel down in the dumps, we will in turn feel more cheerful and less sad.

Several studies have provided experimental support for this speculation (Izard, 1990). For example, in one study subjects were instructed either to suppress or exaggerate the facial expression associated with the fear and discomfort of receiving electric shocks. The researchers monitored physiological arousal during the

Changes in Heart Rate and Skin Temperature for Six Emotions

Specific Emotion	Change in Heart Rate (beats/min.)	Change in Skin Temperature (degrees C)
Anger	+8.0	+.16
Fear	+8.0	-.01
Distress	+6.5	+.01
Joy	+2.0	+.03
Suprise	+1.8	-.01
Disgust	-0.3	-.03

Source: Ekman, Levenson, and Friesen (1983).

FIGURE 9.6

Heart Rate and Skin Temperature

Both heart rate and skin temperature were associated with different acted emotions in Ekman's experiment.

course of shock administration and also obtained written self-reports of the subjects' feelings. The results revealed that subjects who had been told to suppress their facial expression demonstrated lower physiological arousal and reported less negative feelings than the participants who were not instructed to conceal their facial reactions (Lanzetta et al., 1976).

These results should be interpreted with some caution, however. Masking our true feelings may not always be helpful, and in some instances it may actually impede our ability to deal effectively with our feelings. Nevertheless, we all experience circumstances in which we would like to feel just a bit more cheerful. Perhaps in these situations, masquerading the desired emotion may be helpful.

SOLOMON AND CORBIT'S OPPONENT-PROCESS THEORY   One of the authors has a brother who is an avid rock climber. Some years ago he experienced a climbing accident that almost ended his life. However, he is now back rock climbing with just as much zest and enthusiasm as before, perhaps even more. What accounts for his continued participation in a sport that must arouse intense emotion at both ends of the scale—both high fear and ecstatic exhilaration? For that matter, why do people jump out of airplanes with a parachute strapped on their backs, shoot the rapids of wild rivers, ski off extremely steep mountain slopes, or return to a sport that almost killed them?

Some years ago psychologists Richard Solomon and J. D. Corbit (1974) proposed a theory of emotion that attempts to answer these questions. According to their **opponent-process theory of emotion,** people are inclined to maintain a relatively even keel or balance in their emotional lives. When a strong emotional response to a particular stimulus event disrupts this homeostatic balance, an *opponent-process*, or opposite emotional response, is eventually activated to restore equilibrium in our emotional state. Thus if our initial response to being confronted with a class-4 (wild water) rapids is sudden terror, we will probably subsequently experience elation after successfully negotiating the rapids—a positive or opposite emotion that cancels out the original negative emotion, thus restoring us to a neutral or balanced emotional state.

From this perspective, emotions are viewed as possessing *hedonic value*, which is to say they vary from being extremely positive or pleasant to being very negative or unpleasant (Solomon, 1980, 1982). When an emotion of a particular hedonic value is aroused, it will be followed shortly by its hedonic opposite. Thus, when we are elated we can expect that this emotion may eventually give way to feeling somewhat down or depressed. Likewise, fear is replaced with elation (or at least relief), pain with pleasure, anxiety with calm, boredom with interest, and so forth.

Solomon and Corbit theorized that under normal conditions, when we encounter a particular emotion-arousing stimulus only now and then, the opponent emotional states will be sufficiently equalized in intensity to balance each other out. Thus if we go rock climbing only once each year, we can expect to continue experiencing the same relative intensities of high terror and elation that serve to balance our emotional equilibrium. However, what happens if we become avid climbers after our initial encounter with this exhilarating sport? Solomon and Corbit would argue that when we repeatedly expose ourselves to a situation that arouses the same intense emotion, our initial emotional reaction will gradually weaken over time while the opponent emotional reaction will grow stronger. Therefore, we can expect that our terror of heights will gradually diminish to a level of anxiety just sufficient to get the adrenaline pumping. In contrast, our euphoria after successfully negotiating a steep pitch can be expected to become more intense or powerful as time goes on.

This weakening of the initial emotional response together with the eventual dominance of the opponent-process emotion explains why river runners, rock climbers, skydivers, race car drivers, and other risk takers find that the more they engage in their thrilling sports the more enjoyable these activities become. The opponent-process theory has also been used to explain addiction to certain consciousness-altering drugs like heroin and amphetamines. Most people experience intense pleasure and an emotional high during their initial exposure to heroin. However, as any heroin addict can attest, the pleasure associated with using this drug typically decreases with repetitive use (see Figure 9.7).

This reaction is due, at least in part, to a steady increase or intensification of the negative opponent-process feelings associated with coming down from a drug high (Siegel et al., 1978; Siegel et al., 1982). This drug-related phenomenon stands as stark testimony to Solomon's observation that people who seek pleasure often pay for it later, and that with repeated pleasure seeking the pleasure itself often loses much of its intensity. Of course, as previously noted, the reverse is also true, in that the fear component of risky, thrill-seeking activities often diminishes over time as exhilaration and euphoria intensify with each additional experience. It is in this way that the opponent-process theory accounts for the apparent shift in motivation for many activities. For instance, the motivation to use drugs the first few times may be the intense euphoria associated with those drugs. Later, the motivation shifts to the avoidance of the aversive nature of drug withdrawals. Before reading on, try to think of other examples of where the motivation and emotion associated early on with an activity have been replaced by its opposite.

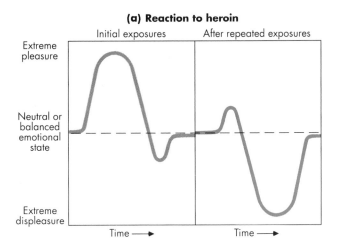

(a) Reaction to heroin

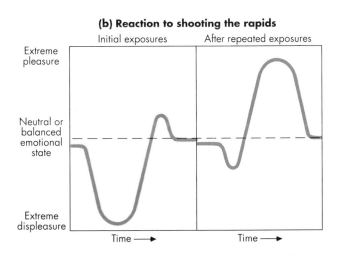

(b) Reaction to shooting the rapids

FIGURE 9.7

Opponent-Processes

Part (a) demonstrates how, with repeated use of heroin, the pleasure decreases while the displeasure associated with withdrawal increases. Part (b) portrays the likely response of a river-runner as he repeatedly shoots the rapids. Each encounter with this sport may result in decreased fear and an increase in the pleasure associated with it.

In concluding our discussion of theories of emotion, we must acknowledge that many questions remain to be answered. Instead of one comprehensive theory that encompasses all human emotional expression, we have discussed several diverse theories. Each theory helps to explain at least a part of the process whereby emotions are activated and all of them are supported to some degree by research. In the next section we will examine one emotion, stress, and its relation to our well-being in more detail.

STRESS

We have all learned that negative emotions such as fear, anxiety, anger, and depression often exact a price in our lives in the form of impaired functioning, fatigue, symptoms of physical discomfort, and even illness. Disruptive, unpleasant emotions play a major role both in contributing to stress and as key components in the manifestation of reactions to stress. Thus we end this chapter with a somewhat detailed discussion of the topic of stress, including comments about the nature of stress and stressors, physiological and psychological responses to stress, and the relationship between stress and illness.

THE NATURE OF STRESS

Although we are all familiar with stress, it is an elusive concept to define. One reason for this is that stress means so many different things to different people, researchers and laypersons alike. Some of us think of stress as sweaty palms, a fast-beating heart, gritted teeth, and a churning stomach. Consistent with this impression, researchers have for many years focused on the physiological changes that accompany stress. More recently, however, the study of stress responses has been expanded to include emotional, cognitive, and behavioral changes as well as physical reactions. Another focus of research explores the stressful environmental events, called *stressors*, that induce stress reactions. When we are feeling stressed we may be more inclined to describe our condition as being unprepared for an exam, feeling crowded in our dorms, or being harassed by a supervisor on the job, rather than focusing on our bodily or psychological responses.

According to Selye, stress from a variety of situations may accumulate to produce the General Adaptation Syndrome.

Most contemporary researchers believe that an adequate definition of stress must take into account the interplay between external stressors and our physical and psychological responses. This relationship is neither simple nor predictable, for it varies from person to person and from day to day. As we see later in our discussion, this variation occurs because stress is inextricably connected to our cognitive appraisals of events. Health psychologist Shelley Taylor (1986) has integrated all of these aspects of stress—stressors, responses to stress, and cognitive appraisal—into one definition. According to Taylor, **stress** is "the process of appraising events (as harmful, threatening, or challenging), of assessing potential responses, and of responding to those events" (p. 146). Taylor notes that those responses may include not just physiological but also emotional, cognitive, and behavioral changes. In the following paragraphs we examine physiological and psychological responses to stress as well as the situations that produce stress. We then explore what we know about the role stress plays in some common illnesses.

PHYSIOLOGICAL RESPONSES TO STRESS

In the 1930s the Canadian researcher Hans Selye was conducting research that he hoped would lead to the discovery of a new sex hormone. The leads were promising so far. When he injected rats with extracts of ovary tissue, the results were consistent: bleeding ulcers in the stomach and small intestine, enlargement of the adrenal cortex, and shrinkage of the thymus gland. Since no hormone was known to produce these effects, Selye was convinced that he was on the track of identifying a new one. His elation was quickly dampened, however, for when he injected extracts from other tissues, the effects were identical. Furthermore, the same thing occurred when he injected toxic fluids that were not derived from tissues.

Selye was devastated by this turn of events. But instead of giving up, he tried to figure out what had happened. The answer occurred to him only when he stopped trying to relate his findings to the discovery of a new sex hormone. In his own words,

> It suddenly struck me that one could look at [my ill-fated experiments] from an entirely different angle. . . .
> [Perhaps] there was such a thing as a single nonspecific reaction of the body to damage of any kind. . . .
> (1976, p. 26)

Selye went on to study how animals responded to a wide range of stressful events other than injections. He exposed rats to a variety of adverse conditions such as extreme cold and fatigue, electric shock, immobilizing restraint, and surgical trauma—and noted the same physiological response pattern as he had originally observed with injections of tissue extracts. As we see later in this chapter, Selye also learned that humans respond to stress with fairly consistent physiological patterns (1936, 1956, 1974, 1976). The awareness that stress can have harmful effects on our bodies has led to many more studies, as well as techniques for reducing the impact of stress on our own lives.

Hans Selye's observations of how his rats responded to stressors led him to formulate the concept of the **general adaptation syndrome (GAS).** According to this notion, when an organism is confronted with a stressor, its body mobilizes for action. This mobilization effort is mediated by the sympathetic nervous system, as we saw in Chapter 3, and it works primarily through the action of specific stress hormones on the body's muscles and organ systems. The response to stress is *nonspecific*, for the same physiological reactions occur regardless of the stressor. Selye also noted that repeated or prolonged exposure to stress that is not adequately managed or reduced results in tissue damage (such as bleeding ulcers), increased susceptibility to disease, and even death in extreme cases.

Hans Selye

FIGURE 9.8

Three Phases of Selye's General Adaptation Syndrome

SOURCE: Adapted from Selye, 1956

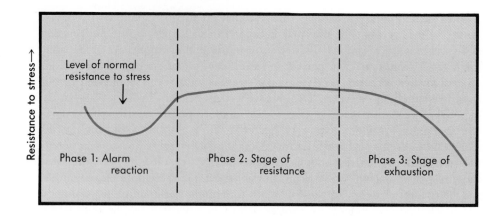

ALARM, RESISTANCE, AND EXHAUSTION Selye described three phases of the general adaption syndrome: alarm, resistance, and exhaustion (see Figure 9.8). When an organism is exposed to a stressful event, it first experiences an *alarm* reaction in which it mobilizes to meet the threat. A sudden arousal of the sympathetic nervous system produces a flood of stress hormones—corticosteroids from the adrenal cortex and epinephrine (often called adrenalin) and norepinephrine from the adrenal medulla.

These hormones prepare the body for "fight or flight" by producing a number of physiological reactions. First, our heart rate is likely to increase, as is blood pressure. This activity forces blood to parts of the body that may need it for strenuous physical activity such as flight away from danger. We experience this response as a pounding heart, like the rapid-fire thumping you may have felt after barely avoiding an accident on the freeway. Sugars and fats also flood the blood to provide fuel for quick energy. This emergency response provides extra reserves, with the result that people are often able to perform seemingly superhuman feats (such as lifting a heavy beam off a person trapped in a mine cave-in) that they could not otherwise perform. Digestion slows or ceases during the alarm stage, making more blood available to the muscles and brain.

Our breathing rate also accelerates to supply increased oxygen to muscles poised for greater than normal output. Thus people often have difficulty catching their breath after a severe fright. Still another response to stress is a tensing of the muscles in preparation for an adaptive response. This explains the stiff neck, sore back, and painful aching legs that many people experience after a long, hard exam or a rough day at work.

We also tend to perspire more when under stress—a response that acts as a kind of built-in air conditioner that cools our energized bodies. It also allows us to burn more energy (which produces heat) when we are faced with emergency situations. This is why many people find themselves drenched with perspiration after giving a speech or undergoing a stressful interview.

Finally, clotting agents are released into the blood when we are under stress, so that our blood will clot more rapidly if we are injured. One reason why we may not notice an injury we receive during an accident or fight is because the wound may have bled very little. Figure 9.9 summarizes these responses to stress.

We are not able to maintain the alarm phase's high level of bodily response or sympathetic activity for very long. Eventually the parasympathetic nervous system comes into play, providing a braking mechanism for the organs activated by the sympathetic system. At this point the organism enters into the second stage of *resistance*. Now the body continues to draw upon resources at an above-normal rate, but it is less aroused than in the alarm state.

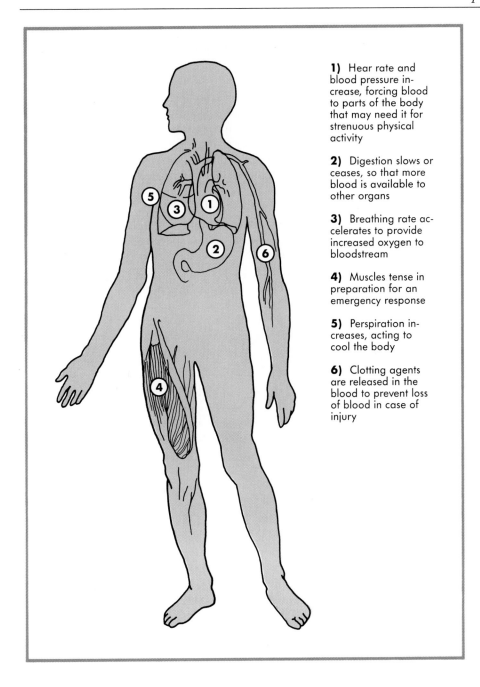

1) Hear rate and blood pressure increase, forcing blood to parts of the body that may need it for strenuous physical activity

2) Digestion slows or ceases, so that more blood is available to other organs

3) Breathing rate accelerates to provide increased oxygen to bloodstream

4) Muscles tense in preparation for an emergency response

5) Perspiration increases, acting to cool the body

6) Clotting agents are released in the blood to prevent loss of blood in case of injury

FIGURE 9.9
Some Physiological Responses to Stress

If the stress is prolonged or repeated, an organism is likely to enter the third stage of *exhaustion*. As a direct result of the continued drain on resources, the body tissues may begin to show signs of wear and tear during the exhaustion stage. Susceptibility to disease also increases, and continued exposure to the stressor is likely to deplete the organism's adaptive energy. The symptoms of the initial alarm reaction are likely to reappear, but resistance is now decreased and the alarm reaction is likely to continue unabated. If the organism is unable to develop strategies to overcome or cope with stress, serious illness or even collapse and death may result.

Selye's model has had a profound impact on our understanding of stress and its links to illness. It not only provides a way of conceptualizing our physiological response to events in the environment, it also provides a plausible explanation for the relationship between stress and disease. Few medical experts today disagree with Selye's basic contention that prolonged stress will often produce bodily wear and tear and erode our ability to resist disease if it is not effectively coped with. However, Selye's theory has also been criticized on a few counts. One criticism is that Selye failed to acknowledge the important role of psychological factors in stress responses. For example, the significant role of cognitive appraisal in determining the extent to which we assess a particular environmental event as stressful. Furthermore, some newer evidence suggesting that particular stressors may be associated with distinctly different physiological responses calls into question Selye's assumption of nonspecificity in reaction to stress (Appley & Trumbull, 1986; Hobfoll, 1989; Lazarus & Folkman, 1984a; Mason, 1974; Taylor, 1990). Although these criticisms have had little impact on Selye's cornerstone position in the field of stress research, health psychologists have become increasingly interested in additional aspects of the experience of stress.

PSYCHOLOGICAL RESPONSES TO STRESS

Most of Selye's work focused on endocrinological responses to stress in nonhuman animals, most notably rats. In recent years, however, increased attention has been directed to assessing the importance of psychological factors in stress reactions. It is now widely recognized that stress affects not only our bodies but also how we think, feel, and behave.

COGNITIVE RESPONSES TO STRESS
If you think back to a situation in which you were under a great deal of stress—after breaking up with a partner, for instance, or perhaps receiving a rejection letter from a special school you were set on—it is quite possible that your cognitive responses stand out more clearly in your memory than your physiological responses. Typical cognitive responses may include reduced ability to concentrate, higher than normal levels of distractibility, impaired performance on cognitive tasks (such as reading or doing your homework), and sometimes a tendency to be plagued by disruptive or morbid thoughts (Cohen, 1980; Taylor, 1986; Zajonc, 1965). People who are under a great deal of stress often find that their attention wanders and that they are easily distracted. It is also common to be troubled by intrusive, repetitive thoughts such as "I'm worthless" or "I just don't have what it takes," especially after experiencing a setback such as the loss of a job.

We often react to stressful events by employing one or more *defense mechanisms,* unconscious strategies for avoiding anxiety. (Defense mechanisms are discussed in Chapter 14.) For example, we may seek to minimize the harm or threat of a stressful event by blocking it from our conscious awareness (a defense mechanism known as *repression*), engaging in *rationalization* (I didn't have a chance to prepare adequately and that is why I failed the test), or *cognitive dissonance* (I had to cheat to keep up with the cheaters in the class), and so forth.

Stress may also result in positive cognitive responses, as we learn new ways to cope with or neutralize the stressful event. For example, you may learn to cope with the stress of getting caught in rush-hour traffic by leaving for class earlier or not scheduling courses at times that coincide with heavy commuter traffic, or you may take a basic course in auto mechanics to avoid the stress of a car that does not operate properly.

Why do some stressful situations produce negative effects, whereas others have a positive outcome? Psychologists Richard Lazarus and Susan Folkman (1984a, 1984b) propose that our cognitive appraisal of a stressor makes a difference in our immediate response as well as our ability to cope with the stressor in the long run. Lazarus and Folkman maintain that when we confront situations which may be potentially stressful, we first engage in a process of *primary appraisal* to determine if the event is positive, neutral, or negative. If we consider an event to be negative, we further appraise it to determine how harmful, threatening, or challenging it is.

For example, suppose your fiance just returned your ring and broke off your engagement. This potentially very stressful event is one you might appraise according to the three dimensions of harm, threat, and challenge. *Harm* is your assessment of the damage inflicted immediately by the event, such as damaged reputation, lowered self-esteem, loss of intimacy, and so forth. *Threat* is your assessment of possible future damage that may result from the unpleasant occurrence, such as a reluctance to develop another close intimate relationship out of fear that the same painful experience will be repeated. Finally, you may appraise your broken engagement in terms of the *challenge* it provides to overcome and profit from the event. Perhaps you had second thoughts yourself about the relationship, and you may see your new unattached status as providing opportunities for other involvements.

Once we complete the process of primary appraisal of potentially stressful events, Lazarus and Folkman suggest that we engage in a *secondary appraisal* to determine whether or not our coping abilities and resources will allow us to overcome the harm or threat and successfully meet the challenge. The end result, in terms of the amount of stress we actually experience, represents a blending or balance between these two processes of primary and secondary appraisal. If we perceive the harm and/or threat to be very high, we are likely to experience a high degree of stress. On the other hand, if we think we can cope with the situation, we are likely to experience far less stress. Figure 9.10 summarizes Lazarus and Folkman's psychological model of stress.

EMOTIONAL RESPONSES TO STRESS Negative emotional states are strongly associated with stress (Watson & Pennebaker, 1989). Emotional responses to stress include such feelings as anxiety, irritability, anger, embarrassment, depression, helplessness, and hostility. Anxiety is potentially one of the most damaging emotional reactions. It is especially likely to develop when we perceive a marked imbalance between the threat posed by a stressor and our personal resources for coping with it. We have seen in previous discussions how devastating anxiety can be. People who are unable to cope effectively with anxiety become physically and psychologically taxed, a condition that increases their susceptibility to a variety of disorders.

BEHAVIORAL RESPONSES TO STRESS There are so many behavioral responses to stress that it is impossible to outline them all here. We have seen, however, that two general classes of adaptive behavioral responses are suggested by the fight or flight pattern. In some cases we take some kind of assertive action (*fight*) to confront stressors. For example, if you find that your home environment is stressful because of a parent who is constantly nagging at you, you may eventually confront the complaining parent. By confronting the source of your stress, you may be able to clear the air and find mutually acceptable ways of reducing or eliminating this stressor in your life. Sometimes, however, people prefer to withdraw from a threatening or harmful situation (*flight*). That is, you may decide you will experience less stress if you move into your own place.

Our strategies for coping with stress are not always either a clear confrontation or a clear withdrawal. A third alternative is to try to *adapt* to the stress. For example, assume you live near elevated train tracks and once every hour, at roughly the same time, you are disturbed by the loud noise caused by a passing train. If you are trying to study in your home, this intrusive noise could be a major source of stress in your life. You might neutralize this stressor simply by taking short hourly study breaks whenever a train passes. The Health Psychology

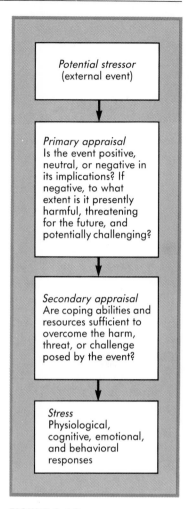

FIGURE 9.10

Lazarus and Folkman's Psychological Model of Stress

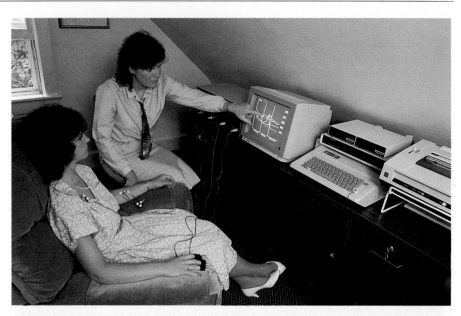

Top: Biofeedback provides individuals with information about their bodily processes that are otherwise unobservable. Subjects may use this information to modify their bodily responses. Here a subject learns to modify her blood pressure.
Bottom: Although exercise is also a kind of stress, the physiological benefits of exercise (eg., increased circulation, decreases in blood cholesterol, strengthening muscles, and weight loss) far outweigh the costs of additional stress.

and Life discussion at the end of this chapter proposes several physiological, cognitive, and behavioral strategies for reducing the effects of stress.

Recent research by Michael Meaney and his colleagues at McGill University suggests that early experiences can have a profound impact upon how an organism responds to stress (Meaney, 1990; Meaney et al., 1988). Meaney and his associates demonstrated that rats gently handled during the first few weeks of life were subsequently better able to turn off physiological responses to stress than a comparable group of animals that were not handled during their early weeks of development. Since the nonhandled rats were unable to turn off the stress response, they were exposed to significantly higher levels of stress hormones throughout their lives than their handled counterparts (the experiment lasted 30 months, roughly the length of a typical rat's lifespan). Extensive exposure to stress hormones can cause degeneration of cells in the hippocampus, a brain structure known to play an important role in learning and memory. This fact is consistent with the research team's finding that older handled animals performed much better on a learning task than older nonhandled rats.

The research of Meaney and his colleagues poses a number of important questions. Can an organism's early experiences influence its ability to cope with stress later in life? Can the capacity to cope with stress predict whether an organism's intellect is impaired at some later point in development? And perhaps most importantly, are humans similar to rats in that individual differences in intellectual functioning among elderly people might be related to their ability to cope with stress? The answer to all of these questions appears to be yes.

We have been looking at the ways we respond to stress, but so far we have said relatively little about the situations or events that produce stress in our lives. Are some kinds of events more likely to cause stress than others? Are stressors always negative events? We explore these questions next.

STRESSORS

FACTORS THAT CONTRIBUTE TO STRESS Our cognitive assessments have a lot to do with the degree of stress an event will produce in our lives, but it is not true to say that all events have the same potential for eliciting stress (Rodin & Salovey, 1989; Taylor, 1990). What characteristics increase the likelihood that we will perceive an event as stressful?

Lack of Control One factor that contributes to the stressfulness of a situation is our lack of control over it. Thus it is much less stressful for you to stick a needle into yourself (for example, when removing a splinter) than to have a physician stick a needle into your arm. Research reveals that uncontrollable or unpredictable events are generally more stressful than those we can control or predict (Fleming et al., 1987; Frankenhaeuser, 1975; Glass & Singer, 1972; Singer et al., 1978; Suls & Mullen, 1981; Thompson, 1981). You might think that certain experiences, such as excessive noise, a nagging parent, or a series of painful rehabilitative exercises after a serious accident, would be stressful for anybody exposed to these events. This conclusion is not necessarily warranted, however. When people believe that they can predict, modify, or end an unpleasant event, they are likely to experience it as being less stressful (even if they take no action to modify it). The knowledge that something can be done may be sufficient to reduce the stress.

Suddenness A second variable influencing how stressful we perceive an event to be is the suddenness with which it overtakes us. When people experience accidents, the sudden death of a loved one, or an unexpected pink slip at work, they may find it very difficult to mobilize adequate coping mechanisms. In general, it is easier to cope with challenges that we can foresee. Thus a person who loses a loved one after a protracted illness, or who loses a job after expecting to be terminated for months, may be much less stressed by these aversive events.

Ambiguity In general, a stressor that we perceive as ambiguous is likely to induce more stress than one that is clear-cut. In well-defined situations we may be able to determine an appropriate course of action (fight, flight, or adapt), but ambiguity forces us to spend resource-depleting energy trying to figure out the nature of the stressor. Research demonstrates that role ambiguity is a major cause of stress on the job (Cooper & Marshall, 1976). If you have a job in which your role is not clearly defined so that you do not know what is expected of you, you are likely to experience far more stress than if your employer's expectations are made clear.

LIFE CHANGES AND STRESS   From our discussion so far, it may seem that all stress is bad and that stressors are always negative events. However, many of the happiest and most positive events in our lives—for instance, acceptance by our first choice college, marriage, having a baby, and receiving a promotion—can also be highly stressful. Although such events often bring out the best in us by mobilizing our energies and providing opportunities for development, they may still place heavy demands on our physiological resources. It is common to experience reactions such as loss of sleep, a feeling of confusion, and even an irritating lack of groundedness because we are too excited to function normally. Even though positive events may be stressful, however, events that we perceive as negative are much more likely to produce both physical and psychological manifestations of stress than are positive events (McFarlane et al., 1980; Sarason et al., 1978; Vinokur & Selzer, 1975).

Some psychologists have attempted to assess how various positive and negative changes in our lives may contribute to stress. An ambitious effort is the Social Readjustment Rating Scale (SRRS) published in the late 1960s (Holmes & Rahe, 1967). This scale, shown in Table 9.1, is based on the assumption that any changes in our life situation, whether for the better or the worse, can produce stress. The SRRS assigns different values to a number of life events. For instance, marriage is assigned a value of 50 stress points (called *life change units*). A person's score is obtained by adding the numbers associated with each event experienced in the last 12 months.

MEASURING STRESS BY LIFE CHANGE UNITS   We have seen that Holmes and Rahe's scale provides a method for assessing stress by looking at life events. Do you think it is an accurate assessment method, or are there other factors (or stressors) that the SRRS does not account for? Consider this question, referring

The death of a loved one taxes physiological coping mechanisms and may result in lowered immunity to disease.

TABLE 9.1 *Social Readjustment Rating Scale*

RANK	LIFE EVENT	MEAN VALUE	RANK	LIFE EVENT	MEAN VALUE
1	Death of spouse	100	24	Trouble with in-laws	29
2	Divorce	73	25	Outstanding personal achievement	28
3	Marital separation	65			
4	Jail term	63	26	Spouse begins or stops work	26
5	Death of close family member	63	27	Begin or end school	26
6	Personal injury or illness	53	28	Change in living condition	25
7	Marriage	50	29	Revision of personal habits	24
8	Fired at work	47	30	Trouble with boss	23
9	Marital reconciliation	45	31	Change in work hours or conditions	20
10	Retirement	45			
11	Change in health of family member	44	32	Change in residence	20
12	Pregnancy	40	33	Change in schools	20
13	Sex difficulties	39	34	Change in recreation	19
14	Gain of new family member	39	35	Change in church activities	19
15	Business readjustment	39	36	Change in social activities	18
16	Change in financial state	38	37	Mortgage or loan less than $10,000	17
17	Death of close friend	37			
18	Change in different line of work	36	38	Change in sleeping habits	16
19	Change in number of arguments with spouse	35	39	Change in number of family get-togethers	15
20	Mortgage over $10,000	31	40	Change in eating habits	15
21	Foreclosure of mortgage or loan	30	41	Vacation	13
22	Change in responsibilities at work	29	42	Christmas	12
23	Son or daughter leaving home	29	43	Minor violations of the law	11

SOURCE: From Holmes &: Rahe, 1967.

if necessary to the earlier discussion of psychological responses to stress, before reading on.

Early research reported positive correlations between SRRS scores and the incidence of physical illnesses. For example, scores in the 200s were linked with about a 50 percent chance of developing a physical illness within the next two years; scores of 300 or higher were associated with about an 80 percent chance of illness (Holmes & Rahe, 1967; Rahe & Arthur, 1978). More recent research, however, has demonstrated that total scores on life-change scales such as the SRRS are not very accurate predictors of future problems with illness and disease (Brett et al., 1990; Krantz et al., 1985; McCrae, 1984; Schroeder & Costa, 1984).

One of the difficulties with trying to predict health problems from supposedly stressful life-change events is that merely adding up values assigned to each event does not take into consideration our cognitive appraisal of the potential stressfulness of events. For example, marriage, divorce, a child leaving home, or retirement might dramatically increase stress for one person while significantly lowering it for another. As we have seen, the amount of stress an event produces is not inherent in the event itself. Instead, our perception of an event as stressful determines how much stress we actually experience.

Even the happiest and most positive events in our lives are a source of stress.

In addition, as Richard Lazarus (1981) has pointed out, it is not just the major life changes that produce stress. Everyday stressors such as traffic jams, arguments with a partner, or a car that does not operate properly may well have a much greater impact on us than the major life-change events listed in scales such as the SRRS.

STRESS AND DISEASE

Stress is widely recognized as a major factor in a wide range of physical illnesses (Carson, 1989; Maddi et al., 1987). It has been estimated that as many as three out of four visits to physicians are prompted by stress-related problems (Charlesworth & Nathan, 1982). Furthermore, stress and stress-related behaviors may be the leading contributers to early death.

Table 9.2 compares the leading causes of death in the United States in the early 1900s and in 1990. The major health problems of the early 1900s were infectious diseases (numbers 2, 3, and 4 in the table are all infectious diseases and total 539 per 100,000), followed by cardiovascular diseases. Today the leading health problems are no longer infectious diseases but cardiovascular diseases, cancers, and strokes. Although these diseases are not new, the proportion of people who die from them has increased dramatically since 1900. Most importantly, these are all diseases that in some part can be attributed to individual behavior and life-style and all of them have been linked to stress. This stress link may be direct through impaired immune function or indirect through cigarette smoking, excessive drinking, poor diet, and/or lack of exercise. In this section we explore the evidence linking stress with three common, but severe, physical disorders: coronary heart disease, hypertension, and cancer.

CORONARY HEART DISEASE **Coronary heart disease (CHD)** is a general label for illnesses that cause a narrowing of the coronary arteries, the vessels that supply the heart with blood. CHD accounts for nearly half of all deaths in the United States each year (Statictical Abstracts, 1992), many of which occur when people are still in the prime of life. Millions of Americans also experience reduced quality of life as a result of the ravages of CHD.

While factors such as smoking, obesity, diabetes, family history, diets high in fat, high serum cholesterol levels, physical inactivity, and high blood pressure are

TABLE 9.2 *The Eight Leading Causes of Death in the United States, 1900 and 1990 (rates per 100,000 population)*

1900	RATE	1990	RATE
1. Cardiovascular diseases (heart disease, stroke)	345	1. Cardiovascular diseases (heart disease, stroke)	367
2. Influenza and pneumonia	202	2. Malignant neoplasms	202
3. Tuberculosis	194	3. Accidents	37
4. Gastritis, duodenitis, enteritis, and colitis	143	4. Chronic obstructive pulmonary diseases	36
5. Accidents	72	5. Influenza and pneumonia	31
6. Malignant neoplasms	64	6. Diabetes mellitus	20
7. Diphtheria	40	7. Suicide	12
8. Typhoid fever	31	8. Chronic liver diseases and cirrhosis	10

SOURCE: Figures for 1900 from *Historical Statistics of the United States: Colonial Times to 1970. Pt 1* by U.S. Bureau of the Census, 1975, Washington. DC: U.S.Government Printing Office. Figures for 1990 from *Statistical Abtracts of the United States* by U.S. Bureau of the Census, 1992, Washington, DC: U.S. Govenment Printing Office.

all linked to CHD, these risk factors considered together account for less than half of all diagnosed cases of CHD (American Heart Association, 1984). Something else besides genetics, diet, exercise, and general health habits must be a factor in CHD, and research over the last three decades has strongly implicated stress.

The story of how stress was first linked with heart disease begins with an unexpected discovery by cardiologists Meyer Friedman and Ray Rosenman (1974). In the late 1950s, Friedman and Rosenman were studying the relationship between eating behavior and disease among a sample of San Francisco couples. They found that although the women consumed amounts of cholesterol and animal fat equal to those consumed by their husbands, the women were dramatically less susceptible to heart disease than the men in the study. Since most of the men were employed and their wives were not, Friedman and Rosenman began to suspect that job-related stress might be implicated in the sex differences in CHD. Following up on this hunch, they mailed questionnaires to hundreds of physicians and business executives, asking them to speculate about what had caused the heart attacks of their patients, friends, and colleagues. Their responses overwhelmingly blamed job-related stress.

The next step was to conduct a field study. A sample of 40 tax accountants was studied over several months, commencing at the first of the year. During the first three months, laboratory measures of two warning indicators, blood-clotting speed and serum cholesterol levels, were generally within the normal range. This changed, however, as the April 15 tax-filing deadline approached. During these few weeks the accountants were under a great deal of pressure to finish their clients' tax returns, and both blood-clotting measures and serum cholesterol rose to dangerous levels. Once the tax-filing crunch passed, both measures returned to normal.

Convinced that responses to stress may be a major contributor to coronary heart disease, Friedman and Rosenman embarked on a nine-year study of several thousand men, ages 35 to 39, who were physically healthy at the outset of their investigation. Each subject was asked specific questions about his work and eating habits and his usual ways of responding to stressful situations. Using subjects' responses as well as observations of their behavior, the researchers divided participants into two groups roughly equal in size. Subjects in the **Type A** group tended to be hard-driving, ambitious, very competitive, easily angered, very time conscious, and demanding of perfection in both themselves and others. In contrast, **Type B** subjects were relaxed, easygoing, not driven to achieve perfection, happy in their jobs, understanding and forgiving, and not easily angered (Friedman & Rosenman, 1974; Friedman & Ulmer, 1984).

By the end of the long-term study, it was clear that Type A subjects were far more prone to heart disease than their Type B counterparts. Over the nine-year period, 257 subjects in the total research population had suffered heart attacks, and approximately 70 percent of these subjects were Type As. In other words, Type A men were more than twice as vulnerable as Type Bs. Subsequent studies by other researchers have also linked Type A behavior to CHD risk, a relationship that seems to be true of women as well as men (Baker et al., 1984; Dressler, 1989; Hatton et al., 1989; Haynes et al., 1980).

More recent studies have also confirmed that there are noteworthy differences between Type A people and Type B people. For example, research comparing Type A and Type B individuals has revealed that the former demonstrate a greater time urgency (Glass et al., 1974); a stronger tendency to think negative thoughts (Henly & Williams, 1986); greater competitive achievement strivings (Glass, 1977; Van Egeren et al., 1982; Vega-Lahr & Field, 1986); a stronger tendency to suppress symptoms of fatigue (Schlegel et al., 1980); a greater probability of experiencing an occupational injury (Niemcryk et al., 1987); and increased expression of aggression and hostility (Carver & Glass, 1978; Van Egeren et al., 1982). While all of these behaviors may increase the risk of CHD, hostility and an aggressively reactive temperament seem to play an especially important role (Carson, 1989; Dembroski et al., 1985; Spielberger et al., 1985). Thus it may be that people who are inclined to lash out at others may also be striking at themselves, placing their own health in jeopardy.

We still do not understand exactly how Type A behavior is linked to coronary heart disease, but a few possibilities have been explored. First, it is possible that Type A people are more likely to engage in behaviors that are known risk factors in CHD, such as drinking more caffeine-containing beverages, sleeping less, exercising less, smoking more, and eating more fatty fast foods (Hicks et al., 1983; Hicks & Pellegrini, 1982). A second possibility is that temperament and physiological responses to stress may also contribute to the proneness of Type A people to heart disease. Several studies have shown Type As to be much more physiologically reactive than Type Bs to potentially stressful situations (Dembroski et al., 1978; Krantz & Manuck, 1984; Manuck et al., 1978). It is also possible that both of these suggested tendencies may interact in some complex fashion to induce heart disease.

Still another line of research suggests that Type A behavior may represent a *response* to rather than a *cause* of excessive physiological reactivity (Krantz & Durel, 1983). One intriguing study revealed that even when unconscious, Type A patients undergoing surgery manifested a greater elevation of blood pressure than Type B patients experiencing the same procedure (Kahn et al., 1980). Since subjects were not able to respond cognitively and emotionally when unconscious, the elevated response of the Type A subjects suggests a possible predisposition to greater than normal physiological responses to stress. If this is the case, it seems possible that Type A behavior may represent a coping response to heightened sympathetic nervous system activity, rather than a cause of this activity.

HYPERTENSION **Hypertension,** commonly referred to as high blood pressure, occurs when blood flow through the vessels is excessive, a condition that may cause both hardening and general deterioration of tissue in the vessel walls. It has been estimated that roughly 30 million Americans suffer from hypertension and that annually about 16,000 die as a direct result of this condition (Taylor, 1986).

A number of physical factors may contribute to hypertension, including such things as obesity, excess salt intake, and genetic predispositions (Shapiro & Goldstein, 1982). However, there is also substantial evidence linking stress to increased blood pressure (Harrell, 1980; Obrist, 1976; Shapiro & Goldstein, 1982; Sommers-Flanagan & Greenberg, 1989). For instance, one study identified areas of high and low stress within the city of Detroit, Michigan (high stress locales were characterized by high poverty, high population density, high crime rates, and high divorce rates), and measured the blood pressure of a representative sample from each area. The highest blood pressure readings were recorded among residents of the high-stress areas (Harburg et al., 1973).

It has been suggested that a variety of personality factors may be linked to hypertension. Most frequently mentioned are a tendency to deal with anger by suppressing it (Gentry et al., 1982; Harrell, 1980) and the Type A behavior pattern discussed in the preceding section.

Some people may also be physically predisposed toward hypertension. Many hypertensive people show a more pronounced blood pressure response to a range of stressors (such as exposure to cold water or participation in a challenging cognitive task) than do people without hypertension (Harrell, 1980). This excess reactivity may to some extent be genetically programmed. In one study, 30 nonhypertensive subjects with a strong family history of hypertension were exposed to a variety of stressful tasks. Most exhibited an elevation of heart and blood pressure rates well above the norms for these tasks, a finding which suggests that a genetically based overreactivity of the sympathetic nervous system to stress may play a role in chronic hypertension (Jorgensen & Houston, 1981).

CANCER Evidence linking stress to cancer is less conclusive and certainly more controversial than that for CHD or hypertension. However, many specialists in the field of behavioral medicine strongly suspect a connection. **Cancer** is a collection of many diseases (over 100), all of which result from a DNA malfunctioning that produces runaway cell growth. Although researchers are still far from understanding all the mechanisms and agents involved in cancer, compelling evidence suggests a relationship between stress and cancer (Baltrusch & Waltz, 1985; Rodin & Salovey, 1989).

Studies of cancer patients often reveal that they have experienced a higher than normal rate of stressful life events prior to the onset of their disease (Sklar & Anisman, 1981). Several studies have also found a high incidence of cancer among people who have experienced prolonged episodes of depression, grieving, or helplessness (Sklar & Anisman, 1981). Stress associated with lack of social support has also been linked to cancer. For example, the lack of close family relations during childhood and the absence of a social support network of friends and family members during adulthood has been linked to a higher than normal cancer incidence (Shaffer et al., 1982; Thomas et al., 1974; Thomas et al., 1979). Indeed, cancer has been found to occur more often among widowed, divorced, or separated adults than among those who are married (Tache et al., 1979).

Animal studies provide information not available in human research. For example, rats who are inoculated with cancerous cells and then exposed to inescapable electric shocks are less able to reject the cancerous cells than are rats who are subjected to escapable shocks (Visintainer et al., 1983). This research suggests that the greater stress associated with an uncontrollable event may have reduced the animals' resistance to cancer. Other studies, in which animals have been exposed to stressors such as crowding, have also reported higher incidences of malignancies than among nonstressed animals (Amkraut & Solomon, 1977).

Another promising line of research has explored the idea of a *cancer-prone personality*. Researchers have long suspected that people who are inhibited, compliant, conforming, inclined to depression, calm, passive, and with strong tendencies to suppress their emotions are particularly prone to developing cancer (Bahnson, 1981; Renneker, 1981). A major methodological problem with many of these studies, however, is that it is often not possible to determine whether this pattern of personality traits triggers cancer or whether it develops as a consequence of the disease.

Assume you are a health psychologist studying the relationship between personality variables and cancer. You find an unusually high incidence of traits such as passivity, compliance, and suppression of emotion among a sample of cancer patients. While these traits may have existed before the cancer and played a role in its development, you suspect that at least some of the traits may have developed as a consequence of the disease. What kind of research design would you use to clarify whether these personality traits are more likely to be a cause or a consequence of cancer? Consider this issue for a moment before reading on.

To differentiate between potential cause and consequence, you would need to apply the longitudinal research design discussed in Chapter 11. Here, you would begin by identifying personality factors in a population of cancer-free people, then follow up over a period of years to determine whether those who subsequently develop cancer have different personality profiles from those who do not. One study that used this methodology did find evidence supporting the idea of a cancer-prone personality. In this investigation, researchers compared personality profiles of patients who had cancer with those who did not, based on scores from a widely used personality inventory, the MMPI (see Chapter 14), which had been administered several years earlier when the subjects were cancer-free. Those subjects who became cancer patients had been shown to be significantly more inclined to suppress their emotions than were those who did not develop this disease (Dattore et al., 1980).

Research also suggests a possible link between personality factors and the course of cancer once it is diagnosed (Levy, 1983). People who are polite, acquiescent, and not emotionally reactive tend to experience a rapid course of illness leading to early death, in contrast to the slower progression of the disease experienced by many people who exhibit anger and combativeness (Derogatis et al., 1979; Rogentine et al., 1979). Research linking personality factors to both the etiology and course of cancer does not necessarily provide evidence that cancer is linked to stress. However, it is quite possible that people who fit the cancer-prone personality profile may be inclined to direct their responses to stress and frustration inwardly.

Researchers have also speculated about the biological mechanisms linking stress to cancer, and several have implicated an impaired immune system (Levy, 1983). As we will see, the immune system guards against invaders and foreign tissue of all kinds, including cancerous or precancerous cells. In fact, the immune system may produce tumor-specific chemicals that attack and destroy cancerous growth (Rogers et al., 1979). Since we know that prolonged or severe stress can suppress immune response, it follows that stress may also allow cancer cells to proliferate more rapidly than might otherwise occur.

STRESS AND THE IMMUNE SYSTEM   The **immune system** is an exceedingly complex surveillance system that guards the body by recognizing and removing bacteria, viruses, cancer cells, and other hazardous foreign substances (Pomerleau & Rodin, 1986). When such substances are detected, our immune systems respond by stimulating *lymphocytes* (white blood cells) to attack and destroy these invaders. The action of the lymphocytes as well as other immune-system responses are delicately regulated in an extremely complex process. If the immune system is suppressed, we become more vulnerable to a variety of infectious organisms and cancers, a fact that has been made painfully clear in recent years with the unfolding story of acquired immunodeficiency syndrome (AIDS), discussed in Chapter 8. Conversely, a breakdown in the body's system of checks and balances may cause the immune system to become overreactive, turning on itself to attack and destroy healthy body tissues. (This phenomenon occurs in autoimmune disorders such as rheumatoid arthritis.) While diet, age, heredity, and general health all affect the functioning of the immune system, stress also exerts a marked influence on *immunocompetence*, the immune system's ability to defend our bodies successfully (Arnetz et al., 1987; Irwin et al., 1987 & 1990; Jemmott & Locke, 1984; Martin, 1987).

For instance, many studies of nonhuman animals have demonstrated that experimentally manipulated stressors, such as separation from mother, isolation from peers, exposure to loud noise, and electric shock, can reduce immunocompetence by suppressing the activity of the lymphocytes (Borysenko & Borysenko, 1982; Esterling & Rabin, 1987; Laudenslager et al., 1982; Monjan & Collecter, 1977; Rogers et al., 1979). Research with human subjects has revealed similar results. Lymphocyte production has been shown to be suppressed following death or prolonged illness of a spouse (Bartrop et al., 1977; Schleifer et al., 1983). Studies of Apollo and Skylab astronauts revealed immunological deficiencies immediately after the stress of reentry and splashdown (Fisher et al., 1972; Kimzey, 1975), and the anticipation of HIV tests results has been shown to be immuno-suppressive (Ironson et al., 1990).

High-stress periods such as final exam week have also been linked to reduced immunocompetence—a finding which helps explain why people may be more likely to become ill during finals (Jemmott et al., 1983). Research with children has revealed an increased incidence of infectious disease when the family is under stress, suggesting a suppression of the immune system (Boyce et al., 1977; Meyer & Haggerty, 1962). Research on adult subjects has also linked symptoms of a variety of infectious diseases, including colds, influenza, herpes, and mononucleosis, to stressful events (Cohen & Williamson, 1991; Jemmott & Locke, 1984).

We still do not know exactly how stress suppresses immunocompetence. However, several lines of evidence suggest that endocrine responses to stress may play a primary role (Arthur, 1987; Martin, P., 1987). Recall from our earlier discussion of Selye's general adaptation syndrome that stress arouses the sympathetic nervous system, triggering the release of stress hormones. It has been shown that the effects of stress hormones—corticosteroids, epinephrine, and nor-epinephrine—on the activity of the immune system depends critically on the type of stress experienced. For instance, immune function may be enhanced following acute fearful stress, but greatly suppressed with the stress of depression and helplessness (O'Leary, 1990). For cancer there is evidence that emotionality and a fighting spirit are beneficial, whereas emotional inexpressiveness and depression are more harmful (Contrada, Leventhal, & O'Leary, 1990).

In summary, there is considerable evidence linking stress with depressed immune function and the onset and progression of certain diseases. Studies with animals have demonstrated strong relationships between the stress of shock, isolation, and loud noise and the ability of the immune system to fight off infectious diseases as well as cancerous tumors. Interpreting data from humans is more difficult, because of the difficulty in controlling for the amount and type of stress, but consistent with animal studies. The suppression in immune function that follows severe stress appears to be mediated by the release of stress hormones.

MANAGING STRESS

Recent evidence linking stress with a variety of illnesses has prompted many health professionals to turn their attention to developing techniques for managing stress. These techniques take aim not only at our physiological, cognitive, and behavioral responses to stress but also at behaviors and thought patterns that may induce or increase stress. The following paragraphs summarize some of the strategies that have been successfully applied in various stress-management programs offered at hospitals, clinics, and corporations. For more information about these techniques or programs, check your library or bookstore for some of the many excellent self-help stress-management books currently available.

HEALTH
PSYCHOLOGY
&
LIFE

MANAGING PHYSIOLOGICAL RESPONSES TO STRESS

Much of the physical damage associated with stress results from our bodies' physiological responses. These include the release of hormones and corticosteroids into the blood resulting in increases in metabolism, heart rate, blood pressure, and muscle tension, and perhaps decreases in the ability of our immune system to respond effectively to invasion.

Many techniques have been developed to minimize these reactions; three of the most effective are biofeedback, relaxation training, and exercise.

BIOFEEDBACK We are seldom aware of the subtle physiological changes that take place when we are under stress, such as rising blood pressure or increased heart rate. The theory behind biofeedback is that if we learn to recognize these destructive changes we can also learn to control them. Biofeedback provides individuals with information about their bodily processes that they can use to modify these processes. For instance, people who suffer from high blood pressure might be hooked up to a biofeedback apparatus that constantly monitors their blood pressure, sounding a tone which changes in pitch as their blood pressure rises or falls. Through this process, they may eventually learn to recognize symptoms of high blood pressure even when they do not hear a tone, so that they can apply techniques to control this response. Although biofeedback is not a panacea for all stress-related disorders, it has been helpful in treating migraine headaches, tension headaches, muscle tension, blood pressure abnormalities (both high and low), and chronic pain (King & Montgomery, 1980; Miller, 1978, 1985; Qualls & Sheehan, 1981; Turk et al., 1979).

RELAXATION TRAINING Virtually every formal stress-management program teaches some kind of relaxation technique. One of these is *progressive relaxation*, in which a person first tightens the muscles in a given area of the body (such as the legs), then relaxes them, then progresses systematically to other body areas until the entire body is relaxed. The idea that physical relaxation can lead to mental relaxation has been supported by experience, and progressive relaxation is now a key element in many stress-management programs.

How effective is relaxation in controlling stress-induced effects such as muscle tension and high blood pressure? In one recent study, several hundred heart attack survivors were randomly assigned to one of two groups. One group received standard advice about proper diet and exercise; the other received the same advice, plus counseling on how to relax and slow down. In the ensuing three years, subjects in the group that received relaxation counseling experienced only half as many recurrent heart attacks as those who had received the standard medical advice (Friedman & Ulmer, 1984).

Relaxation training is also being used with some success in delaying the recurrence of some kinds of terminal cancer. It is believed that relaxation training may play a role in facilitating the body's immune system to fend off the rapid growth of cancer cells. While it is too early at this time to critically evaluate this evidence, a number of treatment programs have begun to adopt relaxation training as part of cancer treatment.

EXERCISE Have you ever noticed that some types of exercise, such as jogging a few miles or playing tennis, can help to relieve stress? Exercise helps to distract us from sources of stress and it can also help to moderate some potentially damaging physical effects of stress by lowering blood pressure, improving circulation, and strengthening the heart muscle (Brown & Lawton, 1986; Roviario et al., 1984). In addition, people who regularly engage in some form of exeercise are more likely to adopt a healthful diet and be non-smokers.

MODIFYING COGNITIVE ANTECEDENTS OF STRESS People involved in stress-management programs learn to pay attention to what they are thinking just before they experience stress. One of the benefits of this self-monitoring is the awareness of how frequently our own upsetting thoughts or negative self-talk trigger our feelings of stress. Negative self-talk such as, "I'll never be able to pass this exam" can make the difference between good performance and failure; it can also help to bring on the elevated physical reactions typical of stress responses (Schuele & Wiesenfeld, 1983).

To modify these common cognitive antecedents of stress, Canadian psychologist Donald Meichenbaum (1977) suggests a technique he calls *stress inoculation*, in which we learn to replace negative self-statements with positive coping statements. For example, when faced with the stress of an exam, we might use positive self-talk such as, "There's no point in imagining the worst; I've prepared as well as anyone and I'll do the best I can." Although it may take some time to learn to alter negative self-talk successfully, the effect can be a reduction in anxiety and stress.

MODIFYING BEHAVIORAL ANTECEDENTS OF STRESS Many of us bring stress on ourselves by certain maladaptive behaviors. For instance, we may use our time poorly and then suddenly find ourselves under pressure, or we may habitually take on too many tasks to accomplish in the time we have. Stress management programs offer a variety of techniques for modifying such stress-producing behaviors. The following abbreviated list illustrates a number of these behaviors, as well as some strategies that are helpful in combating them.

Procrastination. Time-management training can help people pace themselves to avoid leaving too much for the last minute.

The "superperson syndrome." For some people, an important part of stress management is learning to say "no" and to delegate tasks to others. Time-management training can also help people recognize their limits so that they do not commit to more work than they can complete.

Disorganization. Stress-management programs often help people deal with disorganization by providing training in how to set goals for each day, establish priorities, avoid wasting time, and become task-oriented.

Lack of assertiveness. People who have difficulty standing up for their rights may be "boiling inside," generating tremendous amounts of stress. To combat this tendency, many stress-management programs incorporate *assertiveness training*, which teaches people to confront such situations rather than tiptoe around them.

Going it alone. Facing stress alone is much more damaging than facing it with the support of people who care about us (Dressler, 1989; Fontana et al., 1989; Kamarck et al., 1990; Orth-Gomér & Undén, 1990; Rook, 1987). Talking with others provides us with new perspectives; it may also boost our self-esteem and our sense that we are valued (Cohen & Wills, 1985). Thus an important tactic in managing stress is to talk things over with someone. If friends or family members are not able to provide support, a campus counseling center, community health center, or private clinic may be a valuable resource.

SUMMARY

THE COMPONENTS OF EMOTIONS

1. Motivation and emotion are closely connected. Emotions often motivate our actions.
2. Emotions are composed of four integral components: cognitive processes, affect, physiological arousal, and behavioral reactions.

THE RANGE OF HUMAN EMOTIONS

3. According to Plutchik's Emotion Wheel there are eight primary human emotions, which consist of four pairs of opposites: acceptance and disgust, fear and anger, surprise and anticipation, and sadness and joy.

THEORIES OF EMOTION

4. According to the James-Lange theory, environmental stimuli trigger physiological responses from the viscera and muscle movements. These visceral and muscular responses then activate emotional states.
5. Recent evidence has demonstrated that different emotions are associated with similar, but not identical, physiological changes. However, there is little concrete evidence that people are able to make fine discriminations between the varied, often highly similar patterns of physiological and muscular responses to determine what emotions they are experiencing.
6. The Cannon-Bard theory suggests that internal physiological changes and muscular responses are not the cause of emotion, but rather that emotional experiences and physical changes occur simultaneously.
7. The Schachter-Singer theory combines elements from both the James-Lange and Cannon-Bard theories. Schachter and Singer

maintained that emotions depend on a kind of double cognitive interpretation: We appraise the emotion-causing event while also evaluating what is happening physiologically with our bodies.

8. According to the facial feedback theory, facial muscles respond very rapidly and with sufficient differentiation to account for a wide range of emotional experience. Feedback from our own facial expressions helps determine our emotional experiences.

9. Solomon and Corbit's opponent-process theory maintains that when a strong emotional response to a particular stimulus event disrupts emotional balance, an opponent-process is eventually activated to restore equilibrium in one's emotional state. Repeated exposures to stimuli that arouse intense emotions result in a gradual weakening of the initial emotional reaction as the opponent process becomes stronger.

STRESS

10. There is a powerful relationship between emotion and stress. Stress may be defined as the process of appraising events (as harmful, threatening, or challenging), of assessing potential responses, and of responding to those events.

11. Selye's observation of organisms' physiological responses to stress led him to formulate the concept of a general adaptation syndrome (GAS) composed of three phases: alarm, resistance, and exhaustion. The alarm phase is characterized by a flood of stress hormones that prepare the body for fight or flight. In the resistance stage the body returns to a less aroused state, but one in which it continues to draw upon resources at an above-normal rate. If the stress is not alleviated, an organism is likely to enter the third state of exhaustion in which its body tissues begin to show signs of wear and tear, and susceptibility to disease increases.

12. Typical cognitive responses to stress include reduced ability to concentrate, distractibility, impaired performance on cognitive tasks, and a tendency to be plagued by disruptive or morbid thoughts.

13. Emotional responses to stress include such feelings as anxiety, irritability, anger, embarrassment, depression, and hostility.

14. A myriad of possible behavioral responses to stress include assertive action to confront stressors, withdrawal from a stressful situation, and adapting to the source of stress.

15. Factors that contribute to the stressfulness of a situation include our lack of control over it, its sudden onset, and a degree of ambiguity that forces us to spend resource-depleting energy trying to figure out the nature of the stressor.

16. Research has demonstrated that total scores on life change scales are not very accurate predictors of future problems with illness and disease.

17. Response to stress may be a major contributor to coronary heart disease. Type A people, who tend to be hard-driving, ambitious, competitive, and perfectionist, are much more prone to CHD than Type B people, who are more relaxed, easygoing, and not driven to achieve perfection.

18. People who deal with anger by suppressing it and those who exhibit Type A behavior may be particularly predisposed to develop hypertension.

19. Stress hormones appear to exert a pronounced negative effect on immunocompetence—the immune system's ability to defend our bodies successfully against disease.

emotion
James-Lange theory
Cannon-Bard theory
Schachter-Singer theory
facial feedback theory
opponent-process theory of emotion
stress

general adaptation syndrome (GAS)
coronary heart disease (CHD)
Type A
Type B
hypertension
cancer
immune system

CHAPTER 10

Cognition: Thinking and Language

THINKING

Components of Thinking
Concept Formation

PROBLEM SOLVING

Stages of Problem Solving
Strategies for Problem Solving
Characteristics of Difficult Problems

REASONING AND DECISION MAKING

Logical Reasoning for Decisions
Some Common Causes of Reasoning
  Errors
Subjective Probability and Reasoning for
  Decisions

ARTIFICIAL INTELLIGENCE

Expert Systems
General Problem Solvers

LANGUAGE

Psycholinguistics
Theories of Language Acquisition
Brain Mechanisms for Language
Is Language Unique to Humans?

THINKING AND LANGUAGE

Does Language Structure Thought?
Does Thought Structure Language?

*I*n Germany, around the turn of the century, there was a famous horse named Hans who performed amazing intellectual feats. When asked to solve spoken arithmetic problems such as "What is the sum of 5 plus 1?" he consistently signed the correct answer by tapping his hoof the correct number of times. Some cynics declared that Hans was a hoax and that his trainer was somehow cueing the right answer to the horse, but these assertions were dispelled when the horse provided the correct answer even when his trainer was not present.

Many people view abstract thought, problem solving, and language as qualities that set humans apart from other animals. Does Hans provide evidence disproving this belief? To answer this question, let us return to our narrative.

After the critics had seemingly been disproved, someone noticed an odd pattern. Hans had trouble solving math problems if the questioner either did not know the answer or was standing out of sight. What did this mean?

Hans was clever, but, as the saying goes, a horse is a horse. He did not understand either the words or the math problems; instead, he had learned to respond to subtle body language cues. Whenever his trainer or another questioner said something to him in an expectant tone of voice, then leaned forward and tensed up, Hans knew that he should start tapping his hoof on the ground. He would keep striking the ground until the trainer relaxed and stopped leaning forward. Hans knew that if he stopped tapping his hoof at this point, he would receive a carrot as a reward (Fernald, 1984).

In the following pages, we explore thinking, problem solving, reasoning and decision making, and the special qualities of human language. As discussed in Chapter 1, these processes constitute the core topics within the area of *cognitive psychology*. The abilities of Hans demonstrate that cognitive processes can be misinterpreted and often complex behavior of humans and other animals can be reduced to simpler behavioral processes. The cognitive processes discussed in this chapter are not an exception.

Clever Hans with his owner, Mr. van Osten.

THINKING

The term *think* has a variety of meanings. For example, we might remark to a companion, "I can't think of the name of that architectural style" or "I think that car is a terrific buy." Or if a neighbor asks your opinion about the best way to deal with the problem of cars speeding along your quiet street, you may respond, "Let me think about it for a while."

In the first two instances the word think is synonymous with remembering and belief, respectively; in the third example it implies a process of reasoning about a particular situation with the intent of solving a problem. Psychologists who study thought are interested primarily in this latter meaning. Thus we may define **thought** or thinking as a collection of internal processes directed toward solving a problem. When we use symbols or concepts to imagine something internally, and to solve problems, we are said to be thinking. (Note that this definition is somewhat narrow. Broader definitions of the term *thinking* include diverse cognitive processes, including such things as understanding language, memory retrieval, and perceiving patterns in sensory inputs [Houston, 1986; Oden, 1987].)

Thinking is the process that lets us make sense out of our perceptions. Our ability to think also allows us to put what we have learned to use. Perhaps most importantly, thinking allows us to manipulate representations of objects, so that we can solve problems without actually going through any physical motions. For example, an architect working on a design for a new home on a hilltop does not have to draw several sets of plans to determine which will take best advantage of the view. Instead, he or she manipulates the various design features in order to arrive at a solution, even before getting out the drafting paper. Finally, thinking allows us to behave privately without commiting ourselves. In a game of chess we might think about the consequences of several moves before actually moving.

Cognitive psychologists who study thought are interested in determining how people transform and manipulate information to solve problems and make decisions. Before examining what research has revealed about how we accomplish these goals, we first consider a fundamental question: What are the basic components of thinking?

COMPONENTS OF THINKING

THINKING AS BEHAVIOR About half a century ago, many psychologists believed that thinking was essentially a matter of talking to ourselves. The leading proponent of this view was John Watson (1930), the founder of behaviorism. Like other behaviors, Watson argued, thinking involves specific motor actions; the only difference is that the muscular movements involved in thinking are usually much more difficult to observe than those of other kinds of behavior. Watson maintained that tiny movements of the tongue and throat, which he called *subvocal* or *implicit speech*, occur when we think. Watson further argued that there were many muscular combinations, including hand and arm gestures, that could become substitutes for words and therefore were involved in thinking.

Some early evidence supported Watson's view. For example, when researchers used sensitive recording devices, they were able to record very subtle movements of the tongue and throat muscles that occurred when subjects were silently thinking about various problems (Jacobson, 1932). One noteworthy study found that deaf people, who were accustomed to communicating with sign language rather than speech, exhibited muscular activity in their fingers when asked to solve problems (Max, 1937). Such findings certainly supported the notion that some relationship existed between thought and motor action, a relationship you may have noted yourself if you have ever observed people scratching their heads or furrowing their brows as they think. Watson, however, argued that there was more than just a relationship. He believed that subvocal speech and overt motor action were essential for thinking.

Watson's assertion was put to the test in an interesting experiment. The subject (a member of the research team) was injected with *curare*, a drug that temporarily paralyzes all of the skeletal muscles. Since the paralyzed subject could not move any muscles, he was unable to engage in subvocal speech, to breathe, or even to blink. His research associates provided artificial respiration and other vital support services while their colleague was temporarily immobilized. When the drug wore off, the subject reported that his mind had remained clear during the entire procedure, and that he had been able to think not only about questions put to him during the experiment but also about the experimental procedure (Smith et al., 1947). These results were interpreted as evidence against Watson's theory and in support of the idea that thinking can be independent of motor action.

More recent versions of behaviorism continue to argue that thinking is behavior, but on a small scale that is usually verbal and unobservable to others. B.F. Skinner (1974) termed this kind of behavior **covert behavior.** According to Skinner, covert behavior, like thinking, had advantages in that we could act without committing ourselves. In other words, we could revoke the behavior if the private consequences were not reinforcing. In this way a chess player might try a number of covert moves, to test the consequences of each, before committing an overt move.

While it is too early to rule out the behavioral position completely, most psychologists agree that thinking is more than covert behavior. Even Skinner believed that covert behavior was not a complete explanation of thinking.

MENTAL IMAGES If thinking is not solely covert behavior, what else is there? One additional component may be mental images of visual scenes, sounds, or tactile sensations that we manipulate in some systematic or logical fashion (Richardson, 1983; Shepherd & Cooper, 1982).

For example, suppose you are trying to figure out how to assemble a new lawn mower after removing all the parts from the packing crate. You are likely to think about this task by manipulating visual pictures or mental images of the various parts. You might also use mental imagery to associate sounds as you try to recognize a melody, to picture the components of a perfect tennis swing, to figure out the fastest route from your dorm to the laundromat, or if you recall from Chapter 7 (Figure 7.5), identify the correct rotation of a three-dimensional object.

But what are these mental images? Certainly they cannot be mere internal pictures, as this would require another "mind's eye" to interpret them, by perhaps another image. While some cognitive psychologists insist that mental images which represent the spatial properties of real objects exist and are a component of thinking, other psychologists argue that the image analog is misleading and that mental images do not explain our ability to solve spatial or rotational problems (Pylyshyn, 1973, 1984).

Although it appears that mental images of some sort are an element of thought, there is more to thought than representational images of sights, sounds, and touches. Most cognitive psychologists believe that there is another, more abstract or symbolic form of thinking that involves the use of *concepts* (Medin & Smith, 1984).

CONCEPTS Suppose you are the parent of a six-year-old who asks, Where do babies come from? You respond as well as you can by providing a simplified version of a very complex set of emotional and biological processes. This task may not be the easiest you have ever performed, but imagine how difficult it would be to answer this question if your child had not already acquired a representation or conception of the meaning of the terms you used to answer the question—terms like *love*, *feeling good*, *little*, or *seeds*?

In order to think and communicate about the objects, living things, activities, physical properties, and relationships between things we encounter in our daily lives, we learn to simplify and provide order to our world by grouping events, objects, and so forth, into general categories called **concepts.** Concepts thus represent categories or kinds of things and their rules of combination, not just individual cases. Most of our knowledge is in the form of concepts rather than independent, specific items or instances (Bourne et al., 1986). Furthermore, concept formation may be one of the most important cognitive functions that humans perform (Solso, 1991).

A concept may represent a category to which all varieties of one kind of physical object belong. For example, our concept of *car* encompasses everything from a Model T to a Rolls Royce. Concepts also represent kinds of living things (such as *dog*, *plant*, or *person*); types of activities (*reading* and *jogging*); physical properties (*little*, *pungent*, or *square*); and relationships between things (*taller than* or *prettier than*). Concepts may also represent more abstract ideas, such as *feeling good*, *love*, or *morality*.

Our ability to think and function efficiently would be greatly impaired if we were not able to form concepts. Without the general concept *car*, we could never give our children simple instructions such as, "Watch out for cars when you cross the street." Instead, we would have to list every name of every automobile. Without concepts such as *happy* and *sad*, we could not describe someone's emotional behavior without an extended description of that person's facial expressions, vocal inflections, and the nature of communicated messages.

Concepts provide a sense of order to a world filled with unique objects and events, allowing us to group things that share certain features even though they are not identical. They also permit us to categorize most of the new objects or activities that we encounter, even though they may be quite novel. Since we can relate these new situations to objects or events with which we are already familiar, we can immediately understand something about them even though they are new. For instance, chances are that you have never seen a hurdy-gurdy before, as shown in Figure 10.1. However, you probably recognize certain elements—the

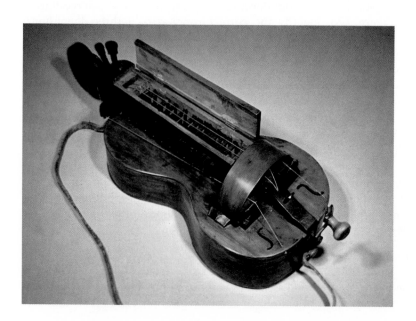

FIGURE 10.1

A Hurdy-Gurdy

Recognizing certain elements leads us to categorize this as a musical instrument even if we have never seen one before.

drum, the crank at the base, and the guitarlike shape—that lead you to categorize this image as a musical instrument.

Concepts range from broad to very specific. Examples of specific, narrow concepts are *sock, golden retriever,* and *red ball.* Examples of broader concepts are *footwear, dog,* and *ball.* We tend to organize concepts into hierarchies, with specific concepts grouped as subcategories within broader concepts. Thus *airplane* represents a broad concept which may be subdivided into more specific lower-level categories, such as *propeller aircraft* and *jet aircraft.* Furthermore, *jet aircraft* may be subdivided into more specific concepts such as *jet fighters, commercial passenger jets,* and so forth.

There seems to be an optimal or *basic level* in each concept hierarchy that we naturally use when we think about objects or events. For example, look at the two objects pictured in Figure 10.2. What were the first labels for each of these objects that came to your mind? The odds are that you probably said, a *house* and a *car.* Certainly it would have been correct to classify them as a *colonial-style house* and a *two-door coupe.* However, these lower-level-category responses provide more detail than you need to think optimally about the objects. Likewise, you would have been correct if you had classified the objects as an *architectural structure* and a *motorized vehicle.* But this concept level would not have been efficient either, because the categorizations are too imprecise.

Research has supported the idea that we rely on basic-level categories most of the time. When subjects are shown a picture of an object and are asked to verify (yes or no) that it illustrates a particular concept, they tend to react fastest at the basic level (Rosch, 1978; Rosch et al., 1976). For example, when shown a picture of a kitchen chair, subjects consistently classify it more quickly at the basic level *(chair)* than at either a subordinate level *(kitchen chair)* or a superordinate level *(piece of furniture).* As children develop and learn to think conceptually about their environments, basic-level categories are probably those they use first as they acquire the ability to name and classify events and objects (Mervis & Crisafi, 1982). Many cognitive psychologists now believe that this dependence on basic levels of concepts continues to be a fundamental aspect of human thought throughout our lives.

FIGURE 10.2
How Do You Describe These Objects?

CONCEPT FORMATION

A number of different theories have been proposed to explain how people form concepts. These include *association theory*, *hypothesis-testing theory*, and *exemplar theory*.

ASSOCIATION THEORY   One theory of how we form concepts was proposed by Clark Hull (1920), who described concept formation as the acquisition of stimulus-response (S-R) associations. According to this view, we learn to associate a single response (the concept) with a set of stimuli that share one or more common elements. Thus we associate the concept response *bird* with a pattern of stimuli (has wings, flies, lays eggs, etc.). We form a representation of a concept that is broad enough to allow us to generalize the response to many different instances of the concept. When we encounter a novel instance of the concept, such as an exotic bird we have never seen before, we respond correctly ("it is a bird") on the basis of stimulus generalization (see Chapter 6).

HYPOTHESIS-TESTING THEORY   Another view, originally proposed by Jerome Bruner and his Harvard colleagues, suggests that we acquire formal concepts in a more or less systematic fashion by forming and testing hypotheses. Thus we develop some type of strategic hypothesis-testing plan for identifying members of a particular category or concept. This plan typically takes the form of speculating about what attribute or attributes are critical for determining whether an item belongs in a particular concept category, generating a hypothesis about how the attribute(s) determines the concept, and maintaining the hypothesis if it leads to a correct decision. If the hypothesis is proved wrong, another is formed, and another, and another, until the concept is learned (Bruner et al., 1956; Medin & Smith, 1984).

Although subjects often seem to use hypothesis testing in laboratory settings, many psychologists have questioned whether this model applies to real life. Laboratory studies are typically based on artificial tasks, using arbitrarily selected attributes that bear little resemblance to the types of natural concepts we encounter in ordinary life (Bourne et al., 1986). Eleanor Rosch (1973, 1978) proposed an alternative explanation of how we form concepts in everyday life.

EXEMPLAR THEORY   According to Rosch's **exemplar theory,** the natural concepts that we learn in everyday life are represented in our memories by examples rather than by abstract rules. Thus our concept of *fish* may be based on images of salmon, trout, or bass — all examples of fish that we have seen rather than arbitrary rules such as "have fins," "breathe through gills," and "live in water." Rosch pointed out that most natural concepts, such as *furniture*, *fish*, *bird*, and *game*, are not easily described as some well-defined combination of discrete attributes; nor are all instances of a natural concept equally good examples of their respective categories. For any given concept category, some examples are more typical and some less typical. Rosch suggests that we often structure our concepts around best instances, or most typical representatives of the category, which she calls **prototypes.** The more closely objects or events match our prototypes for a concept, the more readily we include them in the category (Armstrong et al., 1983).

Suppose, for example, you were asked, "Is a robin a bird?" and "Is a penguin a bird?" You would respond yes to both questions, but you would probably be slower to respond to the second question (Rips et al., 1973). The reason is that robin is more typical of the concept bird than is penguin. (It may, in fact, be the prototype around which you have organized your concept of bird.)

Rosch demonstrated this in an experiment in which she asked people to rank different instances of a given category according to the degree to which the instance typified the concept. For example, when subjects were asked to rank various examples of the concept *furniture*, *chair* and *sofa* received the highest ranks

This three-year-old quickly identifies the seagull as a bird but has more difficulty identifying the penguin as a bird.

(most prototypical), *lamp* and *stool* received intermediate ranking, and *fan* and *telephone* were ranked as least typical of the concept (see Table 10.1). These rankings correlated with reaction time, with the most typical examples producing the fastest responses and the least typical examples resulting in the slowest responses (Rosch, 1975).

TABLE 10.1 *Furniture Items Ranked by Goodness of Example*

MEMBER	GOODNESS OF EXAMPLE RANK	MEMBER	GOODNESS OF EXAMPLE RANK	MEMBER	GOODNESS OF EXAMPLE RANK
chair	1.5	vanity	21	mirror	41
sofa	1.5	bookcase	22	television	42
couch	3.5	lounge	23	bar	43
table	3.5	chaise lounge	24	shelf	44
easy chair	5	ottoman	25	rug	45
dresser	6.5	footstool	26	pillow	46
rocking chair	6.5	cabinet	27	wastebasket	47
coffee table	8	china closet	28	radio	48
rocker	9	bench	29	sewing machine	49
love seat	10	buffet	30	stove	50
chest of drawers	11	lamp	31	counter	51
desk	12	stool	32	clock	52
bed	13	hassock	33	drapes	53
bureau	14	drawers	34	refrigerator	54
davenport	15.5	piano	35	picture	55
end table	15.5	cushion	36	closet	56
divan	17	magazine rack	37	vase	57
night table	18	hi-fi	38	ashtray	58
chest	19	cupboard	39	fan	59
cedar chest	20	stereo	40	telephone	60

SOURCE: From Rosch, 1975.

PROBLEM SOLVING

Imagine that you and a friend have just hiked the last leg of a week-long backpacking trip. You arrive at your parked car hot, thirsty, and anxious to return to civilization, but when you try to start your car, the motor does not turn over. You quickly diagnose the problem: a dead battery. A few other vehicles are parked at the trail head, but nobody is around to provide help. The nearest town is 10 miles away on an absolutely flat country road. You have to be home in six hours for an important engagement, and it is a three-hour drive to your home. You have a problem.

A problem exists when there is a discrepancy between your present status and some goal you wish to obtain, with no obvious way to bridge the gap. The essence of a problem is that you must figure out what can be done to resolve a predicament and to achieve some goal. In this example, your goal is to start your car so that you can get home on time, but the dead battery is preventing you from reaching that goal.

Problem solving is different from simply executing a well-learned response or series of behaviors, as a rat might do when it negotiates a maze to reach a food reward. It is also distinct from learning new information. For instance, you would not be problem solving if some hikers fortuitously returned to their car and told you they could take you to the nearest service station. The essence of all problems is that they require you to supply new knowledge or skills that allows you to achieve your goal.

Problems consist of three components: (1) the *original state* of the situation as it exists at the moment, as perceived by the individual; (2) the *goal state*, which is what the problem solver would like the situation to be; and (3) the *rules* or *restrictions* that govern the possible strategies for moving from the original state to the goal state. To return to the dead battery problem, your perception of the original state might be, "My car won't start because of a dead battery and I am 10 miles from the nearest garage." Your goal would be, "I want to be home in six hours." The rules or restrictions might include: "Walking to the nearest town is unacceptable because it would take too long," and "There are three other cars at the trail head but no people to provide help."

How would you go about solving such a problem? To treat this topic fairly, we have to admit there may be no ideal solution. Instead, there are a number of possibilities, ranging from hitchhiking to borrowing a battery from one of the parked cars so that you can drive your own battery to a service station for recharging. Each of these strategies, however, has its own risks. The solution to this problem (and other problems we discuss later) is not really the issue here. Instead, our concern is the way we approach problems—the strategies that can make problem solving easier, and the potential stumbling blocks which get in the way of problem solving.

STAGES OF PROBLEM SOLVING

Problem-solving behavior generally involves three logical steps or stages: representing or defining the problem, generating possible solutions, and evaluating how well a given solution works.

REPRESENTING THE PROBLEM   Logically, the first step in problem solving is to determine what the problem is and to conceptualize it in familiar terms that will help us better understand and solve it. Consider the following problem:

Two train stations are 50 miles apart. At 2 P.M. one Saturday afternoon two trains start toward each other, one from each station. Just as the trains pull out of the stations, a bird springs into the air in front of the first train and flies ahead to the front of the second train. When the bird reaches the second train it turns back and flies toward the first train. The bird continues to do this until the trains meet. If both trains travel at the rate of 25 miles per hour and the bird flies at 100 miles per hour, how many miles will the bird have flown before the two trains meet? (Posner, 1973)

The manner in which you represent this problem will significantly influence the ease with which you can generate solutions. Some problems can be represented visually. Thus you might be tempted to draw a diagram showing the paths of the two trains and the zigzagging path of the bird as it goes back and forth between them. Unfortunately, this strategy will probably serve to complicate this problem rather than making it easier to solve.

A much more logical approach is to represent the problem mathematically. You know that the bird flies at 100 miles per hour, and that it will keep flying until the trains meet. All you have to do is figure out how long it will take the trains to meet and translate this figure into the bird's flying rate. Since the stations are 50 miles apart, and since each train travels at 25 miles per hour, they will meet at the halfway point between the stations in exactly one hour. Thus the bird will have to fly for one hour, and since it flies at a rate of 100 miles per hour, it will fly exactly 100 miles.

Our understanding of a problem is influenced not only by how we represent it, but also by how the problem is presented to us. The problem shown in Figure 10.3 illustrates this point. Assume you are sitting at the table shown in the figure; on it are a few candles, a pile of tacks, and a box containing some matches. The table is flush against a corkboard wall. You are told to attach a candle to the wall so that no wax will drip on either the table or the floor when the candle is lit. Try to solve this problem, and then check your solution by looking at Figure 10.4.

FIGURE 10.3

The Candle Problem

How can you attach this candle to the wall so it will not drip wax on the floor or the table when it is lit?

SOURCE: Adapted from Bourne et al., 1971

FIGURE 10.4
Solution to the Candle Problem

Research has shown that the candle problem is often quite difficult to solve when the elements (candle, matches, etc.) are presented in the fashion illustrated in Figure 10.3. Cognitive psychologists refer to this kind of difficulty as *functional fixedness* because we tend to make fixed assumptions about the elements of a problem depending upon how they are presented. Now that you know what the solution is, can you think of a different way to present the elements that would make the problem easier to solve? Give some thought to this question before reading on.

One minor variation in the representation of the candle problem can make it much easier to solve. When the matches are removed and scattered on the table, so that the box is presented empty, most people have no trouble solving the problem (Glucksberg & Weisberg, 1966). When the box is shown holding matches as in the figure, however, people have a harder time visualizing it as a separate object that may be used as a platform to mount the candle.

GENERATING POSSIBLE SOLUTIONS   Once we have a clear idea what the problem is, the next step is to generate possible solutions. Sometimes these solutions are easy. For example, if you sit down to begin studying and discover that your notes are missing, you might only need to search your long-term memory: Ah yes, I remember lending the notes to my roommate, who missed yesterday's lecture. Assuming your roommate is nearby, your problem is solved. Other more complicated problems may require you to generate more complex strategies. Consider the following problem:

Find a number such that if 3 more than 4 times the number is divided by 3, the result is the same as 5 less than 2 times the number. (Mayer, 1982, p. 448)

One approach to this problem is to use a trial-and-error strategy, testing different numbers at random. However, this method is highly inefficient. A person who understands algebra might elect to apply an algebraic strategy. This procedure would lead to the formula $(3 + 4 \times X)/3 = 2X - 5$ Solving for X yields the correct answer, 9. This example illustrates once again how representing a problem makes all the difference in the ease with which we can solve it. Subjects who represented the problem as a mathematical formula were able to solve it more readily than those who represented it as a word problem (Mayer, 1982).

EVALUATING THE SOLUTION   The final stage in problem solving is to evaluate your solution. In some cases, this is a simple matter. For example, solving for X in the previous problem and then plugging the obtained value into the original formula would quickly reveal whether or not the solution was correct. That is because the problem is clear-cut, with only one possible solution.

With some other types of problems, the solution may be much more difficult to evaluate. For example, college students often have trouble evaluating their answers to the problem "What should I major in?" The reason for this difficulty has to do with the vague nature of the problem itself. Many students have not yet defined what their goals are, and have only a hazy notion of their options. As a result, many students are not certain that they have made the best choice even after they have selected a major. Problems that are unclear or poorly defined are almost always difficult to evaluate.

Whether a problem is clear-cut or vague, the way we approach it makes a critical difference in our ability to find a workable solution. A number of different strategies can be applied. We consider four common approaches: trial and error, testing hypotheses, algorithms, and heuristics.

STRATEGIES FOR PROBLEM SOLVING

TRIAL AND ERROR   Some problems have such a narrow range of possible solutions that we decide to solve them through **trial and error.** For example, suppose you return to campus late Sunday after a weekend trip, and an acquaintance in your dorm tells you that you had a call from a woman who sounded distraught, insisting that you call immediately upon your return. Unfortunately, your dorm mate cannot find the slip of paper with her name and phone number, and has forgotten her name. The list of women who call you is somewhat limited, so you decide to call them one by one until you find out which one left the message. This trial-and-error process is not a bad strategy for solving the problem of the mystery caller, since the likely solutions are probably few in number.

TESTING HYPOTHESES   A somewhat more systematic approach to problem solving is provided by the strategy of **testing hypotheses.** Assume that the list of possible woman callers is rather lengthy (you are a very social person) and that calling each one on a trial-and-error basis would be too time consuming. Instead, you may formulate specific hypotheses that generate a more efficient approach to solving your problem. For example, it sounds to you as though the person who called is going through a difficult emotional time. Based on this information, you may narrow your choices to those friends whom you know to have recently been distressed or agitated. Thus your first calls would be to a friend whose father has been ill and another whose romance has been on shaky ground lately.

ALGORITHMS   A third possible problem-solving strategy is the **algorithm.** Algorithms involve a systematic exploration of every possible solution until the correct one is found. This strategy originated in the field of mathematics, where its application can produce guaranteed solutions. Algorithms are especially well suited to computers, which can rapidly sort through hundreds, thousands, even millions of possible solutions without growing tired or suffering from boredom (both shortcomings of the human data processor).

Algorithms guarantee a correct solution if you are aware of all the possibilities —but in real life, that is a big "if." For instance, you could not apply an algorithm in solving the problem of the unknown caller, since the caller might have been someone you have never met, or it might be a voice from the distant past that you would never think to include in your list of possibilities. In addition, people try to find shortcuts when faced with complicated problems: Often algorithms simply require too much effort. One type of short-cut strategy we commonly use is called a *heuristic*.

HEURISTICS   **Heuristics** refer to a variety of strategies or sets of empirical rules that may lead to solutions to problems. We all have a repertoire of "rules-of-thumb" methods for approaching problems, based on both experiences with strategies that have worked in the past and our own personal knowledge that can be applied to specific problems.

For example, in a game of chess there is an extremely large number of possible moves during the game. An algorithmic search that examines all alternatives at each point in the game would inevitably lead to a conclusion (either win, lose, or draw). However, even the most sophisticated computer would find this strategy implausible. Alternatively, both humans and chess playing computers use heuristic search methods. These heuristic strategies might include: Attack the opponent's queen, control the center of the board, or exchange pieces on the basis of position advantage. These heuristic strategies greatly reduce the number of alternative moves at any point in the game. Modern chess-playing computers (for example, "Deep Thought") use heuristics that were developed to utilize some of the same strategies that expert chess players use. We will have more to say about how computers solve problems in a moment.

We use several kinds of heuristic strategies. One of the most common, **means–ends analysis,** involves first identifying the difference between the original state and the desired goal state, and then choosing a set of operations that will reduce this difference by progressing through a series of subgoals that systematically move you closer to the final solution (Newell & Simon, 1972). For instance, you would probably use means-ends analysis to solve the anagram

Sophisticated chess-playing computers can now beat the best human players.

teralbay, rather than using the algorithmic strategy to combine and recombine its eight letters 40,320 times (ie., 8!).

To use means-ends analysis, you might begin by defining some subgoals that would help you move to a solution. Perhaps your accumulated knowledge about the English language would first prompt you to focus on certain common letter combinations (such as *ra, be, bay, able,* and *tray*) from the eight-letter anagram, and to exclude combinations that rarely or never occur (such as *aa, lbya, yblt, rtbl*). With these subgoals accomplished, you could then manipulate common letter combinations to seek a final solution. Do words with the combination *bay* in them work? No such luck. How about *able?* Again, no cigar. What about *tray?* This combination is the one: The answer is *betrayal.*

Another common heuristic strategy is **working backward** from a clearly defined goal to the original state (Newell & Simon, 1972). For example, suppose that you decide to stay on campus over the Thanksgiving holiday to study for a major biology exam scheduled for the following week. On Thanksgiving Day you discover that both your textbook and lecture notes are missing. After searching your memory, you remember leaving them in the biology laboratory, which is locked up for the holidays. You also recall that your lab partner is a good friend of the young man who is performing custodial duties in the Science Building. This young man is taking some time off from school to earn money to continue his education, and he lives close to campus. If you can find him, he can probably help you gain access to your books.

You have now defined your goal as getting into the biology lab. The best way to reach it is to work backward from that goal. The final step that will lead to this goal is phoning the janitor and asking if he would kindly take a few minutes to drive to campus and let you into the laboratory. What has to be done before this step? You must get the janitor's phone number from the telephone directory, but to do this you must have his name. You can get his name from your lab partner who is home for the holidays. Thus you must begin by calling your lab partner at home. You now have a reasonable strategy for solving your problem.

Most of us are reasonably successful at solving the kinds of problems we encounter in our everyday lives. However, a number of relatively common situations can create obstacles to effective problem solving. Some of these obstacles have to do with the problem itself; others are the result of the way we approach the problem.

Problems come in many forms and vary greatly in difficulty. Two characteristics that can make a problem difficult to solve are lack of definition and complexity. We next examine each of these issues in turn.

CHARACTERISTICS OF DIFFICULT PROBLEMS

DEFINING PROBLEMS   According to cognitive psychologists, problems exist on a continuum ranging from well-defined to ill-defined. *Well-defined problems* are those in which the original state and goal state are clearly specified, as are the rules for allowable problem-solving operations. Assembling a lawn mower from parts that arrive in a crate, putting together pieces of a jigsaw puzzle, and solving a mathematical problem are all examples of well-defined problems.

As we have already seen in our discussion of evaluating solutions, *ill-defined problems* are often more difficult. With these problems, we usually have a poor conception of our original state and only a vague notion of where we are going and how we can get there; we also have no obvious way of judging whether a solution we might select is correct (Matlin, 1989). For example, it is not uncommon to reach the goal of graduating from college only to face a new problem of vast dimensions: What to do with the rest of our lives? Before we can work effectively toward solving such problems, we need to define our goals more clearly and have a better idea of what means are available to us.

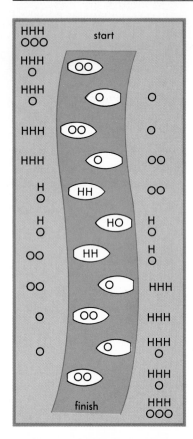

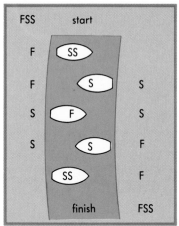

FIGURE 10.5
Solutions to River-Crossing Problems

COMPLEX PROBLEMS Try to solve the following two problems:

Orcs are monsters who eat small humanlike dwarfs called hobbits (characters from Tolkien's *Lord of the Rings*). Three orcs and three hobbits are stranded on one side of a river. They have a small boat that holds a maximum of two creatures. The problem is to transport all six safely to the other side. If at any time orcs outnumber hobbits (on either side of the river), the orcs will dine on the outnumbered hobbit(s). How can all six get across in one piece?

A man and his two sons want to use an available boat to get across a river. The boat has a maximum capacity of 200 pounds. The father weighs 200 pounds and each son tips the scales at 100 pounds. How can all three safely cross the river?

The solutions to these problems are provided in Figure 10.5. If you were able to solve one of these problems successfully, you probably found it relatively easy to solve the other, since both require the same kind of strategy. However, observations of people who work on only one or the other of these problems, but not both, generally reveal that the "man and his sons" version is solved more quickly than the "orcs and hobbits" version. The reason for this difference is related to the number of steps required to solve each version. The father and his sons get across the river in only five steps, compared to 11 steps to get all of the orcs and hobbits across. In sum, complex problems with numerous steps are generally more difficult to solve than problems whose solutions involve fewer steps.

COGNITIVE INFLUENCES ON PROBLEM SOLVING Although complex and ill-defined problems tend to be inherently difficult, sometimes we have only ourselves to blame for the trouble we have solving problems. Three common obstacles that we often create for ourselves are mental set, functional fixedness, and confirmation bias.

Mental Set Suppose you have three containers that have a maximum capacity of 21 ounces, 127 ounces, and 3 ounces, respectively, and a tap from which you can draw water. Your task is to use these three containers to obtain exactly 100 ounces of water. Attempt to solve this problem, as well as the other problems listed in Table 10.2.

How well did you do on these problems? Did you overlook a simpler solution on the sixth water container problem and perhaps get temporarily stymied on the seventh problem? If you answered yes, you have just experienced firsthand how a mental set can inhibit or block effective problem solving. A **mental set** is a tendency to approach a problem in a set or predetermined way regardless of the requirements of the specific problem. When we operate under the influence of a mental set, we apply strategies that have previously helped us to solve similar problems, instead of taking the time to analyze the current problem carefully.

Mental sets often facilitate problem solving, but they can also get in the way. Consider how most people perform on the water container problems in the table. The chances are good that you figured out that the way to obtain 100 ounces is to fill the *B* container with 127 ounces and pour 21 ounces into the *A* container, then fill *C* with 3 ounces twice. Once you solved this problem, you probably applied the same strategy (mathematically represented by the formula $B - A - 2C$) to the next several problems. Thus, this mental set helped you to solve these problems readily. But what about item six? If you are like most people, you probably applied the same formula to this problem as well. It worked, but problem six can also be solved by a simpler and more efficient method, expressed by the formula $A - C$.

It is interesting to note that when these problems are presented to students in a classroom demonstration, many dash along to item seven, at which point they often get stuck and sometimes even declare that it cannot be solved. Even

TABLE 10.2 *Water Container Problems*

| PROBLEM NO. | CONTAINERS WITH CAPACITY IN OUNCES | | | OBTAIN EXACTLY THESE AMOUNTS OF WATER |
	CONTAINER A	CONTAINER B	CONTAINER C	
1	21	127	3	100
2	14	163	25	99
3	18	43	10	5
4	9	42	6	21
5	20	59	4	31
6	23	49	3	20
7	10	36	7	3

SOURCE: From Luchins and Luchins, 1959.

though they are never told to solve all problems in the same way, the $B - A - 2C$ strategy has worked so well that the resulting strong mental set keeps them from considering another approach.

Functional Fixedness A second common obstacle to solving problems is functional fixedness (previously discussed in the candle problem). To see how this factor operates, consider the problem illustrated in Figure 10.6. You are brought into a room where two strings dangle from the ceiling. Your task is to tie the two strings together. Unfortunately, they are just far enough apart so that it is impossible to hold on to one while at the same time stretching out to grasp the other. Several objects are present in the room, as pictured in the figure. Before reading on, take some time to search for a solution to the problem (or solutions, since there are more than one).

FIGURE 10.6
The Two-String Problem

FIGURE 10.7

Solution to the Two-String Problem

One possible solution is illustrated in Figure 10.7. You could tie the end of one string to the pliers and swing the pliers and string like a pendulum. This strategy would allow you to grasp the stationary string in one hand and simply wait until the swinging string comes within easy reach of your free hand. If you did not think of this idea, you may be kicking yourself now for overlooking such a simple solution. However, you may take consolation in knowing that many people faced with this problem also overlook this solution. This failure may be due to what psychologists call **functional fixedness**—the tendency to be so set or fixed in our perception of the proper function of a given object that we are unable to think of using it in a novel way to solve a problem. Thus we may be so fixed in considering that the function of pliers is to grasp and hold that we do not consider using the tool as a potential pendulum weight.

Confirmation Bias   Another relatively common obstacle to problem solving is our inclination to seek out evidence that will confirm our hypothesis, while at the same time overlooking contradictory evidence. This phenomenon, known as **confirmation bias,** was demonstrated in investigations conducted by British researcher Peter Wason (1968). Wason asked his subjects to discover what rule applied to a three-number series. Initially the subjects were provided with one example of a positive instance of the rule to be discovered, such as 2, 4, 6. They were then told to propose additional series to the experimenter, who would indicate whether each did or did not conform to the rule.

Many of Wason's subjects tackled the problem we have just described by hypothesizing a specific rule, such as numbers increasing by 2. They then proposed additional series, such as 4, 6, 8; 10, 12, 14; or 1, 3, 5, to verify their hypothesis. Wason responded that each of these series conformed to the rule. On this basis, many of Wason's subjects concluded that their hypothesis was correct and they were visibly frustrated when told that "numbers increasing by 2" was not the general rule the experimenter had in mind. Can you figure out what they failed to do as they put their hypothesis to the test? Take a moment to consider this question before reading on.

The fact is, Wason's unknown rule was very general—"numbers in increasing order of magnitude." Thus if you had been a subject and your initial hypothesis had been "numbers increasing by two," any series that you proposed (4, 6, 8; 10, 12, 14; or 1, 3, 5), would also have conformed to the unknown rule. The point is that you would never be able to solve this problem if you continued to search only for evidence that would confirm your initial hypothesis. The only way you could discover Wason's general rule would be to seek evidence that would *disprove* your hypothesis. For instance, you might have proposed 4, 6, 7 to disconfirm your "increasing by 2" hypothesis. Discovering that this series also conformed to the rule would allow you to shift your thinking and quickly discover the correct solution.

People often have trouble with such problems for a simple reason: We are naturally more inclined to find instances that verify our hypotheses than those that disprove our theories. It is wise to keep in mind this confirmation bias, and to remember that finding solutions may require us to look not only for what might be correct, but also for what is incorrect.

REASONING AND DECISION MAKING

Life constantly presents us with problems and decisions: how to get to class on time when the car does not start, what field of study to select as a major, what political candidate to support, how to get an *A* in psychology, what to do about an uncomfortable relationship. Our ability to solve problems successfully and make good decisions is greatly influenced by the reasoning processes we use. In this section we consider the ways in which people reason when they make a decision. We also examine some of the common thinking errors that can cloud our reasoning process. We end the section by examining certain aspects of decision making.

We often attribute a poor decision or failure to solve a problem to faulty reasoning, implying that there are normative standards for proper or correct reasoning. Such standards are available; in fact, they emerged ages ago from the discipline of formal logic, a branch of philosophy.

LOGICAL REASONING FOR DECISIONS

You may have already been exposed to the basic tenets of logic in your prior studies. If so, you know that there are two basic types of reasoning: inductive and deductive (Rips, 1990).

In **inductive reasoning,** we reach a general conclusion by generalizing from specific instances. For example, suppose that every male acquaintance expresses an interest in watching TV broadcasts of football games. This information might lead us to conclude that men in general enjoy this activity. With inductive reasoning, however, we can never be absolutely certain that we have reached a correct conclusion: Some day we might meet a man who hates watching TV football. As a result our generalization about males is proven wrong.

When we engage in **deductive reasoning,** we begin with certain general assumptions or premises that we believe to be true, and we use these assumptions as the basis for drawing conclusions that apply to specific instances. For example, given the premise, or assumption, that all birds have feathers, we can conclude that if a specific animal is a bird, it will have feathers. As long as we begin with valid assumptions and follow certain rules of logic, we can be confident that our deductions are valid (Skyrms, 1986). On the other hand, if our premise is wrong we can make faulty conclusions even though we follow the rules of deduction. For instance, if we assume that all birds fly, we might conclude wrongly that a penguin is not a bird.

In real life, most of us tend to use both deductive and inductive reasoning (Halpern, 1984). However, the discipline of formal logic has placed its emphasis primarily on deductive reasoning, providing a set of rules and systematic methods for reaching valid conclusions. A classical model for studying deductive reasoning is provided by the syllogism.

SYLLOGISMS   A **syllogism** is an argument consisting of two (or more) presumably true statements, called *premises*, and a statement of conclusion that may or may not follow logically from the premises. Once the form of a syllogism is established, a person is not asked to decide if the conclusion is factually true, but is asked to decide whether the conclusion is valid. Consider the following examples:

> **All men are humans.**
> **All humans are animals.**
> **Therefore, all men are animals.**
>
> **All women are child abusers.**
> **All child abusers are highly intelligent.**
> **Therefore, all women are highly intelligent.**

The conclusion in the first example follows logically from the two premises; therefore, it is valid. Very few people have a problem with this kind of argument, since its statements seem reasonable and consistent with our collective knowledge of the world. In contrast, the bizarre statements in the second example may have caused you to question the validity of the conclusion. If you rejected the second argument after accepting the first, however, you were not consistent in applying the principles of formal logic to your reasoning process.

As our example illustrates, the content of verbally expressed arguments can misdirect our reasoning processes and lead to faulty conclusions. Thus logicians prefer to express syllogisms in a more abstract way by substituting letters for real words. If we abstract the previous two examples of syllogisms in this fashion, we see that both follow the same form.

> **All *As* are *Bs***
> **All *Bs* are *Cs***
> **Therefore, all *As* are *Cs***

To apply the principles of formal syllogistic reasoning correctly, we must meet the following three requirements: (1) each premise must be considered in terms of all its possible meanings (most premise statements are ambiguous in that they may refer to more than one possible relationship); (2) all of the varied meanings of the premises must be combined in every conceivable way; and (3) a conclusion may be judged to be valid only if it applies to every conceivable combination of all possible meanings of the premises. If we can come up with at least one combination of the premise meanings that is inconsistent with the conclusion, we may judge the syllogism to be erroneous. Figure 10.8 illustrates how these principles may be applied to syllogisms.

SOME COMMON CAUSES OF REASONING ERRORS

If we were able to apply the rules of formal logic consistently and systematically to our reasoning, we would often be successful in solving problems and making decisions. However, even students of logic probably find it difficult to apply these principles with total accuracy to every reasoning problem that occurs in everyday life. We often err because we are too quick to accept faulty premises or because our attitudes or experiences interfere with our ability to think logically.

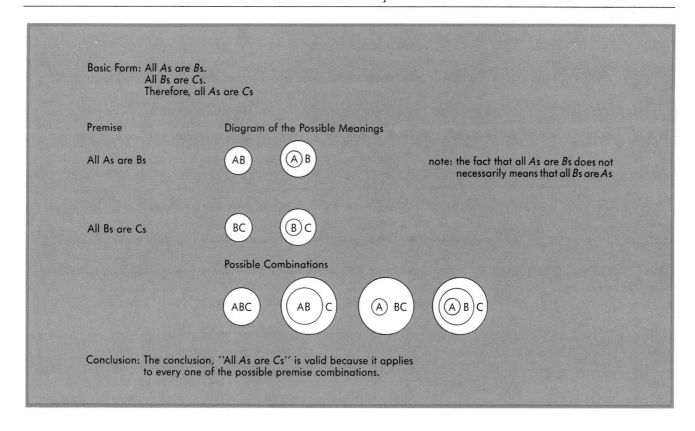

Basic Form: All *As* are *Bs*.
All *Bs* are *Cs*.
Therefore, all *As* are *Cs*

Premise   Diagram of the Possible Meanings

All As are Bs   (AB)   (A) B   note: the fact that all *As* are *Bs* does not
                                                             necessarily means that all *Bs* are *As*

All Bs are Cs   (BC)   (B) C

                            Possible Combinations

                    (ABC)   ((AB) C)   ((A) BC)   ((A) B) C)

Conclusion: The conclusion, ''All *As* are *Cs*'' is valid because it applies
to every one of the possible premise combinations.

FAULTY PREMISES   Consider the following syllogisms:

The job applicant comes from a broken home.
People from broken homes are social misfits.
Therefore, the job applicant is a social misfit.

All women experience mood swings.
People with mood swings are not corporate presidents.
Therefore, women are not corporate presidents.

FIGURE 10.8
Logical Analysis of a Syllogism

In both of these examples the conclusions are false even though the actual syllogisms are logically valid. The problem is that both arguments are based on faulty premises: Many people from broken homes are not social misfits, and not all women experience mood swings (in addition, some corporate presidents surely do experience mood swings). Unfortunately, we are often inclined to make bad judgments, not because we reason incorrectly, but rather because our initial assumptions or premises are false.

BELIEF-BIAS EFFECT   Another possible source of trouble is the tendency to rely on cherished beliefs rather than logical analysis. This **belief-bias effect** may be stated as follows: People tend to accept conclusions that conform to their beliefs and reject conclusions that do not conform, regardless of how logical these conclusions are (Bourne et al., 1986; Matlin, 1989).

A recent study demonstrates this phenomenon. Subjects were asked to evaluate several syllogisms and to decide whether or not the conclusions followed from the premises. The conclusions were sometimes logically valid and sometimes not; in addition, their believability (the key variable in the experiment) varied greatly. Some conclusions were quite believable (for example, "Some good ice skaters are not professional hockey players") and others were unbelievable

("Some professional hockey players are not good ice skaters"). The results indicated that many subjects succumbed to the belief-bias effect, accepting believable but invalid conclusions and rejecting unbelievable but valid conclusions (Evans et al., 1983). We often face conflict between principles of logic and what we believe about the world. This research suggests that too much reliance on preexisting beliefs can impair our ability to think logically and make valid judgments.

SUBJECTIVE PROBABILITY AND REASONING FOR DECISIONS

We have considered a number of situations in which the rules of formal logic have allowed us to decide whether or not a conclusion follows from the given facts. And, assuming that we have correctly applied the principles of logic, our true or false decisions have been relatively straightforward thus far. However, our lives are shaped by many everyday decisions in which the facts as we know them do not dictate a single, logical conclusion. For example, you know of several approaches to losing weight, and you have to select one option on the basis of the evidence at your disposal. *Decision making* is a process that occurs whenever we are faced with an array of alternative choices and we choose one option while rejecting others (Hammond & Arkes, 1986; von Winterfeldt & Edwards, 1986).

Many of our everyday decisions are based on our *estimates of probabilities* of uncertain outcomes. Whether you decide to ask someone for a date, buy a lottery ticket, or plan a weekend camping trip, all depend on estimates of probabilities of success. In some cases our estimates may be based on mathmatical probabilities, but in most cases our estimates are based on past experience. For instance, if the weatherman predicted an 80 percent chance of rain for the weekend you may decide not to go camping. In this case your estimate of success was influenced by a mathmatical probability of rain. Your decision to ask a person for a date, on the other hand, will more likely be influenced by your estimate of success based on past experience. There are several heuristics that appear to influence our estimates of probabilities; in this section we will examine two: representativeness and availability. In addition to these heuristics, we will see how the context in which a problem is formulated or framed influences our decision-making process.

REPRESENTATIVENESS HEURISTIC   Consider the following description of a friend of one of the authors and decide in which of the following two occupations she is most likely to be involved: police officer or host of a local radio talk show oriented to solving relationship problems.

> She is petite, soft spoken, and very gentle. She almost never displays any aggressive or hostile behavior, although she is moderately assertive. She likes to read about psychology and enjoys dealing with people on a personal/emotional level. She is sensitive to others' needs and always willing to listen to viewpoints that may not be her own.

If you were not expecting to be tripped up, you probably guessed that the mystery person earns her living in radio because the description is more representative of your preconceived notion of a person who solves personal problems than of a police officer. The **representative heuristic** strategy entails judging the likelihood of something by intuitively comparing it to our preconceived notion of a few characteristics that represent a given category to us.

For example, most people probably have a stereotype image of a police officer. You might associate characteristics such as "tough," "aggressive," and "nonemotional" with this job. The extent to which our mystery person fits these stereotypes indicates how representative she is of this category: Clearly, the fit is quite poor. On this basis alone, many people would be unlikely to guess that she is indeed a police officer. On the other hand, traits such as "sensitive," "good listener," "likes psychology," and "assertive but not aggressive" do match many people's image of someone who hosts a talk show that focuses on solving relationship problems.

What useful piece of information is likely to be overlooked in the occupation decision problem you just considered? Think about this question before reading on.

Do you think you might have made a different choice if we had suggested that you consider the relative proportion of police officers and talk show hosts in the general population? In the greater metropolitan area of Portland, Oregon, there are over 100 police officers for every talk show host. This information might have influenced you to decide that the woman is probably a police officer (as indeed she is). On the other hand, it might have had no influence at all on your decision.

In one study, college student subjects were presented with a series of brief personality profiles allegedly drawn at random from a sample of 100 attorneys and engineers (Tversky & Kahneman, 1973). They were asked to assign each profile to one job category or the other. Before the task began, they were told the relative proportions of attorneys to engineers in the sample—a proportion that the researchers varied with different groups of subjects, so that it might be 70 to 30 in some trials and 30 to 70 in others. Although you might expect this information about proportions to influence their decisions, it had virtually no impact. If a description stated that a person was politically active, argumentative, and articulate, subjects were likely to assign the profile to the attorney category no matter what the ratio. In this case the subjects overlooked the information about probabilities, basing their decisions instead on how well the profiles matched their own stereotypes.

Another common example of representativeness in estimating outcomes is our tendency to expect randomness in a short run of outcomes. For instance, suppose you observed four heads in four successive tosses of a fair coin. If you had to bet $10 on the fifth coin toss, how would you bet, heads or tails? Many people would bet on tails because "it's about time for tails." In other words, tails seems more representative of the random process than heads even though the outcome on the fifth toss is completely independent of the previous four. This bias in estimation of outcomes is referred to as the *gambler's fallacy*. Do you think that the gambler's fallacy applies to repeated purchases of lottery tickets?

AVAILABILITY HEURISTIC Another factor that influences our estimates is the degree to which we can access information relevant to a decision from our memories. This idea, called the **availability heuristic,** is based on two assumptions: first, that the probability of an event is directly related to the frequency with which it has occurred in the past; and, second, that events occurring more frequently are usually easier to remember than less common events.

For example, our decision to serve hamburgers rather than calamari (squid) to a group of teenagers at a Sunday picnic is no doubt a wise choice based on past experiences with teenagers who enjoy hamburgers but dislike exotic seafood. Similarly, we decide to carry an umbrella on a gray, overcast day because we remember that clouds often bring rain.

On the other hand, the easiest events to remember are not always the most common ones. For example, a person who lives near a nuclear power plant may seriously consider relocating in order to reduce the risk of becoming a victim of a nuclear disaster similar to the one that occurred in 1986 in Chernobyl, U.S.S.R., despite the fact that the chances of its happening are statistically minute. Considering the extensive media attention to the risk of nuclear accidents, it is understandable that many people might decide to move away from the shadow of a nuclear plant. We are not suggesting that this decision would necessarily be irrational. It does, however, illustrate decision making that is influenced by available vivid images rather than by the logical evaluation of probabilities (1973).

This idea was tested in several experiments conducted by Tversky and Kahneman. In one experiment subjects were asked questions like the following:

> Are there more words in the English language that start with the letter "k" or that have the letter "k" as their third letter?

> Which is the more likely cause of death in women — breast cancer or heart attack?

Think about your own answers to these questions before reading on.

In both cases subjects' answers to the questions were generally wrong. When asked about the letter "k," subjects reported that it occurred more frequently when starting a word, not in the third position. Actually the letter "k" occurs much more frequently in the third position but it is much more difficult to identify these words. Likewise, far more women die from heart attacks than from breast cancer, but breast cancer has received more attention in the media than heart attacks. This attention makes it more available to memory, thus influencing our estimate of true probability.

In a similar experiment conducted by Tversky and Kahneman (1973) subjects were asked to read lists of 39 names of well-known people. (The list had 19 names of familiar men and 20 names of familiar women). On one list the names of the women were more famous than the men and on the other list the men were more famous. In both cases subjects overestimated the number of males or females on the lists depending on how famous the names were, even though their frequencies were nearly identical. Why did they do this? According to the researchers, the famous names were more available to memory and therefore influenced subjects' estimates of gender proportions.

FRAMING   An additional factor that can influence subjective probabilities is the way in which a particular problem is formulated or framed. *Framing* entails manipulating the reasoning process by increasing the representativeness or the availability of an outcome (Best, 1992). As we have demonstrated, both representativeness and availability greatly influence our subjective estimates of probability. How can problems be formulated to influence our estimates? Consider the now classic problems proposed by Kahneman and Tversky (1981):

> Imagine the U.S. is preparing for the outbreak of an unusual Asian disease, which is expected to kill 600 people. Two alternative programs to combat the disease have been proposed. Assume that the exact scientific estimates of the consequences of the programs are as follows:
>
> • If Program *A* is adopted, 200 people will be saved.
>
> • If Program *B* is adopted, there is a 1/3 probability that 600 people will be saved and a 2/3 probability that no people will be saved.

Which program would you select if the decision were yours to make? If you were like most (about 72%) of Kahneman and Tversky's subjects you selected Program *A*. Within this frame (where lives are saved or gained), subjects are typically biased towards a sure thing even though statistically the outcomes are the same (200/600 = 1/3 of 600). When decision alternatives are framed in terms of gains, people are more likely to be risk averse. What if the programs were framed as follows:

- If Program *A* is adopted, 400 people will die.

- If Program *B* is adopted, there is a 1/3 probability that nobody will die, and a 2/3 probability that 600 people will die.

In this case the majority (about 78%) of the subjects chose Program *B*, which is the risky choice, even though statistically they are again the same. When decision alternatives are framed in terms of losses, people are more likely to be risk prone.

Suppose that you were given the following decision alternatives framed in terms of gains:

A. You can choose to have $200 immediately, or

B. You can choose to have a 40 percent chance of winning $500.

Which of the above alternatives is most attractive? Now consider similar alternatives framed in terms of losses:

A. You can choose to give me $200 immediately, or

B. You can choose a 40 percent chance of giving me $500.

If you are like most people, you would select *A* when it is framed in terms of gains (risk averse in terms of gains) and *B* when framed in terms of losses (risk prone in terms of losses). Although most of the research presented here is concerned with hypothetical gains and losses, people and other animals appear to behave as Kahneman and Tversky describe even when the gains and losses are real (Rachlin et al., 1986). One of the authors has even demonstrated these framing effects with psychology students "gaining" or "losing" extra credit points!

In the previous section we have seen how probability estimates effect our decisions. In some instances our probability estimates can be inaccurate, leading us to undesirable decision outcomes. Perhaps now that you are aware of the potential shortcomings of your decision processes you will be less likely to be influenced by faulty judgments. On the positive side, representativeness and availability can facilitate decision making and thus serve as heuristics in decision-making processes. In many cases they lead to quick and accurate decisions which serve us well most of the time (cf. Best, 1992).

In this section we have examined several important factors involved in problem solving and decision making by people. In the next section we look at some recent developments in cognitive and computer science in the area of *artificial intelligence*. Will the design of intelligent computers provide us with helpful insights into human cognition? Can computers use heuristics as well as algorithms to solve problems and make decisions?

ARTIFICIAL INTELLIGENCE

Artificial intelligence (AI) is a very broad term which includes a number of approaches to problem solving using computers. In this section we will examine two AI applications to problem solving: expert systems and general problem solvers. AI applications involve several of the problem-solving approaches already described for people, including heuristics and logic. The chess-playing computer Deep Thought uses heuristics based on detailed analyses of expert chess players as opposed to algorithmic search in determining moves.

EXPERT SYSTEMS

Expert systems are computer programs designed to help solve specific problems. For instance, **Deep Thought** is an expert system designed to play chess. Although the design of the program was influenced by strategies and decision processes (heuristics) of expert chess players, Deep Thought was not designed to simulate human players. Rather, it was designed to beat experts by outcomputing them. That is, by computing the outcomes of thousands of possible moves based on the heuristics programmed into it.

Another example of an expert system is the computer program MYCIN that was developed at Stanford University in 1975. **MYCIN** was designed to assist physicians in making diagnoses. A physician enters pertinent symptoms, results of laboratory tests, and patient history. If the computer needs additional information it requests it. MYCIN can diagnose different infectious diseases, prescribe medication, and check for possible drug interactions with other patient medications. This expert system was based on about 250 rules that were identified after extensive interviews with physicians. MYCIN was designed so that the rules could be continually modified as new circumstances arose. For instance, if a patient had a particular allergic reaction, certain medications would not be prescribed unless the potential benefit outweighed the severity of the reaction to the drug.

Expert systems have been designed for a large number of applications in research and industry. They are particularly useful where extensive knowledge within a specific domain is required, like playing chess, diagnosing infectious diseases, and scanning and identifying bad computer boards. Unlike their human counterparts, however, expert systems lack general reasoning abilities and common sense. Although MYCIN was surprisingly powerful, like other expert systems, its expertise alone was not enough. If it were asked about diseases or medical conditions outside of its domain of infectious diseases, it was at a loss. Other AI approaches to problem solving have attempted to design more general problem-solving computers.

GENERAL PROBLEM SOLVERS

Unlike expert systems, **general problem solvers** are being designed to model or simulate human problem-solving abilities. Perhaps the best-known general problem solver is the computer program SOAR developed by Newell, Laird, and Rosenbloom. **SOAR** is a computer program designed to solve problems using heuristics like the means-ends analysis discussed earlier. Programmed with a variety of heuristics and the ability to learn from mistakes, SOAR has recently been proposed as a general (unified) theory of cognition (Newell, 1988; 1992).

How can a computer program become a theory of human cognition? What advantages does a computer program have over plain English? Think about these questions before reading on.

According to Newell, a computer program is the most natural way to do what we want a theory of cognition to do—account for the information processing we do in our brains. Computers are very much like brains in that they process information, even though their organization and structure are quite different. SOAR and other general problem solvers must be more than sets of conventional programming algorithms defining precise procedures for a problem-solving task. Instead, SOAR is a program that is quite flexible. When it encounters an impasse where a rule does not apply, it defines a new rule to obviate the impasse, much like trial-and-error reasoning which draws upon an extensive body of knowledge. The next time SOAR encounters a similar situation it remembers its new rule, thus avoiding the impasse. This ability to learn from experience gives SOAR an individualistic approach to solving a variety of problems. SOAR is certainly an impressive program, yet whether it will serve as a general theory of cognition remains to be seen. At the very least SOAR will provide years of valuable debate between scientists on the qualities and characteristics of human cognition.

LANGUAGE

Our last topic, the ability to use language, is perhaps the most profound indicator of the power of human cognition (Miller, 1981). Although other animals, such as bees, birds, dolphins, monkeys, and apes, demonstrate complex means of communication, the degree of abstraction in human language is far greater. Without language, our ability to communicate our thoughts would be limited to the basic kinds of meanings that we could indicate by nonverbal gestures. We would not be able to establish complex social structures and pass on knowledge from generation to generation. Our ability to remember, to reason, and to solve problems would also be severely curtailed, since so much of human information processing and thinking occurs at the abstract level of language symbols.

Language is the primary means by which we communicate with one another. This is not to say that language and communication are the same thing. An animal on the prairie that emits a cry of warning as a predator approaches, or a bee signaling the direction of a food source, are communicating messages. However, it is the ability to use abstract symbols to convey original messages that lifts human language to its heights.

Psycholinguistics is the study of how we translate sounds and symbols into meaning, and of what processes are involved in the acquisition and use of language. Psycholinguists have devoted considerable effort to studying the structure and rules of language. We begin our discussion at this level.

PSYCHOLINGUISTICS

THE STRUCTURE AND RULES OF LANGUAGE   The people we talk to each day are able to make sense out of what we say to them because we all string sounds together according to a common set of rules. There are actually four levels of rules —phonemes, morphemes, syntax, and semantics—and psycholinguists analyze languages at each of these four levels.

All languages follow the same four levels of rules—phonemes, morphemes, syntax, and semantics.

Phonemes The basic structural elements of spoken language are called **phonemes.** All languages are made up of individual sounds that are recognized as distinct or different. The English language has about 45 phonemes; other languages may have as few as 15 or as many as 85 (Solso, 1991). Most of the phonemes in the English language correspond to the consonant and vowel sounds. For example, in the word *tap* we may identify three separate phonemes, corresponding to the consonant sounds *t* and *p* and the vowel sound *a*. (The letter *a* represents four different vowel sounds, as in *tap*, *pray*, *care*, and *water*.) Some phonemes are represented by letter combinations, such as the *th* sound in *the* and the *sh* in *shout*. In some cases different letters represent the same sounds, such as the *a* in *bay* and the *ei* in *sleigh*. Thus phonemes are not identical to the letters of the alphabet, even though individual letters correspond to many of the sounds unique to our language. Phonemes can be combined in numerous ways to create literally thousands of different words.

In order to represent ideas in our thought processes or to convey meaningful information, we must combine phonemes in ways that produce acceptable words. For instance, you quickly recognize that *dzashp* and *heeoiay* are not acceptable sound combinations in English even though they are pronounceable.

Morphemes A **morpheme** is the smallest unit of meaning in a given language. In the English language almost all morphemes consist of combinations of two or more phonemes (exceptions are the pronoun *I* and the article *a*). Many morphemes, like *book*, *learn*, and *read*, are words that can stand alone. Other morphemes must be attached as prefixes or suffixes to root words. For example, the word *replays* is a word that consists of three morphemes: *play*, which can stand alone; the prefix *re*, meaning "again" or "anew"; and the suffix *s*, which indicates "more than one."

The manner in which morphemes are formed and used also follows distinct rules. In the English language, for example, no more than three consonant sounds can be strung together in one morpheme. Rules also govern the manner in which suffixes can be added to form plurals. Thus the plural forms of *hat* and *bus* are *hats* and *buses*. Morphemes also have fixed positions in the structure of language: A football broadcaster who repeats a critical play for home viewers is presenting a *replay*, not a *playre*.

Syntax Besides learning how to recognize phonemes and use morphemes, we also learn to use **syntax** (commonly known as grammar), the set of language rules that governs how words can be combined to form meaningful phrases and sentences. The sentence "She purchased the dog small" is immediately recognizable as an improper sentence because one of the rules of English syntax is that adjectives generally precede the nouns they modify ("small dog"). If a Spanish-speaking person read this same sentence, translated word for word into Spanish, he or she would consider it to be grammatically correct, since adjectives normally come after nouns, according to Spanish rules of syntax.

Semantics Finally, language is also characterized by a system of rules that helps us to determine the meaning of words and sentences. The study of meaning in language is called **semantics.** For example, sentences may be syntactically correct but semantically incorrect. The grammatically correct sentence, "The dorm food is emotionally disturbed" is quite bizarre from the standpoint of semantics, for food cannot be emotionally disturbed (although some dorm food can lead to disturbed emotions!).

THEORIES OF LANGUAGE ACQUISITION

How do we learn all of these rules? A number of theories have been proposed to explain how we acquire language. Those explanations vary considerably in their emphasis on environment versus innate biological mechanisms.

THE LEARNING PERSPECTIVE At one end of the continuum are theories of language acquisition that emphasize the role of learning. According to behaviorist B. F. Skinner (1957) and social learning theorist Albert Bandura (1971), children learn to shape sounds into words and words into sentences through processes of selective reinforcement and imitation.

This learning perspective is supported by research evidence. For example, babies whose parents reinforce their early attempts at meaningful sounds do tend to vocalize more than institutionalized children who receive less attention (Brodbeck & Irwin, 1946). Small children often imitate the words they hear their parents say, and this behavior is often reinforced. Selective reinforcement and behavioral modeling techniques have also been successful in teaching language to emotionally disturbed or developmentally delayed children (Lovass, 1973, 1987).

Parents play a very important role in shaping language acquisition in their children. Jean Berko Gleason (1990), a Boston University psychologist, is an authority on language development. Her primary research focus has been on how social interaction between children and adults (especially parents) shapes the acquisition of language. Gleason believes that social relationships may be necessary to activate the process of children learning to communicate through language.

The learning perspective does not explain all aspects of human language acquisition. For example, many of the words children spontaneously utter are their own inventions, not imitations of a model. Where do they come from if they are not learned? Again, children typically do not imitate verbally exactly what they hear. Instead, they put words together in their own, often unique, way. Furthermore, even though parents seldom correct their children's syntax, children usually begin to form grammatically correct sentences before formal schooling begins (Stine & Bohannon, 1983; Tartter, 1986). Most importantly, it has been demonstrated that language acquisition follows an invariable sequence among children all over the world, under highly variable conditions (Brown, 1973; Nelson, 1981; Rice, 1989; Tartter, 1986). This finding suggests that there is something innate about language, which is exactly the position championed by psycholinguist Noam Chomsky.

THE NATIVISTIC PERSPECTIVE Just as children are genetically programmed to follow the developmental sequence of sitting, crawling, and walking, Chomsky (1965, 1968, 1980) maintains that the human brain is also programmed to learn speech according to a sequential pattern. This view of language acquisition, sometimes referred to as *nativism*, does not suggest that our brains are programmed to learn a specific language such as English or French. Instead, it argues that a newborn's brain is organized with the ability to recognize phonemes and morphemes and to learn the basic rules of grammar and semantics. Chomsky labeled this innate ability to learn language the **language acquisition device (LAD)**. He believes that without this innate mechanism we would be overwhelmed by the virtually unlimited number of possible variations in combinations of sounds and words, and thus would be unable to understand the rules of language.

How can we possibly understand this limitless number of creative sentences? For instance, how do we know that the meanings of the following sentences are the same: "The young boy chased the girl" and "The girl was chased by the young boy." According to Chomsky our capacity to understand that these sentences have the same meaning is explained not by learning or imitation, but by an innate capacity to grasp the rules that allow us to form sentences and transform them into other sentences with the same meaning. These rules are referred to as *transformational grammar.* Our understanding of the meaning of these two sentences prevails even though the arrangement of the words or morphemes is

Babies whose parents reinforce early attempts at language tend to vocalize more than children who receive less attention.

altered. Chomsky argues that meaning is contained in the *deep structure*, or underlying form, of a sentence, not its surface structure. *Surface structure* refers to the superficial appearance of the sentence. In our example above the surface structure of the sentences was altered but the deep structure remained the same.

This genetic or nativist position has been supported by a variety of data, and "there is strong evidence that the process of learning human speech is largely guided by innate abilities and tendencies" (Gould & Marler, 1987). Certainly, the fact that all normal children progress through the same sequence of language acquisition suggests some basic, genetically shaped biological program. In contrast, according to the learning position we should find considerable individual differences in patterns of language development because of the wide variations that occur in learning histories of people from widely divergent environments. Further support for the nativist position is provided by evidence that human infants recognize virtually all of the consonant sounds characteristic of human speech (Eimas, 1985).

Have you ever had an occasion to listen to preschool-age identical twins communicate with each other? One of the authors attended graduate school with the father of identical twin daughters. These girls, approximately age four, had developed a language that was completely unintelligible to anyone else. Nevertheless, observations of the animated way in which they used their strange lingo indicated they were clearly communicating thoughts that had meaning and clarity for both. Psycholinguists have frequently observed this phenomenon among sets of twins (Carelli & Benelli, 1986; Malmstrom & Silva, 1986). The key finding of these observational studies is that these special languages are not a mere variation on the common language(s) spoken by others in their environments. Furthermore, the private language of twins appears to have the characteristics of other languages, including nouns, verbs, and a definite syntax. Psycholinguists such as Noam Chomsky believe such findings support the view that humans are born with a predisposition for syntax. How else might we explain why the private language of twin sets contains a structure comparable to all known language?

Twins often communicate with their own private language. Originally these twins were believed to be severely retarded, but later it was discovered that their "gibberish" was intelligent and that they understood both English and German.

INTERACTIONIST PERSPECTIVE Most contemporary psychologists look to both the learning position and the nativistic approach to supply pieces of the puzzle of human language. According to the interactionist perspective, language acquisition is the joint product of innate organization and the individual's linguistic environment. Learning helps explain how children learn specific rules of grammar, and it also clarifies why language acquisition may be retarded among children raised in environments that offer few opportunities to observe, imitate, and receive reinforcement. In addition, learning appears to contribute to our rich vocabularies. At the same time genetics explains not only the universal developmental sequence of language acquisition, but also the ease with which children acquire one or more languages despite the enormous complexity of language rules. It seems, then, that genetics and environment interact in some complex fashion that Vivien Tartter (1986) calls a tuneable blueprint to provide us with the necessary foundations for learning language.

NEWBORN LANGUAGE COMPETENCY That "tuneable blueprint" can be traced through several stages in a universal developmental sequence in which children learn language. This section presents a typical timetable. Note that there is considerable individual variation within the normal range of the stages outlined here.

A large body of evidence indicates that human infants are genetically organized to understand and process human speech sounds (Eimas, 1975; Flavell, 1985; Gibson & Spelke, 1983). Even in the earliest stages of infancy, children are able to distinguish speech from nonspeech sounds, and they seem particularly tuned in to speech (de Villiers & de Villiers, 1979). Thus a one-day-old baby rhythmically moves her or his body in accordance with the surrounding speech sounds (Condon & Sander, 1974), and a three-day-old can distinguish the voice of mother from strangers (DeCasper & Fifer, 1980).

By the age of one month, infants are able to distinguish between phonemes and other sounds, even when they are physically and acoustically almost the same (Aslin et al., 1983; Eimas, 1975). This apparently innate perceptual ability may be the portion of Chomsky's language acquisition device that allows children to understand the phonological code of whatever language they are exposed to.

EARLY VOCALIZATIONS *Crying* All children typically progress through the same stages of sound production during their first year (Tartter, 1986). Initially, newborns emit only one sound, that of crying (Hopkins & Palthe, 1987). Even though crying is clearly a very rudimentary form of communication, research has shown that parents of both sexes are generally able to distinguish between taped cries of their own offspring and those of other infants (Roberts, 1987). Some people, particularly parents, also believe that they can distinguish between cries of hunger, pain, or anger by noting different patterns of pitch and intensity. If this were true, we would have to conclude that cries at an early age exhibit semanticity, or special meaning.

You have probably observed parents remarking, in response to the cries of their babies, that "He sounds hungry" or "She's mad because I am ignoring her." Can parents actually determine when a cry means "I'm hungry," "I hurt," or "I'm annoyed?" How would you investigate this question? Can you think of another explanation for why parents often seem able to determine the reasons for their infants' cries? Give these questions some thought before reading on.

One simple way to determine whether parents can distinguish cries in different contexts would be to record the cries of infants in situations where they are clearly hungry, frustrated, or in pain, and then to play the tapes for parents and ask them to identify their baby's condition. An experiment using this methodology demonstrated that parents could not distinguish between different prerecorded cries (Dale, 1976). Under natural conditions, however, they are likely to make much better judgments because they have considerable additional information: They know how long it has been since the last feeding, or that the infant is due for a diaper change, and so forth. A more recent study provided additional evidence supporting the conclusion that infants' cry sounds communicate information about the general distress level of the infant better than information about specific causes (Gustafson & Harris, 1990, p. 144).

Cooing and Babbling Sometime between four and six weeks, infants enter the second stage of vocalization, called *cooing*, in which they emit sounds of pleasure when they are happy. At about six months, sometimes earlier, there is another significant stage referred to as *babbling*. The baby begins to utter repeatedly a variety of simple one-syllable consonant and vowel sounds like da-da-da, ba-ba-ba, or ma-ma-ma. In the first few months of babbling, the infant emits both sounds that are used in the adult language and those that are not. Vivien Tartter (1986) notes that infants at this stage appear "to be playing with the sounds, enjoying the tactile and auditory feel of vocalization" (p. 337).

At about nine or 10 months the babbling becomes intelligible, as babies begin to imitate more purposefully the sounds of the speech of others, even though they may not yet understand them. At this point in language development, these vocalizations begin to approximate the phonemes of the language they hear every day. Thus cooing and babbling provide babies with a basic repertoire of sounds, laying the foundation for real speech.

FIRST WORDS Children usually produce their first one-word utterances sometime around their first birthday (Rice, 1989). They have already learned that sounds can be associated with meanings, and now they begin to use sounds to convey meaning. First words are usually very simple, and they often refer to concrete things like familiar people ("mama," "dada"), toys ("ball"), consumables ("juice"), common implements ("cup"), animals ("da" or "dog"), words for greeting ("hi"), and a few action words ("eat," "up," "more") (Clark, 1983). These words may be oversimplifications of the actual words, but they nevertheless qualify as words if they are used consistently to refer to particular objects or events (thus "ba" for bottle or "nana" for banana).

A child may also use single words in a way that indicates much more. For example, a toddler who tugs on your leg and pleads "up" is probably conveying the meaning "Pick me up," just as a child who points to a balloon and says "ba" with a rising inflection at the end is asking, "Is that a ball?" These single-word utterances designed to express a complete thought are called *holophrases*.

CONDENSED SPEECH Within about six months after the first word is spoken, children develop a vocabulary of about 50 words. Sometime between 18 and 24 months they generally produce their first sentences, which usually consist of two-word utterances like "More milk" or "There ball." These early primitive sentences typically leave out articles (such as "a" and "the"), prepositions ("to," "on"), conjunctions ("and"), and auxiliary verbs ("can," "will") (Flavell, 1985). This pattern of condensed speech is simply a reduction of complex speech and it is typical of the first sentences spoken by children all over the world (Brown, 1973). Young children also have similar meaning in their short utterances, no matter what culture they belong to (Flavell, 1985).

Harvard's Roger Brown (1973) has extensively reviewed data from a number of diverse cultures to determine what early meanings are expressed in children's two-word sentences. He concludes that most two-word sentences are designed to express any of eight common semantic or meaning relations (see Table 10.3).

EXPANDED LANGUAGE From age two, language development progresses rapidly. Children expand their vocabulary at the rate of several hundred words for every six months of age. Children seem to be remarkably adept at determining the meaning of new words they hear from the context in which the word was spoken (Markman, 1987). Two-word sentences give way to meaningful sentences that may lack absolutely correct grammatical structure but nevertheless display a syntax that approximates proper language structure (Valian, 1986). Children begin to make a shift from simple sentence grammar to a more complex syntax sometime between ages two and three (Bloom & Capatides, 1987). By age four or five, most children have learned most of the basic grammatical rules for combining nouns, adjectives, and verbs into meaningful sentences.

As they learn to combine morphemes into more complex words and into still more complex sentences, a number of errors typically occur regardless of what language is being learned. For instance, when children first learn the basic rules of grammar (such as that plurals are formed by adding an *s* and the past tense of many verbs is formed by adding a *d* sound to the end) they may tend to overgeneralize these rules to instances where they do not apply. Thus *oxes* may be used instead of *oxen, deers* instead of *deer,* and "I sleeped in the bed" instead of "I slept in the bed." Children may also overgeneralize by applying concept words too broadly. For instance, a child who learns to recognize police officers by their uniforms may call every person in uniform "police."

Another common error in the early stages of sentence usage is oversimplification—using just enough words to convey a message, without being syntactically correct. For example, when a three-year-old wants to play in the park she might say to her mother, "I go park". Later on she learns to add the articles, prepositions, and other parts of speech that are necessary to form grammatically correct sentences such as "I want to go to the park." Most children are quite successful at mastering these refinements: By the time they enter school, they usually have

TABLE 10.3 *Common Semantic Relations in First Sentences*

DESCRIPTION	EXAMPLE
They name an *actor and an action*	"Daddy eat"
They *modify a noun*	"Bad Doggy"
They *indicate possession*	"Mommy shoe"
They *specify a location*	"Dog outside"
They describe an *action and a location*	"Go home"
They name an *action* and an *object* (leaving out the subject, eg., I)	"Eat lunch"
They describe an *actor and an object* (leaving out the verb, eg., eat)	"Mommy lunch"

SOURCE: Adopted from Gleason and Ratner, 1993.

a good comprehension not only of the general rules of their language, but also of the exceptions.

PRAGMATICS OF LANGUAGE   The rules of sentence structure are not the only rules children learn as they develop language competency. In addition, there are a variety of extralinguistic and pragmatic rules that are also necessary for conversation. For instance, along with sentence structure, a child needs to learn how to develop and maintain a conversation, adjust speech level, react to pauses in speech, and how to intonate speech sounds. Research suggests that children continue to develop these linguistic competencies through feedback from listeners as well as through listening to older models throughout their early school years (Wilkinson et al., 1984).

As children continue to grow and become more interested in their surroundings, we see the language interactions with their parents becoming necessarily more complex. The outcome of this tutorial process is perhaps one of the most impressive developmental feats a child acquires—that is, the ability to communicate (Ashcraft, 1989).

BRAIN MECHANISMS FOR LANGUAGE

In the preceeding sections we have assumed that language exists at two levels: at the level of abstract language symbols in the external world, and at a level within the brain where these abstract symbols and their rules of combination are represented. In this section we will examine several of the major brain structures where language appears to be represented and processed.

Most of what we know about the role of the brain on language processing comes from patients who have suffered from brain injuries or strokes. Sometimes these lesions produce disturbances in the comprehension and formulation of speech referred to as *aphasias*. Aphasias can also occur in nonvocal sign languages. As you recall from Chapter 3, we described two major language areas that are involved in speech: Broca's area and Wernicke's area (see Figure 10.9).

BROCA'S AREA   Damage to **Broca's area,** a small part of the frontal lobe in the left cortex, results in the inability to speak fluently, and is referred to as *Broca's aphasia*. If the damage is more severe and also includes parts of the thalamus and basal ganglia, a more severe long-lasting speech impairment results. This suggests that fluent speech involves all of these areas (Alexander, Benson, & Stuss, 1989).

Another common characteristic of Broca's aphasia is the inability to organize words so sentences follow proper grammatical rules. In addition, patients underuse or fail to use conjunctions *(and, or, if)*, prepositions *(to and from)* and auxiliary verbs *(will and did)*. For instance a patient might say "Go I home tomorrow" instead of "I will go home tomorrow" (Damasio, 1992).

WERNICKE'S AREA   Damage to Wernicke's area, on the other hand, does not disrupt the ability to produce speech, but it does disrupt the ability to comprehend both verbal and written speech. **Wernicke's area** is located in the left temporal cortex below the Sylvian fissure (see Figure 10.9). In many cases people with *Wernicke's aphasia* speak fluently and articulately, but they have difficulty finding appropriate words and understanding speech. A typical sentence produced by an individual with Wernicke's aphasia when asked to name a common object like an apron might sound like this: "Um. . . you see I can't, I can I can barely do; he would give me sort of umm. . ." (Kalat, 1992, p. 179). In this case language is unintelligible because of inappropriate word choice. Often Wernicke's aphasia includes the inability to comprehend language from others.

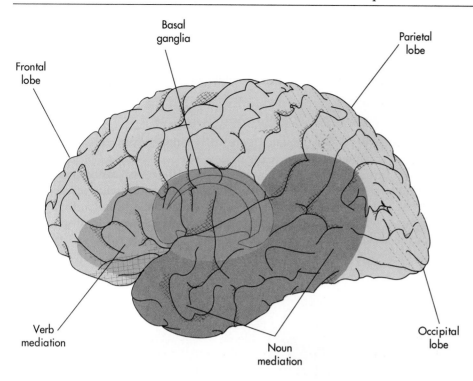

Frontal lobe

Basal ganglia

Parietal lobe

Verb mediation

Noun mediation

Occipital lobe

FIGURE 10.9
The Left Hemisphere of the Brain
This illustration identifies several important language areas of the brain.

Other researchers have identified language disorders that appear to be much more specific. For instance, patients referred to as A.N. and L.R. have difficulty with some concepts; when shown pictures of objects like body parts, vehicles, animals, plants, tools, or human faces, these patients recognize what they are looking at, but have difficulty retrieving names for these entities. They can even define the object's function, habitat, or value. If shown a picture of a raccoon, they might say "Oh! I know what it is—it is a nasty animal. It will come and rummage in your backyard and get into the garbage. The eyes and the rings in the tail give it away. I know it, but I cannot say the name" (Damasio & Damasio, 1992). A.N. and L.R.'s, symptoms, as well as other patients' with similar problems with proper nouns, have been attributed to damage in the anterior and middle regions of the left temporal lobe (see Figure 10.9).

Although patients with temporal lobe damage often have difficulty using nouns to name people and other objects, they have little or no difficulty using verbs. Evidence from PET studies (described in Chapter 3) and patients with brain damage suggest that verb use involves the left frontal lobe (Figure 10.9). People with left frontal lobe damage may have difficulty generating appropriate verbs. For instance, a patient may not be able to generate the verb *running* when shown a picture of a person running.

These studies suggest that the use and comprehension of language involve interconnections between areas within the left temporal lobe, the posterior frontal lobe, and the basal ganglia. Furthermore, different components of speech and grammar appear to be mediated by specific regions within the left hemisphere of the brain.

In the past few years tremendous progress has been made in understanding the brain mechanisms for language. Much more research with both brain-damaged and normal people will be necessary, however, before conclusions about specific brain structures and their role in language can be made.

We have briefly touched upon several important aspects of language processing including its structure, its acquisition, and neural bases. However, a topic of such importance to human behavior deserves much more than we can provide in this context. The analysis of language at all levels continues to be both an active and a vital aspect of psychology and neuroscience. The final section of this chapter examines the topic of language in nonhuman animals. Do other animals possess language?

IS LANGUAGE UNIQUE TO HUMANS?

We have been discussing human language, but nonhuman animals also have methods of communicating. A walk in any forest is likely to produce a cacophony of birdcalls that communicate danger. Monkeys have been shown to produce different sounds to indicate danger approaching from above, such as an eagle, versus danger from below, such as a prowling panther (Marler, 1967). Bees communicate with each other about the nature and location of food sources by engaging in an intricate waggle dance (Moffett, 1990; von Frisch, 1974) (see Figure 10.10). Studies with vervet monkeys indicate that they have a rudimentary

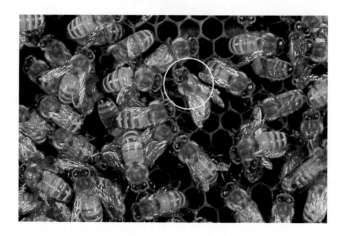

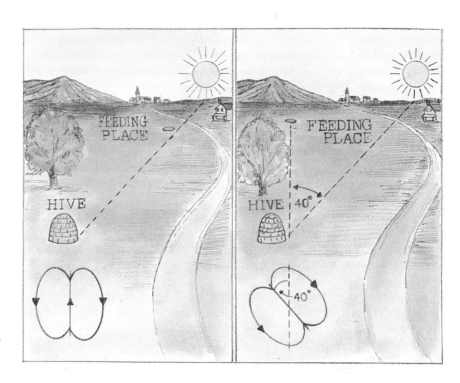

FIGURE 10.10

Honey Bees Communicate the Direction and Distance to a Source of Food

semantic system where specific calls appear to convey special meaning (Seyfarth and Cheney, 1992). Do these methods of communicating qualify as a true language in the sense that they contain the same features as human language? To answer this question, we first need to identify the primary criteria or attributes of all human languages: generativity, specialization, arbitrariness, displacement, and novelty. Table 10.4 defines these five criteria.

If we strictly interpret the criteria in the table, it is quite clear that birdcalls, monkey vocalizations, dolphin whistles, or bee dances do not qualify as language. But this does not rule out the possibility that nonhuman animals may have the ability to learn to use language to communicate abstract thoughts and ideas. Considerable research with apes, in fact, has challenged the view that only humans can communicate with abstract symbols.

Some of the earliest research attempted to teach chimpanzees to talk. These experiments were essentially failures, although one chimpanzee did learn to vocalize four words: "mama," "papa," "cup," and "up" (Hayes, 1951; Kellogg & Kellogg, 1933). Later experiments used another strategy. Speculating that chimpanzees simply did not have the vocal apparatus to communicate verbally, Allen and Beatrice Gardner (1969, 1975) took another route; they taught American Sign Language (ASL) to a chimpanzee named Washoe.

The Gardners began training Washoe when she was eight months old. They used a variety of methods, including modeling and physical guidance (actually moving her hands) and applying operant reinforcement. Washoe spent all of her waking hours with a trainer who communicated with her only through ASL. After four years of training, she could use 132 signs.

Not only was Washoe adept at imitating her trainer's signs, but she also seemed to create her own communications. For example, when she was menaced by an aggressive rhesus monkey, she signed "dirty monkey," and when she saw a swan for the first time, she signed "water bird." Since she already knew the signs for water and bird, her trainer speculated that she understood the meaning of the words and was thus able to combine them creatively. Washoe was never exposed to training in syntax, but she occasionally produced syntactically meaningful phrases like "gimme tickle" (chimpanzees enjoy being tickled). Washoe even

TABLE 10.4 *Attributes of Human Languages*

1. *Generativity:* The ability to provide for a huge variety of meanings in an unlimited number of utterances.
2. *Specialization:* The only purpose of the language is to communicate information to others.
3. *Arbitrariness:* The combinations of sounds selected to refer to objects or events is purely arbitrary. Thus our English word *book* might just as well have been *zock*.
4. *Displacement:* Language can be generated in the absence of any eliciting stimulus. Thus humans can talk about dangerous dogs when no dogs are present, whereas a monkey vocalizes a sound indicating danger only when a predator is observed. Displacement also refers to the ability to communicate about things in the past and future, not just the present.
5. *Novelty:* Humans are able to express themselves with novel phrases and sentences that they have never heard before. Thus human language is more than mere memorization and repetition of word strings.

SOURCE: Adapted from Hockett, 1960.

seemed to be able to string words together in a creative and meaningful fashion, as evidenced by such requests as "You me go out please."

Other studies have used varying approaches, also with success. Psychologist David Premack (1971) used operant and classical conditioning to teach a chimpanzee named Sarah to associate pieces of plastic with different aspects of her environment. The plastic pieces, which differed in size, shape, and color, had magnetic backing so that they could be placed on a metal "language board" to form vertical sentences. Sarah learned a large number of symbols indicating names of trainers, objects, properties of objects (like "color of"), and prepositions; she also learned to combine words in an apparently meaningful fashion (such as "Mary give apple Sarah"). Premack and his associates believed that Sarah could also learn concepts. For example, when she was asked to compare a banana and a yellow ball, she arranged symbols on the magnetic board to indicate "the same." (This correct answer requires an appreciation of the concept of color.)

At the Yerkes Primate Research Center in Atlanta, Georgia, another study attempted to teach chimpanzees "Yerkish", a computer language. The star pupil of this study, Lana, was raised in a room with a computer that she learned to use to obtain food, drink, and so forth. Each key was labeled with a particular symbol that stood for an object or action. (For example, a circle with a dot inside signified juice.) Lana and other chimpanzees learned to use the computer to type requests, answer questions, and even to engage in a complex game with another chimpanzee which required them to use the computer symbols to make statements. Some of Lana's keyboard talk was quite amazing. For example, one day she observed that her trainer had an orange that she wanted, but Lana did not have a symbol for orange in her language repertoire. So Lana improvised and typed "Tim give apple which is orange" (Rumbaugh, 1977; Savage-Rumbaugh et al., 1980, 1983).

The evidence we have just discussed, as well as findings from several other studies, seems to suggest that language is not unique to humans. From your reading of the ape studies and a review of Table 10.4, what is your conclusion? Take a moment to consider this question before reading on.

Upon examination of Table 10.4 it appears that ape communication comes close to our criteria for language. For instance, the criteria of arbitrariness and perhaps novelty have been demonstrated in apes. The criteria of displacement, generating language in the absence of a stimulus, however, has not been adequately demonstrated. One criterion implied by displacement is that humans have a theory of "mind" and can attribute beliefs, knowledge, and emotions to others (Seyfarth and Cheney, 1992). In other words, people can talk about an object in its absence indicating we attribute knowledge of the object to another person. Our warning a child not to venture into the street until the light changes is prompted not by his or her behavior, but by a lack of knowledge about streets we attribute to them. Likewise children learn to attribute beliefs, knowledge, and emotions to others and behave in ways to change or maintain them. To date there have been no convincing studies to indicate that communication by other animals meets this criterion.

To do justice to this issue, we must return again to Clever Hans. According to some critics of ape language studies, the impressive results that we have just described simply show that chimpanzees can learn to respond to trainers in a manner similar to Clever Hans. Some support for this contention is provided by the frequent observation that when apes are tested by people who either are not familiar with the particular language symbols being used or do not know the correct answers, they consistently perform far more poorly than when they are tested by familiar trainers (Tartter, 1986). However, we cannot ignore the fact that this reduced performance may be no different from the common tendency of children to perform worse for strangers than for people they know.

Evidence that a chimpanzee's signs may be nothing more than imitations of a trainer's signs was provided by Herbert Terrace (1979) who carefully analyzed videotapes of chimpanzees signing. Terrace concluded that his top performer, a chimpanzee named Nim Chimpsky (named after linguist Noam Chomsky), was able to use an impressive number of combinations of 125 basic signs, but only in imitative response to his trainer, and not as a means of creatively communicating new information.

It has also been suggested that language researchers, anxious to be vindicated for their enormous investments in time and effort in training their chimpanzees, may fall victim to what has been called the generous interpretation pitfall (Tartter, 1986). We all have a tendency to interpret the words of others as if we were emitting them ourselves. Thus when Washoe signed "water bird" it was natural for a human observer to assume that she was being creative in naming a novel stimulus, a swan, by combining two other words. It has been pointed out, however, that a less generous interpretation would need to acknowledge the possibility that Washoe was first naming the *water* in which the swan was swimming, and then naming the animal, *bird*, both words with which she was familiar (Terrace et al., 1979).

You may agree that the accomplishments of Washoe and Sarah can probably be explained by the Clever Hans phenomenon or by their trainers' generous interpretations, but significant questions are still raised by the Yerkes Primate Research Center studies of computer communications. How can these results be explained? According to behaviorists such as B. F. Skinner and his colleagues at Harvard, the so-called language-driven behaviors of chimpanzees may be explained simply by common principles of learning, such as imitation and reinforcement. They see little difference between pigeons pushing buttons in sequence to get a grain reward and chimpanzees stringing together a series of symbols to obtain a payoff of juice or a tickling session. Epstein, Lanza, and Skinner (1980) used operant conditioning to train two pigeons, Jack and Jill, to perform language-like behaviors in which one pecked colored keys to answer a question selected by the pecks of its partner. These researchers noted, "We have thus demonstrated that pigeons can learn to engage in sustained and natural conversation without human intervention, and that one pigeon can transmit information to another entirely through the use of symbols" (p. 545).

In all, much of the data obtained from the ape language studies can be explained by simpler principles, such as the Clever Hans phenomenon or learning principles—none of which require us to assume that apes have language capabilities. Certainly if we confine our conception of true language ability to the criteria in Table 10.4, we must conclude that humans alone possess language. However, if we define language as the ability to convey meaning through the use of symbols, it is clear that apes and other animals also have this ability. Because this topic has generated considerable debate over the years we refer you to the *Research Perspectives* discussion between Terrace and the Gardners at the end of this chapter .

THINKING AND LANGUAGE

We conclude this chapter with some observations about the relationship between thinking and language. As we discovered earlier, thinking is certainly more than mere silent language or talking to ourselves. It has also been conclusively demonstrated that thought can occur without language (Weiskrantz, 1988). However, the mental imagery we may use in thinking certainly involves language, and a great deal of thinking is in verbal form.

The two questions most widely pondered by cognitive psychologists as they consider the nature of the interrelationship between thinking and language are (1) Does language structure thought? and (2) Does thought structure language? We address both of these questions in the following paragraphs.

DOES LANGUAGE STRUCTURE THOUGHT?

The fact that much of our thinking occurs at the abstract level of language symbols suggests the possibility that language might determine how we think. Anthropologists who study the cultures of different societies in the underdeveloped world have widely reported that languages spoken by people in these diverse societies often have little in common with the more familiar English and European languages. Furthermore, people in these societies are often described as thinking about their worlds in ways very different from Europeans and Americans. Linguist Benjamin Whorf (1956) argued that these variations in the way members of different societies view the world are a function of fundamental differences in the structure of language in these highly varied cultures. He formalized this theoretical conception in what has become known as the **linguistic-relativity hypothesis**—the idea that the language of a particular culture determines the content of thoughts among members of that culture and the way these people perceive and think about their world. For most of us, who speak only English, language may seem to be more a vehicle for expressing our thoughts than a shaper of thinking. Nevertheless, Whorf maintained that people think differently in different languages.

Whorf offered a number of observations to support his contention. For example, he suggested that the American Hopi Indians have difficulty thinking about the past because their language does not provide a past tense. Other evidence marshaled by Whorf is the difference in the ways in which Eskimos and English-speaking people view snow. There is only one English word for snow, whereas Eskimos use several different words, depending on whether the snow is slushy, packed hard, and so forth. Whorf argued that this broader range of descriptive terms, aside from demonstrating the survival value for Eskimos of recognizing snow conditions, illustrates that Eskimos can perceive different snow conditions more accurately than English-speaking residents of, say, California or Oregon.

Would you agree with Whorf that the presence of several words for snow in the Eskimo language actually enhances the clarity of these people's thinking about snow, and thus their ability to discriminate between different snow conditions? This argument supports the notion that language structures thought.

Just because residents of California or Oregon lack a rich vocabulary for describing snow does not necessarily imply that English-speaking non-Eskimos are any less capable of discriminating varied snow conditions. In fact, English-speaking skiers, who benefit from knowledge of different snow conditions, do use several descriptive terms for distinguishing types of snow, such as "sticky snow," "corn," and "powder." This latter example suggests that rather than having their thinking structured by language, Eskimos and skiers first learn to discriminate between varied snow conditions, and then invent a vocabulary for describing these differences.

Perhaps the most rigorous experimental test of Whorf's hypothesis was conducted as part of field research on how people learn natural color concepts. A comparison was made on memory for colors between people from the Dani society in New Guinea and college students in America. The Dani have only two words for colors—one for the darkest colors and one for light warm colors. In contrast, the vocabulary of the English-speaking students included words for 11 basic colors. Each subject was briefly shown a colored chip and then, after a delay of 30 seconds, was asked to pick out a chip of the same color among a set of 40 different colored chips.

Eskimos use several different words to describe snow.

If there is validity to Whorf's linguistic-relativity hypothesis, then a person's color vocabulary should influence memory for colors. Furthermore, we might logically predict that the Dani would have more difficulty with this task: They would be more likely to confuse similar colors of a slightly different hue that they had labeled with the same name than would the English-speaking subjects, whose broader color vocabulary would allow them to code the similar hues verbally into distinct categories. In actuality, the results did not support this prediction. While both American and Dani subjects made many mistakes, there were no significant differences in the rate at which people from each culture confused similar colors in spite of major differences in color vocabularies of the two languages (Heider & Oliver, 1972).

Today there is very little support for the notion that language rigidly structures or restricts thought as originally implied by the linguistic-relativity hypothesis. However, this is not to say that language has no influence on thought. Most cognitive psychologists and psycholinguists agree that languages influence the ease with which people are able to express a particular concept or idea or make distinctions about certain features of their environments. Put another way, it seems reasonable to conclude that it is often easier to express a particular concept or idea in one language as opposed to another. Furthermore, expanding our language comprehension through education and reading no doubt enhances our thinking processes. It does not follow from these observations, however, that our thoughts or perceptions are largely determined or structured by language.

A distinctly different viewpoint about the relationship between thinking and language is the idea that thought has some impact on the structure of language. Advocates of this theoretical position suggest that language takes on a form or structure that reflects, at least to some degree, the developing child's understanding of his or her world. Jean Piaget, a chief proponent of this interpretation, argued that certain words or phrases appear in the verbalizations of a child only after she or he has mastered certain intellectual skills during development (Piaget, 1972; Piaget & Inhelder, 1969).

We defer a detailed discussion of Piaget's theory of cognitive development to Chapter 11. However, one simple example here illustrates his viewpoint that language is structured by thought. By the age of two, most children have mastered the principle of *object permanence*—the realization that objects continue to exist even when they are not immediately in view. Piaget would argue that prior to mastering object permanence, a child's language would be devoid of references to objects not within view in the surrounding environment. Or, put another way, once children's thoughts (cognitions) embrace the understanding that hidden objects continue to exist, they are able to expand their language to conversations about these out-of-sight objects. This interpretation was supported by a study showing that child subjects were able to talk about absent objects only after demonstrating a firm grasp of object permanence (Corrigan, 1978).

Thus we have some evidence that thought does influence the structure of language. However, just as it is invalid to presume that language imposes a rigid structure on thought, it is inaccurate to presume that thought strictly structures language. Rather, in light of current knowledge, it seems more reasonable to conclude that the structure of language may bear some influence on how we think about our world just as our language reflects, to some degree, our understanding of our environment.

In the next chapter we will continue our discussions of thinking and language as we examine the topic of human development. As you will see, a number of issues raised about the roles of genetics and the environment will resurface in these discussions as well.

DOES THOUGHT STRUCTURE LANGUAGE?

SUMMARY

THINKING

1. We may define thought or thinking as a collection of internal processes or behaviors directed toward solving a problem.
2. Research has demonstrated the inaccuracy of John Watson's early contention that subvocal speech was essentially equivalent to thinking.
3. Modern behaviorists argue that thinking involves covert behavior maintained by private reinforcers.
4. One component of thought is mental images of visual scenes and sounds that we manipulate in some systematic or logical fashion.
5. A more abstract or symbolic form of thinking involves the use of concepts. Concepts represent general categories into which we mentally group things (objects, activities, kinds of animals, and so forth) that share certain features even though they are not identical.
6. We tend to organize concepts into hierarchies, ranging from very broad to very specific. There seems to be an optimal or basic level in each concept hierarchy that we naturally use when we think about objects or events.
7. Formal concepts, employed by laboratory researchers, are logical and well-defined with clear, unambiguous rules specifying what features belong to that category.
8. In real life most of the natural concepts that we use to think efficiently about past and present experiences tend to be more ambiguous than formal concepts.
9. A number of different theories have been proposed to explain how people form concepts. These include association theory, hypothesis-testing theory, and exemplar theory.

PROBLEM SOLVING

10. A problem exists when there is a discrepancy between your present status and some goal you wish to obtain, with no obvious way to bridge the gap.
11. Problems consist of three components: the original state of the situation as it exists at the moment; the goal state, which is what the problem solver would like the situation to be; and the rules or restrictions that govern the possible strategies for moving from the original state to the goal state.
12. Problem-solving behavior generally involves three logical stages: representing or defining the problem, generating possible solutions, and evaluating how well a given solution works.
13. Four common strategies for problem solving are trial and error, hypothesis testing, algorithms, and heuristics.
14. A trial-and-error approach is often applied to problems whose likely solutions are probably few in number.
15. When potential solutions to a given problem are more extensive, people often formulate specific hypotheses that generate a more efficient approach to solving a problem.
16. Algorithms involve a systematic exploration of every possible solution to a problem until a correct one is found.
17. Heuristics refer to a variety of rule-of-thumb strategies that may lead to quick solutions but are not guaranteed to produce results. Two commonly employed heuristic strategies are means-ends analysis and working backward.
18. Two characteristics that can make a problem difficult to solve are lack of definition and complexity.

19. Common obstacles we often create for ourselves when engaged in problem solving are mental set, functional fixedness, and confirmation bias.

20. Mental set is a tendency to approach a problem in a set or predetermined way regardless of the requirements of the specific problem.

21. Functional fixedness is the tendency to be so set or fixed in our perception of the proper function of a given object that we are unable to think of using it in a novel way to solve a problem.

22. Confirmation bias refers to our inclination to seek evidence that will confirm our hypothesis at the same time that we overlook contradictory evidence.

23. There are two basic types of reasoning: deductive and inductive. Deductive reasoning involves beginning with certain assumptions we believe to be true and using these assumptions as the basis for drawing conclusions that apply to specific instances. In contrast, inductive reasoning reaches a general conclusion by generalizing from specific instances.

24. A model for studying deductive reasoning is provided by the syllogism, which is an argument consisting of two (or more) presumably true statements, called premises, and a statement of conclusion that may or may not follow logically from the premises.

25. We often err in our deductive reasoning processes because we are too quick to accept faulty premises, because we misinterpret a premise, or because our attitudes or experiences interfere with our ability to think logically.

26. Decision making is a process that occurs whenever we are faced with an array of alternative choices and we choose one option while rejecting others.

27. Subjective probabilities of outcomes influence our decisions. While these estimates can facilitate decision making, they can also lead to undesirable decision outcomes.

28. Two common rules-of-thumb or heuristic approaches to decision making include the representative heuristic and the availability heuristic.

29. Artificial intelligence includes a number of approaches including expert systems and general problem solvers to solve problems and model human behavior with computers and computer programs.

LANGUAGE

30. The ability to use language is perhaps the most profound of all human behaviors.

31. Psycholinguistics is the psychological study of how we translate sounds and symbols into meaning, and of what processes are involved in the acquisition and use of language.

32. The basic structural elements of language are called phonemes.

33. A morpheme is the smallest unit of meaning in a given language.

34. Syntax refers to the set of language rules that govern how words can be combined to form meaningful phrases and sentences.

35. Language is also characterized by a system of rules that help us to determine the meanings of words and sentences. The study of meaning in language is called semantics.

36. Theories of language acquisition include the learning perspective, which emphasizes the role of experience in language acquisition, and the nativistic perspective, which maintains that the human brain is genetically programmed to learn speech. Most

contemporary psychologists believe that genetics and environment interact in a complex fashion to provide us with the necessary foundations for learning language.

37. There appears to be a universal developmental sequence in which children learn language by progressing from crying to cooing to babbling to one-word utterances to two-word utterances, and finally to expanded language using more complex sentences.

38. The major brain areas for language are located in the left hemisphere. These areas include Broca's area and Wernicke's area. Different components of speech and grammar appear to be mediated by specific regions within the brain.

39. Much of the data obtained from primate language studies can be explained by simpler principles, none of which requires us to assume apes have true language capabilities.

40. If we confine our conception of true language ability to the criteria of generativity, specialization, arbitrariness, displacement, and novelty, then we must conclude that humans alone possess language. However, if we define language as the ability to convey meaning through the use of symbols, it is clear that apes and other animals also have this ability.

41. According to Benjamin Whorf's linguistic-relativity hypothesis, people's language determines the content of their thought—so that, for instance, an Eskimo group that had several descriptive words for snow could perceive different types of snow more readily than could people whose language had only a few words for snow. Studies indicate, however, that while language may influence our ability to communicate ideas, it does not determine those perceptions or ideas.

42. Some theorists have argued that thought shapes language. The developmental psychologist Jean Piaget, for instance, noted that children do not develop a language to express concepts or ideas until they achieve mastery of these concepts.

43. While thought seems to influence language to some degree, it is inaccurate to presume that thought strictly structures language any more than language determines thought.

TERMS & CONCEPTS

thought
covert behavior
concepts
exemplar theory
prototypes
trial and error
testing hypotheses
algorithm
heuristics
means–ends analysis
working backward
mental set
functional fixedness

confirmation bias
inductive reasoning
deductive reasoning
syllogism
belief-bias effect
representative heuristic
availability heuristic
artificial intelligence
expert systems
Deep Thought
MYCIN
general problem solvers
SOAR

psycholinguistics
phoneme
morpheme
syntax
semantics

language acquisition device (LAD)
Broca's area
Wernicke's area
linguistic-relativity hypothesis

PERSPECTIVE #1

Dr. Herbert S. Terrace

Herbert S. Terrace is a professor of psychology at Columbia University. He was B.F. Skinner's last doctoral student and has performed research projects on errorless discrimination in pigeons, autoshaping in pigeons and monkeys, and the linguistic competence of apes. He is currently investigating serial memory in pigeons and monkeys. The ability of these species to learn arbitrary lists shows that animals can think without language and that the serial competence needed to acquire a language is a cognitive skill that is phylogenetically quite old.

PERSPECTIVE #1

LANGUAGE COMPETENCE OF APES

Dr. Herbert S. Terrace

Q: Dr. Terrace, do you feel that studying language acquisition in primates will help us understand human language acquisition, or do you think there are important differences in how we and other primates acquire and use language?

A: Some psychologists, including myself, used to think that it would be valuable to study language learning in apes but the results of various ape language projects suggests that language is uniquely human. There are at least two reasons to come to that conclusion: no evidence of spontaneity in combinations and what I would describe as lack of reference for the symbols various apes have been trained to use. The focus of the various ape language projects was, understandably, on grammatical competence. That is understandable because Chomsky and other psycholinguists cited grammar as the crucial feature of language that distinguishes it from other forms of communication. I started my own project, centered around a chimpanzee named Nim, to try to obtain definitive evidence of grammatical competence. Nim was trained to use sign language because of the generally agreed upon limitations of the vocal apparatus of the ape. While looking for regularities in combinations of signs, I initially thought I found the evidence I was seeking. I examined more than 20,000 combinations of two or more signs and noticed that in combinations involving, say, the word "more," "more" would occur in the first position of two sign combinations—"more eat," "more drink," "more play" and so on. Signs like "me" or "Nim" would usually occur in the second position of a two-sign combination. These regularities were the strongest evidence I was aware of that would support the conclusion of the

"The results of various ape language projects suggests that language is uniquely human."

R. Allen Gardner and Beatrix T. Gardner are professors in the Department of Psychology and Fellows of the Center for Advanced Study at the University of Nevada at Reno. In 1966, they began Project Washoe to study the nature of language and intelligence and the relation between human and nonhuman intelligence by cross-fostering an infant chimpanzee in a human environment. The results of their work, and follow-up studies by their colleague Roger Fouts, are described in their 1989 book *Teaching Sign Language to Chimpanzees* (SUNY Press). —

PERSPECTIVE #2
Allen and Beatrix Gardner

use of simple grammatical rules similar to those used by children. Somewhat unexpectedly, while I was looking at video tapes for other reasons, I noticed something I hadn't seen previously. Nim's signing seemed to occur almost exclusively in response to the teacher's signing. So after doing a discourse analysis of a dozen video tapes I had quantitative data showing that his signing was not spontaneous and, in fact, in most instances, it was imitative of what the teacher signed to Nim. This is quite different from the results of a similar analysis that could be done of children first learning to use language. In fact, the discourse analysis I used was modeled after one that's a classic study of language acquisition by children performed by Lois Bloom of Teachers College at Columbia University. That's the first reason I think one has to say that apes lack the human ability to communicate with language.

The second reason is perhaps less obvious but even more fundamental. I think all the investigators studying ape language including myself made a mistake of assuming that the signs of sign language or the symbols used by Rumbaugh and Premack function as words. However, looking at videotape records and films of other projects—for example, Washoe signing with the Gardners—I was struck by the fact that the signs seemed to be tricks that the chimpanzee used as a means to obtain particular kinds of reward, whether the reward was tickling, being chased, getting a banana, getting a drink, and so on. Children, unlike chimps, will use a word to tell you that they have noticed something about the environment. If a child says tree, he doesn't want you to bring the tree over to him, nor does he want a candy for saying tree, but those seem to be the only circumstances under which a chimp would sign. What is missing from apes is the ability

PERSPECTIVE #1

to refer to features of the environment for their own sake, to share curiosity. If you don't have that I can't see why one would even ask about grammatical competence, because I think in the evolution of language, the ability to refer undoubtedly preceded the appearance of grammatical competence. Once our ancestors began referring to features of the environment, there were too many things they had to keep track of. In order to make sense of the various words, symbols, etc., there was pressure to organize them in grammatical rules. So, for the two reasons I have cited, I don't think the communication that has been observed between apes and teachers has very much to do with human language.

Q: Would it then be your contention that apes and other nonhuman primates don't use language in a symbolic way?

A: I think that apes can solve problems that involve symbols that they have to think about or remember. That is, if you show an ape a triangle and, 20 seconds later, ask it to select that triangle from an array of stimuli including circles, squares and so on, I'm certain the chimp can do it. But that doesn't mean that they're using language. That means that they have the ability to represent features of the environment and remember those features in a nonlinguistic way. In fact, for the last ten years I have been studying how an animal thinks without language, and there is no question that animals do think. Descartes' contention that animals lack language and therefore can't think, notwithstanding. The intriguing question is how a nonlinguistic creature can solve problems without simply resorting to conditioned reflexes without language. Curiously, the same problem comes up in the study of human infants. Human infants are not born with language, and yet there is much evidence that they think. What, then, is the medium of their thought before language appears?

Q: Has your research into this area provided you with any clues or any preliminary conclusions about the nature of that kind of thought?

A: Yes. I have been studying how pigeons and, more recently, monkeys learn lists which consist of photographs displayed on video monitors. My initial conclusions are that monkeys, in particular, use a spatial representation of the lists they have to produce in order to keep track of which is first, which is second, which is third, and so on. Animals have an obviously well-developed sense of space that they use while foraging and hunting, so it is not unreasonable to assume that they could use their spatial abilities to represent things like the order of an item in a sequence. I suspect there are other ways that animals represent the world, but this is the subject of much current investigation.

Q: What about studies in which chimps have been shown to converse among themselves or teach other chimpanzees sign language in the absence of human confederates? What do you think is operating in those circumstances, if it is not a form of language which is being used or passed on?

A: Well, it's a question of the quality of that evidence. I have seen Nim sign "hug" to dogs and cats. I mean this is an overtrained, potentially conditioned, response. The reports of Washoe teaching signs to an adopted offspring don't make much sense to me because the most frequent sign the offspring learned was "George," the name of one of the trainers, whom the offspring had never seen. Clearly Washoe was using signs and the offspring was in some interesting sense imitating Washoe but I don't think that was communication. I think what we have is an interesting case of imitation, a phenomenon that is important in its own right. But I don't see that it has anything to do with language.

Q: Do you see any similarity at all between language acquisition in humans and the kinds of activities or actions you've seen among the chimpanzees?

A: No. I think the crucial difference is, as I said earlier, that infants have an essentially innate ability to refer to features of the environment. You can actually see precursors of what I call the ability to refer before the first words are uttered, in shared eye movements. Infants will often look at an object, look at the parent to monitor whether the parent has seen the object, and when they sense that the parent has seen the object, they will smile, to say, "Ah, you see it, I see it." And this is without language. That kind of shared perception, as far as I can determine, is uniquely human. And it is, I think, from that kind of nonverbal communication that words occur in a very straightforward manner. It is very easy to build on that foundation. There are fundamental gaps in this kind of cognitive ability that separate human beings from their closest ape relatives.

Q: Would you say, then, that the acquisition and use of language would be based more upon some kind of prewired structure that humans possess and other animals don't more than through learning?

A: I don't think it's an either/or proposition. I think there is clearly evidence of prewired functions of the brain that are involved in language. One kind of evidence is essentially behavioral. There are generalizations that a child makes, having begun to use language, that cannot be explained by simple learning or conditioning principles. I think Chomsky has very forcefully made that point. So, given the limited input that a child has, there must be some innate machinery that makes use of that input to produce novel constructions. The evidence of aphasia and lateralization is also consistent with the notion that there is hard wiring for language. But I don't think that makes language terribly different from other forms of hard wired functions. We know that there are certain parts of the brain that are dedicated to detecting shapes, contours, colors, and so on, so it's not surprising that in the case of language we have evidence of biological constraints or innate determinants. Clearly, however, a large part of language is learned. That is demonstrated by the fact that children in Germany learn German and children in the United States learn English, so there must be a learned component. That is why I stress that it shouldn't be viewed as an either/or dichotomy.

Q: Can you tell us about the focus of your current research?

A: My current focus really is how thinking occurs without language. I see that animals, particularly primates, are fascinating in the sense that they can illuminate how intelligence evolved. One of the strategies of science is always to simplify one's problem. Primates provide a simplification that allows one to study various forms of cognition without, if you will, the complication of language which is inextricably an element of human thought, at least once a child is two or three years old. So I'm not studying language or communication in apes or other primates, but what I hope to accomplish is to see what intellectual and cognitive abilities had evolved upon which language can build.

Q: Have you had any results in that area that you might be able to share with us?

PERSPECTIVE #1

A: Well the major one is that ability to produce and remember sequences, which is vital to the production of sentences, and is phylogenetically much older than the human species. You can get this in monkeys and you can get it in a simple form even in pigeons. So my current concern is, how does the animal represent the sequence? These are the kinds of questions that don't require language, but certainly require some kind of thinking ability.

Q: Do you think those studies have any implications for thinking and learning in humans?

A: Yes because even though in our conscious awareness we seem always to think in language, it is highly probable that much of our thinking is nonverbal. Much of it is unconscious and if we had a good picture of what the nature of nonverbal thinking is in animals, I'm sure that it didn't stop with the human species. I suspect that ultimately we would find out about a component of human thinking that is very rarely considered.

Q: Are there other implications of the research that you're doing now that you think might have some strong significance in the near future?

A: Well one point I just briefly touched upon is the study of thinking in human infants. That is unfortunately an area that's received very little attention. It's a very difficult area and it poses the same problems as studying thinking in animals. How do you know what a baby is thinking if the baby can't speak? There is a growing body of techniques available that will allow one to examine that problem. Another point that has to be made about an infant's ability to think is that anybody who doubts that an animal can't think because an animal lacks language, should ask themselves, well what about human babies? Do we want to reach the same conclusion about them? I think the answer is clearly no.

PERSPECTIVE #2

LANGUAGE COMPETENCE OF APES

Allen and Beatrix Gardner

Q: Do you feel that studying language acquisition in primates helps us to understand human language acquisition or do you feel there are important differences in how we and other primates acquire and use language?

A: Well, our notion is the modern notion that language is a part of intellectual development. The old notion, almost medieval, is a brain separated into compartments—a language area, a social area, an emotional area, and so on. The modern notion is that the brain is integrated and all aspects of intellectual development are inextricably intertwined. Our idea was to give the chimpanzees a rich intellectual environment like that of a human child and let language develop within that.

Q: So you see language development and acquisition as going hand in hand with the acquisition and development of the other skills which we need for living?

*Evidence cited in this interview appears in Gardner, R.A., Gardner, B.T., and Van Cantfort, T.E. (Eds) (1989). *Teaching sign language to chimpanzees*, Albany: SUNY Press.

PERSPECTIVE #2

A: Yes. Just as with children, a young chimpanzee would have to be familiar with simple tools such as keys and light switches, articles of clothing like shoes, in order to learn the signs for keys, light, opening, or lacing. We kept our laboratory stocked with the objects and activities of a child's world. The chimps learned in that environment the way children learn. They learned to eat human style food, to use a cup and a spoon, clear the table, help wash the dishes. They learned, say, to use the human toilet—including flushing and wiping themselves—and also to use signs to ask to go potty as a way to get out of lessons or postpone a bath. But always the primary objective was to study the patterns of social and intellectual development with sign language as a strand in that development.

Q: In the course of your studies, did you note similarities in the patterns of language acquisition and development between chimpanzees and human children?

A: One of the most important similarities between chimps and children is that both take a long time to grow up. Wild chimpanzees in Africa are only weaned when they are four or five years old. They only start getting adult teeth at age six. They live with their mothers till they are seven to ten years old. Mothers have their first babies when they are between 12 and 15 years old. In labs and zoos chimpanzees live well over 50 years.

So, we can compare patterns of chimpanzee development with patterns of child development. There are some well documented steps in the development of language in human children. For instance, one of the things that has been described very well is the way children answer questions. They go from "what" and "where" to "who" and then on to "whose." The chimpanzees learned the American Sign Language version of these question words. The basic question types that are earlier for signing chimpanzees are also earlier for children. That similarity is very important. But the object of our research went beyond the language. The object was to see how a chimpanzee would develop in a human intellectual environment. The purpose of the sign language was to complete that development. Other psychologists had tried to raise a chimp like a child, but they used English and the chimpanzees couldn't make the sounds of English. You can't really say that you cross-fostered a chimp in a human environment if the chimp can't ask a question or carry on a conversation with you.

Our notion was that the sign language would complete the cross-fostering. So we had to have a naturally occurring language that human children learn. Not an artificial language used only to test some abstract theory. We were using sign language to support the cross-fostering rather than using cross-fostering to support the sign language. But, of course, they interacted and supported each other. We assumed that if we used a suitable language it would come in with the rest of the development. We and other comparative psychologists always understood this. The notion of a great divide between language and the rest of human behavior and between human behavior and the rest of animal behavior is a throwback to scholasticism.

Q: Have you noted similarities in all aspects of language acquisition and development—the acquisition of terms, syntax, usage, and so on?

A: Oh, yes. In traditional Chomskyan linguistics, the child is born with language and then in three years you see all syntax. Back in the 60s and 70s people said things like that. But most scientists understand now that there is a long

"The object was to see how a chimpanzee would develop in a human intellectual environment. The purpose of the sign language was to complete that development."

PERSPECTIVE #2

period of linguistic development in young children. For that matter, high school students haven't quite mastered their native language and even college students still have a lot to learn. This long period of development in human children gives us a scale for comparison. It shows that cross-fostered chimpanzees, up to five or six years old, were developing in a very parallel way. Not as fast; they are behind human children, but the patterns are very similar and, I would say, parallel.

Q: Has the work that you've done recently differed qualitatively in any way from the work that you started doing and if so can you tell us a little bit about your most recent research efforts?

A: We're mainly working on the data from the first five years now, but the chimpanzees are with Roger Fouts at Central Washington University and the work is going on into a second generation. Washoe's own baby died soon after birth but Roger found a 10-month-old infant, Loulis, for Washoe to adopt. Roger then started a project in which the humans never spoke sign language when Loulis was around, which was practically all the time. So the only input Loulis got was from other chimpanzees and he learned over 50 signs which he could only have learned from the other chimps. During this period, that went on for five years, the other chimps went right on as a community of signers even though there was practically no input from human beings. The cross-fostered chimpanzees went right on signing among themselves almost without any human influence.

In the second project with Moja, Pili, Tatu, and Dar we had better human models of sign language than we had in the Washoe days. Everybody knew more signs and there were some deaf people in the foster family who only spoke sign language. Not only did Loulis learn signs from Washoe and the other chimps but Washoe learned some new signs from the chimps of the second project.

In the Reno laboratory, we had several people for each chimp but Roger has several chimps for each person and there are many hours when the chimps are by themselves in a group. Video cameras are rolling to record conversations among the chimps when no human being is present. All sorts of chimp-to-chimp transmissions go on with no human support at all, if you don't count the video cameras. Roger and his students record conversations and topics of conversations and identify the chimps' favorite addressees in elaborate conversations among themselves. Loulis, for instance, switched from Washoe, his mother, as his favorite addressee to Dar, his peer playmate, as the most common addressee. Although the chimpanzees haven't developed entirely new signs among themselves, certain variants of signs have become traditional within the group, for instance, making a quite noisy sign out of the \person\ sign, by adding a slapping movement.

Q: In the observations that were made of chimps who were conversing among themselves, did you see the kind of turn taking and the other dynamics of the pragmatic uses of language in that situation as well as in interaction with the humans?

A: Oh yes, that's one of the things that we saw starting in Reno. Things like tapping you to get your visual attention so they could sign to you, or making some noise to get you to turn around and at that point signing to you. That makes a lot of sense. You don't just put out signs, you want to converse with someone. One of the projects now is nailing down the observations of pragmatics, experimentally. What do signing chimpanzees do when a person or another chimp is facing the other way? What do they do to get a chimp to turn around—the sounds they make, like hand clapping, banging objects? Where in the sequence do they begin signing? They do things like touch each other to get attention and make kissing sounds, and they persist until the addressee responds.

In the formal experiment that is going on right now, one of our students, Mark Bodamer, has a setup to demonstrate this under experimental conditions. He is at a desk working and the chimps are in another room, but they have a place where they can come and get his attention. They are behind a barrier and he sits with his back to them. He has a video camera watching them. They come to the doorway and they do various things to get his attention and distract him from his work, and only when he turns around do they start talking to him. They know enough not to sign to his back.

Q: Does your research suggest to you that all primates have prewired structures in the brain which direct language development? And would you say that there is a heavier learning component for language acquisition, a stronger biological component, or an interaction between the two?

A: Well that's a really good question, a question that shows the advancement of theory in the last twenty or thirty years. The notion of a compartmentalized brain for different functions is really phrenology. Yes, you have visual areas and hearing areas and motor areas but, the more advanced a function, the more generalized the brain. Just as you find that the more primitive the animal, the more prewired it is, the more advanced the animal, the more generalized its brain is—the more different foods it can eat, the more different climates it can live in. The most generalized function of all, of course, is learning. The way human beings are different from other animals is not in having more specialized organs—that would be more primitive. The way human beings are more advanced than other animals is in being more general. We have the widest diet, the widest variety of climates that we live in and the widest number of things that we can learn. And so, in the modern view, the notion is that the most advanced functions are the most general ones. We see everything in modern development as part of the generalized, adaptive learning ability of our species. As primates, we are superb learners.

Q: What do you feel are the more important implications of this research in the teaching and learning of humans? How would this kind of knowledge help people who are trying to find better ways to help human children learn?

A: If you look at Skinnerian behaviorism, what you find is that the more reward and punishment, the stupider the animal gets. Even monkeys and rats, if given less drill, solve more advanced problems. The research in our area that has had negative results has been research in which chimpanzees or other animals have been given Skinnerian reinforcement in order to solve abstract problems, so that in the end all you get is sort of like tricks. We don't just want the chimps to take tests, we want to carry on conversations with them, have them tell us what they saw. This holds true for the education of children, also—the more you emphasize reward and punishment, the narrower, the stupider the behavior. Even in retarded children that fact stands out.

CHAPTER 11

Development 1: Conception through Childhood

CHAPTER 12

Development 2: Adolescence to the End of Life

CHAPTER 13

Intelligence

CHAPTER 14

Personality: Theories and Assessment

PART 4

Developmental Processes and Individual Differences

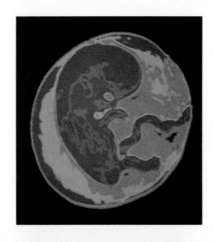

CHAPTER 11

Development 1: Conception through Childhood

DEVELOPMENTAL ISSUES

Heredity and Environment
Continuous versus Stage Development
Critical Periods in Development

DEVELOPMENTAL RESEARCH

The Cross-Sectional Design
The Longitudinal Design
The Cross-Sequential Design

THE BEGINNING OF LIFE

Mechanisms of Heredity
Problems in Inheritance
Genetic Counseling
Genetic Engineering

PRENATAL DEVELOPMENT

PHYSICAL DEVELOPMENT

Development of the Brain
Physical Growth
Motor Development

COGNITIVE DEVELOPMENT

Piaget's Theory of Cognitive
    Development
Gender Differences in Cognitive Abilities

PSYCHOSOCIAL DEVELOPMENT

Attachment
Parenting Styles and Social-Emotional
    Development
Erikson's Theory of Psychosocial
    Development

GENDER IDENTITY

Biological Influences on Gender Identity
Social Learning Influences on Gender
    Identity
The Interaction of Biological and Social
    Influences on Gender Identity
The Socialization of Gender Roles

*W*e are constantly changing, growing, and developing throughout our lives, from conception to old age. At some periods, these changes take place very rapidly, and are clear to anyone who is there to observe them; at other times, particularly later in life, they may not be so obvious. This chapter begins at the beginning as it explores conception, *pre-natal* (before birth) development, and childhood. Chapter 12 continues where this chapter leaves off, exploring adolescence and the adult years. First, we outline some key issues that have been the center of debate among developmental psychologists and examine typical ways in which development is studied.

DEVELOPMENTAL ISSUES

A number of issues have influenced developmental theory and research; we explore three of the most important. The first is the ongoing nature versus nurture controversy: What are the relative influences of heredity and environment on development? A second question has to do with the way in which development proceeds: Do changes take place in a continuous fashion throughout our lives, or do they occur in stages, with qualitatively different changes taking place at different points in our lives? A third issue has to do with critical periods in development: Must certain experiences occur during a specific window of time in our lives in order for development to proceed normally, or can later experiences make up for earlier deficiencies? Because these three questions recur throughout the study of development, we introduce each before proceeding with our discussion of human development.

HEREDITY AND ENVIRONMENT

Some individuals are capable of prodigious intellectual feats; others have only average ability. Some of us are extroverted and outgoing; others are introverted and shy. A few of us are leaders; most are followers. Are such differences due to inheritance or are they learned?

THE NATURE–NURTURE ARGUMENT *Nurture Argument* One answer to this question is that we are products of the experiences that *nurture* our development from conception to death. This view was expressed by the seventeenth-century English philosopher John Locke, who proposed that an infant's mind at birth is a *tabula rasa* or blank slate upon which virtually anything can be written by experience. The behaviorist John Watson updated this view in the 1920s.

> Give me a dozen healthy infants, well-formed and my own specific world to bring them up in and I'll guarantee to take any one at random and train him to become any type of specialist I might select—a doctor, lawyer, artist, merchant-chief and, yes, even beggar-man and thief, regardless of his talents, penchants, tendencies, abilities, vocations and race of his ancestors. (1926, p. 10)

Nature Argument The opposing point of view in the **nature-nurture controversy** is that our genetic endowment, or *nature*, is what makes us who we are. The eighteenth-century French philosopher Jean-Jacques Rousseau saw human development as simply the unfolding of genetically determined attributes; in this century developmental psychologist Arnold Gesell (1928) stated that "It is the hereditary ballast which conserves and stabilizes the growth of each individual infant" (p. 378).

Interaction Argument Neither the nature nor the nurture position is supported today in its extreme form. Instead, contemporary theorists are interested in how genetics and experience interact. Although heredity predisposes us to behave in certain ways (and also sets limits on what we can do), environment is also critical. For example, although genetics determines whether your biological sex is male or female, gender-associated behaviors—from manner of dress, to enjoyment of football, to assertiveness in a relationship—are highly influenced, if not entirely determined, by social learning. We explore the relative influence of heredity and environment on gender identity and gender roles later in this chapter.

Thus human traits develop within the context of our environments. While some behaviors or attributes are largely, if not exclusively, determined by experience, others seem to develop without any specific experience, as long as environmental conditions stay within a normative range. An example is the early stages of language acquisition, as we saw in Chapter 10. Another is the universal developmental sequence through which babies progress, from sitting without support to crawling and ultimately to walking. Virtually all babies crawl, commencing at around 10 months, before they begin to walk at about 13 or 14 months. (Throughout this chapter, we quote average ages for different developmental milestones. Please note that there is a wide range of individual variation around these norms.) This biologically determined sequence occurs even if children are not encouraged to sit, crawl, or walk. Both language acquisition and walking are examples of **maturation,** the orderly unfolding of certain patterns of behavior in accordance with genetic blueprints.

CONTINUOUS VERSUS STAGE DEVELOPMENT

A second issue confronting developmental psychologists concerns the nature of changes that occur over the life span. We all know that adolescents are quite different from infants, and that most elderly people are noticeably different from young adults. Are these differences created by a gradual, cumulative growth, with each new developmental change building upon earlier developments and experiences in a fashion characterized by *continuity?* Or do these changes exhibit *discontinuity*—that is, are the behaviors expressed at each new stage of development qualitatively different from those of the previous stage?

In general, psychologists who emphasize the role of learning have tended to view development as a gradual, continuous process. According to this view, the mechanisms that govern development are relatively constant throughout a person's life: Because individuals accumulate experiences, development is seen as a *quantitative* change (change due to increases in the amount or quantity of experiences). Developmental psychologists who embrace this perspective believe that the only important difference between young people and those who are older is that the latter have experienced more in life and are likely to know more. In contrast, many developmentalists who emphasize maturation view development as a discontinuous process that occurs in a series of steps or stages. A stage is a concept used to describe how a person's manner of thinking and behavior are organized and directed during a particular period.

Stage theorists are inclined to interpret the differences between children and adults as being *qualitative* in nature (differences due to distinctions in the kind and nature of experiences). For instance, adults are viewed as better problem solvers than children not just because they know more, but also because they think differently, in a more logical and systematic fashion. Here and in Chapter 12 we discuss two influential stage theories: Jean Piaget's theory of cognitive development and Erik Erikson's theory of psychosocial development.

Stage theorists see adults as better problem solvers than children, not just because they know more, but because they think differently, in a more logical and systematic fashion.

An important aspect of the continuity-discontinuity issue is the question of whether development from infancy to old age is characterized more by stability or by change. For instance, will an introverted, withdrawn child grow up to be reclusive as an adult? How much can we rely on a person's present behavior to predict what that person will be like in the future? Many of us grow up to be older versions of our childhood selves. Stability is not inevitable, however, and at least some people develop into persons quite different from their earlier selves.

A third developmental issue is the relative importance of different periods of development. Is the timing of training essential for optimal acquisition of certain skills and is timing also necessary for the development of behavioral traits? Is it necessary to have certain experiences early in life to ensure normal development later on?

According to one point of view, there are **critical periods** during which an infant or child must experience certain kinds of social and sensory experiences. If

CRITICAL PERIODS IN DEVELOPMENT

In a series of experiments, Konrad Lorenz demonstrated that newly hatched ducklings will begin to follow the first moving object they see, whether it was their mother or Lorenz himself.

the proper experiences are not provided at the right time, later experiences will not be able to make up for earlier deficiencies. Psychologists who argue for critical periods often cite animal research for support. One widely quoted source of evidence is the research of biologist Konrad Lorenz (1937), who was curious about why baby ducks begin to follow their mothers shortly after they are hatched. In a series of experiments he demonstrated that newly hatched ducklings will begin to follow the first moving thing they see—their mother, a member of another species like a goose, or even Lorenz himself (see photo). Lorenz labeled this phenomenon **imprinting.**

Another famous study was conducted by psychologist Harry Harlow and his associates at the University of Wisconsin. Harlow found that when baby monkeys are deprived of "contact comfort" with their mothers during early development, the result is emotional and social impairment. For instance, infant monkeys who were reared in isolation for the first six months or more showed severely disturbed behavior such as incessant rocking, timidity, and inappropriate displays of aggression—behaviors that persisted into adulthood, even after the imposed isolation was ended (Suomi & Harlow, 1978). We discuss this research in more detail later in this chapter.

The evidence of critical periods in human development is inconsistent. One widely quoted early study reported that institutionalized infants who were deprived of loving, responsive care during their first six months were significantly more likely to be emotionally and socially maladjusted than infants who were institutionalized after they had experienced a period of close contact with responsive caregivers during the early months of their lives (Goldfarb, 1945). Some psychologists saw this study as evidence that the first six months are a critical period for starting a child on the proper path toward healthy emotional and social adjustment.

However, other studies have had very different findings. In one, for example, infants who had been subjected to a profoundly impoverished orphanage environment for most of their first two years were then transferred to another institution where they received one-on-one contact with loving caregivers. Despite the early lack of love and stimulation, these infants developed into well-adjusted adults without identifiable behavioral problems (Skeels, 1966; see Chapter 13 for a more detailed discussion of this classic study). Numerous other investigations have shown that children adopted after infancy and raised by loving parents can often overcome early disadvantages associated with severely deprived environments (Kagan et al., 1978; Maccoby, 1980; Yarrow et al., 1973).

Even Harlow's monkey studies cast doubt on the critical-period theory. If monkeys who had been deprived of contact comfort during infancy were later provided extensive contact with therapist monkeys (infant monkeys, still in the clinging stage, who provided extensive contact comfort to the older monkeys—see Figure 11.1), their behavioral deficits could be almost entirely overcome. Monkeys exposed to longer periods of isolation (12 months instead of 6 months) also responded to this unusual therapy, but their recovery was not as complete (Novak & Harlow, 1975; Suomi & Harlow, 1972).

Another question related to the critical-period issue is whether bonding between parent and infant must take place at a certain point in early development. Most nonhuman mammals lick and groom their offspring during the first hours after birth, often rejecting their young if this early "getting acquainted" session is somehow prevented. Some child specialists have suggested that a similar critical period exists for humans in the first hours after birth, and that if contact is prevented, mother-infant bonding will not develop adequately (Klaus & Kennell, 1982). This notion has received little support from research, however (Goldberg, 1983; Lamb, 1982; Myers, B., 1984; Singer et al., 1985). Instead, the parent-child relationship seems to be malleable, with plenty of opportunity to establish attachment throughout development.

FIGURE 11.1

A Young Monkey Still in the Clinging Stage Acts as a "Therapist" for an Older Monkey

In all, the evidence suggests that most effects of adverse early experience can be modified, if not overcome, by later experience. Certainly the kinds of experiences we have during our early development may strongly influence our feelings about ourselves and others, our styles of relating to people, our mode of expressing emotions, the degree to which we realize our intellectual potential, and countless other aspects of our adjustment. Most contemporary psychologists agree, however, that the concept of critical periods in infant development, at least when applied to emotional, intellectual, and behavioral traits, lacks supporting evidence.

DEVELOPMENTAL RESEARCH

The task of developmental psychology is to describe and attempt to explain the nature of behavioral changes that occur throughout the life span. To realize this aim, researchers need to gather information about individuals at different points in their development. Three research designs have been developed for this purpose: the cross-sectional, longitudinal, and cross-sequential methods.

THE CROSS-SECTIONAL DESIGN

The most widely used research method in developmental psychology is the **cross-sectional design.** Groups of subjects of different ages are assessed and compared at one point in time, and the researcher draws conclusions about behavior differences that may be related to age differences. For example, suppose we want to determine whether there are age differences in television-viewing habits. Using the cross-sectional method, we might attach program-monitoring devices to the television sets of a sample population ranging from young adults to retirees, then analyze several months of viewing records. The result would be a profile of viewing habits of different age groups.

The cross-sectional study gives an accurate "snapshot" of one point in time, but it leaves an important question unanswered: Do its findings reflect developmental differences or changes in the environment? For instance, suppose we discover that young adults watch very few comedies whereas older adults spend most of their television time viewing comedies. Does this mean that when the young people in our sample grow older, they will spend more time viewing comedies, or does it simply reflect the fact that the older subjects developed their viewing habits in an era when situation comedies were featured in television programming? One way to find out if a behavioral change is related to development is to conduct a longitudinal study.

THE LONGITUDINAL DESIGN

The **longitudinal design** evaluates behavior in the same group of people at several points in time to assess what kinds of changes occur over the long term. To apply this method to the study of age-related television preferences, we might begin by monitoring the viewing habits of a group of young adults at age 20. The same subjects might then be repeatedly observed at five-year intervals over the next 50 years. This method would allow us to assess reliably whether or not the television consumption habits of our subjects actually change with age, and if so, in what direction.

A famous example of a longitudinal investigation is Lewis Terman's long-term study of gifted children with IQs above 135. A Stanford University psychologist, Terman began his research in the early 1920s with a sample of 1,528 gifted boys and girls of grade-school age. These subjects were evaluated and tested at regular intervals, first to see if they would maintain their intellectual superiority, and later to see how well they adjusted to life. Although Terman died in 1956, his research was continued by Stanford psychologists Robert Sears and Pauline Sears. The Terman "whiz kids" are now approaching their eighties.

This classic study has provided a wealth of information about the impact of superior intelligence on life satisfaction and on the course of development. Over time, Terman's gifted subjects have been shown to be healthier, happier, more socially adept, and more successful in their careers than are comparably aged people of average intelligence. They have also exhibited a much lower than average incidence of emotional disorders, substance abuse, suicide, and divorce (Sears, 1977; Sears & Barbee, 1977; Terman, 1925, 1954). These findings have helped dispel the common myth that people of very high intelligence are more likely to exhibit severe behavior disorders than are people of average intelligence.

Unlike the cross-sectional design, the longitudinal approach allows researchers to track an individual's changes over time. However, the longitudinal approach does have some drawbacks. One is the large investment of time that it requires: Relatively few researchers are ready to embark on a Terman-like study whose results will not be evident for years. Another problem is the shrinking sample. Over time, subjects may drop out of the study as they move away, die, or simply lose interest.

Finally, environmental factors still play a role in longitudinal studies, and so researchers must be cautious in generalizing their findings. For example, suppose that as part of a longitudinal study you interview a group of college students in 1960 and then again survey the same group in 1990, asking them their opinions about abortion. You might find that as middle-aged adults these subjects expressed more support for a woman's right to choose abortion than they did as young adults. Does this mean that attitudes toward abortion become more liberalized in the period between early and mature adulthood? Such a conclusion would overlook the dramatic social changes that have taken place in the last 10 to 20 years. The attitudinal changes in our study group might well reflect social changes rather than a normal developmental pattern.

THE CROSS-SEQUENTIAL DESIGN

In an attempt to overcome some of the drawbacks of both the cross-sectional and longitudinal designs, researchers have combined the best features of each in a **cross-sequential design.** Subjects in a cross-sectional design are observed more than once, but over a shorter span of time than is typical of longitudinal studies. Subjects in cross-sequential studies with the same year of birth are said to belong to the same *birth cohort*. Developmental psychologists who use this research design generally choose cohorts whose ages will overlap during the course of the study. This method helps to avoid both the longitudinal shortcoming of limited generalizability of findings and the potential cross-sectional problem of confusing the effects of growth with those of societal conditions.

THE BEGINNING OF LIFE

For all of us, life begins in the same way. Shortly after a ripened ovum is released from one of our mother's ovaries, a sperm cell penetrates the ovum, fertilizing it. The sperm and ovum, collectively called **gametes** or **germ cells,** normally unite in the upper portion of the *fallopian tube*. The resulting new cell, called a **zygote,** then travels downward through the fallopian tube to the *uterus* or womb (see Figure 11.2).

The nuclei of the sperm and ovum each contain 23 rodlike structures called **chromosomes,** 22 of which are autosomes (not sex-determining) and one of

which is a sex chromosome. After fertilization, the zygote contains a complement of 46 chromosomes arranged in 23 pairs, one chromosome in each pair
from the sperm and one from the egg (see Figure 11.3).

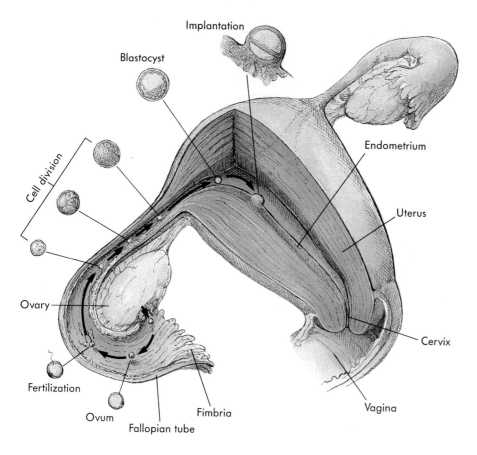

FIGURE 11.2

From Ovulation to Fertilization

The egg travels to the fallopian tube where fertilization occurs. The fertilized ovum divides as it travels towards the uterus where it becomes implanted.

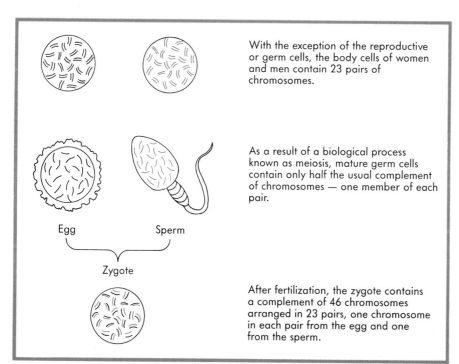

With the exception of the reproductive or germ cells, the body cells of women and men contain 23 pairs of chromosomes.

As a result of a biological process known as meiosis, mature germ cells contain only half the usual complement of chromosomes — one member of each pair.

After fertilization, the zygote contains a complement of 46 chromosomes arranged in 23 pairs, one chromosome in each pair from the egg and one from the sperm.

FIGURE 11.3

Chromosome Complement of the Zygote after Fertilization

MECHANISMS OF HEREDITY

GENES AND CHROMOSOMES Chromosomes are composed of thousands of **genes,** the chemical blueprints of all living things. Genes determine physical traits such as eye color, blood type, and bone structure; they also have a significant impact on behavioral traits such as intelligence, temperament, and sociability.

Genes are made of **DNA (deoxyribonucleic acid)** molecules. Under high amplification, a DNA molecule looks like a long double strand arranged in a spiraling staircase fashion. Although DNA molecules are composed of the same chemical bases, the exact arrangement of chemicals varies, causing different DNA molecules to have different effects. A person's genetic code thus consists of a variety of patterns of DNA molecules arranged in gene groupings on specific chromosomes within a cell's nucleus. Each individual's genetic code is unique.

The exception, of course, is **identical twins** (also called **monozygotic** or one-egg twins), who share the same genetic code. Identical twins originate from a single fertilized ovum that divides into two separate entities with identical genetic codes. Identical twins are always same-sex individuals who physically appear to be carbon copies of each other. Since they have the same genes, any differences between them must be due to environmental influences.

Identical twins may not be as identical as researchers assume, however. Recent genetics research suggests that identical twins may result from tiny genetic mutations that lead one part of the developing embryo to reject the other part, resulting in two nearly identical embryos (Hall, 1992). At present it is too early to know the significance of these genetic differences on human development and behavior.

In contrast, **fraternal twins** (also known as **dizygotic** or two-egg twins) occur when the woman's ovaries release two ova, each of which is fertilized by a different sperm cell. Since fraternal twins result from the fusion of different germ cells, their genetic makeup is no more alike than that of any other siblings. Physical and behavioral differences between fraternal twins may be due to genetic factors, environmental influences, or a combination of the two.

Psychologists who seek to understand the relative roles of genetics and environment in determining behavioral traits often compare the degree to which a particular trait is expressed by both members of a twin pair. When identical twins are more alike **(concordant)** than fraternal twins in a particular trait, we can assume that the attribute has a strong genetic basis. Conversely, when a trait shows a comparable degree of concordance in both types of twins, we can reasonably assume that environment is exerting the greater influence. We will have more to say about twin studies throughout the remaining chapters of this text.

GENOTYPES AND PHENOTYPES The assortment of genes we inherit at conception is known as our **genotype;** the characteristics that result from the expression of various genotypes are known as **phenotypes.** Sometimes genotypes and phenotypes are consistent, as when a person with brown eyes (phenotype) carries only genes for brown eye color (genotype). However, a phenotype is often inconsistent with its genotype, so that a person with brown eyes may carry a blue eye gene as well as a brown eye gene. This happens because genes occur in pairs, one of which is contributed by the mother and one by the father.

If your genetic blueprint contains different genes for a trait, you are said to be **heterozygous** for that trait. In contrast, if you inherit identical genes from both your parents, you are **homozygous** for that trait. What determines how a phenotype will be expressed when a person is heterozygous for a particular trait?

DOMINANCE AND RECESSIVENESS Suppose you received a gene for brown eyes from one parent and a gene for blue eyes from the other. The principles of *dominance* and *recessiveness* would allow us to predict that the actual color of your eyes would be brown because genes for brown eyes are dominant over blue eye genes. A **dominant gene** is one that is always expressed in the phenotype; it is the gene that prevails when paired with a subordinate or recessive gene. A **recessive gene** is one that may be expressed only in the absence of a dominant gene, or when it is paired with a similar recessive gene. Table 11.1 lists some dominant and recessive traits.

Not all human traits can be predicted as easily as eye color. Several traits, such as growth or metabolic rate, result from gene pairs working in consort with each other. This more complicated form of genetic transmission, in which several gene pairs interact, is called **multifactorial inheritance.**

SEX-LINKED INHERITANCE   You may be aware that certain undesirable traits, such as red-green color blindness and hemophilia (abnormal bleeding) are far more common among males than females. Have you ever wondered why males are more susceptible to these and other diseases that demonstrate **sex-linked inheritance?** The answer lies in the fact that the smaller Y chromosome carries fewer genes than the much larger X chromosome. (The sex chromosome pair in males is XY; in females it is XX.) The genes that determine whether or not a person develops these diseases are carried only on the X chromosome.

In the case of hemophilia, as long as a person has at least one dominant gene for normal blood clotting (which we designate as H: geneticists use uppercase letters to denote dominant genes and lowercase letters for recessive genes), the disease will not be expressed. Thus a female can carry the recessive gene for hemophilia (h) on one of her X chromosomes but nevertheless have blood that clots normally due to the presence of a dominant H on the other member of her XX pair. A male, however, will be a bleeder if he inherits only one h gene from his mother, since the gene-deficient Y chromosome does not carry a gene that regulates blood clotting.

TABLE 11.1   *Some Common Dominant and Recessive Traits*

DOMINANT TRAITS	RECESSIVE TRAITS
Dark hair	Light hair
Nonred hair (brunette or blond)	Red hair
Normal hair growth	Baldness
Curly hair	Straight hair
Brown eyes	Blue, green, hazel, or gray eyes
Normal color vision	Red-green color blindness
Normal visual acuity	Nearsightedness
Normal protein metabolism	Phenylketonuria (inability to convert phenylalanine into tyrosine)
Type A or type B blood	Type O blood
Normal blood clotting	Hemophilia
Normal blood cells	Sickle-cell anemia
Normal skin coloring	Albinism (lack of pigment)
Double-jointedness	Normal joints
Huntington's disease	Normal health
Abnormal digits in fingers or toes (extras, fused, stumps, etc.)	Normal digits

FIGURE 11.4

Sex-Linked Inheritance of Hemophilia

A female can carry a recessive gene for hemophilia (h), a blood clotting disorder, on one of her X chromosomes but not express the disease. A male, however, will express hemophilia if he inherits only one (h) gene from his mother since the Y chromosome does not carry a gene that regulates blood clotting. The probability of a male inheriting this disease under these conditions is 0.50, or 50 percent.

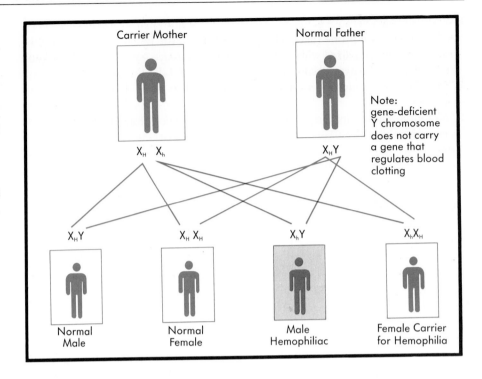

A woman who carries the hemophilia trait can pass her defective gene to her children. If the offspring is a male, there is a 50 percent probability that he will inherit the disease, since there is no dominant H gene present on the smaller Y chromosome to block the expression of the disorder. Figure 11.4 illustrates the sex-linked inheritance of hemophilia.

PROBLEMS IN INHERITANCE

Perhaps the greatest hope of most expectant parents is that their baby will be born healthy and normal. Thankfully, the odds are very high, about 97 percent, that this wish will be granted (Koop & Kaler, 1989). This statistic means, however, that about 3 percent of all babies born each year in the United States have some gene defect or chromosomal abnormality that produces a major physical and/or mental handicap. Some of these defects are apparent at birth or shortly thereafter; others do not show up until later in life. The following paragraphs describe some inherited abnormalities.

HUNTINGTON'S DISEASE Huntington's disease, or Huntington's chorea, is one of the cruelest of all genetic diseases. This incurable disorder, which killed folksinger Woody Guthrie, progressively destroys brain cells (Ferrante et al., 1987; Goto et al., 1989; Mazziotta et al., 1987; Mendez et al., 1989; Shoulson et al., 1989). Common symptoms include jerky, uncontrollable movements, loss of balance, intellectual impairment, and emotional disturbance (depression, irritability, etc.). Not uncommonly the disease is confused with disorders such as Parkinson's disease, Alzheimer's disease, and schizophrenia.

Huntington's disease is caused by a dominant gene that does not produce symptoms until a person is 35 to 45 years old. Unfortunately, by that age a person is likely to have already had children, unaware that each child has a 50 percent chance of inheriting the illness. (Figure 11.5 illustrates the genetic transmission of Huntington's disease.)

The National Huntington's Disease Association has reported that at least 25,000 Americans have the illness, and that an additional 50,000 to 100,000 people may have inherited the disease but do not yet know that they have it. Until recently there was no way to identify people who had inherited the gene until symptoms began to appear. However, in the early 1980s Harvard molecular biologist and geneticist James Gusella and his colleagues (1983) announced that they had located a genetic marker for Huntington's disease on chromosome 4.

Gusella made his discovery by applying **recombinant DNA technology,** sometimes called gene splicing. This extremely complex technique allows researchers to examine microscopic strands of genetic material for indicators of disease. Researchers use chemicals called restriction enzymes to cut apart and reassemble sections of DNA strands in different ways so they can look at genetic information that is passed along in a family. Analysis of these DNA fragments has revealed many variations in DNA scattered throughout the chromosomes. Some of these DNA variants are close enough to a defective gene to travel along with it and can be used as genetic markers of the disease (Breakerfield & Cambi, 1987; Martin, J., 1987).

Since individual differences in DNA patterns run in families, Gusella reasoned that a particular DNA pattern might be linked with Huntington's disease. He tested his theory on blood samples from 25 living members of an American family known to have a high incidence of the disease. Gusella quickly located a marker for the disease, and his findings were later corroborated in a much larger sample of over 500 people from a small community in Venezuela where the disease is rampant (Miller, J., 1983). Once the location of a marker for the Huntington's disease gene was established, researchers were able, by the late 1980s, to forge ahead and develop a test to determine whether a person has inherited it before symptoms appear. Medical geneticists are hopeful that now that they have isolated the Huntington's gene, they will be able to alter its deadly message through a process of genetic engineering or gene therapy, discussed later in this chapter.

Many geneticists and physicians welcome the development of tests for genes that cause such devastating diseases as muscular dystrophy, cystic fibrosis, and Huntington's disease. These tests represent marvelous breakthroughs that provide the potential for alleviating much pain and suffering, ideally through gene engineering or, in the absence of such therapeutic intervention, either through the abortion of fetuses doomed to live shortened, painful lives or by alerting and motivating individuals who carry major defect genes to forgo biological parenthood.

The rapid emergence of genetic tests has also raised serious ethical dilemmas for health practitioners. If a genetic test indicates that a child will develop a deadly illness which will result in a painful and/or premature death, should that child be told his or her fate? Should such a test even be performed? Genetic counselors who struggle with these issues note that many people at risk for a serious genetic disease do not want to know if they carry a life-ending defective gene, for fear that such depressing news will be a blight on whatever healthy years remain. However, what if these at-risk individuals choose to have children while electing to remain ignorant about their chances of passing a defect on to their offspring? Does society have the responsibility or right to take steps to ensure against this eventuality? What kinds of legal and ethical issues might be encountered by people who, in spite of being aware of their genetic flaws and the associated risks, opt to become parents? Should insurance companies be allowed to withhold medical insurance from people whose medical records reveal they carry a gene that one day will be a cause of major medical expenses?

The ethical dilemmas just described are only a sample of issues that medical ethicists, genetic researchers and other concerned professionals discuss and debate as they seek to deal with the social, ethical, and moral issues that accompany the emergence of amazing new genetic technologies. As researchers work to understand what the genes can tell about predicting and someday curing inherited

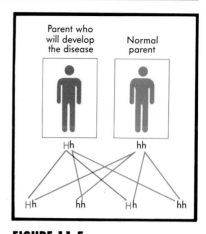

FIGURE 11.5

Genetic Transmission of Huntington's Disease

One parent who will eventually develop Huntington's disease (usually by age 45) has a single faulty gene (H) that dominates its normal counterpart (h). The probability that a child from this union will inherit Huntington's disease is 0.50, or 50 percent.

A child with Down syndrome

diseases, geneticists, lawyers, and counselors grapple with the many ethical questions in an effort to help people take advantage of the genetic revolution without falling prey to its pitfalls (Barinaga, 1989, p. 1).

PHENYLKETONURIA   **Phenylketonuria (PKU)** is another potentially devastating genetic disease. PKU is caused by a recessive gene that, when present in a double dose, results in the absence of an enzyme necessary to metabolize the protein phenylalanine found in milk. A newborn with phenylketonuria cannot metabolize milk to form phenylalanine. Unmetabolized phenylalanine converts to phenylpyruvic acid. The consequence is an excessive accumulation of phenyl-pyruvic acid, which damages the baby's developing nervous system and can lead to mental retardation and a variety of other disruptive symptoms.

Fortunately, a routine screening process can be used to test levels of phenylpyruvic acid shortly after birth. Infants who show high levels of phenyl-pyruvic acid test positive for PKU, and they can be placed on milk substitutes. They must remain on the diet for several years until their brains have developed to the point that they can no longer be damaged by the acid.

There are many other examples of diseases caused by genetic defects. These include such conditions as *muscular dystrophy, cystic fibrosis, sickle-cell anemia* (a blood disorder that primarily affects blacks), and *Tay-Sachs disease* (a disorder characterized by progressive degeneration of the central nervous system that occurs primarily in Jewish people of Eastern European origin). However, many inherited diseases are caused not by the transmission of faulty genes but rather by chromosomal abnormalities. One of the best-known conditions caused by chromosomal abnormalities is Down syndrome (previously called Down's syndrome).

DOWN SYNDROME   **Down syndrome** is the most common chromosomal disorder. It is characterized by a distinctive physical appearance—short stature, small round head, flattened skull and nose, oval-shaped eyes with an extra fold of skin over the eyelid, a short neck, a protruding tongue, and sometimes webbed fingers or toes. People with this syndrome also demonstrate marked mental retardation. Down syndrome children tend to be cheerful, affectionate, and sociable. Most are educable, and some acquire simple skills that allow them to earn an income and live independently in special environments.

Down syndrome is an autosomal chromosome disorder in which the 21st chromosome pair has an additional chromosome attached to it. A person with Down syndrome thus has 47 chromosomes rather than the normal 46. While there is inconclusive evidence that a small percentage of Down syndrome cases may have a genetic basis, most if not all instances of this disorder are caused by a chromosomal accident (Hamamy et al., 1990; Smith & Wilson, 1973). Older women are at greater risk of bearing Down syndrome children, a fact that has led many researchers to attribute this disorder primarily to deterioration of the mother's ova with age. However, evidence suggests that the syndrome may also be caused by a defect in the father's sperm (Abroms & Bennett, 1981).

GENETIC COUNSELING

The idea behind **genetic counseling** is that it is often possible to estimate the odds that a couple will have children with certain disorders. A genetic counselor, who may be a genetic specialist, obstetrician, pediatrician, or family practice physician, can often make such predictions based on a detailed study of family histories and medical examinations of both partners. Laboratory investigations may use urine, blood, and skin samples. Chromosomes obtained from tissue samples are often photographed, and the photos are cut and rearranged so that the chromosomes are organized according to size and structure on a chart called a **karotype.** A karotype often reveals any chromosomal abnormalities that may exist.

A genetic counselor can only estimate the probability of having children with a disorder. The couple must decide if the risks are great enough to elect not to have children. In such a case, many alternatives are available. The partner with the defective gene may choose to be sterilized, and the couple may wish to consider adoption or a variety of other alternatives. For example, if the man carries the genetic defect, a viable option may be **artificial insemination** in which semen from a donor is mechanically introduced into the woman's vagina or in some cases, after being specially prepared, directly into her uterus. If the genetic defect is carried by the woman, the man's sperm may be used to fertilize a female donor's ovum. In this process, called **embryo transfer** or *artificial embryonation*, a female volunteer is artificially inseminated with sperm, and approximately five days after fertilization the tiny embryo is removed from the woman donor and transferred surgically into the uterus of the mother-to-be, who then carries the pregnancy.

The recent development of several revolutionary techniques for assessing fetal development and diagnosing birth defects *in utero*, together with the legalization of abortion, have encouraged some couples with a history of genetic disease to take a chance on a pregnancy. One of these techniques is a reliable and accurate method of prenatal screening known as **amniocentesis** (Brandenburg et al., 1990; Simoni et al., 1990). If a woman and her physician have some reason to suspect that there may be fetal abnormalities, amniocentesis can help establish whether a problem exists. As Figure 11.6 illustrates, a needle is inserted through

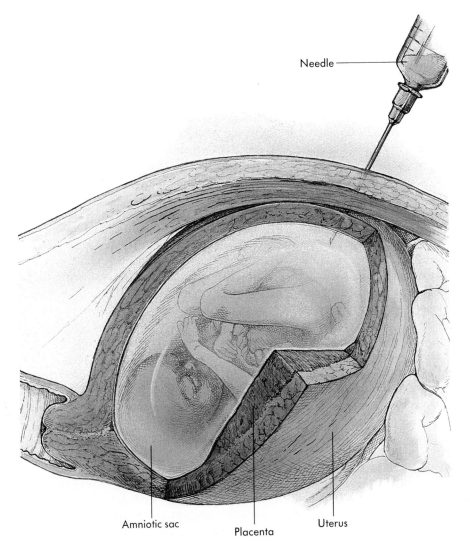

Needle

Amniotic sac

Placenta

Uterus

FIGURE 11.6

Amniocentesis Procedure

This procedure consists of inserting a needle through the woman's abdominal wall into the uterine cavity to draw out a sample of amniotic fluid (fluid surrounding the fetus). Fetal cells from the fluid are cultured for chromosomal analysis.

the woman's abdominal wall and into the uterus to draw out a sample of the *amniotic fluid* (fluid surrounding the fetus). Fetal cells from the fluid are cultured for chromosome analysis and the fluid is then tested, using procedures that take two to three weeks. A variety of birth defects can be detected by this means. Although amniocentesis cannot detect all fetal abnormalities, the number is increasing as techniques become more sophisticated.

Another technique for detecting birth defects is **chorionic villi sampling (CVS)** (Brandenburg et al., 1990; Huggins, 1989; Simoni et al., 1990). The chorionic villi are threadlike protrusions on a membrane surrounding the fetus that are made up of rapidly developing fetal cells. This test involves inserting a thin catheter through the vagina and the cervix into the uterus and taking a small sample of the chorionic villi. This procedure has an advantage over amniocentesis: It can be done as early as the ninth week instead of the fourteenth (Greenwood, 1989). Both amniocentesis and CVS involve some risks, including damage to the fetus, induced miscarriage, and infection. For this reason, the procedures are not used unless there is a likelihood of a problem.

Prenatal screening through either amniocentesis or CVS cannot detect all birth defects. However, rapidly improving technologies for detecting faulty genes, such as the recombinant DNA procedure for detecting the presence of the Huntington's gene, suggest that prenatal screening will prove increasingly helpful in the years to come. At the present time several hereditary diseases caused by defective genes may be diagnosed prenatally via *in utero* testing (Pardes et al., 1989).

GENETIC ENGINEERING

The most controversial new technology is the developing science of **genetic engineering,** sometimes called **gene therapy** (Friedman, 1989; Hirschhorn, 1987; Pardes et al., 1989). Genetic engineering involves using recombinant DNA techniques both to identify gene defects and to insert a new gene into cells to alter and correct a defective genetic code. The artificially introduced gene instructs the recipient cells to begin manufacturing a substance they might not otherwise produce because of a genetic error. Most of the genetic engineering research to date has been conducted with nonhuman subjects such as mice and monkeys. For example, scientists recently reported success using this technique to treat an inherited disorder in mice that is characterized by violent shivering, convulsions, and death within three to four months of birth (Readhead et al., 1987).

In March of 1990, a panel of scientists and lay persons from the National Institutes of Health held the first public hearing in the United States on a human gene therapy project. They approved it as safe. In this project, a medical team will attempt to successfully cure young children suffering from *adenosine deaminase deficiency (ADA)*, a genetic disorder that destroys immune systems. Six other federal regulatory panels still must approve the project before it is attempted. However, if this initial human gene therapy experiment ultimately proves successful, it will undoubtedly open the door to new and powerful methods for treating hereditary diseases.

At the present time, human research efforts are focused on the *somatic* or nonreproductive body cells so that any genetic changes that do occur will not be passed on to children. Thus, while a person might be cured of an inherited disease, he or she would still have the risk of passing the defect on to children. To prevent this outcome, genetic engineers would have to alter the reproductive cells—a procedure that for ethical reasons is probably still years away (Annas & Elias, 1990; Friedman, 1989; Young, 1985).

Recent evidence suggests that gene therapy in humans may prove effective in averting the detrimental effects of a variety of diseases including disorders of the bone marrow, liver, central nervous system, some kinds of cancers, and deficiencies of circulating enzymes, hormones, and blood coagulation factors (Friedman,

1989). At the time of this writing, studies are under way in which researchers are exploring ways to utilize gene therapy in the treatment of Alzheimer's disease and Parkinson's disease.

PRENATAL DEVELOPMENT

The nine months or approximately 266 days of prenatal development take place in three stages: germinal, embryonic, and fetal. These stages of prenatal development are not to be confused with the customary convention of dividing pregnancy into three-month segments called *trimesters.*

GERMINAL STAGE   During the **germinal** or **zygote stage** (the first two weeks after fertilization), the zygote develops rapidly as it becomes attached to the walls of the uterus. By the end of the second week, various auxiliary structures—the amniotic sac, umbilical cord, and placenta—are well established and the cell mass is called an **embryo.**

EMBRYONIC STAGE   The second stage, the **embryonic stage,** lasts from the beginning of the third week to the end of the eighth. It is characterized by very fast growth and differentiation of the heart, lungs, pancreas, and other vital organs as well as the major body systems. During this stage, the embryo is extremely vulnerable to negative environmental influences such as faulty nutrition, drugs, or maternal disease. Because any of these environmental insults may have devastating, irreversible effects on the developing baby, the embryonic period is viewed as a critical stage of development. The vast majority of environmentally induced prenatal development defects, as well as most spontaneous abortions (miscarriages), occur during this period. By the end of the embryonic stage almost all of the baby's structures and organs are formed and a few organs, like the heart, are already functioning. By the end of eight weeks the baby, now called a **fetus,** has clearly discernible features and a prominent head.

FETAL STAGE   During the final **fetal stage,** which extends from the beginning of the third month to birth, bone and muscle tissue form and the various organs and body systems continue to mature and develop. By the end of four months, external body parts—including fingernails, eyebrows, and eyelashes—are clearly formed. Fetal movement may be felt at this time. Future prenatal development consists primarily of growth in size and refinement of the features that already exist. (Figures 11.7 and 11.8 portray prenatal development at 5 and 14 weeks, respectively.)

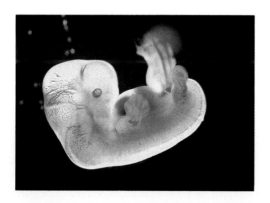

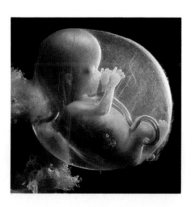

FIGURE 11.7 (left)
Prenatal Development at 5 Weeks

FIGURE 11.8 (right)
Prenatal Development at 14 Weeks

Throughout pregnancy, the fetus depends on the mother for nutrients, oxygen, and waste elimination as substances pass through the placenta and the umbilical cord to the fetus. Fetal and maternal blood do not mix. Fetal blood circulates independently within the closed system of the fetus and inner part of the placenta; maternal blood flows in the uterine walls and outer part of the placenta. All exchanges between fetal and maternal blood systems take place as substances pass through the walls of the blood vessels.

PHYSICAL DEVELOPMENT

The period from *infancy* (birth to roughly the toddler stage) through *childhood* (toddlerhood to the onset of adolescence) is marked by many important developmental changes. The remainder of this chapter deals with various aspects of physical, cognitive, and psychosocial development that occur during the first 12 or 13 years. We begin by discussing physical development, including development of the brain, physical growth, and motor development.

DEVELOPMENT OF THE BRAIN

A newborn's brain has most, if not all, of the neurons it will ever have. However, it is still far from mature. At birth, the brain is only about 25 percent of its adult weight, and the complex neural networks that form the basis for our skills and memories are just beginning to form. Growth occurs rapidly: By six months the brain is 50 percent of its adult weight; at two years, 75 percent; and at five years, 90 percent of its adult weight. At age 10, the figure is 95 percent. These figures stand in sharp contrast to the weight of the entire body, which at birth is only about 5 percent of adult weight and at 10 years is only about 50 percent (Peacock, 1986). During this period of rapid growth (and to a lesser extent in the years that follow), neural networks become increasingly complex as changes take place in the size, shape, and density of interconnections among neurons (see Figure 11.9).

The brain develops in an orderly fashion after birth. In the first few months the primary motor area of the cerebral cortex develops rapidly as the infant progresses from involuntary reflexive activity to voluntary control over motor movements. The cortical areas that control vision and hearing develop somewhat more slowly. By three months, however, these sensory areas, particularly those controlling visual perception, are more fully developed, so that infants can reach out and touch objects that they see. In the ensuing months, further development and refinement of sensory and motor capabilities are closely linked to changes in the brain and the rest of the nervous system.

Recall from Chapter 3 that certain cognitive functions tend to be localized in one of the cerebral hemispheres. At one time it was believed that much of this hemispheric specialization or localization of cortical functions occurs gradually throughout childhood (Lenneberg, 1967). Recent evidence suggests, however, that this specialization begins very early (Bryden & Saxby, 1985; Meerwaldt & van Dongen, 1989). One study demonstrated that most newborns are better able to process speech syllables in their left than right hemispheres (Molfese & Molfese, 1979). (Remember that verbal functions tend to be localized in the left hemispheres of most people.) By age three, nine out of 10 children show this specialization for verbal processing. Left- or right-handedness also develops early, providing further evidence of hemispheric specialization during infancy (Bryden & Saxby, 1985; Hawn & Harris, 1983).

EFFECTS OF EXPERIENCES ON BRAIN DEVELOPMENT   Do our early experiences influence the way our brains develop? Some experiments performed in the late 1960s indicate that they do. Mark Rosenzweig and his colleagues at the Univer-

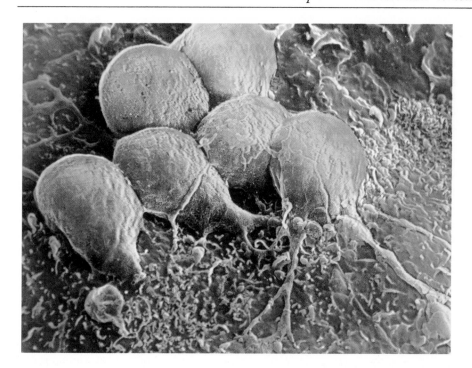

FIGURE 11.9
Neural Development

Neural development continues throughout life and consists of the growth of dendrites and synaptic connections. By age 10 the brain is about 95 percent of adult size. This electron micrographic shows a group of cell bodies with numerous dendritic connections.

sity of California at Berkeley conducted a series of experiments to compare how being raised in enriched as opposed to impoverished environments affected rats (Rosenzweig, 1966). Some of the rats were reared in sterile, dimly lit, individual cages with solid side walls that prevented them from seeing or touching other animals; others were raised in a large cage with 10 to 12 other rats and plenty of toys such as ladders, wheels, and boxes (see Figure 11.10).

The researchers were not originally looking for significant brain differences: Most psychologists at the time had not considered that experience might alter brain anatomy. However, Rosenzweig and his associates routinely recorded brain

Impoverished environment

Enriched environment

FIGURE 11.10
The Environment Has a Profound Effect on the Development of the Brain

Mark Rosenzweig and his colleagues found that rats reared in enriched environments developed larger brains with thicker cerebral cortexes than rats reared in impoverished environments.

weights as part of their research, and as a result they made an important discovery: The brains of the rats reared in the enriched environments were heavier than those of rats raised in solitary confinement. These variations were most pronounced in the cerebral cortex, where the average weight difference was 4 percent. Rats raised in the impoverished, sterile environments tended to develop a lighter and thinner cortex, with smaller-than-normal neurons (Rosenzweig et al., 1972).

Other evidence provided by researchers at the University of Illinois has supported these findings, linking enriched early experiences with expanded networks of dendrites in the precise areas of the brain where the experiences are processed (Greenough & Green, 1981). The increased number of dendrites seems to preserve newly established neural networks. More branches mean more synapses, suggesting that greater amounts of information can be transmitted more efficiently in these animals' brains.

Early experience seems to affect brain biochemistry as well as anatomy. In the enriched rats, Rosenzweig and his colleagues also found a significant increase in the activity of two enzymes, acetylcholinesterase and cholinesterase, both of which play an important role in the synaptic transmission of neural messages (Rosenzweig et al., 1972).

In both the Berkeley and University of Illinois studies, the anatomical and biochemical effects were not restricted to the earliest periods of development. Rats who were reared under normal laboratory conditions in their early days and then subjected to either impoverished or enriched environments showed similar weight and biochemical changes in their brains. Although the effects of environmental stimulation may be greater during early development, these findings indicate that the brains of rats, and possibly humans, are malleable throughout development.

Research during the past ten years has confirmed that the development of the brain is not predetermined by some genetic blueprint waiting to be completed as development progresses. Rather, brain development, including the elaborate interconnections between neurons, depends upon neural stimulation. Even though humans are born with almost all of the 100 billion neurons they will ever have, the mass of their brain is only about one fourth that of an adult. The brain becomes bigger, not because more neurons develop, but because the existing neurons get larger. Both the number of axons and dendrites, as well as the complexity of their connections, continue to increase.

How are neural connections increased? What is the mechanism that allows experience to rewire the brain? These questions are partially answered by the mechanism proposed by Donald Hebb over 40 years ago, now referred to as *Hebbian synapses*. Hebbian synapses were described in considerable detail in Chapter 7 as a neural mechanism for memory. As you may recall, Hebbian synapses refer to long-term changes in synaptic connections that are dependent upon particular patterns of neuronal activity. In a sense, cells that fire together get wired together. Recent research on neural development has confirmed that neural activity (action potentials) is critical for many aspects of development (Kalil, 1989; Shatz, 1992).

PHYSICAL GROWTH

Changes that take place in the brain are only part of the picture of what happens during development. Another significant change is physical growth. Children grow more rapidly during the first few years than at any other time. During the first six months, in fact, infants more than double their weight, and by their first birthday most infants have tripled their birth weight (the average newborn weighs seven pounds) and increased their birth height by 50 percent. In the next two years they gain another eight inches and 10 pounds, on the average. After their third birthday, this early growth levels off somewhat to a more steady two or three inches per year, until the adolescent growth spurt.

Both physical growth and motor development follow two basic patterns. The first pattern is **cephalocaudal** (that is, from head to foot); the second pattern is **proximodistal** (inner to outer) (Hall, 1987). The cephalocaudal pattern of development occurs first and most rapidly in the head and upper body, which is why newborns have large heads. It is also why a one year old's brain weighs approximately two-thirds of its eventual adult weight while the rest of the body is a much smaller proportion of its adult size. The cephalocaudal principle also explains why babies can track things with their eyes before they can effectively move their trunks, and why they can do many things with their hands before they can use their legs. Because development is also proximodistal, infants gain control over the upper portions of their arms and legs, which are closer to the center of the body, before they can control their forearms and forelegs. Control of the hands, feet, fingers, and toes comes last.

MOTOR DEVELOPMENT

Another basic rule of development is that it proceeds from the simple to the more complex. This progression is particularly apparent in the acquisition of motor skills. The motor movements of young babies are dominated by a number of involuntary reflexes that offer either protection or help in securing nourishment. An example is the *rooting reflex:* When babies are stroked on the cheek, they turn their heads toward the sensation, vigorously "rooting" for a nipple (see Figure 11.11 on page 422). Other common reflexes are listed in Table 11.2. As

TABLE 11.2 *Primitive Reflexes in Human Infants*

NAME OF REFLEX	STIMULATION	BEHAVIOR	AGE OF DROPPING OUT
Rooting	Cheek stroked with finger or nipple	Head turns, mouth opens, sucking movements begin	9 months
Moro (startle)	Sudden stimulus such as gunshot or being dropped	Extends legs, arms, and fingers, arches back, draws back head	3 months
Darwinian (grasping)	Palm of hand stroked	Makes such a strong fist that baby can be raised to standing position if both fists are closed around a stick	2 months
Swimming	Put in water face down	Well-coordinated swimming movements	6 months
Tonic neck	Laid down on back	Turns head to one side, assumes "fencer" position, extends arms and legs on preferred side, flexes opposite limbs	2 months
Babinski	Sole of foot stroked	Toes fan out, foot twists in	6–9 months
Walking	Held under arm, with bare feet touching flat surface	Makes steplike motions that look like well-coordinated walking	2 months
Placing	Backs of feet drawn against edge of flat surface	Withdraws foot	1 month

SOURCE: Papalia and Olds, 1986

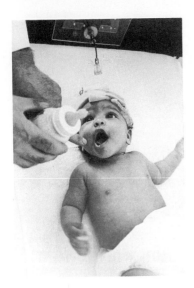

FIGURE 11.11
The Rooting Reflex

When babies are touched on the cheek they turn their heads toward the touch and begin to "root" for a nipple to suck on.

development progresses, voluntary, cortically controlled movements begin to take over, and the primitive reflexes disappear according to the timetable shown in the table. Some reflexes, such as coughing, sneezing, gagging, and the eyeblink, remain with us throughout our lives.

As the nervous system and muscles mature, more complicated motor movements and skills begin to emerge. There is wide variation in the ages at which babies are able to roll over, sit without support, stand, and walk, but the sequence of these developments is universal.

Can different environmental experiences influence the rate at which we acquire motor skills? A number of studies have explored this question, and within a normal range of experiences, the answer seems to be no. As long as children are well fed, healthy, and free to initiate motor skills when they are ready, the role of environmental influences on motor development is quite limited (Clarke-Stewart, 1977; Ridenour, 1982). For example, regardless of the amount of training or encouragement children receive, they will not walk until the cerebellum has matured enough to create a readiness for walking, an event that occurs at about age one.

In certain Native American cultures, infants are wrapped in swaddling clothes and bound to cradleboards during most of their waking hours for the first 12 or more months of their lives. We have just seen that children will not walk until they reach a certain level of biological readiness. Is the converse true? Will children begin to walk when their biological clocks reach a certain point, even if they have not had earlier opportunities to crawl and otherwise move about on their own? Make a reasoned prediction before reading on.

In the discussion of maturation earlier in this chapter (see "Heredity and Environment"), we noted that certain biologically determined sequences occur even if children do not receive encouragement. As we have noted, studies have shown that babies who have been virtually immobilized on cradleboards during their first year typically begin to walk at about the same age as infants from other cultures who are free to practice sitting, crawling, and pulling themselves up on furniture (Orlansky, 1949). This finding does not mean that the environment has no influence at all. Babies that spend most of their first year of life lying in a crib develop abnormally slowly. Other studies of children raised with insufficient love, stimulation, or proper nutrition often show profound physical and mental retardation.

If early training does not significantly accelerate the rate at which children master motor skills such as standing or walking, does the same rule apply to other physical skills such as bowel and bladder control? A classic early study assessed the effect of differential toilet training on twin boys. One was placed on a toilet once on the hour every day from two months of age, while the other did not begin training until age 23 months. The first twin did not demonstrate any control until 20 months, but by 23 months he had mastered bladder and bowel control. The other twin, with no prior training, caught up in short order as soon as training began (McGraw, 1940).

Later research has generally confirmed this finding, and it is now widely recognized that no amount of encouragement, reinforcement, punishment, or pleading will induce successful toilet training until the necessary muscular and neurological maturation has occurred (usually sometime between 15 and 24 months of age). Unfortunately, toilet training is often begun long before an infant can voluntarily control the sphincter muscles in order to retain waste. While an early start does not hasten toilet training, it may result in emotional strain, particularly if parents put too much pressure on a child.

Although the milestones are no longer so dramatic, motor development continues beyond infancy and early childhood. Parents are sometimes amazed to realize one day that the awkward child they observed banging around the house has been transformed into a coordinated athlete who performs with distinction.

COGNITIVE DEVELOPMENT ------------------

Cognitive development refers to the development of various behaviors such as perceiving, remembering, reasoning, and problem solving. When do children begin to remember? How do they categorize experiences? When can they see things from another's perspective, reason logically, and think symbolically? Most efforts to answer such questions lead inevitably to the writings of the late Swiss psychologist Jean Piaget.

No one has provided more insights into cognitive development than Jean Piaget (1970, 1972). Piaget became interested in how children think in the early 1920s, when he was working with Alfred Binet in Paris on standardizing children's intelligence tests. At first, his goal was to find certain questions that the average child of a specific age could answer correctly. However, Piaget soon became intrigued with another finding: The mistakes made by many children of the same age were often strikingly similar (and strikingly different from those made by children of other ages). It occurred to Piaget that children's cognitive strategies are age-related, and that the way children think about things changes with age regardless of the specific nature of what they are thinking about. These observations led Piaget to refocus his research. From this point until his death in 1980, he devoted his efforts to understanding how cognitive abilities develop. Piaget's theory gradually evolved from years of carefully observing and questioning individual children, including his own three offspring. The following paragraphs provide an overview of his major themes.

PIAGET'S THEORY OF COGNITIVE DEVELOPMENT

SCHEMAS According to Piaget, the impetus behind human intellectual development is an urge to make sense out of our world. To accomplish this goal, he theorized, our maturing brains form "mental" structures or **schemas** which assimilate and organize processed information. These schemas guide future behavior while providing a framework for making sense out of new information.

Newborns are equipped with only primitive schemas that guide certain basic sensorimotor sequences such as sucking, looking, and grasping. According to Piaget, these early schemas become activated only when certain objects are present —for example, things that can be looked at, grasped, or sucked. However, as an infant evolves into a child and later an adult, these schemas become increasingly complex, often substituting symbolic representations for objects that are physically present (Piaget, 1977).

By the time we reach adulthood, our brains are filled with countless schemas or ways of organizing information that range from our knowledge of how to play a tune to the fantasies we concoct when we are bored. To Piaget, cognitive growth involves a constant process of modifying and adapting our schemas to account for new experiences. This adaptation takes place through two processes: assimilation and accommodation.

ASSIMILATION AND ACCOMMODATION **Assimilation** is the process by which we interpret new information in accordance with our existing knowledge or schemas. In this ongoing process, we may find it necessary to modify the information we assimilate in order to fit it into our existing schemas. At the same time, however, we adjust or restructure what we already know so that new information can fit in better—a process Piaget called **accommodation.**

For instance, an infant who is accustomed to taking its nourishment from the breast uses a simple "suck and swallow" schema to guide this basic sensorimotor sequence. When it is switched from the breast to the bottle, the infant assimilates this new experience into the existing schema and continues to suck and

Jean Piaget

swallow. What happens when the parents introduce a notable variation by filling the formula bottle with apple juice instead of milk? The baby's initial reaction may be to spit out the strange new substance. With time, the infant may come to like apple juice but dislike other types of juice. Basically the infant has accommodated the new information by modifying the suck and swallow schema to one of "suck, taste, and swallow (maybe)."

Piaget believed that we learn to understand our world as we constantly adapt and modify our mental structures through assimilation and accommodation. As we develop, assimilation allows us to maintain important connections with the past while accommodation helps us to adapt and change as we gain new experiences.

FOUR STAGES OF COGNITIVE DEVELOPMENT Piaget viewed cognitive growth as a four-stage process with qualitatively different kinds of thinking occurring in each of these stages. Although all people progress through these stages in the same sequence, Piaget noted that the speed of this progression may vary from person to person. Table 11.3 outlines these four stages: the sensorimotor, preoperational, concrete operations, and formal operations.

Sensorimotor Stage (Birth to About 24 Months) During the **sensorimotor stage,** infants learn about their worlds primarily through their senses and actions. Instead of thinking about what is going on around them, infants discover by sensing (sensori-) and doing (motor). They learn by their actions, which gradually evolve from reflexes to more purposeful behaviors. For example, an infant might learn that shaking a rattle produces a sound or that crying at night produces parents. Thus some of the schemas that develop during this stage are organized around the principle of causality, as the infant begins to perform cognitively organized goal-directed behaviors.

Another key aspect of the sensorimotor stage is the gradual development of **object permanence**—the realization that objects (or people) continue to exist even when they are not immediately in view. Up to about the age of four months, an object ceases to exist for the infant when it is out of sight (see Figure 11.12). After about four months babies begin to look for objects they no longer see, and sometime between eight and 12 months they begin to retrieve objects they see being hidden manually. By age two, most children are able to incorporate into their schemas symbolic representation of objects which are clearly independent of their perception of these articles. At this point in development toddlers gleefully and systematically search all kinds of possible hiding places for objects they have not seen hidden. Research by University of Illinois psychologist Rene Baillargeon (1987) revealed that object permanence in infants may occur as early as age three-and-one-half months.

Another important cognitive skill of the sensorimotor stage is imitation. Even a tiny baby may try to imitate the facial expression of an older person. Under

FIGURE 11.12

Object Permanence

Up to about four months of age an object ceases to exist when it is out of sight. After four months of age babies begin to look for hidden objects.

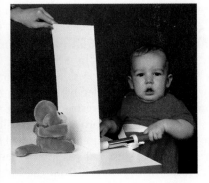

TABLE 11.3 *Piaget's Four Stages of Cognitive Development*

COGNITIVE DEVELOPMENT STAGE	APPROXIMATE AGE	GENERAL CHARACTERISTICS
Sensorimotor	Birth to about 24 months	Infants experience world primarily by sensing and doing. They learn by their actions, which gradually evolve from reflexes to more purposeful behaviors. Cognitive growth marked by improving ability to imitate behavior and gradual development of object permanence.
Preoperational	2–7 years	The child begins to acquire the ability to use symbols to represent people, objects, and events. However the child cannot reason logically and thought tends to be limited by the inability to take into account more than one perceptual factor at the same time and to perceive the world from any perspective other than one's own.
Concrete operations	7–12 years	The child makes a major transition in cognitive development by shifting from a single-dimensional emphasis on perception to a greater reliance on logical thinking about concrete events. During this stage children master the principle of conservation.
Formal operations	12 years and older	Abstract reasoning emerges during this stage. Teenagers acquire the ability to make complex deductions and solve problems by systematically testing hypothetical solutions.

controlled laboratory conditions, researchers have found that attempts at imitation are clearly present even among newborns 7 to 72 hours old (Meltzoff & Moore, 1983). For example, when an experimenter stuck his tongue out at a newborn, the infant responded in kind! This cognitive skill continues to be refined, so that by the end of the sensorimotor period children imitate all kinds of behaviors.

Preoperational Stage (Ages Two to Seven) As children move beyond their second birthday, they increasingly use symbolic thought. Having mastered object permanence, they are now ready to think representatively, using symbols rather than depending on what they see or touch. The ability to use words to represent people, objects, and events allows children to make giant steps in cognitive development. Imagination becomes important as children's play activities become increasingly focused on make-believe. Three and four year olds can now imitate another person's behavior after a lapse of time—a qualitative change from the immediate imitation that took place during the sensorimotor stage. The use of language, imaginative play, and delayed imitation all demonstrate an increasing sophistication.

Despite these advances, however, preoperational thought remains somewhat limited, for it depends largely on how things appear or seem to be. Children at this stage have yet to master logical reasoning processes based on rules and concepts, which is why Piaget used the term **preoperational stage:** Young children are able to develop only immature concepts, or *preconcepts*, in their effort to understand the world. For example, an adult has no problem distinguishing between a sports car and a sedan, or a new versus an old car. However, a small child has only a ill-defined, immature concept of a car—something that has wheels and doors and goes *vroooom!*

Another limitation of preoperational thought is apparent in the phenomenon of **centration**—the inability to take into account more than one perceptual factor at the same time. (The ability to evaluate two or more physical dimensions simultaneously, a process called **decentration,** does not emerge until the end of the preoperational period.)

Piaget demonstrated centration and decentration in a simple experiment. When he poured equal amounts of liquid into two identical glasses, five-, six-, and seven-year-old children all reported that the glasses contained equal amounts. However, when the liquid from one glass was poured into a taller, narrower glass, the children had different opinions about which of the two glasses contained the most liquid. The five and six year olds knew that it was the same liquid, but they were unable to generalize beyond the central perceptual factor of greater height, which normally indicates "more." Thus they indicated that the tall glass had more juice. In contrast, the seven year olds generally reported there was no difference, a fact they knew to be true since they were able to decentrate, or simultaneously take into account the two physical dimensions of height and width.

The ability to decentrate enables children to master **conservation,** the understanding that changing something's form does not necessarily change its essential character. Research conducted by Piaget and others has demonstrated that children do not understand the principle of conservation until the concrete-operations stage of cognitive development.

Piaget also stressed the egocentric nature of preoperational thinking. **Egocentrism** does not imply selfishness, but rather the inability to perceive the world from any perspective other than one's own. In essence, Piaget said that preoperational children view life as though everyone else were looking at it from their perspective.

In recent years, Piaget's conclusions about the degree of egocentric thinking in young children have been challenged (Ford, 1985; Moore et al., 1987). Did his young subjects perform poorly because their thinking was egocentric, or because the problem was too difficult? Some later studies have shown that even three and four year olds can successfully manipulate movable versions of simple scenes to show another's view (Borke, 1975). Researchers have also noted that four year olds seem to understand that two year olds perceive things differently, since they change their way of speaking when conversing with toddlers (Shatz & Gelman, 1973).

Although preoperational children are not necessarily incapable of viewing things from the perspectives of others, it is generally agreed that young children tend to be egocentric, as Piaget suggested. This explains why children, who see themselves as central to all events in their world, often view themselves as causing certain outcomes. For example, young children of divorcing parents may think that they are the cause of the estrangement. Needless to say, children in such highly vulnerable situations may require a great deal of assurance that they are not the cause of calamitous events such as divorce.

Concrete Operations Stage (Ages Seven to 12) Between ages seven and 12, children again make a qualitative leap as they learn to engage in decentration and to shed their egocentrism. Whereas the preoperational stage is characterized by intuitive thinking and a dependence on imagination and the senses, children in the **concrete operations stage** begin to use *logical operations* or rules. This

A liquid conservation test. When the same amount of liquid was poured into a tall narrow glass the five-year-old boy thought it contained more liquid. The seven-year-old girl believed that the tall narrow glass held the same as the shorter wide glass.

shift from a single-dimensional emphasis on perception to a greater reliance on logic is a major transition in cognitive development.

As we saw earlier, Piaget viewed mastery of the concept of conservation as a milestone of the concrete operations stage. Children master different aspects of conservation at various times during the concrete operations stage. For example, a child who understands conservation of substance will realize that a ball of clay rolled into the shape of a hot dog still has the same amount of clay. However, when the same child sees two identical clay balls weighed on a balance scale, and then watches as one of the balls is rolled into a hot dog shape, a strange thing may happen. Although the child understands conservation of substance, he or she may not yet understand the more abstract principle of conservation of weight—and thus does not realize the hot dog and ball will weigh the same. By the end of the concrete operations stage, children typically master all of the various dimensions of conservation: substance, length, number, weight, and volume.

Throughout this stage, thinking is still somewhat restricted by a tendency to limit the use of logical operations to concrete situations and objects in the visible world. For example, if you played the game 20 questions with an eight year old, the child would be likely to stick with concrete questions that, if correct, would solve the problem ("Is it a carrot?" "Is it a rabbit?"). In contrast, older children in the final stage of cognitive development might approach the problem more abstractly, asking general questions such as, "Is it vegetable?" or "Is it animal?" before making specific guesses.

In the concrete operations stage, children are not yet able to deal with completely hypothetical problems of a "what if" nature in which they must compare what they know to be true with what may be true. For instance, if you ask concrete operational children what it would be like if people could fly, their answers would probably reflect what they have actually seen (in cartoons and movies as well as in real life) rather than total abstractions. Thus you might be told that people would look funny with wings or that people cannot fly. In contrast, older children are more able to imagine things beyond their own experiences. Thus a teenager might tell you that if people could fly, department stores would no longer need elevators, or that no one would need to take drugs to "get high."

Formal Operations Stage (Age 12 and Older) In the **formal operations stage,** individuals acquire the ability to make complex deductions and solve problems by systematically testing hypothetical solutions. Adolescents can now think about abstract problems. For example, younger children in the concrete operations stage would indignantly reject the syllogism, "People are faster than horses, and horses are faster than cars; therefore people are faster than cars" because it runs counter to concrete, observable facts: They *know* cars are faster than humans. In contrast, adolescents in the formal operations stage are able to evaluate the logic of this syllogism separately from its content.

Although Piaget originally believed that the formal operations stage almost always begins at about the age of 12, he later revised this position to allow for a variety of situations that could either postpone or prevent the arrival of this stage. Piaget did maintain that once children enter the stage of formal operations, there are no longer any qualitative differences between their thought processes and those of older teenagers or adults. Any further advances in cognitive functions are merely refinements in the ability to think logically and reason abstractly.

This stage of cognitive development is marked by the emergence of the capacity to manipulate object representations, when they are not physically present, and by the ability to engage in deductive reasoning. Deductive reasoning requires manipulations of complex thoughts and concepts. Piaget devised the pendulum problem to illustrate deductive reasoning in the formal operations stage. A child is shown a pendulum consisting of an object suspended from a string. The child is then shown how to manipulate four variables: the length of the string, the weight of the suspended object, the height in the pendulum arc from which the object is released, and the force with which the object is pushed. Then the child is instructed to determine which of these factors, singly or in combination, influences how fast the object swings.

EVALUATION OF PIAGET'S THEORY Piaget discovered that typical seven or eight year olds try to solve the problem by physically manipulating the four variables in a random fashion. For instance, they might release a light weight from high in the arc, then release a heavy weight from a low point in the arc. Because they did not test each variable systematically, these younger children often arrived at erroneous conclusions (and then insisted that their answers were correct!). At age 10 or 11, children are more systematic in their approach, but they still lack the capacity to engage in careful hypothesis testing and deductive logic.

By adolescence, perhaps as early as age 12, children's strategies change radically. Now they systematically keep one variable constant while manipulating the others. In this fashion, they can deduce that only one factor (the length of the string) determines how fast the pendulum swings. Formal operations adolescents also tend to work out a plan or strategy for approaching the pendulum problem before commencing their tests. The ability to think a problem through before actually performing any concrete physical manipulations represents a major qualitative change in cognitive functioning. (See Table 11.3.)

Piaget's theory of cognitive development has been criticized for placing too much emphasis on the maturation of biologically based cognitive structures while understating the importance of environment and experience. He has also been criticized for ignoring individual differences in his attempt to portray developmental norms. Despite these criticisms, however, his theory has had a profound impact on developmental psychology and on educational procedures in the Western world. Its basic tenets have been repeatedly tested and largely supported. Particularly noteworthy is recent research revealing that the occurrence of growth spurts in the development of human cerebral hemispheres tends to overlap with the timing of the major developmental stages described by Piaget (Thatcher et al., 1987). These findings add credibility to Piaget's assertion that biological maturation and cognitive development are closely associated. In conclusion, we can say that Piaget's theory has provided immense insights into understanding the development of thought, stimulating more research than any other developmental theory and providing the impetus for many valuable changes in both education and child care.

GENDER DIFFERENCES IN COGNITIVE ABILITIES

People have had questions pertaining to differences in the cognitive abilities of males and females for as long as human history has been recorded. Even today, after a century of research, many questions remain about the nature and origins of cognitive gender differences. In the following paragraphs we examine what research has revealed.

In the early 1970s, psychologists Eleanor Maccoby and Carol Jacklin (1974) conducted an exhaustive review of the psychological literature on gender differences in which they analyzed, compared, and tabulated findings reported in over 2,000 journal articles. They concluded that cognitive gender differences were clearly demonstrable in only three areas: (1) females surpass males in verbal skills; (2) males have greater spatial skills; and (3) males excel in mathematical ability. Several years later, Janet Hyde (1981) reanalyzed the studies of verbal, mathematical, and spatial abilities included in Maccoby and Jacklin's original survey. Using a statistical technique called *meta-analysis* (a complex statistical procedure whereby data from many studies are combined and collectively analyzed), Hyde collectively analyzed data from several studies and found that the cognitive gender differences reported by Maccoby and Jacklin were in fact quite small. Hyde concluded that gender differences "appear to account for no more than 1% to 5% of the population variance" (p. 894). In recent years psychologists have been increasingly cautious about assuming that these cognitive gender differences are significant. We examine each of these areas with particular attention to data that have emerged in recent years.

VERBAL SKILLS Verbal skills encompass such things as word knowledge and usage, grammar, spelling, and understanding analogies. Until recently, a preponderance of evidence suggested that females score higher than males on tests of verbal abilities (Halpern, 1986).

If females are superior in verbal skills, it is possible that this superiority may result from inborn biological factors. As we discuss later in this chapter, some evidence suggests that there may be differences between male and female brains which favor females in verbal skills. However, we might argue just as convincingly that girls may have the edge in verbal abilities because of socialization practices. Many of us grow up thinking that writing and reading are girls' subjects. It seems plausible that such stereotyped notions may discourage boys from giving English classes their best shot. Furthermore, while girls are often encouraged to use standard language, boys are more likely to get away with using nonstructured language, such as slang and swearing.

SPATIAL ABILITIES Spatial aptitudes encompass the related abilities to perceive the position and configuration of objects in space and to manipulate these objects while maintaining a representation of their relationship. Spatial skills are used in such tasks as negotiating mazes, aiming at a target, arranging blocks to match geometric designs, visualizing how an object would look from a different perspective—even figuring out how to fit several odd-shaped suitcases into the trunk of a car.

Evidence suggests that the spatial skills of males are superior to those of females. Why? Some theorists propose a biological explanation, noting that the portion of the brain most involved in spatial tasks (the right cerebral hemisphere) is more developed in males. As in verbal differences, however, we cannot rule out the impact of socialization. During the developmental years, boys are typically provided with more opportunities to develop spatial skills. They are more likely to own toys they can take apart, such as Erector™ sets, Legos,™ and models, all of which serve to sharpen design and construction skills. Boys are also more likely to participate in athletic activities that place a premium on spatial skills (aiming at goals, visualizing patterns in set plays, and so forth). These visual-manipulative experiences certainly contribute more to understanding the relationships between objects in space than do traditional feminine activities such as playing house and cutting out paper dolls.

MATHEMATICAL SKILLS   Gender differences in mathematical abilities have been widely reported (Benbow & Stanley, 1980; Halpern, 1986). Various explanations have included females' weaker analytic ability, poorer visual-spatial skills, the conditioning of more math avoidance behavior in females, and socialization processes that encourage people to view math interest or ability as inappropriate for females.

Researchers Doris Entwisle and David Baker (1983) theorized that differential socialization in the early years may contribute to gender differences in math skills. These investigators hypothesized that boys develop higher expectations for their own math performance than do girls, probably in response to their parents' stereotyped expectations. Entwisle and Baker tested their hypothesis on approximately 1,100 Baltimore schoolchildren. In this population, they found not only that boys in the sample consistently registered higher expectations for their own math performance than did the girls, but that parents demonstrated markedly higher expectations for the performance of sons than daughters. The researchers concluded that parents' different expectations for boys and girls is an important early influence that is ultimately reflected years later in math performance.

Thus it seems likely that gender differences in mathematical abilities are not inevitable, and that if socialization practices are changed, these differences may ultimately disappear. Support for this notion was provided by a study conducted by psychologists Karen Paulsen and Margaret Johnson (1983), who evaluated attitudes toward and aptitude for mathematics in a high socioeconomic sample of approximately 500 fourth-, eighth-, and eleventh-grade students. The researchers found no gender-related differences in math abilities at any level. A possible explanation for this finding lies in the attitudes of these subjects toward mathematics. The girls in the sample tended to express positive attitudes toward math at all grade levels, even more so than their male counterparts at the eleventh-grade level. Paulsen and Johnson speculated that the high socioeconomic level of their subjects may have resulted in female children being encouraged as much as male children to succeed even in math.

A recent meta-analysis of 100 studies of gender differences in mathematics, conducted by Janet Hyde and her colleagues (1990), casts serious doubt on the widespread assumption that males perform better than females on mathematics tests. These researchers reported that the data derived from these combined studies revealed that during the elementary- and middle-school years there were no gender differences in problem solving and understanding mathematical concepts, and that females actually demonstrated a slight superiority in computation. However, small gender differences in problem solving that favored males were shown to emerge in high school and college. Hyde and her associates speculated that this latter finding may be due, at least in part, to the fact that high school and college "are precisely the years when students are permitted to select their own courses, and females elect somewhat fewer mathematics courses than do males" (p. 150). Other researchers argue that females tend to outperform males on mathematical computation tests (arithmetic problems), but males outperform females on mathematical reasoning tasks (story-type problems) (Kimura, 1992).

TRENDS IN GENDER DIFFERENCES In recent years research has suggested that gender differences in verbal, spatial, and mathematic abilities have declined sharply. Based on a review of gender differences in test scores on the Differential Aptitude Tests (DAT) and Preliminary Scholastic Aptitude Test/Scholastic Aptitude Test (PSAT/SAT) from the 1940s to the 1980s, Yale psychologist Alan Feingold (1988) recently suggested that cognitive gender differences have declined precipitously and are disappearing.

Feingold's conclusions were supported by researchers Marcia Linn and Janet Hyde (1989). Using the statistical technique of meta-analysis to analyze hundreds of studies, these researchers found a marked narrowing of gender differences in all cognitive abilities. Another study compared the performance of 74,000 13 year olds in 20 nations on an identical battery of cognitive skills tests (Hanna, 1988). No significant gender differences were found in algebra performance, and in half of the countries boys had only a slight edge in geometry and measurement scores. Among 6,600 U.S. adolescents tested, boys scored only 2 percent better in geometry and measurement tests, and both sexes performed equally in algebra, arithmetic, and statistics.

In spite of indications that cognitive gender differences are diminishing, some researchers maintain that these differences are still very much evident (Halpern, 1989; Kimura, 1992). We expect debate to continue in this area as new research sheds light on the controversy. However, we are inclined to agree with an opinion voiced by several influential theorists (Feingold, 1988; Geary, 1989; Hanna, 1988; Linn & Hyde, 1989) that while cognitive gender differences may have a basis in biology, psychosocial factors such as different experiences and expectations also play a role. Certainly, an abundance of evidence indicates that cognitive skills are readily trainable in both sexes. If the present trend continues and boys and girls increasingly focus on the same types of activities (course work, sports participation, etc.), we might expect a further eroding of cognitive gender differences.

PSYCHOSOCIAL DEVELOPMENT

Children's physical and cognitive growth is accompanied by psychosocial development—changes in the way they think, feel, and relate to their world and the people in it. This section first describes two areas of psychosocial development, the establishment of attachment and the impact of parenting styles, then concludes with Erik Erikson's theory of psychosocial development.

ATTACHMENT

You may have observed babies at the age of seven or eight months and up to 18 months who are content as long as a parent is nearby, but who cry virtually inconsolably if the parent leaves the room. Many a babysitter has spent frustrating hours cuddling, bouncing, and singing to a baby who refuses to take comfort from anyone but the real thing—Mom or Dad.

Such experiences demonstrate one of the earliest and most profound aspects of early psychosocial development: **attachment.** Attachment is the term applied to the intense emotional tie that develops between two individuals, in this case an infant and a parent. Attachment has clear survival value in that it motivates infants to remain close to their parents or other caregivers who protect them from danger. Infants may establish intense, affectionate, reciprocal relationships with their parents, older siblings, grandparents, or any other consistent caregiver. However, the most intense attachment relationship that typically occurs in the early stages of development is between mother and child, and most of the available research has focused on the development of this bond (Cohn & Tronick, 1987; Field et al., 1987; Rutter & Durkin, 1987).

Attachment develops according to a typical sequence (Ainsworth, 1963; Schaffer & Emerson, 1964). During the first few months, babies exhibit **indiscriminate attachment:** Social behaviors such as smiling, nestling, and gurgling are typically directed to just about anyone. This pattern continues for about six to seven months, when babies begin to develop selective, **specific attachments.** At this time, they often show increased responsiveness to their parents or other regular caregivers by smiling more, holding out their arms to be picked up, and vocalizing more than to other people. This specific attachment is likely to become so strong that infants will show great distress when separated from their parents. When strangers attempt to offer solace, their overtures may be merely tolerated or perhaps overtly rejected.

Fortunately for the countless babysitters, grandparents, and friends who are distressed to be rejected, most infants progress to a third stage of **separate attachments** by about 12 to 18 months. During this stage infants take an active social interest in people other than their mothers or fathers. Fear of strangers also typically diminishes during this period.

HOW ATTACHMENT DEVELOPS How do babies form attachments to primary caregivers? A number of early developmental theorists believed that feeding was the key ingredient in the development of attachment. Because the mother provides nourishment, so the reasoning went, the baby learns to associate mother with a sense of well-being and consequently wants her to remain close at hand. This idea was popular until a series of landmark studies were released by Harry Harlow and his associates (Harlow & Zimmerman, 1958; Harlow & Harlow, 1966; Harlow et al., 1971).

Harlow's research began as the study of learning abilities in rhesus monkeys. To eliminate the possible variable input of early experiences, he separated baby monkeys from their mothers shortly after birth and raised them in individual cages which were equipped with soft blankets. Unexpectedly, the monkeys became intensely attached to the blankets, showing extreme distress when they were removed for laundering. The behavior was comparable to that of baby monkeys when they are separated from their mothers.

Harlow and his colleagues were intrigued, for this finding contradicted the notion that attachment develops through feeding. The researchers decided to conduct some experiments to find out whether contact comfort is more important than food in developing attachment. They separated infant monkeys from their mothers, rearing them in cages containing two artificial "mothers." One was made of a wire mesh cylinder; the other was a similar wire cylinder wrapped with foam rubber and covered with terry cloth to which the infant could cling. A bottle could be attached to either artificial mother so that it could serve as the monkey's source of food.

If attachment were linked to feeding, we would expect the monkeys to form attachments consistently with the "mother" hooked up to the bottle. This anticipated outcome was not what happened, however. Monkeys who were reared with a nourishing wire mother and a nonnourishing cloth mother clearly preferred the latter, spending much more time clinging to their contact-comfort mother. Even while they were obtaining nourishment from the wire mother, the monkeys often maintained simultaneous contact with the cloth mother (see Figure 11.13). The cloth mother also provided the baby monkeys with a secure base for exploring new situations. When novel stimuli were introduced, the babies would gradually venture away from their cloth mothers to explore, often returning to home base before exploring further. When a fear stimulus (such as a toy bear beating loudly on a drum) was introduced, the frightened infants would rush to their cloth mothers for security. If their cloth mothers were absent, the babies would freeze into immobility or cry and dash aimlessly around the cage.

The researchers concluded that the satisfaction of contact comfort was more important in establishing attachment than the gratification of being fed. When other qualities were added to the cloth mother, such as warmth, mechanical rocking, and feeding, the bonding was even more intense. Clearly, a strong parallel exists between this artificial situation and what often occurs when human infants have contact with the warm bodies of parents who cuddle, rock, and feed them. Harlow's demonstration that attachment does not depend on feeding should be reassuring to fathers of breast-fed babies.

EFFECTS OF ATTACHMENT DEPRIVATION   Although Harlow's experiments were aimed at determining whether food was the crucial element in forming attachments, they also provided some valuable information about emotional and social development. One particularly interesting finding has to do with the long-term effects of being raised without a real mother.

The young monkeys in Harlow's experiments seemed to develop normally at first. However, a different picture emerged when the females reached sexual maturity. Despite elaborate efforts to create ideal mating circumstances, most of them rejected the advances of male monkeys, and only four out of 18 females conceived as a result of natural insemination (many more were artificially inseminated). Most of these unmothered mothers rejected their young; some were

FIGURE 11.13

Monkeys in Harlow's Experiment

Infants maintained contact with the terrycloth "mother" even when they obtained nourishment from the wire mesh "mother."

merely indifferent, while others pushed their babies away. In spite of this rejection, the babies persisted in their attempts to establish a bond with their mothers (and in some situations, they actually succeeded). In subsequent pregnancies, these deprived mothers became more adept at nurturing their offspring.

How does this finding relate to human behavior? Do human infants deprived of attachment with nurturing caregivers develop in a similar way, and if so, are the emotional scars permanent? Up until the 1970s most developmental psychologists were inclined to answer yes to both of these questions, citing numerous studies of infants raised from birth in orphanages (Bowlby, 1965; Goldfarb, 1945; Ribble, 1943; Spitz, 1945). These studies found that orphanage children who were provided adequate physical care and nutrition but were deprived of close nurturing relationships with adult caregivers often developed problems such as physical diseases of unknown origin, retarded physical and motor development, and impaired emotional and social development. In one study of 91 orphanage infants in the United States and Canada, over one-third died before reaching their first birthday, despite good nutrition and medical care (Spitz & Wolff, 1946).

These studies clearly demonstrate that an early lack of nurturance can have devastating effects. More recent evidence, however, adds some significant corollaries. Several studies conducted in the 1970s indicate that damage associated with emotional and social deprivation in early infancy can be overcome if the child later receives plenty of loving nurturance (Clarke & Clarke, 1976). Furthermore, as we saw earlier, Harlow found that he could reverse, or at least moderate, the effects of early environmental impoverishment by providing deprived monkeys with extensive contact with "therapist monkeys" (Novak & Harlow, 1975).

One of the most impressive indications that there is hope for babies deprived of early bonding was provided by evidence collected by Harvard University's Jerome Kagan and his associates. This research team studied a Guatemalan Indian society in which infants routinely spend the first year of their lives confined to small, windowless huts. (Their parents believe that sunlight and fresh air are harmful to babies.) Since the parents are occupied with subsistence tasks, they rarely cuddle, play with, or talk to their babies. The infants are listless, unresponsive, and intellectually retarded, as judged by standards of normal development. However, when they emerge from the dark huts shortly after their first birthdays, they rapidly evolve into youngsters who play, laugh, explore, and become attached just like youngsters who have not been similarly deprived (Kagan & Klein, 1973).

We do not mean to suggest that the effects of early deprivation are always transitory. There is a big difference between being raised from infancy to childhood in a sterile orphanage environment and receiving loving care at age six months, one year, or two years. It is also important to note that all infants who do establish early attachments do not necessarily express this bonding in the same manner. As the following discussion points out, some attachments are more secure than others.

SECURE AND INSECURE ATTACHMENTS   In the effort to find out more about infants' attachments, developmental psychologist Mary Ainsworth (1979) used a laboratory procedure that she labeled the "strange situation." In this procedure, a one-year-old infant's behavior in an unfamiliar environment is assessed under various circumstances—with the mother present, with the mother and a stranger present, with only a stranger present, and totally alone.

Ainsworth discovered that infants react differently to these strange situations. Some, whom she labeled *securely attached*, would use their mothers as a safe base

Infants act differently in "strange situations."

for happily exploring the new environment and playing with the toys in the room. When separated from their mothers they expressed moderate distress, and when reunited they would seek contact, and subsequently stay closer to their mothers. *Insecurely attached* infants reacted differently. They showed more apprehension and less tendency to leave their mothers' sides to explore. They were severely distressed when their mothers left, often crying loudly, and when she returned they often seemed angry, behaving with hostility or indifference.

What accounts for these differences? The answer probably lies in a combination of two factors: parenting practices and the inborn differences among infants themselves. There is good evidence that some infants may be innately predisposed to form more secure attachments than others, just as some newborns seem to respond more positively to being held and cuddled (Thomas & Chess, 1977). A second factor in the babies' different reactions was the way in which their mothers responded to them at home. Mothers of the securely attached babies were inclined to be sensitive and responsive to their babies, noticing what they were doing and responding accordingly. For example, they would feed their infants when they were hungry, rather than following a set schedule. They also tended to cuddle their babies at times other than when feeding and diapering. In contrast, mothers of insecurely attached babies tended to be less sensitive and responsive. For example, they might feed their babies when they felt like it and perhaps ignore the child's cries of hunger at other times. These mothers also tended to avoid close physical contact with their babies. Recent research has also shown that mothers of anxious, insecurely attached children are less likely to become actively involved in the play of their offspring than are mothers of securely attached children (Roggman et al., 1987; Slade, 1987).

The establishment of a trusting, secure attachment between child and parent appears to have demonstrable effects on a child's later development. Several studies have indicated that children who are securely attached by 18 months are likely to demonstrate much greater social competence as two to five year olds than are insecurely attached babies. In general, securely attached children have been found to be more enthusiastic, persistent, cooperative, curious, outgoing, socially involved, competent, and appropriately independent (Arend et al., 1979; Matas et al., 1978; Sroufe, 1985; Sroufe et al., 1983; Waters et al., 1979).

FATHER–CHILD ATTACHMENT   We have seen that most investigations of attachment have focused on the mother–child bond. This tendency to overlook fathers probably reflects, at least in part, a general societal conception of fathers as less interested in or capable of providing quality child care. In recent years, however, these notions have begun to change, and researchers have turned their attention to the role of fathers in their children's early lives (Ainsworth, 1989).

They have discovered that many fathers form close bonds with their offspring shortly after birth (Greenberg & Morris, 1974), and that most infants form specific attachments to their fathers at about the same time as they establish these relationships with their mothers. This seems to be true even in families in which fathers play only a minor role in child care (Lamb, 1979). In one study of interactions between babies aged 12 months or older and their parents, almost half of the infants were equally or more attached to their fathers as to their mothers (Kotelchuck, 1976).

Fathers tend to interact with their children somewhat differently than mothers. They often spend less time with their children, and that time is more likely to be devoted to play, often of a boisterous nature, than to providing care (Clarke-Stewart, 1978; Easterbrooks & Goldberg, 1984; Lamb, 1979). The differences between maternal and paternal parenting styles seem to be much more related to societal roles than to biologically based sex differences (Lamb, 1981). In fact, when fathers become the primary caregivers, they interact with their babies in the nurturing, gentle fashion typical of mothers (Field, 1978).

PARENTING STYLES AND SOCIAL-EMOTIONAL DEVELOPMENT

Most parents, naturally, want their children to grow up to be socially and emotionally competent. Certainly there is no shortage of "expert" child-rearing advice, from talk shows, how-to books, parents and in-laws, and well-meaning friends. Unfortunately, much of this advice is based on armchair logic rather than solid empirical evidence. However, a good deal of psychological research provides important insights into how different parenting styles affect a child's social and emotional development. We briefly summarize the evidence here. Research conducted by Stanley Coopersmith (1967) and Diana Baumrind (1971) identified three specific styles of parenting: permissive, authoritarian, and authoritative.

PERMISSIVE PARENTS   **Permissive** parents are inclined not to control their children, preferring instead to adopt a hands-off policy. They make few demands and are reluctant to punish inappropriate behavior. Permissiveness sometimes stems at least in part from the parents' indifference or preoccupation with other functions. More commonly, however, permissive parents hope that providing their children with plenty of freedom will encourage the development of self-reliance and initiative.

AUTHORITARIAN PARENTS   In sharp contrast to the permissive style, **authoritarian** parents rely on strictly enforced rules as they try to make their children adhere to their standards. Authoritarian parents tend to be autocratic, leaving little room for discussion of alternative points of view and often using punishments to ensure compliance. Authoritarian parents generally direct minimal warmth, nurturance, or communication toward their children.

AUTHORITATIVE PARENTS   The third type of parents, **authoritative** parents, also have definite standards or rules that children are expected to meet. Unlike authoritarian parents, however, they typically solicit their children's opinions during open discussions and rule-making sessions. Although children understand that certain standards of behavior are expected, they are also encouraged to think independently, and they acquire a sense that their viewpoints carry some weight. Both authoritarian and authoritative parenting styles seek to control children's behaviors. However, the former tries to achieve this goal through restrictive control without open communication, while the latter establishes reasonable rules in an atmosphere of warmth and open dialogue.

There is convincing evidence that neither the permissive nor the authoritarian parenting styles are conducive to developing social and emotional competence in children. Children of permissive parents tend to be immature, impulsive, dependent on others, and low in self-esteem. Since they have received so little guidance, they are often indecisive in new situations. Children from authoritarian homes may also have difficulty deciding how to behave, because they are worried about their parents' reactions. Authoritarian-reared children are also less likely to express curiosity and positive emotions, and they tend to have few friends.

It is probably no surprise to you that the most well-adjusted children in these studies tended to be those of authoritative parents. This style of parenting provides a structure reflecting parent's reasonable expectations and realistic standards within an overall atmosphere of love and trust. Perhaps one of the primary advantages of this style is that it provides children the greatest sense of control over their lives. Their participation in family discussions means that the rules which ultimately emerge have been negotiated, rather than being arbitrarily imposed. Also, since authoritative parents tend to enforce rules with consistent, predictable discipline, children are more likely to acquire a sense of control over the consequences of their actions.

We have seen that parenting styles seem to influence the behaviors children express as they develop. The evidence is of a correlational nature, however, and, as we learned in Chapter 2, correlation does not necessarily imply cause and effect. Perhaps authoritatively reared children are more socially and emotionally competent because of the manner in which they have been reared. However, it is also possible that some other characteristic coincidentally associated with authoritative parents may be the key factor. For example, parents who raise children in such a reasonable fashion may also have better relationships with one another; thus their children's emotional and social development is likely to progress in a healthy fashion free of the stresses imposed by family conflicts.

It has also been suggested that some of Baumrind's findings could reflect child-to-parent effects rather than parent-to-child effects (Lewis, 1981). Perhaps children who are socially and emotionally well adjusted, for reasons other than parenting practices, may elicit more reasonable, democratic responses from their parents than do children who are less competent and more belligerent.

In all, we cannot conclude with absolute certainty that child-rearing practices influence the social and emotional competence of children. Nevertheless, the evidence certainly indicates a high probability that this is the case.

ERIKSON'S THEORY OF PSYCHOSOCIAL DEVELOPMENT

Our discussion of psychosocial development would not be complete without a brief outline of Erik Erikson's stage theory (1963). Erikson has proposed the only theory of normal psychosocial development that covers the entire life span. He outlined eight stages, each of which involves specific personal and social tasks that must be accomplished if development is to proceed in a healthy fashion. Each of the eight stages is defined by a major crisis or conflict, suggesting that an individual's personality is greatly influenced by the success with which each of these sequential conflicts is resolved.

Only the first four stages in Erikson's theory apply strictly to the years of infancy and childhood. We briefly outline all eight stages here, however, providing a look ahead to Chapter 12, in which Erikson's thoughts regarding psychosocial development during adulthood are discussed.

Erik Erikson

STAGE 1: TRUST VERSUS MISTRUST   During the first stage, which covers the first 12 to 18 months of life, infants acquire either a sense of *basic trust* or a sense of *mistrust*. In this stage, infants acquire a feeling of whether the world is to be trusted, a conclusion that is shaped largely by the manner in which their needs are satisfied. If they are cuddled, comforted, talked to, and fed when hungry, infants are likely to learn to trust their world, but if these interactions are not provided, they will probably become fearful and mistrusting.

STAGE 2: AUTONOMY VERSUS SHAME AND DOUBT   Erikson's next major stage occurs between 18 months and three years, when children who have developed a basic trust become ready to assert some of their independence and individuality. How well this task is accomplished determines whether the child will achieve a sense of *autonomy* or a sense of *shame and doubt*.

During this stage, children learn to walk, talk, and do other things for themselves. Parents who encourage and reinforce these efforts can foster a sense of autonomy and independence. In contrast, when parents are overprotective, or when they disapprove of a child's initiative, the child is likely to become doubtful, hesitant, and perhaps ashamed.

STAGE 3: INITIATIVE VERSUS GUILT   Between about ages three and five, children broaden their horizons by exploring new situations and meeting new people. During this stage, a conflict exists between children's taking the *initiative* to strike out on their own, and the potential *guilt* they will feel if this behavior offends their parents. Parents who encourage inquisitiveness make it easier for a child to express such healthy behaviors, whereas those who actively discourage such actions may contribute to their children's ambivalence or even guilt about striking out on their own.

STAGE 4: INDUSTRY VERSUS INFERIORITY   The next stage extends from about age six to 11. At this point, children are much more involved in learning to master intellectual, social, and physical skills. The peer group becomes much more important during this time as children constantly evaluate their abilities and compare them to those of their peers. If their assessments are positive, they may contribute to a sense of *industry* or achievement. In contrast, a poor self-assessment is likely to induce feelings of *inferiority*. Parents and other adult caregivers can help a child develop a sense of industry by encouraging participation in a variety of tasks that are challenging without being too difficult, and by reinforcing a child for completing such tasks.

STAGE 5: IDENTITY VERSUS ROLE CONFUSION   The next conflict occurs during adolescence, from approximately ages 12 to 18. Now an individual's major task is to secure a stable *identity*. According to Erikson, this stage is when we must integrate all of our experiences in order to develop a sense of "who I am." Young people who are unable to reconcile all of their various roles (as a dependent child, independent initiator of industrious actions, and so forth) into one enduring, stable identity experience *role confusion*.

STAGE 6: INTIMACY VERSUS ISOLATION   As adolescents emerge into young adulthood, they now face the task of achieving *intimacy*. According to Erikson, an adult who has previously achieved a stable identity is often able to form close, meaningful relationships in which intimacy can be shared with significant others. Failure to achieve intimacy is likely to result in a sense of *isolation* in which the young adult may be reluctant to establish close ties with anyone else.

STAGE 7: GENERATIVITY VERSUS STAGNATION The middle years of adulthood are characterized by still another conflict, this one between *generativity* and *stagnation*. Here, our central task is to determine our purpose or goal in life, and to focus on achieving aims and contributing to the well-being of others, particularly children. People who successfully resolve this conflict establish clear guidelines for their lives and are generally productive and happy within this directive framework. In contrast, individuals who fail to accomplish these goals by the middle years of life are likely to become self-centered and stagnated in personal growth.

STAGE 8: EGO INTEGRITY VERSUS DESPAIR Erikson's final stage extends into the older years of life. This phase of development is characterized by extensive reflection on our past accomplishments and failures. According to Erikson, individuals who can reflect on a lifetime of purpose, accomplishments, and warm, intimate relationships will find *ego integrity* in their final years. In contrast, people whose lives have been characterized by lack of purpose, disappointments, and failures are likely to develop a strong sense of *despair*.

Erikson's theory has been praised for recognizing the importance of sociocultural influences on development, and because it encompasses the entire life span. However, many of Erikson's assertions are so nebulous that they are virtually impossible to test.

GENDER IDENTITY

Gender identity refers to each person's subjective sense that "I am a male" or "I am a female," an identity that most of us form in the first few years of life. How do we come to think of ourselves as male or female? This question has at least two answers. The first centers on biological factors: The most obvious reason we think of ourselves as male or female is our biological sex. The second answer is based on social-learning theory, which says that our identification as either masculine or feminine results primarily from social and cultural influences during early development.

It seems clear that both biology and social learning help form our gender identity. Certainly there is a wealth of evidence implicating the important role of multiple biological factors in shaping our sense of maleness or femaleness. However, extensive evidence also supports the role of social learning in shaping our gender identity. In this final section we attempt to unravel some of the mysteries surrounding gender identity formation. We begin our discussion by considering biological influences; then we look at social-learning factors in gender identity formation. We end this section with a discussion of the socialization of gender roles.

NORMAL PRENATAL DIFFERENTIATION Research efforts to isolate the many biological factors that influence gender identity have resulted in the identification of six biological categories, or levels: chromosomal sex, gonadal sex, hormonal sex, sex of the internal reproductive structures, sex of the external genitals, and sex differentiation of the brain.

Chromosomal Sex At the first level of differentiation, our biological sex is determined by the sex chromosomes present in the reproductive cells. We have seen that females have two similar chromosomes labeled XX, whereas males have

BIOLOGICAL INFLUENCES ON GENDER IDENTITY

dissimilar chromosomes labeled XY. Although science is far from a complete understanding of the role of sex chromosomes in determining biological sex, certain facts seem well established. The Y chromosome must be present to ensure the complete development of internal and external male sex organs (Kolata, 1986; Page et al., 1987); in the absence of a Y chromosome, an individual will develop female external genitals. The presence of at least one Y chromosome (regardless of the number of X chromosomes) allows the development of male structures. Recent research has demonstrated that "only a small region of the Y, perhaps a single gene, is responsible for initiating the sequence of events that lead to testis formation and hence to male development. In the absence of this gene, called *TDF* (for *testis-determining factor*), female development ensues" (Hodgkin, 1988, p. 300). However, two X chromosomes are needed for the complete development of both internal and external female structures.

Gonadal Sex   During the first weeks of prenatal development, the **gonads**— the structures containing the future reproductive cells—have the capacity to become either testes or ovaries. Without specific masculinizing signals, the gonads develop as ovaries. Recent evidence implicates a substance called **H-Y antigen,** which appears to be under the control of male-determining genes on the Y chromosome. This substance triggers the transformation of the embryonic gonads into testes (Amice et al., 1989; Bernstein, 1981; Haseltine & Ohno, 1981). In the absence of H-Y antigen, the undifferentiated gonadal tissue develops into ovaries. Thus the presence of a Y chromosome causes the gonads to develop into testes.

Hormonal Sex   As soon as the gonads differentiate into testes or ovaries, the control of biological sex determination passes to the sex hormones, and genetic influence ceases. Recall from Chapter 3 that the major gonadal sex hormones are the ovarian estrogens and the androgens produced by the testes, the most important of which is testosterone.

Considerable research has shown how sex hormones contribute to differentiation of the internal and external sex structures. If fetal gonads differentiate into testes, they soon begin to secrete androgens, which in turn stimulate the development of male structures. If for some reason a male fetus does not produce enough androgen, its sex organs will develop as female in form and appearance, despite the presence of the male chromosome (Money, 1968). Thus maleness depends on the secretion of the right amount of androgen at a crucial time. In contrast, a specific female hormone is not necessary for female structures to develop; in the absence of male hormones, the developmental pattern is female.

Under the influence of testosterone produced by the testes, the internal and external sex structures of chromosomal males differentiate in a male direction. In the absence of testosterone, female structures develop. Thus the human form is biologically female until critical physiological events in the early stages of prenatal development begin the complex process of sex differentiation.

SEX DIFFERENTIATION OF THE BRAIN   Evidence suggests that some important structural and functional differences exist in the brains of males and females. Like the development of sex structures, this sex differentiation process occurs largely, if not exclusively, during prenatal development. At least two major brain areas are involved: the hypothalamus and the left and right cerebral hemispheres. Most evidence for sex differentiation of the brain comes from studies of nonhuman animals, particularly rats. However, "it seems likely that similar sex differences exist in the brains of all mammals" (Thompson, 1985, p. 164).

In addition to other functions outlined in Chapter 3, the hypothalamus plays a major role in controlling the production of sex hormones and in mediating fertility and menstrual cycles through its interaction with the pituitary gland. The consequences of prenatal sex differentiation of the hypothalamus become most apparent at puberty. The female hypothalamus directs the pituitary to release sex hormones cyclically, creating the menstrual cycle, whereas the male hypothalamus directs a relatively steady hormone production. Thus hypothalamic sex differences are the reason why female fertility is cyclic and male fertility is not.

Not only are there differences in hypothalamic function, the hypothalamus is structurally different in males and females. For instance, in males the preoptic area of the hypothalamus is about twice as large and contains far more neurons than the preoptic area in females. This increase in size is promoted by the presence of androgens in the brain (Gorski, 1985; Kimura, 1992).

Several researchers have reported sex differences in the structure of the two cerebral hemispheres, suggesting a possible biological basis for differences in the skills of males and females. This **sexual differentiation** is partially explained by the differences in the thickness of the cerebral cortex. Females generally have thicker left hemispheres while males have thicker right hemispheres. The sex hormone *estradiol* influences the development of the cerebral cortex by increasing the rate of cell loss in areas where estradiol is present. Females have more estradiol in their right hemisphere, thus a greater cell loss, and males have more in their left hemisphere during development (Sandhu, Cook, and Diamond, 1986).

ABNORMAL PRENATAL DIFFERENTIATION   We have seen that the differentiation of internal and external sex structures occurs under the influence of biological cues. When these signals deviate from normal patterns, the end result can be ambiguous biological sex. People with ambiguous or contradictory sex characteristics are sometimes called **hermaphrodites** (a term derived from the mythical Greek deity Hermaphroditus, who was thought to possess attributes of both sexes). This unusual situation can result from a variety of biological errors that produce markedly atypical patterns of hormonally induced prenatal sex differentiation.

We can distinguish between *true hermaphrodites* and *pseudohermaphrodites.* True hermaphrodites, who have both ovarian and testicular tissue in their bodies, are exceedingly rare. Their external genitals are often a mixture of male and female structures. Pseudohermaphrodites are much more common in nature. They also possess ambiguous internal and external reproductive anatomy, but unlike true hermaphrodites, pseudohermaphrodites are born with gonads that match their chromosomal sex. Studies of pseudohermaphrodites have helped to clarify the relative roles of biology and social learning in the formation of gender identity. We consider evidence from three varieties of pseudohermaphrodites: fetally androgenized females, androgen-insensitive males, and DHT-deficient males.

Fetally Androgenized Females   Occasionally a chromosomally normal female (XX) is exposed to an excessive amount of androgens or androgenlike substances during the critical period of prenatal sex differentiation. These androgens may have two possible sources. First, the female fetus' own adrenal glands may malfunction, producing abnormally high levels of androgens. Alternately, androgens may be introduced by drugs the mother takes during pregnancy. (In the 1950s, for instance, some pregnant women were administered androgenlike synthetic hormones to reduce the risk of miscarriage.)

Regardless of the source, the effect of these prenatal androgens is similar. The internal reproductive structures of these chromosomal females do not appear to be affected, but the external genitals resemble those of male infants. The clitoris is often enlarged and may be mistaken for a penis, and the labia are frequently fused so they look like a scrotum. Physicians faced with such gender ambiguities typically obtain additional information about the composition of the chromosomes and the nature of the gonads. Thus most of these **fetally androgenized**

females are correctly identified and reared as girls. Usually only a relatively minor amount of surgery and hormone therapy is necessary to make the appearance of their external genitals consistent with their internal sex structures and chromosomes.

Some years ago John Money and Anke Ehrhardt (1972) provided some fascinating data from an extensive study of 25 fetally androgenized females. Their subjects, all of whom had received appropriate medical treatment and had been reared from infancy as girls, were matched with a group of nonandrogenized girls who shared similar characteristics of age, race, and socioeconomic status. Would you expect that differences were found in the behavior of the fetally androgenized females as compared to those in the nonandrogenized group? Why or why not? Take a few minutes to consider this question before reading on.

Money and Ehrhardt found marked differences in the behaviors of these two groups. Of the 25 fetally androgenized girls, 20 identified themselves as "tomboys"—a label with which their parents and friends concurred. These girls tended to be active and aggressive and to engage in traditionally male activities such as rough-and-tumble athletics and pushing trucks in dirt piles. They demonstrated little interest in bride and mother roles, disliked handling infants, and were uninterested in makeup, hairstyling, and jewelry. In contrast, only a few of the girls in the matched group of nonandrogenized girls claimed to be tomboys.

Androgen Insensitivity Syndrome A second pseudohermaphroditic condition is **androgen insensitivity syndrome (AIS).** A chromosomally normal (XY) male fetus develops testes that produce normal levels of prenatal androgens. However, as a result of a genetic defect, his body cells are insensitive to the action of testosterone and other androgens, with the result that prenatal development is feminized. Internal reproductive structures of either sex do not develop, the external genitals fail to differentiate into a penis and a scrotum, and the testes do not descend. (Testes normally descend from their position inside the abdomen to the scrotum during the seventh month of prenatal development.) Instead, the newborn has normal-looking female external genitals and a shallow vagina. (Remember, in the absence of male hormones—or in this case, insensitivity to androgen—the developmental pattern is female.) Nothing unusual is suspected, and such babies are classified as girls and reared accordingly.

At puberty, breast development and other signs of normal sexual maturation appear, the result of estrogen production from the undescended testes. The error may not be discovered until adolescence or later, often as a result of medical consultation to determine why menstruation has not occurred.

Money and his colleagues (1968) reported an in-depth study of 10 AIS individuals who had been reared as girls. Only one, a young girl with a very disturbed family background, showed any gender-identity confusion. The other nine were strongly identified as female by themselves and others, demonstrating strong preferences for the role of homemaker, fantasizing about becoming pregnant and raising a family, and engaging in typically female play with traditional girls' toys such as dolls. In a word, there was nothing that could be viewed as traditionally masculine in the way these girls behaved, despite their XY chromosomes and male gonads.

This example contrasts markedly with our first example. Whereas the behavior of fetally androgenized females seems to reflect biological factors, it is social-learning factors that seem to have played the decisive role in determining behavior of individuals with androgen insensitivity syndrome.

DHT-Deficient Males Still other evidence comes from a genetic disorder that prevents the prenatal conversion of testosterone into *dihydrotestosterone (DHT)*, a hormone that is necessary for normal development of male external genitals. A team of Cornell University researchers studied 18 DHT-deficient boys raised in two rural communities in the Dominican Republic (Imperato-McGinley et al., 1979). In all of these boys, the internal sex structures had developed normally, and appropriate prenatal androgen levels were present. However, their testicles were undescended at birth, their stunted penises resembled clitorises, and they had partially formed vaginas and incompletely formed scrotums that looked like labia, features that caused them to be incorrectly identified as female and raised as girls. At puberty, however, their as-yet-undescended testes began accelerated testosterone production, causing the most amazing things to happen: Their voices deepened, their clitoris-like organs enlarged and became penises, and their testes finally descended.

In response to these marked biological changes in their bodies, all but two of the 18 adopted the culturally mandated male gender roles, including occupational inclinations and patterns of sexual activity. Of the remaining two, one acknowledged that he was male but continued to dress as a woman; the other maintained a female gender identity, married, and sought a sex-change operation.

The Dominican study challenged some widely held assumptions of psychologists, most notably the notions that gender identity is primarily learned, and that once it is established during the critical early years of life it cannot be changed without creating severe emotional problems. Certainly, this important research suggests that gender identity may be more malleable than previously thought. However, important questions remain unanswered about the environments of these Dominican youths. For example, because the study was conducted after the subjects had become adults, we cannot be sure that their early gender socialization was unambiguously female. Furthermore, we must consider the possibility that these individuals converted to a male identity because of extreme social pressure (locals sometimes made the boys objects of ridicule ad referred to them as *quevote*, "penis at 12" or *machihembra*, "first woman, then man") or because the environment in this Caribbean country is so openly male-biased. (Some of the parents were proud to discover that their daughter was actually their son.)

Support for a sociocultural explanation of why the Dominican Republic youths were able to successfully change from a female to a male gender identity is provided by a second investigation of DHT-deficient males, this one among the Sambia society of Papua, New Guinea. The authors of this study, Gilbert Herdt and Julian Davidson (1988), assert that sociocultural factors play a primary role in facilitating gender-identity change in DHT-deficient males. They conclude that "Cultural valuation of the male role makes gender-switching from female to male pragmatically adaptive" (p. 33).

DIFFERENTIATION ERRORS AND GENDER IDENTITY: A CRITIQUE The three examples of hormone-based differentiation errors just described provide seemingly contradictory evidence. In the first case, chromosomal females who were masculinized before birth by excessive androgens tended to manifest typically masculine behavior despite having been raised as girls. In contrast, the chromosomal males in the second example who were insensitive to androgens behaved in a typically feminine manner, consistent with their socialization. And in the third case, chromosomal males whose biological maleness did not become known until puberty were able successfully to alter their gender identity to male, even though they had apparently been reared as girls. Are the results of these investigations at odds with one another? Or is there a way to explain the apparent inconsistencies in these varied results? Think about these questions for a couple of minutes before reading on.

These apparent inconsistencies may not be contradictory at all when evaluated from a biological perspective. As we discussed earlier, mounting evidence suggests that prenatal androgens play a key role in prenatal sex differentiation of the human brain. Using this evidence as a foundation, we might theorize that prenatal androgens also masculinize the brain just as they trigger masculinization of the sex structures. This hypothesis could explain the masculine behavior of fetally androgenized females. Furthermore, the same genetic defect that prevents masculinization of the genitals of individuals with AIS may also prevent the masculinization of their brains.

What about the Dominican and Sambia boys who seem to have converted so smoothly from a female to a male gender identity? Presumably, these individuals had normal androgen levels during critical prenatal stages of development and were able to respond normally to these hormones; the lack of DHT affected only their external genital development. Thus their brains might already have been programmed along male lines by prenatal androgens. It seems plausible that prenatal androgens, besides instigating proper differentiation of biological sex, may also masculinize the brain, thereby predisposing a person toward a male gender identity.

The results of the investigations of these varied biological accidents raise a fundamental question. Just what makes us male or female? Our chromosomes? Our hormones? The characteristics of our sexual structures? The sex we are assigned at birth? Clearly, there is no simple answer. Biological sex is determined by a complex process involving several interacting levels. Many steps, each susceptible to errors, are involved in sex differentiation prior to birth. We now turn our attention to the social-learning factors that influence gender-identity formation *after* birth.

SOCIAL LEARNING INFLUENCES ON GENDER IDENTITY

As we have seen, our sense of maleness or femaleness is not based exclusively on biological conditions. The social-learning perspective provides an additional explanation, suggesting that our identification with either masculine or feminine roles or a combination thereof *(androgyny)* also results from the social and cultural models and influences to which we are exposed during early development.

At birth, parents label their children as male or female with the announcement, "It's a boy!" or "It's a girl!" From this point on, people react to children in a manner dictated by their *gender-role expectations* (sex-related behavioral expectations that people are expected to fulfill) (Sedney, 1987). Parents typically dress boys and girls differently, decorate their rooms differently, provide them with different toys, and even respond to them differently. Parents and others actively teach little boys and girls what gender they are by how they describe them. Expressions such as, "You are a sweet little girl" or "You are a bright little boy" are common. Small children may not comprehend what makes them biologically male or female, but they definitely are not confused about whether they are boys or girls. Just try calling a two-year-old boy a girl, or vice versa, and observe the indignant manner in which you are set straight.

A child's own actions probably strongly influence the process whereby his or her gender identity is established. Most children have developed a firm sense of being a boy or a girl by the age of 18 months. Once this takes place, they typically acquire a strong desire to adopt behaviors appropriate for their sex (Kohlberg, 1966; Sedney, 1987).

Anthropological studies of other cultures support a social-learning interpretation. In several societies, the differences between males and females that we often assume to be innate are simply not evident. Margaret Mead's classic book *Sex and Temperament in Three Primitive Societies* (1963) reveals that other societies may have very different views of femininity or masculinity. Mead discusses two New Guinea societies that minimize differences between the sexes. Among the Mundugumor, both sexes exhibit aggressive, nonnurturing behaviors that would be considered masculine by our society's norms. In contrast, both males and females of the Arapesh society exhibit gentleness, nurturing, and nonaggressive behaviors, traits many Americans would consider feminine. In a third New Guinea society, the Tchambuli, Mead observed an actual reversal of our typical masculine and feminine gender roles. Tchambuli women tend to be dominant and assertive, whereas men are quiet, undemanding, and emotionally dependent. Because there is no evidence that people in these societies are biologically different from Americans, their often diametrically different interpretations of what is masculine and what is feminine seem to result from different processes of social learning.

Some of the most impressive support for the social-learning viewpoint has emerged from the research of John Money and his colleagues. In most of their studies of children whose biological sex was ambiguous, Money and his coworkers found that children whose assigned sex did not match their chromosomal sex developed a gender identity consistent with their socialization (Hampson & Hampson, 1961; Money, 1965; Money et al., 1955; Money & Ehrhardt, 1972). (Although fetally androgenized females tend to manifest some dissatisfaction with their gender identity, they do not express a desire to actually change their sex.)

One particularly unusual study of two identical twin boys (Money, 1975; Money & Ehrhardt, 1972) is often cited in support of the social-learning interpretation. At the age of seven months, a circumcision accident destroyed most of the penile tissue of one boy. Because no amount of plastic surgery could adequately reconstruct the severely damaged penis, it was recommended that the child be raised as a female and receive appropriate sex-change surgery. When the child was 17 months old, the parents decided to begin raising him as a girl, and genital surgery was performed shortly thereafter. Initial follow-up studies revealed that, despite possessing identical genetic materials, the twins responded to their separate social-learning experiences by developing opposite gender identities. Furthermore, the child reassigned to the female gender appeared to demonstrate no confusion about her identity during her early developmental years.

If the story ended here, we would have strong evidence of the dominant role of social learning in gender-identity formation. However, in 1979 the psychiatrist following this case revealed that the assigned female twin was experiencing considerable difficulty in adjusting as a woman (Williams & Smith, 1979). Apparently, her appearance and behavior was so unfeminine during her school years that classmates taunted her as a "cave woman" (Diamond, 1982). Thus the efforts to alter her biological potential as a male appear not completely successful. The reasons for this circumstance are not entirely clear. Perhaps her parents waited too long to make their decision: The probability of successful reassignment of sex diminishes with increasing age. Perhaps prenatal masculinization of the brain by androgens was a factor. If biological and social-learning factors interact in the formation of gender identity after birth, the unfolding results of this twin study become more understandable (and perhaps even predictable). In the next section, we briefly present an interactional interpretation of gender-identity formation.

Perhaps you have already surmised, quite correctly, that an explanation of how we acquire our gender identity must involve both biology and social learning. Many social scientists have tended to deemphasize the biological evidence—in some cases, because of a propensity to emphasize learned over biological causes of behavior, and in others perhaps because of a fear that acknowledging the role of biology implies that gender-based behavioral patterns are unchangeable. Few psychologists would take the exclusively biological position that biology denies the importance of life experiences in establishing our own subjective sense of masculinity or femininity. The evidence supporting the role of social learning is simply too pervasive.

THE INTERACTION OF BIOLOGICAL AND SOCIAL INFLUENCES ON GENDER IDENTITY

Today, virtually all researchers and theorists embrace the *interactional position*, wherein gender identity is considered to result from a complex interplay of biological and social-learning factors. The question of which plays the greater role in shaping gender identity undoubtedly will be debated for years to come as new evidence is gathered.

THE SOCIALIZATION OF GENDER ROLES

The issue of gender goes beyond the processes by which we acquire a male or female identity. Society dictates a set of behaviors that are considered normal and appropriate for each sex. These standards are typically labeled **gender roles** or sex roles. How do gender roles arise? Are they biologically mandated, or are they learned? It seems reasonable to suspect that at least some of the behavioral differences between males and females may be related to biological factors—such as differences in muscle mass, hormonal variations, and brain differences (Bloom et al., 1985; Diamond, 1977, 1979; Diamond & Karlen, 1980). Nevertheless, most theorists believe that gender roles result largely from the manner in which we are socialized as males and females. **Socialization** refers to the process whereby society conveys behavioral expectations to the individual. In the following paragraphs, we examine the influence of the most important agents of socialization: parents, peers, schools, and television.

THE INFLUENCE OF PARENTS ON GENDER ROLES

Parents play a powerful role in the socialization of gender roles (Sedney, 1987). Many parents have certain preconceived ideas about how boys and girls differ, and they communicate these views to their children from the very beginning. For example, in one study (Rubin et al., 1974) parents were asked to describe their infants within 24 hours of birth. All babies included in this sample were of approximately the same height, weight, and muscle tone. Yet parents of girls tended to describe their daughters as soft, sweet, fine-featured, and delicate, whereas parents of boys used terms like strong, well coordinated, active, and robust. Such perceptions may well influence the way children learn to think of themselves.

Parents often interact differently with boys and girls also. Baby girls are often treated as if they were more fragile than boys (Doyle, 1985; Jacklin et al., 1984; Ross & Taylor, 1989; Tauber, 1979), and they may receive more attention than boy babies (Thoman et al., 1972). Parents often encourage boys to suppress emotion and to be independent, nonnurturant, and aggressive, while girls are expected to display the opposite characteristics (Armentrout & Burger, 1972; Gagnon, 1977; Hyde, 1985; Mosher & Tomkins, 1988; Siegel, 1987).

Although increasing numbers of parents are becoming sensitive to the gender-role implications of a child's playthings, many others still encourage their children to play with toys and engage in activities that help prepare them for specific adult gender roles. Tea sets, miniature ovens, dolls, and dollhouses are still common girls' toys, while boys often receive trucks, toy guns, and footballs. Such parental influences may combine to produce men who are comfortable being assertive and competitive and women who are inclined to be nonassertive and nurturing.

THE INFLUENCE OF PEER GROUPS

The peer group is another agent of socialization, particularly during late childhood and adolescence (Adams, 1973; Doyle, 1985; Hyde, 1985). Most youths have fairly rigid views of what is gender appropriate and what is not. For girls, being popular and attractive may be very important. In contrast, boys may try to prove their worth on the athletic field. Individuals who do not conform to these traditional roles may be subjected to considerable pressure.

Psychologist Eleanor Maccoby (1985) has noted a pronounced segregation between the sexes that begins very early in life. This separation of the sexes is another aspect of the peer group structure among American children that helps perpetuate traditional gender roles. Research conducted by Maccoby and Carol Jacklin (1987) suggests that even preschool children select same-sex playmates about 80 percent of the time. By the time they enter the first grade, children voluntarily select other-sex playmates only about 5 percent of the time.

THE INFLUENCE OF SCHOOLS ON GENDER ROLES   Still another influence in the development and perpetuation of gender roles is the school. Teachers' responses to their students are often guided by their own stereotypes about males and females (Rogers, 1987). It is common for instructors to expect girls to excel in subjects like English and literature, whereas boys are often believed to be more proficient in math and science. Guided by such assumptions, teachers may differentially encourage and reward boys' and girls' performances in these particular subjects. Furthermore, girls often learn that hanging around their teachers and acting dependent is a good way to get their attention, whereas boys learn that independent or aggressive behavior works better (Serbin, 1980). Research also shows that elementary school boys are much more likely to receive praise, criticism, and/or remedial help from their teachers than are elementary school girls (Sadker & Sadker, 1985).

THE INFLUENCE OF TELEVISION AND FILM ON GENDER ROLES   Children regularly spend long hours in front of the TV, and it would hardly be surprising to discover that television portrayals of men and women influence their learning of gender-role behaviors. Television and film are often quite blatant in depicting stereotyped gender roles. In a major investigation during the mid-1970s, commercials were found to depict men as authoritative sources on most topics (McArthur & Resko, 1975). A study of prime-time shows also found that women were commonly portrayed as seductive sex objects who were incompetent, domestically inclined, passive, and unintelligent. In contrast, men were typically

Gender roles appear to be learned.

Does television currently depict women as competent, assertive, and independent, or does it portray them as sensuous and incompetent?

shown as competent, intelligent, brave, adventurous, active, and in charge (Women on Words and Images, 1975).

Recent years have witnessed a change in prime-time television and film, characterized by the portrayal of women in some lead roles as active, assertive, independent, and effective. At the time of this writing, some of television's hottest series feature women in central roles, including such characters as Murphy Brown, Roseanne, and Star Trek's Major Nerys and Lieutenant Dax. In addition, several popular shows feature virtually all-women casts—series such as "Designing Women" (women in business) and "The Golden Girls" (women in retirement). The portrayal of powerful women on television reflects in large part a demographic shift in which female viewers have seized control of the prime-time dial (Waters & Huck, 1989, p. 48). Market research also suggests that products advertised on television are more likely to be purchased by women than men. Hence, the presence of women in leading roles may have more to do with ratings and product marketing than with efforts to reverse the negative effects of traditional gender-role typecasting. Anyone who watches movies or television knows, however, that there are plenty of TV shows and films that still portray females as seductive and less competent than males.

Throughout this chapter we have focused on the factors that influence human development and behavior from conception through childhood. We have seen that both genetics and the environment contribute to all aspects of development including the developing brain. In the next chapter we will focus on developmental changes that occur from adolescence through old age.

SUMMARY

DEVELOPMENT ISSUES

1. Contemporary developmental psychologists believe that humans are the products of both nature and nurture, and they are interested in how genetics and experience interact to shape development and the expression of human behavior.

2. Psychologists who emphasize the role of learning have tended to view development as a gradual, continuous process in which individuals undergo qualitative changes over the life span as they accumulate experiences. In contrast, psychologists who emphasize maturation (the orderly unfolding of certain genetically determined behaviors) view development as a discontinuous process that occurs in a series of stages.

3. Most contemporary psychologists agree that the concept of critical periods in infant development, at least when applied to emotional,

intellectual, and behavioral traits, lacks supporting evidence.

4. Three research designs have been widely used in the study of development: the cross-sectional, longitudinal, and cross-sequential methods.

THE BEGINNINGS OF LIFE

5. Life begins when the germ cells (sperm and ovum) unite to produce a zygote. The zygote contains a complement of 46 chromosomes arranged in 23 pairs, one chromosome in each pair from the sperm and one from the egg.

6. Chromosomes are composed of thousands of genes, the chemical blueprints that determine physical characteristics and influence behavioral traits.

7. The assortment of genes we inherit at conception is known as our genotype; the characteristics that result from expression of

various genotypes are known as phenotypes.

8. A dominant gene is one that is always expressed in the phenotype; a recessive gene is one that may be expressed only in the absence of a dominant gene, or when it is paired with a similar recessive gene.

9. Many sex-linked diseases are more common in males than females because only a single dose of the defect-causing gene on the X chromosome is necessary to cause the disease. (The gene-deficient Y chromosome does not carry a gene that may counteract this adverse factor.)

10. About 3 percent of babies born each year in the United States have some gene defect or chromosomal abnormality that produces a physical and/or mental handicap.

11. Huntington's disease is caused by a dominant gene that does not cause symptoms until a person is 35 to 45 years old.

12. Recombinant DNA technology allows researchers to map microscopic strands of genetic material for indicators of disease.

13. Phenylketonuria (PKU) is a potentially devastating genetic disease, characterized by mental retardation and other disruptive symptoms, that is caused by a recessive gene.

14. Down syndrome, the most common chromosomal disorder, is an autosomal chromosome disorder in which the 21st chromosome pair has an additional chromosome attached to it.

15. The idea behind genetic counseling is to estimate, if possible, the odds that a couple will have children with certain disorders.

16. Techniques for assessing fetal development and diagnosing birth defects *in utero* include amniocentesis and chorionic villi sampling (CVS).

17. Genetic engineering, sometimes called gene therapy, involves using recombinant DNA techniques to insert a new gene into cells to alter and correct a defective genetic code.

PRENATAL DEVELOPMENT

18. The approximately nine months of prenatal development takes place in three stages: germinal (the first two weeks after fertilization), embryonic (beginning of the third week to the end of the eighth), and fetal (from the beginning of the third month to birth).

19. Addictive drugs, alcohol, tobacco, and a multitude of medications can cross through the placenta and damage the developing fetus. No drugs should be used during pregnancy unless absolutely necessary and taken under close medical supervision.

PHYSICAL DEVELOPMENT

20. Brain growth is very rapid in the early years of life. At age six months the brain is 50 percent of its adult size; by age five it has reached 90 percent of its adult size.

21. Research has revealed anatomical and biochemical brain changes associated with improved cortical functioning in animals exposed to environmental enrichment.

22. Both physical growth and motor development follow two basic patterns: cephalocaudal (that is, from head to foot), and proximodistal (inner to outer).

23. Motor development follows a pattern of progression from the simple to the more complex.

24. Within a normal range of experiences, the role of environmental influences on motor development is quite limited.

COGNITIVE DEVELOPMENT

25. Piaget formulated the concepts of schemas, assimilation, and accommodation to explain how we

organize incoming information (schemas), interpret it in accordance with existing schemas (assimilation), and restructure it to fit better with already existing schemas (accommodation).

26. Piaget viewed cognitive growth as a four-stage process with qualitatively different kinds of thinking occurring in each of these four stages: the sensorimotor, preoperational, concrete operations, and formal operations.

27. During the sensorimotor stage (birth to about 24 months), infants learn about their worlds primarily through their senses and actions.

28. The preoperational stage (ages two to seven) is characterized by an increasing use of symbolic thought, language, and imaginative play. However, children at this stage have yet to master logical reasoning processes based on rules and concepts and have difficulty taking into account more than one perceptual factor at the same time.

29. Between ages seven and 12, children in the concrete operations stage again make a qualitative leap as they begin to use logical mental operations or rules. However, children in this stage are not yet able to deal with completely hypothetical problems.

30. In the formal operations stage (ages 12 and older) individuals acquire the ability to think abstractly and to make complex deductions and solve problems by systematically testing hypothetical solutions.

PSYCHOSOCIAL DEVELOPMENT

31. Attachment is the term applied to the intense emotional tie that develops between infants and their parents or other consistent caregivers. The most intense attachment relationship that typically occurs in the early stages of development is between mother and child.

32. Research suggests that satisfaction of contact comfort is more important in establishing attachment than is gratification of being fed.

33. Infants deprived of early attachment with nurturing caregivers may suffer serious development difficulties. However, there is evidence that damage associated with deprivation in early infancy can be overcome by ample loving nurturance during childhood.

34. In general, children who are securely attached to their mothers or other caregivers demonstrate a more healthy picture of psychosocial adjustment than children who are insecurely attached.

35. Research has shown that most infants form specific attachments to their fathers at about the same time as they establish these relationships with their mothers.

36. The authoritative style of parenting is much more conducive to the development of social and emotional competence in children than either the permissive or authoritarian parenting style.

37. Erik Erikson's theory of psychosocial development outlines eight stages that people pass through during their journey through life: trust versus mistrust (birth to 18 months); autonomy versus shame and doubt (18 months to three years); initiative versus guilt (ages three to five); industry versus inferiority (ages six to 11); identity versus role confusion (ages 12 to 18); intimacy versus isolation (early adulthood); generativity versus stagnation (midlife); and ego integrity versus despair (older years).

GENDER IDENTITY

38. The formation of gender identity (a person's subjective sense of maleness or femaleness) occurs in the first few years of life as the result of a complex interplay of biological and social-learning factors.

39. Research efforts to isolate the many biological factors that influence a person's gender identity have resulted in the identification of six biological categories, or levels: chromosomal sex, gonadal sex, hormonal sex, sex of the internal reproductive structures, sex of the external genitals, and sex differentiation of the brain.

40. Under normal conditions these biological variables interact harmoniously to determine our biological sex. However, errors may occur at any of the six levels. The resulting abnormalities in the development of a person's biological sex may seriously complicate acquisition of a gender identity.

41. The social-learning interpretation of gender-identity formation suggests that our identification with either masculine or feminine roles results primarily from the social and cultural models and influences to which we are exposed.

42. Most contemporary theorists embrace an interactional model in which gender identity is seen as a result of a complex interplay of biology and social-learning factors.

43. Socialization refers to the process whereby society conveys its behavioral expectations to us. Parents, peers, schools, textbooks, and television all act as agents in the socialization of gender roles.

TERMS AND CONCEPTS

nature-nurture controversy
maturation
critical periods
imprinting
cross-sectional design
longitudinal design
cross-sequential design
gametes (germ cells)
zygote
chromosome
genes
DNA (deoxyribonucleic acid)
identical (monozygotic) twins
fraternal (dizygotic) twins
concordant
genotype
phenotype
heterozygous
homozygous
dominant gene
recessive gene
multifactorial inheritance
sex-linked inheritance
Huntington's disease
recombinant DNA technology
phenylketonuria (PKU)
Down syndrome
genetic counseling
karotype
artificial insemination
embryo transfer
amniocentesis
chorionic villi sampling (CVS)
genetic engineering (gene therapy)
germinal (zygote) stage

embryo
embryonic stage
fetus
fetal stage
cephalocaudal
proximodistal
schemas
assimilation
accommodation
sensorimotor stage
object permanence
preoperational stage
centration
decentration
conservation
egocentrism
concrete operations stage
formal operations stage
attachment
indiscriminate attachment
specific attachments
separate attachments
permissive
authoritarian
authoritative
gender identity
gonads
H-Y antigen
sexual differentiation
hermaphrodite
fetally androgenized females
androgen insensitivity syndrome (AIS)
gender roles
socialization

CHAPTER 12

Development 2: Adolescence to the End of Life

ADOLESCENCE

Physical Development during
    Adolescence
Cognitive Development during
    Adolescence
Moral Development during Adolescence
Psychosocial Development during
    Adolescence

ADULTHOOD

Physical Development in Early and
    Middle Adulthood

Cognitive Development in Early and
    Middle Adulthood
Psychosocial Development in Early and
    Middle Adulthood

THE OLDER YEARS

The Graying of America
Physical Development in the Older Years
Cognitive Development in the Older
    Years
Psychosocial Development in the Older
    Years

My teenage years were the worst years of my life. It seemed to me that my life just couldn't work out. I didn't feel very smart, I wasn't attractive, and there was really nothing that distinguished me from my peers. At this time my parents were going through a messy divorce that left me feeling both guilty for their unhappiness and mad at them for mine. My emotions were always on a rollercoaster. I was either so in love that I couldn't concentrate on anything else or I was depressed and couldn't care less. Thoughts of suicide were not uncommon, especially after breaking up with my girlfriend my junior year. At that time I couldn't imagine life getting any worse and at that time perhaps it couldn't have.

*A*lthough the experiences expressed above are not common to all adolescents in our society (we see in this chapter that there is no such thing as a typical adolescence), it is probably fair to say that most of us have some painful memories of our teenage years. It is also a fair prediction that most of us will experience a certain degree of conflict at other transitions in our lives, for the ages of 30, 40, 60, and so on, are all milestones that may seem to us to mark the closing of one phase of our lives or the entrance into another.

Whether the transition be the entrance into adulthood, middle age, or the older years, much of the conflict we experience has to do with our images or expectations for the new era we are entering. How accurate are these images? Certainly not all adolescents go through a period of storm and stress, nor do all young adults embark on a career and start a family. For that matter, not all older adults fit our society's characterizations of old age. As we explore adolescent and adult development in this chapter, we note the diversity with which individuals experience various ages and stages. Perhaps the most striking diversity occurs during adolescence, and we begin by examining this transitional period.

ADOLESCENCE

Adolescence is a time of dramatic physiological change and social-role development. In Western societies, it is the transition between childhood and adulthood that typically spans ages 12 to 20. Although most major physical changes take place during the first few years of adolescence, important and often profound changes in behavior and expectations occur throughout the period.

By cross-cultural standards, the prolonged period of adolescence in America and other modern Western societies is unusual. In many nonindustrial societies, adolescence is considered to be either nonexistent or nothing more than a period of rapid physical changes leading to sexual maturity. In such societies, the transition from child to adult is often marked by some sort of "rite of passage" (Dunham et al., 1986). Even in our own society, adolescence is a relatively recent phenomenon. Before schooling requirements were extended through high school, early in this century, children were often expected to join the work force when they became teenagers.

Our society has no single initiation rite that signals passage into adulthood. Instead, a variety of signposts may herald this transition, including graduation from high school or college, moving away from home, securing a full-time job, or establishing an intimate, monogamous relationship.

Just as there is no one rite of passage into adulthood, in many ways there is no typical adolescence. Much has been written about the many conflicts and dilemmas faced by teenagers. However, the teenage years can also be a rewarding, relaxing, and exciting time of life, free from the stresses and responsibilities that come with adulthood. For most of us, adolescence probably varied between a time of anxiety and stress and a time of freedom and optimism, depending on what day we were asked. Although we cannot describe a typical adolescence, we can describe some of the common physical, cognitive, and psychosocial changes that most teenagers experience.

PHYSICAL DEVELOPMENT DURING ADOLESCENCE

Puberty (from the Latin *pubescere,* to be covered with hair) describes the approximately two-year period of rapid physical changes that culminate in sexual maturity. In our society, the onset of puberty in girls generally occurs sometime between ages 7 and 14, with the average about age 10. Boys typically enter puberty two years later at about age 12, with a normal range of 9 to 16 (Chumlea, 1982).

PHYSICAL CHANGES DURING PUBERTY As we saw in Chapter 11, the first few years of life are marked by rapid growth. With adolescence, children enter a second period of accelerated growth, often called the **adolescent growth spurt,** which usually runs its course in the two years following the onset of puberty. Sexual maturity is reached soon after the growth spurt ends.

The physical changes that occur during puberty are quite dramatic and rapid. Suddenly the body a person has inhabited for years undergoes a mysterious transformation. What causes these changes? One important factor is a genetically determined timetable that causes the pituitary gland to release a growth hormone which triggers the rapid growth that takes place at the start of adolescence (Gormly & Brodzinsky, 1989). The hypothalamus also increases production of chemicals that stimulate the pituitary to release larger amounts of **gonadotropins**—hormones that stimulate production of testosterone in men and estrogen in women. The resulting developments (breasts, deepened voice, and facial, body, and pubic hair) are called **secondary sex characteristics.** The timetable that governs these processes may also be influenced by environmental factors as well as by an individual's health.

There is considerable variation in the rates of growth and development in different societies around the world. We cannot be certain about what causes these changes in human physical growth patterns (including height, weight, and rates of maturation) measured in sample populations throughout the world. However, the most likely cause is the improved standard of living in societies where these changes have been observed. Over the last several decades, children in such diverse places as Japan, New Zealand, China, the United States, and Western Europe have experienced increasingly better nourishment and improved health care during their childhood years. The fact that physical and sexual maturity is taking place at a later age in many preindustrial societies today tends to support the view that **secular growth trends** in the West are related to improved nourishment and health care (Eveleth & Tanner, 1976; Hamburg & Takanishi, 1989).

EFFECTS OF EARLY AND LATE MATURATION Adolescents are often very concerned with what other people think of them, and anything that sets them apart from the crowd is likely to have a notable impact on their psychosocial adjustment. Thus it is not surprising that being either the first or the last to go through puberty can cause a good deal of self-consciousness. The timing of physical and sexual maturity may also have an important influence on psychosocial adjustment, especially for males.

A number of studies have shown that early maturation often holds some advantages for boys. Males who mature early tend to be more poised, easygoing, and good-natured; they are also more likely to be school leaders, better at sports,

Early maturing girls are bigger than most boys of the same age.

more popular, and more successful academically (and later vocationally). However, early maturers may find it difficult to live up to expectations that they should act mature just because they happen to have adultlike bodies. In addition, being thrust into adolescence at such an early age shortens the period of transition from childhood. Early maturers tend to be more bound by rules and routines, more conventional in career and life-style choices, more cautious, and more inclined to worry about what other people think of them (Jones, 1957, 1958; Mussen & Jones, 1957; Peskin, 1973; Siegel, 1982).

In general, late-maturing boys are more likely to be inappropriately aggressive and rebellious against adult authority; they may also lack self-confidence, feeling inadequate and insecure. On the other hand, late-maturing males tend to be more flexible during their youth and more insightful, independent, and less bound to conventional life-styles and routines later on (Livson & Peskin, 1980; Mussen & Jones, 1957; Peskin, 1967, 1973; Siegel, 1982). A few of the differences between early and late maturers may persist into the adult years, but most disappear or are compensated for by the development of other traits.

For girls, early maturation generally seems to be less advantageous than for boys (Brooks-Gunn & Peterson, 1983; Peterson, 1979). Early-maturing girls are bigger than practically all the boys their age; they also look more grown-up than most of the girls their age. As a consequence, they may feel terribly conspicuous at a time of life when they would most like to blend in with the crowd. Because they are so advanced physically, they are often shunned by their peers. As a result, many early-maturing girls tend to be more introverted and less sociable than girls who mature at a later age (Jones, 1958; Peskin, 1973). They also may have to deal with parents and other caregivers who react to their early sexual development by being overly restrictive. However, these disadvantages are short-lived, and early-maturing girls often are as well (or even better) adjusted in their adult years as girls who mature later (Jones & Mussen, 1958; Livson & Peskin, 1980; Peskin, 1973).

Although the most obvious changes of adolescence are physical, significant changes also take place in the way we think. With adolescence, individuals acquire the ability to think abstractly. Teenagers can engage in hypothetical reasoning, imagining all kinds of possibilities in a given situation. They also begin

COGNITIVE DEVELOPMENT DURING ADOLESCENCE

to approach problems more systematically and logically, rather than relying on trial-and-error strategies.

PIAGET'S FORMAL OPERATIONS STAGE   As we saw in Chapter 11, Piaget maintained that most people enter the formal operations stage sometime around age 12. This stage of cognitive development is marked by the emergence of the capacity to manipulate representations of objects, even when they are not physically present, and by the ability to engage in deductive reasoning. These newfound cognitive abilities have important implications for the way adolescents perceive their world. With their increased ability to think logically and abstractly, teenagers often detect what they consider to be logical inconsistencies in other people's thinking, and they may be impatient with the thought processes and decisions of others. Adolescents also may question their own judgments, and the result is often confusion.

Adolescence is also a time when individuals begin to ponder and debate such complex issues as social justice, the meaning of life, the validity of religious dogma, and the value of material wealth. No longer constrained by personal experiences and concrete reality, teenagers can explore all kinds of "what if" possibilities. They may feel compelled to contribute to ending human misery, poverty, social injustice, and war. As adolescents grow older, however, much of their idealism is replaced with a more pragmatic or practical view.

CRITIQUE OF FORMAL OPERATIONS STAGE   In Chapter 11 we explored some criticisms of Piaget's theory, but we did not specifically discuss criticisms of his formal operations stage. A number of developmentalists have challenged Piaget's ideas about the timing of this stage. Researchers have found that the transition to formal operations does not necessarily occur rather abruptly at the onset of adolescence, for even relatively young children often demonstrate rudiments of logical thinking (Ennis, 1982; Keating, 1980). In addition, adolescents (and even adults) often revert to nonlogical thinking as they deal with issues and problems. Thus, unlike the sudden and dramatic physical changes of adolescence, the shift to formal operations is often gradual, spanning late childhood and adolescence and perhaps even extending into the adult years.

Some critics have also argued that many adolescents and adults never attain the level of formal operations logic (Kohlberg & Gilligan, 1971; Scribner, 1977). A number of studies in the United States have shown that only about 50 percent of college students attain the formal operations stage of cognitive development (Lindgren & Suter, 1985; Mwamwenda & Mwamwenda, 1989; Reilly & Lewis, 1983). Piaget anticipated this criticism by noting that even though adolescents may attain the level of brain maturation necessary for abstract reasoning and logical thinking, they may never achieve the formal operations stage unless they are provided with adult models of formal reasoning and are schooled in the principles of logic. Thus, both neurological maturation and specific training may be necessary for higher cognitive development. As we see in the following section, whether we reach formal operations or not may have a profound influence on another area: moral development.

MORAL DEVELOPMENT DURING ADOLESCENCE

When we begin life, we are all *amoral*: We do not yet have even the rudiments of moral judgment. By the time we become adults, however, most of us possess a complex notion of *morality*. Morality is a system of personal values and judgments about the fundamental rightness or wrongness of acts, and of our obligations to behave in just ways that do not interfere with the rights of others. How do we evolve from amoral to moral, from a total lack of understanding our responsibilities to a complex perception of right and wrong?

KOHLBERG'S THEORY OF MORAL DEVELOPMENT The question of how moral development occurs has occupied the attention of a number of developmental theorists, most notably Lawrence Kohlberg (1964, 1968, 1969, 1981, 1984). Kohlberg was more interested in the ways in which thinking about right and wrong change with age than the specific things that children might consider to be right or wrong. For example, whether we are 8, 16, or 32, most of us would say that it is wrong to break our society's laws. However, our reasons for not breaking the law, as well as our views about whether we might be justified in breaking the law under some circumstances, might change drastically as we develop.

To learn how this change takes place, Kohlberg devised a series of moral dilemmas that typically involved a choice between two alternatives, both of which would be considered generally unacceptable by society's standards. Heinz's dilemma is an example.

> In Europe a woman was near death from a special kind of cancer. There was one drug that the doctors thought might save her. It was a form of radium that a druggist in the same town had recently discovered. The drug was expensive to make, but the druggist was charging ten times what the drug cost him to make. He paid $200 for the radium and charged $2,000 for a small dose of the drug. The sick woman's husband, Heinz, went to everyone he knew to borrow the money, but he could only get together $1,000 which is half of what it cost. He told the druggist that his wife was dying and asked him to sell it cheaper or let him pay later. But the druggist said, No, I discovered the drug, and I am going to make money from it. So Heinz got desperate and broke into the man's store to steal the drug for his wife. (1969, p. 379)

What is your reaction to this story? Kohlberg would not be interested in whether you thought Heinz was right or wrong. (In fact, either answer could demonstrate the same level of moral development.) Instead, Kohlberg was interested in the process you used to reach your judgment, for your reasoning would indicate how advanced your moral thinking is.

Kohlberg asked his subjects a series of questions about each moral dilemma, then used a complex scoring system to assign a subject to a particular category or stage of moral reasoning. This approach led him to formulate a theory of moral development in which he proposed that we move through as many as six stages of moral reasoning that traverse three basic levels: preconventional, conventional, and postconventional.

According to Kohlberg, most children between ages four and 10 have a **preconventional morality,** a kind of self-serving approach to right and wrong. In *stage 1* of preconventional morality, children behave in certain ways in order to avoid being punished; during *stage 2,* they behave in certain ways to obtain rewards. At this lowest level of moral development, children have not internalized a personal code of morality. Rather, they are molded by the standards of adult caregivers and the consequences of adhering to or rejecting these rules.

By late childhood or early adolescence, a person's sense of right and wrong typically matures to the level of **conventional morality.** Here, the motivating force behind behaving in a just or moral fashion is the desire either to help others and gain their approval *(stage 3)* or to help maintain the social order *(stage 4).* As children and young adolescents progress through these stages, they begin to internalize the moral standards of valued adult role models.

A few individuals, particularly those who become adept at the abstract reasoning of formal operational thought, may progress to the final level of **postconventional morality.** *Stage 5* of postconventional morality affirms values agreed on by society, including individual rights and the need for democratically determined rules; in *stage 6,* individuals are guided by universal ethical principles in which they do what they think is right as a matter of conscience, even if their acts conflict with society's rules. Table 12.1 summarizes Kohlberg's six stages of moral reasoning and illustrates how an individual at each stage might respond to Heinz's dilemma.

TABLE 12.1   *Kohlberg's Levels and Stages of Moral Development with Stage-Graded Answers to the Story of Heinz*

STAGE DESCRIPTION	EXAMPLES OF MORAL REASONING FAVORING HEINZ'S THEORY	EXAMPLES OF MORAL REASONING OPPOSING HEINZ'S THEORY
Level One—Preconventional Morality		
Stage 1: Punishment and Obedience Orientation (the consequences of acts determines if they are good or bad)	He should steal the drug because he offered to pay for it and because it is only worth $200 and not the $2,000 the druggist was charging. He should steal it because if he lets his wife die he would get in trouble.	He shouldn't steal the drug because it is a big crime. He shouldn't steal the drug because he would get caught and sent to jail.
Stage 2: Instrumental Orientation (an act is moral if it satisfies one's needs)	It is all right to steal the drug because his wife needs it to live and he needs her companionship. He should steal the drug because his wife needs it and he isn't doing any harm to the druggist because he can pay him back later.	He shouldn't steal the drug because he might get caught and his wife would probably die before he gets out of prison, so it wouldn't do much good. He shouldn't steal it because the druggist was not doing a bad thing by wanting to make a profit.
Level Two—Conventional Morality		
Stage 3: Good Person Orientation (an action is moral if it pleases or helps others and leads to approval)	He should steal the drug because society expects a loving husband to help his wife regardless of the consequences. He should steal the drug because if he didn't his family and others would think he was an inhuman, uncaring husband.	He shouldn't steal the drug because he will bring dishonor on his family and they will be ashamed of him. He shouldn't steal the drug because no one would blame him for doing everything that he could legally. The druggist, and not Heinz, will be considered to be the heartless one.
Stage 4: Maintaining the Social Order Orientation (moral people are those who do their duty in order to maintain the social order)	He should steal the drug because if he did nothing he would be responsible for his wife's death. He should take it with the idea of paying the druggist back. He should steal the drug because if people like the druggist are allowed to get away with being greedy and selfish, society would eventually break down.	He should not steal the drug because if people are allowed to take the law into their own hands, regardless of how justified such an act might be, the social order would soon break down. He shouldn't steal the drug because it's still always wrong to steal and his law-breaking would cause him to feel guilty.

TABLE 12.1 *Kohlberg's Levels and Stages of Moral Development with Stage-Graded Answers to the Story of Heinz* (Cont.)

STAGE DESCRIPTION	EXAMPLES OF MORAL REASONING FAVORING HEINZ'S THEORY	EXAMPLES OF MORAL REASONING OPPOSING HEINZ'S THEORY
Level Three — Postconventional Morality		
Stage 5: Social Contract and Individual Rights Orientation (a moral person carefully weighs individual rights against society's needs for consensus rules)	The theft is justified because the law is not set up to deal with circumstances in which obeying it would cost a human life. It is not reasonable to say the stealing is wrong, because the law should not allow the druggist to deny someone's access to a life-saving treatment. In this case it is more reasonable for him to steal the drug than to obey the law.	You could not really blame him for stealing the drug, but even such extreme circumstances do not justify a person taking the law into his own hands. The ends do not always justify the means. He shouldn't steal the drug because eventually he would pay the price of loss of self-respect for disregarding society's rules.
Stage 6: Universal Ethical Principles Orientation (the ultimate judge of what is moral is a person's own conscience operating in accordance with certain universal principles. Society's rules are arbitrary and they may be broken when they conflict with universal moral principles.)	He must steal the drug because when a choice must be made between disobeying a law and saving a life, one must act in accordance with the higher principle of preserving and respecting life. Heinz is justified in stealing the drug because if he had failed to act in this fashion to save his wife, he would not have lived up to his own standards of conscience.	Heinz must consider the other people who need the drug just as much as his wife. By stealing the drug he would be acting in accordance with his own particular feelings with utter disregard for the value of all the lives involved. He should not steal the drug because, though he would probably not be blamed by others, he would have to deal with his own self-condemnation because he did not live up to his own conscience and standards of honesty.

A person may progress from conventional to postconventional morality any time during adolescence. However, Kohlberg maintained that only about 25 percent of adults in our society progress beyond *stage 4*, and that most of these individuals do so sometime during their adult years.

EVALUATING KOHLBERG'S THEORY Kohlberg's theory is an impressive attempt to account systematically for the development of moral reasoning. His writings have also provided some guidelines for implementing moral education for children and adolescents. He suggests that people are often encouraged to advance to higher, more mature levels of moral reasoning through exposure to the more advanced moral reasoning of others, and that moral reasoning may develop at a faster rate and achieve a higher pinnacle if children have frequent opportunities to confront moral challenges. Parents and educators might take a cue from these suggestions by arranging for frequent moral consciousness-raising experiences during the developmental years of childhood and adolescence.

Recently John Snarey (1987) reported his evaluation of data obtained from 45 studies conducted in 27 diverse world cultures that provide striking support for the universality of Kohlberg's first four stages. However, Snarey did find some cultural diversity in the expression of moral principles beyond *stage 4.*

Kohlberg's theory has been criticized for a number of reasons. Some critics argue that a high level of moral reasoning does not necessarily go hand in hand with moral actions, especially if a person is under strong social pressure (Blasi, 1980; Kurtines & Greif, 1974). This viewpoint was demonstrated in an experiment conducted by Stanford's David Rosenhan (1973). At the first stage of the study, Kohlberg's assessment procedures were used to classify subjects according to their level of moral reasoning. Next, each subject became the "teacher" in a replication of Stanley Milgram's classic study of obedience (see Chapter 2), in which "teacher"-subjects administered what they thought were electric shocks to learners who gave incorrect answers. Rosenhan found that even some subjects who scored at the highest level of moral development, *stage 6,* still delivered the full 450 volts to learners who gave incorrect responses. (In all fairness to Kohlberg, we must point out that *stage 6* subjects were less likely to continue to the maximum of 450 volts than were subjects at the lowest stages of Kohlberg's scheme.)

Other critics take issue with Kohlberg's assertion that postconventional morality is somehow preferable to conventional morality. Since most adults in our society never reach these stages, critics argue that widespread moral education programs designed to take people to the sixth stage of moral development could have disastrous results. They ask where we would be if most people chose to act according to individual moral principles with little regard for society's rules (Shweder, 1982).

PSYCHOSOCIAL DEVELOPMENT DURING ADOLESCENCE

In addition to the physical, cognitive, and moral development of adolescence, there are also significant social and behavioral changes. During this period, relationships with parents may be under stress, the peer group may become of paramount importance in influencing behavior, and there is an increased interest in sexual behavior. Perhaps the most important task an adolescent faces is to answer the question, "Who am I?"

IDENTITY FORMATION Considering the tremendous diversity of possible answers to questions such as, "Who am I?" and "Where am I headed?," it is understandable that a great deal of experimentation takes place during adolescence. This experimentation often takes the form of trying out different roles or "selves"—which explains the unpredictability of many teenagers who behave in different ways from one day to the next.

By experimenting with different roles, many adolescents eventually forge a functional and comfortable sense of self. For some, this process takes place with little conflict or confusion. Parents of these young people may wonder why such a fuss is made over the supposedly rebellious teenage years. Other parents may feel like tearing out their hair as their adolescent children blaze their own trails in unexpected directions.

The rapid social changes in contemporary society have greatly complicated the task of achieving a sense of identity. Not only traditional gender roles, but also values associated with religion, marriage, and patriotism are being challenged in society today. Perhaps as a result, several recent studies have found that contemporary adolescents continue to struggle with their identity crises well into their college years (Archer, 1982; Waterman, 1982). In fact, as we see in this chapter, our sense of identity is likely to be modified and recast throughout our lives. However, it is during the glorious and confusing years of our adolescence that most of us first acquire a genuine appreciation of who we are and what we might become.

THE ROLE OF PARENTS AND THE PEER GROUP An important part of establishing an identity is gaining independence from parents (Douvan, 1986). Although this process begins long before adolescence, it is accelerated during the teenage years. As parental influence diminishes, the peer group's influence grows (Brown et al., 1986a, 1986b). But relationships between parents and their teenage children do not necessarily take a nose dive. The popular image of the teenage years as a time of rebellion and intergenerational warfare is more myth than fact, and most teenagers and parents resolve their conflicts with a minimum of fireworks.

The process of becoming a separate, unique individual is a natural part of the transition from child to adult. Certainly most parents would be distressed if their grown children still depended on them for their sense of self and direction in life. However, the process of separation may give rise to difficulties. Parents may feel that their values are being rejected, and adolescents may be torn between the need to be dependent and the need to be independent.

When conflicts increase, family tension often rises. Culturally defined adult behaviors, such as driving, drinking, and smoking, are sometimes used by adolescents as symbols of maturity or as a form of rebellion. Adolescents may reason that they are not children anymore as they seek to become increasingly independent of their parents' authority. However, they still need support from others. This need may be greater now than ever before, considering the profound physical and behavioral changes they are experiencing. In a sense it is paradoxical that adolescents' driving needs for independence force them to retreat from the very people who are likely to be the most supportive and nurturing. To satisfy their needs for both support and independence from their family, teenagers typically turn to other people who are in the same boat—namely, their peers.

Adolescent friendships are typically much closer and more intense than at any previous time in development (Fischer et al., 1986). American teenagers spend over half their waking hours talking to and doing things with friends of the same age group (see Figure 12.1). They tend to identify more with their peers than with adults, and most rate themselves as happiest when they are with their friends. Adolescents are also more inclined to share intimate information with

Adolescents may engage in culturally defined "adult" behaviors such as drinking or smoking.

FIGURE 12.1

With Whom Do Adolescents Spend Their Time?

SOURCE: Adapted from Csikzentmihalyi & Larson, 1984)

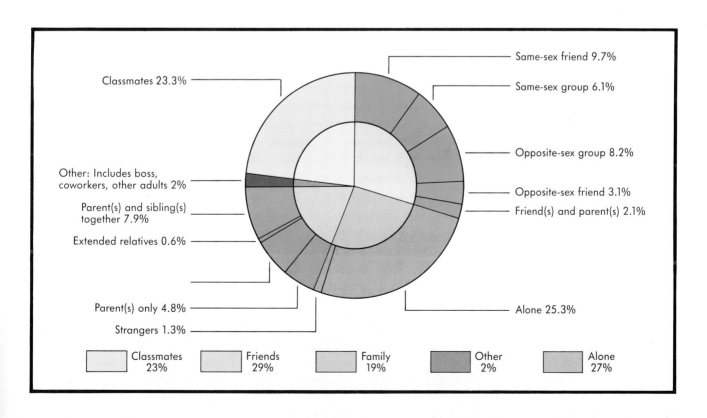

Same-sex friend 9.7%
Same-sex group 6.1%
Opposite-sex group 8.2%
Opposite-sex friend 3.1%
Friend(s) and parent(s) 2.1%
Alone 25.3%
Classmates 23.3%
Other: Includes boss, coworkers, other adults 2%
Parent(s) and sibling(s) together 7.9%
Extended relatives 0.6%
Parent(s) only 4.8%
Strangers 1.3%

| Classmates 23% | Friends 29% | Family 19% | Other 2% | Alone 27% |

Adolescents often identify with a peer group by dressing the same or by having similar hairstyles.

peers than with parents or other adults (Berndt, 1982; Csikszentmihalyi & Larson, 1984). The important role of peers in adolescent development appears to be a worldwide phenomenon (Newman, 1982).

Young people may find it reassuring to be with friends who are experiencing the same kinds of awkward physical changes. Having friends the same age to go to for advice allows teenagers to get support and counsel without short-circuiting their independence from their parents. The peer group also provides a sounding board for trying out new ideas and behaviors. Finally, it is comforting for teenagers to feel they belong to a world of their own rather than being minor players in the adult world.

It is not surprising, then, that adolescents are strongly inclined to conform to the standards of their peer group in order to gain approval. This conformity may sometimes be taken to extremes in which they radically change their manner of dress, hairstyle, and behaviors. If they identify with a group whose values and behavioral styles are dramatically different from those of their parents, considerable strife and stress may result (Newman, 1982). Of course, parents' horrified responses are often welcomed by teenagers as evidence that their rebellion has succeeded!

Despite the increased influence of peers and occasionally extreme acts of independence, however, the so-called generation gap between parents and teens is rather small. Parents continue to exert a strong influence on their teenagers' attitudes and values, and, in fact, adolescents are often more inclined to accept their parents' values and opinions than those of their peers (Brittain, 1963; Emmerick, 1978, Offer & Offer, 1975; Youniss & Ketterlinus, 1987). Peer influence is greatest in matters of dress and hairstyles, problems related to school and dating, and minor day-to-day concerns, but teenagers appear to be more influenced by their parents in issues of politics, religion, morality, and major decisions such as career choices (Emmerick, 1978; Gallatin, 1980; Lerner & Spanier, 1980).

SEXUAL DEVELOPMENT   It is impossible to explore the psychosocial development of adolescence without taking notice of the changes that take place in sexual behavior. While much of teenage sexuality represents a progression from childhood behavior, a new significance is often attached to sexual expression. Two pervasive influences on adolescent sexuality are the male–female double standard and so-called sexual liberation.

The Double Standard during Adolescence   Although children have been exposed to gender-role socialization since infancy, the emphasis on gender-role differentiation often increases during adolescence. Thus in our society teenagers receive the full brunt of the double standard. For males, the focus of sexuality may be sexual conquest, to the point that young men who are nonexploitative or inexperienced may be labeled with highly negative terms like "sissy." For females, the message and the expectations are often very different. Many girls learn to appear "sexy" to attract males, yet they often experience ambivalence about overt sexual behavior. If they do not have sexual relations, they worry that a boyfriend will lose interest. On the other hand, having sex might make a boy think they are "easy."

Despite the double standard, early sexual experiences today are more likely to be shared within the context of an ongoing relationship than they were a few decades earlier. It appears that contemporary adolescents are most likely to be sexually intimate with someone they love or feel emotionally attached to, and changes in both sexes are narrowing the gender gap (Christopher, 1988; Christopher & Cate, 1984). For instance, adolescent females seem to be more comfortable having sex with someone for whom they feel affection rather than feeling they need to "save themselves" for a love relationship, whereas teenage males are becoming increasingly inclined to have sex with someone they like rather than engaging in sex with a casual acquaintance or stranger (Delamater & Mac-Corquodale, 1979; Sorenson, 1973; Zabin et al., 1984).

Peer Pressure and Sexual Liberation   While the double standard is still influential, both males and females today are also affected by another societal influence: increasingly permissive attitudes toward sex. The greater tolerance for and increased expectation of sexual behavior sometimes goes by the label *sexual liberation*. A dimension of this so-called liberation is considerable pressure to be sexually active. Teenagers who resist the pressure to become sexually experienced run the risk of being labeled uptight or old-fashioned. On the other hand, teenagers who become sexually active may feel anxious, confused, guilty, or inadequate.

In view of these kinds of pressures, how appropriate is the term sexual liberation? It is our belief that true liberation means promotion of choice rather than coercion to say yes to sexual intercourse or other activities. Given the current pressure in some peer groups, however, saying no is often difficult.

Nevertheless, even today many adolescents have not experienced premarital sexual intercourse, although the results of five major nationwide surveys of adolescent sexual behaviors reveal a strong upward trend over the last four decades (see Table 12.2). However, a large-scale survey by Mott and Haurin (1988) suggests that this trend leveled off in the late 1980s, and further evidence is provided by a number of other studies (Gerrard, 1987; Hofferth et al., 1987; O'Connell & Rogers, 1984; Ostrov et al., 1986; Pratt et al., 1984). Sexual surveys conducted at one of the authors' institutions between 1989 and 1993 show no increasing trend, with about 80 percent of students becoming sexually active by age 19. There is, however, some indication that this leveling effect is not occurring among very young females, under age 15, who are engaging in intercourse in increasing proportions (Hofferth et al., 1987).

In broad terms we can briefly summarize the major changes in adolescent coital activities in the last four decades. First, there has been an increase in the percentages of both young men and young women who have experienced premarital intercourse. Second, these increases have been considerably larger for females than for males. Finally, there are still fewer women than men who experience premarital intercourse. However, this difference between the sexes has been diminishing at a very rapid rate.

The Effect of AIDS on Premarital Sex   A number of health professionals knowledgeable about AIDS are concerned that American teenagers are particularly at risk for contracting AIDS (Hein, 1989; Broering et al., 1989). Behaviors that put young people at risk for becoming infected with the AIDS virus include a propensity to engage in unprotected intercourse; widespread use of alcohol, cocaine, and other drugs that impair judgment and reduce impulse control,

TABLE 12.2   *Percentage of Adolescents Who Reported Having Premarital Intercourse by Age 19*

	FEMALES	MALES
Kinsey et al. (1948, 1953)	20%	45%
Sorenson (1973)	45%	59%
Zelnik & Kantner (1977)	55%	No males in study
Zelnik & Kantner (1980)	69%	77%
Mott & Haurin (1988)	68%	78%

thereby increasing one's inclination to engage in hazardous sexual activity; and needle sharing among intravenous drug users (Belfer et al., 1988; Broering et al., 1989; Chitwood & Comerford, 1990; Leigh, 1990; McCoy et al., 1990). A reduction in sexual activity among teenagers together with a move toward safer sexual practices might lower adolescents' risk for contracting AIDS while also reducing premarital sex rates. However, many experts in this area fear that AIDS virus infections will increase in the teen population.

A number of studies of high school and college-age youths seem to support these fears. They suggest that most teenagers do not feel that they are at risk for contracting AIDS, and that even when relatively knowledgeable about the disease, adolescents are not inclined to engage in safer sexual practices or to reduce their level of sexual activity. For example, a recent survey of 860 randomly selected adolescents, aged 16 to 19, revealed that over half were unconcerned about contracting AIDS, and only 15 percent indicated that they had altered their sexual practices because of concern about the disease (Strunin & Hingson, 1987). Another survey of undergraduate students at an Oregon university discovered that most respondents, while reasonably informed about AIDS, did not feel at risk for the disease, were not inclined to communicate with one another about risk for AIDS prior to sexual activity with a new partner, and frequently engaged in intercourse without using a condom (Gray, 1988). Still another survey of undergraduates at a university in southern California revealed that having accurate knowledge about how AIDS is transmitted generally did not induce these individuals to engage in fewer or safer sexual acts (Baldwin & Baldwin, 1988). Finally, a survey of several hundred undergraduate students at an eastern university failed to demonstrate clear evidence of behavioral change despite widespread expressed concern about AIDS (Carroll, 1988).

ADULTHOOD

If you have recently entered adulthood or are presently making this important transition, you may be wondering what lies ahead in the remaining 70 percent of your life. Will you continue to grow and change, or has the die already been cast? Will you be the same person at age 40, or age 70, that you are now at age 19 or 20?

It is now widely acknowledged that development continues throughout life, and that this growth is not limited merely to physical changes. Contemporary developmentalists have been amazed at the extent of psychosocial change, and to a lesser degree cognitive development, that continues during the adult years. In all, we can say with some confidence that you will not be the same person at age 40 that you are at 19 or 20.

Most developmentalists divide the adult years into three periods: early adulthood (roughly 20 to 40), middle adulthood (40 to about 65), and late adulthood (after 65). Although these categories are convenient, they are somewhat arbitrary and carry the danger of promoting the notion of age-based expectations (the tendency to associate certain developmental tasks or appropriate behaviors with each phase of adult life). Young adults may be expected to marry and start families, and people in the middle adult years are often expected to reach the top of their careers. However, as we noted at the beginning of this chapter, not all of us experience the phases of our lives in the same orderly fashion.

In fact, many age-based expectations in our society have begun to break down (Neugarten & Neugarten, 1987). People often postpone marriage or decide not to marry at all; in addition, many people are becoming first-time parents in middle adulthood, and gray-haired retirees are now a common sight in many college classrooms. In all, we seem to be moving in the direction of what might be called an age-irrelevant society; and it can be argued that age, like race or sex, is diminishing in importance as a regulator of behavior (Neugarten & Hagestad, 1976, p. 52).

One reason for this shift is that age, per se, is not the cause of changes in our lives. A 30-year-old advertising executive is not more mature than she was as a college student simply because she is older. Rather, her increased maturity reflects the experiences she has encountered in her personal and professional life. Thus, instead of measuring development only by age categories, many of us find it useful to define our phase of adult development in terms of *perceived age*—how old we feel (Gormly & Brodzinsky, 1989).

In keeping with this reduced emphasis on age, the following sections describe physical, cognitive, and social development in fairly general terms during the years between the twenties and the sixties. We begin with the physical changes that take place during adulthood.

During early adulthood—the twenties and thirties—people reach the peak of their biological efficiency. These are typically years of good health and high energy, which is fortunate considering that this is the time of life when most of us are busy establishing careers, adjusting to marriage, and perhaps responding to the boundless needs of small children.

PHYSICAL DEVELOPMENT IN EARLY AND MIDDLE ADULTHOOD

PHYSICAL CAPACITIES   A number of physical attributes are likely to reach their high point during early adulthood. During this period most of us reach the peak of our reproductive capacities and enjoy the best health of any time of our lives. The speed with which we can react to complex stimuli is fastest at around age 20, then gradually declines from the mid-twenties on. However, simple reflex time (such as the knee jerk when tapped with a mallet) remains relatively constant from age 20 to 80 (Gormly & Brodzinsky, 1989; Hodgkins, 1962). Vision and hearing are at their best at around age 20; as we move into our middle adult years, we can expect to become gradually more farsighted and to lose our ability to hear higher notes. Taste and smell sensitivity also decline with age. Sweet and salty taste decrease most rapidly while the tastes of bitter and sour are actually heightened. There is about a tenfold increase in smell thresholds from age 20 to age 80, with most of this increase occurring after age 50 (Shiffman, 1990).

Physical strength also tends to peak sometime in the mid- to late twenties. It then declines gradually, dropping about 10 percent between ages 30 and 60 (Bischoff, 1976; Troll, 1975). Unless you happen to compete in swimming, cycling, running, or some other athletic endeavor requiring peak performance, you may hardly notice the barely perceptible decline in physical strength, stamina, and cardiac output over the third and fourth decades of your life. In fact a number of world-class endurance athletes remain quite competitive throughout their forties. However, sometime in your late forties or early fifties you may notice a slight decline. Among endurance athletes the decrease in VO_2max (a measure of oxygen utilization) between 24 and 50 years of age is only about 4 percent. In addition, individuals who maintain fitness can expect to have VO_2max values far higher than younger, less athletic individuals (Wilmore & Costill, 1988). Maintaining a level of physical fitness may also contribute to fewer health problems and a reduction in the brain cell loss that normally occurs during aging.

Over time, however, middle adulthood brings a gradual decline in physical functioning and perhaps a corresponding increase in health problems. We may begin to notice that it is not so easy to rebound the morning after a late party, or that the body protests more after a hard workout on the tennis courts. Some of the most notable changes, particularly for women, have to do with changing hormonal patterns that, among other things, alter reproductive capacity.

Sexual attractiveness is often related to age.

HORMONAL CHANGES AND THE CLIMACTERIC The term **climacteric** refers to the physiological changes that occur during a woman's transition from fertility to infertility. **Menopause,** one of the events of the female climacteric, refers to the cessation of menstruation. Menopause results from certain physiological changes, most notably a reduction in estrogen levels. It can take place anytime between 40 and 60, but most commonly occurs between 45 and 50 (Crooks & Baur, 1990). Many women consider the cessation of menstruation and fertility to be the most significant biological change related to aging.

Do men also undergo a climacteric? Not in the same sense as women. For one thing, men often retain their reproductive capacity well into the older years (although with declining fertility). The hormonal changes men undergo are much more gradual. Male hormone levels usually reach their peak sometime between ages 17 and 20, then steadily but slowly decline until around age 60, when they level off. Middle-aged and older men are somewhat more likely than younger men to experience depression, irritability, headaches, and insomnia, but researchers have found no links between these changes and altered hormone levels (Doering et al., 1975; Henker, 1981).

THE DOUBLE STANDARD OF AGING In a society that places a premium on youth, it can be difficult for both men and women to grow older. This process is usually more difficult for women than for men because of another double standard of our society—this one related to aging. Although a woman's erotic and orgasmic capabilities continue after menopause, it is not uncommon for her to be considered past her sexual prime relatively early in the aging process. The cultural image of an erotically appealing woman is commonly one of youth. As a woman grows away from this image, she is usually considered less and less attractive. Cosmetics, specially designed clothing, and even surgery are often used to maintain a youthful appearance for as long as possible.

In contrast, men's physical and sexual attractiveness is often considered to be enhanced by age. Gray hairs and wrinkles may be thought to look "distinguished" on men, signs of accumulated life experience and wisdom. Likewise, while the professional achievements of women may be perceived as threatening to some males, a man's sexual attractiveness is often closely associated with his achievements and social status, both of which may increase with age.

It is our opinion that exaggerated attempts at remaining perpetually youthful are both a losing battle and a denial of a woman's full humanity. Susan Sontag (1972) describes the following alternative:

> Women have another option. They can aspire to be wise, not merely nice; to be competent, not merely helpful; to be strong, not merely graceful; to be ambitious for themselves, not merely themselves in relation to men and children. They can let themselves age naturally and without embarrassment, actively protesting and disobeying the conventions that stem from this society's double standard about aging. Instead of being girls, girls as long as possible, who then age humiliatingly into middle-aged women and then obscenely into old women, they can become women much earlier and remain active adults, enjoying the long, erotic career of which women are capable, for longer. Women should allow their faces to show the lives they have lived. (p. 38)

COGNITIVE DEVELOPMENT IN EARLY AND MIDDLE ADULTHOOD

INTELLIGENCE At one time, intellectual ability was believed to peak in young adulthood just as do most aspects of physical functioning. This view was supported by an early large-scale study which administered standardized intelligence tests to large samples of adults of varying ages. Young adults were found to score higher than middle-aged adults, who in turn outperformed older adults (Jones & Conrad, 1933). A more recent cross-sectional study reported a somewhat later peak of intelligence, in the late twenties or early thirties, but it also showed middle-aged and older subjects scoring lower than younger adults (Schaie, 1975).

Does intelligence decline with age? Both of the studies we just cited, which reported a decline in intelligence with age, employed a cross-sectional design. Can we assume that the intelligence differences between age groups in these two sample populations were due solely to aging? Are there other factors that might account for these differences? As you think about this question, you may wish to review the methodological shortcomings of the cross-sectional design outlined in Chapter 11.

The cross-sectional design involves evaluating people of different ages at one point in time. As we saw in Chapter 11, the major shortcoming of this method is that it cannot rule out a possible generational influence: Subjects were born at different times and thus have experienced varied cultural conditions (Flynn, 1987). For example, the older group may have experienced less formal education, poorer nutrition, less childhood exposure to intellectually stimulating events, or even fewer experiences with this kind of standardized test than the younger subjects. Unless we know what 60 year olds scored when they were 40 and 20, we cannot determine that intelligence declines with age.

In fact, a number of longitudinal studies have generally contradicted the results of the cross-sectional studies, suggesting that people retain their intellect well into middle age. In fact, in two well-designed longitudinal studies subjects achieved slightly higher scores in middle age than in early adulthood (Eichorn et al., 1981; Nisbet, 1957). One recent cross-sequential study showed no significant declines in most areas of intellectual functioning until age 60 or older (Schaie & Hertzog, 1983).

CRYSTALLIZED VERSUS FLUID INTELLIGENCE Some changes in specific kinds of intelligence do appear to be age-related, however. Psychologists distinguish between crystallized and fluid intelligence (Horn, 1982). **Crystallized intelligence** results from accumulated knowledge, including a knowledge of how to reason, language skills, and understanding of technology; it is linked closely to education, experience, and cultural background. Crystallized intelligence is measured by tests of general information. Research indicates that crystallized intelligence increases with age, and that people tend to continue improving their performance on tests of this form of intelligence until near the ends of their lives (Horn, 1982; Horn & Donaldson, 1980).

Fluid intelligence allows us to perceive and draw inferences about relationships among patterns of stimuli, to conceptualize abstract information, and to solve problems. It is measured by various kinds of test problems to which people are unlikely to have been exposed previously, such as grouping numbers and symbols according to some abstract principle. Fluid intelligence seems to be relatively independent of education and cultural influences. It peaks sometime between ages 20 and 30 and declines steadily thereafter (Horn, 1982; Horn & Donaldson, 1980).

It is possible that these age-related differences may somehow be an artifact of the research strategy used, since much of the basic research on crystallized and fluid intelligence has relied on the cross-sectional approach. However, since fluid intelligence depends more on optimal neurological functioning than does crystallized intelligence, it seems likely that it is more adversely influenced by age-associated neurological declines.

A FIFTH STAGE OF COGNITIVE DEVELOPMENT Recall that Piaget saw formal operations as the highest level of cognitive functioning. Some critics disagree, maintaining that many adults progress beyond formal operations to what might be called a fifth stage of intellectual development. One theorist, P. A. Arlin (1975, 1977), believes that adults develop cognitively to the level of **problem finding.** Someone at the problem-finding stage is concerned with posing new questions about the world and trying to discover novel solutions to old problems. Arlin believes that problem finding allows intellectually maturing adults to progress beyond Piaget's formal operations to the level of creative thinking.

Klaus Riegel (1973) offers another interpretation of the fifth stage of cognitive development. Riegel believes the mature mind appreciates the dialectical process that results when two or more incompatible viewpoints oppose one another. Have you ever discussed contradictory religious philosophies or political views with friends? If so, you have engaged in what Riegel would label **dialectic operations.** For Riegel, this dialectic operations stage represents the final stage of cognitive development, when the mature adult thinker realizes and accepts that conflict and contradiction in such areas as morality, politics, and religion are natural consequences of living.

Neither Arlin's problem finding nor Riegel's dialectic operations are widely recognized as a fifth stage of adult cognitive development. However, there is increasing evidence of changes in adult thinking that are not easily accounted for within Piaget's framework (Commons et al., 1982; Kramer, 1983). The way in which we think about things, whether we are defining new problems or dealing with contradictions, continues to change well into our adult years.

PSYCHOSOCIAL DEVELOPMENT IN EARLY AND MIDDLE ADULTHOOD

We saw in Chapter 11 that Erik Erikson described two primary developmental tasks in early and middle adulthood: first the establishment of intimacy, and then the achievement of generativity through commitments to family, work, and future generations. The two major topics in this section, "Single and Married Life-styles" and "Commitments to Parenting and Work," explore some of the ways in which people respond to these challenges.

SINGLE AND MARRIED LIFE-STYLES   As we make the transition from adolescent to young adult, the central focus of our psychosocial adjustment is likely to shift from wanting to be liked by people to needing a loving relationship with someone special. Establishing an intimate relationship requires courage, moral fiber, and a certain amount of self-abandon and willingness to compromise personal preferences. In Erikson's view, two people who achieve true intimacy are able to fuse their identities while at the same time retaining a sense of self. Too much independence may prevent the establishment of intimacy and result in a state of isolation.

Erikson emphasized traditional marriage as a vehicle for fulfilling intimacy needs, but there is plenty of statistical evidence that the commitment to marriage is changing in our society. Can the decision to remain single or cohabit also provide a satisfactory adjustment? The following discussions explore the evidence.

Single Living   Increasing numbers of young and middle-aged adults in our society live alone, many out of choice. This increase is most pronounced among people in their twenties and early thirties. For example, a comparison of 1970 and 1991 census figures reveals that the percentage of men who have never been married has increased from 23.8 percent in 1980 to 26.1 percent in 1991. Comparable figures for women demonstrated an increase from 17.1 percent in 1980 to 19.3 percent in 1991. The number of American households composed of only one person more than doubled between 1970 and 1991 (Statistical Abstracts, 1992).

Although single life is still often seen as the period before, in between, or after marriage, these societal attitudes may be changing. Until recently in the United

States a stigma was often attached to remaining single, especially for women. Today it seems quite possible that more and more people will remain single, either as an option to marriage or following a divorce. There may also be a reduction in the number of people who marry primarily for convention's sake.

Various conditions contribute to the increasing numbers of single adults. These factors include people marrying at a later age, more women placing career objectives ahead of marriage, an increase in the number of cohabiting couples, high divorce rates, a greater emphasis on advanced education, and an increase in the number of women who need not depend on marriage to ensure economic stability (Statistical Abstracts, 1992; Riche, 1988).

A survey of 482 single Canadian adults in several major population centers tells us something about why people choose to remain single and also how satisfied they are with single life (Austrom & Hanel, 1985). In this study, almost half of the subjects said they were single by choice. The vast majority denied that they were single because they were reluctant to be committed to an exclusive relationship, because they lacked desire for sexual relations with the other sex, or because high divorce rates made them apprehensive about marriage. Instead, most were unmarried "simply because they had not met the right person and also because their expectations of a marriage partner were very high" (p. 17).

Many of these single subjects were able to fulfill their intimacy needs, at least to some extent, without cohabiting or marrying. The study linked satisfaction with single life to the number and types of friendships described by the respondents. Those who reported having socially and emotionally supportive relationships were especially inclined to value their life-style. This observation provides us food for thought when we compare it to Erikson's emphasis on traditional marriage for fulfilling intimacy needs.

Although single living is becoming more acceptable in our society, most adults still choose to enter into a long-term relationship with a partner, even though it may not be a lifelong bond. There are several kinds of long-term intimate relationships; we will look at the most common: cohabitation and marriage.

Cohabitation   Attitudes toward **cohabitation** (living together in a sexual relationship without being married) have only recently begun to undergo change. The past few decades have seen a significant increase in both the number of people choosing this living arrangement and societal acceptance of what was once an unconventional practice. U.S. Census Bureau figures reveal that 40 percent of women cohabit at some point and 25.7 percent cohabited before marriage (Statistical Abstracts, 1992).

This dramatic increase in cohabitation has been attributed to a growing inclination to question traditional mores, particularly those pertaining to marriage. Today many people believe that sexuality is an important part of life, and that marriage is not the only life-style that legitimizes sexual relations.

DOES COHABITATION LEAD TO BETTER MARRIAGES?   Does the experience of living together have a measurable effect on the longevity and happiness of a subsequent marriage? There are two opposing views, one arguing that living together has a positive effect on marriage and the other arguing just the opposite, that cohabitation leads to less stable marriages. What do you think? Can you think of arguments to support each of these opposing viewpoints? Consider these questions before reading on.

The more popular point of view among college students is that living together will result in happier and more stable marriages. In this view, cohabiting allows the couple to explore their compatibility before making a long-term commitment. Trial experiences with the struggles and joys of an everyday relationship allow individuals to identify their own needs and expectations.

The opposing view suggests that living together will have an overall negative impact on the institution of marriage, particularly its long-term stability. Faced with conflict, a couple who are living together may find it easier to end the relationship than to make a grand effort to resolve their problems. Once the pattern of breaking up has been established, people may be more likely to respond to marital conflict in the same way.

Perhaps neither of these views is correct, and cohabitation has no demonstrable effect on marriage. U.S. Census data on the outcome of a woman's first cohabitation reveal that nearly 53 percent enter marriage after cohabitation. Of these marriages only about 40 percent were still intact (Statistical Abstracts, 1992). Other evidence supports these statistics. For instance, data obtained from the National Survey of Families and Households revealed that 53 percent of first marriages preceded by cohabitation fail within 10 years in contrast to a 28 percent failure rate for marriages not preceded by cohabitation (Riche, 1988).

Another study of university students examined whether cohabitation (with either the future spouse or someone else) had any influence on subsequent marital happiness. It found no differences on several measures, including indicators of relationship stability, sexual satisfaction, physical intimacy, and openness of communication (Jacques & Chason, 1979). A third study, in which couples were evaluated in the fourth year of their marriages, demonstrated that the premarital relationship of these pairs, whether traditional courtship or cohabitation, did not have a long-term effect on the marital adjustment of these individuals (Watson & DeMeo, 1987). In summary, we can conclude that cohabitation before marriage does not lead to happier, more stable marriages. On the contrary, divorce rates among marriages preceded by cohabitation are consistently higher than those not preceded by cohabitation.

Marriage In spite of rapidly changing mores, people do not seem to be permanently substituting single living, cohabitation, or other alternative life-styles for traditional marriage. Census Bureau statistics reveal that about nine out of every 10 adults in the United States marry, some more than once. Recent statistics show that the number of new marriages each year per 1,000 resident U.S. population has remained relatively stable over the 20-year period from 1970 to 1990, only slightly decreasing from 1980 to 1990 (see Table 12.3). Divorce rates during this period have also remained fairly constant with slight decreases since 1980.

There are good reasons why the institution of marriage is found in virtually every society, for it serves several personal and social functions. It provides societies with stable family units that help to perpetuate social norms, as children learn society's rules and expectations from parents or kinship groups. It also structures an economic partnership that ties child support and subsistence tasks into one family unit. Marriage regulates sexual behavior and also provides a framework for fulfilling people's needs for social and emotional support.

Historically, the function of marriage has been to provide a stable economic unit in which to raise children. In many societies, and in some groups within our own society in the past, marriages were arranged through contracts between parents; romance was not expected to play a part. Today, however, most people expect more from the marriage relationship, seeking fulfillment for their social, emotional, financial, and sexual needs. Happiness itself is sometimes thought to be an automatic outcome of marriage. These are high expectations, and they are difficult to meet. As one observer states, "Marriage was not designed as a mechanism for providing friendship, erotic experience, romantic love, personal fulfillment, continuous lay psychotherapy or recreation" (Cadwallader, 1975, p. 134). However, many couples expect all these benefits from the marital relationship.

While people's expectations for marriage have increased, our society's supportive network for marriage has decreased. In a mobile, urban society in which a

TABLE 12.3 *Number of Marriages and Divorces per 1,000 Resident Population, 1970–1990*

	1970	1975	1980	1985	1990
Marriages	10.6	10.0	10.6	10.1	9.8
Divorces	3.5	4.8	5.2	5.0	4.7

SOURCE: Statistical Abstracts, 1992

couple often settle down far from their extended families, many married couples are isolated from their families and neighbors. This geographical distance places further demands on the marriage, for there is often no place else to turn for such things as child-care assistance, emotional support, and financial or household help.

Another development influencing marital patterns is increased longevity. "Till death do us part" now means many more years than it did in the past, raising the question of how long even the best marriage can be expected to fulfill so many functions.

Despite all these pressures, marriage still succeeds in fulfilling many people's needs for intimacy. What makes a successful marriage? Francine Klagsbrun (1985) recently conducted in-depth interviews with 90 couples married 15 years or more who rated their marriages as happy and successful. Some of the traits she found to be associated with good marriages included spending focused time together, sharing values (more important than sharing interests), and flexibility (that is, a willingness to accept change both in one's partner and in the nature of the relationship). Other studies link marital happiness to positive communication, high levels of physical intimacy, and perceptions of emotional closeness and mutual empathy (Lauer & Lauer, 1985; Tolstedt & Stokes, 1983; Zimmer, 1983).

COMMITMENTS TO PARENTING AND WORK We have been looking at the task of establishing intimacy, but another important challenge of adulthood is to focus on things beyond the self. This is most often expressed as a commitment to family and work during our thirties and forties. Erikson suggested that the most important expression of generativity involves molding and nurturing our own children, but he also acknowledged the great potential of work for satisfying this need. In the following paragraphs we consider each of these areas.

Having Children Until recently, parenthood was an expected consequence of marriage, and most married couples still have one or more children. Today, however, effective birth control methods give adults more choice about becoming parents, and more married people are deciding not to have children at all. How does either having or not having children affect psychosocial development? There is too little evidence to reach a clear-cut answer. Investigations of parenthood have traditionally focused almost exclusively on the question of how parenting styles affect children. Only recently have they begun exploring the reverse question—how having children influences an adult.

We do know of many potential advantages to having children. Parenthood may enhance a couple's love and intimacy as they share in the experiences of raising their offspring. Managing the challenge of parenthood can also be a source of self-esteem, providing a sense of accomplishment. Many parents believe that their children provide them not only with reciprocal love but also with a sense of purpose (Hoffman & Manis, 1979).

Parenthood is often an opportunity for discovering new and untapped dimensions of oneself that can give life greater meaning and satisfaction. Many parents say that they have become better people through parenthood, and according to at least one major study, most indicate that being a parent is a major source of satisfaction (Veroff et al., 1981). Children offer ongoing stimulation and change, and they may also provide financial or emotional support in their parents' older years (Mayleas, 1980).

Some people prefer not to have children, however. These individuals and couples have much more time for themselves and do not have to worry about providing for the needs of children. Recreational and social patterns can be more spontaneous, and adults can more fully pursue careers that also provide challenge and fulfillment. Couples without children usually have more time and energy for companionship, and there is often less stress on their marriages. Some studies show that marriages without children are happier and more satisfying than marriages with children (Campbell, 1975; White & Booth, 1986).

Children absorb time as well as emotional and financial resources—strains that often increase over time (Feshbach, 1985; Rollins & Galligan, 1978). Research reveals that women typically experience more stress than men in the transition to parenthood, perhaps because "Mothers feel responsible for the continuing success and happiness of their children and are often blamed when anything goes wrong in their children's lives" (McBride, 1990, p. 381). Couples who become parents may discover that children can place unexpected strains on their relationship, in addition to interfering with their privacy and spontaneity (Kohn, 1987; Lewis, 1988; Sanders & Cairns, 1987). The result may be a decrease in marital happiness that commences with the birth of the first child, but often reverses itself when all the children have reached adulthood and left the home (Belsky & Rovine, 1990; Datan & Thomas, 1984; Gotlib, 1990; Reinke et al., 1985).

In all, there are no guarantees that the benefits of either having children or childless living will meet one's expectations. Still, it is important to assess the choice of parenthood carefully, for it is a permanent and major life decision.

The World of Work If you were to pick at random any young or middle-aged adult today and ask, "Who are you?," the chances are good that most would reply, "I am a teacher" (or computer programmer, medical technologist, or some other profession). Adults are inclined to define or identify who they are by what they do. This tendency has probably always been true of men; now it is also true of most women, since the majority of adult American women have occupations outside the home. Beyond the sense of competence that successful parenting can provide, much of what people do to fulfill generativity needs involves their work.

During late adolescence, many individuals struggle with developing a career track—one reason why so many college students change their majors one or more times. By young adulthood, most of us accomplish the crucial task of choosing a career. In some ways, careers have become more accessible to both sexes than at any previous time in history. Earlier in this century advanced education was a privilege enjoyed mostly by the affluent, but today almost any motivated high school graduate can attend college. Traditional pressures for sons to follow in their fathers' footsteps and for women to become homemakers are diminishing, and new fields of specialization provide many more potential careers for both sexes.

This increased freedom has also been the source of new frustrations and anxieties, however. As we saw in the discussion of decision making in Chapter 10, virtually unlimited opportunities can seem overwhelming, and young adults are often unsure what to do about their careers. This uncertainty may carry over into the work situation and contribute to a tendency of young workers to be less satisfied with their jobs than middle-aged or older adults (Bass & Ryterband, 1979; Janson & Martin, 1982; Quinn et al., 1974).

How many Americans are satisfied with their jobs? According to one major survey, almost nine out of 10 respondents answered yes to the question, "Are you satisfied with your job?" However, when the same subjects were asked, "If you could start over, would you seek the same job you have now?," less than half of those with white-collar jobs and only a quarter of the blue-collar workers said yes (Weaver, 1980). These findings indicate that job satisfaction is less than optimal for many, if not most, workers. People who are generally satisfied with their jobs also tend to be satisfied with their lives (Keon & McDonald, 1982).

JOB SATISFACTION AND AGE   On the whole, job satisfaction tends to be lower among young adults than middle-aged or older workers. Can you think of possible explanations for this finding? Do young people's work expectations differ significantly from those of older workers, or are there other generational factors that might account for this difference? Think about these questions before reading on.

One common explanation is that young adults earn less money, have fewer responsibilities, and are less challenged than their older counterparts. Certainly these factors may contribute to lower job satisfaction, but other factors may also play a role. One is the reality shock many individuals feel when they discover that their initial career choice is not at all what they expected. For example, individuals who have chosen a college major in a "practical field" like accounting or nursing because these professions seemed to fit their self-concept may find that the nature of the work does not match up at all with their expectations, interests, or self-perception. Such a circumstance often contributes to higher job turnover and lower satisfaction among younger workers (Havinghurst, 1982; Ritzer, 1977). Presumably, most people eventually figure out what they want to do and find more suitable jobs as they grow older, and thus experience improved job satisfaction.

Another possible explanation is that many young, newly hired workers have had little or no prior experience with working 40 or more hours per week, with no end in sight. Young people who have not yet adjusted to this routine may be dissatisfied with any job, regardless of its potential to fulfill their expectations or promote a positive self-identity.

Finally, since most of the research in this area is cross-sectional, it is possible that generational effects may contribute to age-graded differences in job satisfaction. The greater emphasis that is placed on education and careers today may influence both sexes to have higher career expectations and feel more pressure to succeed—a setup for stress and disillusionment. Also, since young adults today tend to be better educated than older generations, they may be harder to please.

One of the most noteworthy recent trends is the dramatic increase in the number of women in the work force (Glick, 1989). Today roughly two out of every three women age 25 to 44 work outside the home, a figure that has doubled since the early 1950s. More than half of mothers with children under 18 are participating in the labor force, more than triple the number three decades ago. Current estimates indicate that in 2005 approximately 63 percent of mothers with preschoolers will have jobs that require placing their children in some kind of daycare (Schacheve, 1990; Statistical Abstracts, 1992).

A number of social trends contribute to this increase. For one, traditional social taboos against mothers working outside the home have largely disappeared.

Another factor is that more women are now attending college, and higher education tends to create a desire to apply one's accumulated wisdom in a career. Furthermore, many professions once considered the exclusive domain of men are now more accessible to women.

There are also important practical benefits to working. A job provides a way to broaden social networks, as well as an escape from the sense of isolation that many nonworking women experience. Another benefit is the increased financial security provided by two incomes. Dual-career families are better able to afford the extras that add to enjoyment of life and are less likely to be confronted with the stress of financial crises. Finally, Erikson's assertion that a man's sense of identity and self-worth is strongly influenced by his work also applies to women. A number of studies have shown that women who enjoy their work have higher self-esteem, a greater sense of pride and power, better emotional and physical health, and a greater sense of overall life satisfaction than women who do not work outside the home (Hoffman, 1974, 1979).

Dual-provider families also face some potential disadvantages, however. One of the biggest problems is finding enough time for everything. At the end of the work day the couple must face mundane tasks such as paying the bills, doing housework, washing clothes, and preparing meals. If they have children, there are additional demands that may make it difficult to spend quality time together or to enjoy leisure activities (Moen, 1982). This schedule can exact a high price both in diminished energy levels and downgraded quality of a relationship. Unfortunately, women seem to bear the brunt of these increased pressures, and they often must contend with role overload if husbands neglect to share domestic duties equally (Pleck, 1977; Slocum & Nye, 1976).

THE OLDER YEARS

What kinds of associations or images come to your mind when you hear the words *old people* or *old age?* If you are like most Americans, young and old alike, you are likely to think of old people as forgetful, cranky, touchy, depressed, frail, unhealthy, poorly coordinated, and not as smart as when they were younger. You are also likely to view the older years as a time when people become more dependent on others, less interested in sex, obsessed with physical complaints, more isolated from friends and family, unreliable, and likely to be institutionalized in nursing homes. Are these stereotypes more myth than fact? In the remaining pages of this chapter we explore the evidence about the physical, cognitive, and psychosocial developments that accompany older adulthood.

THE GRAYING OF AMERICA

People today are living longer and retaining their health and vigor longer than previous generations. In fact, the proportion of older people in the American population has increased quite dramatically in recent years. Whereas in 1900 the average life expectancy was slightly less than 50 years, by the 1990s it had increased to approximately age 75. Only 4 percent of the American populace was over 65 in 1900, but in 1991 this figure had tripled to 12.6 percent (more than 31.7 million people). Over the last few decades, the proportion of American people 65 and older has grown at twice the rate of the rest of our population. By the year 2030, more than 20 percent of the American population will be 65 and older (Horn & Meer, 1987; Statistical Abstracts, 1992).

The so-called graying of America may be attributed to a number of factors. To some extent, it is a function of an increased birthrate that commenced around the turn of the century, combined with higher immigration rates early in this century. However, much of this trend is caused by technological changes since

1900 that have resulted in longer life spans and lower mortality rates for the elderly. Improved medications and medical procedures prolong the lives of many older people.

The graying of America has significant implications for changing family patterns, employment trends, social policies, and political trends, but our concern is with the individuals who are experiencing longer life spans. Does a longer life mean a welcome prolongation of life's so-called "golden years," or has technology merely expanded the pain and travail of life on a downward slide?

PHYSICAL DEVELOPMENT IN THE OLDER YEARS

We noted earlier that physical decline in such things as muscle strength, vision, and hearing begins in early to middle adulthood. While many of these changes are barely noticeable in the middle years, they often are disturbingly obvious as we grow older. One area in which there are often sharp declines is vision. Older people may become more farsighted; they may also have trouble perceiving color and depth and adapting to changes in lighting. (Night vision commonly declines with age.) The changes in vision are largely caused by a reduction in the elasticity of the lens. This makes it more difficult for the ciliary muscles to change the shape of the lens. As a result, older people often need to hold reading material further away to keep it in focus.

Hearing loss is also common: Many older people have difficulty following a conversation, particularly when there is competing noise from television, radio, or other background sound. This decline can increase a sense of isolation and perhaps even contribute to mild paranoia if older people assume that others are trying to hide something from them by whispering (Zimbardo et al., 1981). Other frequent accompaniments to aging are reduction in taste and smell sensitivity (which explains why food often does not taste as good to older people). About 25 percent of people between 65 and 68 have no sense of smell and by age 80, this increases to over 50 percent (Shiffman, 1990). There is also a diminution of the body senses of kinesthesis and equilibrium (see Chapter 4), which may be one reason why older people are more likely to lose their balance and fall.

The organ systems also show a decline in functional efficiency with age. When we are young, our hearts, lungs, kidneys, and other organs have the potential to increase their outputs to a level several times greater than normal under emergency conditions, a capacity that is known as **organ reserve.** For example, strenuous physical activity can cause a young heart to work six times harder than normal. As we grow older, organ reserve is reduced. The heart's ability to pump blood declines by about 1 percent per year from the early twenties on, and by age 60 blood flow from the arms to the legs is slower than at age 25 (Brody, 1986). By age 75 there has been an average decline in lung capacity of approximately 50 percent in men and 30 percent in women. Furthermore, muscle fibers decrease in number at an average rate of 3 to 5 percent per decade after age 30 (Brody, 1986).

Although the statistics we have just cited may seem to paint a rather depressing picture, there is a brighter side to the story. Many of the visual and hearing difficulties of older people can be adequately compensated for by glasses, hearing aids, and other medical procedures. There is also evidence that regular exercise can significantly reduce deterioration of many bodily functions that accompanies aging. It has been estimated that disuse accounts for about half of the functional decline that occurs between ages 30 and 70 (Brody, 1986). It would appear that the advice "use it or lose it" has some validity.

Despite the declines associated with the older years, widespread evidence indicates that most older people enjoy reasonably good health, some virtually to the ends of their lives (Horn & Meer, 1987; Neugarten & Neugarten, 1987). While it is true that people over 65 are more subject to chronic long-term ailments, such as arthritis, rheumatism, and hypertension, they are also less likely than

It is becoming more common to see older people engaged in physical activities and sports.

younger people to be troubled by short-term acute ailments like colds, flu, and digestive problems (Palmore, 1981). According to a 1983 survey by the U.S. Census Bureau, four out of five people over 65 report their health to be good or excellent.

NEURONAL CHANGES DURING AGING   In the previous section we reviewed a number of sensory and structural changes that occur during later years. What about the brain? Does it change too? Normally, the effects of aging on the brain are not noticeable until we reach about 50 to 60 years of age. At this time the brain begins to decrease in size as a result of both neuron and glial cell loss. For instance, normal young adults may have in excess of 400,000 dopamine neurons in their brains. By the time they reach 80 years of age this number is reduced by one half (Groves & Rebec, 1992). In addition to cell loss, there is a marked reduction in the number of synaptic connections throughout the brain. Figure 12.2 shows this decrease in neuronal connections.

As with other bodily functions, the normal deterioration in the brain can be significantly reduced by both physical exercise, which increases blood flow to the brain, and by using your brain. Experiments with aging rats has demonstrated new cell growth and synapse formation after exposure to a stimulating environment (Greenough et al., 1986). It is believed that people who continually engage in stimulating activities such as reading can greatly reduce the rate of normal cell deterioration.

FIGURE 12.2

Photomicrographs of Neurons in the Cerebellum Showing the Cell Bodies, Axons, and Dendrites Branching

Notice the cell loss due to aging in the photo on the right.

(From *The Mind* by Restak, R.M., 1988, Bantam Press, p. 72–73.)

THEORIES OF AGING   Why do people age? People have long wondered why our bodies lose their capacity to function efficiently as we grow older. Most investigators agree that aging is influenced by several factors, including heredity, physical activity, nutrition, disease, and a host of environmental factors. However, science has yet to discover exactly why body cells age and cease to function properly.

Over the years there have been two major theories of aging. One, the **genetic clock** or **programmed theory**, maintains that life itself is a terminal disease: Ag-

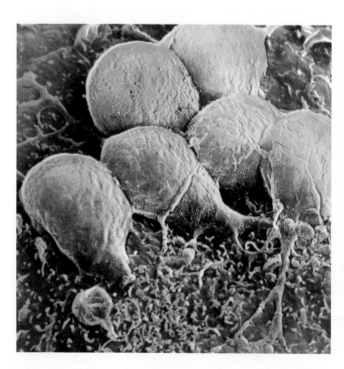

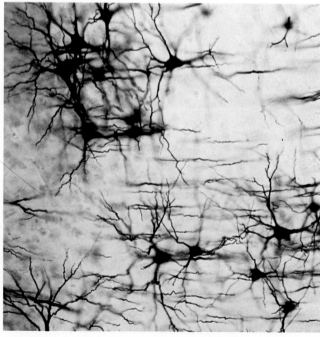

ing is built into every organism through a genetic code that instructs the body cells when it is time to call it a day. Support for this theory was provided by research conducted by Leonard Hayflick (1974), whose investigations of cellular processes in a variety of species revealed that body cells will divide only a preordained number of times (about 50 in the case of humans). The fact that identical twins have very similar life spans seems to support the genetic clock theory. Furthermore, we know that a number of rare human conditions involving accelerated aging are the result of defective genes (Eckholm, 1986).

An alternative **accumulating damages theory** sees aging as a consequence of damages that emerge from the wear and tear of living (Holiday, 1987). Our bodies, like machines, eventually wear out as a result of accumulated insults and damages from continued, nonstop use. As we grow older, our worn-out body cells eventually lose their ability to repair or replace damaged components, and thus they eventually cease to function.

These two theories have different implications for those who are interested in counteracting the ravages of aging. People who believe we age only because things wear out might focus on reducing the stresses that produce damage and on avoiding harmful substances that might aggravate the wearing-out process. Those who lean toward the genetic clock view are probably less optimistic about our ability to alter the aging process. However, thanks to recent advances in genetic engineering (see Chapter 11), it now seems possible that genetic alterations might lead to prolonged life spans. Recently a molecular biologist at the University of California at Irvine was able to increase markedly the life span of a species of roundworm by altering a single gene (Johnson, 1986).

A complete understanding of why we age will probably eventually involve aspects of both the genetic clock and accumulated damages theories, with a gradual blurring of the distinction between the two.

COGNITIVE DEVELOPMENT IN THE OLDER YEARS

It is often said that old people have poor memories, and that intelligence declines sharply in the later years. How accurate is this picture? For most people, the ability to learn and retain meaningful information declines only slightly in the later years (Labouvie-Vief & Schell, 1982; Perlmutter, 1983). The characterization of old age as a time of cognitive decline may be related to a few conditions. One of these is a decline of fluid intelligence that usually does accompany aging; another is the highly visible condition of senility that affects a relatively small percentage of older people. Let us look at both of these factors.

INTELLIGENCE AND AGING   As we saw earlier in this chapter, there seem to be two types of intelligence. Crystallized intelligence tends to hold steady or perhaps even improve somewhat in the later years—a finding that is consistent with our tendency to continue to add to our storehouse of knowledge as we grow older, often up to the end of our lives. In contrast, fluid intelligence declines with age, a process that may be related to reduced efficiency of neurological functioning.

There is another possible explanation for the discrepancy between crystallized and fluid intelligence in the later years. People may be more likely to maintain crystallized abilities because they are exercised or used on a regular basis, whereas older people may be less frequently challenged to use their fluid abilities (Denney & Palmer, 1981). This suggestion presents another version of the "use it or lose it" concept mentioned earlier.

SENILE DEMENTIA   For a small number of people, old age brings a nightmare of deteriorating cognitive functions known commonly as senility or more technically as **senile dementia** (a collective term that describes a variety of conditions characterized by memory deficits, forgetfulness, disorientation for time and place, decline in the ability to think, impaired attention, altered personality, and difficulties in relating to others). Approximately four million Americans are afflicted with senile dementia (Gall & Black, 1989). Dementia has many causes, some treatable and some that cannot be remedied at the present time (Henderson, 1990). Occasionally the confusion characteristic of dementia can be attributed to improper use of medications, hormonal abnormalities, infectious diseases, or metabolic disorders. (Dementia resulting from these causes may often be remedied by medical treatment.) More commonly it is associated with a series of small strokes, brain tumors, neurological disorders, or chronic alcoholism—all of which can result in irreversible loss of brain neurons.

The most common form of senile dementia is **Alzheimer's disease** (Katzman et al., 1989), a currently incurable condition that robs individuals of the capacity to remember, think, relate to others, care for themselves, and even to be aware of their own existence. In the mid-1980s, the National Alzheimer's Disease and Related Disorders Association estimated that roughly 2.5 million Americans, most of whom are over 60, have this dreadful illness. Current estimates suggest that approximately 10 percent of people over 65 and 47 percent of people over 85 years of age are victims of Alzheimer's disease (Statistical Abstracts, 1992). Alzheimer's disease alone accounts for 60 percent of all cases of senile dementia in people over age 65 (Wragg & Jeste, 1989).

A tremendous amount of research is currently underway to determine the cause(s) of this disease, and some clues have been uncovered. One line of evidence suggests that victims of Alzheimer's disease may lack a specific brain enzyme necessary for the successful function of brain cells that produce the neurotransmitter acetylcholine (Sirvioö et al., 1989; Tamminga et al., 1987; Tucek et al., 1990; Wurtman et al., 1990). Research has also linked Alzheimer's disease to the presence of a protein substance referred to as β amyloid protein (Clark et al., 1989; DeLaber et al., 1987; Kang et al., 1987; Masters & Beyreuther, 1990; Tanzi et al., 1987). Amyloid proteins duplicate themselves to such an excessive extent in people with Alzheimer's disease that they create tangled webs, known as amyloid webs, which produce massive neurological damage and ultimately choke the life out of affected brain cells. Amyloid webs have been detected in the brain cells of people who die of Alzheimer's disease and some other brain-destroying ailments (Gall & Black, 1989; Perlman, 1985).

Another line of research has looked for genetic clues. Recently members of a research team headed by Peter St. George–Hyslop (1987) identified the location of a defective gene that causes the familial or inherited form of Alzheimer's disease. This genetic defect is located on chromosome 21—interestingly, the same chromosome that exists in triplicate in Down syndrome (see Chapter 11). (People with Down syndrome typically develop a brain pathology that is indistinguishable from Alzheimer's disease by the time they reach age 60 [Anderton, 1987].) The genetic defect in Alzheimer's disease identified by the St. George–Hyslop research team is located on the same region of chromosome 21 that contains the gene coding for the β amyloid protein (Barnes, 1987a; Goldgaber & Schmechel, 1990; St. George–Hyslop et al., 1987; Tanzi et al., 1987).

Although some studies have failed to detect linkage to chromosome 21 for Alzheimer's disease (Roses et al., 1987 & 1990; Schellenberg et al., 1988), a recent study did find a link between a gene causing Alzheimer's disease and chromosome 21 (Goate et al., 1990). Today, the original report of linkage to chromosome 21, though beleaguered, is standing (Heston, 1990, p. 8).

What about the cases of Alzheimer's disease that are not familial? (At the present time, researchers are uncertain what proportion of cases of Alzheimer's disease are inherited, with estimates ranging from only 5 percent to almost 100 percent [Farrer et al., 1989].) Another research team, led by Dmitry Goldgaber (1987), located a genetic defect that appears to be linked with nonfamilial cases of Alzheimer's disease. This defect is located in the same region of chromosome 21 as the defect associated with the familial form of the disease, suggesting that both forms of Alzheimer's disease may result from a defect of the same gene that contains the coding of the β amyloid protein.

Researchers continue to study the relationship between the defective genetic coding on chromosome 21 and the brain pathology associated with Alzheimer's disease. Scientists hope that this ongoing research will eventually unravel the mystery of Alzheimer's disease and lead to the development of effective preventive or treatment procedures. Despite the wide publicity received by Alzheimer's disease in recent years, 90 percent or more of people over 65 show little or no cognitive deterioration.

PSYCHOSOCIAL DEVELOPMENT IN THE OLDER YEARS

We have seen that the popular stereotype of old age as a time of rapidly deteriorating physical and cognitive functioning is much more myth than fact. But what about the health of older people? Is aging associated with depression, despair, dissatisfaction, unhappiness, and a breakdown of interpersonal relationships? Fortunately, this generalization is true of only a small proportion of aging people.

In reality, the older years do tend to be the golden years for a large number of individuals. Several major national surveys have found that satisfaction with life in general, feelings of well-being, and marital satisfaction actually tend to be higher among the aged than among younger adults (Dickie et al., 1979; Herzog et al., 1982). Despite the common misconception that many older people end up in institutions for the aged, only about 5 percent of America's aged population live in institutions. For most, old age is a time of continued independence, with the additional freedom from the burdens of job and family obligations.

This situation is not always the case, however. Some older people who are widowed, isolated from friends, in poor health, economically disadvantaged, or resentful of being forced to retire may find the older years to be far from golden. Admittedly, some of these factors are beyond most individuals' control, but in many ways our satisfaction in old age is the product of our own attitudes and behaviors.

SUCCESSFUL AGING   Many Americans see continued active involvement in life as the best road to successful aging. Older people are encouraged to remain active and not to retire from their lives when they retire from their jobs. But might there not also be advantages to cutting back, relaxing, and gracefully withdrawing from the bustle of life?

These descriptions summarize two popular theories of successful aging that have generated considerable discussion and research. According to the *activity theory*, the more involved and active older people remain, the more happy and fulfilled they will be. Thus older people should pursue hobbies, travel, do volunteer work, engage in active grandparenting, or involve themselves in other endeavors that help to sustain a relatively high level of activity. In contrast, the *disengagement theory* suggests that we are more likely to be happy in our older years if we cut back on the stresses associated with an active life, taking time to relax, reduce social obligations, and enjoy the tranquility of peaceful reflections.

Which of these prescriptions should a person follow? In general, we can safely say that neither life-style provides a guarantee of successful, happy aging. There is evidence that people's happiness may have little connection with how active they happen to be (Lemon et al., 1972). Furthermore, the process of disengagement, at least when carried to the extreme, seems to be more related to preparation for imminent death than it does to successful aging (Lieberman & Coplan, 1970). Just as happiness for you or us is not strongly correlated with a particular life-style, the same is true for older people. Some are happiest when they are

B.F. Skinner was intellectually active throughout his life.

busy and socially involved, while others may enjoy indulging in plenty of relaxation, perhaps for the first time in their lives (Neugarten, 1972; Neugarten et al., 1965; Reichard et al., 1962). Bernice Neugarten (1972) has suggested that most older people tend to select a life-style that reflects their personality and the kinds of activities they engaged in while they were younger.

As people age, however, they may no longer find the consequences of these activities as rewarding as they once were. Aging not only makes many activities more difficult because of the changes in sensory abilities (like vision, audition, and taste), but it makes the consequences more aversive. For instance, playing tennis or going on long walks may result in fatigue and sore muscles and engaging in intellectual activities may result in embarrassment from a failing memory. For these reasons many people may abandon activities they enjoyed earlier. B.F. Skinner offers some particularly useful advice on how the aging intellectual can compensate for some of these changes (c.f. Skinner, 1987). It is perhaps this advice that kept him intellectually active through the last months of his long and productive life.

Recall that Erik Erikson viewed successful aging as conditional upon achieving integrity. He believed that people who are able to view their lives retrospectively with a sense of satisfaction and accomplishment are likely to achieve a sense of unity or integrity. In contrast, people who view their lives as a series of disappointments and failures are likely to experience unhappiness and despair. Robert Butler (1961) agrees that older people often conduct a *life review* in which they reminisce about their past, sorting out their accomplishments and their disappointments. In addition to allowing older people to achieve a state of integrity, this life review may also provide a new focus for the future. Recall Ebenezer Scrooge in Charles Dickens' *A Christmas Carol*, whose forced life review produced a dramatically more optimistic focus to his life in his remaining years.

The importance of security and close relationships in successful aging should also be noted. Research indicates that those individuals who make the best psychosocial adjustments to the older years tend to be in good health, to be financially secure, and to have close ties with family and friends (Dickie et al., 1979; Herzog et al., 1982). Furthermore, evidence suggests that the process of finding meaning and purpose in life in the older years can help promote health and wellness, whereas in contrast, a sense of meaninglessness may lead to the onset of such negative conditions as anxiety, depression, and/or physical decline (Reker et al., 1987).

Maintaining close personal relationships has been shown to be especially important for maintaining health and recovering from illness in the elderly. A number of studies have demonstrated the health benefits of **social support** from family, friends, and health care providers in reducing risks of disease and prolonging life. For instance, in a large study conducted in Finland, men with few or no social contacts were two times more likely to die from all causes (particularly heart disease) than men with social contacts (Kaplan et al., 1988). Women with few or no social contacts were not found to be at risk. In another study married men were shown to recover more quickly from coronary bypass surgery than unmarried men (Kulik & Mahler, 1989).

How does social support facilitate recovery from surgery and disease as well as prolong life? How might **social isolation** increase an individual's risk of disease? Think about these questions before reading on.

There are several possible ways that social support might influence health. First, it has been suggested that people who live in isolation live in physically different circumstances and it is these circumstances that influence health. These conditions might include the type and location of housing, diet, and opportunities for physical exercise. Another possibility is that social support acts as a buffer to life stressors. This buffering hypothesis argues that people with social contacts are protected (or buffered) from the harmful effects of stress. In addition, people with social contacts are more likely to receive advice about good health practices, receive encouragement, be physically active, and have a greater sense of personal control (Brannon & Feist, 1992).

In this chapter we reviewed the developmental changes that occur during adulthood. Physical, cognitive, and psychosocial changes continue throughout our lives. During these later years there is considerable variability between individuals in how quickly these changes occur. It appears that maintaining a physically active and cognitively stimulating life-style can greatly reduce the rate of detrimental changes in late adulthood. In addition, maintaining close social contacts throughout our lives may contribute to health and longevity.

SUMMARY

ADOLESCENCE

1. In America and other modern Western societies the period of adolescence is prolonged. Unlike many nonindustrial societies, our society has no single initiation rite that signals passage into adulthood.

2. Puberty is the approximately two-year period of rapid physical changes that culminates in sexual maturity. The adolescent growth spurt usually runs its course in the two years following the onset of puberty.

3. Secular growth trends refer to changes in human physical growth patterns in many societies around the world that appear to be caused by improved standards of living.

4. In general, research has shown that early maturation holds some advantages for boys and some disadvantages for girls.

5. The onset of adolescence is marked by the emergence of the capacity to manipulate objects mentally that are not physically present and by the ability to engage in deductive reasoning, both traits Piaget associated with the formal operations stage of cognitive development.

6. According to Lawrence Kohlberg's theory of moral development, most children between the ages four and 10 exhibit a preconventional morality in which they behave in certain ways to avoid being punished or to obtain rewards. By late childhood or early adolescence we achieve the level of conventional morality exemplified by the desire either to help others or to help maintain the social order. Some adults progress to the final level of postconventional morality, in which they affirm individual rights and perhaps are guided by universal moral principles that may conflict with society's rules.

7. It is during our adolescence that most of us first acquire an identity or sense of self. An important part of establishing an identity is gaining independence from parents. As parental influence diminishes, the peer group's influence grows.

8. American teenagers spend over half their waking hours with friends of the same age. They tend to identify more with their peers, and they rate themselves as happiest when they are with friends.

9. Adolescent sexuality in America is marked by the double standard, considerable pressure to be sexually active, and not infrequently, anxiety, confusion, guilt, and feelings of inadequacy.

10. Over the last four decades there has been a strong upward trend in the numbers of adolescents who experience sexual

intercourse. These increases have been considerably larger for females than males. Fewer adolescent women than men experience premarital intercourse, but the difference between the sexes has been diminishing rapidly.

11. Although sexually active teenagers are at risk for contracting AIDS, research suggests that most adolescents have not modified their sexual behavior by engaging in safer sexual practices.

ADULTHOOD

12. Many age-based expectations (the tendency to associate certain developmental tasks or appropriate behaviors with each phase of adult life) have begun to break down in contemporary society. We appear to be moving in the direction of an age-irrelevant society in which such attributes as age, race, or sex are diminishing in importance as regulators of behavior.

13. During early adulthood (the twenties and thirties) people reach the peak of their biological efficiency. During this time most of us enjoy the best health of any time in our lives.

14. Middle adulthood (the forties and fifties) brings a gradual decline in physical functioning and perhaps a corresponding increase in health problems.

15. Our society has a double standard of aging that tends to regard postmenopausal women as past their sexual prime, whereas men's physical and sexual attractiveness is often considered to be enhanced by the aging process.

16. Research has shown that people retain their intellectual abilities well into middle age and beyond. Some changes in specific kinds of intelligence do appear to be age related. Crystallized intelligence, which results from accumulated knowledge, tends to increase with age. In contrast, fluid intelli-

gence, or the ability to conceptualize abstract information and to solve problems, tends to decline after age 30.

17. Two primary developmental tasks in early and middle adulthood are the establishment of intimacy and the achievement of generativity through commitments to family, work, and future generations.

18. Erik Erikson identified traditional marriage as the avenue for fulfilling intimacy needs. Today, however, an increasing number of people remain unmarried, and many are able to fulfill their intimacy needs through close friendships and/or cohabitation relationships.

19. Over the years the expectations Americans have had for marriage have increased while society's supportive network for marriage has decreased.

20. Studies have linked marital happiness to positive communication, high levels of physical intimacy, mutual empathy, spending focused time together, sharing values, and flexibility.

21. Having children may be associated with both positive and negative consequences. On the positive side, parenthood may enhance a couple's love and intimacy and provide them with a sense of accomplishment and a chance to discover untapped personal dimensions and resources. On the debit side, children often sap energy, reduce time for each other, and place a drain on emotional and financial resources.

22. Aside from parenting, much of what people do to fulfill generativity needs involves their work.

23. Young workers generally tend to be less satisfied with their jobs than middle-aged or older adults. People who are satisfied with their jobs also tend to be satisfied with their lives.

24. One of the most noteworthy trends in the world of work is the

dramatic increase in the number of women in the work force.

THE OLDER YEARS

25. Over the last few decades, the proportion of American people 65 and older has grown at twice the rate of the rest of our population.

26. In the older years people experience a decline in all sensory functions together with a reduction in organ reserve (the capacity of organs like the heart and lungs to increase their outputs under emergency conditions).

27. There is ample evidence that regular exercise can significantly reduce the deterioration of both physical and cognitive functions that accompany aging.

28. The two major explanations of why people age are the genetic clock theory, which maintains that aging is built into the body cells through a genetic code, and the accumulating damages interpretation, which suggests that our bodies eventually wear out as a result of accumulated insults and damages from continued, nonstop use.

29. For most people, the ability to learn and retain meaningful information declines only slightly in the later years.

30. The most common form of senile dementia is Alzheimer's disease, which has been linked with neurons containing the neurotransmitter acetylcholine. Research has also linked this disease to the presence of a protein that creates tangled amyloid webs that destroy brain cells. Finally, both familial and nonfamilial Alzheimer's disease are associated with a genetic defect on chromosome 21.

31. Even in old age the neurons of the cerebral cortex seem capable of forming additional functional connections with other neurons.

32. Studies have shown that satisfaction with life in general and feelings of well-being tend to be higher among the aged than among younger adults.

33. Happiness in the later years does not appear to be correlated with a particular life-style. Some older people are happiest when they are busy and socially involved; others may enjoy indulging in plenty of relaxation. Most older people tend to select a life-style that reflects their personality and the kinds of activities they engaged in while they were younger.

34. Maintaining a network of social support seems especially important for the health of older adults. Social isolation is associated with a greater risk of disease and prolonged recovery from illness.

TERMS AND CONCEPTS

puberty
adolescent growth spurt
gonadotropins
secondary sex characteristics
secular growth trends
preconventional morality
conventional morality
postconventional morality
climacteric
menopause
crystallized intelligence
fluid intelligence
problem finding
dialectic operations
cohabitation
organ reserve
genetic clock (programmed) theory
accumulating damages theory
senile dementia
Alzheimer's disease
social support
social isolation

Intelligence

DEFINING INTELLIGENCE

MEASURING INTELLIGENCE

Binet and Intelligence Testing
The Stanford-Binet Intelligence Scale
The Wechsler Adult Intelligence Scale
Group versus Individual Intelligence
    Tests

EVALUATING INTELLIGENCE TESTS

How Intelligence Tests are Developed
Test Reliability and Validity
Achievement and Aptitude Tests

THEORIES OF INTELLIGENCE

Factorial Theories
Process Theories

BIAS IN INTELLIGENCE TESTING

HEREDITARY AND ENVIRONMENTAL INFLUENCES ON INTELLIGENCE

Isolating Contributions to Intelligence
Twin Studies
Adoption Studies
Orphanage and Environmental
    Enrichment Studies
Birth-Order Studies
Animal Research
Evaluating the Hereditary and Environ-
    mental Evidence
Within- and Between-Group Differences
    and Intelligence

RACIAL DIFFERENCES IN INTELLIGENCE

People have always been aware of differences in intelligence between individuals, but not until the closing decades of the 1800s were any efforts made to quantify or measure people's intelligence. The story of how and why the intelligence testing movement began is an interesting one, and it is a good place to start this chapter.

The story centers around Sir Francis Galton, a British biologist who also happened to be the cousin of Charles Darwin. Galton was very much influenced by his cousin's theory of natural selection (see Chapter 1), and he saw the process of survival of the fittest at work in British society. He declared that among humans, the "most fit" were those with high intelligence. But how could we tell who these superior people were? Independently wealthy himself, Galton assumed that those individuals in the upper stratum of society must be the most intelligent. The very fact that they had risen to the top was evidence that they had adapted most successfully to their environment. (No matter that the upper classes were born with a head start denied to the rest of society! Since Galton believed that intelligence was inherited, this detail was of minor importance, for a son would inherit his father's intelligence as well as his hard-earned wealth.) Galton also believed that men were intellectually superior to women, and that Caucasians were superior to other races.

Galton was not satisfied merely to assume that the upper classes were intellectually superior to the rest of society. As biologist Stephen Jay Gould has noted, "quantification was Galton's god" (1981, p. 76), and Galton would not rest until he had proven his theory by measuring people's intelligence. Galton designed a number of procedures (including simple tests of sensory acuity and reaction time as well as some very precise skull measurements) to measure attributes that he thought were the basis of human intelligence. The 1884 International Exposition was taking place in London, and so Galton set up a laboratory there. For threepence, visitors could expose themselves to Galton's procedures and find out how they rated.

Thus the first intelligence test was conducted on some 10,000 visitors to the exposition. The results may have disappointed Galton, for they documented neither the superiority of the upper classes nor even the superiority of the Caucasian male. However, this episode marked the beginning of scientific efforts to determine what intelligence is and how to measure it. Although our understanding of intelligence and our ability to measure it have come a long way since Galton's time, we see in this chapter that intelligence is still an elusive concept. (We also meet up with Francis Galton a few more times, for several of his observations about intelligence are still relevant today.)

We begin by trying to define intelligence, and then move on to explore some of the methods that are used to measure people's intelligence. Several theories of intelligence will be reviewed and we also discuss one of psychology's most debated controversies: To what degree is intelligence a product of heredity, and to what degree is it a product of the environment?

DEFINING INTELLIGENCE

Virtually all of us have used the term "intelligent" to describe friends and acquaintances, but what is intelligence? What attributes must a person display to earn the label intelligent? Consider the personal traits ascribed to the following

Sir Francis Galton

two hypothetical people and decide which person sounds more intelligent to you:

PERSON A

1. Speaks clearly and articulately
2. Sees all aspects of a problem
3. Is a good source of ideas
4. Deals effectively with people
5. Makes good decisions
6. Deals with problems resourcefully
7. Is sensitive to other people's needs and desires
8. Thinks before speaking and doing

PERSON B

1. Displays a good vocabulary
2. Is intellectually curious
3. Learns rapidly
4. Thinks deeply
5. Solves problems well
6. Displays logical reasoning
7. Displays interest in the world at large
8. Is verbally fluent

Admittedly, making a judgment based on this limited information is not easy. Nevertheless, there is reason to believe that you may have found yourself favoring person *A*. This prediction is based on research conducted a few years ago by Yale psychologist Robert Sternberg and his colleagues (Sternberg et al., 1981). Sternberg's group surveyed several hundred laypeople representing a broad spectrum of society, as well as over 100 psychologists with a special interest in intelligence. Both the nonpsychologists and the specialists were asked to list specific kinds of behavior that they thought were indicative of intelligence or the lack of intelligence. A list of 170 indicators emerged from this study.

Most of these behaviors fall into one of three categories: *verbal ability* (speaks clearly and articulately; is verbally fluent), *practical problem-solving ability* (sees all aspects of a problem; is able to apply knowledge to problems at hand), and *social competence* (is sensitive to other people's needs and desires; thinks before speaking and doing). The nonpsychologists and the experts had remarkably similar views, with one major difference: Laypeople were much more inclined than the research psychologists to include dimensions of social competence as attributes of intelligence. Since social competence traits were ascribed only to person *A* (items 4, 7, and 8), we predicted that you would be likely to consider person *A* more intelligent than person *B*.

We have mentioned a number of important attributes of intelligence, but how do these attributes relate to the concept of intelligence? Can we define it precisely? Several psychologists have risen to this challenge. Lewis Terman (1921), an influential pioneer in intelligence research and testing, defined **intelligence** as the ability to think abstractly. David Wechsler (1944), who developed tests that are used widely today to measure intelligence, considered intelligence to be the ability to act purposefully, to think rationally, and to deal effectively with the environment. More recently, Robert Sternberg and William Salter (1982) reported that most experts view intelligence as a person's capacity for goal-directed adaptive behavior.

All of these definitions seem reasonable and they are acceptable to many people, including many psychologists. However, they each pose additional problems.

What does it mean to think abstractly, act purposefully, or engage in goal-directed, adaptive behavior? Because these descriptions are ambiguous, these definitions may mean different things to different people.

Virtually all intelligence researchers agree that intelligence is not a precisely measurable commodity that we possess. Rather, it is a concept or label invented to describe differences in individual behavior. If you wanted to conduct research in which intelligence was one of your key variables (for example, a study of the relationship between birth order and intelligence), you would need to define intelligence operationally. How would you develop a precise operational definition of intelligence that would allow you to quantify and measure this variable? Can intelligence be defined operationally? Take a couple of minutes to consider this question before reading on. (You may wish to review the information about operational definitions in Chapter 2.)

Unfortunately, the only operational definition of intelligence that most psychologists have agreed on to date may be stated as follows: Intelligence is what intelligence tests measure. Virtually all intelligence research to date, whether it be of a correlational or experimental nature, has used test scores to measure intelligence. To make a reasonable judgment about how sound this practice is, you need more information about how intelligence is measured.

MEASURING INTELLIGENCE

We saw at the beginning of this chapter that Sir Francis Galton's early intelligence-testing efforts had disappointing results because they failed to support his beliefs about the superiority of the upper-class Caucasian male. The story did not end there, however. Galton was followed by others who also sought to use science to justify class, racial, and gender biases. Over a period of many years, procedures for measuring intelligence evolved considerably, so that today there are a number of highly regarded devices for measuring intelligence. We'll see also that issues regarding the misuse and biases in intelligence testing are still with us. This section provides a brief overview of what has happened since Galton.

BINET AND INTELLIGENCE TESTING

The so-called modern intelligence testing movement was launched around the turn of the century by French psychologist Alfred Binet in response to an urgent need to ease problems of overcrowding in French schools. The French government had recently made education compulsory for all children, but it had not anticipated two outcomes of this edict. First, the classrooms were filled to overflowing, and second, teachers now had to cope with a much wider range of differences in students' abilities than ever before. It soon became apparent that a sizable number of children needed special classes.

How could these children with special needs be identified? Since Binet was the leading French psychologist at the time, he was asked to develop an objective test to identify such students. With a number of collaborators, most notably Theodore Simon, Binet set out to devise a measure for children's intellectual skills.

Binet and his collaborators reasoned that virtually all children follow essentially the same course of intellectual development, but that some progress more rapidly than others. Thus children of subnormal intelligence were presumed to be merely "retarded" in their development. Taking this reasoning one step further, Binet theorized that a child of low intelligence should perform on tests of

Alfred Binet

intellect like a normal child of a younger age—and conversely, that a precocious child should perform like an older child of average intelligence. Binet coined the term *mental level* to express a child's composite test score. This term, later referred to as **mental age,** corresponds to the chronological (calendar) age of children who, on the average, receive a similar test score. Thus a six year old who scored as well as an average eight year old would be said to have a mental age of eight. Binet and his collaborators reasoned that it would be possible to obtain accurate estimates of children's ability to profit from the standard school curriculum by comparing their mental age to their chronological age (Binet & Simon, 1905).

Guided by this theoretical perspective, Binet and his associates developed a series of subtests covering a range of reasoning and problem-solving abilities. (Subtests are discrete groups of test items used to measure a particular skill or aptitude, which when evaluated together form an entire test.) The end result was a fairly elaborate test that first appeared in 1905, followed by a major revision three years later. Unlike Galton's attempt to differentiate between "superior" and "inferior" people, the Binet test was quite successful in evaluating the intellectual level of Parisian schoolchildren, and it was generally reliable as a predictor of children's success in regular schoolwork.

THE INTELLIGENCE QUOTIENT A few years after Binet's pioneering efforts, the German psychologist L. Wilhelm Stern devised a simple formula to avoid the problem of dealing with fractions that arose when mental age was compared to chronological age. His formula, MA *(mental age)*/CA *(chronological age)* × 100, yielded an **intelligence quotient** or **IQ** score, which provided a rough index of how dull or bright a child was compared to her or his peers. For example, a child with a mental age of seven and a chronological age of five has an IQ of 140 (7/5 × 100 = 140).

Do you think that this IQ formula (MA/CA × 100) is applicable to adults? Why or why not? Can you think of an alternative approach to calculating adult IQs? Give these questions some thought before reading on.

An average six year old can do certain things—like telling the difference between a slipper and a boot—that most four and five year olds cannot do. Consequently, such items became six-year-level subtest items. In similar fashion, Binet and later Lewis Terman (whom we discuss in the next section) were able to select items that differentiated between average seven and eight year olds, nine and 10 year olds, and so forth. However, as they moved up the chronological age scale, it became increasingly difficult to find items that would demonstrate proportionate age differences while maintaining the integrity of the IQ formula.

The credibility of the original formulation completely breaks down in the adult age range. Consider, for example, a 20 year old who performs on an IQ test as well as an average 36 year old. Would it be logical to conclude that the younger person has an IQ of 180 ($36/20 \times 100 = 180$)?

The fact that this conclusion is clearly not justifiable indicates why psychologists needed to devise an alternative method for computing adult IQs. As we see shortly, they resolved the problem by designing adult intelligence tests in which IQ is determined by comparing a subject's performance to the average performance of others in the same age bracket. This approach is now also utilized in the calculation of children's IQ scores, since the original IQ formulation is no longer considered to be applicable to any age group.

THE STANFORD-BINET INTELLIGENCE SCALE

Stanford University psychologist Lewis Terman imported Binet's test to America shortly after Binet's death in 1911. Terman discovered that the age norms developed for French students did not work very well with American children. Consequently, he revised Binet's scale as he translated many of the original items, added some new questions, and established new age norms using Caucasian California students to evaluate how effective test items were for measuring age-related changes. Terman labeled the revised test the **Stanford-Binet test,** a name it still retains over 75 years and several revisions later.

The individually administered Stanford-Binet test has undergone a number of revisions since it first appeared in 1916. In 1937 Terman and his associates introduced two alternate forms of the test, and later revisions in 1960 and 1985 updated some items and introduced a change in the scoring scheme.

The concept of designing different test items or questions appropriate for different age levels reflects Binet's original conception that average children of different ages have different capabilities. Although the test is used primarily for children, some subtests are also designed for adults.

The Stanford-Binet has been widely used for a longer period of time than any other test of intelligence, and it is still highly regarded by most specialists in the testing field. It possesses impressive predictive ability, providing reasonably good estimates of a child's ability to do well in school. A number of studies have shown substantial positive correlations between Stanford-Binet IQ scores and grade school, high school, and college grades. The correlations are generally stronger at the lower grade levels.

THE WECHSLER ADULT INTELLIGENCE SCALE

Since the early days of its use, one of the most frequent criticisms of the Stanford-Binet test has been that it places too much emphasis on verbal abilities such as word knowledge, sentence interpretation, and so forth. In so doing, the test discriminates against people for whom English is a second language as well as members of American subcultures who have their own unique style of verbal communication. Another criticism of the Stanford-Binet test has been that it was originally designed for children and still remains far more applicable to children than adults.

In the late 1930s, psychologist David Wechsler developed a new kind of intelligence test to avoid these two problems. His initial product, published in 1939, was a test designed exclusively for people in late adolescence or adulthood. This test, now called the **Wechsler Adult Intelligence Scale (WAIS),** includes 11

TABLE 13.1 *Verbal and Performance Subtests from the Wechsler Adult Intelligence Scale (WAIS-R, 1981)*

VERBAL SUBTESTS	PERFORMANCE SUBTESTS
1. *Information:* "What is the capital of the United States?" "Who was Shakespeare?"	7. *Digit Symbol:* Learning and drawing meaningless figures that are not associated with numbers.
2. *Comprehension:* "Why do we have zip codes?" "What does 'A stitch in time saves nine' mean?"	8. *Picture Completion:* Pointing to the missing part of a picture.
3. *Arithmetic:* "If three candy bars cost 25 cents, how much will 18 candy bars cost?"	9. *Block Design:* Copying pictures of geometric designs using multicolored blocks.
4. *Similarities:* "How are good and bad alike?"	10. *Picture Arrangement:* Arranging cartoon pictures in sequence so that they tell a meaningful story.
5. *Digit Span:* Repeating series of numbers forwards and backwards.	11. *Object Assembly:* Putting pieces of a puzle together so that they form a meaningful object.
6. *Vocabulary:* "What does *canal* mean?"	

Items for subtests 1, 2, 3, 4, and 6, are similar, but not identical to, actual test items.

subtests which are arranged according to the aptitude being tested rather than the subject's age level. These subtests are grouped into two major categories or scales: a *verbal scale* made up of six subtests, and a *performance (nonverbal) scale* comprising the other five subtests. (Table 13.1 provides examples of subtests from a recent revision of the WAIS.) This division allows for the calculation of separate verbal and performance IQ scores as well as an overall IQ, a feature that was warmly received by professionals in the testing field. For the first time, it was possible to identify individuals with special strengths in nonverbal areas and to detect superior intelligence even in people who might have had limited opportunities to develop verbal skills.

GROUP VERSUS INDIVIDUAL INTELLIGENCE TESTS

Both the Stanford-Binet test and the Wechsler Intelligence Scale are individual intelligence tests. That is, they are administered to one subject at a time by a specially trained tester who can use clinical insight in evaluating the subject's performance.

Many other intelligence tests are administered collectively to a group of subjects. These group IQ tests originated in the early 1900s in this country with mass intelligence testing of World War I recruits. The American Psychological Association developed two group IQ tests: the **Army Alpha test** (for recruits who could read) and the **Army Beta test** (for illiterate and non-English-speaking subjects). The original purpose of these two tests was to enable the army to assign soldiers to appropriate jobs, but they were also used to demonstrate the inferiority of Southern and Eastern European immigrants after World War I. Although the differences in intelligence test scores between the Americans and the Southern and Eastern European immigrants could easily be accounted for by the length of time they had been in the United States, the Immigration Act of 1924 was an attempt to minimize the influx of "weaker stock" based on these test score differences.

Dozens of group intelligence tests are in use today, primarily in educational settings. The name most commonly associated with the development of group IQ tests is Arthur Otis, a former student of Stanford's Lewis Terman. The **Otis-Lennon School Ability Test (OLSAT),** appropriate for children of all school ages, is widely used. Another group intelligence test popular in many school systems is the **Cognitive Abilities Test (CAT),** which is actually a series of tests, each appropriate for a specific age level from kindergarten through high school.

Group tests have certain obvious advantages over individual tests. They are cheaper, quicker, and easier to administer. Since good norms are available for the widely used group intelligence tests, they may be scored quickly and accurately, with no need for the kind of clinical interpretation by trained testers that individual tests demand. On the other hand, group tests also have potential limitations. When many people take a test in a group setting, such as a full classroom, it is impossible for the tester to be certain that all subjects understand directions, feel comfortable with the testing situation, and are motivated to do their best. Thus a child or adult who is not feeling well or whose mind is preoccupied may perform well below her or his potential. Although individual tests take more time to administer and score, they allow for the establishment of rapport and they also are more likely to encourage the best performance from subjects.

EVALUATING INTELLIGENCE TESTS

Earlier in this chapter we asked whether intelligence could be defined operationally, and we had to settle for the operational definition that intelligence is "what intelligence tests measure." We now know something about intelligence tests, but we still do not have enough information about the dependability of these tests to evaluate our operational definition.

To be a good measure of intelligence, a test must be well designed, reliable, and a valid instrument for assessing the particular abilities that indicate intelligence. A look at the processes by which IQ tests are constructed and evaluated can help us determine how effective modern intelligence tests are.

HOW INTELLIGENCE TESTS ARE DEVELOPED

The process by which IQ tests (as well as other assessment methods) are developed can be simplified into four steps: developing test items, evaluating these test items, standardizing the test, and establishing norms. We take a brief look at this process.

DEVELOPING A POOL OF TEST ITEMS   Test constructors generally begin by developing a large pool of potential test items that seem to fit their particular testing needs. For example, the developers of the original Stanford-Binet scales started out with many items that seemed able to differentiate between the intellect of children of different ages. These items were based on such things as common sense and direct observation. Since children's abilities to construct things out of blocks were known to improve with age, for instance, several kinds of block-building tasks of varying complexity were included in the original test item pool.

Most intelligence tests require some type of block-building or picture-completion tasks.

And since the ability to repeat digits from memory also reflected age-graded differences in intellect, measures of these abilities were also included in the test item pool. Test constructors today may invent new test items, or they may modify existing ones from other tests.

EVALUATING THE TEST ITEMS   The next step in test construction is to separate the effective test items from those that are ineffective or misleading. To accomplish this task, all the items in the test pool are administered to large numbers of subjects who are representative of the intended test population. For example, since the developers of the Stanford-Binet were trying to differentiate between high, average, and low intelligence among a broad spectrum of children, they administered their pool of items to thousands of preschool children. They found that some items were effective in reliably differentiating between children of different age levels, and others were not. The test items that were ineffective were discarded.

STANDARDIZING THE TEST   As test items are being evaluated and selected, test constructors must also develop **standardization procedures,** uniform and consistent procedures for both administering and scoring a test. Why are uniform procedures so crucial?

Suppose you are developing a Binet-type intelligence test and one of your subtests evaluates the ability of young children to build a bridge out of wooden blocks, guided only by a pictorial model. An average six year old can master this task, but it is too difficult for the average five year old unless the examiner provides some hints or directives. If testers administered this kind of item in an inconsistent fashion, providing additional hints to some subjects but not to others, two kinds of errors might result. First, during the development stage the test designers might make errors in age-grading the difficulties of the item, assuming that younger children were able to perform the task. Later, after the test had already been developed, errors could be made in assessing the intellect of a child subject.

The purpose of standardization procedures is to avoid these kinds of errors. A standardized test includes instructions that spell out precisely how it should be administered and scored, so that the testing situations are as identical as possible for all subjects. Thus all testers are required to use the same demonstrations, impose the same time limits, and provide the same directions (no random helpful hints). Testers who provide hints that other testers do not provide can give their subjects an edge over other testers' subjects.

ESTABLISHING NORMS   Once the items for an intelligence test have been selected and standardization procedures implemented, the final step is to establish norms. A **norm** reflects the normal or average performance of a particular group of people. For example, if you developed an intelligence test for adults and found that the average score of 20 to 25 year olds was 185 points, a score of 185 would become your basic norm or standard of performance for people in this age category. Similarly, if 40 to 45 year olds scored 169 on the average, 169 would be the norm for this age group. The frequency and magnitude of scores that deviate from these norms are then analyzed to provide a basis for evaluating other levels of performance.

Most intelligence tests assign IQ scores of 85 and 115 to performances that fall one standard deviation below or above the norm for a particular age group. (See Chapter 2 and the Statistics Appendix for a discussion of *standard deviation,* a statistical measure that indicates the degree to which scores are dispersed around an average.) Approximately 68 percent of people who take an IQ test

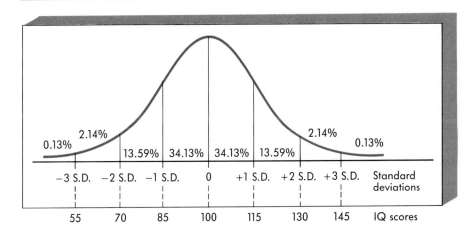

FIGURE 13.1

A Typical Normal Distribution of IQ Scores

achieve scores within a narrow range of about 85 to 115. About 95 percent of IQ scores fall between 70 and 130, and almost all (99.7 percent) are within a range of 55 to 145.

This method of assigning IQ scores is based on the concept of a normal distribution. Recall from Chapter 2 that a normal distribution forms a bell-shaped or normal curve. Many human attributes, including intelligence, are distributed along a normal or bell-shaped curve. Figure 13.1 demonstrates a typical distribution curve of IQ scores. This curve provides the basis for determining where a particular score falls relative to other scores. Thus, if you achieved an IQ of 130 on the test that provided the basis for the curve shown in the figure, approximately 98 percent of subjects would achieve an IQ score lower than you on the test. That is because only a fraction over 2 percent of subjects scored higher than 130. Similarly, if you scored 85, you might expect that about 84 percent of subjects would score higher than you.

The procedures we have just described are designed toward one end: developing a test that will provide a sound, accurate measure of intelligence for the intended subjects. A test that meets this criterion is said to possess two qualities, reliability and validity, and psychologists use a number of methods to check for these qualities.

TEST RELIABILITY AND VALIDITY

DETERMINING TEST RELIABILITY A good test must measure, with dependable consistency, a quality called **reliability.** Since a person's intelligence does not fluctuate widely over time, developers of IQ tests hope to achieve a quantitative consistency in the scores people obtain on their tests. This consistency may be assessed in a variety of ways.

One common method for evaluating test reliability is to give the same person or group of people the same test more than once. This procedure yields a measure of **test-retest reliability.** However, this method may itself be unreliable: People often score better the second time they take a test simply because they are more familiar with the test items or the test routine. One way to minimize this problem is to use an **alternate-forms reliability** check. Subjects take two different forms of a test that are as similar as possible, but not identical, in content and level of difficulty. This approach eliminates the possibility that a subject will score higher because of familiarity with specific test items, but it does not avoid score improvements that might result from practice taking a particular kind of test. Even practice effects can be averted, however, by calculating **split-half reliability.** The reliability of a subject's performance on a single administration of a test is assessed by comparing performance on half of the test items with performance on the other half (most commonly, scores for the odd- and even-numbered questions are compared). If the two scores obtained by any of these three methods generally agree, a test is considered to be reliable.

ASSESSING TEST VALIDITY   Suppose that you construct a simple test of intelligence based on manual dexterity. You design a pegboard task in which subjects' scores are based on the speed with which they insert pegs of varied diameters into holes with comparable dimensions. Assume further that you design two alternate forms of this test that are comparable in format and level of difficulty. You administer both forms of the test to several hundred children and adults and determine that the alternate forms reliability is very high. Does this outcome mean that you have made an important breakthrough in intelligence testing?

Not necessarily. Just because a test is reliable does not necessarily mean that it also has **validity**. A test is considered valid if it accurately measures what it is supposed to measure. All you have measured in your test is the speed with which people can fit pegs into holes—a skill that may be completely unrelated to their level of intelligence.

MEASURING TEST VALIDITY   How would you go about finding out if fast peg fitters are more intelligent than slow peg fitters? In other words, how do you measure the validity of your test (or any other test for that matter)? Take a few moments to see what ideas you can come up with before reading on.

One of the simplest ways to assess whether a test measures what it is supposed to measure is to compare peoples' test scores with their scores on other measures or criteria that are known to be good indicators of the skill or trait being assessed. This technique is called **criterion-related validity.**

There are two types of criterion-related validity: concurrent and predictive. **Concurrent validity** involves comparing test performance to other criteria that are currently available. For example, you might compare subjects' scores on your peg task to their IQ scores as assessed by established intelligence tests whose validity is recognized. If you found that high, average, and low scores on your manual dexterity task were consistently associated with correspondingly high, average, or low IQ scores, you might reasonably conclude that your test is a valid measure of intelligence.

Predictive validity is assessed by determining the accuracy with which tests predict performance in some future situation—for example, how well the Stanford-Binet scores of grade school children predict their high school grades or how precisely Scholastic Aptitude Test (SAT) scores predict a student's scholastic standing after one year of college. In most cases these tests do have predictive validity in that they do quite well in predicting academic success. In some colleges and universities SAT scores are used to determine eligibility for admission; in other schools they are used for academic advising and placement in some courses.

ACHIEVEMENT AND APTITUDE TESTS

We live in a society that places a good deal of emphasis on intelligence and aptitude testing (Linn, 1986). Whether or not you have taken any of the intelligence tests we have mentioned, the odds are that you have experienced plenty of tests, mostly in educational settings.

Many students are confused about the difference between aptitude tests and achievement tests. IQ tests and college entrance exams are generally classified as **aptitude tests**—tests designed to predict your ability to learn new information or a new skill. In contrast, **achievement tests** are intended to measure what you have already learned. Examples of achievement tests are final exams that test what you have learned in your various courses.

Although most psychologists distinguish between aptitude and achievement tests, they are quick to acknowledge that the differences are far from clear-cut. For example, it is reasonable to assume that your scores on the achievement exams given in this course will reflect not only your mastery of general psychology but also your aptitude for learning. The reverse is also true. A test such as the Wechsler Adult Intelligence Scale contains many subtests that measure a range of specific skills or aptitudes, a composite of which presumably reflects overall intelligence. However, many of the items also measure what you have already learned or achieved. For example, your ability to define words (vocabulary) or figure out what is missing from a picture (picture completion) is related to how much you have learned by exposure to previous information. Unfortunately, most items on widely used IQ tests reflect, at least to some degree, what we have already learned. Furthermore, since intelligence test constructors are typically middle- and upper-middle-class whites, these items may also reflect cultural biases. As we see later, this drawback raises some fundamental questions about the tests' applicability for members of racial minorities or lower socioeconomic levels.

There have been several attempts to design tests to measure a kind of pure intelligence, that is, a person's basic capacity to behave intelligently rather than a reflection of how much that person has learned from previous experiences. Unfortunately, these efforts have fallen short of expectations, and to date there is still no clear measure of people's aptitudes as distinct from what they have already learned.

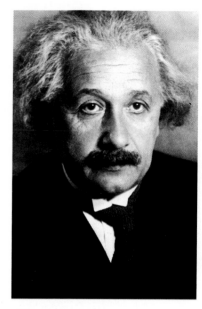

Albert Einstein was not an outstanding student.

THEORIES OF INTELLIGENCE

A number of different theories of intelligence have emerged since Galton's original attempts to measure intelligence. The earliest theories were based on statistical similarities between a variety of tasks. These groups of similar abilities were refered to as *factors*. Different theorists proposed that different factors, or abilities, contributed to our intelligence. Later, theorists began to look at intelligence more as a process for approaching and solving problems. We will first examine some of the older structural theories that conceptualize intelligence as a combination of several abilities.

FACTORIAL THEORIES

Many theorists have been concerned with the *structure* of intelligence—that is, the skills and abilities that it comprises. This focus is true of the first widely influential theory of intelligence, proposed in 1904 by Charles Spearman.

SPEARMAN'S TWO-FACTOR THEORY Spearman's view of intelligence reflected his use of *factor analysis*, a statistical procedure that enables researchers to identify groupings of test items that seem to tap a common ability or factor. For example, people who are quickly able to assemble colored blocks to match pictures of complex designs also tend to perform well when asked to assemble pieces of a puzzle. We could view these two behaviors, as well as other behaviors that reflect an ability to visualize and manipulate patterns and forms in space, as defining a spatial ability factor. Spearman developed his model of intelligence by applying a statistical procedure called factor analysis to the scores of a large number of subjects on diverse tests that assessed many different intellectual skills and abilities. Factor analysis allowed him to assess which of these skills were related to each other.

Spearman noted that some subjects consistently scored high on all of the various tests, regardless of what they were supposed to be measuring, and that a roughly equal number could be counted on to score low. People who scored high (or low) on one kind of test also tended to score at a similar level on other tests, but their scores on various skill tests did tend to differ somewhat.

These statistical observations prompted Spearman to propose that intelligence is made up of two components: a **g-factor,** or general intelligence, and a collection of specific intellectual abilities that he labeled **s-factors.** According to his view, we all have a certain level of general intelligence (g-factor), probably genetically determined, that underlies all of our intelligent behavior. We also have specific abilities (s-factors) that are more useful on some tasks than on others. This theoretical perspective leads to the prediction that a person with a high g-factor will score higher on most skill tests than a person with an average level of general intelligence. It would not be particularly surprising, however, for individuals with average general intelligence to score higher on some specific skills because of a particular strength in their s-factors.

THURSTONE'S PRIMARY MENTAL ABILITIES   One of Spearman's strongest critics was L.L. Thurstone (1938). Thurstone used factor analysis on the scores of a large number of subjects on over 50 different ability tests, but he found no evidence for a general intelligence ability as Spearman had proposed. Instead, he declared that human intelligence is a composite of seven **primary mental abilities:** verbal comprehension, numerical ability, spatial relations, perceptual speed, word fluency, memory, and inductive reasoning. Table 13.2 provides a summary.

Thurstone considered each mental ability to be independent, so that it could be measured separately from other abilities. Unlike Spearman, Thurstone did not believe that a person's intelligence could be expressed as a single score. Rather, assessing any person's intelligence would require measuring all seven of these primary abilities.

GUILFORD'S STRUCTURE OF INTELLECT   Since Thurstone's time, there have been many attempts to isolate different kinds of intellectual attributes. One of the most ambitious efforts is that of J. P. Guilford (1967, 1977, 1982) who also bases his model of intelligence on factor analysis. Guilford proposes that intelligence consists of 150 separate abilities, with no overall general intelligence factor.

Guilford believes that any intellectual task can be analyzed in terms of three major intellectual functions: the mental *operations* that are used (how we think); the *content* upon which those operations are performed (what we think about); and the *products* of applying a particular operation to a particular content. Each of these three functions is divided into a number of subfunctions, and there are 150 possible interactions or combinations of these subfunctions. Guilford thus maintains that he has isolated 150 kinds of intelligence.

The factorial approaches of Spearman, Thurstone, and Guilford served two important purposes. First, they provided logical models of the structure of human intellect. And second, they established that intelligence may be conceptualized as comprising many separate abilities that operate more or less independently. However, none of these approaches addressed the very important question of *how* people solve problems and interact effectively (i.e., intelligently) with their environments. In the last decade, two new theoretical models of intelligence have emerged, both of which seek to understand intelligence as a *process*. These two models were developed by Robert Sternberg and Howard Gardner.

PROCESS THEORIES

STERNBERG'S INFORMATION-PROCESSING APPROACH   Sternberg's initial approach to developing a theory of what he calls "practical intelligence" (1979, 1981, 1982) focused on how people process information in order to solve problems and deal effectively with their environments. Sternberg conducted a num-

TABLE 13.2 *L. L. Thurstone's Seven Primary Mental Abilities*

ABILITY	BRIEF DESCRIPTION
Verbal comprehension	The ability to understand the meaning of words, concepts, and ideas.
Numerical ability	The ability to use numbers quickly to compute answers to problems.
Spatial relations	The ability to visualize and manipulate patterns and forms in space.
Perceptual speed	The ability to grasp perceptual details quickly and accurately and to determine similarities and differences between stimuli.
Word fluency	The ability to use words quickly and fluently in performing such tasks as rhyming, solving anagrams, and doing crossword puzzles.
Memory	The ability to recall information such as lists of words, mathematical formulas, definitions, etc.
Inductive reasoning	The ability to derive general rules and principles from presented information.

ber of experiments to study the steps people go through when solving the kinds of problems typically encountered in intelligence tests. He has identified the following six steps:

1. *Encoding:* Identifying the key terms or concepts in the problem and retrieving any relevant information from long-term memory.
2. *Inferring:* Determining the nature of relationships that exist between these terms or concepts.
3. *Mapping:* Clarifying the relationship between previous situations and the present one.
4. *Application:* Deciding if the information about known relationships can be applied to the present problem.
5. *Justification:* Deciding if the answer can be justified.
6. *Response:* Providing the answer that seems best, based on proper information processing at each of the previous stages.

One of Sternberg's most interesting findings is that good problem solvers who score high on intelligence tests spend more time analyzing a question, particularly in the encoding stage, than those who score lower. He reached this conclusion by presenting a subject with a problem, such as "Washington is to one as Lincoln is to_____," and then measuring how long it took a person to indicate comprehension of the question. Then he showed the subject the answer choices—(*a*) 5; (*b*) 10; (*c*) 15; (*d*) 50—and recorded how long it took to obtain an answer. If you remembered that George Washington's picture is on a one-dollar bill and Abraham Lincoln's is on a five, you may have realized that the correct answer is *a*. Sternberg discovered that his highly intelligent subjects spent longer than average analyzing a question before signaling that they understood it, but were able to recognize the correct answer more quickly than subjects with average intelligence (Sternberg, 1984).

Perhaps you have noticed that students who earn top grades are often among the last to finish an exam. These slow finishers sometimes express embarrassment or concern that their slowness reflects some intellectual inadequacy. Now, thanks to Sternberg's model, we have evidence that intelligence does not necessarily equal speed, and that people who score highest on tests often take a sufficient amount of time to analyze problems carefully.

Sternberg's research has some practical implications. If we can analyze how people use the various steps to process information and solve problems, it may be possible to teach them strategies for improving their performances. For example, a common factor in low test scores is the tendency of some students to rush through a test without carefully analyzing each question and considering a range of options. Such people have a tendency merely to grab on to the first answer that seems halfway reasonable. We have found that the exam scores of these speedy test takers can sometimes be improved by suggesting that they take their finished exams back to their desks and spend the remainder of the test period carefully considering their answers.

By learning to think about how they approach problems and how to function more effectively, Sternberg believes people can be taught to construct their own problem-solving strategies. In this sense, people's intelligence, at least as it is measured by intelligence tests, can be increased by teaching them to apply problem-solving strategies more effectively. A good deal of formal education seems to focus on teaching people lots of facts rather than teaching them how to think. Perhaps with more emphasis on the latter, we might increase the intelligence scores of our students.

Sternberg (1985, 1986) has recently expanded his information-processing approach into what he calls the **triarchic theory of intelligence.** According to this theory, intelligence is a multidimensional trait comprised of three different abilities: componential, experiential, and contextual. The componential aspect of intelligence involves mastering a sequence of components or steps in the process of solving complex verbal, mathematical, or spatial reasoning problems. This analytical ability is heavily emphasized in most contemporary intelligence tests. People with highly developed componential intelligence often do well in academic settings and score high on achievement tests and standard IQ tests. However, such individuals do not necessarily exhibit unusual creativity or insight.

These latter characteristics are more likely to be manifested by individuals endowed with high levels of *experiential* intelligence, which is the ability to combine experiences in insightful ways that lead to novel or creative solutions to complex problems. Sternberg believes that people with only average componential intelligence may score very high on the experiential aspect of intellect and vice versa.

Finally, Sternberg has observed that some people, like a street smart individual, may be highly adept at manipulating and/or adapting to their environments. This component, labeled *contextual* intelligence, is also exemplified in people who always seem to be in the right place at the right time, such as the employee who seems to have an uncanny knack to cultivate the right people or personal image in order to achieve promotions. Sternberg believes that while people vary in their capacity to use each of these three forms of intelligence, all are important in our daily functioning. Furthermore, all people, including those with high IQ scores on standard tests, can benefit from training designed to strengthen each of these three aspects or components of intelligence. The interview with Sternberg in the "Research Perspectives" discussion on pages 514–518 provides an elaboration on Sternberg's ideas.

GARDNER'S THEORY OF MULTIPLE INTELLIGENCES
Harvard University's Howard Gardner (1983, 1990) outlined a view of human intelligence that reflects both his dissatisfaction with the idea that intelligence is a single trait that can be mea-

sured with an IQ test and his belief that the factorial approach to describing the structure of human intellect fails to capture the complexity, diversity, and practicality of human intelligence. In this sense, Gardner is philosophically aligned with Sternberg.

However, Gardner's view of intelligence differs from Sternberg's in another important respect, for he advocates the inclusion of certain kinds of mental abilities that fall well outside the realm of what has traditionally been labeled as intelligence. Gardner observes that in the world community there are many different kinds of things people can do well that are assigned different values in different cultures. To reflect this diversity, Gardner has proposed that humans have seven kinds of intelligence which are independent of each other.

The first form of human intellect in Gardner's theory of multiple intelligences is *linguistic intelligence*. Linguistic intelligence includes the kind of verbal ability or skill with words that writers or orators display. A second form of intelligence, *logical-mathematic intelligence*, is typical of scientists, logicians, and mathematicians. A third type of intellect is *spatial intelligence*, the ability to think accurately about the spatial aspects of the surrounding environment.

Mikhail Baryshnikov would have a high degree of what Gardner refers to as bodily kinesthetic intelligence.

These first three types of mental abilities probably fit your own notion of intelligence. Indeed, all three fall within the category of what has traditionally been viewed as intelligence, and they are the types of skills that are tested on most formal measures of intelligence. However, Gardner does not stop here. He proposes four additional types of intelligence, each of which he considers as important as the first three. Thus *musical intelligence* is the type of intelligence manifested by musicians, composers, or other individuals who can think and express themselves musically. *Bodily kinesthetic intelligence*, another mental ability that is overlooked in traditional definitions of intelligence, involves using one's body or parts of the body to make something or solve a problem. Accomplished dancers, athletes, and craftpersons would have a high degree of bodily kinesthetic intelligence. *Interpersonal intelligence* is the capacity to perceive and understand the needs, motives, and behaviors of other people. This kind of personal intelligence might be particularly noteworthy in accomplished therapists and teachers. And finally, *intrapersonal intelligence* is manifested by people who can accurately assess and understand their own needs and abilities, and who use this knowledge to function effectively.

Gardner's conceptualization serves to humanize or democratize our view of human intelligence by broadening its definition. Instead of equating intelligence with IQ scores or the kinds of abilities listed in Table 13.2, Gardner stresses the importance of certain other components of successful functioning components that are overlooked in more traditional definitions. Yet over the course of human history, Gardner reminds us, skills such as bodily kinesthetic skill, interpersonal intelligence, and musical ability probably have had more value in human culture than the types of verbal, mathematical, or spatial abilities that are commonly equated with intelligence. Again, refer to the "Research Perspectives" on pages 518–521 for an additional discussion of Gardner's views.

BIAS IN INTELLIGENCE TESTING

Despite the care taken in designing a test, evaluating test items, and assessing validity and reliability, it is virtually impossible to avoid some built-in biases that may favor some subjects and place others at a disadvantage (Snyderman & Rothman, 1987). Any intelligence test is bound to reflect the cultural experiences of the test constructors. Subjects who are not from the dominant cultural segment of the population that a test is primarily designed to serve may be at some disadvantage in their ability to understand and interpret test items.

Since IQ tests are typically constructed by white, middle-class city dwellers, it is not surprising that test questions often reflect the mainstream values and experiences of this segment of American culture. For example, a WAIS question such as, "Why do people buy fire insurance?" may have no relevance for minority group members raised in poor inner-city or rural environments.

This type of cultural bias is not unique to American tests or subcultures. Anne Anastasi (1976), a renowned specialist in psychological testing, reported an interesting situation in Israel in which Oriental immigrant children were asked to decide what was missing from a picture of a face with no mouth. Since their cultural background had not provided them opportunities to consider a drawing of a head as a complete picture, they typically answered "incorrectly" that the body was missing. This mistake did not mean that they were less intelligent than native-born Israeli children who typically responded that the mouth was missing. Instead, it indicates how difficult it is to avoid cultural bias in designing intelligence tests.

What are the implications of this kind of bias? In an effort to demonstrate how the white, middle-class slant of mainstream American IQ tests affects minority subjects, two concerned social scientists decided to turn the tables. They designed black alternative IQ tests that drew primarily upon black experience. One test, designed by Robert Williams (1972), is titled the Black Intelligence Test of Cultural Homogeneity (BITCH). The average BITCH score for a group of 100 black teenagers was 30 points higher, on the average, than for a group of same-age whites. Adrian Dove (1968) created a similar test, the Counterbalanced General Intelligence Test.

Sample questions from each of these tests are included in Figure 13.2. See how you fare on these items. If you are a white member of the middle class, you

FIGURE 13.2

Cultural Bias in IQ Testing

The first four items were taken from the BITCH test developed by Robert Williams (1972) and the second four items were taken from the Counterbalanced General Intelligence Test developed by Adrian Dove (1968). The answers are presented below question 8.

1. "Boogie Jugie" means the same as
   (a) tired (b) worthless (c) old (d) well put together
2. Black Draught is a
   (a) winter's cold wind (b) laxative (c) black soldier
   (d) dark beer
3. An alley apple is a
   (a) brick (b) piece of fruit (c) dog (d) horse
4. "Boot" refers to
   (a) a cotton farmer (b) a Black (c) an Indian
   (d) a Vietnamese citizen
5. If you throw the dice and 7 is showing on the top, what is facing down?
   (a) 7 (b) "snake eyes" (c) "Boxcars" (d) "Little Joes"
   (e) 11
6. Jazz pianist Ahmad Jamal took an Arabic name after becoming really famous. Previously, he had some fame with what he called his "slave name." What was his previous name?
   (a) Willie Lee Jackson (b) Le Roi Jones
   (c) Wilber McDougal (d) Fritz Jones (e) Andy Johnson
7. A "gas-head" is a person who has a
   (a) fast-moving car (b) stable of "lace" (c) process
   (d) habit of stealing cars (e) long jail record for arson
8. A handkerchief head is
   (a) a cool cat (b) a porter (c) an Uncle Tom (d) a hoddi
   (e) a preacher

Answers: 1. b 2. b 3. a 4. b 5. a 6. d 7. c 8. c

will probably perform like most college students in this category, not very well. Neither of these tests has been seriously considered as a substitute for traditional IQ testing among black populations. However, the publicity associated with their introduction has dramatically highlighted the problems associated with cultural bias in IQ testing. As one observer noted, "By showing educated whites an intellectual task on which they do poorly, BITCH challenges whites to defend the functional worth of other tests loaded with culture-specific tasks" (Cronbach, 1978, p. 250).

HEREDITARY AND ENVIRONMENTAL INFLUENCES ON INTELLIGENCE

What determines intelligence? Although we may disagree with many of Sir Francis Galton's early ideas about intelligence, most of us would probably agree with one of his observations: Intelligence tends to run in families. You may have noticed that some of your brightest friends seem to have highly intelligent parents, while those with more average abilities often are offspring of parents who seem to be of average intelligence.

The degree of relationship or correlation between the IQs of parents and their children has been shown to be approximately 0.35 (See Table 13.3. Recall from Chapter 2 that a coefficient of correlation always falls between −1.00 and +1.00,

TABLE 13.3 *Approximate Correlation Coefficients between IQ Scores of Persons with Different Amounts of Genetic and Environmental Similarity*

RELATIONSHIP	MEDIAN CORRELATION
Identical (monozygotic) twins	
reared together	.86
reared apart	.72
Fraternal (dizygotic) twins	
reared together	
same sex	.62
opposite sex	.62
reared apart	(no data available)
Siblings	
reared together	.38
reared apart	.24
Parent and child	
live together	.35
separated by adoption	.31
Genetically unrelated persons	
unrelated children reared together	.25
adoptive parent and adopted child	.15

These data were obtained from a variety of studies, most of which were relatively recent investigatons. The correlations in the table reflect the median of a range of correlations obtained from several individual studies. Note that as the degree of genetic similarity decreases, so does the magnitude of obtained correlations. It is also noteworthy that a shared environment increases the IQ correlations in all cases where applicable.

SOURCE: Adapted from Henderson, 1982, and Plomin & Defries, 1980.

and that the closer it is to 1.00, the stronger is the relationship between two variables.) Researchers have found that parents with high IQs tend to have children with high IQs, and parents with low IQs are somewhat prone to have children with relatively low IQs. This finding lends credence to the widespread assumption that intelligence does indeed run in families.

Was Galton correct in saying that intelligence is largely inherited? From our previous discussions of the nature–nurture controversy (see Chapters 1 and 11), you are probably aware that environment as well as heredity contribute to most individual traits. Indeed, nowhere does the nature versus nurture controversy rage more actively than in the question of intellect (Dudley, 1991; Weinberg, 1989; Plomin & Bergman, 1991).

According to the hereditarian view, genetics determines the structural and functional efficiency of the brain, which in turn clearly influences intellectual functioning. In contrast, the environmentalist view says that environment plays a greater role than genes in shaping human intellect, and that the positive relationship in parent–child IQs reflects the fact that adults tend to create home environments which are similar to those they experienced in their own childhood. With comparable sources of intellectual stimulation, an environmentalist would argue that it is not surprising that children develop a level of intelligence similar to that of their parents.

Which point of view is more accurate? Even after years of research, we still are not certain exactly what relative influences heredity and environment have on intelligence.

ISOLATING CONTRIBUTIONS TO INTELLIGENCE

How can we determine to what extent intelligence (or any other human attribute) is influenced by heredity or by environment? Take a moment to consider what research strategies might effectively be used to answer this question before reading on.

If ethics were not a consideration, an obvious choice might be to take people with clearly different genetic makeups (for example, unrelated children) and raise them in identical environments. If we could orchestrate this situation, and all our identically reared children developed similar IQs, we could then conclude with confidence that genetic differences have little or no influence on intelligence, and that environment is the major determinant of intellect.

For obvious reasons, such an experiment has never been conducted. Most parents would not permit their children to be taken from them at an early age so that they might be raised in a controlled environment. Even if we were able to obtain a sample group and create a special environment for them, it is impossible to ensure that two people's experiences are identical. Even identical twins who grow up together do not have exactly the same environments, for each twin may relate differently to other family members and to individuals outside the home.

Since psychologists must work within both ethical and practical constraints, research into the relative impact of heredity and genetics has taken several forms other than the hypothetical method we just described. The following paragraphs highlight what researchers have been able to discover through a number of studies of twins, adopted children, orphanage and environmental enrichment programs, birth order studies, and even some animal research.

TWIN STUDIES

The intellectual differences that exist among all of us are a product of only two factors: genes and environment. Identical twins are unique in that only one of these factors, environment, contributes to differences in intelligence between members of a twin pair. Thus a considerable amount of attention has focused on twin studies.

A hereditarian who discounts the role of environment in determining intelligence would predict a very high positive correlation between the IQs of identical twins, whether they were raised together or in separate environments. Environmentalists, in contrast, would predict a much lower IQ correlation for separated identical twins than for twins reared together, since they place greater weight on environment in determining IQ scores.

What has the evidence shown? Table 13.3 presents the median IQ correlation coefficients for a variety of relationships as determined by a number of studies. You can see that identical twins reared together are highly similar in tested intelligence (.86), and that the second highest degree of correlation is demonstrated by identical twins reared separately (.72).

The slight decline in the degree of IQ correlation among sets of separated identical twins provides some evidence for the environmentalist prediction that IQ correlation will be reduced by differences in the environment. However, identical twins reared separately are still more similar in IQ than fraternal twins of the same sex who are reared together (.62). This finding seems to undermine the environmentalist view that fraternal twins reared together should have a higher degree of IQ correlation than identical twins raised apart. Indeed, research suggests that IQ correlations of same-sex fraternal twins reared together may be even less than the .62 figure shown in Table 13.3. These studies yielded correlations ranging from .38 to .61, with a median of .47 (Nathan & Guttman, 1984; Segal, 1985; Stevenson et al., 1987; Tambs et al., 1984; Wilson, 1986).

For years, many psychologists viewed such findings as evidence that heredity plays an exceedingly large role in determining intelligence. The most widely quoted and best known of these studies was conducted by the late English psychologist Sir Cyril Burt (1966), who reported remarkable IQ similarities between 53 pairs of separated identical twins purportedly reared in totally different environments. In the early 1970s, however, American psychologist Leon Kamin (1974) became suspicious when he noticed several peculiarities in Burt's data and procedures. Shortly after, an investigative reporter for the *London Sunday Times* discovered that two of Burt's collaborators who had supposedly collected much of his data never existed (Gillie, 1976). By the end of the 1970s, even Burt's most staunch supporters conceded that his research was fraudulent and that he had perpetrated a massive hoax on the world scientific community (Hearnshaw, 1979). (The spurious data from Burt's research are not included in Table 13.3.)

This unfortunate episode demonstrates that ethical standards are not always maintained by scientists engaged in research. However, Burt's fraud did not seriously weaken the hereditarian case, since other studies of identical twins reared apart have reported similarly high IQ correlations. Investigations conducted by James Shields (1962) and Horatio Newman and his colleagues (1937) are representative of other research in this area. Both studies reported very high IQ correlations among sets of identical twins reared apart. A recent review of twin IQ studies conducted in the 1980s revealed evidence indicating that "separated identical twins are almost as similar as identicals reared together" (Loehlin et al., 1988).

Psychologists continue to study twins in the hope that such research will lead to a better understanding of the relative contributions of heredity. For instance, research conducted by Bouchard on several sets of identical and fraternal twins reared apart indicate a much greater degree of similarity in identical than fraternal twins in a wide range of intellectual, emotional, and behavioral attributes (Bouchard, 1984; Tellegen et al., 1988). This evidence suggests that genetic factors are important in producing differences in intelligence between people — but again, environmentalists can also find some support in these same data. For example, preliminary findings have revealed that when identical twins were reared in dramatically different environments, the spread between their respective IQs widened to as great as 20 points in one case. Thus the debate rages on (see

Plomin & Bergman, 1991; Dudley, 1991). Hopefully, when enough reliable data are collected, psychologists may be able to reach some consensus on the implications of twin study findings.

ADOPTION STUDIES

Other evidence concerning the influence of nature and nurture on intelligence is provided by studies of adopted children. Here, a few research approaches have been used. One is to measure the degree of correlation between the IQs of children adopted in infancy and those of their adoptive parents. This measure is then compared with a similar correlation statistic from studies of children raised by their biological parents. Whereas children reared by their natural parents may be similar to them because of both genetic and environmental factors, similarities between adopted children and their genetically unrelated parents can only be accounted for by environmental factors.

An environmentalist would predict that the relationship between the IQs of children and the parents who raise them would be similar regardless of whether or not a biological relationship exists. However, a number of studies have found that children are significantly more similar in intelligence to their biological parents who rear them than are adopted children to their adoptive parents. Several studies have also shown that adopted children's IQ scores are more similar to those of their biological parents than of their adoptive parents (Fulker et al., 1988; Plomin et al., 1988; Scarr & Carter-Salzman, 1983).

One problem with adoption studies is the difficulty in assessing the degree of similarity between the home environments of adoptive and biological parents. When major discrepancies exist, there is some indication that environment may play a greater role than otherwise. For example, when children of poor, undereducated parents are adopted into a family of high socioeconomic status, the children may exhibit very substantial increases in IQ scores, a finding which suggests that environment has a significant impact on intelligence (Scarr & Weinberg, 1976). Data from a recent study of French adoptees also lend support to the environmental position. This investigation revealed that the average IQs of adoptees reared by parents with high socioeconomic status were approximately 12 points higher than adoptees raised by parents of low socioeconomic status, irrespective of biological background (Capron & Duyme, 1989). When the socioeconomic status of both biological and adoptive parents is about equal, however, the IQs of adopted children tend to be much more similar to those of their biological parents than of their adoptive parents (Scarr & Weinberg, 1978). This latter finding suggests the importance of heredity in determining intelligence.

ORPHANAGE AND ENVIRONMENTAL ENRICHMENT STUDIES

Some of the strongest support for the environmentalist position has come from studies of children reared in orphanages. The classic experiment in this area was begun in the 1930s under the guidance of H. M. Skeels (1966). Thirteen apparently retarded two year olds, who were living in an orphanage in Iowa, were transferred to an institution that housed mentally retarded women. Each child was placed in the care of a young woman resident who spent much of her time nurturing her foster child. Within a relatively brief period of four years, these children had gained an average of about 30 IQ points—compared to a control group of 12 children remaining in the orphanage, who had lost an average of 20 IQ points. Twenty years later, Skeels reevaluated these children and found that the differences between the two groups were still profound. Most of the 13 raised by the retarded foster mothers had graduated from high school, found jobs, and married. The 12 reared in the orphanage did not fare so well: Most were grade school dropouts, and several were either still institutionalized or not self-supporting.

ENRICHMENT PROGRAMS In a more recent study, psychologist J. McVicker Hunt (1982) assessed the effects of environmental enrichment on 11 children living in an Iranian orphanage. Before entering the enrichment program as infants, all of these children were developmentally and emotionally retarded, passive, and unresponsive to their environments. In the program, trained caregivers provided special attention to the infants, playing vocal games with them, responding to any signs of distress, and so forth. As in the Skeels study, the impact of this environmental enrichment was dramatic. All 11 infants demonstrated marked acceleration in acquiring language skills. They also became much more animated in their reactions to people and events, and in general began to behave in a more intelligent fashion typical of children raised in natural home environments.

In the United States, the most extensive educational and environmental enrichment program has been Project Head Start, a federally funded program launched in 1965 to provide special intellectual and social skills training for children from disadvantaged environments. Typically, a child enrolled in the Head Start program is provided one to two years of compensatory education and environmental enrichment beginning at age four.

The program has been closely watched, and hundreds of research studies have been conducted. Initial findings showed significant short-term IQ gains, generating a great deal of optimism among researchers and educators connected with the program. Unfortunately, however, later follow-up studies revealed that the earlier IQ gains did not hold up over longer periods after children had entered the mainstream educational system.

The program has continued, however, and the consensus today is that Project Head Start has been a qualified success. Although Head Start children typically do not exhibit large, enduring IQ gains, they do fare better on many other measures than disadvantaged children who do not participate in the program. For example, Head Start children are less likely to require special remedial classes and are less likely to fail grades. They also tend to adjust better to the school environment, exhibit better social skills, and, perhaps most importantly, enjoy more positive self-esteem (Collins, 1983, 1984; McKey et al., 1985; Zigler & Berman, 1983).

A number of psychologists have questioned the use of IQ scores as outcome measures in evaluating the effectiveness of the Head Start program (Weinberg, 1979, 1989). These critics suggest that measures which reflect social competence, adaptability, and emotional health might provide a better barometer of the success of such social intervention programs (Christenson et al., 1986; Scarr, 1981, 1986; Zigler & Seitz, 1982).

In evaluating the Head Start program, it is important to remember that unlike the studies of Skeels and Hunt, in which children were rescued from the damaging effects of impoverished orphanage environments in the first year or two of their lives, the children who enter the Head Start program have already experienced four years of an impoverished environment. Hunt (1982) believes that much intellectual and emotional damage has already been incurred by age four, and that enrichment programs such as Head Start should be implemented at birth. This bold approach would surely be controversial, but perhaps it might result in more pronounced and enduring benefits.

The Head Start studies and the orphanage studies provide evidence of the role of environment in intellectual development. In most of these cases, however, the children had previously been subjected to less than optimal environmental conditions. Many researchers believe that the impact of environment on intelligence is far less pronounced among children who experience adequate human contact and normal exposure to environmental stimulation (Scarr, 1984). This suggests that special enrichment programs are likely to have less impact on the intellectual development of children reared in normal environments than on children from disadvantaged environments. This is not to say, of course, that outside of marked neglect, parenting patterns have no impact on children's intellectual growth.

BIRTH-ORDER STUDIES

For further evidence on the influence of heredity and environment, we return to Sir Francis Galton. Galton made still another intriguing observation that we have not yet discussed. He noted a connection between intelligence and the order in which children were born, reporting that an unusual number of eminent British scientists were firstborn children. In the years following Galton's observation, a number of studies have revealed that firstborn children do, in fact, tend to score higher on IQ tests than those born later (Zajonc & Markus, 1975). A recent study revealed that an unusually high number of firstborns were among the prominent figures in the history of psychology! (Terry, 1989).

How would you explain the fact that firstborns typically score higher on IQ tests than their later-born siblings? What is the implication of this evidence for the nature-nurture controversy? Take a moment to consider your answers before reading on.

The meaning of birth order data is not entirely clear. However, some psychologists believe that family size influences the amount of stimulation available in the home environment, and that this is reflected in the relationship between birth order and intelligence. According to this view, firstborns do not have to compete with other siblings for parental attention. Thus they experience a more stimulating environment with extensive individual attention. In contrast, their later-born siblings receive less parental attention, for they must compete with brothers and sisters. If this line of reasoning is valid, we might infer that second-born children will tend to have higher IQs than third-born, third higher than fourth, and so on, for the more siblings there are, the greater the competition. In fact, some research has supported this interpretation.

Robert Zajonc and Gregory Markus (1975) studied a wide range of children from families of different sizes. Overall, they found a close agreement between birth order and the average IQs of children in their sample groups, with IQs dropping with each subsequent child. (Interestingly, the progressive reduction in IQs of later-born siblings reversed itself, commencing with the eighth child. As older siblings approach or enter their teenage years, they are evidently able to contribute to a more intellectually stimulating environment for the youngest brothers or sisters.) It is important to note that Zajonc and Markus were dealing with average values. As you might expect, there were many cases in which younger children had IQs higher than their older siblings.

Some other research findings have supported those of Zajonc and Markus. A major Israeli study of about 200,000 subjects from large families found that first-borns had higher IQs than second children, who in turn exceeded third children, and so on, to the seventh child. At this point, the trend reversed itself. Eighth-born children demonstrated higher IQs than seventh children, ninth higher than eighth, and tenth slightly higher still (Davis et al., 1977).

These studies of birth order and intelligence support the importance of environment in fostering intellectual growth. Of course, we might argue that children who are born later might show lower IQ scores as a result of other effects. For instance, an older mother's uterus might be less conducive to optimal prenatal growth than might have been the case during earlier pregnancies when she was younger and perhaps healthier. However, this biologically based argument does not explain the apparent reversal in the trend that occurs beginning with the eighth child. In balance, then, studies of the relationship between birth order and intelligence suggest that environment is an important factor in intellectual development.

Another source of evidence regarding the influence of environment and heredity has been animal studies. The most notable research is a classic selective-breeding experiment conducted by Robert Tryon (1940) of the University of California at Berkeley. Tryon developed a kind of IQ test for rats in which he measured their ability to learn a complicated maze. Rats who performed very well on this task were mated with other animals who performed similarly; rats who made many errors were mated with animals that also performed poorly. After many generations of selective breeding (with careful attention to make sure that environments were identical for all rats), the result was two strains of rats that demonstrated substantial differences in the number of errors they made while negotiating the maze. Tryon labeled these distinct strains "maze-bright" and "maze-dull."

This study seems to support the hereditarian view, for despite comparable environments, the rats differed substantially in at least this one measure of intelligence. However, other studies with Tryon's maze-bright and maze-dull rats have shown that the former are not necessarily superior to the latter in all learning tasks. Thus, just as with the other studies we have explored in this section, we must be cautious in interpreting this important evidence.

In another study conducted by Cooper and Zubek (1958) performance of maze-bright and maze-dull rats was shown to depend upon both heredity and environment. In their study, groups of bright and dull rats were reared in enriched, standard, or impoverished environments. Both bright and dull rats reared in impoverished environments performed poorly with little difference between them. Groups reared in enriched environments outperformed their counterparts reared in impoverished conditions but the bright rats only slightly outperformed the dull rats. The only condition where bright and dull rats differed significantly was when they were reared in standard lab environments. This study suggests that both environmental and hereditary factors interact to determine performance.

ANIMAL RESEARCH

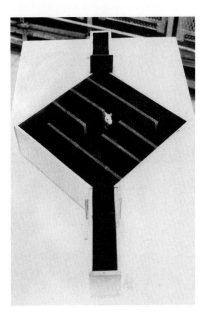

Maze-bright rats learn their way through such mazes more quickly than maze-dull rats.

EVALUATING THE HEREDITARY AND ENVIRONMENTAL EVIDENCE

We have explored a considerable range of evidence in the previous discussions, some of which seems to support each side of the nature-nurture controversy. Many of the twin, adoption, and selective-breeding studies provide strong indications of the role of heredity in determining intelligence. However, some of these investigations, plus evidence from orphanage, birth-order studies, and animal studies suggest that the environment is also important. We could continue exploring this controversy by examining still more evidence. Yet, no matter how much more research we study, most of us would still reach the same conclusion: It is simply not possible, in light of our current state of knowledge, to determine precisely what percentage of our IQs is attributable to genes and what percentage is the product of experience.

Today it is widely recognized that nature and nurture interact in determining intelligence. An excellent description of this process is provided by a prominent researcher in the field, Richard Weinberg (1989):

> Genes do not fix behavior. Rather, they establish a range of possible reactions to the range of possible experiences that environments can provide. Environments also can affect whether the full range of gene reactivity is expressed. Thus how people behave or what their measured IQs turn out to be or how quickly they learn depends on the nature of their environments and on their genetic endowments bestowed at conception. (p. 101)

A continuing debate within this highly controversial area focuses on the ongoing efforts to ascertain the relative contributions of nature and nurture in shaping human intelligence. In a recent survey of several hundred psychologists and

Arthur Jenson

educational specialists with expertise in areas related to intelligence testing, these experts believed the heritability of intelligence to be roughly 60 percent (Snyderman & Rothman, 1987). **Heritability** is a statistical concept which estimates the relative contribution of genetic factors to variability in measures of a particular trait found among members of a sample population. Even if this estimate is accurate, we should not conclude that heredity accounts for 60 percent of our intelligence and environment the rest. Rather than estimates of the percentage of our intellects that is due to heredity, heritability percentages provide estimates of the amount of variation in intelligence that may be attributed to heredity among individuals within a population.

Some researchers have provided somewhat higher estimates of the heritability of intelligence. Arthur Jensen, an educational psychologist and hereditarian, is probably the most controversial advocate of the viewpoint that IQ differences are due primarily to heredity. In 1969 he published an article in the *Harvard Education Review* concluding that heredity accounts for approximately 80 percent of the differences in IQ scores among individuals, an extreme position that has not been supported by mainstream psychologists. Many of his arguments have been sharply criticized (Loehlin et al., 1975).

Jensen took his argument one step further. He reasoned that if IQ differences between people were largely due to genetic factors, it might also be true for IQ differences between races. This perspective led him to assert that differences in IQ scores between Blacks and Whites are very likely attributable to genetic factors. Needless to say, this controversial view has been challenged by members of both the scientific community and the general public. One way Jensen's argument has been challenged is his use of **within-group differences** to explain **between-group differences.**

WITHIN- AND BETWEEN-GROUP DIFFERENCES AND INTELLIGENCE

While many psychologists agree that differences within groups (i.e., within the White population) can be partially attributed to hereditary factors, this does not lead to the conclusion that differences between groups (e.g., Whites and Blacks) are attributable to hereditary factors, as Jensen assumed. A useful analogy has been proposed to illustrate Jenson's error. Imagine drawing two random samples of seeds from a bag containing several genetically different varieties (see Figure 13.3). One sample is planted in enriched soil, the other sample in regular soil.

FIGURE 13.3

Within-Group and Between-Group Differences

The variability within groups (different sizes and shapes) results from the genetic variability within the seeds only because the soil was the same. The variability between groups (also different sizes and shapes) results from both genetic variability (within-group variability) and environmental conditions that differed between groups (the soil condition).

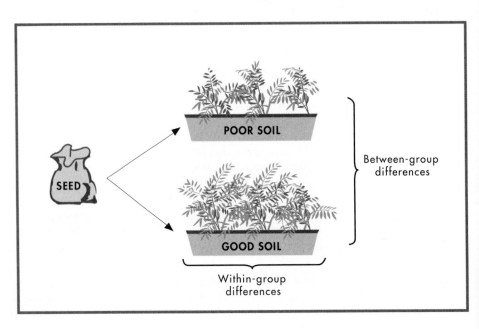

The plants within each planter will differ somewhat. This within-group difference is attributable to genetic differences within each random sample of seeds. The plants grown in the different soils (environmental conditions) will also differ. Most likely the plants grown in the enriched soil will be much taller than the ones grown in regular soil. This difference is a between-group difference and it is attributable to both random genetic differences and the different environmental (soil) conditions. It would be a mistake to claim the differences in height between the two groups of plants was attributable to the genetic differences in the samples alone (Lewontin, 1976).

RACIAL DIFFERENCES IN INTELLIGENCE

Numerous studies conducted over the last 50 to 60 years have found that American blacks score an average of about 15 IQ points (one standard deviation) below American whites on standard tests of intelligence. For instance, on the Stanford-Binet test the difference between American blacks and whites was 17.4 IQ points for the age group 12 to 23 years (Thorndike, 1986). However, as Figure 13.4 reveals, the scores of significant numbers of both black and white individuals fall at all points in the distribution, and there is a great deal of overlap between the two races on IQ scores. Furthermore, the fact that the range of scores for both groups extends from very low to very high indicates that the IQ differences among individuals within one racial group are profoundly greater than differences between the average scores of the two groups. Finally, a substantial number of Blacks have IQs that far exceed the average IQ for Whites.

In view of the comparably wide distribution of IQ scores in both populations and the great overlap between each, we must conclude that knowing if a person is White or Black provides little basis for predicting his or her IQ. Even Arthur Jensen conceded that all levels of human intellect are present among both races. Still, we are left with the puzzling matter of a 15-point spread between the two races.

Psychologists do not dispute the fact that Blacks, on the average, score lower than Whites on IQ tests. The question is, why? We have already seen evidence that most of the IQ tests commonly used today may place blacks at a disadvantage. Can you think of any other factors that might contribute to this difference, or do you agree with Jensen that these differences reflect genetic factors? Consider these questions before reading on.

One of the saddest aspects of American culture is the irrefutable fact that Blacks are socioeconomically and educationally disadvantaged in comparison with Whites. Blacks have been subjected to discrimination and deprivation dating to the time they were first forceably brought to the United States, and it is impossible to discount the influence of this experience on their intellectual development. Perhaps what is truly remarkable is that so many brilliant Blacks have emerged from less than advantageous environments.

Today a widespread opinion among psychologists is that intelligence differences between racial groups are largely, if not exclusively, the result of environmental factors. The findings on which this conclusion is based come from a variety of research studies.

One line of research has explored educational differences between blacks and whites. Many years ago, researchers noted that IQ scores of black children from the rural South increased after they moved to northern cities, and that the extent of their IQ improvement was positively correlated with the number of years they

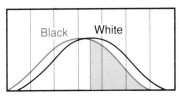

FIGURE 13.4

The Large Degree of Overlap Between the Distributions of IQ Scores for Blacks and Whites

The difference between the mean IQ scores for Blacks and Whites is about 15 points.

spent in northern schools (Klineberg, 1935; Lee, 1951). Presumably, this improvement was a direct result of exposure to educational environments that were far superior to the notoriously limited environments of southern country schools for Blacks only.

Interestingly, a similar argument has been used to explain another racial difference that has been noted in IQ scores—that children in Japan tend to outscore American white children by several IQ points (Mohs, 1982). Although a few researchers suggest that these differences may be due to genetic factors, most believe this gap is attributable to the superior Japanese school system (Stevenson, 1983). The academic year for Japanese elementary school students is 30 percent longer than the typical American school schedule, and Japanese pupils average about twice the homework of American students. Perhaps most importantly, however, is the fact that the Japanese school system fosters a greater positive attitude towards education than do American schools. This attitude is facilitated by innovative teaching styles that makes education both challenging and enjoyable (Stevenson, 1992).

As you might expect, numerous studies have shown a relationship between IQ scores and socioeconomic status similar to that between intelligence and quality of education. For example, James Coleman (1966) found that children from low socioeconomic groups score well below the national average on tests of intellectual ability. Needless to say, blacks are disproportionately overrepresented among families of low socioeconomic status.

Research also suggests that an enriched environment can have a significant positive impact on IQ scores. The work of Sandra Scarr and Richard Weinberg (1976) was mentioned earlier in the discussion of adoption studies, and it is also relevant here. These researchers studied 99 black children in Minneapolis who were adopted by white middle-class parents and raised in environments more affluent and advantaged than the ones in which they were born. The average IQ of these black children was about 106, which is equivalent to the typical IQ of white children adopted into similarly privileged families and above the average for white children in general. In contrast, the average of 106 is significantly higher than the average IQ of 90 for black children reared in their own homes in the Minneapolis area.

Note that this difference of 16 IQ points is approximately equal to the gap between whites and blacks in general mentioned earlier. This similarity provides strong evidence for the role of environment in racial IQ differences. Scarr and Weinberg found that the younger the children were at the age of adoption, the higher their IQs tended to be—a finding that underscores the importance of early experiences in fostering intellectual growth.

This latter finding is not surprising in view of evidence that IQ differences between very young black and white children are minimal, but as the children grow older the gap substantially widens (Osborne, 1960). It appears that the negative effects of disadvantaged, impoverished environments have a cumulative effect on intellectual growth, and that these effects are much more adverse for black children whose environments tend to be more impoverished than those of white children.

Even Arthur Jensen provided some evidence supporting environmental explanations for racial IQ differences. In 1977 he reported the results of an investigation of IQ scores of white and black children in rural Georgia, where blacks were greatly disadvantaged, both educationally and socioeconomically. He found evidence of a steady and substantial decline in the IQ scores of black children as they grew older, from age five to 16. Comparable declines for whites were not observed. Jensen admitted that this cumulative deficit found only among blacks could not be explained solely by genetic factors. Rather, this finding indicates that impoverished educational and economic environments severely curtail the opportunities for intellectual growth.

In concluding this discussion, the safest thing to say is that neither genetics nor environmental conditions alone account for the differences in intelligence observed either within or between groups of individuals. Experiments with animals and correlational studies with people seem to suggest that genetic differences can be overridden by environmental circumstances. Unfortunately the history of intelligence testing has been largely motivated by attempts to justify racial attitudes. Given these suspicious beginnings, test biases and the role of heredity versus environment will continue to be actively discussed. In the next chapter we will confront some of these same issues as we examine the determinants and the assessment of personality.

SUMMARY

DEFINING INTELLIGENCE

1. Both psychologists and laypersons have similar views about what constitutes intelligence, except that laypersons are more likely to include social competence in their list of attributes.

2. The only operational definition of intelligence that psychologists have agreed on is that intelligence is what intelligence tests measure.

MEASURING INTELLIGENCE

3. The modern intelligence testing movement was launched by Alfred Binet and his associates, who devised a test to measure French schoolchildren's intellectual skills.

4. Terman revised the original Binet test to make it applicable to American children. The resulting test, called the Stanford-Binet, was most recently revised in 1986.

5. The Stanford-Binet is an individually administered IQ test comprising a series of subtests that are graded by age level.

6. Studies have demonstrated substantial positive correlations between Stanford-Binet IQ scores and school grades.

7. The Wechsler Adult Intelligence Scale (WAIS) is an individually administered IQ test for people in late adolescence or adulthood that includes 11 subtests grouped into two major categories or scales—a verbal scale and a performance scale.

8. Group intelligence tests, which are widely used today, are cheaper, quicker, and easier to administer than individual tests like the Stanford-Binet or WAIS. However, group tests are limited by the inability of the tester to determine accurately subjects' level of comprehension of directions and motivation to perform well.

9. Aptitude tests are designed to predict the ability to learn new information or a new skill, whereas achievement tests are intended to measure what has already been learned. Intelligence tests tend to measure both aptitude and achievement.

EVALUATING INTELLIGENCE TESTS

10. The process by which IQ tests are developed can be simplified into four steps: developing test items, evaluating these test items, standardizing the test, and establishing norms.

11. Good tests of IQ (or any other psychological assessment device) must possess both reliability and validity. Reliability refers to measuring a trait with dependable consistency. A test that possesses validity is able to measure accurately what it is supposed to measure.

12. Thus far it has been impossible to eliminate cultural bias from IQ

tests. Test questions often reflect the mainstream values and experiences of White middle-class city dwellers.

THEORIES OF INTELLIGENCE

13. Factorial models of intelligence are concerned with the structure of intelligence. Factorial models have been proposed by Spearman, Thurstone, and more recently, Guilford.

14. Spearman proposed that intelligence is made up of two components: a g-factor, or general intelligence, and a collection of specific intellectual abilities that he labeled s-factors.

15. Thurstone proposed that human intelligence is a composite of seven primary mental abilities: verbal comprehension, numerical ability, spatial relations, perceptual speed, word fluency, memory, and inductive reasoning.

16. Guilford's structure of intellect model proposes that intelligence consists of 150 separate abilities, with no overall general intelligence factor.

17. Unlike the factorial models, Sternberg's information-processing model of intelligence is concerned with the process of intelligence. It identifies six steps that people generally go through when solving problems typically encountered on intelligence tests. These steps are encoding, inferring, mapping, applications, justification, and response.

18. Sternberg has found that people who score high on intelligence tests typically spend more time analyzing a question than those who score lower.

19. Recently Sternberg expanded his information-processing approach into what he calls the triarchic theory of intelligence, which maintains that intelligence is a multidimensional trait comprising three different abilities: com-

ponential, experiential, and contextual.

20. Gardner proposes a theory of multiple intelligences, suggesting that there are seven kinds of intelligence. In addition to the linguistic, logical-mathematical, and spatial intelligences that are included in traditional definitions, Gardner gives equal billing to musical intelligence, bodily kinesthetic intelligence, and inter- and intrapersonal intelligence.

HEREDITARY AND ENVIRONMENTAL INFLUENCES ON INTELLIGENCE

21. Evidence from twin and adoption studies, and from selective-breeding studies of animals, has been used to support the role of heredity in determining intelligence. However, other experiments, together with evidence from orphanage and birth order studies, suggest that environment is also important.

22. Heritability percentages provide estimates of the amount of variation in intelligence that may be attributed to heredity.

EVALUATING THE HEREDITARY AND ENVIRONMENTAL EVIDENCE

23. Heritability studies may falsely assume that heredity and environment are additive in their contributions to intelligence. Some psychologists argue that heredity and the environment interact throughout development to determine intelligence.

24. It is argued that within-group differences in intelligence cannot be used to explain between-group (racial) differences.

RACIAL DIFFERENCES IN INTELLIGENCE

25. Significant numbers of both Blacks' and Whites' scores fall at all points in distributions of IQ scores, and there is considerable

overlap between the two races on IQ scores.

26. The fact that Blacks score somewhat lower on IQ tests than Whites, on the average, may be attributed to the higher incidence of socioeconomic and educational disadvantages in the Black versus White population.

27. When social and educational deficits in the lives of Blacks are corrected (through such things as geographical relocation and adoption into more socioeconomically advantaged environments), IQ differences between the races decrease.

TERMS AND CONCEPTS

intelligence
mental age
intelligence quotient (IQ)
Stanford-Binet test
Wechsler Adult Intelligence Scale (WAIS)
Army Alpha test
Army Beta test
Otis-Lennon School Ability Test (OLSAT)
Cognitive Abilities Test (CAT)
standardization procedures
norm
reliability
test–retest reliability

alternate-forms reliability
split-half reliability
validity
criterion-related validity
concurrent validity
predictive validity
aptitude tests
achievement tests
g-factor
s-factors
primary mental abilities
triarchic theory of intelligence
heritability
within-group differences
between-group differences

PERSPECTIVE #1

Dr. Robert Sternberg

Dr. Robert Sternberg grew up in Maplewood, New Jersey, went to Yale University for an undergraduate degree in psychology, and then went to Stanford University where he received his Ph.D. in experimental psychology in 1975. After graduating, he took a position at Yale and is now a professor of psychology. Dr. Sternberg has developed an information-processing approach to intelligence and has been studying the limitations of traditional intelligence testing and creating measures for what he calls "practical intelligence"—the ability "to go into an environment and figure out what you need to know in it, and then work effectively within that environment."

PERSPECTIVE #1

ARE INTELLIGENCE TESTS INTELLIGENT?

Dr. Robert Sternberg

Q: Dr. Sternberg, do you view intelligence as a fixed ability or do you think that it changes considerably throughout our lifetime?

A: I think it changes. It changes in two ways. One is—clearly it develops. As children get older they become more intelligent. And also it's possible to develop it through interventions, through having a better environment, or through programs that directly teach intellectual skills. So I see it as a flexible kind of ability.

Q: Do you think that there is any genetic component that is at all significant?

A: I think that there is a genetic component. And there is also an environmental one and, as most people believe, I think they're interactive. But one of the goals of my own research is devising programs to help people develop their intelligence. I have a book called *Intelligence Applied*, which is a program for developing intellectual skills according to the triarchic model—analytic, creative, and practical skills. Right now we also have a program called "Developing Practical and Creative Intelligence for Schools." So in general I think it's something that can be developed and I believe the data are consistent with that point of view.

Q: Do you feel that the environmental component is the one that has the most impact on intellectual development?

514

Howard Gardner is Professor of Education and Co-Director of Project Zero at Harvard University. Trained in developmental psychology and neuropsychology, he has for over twenty years been investigating the development and breakdown of symbol-using skills, with a special emphasis on artistic thinking. More recently, he has carried out investigations in the areas of creativity and intelligence, culminating in the books mentioned in the interview. At present, he is engaged in efforts at school reform in the United States. In 1981 he was awarded a MacArthur Prize Fellowship and in 1990 he became the first American to win the University of Louisville Grawmeyer Award in Education.

PERSPECTIVE #2
Dr. Howard Gardner

A: Well, I think that relates to questions about environment versus heritability. However, the genetic component you can't do a whole lot about. As I said, I believe there is a genetic component but that it's a given. What you can do is maximize the quality of the environment. That is something you can do something about. Height is frequently given as an example of how environment can influence a highly heritable trait. Height is partially genetic—it's largely genetic—but environmental intervention can certainly increase height.

Q: That brings up the question of twin studies. Do you think that there is a great deal we can learn from investigating differences in twin intelligence?

A: I think that twin studies are useful if your question is on specific cognitive tests such as psychometric intelligence tests. What is the proportion of individual difference variation that's heritable? The thing to remember is, first of all, that intelligence is broader than what is measured by most of the tests so you're only looking at a portion of intelligence through the tests that are used. The second thing is that heritability can vary with place and time and group. In other words, there's not one heritability for intelligence. It's different in different countries, it's different in different periods, it's different for different ethnic groups. So it's not like there is a fixed n^2, contrary to what many people think. So I think that there is some usefulness in twin studies, but you have to understand what questions they answer.

Q: Do you have any theories or hypotheses about why there might be differences in heritability and intelligence from one culture to another?

PERSPECTIVE #1

A: I think that it depends on a lot of factors. It depends on the amount of variation in the population, in the gene pool. It depends on the amount of variation in the environment. It depends on how much difference there is in opportunities and in how much potential mobility there is in a society. So I think that there are a lot of factors that can affect heritability.

Q: There has been a lot of recent interest in the area of crystalized versus fluid intelligence, especially in the elderly. Is there any evidence to suggest that there is more flexibility in fluid intelligence as we age than had previously been thought?

A: Well, the going view is that crystalized ability tends to increase across the life span and that fluid abilities tend to level off and then to decline. I think that the evidence on that is in favor of this view. But there are two factors that need to be taken into account. One is compensation. As you grow older and develop more crystalized skills you can compensate for things you can't do in other ways. So less fluid ability doesn't necessarily imply that your total performance is any less. Even before you're older, there are some things you just stop liking to do—you no longer want to do them—and so you find ways of having other people do them or ways around them or ways to make them easier for yourself. Part of what life is about is working out compensatory mechanisms for the things that you either don't like or don't do well. At the same time you capitalize on your strengths. So by a pattern of capitalizing on your strengths and compensating for your weaknesses—even though it's probably the case that fluid ability at some point starts to decline—performance doesn't necessarily decline.

The other thing I want to mention is that in a study we did on creativity, rated creativity of products started to decline roughly at about age 40. However, when we compared the ages of the people rating creativity with the ages of the people being rated we found cohort matching, meaning that people tended to rate as more creative products of their own age cohort. And that would mean that people who are older or younger than the raters would tend to be rated lower because of the age mismatch. In other words, what constitutes intelligence changes with age and in our assessments we may be using a standard that doesn't apply as well as older people as it does to younger ones. Our life tasks change over time and so what it means to be intelligent may change as well. As an adult, what I need to succeed is not the same as what a student needs to succeed in school. At the same time, the kid who can be a straight *A* student in school is not necessarily the best person in the world of work. So our developmental tasks change, and I think we need to recognize that what it means to be intelligent can also change with age.

Q: That brings up an interesting point about the relationship between creativity and intelligence. How closely related do you think they are?

A: Well, according to my own theories, intelligence is one component of creativity and there's also a creative part of intelligence, so they're like overlapping circles.

Q: Do you think creativity is an ability that can be increased or fostered through some type of intervention or training?

A: Yes, absolutely. As I said, we have programs for teaching creative intelligence in school. I don't know if you know my investment model, but every element in that theory is trainable. Basically the idea of the investment model is that creative people buy low and sell high. In other words, they come up with ideas that aren't very popular at the time. Then, once they have convinced people of the worth of those ideas, they move on to the next idea. They go against the crowd; they're contrarians. And that's a style that can be taught. In other words, don't always follow others but follow your own beliefs and ideas.

Q: This question of the role of genetics versus environment touches upon the subject of intelligence testing. Such tests have been used by some to support contentions of racial differences in intelligence. What is your view of such tests?

A: Any technology is misused from time to time. So the biggest problem is not so much in the tests but in overinterpretation of them. In other words, making too much of differences or misconceiving differences. So the problem is not with the method, it's with what people do with the method. In terms of racial differences, there *are* differences in scores. The disagreement is as to *why* there are those differences. In my own research I emphasize socialization. When I say socialization, I mean that parents want to have smart kids. They try to socialize their kids to be smart. But people are brought up in different ways and sometimes the concept of intelligence in a group does not correspond to the IQ test concept, or the school conception of intelligence. You may have kids who are smart who are socialized to be smart in their home environment or community environment, but that doesn't match with what the school or the test is looking for. So you may see differences in test scores but those tests are based on particular sets of skills. If, for example, I were to go into a hunting and gathering culture, I might not look very smart there. I don't expect that I would be terribly successful in what's required for adaptation in that kind of culture. Different cultures mean different things by "smart person."

Q: Given that fact, do you think there is any validity in trying to develop so-called "culture-free" intelligence tests?

A: No, I think it's impossible. Intelligence manifests itself in a culture. It exhibits itself, and you can't speak of intelligence outside of culture because we define what we mean by intelligence in terms of cultural acts. What we put on tests is not culture free. Rather, the content reflects what we value. So to talk about intelligence outside of culture doesn't make sense. There are certain processes that are intelligent in any culture but the way they're manifested differs from culture to culture. For example, take something like setting up a strategy to solve problems. This process is an important aspect of intelligence in any culture; it's universal. But the strategies that are considered to be intelligent may vary from one culture to another. Use of time and being able to allocate resources well are aspects of intelligence in any culture. But what's considered good time allocation may vary from one culture to another.

Q: Are you doing any research right now that bears on the question of intelligence testing that you might be willing to share with us?

A: Well, I used the pilot version of my own test in a program for selecting gifted high school kids for a program this summer. There was an analytical section which is more like an SAT, but there was also a creative section and a practical section. And so rather than just selecting kids because they're good at one thing, we selected kids who are good at any one of those three. And the interesting thing relevant to all these questions about group differences is that we had a

"You can't speak of intelligence outside of culture because we define what we mean by intelligence in terms of cultural acts."

PERSPECTIVE #1

very heterogeneous group with respect to ethnic diversity. I think part of the reason for that was precisely that we did look for a broader range of abilities and not just IQ. We're analyzing the data right now. We hope to issue a report in a couple of months.

PERSPECTIVE #2

ARE INTELLIGENCE TESTS INTELLIGENT?

Dr. Howard Gardner

Q: Dr. Gardner, do you view intelligence as a fixed ability or do you feel it changes considerably throughout our lifetime?

A: Well, of course that question presupposes I believe there's a single thing called intelligence, and I don't. To be sure, in fact both common language and scientific tradition defend the notion that there's such a thing as a single intelligence. People who believe there's a single intelligence can cite as evidence for the fixed nature of that intelligence the fact that there's a high degree of heritability, meaning that people who share all the genes in common are very likely to have similar intelligences and people who share half their genes in common are more likely to have similar intelligences than people who are genetically unrelated. But the whole thrust of my work going on the past 15 years has been to challenge the notion of there being a single kind of intelligence.

Q: Could you kind of give us a brief overview of some of the components that you see as going into intelligence?

A: Even using the word "components" assumes there's a single thing called intelligence. That's sort of what Robert Sternberg's position would be. He would say, yes there's intelligence but it is composed of many different components. I say there are in fact at least seven different intelligences. And I claim that, as a species, human beings have evolved over thousands, maybe millions, of years and developed this set of intelligences. Everybody has all of them, but no two people have exactly the same blend or combination. The first two intelligences, linguistic and logical mathematical, are the ones which are usually valued in school and tested in standard tests. So when people on the street say "intelligence," they usually mean some kind of a blend of language and logic. I often say it needs to be a *superficial* blend of language and logic because the instruments test how quickly you can switch from one thing to the other, which is a test of superficiality, not necessarily of depth. But I claim there are five other intelligences: musical, spatial, bodily kinesthetic, interpersonal (understanding of other people), and intrapersonal (understanding of yourself). And those aren't components of intelligence, those are seven separate intelligences.

I challenge the notion of a single thing called intelligence on the basis both of biology—what we understand about the brain and how it's evolved—and on the basis of what we know about human abilities as they play out in different cultures. I think many of the kinds of things we look at in standard intelligence tests in our culture don't even exist elsewhere. Conversely, survival in a sailing culture would depend on whether you could find your way around without tipping over or getting knocked out by storms and we have no way of knowing from our intelligence tests whether people in our culture whom we call intelligent could do that at all. So I reject the notion that tests of intelligence do more than predict a certain kind of scholastic skill.

Q: What, then, is your view of the practicality of developing culture-free intelligence tests as alternatives to some of the standard intelligence and IQ tests that are administered today?

A: I think the most you could hope to do, given that you believe in testing at all, is to develop an instrument which is in no obvious way biased within a particular culture. So let's just say we might, over the long run, be able to produce in North America a test which does not seem to be skewed for or against any particular group within that culture. The notion that we could somehow produce something that would be usable around the world is, I think, preposterous. You have to be very naive to think that anything that we do around here just happens to be culture free.

Q: Have you conducted any research or are you in the process of conducting any research that bears upon some of the applications of your work, for instance, developing learning environments?

A: I published my book *Frames of Mind* in 1983 and I saw that as basically a contribution to the field of psychology. In fact, it has had some influence in psychology and it's been controversial. Overwhelmingly, it's biggest impact has been in the educational arena. So I have really been devoting my efforts in the last ten years to exploring the educational implications of this theory. How do you assess intelligences? What kind of curricula do you set up? Which environments are productive for the enhancement of intelligences? I now have about 50 people working with me on those questions, and there are literally hundreds of schools in the country which are exploring educational implications of the theory and some of them are doing research. My 1993 book, *Multiple Intelligences in Theory and Practice* describes what people are actually doing with the theory. While I do talk about museums and apprenticeships and things like that, most of it is about the implications in the school. To give you one specific example, we have a project called Spectrum, which was started about ten years ago in an effort to figure out whether, as young as the age of 3 or 4, kids already have different intellectual profiles from one another. We find that some kids will be strong in one intelligence and others in another, and there's no question that as young as 3 or 4 kids have very different profiles of intelligence. It's not the case that we're all alike until 5 and then we begin to differentiate.

We created a very rich environment which we call a Spectrum classroom, which is as much like a children's museum as like a classroom. Over the course of a year we watched how kids interact with the materials in that classroom: musical instruments, all kinds of games, stuff to take apart and put together again, different learning centers. We even have a miniature version of the classroom which kids take apart and put together so that it will look like the regular class. And we have little photographs of all the kids and teachers on pieces of wood and we look at the kids' personal intelligences by the way that they can identify and reconstruct the habits of kids in the classroom.

PERSPECTIVE #2

So there's two points. One is, you can do research in intelligences and you can find evidence for them very early. The second is, you don't have to do standard tests. You can create environments which themselves allow you to look at people's profiles of intelligence.

Q: You mentioned that your research has shown that there are noticeable differences in intelligence profiles between one individual and another at an early age. Have you made any recommendations based upon that in terms of educational environments or tracking people into certain educational areas?

A: That's a very interesting question because when I wrote *Frames of Mind* I did not particularly have special educational interventions in mind. What happened was, many people read the book and it became like a Rorschach inkblot test. And so you had some people reading the book that said what we need to do is to find people's talents as early as possible and to stream them and track them as much as possible. Other people said you need to find a kid's weaknesses as early as possible and really try to shore them up. And still other people, like the Key School in Indianapolis, said that we ought to give every kid exactly the same amount of time each day in each intelligence. So it's quite clear the theory itself doesn't contain within it a particular recipe.

What we've done in Spectrum is to write a little essay for parents on the kids' particular strengths and weaknesses, and actually suggest what might be done either if you, as a parent, wanted to play for strength or if you want to shore up weaknesses. Initially we just told what to do to build on strengths. However, many parents said they wanted to know about the weaknesses, so we felt we should tell them. I then came to the conclusion that whether to build strengths or shore up weaknesses is really a value judgment. And I don't think it's appropriate for psychologists to say you should do one or the other.

Let me give you a concrete example why. If you're a recent immigrant from southeast Asia and you have a kid who's very strong in an area, you're probably going to want to push that as far as you can, because that's going to be his or her meal ticket to being successful in America. If, however, you are very comfortably middle class and there's no problem that your kid is ever going to be able to make a living, you might want to have a much more rounded child or even work in areas of weakness. And you can see why if I as a psychologist recommended only one of those, I would not be doing a service to somebody whose set of needs and priorities are very different.

Q: Another topic that comes to mind when discussing intelligence is the topic of creativity. How would you describe the relationship between different intelligences and a person's creative ability? Are they linked in any way?

A: That's an area that I'm totally involved in at the present time, so this is very close to the center of my work. Just as I don't believe there's a general intelligence, I don't believe there's a general creativity. People are creative or not creative in particular domains within a society. And those domains map roughly into the intelligences. Some people are creative in music, some are creative in math and so on. Second of all, and more complexly, creativity is not something that's in somebody's head. It's always an interaction between whatever abilities you have, whatever domains exist in the culture, and judgments made of the quality and originality of your work. So we can't talk about X or Y being creative in an area alone. We have to say, How do people assess that person's work? And although that judgment may be faulty in the short run, over the long run we hope it will be less faulty. There are people like Emily Dickinson or Gregor Mendel whose work was not appreciated during their lifetime. We don't therefore conclude they weren't creative. We conclude they needed to have an audience that was receptive to what they did.

My general belief about the relationship between intelligence and creativities is as follows: In order to be creative, you have to have a certain kind of personality. And you have to have a sense of what kinds of ideas or products might possibly find a future audience, though it may not necessarily find an audience now. This is important because you can have a terrific brain and a terrific set of intelligences, but if you want to be accepted and you want to do what people are going to like, you'll never be creative. You've got to have the kind of personality that's willing to take risks, to be knocked down, to be criticized, and keep on going. This doesn't mean that you pay no attention to the criticism, but you can't be floored by it. So there are many people who are highly intelligent in any definition, who never do anything creative because they don't want to take a chance. There are some people who are highly intelligent and who are willing to take a chance but their work is never appreciated so we have to assume it's not creative. So this is a quite different way of thinking about creativity. I have another 1993 book, *Creating Minds: The Anatomy of Creativity as Seen through the Lives of Freud, Einstein, Picasso, Stravinsky, Eliot, Graham, and Gandhi*, where I lay out that argument in some detail. I'm sure it's going to cause hackles to rise.

Q: Do you think that creativity can be fostered or increased in any way through intervention?

A: Definitely, but it's even easier to abolish. I mean if you chastise people or kill them if they do original kinds of things, you simply destroy creativity. Most cultures throughout history have wanted to get rid of creativity because it's a destabilizing kind of influence. The most creative societies have exploded pretty quickly because there wasn't enough stability: Florence in the Renaissance, Greece in classical times, and so on.

After 25 years in education I've boiled down my educational recipe to three points: Model and practice with feedback. If you want kids to be creative, you've got to model what it's like to pursue new questions, to make mistakes, to take a chance. You've got to give kids plenty of practice in doing that and you've got to let them know how they're doing. So creativity is very much a sociological issue as well as a psychological and biological issue. You could look at a person's brain and know where every single wiring was and it wouldn't tell you the faintest thing about whether they were creative or not. You'd have to see what they do living in a certain culture and how it's valued by people in that culture.

"If you want kids to be creative, you've got to model what it's like to pursue new questions, to make mistakes, to take a chance."

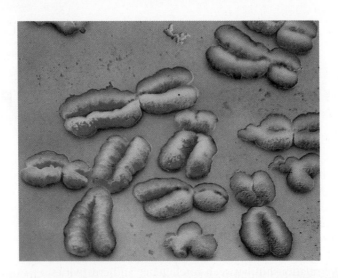

C H A P T E R 1 4

Personality: Theories and Assessment

DEFINING PERSONALITY

THEORIES OF PERSONALITY

Trait Theories
Evaluating the Trait Theories

PSYCHOANALYTIC THEORY

The Historical Context of Freud's
   Theory
Personality and the Unconscious
The Structure of Personality
Personality Dynamics
Freud's View of Personality Development
Evaluating Freud's Psychoanalytic Theory
Other Psychodynamic Theorists: The
   Neo-Freudians

**HUMANISTIC THEORIES OF
PERSONALITY**

Rogers: The Concept of Self
Maslow: Self-Actualization
Evaluating Humanistic Theories

**BEHAVIORAL, SOCIAL-
LEARNING, AND BIOLOGICAL
THEORIES OF PERSONALITY**

The Behavioral Perspective
The Social-Learning Perspective
Evaluating Behavioral and Social-
   Learning Theories
Biological Determinants of Personality

**THE ASSESSMENT OF
PERSONALITY**

Behavioral Observation
Interviews
Questionnaires
Projective Tests

*W*hat makes people different from one another? The ancient Greeks thought the answer had something to do with the four basic body fluids or *humors:* blood, phlegm, black bile, and yellow bile. According to the Greek physician Hippocrates (460–371 B.C.), there were four possible personality types. *Sanguine* individuals had an abundance of blood; they tended to be cheerful, optimistic, and active. *Phlegmatic* people were listless, sluggish, and tired because they had too much phlegm. Sad, brooding, *melancholic* temperaments resulted from too much black bile, and *choleric* (excitable, easy to anger) personalities resulted from an excess of yellow bile (see Figure 14.1).

Although Hippocrates' terminology still survives in descriptive adjectives that we use today, both the typologies psychologists use to distinguish personalities and the explanations of what causes personality differences have changed considerably in the last 2,300 years. In this chapter we look at some more contemporary conceptions of personality, including both theories that describe personality traits and the psychoanalytic, behavioral, and humanistic explanations of what makes each of us unique. Like Chapter 13, this chapter also describes assessment techniques, although here our interest is in assessing people's personalities instead of their intelligence.

DEFINING PERSONALITY

You have often heard statements like "Mary has a great personality" or "John has no personality at all." Do these statements reflect logical observations about human personality? Consider this question and formulate a response before reading on.

The notion of personality as an attribute that people possess in varying amounts is a common one. However, personality is not something we possess in large or small quantities, nor is it a concrete trait that is easily observable, such as blue eyes or blond hair. Rather, personality is what we are, a collection of many traits and attributes, the sum total of which constitutes a unique person unlike anyone else. We begin this chapter by trying to define personality.

Although personality psychologists have not reached a general consensus on a formal definition of **personality,** a common theme can be found in most definitions. A leading personality theorist of our time, Columbia University's Walter Mischel (1986), notes this common theme by observing that "personality usually refers to the distinctive patterns of behavior (including thoughts and emotions)

FIGURE 14.1
According to ancient Greeks, different behaviors were attributed to four basic humors or fluids. The effects of these humors are depicted by these illustrations. From left to right they include: choleric, melancholic, phlegmatic, and sanguine behavior.

that characterize each individual's adaptation to the situations of his or her life." We use Mischel's formulation as a working definition in this chapter.

A key aspect of virtually all definitions of personality is their emphasis on the individual. We may best describe *personality psychology* as the study of individuals —their distinctive characteristics and traits and the manner in which they integrate all aspects of their functioning as they adapt to their environments.

Since for most personality theorists the focus of personality research is nothing less than the total person, it is not surprising that personality psychology's domain is very broad. You will find that many of the discussions in the following pages relate closely to other chapters in this book, particularly discussions of development, learning, behavioral disorders, and assessment techniques.

THEORIES OF PERSONALITY

In view of the far-reaching nature of personality psychology, it is common for personality theorists to attempt to integrate most or all aspects of human behavior into a single theoretical framework. A number of theories have been developed in this attempt. Virtually all of these theoretical perspectives share a focus on the whole person, although they take different approaches. The *trait theories* are primarily descriptive theories in that they attempt to identify specific dimensions or characteristics that are associated with different personalities. It is important to remember here that identifying and describing personality characteristics is not the same as explaining them. As with other branches of science, classification and description often precede explanation.

Other theories make an attempt to explain personality differences in terms of unconscious motivation, learning, self-actualization, or the heritability of personality. Predictably, the major viewpoints are the *psychoanalytic theory* of Sigmund Freud and his followers, with its emphasis on the role of unconscious motivation in personality; the attempts of *behavioral* and *social-learning theories* to explain how our personalities are shaped by interacting with our environments; the *humanistic* view of personality as molded by our capacities for personal growth and self-actualization; and biological approaches that attribute personality to inherited dispositions. Because the trait theories help to describe and characterize personality, we begin with them.

TRAIT THEORIES

A number of theorists have tried to identify the behavioral traits that are the building blocks of personality (Buss & Finn, 1987). How do these trait theorists determine what traits are relevant in describing personality? A few different approaches have been used. One approach, known as the *idiographic approach*, defines traits by studying individuals in depth and focusing on the distinctive qualities of their personalities. A second approach, known as the *nomothetic approach*, studies groups of people in the attempt to identify personality traits that tend to appear in clusters. This approach uses the factor analysis technique we learned about in Chapter 13. We look at one representative of each method: First, the idiographic approach of Gordon Allport, and next, the nomothetic approach of Raymond Cattell.

ALLPORT'S CARDINAL, CENTRAL, AND SECONDARY TRAITS Gordon Allport (1897–1967) considered patterns of traits to be unique attributes of individuals. Thus Allport conducted thorough and detailed studies of individuals in depth, often through long-term case studies. His research led him to conclude that all people have certain *traits* or personal dispositions that are the building blocks of personality (1937, 1961, 1965, 1966). He described these traits as "predispositions to respond" or "generalized action tendencies." He further maintained that "it is these bona fide mental structures in each personality that account for the consistency of its behavior" (1937).

Why do traits produce consistencies in behavior? According to Allport, traits are both enduring and broad in scope, and so they act to unify a person's responses to a variety of stimulus situations. For example, a person with the trait of friendliness might be expected to be pleasant and sociable when meeting strangers, helpful and supportive on the job, and warm and sensitive when relating to family members (see Figure 14.2). Allport believed that our personality traits determine our unique patterns of response to environmental events. Thus the same stimuli might be expected to produce quite a different response in different people. For example, a person with the trait of shyness might react to meeting strangers by acting in a withdrawn, noncommunicative manner—a very different reaction from that of the person with the friendliness trait.

Allport described three types of traits that operate to provide a person's own unique personality structure. A **cardinal trait** is a powerful, dominating behavioral predisposition that seems to provide the pivot point in a person's entire life. For example, if you are the kind of individual who organizes your life around competitiveness—beating classmates on exams, being the fastest down the ski slope, and so forth—we might say that competitiveness is your cardinal trait. Allport recognized that only a very small number of people have cardinal traits. Some famous and infamous examples that come to mind are Adolf Hitler (hatred), the Marquis de Sade (cruelty), Don Juan (lust), and Albert Schweitzer (reverence for life).

All of us possess Allport's second type of trait, the **central trait**. Central traits are major characteristics of our personalities, such as sensitivity, honesty, and generosity. While less pervasive than cardinal traits, central traits are quite generalized and enduring, and it is these traits that form the building blocks of our

Gordon Allport

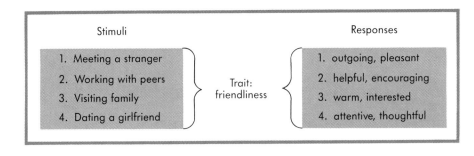

Stimuli		Responses
1. Meeting a stranger	Trait: friendliness	1. outgoing, pleasant
2. Working with peers		2. helpful, encouraging
3. Visiting family		3. warm, interested
4. Dating a girlfriend		4. attentive, thoughtful

FIGURE 14.2

How a Central Personality Trait Unifies a Person's Response to a Variety of Situations

According to Allport, few people have cardinal traits—powerful, dominating behavioral dispositions that seem to pervade a person's entire life. Hitler was believed to have the cardinal trait of hatred.

Raymond Cattell

personalities. Allport found that most people could be characterized by a fairly small number of central traits (usually five to 10).

Finally, we also have a number of less generalized and far less enduring **secondary traits** that affect our behaviors in specific circumstances. Examples of secondary traits might include our dress style preferences or patterns of exercise, both of which are quite changeable and thus not central or enduring aspects of personality.

CATTELL'S SIXTEEN PERSONALITY FACTORS   Raymond Cattell (b. 1905) took just the opposite approach from Allport, studying groups of people rather than individuals. He began his work by identifying certain obvious personality traits, such as integrity, friendliness, and tidiness (1950, 1965, 1973, 1982). He called these dimensions of personality **surface traits.** He then used both direct observations of behavior in everyday situations (what he called "life records") and a variety of questionnaires to obtain extensive data about surface traits from a large number of people. Statistical analysis of these data revealed that certain surface traits seemed to occur in clusters, and Cattell theorized that these clusters probably indicated the operation of a single underlying trait. Cattell applied factor analysis to determine what the surface trait clusters had in common. This analysis yielded a list of 16 primary or **source traits** which he considered to be at the center or core of personality. He listed each of these traits as a pair of polar opposites, such as trusting versus suspicious.

Cattell and his colleagues developed a questionnaire called the *16 Personality Factor Questionnaire* (or the *16 PF*) to measure these source traits. Figure 14.3 shows samples of these profiles for subjects from three different occupational groups: writers, artists, and airline pilots. As you might expect, Cattell and his associates found that writers and artists have more in common than either group has with pilots.

Cattell demonstrated a number of potential applications of his trait theory and the questionnaire he designed to measure source traits. For example, in one study of 180 married couples, he found that the most satisfied couples were those

FIGURE 14.3

Personality Profiles, Based on Cattell's 16PF Questionnaire, for Three Occupational Groups

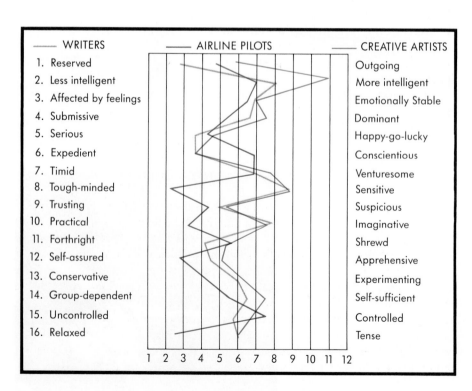

that were most alike in their personality profiles derived from the 16 PF (Cattell, 1973).

Trait theories offer the distinct advantage of providing specific methods for measuring or assessing basic characteristics that can be used in comparing individuals. While they often disagree about which basic traits are needed to describe personality, these theories share a common assumption that traits may be used to explain consistencies in behavior and to explain why different people tend to react differently to the same situations (Mischel, 1986).

EVALUATING THE TRAIT THEORIES

DESCRIPTIONS VERSUS EXPLANATIONS OF BEHAVIOR A trait theorist such as Allport might observe that a woman who returns excess change to a cashier, admits to damaging a fixture in a motel, and refuses to accept help from a classmate during an exam behaves in these ways because she has the trait of honesty. What is the problem with this kind of reasoning? Think about this question before reading on.

How do we know that the woman just described has the trait of honesty, and that this trait is the cause of her behavior? The only answer Allport or other trait theorists might provide is "because she is honest in much of her behavior." If you have taken any logic courses, you may recognize this response as an example of circular reasoning: We first deduce the existence of a trait from observing a behavior, then use our deduction to explain the behavior. For instance, if we observe the woman returning extra money to a cashier we might conclude she is honest. *Honest* is a description of her behavior; it cannot be used to explain why she returned the money. For this reason, most psychologists insist that traits are only descriptions, not explanations.

Related to this point are criticisms of the view that traits produce consistent behavior from one situation to the next. Cattell went so far as to contend that a person's 16 PF Questionnaire scores can be used to predict such diverse things as success in school, accident-proneness, or marital happiness (Cattell, 1973).

A number of psychologists, most notably Walter Mischel (1968, 1979, 1984), have argued that while people may possess certain enduring behavioral predispositions, they do not act with consistency from one situation to the next. You may have noticed that you are shy in some kinds of situations and more assertive in others. Such inconsistencies are common to many of us, and a considerable body of research indicates that many personality "traits" may be situationally, or state, dependent.

One early study observed over 10,000 children who were given opportunities to steal, cheat, or lie in a variety of contrived situations at home, in the classroom, and on the playground (Hartshorne & May, 1928). It found very little consistency in the behavior of subjects: Most of the children would lie, steal, or cheat in some circumstances, but not in others. The researchers thus concluded that the so-called trait of honesty was actually a collection of *situation-specific habits.*

Later studies have reported similar inconsistencies in behavior. For example, a study of punctuality among several hundred college students revealed virtually no consistency in their time of arrival at a variety of college-related events (Dudycha, 1936). Walter Mischel's (1968) more recent investigation of college students' conscientiousness (turning in assignments on time, arriving before a lecture begins, and so forth) revealed a similar lack of situational consistency. Mischel went on to examine the research literature on this topic, and found very little evidence that behavior is consistent across diverse circumstances.

A number of personality psychologists have objected to this criticism, however. As one observer notes, trying to predict a person's behavior in a specific situation, based on either a questionnaire score or past observations, is like trying to predict how carefully you will check your next English composition for errors, based on the care you took in reviewing your answers on a previous psychology exam (Epstein, S., 1983). People's behavior in any given situation depends on many factors, from the amount of sleep they have had, to whether they are in a good mood, to their past experiences in similar situations.

Some of the debate over the consistency issue may stem, at least in part, from the fact that some individuals may be more consistent than others. According to one observer, if you think of yourself as a person who behaves according to your true feelings and attitudes, you will be inclined to act consistently in different situations. In contrast, if you perceive yourself as acting like a different person in different circumstances, your behavior is more likely to be inconsistent (Snyder, 1983). Thus if you perceive yourself as an honest person, you are more likely to demonstrate this trait consistently than if you do not have a clear sense of yourself as honest. It is also possible that people may be consistent in some traits and not in others—that people show situational consistency only in those trait behaviors in which they perceive themselves as being consistent (Bem, 1983).

Despite situational variance in behavior, however, our tendency to be honest (or happy, shy, outgoing, or any other quality) over a variety of situations is somewhat predictable. If we average out our behaviors across a range of situations, at least some of our most distinctive personality traits contribute to a consistency that tends to be enduring over the life span. For example, a child who is gregarious during her early developmental years is likely to remain friendly and outgoing throughout her life. Research indicates that threads of behavioral continuity do emerge when people are examined over long time spans (Arend et al., 1979; Block, 1971).

Where did these traits come from in the first place? This question leads to a final criticism of trait theories—that they offer essentially no understanding of how personality develops. Instead of telling us about the origin of traits, how they are learned, how they may be changed, and how they interact to shape behavior, these theories offer little more than a rather static view of personality as a collection of characteristics or behaviors. For answers to the question of where traits come from, we turn to the psychoanalytic, behavioral, humanistic, and biological theories.

PSYCHOANALYTIC THEORY

The most influential, most comprehensive and systematic, and most widely studied personality theory of all time is the psychoanalytic theory of the Viennese physician Sigmund Freud (1856–1939). It is impossible to do justice in a few pages to Freud's theoretical interpretations, originally published in 24 volumes between 1888 and 1939. However, we attempt to acquaint you with some of the most important features of his theory.

THE HISTORICAL CONTEXT OF FREUD'S THEORY

Although Freud presented the Western world with a bold new vision of human nature, his views also reflected his own upbringing in the Victorian climate of nineteenth-century Austria. Freud was the firstborn child in a large, middle-class Jewish family. Almost his entire life was spent in Vienna where, as a young man, he received a medical degree and entered private practice as a neurologist. The Victorian climate strongly influenced attitudes towards sexual behavior, particularly among women. Women were not encouraged to behave sexually or enjoy sexual relations. As well, women were relatively oppressed compared to women today in most of the Western world. Men held most of the powerful positions, had money and prestige, and were envied by aspiring women. The development of Freud's theory was influenced by these times and his female patients. As you read this section on Freud's ideas keep these things in mind.

Freud's interest was in nervous disorders, but early in his medical career he noticed that many of his patients showed no evidence of nervous system pathology. A patient might be unable to walk, see, or hear but no neurological impairment could be found. Freud suspected that such symptoms might be psychological rather than physical. After observing neurologists such as Jean Charcot and Freud's colleague Joseph Breuer, both of whom were using hypnosis to treat cases similar to his own, Freud incorporated Breuer's *cathartic* method into his treatment regimen. This approach involved hypnotizing patients, then encouraging them to recall the first time their symptoms were experienced and to talk freely about the circumstances surrounding this occurrence. When such experiences could be relieved, the effect was often a release of bottled-up emotions in a kind of cathartic experience, followed by a marked reduction of the symptoms. Eventually, Freud dispensed with hypnosis, expanding the cathartic technique into a method known as **free association.** Freud encouraged patients to relax and to say whatever came to their minds, no matter how embarrassing, painful, or trivial.

Sigmund Freud

- -

PERSONALITY AND THE UNCONSCIOUS

Through listening to his patients free-associate about their early experiences, fears, and concerns, Freud gradually began to formulate a concept of the **unconscious** mind, which ultimately became central to his personality theory. He envisioned the mind as being like an iceberg, with most of it hidden beneath the surface in the vast reservoir of the unconscious. He theorized that memories and feelings are repressed or submerged in the unconscious because they are too painful or anxiety-producing to be tolerated in conscious thoughts. Free association was able to open a door to the unconscious, allowing a person to release or express its contents.

Freud used the term **psychoanalysis** to describe his interpretation of a patient's revelations of normally unconscious cognitions. The psychoanalytic theory of personality gradually evolved from his attempts to explain certain recurrent themes that emerged from his use of psychoanalysis. Thus the psychoanalytic perspective provides both a theory of personality and a method for treating behavioral disorders. (We discuss the therapy side of psychoanalysis in Chapter 16.)

The more Freud listened to his patients, the more convinced he became that unconscious thoughts and feelings are powerful molders of personality. He believed that these ever-present forces emerge into consciousness in disguised form, influencing our relationships with others, the kind of work we do, the beliefs we hold, and the symptoms of emotional disorders. Freud believed that the workings of the unconscious can be seen in the kinds of dreams we have. As you may recall from Chapter 5, Freud was particularly fond of analyzing dreams, which he considered to be a major outlet for unconscious wishes. Freud also believed that slips of the tongue or pen can provide insights into the unconscious. For example, the woman who describes her father as "kind, generous, and insensitive" (instead of "sensitive") may be expressing thinly disguised, repressed hostility.

Freud's training in physiology and medicine led him to conclude that we are biological organisms dominated by biological needs, especially sexual, that must be controlled if we are to become civilized human beings. In his view, our perpetual struggle to tame these impulses leads to the emotional conflicts that so profoundly shape our personalities. Considering the extreme sexual repression of the Victorian period, it is not surprising that Freud's initial theories of personality placed such an emphasis on conflicts surrounding sexual urges. Many years later, the death of millions of people in World War I also had a profound impact on Freud, and he modified his theory to include an equally strong emphasis on aggressive urges in molding personality. Thus the **psychoanalytic theory** depicts personality as shaped by an ongoing conflict between people's primary drives, particularly sex and aggression, and the social pressures of civilized society.

Freud also theorized that early childhood experiences play a major role in molding personality. After listening to countless revelations of what he considered to be profoundly significant events in his patients' early years, he concluded that such experiences place an indelible stamp on personality and behavior. In the next several paragraphs, we explore Freud's view of the structure, dynamics, and development of personality.

THE STRUCTURE OF PERSONALITY

One of the best known aspects of Freud's theory is his conceptualization of human personality as composed of three interacting systems or structures: the id, ego, and superego. These structures are not physically present in the brain; they are psychological concepts or constructs that Freud invented to help explain certain aspects of human behavior. These three systems are interrelated and interactive, but each has its own characteristics, as Table 14.1 illustrates.

THE ID According to Freud, the **id** is basically the biological component of personality. It consists of a vast reservoir of instinctual drives which Freud called the *life instincts* (such as hunger, thirst, and sex); it also includes the *death instinct*, which is responsible for aggressiveness and destruction. The id is fueled primarily by a form of energy called **libido** that motivates all behavior. It operates according to the **pleasure principle**, seeking immediate gratification of all instinctive drives—regardless of reason, logic, or the probable impact of the behaviors it motivates. Freud believed that only the id is present at birth; thus a newborn's behaviors are dominated by the id. This viewpoint has a ring of truth for anyone who has observed a hungry infant's demanding cry for attention regardless of what important tasks Mom or Dad is engaged in.

The id cannot tolerate any tension, and so it seeks immediate gratification. However, since it operates at an essentially unconscious level, it is not able to interact effectively with external reality to achieve gratification. The newborn is largely helpless, driven by basic instincts but dependent on others for fulfilling these needs. Freud believed that the id seeks to discharge tension by conjuring up mental images of the object it desires. Thus a hungry baby might form an internal image of the mother's breast, or we might have dreams about sex. Freud called this wish-fulfilling mental imagery **primary process thinking.**

In sum, the id is the storehouse of largely unconscious, biologically based, instinctive drives that provide the basic energy source for the entire personality system. It is also the foundation from which the ego and superego later evolve.

THE EGO A newborn's world is not designed to serve his or her every need. No matter how much a baby cries or carries on, a mother's breast or a bottle does not always appear magically. Thus infants soon come to realize that immediate gratification is not always possible. According to Freud, such discoveries prompt the development of the **ego** as an outgrowth of the id. The ego develops gradually as the infant learns to cope with the real world. It functions as an intermediary between the instinctual demands of the id and the reality of the world. Freud's concept of the ego explained how the id-dominated infant who might lie helplessly crying for food gradually evolves into a toddler who is able to reach into the cookie jar or say the word "milk."

The ego operates according to the **reality principle.** That is, it seeks to satisfy the id's wants and needs in ways that are consistent with reality. To accomplish

TABLE 14.1 *Mental Structure According to Freud*

STRUCTURE	CONSCIOUSNESS	CONTENTS AND FUNCTION
Id	Unconscious	Basic impulses (sex and aggression); seeks immediate gratification regardless of consequences; impervious to reason and logic; immediate, irrational, impulsive.
Ego	Predominantly conscious	Executive mediating between id impulses and superego inhibitions; tests reality; seeks safety and survival; rational, logical taking account of space and time.
Superego	Both conscious and unconscious	Ideals and morals; strives for perfection; observes, dictates, criticizes, and prohibits; imposes limitations on satisfactions; becomes the conscience of the individual.

this goal, the ego must be largely conscious and in direct contact with the external world. Furthermore, to carry out its executive functions of screening the id's impulses, the ego system must include our abilities to perceive, think, learn, and remember. Thus what psychologists now call cognitive processes were considered by Freud to be functions of the ego.

THE SUPEREGO In the early years of life, the ego only needs to check external reality to determine whether a particular id impulse may be expressed: Morality has no influence at all. Thus if a toddler is hungry and a freshly baked cake that Mom baked for the school fund-raiser is within reach, the outcome is predictable even though such behavior is "wrong."

As the infant becomes a child, however, Freud theorized that a third system of personality emerges. The **superego** is a composite of the moral values and standards of parents and society that we incorporate into our personalities as we develop. While the id is driven to seek pleasure and the ego to test reality, the superego is concerned with striving for perfection. The superego makes the task of the ego much harder by forcing it to consider not just what is real, but also what is right.

According to Freud, the superego includes two distinct subsystems. The first, the *conscience*, consists of the moral inhibitions or "should nots" of behavior that stem from punishment (either parental punishment or punishing ourselves through guilt). The second subsystem, the *ego-ideal*, is the "shoulds" of behavior for which we receive approval and/or reinforcement, and to which we aspire. Freud believed that emotions such as guilt and pride are essential in the functioning of our superegos. He particularly emphasized the role of guilt both in inhibiting id impulses and in contributing to many personality disorders.

The superego, then, is the moral arm of personality that tries to prevent the id from expressing its primitive impulses. Even though the superego shares some characteristics with the id (for instance, it is nonrational) and the ego (it is controlling), it nevertheless stands in opposition to both of them. Unlike the ego, which merely suppresses the id long enough to find a rational way to satisfy its needs, the superego tries to block id impulses totally. In this sense, it is the original "spoilsport." If the superego is too successful in its task, the end result is a rigid, guilt-ridden, inhibited personality. But if the superego consistently plays a weak hand, the result is a self-centered, self-indulgent, antisocial personality.

PERSONALITY DYNAMICS

Personality theorists use the term *dynamics* to refer to the forces that shape personality. According to Freud, the dynamics of personality reside in the continuous interaction and clash between the impulse-driven id, the guilt-inducing superego, and the ego, which acts as mediator by reconciling reality with the demands of both the id and the superego. The interplay among these personality forces requires a delicate balance that is difficult to achieve. No matter how well we have adjusted to external reality and integrated a system of morality into our daily lives, Freud maintained that the id's primitive urges inevitably create conflicts that upset this balance. A severe breakdown of this balance may result in various forms of behavioral disorders, such as amnesia, paralysis, or blindness — just the kinds of symptoms that aroused Freud's interest in the first place.

When the ego is faced with conflicts that threaten to disrupt the balance among the systems of personality, it sounds an alarm in the form of anxiety which, in turn, induces it to fall back on a variety of mechanisms designed to control this anxiety.

ANXIETY AND THE DEFENSE MECHANISMS **Anxiety** is a kind of free-floating fear with no easily identifiable source. Since its source is abstract, a person with anxiety cannot act to eliminate the cause, which is why anxiety can be such a devastating emotion. Freud maintained that anxiety stems primarily from an unconscious fear that our id will cause us to do something that will result in punishment or guilt. (In terms of the three systems of personality, the ego experiences anxiety when an impulse that is unacceptable to the superego threatens to be expressed in overt behavior.) When the ego is not able to relieve this anxiety through rational, problem-solving methods, Freud suggested that it resorts to certain less rational maneuvers called defense mechanisms. The purpose of the **defense mechanisms** is to shield the ego from some of the harsh aspects of reality (see Figure 14.4).

All defense mechanisms share two characteristics. They protect the ego from anxiety by denying or distorting reality and they operate unconsciously so we are not aware that a distortion of reality has taken place. Thus defense mechanisms are not subject to the normal checks and balances of rational, conscious reasoning — a limitation that causes people who are using defense mechanisms to be absolutely convinced of the correctness of their viewpoint.

People often assume that using a defense mechanism is a sign of weakness, or of a disturbed personality. According to Freud, all of us, well-adjusted and otherwise, use the common defense mechanisms in our everyday lives. Therefore, if you recognize yourself in some of the examples of defense mechanisms in the following paragraphs, do not conclude that you are "weak." Most of us occasionally resort to such defensive maneuvers. In fact, in some situations the ability to deceive ourselves by using repression or some other defense mechanism may actually be helpful (Goleman, 1987). Because they are beyond the reality checks of conscious awareness, however, the potential danger exists that one or more of these defenses may become habitual. We look here at a number of defense mechanisms, including repression, rationalization, projection, displacement, regression, and reaction formation.

Repression The ego's first line of defense against anxiety is often **repression.** This defense mechanism involves holding back or banishing from consciousness a variety of unacceptable impulses and disturbing memories. For example, you

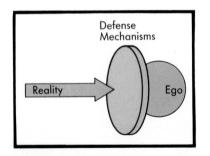

FIGURE 14.4

The Purpose of Defense Mechanisms

Defense mechanisms serve to shield the ego from the harsh aspects of reality.

might repress the aggressive impulses you feel toward a teacher or employer because these feelings are unacceptable and therefore anxiety-provoking.

Freud believed that all defensive reactions to anxiety first begin with a massive inhibition or repression of id urges: We first attempt to fend off anxiety-arousing thoughts and feelings by blocking them out. Repression is the most basic and pervasive of the defenses against anxiety, and it underlies all other defense mechanisms. Since the id has such an overwhelming number of disruptive urges, however, this primary defense mechanism is unable to contain them all. Thus we use other secondary defense mechanisms.

When we repress an impulse or feeling, such as hostility toward a parent, we block it from our conscious awareness because it is too painful or threatening to face directly. This mechanism is involuntary and we are unaware of the process. In contrast, when we *suppress* something, such as an urge to hit back after being slapped, we are fully aware of our impulse, and we voluntarily hold it in check. Although the end result of each process may be the same—namely, blockage of a particular behavior—there is a considerable difference between the two.

Rationalization   Another widely used defense mechanism is **rationalization,** in which we substitute self-justifying excuses or explanations for the real reasons for our behaviors. For example, the parent who severely disciplines a child with physical punishment may rationalize this behavior by invoking the old saying "Spare the rod, spoil the child." The real motive, however, may be to vent repressed aggression and hostility.

College students often rationalize their poor performance on an exam by stating that they had too many distractions to study adequately, that they had worked hard all semester and deserved a chance to have a little fun, or that they just could not get into the subject matter. What is the harm in these excuses? Not much, probably—as long as the excuses do not become a habit. After all, it would be a grim world if we came away from every unsuccessful event with a deep sense of failure. However, an overdependence on rationalization, or any other defense mechanism for that matter, may lead to serious problems.

Consider the case of a student we know who began and dropped an introductory psychology class four times. Each time he had a supposedly legitimate excuse. During one term, he had to drop out because his sick mother needed extra attention; another time financial problems caused him to lighten his class load so he could work longer hours. A look into his background revealed that quitting was a common occurrence. When this pattern was called to his attention, he denied that he was a dropout by choice; instead, he was a victim of circumstances, and it is likely that he truly believed in his own excuses. In-depth counseling revealed that the student had a deeply rooted fear of failure, and that he had been withdrawing from challenging situations to avoid the profoundly disturbing possibility of failing.

Projection   A third defense mechanism, **projection,** occurs when we reduce the anxiety created by our own unacceptable impulses by attributing these impulses to someone else. An example is the married woman who blames an extramarital sexual affair on the man who "led me on." In addition to allowing us to project our unacceptable impulses onto another, projection provides a mechanism for blaming others for our own shortcomings. For example, a student might project the blame for a poor exam performance onto a "devious professor who purposely writes ambiguous questions just to make students squirm."

Displacement   In the defense mechanism known as **displacement,** individuals divert their impulse-driven behavior from primary targets to secondary ones that will arouse less anxiety. Thus a student who does not want to risk expressing anger toward a professor may come home and pick a fight with his roommate instead.

According to Freudian Theory, displacement occurs when impulse-driven behavior, such as anger, is directed at a secondary target that arouses less anxiety. Perhaps you have found yourself directing anger aroused in one situation towards another.

Displacement can sometimes produce a socially valued accomplishment. When it does, it is called **sublimation.** Freud believed sublimation is a mechanism that provides a major impetus for the development of culture and the production of artistic endeavors. He suggested that Leonardo da Vinci's paintings of madonnas resulted from a displacement or redirection of da Vinci's impulse to achieve intimacy with his mother, from whom he had been separated in early childhood (see Figure 14.5). Freud also maintained that many repressed sexual

FIGURE 14.5

The Psychodynamic Transformation of Motives: Displacement in the Form of Sublimation

urges of youth, particularly those centered on masturbation, are transformed or sublimated into such socially acceptable activities as athletics, music, art, or horseback riding.

Regression   Sometimes people may attempt to cope with anxiety-producing situations by retreating to an earlier stage of development in an effort to recapture the security they remember. This defense mechanism of **regression** may be expressed in such familiar behavior as a child returning to the infantile pattern of thumb sucking on the first day of school or a newlywed running home to Mom and Dad after the first serious argument with the new spouse.

Reaction Formation   In **reaction formation,** the ego unconsciously replaces unacceptable impulses with their opposites. Thus a person with a barely controllable fascination with obscene literature and films may become involved in an obscenity-fighting group that actively reviews and censors sexually explicit literature and movies. In this fashion the id impulses may be expressed, but in a disguised form that is acceptable to the ego.

- -

Freud's experiences in conducting psychotherapy convinced him that personality is essentially formed within the first few years of life. He believed that most of his patients' symptoms stemmed from unresolved conflicts, particularly conflicts involving sexual themes that emerged in the early years.

FREUD'S VIEW OF PERSONALITY DEVELOPMENT

PSYCHOSEXUAL DEVELOPMENT   At the time Freud formulated his theory, it was traditional to view childhood as a period when sexuality remains unexpressed. Freud challenged this thinking, asserting that a child is very aware of the sexual pleasure inherent in body stimulation. His concept of this sexual urge was quite broad, dealing with several different parts of the body (called *erogenous zones*) that play key roles in the arousal and gratification of sexual drive. Freud theorized that a child progresses through a series of stages of **psychosexual development** in which the focus of sexual gratification shifts from one body site to another. The manner in which a child goes through these stages, said Freud, is a major determinant of the personality that emerges as development progresses. Table 14.2 summarizes these stages.

TABLE 14.2   *Freud's Stages of Psychosexual Development*

STAGE	TIME SPAN	FOCUS OF SEXUAL GRATIFICATION
Oral	Birth through first 12 to 18 months	Lips and mouth
Anal	12 to 18 months to age three	Anal area
Phallic	Age three to age five or six	Genitals
Latency	Age five or six to puberty	No focus—sexual drives unexpressed
Genital	From puberty on	Sexual relations with people outside the family

The first phase of psychosexual development is the **oral stage,** spanning the first 12 to 18 months of life. During this stage, the lips and mouth are the erogenous zone and the id's pleasure-seeking energies find an outlet in sucking, chewing, and biting. Thus babies suck not just because they are hungry, but also because they find such activity to be sensually pleasurable.

At some point during the second year of development the erogenous zone shifts from the mouth to the **anal area.** This shift coincides with the neurological development of the anal sphincter muscles, and it marks the beginning of the anal stage (12 to 18 months to age three). Freud believed that the nature of toilet training during this stage could have serious ramifications for later adult personality. (We elaborate on this point later.)

The third phase of psychosexual development, the **phallic stage,** occurs from the age of three to age five or six. During this time the focus of sexual gratification shifts to genital stimulation. At the same time, the so-called family romance may emerge in which a child feels sexual attraction to the parent of the other sex, and also experiences jealousy of the same-sex parent. Freud coined the term **Oedipus complex** to describe this reaction. He believed that most children find this situation stressful, so they resolve it by repressing their feelings of sexual attraction and identifying with the same-sex parent.

The fourth stage of psychosexual development, the **latency period,** extends from age five or six to puberty. Freud believed that sexual drives remain unexpressed, or latent, during this period. Finally, during the last phase of sexual development, the **genital stage** (from puberty on), sexual feelings that were dormant during the latency period reemerge in full force. Adolescents and adults seek to gratify these drives through sexual relations with people outside the family.

FIXATION   Freud believed that a child may experience an arrest in development at one of the early stages of psychosexual development as a result of exposure to too little or too much gratification. This phenomenon is called **fixation,** and it can influence adult personality.

Fixation at the Oral Stage   According to Freud, children thwarted from experiencing oral stimulation (sucking, biting, eating) may be inclined to eat excessively or smoke as adults. Frustration during the oral stage might also lead to a later lack of trust of others, or to certain aggressive oral behaviors such as verbal hostility. Excessive gratification can also affect personality, so that infants who are always given a bottle or pacifier may be overly dependent as adults, or toddlers who are subjected to very early and stressful toilet training (before adequate anal sphincter muscle development) may as adults be obsessively concerned with cleanliness and orderliness.

Freud never explained clearly the precise mechanism whereby fixation occurs, and few of the predictions stemming from this concept have been supported by research.

EVALUATING FREUD'S PSYCHOANALYTIC THEORY

Freud based his theory on his own analysis of his patients' free associations and dreams. Therefore, it is not surprising that perhaps the most serious shortcoming of Freud's theory is the difficulty in testing it empirically. As we saw in Chapter 2, a good scientific theory contains terms that may be defined operationally and is constructed in such a way that it generates hypotheses or predictions about behavior that can be confirmed or disproved by empirical tests. Freud's vague pronouncements about personality meet neither of these requirements, and terms such as "primary process thinking" and "oral dependent personality" are virtually impossible to define operationally. Although many experiments have attempted to prove or disprove Freud's basic ideas, the collective results have been ambiguous (Fisher & Greenberg, 1977; Ross, 1987).

Another difficulty broached by critics has to do with predicting behavior. Psychoanalytic theory provides no clear predictions about how a particular collection of experiences will affect personality and behavior. For example, punitive toilet training might produce a compulsively neat personality, but then again it could also result in an excessively sloppy individual. Freud did recognize this limitation of his theory, particularly as it related to predicting adult personality from childhood experiences. He admitted, "We never know beforehand which of the determining factors will prove the weaker or the stronger. We can only say at the end that those which succeeded must have been the stronger" (1933, p. 227).

Freud has also been criticized regarding the sample of individuals who served as the basis for much of his theory. Freud based virtually his entire theory on his observations of a relatively small number of troubled patients, primarily middle- and upper-class Austrian women. How might such a limited sample have influenced his theorizing? Think about this question for a moment before reading on.

Perhaps Freud's failure to appreciate the strengths of healthy personalities resulted in a theory that tended to emphasize the negative and irrational components of human behavior. Freud's patients were also the products of a sexually repressed Victorian society. Thus it seems likely that this group of people collectively experienced a far greater number of sexual conflicts than we might expect to find in a sample of contemporary Austrian or American people. Today, there is widespread agreement among Freud's supporters as well as his detractors that his theory placed far too much emphasis on sex as a dominant motivating force throughout life.

Another area of criticism is Freud's emphasis on the importance of early experience. As we saw in Chapters 11 and 12, behavior and personality are shaped throughout the life cycle. Freud did teach us, however, to recognize the importance of childhood experiences in molding personality and influencing our thoughts, feelings, and behaviors at later points in our development.

Freud also incorrectly assumed that women are inferior to men in a number of ways: sexually (because they do not have a penis and because they often lack the "maturity" to transfer their erotic sensitivity from the clitoris to the vagina); morally (because the Oedipus complex creates a more severe conflict in women than in men); and culturally (because women's weaker superegos result in less sublimation of primitive urges into creative endeavors).

All these criticisms are valid, and from the perspective of the 1990s it is relatively easy to recognize Freud's shortcomings. We must keep in mind, however, that Freud developed his theory in a virtual vacuum of data about human development, thinking, emotions, and social behavior. From this perspective, it is remarkable that several of his theoretical perspectives continue to be supported by mainstream psychology today. We have Freud to thank for the concept of the unconscious. (However, most modern theorists do not believe that the unconscious plays a much greater role than the conscious mind in shaping behavior.) We also must credit Freud for the understanding that unresolved conflicts are central to many behavioral problems; for making sexuality from childhood through adulthood a legitimate topic for psychological research; and for introducing the concept of defense mechanisms.

In all, Freud created a theory of momentous proportions that has irrevocably influenced our view of human nature. While few people today agree with all of Freud's basic premises, no one suggests that his ideas were anything less than bold, creative, and highly courageous, considering the cultural context within which he worked. We can expect that Freud's personality theory will continue to influence the views of future generations, primarily because psychology has emerged from years of storm and controversy over Freudian doctrine with the somewhat pragmatic conclusion that psychoanalytic theory "is not an entity that must be totally accepted or rejected as a package. It is a complex structure consisting of many parts, some of which should be accepted, others rejected, and the rest at least partially reshaped" (Fisher & Greenberg, 1977, p. 28).

OTHER PSYCHODYNAMIC THEORISTS: THE NEO-FREUDIANS

Freud was a very dynamic and influential theorist who attracted many students who were strongly affected by his psychoanalytic theory of personality. Some of these followers were highly creative, thoughtful individuals who, because of disagreement with some of Freud's pronouncements, eventually developed new interpretations of the psychodynamic forces that help to shape human personality. Freud's disciples and dissenters, or **neo-Freudians** as they were called, were in general agreement with Freud's basic interpretation of the structure of personality, his focus on the key role of unconscious forces in personality formation, and the importance of childhood experiences. As a group, however, the neo-Freudians agreed that Freud's theory placed too much emphasis on aggressive impulses and unconscious sexual conflicts, overstated the impact of biological determinants of personality, and failed to recognize the importance of social influences such as significant interpersonal relationships. Among the most influential of the neo-Freudians were Carl Jung, Alfred Adler, and Karen Horney. We briefly consider what each of these theorists added to the psychoanalytic perspective on human personality.

CARL JUNG   Carl Jung (1875–1961) was once one of Freud's most avid students as well as his good friend. However, over the course of a seven-year relationship, he gradually evolved from a staunch supporter to an outspoken critic of certain aspects of Freud's brand of psychoanalytic theory. Jung (1916, 1933, 1953) objected to what he considered to be Freud's overemphasis on sexual motivation. He also came to believe that the unconscious contains much more than repressed thoughts, feelings, and impulses. Jung distinguished between what he called the **personal unconscious**—which is akin to Freud's concept of a reservoir of all repressed thoughts and feelings—and the **collective unconscious,** a kind of universal memory bank that contains all the ancestral memories, images, symbols, and ideas that humankind has accumulated throughout its evolvement. Jung used the term *collective* to stress that the content of this part of the unconscious mind is the same for all humans. He placed particular emphasis on one key component of the collective unconscious called **archetypes,** which consist of powerful, emotionally charged, universal images or concepts of such things as *mother* (a nurturing figure) and *shadow* (similar to Freud's notion of the id, which Jung later equated with the universal notion of sin).

One other important contribution of Jung that has endured and been incorporated into mainstream psychology as well as popular language was his description of two opposite personality traits: **introversion** and **extroversion.** Introversion is expressed as shyness, reclusiveness, and inner-directedness (or preoccupation with the inner world of our own thoughts, memories, and feelings), whereas extroversion is manifested by friendliness, sociability, and interest in people and events in the external world. Jung maintained that all of us contain the underpinnings of tendencies to be both introverted as well as extroverted. A healthy person, Jung argued, could strike a balance between these polar opposite traits by maintaining an interest in things and people in the surrounding environment while not losing touch with his or her own unique individuality.

ALFRED ADLER   Alfred Adler (1870–1937), like Jung, also felt that Freud was mistaken in centering his theory around the concept of repressed sexual and aggression conflicts. From his perspective, the single most important driving force in shaping human personality is not striving for ways to satisfy sexual and aggres-

Carl Jung

sive urges, as suggested by Freud, but rather striving for perfection or superiority (Adler, 1917, 1927, 1930). This quest for superiority did not necessarily mean achieving social distinction or professional eminence. Instead, Adler conceptualized **striving for superiority** as a universal urge to achieve self-perfection through successful adaptation to life's circumstances, meeting and mastering challenges, and personal growth. Adler theorized that all people acquire feelings of inferiority early in childhood as a result of their small stature, limited knowledge, dependency on adults, and lack of physical and social power. He suggested that we learn to compensate for or overcome this perceived inferiority by striving to bolster our self-sufficiency and to develop our abilities as quickly and successfully as possible.

A pitfall encountered by some individuals in the course of personality development is the inability to compensate successfully for early feelings of inferiority, an occurrence that can result in the formation of an *inferiority complex*—an exaggerated sense of personal incompetence and weakness. Adler considered inadequate parenting, particularly in the early formative years, to be the primary culprit in the development of an inferiority complex. In this sense he agreed with Freud's emphasis on the importance of early childhood experiences. However, instead of focusing on such troublesome points as arrested psychosexual development, Adler noted the adverse impact of overindulgent or neglectful parents. He believed that the manner in which parents interact with their children has a profound impact on how successful children are in overcoming their feelings of inferiority by becoming competent human beings. Thus Adler anticipated a strong focus in contemporary psychology on the role of early social relationships as important shapers of human personality.

Alfred Adler

Adler asserted that people are inclined to behave in a neurotic or maladaptive manner because they have not been successful in overcoming feelings of inferiority. Personality disturbances arise when an inferiority complex erodes or blocks healthy striving for superiority. For example, Adler wrote about people who tend to engage in a kind of unconscious self-deception, or *overcompensation*, by acquiring power, financial status, impressive houses, and other superficial indicators of success as a way to cover up or conceal (even from themselves) their powerful feelings of inferiority.

KAREN HORNEY Karen Horney (1885–1952) agreed with Freud that childhood is very important in the formation of personality. However, Horney (1939, 1945, 1950) emphasized the social relationships of children, particularly their relationships with their parents; like Jung and Adler, she objected to Freud's preoccupation with sexual conflicts. Horney believed that a child's primary need is for security, which represents a human striving that is far more significant than efforts to resolve conflicts between the id and superego. Children who are fortunate enough to be reared in a home environment rich with love, caring, and good parenting practices will feel secure and thus be able to develop the positive aspects of their personalities. However, when children perceive their parents as being indifferent, harsh, disparaging, or erratic in their responses to them, they are likely to lose confidence in parental love and to feel alone, helpless, and insecure. This situation leads to a state Horney labeled **basic anxiety.**

An insecure, lonely child is also likely to feel deep resentment toward his or her parents, an attitude state labeled **basic hostility.** Understandably, most children are unable to express this hostility directly: Not only do they fear their more powerful parents, but they are loath to jeopardize their quest for the love they desperately need. The consequent conflict between need for security, arising out of basic anxiety, and hostile feelings toward parents may lead the child, and later the maladjusted adult, to adopt one or more of three distinct patterns of social interaction. In one pattern, *moving against* others, the individual attempts to gain some sense of security by achieving domination over others. A

Karen Horney

second pattern, *moving away* from others, is reflected in people who try to find a sense of security by rejecting their need for others, becoming aloof and withdrawn, and focusing only on themselves. Finally, a third pattern of maladaptive social interaction is *moving toward* others, exhibited by persons who are overly compliant and subservient in their neurotic need to please and gain affection and approval from others. Each of these ineffectual ways of achieving security is more likely to create interpersonal problems than to promote a lasting sense of being loved and appreciated.

In conclusion, psychoanalytic approaches have contributed more to psychology's past than to its present. Psychoanalytic theories are not useful scientific theories because they are often vague and lack the ability to predict behavior from specific past histories. They also fail in describing how past experiences affect future behavior. Psychoanalytic theories are discussed at length here because of their historical significance and because they are not emphasized in other chapters. In the next section we examine several contemporary theories of personality development.

HUMANISTIC THEORIES OF PERSONALITY

The humanistic personality theorists—so-called because of their emphasis on the unique characteristics of humanity and their rejection of animal models of behavior—emerged in the late 1950s and early 1960s as a third force in personality theorizing. This movement grew in part out of the humanists' dissatisfaction with the idea that personality is molded by either unconscious drives or the environment. The alternative view presented by the humanists is a much more optimistic interpretation of human nature.

Although the humanistic perspective encompasses a range of viewpoints, its theorists agree on several points. First, virtually all humanistic theorists agree that a primary motivation for behavior comes from each person's strivings to develop, change, and grow in pursuit of full realization of human potential (recall Maslow's concept of self-actualization discussed in Chapter 8). Second, humanists collectively reject the notion that personalities are significantly influenced by the kinds of basic impulses postulated by Freud and his followers. Third, humanistic theories also tend to be *phenomenological*, emphasizing a subjective view of reality as seen from the individual's own frame of reference. We can learn more about personality from understanding what it is like to be "in the other person's shoes," argue the humanists, than from objectively observing and analyzing what people say and do. For humanists, the "stuff" of personality consists of our own subjective, personal view of the world, including our attitudes, beliefs, and feelings. The theories of the two most influential humanists, Carl Rogers and Abraham Maslow, both illustrate these features.

ROGERS: THE CONCEPT OF SELF

Carl Rogers (1902–1987) began his professional career as a practicing psychotherapist in the late 1920s. Like Freud, his eventual emergence as a personality theorist was stimulated by what he observed in his patients' revelations. However, Rogers' reading was quite different from that of Freud. Instead of seeing people as driven by sexual and aggressive impulses, Rogers saw the inherent potential for good in each of us (1961, 1977, 1980). Through listening to his clients, he became convinced that the most enduring, driving force in people's lives is their constant striving toward self-fulfillment and the realization of their own unique potential. He considered this striving to be a positive, constructive force motivating us to engage in healthy behaviors that enhance our sense of self.

Central to Rogers' theory of personality is the concept of self, the basic core of our beings that glues the elements of our personalities together. The self is the central organizing, all-encompassing structure that accounts for the coherence and stability of our personalities. Rogers did not claim to have invented the concept of self—it was the Greeks who first provided us with the mandate "know thyself." What Rogers did was to sensitize psychology to the role of this ancient maxim in the evolution and expression of human personality. "At bottom, each person is asking, Who am I, really? How can I get in touch with this real self, underlying all my surface behavior? How can I become myself?" (1961, p. 108).

In response to the question, "Who am I?" Rogers maintains that we derive a self-concept, or image of ourselves, that determines how we perceive and respond to the world. If we see ourselves as being likeable and attractive, we are likely to approach the intriguing person we see at a party. If, on the other hand, we see ourselves as boring and unattractive, we are less likely to make overtures.

Rogers believes that the key to healthy adjustment and happiness is a consistency or *congruence* between our self-concept and our experiences. Thus, if you consider yourself to be likeable and easy to get along with, this image will be bolstered by your good relationship with your friends. The opposite is true when your experiences are not congruent with your self-concept. For instance, if you find one year that you cannot seem to get along with either your roommate or neighbors, you will probably feel anxious and troubled. In Rogers' view, such incongruence between self-concept and experiences is often an important factor in maladjustment. To regain a sense of congruence, you must change either your behaviors or your self-concept.

In addition to the interrelationship between the self and the outside world, Rogers suggests that all of us are possessed of a sense of the *ideal self*, what we would like to be. Just as maladjustment can be caused by experiences that contradict our self-concept, it can also be caused by a discordance between the ideal self and the *real self* (our perception of ourselves as we really are).

Since Rogers' primary endeavor was as a psychotherapist, he was involved in treating the maladjustment that results from a poor fit between either the self and external reality or the ideal self and the real self. His therapy strategy was to help people initiate behavior changes where necessary, and ultimately to come to know, accept, and be true to themselves. We say more about Rogers' therapeutic rationale in Chapter 16.

MASLOW: SELF-ACTUALIZATION

Abraham Maslow's (1908–1970) initial training as a psychologist was in the behaviorist tradition. However, early in his career he began to question the idea that human actions can be explained solely in terms of reinforcement and punishment. This attitude eventually led him to move in the direction of humanistic psychology, which he named the "third force" (with psychoanalytic theory and behaviorism being the other two forces) (1968, 1970, 1971).

Most of Maslow's life was spent developing and expanding a theory of motivation and personality that emphasized people's positive strivings toward intimacy, joy, love, a sense of belonging, self-esteem, and fulfillment of their highest potential. As we saw in Chapter 8, Maslow proposed that we are motivated by a hierarchy of needs (see Figure 8.1). When our basic needs for such things as food, warmth, and security are met, we are then motivated toward higher needs, first for love and self-esteem, and then, for some people, for self-actualization (the need to reach our own highest potential and to do the things we do best in our own unique way).

Maslow derived his ideas about human motivation and personality from the study of healthy people rather than from disturbed people observed in clinical settings. Perhaps it was his intense interest in creative, vibrant, well-adjusted people that led him to place a strong emphasis on such positive human qualities as joy, love, enthusiasm, creativity, and humor while largely ignoring other forces like guilt, anger, shame, conflict, and hostility. Maslow was influenced and inspired by his study of a number of historical and contemporary public figures whom he believed exemplified his concept of self-actualization. In 1950 he identified 38 people he assessed as having reached their fullest potential. This select group included a number of lesser known people Maslow knew personally, as well as many historical luminaries such as Ludwig van Beethoven, William James, Abraham Lincoln, Jane Addams, Albert Schweitzer, Albert Einstein, and Eleanor Roosevelt.

Maslow identified 16 individual characteristics of the self-actualized person. If you would like to see how closely you fit his conception of a completely fulfilled person, take a look at his characteristics as listed here. The self-actualized person:

Is accepting of self and others.

Takes a realistic, nonfanciful view of life.

Is inclined to appreciate people and new ideas, and is not inclined to view them in a stereotypical fashion.

Enjoys intimate and loving relationships with a few people.

Has a lively sense of humor.

Is disinclined to go along with tradition just for the sake of conformity.

Shows the ability to expand and improve the environment rather than merely adjust to it.

Is creative.

Has democratic values.

Is problem-centered rather than self-centered.

Is independent and able to function without being hindered by the opinions of others.

Is open and spontaneous.

Is inclined to seek privacy and is content spending time alone.

Feels a strong identification with the plight of all human beings.

Has the ability to separate means from ends.

Has a history of peak experiences (moments of profound intellectual insight or intense appreciation of music or art).

EVALUATING HUMANISTIC THEORIES

Humanistic theories of personality have inspired psychologists and laypersons alike to consider the positive dimensions of human personality. This approach provides a welcome focus on the healthy personality that has helped to broaden our perspectives on human nature. The humanistic view of the self or self-concept as a central component of human personality has added a valuable dimension in our understanding of personality. The current emphasis on fostering personal growth and a positive sense of self that we see in such diverse areas as counseling, education, child-rearing, and even occasionally in management policies is due at least in part to the pervasive influence of Rogers and Maslow. A number of valid criticisms have challenged the humanistic perspective, however.

One key objection has to do with the vague, subjective nature of many humanistic concepts. The humanists have been criticized for basing their theories on subjective, nonverifiable observations of people in clinical or natural settings.

Rogers' concept of *self* and Maslow's principle of *self-actualization* are both terms that defy objective, operational descriptions. If you cannot describe something operationally, how can you conduct empirical research to test its validity? The fact that many humanists are demonstrably unconcerned about putting their ideas to empirical tests does not add to their credibility among psychologists who value verifiable evidence. Critics also claim that a theoretical perspective centered on such nebulous concepts as self-perception, the individual's subjective assessment of the world, and the meaning of his or her experiences does not add to our ability to explain behavior. In the view of one pair of critics, "Explaining personality on the basis of hypothesized self-tendencies is reassuring doubletalk, not explanation" (Liebert & Spiegler, 1982, p. 411).

Humanistic theories have also been criticized for focusing so closely on the individual and the role of the self that they have largely ignored the impact of environmental factors in shaping behavior. Finally, a few psychologists have expressed concern that the humanistic perspective places so much emphasis on being in touch with the self, being true to the self, and striving to fulfill one's potential, that it promotes a "me first" philosophy that encourages selfishness and self-indulgence (Campbell & Specht, 1985; Wallach & Wallach, 1983, 1985).

Finally, the humanistic perspective evolved out of a dissatisfaction with scientific approaches to animal and human behavior (see Chapter 1). As a result, humanistic theories were not intended to be evaluated by experimental verification. Humanistic theories are inherently untestable because of the vagueness of concepts and the lack of detail about how behavior results from specific situations or needs.

BEHAVIORAL, SOCIAL-LEARNING, AND BIOLOGICAL THEORIES OF PERSONALITY

Whereas the psychoanalytic perspective looks to internal mechanisms to explain personality and humanistic theories look to the satisfaction of inner needs, behavioral and social-learning theories take a distinctly different approach. These theories emphasize the role of external events in determining personality. We look first at the behavioral position, then at the perspective of social-learning theory.

THE BEHAVIORAL PERSPECTIVE

We have discussed the views of B. F. Skinner (1904–1990) and other behaviorists in previous chapters, so it should come as no surprise that these theorists reject the psychoanalytic notion that internal forces are the primary instigators of behaviors. To the extent that an individual has identifiable characteristics, behaviorists maintain that they are merely products of external environmental forces in the form of reinforcement contingencies.

According to Skinner, we do not need to assume that a man is a nonstop smoker because he was fed irregularly during infancy. His behavior can be explained, says Skinner, by noting the contingencies of reinforcement that have been associated with it. Not only is it a waste of time to search for personality structures in the form of internal forces, argues Skinner, it may also impede our efforts to understand the true causes of personality.

> The practice of looking inside the organism for an explanation of behavior has tended to obscure the variables which are immediately available for a scientific analysis. These variables lie outside the organism, in its immediate environment and in its environmental history. (1953, p. 31)

To Skinner, our personalities are the sum total of our overt and covert responses to the world around us. Furthermore, our patterns of responding to the environment are a direct outgrowth of the contingencies of reinforcement we have experienced in the past. We are unique individuals because no two people share identical reinforcement histories. Thus from the perspective of behaviorism, conditioning (defined in Chapter 6) is responsible for the development of personality. The reason why two people act differently in the same situation is not because they have different traits, as trait theorists would argue, or because they have stronger or weaker superegos, as Freud would argue, but rather because of their unique histories of operant and classical conditioning. The behavioral position argues that explanations of behavior in terms of inner traits are not explanations at all since the traits themselves are descriptions of the behavior. Essentially, any trait theory of personality will be circular.

Skinner and other behaviorists challenge the notion that enduring traits are evidence of some underlying behavioral predisposition, as trait theorists would claim. Instead, they suggest that the reason some so-called traits appear to be stable is because the environment is itself relatively stable: People are often subjected to a consistent pattern of reinforcement contingencies. As we saw in Chapter 6, relatively simple schedules of reinforcement can produce remarkably stable behavior patterns.

On the other hand, if sufficient changes are made in the environment (either the contingencies of reinforcement are changed or eliminated), the behaviorists note that certain enduring aspects of personality may undergo dramatic change. For example, suppose you become the new foster parent of an 11-year-old boy who is submissive and *introverted* (socially withdrawn and emotionally reserved). You check with the child welfare agency who placed the child with you, and find that these behavioral patterns were first noted in his case file record several years ago. Does this history mean you should expect these qualities to endure?

The behavioral view says no: If you change the boy's environment by reinforcing even the slightest indications of sociability (for instance, smiling at you) and assertiveness (such as his meekly saying he likes his eggs scrambled rather than fried), you will probably be able to increase the frequency of these behaviors gradually, using the operant principle of shaping (see Chapter 6). These environmental modifications are likely to change his personality by replacing his introversion and submissiveness with more sociable and assertive behavior patterns. As we shall see in Chapter 16, some of the most effective methods for changing the behaviors of unhealthy personalities and behavior patterns have evolved out of the behavioral approach.

THE SOCIAL-LEARNING PERSPECTIVE

Like the behaviorists, social-learning theorists believe that external events are important determiners of personality. However, they part company with Skinner and other behaviorists on the issue of cognitive processes. Whereas Skinner asserts that internal cognitive processes such as thinking, perceiving, and feeling are not causes of behavior and personality, social-learning theorists emphasize our cognitive interpretations of external events to fit our memories, beliefs, and expectations.

A basic tenet of the social-learning approach is that cognitive processes greatly influence the molding of personality by mediating between external environmental events and behavior. Thus, unlike the more traditional behavioral approach, the social-learning perspective stresses the role of our thoughts, perceptions, and feelings in acquiring and maintaining our behavior patterns (which in the final analysis represent our personalities). Thus, instead of emphasizing how we are controlled by our environments, social-learning theory focuses on the interaction between cognition and environment in shaping personality.

Because of its emphasis on cognitive processes, the social-learning approach is sometimes referred to as the *social-cognitive perspective.* The following paragraphs outline the key tenets of Albert Bandura, the most influential representative of this perspective.

BANDURA'S SOCIAL-COGNITIVE PERSPECTIVE Albert Bandura (b. 1925) is perhaps the most eloquent spokesman for the viewpoint that observational learning strongly influences our behaviors (1982, 1983, 1986). Recall from Chapter 6 that observational learning is the process whereby we learn patterns of behavior simply by observing people *(models)*. This process allows us to acquire cognitive representations of the behaviors of others, which may then serve as models for our own actions. Bandura maintains that throughout both childhood and adulthood, our observations of which behaviors are rewarded and which are punished or ignored provide us with many such cognitive representations. Accordingly, our own consistent patterns of responding to various situations—in other words, our personality styles—reflect our observational learning.

Bandura has conducted numerous experiments which he believes demonstrate that children may learn "personality traits" through observation. Chapter 6 discussed his famous BoBo doll study, which demonstrated that children displayed increased aggression after observing an aggressive model. Another of Bandura's more interesting experiments concerned the ability to delay gratification, a propensity that many people would consider to be a basic personality trait.

Bandura and Walter Mischel (1965) conducted an experiment with nine and 10 year olds to find out whether this trait can be manipulated by observational learning. The experimenters wanted to see if they could modify children's inclinations to prefer immediate or delayed gratification by exposing them to adult models. Their first step was to determine each subject's preference for high or low delay of reinforcement. They provided each child with a series of test situations in which they could choose between small, immediate reinforcers or larger payoffs that they had to wait for. The next step was to assign a child to one of three conditions: a live adult that modeled behavior opposite to the child's demonstrated preference; a symbolic model (written information) supporting a contrary position; or no model at all. After this phase was completed, the children's preferences were again evaluated by a second series of test situations. Finally, one month later their preferences were again evaluated to see if any effects of the modeling persisted.

The results, presented in Figure 14.6, reveal that both live and symbolic models were effective in causing children to change their preferences, and that these personality changes tended to persist for at least a month. Of added interest is recent evidence that children who delay gratification in certain laboratory settings (in contrast to those who prefer immediate reinforcement) tend to develop into more cognitively and socially competent adolescents (Mischel et al., 1989).

Albert Bandura

FIGURE 14.6

Models as Agents of Change for a Personality Trait

Graph A demonstrates the average change of response in children who initially preferred immediate reinforcement. Graph B shows average change of response in children who initially preferred delayed rewards. Both live and symbolic models were effective in bringing about change in behavior.

SOURCE: Bandura & Mischel, 1965

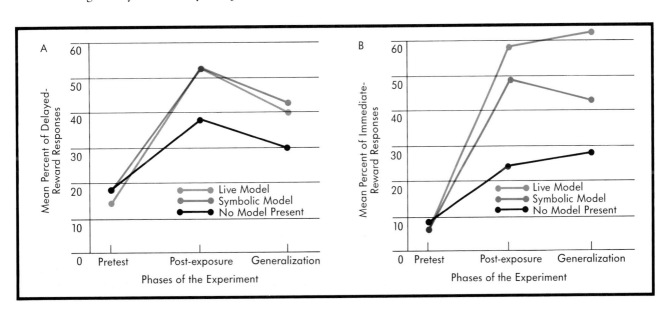

Another keystone of Bandura's social-cognitive perspective is his concept of **reciprocal determinism.** According to this principle, our behaviors and thus our personalities are shaped by the interaction between cognitive factors (such as thoughts, feelings, and perceptions) and environmental factors. For example, our response to first meeting our sweetheart's family is likely to be influenced not only by environmental factors (such as whether we meet at their home or in an environment with which we are familiar, such as the campus) but also by personal-cognitive factors such as our past experiences meeting strangers, our degree of anxiety about making a good impression, and our sense of self-worth.

Each of these two sets of factors can influence and change the other, and the direction of change is typically reciprocal rather than one-way. If we have a history of reinforcing experiences of meeting people for the first time, we are likely to perceive our present situation in a positive way and thus act in a sociable manner. Our actions might also have a decided effect on the environment—for instance, if our sweetheart's parents are so charmed by our friendliness that they quickly shift from aloofness to warm sociability. Thus environmental stimuli, internal cognitive factors, and behavior all operate as reciprocal determinants of each other.

One final element of the social-cognitive perspective deserves mention. In recent years Bandura has made the concept of self-efficacy a central component of his theory. **Self-efficacy** is described as our belief that we can perform adequately and deal effectively with a particular situation. Bandura believes that our sense of self-efficacy greatly influences personality development by affecting whether or not we will even try to behave in a certain way. For example, if we think that we are socially inept and boring, we are inclined to avoid social interactions with people. This behavior may cause others to view us as aloof or withdrawn, even further reducing our sense of social self-efficacy.

The concept of self-efficacy is sometimes confused with self-esteem, but Bandura does not equate the two. He views self-efficacy as a collection of specific evaluations that we make about our sense of adequacy in a variety of situations. Thus a person who feels socially inept may at the same time have a strong sense of artistic self-efficacy.

Self-efficacy arises from a variety of experiences, including our past successes or failures, our observations of the performances of others ("Gee, I think I can do that" or "That looks too hard for me"), and our own particular feelings as we contemplate a task. (Anxiety or depression lowers self-efficacy; excitement and anticipation tend to elevate expectations of good performances.)

Besides influencing what activities or situations we become involved in, our self-efficacy judgments are likely to influence the amount of effort we exert. For instance, if you perceive yourself as a good student, you will probably be more likely to persist in your efforts to understand a difficult intellectual concept than a student with a lower sense of self-efficacy.

In summary, Bandura's social-cognitive perspective stresses the reciprocal interaction between environmental conditions and our beliefs and expectations. Bandura views people not as slaves to environmental contingencies, but rather as individuals capable of assessing situations based on previous experiences, judging their own capability to deal effectively with these situations, and choosing their behavior accordingly.

EVALUATING BEHAVIORAL AND SOCIAL-LEARNING THEORIES

Both the behavioral and social-learning approaches focus on the important role of external events in shaping and molding our personalities. Bandura's social-cognitive theory extends this focus to include the reciprocal influence of cognitive behavior and external events.

An important contribution of behavioral and social-learning theories to the field of personality research is their emphasis on rigorous experimental research in testing personality theory. These two perspectives have helped foster a climate of empirical science that is sorely lacking in many other areas of personality theory.

Behavioral and social-learning theories have also provided important insights into why behavior may change from situation to situation, and why certain presumably enduring aspects of personality may not be so enduring after all. As we see in Chapter 16, the behavioral perspective has been the basis of some of our most effective models for altering dysfunctional behavior.

Behavioral theories have also received considerable criticism. As you might expect, much of this criticism comes from psychoanalytic and humanistic psychologists who emphasize the role of inner drives and needs in determining behavior. Other criticism comes from those who argue that personality is largely determined by genetics. Although Skinner and other behavioral theorists don't discount the role of genetic factors in personality, they consider genetic factors to be less important in determining individual differences in personality than environmental influences. In the next section we will examine some of the evidence for the heritability of certain personality characteristics.

In Chapter 13 we discussed at length the issues surrounding the **heritability** of intelligence. Do the same issues apply to personality? How much of our personality is determined by genetic factors and how much is determined by the environment? Think about these questions before reading on.

BIOLOGICAL DETERMINANTS OF PERSONALITY

HERITABILITY STUDIES WITH TWINS   As you might expect, there are no clear answers here either. Trait theorists like Cattell and Allport maintained that genetics played an important role in determining personality differences and numerous studies tend to support this view, at least for certain personality traits. In most heritability studies the contributions of genetic and environmental factors are estimated using statistical procedures that compare personality measures from two identical twins that are reared apart. For instance, in a study conducted by Tellegen et al., (1988) on identical (monozygotic) twins, heritability estimates on a wide range of personality measures ranged from 39 to 58 percent. In a similar study conducted in Australia by Heath et al. (1989), the heritability of traits for extroversion and neuroticism, in about 3000 identical twins, ranged between 47 and 53 percent. These values are similar to those obtained from more recent studies measuring the heritability of extroversion, activity, and task orientation in infants (Braungart et al., 1992).

How similar are the personalities of identical twins reared apart compared to those that are reared together? Several studies suggest that there is really no difference. According to Plomin et al. (1988) and Bouchard et al. (1990), behavioral dispositions like emotionality, sociability, and activity are no more similar in twins reared together than in twins reared apart. In both cases the heritability of these personality traits is approximately 50 percent. Furthermore, environmental influences on personality tend to diminish as twins get older.

What are we to conclude from these studies? Can we conclude that our genes contribute about 50 percent to many behavioral traits as these studies imply? From this discussion it would appear that much of human personality is determined by genetic factors.

CRITICISM OF HERITABILITY STUDIES   Many psychologists disagree with heritability studies that assume genetic and environmental factors contribute to behavioral dispositions, such as personality and intelligence, in an additive way (genes + environment). Rather, they argue that all levels of biological organization, including behavior, have a genetic basis that is expressed only through the interaction of genes with the environment (genes × environment) during development. From this perspective, beginning with the moment of conception, an individual's genes help to determine the developmental environment (at this stage it is the uterine environment) and this in turn helps to determine further genetic expression, and so on throughout development. In other words, behavioral dispositions do not just appear because they are genetically determined, they are nurtured into being as is every outcome of human development. There is little doubt among behavioral scientists that nearly every human characteristic has some genetic influence. The concern is that heritability measures are not accurate reflections of the ways genes and the environment interact to determine behavior.

THE ASSESSMENT OF PERSONALITY

In our overview of trait theories and the psychoanalytic, humanistic, behavioral, and biological perspectives, we have seen a variety of descriptions and explanations of human personality. Thus it should come as no surprise that *personality assessment*, the measurement or assessment of personality, has been approached in a variety of ways.

Indeed, personality assessment is far from an exact science, and the reason has to do with the difficulty in pinpointing the subject matter. If psychologists limited their interests in human personality only to those overt behaviors that can be directly observed, the task of personality assessment would be relatively straightforward. However, as we have learned, personality theorists are also interested in the unconscious mechanisms, behavioral predispositions, and traits that presumably underlie our actions. How can abstractions like repression, anxiety, introversion, dominance, the self, and self-actualization be measured? Psychologists have devised a variety of methods for at least obtaining glimpses of these seemingly intangible dimensions. We comment on how well they have succeeded as we outline four of the most important methods: behavioral observation, interviews, paper-and-pencil questionnaires, and projective tests.

BEHAVIORAL OBSERVATION

If you notice that a classmate always sits alone and appears flustered when a question is directed his way, you probably infer that he is shy and withdrawn. Similarly, if a roommate always remembers to deliver phone messages and clean up after herself, you may conclude that she is a responsible person. Virtually all of us develop impressions of people by observing how they act. This process is the essence of one personality assessment method, **behavioral observation.** The assumption underlying this technique is that personality is best assessed within the environment in which behavior occurs. This method is favored by behavioral and social-learning theorists who emphasize people's interactions with their environments. In their view, this technique is the best and most logical procedure for identifying the environmental events associated with particular types of behaviors.

Clinical psychologists, clinical social workers, and psychiatrists also use this method to gain insight into their clients' personalities. For example, a client's gestures, manner of speaking, facial expressions, and reactions to the clinician's questions can all provide important information.

As logical and practical as this technique may seem, however, it also can be misleading. Certainly all of us have discovered from time to time that our initial conclusions about people do not always hold up over time. For example, you might be surprised to observe your shy, introverted classmate talking animatedly and dancing up a storm at a party. Our observations of people can be misleading because they typically provide an opportunity to observe behavior in only a limited range of circumstances. The behavior we happen to observe in any given situation may not be at all typical of an individual's personality.

Can you think of any techniques that could make the behavioral observation method a more reliable tool for assessing personality? Take a moment to consider this question before reading on.

Psychologists sometimes go to considerable lengths to engage in more structured observations of behavior in a variety of situations. For example, a child psychologist interested in studying personality development in small children might observe a child's behavior in the natural setting of the classroom, playground, and at home with family. By carefully recording the times and places certain behaviors occur (such as sharing things with others, engaging in aggressive behavior, acting in a submissive manner, or displaying dependency behaviors), important information might be obtained about the role of the environment in shaping certain personality traits.

This more structured approach to behavioral observation improves the reliability and precision of measurement. But as we saw in Chapter 2, it is also limited because an observer's presence may influence the subject's behavior, and any one observer's interpretation of behavior may reflect his or her own biases. Furthermore, as a matter of practicality, any observer is generally able to sample only a relatively limited range of a subject's behaviors in only a few situations.

INTERVIEWS

Another valuable method of learning about an individual's personality is to ask that person questions. Freud relied heavily on the **interview** approach, and today it is used by advocates of all the theoretical perspectives we have considered, including the behaviorists. Interviews range from informal, unstructured exchanges in which an interviewer asks a few broad questions and encourages the subject to talk extensively, to much more structured procedures in which very specific questions are asked in a prescribed sequence.

An important advantage of the interview technique is its flexibility. If some questions are confusing, the interviewer can clarify them; their sequence can also be varied to meet the subject's needs. A competent interviewer can establish a sense of rapport that may encourage more candor than that produced by less personal assessment methods such as questionnaires. This technique also allows interviewers to delve into whatever areas of personality interest them. Unstructured interviews also provide the option of pursuing or dropping a particular line of questioning depending on the amount of useful information that is being produced. Furthermore, an interview allows an interviewer to assess not only what a subject says, but also how it is said.

The interview method also has its limitations (Anastasi, 1988). The basic data of interviews—what people say about themselves—is virtually impossible to quantify. As a result, what gets recorded are largely the interviewer's impressions and inferences, and these are subject to observer bias. Secondly, since there is no standard way of conducting an interview, an interviewer's personal style may significantly influence the subject's responses. The same subject may respond gregariously to a warm, affable interviewer but hold back information when interviewed by someone with a less approachable style. Extensive clinical evidence suggests that an interviewer's approach may also influence the subject. It is noteworthy that interviewers who have a strong theoretical perspective on personality may influence subjects to respond in ways that are supportive of the interviewer's position (Feshbach & Weiner, 1982).

QUESTIONNAIRES

While the observational and interview methods have strengths, neither is as standardized or objective as personality psychologists would like them to be. And while both techniques allow psychologists to observe what people do or say, there is always the concern that knowing how people behave may not reveal what they are thinking or feeling. To compensate for these shortcomings, psychologists have developed a number of **paper-and-pencil questionnaires:** objective, self-report inventories designed to measure scientifically the variety of characteristics or traits that make up personality.

Most paper-and-pencil questionnaires ask subjects to rate as true or false a collection of statements about their thoughts, feelings, and behaviors. Some of these questionnaires are designed to measure a very limited range of traits or only a single personality characteristic such as anxiety, self-concept, or introversion-extroversion. Others are designed to provide more global measures of personality. Two noteworthy examples of questionnaires are the Minnesota Multiphasic Personality Inventory and the California Psychological Inventory.

MINNESOTA MULTIPHASIC PERSONALITY INVENTORY   The best known and most widely used objective personality inventory is the *Minnesota Multiphasic Personality Inventory (MMPI)* (Hathaway & McKinley, 1942). Originally designed to help diagnose and classify persons with behavioral disorders, its developers started with a pool of 1,000 possible test-item statements describing mood states, attitudes, and overt behavior. These statements were drawn from such sources as existing tests and psychiatry and psychology textbooks. Following a test development procedure similar to that described in Chapter 13 (see "How Intelligence Tests Are Developed"), the researchers administered these items to a standardization group of approximately 200 psychiatric patients with a variety of diagnosed disorders and to 724 so-called normal individuals recruited from university applicants, hospital visitors, and residents of Minneapolis.

This procedure resulted in a final version of the MMPI that consisted of 566 statements about behavior, thoughts, or emotional reactions that subjects rate as "true" of themselves, "false," or "cannot say" (undecided about the truth of the statement). Examples of the kinds of items found on the MMPI include "I am basically a happy person"; "I believe people are plotting against me"; "Sometimes I disobey laws"; and "I worry a lot about sex." (These examples are not exact replicas of MMPI items.)

The MMPI is referred to as a **criterion-keyed test** because each of the 566 items is referenced to one of the original criterion groups that were used in developing the test—either the 724 nonpatients or the subjects who had been diagnosed as having a particular psychiatric disorder. For example, most people would respond "false" to an item like "I believe people are plotting against me." On the other hand, a person with a *paranoid disorder* (characterized by delusions of persecution and/or grandeur) would be more likely to respond "true." Thus this item is referenced to the paranoid criterion group. It is not possible to make a diagnosis based on just one item, so the developers of the MMPI used statistical procedures to group together items which clearly relate to a particular clinical condition or criterion group. For example, a paranoia scale contains items that people with diagnosed paranoia respond to differently than either normal subjects or subjects with other diagnosed disorders.

The MMPI contains 10 clinical scales designed to measure such conditions as depression, social introversion, schizophrenia, paranoia, and psychopathic personality. It also includes four validity scales designed to assess whether subjects have falsified or faked their answers. Table 14.3 lists all 14 clinical and validity scales on the MMPI.

TABLE 14.3 *MMPI Scales and Descriptions*

SCALE	ABBREVIATION	DEFINITION
Validity Scales		
Question	?	Corresponds to number of items left unanswered
Lie	L	Lies or is highly conventional
Frequency	F	Exaggerates complaints, answers haphazardly
Correction	K	Denies problems
Clinical Scales		
Hypochondriasis	Hs	Expresses bodily concerns and complaints
Depression	D	Is depressed, pessimistic, guilty
Hysteria	Hy	Reacts to stress with physical symptoms, lacks insight
Psychopathic deviate	Pd	Is immoral, in conflict with the law, involved in stormy relationships
Masculinity femininity	Mf	Has interests characteristic of stereotypical sex roles
Paranoia	Pa	Is suspicious, resentful
Psychasthenia	Pt	Is anxious, worried, high-strung
Schizophrenia	Sc	Is confused, disorganized, disoriented
Hypomania	Ma	Is energetic, active, easily bored, restless
Social Introversion	Si	Is introverted, timid, shy, lacking self-confidence

The MMPI is widely used for its original purpose of diagnosing behavioral disorders. Many clinical psychologists today find it helpful as an aid to the diagnostic process, and personality psychologists have also found it a useful source of information about the personalities of normal people. However, the MMPI has been widely criticized for a number of reasons.

First, some psychologists have expressed reservations about the original sample group of disturbed individuals because it was severely limited in both size and geographic representation. Recall that the standardization sample included only 200 disturbed patients, and that the normal group was drawn from a limited population within Minneapolis.

Of even greater concern are questions about the reliability and validity of clinical diagnoses of the original psychiatric sample used in standardizing the MMPI (Ross, 1987). Since the decision process by which these diagnoses were made has not been well documented, we cannot be certain that all or the great majority of the patients in these criterion groups were correctly diagnosed. To the extent that at least some members of the original patient population were misdiagnosed, the validity of the MMPI itself would need to be questioned. The MMPI has also been criticized because some of its items, particularly those dealing with sex and religion, represent an invasion of privacy, and because its excessive length causes at least some subjects to get sloppy in their haste to finish the process. In addition, low test–retest reliability has been a problem.

The MMPI has been shown to be a good device for differentiating disturbed from normal people, but it lacks the capacity to differentiate reliably between people within each of these categories (Kleinmuntz, 1982; Ross, 1987). This major limitation renders the MMPI less than useful to personality researchers interested in assessing individual differences.

In 1989 the first revision of the MMPI after half a century of use was released. The MMPI-2 employs restandardized norms in which 2,600 individuals from Minnesota and six other states now constitute the so-called normal or nonpatient group. These people were selected to represent the cultural and ethnic diversity in the United States as revealed in the 1980 U.S. Census. Consequently, the MMPI-2 norms are much more representative of the present population than the original norms. In addition, the MMPI-2 drops sexist language, cultural bias, and some questions about sex, religion, and bowel and bladder habits that were deemed too intrusive or offensive in the original release (Brataas, 1989). The total number of items has only been increased by one to 567 and the vast majority of core statements are unchanged, thus assuring continuity between the original and revised versions of the MMPI.

CALIFORNIA PSYCHOLOGICAL INVENTORY A few global personality questionnaires have been designed specifically for use with normal populations. Perhaps the most exemplary of this group is the *California Psychological Inventory (CPI)* (Gough, 1957, 1975). The format of this questionnaire is similar to that of the MMPI, and it also is criterion keyed, but here, the criteria are 15 "normal" personality traits: dominance, sociability, self-acceptance, social presence, self-control, achievement via conformance, achievement via independence, responsibility, intellectual efficiency, flexibility, socialization, femininity, capacity for status, psychological mindedness, and tolerance.

The CPI was developed by selecting test items from a pool of statements administered to people known to differ on some personality trait. For example, if an item differentiated between people known to have high or low levels of self-acceptance (based on self-reports and the ratings of others who knew them well), it was included in a final self-acceptance scale. In this manner, a total of 15 "normal" personality traits and three response-bias scales were included in the final instrument.

The CPI has a much larger standardization group (7,000 females and 6,000 males) than the MMPI, and much greater care was taken in controlling for factors such as social status, geographical locale, and age. Furthermore, in contrast to the relatively low test–retest reliability of the MMPI, the CPI has a test–retest reliability of approximately .90 (Ross, 1987). Finally, this questionnaire has been shown to have good predictive validity for a variety of purposes, such as predicting school and job success, leadership, conformity, and reactions to stress (Megargee, 1972; Ross, 1987). From an overall perspective then, the CPI is in many ways a more valid instrument than the MMPI, even though it is much less widely used.

PROJECTIVE TESTS

Paper-and-pencil questionnaires such as the MMPI and CPI are relatively easy to standardize, administer, and score because they are highly structured and empirically constructed. Their tight structure, however, can also be a liability, particularly because subjects must limit responses to "true," "false," or "cannot say." Partly in response to this limitation and partly out of a desire to tap unconscious thoughts and feelings, psychologists have developed projective tests.

Projective tests are collectively distinguished by a loose structure and unclear or ambiguous stimuli that allow respondents a wide latitude of response. Because the tests do not have obviously correct or socially more or less desirable responses, it is assumed that subjects "project" their own thoughts or feelings into their responses—hence the name projective tests or techniques. The underlying rationale, manner of development, and application of projective techniques is based primarily on psychoanalytic theory, which predicts that people will resort to hidden or inner processes to project structure onto ambiguous stimuli. A trained examiner then applies subjective clinical judgment to draw inferences about such dimensions of personality as unconscious conflicts, repressed impulses, hidden fears, and ego defenses. The two most commonly used projective techniques are the Rorschach inkblot test and the Thematic Apperception Test.

THE RORSCHACH INKBLOT TEST The **Rorschach inkblot test,** developed in 1921 by the Swiss psychiatrist Hermann Rorschach, consists of 10 cards showing ink blots, such as the one in Figure 14.7. Blots are presented to a subject one at a time in an order prescribed by Rorschach. The subject is asked to examine each of the blots and say what it looks like or brings to mind.

Scoring of the Rorschach is highly complex, involving extensive training in one of several systems by which the responses are coded, scored, and interpreted. However, all of the various systems agree that the major scoring categories for each response include its *location* (where the subject focuses attention), its *determinants* (color, implied movement, shading, particular form, etc.), and its *content* (human, nonhuman animal, or object). Various interpretations may be assigned to a subject's responses. For example, if a person focuses on only a small portion of a blot, this tendency might indicate that this person pays attention to the little details and likes things to be neat and orderly. A person who gives very unusual or unique responses might be considered to be overly concerned with asserting independence and individuality, whereas someone who gives many obvious and common responses might be considered to be conventional and anxious to blend in with the crowd. These interpretations are very subjective, however, and even the experts who work with the Rorschach all the time do not always agree on how various responses should be interpreted.

The fact that clinicians who regularly use the Rorschach often disagree in their interpretations raises serious doubts about its validity as a diagnostic instrument. One of the problems in assessing the validity of the Rorschach test is that most clinicians use it along with several other diagnostic procedures. Thus they typically interpret a person's Rorschach responses in the context of information obtained from such sources as interviews, family members, and other kinds of tests. As a result, it is very difficult to assess the capacity of this instrument by itself to provide valid personality assessments and accurate predictions of behavior. When researchers have attempted to study the diagnostic and predictive accuracy of Rorschach scores in isolation from other sources of information, they have found them to have little or no predictive validity (Kleinmuntz, 1982).

Despite this liability, the Rorschach continues to be a widely used instrument for clinical diagnosis and personality assessment. Many clinical practitioners

FIGURE 14.7
A Sample Rorschach Inkblot
What does this image make you think of?

point out that the validity studies are not a fair representation of the manner in which they use the Rorschach in their practices. They claim that the Rorschach is just one of many assessment devices they use to evaluate their clients, and as such it continues to be a valuable diagnostic resource.

THE THEMATIC APPERCEPTION TEST You may recall being introduced to the **Thematic Apperception Test (TAT)** in Chapter 8, where we discussed its application in assessing achievement needs. The TAT consists of 30 cards that depict various scenes and one blank card (a redrawn example is shown in Figure 14.8). While recognizable, all the pictures are vague and ambiguous. In the standard administration of the TAT, the tester selects 20 cards on the basis of the sex and age of the subject, who is then shown the cards one at a time and asked to describe what is going on in each scene, what the characters are thinking and feeling, what led up to the portrayed situation, and what its outcome will be.

Like the Rorschach inkblot test, the TAT is based on the assumption that when people are asked to respond to unstructured stimuli, they will reveal certain aspects of their inner selves that they normally keep to themselves. As one of the developers of the TAT observed, "The test is based on the well-recognized fact that when a person interprets an ambiguous social situation he is apt to expose his own personality as much as the phenomenon to which he is attending" (Murray, 1938, p. 530).

Formal systems for scoring and interpreting TAT responses are available. However, most clinicians tend to disregard these systems, relying instead on their own impressionistic, subjective assessments. Typically clinicians look for common themes that run through the stories (hence the term *thematic*). For example, if a person told several stories with themes of loneliness or isolation, an examiner might interpret this response as a sign of depression or alienation.

FIGURE 14.8

A Sample Redrawn from One Card in the Thematic Apperception Test (TAT)

After examining the drawing, write a brief description of the scene.

How valid is the TAT for clinical diagnosis? Many examiners use only a few cards that they think will be most productive in revealing aspects of a particular client's personality. This preselection compromises efforts to assess the test's validity because the clinician is likely to draw upon other sources of information in making the initial judgment about which cards to use. Furthermore, scoring tends to be highly subjective, based on an examiner's experience and clinical judgment which has already been influenced by knowledge of the subject. However, when the TAT has been used as a research tool in controlled experiments, it has demonstrated adequate levels of validity. An example is the research discussed in Chapter 8 that measured the relationship between need to achieve and various behaviors, in which the TAT was used to measure achievement motivation.

In all, although a wide range of methods are used to assess personality, none is without limitations. Most psychologists agree, however, that it is important to continue our efforts to understand the distinctive needs, values, and patterns of behavior that characterize individuals' adaptations to the situations of their lives. Therefore we can expect that personality assessment devices will continue to evolve.

In the next chapter we will continue with the topic of personality as we examine some of the most common personality and behavioral disorders. As we will see, the issues of definition, assessment, and genetic versus environmental determination that we discussed in this chapter will resurface.

SUMMARY

DEFINING PERSONALITY

1. Personality is not an attribute that people possess in varying amounts. Rather, personality refers to the distinctive patterns of behavior that characterize each individual's adaptation to life situations.

2. We may best describe personality psychology as the study of individuals, their distinctive characteristics and traits, and the manner in which they integrate all aspects of their psychological functioning as they adapt to their environments.

TRAIT THEORIES

3. Trait theorists attempt to identify the behavioral traits that are the building blocks of personality.

4. Two approaches to determining personality traits are the idiographic approach, which defines traits by studying individuals in depth to determine the distinctive qualities of their personalities, and the nomothetic approach, which studies groups of people in the attempt to identify personality traits that tend to appear in clusters.

5. Allport's application of the idiographic approach led to a description of three types of traits that operate to produce an individual's unique personality structure. A cardinal trait is a dominating behavioral predisposition that provides the pivotal point in a person's life. Central traits are major characteristics of someone's personality, such as honesty or generosity. Finally, secondary traits are less enduring behavioral tendencies such as dress style preference.

6. Cattell's nomothetic approach has yielded a list of 16 primary or source traits which he considers to be the center or core of

personality. He lists each of these traits as a pair of polar opposites, such as trusting versus suspicious.

7. Critics of trait theories maintain that traits are only descriptions, not explanations, that so-called personality traits may be situationally dependent, and that trait theories offer essentially no understanding of how personality develops.

PSYCHOANALYTIC THEORY

8. Freud's psychoanalytic theory of personality evolved from his attempts to explain certain recurrent themes that emerged from his psychoanalysis of patients.

9. The psychoanalytic theory of personality depicts people as shaped by ongoing conflict between their primary drives, particularly sex and aggression, and the social pressures of civilized society. Freud also theorized that early childhood experiences play a major role in molding personality.

10. According to Freud, the dynamics of personality reside in the continuous interactions of the impulse-driven id, the guilt-inducing superego, and the ego, which acts as mediator by reconciling reality with the demands of both the id and the superego.

11. Freud maintained that the ego experiences anxiety when an impulse that is unacceptable to the superego threatens to be expressed in overt behavior. When the ego is not able to relieve this anxiety through rational methods, it resorts to certain less rational maneuvers called defense mechanisms, which include repression, rationalization, projection, displacement, sublimation, regression, and reaction formation.

12. Freud theorized that a child progresses through a series of stages of psychosexual development in which the focus of sexual gratification shifts from one body site (erogenous zone) to another. During the first phase, the oral stage (from birth to 12 to 18 months), the lips and the mouth are the erogenous zone. During the second or anal stage (12 to 18 months to age three), the erogenous zone shifts from the mouth to the anal area. During the third, phallic, stage (ages three to five or six), the focus of sexual gratification shifts to genital stimulation. The latency period (age five or six to puberty) is characterized by unexpressed or latent sexual drives. Finally, during the genital stage (from puberty on), sexual feelings are expressed in sexual relations with people outside the family.

13. Too much or too little gratification can result in a child becoming arrested or fixated at an early stage of psychosexual development.

14. Criticisms of psychoanalytic theory include concern about the inability to define operationally and test some of its basic tenets, its lack of clear-cut predictions about how specific experiences will affect personality and behavior, its failure to appreciate the strengths of healthy personalities, its overemphasis on the importance of early experiences, and the inherent assumption that women are inferior to men in a number of ways.

15. The neo-Freudians were a group of individuals, originally disciples of Freud, whose disagreement with some of Freud's basic tenets led them to develop their own psychoanalytic perspectives on human personality.

16. Carl Jung's major contribution was his concept of the collective unconscious, a storehouse of universal images or thoughts possessed by all humans. Jung also provided psychology with the concept of two opposite person-

ality traits, introversion and extroversion.

17. Alfred Adler conceptualized striving for superiority as a universal urge to achieve self-perfection that emerges from childhood feelings of inferiority.

18. Karen Horney maintained that a child's basic need is for security, the absence of which can result in both anxiety and an attitude of hostility toward parents.

HUMANISTIC THEORIES OF PERSONALITY

19. The humanistic personality theorists agree that a primary motivation for behavior comes from each person's strivings to develop, change, and grow in pursuit of the full realization of human potential.

20. Central to Rogers' theory of personality is the concept of the self, the basic core of our being which is the central organizing, all-encompassing structure that accounts for the coherence and stability of our personalities.

21. Rogers believes that the key to healthy adjustment and happiness is a consistency or congruence between our self-concept and our experiences.

22. Maslow's theory of motivation and personality emphasizes people's positive strivings toward intimacy, joy, love, a sense of belonging, self-esteem, and fulfillment of their highest potential.

23. Critics have objected to the vague, subjective nature of many humanistic concepts, and the humanists have been criticized for basing theories on subjective, nonverifiable observations of people in clinical or natural settings. The humanists have also been criticized for focusing so closely on the individual and the role of the self that they have

largely ignored the impact of environmental factors in shaping behavior.

BEHAVIORAL, SOCIAL-LEARNING, AND BIOLOGICAL THEORIES OF PERSONALITY

24. According to the behavioral position, our personalities are characterized by the sum total of our overt and covert responses to the world around us. Personalities do not cause our behavior, rather they are descriptions of our behavior.

25. From the perspective of behaviorism, each person's own unique history of operant and classical conditioning is the major contributer to the development of his or her unique personality.

26. Social-learning theorists also believe that external events are important determiners of personality. However, unlike traditional behaviorists, social-learning theorists emphasize our cognitive interpretations of external events to fit our memories, beliefs, and expectations.

27. According to Bandura, our own consistent patterns of responding to various situations—in other words, our personality styles—reflect our observational learning (the process whereby we learn patterns of behavior simply by observing people).

28. Another keystone of Bandura's social-cognitive perspective is his concept of reciprocal determinism, which suggests that our personalities are shaped by the interaction between cognitive factors and environmental factors.

29. Bandura also believes that self-efficacy, or our belief that we can perform adequately and deal effectively with situations, greatly influences personality development by affecting whether or not we will even try to behave in a certain way.

30. Heritability studies suggest that there is a strong genetic determinism for personality.
31. Critics of heritability studies argue that, because genetic and environmental factors interact throughout development, parsing out genetic contributions to personality is misleading.

THE ASSESSMENT OF PERSONALITY

32. Four of the most important methods for assessing personality include behavioral observations, interviews, paper-and-pencil questionnaires, and projective tests.
33. The assumption underlying behavioral observation is that personality is best assessed within the environment in which behavior occurs. Limitations of this method include the fact that an observer's presence may influence the subject's behavior, and that any one observer's interpretations of behavior may reflect his or her own biases. To remedy these shortcomings, psychologists employ rating scales that several people who know a subject can use to indicate the degree to which particular traits are evident in her or his personality.
34. Interviews, which range from informal, unstructured exchanges to much more structured procedures, have the important advantage of flexibility (questions can be clarified, sequence varied, etc.). However, it is virtually impossible to quantify the basic data of the interviewer's impressions and inferences, both of which are subject to observer bias.
35. Paper-and-pencil questionnaires are objective self-report inventories that typically ask subjects to rate as true or false a collection of statements about their thoughts, feelings, and behaviors.
36. The best known and most widely used objective personality inventory is the Minnesota Multiphasic Personality Inventory (MMPI), which is designed to measure a variety of clinical conditions such as depression and paranoia. The MMPI is widely used for diagnosing psychological disorders. Criticisms of the MMPI concern its original standardization group, its reliability and validity, and its tendency to invade the privacy of the test taker. MMPI-2, the first revision of the original MMPI, employs restandardized norms that are more representative of the present population than the original norms.
37. The most exemplary of the global personality questionnaires designed for use with normal populations is the California Psychological Inventory (CPI), which is designed to measure 15 so-called normal personality traits, such as sociability and self-control. This questionnaire has been shown to have good predictive validity for a variety of purposes, such as predicting school and job success.
38. Projective tests are collectively distinguished by a loose structure and ambiguous stimuli that allow respondents to project their own thoughts or feelings into their responses.
39. The Rorschach inkblot test, which consists of 10 cards showing inkblots, has little or no predictive validity when considered in isolation from other sources of information.
40. The Thematic Apperception Test (TAT), which consists of a series of cards that depict various scenes, allows clinicians to look for common themes that run through the stories subjects tell about each scene. When the TAT has been used as a research tool in controlled experiments, it has demonstrated adequate validity.

personality
cardinal trait
central trait
secondary trait
surface trait
source trait
free association
unconscious
psychoanalysis
psychoanalytic theory
id
libido
pleasure principle
primary process thinking
ego
reality principle
superego
anxiety
defense mechanisms
repression
rationalization
projection
displacement
sublimation
regression
reaction formation
psychosexual development

oral stage
anal stage
phallic stage
Oedipus complex
latency period
genital stage
fixation
neo-Freudians
personal unconscious
collective unconscious
archetypes
introversion
extroversion
striving for superiority
basic anxiety
basic hostility
reciprocal determinism
self-efficacy
heritability
behavioral observation
interview
paper-and-pencil questionnaire
criterion-keyed test
projective test
Rorschach inkblot test
Thematic Apperception Test (TAT)

CHAPTER 15
Behavioral Disorders

CHAPTER 16
Treatment of Behavioral Disorders

PART 5

The Nature and Treatment of Behavioral Disorders

CHAPTER 15

Behavioral Disorders

DEFINING ABNORMAL BEHAVIOR

CLASSIFYING BEHAVIORAL DISORDERS

ANXIETY DISORDERS

Panic Disorders
Social Phobias
Specific Phobias
Obsessive-Compulsive Disorder
Posttraumatic Stress Disorder
Generalized Anxiety Disorder
Theoretical Perspectives on Anxiety
    Disorders

SOMATOFORM DISORDERS

Somatization Disorder
Hypochondriasis
Conversion Disorder
Theoretical Perspectives on Somataform
    Disorders

DISSOCIATIVE DISORDERS

Dissociative Amnesia
Dissociative Fugue
Dissociative Identity Disorder
Theoretical Perspectives on Dissociative
    Disorders

MOOD DISORDERS

Major Depressive Disorder
Bipolar (Manic-Depressive) Disorder
Seasonal Affective Disorder
Theoretical Perspectives on Mood
    Disorders

SCHIZOPHRENIA

Primary Symptoms of Schizophrenia
Subtypes of Schizophrenia
Theoretical Perspectives on
    Schizophrenia

PERSONALITY DISORDERS

Antisocial Personality Disorder
Theoretical Perspectives on Antisocial
    Personality Disorder

The letter in Figure 15.1 was written to the director of a state hospital by a patient who was being treated for a severe mood disorder (bipolar disorder). This patient made repeated attempts for release as well as numerous claims that his psychologist was a communist who beat and starved patients. Notice that, although there is evidence of distorted thought, the writing is mostly coherent and organized. The style of writing here is also characteristic of severe mood disorder in that it is forceful and directed off the page.

Figure 15.2 on page 564 represents a sample of doodlings made by a patient at the same hospital diagnosed with schizophrenia. Notice here that the writing is not very coherent and that there are numerous references to Christianity and sex. These kinds of references are not uncommon with schizophrenic disorders.

Although these samples of behavior are not sufficient for a diagnosis, it is not difficult to see that these patients are severely disturbed. In fact, when someone's behavior deviates extremely from the way people customarily behave or speak, no one would question labeling their behavior abnormal.

But what about the schoolteacher who functions well in his everyday life but confides in a friend that sometimes he hears the voice of his deceased child? Or the woman who becomes so melancholic in the winter that she spends most of her day sleeping. Or the person who seems normal but refuses to ride in elevators? Are these also examples of abnormal behavior? Defining abnormality is not always an easy task. There are shades of gray on the continuum from normal to abnormal, and it is often difficult to know where to draw the line.

Psychology and psychiatry have a long history of debate in the interrelated areas of defining abnormality and classifying behavioral disorders. However, after extensive discussions and many changes,

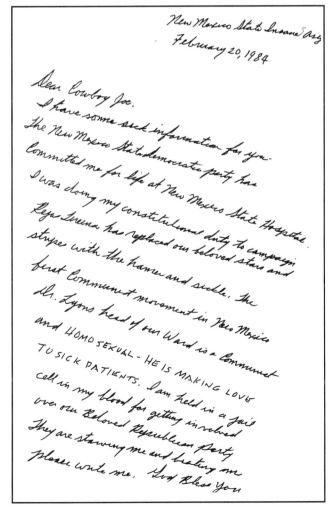

FIGURE 15.1

Letter from a Mental Patient to the Director of the State Hospital Where He Was Being Treated for a Severe Mood Disorder

clinicians are beginning to reach some consensus about what constitutes disordered behavior. In this chapter we first look at the criteria for defining ab-normality and the classification of behavioral disorders; then we look more closely at some specific behavioral disorders.

FIGURE 15.2

Doodlings Produced by a Patient Diagnosed with Schizophrenia

Note references to Christianity and sex.

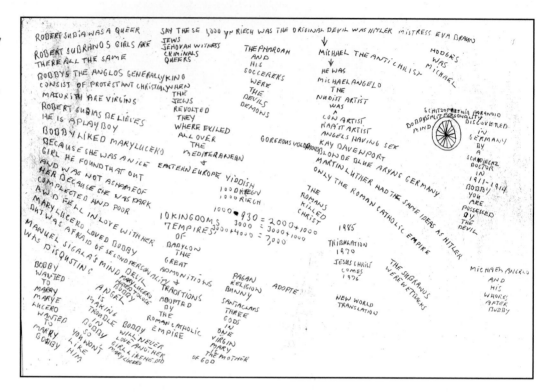

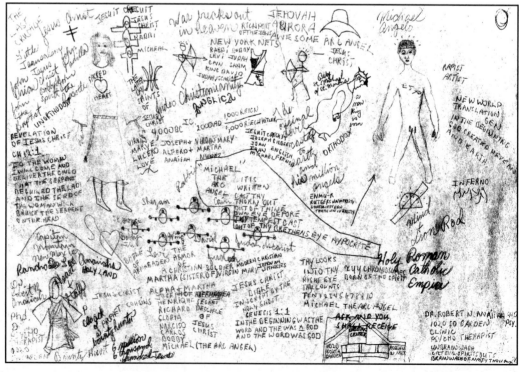

DEFINING ABNORMAL BEHAVIOR

There is no universally accepted definition of abnormality. However, psychologists who specialize in studying abnormal behavior tend to emphasize a common core of four criteria that may be used to distinguish between normal and **abnormal behavior:** atypicality, maladaptivity, emotional discomfort, and social unacceptability.

The behavior of the people described in the opening account is certainly *atypical,* and indeed all of the behavioral disorders that we consider in this chapter are atypical in a statistical sense. However, rarity alone is not a sufficient criterion for determining that a behavior is abnormal or disordered. If it were, we would have to conclude that people like Albert Einstein and Leonardo da Vinci were behaviorally disordered. More important from a psychological perspective is that the behaviors associated with behavioral disorders are often *maladaptive.* That is, the individual's ability to function adequately in everyday social and occupational roles is impaired. The degree of maladaptivity in behavioral disorders varies from relatively minor to so severe that a person may need to be hospitalized. Some psychologists believe that maladaptivity may be the most important criterion for distinguishing behavioral disorders (Coleman et al., 1984).

Despite the myth that severely disordered people are in their own little worlds that may be more comforting than the real world, people with behavioral disorders often experience a great deal of *emotional discomfort.* This third criterion may take the form of anxiety, depression, or agitation. Finally, the behaviors of behaviorally disordered people are often judged to be *socially unacceptable.* Few people would consider tearing up a hospital robe and screaming out the window to be acceptable behavior.

It is important to note that to a certain extent, definitions of what is normal are both culturally based and era dependent. For example, while we may consider talking to oneself or hallucinating imaginary visions to be clear signs of a serious behavioral disorder, these same behaviors are viewed by people in certain Polynesian and South American societies as indications of a great gift or special status among deities.

All four characteristics of abnormality are not necessarily evident in all behavioral disorders. Aside from the fact that they are all atypical or uncommon, any given disorder may reflect only one or a combination of the characteristics of maladaptivity, emotional discomfort, and social unacceptability. Specific symptoms also vary according to the disorder, and these symptoms form the basis for classifying disorders.

Talking to a statue might be considered abnormal behavior, particularly if it were to occur frequently.

CLASSIFYING BEHAVIORAL DISORDERS

The first widely accepted system for classifying behavioral disorders was published in 1952 by the American Psychiatric Association in the *Diagnostic and Statistical Manual of Mental Disorders*, conveniently shortened to *DSM-I*. This scheme, which listed the symptoms of 60 disorders, was poorly organized and widely criticized. An improved version, *DSM-II*, was published in 1968. DSM-II attempted to provide some definitive diagnostic categories, delineating 145 types and subtypes of disorders.

Both DSM-I and DSM-II divided mental disorders into two broad categories: neuroses and psychoses. Freud had used the term **neurosis** to describe anxiety disorders, and from Freud's time until the publication of the third *Diagnostic and Statistical Manual (DSM-III)* in 1980, the term neurosis was widely used to describe a range of behavioral disorders that are distressing and often debilitating, but are not characterized by a loss of contact with reality, severe thinking disturbances, or inability to carry on the tasks of daily living. The term **psychosis** was used to describe more severe disorders that involve disturbances of thinking, reduced contact with reality, loss of ability to function socially, and other bizarre behaviors.

DSM-I and DSM-II's general organization was widely criticized, mainly because extremely diverse conditions were grouped together under the labels neurosis and psychosis. Therefore, when DSM-III was published in 1980, it dispensed with these two broad divisions and used more specifically defined diagnostic categories instead.

In 1987 the American Psychiatric Association published a revision of the DSM-III (DSM-III-R) which provided even more precise behavioral criteria for diagnosing a broad array of behavioral disorders. DSM-III-R has been the most widely used scheme for diagnosing and classifying behavioral disorders throughout the world. In 1994 the American Psychiatric Association released DSM-IV which, like its predecessor, relied extensively on empirical research on the diagnosis of behavioral disorders. Some of the major changes found in DSM-IV include the reclassification of developmental disorders, the inclusion of a major category for substance-related disorders (drug and alcohol related disorders), and the elimination of the category Organic Mental Disorders which, according to the authors, implied that disorders not included within this category had no biological foundation. We have elected to discuss several major categories based on DSM-IV criteria in depth rather than summarizing all of the diagnostic categories found in DSM-IV. The behavioral disorders presented here include: anxiety disorders, somatoform disorders, dissociative disorders, mood disorders, schizophrenia, and personality disorders. These disorders were selected because they are among the most common of the behavioral disorders or because they are unusual and interesting.

It is possible that some of the behaviors described in this chapter may not be all that different from those of your friends, loved ones, or even yourself. Does this similarity mean that people you know who share some of these symptoms are disordered? Although we all have times when we are depressed, anxious, or somewhat disorganized in our thinking, the key to diagnosis of a behavioral disorder is the possession of a cluster of symptoms that are persistent rather than transitory. Therefore, do not be too hard on yourself (or your friends). It has been estimated, however, that as many as 70 million U.S. citizens now living will experience a diagnosable behavioral disorder at some point in their lives (Goldstein et al., 1986).

We end our discussion of each major category of disorder with an overview of theoretical explanations. Space limitations prevent us from considering them all.

Therefore, each discussion includes a brief summary of the three best known *etiological* (explanatory) perspectives: psychoanalytic theory, behavioral explanations, and biological explanations. Chapter 16 discusses therapeutic intervention techniques for treating behavioral disorders.

ANXIETY DISORDERS

Anxiety may be described as a generalized feeling of dread or apprehension typically accompanied by a variety of physiological reactions including increased heart rate, rapid shallow breathing, sweating, muscle tension, and drying of the mouth. Anxiety differs from fear in one important respect. Fear has an obvious cause, and once that cause is eliminated, the fear will subside. In contrast, anxiety is less clearly linked to specific events or stimuli. Therefore, it tends to be more pervasive and less responsive to changes in the environment.

We all experience occasional episodes of anxiety. For approximately one out of every 10 to 15 Americans, however, anxiety is such a pervasive condition that they are said to suffer from an **anxiety disorder** (Freedman, 1984; Regier et al., 1984). Anxiety disorders are the most common behavioral disorders in the United States (Gorman et al., 1989). Anxiety is also present in many of the other behavioral disorders we discuss in this chapter, but it is typically most pronounced in the various anxiety disorders.

DSM-IV describes several categories of anxiety disorders including: panic disorder (with or without agoraphobia); agoraphobia without history of panic disorder; specific phobia; social phobia; obsessive-compulsive disorder; posttraumatic stress disorder; acute stress disorder; generalized anxiety disorder; anxiety disorder due to a general medical condition; and substance-induced anxiety disorder. In this section we will not discuss anxiety disorders associated with a medical condition or those induced by drugs.

PANIC DISORDERS

Have you ever had an experience in which everything was fine one moment, and then for no apparent reason you suddenly felt an intense apprehension and overwhelming terror that caused your heart to pound, your breathing to become labored, and your hands to tremble? If your answer is yes, you have probably experienced a panic attack. There is good evidence that many people have occasional panic attacks. In one recent survey of over 2,000 college students, 12 percent of the sample had experienced at least one panic attack and 2.4 percent met the criteria for panic disorder (Telch et al., 1989). Two additional surveys of young adults, with sample sizes of 186 and 256, revealed that approximately one in three in each of these populations had experienced one or more panic attacks in the preceding year (Norton et al., 1985, 1986).

Having an occasional panic attack does not necessarily mean that you suffer from a **panic disorder.** DSM-IV stipulates that a person experience recurrent, unexpected panic attacks and that at least one of the attacks be followed by a month or more of persistant concern about having additional attacks before being diagnosed with panic disorder. The incidence of this disorder in America falls somewhere in the range of 1 to 2 percent of the population (Black & Robbins, 1990; Dilsaver, 1989; Karno et al., 1987; Telch et al., 1989). A recent research report revealed that panic disorder led the list of behavioral disorders for which people in five American urban centers sought mental health services (Boyd, 1986).

Panic attacks sometimes occur during sleep (Craske & Barlow, 1989; Dilsaver, 1989) and thus may be confused with sleep terrors (see Chapter 5), which also induce intense emotional responses. However, nocturnal panic attacks differ from sleep terrors in that the latter are typically followed by a quick return to peaceful sleep, with no later recall, whereas panic attacks are usually vividly recalled and are rarely followed by a quick return to sleep (Craske & Barlow, 1989).

The panic attacks associated with a panic disorder can be so overwhelmingly terrifying that a person may feel driven to attempt suicide. (Recently it was reported that people who experience recurring panic attacks are 18 times more likely to attempt suicide than people with no diagnosed behavioral disorder [Weissman et al., 1989].) During an attack, people may think they are going crazy or that death from a heart attack is likely. Sometimes an individual may have a sense of *derealization* (the feeling that the world is not real), or *depersonalization* (loss of a sense of personal identity manifested as feeling detached from one's body). Physical symptoms include erratic or pounding heartbeats, labored breathing, dizziness, chest pain, sweating and trembling, and feelings of choking and suffocating. The following account provides a vivid description of a panic attack:

> I remember walking up the street, the moon was shining and suddenly everything around me seemed unfamiliar, as it would be in a dream. I felt panic rising inside me, but managed to push it away and carry on. I walked a quarter of a mile or so, with the panic getting worse every minute. . . . By now, I was sweating, yet trembling: my heart was pounding and my legs felt like jelly. (Melville, 1977, p. 1)

In the majority of panic disorder cases seen by clinicians, the subject also exhibits symptoms of **agoraphobia** (American Psychiatric Association, 1987). Agoraphobia is characterized by intense fear of being in places or situations from which escape might be difficult or in which help might not be available in the event of a panic attack. Common focal points for agoraphobic fear are being outside the home alone or being in open, public places such as stores, theaters, buses, and trains. To avoid these situations, individuals with this disorder may stay away from all public places and, in extreme cases, become virtual prisoners in their own homes (Dilsaver, 1989).

Less commonly, individuals may suffer a panic disorder without related symptoms of agoraphobia (Gelder, 1989). Conversely, in some cases agoraphobia exists without any symptoms or prior history of panic disorder (American Psychiatric Association, 1987). The available data do not adequately explain why some people develop agoraphobia manifested as phobic avoidance behaviors while others do not (Gorman et al., 1989). Agoraphobia is but one of several kinds of **phobias,** disorders characterized by a persistent fear of and consequent avoidance of a specific object or situation. Individuals with phobic disorders may be terrified of spiders, snakes, heights, open spaces, being alone, or numerous other objects or situations. Although they usually realize that their fear is far out of proportion to any actual danger, this understanding does little to reduce the fear.

Phobias are among the most common behavioral disorders; approximately 14 percent of the general population have been estimated to have a phobia (Robins et al., 1984). This estimate is inexact, however. Since less than 10 percent of these phobias are serious enough to be considered significantly disruptive (Duke & Nowicki, 1986), most go untreated. A person who is afraid of heights may be more inclined simply to avoid climbing ladders or hiking along high mountain trails than to seek professional help. In addition to agoraphobia, DSM-IV provides diagnostic categories for social phobias and specific phobias.

SOCIAL PHOBIAS

A **social phobia** is a persistent, irrational fear of performing some specific behavior, such as talking, writing, eating, drinking, or using public lavatories, in the presence of other people. People with social phobias are compelled to avoid situations in which they may be observed behaving in an ineffective or embarrassing manner. Many social phobics are particularly fearful of interaction with authority figures such as teachers, employers, or police officers. Some social phobics have a poor self-image with regard to their physical appearance, and they may seek to correct what they perceive to be defects in their anatomy, even to the extent of undergoing elective plastic surgery.

A distinction is sometimes made between two forms of social phobia. One kind, called *discrete performance anxiety*, reflects fear of specific situations—such as speaking or acting—in which the individual must perform before an audience. This kind of social phobia is manageable in that the individual can lead a relatively normal social life by simply avoiding such situations. However, a performance-oriented social phobia can limit career options or professional growth. The second type of social phobia, *generalized social anxiety*, may impose more serious limitations by causing individuals to avoid all kinds of social situations in both professional and personal activities. Individuals with this phobia have difficulty making new acquaintances, interacting with peers and supervisors on the job, enjoying recreational pursuits with others, attending social functions, and so forth. "In extreme cases, victims fear contact with anyone outside their families" (Liebowitz, 1989).

SPECIFIC PHOBIAS

In **specific phobias**, the source of the irrational fear is a specific situation or object, such as heights, small closed places, various living things, (particularly dogs, cats, snakes, mice, and spiders), transportation (flying, cars, trains), thunder, and darkness (see Table 15.1). Although the specific phobias are the most common phobic disorders, they are also the least disruptive. Therefore, they are only infrequently seen in clinical settings.

OBSESSIVE-COMPULSIVE DISORDER

If you have ever had the experience of not being able to get a catchy, repetitive jingle out of your mind, or of needing to go back and make sure you have locked all the doors even though you are sure you have, you should have a sense of what it is like to have an **obsessive-compulsive disorder.** Here, a person's profound sense of anxiety is reflected in persistent, unwanted, and unshakable thoughts and/or irresistible, habitual repeated actions. Although the approximately 2.5

TABLE 15.1 *Some Varieties of Specific Phobias*

NAME	OBJECT(S) FEARED	NAME	OBJECT(S) FEARED
Acrophobia	High places	Monophobia	Being alone
Agoraphobia	Open places	Mysophobia	Contamination
Ailurophobia	Cats	Nyctophobia	Darkness
Algophobia	Pain	Ocholophobia	Crowds
Anthropophobia	Men	Pathophobia	Disease
Aquaphobia	Water	Pyrophobia	Fire
Astraphobia	Storms, thunder, and lightning	Syphilophobia	Syphilis
		Thanatophobia	Death
Claustrophobia	Closed places	Xenophobia	Strangers
Cynophobia	Dogs	Zoophobia	Animals or a single animal
Hematophobia	Blood		

Lady Macbeth repeatedly washed her hands after helping to murder the king. Hand washing is one of the most frequent compulsions associated with obsessive-compulsive behavior.

percent of Americans who have this disorder (Robins et al., 1984) usually know that their obsessive thoughts or compulsive actions are irrational, they still cannot block out their thoughts or keep themselves from performing the repetitious act, often an extreme number of times (March et al., 1989; Rapoport, 1989; Swedo et al., 1989). There is one report of a woman who washed her hands over 500 times per day (Davison & Neale, 1990). (The hand-washing compulsion which Lady Macbeth acquired after helping her husband murder the king of Scotland is one of the most common compulsions reported.) The senseless, repetitious behavior seems to ward off a flood of overwhelming anxiety that would result if the compulsive acts were terminated.

In the classic manifestation of this disorder, obsessive thoughts lead to compulsive actions. The following case illustrates this connection:

> Shirley K., a twenty-three-year-old housewife, came to the clinic with a complaint of frequent attacks of headaches and dizziness. During the preceding three months she had been disturbed by recurring thoughts that she might harm her two-year-old son, Saul, either by stabbing or choking him (the obsessive thought). She constantly had to go into his room, touch the baby and feel him breathe in order to reassure herself that Saul was still alive (the compulsive act); otherwise she became unbearably anxious. If she read a report in the daily paper of the murder of a child, she would become agitated, since this reinforced her fear that she too might act on her impulse. Shirley turned to the interviewer and asked, with desperation, whether this meant that she was going crazy. (Goldstein & Palmer, 1975, p. 155)

In the case just described, it appears that by constantly checking on her son's well-being this woman was able to relieve temporarily the anxiety caused by her thoughts about harming her son. Most people who manifest this disorder demonstrate the components of both obsessions and compulsions. However, about 15 percent of cases experience only obsessive thoughts that are not accompanied by compulsive acts (March et al., 1989).

POSTTRAUMATIC STRESS DISORDER

People who experience a profoundly traumatic event, such as an assault, an accident, or wartime combat, often exhibit a range of severely distressing symptoms as an aftermath to the occurrence. For example, a rape survivor may have vivid flashbacks of the attack in which she reexperiences all the terror of the assault. Many war veterans also have flashbacks of traumatic war experiences as an aftermath of their participation in that conflict (Faustman & White, 1989; Green et al., 1989; Paige et al., 1990; Pitman et al., 1990; Solomon et al., 1987). A similar kind of reliving the trauma often occurs among survivors of severe accidents. In one study, all 10 survivors of a plane crash that left 127 dead relived the tragedy over and over again in the form of dreams, nightmares, or panic attacks (Krupnick & Horowitz, 1981).

These symptoms are typical of **posttraumatic stress disorder (PTSD).** According to DSM-IV, PTSD develops after a person has experienced, witnessed, or been confronted with an event that involved actual or threatened death or serious injury. In response to this traumatic event the person must have also experienced intense fear, helplessness, or horror. Characteristic symptoms of PTSD include recurrent distressing recollections or dreams of the traumatic event, acting or feeling as if the traumatic event were recurring, and intense distress associated with exposure to cues related to the traumatic event (American Psychiatric Association, 1993).

Posttraumatic stress disorder differs from other anxiety disorders in that it can be explained largely if not solely on environmental grounds. An examination of the life histories of people who have conditions such as phobias or obsessive-compulsive disorders does not reveal a consistent pattern of background factors. In contrast, all victims of PTSD, while certainly different from one another in many ways, share experiences with a profoundly traumatizing event(s).

For instance, war veterans most likely to manifest severe symptoms of PTSD are those who are exposed to frequent, intense combat and/or who participate in atrocities such as the killing of civilians (Breslau & Davis, 1987; Green et al., 1989). PTSD has also been diagnosed in veterans who were prisoners of war (POWs). A recent follow-up study of 62 former World War II POWs revealed that half experienced PTSD after repatriation, and that 18 (29 percent) continued to meet the criteria for PTSD 40 years later (Speed et al., 1989).

GENERALIZED ANXIETY DISORDER

Generalized anxiety disorder is a chronic state of anxiety so pervasive that it is often referred to as free-floating anxiety. The anxiety is so omnipresent across a wide range of situations that many clinicians think it is fruitless to attempt to link it to specific eliciting stimuli. Thus the individual is unable to take any concrete avoidance actions to cope with it. This condition has been compared to what it must be like to be a soldier on the alert for attack: There is a constant sense of danger, but its source cannot be identified (Goldstein et al., 1986).

Symptoms of generalized anxiety disorder include restlessness or feeling on edge, being easily fatigued, difficulty with concentration, irritability, muscle tension, and sleep disturbances. According to DSM-IV, three or more of these symptoms must be present for the past six months for generalized anxiety disorder to apply.

THEORETICAL PERSPECTIVES ON ANXIETY DISORDERS

How can anxiety disorders be explained? Psychoanalytic theory, the behavioral (learning) perspective, and biological explanations all provide some insight into these disorders. We look briefly at each perspective.

THE PSYCHOANALYTIC PERSPECTIVE

Freud (1936) explained the anxiety disorders as a result of internal conflicts, particularly those involving sexual or aggressive impulses. Recall from Chapter 14 that Freud saw the ego's primary function as protecting a person from severe anxiety. It does this by mediating among the id's impulses, the superego's demands, and reality, often relying on the ego defense mechanisms. According to psychoanalytic theory, anxiety and the symptoms of anxiety disorders appear when these defenses are overused or rigidly applied, or when they fail.

This perspective explains generalized anxiety disorders as the result of unacceptable impulses that the ego has blocked. These impulses are powerful enough to produce a constant state of tension and apprehension, but since they are unconscious, the person is unaware of the source of the anxiety.

Phobias may occur if the individual *displaces* this anxiety to some object, situation, or social function which can be avoided (Nemiah, 1981). Consider one of Freud's most famous cases, that of a five-year-old boy known as Little Hans, whose phobic fear of horses kept him from going outside his house. Freud concluded that Hans' fear of horses was an expression of anxieties related to an Oedipal complex: He unconsciously feared and hated his father (whom he perceived as a rival for his mother's affections), and he displaced this fear onto horses, which he could avoid more easily than his father.

Psychoanalytic theory has a different explanation for panic disorders and agoraphobia. According to this perspective, these disorders may both be rooted in an unresolved separation anxiety (a fear of being separated from parents) early in life (Klein & Rabkin, 1981). People who have learned during childhood to protest intensely when they are threatened with separation from a parental figure may experience panic attacks later in life when they either perceive a threat of separation or actually experience removal of a significant other.

Still another explanation is suggested for obsessive-compulsive disorder, which is seen as the result of a fixation at the anal stage of psychosexual development. Freud believed that when children are subjected to harsh toilet-training experiences, they react with anger and aggressive urges that must be controlled if punishment is to be avoided. The persistent thoughts or repetitive behavioral rituals associated with this disorder serve to dissipate angry feelings before they can be translated into aggressive acts. The fact that compulsive behavior rituals often involve cleanliness themes lends support to Freud's contention that such neurotic acts reflect fixation during the anal period, a time focused on mastering "unclean" bowel and bladder functions.

THE BEHAVIORAL PERSPECTIVE   During the 1960s several behavioral theorists (Bandura, 1969; Wolpe & Rachman, 1960) carefully analyzed Freud's published account of Little Hans and noted that his phobic response occurred only in the presence of a large horse pulling a heavily loaded cart at high speed. They further noted that Hans' phobia originally appeared after he had witnessed a terrible accident involving a horse pulling a cart at high speed. Not surprisingly, these observations led behaviorists to a different explanation than Freud's: Hans' phobia was a classically conditioned fear that had nothing to do with Oedipal complexes or displacement. Behavioral psychologists see conditioning, discussed in Chapter 6, as the source of anxiety disorders.

Classical conditioning seems to provide a reasonable explanation: Phobias are the result of learned associations between previously neutral stimuli and frightening events. Thus we might argue that a person develops a fear of strangers after being assaulted, or a fear of riding in cars after being in a bad automobile accident, or fears elevators after an aversive experience in a confined space. Once fear or anxiety is conditioned to certain stimuli, people may then learn to reduce this conditioned fear by avoiding the fear stimulus. This kind of conditioning was referred to as *two-factor learning* in Chapter 6. For instance, a person with a strong fear of elevators may avoid them by using stairs instead. The avoidance behavior here is maintained by negative reinforcement (fear reduction). Through the process of *stimulus generalization* (also discussed in Chapter 6) a variety of situations may serve to elicit fear and anxiety.

Why don't all people with fearful experiences develop phobias or severe anxiety? The answer to this question may be that certain brain structures involved in mediating conditioned fear, including the amygdala and the prefrontal cortex, don't turn off normally in some people. Recent experimental work with animals supports this idea. For instance, work with animals has demonstrated that the *amygdala* (see Chapter 3) is essential for the development of conditioned fear responses. In addition, during the course of fear conditioning, cells in the amygdala begin to fire with the onset of a CS (conditioned stimulus) that precedes shock. On the other hand, damage to the amygdala prevents fear conditioning in animals (Davis, 1992).

While the amygdala appears to be important in the acquisition of conditioned fear, the *prefrontal cortex* seems to be responsible for the extinction of conditioned fear. Animals with prefrontal cortex damage fail to extinguish conditioned fear when the unconditioned stimulus (shock) is no longer presented. People with posttraumatic stress syndrome also show a failure to extinguish conditioned fear responses (see Figure 15.3). Perhaps anxiety disorders result when people can no longer turn off or inhibit conditioned fear responses (Davis, 1992; LeDoux, 1992).

Although both classical conditioning and operant conditioning account for many kinds of anxiety disorders, some questions may remain unanswered. How can we explain the fact that many people who have phobias have had no frightening experiences with the object or situation that they fear so greatly? Furthermore, although there are quite a few different kinds of phobias, the objects of these phobias tend to be limited to a fairly narrow range of stimuli (Goldstein et al., 1986). By far the most common phobias are *zoophobias* (fear of particular animals, such as snakes or mice). Yet in our own society today, we are exposed far more to motor vehicles and machines than we are to snakes. Why don't we develop proportionately more phobias to these objects?

Different theorists have approached our question about phobias in different ways; two answers are particularly interesting. The first argument is that evolution has built into humans a biological predisposition to react fearfully to certain

FIGURE 15.3

An Experiment to Measure Fear Conditioning and Extinction in Human Subjects

Tones precede mild shocks to the forearm. Conditioned responses include facial movements which are recorded by the electric leads.

classes of potentially dangerous stimuli, such as snakes and spiders. It is not difficult to believe that a natural wariness can have some adaptive advantage to humans, but is there any objective evidence to support this notion? The answer is a tentative yes. One series of experiments attempted to classically condition fear responses to both "evolutionarily prepared stimuli" such as spiders and snakes, and to innocuous stimuli such as mushrooms. It found not only that fear responses to evolutionarily prepared stimuli were much more easily established (often in only one trial), but also that these responses were very difficult to extinguish (Ohman, 1979).

Not all theorists agree that biological predispositions explain why some phobias occur more readily than others. Social-learning theorist Albert Bandura (1969) believes that modeling, or imitating the behavior of others, provides a more likely explanation for the acquisition of some anxiety disorders. For example, a child who observes a parent reacting anxiously to dogs or thunderstorms may also acquire a phobic fear of dogs or thunder. In this manner phobias may be transmitted from one generation to the next. This interpretation is supported by evidence that animal phobias typically occur in children who are about age five and whose mothers have the same phobia (Klein, 1981). Thus the fact that a relatively narrow range of stimuli become phobic objects may be due to social-learning mechanisms rather than biological predispositions.

How do behavioral theorists explain other anxiety disorders? Posttraumatic stress disorders, as we have seen, are clearly linked to traumatizing experiences and possibly the failure to inhibit conditioned fear responses. The behavioral explanation of obsessive-compulsive disorders is more complex. Some argue that compulsive, repetitious acts such as hand washing occur repeatedly because they provide a temporary reduction in anxiety. According to this argument compulsive behaviors are maintained by negative reinforcement.

Finally, in the case of panic attacks with accompanying agoraphobia, it has been suggested that individuals who experience sudden panic attacks develop a kind of anticipatory anxiety attached to situations in which they have previously experienced attacks. Indeed, they may become so fearful of future attacks that they subsequently avoid what they perceive as dangerous situations. Such phobic avoidance behaviors are then reinforced by a reduction in fear. (Gorman et al., 1989). However, this perspective does not provide an explanation of what causes the initial panic reactions. One possible explanation is that certain underlying physiological and biochemical anomalies affect the autonomic nervous system in such a way as to predispose certain individuals to experience panic attacks (e.g., an amygdala that is overactive). These unanticipated attacks lead to fearful attitudes which help to maintain the disorder via phobic avoidance behaviors (Clark et al., 1988). In this sense, we might view panic disorder with agoraphobia as resulting from an interaction of biological and psychological causes (Gelder, 1989). The following discussion explores some of the suggested biological causes of anxiety disorders.

THE BIOLOGICAL PERSPECTIVE Perhaps the best place to start is with a notion that has been suggested by several researchers—that some individuals with unusually responsive nervous systems may be biologically predisposed to develop certain anxiety disorders, particularly panic, phobic, and generalized anxiety disorders. Some evidence suggests that the autonomic nervous systems of individuals with anxiety disorders are more easily aroused by environmental stimuli, a condition known as *autonomic lability*. This condition might contribute to a tendency to be jumpy, anxious, or apprehensive (Ciesielski et al., 1981; Lacey, 1967; Turner et al., 1985). There is also evidence that some people may be biochemically predisposed to at least some types of anxiety disorders (Gaffney et al., 1988; Liebowitz et al., 1984).

In addition, studies have linked anxiety disorders to atypical EEGs (Edlund et al., 1987; Weilburg et al., 1987); abnormal neural discharge and functional abnormalities in various brain structures (Fontaine et al., 1990; Gorman et al., 1989; Swedo et al., 1989); hypersensitivity and instability of the limbic system (Everly, 1989); and deficits of the neurotransmitter serotonin (March et al., 1989). The role of the amygdala and the prefrontal cortex in conditioning fear and anxiety was discussed in the previous section.

One of the most fascinating new lines of evidence pertaining to the biological perspective on anxiety disorders is represented by the research program of Judith Rapoport and her colleagues (1989; 1991), who have investigated the biology of obsessive-compulsive disorder. Data from a number of studies have led Rapoport to postulate a biological model to explain this disorder. Her central thesis is that certain behavioral subroutines related to such things as grooming, cleanliness, and checking key elements within one's territory are programmed or hard-wired into the human brain over the course of evolution. Such behavioral packages are believed to have served crucial functions during the evolution of the human species. The repository of these hard-wired behavioral packages is presumed to be located within the **basal ganglia,** a group of brain structures that lie under the cerebral cortex and function as "way stations" between the input of sensory messages and resulting cortically initiated motor or cognitive outputs (refer to Chapter 3). Rapoport theorizes that "in obsessive-compulsive patients disturbances in these way stations have somehow short-circuited the loop that normally connects sensory input with behavioral output, thereby releasing stored, hard-wired behavioral packages" (Rapoport, 1991).

For most of us, evidence provided by our senses and interpreted by higher brain centers (that we are clean or that the windows are locked, for instance) is sufficient to keep us from engaging in compulsive routines related to these concerns. According to Rapoport's model, however, people with such short-circuited loops feel compelled to engage in such things as handwashing (cleanliness subroutine) and repetitively checking the windows (territory subroutine). While Rapoport and her colleagues have gathered an impressive array of evidence to support this intriguing biological theory, we must await further supporting evidence before concluding that obsessive-compulsive disorder is reliably related to dysfunction of the basal ganglia. Figure 15.4 shows a PET scan of an obsessive-compulsive patient compared to a normal subject. The middle image shows increased activity in the area of the basal ganglia.

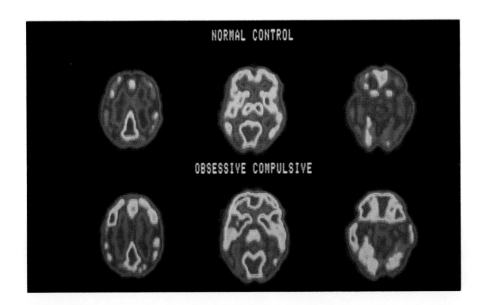

FIGURE 15.4
PET Scans Comparing a Patient with Obsessive-Compulsive Disorder with a Normal Subject

Note the higher levels of metabolic activity in several areas.

If certain people are biologically predisposed to some anxiety disorders, it follows that there may be a genetic basis for these disorders. In fact, extensive evidence seems to support this conjecture. One study measured the incidence of anxiety disorders among siblings, mothers, and fathers of three groups of subjects: agoraphobics, panic-disordered individuals, and a control group with no diagnosed anxiety disorders. As Table 15.2 shows, the relatives of both groups of anxiety-disordered subjects showed more than double the incidence of anxiety disorders that were found among relatives of the control group (Harris et al., 1983). Other research has also reported a higher than normal incidence of anxiety disorders among relatives of people with diagnosed panic disorders (Balon et al., 1989; Cloninger et al., 1981; Crowe et al., 1987).

The studies just described suggest a genetic component in anxiety disorders. But does the evidence point clearly to a hereditary explanation, or is there another possible explanation for these findings? What other types of research besides family studies might provide more clear-cut evidence? Give these questions some thought before reading on.

As we noted in Chapters 13 and 14, the fact that a particular trait or condition runs in a family does not prove it has a genetic basis. Another interpretation might be that environmental factors which give rise to a disorder in one person are likely to have a similar effect on relatives who share the same environment.

A more reliable source of evidence about the role of genetic transmission is twin studies. So far, the information gathered from this source does seem to point to a genetic link for anxiety disorders. A major study conducted in Norway reported a much higher concordance rate among identical twins (45 percent) than fraternal twins (15 percent) for a grouping of anxiety disorders that included agoraphobia, panic disorders, obsessive-compulsive disorders, and social phobias (Torgersen, 1983). Other studies have reported similar concordance rates for anxiety disorders among identical and fraternal twins (Katschnig & Shepherd, 1978; Rosenthal, 1970). Slater and Shields (1969) reported concordance rates of 49 percent for generalized anxiety disorders among identical twins

TABLE 15.2 *Risk for Several Types of Anxiety-Based Disorders in Siblings and Parents of Agoraphobics, Panic-Disordered, and Nonanxious Controls*

	PATIENT STATUS		
	AGORAPHOBIA	PANIC	CONTROLS
	Incidence (%) in first degree relatives for the disorder:		
Agoraphobia	8.6	1.9	4.2
Panic disorder	7.7	20.5	4.2
Generalized anxiety	5.1	6.5	5.3
Atypical anxiety	2.6	3.7	0.0
Social phobia	3.4	0.0	1.1
Specific phobia	2.6	0.0	0.0
Obsessive-compulsive	1.7	0.0	0.0
Total of all anxiety-based disorders	31.7	32.6	14.8

SOURCE: From Harris et al., 1983

and only 4 percent among fraternal twins. Thus the evidence points strongly toward genetic factors in various anxiety disorders. However, as you recall from our discussion in Chapter 14, partitioning the relative contributions of genetics and the environment misrepresents the importance of the ongoing interaction between genes and the environment in determining behavior. Many psychologists argue that concordance rates provide little interesting or useful information about the origins of behavioral dispositions.

SOMATOFORM DISORDERS

Whereas the primary symptom of anxiety disorders is psychological distress, the **somatoform disorders** are expressed through *somatic* or physical symptoms. Dizziness, stomach pain, vomiting, breathing difficulties, difficulty in swallowing, impaired vision, inability to move the legs, numbness of the hands, and sexual dysfunctions are common symptoms of somatoform disorders. In all cases, however, the symptoms have no physiological basis.

The somatoform disorders affect a much smaller portion of the population than anxiety disorders—less than 1 percent (Robins et al., 1984). DSM-IV classifies several types of somatoform disorders. We look at three: *somatization disorder, hypochondriasis,* and *conversion disorder.*

SOMATIZATION DISORDER

A person with **somatization disorder** typically has multiple and recurrent physical symptoms that have no physical cause, but for which medical attention is repeatedly sought. People who have this disorder commonly complain about chest, stomach, and back pain, headaches, heart palpitations, vomiting, dizziness, and fainting, and genitourinary symptoms. Table 15.3 indicates the type and frequency of symptoms reported by a sample of people with somatization disorder. Patients typically present their complaints in such a convincing fashion that medications and medical procedures are provided, including unnecessary surgery in some cases. This disorder typically begins in the late teenage years, and is more common among women than men (Kroll et al., 1979). Recent data suggest that approximately one person in 250 manifests this disorder (Swartz et al., 1986).

TABLE 15.3 *Various Symptoms and Their Frequency as Reported by a Sample of Patients with Somatization Disorder*

SYMPTOM	PERCENTAGE REPORTING	SYMPTOM	PERCENTAGE REPORTING	SYMPTOM	PERCENTAGE REPORTING
Dyspnea (labored breathing)	72	Anorexia	60	Back pain	88
Palpitation	60	Nausea	80	Joint pain	84
Chest pain	72	Vomiting	32	Extremity pain	84
Dizziness	84	Abdominal pain	80	Burning pains in rectum, vagina, mouth	28
Headache	80	Abdominal bloating	68		
Anxiety attacks	64	Food intolerances	48	Other bodily pain	36
Fatigue	84	Diarrhea	20	Depressed feelings	64
		Constipation	64		

(Continued)

TABLE 15.3 *Various Symptoms and Their Frequency as Reported by a Sample of Patients with Somatization Disorder (Cont'd)*

SYMPTOM	PERCENTAGE REPORTING	SYMPTOM	PERCENTAGE REPORTING	SYMPTOM	PERCENTAGE REPORTING
Blindness	20	Dysuria (painful urination)	44	Phobias	48
Paralysis	12	Urinary retention	8	Vomiting all nine months of pregnancy	20
Anesthesia	32	Dysmenorrhea (painful menstruation, premarital only)	4	Nervous	92
Aphonia (loss of voice above a whisper)	44	Dysmenorrhea (pre-pregnancy only)	8	Had to quit working because felt bad	44
Lump in throat	28	Dysmenorrhea (other)	48	Trouble doing anything because felt bad	72
Fits or convulsions	20	Menstrual irregularity	48	Cried a lot	70
Faints	56	Excessive menstrual bleeding	48	Felt life was hopeless	28
Unconsciousness	16	Sexual indifference	44	Always sickly (most of life)	40
Amnesia	8	Inability to experience orgasm	24	Thought of dying	48
Visual blurring	64	Dyspareunia (painful sexual intercourse)	52	Wanted to die	36
Visual hallucination	12			Thought of suicide	28
Deafness	4			Attempted suicide	12
Olfactory hallucination	16				
Weakness	84				
Weight loss	28				
Sudden fluctuations in weight	16				

SOURCE: From Perley & Guze, 1962.

HYPOCHONDRIASIS

Like somatization-disordered individuals, people with **hypochondriasis** also complain about a variety of physical difficulties (most commonly stomach and heart problems). The primary difference between the two conditions is that individuals with hypochondriasis are fearful that their symptoms indicate a serious disease, whereas those with somatization disorder typically do not progress beyond a concern with the symptoms themselves. A hypochondriac who notices a minor heart palpitation may be convinced it is a sign of severe cardiac disease, or may interpret a cough as a sign of lung cancer. Hypochondriacs have also been shown to be excessively fearful about death and often spend an inordinate amount of time consulting with physicians about imaginary symptoms of physical illness (Kellner et al., 1987).

CONVERSION DISORDER

A third somatoform disorder, **conversion disorder,** is typically manifested as a sensory or motor-system disturbance for which there is no known organic cause. Unlike the two previous categories of somatoform disorders, conversion disorders are seldom confused with genuine physical disease because their symptom patterns make no anatomical sense. In the condition known as *sensory conversion*, for example, individuals may lose sensitivity in specific parts of their bodies in which the loss-of-feeling pattern is neurologically impossible (see Figure 15.5).

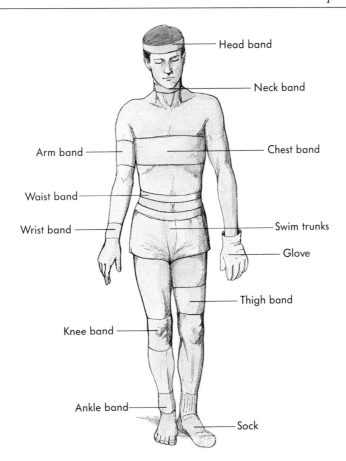

Head band

Neck band

Arm band

Chest band

Waist band

Wrist band

Swim trunks

Glove

Thigh band

Knee band

Ankle band

Sock

FIGURE 15.5
Common Sites for Sensory Conversions That Reflect Neurologically Impossible Loss-of-Feeling Patterns

Other forms of sensory conversion may be reflected in loss of sensitivity to pain, impaired vision or hearing, and, in some cases, heightened sensitivity to touch. In another related condition, *motor conversion*, an individual may experience paralysis in some part of the body, usually a limb, or experience uncontrollable tremors or twitches.

Conversion disorders typically surface after a person has experienced serious stress or conflict, and the symptoms appear to allow the person to escape from or avoid that stress or conflict. This situation is apparent in the following case, in which a man developed a sensory conversion to escape from a nagging wife and mother-in-law:

Phil, forty years of age, had a history of marginal work adjustment since his discharge from the Army at age twenty-five. In the fifteen years since discharge, he had depended on public assistance and financial aid from relatives to get by. He painted a very dismal picture of his married life, as one of almost constant harassment from his wife and mother-in-law. He had a history of minor illnesses involving his eyes, none of which had grossly affected his visual acuity.

During the Christmas season his wife and mother-in-law were being more demanding than usual, requiring him to work nights and weekends at various chores under their foremanship. Three days before Christmas, while shopping with his wife and mother-in-law, Phil suddenly became blind in both eyes.

Neurological and ophthalmological exams were essentially negative in accounting for his blindness, and a diagnosis of conversion disorder was made. At this time, Phil did not seem greatly alarmed by his loss of sight, but instead displayed an attitude of patient forbearance. Observers in the hospital noticed that Phil could get about in the ward better than expected for a totally blind man. He was not concerned with this, but felt hurt and unjustly accused when other patients pointed out the discrepancy to him. (Adapted from Brady & Lind, 1965, p. 762)

Phil's apparent lack of concern about his condition is fairly common among people with conversion disorders. The French psychiatrist Pierre Janet (1929) labeled this blasé attitude *la belle indifference*, or the noble lack of concern. Observers may incorrectly assume that a person with a conversion disorder is malingering, or deliberately faking symptoms. However, unlike malingerers, who tend to be cautious about discussing their symptoms for fear that their pretense will be discovered, individuals with a conversion disorder appear eager to talk at great length about their symptoms.

THEORETICAL PERSPECTIVES ON SOMATOFORM DISORDERS

Recall from Chapter 14 that Freud was profoundly influenced by experiences with patients whose physically manifested symptoms had no neurological basis. Freud thought such problems stemmed from unresolved sexual impulses, particularly Oedipal complexes. These unresolved incestuous yearnings, said Freud, produce intense anxiety, which the individual may then convert into physical symptoms. This conversion reduces the anxiety associated with repressed id impulses, a process Freud called *primary gain*. Freud noted that such disorders might also produce some *secondary gain*, allowing the person to avoid or escape from some currently stressful life situation.

Freud's concept of secondary gain is similar to the interpretation of somatoform disorders offered by some behavioral theorists. According to their viewpoint, the symptoms of a somatoform disorder are reinforced if they allow a person to escape from or avoid the negative reinforcer of anxiety. Reinforcement in the form of sickness, benefit, or disability insurance has also been noted to play a role in somatoform disorder (Kellner, 1990). There is some evidence that biological predispositions or genetic factors may play a noteworthy role in the somatoform disorders (Kellner, 1990).

DISSOCIATIVE DISORDERS

In the **dissociative disorders,** the thoughts and feelings that generate anxiety are separated, or *dissociated,* from conscious awareness by memory loss or a change in identity. These uncommon disorders usually take the form of *dissociative amnesia, dissociative fugue,* or *dissociative identity.*

DISSOCIATIVE AMNESIA

The most common dissociative disorder is **dissociative amnesia.** Here, a person experiences sudden loss of memory, usually after a particularly stressful or traumatic event. The most typical manifestation is loss of memory for all events for a specified period of time. For example, a person involved in a terrible accident might block out all memory of the accident as well as everything that happened just before or after it. Less commonly, a person may develop total amnesia for all prior experiences, and will be unable to recognize relatives, friends, and familiar places. (In these cases, the individual usually retains reasoning and verbal abilities, talents such as the ability to play a musical instrument, and general knowledge.) Episodes of dissociative amnesia may last from several hours to many years. They typically disappear as suddenly as they appeared, and they rarely recur.

Memory loss may also result from organic brain disease associated with such illnesses as chronic alcoholism and Alzheimer's disease, as we saw in Chapters 7 and 12. However, *dissociative amnesia* is easily distinguished from organic amnesia, in that memory loss due to organic causes (diseases, injury, or aging) is generally a gradual process which is not connected with traumatic events.

DISSOCIATIVE FUGUE

Whereas a person with dissociative amnesia escapes from a stressful situation by blocking it out of awareness, **dissociative fugue disorder** combines amnesia with a more radical defensive maneuver—a flight away from an intolerable situation (the word fugue comes from the Latin *fuga*, or flight). Typically, the fugue state is of relatively brief duration in which a person travels from place to place in an apparently purposeful fashion but has little social contact with other people. It is likely that many of the supposed amnesia victims who end up in police reports or local newspaper accounts are experiencing dissociative fugue disorder.

Less frequently, a person may relocate to another part of the country and assume a new identity complete with new name, job, and perhaps a new family. All this behavior may be accomplished without the individual ever seriously questioning her or his inability to remember the past.

DISSOCIATIVE IDENTITY DISORDER

Dissociative identity disorder or multiple personality is a very uncommon form of dissociative disorder in which the individual alternates between an original or primary personality and one or more secondary or subordinate personalities. Usually the subordinate personality is aware of the primary personality but not vice versa.

In a sense, we all have multiple personalities in that we have conflicting behavioral tendencies—for instance, between the part of us that is socially conforming and the part that likes to cut loose. Most of us are able to find appropriate outlets for expressing different aspects of our personalities. However, not everyone is able to achieve a satisfactory synthesis. Multiple personality disorder seems to provide an outlet for these different selves, by separating the conflicting parts and elaborating each into an essentially autonomous personality. Frequently the separated personalities represent two extremes, from responsible and conforming to irresponsible and "naughty."

An analysis of 100 recently reported cases of multiple personality disorder revealed that 83 percent of these disturbed individuals had in common "histories of significant childhood trauma, primarily sexual abuse" (Putnam et al., 1986, p. 292). The individuals in this sample also displayed a core of clinical symptoms including depression, substance abuse, insomnia, sexual dysfunction, and suicidal or other self-destructive behaviors.

An interesting case of multiple personality disorder that appears to have followed a long history of sexual abuse is the case of Truddi Chase (Figure 15.6) who supposedly displayed 92 separate personalities. Apparently these personalities began to emerge at the age of two and they replaced Truddi (the original personality) who was "asleep." Truddi's alternate personalities were referred to as her "troops" in the book *When Rabbit Howls*, (Chase, 1990). The main personality of Truddi is a divorced mother of one child. Before treatment, Truddi supposedly knew nothing of the other personalities (troops), which were drawn out and actually participated in her treatment. Some of these other personalities included: Rabbit—a character who only communicated through howls of pain; Miss Wonderful—a character who played the perfect woman; Sewer Mouth—a character who played a vulgar woman; Mean Joe—an 11-foot protector of the troops; Elvira—an irresponsible carefree character; Twelve—an artistic, sensitive child; and The Front Runner—a character who kept track of all the other troops.

Multiple personality disorder seems to occur more frequently in women than men, with nine times more women affected than men (Putnam et al., 1986; Ross, 1989). It has been widely assumed that multiple personality is very rare: According to one estimate, only about 300 cases had been reported in the world's professional literature prior to 1970 (Bliss, 1984). In recent years, however, the

FIGURE 15.6
Truddi Chase, Author of When Rabbit Howls

This book describes her "troops" who were identified as 92 separate personalities. Truddi's history of sexual abuse may have contributed to the development of her multiple personalities.

reported incidence of this disorder has been on the rise (Boor, 1982; Putnam et al., 1986). One clinician reported seeing more than 100 cases of multiple personality between 1980 and 1984 (Bliss, 1984). Ross (1989) argues that this increasing trend may be the result of an increasingly sick society in which child abuse is increasing at a high rate. The incidence of child abuse of females is also much higher than for males. Although child abuse, particularly sexual abuse, appears to be associated with multiple personality disorder, not all psychologists agree that this is a causal relation.

Caution should also be exercised in diagnosing a multiple personality disorder, especially when the diagnosis may produce secondary gains (Thigpen & Cleckley, 1984). This issue was brought to public attention recently by the case of Kenneth Bianchi (the Los Angeles "Hillside Strangler") who manifested what appeared to be a multiple personality disorder. The primary personality of Kenneth claimed no awareness of two underlying or subordinate personalities: "Steve," who claimed responsibility for a number of rape–murders, and "Billy," who was allegedly responsible for thefts and forgeries. At first, examining clinicians diagnosed Bianchi as having a genuine multiple personality disorder that would make him legally insane (Watkins, 1984). However, later findings (including a lack of consistency in the structure and content of the personalities over time and the inability of Bianchi's acquaintances to support his claims) led to the conclusion that Bianchi was simulating a multiple personality in order to avoid the death penalty (Orne et al., 1984). Bianchi was diagnosed as having an antisocial (psychopathic) personality with sexual sadism, and the court held him responsible for his actions.

THEORETICAL PERSPECTIVES ON DISSOCIATIVE DISORDERS

Dissociative disorders are among the least understood of all behavioral disorders. Thus explanations are highly speculative. In some ways, all three of the dissociative disorders we have discussed—amnesia, fugue, and multiple personality—seem to provide strong support for Freud's view that excessive application of the defense mechanisms can lead to serious disorders.

Psychoanalytic theory sees all of these conditions as resulting from massive reliance on repression to ward off unacceptable impulses, particularly those of a sexual nature. These yearnings increase during adolescence and adulthood, until they are finally expressed, often in a guilt-inducing sexual act. Normal forms of repression are not effective in blocking out this guilt, and so the person blocks the acts and related thoughts entirely from consciousness by developing amnesia or acquiring a new identity for the dissociated "bad" part of self.

Behavioral theory does not offer a well-developed and cohesive explanation for dissociative disorders. A number of theorists within this perspective suggest, however, that the dissociative reactions may involve operant avoidance responses that are reinforced because they allow an individual to avoid anxiety associated with highly stressful events, such as early childhood abuse. There is no evidence that genetic factors or biological predispositions play a significant role in the development of dissociative disorders.

MOOD DISORDERS

I do not care for anything. I do not care to ride, for the exercise is too violent. I do not care to walk, walking is too strenuous. I do not care to lie down, for I should either have to remain lying, and I do not care to do that, or I should have to get up again, and I do not care to do that either. I do not care at all. (Kierkegaard, 1844, p. 19)

This account was written by the nineteenth-century Danish philosopher Søren Kierkegaard, who was subject to recurring bouts of severe depression. It provides a firsthand description of some of the characteristics of depression, the primary symptom of the **mood disorders.**

We have all experienced depression on occasion, as a natural response to setbacks such as failing an exam, ending a relationship, or being rejected by a potential employer. Fortunately for most of us, depression is a transitory state that generally lifts in short order as life goes on. However, when feelings of sadness, dejection, and hopelessness persist longer than a few weeks and when these feelings are severe enough to disrupt everyday functioning, the depression is considered to be an abnormal behavioral state.

The common symptoms or signs of depression include a variety of psychological, psychomotor, and physical manifestations, such as severe and prolonged feelings of sadness, hopelessness, and despair; low self-esteem; a sense of worthlessness; eating disturbances (either undereating or overeating); sleep disturbances (either insomnia or excessive sleep); psychomotor disturbances characterized by a marked shift in activity level; a variety of somatic or bodily complaints; lack of energy with accompanying fatigue; loss of interest in and enjoyment of everyday activities; indecisiveness; difficulty in concentrating; and persistent thoughts of suicide and death.

Like anxiety, depression is associated with many varieties of behavioral disorders, including the anxiety and somatoform disorders, substance-related disorders such as alcoholism (discussed in Chapter 3), and schizophrenia, which we discuss later in this chapter. In these and related conditions, depression is secondary to other symptoms. In contrast, depression is the primary problem in the mood disorders.

DSM-IV distinguishes two major mood disorders: **major depressive disorder** and **bipolar disorder.** A major depressive episode is characterized by depressed mood, diminished interest in activities, significant weight loss or gain, sleep disturbances, restlessness, fatigue, diminished ability to concentrate, and/or recurrent thoughts of suicide. In addition, some or all of these symptoms must be severe enough to impair social or occupational functioning.

Bipolar disorder (sometimes called manic depression) is characterized by intermittent episodes of both depression and *mania.* Mania is a highly energized state characterized by an inflated self-esteem, decreased need for sleep, increased pressure to talk, racing thoughts, distractibility, and/or increases in directed activity. These symptoms, as well as those for the depressive episode, must be severe enough to impair social or occupational functioning to warrant the diagnosis of bipolar disorder.

The distinction between major depressive disorder and bipolar disorder is an important one that is based on different symptomatology as well as different etiology. Bipolar disorder generally appears during a person's twenties, whereas major depressive disorder is more likely to develop later, often in a person's thirties. However, major depressive disorder may occur in children, adolescents, or young adults, and recent research provides evidence of an increased rate in younger people (Weissman, 1987). Symptoms of depression may vary somewhat according to the disorder. The depression associated with bipolar disorder typically causes a person to become lethargic and sleep more. In contrast, major depressive disorder is characterized by insomnia and agitation (Wehr et al., 1987a). These two different types of mood disorders also respond quite differently to various treatments.

As many as one out of five Americans may experience a severe depressive episode at any point in time (Boyd & Weissman, 1981), but only 1 percent of the population has been diagnosed with bipolar disorder (Davison & Neale, 1990).

Evidence suggests that the incidence of mood disorders has been progressively increasing over the last few decades (Gershon et al., 1987). It is now estimated that 18 million people suffer from a depression severe enough to interfere with their life each year.

MAJOR DEPRESSIVE DISORDER

People diagnosed as having major depressive disorder typically manifest their symptoms over an extended period, from several months to a year or longer, and their ability to function effectively may be so impaired that hospitalization is warranted. The following brief case study illustrates some of the common symptoms of severe depression:

> On admission to the hospital, the patient sat slumped in a chair, frowning deeply, staring at the floor, his face looking sad and drawn. When questioned he answered without looking up, slowly and in a monotone. Sometimes there was such a long pause between question and reply that the patient seemed not to have heard. Every now and then he shifted his position a little, sighed heavily and shook his head from side to side. His first verbal response was, "It's no use. I'm through. All I can think is I won't be any good again." In response to further inquiries he made the following comments, relapsing into silence after each short statement until again asked a question. "I feel like I'm dead inside, like a piece of wood. I don't have any feeling about anything, it's not like living anymore. I'm past hope, there's nothing to tell." (Cameron, 1947, p. 508)

Earlier we mentioned that the depression in major depressive disorder is more likely to be accompanied by agitation than it is in bipolar disorder. This state may cause people to pace, wring their hands, or cry out and moan loudly. Depressed people who express this heightened motor activity continue to feel worthless and without hope.

Not surprisingly, people with major depressive disorder almost inevitably experience a breakdown in interpersonal relationships. Most of us do not enjoy being around irritable people, and since many depressed people are irritable, it is understandable that friends, associates, and even family members may eventually gravitate away from such people. In addition, depressed people often seek guidance and support from others, and it can be very frustrating for friends to observe that their efforts to provide help often seem to have no effect. Sometimes people may avoid depressed individuals because such interactions often make them feel gloomy or depressed (Hammen & Peters, 1978).

Although often incapacitating and sometimes even life threatening (individuals who contemplate suicide are often deeply depressed), episodes of major depression are generally transitory in nature. In most cases the depression lifts over a period of months, regardless of whether or not it is treated. However, most people with diagnosed major depressive disorder experience one or more recurrence(s) of major depression later on in their lives. Research has linked certain key variables with the recurrences of major depression. Factors predictive of relapse include (1) early onset (before age 20) of initial episode of major depression, (2) marital distress, and (3) relatives who express critical or hostile attitudes toward the recovered depressive (Giles et al., 1989; Hooley & Teasdale, 1989).

BIPOLAR (MANIC-DEPRESSIVE) DISORDER

In contrast to major depressive disorder, bipolar disorder is characterized by extreme mood swings, from immobilizing depression to euphoria and frantic activity. In some cases, episodes of depression and elation may alternate regularly, with months or years of symptom-free normal functioning between the disordered mood states. Other cases may be characterized by a series of intermittent manic episodes followed by a period of depression. Unlike the normal highs and lows most of us experience in response to life events, the depression and mania associated with bipolar disorder do not seem to be triggered by identifiable events. In some manic-depressives, depressive symptoms may occur concurrently with classic manic features, a condition referred to as *mixed mania*.

About one in 100 people suffer from bipolar disorder, a rate comparable to that of schizophrenia but far lower than the incidence of major depression (Kolata, 1986, 1987b; Robertson, 1987). Men and women are equally likely to develop bipolar disorder. Since the depression experienced in bipolar disorder is quite similar to what we already described as experienced in major depression (with noteworthy differences in sleep and activity level), we focus here on the manic symptoms of the disorder.

According to DSM-IV, manic episodes are characterized by "inflated self-esteem or grandiosity (which may be delusional), decreased need for sleep, pressure of speech, flight of ideas, distractibility, increased involvement in goal-directed activity, psychomotor agitation, and excessive involvement in pleasurable activities which have a high potential for painful consequences that the person often does not recognize" (American Psychiatric Association, 1993). Manic episodes often begin suddenly and escalate rapidly, as revealed in the following case:

> Mr. M., a thirty-two-year-old postal worker, had been married for eight years. He and his wife lived comfortably and happily in a middle-class neighborhood with their two children. In retrospect there appeared to be no warning for what was to happen. On February the twelfth Mr. M. let his wife know that he was bursting with energy and ideas, that his job as a mail carrier was unfulfilling, and that he was just wasting his talent. That night he slept little, spending most of the time at a desk, writing furiously. The next morning he left for work at the usual time but returned home at eleven A.M., his car filled to overflowing with aquaria and other equipment for tropical fish. He had quit his job and then withdrawn all the money from the family's savings account. The money had been spent on tropical fish equipment. Mr. M. reported that the previous night he had worked out a way to modify existing equipment so that "the fish won't die anymore. We'll be millionaires." After loading the paraphernalia, Mr. M. set off to canvas the neighborhood for possible buyers, going door to door and talking to anyone who would listen.
>
> The following bit of conversation from the period after Mr. M. entered treatment indicates his incorrigible optimism and provocativeness.
>
> *Therapist:* Well, you seem pretty happy today.
>
> *Client:* Happy! Happy! You certainly are a master of understatement, you rogue! (Shouting, literally jumping out of his seat). Why I'm ecstatic, I'm leaving for the West Coast today, on my daughter's bicycle. Only 3100 miles. That's nothing, you know. I could probably walk, but I want to get there by next week. And along the way I plan to contact a lot of people about investing in my fish equipment. I'll get to know more people that way—you know, Doc, "know" in the biblical sense (leering at therapist seductively). Oh, God, how good it feels. (Davison & Neale, 1986, p. 196)

A manic episode often follows a three-stage course of accelerating intensity (Carlson & Goodwin, 1973). In the first stage, *hypomania*, individuals typically retain their capacity to function in their daily lives, and may even exhibit high levels of productivity. However, as they progress through the second and third stages of *mania* and *severe mania*, their thinking becomes more disorganized, and their behavior often takes on a bizarre psychotic-like quality. These advanced stages may be accompanied by both **delusions** (exaggerated and rigidly held beliefs that have little or no basis in fact, such as Mr. M.'s belief that he had found a way to keep tropical fish alive forever) and **hallucinations** (false perceptions that lack a sensory basis, such as hearing or seeing imaginary voices or images). Bizarre symptoms such as those described in this chapter's opening case are not often manifested, since modern drugs are quite effective in controlling such behaviors.

A number of studies have shown a disproportionately high incidence of bipolar disorder among creative individuals. One of the first studies to demonstrate

TABLE 15.4 *Suicide Facts*

1. Approximately 30,000 people in the United States take their own lives each year (probably an underestimation, since many suicides are not officially recorded).
2. For every successful suicide there are at least eight attempts. This translates to approximately a quarter of a million suicide attempts each year in this country.
3. Somewhere between 50 and 80 percent of people who complete suicides have made one or more previous attempts.
4. Two to three times more men than women succeed in committing suicide, although over three times as many women as men attempt suicide. Men often use absolute and irreversible methods, such as guns and hanging, to kill themselves, whereas women are more likely to use drugs, gas, or poison.
5. Suicide rates by age group rise steadily from adolescence, peaking in the 45+ group. The suicide rate among Americans aged 65 and older steadily increased during the 1980s. Recent evidence also indicates a rising incidence of suicide among adolescents and young adults.
6. Suicide ranks as the ninth leading cause of death among all American adults, but it is second only to accidents as a cause of death among college students.
7. Divorced people, particularly men, are more likely to commit suicide than married people.
8. Suicide is found among all socioeconomic levels, but certain professionals, including physicians (particularly psychiatrists), psychologists, and attorneys, have a disproportionately high incidence.
9. In the United States and many other countries, May and October are times of peak incidence of suicides. These findings are consistent with seasonality data for mood disorders, particularly bipolar disorders.
10. About 80 percent of people who kill themselves provide ample verbal or other behavior clues beforehand.
11. It is believed that more than half of the people who commit suicide are seriously depressed at the time of the act. However, many people who kill themselves do not have a diagnosable psychological disorder.
12. Surveys of people who have survived suicide attempts indicate a range of motives, including loneliness, powerlessness, a feeling that no one can help to ease the pain, depression, poor health, conflicts involving spouses or other people, unhappiness, and loss of a close relative or a friend.

SOURCES: Beck et al., 1990; Cole, 1989; Davison & Neale, 1990; Dorpat & Ripley, 1967; Duke & Nowicki, 1986; Goldstein et al., 1986; Goodwin & Jamison, 1986; Holinger, 1979, 1980; Kaprio et al., 1987; Lester, 1989; Lester & Smith, 1989; Michel, 1987; Miles, 1977; Schneidman, 1974, 1987; Schneidman et al., 1970; Seiden, 1974; Tolchin, 1989.

this apparent connection found almost five times the incidence of mood disorder in a sample of American creative writers as in a matched control group (Andreasen & Carter, 1974). A more recent study of 47 award-winning British writers and artists revealed that 38 percent had been treated for mood disorders (Jamison, 1989).

Episodes of either mania or depression tend to last only a few weeks or months. When they lift, the person recovers and returns to a symptom-free life. Unfortunately, however, the symptoms tend to recur, and many people require periodic treatment and sometimes maintenance medication throughout their lives (Coryell et al., 1989). This pattern takes its toll in the form of alienated friends and loved ones, financial problems, and careers that remain on hold due to the unpredictable nature of symptoms. One of the most devastating aspects of this disorder is the high risk of suicide associated with it (see Table 15.4). Available evidence indicates that people with bipolar disorders are more likely to kill themselves than any other group of people with a behavioral disorder (Goldstein et al., 1986).

SEASONAL AFFECTIVE DISORDER

In the last 10 years mental health professionals seem to have rediscovered what was once central to many ancient theories about the causes of diseases: namely, that seasons influence mood and shape mental health. It is now recognized that some people suffer from **seasonal affective disorder (SAD),** and DSM-IV applies the designation "with seasonal pattern" whenever appropriate as a supplement to the diagnosis of major depressive disorder or bipolar disorder. There are actually two kinds of SAD, manifested as recurrent winter depression or recurrent summer depression (Boyce & Parker, 1988; Wehr & Rosenthal, 1989; Wehr et al., 1989).

These two subtypes of SAD have opposite kinds of symptoms. People with *winter depression* exhibit a typical constellation of additional symptoms including craving for carbohydrates, overeating, weight gain, and oversleeping (Garvey et al., 1988; Thompson & Isaacs, 1988; Wehr & Rosenthal, 1989; Wurtman & Wurtman, 1989). In contrast, *summer depression* is associated with loss of appetite, weight loss, and insomnia (Boyce & Parker, 1988; Wehr et al., 1989a).

Winter depression appears to be caused by deficient exposure to light (Rosenthal et al., 1985; Terman, 1988; Wehr & Rosenthal, 1989). Researchers are less certain about the cause of summer depression, but some evidence implicates heat as a possible triggering factor (Wehr et al., 1987; Wehr et al., 1989b).

The fact that depression is influenced by seasons suggests possible treatments for winter SAD. Can you think of potentially beneficial therapies for this disorder that build on the known relationship between mood states and climate? Give this question some thought before reading on.

The concept of *climatotherapy*, which involves suggesting that a person move to a different climate to avert the onset of depression, is certainly not a new idea. For instance, the nineteenth-century French physician Esquirol (1845) successfully treated a man's winter depression by mandating that he be in Italy before the close of October, "from whence you must not return until the month of May" (p. 226). Unfortunately, most people who suffer from winter depression are not able to make an annual move to a more sunny climate prior to the onset of each winter season.

What other option(s) exist for these people? A clue for an alternative treatment was contained in the previously stated observation that winter SAD appears to be precipitated by light deficiency. Perhaps exposure to artificial light (or *phototherapy*) might provide a more convenient and practical access to the benefits associated with exposure to bright, sunny climates. An abundance of research has confirmed this hypothesis. Daily exposure to bright artificial light acts as an effective antidepressant in most individuals with winter SAD (Lewy et al., 1987; Sack et al., 1990; Thompson & Isaacs, 1988; Wehr & Rosenthal, 1989).

A number of studies have provided guidelines for the effective application of phototherapy. Winter SAD sufferers should have their eyes exposed to 2,500 lux of full-spectrum visible light for at least two hours every day during the season of risk. (A lux is a unit of light equivalent to the illumination cast by one candle on a surface one meter away.) Morning treatments tend to be most effective, although evening phototherapy sessions may also be helpful in some cases (Sack et al., 1990; Wehr & Rosenthal, 1989).

Most theorists have speculated that SAD has its basis in biological mechanisms and that phototherapy produces its therapeutic effect by acting upon these underlying biological mechanisms. We discuss the hypothesized biological basis of SAD in a later section.

THEORETICAL PERSPECTIVES ON MOOD DISORDERS

Psychoanalytic theory, the behavioral/learning perspective, and biological explanations provide different insights into the causes of mood disorders. We look at each in turn.

THE PSYCHOANALYTIC PERSPECTIVE

The first detailed theoretical interpretation of depression was offered by Karl Abraham (1911), a psychoanalyst who was once a student of Freud. Abraham suggested that mood disorders are rooted in an oral fixation. Frustrated in their efforts to achieve gratification at the oral stage of psychosexual development, individuals develop ambivalent feelings toward their mothers, which eventually transfer to other loved ones so that they are unable to relate successfully to people they love. The consequence is a regression back to the oral level, where these individuals can direct their original love/hate ambivalence toward the self. At times they excessively love themselves (mania), whereas at other times they experience exaggerated self-hatred (depression).

In addition to emphasizing the love/hate ambivalence suggested by Abraham, Freud (1917) theorized that the fixation also causes a person to depend too heavily on others for gratification of basic needs and for maintaining self-esteem. Freud thought mood disorders were rooted in relationships involving overdependency and ambivalent feelings of love and hate. When a person experiences loss (or even the threat of loss) of such a relationship, the unconscious hostility toward the lost person surfaces as anger that is turned back against oneself. This anger takes the form of despair that may be so intense as to motivate suicide, the ultimate form of aggression turned inward.

Many critics ask why only the hate component of a person's love/hate ambivalence is turned inward. Presumably, if positive feelings were turned inward, a person would emerge from mourning with happy memories. Psychoanalytic theorists explain this paradox by arguing that loss of a loved one through death or separation is likely to be interpreted as rejection by a person who already feels ambivalent and emotionally dependent. Accordingly, an intense negative emotional state is a more likely consequence than happy memories.

What little research there is does not support Freud's speculations. Researchers have analyzed the dreams of depressed people and found that they reflect themes of disappointment, failure, and loss rather than anger, hostility, and aggression (Beck & Ward, 1961). Furthermore, if depressed people do turn their anger inward, we should not expect to find much evidence of overt hostility to others. In fact, studies have revealed that depressed people often direct excessive amounts of hostility toward people who are close to them (Weissman & Paykel, 1974; Weissman et al., 1971). Finally, there is a lack of direct evidence that depressed people interpret the death of a loved one as rejection of themselves (Davison & Neale, 1990).

THE BEHAVIORAL PERSPECTIVE

Behavioral and learning theorists tend to view depression in a different light. They note that death of or separation from a loved one means the loss of a primary source of positive reinforcement (Ferster, 1965). Thus a person whose spouse has recently died or who has just divorced may sit at home alone. With no one there to provide ongoing positive reinforcement, he or she may fall into a rut, participating in fewer social and leisure activities that would normally function as primary sources of reinforcement.

Peter Lewinsohn (1974) has expanded this behavioral explanation, noting that depressed behaviors themselves may be reinforced by friends' concern, sympathy, increased attention, and perhaps lowered expectations for the individual's performance. Lewinsohn also suggests that people who lack social skills are prime candidates for depression, because their social ineptness is unlikely to produce much positive reinforcement from others. Lewinsohn's model of depression (see Figure 15.7) takes into account both the reduction of positive reinforcers that result from decreased activities, such as going out with friends, and also increased expressions of concern from others, which he sees as a reinforcer for depression.

Behavior theory suggests that depression can have other sources besides the loss of a loved one. Loss of a job, a move to a different geographic area that cuts us off from a primary circle of friends (for example, going away to college), or a prolonged illness can all substantially reduce opportunities for positive reinforcement; thus all may be linked to depression.

Contrary to Lewinsohn's hypothesis, depressed people seem more likely to elicit negative responses than expressions of concern from people they interact with (Coyne, 1976; Gotlib & Robinson, 1982; Hammen & Peters, 1978). In addition, investigators have reported that depressed people tend to confirm their negative self-opinions by seeking out negative comments from others. For instance, Swann et al. (1990; 1992) have conducted experiments demonstrating that depressed people prefer to interact with someone giving them unfavorable feedback, even when it makes them feel unhappy, rather than someone who gives them positive feedback. Other research suggests that depressed people indicate having fewer pleasant experiences than nondepressed people (MacPhillamy & Lewinsohn, 1974), and that the more depressed a person is, the fewer pleasant experiences are likely to be reported (Lewinsohn & Libet, 1972). This evidence, however, does not rule out the possibility that depressed behavior precedes rather than follows a reduction in reinforcing experiences. It certainly seems plausible that people who become depressed may curtail their participation in reinforcing events. Thus we are left with a chicken-and-egg question: Which comes first?

Another behavioral perspective on depression is Seligman's theory of **learned helplessness** (Garber & Seligman, 1980; Peterson & Seligman, 1984; Seligman,

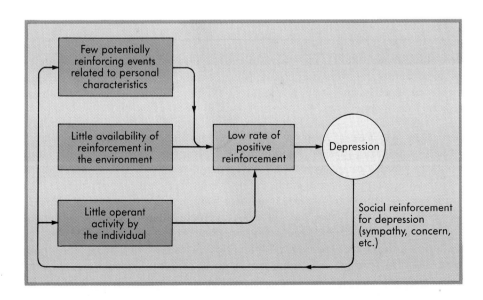

FIGURE 15.7

Lewinsohn's model of depression takes into account both the reduction in positive reinforcement and increases in concern from others which may reinforce depressed behavior.

SOURCE: From Lewinsohn, 1974.

1975; Seligman et al., 1979). This theory, which suggests that people become depressed when they believe they have no control over the reinforcers and punishers in their lives, evolved out of a series of experiments with animals. For example, in one study Seligman and Maier (1967) used dogs as subjects, assigning the dogs to one of three groups. Subjects in one group, the *escape group*, quickly learned to escape from repeated electric shocks by using their noses to press a panel. In contrast, animals in the *inescapable group* were exposed to the same pattern of shocks but were not provided with an escape response. Termination of the shock was independent of any actions taken by these dogs. Dogs in a third *control group* were placed in the same apparatus but not shocked. Animals in the inescapable group appeared to acquire a sense of passive resignation to the unavoidable shock.

In a later phase of the experiment, dogs from all three groups were placed in another experimental situation in which they could avoid a shock merely by jumping over a hurdle to a safe compartment after hearing a warning signal. This avoidance task was easily mastered by dogs previously assigned to either the escape or control conditions. Animals in the inescapable group, however, merely sat passively, making no effort to escape the shocks. Seligman and his colleagues labeled this phenomenon "learned helplessness."

What does this experiment have to do with human depression? Seligman argues that humans, like the dogs in the inescapable group, learn from past situations that their actions will be fruitless in producing desirable change in their environments. When individuals feel helpless to influence their encounters with reinforcers and punishers, the result is depression. According to Seligman, people are most inclined to become depressed if they attribute their helplessness and failure to internal inadequacies (such as a lack of ability, social incompetence, etc.) that are unlikely to change in the future instead of external environmental conditions that are changeable.

Support for Seligman's perspective on depression has been somewhat inconsistent. Some studies have demonstrated that mildly depressed people do tend to express defeatist, helpless behaviors (Peterson & Seligman, 1984). However, other studies of people hospitalized with severe depression demonstrate that although helplessness often accompanies depressive episodes, this pattern changes once patients' depressive episodes end. Such research has found that these formerly depressed subjects are no different from never-depressed control subjects in their tendency to view negative events with an attitude of helpless resignation (Barnett & Gottlib, 1988; Hamilton & Abramson, 1983; Fennell & Campbell, 1984). This finding suggests that an attitude of helplessness may be a symptom rather than a cause of depression.

THE BIOLOGICAL PERSPECTIVE   Considerable evidence points toward the role biological factors in affective disorders. Most of these findings are concentrated in two areas: genetics and brain biochemistry. We first look at the evidence suggesting the role of genetics.

Genetics   Some of the most compelling evidence linking genetics to mood disorders comes from that old standby of nature-nurture research, the twin study. Table 15.5 provides an overview of concordance rates among identical and fraternal twins found in several studies. The average concordance rate for identical twins in these studies (65 percent) is almost five times that for fraternal twins (14 percent). The concordance rates in this table include both unipolar and bipolar forms of mood disorders. If the data are further broken down according to type of disorder, the concordance rates for identical twins are much higher for bipolar than unipolar disorders—72 percent versus 40 percent. Concordance rates for fraternal twins are approximately equal for the two disorders (Allen, 1976). It has

TABLE 15.5 *Concordance of Affective Disorders in Identical and Fraternal Twins*

INVESTIGATOR	NUMBER OF PAIRS IN SAMPLE	CONCORDANCE AMONG IDENTICAL TWINS (%)	NUMBER OF PAIRS IN SAMPLE	CONCORDANCE AMONG FRATERNAL TWINS (%)
Luxenberger (1930)	4	75	13	0
Rosanoff et al. (1935)	23	70	67	16
Slater (1953)	7	57	17	24
Kallman (1954)	27	93	55	24
Harvald & Hauge (1965)	15	67	40	5
Allen et al. (1974)	15	33	34	0
Bertelsen (1979)	55	58	52	17
	Total 146	Average 65	Total 278	Average 14

SOURCE: Adapted from Nurnberger & Gershon, 1982.

also been demonstrated that concordance rates among identical twins are higher in severe than in milder forms of mood disorders (Nurnberger & Gershon, 1982).

For the last several years, genetic researchers have been applying a recently developed technology involving the use of DNA markers to pinpoint the location of genes that induce a variety of diseases. The idea behind this approach is to trace the inheritance of a given disease within large high-risk families and to look for a DNA segment that is inherited along with a predisposition to develop the disease.

A team of researchers headed by Janice Egeland (1987) reported that they had located two genetic markers for bipolar disorder. The subjects were 81 people selected from four high-risk families, all parts of an Old Order Amish community in Pennsylvania. Of the total group of 81, 14 were diagnosed as having a bipolar disorder, and all 14 were shown to have the genetic markers on chromosome 11. Although Egeland and her colleagues were unable to identify a specific

Severe mood disorders, such as bipolar disorder, appear to have high concordance rates among blood relatives. This family has a history of bipolar disorder spanning four generations, including the woman in the photo and her son, as well as her mother and grandmother.

bipolar gene, they found it noteworthy that another gene located in the same region of chromosome 11 is known to be involved in the synthesis of neurotransmitters known as the catecholamines (including norepinephrine, epinephrine, and dopamine). Disturbances in the function of these neurotransmitters have also been implicated in a broad array of behavioral disorders.

Other research teams have attempted to corroborate this finding in two other subject populations in which bipolar disorder appears to be inherited—a group of three large Icelandic families (Hodgkinson et al., 1987) and a group of three North American families (Detera-Wadleigh et al., 1987). Although neither study found evidence of chromosome 11 linkage, they suggested that at least two or more different genes may produce predispositions to bipolar disorder (Kolata, 1987b; Robertson, 1987). This interpretation was supported by a study in Israel which claimed to have isolated a second gene, located on the X chromosome, that causes bipolar disorder (Baron et al., 1987). More recently, studies have begun to question Egeland's interpretation of the role of chromosome 11 (or another chromosome) in bipolar disorders, arguing that the evidence is either unclear or nonexistent (Barinaga, 1989; Mendlewicz, 1991).

How should we interpret these conflicting interpretations of genetic linkages for bipolar disorder? At present we recommend a cautious interpretation. Until further research confirms the location of the gene or genes, it appears premature to claim it is located on chromosome 11, or any other chromosome. On the other hand, heritability studies do suggest that there may be a genetic disposition toward bipolar disorder.

Numerous family studies have shown that siblings and parents of people with mood disorders are from two to five times more likely to have unipolar and bipolar disorders than subjects whose close relations have no diagnosed mood disorders (Nurnberger & Gershon, 1982; Weissman, 1987; Weissman et al., 1982). Adoption studies provide further support; in one study, adoptees who had a biological parent or parents diagnosed as having a mood disorder were much more likely to develop the illness themselves than adoptees whose biological parents were free of the disorder (Cadoret, 1978). Two other studies of adoptees with diagnosed bipolar disorder found a considerably higher incidence of this disorder among biological than adoptive parents (Mendlewicz & Rainer, 1977; Wender et al., 1986).

Virtually all researchers studying the causes of mood disorders currently agree that the data from twin, family, and adoption studies present compelling evidence for a strong genetic factor in vulnerability to mood disorders. The exact mode of transmission is unknown, but it is presumed to be quite complex, considering the wide variation in the degree of severity and manner of expression of the mood disorders.

Brain Biochemistry   If mood disorders can be genetically transmitted, this trait must be expressed through some physiological mechanism that makes a person vulnerable to mood disorders. Present evidence strongly suggests that this physiological expression takes the form of altered levels of neurotransmitters in the brain. Recall from Chapter 3 that neurotransmitters are chemical messengers that enable nerve impulses to be transmitted from one neuron to another. The level of certain critical neurotransmitters is strongly linked to mood disorders.

The search for a link between neurotransmitters and mood disorders began in the 1950s, when it was learned that two classes of drugs, the *monoamine oxidase inhibitors (MAO inhibitors)* and the *tricyclics*, often alleviated the symptoms of depression. Subsequent studies of nonhuman subjects revealed that both of these drugs act to increase the brain levels of two neurotransmitters, norepinephrine and serotonin. Thus it seemed that low levels of these neurotransmitters might contribute to depression. This and other research led to the first formal biochemical *theory* of mood disorders, known as the *norepinephrine theory* (Schild-kraut, 1970). This theory proposed that depression is related to reduced amounts of norepinephrine, and that the manic side of bipolar disorder results from an excess of this neurotransmitter.

The norepinephrine theory was supported by a number of studies. In addition to the evidence that drugs which increase norepinephrine levels often reduce depression (Maas et al., 1972; Teuting et al., 1981), lower-than-normal levels of norepinephrine were found in the urine of depressed people, and abnormally high levels were found in the urine of manic patients (Kety, 1975). In one interesting series of studies, researchers monitored urinary levels of norepinephrine in a sample of bipolar patients as they cycled through the stages of depression, normalcy, and mania. They found that the norepinephrine levels decreased as the subjects entered depression and increased when they became manic (Bunney et al., 1970, 1972). The drug lithium carbonate, now widely used to treat the manic side of bipolar disorder, has been shown to reduce norepinephrine levels significantly at certain synapses in the brain (Teuting et al., 1981).

Abnormalities in serotonin levels also seem to be related to mood disorders, but in a different way. Studies have found low serotonin levels in depressed people (Goodwin et al., 1978; Shaw et al., 1967; Zubenki et al., 1990) as well as in manic people (Coppen, 1972; Van Praag, 1981).

The *amine theory of mood disorders* (Kety, 1975; Prange et al., 1974) attempts to integrate the different patterns of norepinephrine and serotonin into a cohesive explanation. According to this theory, serotonin places limits on the range of variations possible in norepinephrine levels. When serotonin levels are normal, norepinephrine levels also remain within a normal range, and the person experiences only normal highs and lows. However, a deficiency in serotonin causes a breakdown in its stabilizing functions, allowing norepinephrine levels to fluctuate beyond the normal high and low boundaries. This imbalance can result in deep depression or excessive mania (see Figure 15.8).

The amine theory seems to make sense, but is it supported by research? As with the other disorders we have discussed in this chapter, the evidence is not entirely conclusive. Recall the two drugs, tricyclics and MAO inhibitors, that

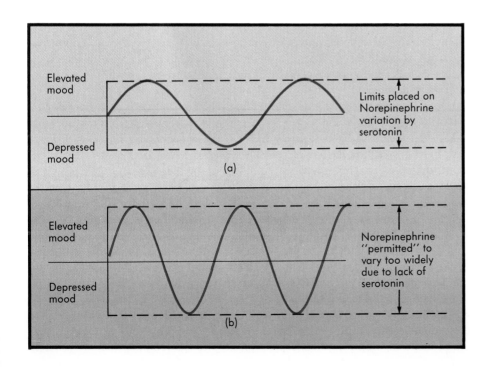

FIGURE 15.8

A Schematic Representation of the Amine Theory of Depression

Normal levels of serotonin limit fluctuations in norepinephrine levels. When serotonin levels are low, norepinephrine levels vary widely.

were found in the 1950s to alleviate depression. We reported that these drugs act to increase the brain levels of norepinephrine and serotonin. However, this effect occurs only in the period immediately after drug therapy begins: Within a few days these two neurotransmitters return to their level prior to drug therapy.

This finding would not present a problem for the amine theory if the antidepressant effect of the drugs also occurred during the brief period when transmitter levels are elevated. However, such is not the case. Both tricyclics and MAO inhibitors generally take from one to two weeks to relieve depression. Contrary to the amine theory, then, it appears that the effectiveness of these drugs in alleviating depression cannot be explained merely by a change in neurotransmitter levels (Heninger et al., 1983). Then what is it due to? Researchers have speculated that the MAO inhibitors and tricyclic drugs may reduce depression by increasing the sensitivity of both norepinephrine and serotonin receptors in receiving neurons. The increased sensitivity would allow receptors to utilize better what limited supplies of neurotransmitters are available, thus relieving the depression (Charney et al., 1984; Heninger et al., 1983). Although researchers still do not know exactly why antidepressant drugs are effective, it is clear that biochemical factors are strongly implicated in mood disorders.

Recent evidence suggests that the winter form of SAD may be induced by biochemical disturbances in two separate biological systems. One system involves the neurotransmitter serotonin, whose relationship to depression has been previously discussed. Drugs and a high carbohydrate diet which increase the availability of serotonin often alleviate the symptoms of winter depression (Wurtman & Wurtman, 1989). A second biological system implicated in winter SAD is one that involves the hormone *melatonin*, a substance secreted by the brain's pineal gland that affects mood and subjective energy levels. Research suggests that winter SAD may be induced by too much melatonin or by excessively prolonged secretions of melatonin (Wehr & Rosenthal, 1989; Wurtman & Wurtman, 1989). Both serotonin and melatonin systems are influenced by *photoperiodism*, the earth's daily dark-light cycle (Wurtman & Wurtman, 1989, p. 68). To the extent that SAD is related to disturbances in the earth's dark-light cycle, it seems logical to speculate that phototherapy may be effective in treating winter depression by acting to correct abnormalities in one or both of these two distinct biological systems.

As persuasive as the biological evidence is, can we explain mood disorders solely in terms of genetics and brain biochemistry? Many psychologists now believe that vulnerability to mood disorders involves an interaction of biological predispositions and environmental factors, and a number of studies support this interactive model.

In one fascinating study, monkeys were subjected to a range of developmental conditions including being raised by their mothers, removed from mothers and raised with peers with no separations from these peers, and raised with peers with intermittent separations of variable frequency. At a later stage of development, the monkeys were given variable doses of a drug known to reduce norepinephrine levels in the brain; then their behaviors were monitored for signs of depression (such as decreased activity or huddling behaviors). The researchers found that monkeys who had remained with their mothers required up to eight times as much drug to produce depression symptoms as monkeys reared only with peers. And of the two groups of peer-reared monkeys, those that had experienced frequent separations from their companions were more susceptible to the depressant effects of the drug than those who experienced few or no separations (Kraemer & McKinney, 1979).

This study suggests that both environment and biological factors interact to determine susceptibility to depression. But how does this finding relate to humans, many of whom develop depression despite stable home lives? One interesting finding, for instance, is that as many as six times more women than men in this country are diagnosed as depressive (Duke & Nowicki, 1986), a finding that has been corroborated in other societies as well (Goldstein et al., 1986).

SEX DIFFERENCES AND DEPRESSION   Evidence indicates that women are more likely than men to experience major depression (Nolen-Hoeksema, 1987; Wilhelm & Parker, 1989). What accounts for this sex difference in the incidence of depressive disorder? Are women more biologically prone to depression than men? And if they are, what is the biological mechanism—genetics, hormones, or something else? Or is it possible that other nonbiological factors may contribute to this sex difference? Consider this issue before reading on.

There is evidence that some women experience depression as part of a generalized *premenstrual syndrome (PMS)* (Boyle et al., 1987; Hamilton et al., 1989), a term used to identify a myriad of symptoms that precede each menstrual period and are occasionally severe enough to interfere with some aspects of daily functioning. Some studies have also shown an increase in depression in women taking oral contraceptives (Hatcher et al., 1988). Other studies have found a higher incidence of depression among women with PMS (Cumming et al., 1991). In addition, studies have demonstrated that PMS is associated with lower brain levels of serotonin, a neurotransmitter implicated in depression, and that drugs designed to elevate serotonin levels appear to alleviate depression associated with PMS (Moller, 1991). This finding suggests that the tendency for many women with PMS to crave carbohydrates may be negatively reinforced by the alleviation of depression.

The contributions of PMS to depression in women does not account for the large differences in depression among men and women, however. Recently, published results of a five-year study of depression incidence among a sample of men and women suggested the possible irrelevance of biological factors in determining sex differences in depression, while indicating that "social factors are of key relevance in determining any female preponderance in depression described in general population studies" (Wilhelm & Parker, 1989, p. 401).

What are these social factors that may account for sex differences in the incidence of depression? A number of theorists have looked into the role of cultural conditioning. When this issue is put to students, many of them speculate that the high incidence of depression among women has something to do with the housewife role, which may cause them to feel isolated from the mainstream of life. However, there is evidence not only that married women with careers are no less depressed than housewives, but also that married women with careers have much higher rates of depression than married men with careers (Radloff, 1975). In summary, we cannot adequately account for the difference in the incidence of depression among men and women. In fact, a recent longitudinal study of grade school children indicates that it is boys, not girls, that display a higher incidence of depressive symptoms (Nolen-Hoeksema et al., 1991). It will be interesting to follow these children to see if this pattern switches later in life.

SCHIZOPHRENIA

When my first episode of schizophrenia occurred, I was 21, a senior in college. . . . Everything in my life was just perfect. I had a boyfriend whom I liked a lot, a part-time job tutoring Spanish, and was about to run for the Ms. Senior pageant.

All of a sudden things weren't going so well. I began to lose control of my life and, most of all, myself. I couldn't concentrate on my schoolwork, I couldn't sleep, and when I did sleep, I had dreams about dying.

I was afraid to go to class, imagined that people were talking about me, and on top of that I heard voices. . . I moved [off campus to live] . . . with my sister, [but] things got worse. I was afraid to go outside and when I looked out of the window, it seemed that everyone outside was yelling, "kill her, kill her. . . ." I imagined that I had a foul body odor and I sometimes took up to six showers a day. . . . I couldn't remember a thing. I had a notebook full of reminders telling me what to do on that particular day. I couldn't remember my schoolwork, and I would study from 6:00 P.M. until 4:00 A.M., but never had the courage to go to class on the following day. I tried to tell my sister about it, but she didn't understand. She suggested that I see a psychiatrist, but I was afraid to go out of the house to see him.

One day I decided that I couldn't take this trauma anymore, so I took an overdose of 35 Darvon pills. At the same moment, a voice inside me said, "What did you do that for? Now you won't go to heaven." At that instant I realized that I really didn't want to die, I wanted to live, and I was afraid. I got on the phone and called the psychiatrist. . . . I told him that I had taken an overdose of Darvon and that I was afraid. He told me to take a taxi to the hospital. . . . Somehow I just couldn't accept the fact that I was really going to see a psychiatrist. I thought that psychiatrists were only for crazy people, and I definitely didn't think I was crazy yet. As a result, . . . I left the hospital and ended up meeting my sister on the way home. She told me to turn right back around, because I was definitely going to be admitted. (O'Neal, 1984, pp. 109–110)

The young woman who related this account was diagnosed as having **schizophrenia**. Schizophrenia is one of the most severe and disabling of all mental disorders, characterized by extreme disruptions of perceptions, thoughts, emotions, and behavior. At any point in time it affects about 1 percent of people throughout the world, and it is estimated that as many as three out of every 100 people may experience this disorder at some time during their lives (Reiger et al., 1984). Approximately 600,000 people receive treatment for schizophrenia annually in the United States. This disorder occurs with equal frequency in both sexes.

Schizophrenia was once called *dementia praecox* (Kraeplin, 1918), because the disorder typically has an early *(praecox)* onset in the teenage or young adult years and is characterized by a progressive intellectual deterioration, or *dementia*. The term *schizophrenia* was later coined by Eugene Bleuler (1950) to describe what he saw as the primary symptom of this disorder: a dissociation of thoughts from appropriate emotions caused by a splitting off (the Greek *schizo*, or split) of parts of the mind (the Greek *phrenum*, or mind). Laypersons often confuse schizophrenia with multiple personality, an entirely different disorder. Whereas the split in multiple personality disorder is between different personalities, all of which are capable of maintaining contact with reality, the split in schizophrenia is between thoughts and feelings. The result is often bizarre behavior that is highly dysfunctional.

Schizophrenia is distinguished from other behavioral disorders primarily by the characteristically extreme disturbances in thinking that cause people to behave in maladaptive ways. In addition to these thought disturbances, a constellation of other symptoms are used to diagnose this disorder. People diagnosed as schizophrenic may show considerable diversity of symptoms. They typically exhibit most but not necessarily all of a *primary* core of symptoms as well as one or more *secondary* symptoms that are used to assign the individual to a particular subtype of schizophrenia. We look at the primary symptoms that typify all forms of schizophrenia, then at the secondary symptoms of each subtype.

PRIMARY SYMPTOMS OF SCHIZOPHRENIA

The collection of primary or core symptoms that are characteristic of many forms of schizophrenia include disturbances in thought, perception, emotional expression, and speech, together with social withdrawal and diminished motivation.

TABLE 15.6 *Several Varieties of Delusional Thoughts That May Be Associated with Schizophrenia*

Delusion of influence	A belief that others are influencing one by means of wires, TV, and so on, making one do things against one's will.
Delusion of grandeur	The belief that one is in actuality some great world or historical figure, such as Napoleon, Queen Victoria, or the president of the United States.
Delusion of persecution	The belief that one is being persecuted, hunted, or interfered with by certain individuals or organized groups.
Delusion of reference	The belief that others are talking about one, that one is being included in TV shows or plays or referred to in news articles, and so on.
Delusion of bodily change	The belief that one's body is changing in some unusual way—for example, that the blood is turning to snakes or the flesh to concrete.
Delusion of nihilism	The belief that nothing really exists, that all things are simply shadows; also common is the idea that one has really been dead for many years and is observing the world from afar.

Delusions and Disturbances of Thought Thought disturbances associated with schizophrenia tend to be of two basic types: disturbances of *content* (that is, the actual ideas expressed), and disturbances of *form* (the manner in which ideas are organized).

Most individuals with schizophrenia demonstrate marked disturbances in the content of their thoughts. These disturbances may be evident from a few characteristic symptoms. One is a lack of awareness of some of the basic realities of life, such as what is going on around them and the nature of their condition. Another disturbance in the content of thought is delusions. Table 15.6 describes several varieties of delusional thoughts that may be associated with schizophrenia.

Disturbances in the form of thought may be evident in the incoherence of the ideas a person verbalizes. For example, consider the following account of a conversation between a schizophrenic patient and a clinician:

THERAPIST: How old are you?

CLIENT: Why I am centuries old, sir.

THERAPIST: How long have you been here?

CLIENT: I've been now on this property on and off for a long time. I cannot say the exact time because we are absorbed by the air at night, and they bring back people. They kill up everything: they can make you lie; they can talk through your throat.

THERAPIST: Who is this?

CLIENT: Why, the air.

THERAPIST: What is the name of this place?

CLIENT: This place is called a star.

THERAPIST: Who is the doctor in charge of your ward?

CLIENT: A body just like yours, sir. They can make you black and white. I say good morning, but he just comes through there. At first it was a colony. They said it was heaven. These buildings were not solid at the time, and I am positive that this is the same place. They have others just like it. People die, and all the microbes talk over there, and prestigitis you know is sending you from here to another world. I was sent by the government to the United States to Washington to some star, and they had a pretty nice country there. Now you have a body like a young man who says he is of the prestigitis.

THERAPIST: Who was this prestigitis?

CLIENT: Why, you are yourself. You can be prestigitis. They make you say bad things; they can read you; they bring back Negroes from the dead. (White, 1932, p. 228)

It is common for schizophrenics to invent new words, or **neologisms,** like the word "prestigitis" in the preceding passage. Another anomaly in the form of schizophrenic thoughts is *loose associations*, in which ideas shift from one topic to another so that it is very difficult for a listener to follow the train of thought.

Hallucinations and Disturbance of Perception   A second primary symptom, disturbed perception, may include changes in how the body feels (including numbness, tingling, or burning sensations, or the feeling that organs are deteriorating or that parts of the body are too large or small), or a feeling of depersonalization that makes a person feel separated from his or her body. Many schizophrenics report changed perceptions of their external environment. For some, everything may appear two-dimensional and colorless; others report that they are hypersensitive to light, sounds, or touch. Research also demonstrates that schizophrenics have considerable difficulty properly focusing their attention as they process sensory stimulation and that they are often unable to filter out irrelevant information (Braff & Geyer, 1990; Grillon et al., 1990; Harris et al., 1990).

The most common altered perceptions in schizophrenia are hallucinations. Hallucinations may occur in any of the sense modalities, but most often a schizophrenic person hears voices that seem to be coming from outside the person's head. It has been suggested that at least some of the auditory hallucinations experienced by schizophrenics may be projections of their own thoughts (Bick & Kinsbourne, 1987). These voices may give commands ("take off your clothes"; "kill corrupting prostitutes") that are sometimes obeyed with disturbing or tragic consequences. More commonly the imagined voices may make insulting comments about the person's character or behavior (illustrated in the following account):

A forty-one-year-old housewife heard a voice coming from a house across the road. The voice went on incessantly in a flat monotone describing everything she was doing with an admixture of critical comments. "She is peeling potatoes, got hold of the peeler, she does not want that potato, she is putting it back, because she thinks it has a knobble like a penis, she has a dirty mind, she is peeling potatoes, now she is washing them. . . ." (Mellor, 1970, p. 16)

Disturbance in Emotional Expression   A third common symptom of schizophrenia is a disturbance in emotional expression. This symptom may take the form of a *blunted* or *flat affect*, characterized by a dramatic lack of emotional expression. The person may stare vacantly with listless eyes, speak in a monotone, and show no facial expression. Differing theories have been offered to explain this lack of affect, including the possibility that schizophrenic people may be so absorbed in responding to internal stimuli that they are unresponsive to outside stimuli (Venables & Wing, 1962). It has also been suggested that by turning themselves off, schizophrenics are able to protect themselves from stimuli with which they feel incapable of coping (Mednick, 1958).

Perhaps even more common than flat affect are inappropriate emotional responses, in which the emotional expression is incongruous with its context. For example, a schizophrenic person may laugh upon hearing of the death of a loved one, or may fly into a rage when asked an innocuous question such as, "Did you enjoy your dinner?" Mood states may shift rapidly for no discernible reason.

Disturbances in Speech   In addition to abnormal speech patterns (such as incoherence and loose associations) that result from thought disturbances, two verbal dysfunctions may be viewed as primary examples of speech disturbances linked with schizophrenia. In **mutism,** the person may not utter a sound for hours or days regardless of how much encouragement or prodding is provided. In the other disturbance, **echolalia,** a person might answer a question by repeating it verbatim or might repeat virtually every statement he or she hears uttered.

Disorganized or Catatonic Behavior   A fifth symptom of schizophrenia is grossly disorganized or catatonic behavior. Catatonic behavior is characterized by a severe rigidness of posture which may be maintained for hours. In addition, catatonic postures can be molded into new and unusual positions. Throughout an episode of catatonia an individual may be completely unresponsive even though they are often fully aware of what is going on around them.

For a diagnosis of schizophrenia, at least two of the above five symptoms must have been present during the preceding month. In addition, these symptoms must have been severe enough to disrupt social or occupational functioning (American Psychiatric Association, 1993).

THE DEVELOPMENT OF SCHIZOPHRENIA   *Prodromal Stage*   The first signs of a schizophrenic disorder appear during the *prodromal stage*, usually during late adolescence or early adulthood. Early symptoms often include diminished interest in work, school, and leisure activities; lowered productivity; social withdrawal; and a deterioration in health and grooming habits. The prodromal phase may last for months or even years.

Active Stage   The major symptoms of schizophrenia appear during the second phase, the active stage. The duration of this phase is highly variable, ranging from months to most of a lifetime.

Residual Stage   When and if the active phase subsides, either spontaneously or as a result of treatment, the person enters the third, or residual phase, in which the major symptoms are absent or markedly diminished. During this gradual recovery, residual symptoms, such as continued difficulty establishing social contacts, low motivation, somewhat blunted or inappropriate affect, and unusual perceptual experiences, may linger.

Although the primary symptoms of schizophrenia are common in all the various subtypes of this disorder, the secondary symptoms make these subtypes appear very different from one another. DSM-IV distinguishes five subtypes or varieties of schizophrenia: *disorganized (hebephrenic), catatonic, paranoid, undifferentiated,* and *residual.*

SUBTYPES OF SCHIZOPHRENIA

DISORGANIZED SCHIZOPHRENIA   Personality disintegration is generally most severe in **disorganized schizophrenia.** This subtype is characterized by marked disorganization and regression in thinking and behavioral patterns. Hallucinations and delusions are very common, often with sexual, religious, or hypochondriacal themes. Emotional moods change constantly, with wild swings from fits of crying to episodes of uncontrollable giggling. A person with disorganized schizophrenia often behaves in an infantile manner, neglecting personal hygiene and sometimes even engaging publicly in bladder and bowel functions. Speech is often incoherent, marked by stringing together similar-sounding or rhyming words or phrases (this thinking distortion is called a *clang*) and neologisms. The term *word salad* has been used to describe the bombastic, illogical flood of words that streams forth from the mouths of disorganized schizophrenics.

CATATONIC SCHIZOPHRENIA   The distinguishing symptoms of **catatonic schizophrenia** are extreme psychomotor disturbances, which may range from stuporous immobility to wild excitement and agitation. In the stuporous state of catatonic immobility, a person may adopt a strange posture that is held for prolonged periods of time, sometimes even after the limbs become stiff, blue, and swollen from lack of movement. The person's limbs often exhibit a kind of *waxy flexibility*, so that another person can move them about and put them in new positions which are then maintained. Although people in this stage appear totally oblivious to what is going on around them, interviews with recovered catatonics show that many have excellent recall for what occurred around them during their episodes of stupor.

Agitated catatonia is characterized by extreme motor excitement in which the person thrashes about, shouts, talks continuously and incoherently, or runs about wildly. Sometimes stuporous catatonics will suddenly, without warning, blast out

Patients with catatonic schizophrenia may adopt a rigid posture for extended periods of time.

of their immobility into frenzied activity. During this state of great agitation individuals can do considerable damage to themselves, nearby objects, and other people. These bizarre motor symptoms are fairly uncommon today, thanks to effective drug therapy.

PARANOID SCHIZOPHRENIA   Of all of the subtypes of schizophrenia, people with **paranoid schizophrenia** demonstrate the highest level of awareness and the least impairment of the ability to carry out daily functions. However, this disorder is also a profound disturbance. Its dominant symptom is the presence of well-organized delusional thoughts, such as those described earlier in Table 15.6. Vivid auditory, visual, or olfactory hallucinations are also common in this condition. Paranoid schizophrenics often appear agitated, angry, argumentative, and sometimes violent. They may become particularly dangerous if they decide to destroy their supposed persecutors.

UNDIFFERENTIATED AND RESIDUAL SCHIZOPHRENIA   **Undifferentiated schizophrenia** is a kind of catchall category to which schizophrenics are assigned if they do not manifest the specific symptom patterns of disorganized, catatonic, or paranoid forms of the disorder. However, the primary core of symptoms, such as disturbance of thought, perception, and emotional expression, are present. The final category, **residual schizophrenia,** is a label used for schizophrenics in the final phase as described earlier.

Schizophrenia has spawned more research into causes and treatments than any other behavioral disorder. We shall look at the psychoanalytic, behavioral, and biological perspectives, then present a model that accounts for both biological and psychological factors.

THEORETICAL PERSPECTIVES ON SCHIZOPHRENIA

THE PSYCHOANALYTIC PERSPECTIVE   Freud believed that schizophrenia occurs when a person's ego either becomes overwhelmed with id demands or is besieged by unbearable guilt. In both cases, the ego elects to retreat rather than attempt to set things straight, and the person undergoes a massive regression back to the oral stage of psychosexual development. In the first phase of this retreat, *regressive symptoms* demonstrate a return to the infantile. A person may return to primary process thinking (see Chapter 14) and may experience delusions of self-importance. Eventually the regression becomes so extensive that all contact with reality is lost. At this point, the schizophrenic begins a struggle to regain reality. *Restitutional symptoms* appear, such as hallucinations, delusions, and bizarre speech patterns that reflect an effort to reestablish verbal communication with other people. Today only a very few psychoanalytic theorists place much credibility in Freud's explanation of schizophrenia.

THE BEHAVIORAL PERSPECTIVE   It is difficult to see how behavioral principles such as reinforcement and modeling contribute to the symptoms of people who are as out of touch with reality as schizophrenics are. However, learning theorists Leonard Ullman and Leonard Krasner (1975) propose that schizophrenics either have not been reinforced adequately for responding to normal social stimuli, or perhaps have even been punished for such responses. As a consequence, normal patterns of attending to or reacting to appropriate social cues are extinguished or suppressed. To fill the resulting void, they begin to respond to inappropriate stimuli, such as imaginary voices emanating from the coffeepot. Other people's responses to these bizarre behaviors may then further reinforce these patterns.

In fact, the worsening of schizophrenic symptoms can often be attributed to the consequences of these behaviors. While behavioral theory may have some difficulty explaining why some people become schizophrenic, as you will see in the next chapter, it has been a useful approach in the treatment of schizophrenic behavior.

THE BIOLOGICAL PERSPECTIVE A stronger explanation for schizophrenia is provided by the biological perspective. As with mood disorders, substantial clues point toward both genetics and brain biochemistry.

Genetics An extensive body of research indicates that certain people are genetically predisposed to develop schizophrenia (Barnes, 1987b; Gottesman et al., 1987; Kendler, 1986; Pardes et al., 1989). Table 15.7 summarizes some of these data from a number of twin studies. Note that the concordance rate for identical twins runs two to four times higher than that reported for fraternal twins. Studies have also demonstrated that concordance rates among identical twins are higher in severe than in milder forms of schizophrenia (Gottesman & Shields, 1982).

Family studies have shown a substantially higher incidence of schizophrenia among relatives of schizophrenics than among the general population (Baron et al., 1985; Kendler et al., 1985; Loehlin et al., 1988; Mayer-Gross et al., 1969; Rosenthal, 1971; Slater & Cowie, 1971). Adoption studies have provided further evidence: Several investigators have found that adoptees whose biological parent or parents were diagnosed as schizophrenic were considerably more likely to develop the disorder than adoptees whose biological parents were free of the illness (Kety et al., 1975; Rosenthal, 1977; Rosenthal et al., 1971).

One investigation suggested a possible linkage between genetic markers on chromosome 5 and schizophrenia (Sherrington et al., 1988). In this study, members of seven families appeared to carry a single dominant gene for schizophrenia on chromosome 5. Another more recent investigation of one family provided

TABLE 15.7 *Concordance Rates of Schizophrenia among Identical and Fraternal Twins*

INVESTIGATOR	COUNTRY	IDENTICAL TWINS		FRATERNAL TWINS	
		NUMBER OF PAIRS IN SAMPLE	PERCENTAGE CONCORDANCE RATE	NUMBER OF PAIRS IN SAMPLE	PERCENTAGE CONCORDANCE RATE
Gottesman & Shields	England	22	40–50*	33	9–19
Pollin et al.	U.S.A.	95	14–27	125	4–8
Fischer	Denmark	21	24–48	41	10–19
Kringlen	Norway	55	23–38	90	4–10
Tienari	Finland	17	0–36	20	5–14

*The range in the concordance rate figures reflects different estimates of what would constitute a concordant pair, which vary depending on how narrowly or broadly schizophrenia is defined. The lower figure is for the narrower definition, which requires a majority of the major symptoms of schizophrenia to be present.
SOURCE: Adapted from Gottesman & Shields, 1982.

The Genain sisters have all been diagnosed with schizophrenia.

further evidence of a possible linkage of schizophrenia to a single major gene on chromosome 5 (McGillivry et al., 1990). However, another study of a large multigenerational family failed to find evidence linking schizophrenia to markers on chromosome 5 (Kennedy et al., 1988). Taken together, these three investigations indicate that schizophrenia does not follow the same pattern of inheritance in every family that is affected. Rather, it seems likely that schizophrenia is genetically heterogeneous (that is, it can be caused by different single major genes) or that it is caused by multiple genetic and environmental factors (Loehlin et al., 1988).

In all, while there is abundant evidence that genetics is an important factor in the development of schizophrenia, it seems unlikely that genes alone cause this disorder. If that were the case, the concordance rate between twins would be virtually 100 percent. Furthermore, even when both parents have schizophrenia, the odds are better than 50–50 that their offspring will not develop the disorder. Several schizophrenia researchers explain this discrepancy by theorizing that a genetic predisposition toward schizophrenia is by no means a sufficient condition to produce this disorder, and that certain environmental stresses must also be present (Kessler, 1980; Mirsky & Duncan, 1986). We return to this interaction hypothesis after considering some additional evidence of biological factors.

Brain Biochemistry As with the mood disorders, researchers studying schizophrenia have focused considerable attention on biochemical abnormalities and mechanisms of drug action to explain schizophrenia. Although several different biochemical hypotheses have been proposed over the years the dopamine hypothesis appears to be the most promising. The *dopamine hypothesis* suggests that schizophrenia is caused either by abnormally high levels of the neurotransmitter dopamine or by above-normal reactivity to this chemical due to an increased number of receptors for dopamine (Barnes, 1987b; Grey et al., 1991; Wong et al., 1986).

This hypothesis is supported by research. For example, it is known that the *phenothiazines* (drugs that alleviate some of the symptoms of schizophrenia) reduce the activity of dopamine by blocking postsynaptic dopamine receptors (Kimble, 1988; Lipper, 1985; Wolkin et al., 1989). In addition, postmortem

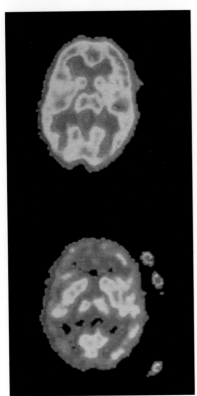

FIGURE 15.9

PET Scans Comparing a Patient Diagnosed with Schizophrenia (top) *with a Normal Subject* (bottom).

Note the difference in activity of the frontal cortex. Some studies suggest that schizophrenics have lower levels of frontal cortex activity than normal subjects.

brain analyses have found an abnormal number of dopamine receptors in the brains of some schizophrenics (Wong et al., 1986), as well as abnormally high levels of dopamine in certain areas of schizophrenic brains (Bird et al., 1979; Stein & Wise, 1971). Considered together, these findings provide strong evidence linking either excessive dopamine levels or abnormal sensitivity to dopamine (or perhaps both) to schizophrenia (Carlsson, 1977; Cortes et al., 1989; Grey et al., 1991).

Brain Structural Abnormalities There is also extensive evidence of structural abnormalities in the brains of schizophrenics. These findings, considered in tandem with data concerning biochemical irregularities, provide powerful evidence that schizophrenia is a brain disease (Johnson, 1989). Several of the new techniques for observing living brains, such as CAT and PET scans and magnetic resonance imaging (see Chapter 3), have provided evidence of various kinds of physical abnormalities in the brains of individuals diagnosed as having schizophrenia. These structural abnormalities include unusually large ventricles (hollow spaces within the brain filled with cerebrospinal fluid) (Andreasen et al., 1990; Johnstone et al., 1989; Kaplan et al., 1990; Rossi et al., 1989a, 1989b; Weinberger et al., 1990; Woods et al., 1990); reduced volume of temporal lobe gray matter (Rossi et al., 1990; Suddath et al., 1989; Weinberger et al., 1990); unusually small corpus callosums (Rossi et al., 1989a); and high densities of white matter in the right frontal lobe and right parietal lobe (Rossi et al., 1989b). The PET scans in Figure 15.9 show some of these abnormalities.

At the present time researchers are uncertain about both the causes of these varied brain abnormalities and their relationship to various types of schizophrenia. It remains to be seen whether one complex pattern of structural brain irregularities characterizes all schizophrenics, or whether a distinct pattern is associated with each subtype. Furthermore, additional research is necessary to reveal whether brain structural abnormalities are characteristic of all forms of schizophrenia.

Throughout this text we have emphasized the role of genetic (biological) and environmental interactions in determining behavioral dispositions. Our discussion of schizophrenia is no exception. As strong as the biological evidence is, the fact remains that not everyone who is genetically predisposed toward schizophrenia becomes schizophrenic. On the other hand, we cannot simply ignore the strong evidence for some degree of heritability for schizophrenia. For further discussion of the biological determinants of schizophrenia, refer to the Research Perspectives segment at the end of this chapter.

We hope that continued research will eventually provide a clearer explanation of the causes of schizophrenia. Until that time, theorists will continue their attempts to explain schizophrenia in terms of both biological dispositions and environmental factors.

PERSONALITY DISORDERS

We end our discussion of behavioral disorders with a brief look at the diverse array of disorders grouped under Personality Disorders. DSM-IV identifies 10 related personality disorders that are grouped into three clusters (A–C), outlined in Table 15.8. Cluster A disorders are all characterized by odd and/or eccentric behavior; Cluster B disorders are characterized by dramatic, emotional, or erratic behavior; and Cluster C disorders are characterized by anxious or fearful behavior.

TABLE 15.8 *Personality Disorders*

CLUSTER A: DISORDERS OF ODD OR ECCENTRIC BEHAVIOR

Paranoid Personality Disorder
Extreme and pervasive suspiciousness, mistrust, and envy of others; hypersensitivity and difficulty in getting along with others; restricted expresssion of emotion; inclined to avoid intimacy.

Schizoid Personality Disorder
Very cold, aloof, and socially isolated; unable to form close relationships; humorless; appears to be indifferent to praise or criticism.

Schizotypal Personality Disorder
Oddities or eccentricities in thought, perception, speech, or behavior not severe enough to be diagnosd as schizophrenic; extreme social isolation; strong tendency toward egocentrism.

CLUSTER B: DISORDERS OF DRAMATIC, EMOTIONAL, OR ERRATIC BEHAVIOR

Antisocial Personality Disorder
A continuous pattern of utter disregard for the rights of others and the rules of society; antisocial acts usually commence before age 15; often unable to perform adequately on the job or in relationships; a strong tendency to engage in exciting, impulsive behavior with little attention to the consequences.

Borderline Personality Disorder
This condition is not associated with a characteristic pattern of behavior that is invariably present, and it is often associated with other personality disorders (hence the label "borderline"); instability in several areas including mood, self-image, behavior, and interpersonal relationships; a chronic inclination to be indecisive and uncertain about a variety of important life issues.

Histrionic Personality Disorder
Overly dramatic behavior, frequently expressed as drawing attention to oneself and/or overreacting to minor events of small consequence; self-centered, self-indulgent, vain, manipulative, and inconsiderate; tendency to be dependent on others but poor interpersonal skills.

Narcissistic Personality Disorder
Grandiose sense of self-importance; preoccupied with fantasies of great achievements; childish demands for constant attention and special favors; little empathy for others.

CLUSTER C: DISORDERS INVOLVING ANXIOUS OR FEARFUL BEHAVIOR

Avoidant Personality Disorder
Hypersensitive to the possibility of being rejected by others; a desire for close social relationships but unable to reach out to others because of fear of rejection; very low self-esteem.

Dependent Personality Disorder
Extremely poor self-image and a lack of self-confidence; depends upon others to make all major decisions; subordinates personal needs to avoid alienating people depended upon; unable to tolerate being alone.

Obsessive-Compulsive Personality Disorder
Excessive preoccupation with rules and regulations and the need to do things "by the book"; inflexible, stiff workaholic; limited ability to express tender emotions such as warmth, caring, and love.

SOURCE: Adapted from DSM-IV, American Psychiatry Association, 1993.

The various personality disorders are linked by a number of shared characteristics. First, most tend to show up at an early age, usually no later than adolescence, and the characteristic maladaptive behaviors often tend to become more deeply ingrained over the years. Another common feature is that very few individuals diagnosed as having a personality disorder ever seem to believe that there is something wrong with the way they are functioning. Third, there is a strong tendency for the various personality-disordered behaviors to be rigidly ingrained, highly repetitive, and ultimately self-defeating. Finally, the prognosis for overcoming any of the personality disorders is rather poor, perhaps because individuals with personality disorders are generally more inclined to refuse therapy than are people with the other behavioral disorders outlined in this chapter (Vaillant & Perry, 1985). The antisocial personality disorder has been the subject of more research and theorizing than any of the other 10 personality disorders; therefore, it is the focus of our discussion.

ANTISOCIAL PERSONALITY DISORDER

From the point of view of society at large, the most disruptive of the personality disorders is the **antisocial personality disorder,** also referred to as psychopathic or sociopathic personality disorder. Recent estimates indicate that almost 3 percent of the population have antisocial personalities, with six times as many men as women included in this diagnostic category (Robins, 1987). Perhaps the best clinical description of this disorder was provided by Hervey Cleckley in his book *The Mask of Sanity* (1976). The following list summarizes some of the most prominent characteristics of an antisocial personality as outlined by DSM-IV:

1. A history dating back to before age 15 that demonstrates a repetitive and persistent pattern of behavior in which either the basic rights of others or major age-appropriate societal norms or rules are violated. Commonly occurring behavior includes intimidation of others, physical fights, use of weapons, thievery or robbery, physical cruelty to people and animals, rape, persistent lying, arson, vandalism, and/or truancy.
2. A pervasive pattern of disregard for and violation of the rights of others occurring since age 15. Behaviors consistent with a diagnosis of antisocial personality disorder include unlawful behavior, aggressiveness and physical fighting, consistent irresponsibility, impulsivity or failure to plan, deceitfulness, disregard for the safety of self and others, and a lack of remorse for the mistreatment of others (American Psychiatric Association, 1993).

A number of these characteristics are apparent in the following account of an interview with a man diagnosed as having an antisocial personality disorder:

In the early 1950s, I interviewed a 20-year-old man on the prison ward at Bellevue Psychiatric Hospital who had planned, conspired, and helped commit a double murder with ruthless disregard for the consequences of his actions. In a very businesslike way he had persuaded a companion, a schizophrenic who was the only son of two physicians, to poison them by having them both drink champagne, which the instigator had filled with arsenic, on the parents' wedding anniversary night at a celebration by this foursome. The police listed their deaths as a double suicide for more than a year. Meanwhile, a life insurance policy of $150,000 was shared by the two youths. The reason for their eventual arrest was my patient's need to impress his girlfriend by constantly boasting of his role in killing his friend's parents; she eventually informed the police about the crime. As a result, both young men were placed on the prison ward for examination and observation. The couple's son was diagnosed as a schizophrenic and my patient as a "psychopathic personality."

During my psychiatric interviews with him, he neither showed conscious remorse, guilt, shame, nor anxiety, nor did he admit feeling any of these emotions. He admitted readily to his part in the murder which he said was, to him, an experience similar to Oscar Wilde's "In Search of a New Experience." He did not have any remorse about his actions, except for the regret he felt about being apprehended and imprisoned. He admitted seeing nothing wrong with murder, stealing, or any other immoral or amoral actions, provided he or anyone else could get away with it. He showed no psychotic illness or symptoms. (Hott, 1979)

In spite of several decades of extensive research, we still do not have a clear understanding of the origins of the antisocial personality disorder. The following paragraphs briefly consider the psychoanalytic, behavioral, and biological perspectives on the etiology of this condition.

The psychoanalytic perspective looks to the childhood development of personality dynamics. Recall that Freud and his followers maintained that our sense of right and wrong emerges with the development of the superego sometime during the childhood years. It is the superego that places moral and ethical restraints on one's actions. Theorists with a psychoanalytic orientation suggest that because of some aberration in the normal course of early personality development, a person with an antisocial personality disorder fails to acquire a superego. Consequently, he or she acts to satisfy id instincts without regard for social mores and unhindered by guilt or shame.

Behavioral theorists propose a number of interpretations; perhaps the most prominent is the view that people with antisocial personality disorder act impulsively and repeatedly manifest antisocial misbehavior because they have not learned to avoid punishment. Such inappropriate behaviors persist despite repeated social and/or legal sanctions.

What is the source of this apparent indifference to punishment? Psychologist David Lykken (1957) reasoned that people with antisocial personality disorder may have far less anxiety about the possible consequences of punishment than most people. To test this hypothesis, Lykken devised a complex learning task in which three groups of male subjects (imprisoned sociopaths, nonsociopathic inmates, and college students) were told that electric shocks would be randomly administered for incorrect responses as a stimulant for good performance. Successful mastery of the task was not made contingent on avoiding shocks, and subjects were not told that avoiding shock was desirable or even possible. (In actuality, it was possible to learn to avoid shocks while mastering the task.) Although all three groups performed equally well on the learning task, there were considerable differences in the way they responded to the shocks. The college men eventually figured out how to respond in such a way as to decrease their chance of receiving a shock, but individuals with antisocial personality disorder demonstrated little or no such learning. (The nonsociopathic inmates exhibited shock-avoidance behavior that fell between these two extremes.) Lykken's findings have been supported by other research (Chesno & Kilman, 1975; Schachter & Latané, 1964), and other studies have also shown that antisocial personalities demonstrate considerably less emotional responsiveness to threatened pain than nondisordered individuals (Borkovec, 1970; Hare, 1975; Hare et al., 1978; Mednick et al., 1982). Considered collectively, such findings suggest that punishments may have little meaning for people with antisocial personality disorder. Perhaps because of their lower degree of anticipatory anxiety, such people seem to express the attitude "You can't hurt me because I have little fear of pain."

Finally, we turn to the biological perspective on antisocial personality disorder. Several investigations have shown that 50 to 60 percent of people with antisocial personality disorder exhibit abnormal brain waves, compared to 10 to 15 percent of nondisordered people (Hare, 1970; Mednick et al., 1982; Syndulko, 1978). The most frequent of these aberrations in electroencephalogram (EEG) readings is an abnormally excessive amount of very slow brain-wave activity (5 to 8 cycles per second) (Mednick et al., 1981). Since this pattern is more typical of children

THEORETICAL PERSPECTIVES ON ANTISOCIAL PERSONALITY DISORDER

than adults, some theorists have suggested that higher brain centers mature more slowly in antisocial personalities. One consequence of this difference in maturation time might be reduced cortical control over impulsive actions.

The biological perspective is also supported by evidence linking this disorder to genetic factors. For example, some investigators have reported a much higher concordance rate for antisocial personality disorder among identical than among fraternal twins (Slater & Cowie, 1971). A number of studies have also shown that adoptees whose biological parent or parents were diagnosed as having an antisocial personality disorder were considerably more likely to develop the disorder than adoptees whose biological parents were free of behavioral disorders (Cadoret et al., 1987; Crowe, 1974; Hutchings & Mednick, 1974; Mednick et al., 1984; Schulsinger, 1972).

In this chapter we have defined, characterized, and discussed possible causes of the major behavioral disorders. Although considerable progress has been made in identifying causal factors in these disorders, this continues to be an active area of research from several theoretical perspectives. We can continue to expect that our understanding of these disorders will increase as this research progresses. In the next chapter we will see how psychologists and other professionals treat behavioral disorders.

SUMMARY

DEFINING ABNORMAL BEHAVIOR

1. While there is no universally accepted definition of abnormality, psychologists emphasize a common core of four criteria that distinguish between normal and abnormal behavior: atypicality, maladaptivity, emotional discomfort, and social unacceptability.

2. Any given behavioral disorder may reflect only one or a combination of these four criteria.

CLASSIFYING BEHAVIORAL DISORDERS

3. DSM-IV is the most widely used scheme today for classifying and diagnosing behavioral disorders throughout the world.

ANXIETY DISORDERS

4. A panic disorder is characterized by episodes of intense apprehension and overwhelming terror that occur as often as four or more times in a four-week period.

5. Most people who have a panic disorder also exhibit symptoms of agoraphobia. Agoraphobia is characterized by intense fear of being in places or situations from which escape might be difficult or in which help might not be available in the event of a panic attack.

6. Less commonly people may suffer a panic disorder without symptoms of agoraphobia. In some cases, agoraphobia exists without any symptoms or prior history of panic disorder.

7. Phobias, characterized by a persistent fear of and consequent avoidance of a specific object or situation, are among the most common behavioral disorders.

8. A social phobia is a persistent, irrational fear of performing some specific behavior in the presence of other people. A distinction is made between discrete performance anxiety and generalized social anxiety.

9. A specific phobia is an irrational fear of a specific situation or object such as closed places or spiders.

10. An obsessive-compulsive disorder is characterized by a profound sense of anxiety that is reflected in persistent, unwanted, and un-

shakable thoughts and/or irresistible habitual actions in which the individual repeatedly engages in some ritualistic act.

11. Posttraumatic stress disorder occurs after a person experiences a psychologically traumatic event (or events) outside the normal range of human experience. PTSD is characterized by vivid flashbacks and avoidance of stimuli associated with the traumatic event or numbing of general responsiveness.

12. Generalized anxiety disorder is characterized by a chronic state of anxiety that is omnipresent across a wide range of situations.

13. Freud explained the anxiety disorders as a result of internal conflicts, particularly those involving sexual or aggressive impulses.

14. Behavioral theorists see classical conditioning as the source of the anxiety disorders.

15. The biological perspective on anxiety disorders presents evidence that genetic factors play a role in these disorders, that some people with unusually responsive nervous systems may be biologically predisposed to develop anxiety disorders, and short-circuiting of hard-wired behavioral subroutines stored in the basal ganglia may be a cause of obsessive-compulsive disorder.

SOMATOFORM DISORDERS

16. A person with somatization disorder typically has multiple and recurrent physical symptoms for which medical attention is repeatedly sought, but which have no physical cause.

17. People with hypochondriasis also complain about a variety of physical difficulties. The primary difference between hypochondriasis and somatization disorder is that people manifesting the former are fearful that their symptoms indicate a serious disease(s), whereas those with somatization

disorder typically do not progress beyond a concern with the symptoms themselves.

18. Conversion disorder is typically manifested as a sensory or motor system disturbance for which there is no known organic cause.

19. Freud believed that somatoform disorders stem from unresolved sexual impulses. According to the behavioral/learning perspective, a somatoform disorder allows a person to escape from or avoid the negative reinforcer of anxiety. There is little evidence of biological factors in somatoform disorders.

DISSOCIATIVE DISORDERS

20. A person with psychogenic amnesia experiences sudden loss of memory, usually after a particularly stressful or traumatic event.

21. Psychogenic fugue disorder combines amnesia with a more radical defensive maneuver—a flight away from an intolerable situation.

22. A person with a multiple personality disorder alternates between an original or primary personality and one or more secondary or subordinate personalities.

23. Personality disorders are associated with some individuals who have experienced extreme physical and emotional abuse during childhood.

24. Psychoanalytic theory considers all dissociative disorders to be the result of massive reliance on repression to ward off unacceptable impulses, particularly those of a sexual nature. Behavioral/learning theory suggests that dissociative reactions may involve operant avoidance responses that are reinforced because they allow an individual to avoid anxiety associated with stressful events. There is no evidence linking biological factors to development of these disorders.

MOOD DISORDERS

25. DSM-IV distinguishes two major mood disorders: major depressive disorder and bipolar (manic-depressive) disorder.

26. Major depressive disorder is distinguished by deep depression. In contrast, bipolar disorder is characterized by intermittent episodes of both depression and mania (highly energized, euphoric behavior and excessive activity).

27. People with major depressive disorder typically manifest their symptoms over an extended period (from months to a year or longer), are unable to function effectively, and experience a breakdown in interpersonal relationships.

28. In some cases of bipolar disorder, episodes of depression and mania may alternate regularly, with months or years of symptom-free normal functioning between the disordered mood states.

29. A manic episode often follows a three-stage course of accelerating intensity (mania, hypomania, and severe mania) in which the individual's thinking and behavior become progressively more disorganized and psychotic-like.

30. Seasons influence people's moods. Of the two subtypes of seasonal affective disorder (SAD), recurrent winter depression seems to be linked to deficient exposure to light, whereas the causes of recurrent summer depression are not as certain.

31. According to the psychoanalytic perspective, mood disorders are rooted in relationships involving overdependency and ambivalent feelings of love and hate. When a person experiences actual (or threatened) loss of such a relationship, the unconscious hostility toward the lost person surfaces as anger that is turned back against oneself in the form of depression.

32. Behavioral and learning theorists see depression as emerging from the loss of a primary source of positive reinforcement through such things as separation from or death of a loved one or loss of job.

33. Seligman's cognitive learning perspective suggests a theory of learned helplessness, which links depression to people's belief that they have no control over the reinforcers and punishers in their lives.

34. There is compelling evidence linking altered brain chemistry to severe mood disorders.

35. The amine theory of mood disorders suggests that a deficiency in serotonin and/or norepinephrine results in depression.

SCHIZOPHRENIA

36. A collection of primary or core symptoms that characterize many forms of schizophrenia includes disturbances in thought, perception, emotional expression, and speech, together with social withdrawal and diminished motivation.

37. Disorganized schizophrenia is indicated by marked disorganization and regression in thinking and behavioral patterns. A person with this disorder often behaves in an infantile manner and expresses wild swings in mood from fits of crying to episodes of uncontrollable giggling.

38. The distinguishing symptoms of catatonic schizophrenia are extreme psychomotor disturbances, which may range from stuporous immobility to wild excitement and agitation.

39. The dominant symptom of paranoid schizophrenia is the presence of well-organized delusional thoughts.

40. Freud believed that schizophrenia occurs when a person's ego either becomes overwhelmed with id demands or is besieged by un-

bearable guilt. In both cases, the person undergoes a massive regression back to the oral stage of psychosexual development.

41. One behavioral/learning view suggests that schizophrenics either have not been reinforced adequately for responding to normal social stimuli, or perhaps have even been punished for such responses. As a consequence, normal patterns of responding are extinguished or suppressed, and the schizophrenic instead begins to respond to inappropriate stimuli, such as imaginary voices.

42. An extensive body of research indicates that certain people are genetically predisposed to develop schizophrenia.

43. There is biochemical evidence that schizophrenia may be caused by elevated levels of dopamine or a heightened sensitivity to dopamine.

44. There is also substantial evidence of structural abnormalities in the brains of schizophrenics.

45. According to the interactional model, two factors are necessary for schizophrenia to develop. The first is a biological vulnerability to schizophrenia; the second is severe life stresses.

PERSONALITY DISORDERS

46. Personality disorders are grouped into three clusters: Disorders in the first cluster are characterized by odd and/or eccentric behavior; those in the second cluster share a common denominator of dramatic, emotional, or erratic behavior; and those in the third cluster are all characterized by anxious or fearful behavior.

47. Common characteristics of antisocial disorder include a history dating back to or before age 15, lack of remorse or guilt over antisocial acts, repeated academic, vocational, and relationship failures, lack of insight, superficial charm, manipulative behavior, and extreme egocentricity.

48. Psychoanalytic theorists associate antisocial personality disorder with the failure to acquire a superego during early childhood development. Learning theorists suggest that antisocial personalities have not learned to avoid punishment. The biological perspective speculates both that higher brain centers may mature more slowly in antisocial personalities, and that this disorder may be linked to genetic factors.

TERMS AND CONCEPTS

abnormal behavior
neurosis
psychosis
anxiety disorder
panic disorder
agoraphobia
phobia
social phobia
specific phobia
obsessive-compulsive disorder
posttraumatic stress disorder (PTSD)
generalized anxiety disorder
somatoform disorder
somatization disorder
hypochondriasis
conversion disorder
dissociative disorder
dissociative amnesia
dissociative fugue disorder

dissociative identity disorder
mood disorder
major depressive disorder
bipolar (manic-depressive) disorder
delusions
hallucinations
seasonal affective disorder (SAD)
learned helplessness
schizophrenia
neologism
mutism
echolalia
disorganized schizophrenia
catatonic schizophrenia
paranoid schizophrenia
undifferentiated schizophrenia
residual schizophrenia
personality disorder
antisocial personality disorder

PERSPECTIVE #1

Dr. Irving I. Gottesman

Irving I. Gottesman has been Commonwealth Professor of Psychology at the University of Virginia since 1985, after serving five years as Professor of Psychiatric Genetics at the Washington University School of Medicine in St. Louis. He received his Ph.D. in clinical and developmental psychology from the University of Minnesota in 1960. His many awards and honors include the American Psychological Association's Hofheimer Prize for Research for his work with the late James Shields on the genetics of schizophrenia in twins. Dr. Gottesman is past president of the Behavior Genetics Association and currently serves as President of the Society for Research in Psychopathology.

PERSPECTIVE #1
VIEWS ON THE BIOLOGICAL BASES OF BEHAVIORAL DISORDERS

Dr. Irving I. Gottesman

Q: Dr. Gottesman, is there evidence that severe mental disorders such as schizophrenia and chronic depression are caused by abnormalities in brain structure and functions?

A: Some of the evidence for that is direct and involves looking at the brain and looking at the way human beings with these disorders respond to biological intervention. In other words, they take medication or are the recipients of particular kinds of somatic treatments such as electroconvulsive therapy in the case of depression. The other reason why we are so fond of biological and genetic explanations for the major mental disorders is that alternative explanations—sociological, anthropological, the "soft side" of psychology, including psychodynamic or Freudian explanations—have been found so wanting. So we have another large group of studies that provide indirect evidence of the importance of genetic and biological factors.

Q: Can you describe some of the research which you've done along those lines?

A: I have been involved for many years, going back to the late 1950s and continuing up to the present, with studies using twins as a main strategy. I have also been involved in family studies of major mental disorders including an important strategy of adoption studies. I think that the twin studies and adoption studies

PERSPECTIVE #2

Dr. Kurt Salzinger

Kurt Salzinger, Ph.D., Professor of Psychology and Director of the Combined Ph.D. Program in Clinical and School Psychology at Hofstra University, just wrote an article ("Connections: A search for bridges between behavior and the nervous system," ANNALS OF THE NEW YORK ACADEMY OF SCIENCES 658 (1992), 276–286) dealing with the question of how to relate body to behavior. He is the author of *Schizophrenia* (New York: John Wiley and Sons, 1973), past president of the New York Academy of Sciences, and winner of the Stratton Award from the American Psychopathological Association for his work in schizophrenia.

have really had a major impact on the way psychologists, psychiatrists, and students in those areas have come to think about the causes of these major disorders.

Q: Can you describe some of the results that you've seen?

A: Yes. I would go back to one study that has stood the test of time and involves research that I did in London in the early 1960s. I had been invited over by one of the major figures in psychiatric genetics to the Maudsley Hospital in London where Eliot Slater had maintained a register of all twins who had been admitted to the outpatient or the inpatient departments. We only looked at same-sex pairs, that is, brothers and brothers, and sisters and sisters. So we were able to conduct the first modern post-war studies of the genetics of schizophrenia using the twin method. We ended up with 24 pairs of identical twins where at least one of the members of the pair had schizophrenia, and 33 pairs of fraternal twins where at least one of the members of each pair had a diagnosis of schizophrenia. What we found at the end of our first period of investigation was that there was overwhelming but indirect evidence for the strong role of specific genetic factors in causing the differences that we observed between the rates of schizophrenia in the identical co-twins compared to the rates observed in the fraternal co-twins. It turned out that if one identical twin was schizophrenic, then 58 percent of their co-twins were also schizophrenic. In the fraternal sample, when the first twin was schizophrenic, then 12 percent of the fraternal co-twins were also schizophrenic. These numbers are to be compared with the expectation of developing schizophrenia in the general population, which is 1 percent. So you have this really striking finding that if you are the identical twin of a schizophrenic, then your chance of developing schizophrenia is 58 times

PERSPECTIVE #1

what it would be if you were a member of the general population. And it's this contrast between the rates in identical co-twins and fraternal co-twins compared to the general population rate that puts you on a firm footing with regard to inferring the importance of genetics and therefore biological factors in causing schizophrenia. The same strategies, I might add here, have been applied to the affective disorders—bipolar disorders where you have both depression and mania at different times, and affective disorder where you have recurring depressions. For both of those disorders similar findings have been generated in different centers throughout the world.

Q: In any of your follow-up research since those early studies, have you been successful in identifying any of the specific genetic factors that might be responsible for them?

A: That's where the difficulty comes in. Making that leap from the indirect evidence using what are called population genetic approaches to the molecular genetic level where you would actually get at the genes involved or the biochemistry that must necessarily be involved. In order to do that, I began a new twin study in the middle 1980s with a colleague at St. Elizabeth's Hospital in Washington, D.C., Dr. E. Fuller Torrey. We have collected a nationwide sample of identical twins where one twin has schizophrenia and the other twin apparently does not. We also collected control pairs of identical twins where both have schizophrenia, a small sample where both are normal, and then another small sample where one has bipolar disorder and the twin is normal. These results that I mention are still preliminary. But in one of the first published papers by the group at St. Elizabeth's Hospital, they were able to show, using the technique of magnetic resonance imaging, at least for the first 14 pairs or so in the discordant twin series, that in all but one pair, the twin who was schizophrenic had enlarged ventricles in the brain compared to the normal co-twin. Now the difference was often very, very small and subtle and the only way you could see it was by looking at the images of both brains simultaneously, so that an outsider coming in and looking at the twin who has schizophrenia might not reach the conclusion that this twin had anything unusual in regard to the size of his or her ventricles. It's therefore a subtle difference, but it was so consistent that the statistical tests were something to knock your socks off. This is just the beginning on what will be done with these discordant twins using modern techniques. Another group connected to the project is using PET scans—positron emission tomography—and this will give us a view of the way the brain metabolizes glucose in order to see whether or not the energy consumption in the brain is different in the twin who is schizophrenic compared to the twin who is well.

Q: Does your research or research of others suggest ways of trying to make any earlier determination of whether a person may have a hereditary disposition to schizophrenia or any of the major affective disorders?

A: It's very definitely part of the research and we go about that in two ways. One way is to collect careful retrospective accounts of the lives of these individuals who are adults at the time we encounter them. We do that not only by taking their word for what happened to them while they were growing up but by trying to collect information from their parents, especially the mothers, who would tell us such things as how much the person weighed when he or she was a baby, were there any complications that you were aware of in the delivery of this child, and so forth. The other strategy that is very important, and one with which I'm also connected, is what's called the high risk strategy using a prospective longitudinal design. You start out with mothers—sometimes you can have fathers—who are schizophrenic and who then happen to have children and you study their children from early in life and observe them over a long period of time, waiting, so to speak, for the other shoe to drop. We know that approximately 12 to 15 percent of the children of schizophrenic parents will eventually develop schizophrenia themselves. So you're in the position of observing infants who are apparently normal and watching them over time knowing that if you have 100 such infants born to a schizophrenic mother or father that by the time this group of 100 reaches the age of, say, 55, 15 of them or so will develop overt schizophrenia and others will develop what has come to be called schizophrenia spectrum disorders, that is, not the full blown manifestation of schizophrenia but certain abnormalities or aberrations in personality that still allow you to attach a description as schizotypal personality, paranoid personality or schizoid personality.

Q: Do you think that we are progressing to a point where, in the near future, we might be able to identify those people who are most at risk for developing schizophrenia and have some type of program of intervention?

A: That's one of the major goals. Now you run into an ethical bind here because when you start to notice beginning significant symptoms that may be related to the development of schizophrenia you can't just sit idly by and watch the person develop into a full-blown case. So you inevitably get involved in recommending intervention, not by the project itself but by referring these people for care. So you have this ethical obligation to refer individuals who start to show the symptoms. You know already that they're at high risk based on earlier work, but now when you are actually meeting these children and having to continually talk to their parents about what you may be finding, there's no way out other than to try to prevent the further development of the disorder. I do think that we're not too far off from being able to identify children who are at much higher risk than others. This is not the same as saying that they will develop schizophrenia, but it's the same as saying we know something about these individuals and therefore we ought to educate them at least in regard to the avoidance of certain environmental stressors that may be triggers for developing schizophrenia. Among these, my favorite candidates would be street drugs, especially PCP, LSD, cocaine, and things that have amphetamines. Those things are known to irritate, so to speak, the dopaminergic system of the brain. And we know dopamine is somehow involved in the neurochemistry of schizophrenia, because all the medications that work to alleviate the symptoms of schizophrenia involve blocking of dopaminergic transmission in the brain.

Q: What, in your opinion, is the role, if any, of psychotherapy in treating any of these disorders, especially disorders like depression which people would feel are treatable by a psychotherapeutic approach?

A: Well, once you give up a strict analogy between major mental disorder and an infectious disease, which I'm quite willing to do, then you're talking about disorders that are multifactorially determined. In other words, we're dealing with some kind of combination of genetic predisposing factors, together with unknown environmental factors which may be in the physical environment as well as in the psychological environment which combine to trigger episodes of

"I do think that we're not too far off from being able to identify children who are at much higher risk than others."

PERSPECTIVE #1

major mental disorders such as schizophrenia and the affective disorders. This means you would be naive and foolish to omit from consideration the effects of psychotherapeutic intervention for individuals who have already developed the disorder. This is not the same as saying that psychotherapeutic intervention alone would very often be an efficient way of treatment, but in conjunction with the medication that has been found so useful for schizophrenia and for the major affective disorders it's also quite clear that by adding to the therapeutic regime some form of psychotherapy, you add tremendously to the ability of these medications to maintain a remission and to prevent recurrence of the episodes. There are whole series of studies coming out of centers in England and in California and in Pittsburgh which show that even when schizophrenics are maintained on antipsychotic medication that, if you have that as your only way of intervening, those individuals still have a very high rate of relapse. Now the highest relapse rate of all, of course, comes from those individuals who stop taking their medication. If they are further exposed to psychological stressors of fairly specific kinds, those individuals have almost a 100 percent rate of relapse. So when it comes to talking about helpful intervention, we're looking for a combination of antipsychotic medication plus—I'll call it common sense intervention—in order to get the best effect. Psychotherapy for schizophrenia is not the same as psychotherapy that is so familiar with regard to such things as neurosis. We're looking here at many studies—between a half dozen and a dozen—which say that the kind of intervention to use psychotherapeutically *does not* involve the psychodynamic approach made popular by Freud and his followers. Instead it makes relevant an approach which has been called family therapy combined with education.

PERSPECTIVE #2

VIEWS ON THE BIOLOGICAL BASES OF BEHAVIORAL DISORDERS

Dr. Kurt Salzinger

Q: Dr. Salzinger, is there evidence that severe mental disorders such as schizophrenia or chronic depression are caused by abnormalities in brain structure and function?

A: The answer is yes, in the sense that for many years people have been looking at such facts as the first and most important aspect of the genetic findings. Twin studies originally and, more recently, adoption studies, have shown that there is some genetic component which makes it more likely that individuals who come from families that have schizophrenia will develop schizophrenia and individuals who come from families that have depression will have a greater likelihood of depression. The next question, then, is why it doesn't occur more consistently in people, like transmission of eye color. As far as actual neural structure is concerned, there the evidence is perhaps less balanced but, in schizophrenia

PERSPECTIVE #2

for example, there is evidence that suggests that the ventricles—open spaces in the brain—are larger. But the question is, larger than what percent of the population? And in fact, if you find that if you examine discordant identical twins, people who have exactly the same genetic makeup, but one has schizophrenia and the other one does not, you find that the twin with schizophrenia has a larger ventricle than the individual who is normal. However, if you just look at the general population, normal individuals who have larger ventricles appear similar to schizophrenic patients, so you can't find any difference. The real problem as I see it is not merely to look for some kind of physiological factor or biochemical factor or anatomical factor. The real problem is trying to relate those differences to behavioral differences and then find which came first, so-called biological factors or behavioral factors.

Q: Are you now or have you been involved in research to explore that question?

A: Well, I'm not a physiological psychologist. On the other hand, I have been putting forth a theory of schizophrenia called the immediacy theory, which is based on the notion that, put most simply, schizophrenic patients differ from normal individuals in terms of responding to stimuli which are close in time. This means that a remote stimulus has less control over the behavior of a schizophrenic patient—it's less likely to influence his behavior than the behavior of a normal individual. Those stimuli that are around at the time will have the greatest effects on behavior. This factor I have been able to relate to the difference in the neurotransmitter dopamine. There is a dopamine theory in schizophrenia which says that schizophrenic patients have more dopamine in the synaptic gap than do normal individuals. What would the effect of that be? Well, if there's more dopamine there, that suggests that impulses go from neuron to neuron more quickly and that suggests that in such a person the responses to immediate stimuli will come much more quickly than in an individual that doesn't have all that dopamine waiting for the slightest kind of stimulation to go on and do something. So here is a case where you can talk about relating behavioral effects to physiology. The immediacy hypothesis also says that if an individual has a tendency to respond quickly to stimuli that are close in time, that means that such an individual will be more likely to speak in ways that are puzzling because words that follow one another closely will, in fact, relate to one another, but words that follow one another over a longer period of time will not. What I'm talking about here is going off on tangents. To give you one example in a sentence, the word "mine" can be a possessive pronoun or it can also, of course, refer to the places where miners go and extract ore. Now if you look at the word mine out of context, that is, just as the word mine, you can use it either way. You can then see why schizophrenic patients may speak in ways that make other individuals say "What? What? How did you get to that?"

Q: Does this theory provide any clues to identifying people who might have a predisposition for schizophrenia before the onset of the more severe symptoms, or determining the chance that a person would develop schizophrenia at a later time in their life?

A: Well, the fact of the matter is that the best predictor at this point is, in fact, genetics. That is to say, if the individual is a child of a schizophrenic mother,

PERSPECTIVE #2

then there is a higher probability that that child will become a schizophrenic than someone from the population at large. Now that probability isn't very great —the general predictability of schizophrenia in the population is about 1 percent—but it is several times larger than that. I haven't had a chance to study it, but it would be very interesting to look at children who are high risk and then see whether they do have a tendency to respond to stimuli closer in time to them. If they did respond to such stimuli, the reason that nobody says anything, for most people don't look at it being peculiar, is that we make allowances for children, we laugh about it, you know, because with a child you can take into account that something else is involved. Because it takes a while to notice a pattern and because one makes allowances for younger people, if there is a tendency to respond in this manner, it will not be noticed until there comes a time when obviously it makes a difference in the child's ability to plan. If a child has difficulty planning tasks and begins to respond to stimuli in ways that are peculiar, well here's a good tip off for that. But the important thing always in my way of thinking is to say, just to take my theory for the moment as if the immediacy is important, you then have to say "How does this interact with the conditions surrounding the individual?" Well, while other things have happened to make you learn, how do you learn? You learn through reinforcement. You do things and the consequences are rewarding to the individual. Well if the only items that are going to be rewarding are predominantly items that have to be close in time, then you can see that this individual can be conditioned in a peculiar way. In other words, if I do something and a week later something wonderful happens, I don't associate the two and I will not be conditioned as a function of that event. To me the important thing will be what happens in the next 15 minutes. If nothing happens my behavior will be affected because if I can't distinguish a relationship between the two events, I will be conditioned to do things which require immediate response or reinforcement.

Q: Given the fact that the primary treatments for schizophrenia are pharmacological, do you see any possible efficacy for earlier pharmacological interventions along with behavioral interventions?

A: There's a possibility. There's always a danger, of course, because anybiochemical intervention has side effects. It might be useful, but I would be very much concerned that we have good evidence that the children were truly showing some of the symptoms of schizophrenic behavior. We still have to be concerned about the question of the reliability of the diagnosis. The DSM-III-R and DSM-IV have made the diagnosis of schizophrenia narrower and narrower, and that in essence is a good thing. At the same time, the follow-up of high risk populations, and genetic studies following up children and others who have been diagnosed as having schizophrenia, have given rise to a new diagnosis called "spectrum." This, in fact, is just another way of saying that some of these children do not have schizophrenia; what they have is an increase in criminal activity; what they have is schizoid behavior; what they have is other manifestations of psychological dysfunction. And it's almost forcing a result to say, "Oh yes, genetic effects are very powerful, look at this, what we have is a spectrum of schizophrenics, and we also have schizophrenia." But it's a good example of another change of course about what we are to call schizophrenic behavior. That's what makes me uneasy about the intervention, and that's where we have to be careful.

Q: What does evidence about the biological bases for these disorders suggest about the efficacy of psychotherapy in treating them?

A: Well, that's an interesting question because there are two recent developments in the field of medicine. In all fields of medicine, aside from psychiatry, there has been an increased interest in and use of behavioral intervention. Prevention has become the word in medicine. A few years ago, the National Academy of Medicine said the one thing which we can do to prevent or have any affect on disease is changing behavior. Whether you're talking about running or whether you're talking about slowing down Type A kinds of behavior, these are profound effects and we continue this in medicine. People are now doing experiments in which they are taking wings of hospitals and changing the environment of the rooms that were really terrible and making them like home and finding that these people respond much faster to drugs, require fewer drugs, respond better to operations and on and on and on. In psychiatry, on the other hand, everybody is going to neurosciences, which means primarily studying the cell structure of the brain, so there's an interesting contradiction here. If medical illnesses, including cancer, AIDS, pneumonia, etc., are affected by behavioral intervention, then it makes sense to believe that behavioral disturbances will be affected by behavioral interventions. So I think we must go away from the notion of quick fix, which is typically the drug; the notion that, "Something's wrong, give me this thing so tomorrow I'll be better." Behavioral intervention takes a little longer. Even if the drug helps, you need behavioral intervention. For example, when you talk about schizophrenia, it certainly is useful not to have somebody who is terrified of voices continue in that state, because you can't work with such a person in a behavioral intervention. At the same time, somebody who is given a diagnosis of schizophrenia has had a very strange kind of life, and no matter what the drugs do, this person has to be conditioned in some way. Since one of the aspects of schizophrenia is that the individual has no friends, you have to teach that person such things as social skills: how do you make friends, how do you call up a member of the opposite sex and get a date, what do you say to them? So no matter what the drugs do, they don't provide behavioral repertoires and those have to be provided to facilitate prevention. So I think it is not only that behavioral intervention is needed as a substitute for pharmacology—in some cases it's used that way—but in the cases where pharmacology is in fact successful there's even a greater call for behavioral intervention to really have it succeed.

"I think we must go away from the notion of the quick fix, which is typically the drug."

CHAPTER 16

Treatment of Behavioral Disorders

PSYCHOLOGICAL THERAPIES

Psychoanalysis
Techniques of Psychoanalysis
The Present Status of Psychoanalysis
Humanistic Therapies
Cognitive Therapies
Behavioral Therapies
Group Therapies

EVALUATING PSYCHOTHERAPY

Is Psychotherapy More Beneficial Than
    No Therapy?

Is One Type of Psychotherapy More
    Effective Than Another?
Common Features of Psychotherapeutic
    Approaches

BIOLOGICALLY-BASED THERAPIES

Psychosurgery
Electroconvulsive Therapy
Psychoactive Drugs

*C*hapter 15 discussed a variety of behavioral disorders. The treatment of these disorders is the topic of this chapter, which describes the kinds of therapeutic interventions used to help people overcome or at least better cope with behavioral problems. Our primary focus in this chapter is on psychological therapies, or **psychotherapy** — any nonbiological, noninvasive technique or procedure designed to improve a person's adjustment to life. *Noninvasive* means that no attempt is made to alter body physiology or function, as occurs with biomedical therapies.

The final section of this chapter deals with biological treatments such as surgery, shock therapy, and drug therapy. We will discover that therapy may take many different forms; we will also see that these varied approaches share many common themes. Today, treatment for behavioral disorders is provided by a variety of clinicians, including clinical psychologists, clinical social workers, psychiatrists, medical doctors, and family, marital, school, and pastoral counselors. We will begin with an overview of psychological therapies.

PSYCHOLOGICAL THERAPIES

In the following pages we discuss several different forms of noninvasive therapy, including psychoanalysis, humanistic therapy, cognitive therapy, behavioral therapy, and therapies for interpersonal relationships. (Table 16.3 on page 640 provides a summary comparison of some of the major therapies we discuss.) We begin this section with an overview of psychoanalysis.

The first formal model of psychotherapy was developed by Sigmund Freud at the end of the last century. Freud's technique, which became known as **psychoanalysis,** spawned a vast collection of observations and insights into the human condition that were eventually organized in the psychoanalytic theory of personality discussed in some detail in Chapter 14.

Psychoanalysis is based on a number of assumptions; the most fundamental is that disordered behavior results from unconscious conflicts and repressed urges, most of which are rooted in childhood experiences. A primary theme in many of these conflicts is the struggle between the id's sexual and aggressive impulses and the superego's moralistic commands. These conflicts generate anxiety, which the ego defense mechanisms may not be able to ward off. As the individual tries more desperate strategies for coping with anxiety, symptoms of behavioral disturbances, such as phobias and conversion disorders, begin to appear. At this point the person is likely to seek psychotherapy.

Freud believed that the only way to help people gain true relief from severe anxiety was to enter their unconscious, search out the anxiety-causing conflict(s), and help them gain *insight* or conscious awareness of the repressed conflict. Only then can the conflict be resolved. Put another way, the aim of psychoanalysis is to make the unconscious conscious (Kutash & Wolf, 1986). To accomplish this goal, Freud developed a number of therapeutic techniques.

PSYCHOANALYSIS

Classical Freudian psychoanalysis was organized around several major techniques. Probably the most important of these methods are free association,

TECHNIQUES OF PSYCHOANALYSIS

Sigmund Freud's office. Notice that Freud would sit out of view of his patients, who would lie down on a couch.

dream analysis, and interpretations of resistance and transference (Blum, 1986; Kutash & Wolf, 1986; Phares, 1988).

Free Association   If you visited Freud as a patient, you would be asked to lie down on a comfortable couch. Freud would sit behind you, out of your line of vision — a practice Freud believed helped to reduce distractions that might interfere with his patients' concentration. He would encourage you to say whatever came into your mind, no matter how silly or frivolous it might seem. As we saw in Chapter 14, Freud believed that through the process of **free association,** he could obtain glimpses of the unconscious conflicts and desires boiling below the surface of conscious awareness. He also believed that the actual process of venting repressed feelings *(catharsis)* can result in at least a temporary reduction in tension. Freud realized that free association is not an easy process, and that it often takes several sessions before a person begins to open up.

Dream Analysis   Freud placed great emphasis on **dream analysis,** or interpretation of dreams. He believed that dreams are the "royal road to the unconscious" and thus a rich source of information about the hidden aspects of personality. Freud provided his patients with suggestions on how to remember their dreams. During a session of analysis patients were encouraged to report the apparent or *manifest* content of their dreams, then to work with Freud to uncover the hidden or *latent* content that often revealed the workings of the unconscious mind.

Resistance   Freud believed that what a patient does not say is as important as what is verbalized. He noted that his patients often exhibited **resistance,** or an unwillingness to discuss freely some aspects of their lives. Resistance can take many forms, including disrupting a session or changing the subject whenever a certain topic came up, consistently joking about something as though it were unimportant (or avoiding the topic altogether), or missing appointments or arriving late. Freud believed that it was only natural to resist delving into certain areas, because it is often very painful to bring unconscious conflicts into conscious awareness. Resistance was thus viewed as a sign that the therapist was getting close to the problem and the unconscious was struggling to avoid giving up its secrets. One of the major goals of Freudian psychoanalysis was to detect and break through these resistances.

Transference   People who undergo long-term psychotherapy often begin to relate to their therapists in much the same way as they do to a parent, lover, or some other important person in their lives. Thus feelings such as anger, love, hostility, and dependency that characterize a person's relationships with other important people might be transferred to the therapist. Freud believed that this process of **transference** exposes long-repressed feelings, which the patient can then work through with the help of the analyst.

Freud used transference as a model to gain insight into the significant relationships of his patients. He wrote extensively about the benefits of transference as a way of making a patient's strong feelings more accessible and thus easier to interpret and work through. (He also wrote about the potential dangers of therapists doing the same thing—of letting their relationships with their patients become complicated by their own past experiences and emotional histories, a process he called *countertransference*.)

Interpretation   To Freud it was important for analysts to interpret for patients the underlying meaning of their experiences, resistances, transferences, and dreams. He believed that such interpretations would help break through patients' defenses, providing them with insight into the causes of their neurotic behavior. This insight was also viewed as an excellent motivator to encourage a patient's active and willing participation in the therapeutic process. In the words of a contemporary psychoanalyst, "The acquisition of insight, the experiences of new and affectively meaningful understanding, has a powerful impact on the patient's continuing interest and investment in the analytic process" (Blum, 1986, p. 5). An example of psychoanalytic interpretation is provided in the following excerpt from a psychoanalytic therapy session:

> The patient is a middle-aged businessman whose marriage had been marked by repeated strife and quarrels. His sexual potency has become tenuous. At times he has suffered from premature ejaculation. At the beginning of one session, he began to complain about having to return to treatment after a long holiday weekend. He said, "I'm not so sure I'm glad to be back in treatment even though I didn't enjoy my visit to my parents. I feel I just have to be free." He then continued with a description of his home visit, which he said had been depressing. His mother was bossy, aggressive, manipulative, as always. He feels sorry for his father. She has a sharp tongue and a cruel mouth. "Each time I see my father he seems to be getting smaller; pretty soon he will disappear and there will be nothing left of him. She does that to people. I always feel that she is hovering over me ready to swoop down on me. She has me intimidated just like my wife."

> "I was furious this morning. When I came to get my car, I found that someone had parked in such a way that it was hemmed in. I feel restrained by the city. I hate the feeling of being stuck in an office from nine until five."

> At this point, the therapist called to the patient's attention the fact that throughout the material, in many different ways, the patient was describing how he feared confinement, that he had a sense of being trapped.

> The patient continued, "You know I have the same feeling about starting an affair with Mrs. X. She wants to and I guess I want to also. Getting involved is easy. It's getting uninvolved that concerns me."

> In this material, the patient associates being trapped in a confined space with being trapped in the analysis and with being trapped in an affair with a woman.

> At this point, the analyst is able to tell the patient that his fear of being trapped in an enclosed space is the conscious derivative of an unconscious fantasy in which he imagines that if he enters the woman's body with his penis, it will get stuck; he will not be able to extricate it; he may lose it.

The analyst goes on to say that one important goal of therapy would consist of making the patient aware of childhood sexual strivings towards his mother, of a wish to have relations with her, and of a concomitant fear growing out of the threatening nature of her personality, and that, like a hawk, she would swoop down upon him and devour him. These interpretations would give him insight into the causes of his impotence and his stormy relations with women, particularly his wife. (Arlow, 1984, pp. 37–39)

Reproduced by permission of the publisher, F. E. Peacock Publishers, Inc., Itasca, Illinois. From Raymond J. Corsini, *Current Contents in Psychotherapies*, 3rd Edition, copyright 1984, pp. 37–39.

THE PRESENT STATUS OF PSYCHOANALYSIS

Earlier in this century psychoanalysis was the only form of psychotherapy available, and it remained the dominant force in psychotherapy until the early 1950s. Since that time, however, its popularity and influence have steadily declined, and today very few psychotherapists practice classical psychoanalysis as developed by Freud. Instead, psychoanalytically oriented therapists are likely to practice a modified version in which patients sit in a chair and face the therapist rather than lie on a couch. In addition, treatment tends to be briefer in duration, with less emphasis on restructuring a person's entire personality and more attention directed to the patient's current life and relationships. Contemporary psychoanalysts still attempt to help people gain insights into the unconscious roots of their problems, but early childhood conflicts are not emphasized as much. One aspect of psychoanalysis which has not changed from the time of Freud is that the treatment simply does not work with severely disturbed or noncommunicative people. The best candidates for this type of therapy seem to be relatively young, intelligent, successful, and highly verbal individuals. As you might guess, the same observation might be made for several other forms of psychotherapy.

HUMANISTIC THERAPIES

Whereas the psychoanalytic perspective tends to take a pessimistic view of humans, considering people who seek treatment to be sick patients in need of a doctor's care, humanistic therapists are much more optimistic about the individual's potential for self-examination, personal growth, and self-fulfillment. People undergoing humanistic therapy are called clients rather than patients, and they are treated as partners in the endeavor of therapy. Responsibility for the success of therapy is placed more on the shoulders of the client than on the therapist. Humanistic therapists see their primary goal as fostering psychological growth. This is accomplished in a special supportive environment that permits the client to achieve greater self-awareness, self-acceptance, personal fulfillment, and self-actualization. Therapists who operate within this theoretical framework tend to focus on the present rather than the past, and on conscious thoughts and feelings rather than repressed conflicts. They also believe that clients can take charge of their lives and be responsible for their actions rather than be victimized by obstacles outside of their awareness or control.

This philosophical framework has given rise to a number of specific therapeutic models. We consider two: the person-centered approach of Carl Rogers, and Gestalt therapy, founded by Frederick Perls.

PERSON-CENTERED THERAPY   **Person-centered therapy,** a continually evolving and changing approach to psychotherapy, was first introduced in the 1940s by Carl Rogers. Rogers originally called his approach client-centered therapy, but in 1974 he and his colleagues changed the name to person-centered therapy in order to focus more clearly on the human values emphasized by this approach

Carl Rogers

(Meador & Rogers, 1984). The central premise is summarized in Rogers' own words as follows:

> It is that the individual has within himself or herself vast resources for self-understanding, for altering his or her self-concept, attitudes, and self-directing behavior — and that these resources can be tapped if only a definable climate of facilitative attitudes can be provided. (1986, p. 197)

This "definable climate" consists of three major elements: genuineness, a deep caring expressed as unconditional positive regard, and an empathic understanding.

Genuineness   **Genuineness** is the ability of therapists to be in touch with their own current feelings or attitudes, and to allow these inner experiences to be apparent to the client. Therapists are closely attuned to what the client is expressing from moment to moment, and they openly share their immediate responses with the client. With such an approach to therapy, it is impossible for the therapist to put on a professional facade and play the objective observer.

Unconditional Positive Regard   The second essential ingredient in creating a climate for change is an attitude of **unconditional positive regard** on the part of person-centered therapists. This means that therapists exhibit a genuine, unconditionally accepting attitude toward whatever the client is at the moment, regardless of what the client may say or do. Therapists do not express approval or disapproval, only acceptance. Rather than offering interpretations or advice, therapists trust their clients' ability to draw upon inner resources for self-understanding, and to initiate positive changes for self-growth. The theory is that if clients can clearly see that someone else believes in their ability to grow, they may begin to believe in themselves (Meador & Rogers, 1984).

Empathic Understanding   The third key element in the therapeutic environment is **empathic understanding** of the world as experienced by the client. This process involves more than merely understanding the client's words. The therapist, in effect, tries to get under the skin of the client, to the point where the therapist may be cognizant of feelings or meanings of which even the client is not yet aware. To accomplish this goal, the therapist uses a special technique known as **active listening.** Rogers called active listening "one of the most potent forces for change that I know" (1986, p. 198). It is used to indicate therapists' acceptance and understanding of what the client is saying, and it involves restating or responding to feelings the client is expressing but may not be fully aware of.

Active listening accomplishes a dual purpose. First, it may help clients better understand or clarify their feelings. Second, it lets the client know that the therapist both understands and accepts what he or she is saying. A person-centered therapist may ask for clarification now and then, but does not offer direct advice or interpretations. Rogers trusts the individual to discover his or her own capacity to resolve difficulties and experience self-growth: What is necessary is not someone to tell clients how to accomplish this goal, but simply the provision of a special environment in which clients may tap into their own resources.

A brief excerpt from one of Rogers' therapy sessions with a client called Jan illustrates his technique of active listening. At this point in the session, Jan is expressing concern about growing older, an issue that appears to involve impressions about how her mother lived and died, and Jan's own fear of marriage.

JAN: Well, my mother died at 53. [CARL: Mm-hmm.] and she was a very young and very bright woman in many ways. But I think maybe that has something to do with it. I don't know.

CARL: You sort of felt that if your mother died at that early age, that was a possibility for you, too. *[Pause]* And time began to seem a lot shorter.

JAN: Right! When I look at my mother's life — and she had many talents — she unfortunately, towards the end, became a bitter woman. The world owed her a living. Now I don't want ever to be in that situation. And at this point in time, I'm not. I've had a very full life — both very exciting and very sad at times. I've learned a lot and I've a lot to learn. But — I *do* feel what happened to my mother is happening to me.

CARL: So that remains sort of a specter. Part of your fear is: "Look what happened to my mother, and am I following in the same path [JAN: Right.] and will I feel that same fruitlessness, perhaps?"

JAN: *[Long pause]* Do you want to ask me some more questions, because I think that will help you to draw information out of me? I just can't — everything is a whirlwind [CARL: Mm-hmm.], going around in circles.

CARL: Things are just going around so fast inside of you, you don't quite know where to — [JAN: Where to begin.] — take hold. I don't know whether you want to talk anymore about your relationship to your mother's life, your fear of that, or what? *[A long pause]*

JAN: The older I get, though, the stronger I feel about the marriage situation. Now whether the two are related, I don't know. But the fear of getting married, and being committed, and children — I find very, very frightening. And it's getting stronger as I get older —

CARL: It's a fear of commitment, and a fear of having children? And all that seems to be a growing fear, all those fears seem to keep increasing.

JAN: Yes. I'm not afraid of commitment. For instance, when it comes to my work, to friendship, to doing certain things. But to me marriage is very —

CARL: So you're not a person who's irresponsible or anything like that — [JAN: No, not at all.] — you're committed to your work, you're committed to friends. It's just that the notion of being tied into marriage — that's scary as hell. (Rogers, 1986, pp. 200–202)

GESTALT THERAPY Frederick (Fritz) Perls (1948, 1973) took a somewhat different approach to therapy than Rogers. He believed that behavioral problems often stem from people's inability to integrate the various parts of their personalities (such as thoughts, feelings, and actions) into a healthy, well-organized whole. His **Gestalt therapy** borrows the term *Gestalt*, from the psychology of perception, for this collection of therapeutic techniques is designed to help a person bring together the alienated fragments of self into an integrated, unified whole. (Recall from Chapter 4 that Gestalt refers to the fact that the whole is different from the sum of its parts.)

Perls was originally trained as a Freudian psychoanalyst, and some of this tradition is reflected in his emphasis on bringing unconscious feelings and unresolved conflicts into awareness. However, unlike the psychoanalysts, he believed that therapy should focus on the present rather than the past. Therefore, whatever unresolved conflicts might linger in a person's unconscious should be uncovered and brought to bear on the here and now.

The primary focus in Gestalt therapy is on moment-to-moment awareness of oneself (Simkin et al., 1986). The therapist's role is one of active *coexplorer* with clients, encouraging them to break through whatever defenses are preventing them from fully experiencing their feelings and thoughts. Gestalt therapists use a number of techniques to help people to become aware of who they are and what they are feeling. In *role playing*, for example, clients might act out feelings about significant others in their lives, or perhaps the therapist may assume the role of someone who is integral to a conflict in the client's life. Another common technique to help clients recognize and take responsibility for their own feelings is to train them to speak in the first person. For example, a client who says, "Sometimes people are afraid to take that first step in initiating a relationship for fear of being rejected," would be encouraged to restate this concern by saying something like, "I am afraid to reach out to another because I am afraid of being rejected."

As in person-centered therapy, the goal of Gestalt therapy is to help the person become his or her true self. However, the Gestaltists tend to be much more direct in their effort to achieve this end. They do not hesitate to point out an incongruence or discrepancy between what the client says and does. For instance, if a client protests that he is not angry even though his face is flushed and fists are clenched, the therapist might say something like, "Get serious. Look at your clenched fists. Your face is red. I know an angry person when I see one, and you are angry. In fact, you're steaming!" Gestalt therapists are also not opposed to interpreting a client's verbal and nonverbal expressions, and they provide considerably more feedback than the person-centered therapists.

The following brief excerpt from a therapy session illustrates some of the important features of Gestalt therapy, including interpretation and phrasing of feelings in the first person. The therapist is James Simkin, a respected Gestalt therapist who directed the Simkin Training Center in Gestalt Therapy up to his death in 1984. The client, Florence, is a 51-year-old marriage counselor who was previously married to an alcoholic. We pick up the therapy at a point where Florence is dealing with feeling old, lonely, and useless.

FLORENCE: I would like to be more comfortable.

JIM: What would you like me to do as you're getting yourself more comfortable?

FLORENCE: I, let's see, what do I want from you? I would like to explore with you inner structure — which procedure or structure or program to use — *[Sighs]* I'm split. *[Sounds teary]* *I don't want to do what I am doing.*

JIM: Right now?

FLORENCE: Right now, which is crying, *[Sighs]* and that other split part of me, I want to — I will get on and listen.

JIM: Uh-huh. If this feels right to you, I want you to say: "I don't want to cry and I am crying."

FLORENCE: I don't want to cry and I am crying.

JIM: "And I want to get on with living."

FLORENCE: And I want to get on with living. I don't want to cry and I am crying, and I want to get on with living.

JIM: How can I be useful, or how do you want to use me in this process?

FLORENCE: When I think of getting on with living, I think of Chet and I start to cry. When I am away from here. That is the only time I cry.

JIM: When you think of getting on with living and you think of Chet, you start to cry. Does Chet have anything to do with living, getting on with living?

FLORENCE: No. Well, nothing that comes to my head, I guess.

JIM: "Chet, I am interested in getting on with living, and when I think of you, I start to cry."

FLORENCE: "And crying is part of my living," I would say to finish that sentence. (Simkin et al., 1986, p. 211)

EVALUATING HUMANISTIC THERAPIES   As we mentioned in Chapter 1, humanistic psychologists have been criticized for their lack of a systematic and scientific approach to human behavior. Without a theoretical framework from which to view the determinants of behavior or, for that matter, the outcomes of therapy, it is difficult to evaluate the effectiveness of these approaches. Research on the effectiveness of humanistic therapies is quite rare and inconsistent (Carson & Butcher, 1992). On the other hand, because the varieties and degrees of behavioral disorders are so extensive, some therapists argue that humanistic therapies are appropriate for some individuals.

COGNITIVE THERAPIES

The **cognitive therapies** (often called *cognitive-behavioral therapies*) are based on the premise that most behavioral disorders result from distortions in a person's cognitions or thoughts. Psychotherapists who operate within the cognitive framework attempt to demonstrate to their clients how their distorted or irrational thoughts have contributed to their difficulties, and they use a variety of techniques to help them change these cognitions to more appropriate ones. Thus while the goal of therapy may be to change people's maladaptive behavior, the method is to change what they think.

Over the last two decades, many psychotherapists have incorporated a cognitive orientation into their therapy practices. The primary models for the cognitive focus are provided by Albert Ellis' rational-emotive therapy and Aaron Beck's cognitive restructing therapy.

RATIONAL-EMOTIVE THERAPY Rational-emotive therapy (RET) was developed in the 1950s by Albert Ellis (1962, 1984), who was originally trained as a psychoanalyst. After years of "being allergic to the passivity of psychoanalysis" (1984, p. 27) and frustrated in his efforts to reform the Freudian approach to therapy, Ellis began experimenting with new methods. His efforts eventually culminated in his highly influential RET approach.

Rational-emotive therapy (RET) is based on the premise that behavioral problems result when people interpret their experiences on the basis of certain self-defeating, irrational beliefs. The therapist's approach is to help people find the flaws in their thinking, to challenge or dispute these maladaptive cognitions (in Ellis' words, to "make mincemeat" of them), and then to guide clients to substitute more logical or realistic thoughts. Ellis provides a brief summation of this model in the following quote:

> Rational-emotive therapy holds that when a highly charged emotional consequence (C) follows a significant activating event (A), A may seem to, but actually does not, cause C. Instead, emotional consequences are largely created by B — the individual's *belief system.* When an undesirable emotional consequence occurs, such as severe anxiety, this can usually be traced to the person's irrational beliefs, and when these beliefs are effectively disputed (at point D), by challenging them rationally, the disturbed consequences disappear and eventually cease to recur. (Ellis, 1984, p. 196)

Figure 16.1 summarizes this model. A number of self-defeating, irrational beliefs that Ellis has found to be particularly disruptive are listed in Table 16.1.

Ellis and other RET therapists take a much more active or directive role than either the psychoanalytic or humanistic therapists. To minimize a client's self-defeating outlook, RET therapists employ an eclectic, or highly varied, collection of therapeutic techniques, including such things as confrontation, persuasion, role playing, interpretation, behavior modification, and reflection of feelings. The focus of therapy is on the here-and-now, rather than on the client's history. In Ellis' words, "rational-emotive therapists do not spend a great deal of time . . . encouraging long tales of woes, sympathetically getting in tune with emotionalizing, or carefully and incisively reflecting feelings" (Ellis, 1984, p. 214). All of these methods may be used occasionally and briefly, but RET therapists shy away from what Ellis calls "long-winded dialogues," viewing them as indulgent. Rather than helping the client *feel* better during a therapy session, Ellis is more interested in helping clients *get* better.

Albert Ellis

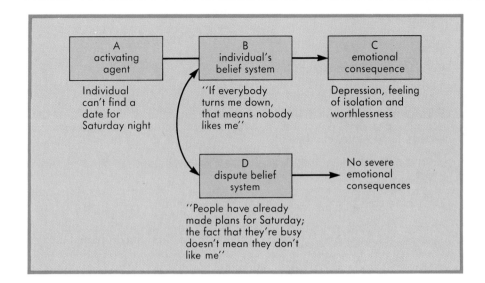

FIGURE 16.1
Ellis' Model of How Psychological Problems Arise

TABLE 16.1 *Some Self-Defeating Beliefs (According to Albert Ellis' Rational–Emotive Perspective)*

1. The idea that you can give yourself a global rating as a human and that your general worth and self-acceptance depend on the goodness of your performance and the degree that people approve of you.
2. The idea that you must have sincere love and approval almost all of the time from all the people you find significant.
3. The idea that emotional misery comes from external pressures and that you have little ability to control your feelings or rid yourself of depression and hostility.
4. The idea that people and things should turn out better than they do, and that you have to view it as awful and horrible if you do not quickly find good solutions to life's hassles.
5. The idea that life proves awful, terrible, horrible, or catastrophic when things do not go the way you would like them to go.
6. The idea that your past remains all-important and that because something once strongly influenced your life, it has to keep determining your feelings and behavior today.

SOURCE: Adapted from Ellis, 1962, 1975; Ellis & Harper, 1975.

In most cases rational-emotive therapists use a rapid-fire directive approach, quickly pinning the client down to a few irrational beliefs. This technique is demonstrated in the following excerpt from an initial session with a 25-year-old single woman who manages a computer programming department:

ELLIS: [reading from the biographical information form that the clients at the Institute for Rational-Emotive Therapy in New York City fill out before their first session]: Inability to control emotions; tremendous feelings of guilt, unworthiness, insecurity; constant depression; conflict between inner and outer self; overeating; drinking; diet pills. All right, what would you like me to start on first?

CLIENT: I don't know. I'm petrified at the moment!

ELLIS: You're petrified — of what?

CLIENT: Of you!

ELLIS: No, surely not of me — perhaps of yourself!

CLIENT: *[laughs nervously]*

ELLIS: Because of what I am going to do to you?

CLIENT: Right! You are threatening me, I guess.

ELLIS: But how? What am I doing? Obviously, I'm not going to take a knife and stab you. Now, in what way am I threatening you?

CLIENT: I guess I'm afraid, perhaps, of what I'm going to find out — about me.

ELLIS: Well, so let's suppose you find out something *dreadful* about you — that you're thinking foolishly, or something. Now why would that be awful?

CLIENT: Because I, I guess I'm the most important thing to me at the moment.

ELLIS: No, I don't think that's the answer. It's, I believe, the opposite! You're really the *least* important thing to you. You are prepared to beat yourself over the head if I tell you that you're acting foolishly. If you were not a self-*blamer,* then you wouldn't care what I said. It would be important to you — but you'd just go around correcting it. But if I tell you something really negative about you, you're going to beat yourself mercilessly. Aren't you?

CLIENT: Yes, I generally do.

ELLIS: All right. So perhaps *that's* what you're really afraid of. You're not afraid of me. You're afraid of *your* own self-criticism.

CLIENT: *[sighs]* All right.

ELLIS: So why do you have to criticize yourself? Suppose I find you're the worst person I ever met? Let's just suppose that. All right, now *why* would you have to criticize yourself?

CLIENT: *[pause]* I'd have to. I don't know any other behavior pattern, I guess, in this point of time. I always do. . . .

ELLIS: Yeah. But that, that isn't so. If you don't know how to ski or swim, you could learn. You can also learn not to condemn yourself, no matter what you do.

CLIENT: I don't know.

ELLIS: Well, the answer is: you don't know how. . . . Now, what are you *mainly* putting yourself down for right now?

CLIENT: I don't seem quite able, in this point of time, to break it down very neatly. The form gave me a great deal of trouble. Because my tendency is to say *everything.* I want to change everything; I'm depressed about everything.

ELLIS: Give me a couple of things, for example.

CLIENT: What I'm depressed about? I, uh, don't know that I have any purpose in life. I don't know what I — what I am. And I don't know in what direction I'm going.

ELLIS: Yeah. But that's — so you're saying "I'm ignorant!" *[client nods]* Well, what's so awful about being ignorant? It's too bad you're ignorant. It would be nicer if you weren't — if you *had* a purpose and *knew* where you were going. But just let's suppose the worst: for the rest of your life you didn't have a purpose, and you stayed this way. Let's suppose that. Now, why would *you* be so bad?

CLIENT: Because everyone *should* have a purpose!

ELLIS: Where did you get the *should?*

CLIENT: 'Cause it's what I believe in. *[silence for a while]*

ELLIS: I know. But think about it for a minute. You're obviously a bright woman; now, where did that *should* come from?

CLIENT: I, I don't know! I'm not thinking clearly at the moment. I'm too nervous! I'm sorry.

ELLIS: Well, but you *can* think clearly. "What [an idiot] I am for not thinking clearly!" You see you're blaming yourself for *that*. (Ellis, 1984, pp. 215–216)

Reprinted by permission of the publisher, F.E. Peacock Publishers, Inc., Itasca, Illinois. From Raymond J. Corsini, *Current Contents in Psychotherapy*, 3rd Edition, copyright 1984, pp. 215–216.

You can see in this account that Ellis attempts to get the client to recognize her irrational ideas, such as the belief that it would be terrible if someone did not like her, and the idea that she is an inadequate person for not having a clear purpose in life. It is also apparent that Ellis is attempting to break down her tendency to be a self-blamer, and to get her to realize that even if her behavior is not what she would like it to be, it in no way reduces her value as a person.

COGNITIVE RESTRUCTURING THERAPY   Like the rational-emotive approach, **cognitive restructuring therapy** approaches therapy with the premise that behavioral problems stem primarily from a few irrational beliefs that cause people to behave and emote in maladaptive ways. Aaron Beck, who developed cognitive restructuring therapy, believes that disturbed people typically have very negative self-images based on highly negative self-labels (1976).

For example, a recent college graduate may be depressed and plagued with a defeatist, "What's the use?" attitude based on the belief that he is a mediocre person who is boring and unattractive to the other sex. Beck believes that people who do not value themselves have a tendency to overgeneralize from their experiences, and unconsciously seek out other experiences that will confirm their poor self-image. Thus if our hypothetical graduate were turned down on his first job interview and rebuffed by the attractive woman he met at a recent party, he may go on to apply for jobs that he is clearly not qualified for and perhaps to approach women that he senses are not interested in him—efforts that will validate his poor self-image because they will result in rejection. Such people are likely to continue to be victimized by their own self-defeating behaviors unless salvaged through therapeutic intervention.

Like Ellis, Beck's aim is to get his clients to restructure their thinking, particularly their negative self-labels. His methods, however, tend to be less confrontational and more experiential. A common strategy is for the therapist and client to make a list of the client's misguided self-impressions (although, at this point, the client is not likely to consider them to be misguided), and then to agree on some experiments to test these assumptions. For example, a therapist working with our college graduate might suggest that he obtain several job interviews for positions well within his level of expertise. Since the therapist is interested in setting up experiments that will disprove rather than confirm the client's negative self-image, some time might be spent providing guidance on how the client can conduct himself effectively in an interview session. Some efforts might also be made to change the client's thoughts about unsuccessful interviews from such negative statements as "I'll never get a good job," or "This rejection proves I am a mediocre person," to "Looks like I may have some difficulty getting the job I want," or "How annoying to be turned down."

Aaron Beck

EVALUATING COGNITIVE THERAPIES Research on the outcomes of cognitive therapies suggest that, at least for some behavioral disorders, these methods can be quite effective. For instance, several studies evaluating therapy outcomes suggest that cognitive approaches are very effective in the treatment of depression (Hollon & Garber, 1990; Robinson et al., 1990). Interestingly, there is some debate as to whether these positive outcomes can be attributed to "cognitive" or "behavioral" change (Hollon et al., 1987). We next examine behavioral therapies.

BEHAVIORAL THERAPIES

Traditional models of psychotherapy have emphasized the underlying causes of behavioral disorders, which are viewed as distinct from those that mold so-called normal behavior. For example, disordered behavior is viewed as the result of either unresolved conflicts or disordered thought processes. **Behavior therapy** departs from this traditional conception. Its central thesis is that maladaptive behavior has been learned and maintained by a history of reinforcement and/or punishment, and therefore it can be unlearned. The same principles that govern the learning and maintenance of normal behavior also determine the acquisition and maintenance of abnormal behaviors. Behavior therapy draws heavily upon the extensive body of laboratory research on human and animal learning to devise strategies for helping people to unlearn maladaptive behavior patterns at the same time that they learn more adaptive behavior patterns.

Behavior therapy focuses on a person's behavior as being the source of the problem rather than attempting to identify underlying personalities, repressed conflicts, or unconscious motives that are causing maladaptive behavior. To change these disruptive behaviors, they enact appropriate changes in the interaction between the client and his or her environment (Kuehnel & Liberman, 1986).

For example, a person with a disabling fear of hospitals and medical personnel might be helped to gain exposure gradually to these feared situations until the anxiety is reduced to manageable levels. Parents of children who fight or squabble incessantly might be shown how to extinguish these inappropriate behaviors by no longer providing the inadvertent reinforcers of paying attention to them. A person who responds sexually to inappropriate stimuli, such as small children, might be treated through repeated exposures to an aversive stimulus paired with the stimuli that elicit the deviant arousal pattern. The following paragraphs outline some of the more commonly employed behavior therapies.

CLASSICAL CONDITIONING THERAPIES You may recall the Chapter 6 account of the woman who was afraid of the biology laboratory. Her fear had been classically conditioned. Fears may often be acquired as a result of a traumatic experience. It follows, then, that classical conditioning principles should also be able to help people *un*learn fears—and this is the basic premise of **classical conditioning therapy.**

For example, suppose you are afraid of the dark as a result of a particularly frightening experience in a darkened room that occurred some years ago. Before this experience, darkness (the conditioned stimulus) was a neutral or nonfrightening stimulus, but now due to the pairing of the CS with the frightening event (an unconditioned stimulus), fear has been learned as a conditioned response.

We know that repeated exposures to darkness without the association of a frightening experience will eventually cause a conditioned fear response to extinguish. However, you would probably be unwilling to expose yourself to solitary darkness long enough to extinguish your fear response. In view of this limitation, behavior therapists have devised a number of *counterconditioning* strategies in which a client learns a new response (one that is incompatible with fear) to the threatening stimulus.

Systematic Desensitization Perhaps the most widely used behavioral therapy technique is **systematic desensitization,** a strategy developed in the late 1950s by Joseph Wolpe (1958, 1985) to treat people who respond to specific stimulus situations with excessive anxiety or phobic fear. Wolpe's therapy method is based on the premise that people cannot be both relaxed and anxious at the same time. Therefore, he reasoned, if individuals can be trained to relax when confronted with fear-inducing stimuli, they will be able to overcome their anxiety. The key is to proceed slowly and systematically.

For instance, in one case known to the authors, a young woman in her mid-twenties sought treatment at the urging of her husband, who was tired of sleeping "with a searchlight on every night." The woman had a deeply rooted fear of darkness that had generalized to situations other than just being in bed with the lights off. She was afraid to go anywhere if it was likely to be dark, particularly if she had to go alone.

The first step in treatment was to analyze her problem carefully, step by step. The goal of treatment was for the client to be unafraid of the dark no matter where she might encounter it—at home in bed, outside at night walking to a friend's house, and so forth. The next step was to construct a hierarchy of situations that triggered her fear of darkness, with the most intense fear-inducing situation at the top of the list and the least at the bottom. As Table 16.2 shows, this woman's fear hierarchy ranged from a mildly anxiety-provoking situation of walking in a commercial area at dusk with a companion to the intensely frightening situation of being in bed alone with no lights on.

The next phase of treatment was to teach her how to relax by training her first to recognize muscle tension in various parts of her body and then to relax all of the various muscle groups in a progressive fashion until she was in a state of complete, tranquil relaxation. Finally, when the client was fully relaxed, she was told to imagine as vividly as possible the scene at the bottom of her anxiety hierarchy. If at any time she found herself becoming anxious, she was instructed to signal, by raising a finger, her desire to switch off the image immediately, and to concentrate again on becoming deeply relaxed. When she was able to imagine this mildly threatening situation repeatedly without experiencing any anxiety, her attention was directed to the next image in the hierarchy. In this fashion, she was able to move up the hierarchy gradually and systematically until, after several sessions, she could imagine any of the scenes on her list with no discomfort.

TABLE 16.2 *An Anxiety Hierarchy in Descending Order of Intensity*

1. At home at night, alone in bed, no light
2. Outside at night, alone, walking in a poorly lighted residential area
3. At home, at night, alone, not in bed, power failure
4. At home, at night, in bed with husband, no light.
5. Outside at night, with a friend or husband, walking in a poorly lighted residential area
6. At home at night, husband present, not in bed, power failure
7. Outside at night, alone, walking in a well-lighted commercial area
8. Outside at night, with a friend or husband, walking in a well-lighted commercial area
9. Outside at dusk, walking alone in a residential area
10. Outside at dusk, with a friend or husband, walking in a residential area
11. Outside at dusk, with a friend or husband, walking in a commercial area

The final phase of treatment was to instruct her to confront the anxiety-producing stimuli in the real world. Here again, she was encouraged to move slowly, starting with situations at the bottom of her anxiety hierarchy. As she received firsthand evidence that she was able to apply her newly acquired ability to relax in real life, she was encouraged to expose herself gradually to even the most fearful situation listed in the hierarchy. The treatment was successful: Several months after therapy was terminated, there was still no "searchlight" in the couple's bedroom at night.

Research has shown that systematic desensitization is often effective in dealing with specific fears and anxieties, such as those that occur in many phobic disorders. It is less effective in treating the diffuse fear that accompanies conditions such as generalized anxiety disorder. This may be because individuals with generalized anxiety or posttraumatic stress syndrome do not undergo extinction of conditioned fear as normal subjects do (see Chapter 15 for more discussion of this idea). Compared with other therapeutic approaches to dealing with specific fears and phobias, systematic desensitization often fares best.

Aversive Conditioning   Aversive conditioning is another variety of classical conditioning behavior therapy that is quite different from systematic desensitization. In aversion therapy the goal is to condition an aversion to some specific stimulus such as alcohol or cigarette smoking.

For example, an alcoholic's behavior is normally characterized by excessive attraction to the stimulus of alcoholic drinks. However, suppose a chronic drinker is given a drug that induces nausea and vomiting when combined with alcohol. The drug alone will not make the person sick, but immediately after alcohol enters the system, the person experiences violent nausea and vomiting. It does not take many pairings of the CS, alcohol, and the UCS, sickness, before the alcohol begins to elicit an aversion response (CR). This conditioned aversion may generalize to a variety of alcohol-related stimuli including the taste and smell of alcohol and visual displays of containers of alcohol. (Effective therapeutic intervention using this strategy actually combines both classical and operant conditioning. Once the classically conditioned fear of alcohol is established, an alcoholic is inclined to avoid future contact with alcohol [an operant response maintained by negative reinforcement] to alleviate his or her fear of this substance. This sequence is a form of two-factor learning, described in Chapter 6.)

Aversive conditioning is not a pleasant experience, and you may wonder why anyone would undergo it voluntarily. The answer is that people who are desperate to overcome their alcohol dependency, or highly motivated to stop smoking, may consider continuation of the undesired behavior to be more aversive than the treatment. Clearly, aversive conditioning is not an appropriate treatment strategy unless the client consents to it.

Aside from any ethical issues that may have been raised in your mind by our discussion of aversive conditioning, can you think of any pragmatic issues, related to persistence of therapeutic effects, that this approach to therapy raises? Think a moment before reading on.

Common sense might suggest that any beneficial effects associated with aversive therapy would be only short-lived. People have the ability to discriminate between the clinical situation in which the aversive condition occurs and situations in the real world. Thus why not expect clients to resume the harmful behavior as soon as treatment ends?

To answer this question, let us consider a hypothetical example. If you ever have overindulged in a favorite food and then become violently ill, the odds are good that you acquired an aversion for the food even though you knew that you got sick only because you ate too much. Such a classically conditioned fear or aversion is often highly resistant to extinction, and that is one reason why this treatment is effective. (Nevertheless, when the motivation to engage in the inappropriate behavior is very strong, it is still possible to overcome the aversive conditioning effect.) On the other hand, if one has had numerous reinforcing experiences with a stimulus (for example, alcohol or tobacco) it is much more difficult to condition aversions to it.

A number of studies have provided encouraging findings about the use of this therapeutic intervention in treating alcohol or nicotine addiction. For example, one study of 685 alcoholics who underwent an intensive aversive therapy program, followed by several booster treatments (additional conditioning trials) over a period of several months, showed that 63 percent still avoided alcohol one year later. Three years later this figure had changed to approximately one-third still abstaining (Wiens & Menustik, 1983). A 30 percent success rate over a period of four years is significant in an area of treatment characterized by high recidivism rates.

OPERANT CONDITIONING THERAPIES   We learned in Chapter 6 that our behaviors are strongly influenced by their consequences. Reinforcers are powerful determinants of behavior, and by manipulating contingencies of reinforcement, behavior therapists are often able to exert a strong influence on behavior. Three versions of **operant conditioning therapies** (sometimes called *behavior modification* techniques) include attempting to induce desired behavior through *positive reinforcement*, or striving to eliminate undesirable or maladaptive behavior through either *extinction* or *punishment*.

Positive Reinforcement   The positive reinforcement therapy technique is based on the fact that people behave in ways that produce positive consequences or reinforcers. This approach to behavior therapy involves identifying the desired behavior and determining one or more reinforcers that will be effective in maintaining it, then providing reinforcers contingent upon the client's voluntarily manifesting the desired behavior.

For instance, in one case reported by Arthur Bachrach and his associates (1965), a young anorexic woman had so drastically curtailed her eating that she was hospitalized, in danger of dying. When all else had failed, behavior therapy was applied to the woman, who now weighed only 47 pounds.

How would you apply positive reinforcement to ensure proper eating behavior in this severely emaciated person? What steps would you follow? Consider this question for a few moments before reading on.

In the first step of treatment, the therapist determined an appropriate reinforcer that could be made contingent upon eating. A social reinforcer was chosen: The therapist sat with her when a meal was delivered, and each time she swallowed a bite of food, the therapist reinforced her by talking to her and generally being attentive. If she refused to eat, the therapist left the room and she remained alone until the next meal was served. In this manner her eating behavior was gradually increased, and other reinforcers were introduced contingent upon her continuing to eat and gain weight. For example, other people joined her at mealtime, or she was reinforced by having her hair done after an appropriate gain in weight. This positive reinforcement method succeeded in inducing a dramatic gain in weight, and she was eventually discharged from the hospital. Her parents were instructed in ways to continue reinforcing her for appropriate eating behaviors, and a follow-up almost three years later revealed that she was maintaining an adequate weight.

Positive reinforcement is also a powerful tool for shaping desirable behaviors in everyday life. For example, a parent who wishes a child to use better table manners, or to be more responsible about room-cleaning chores, will probably find that reinforcing appropriate efforts in this direction will be a more effective agent of behavior change than punishment. As we saw in Chapter 6, the most effective approach is often *shaping*, which involves systematically reinforcing closer and closer approximations to the final desired behavior. For example, a child who picks up only a few toys might first be provided praise, then later the reinforcer might be made contingent upon picking up more and more toys until eventually only a complete room cleaning is reinforced.

Extinction Technique   Just as positive reinforcement may be used to establish appropriate behaviors, it may also be possible to eliminate undesired behaviors by eliminating the reinforcers that maintain them. For this technique to be effective, the behavior therapist must be able both to identify and to eliminate the reinforcer(s) maintaining the maladaptive behavior.

This procedure may not always be as easy as it sounds. An example is the case of Norma (not her real name), a 20-year-old woman known to the authors. Norma reluctantly sought help for a problem described by her parents as "compulsive face picking." According to both her parents and fiancé, Norma could not seem to keep her hands off her face. Whenever she found some little blemish or pimple, she would pick and scratch at it until it became a bleeding sore. As a result, her face was marked by several unsightly sores. This situation greatly distressed everybody but Norma, who seemed remarkably unconcerned. Both the parents and the fiancé had tried several tactics to get Norma to stop picking her face, including appealing to her vanity ("You are such an attractive person when your face is clear"), pleading ("I can't stand to see you do that to yourself"), and threats ("I won't be seen with you in public with your face in such a bad state").

What possible reinforcers could be maintaining Norma's behavior? Think about this question for a minute or two before reading on.

As we learned in Chapter 6, attention can be a powerful reinforcer for behavior, even when the actual form of the attention may be negative. In this case, too, the therapist determined that Norma's face picking was maintained by the considerable attention that both her parents and her fiancé directed toward this behavior. As long as Norma continued picking at her face, the pattern of inadvertent reinforcement was maintained, and she would likely remain the center of attention.

Realizing this pattern, the therapist instructed Norma's parents and fiancé to ignore her face picking entirely. They were cautioned that it would probably get worse before improving. (At the beginning of extinction training, people and other animals typically increase the intensity of no-longer-reinforced behaviors before discarding them.) True to prediction, Norma did exhibit a temporary increase in her face picking. However, it was quickly extinguished. (To prevent it from reappearing, the therapist encouraged both parents and fiancé to provide plenty of loving attention and support to Norma contingent upon a variety of healthy, adaptive behaviors.)

Punishment   In Chapter 6 we discussed how the use of an aversive stimulus such as an electric shock can be used in aversion therapy to classically condition an aversion response to an attractive but harmful stimulus. Aversive stimuli can also be used to punish voluntary maladaptive responses.

An example is the case of a nine-month-old infant, whose life was endangered by a chronic pattern of vomiting and regurgitating food (Lang & Melamed, 1969). From a six-month weight of 17 pounds, the infant had dropped to an emaciated 12 pounds. Attempts to feed him through a tube inserted through his nasal passage were a losing cause, since he continued to regurgitate his food within minutes. The behavior therapists assigned to this case carefully evaluated the vomiting behavior. Using electrical recordings of muscular activity, they found they could detect when the infant was about to vomit. On this basis they designed a treatment strategy. Each time electrical recordings signaled that the infant was about to vomit, the therapists delivered a brief shock to his leg. This electrical shock was immediately effective in reducing the vomiting, and after a few short training sessions the undesirable behavior had completely ceased. Within a relatively short period the child had gained considerable weight and was well enough to be discharged from the hospital (see Figure 16.2). A follow-up one year later revealed continued healthy development, with no recurrences of the vomiting behavior.

Students are often disturbed by this case, on two counts. The first disturbing aspect is ethical. Many people cringe at the prospect of a helpless infant receiving electric shocks. It is true that there are ethical implications of using punishment to modify behavior, and such an approach should only be given consideration as a last resort. Nevertheless, in view of the fact that the infant was dangerously close to dying, we believe that this drastic approach to treatment was justified.

The second reservation expressed by many students is a practical one. We have learned that punishment generally produces only a temporary suppression of undesirable behavior unless punishment is continued or another behavior pattern is reinforced in its place. Why was punishment so effective in this case? We can assume that the infant's reduced hunger and improved physical well-being provided adequate reinforcement to maintain the new behavior pattern. Thus there was no return to the vomiting behavior even after the electric shocks ceased.

Modeling   As we saw in Chapter 6, learning theorists have demonstrated that some kinds of learning appear to be learned through modeling. Modeling can be a helpful therapy technique for extinguishing irrational fears or for establishing new, more adaptive behaviors.

For example, suppose you are deathly afraid of the dark. Although this phobia might be treated by systematic desensitization as we described earlier, modeling might also be effective: You might observe others entering the dark with no visible adverse effects. Modeling may be live, or it may take place through films or videotapes. The beneficial, antiphobia effects of modeling techniques may be enhanced even further if relaxation training is also used to ensure the client is in a calm, tranquil state while observing the models.

Modeling has wide application in treating people with phobias. In one study, children who were extremely fearful about undergoing a dental exam were first exposed to a 10-minute videotape in which a child model appeared to be happy and relaxed while experiencing several dental procedures such as X-rays and oral exams. These children exhibited markedly fewer signs of distress during the actual exam than a matched control group of children who were not exposed to the modeling procedure (Crooks, 1969).

Modeling may also be helpful in establishing new, more appropriate responses. For example, people who are shy or nonassertive may observe live or filmed vignettes of models acting out scenes in which people effectively initiate social contacts or behave in an appropriately assertive way. Ideally, these behaviors are shown to produce reinforcers, so that the observers may achieve a kind of vicarious reinforcement by identifying with the model (this is also how advertising works). Clients are often asked to participate actively in the desired behavior after viewing the models. In one study, modeling and active role playing were found to be considerably more effective than cognitive therapy in establishing appropriate assertive behaviors (Gormally et al., 1975).

Token Economies   Another way that reinforcement can be applied to maintain adaptive behavior patterns is through the use of tokens that can later be exchanged for desired objects or privileges. The goal of token economies is to bring the desired pattern of behavior to a level where more natural contingencies maintain it indefinitely. Token economies have proven very successful in the

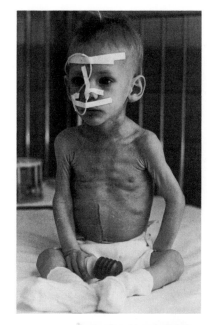

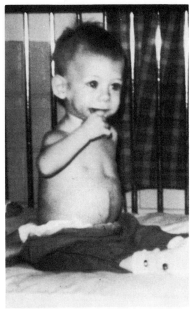

FIGURE 16.2

The Appearance of a Nine-Month Infant Before and After Punishment Therapy

SOURCE: From Lang & Melamed, 1969; courtesy of Peter Lang)

treatment of a variety of severe behavioral disorders including mental retardation, autism, chronic schizophrenia, eating disorders, and severe mood disorders. In a token economy patients are reinforced with tokens for demonstrating appropriate behavior. For instance, a patient may be reinforced with tokens for dressing appropriately and interacting with other patients and staff. These tokens can later be exchanged for the privilege of seeing a movie or having visitors. The major advantage of token economies is that appropriate behaviors can be immediately reinforced and there is little satiation to the reinforcer as there is with other primary reinforcers.

EVALUATING BEHAVIORAL THERAPIES   Of all the psychological therapies, behavioral therapies appear to be the most effective for a wide range of behavioral disorders, especially those with definable symptoms. There are several reasons for this success. First, because behavioral therapies focus on specific disordered behaviors it is very easy to monitor outcomes throughout therapy. If appropriate changes are not occurring immediately, the approach can be modified to bring about desired changes. Second, behavior therapies are based upon well-defined and understood principles of human and animal learning and behavior (see, e.g., Domjan, 1993). No other therapeutic approach is based upon such an extensive research base.

GROUP THERAPIES

To this point in the chapter, we have been discussing individual therapy in which one client meets alone with a therapist. However, virtually all the major schools of psychotherapy also treat people in groups of three or more. This form of therapy, known as **group therapy,** varies widely according to group composition. Large groups may consist of one or two group leaders and five to seven clients, who may represent a heterogeneous mix of different problems or a more homogeneous group of people with the same basic problems (such as drug abusers, people with eating disorders, or sex offenders). Groups may also be composed of entire families or a couple being treated, usually by only one therapist. Available data indicate that more people are now treated via some form of group therapy than through individual therapy (Harvard Medical School, 1989).

One of the greatest advantages of group therapy is simply that it operates in a group setting (Fuhriman & Burlingame, 1990). Many of the problems that lead people to seek therapy in the first place involve getting along with others, and these problems can often be brought out into the open more easily within a group environment.

This setting also has advantages for individual members of a group. Many participants in groups are immediately struck by the realization that they are not alone—a "my gosh, other people are just as fouled up as me" awareness. This sense of solidarity with others, together with feelings of safety and support, can be very comforting, encouraging participants to open up and share their problems more readily than they might in individual therapy.

Group therapy participants have the advantage of receiving feedback not only from the group leader, but also from other members of the group, whose insights and observations can be very beneficial. Groups can provide a much more true-to-life environment than individual therapy for trying out new behaviors and ways of relating to others. The feedback from other group members, which is often considerably more direct than in the outside world, may be extremely helpful in modifying flaws in interpersonal skills.

In addition to receiving advice and suggestions, group members also have an opportunity to observe how others work out their problems. Participants in groups may also experience a boost to their self-esteem as a result of helping other members.

Group therapy sessions are often conducted informally with individuals seated in a circle. Sessions are typically conducted weekly for several months.

A final advantage of group therapy is a practical one. Therapy can be expensive, particularly when it extends over many months: Six months of weekly individual sessions with a psychologist or psychiatrist may cost as much as $1,200 to $2,400. The cost of group therapy, shared across several clients, is likely to be considerably less. Furthermore, since groups typically meet once a week for one and a half to two hours, the amount of time spent in a therapeutic setting is increased by 50 to 100 percent over individual therapy. (Of course, it is also true that the amount of individual attention is considerably less than in one-on-one therapy.)

A variety of problems may be effectively treated in a group setting, including substance abuse, eating disorders, child and sexual abuse, the effects of sexual victimization, problems expressing feelings to others, shyness and lack of assertiveness, social incompetence, compulsive gambling, and difficulties in being intimate with others. People most likely to benefit from group therapy are those who can communicate thoughts and feelings and who are motivated to be active participants. Poor candidates are people who are withdrawn, uncommunicative, combative, antisocial, or so depressed or unreachable that they are likely to frustrate other group members (Bloch, 1979; Harvard Medical School, 1989). We now look at two different forms of group therapy: family therapy and couple therapy.

FAMILY THERAPY **Family therapy** has gained steadily in popularity and respect over the last few decades. It differs from therapy with groups of unrelated individuals because family units bring to the experience a shared history of patterns of interrelationships. The family therapist is more likely to take an active role as model or teacher than other group leaders, who frequently define their role as facilitator rather than director (Yalom, 1975).

Family therapy is based on the premise that an individual's behavioral adjustment is profoundly influenced by patterns of social interaction within the family unit. Families characterized by strife, poor communication, and pathological interaction patterns can foster behavioral difficulties in one or more individual members. The assumption that individual pathology has its roots in a disturbed family leads logically to the deduction that changing patterns of interaction in a disturbed family will affect those family members who have adjustment problems (Kutash & Wolf, 1986; Levene et al., 1990). Thus the task of the family therapist is to alter maladaptive relationship patterns so that symptoms of disturbed behavior diminish or disappear (Foley, 1984).

Family therapists use a number of techniques to change maladaptive patterns in a disturbed family. One strategy may be to alter patterns of alliances that are

TABLE 16.3 *A Comparison of Several Different Forms of Therapy*

TYPE OF PSYCHOTHERAPY	PRIMARY FOUNDER(S)	INTERPRETATION OF CAUSE(S) OF DISORDERS
Psychoanalysis	Sigmund Freud	Disordered behavior results from unconscious conflicts and repressed urges, which are rooted in childhood experiences.
Person-Centered	Carl Rogers	Poor psychological adjustment results from an incongruence between individuals' self-concepts and their experiences.
Gestalt	Frederick Perls	Psychological problems stem from people's inability to integrate the various parts of their personalities (such as thoughts, feelings, and actions) into a healthy, well-organized whole.
Rational-Emotive	Albert Ellis	Psychological problems result when people interpret their experiences on the basis of certain self-defeating, irrational beliefs.
Cognitive Restructuring	Aaron Beck	Psychological problems stem primarily from a few irrational beliefs that cause people to behave and emote in maladaptive ways.
Behavior	Joseph Wolpe, Albert Bandura, and others.	Disordered or maladaptive behaviors result from learning.
Biomedical	Antonio de Egas Moniz, James Watts, Ugo Cerletti, Lucino Bino, and others.	Many psychological problems result from biological abnormalities.

damaging to one or more family members. For instance, suppose an alliance has formed between a mother and her son, so that the father feels left out, angry, and depressed—feelings that may cause the father to display hostility toward his son and to withdraw from his wife. The therapist may seek to restructure patterns of family interaction by encouraging the father to take a more active interest in his son's experiences and to be more involved in making decisions that directly affect his son (Kendall & Norton-Ford, 1982).

Family therapists also aim to have all family members redefine problems as a family responsibility rather than projecting the blame onto only one member. For example, a teenage daughter's school truancy and drug use might be viewed as reflecting problem behavior of all family members. Perhaps she has reasoned that if she acts bad enough, her feuding parents will be forced to focus on her problems and thus stop battling with each other.

In summary, family therapists treat the entire family as the patient as they seek to educate all members about what kinds of maladaptive patterns are occurring within the family unit, how each member contributes to these problems, and what can be done to change the disruptive patterns to a more healthy system of interrelationships. Family therapy often tends to be relatively short term, consisting of once-a-week sessions for several weeks or a few months. The family may always be seen as an entire unit, although occasionally separate sessions may be scheduled for one or more members.

COUPLE THERAPY Assume that you are having serious conflicts with your spouse or partner. Perhaps you are struggling with role definitions, a breakdown in communication, financial decisions, or matters related to expressing intimacy.

FOCUS/GOALS OF THERAPY	METHODS OF THERAPY
To enter the unconscious of disturbed people, search out the anxiety-causing conflict(s), and help these individuals gain insight or conscious awareness of the repressed conflicts.	Techniques include free association, dream analysis, and interpretation of resistance and transference.
To create a therapeutic environment that enhances individuals' potential for self-examination, personal growth, and self-fulfillment and reduces incongruence between their self-concept and experience.	Genuineness, unconditional positive regard, and an empathic understanding.
To help people bring together the alienated fragments of self into an integrated unified whole. The primary focus is on moment-to-moment awareness of oneself.	Role playing, training clients to speak in the first person, and pointing out incongruences or discrepancies between what clients say and do.
To help people find the flaws in their thinking, to challenge or dispute these maladaptive cognitions, and then to guide clients to substitute more logical or realistic thoughts.	Confrontation, persuasion, role playing, interptretation, behavior modification, and reflection of feelings.
To help clients restructure their thinking, particularly their negative self-labels.	Structure certain "experiments" or experiences to disprove a client's misguided self-impressions.
To focus on people's current behaviors that are creating problems and help them unlearn maladaptive behavior patterns while learning more adaptive behavior.	Systematic desensitization, aversive conditioning, positive reinforcement, extinction, and punishment.
To eliminate symptoms of psychological disorders through biological intervention.	Psychosurgery, electroconvulsive therapy, and psychoactive drugs.

You are determined to get help but do not know whether you should seek treatment as an individual, encourage your partner to get help (maybe you think the problem is primarily his or hers), or go for treatment together. Therapists who practice couple therapy agree with the underlying premise of family therapy: Difficulties that exist within a primary unit, in this case a couple, are best treated within the context of the unit rather than through individual therapy. Today conjoint or **couple therapy** (working with the two partners together) has become the most common approach for treating relationship problems within a primary couple, married or unmarried (Sager, 1986).

Because unclear, ambiguous, or mixed messages often contribute to relationship conflicts, couple therapists often focus on improving communication between partners (Holmes & Boon, 1990). However, the fact that a couple knows how to communicate effectively is no guarantee that they will apply this knowledge in their relationship. Therapists often need to probe for hidden agendas or underlying reasons why one or both partners seem unwilling or unable to explore ways to improve the level of verbal, emotional, and physical intimacy between them.

EVALUATING PSYCHOTHERAPY

We have explored several approaches to psychotherapy without stopping to discuss whether one approach is more effective than another. These therapies are summarized in Table 16.3. This section first deals with whether psychotherapy is more beneficial than no therapy at all and whether one type of psychotherapy is better than another. It concludes by describing common features that are shared by the various approaches to psychotherapy.

IS PSYCHOTHERAPY MORE BENEFICIAL THAN NO THERAPY?

You may have heard people criticize psychotherapy, saying that with a little bit of gumption, people can get well on their own. Even though many people who have gone through therapy swear by it, these critics answer that it is normal for people to defend an investment of so much time and money. Indeed, it has been shown that clients may work very hard to find something positive to say about their therapists (Zilbergeld, 1983). What does the record say—are people with adjustment problems just as well off if they do not see a therapist?

In the effort to answer this question, a number of controlled research studies have attempted to evaluate psychotherapy. The first of these studies was published in 1952 by an English psychologist, Hans Eysenck. Eysenck was well aware that many people with behavioral problems get well on their own without any formal treatment, a phenomenon called *spontaneous remission*. Therefore he compared the success rates of psychotherapy reported in 24 studies with spontaneous remission rates among untreated behaviorally disturbed individuals. (He collected data such as the number of people on waiting lists for treatment who spontaneously improved and therefore removed themselves as candidates for psychotherapy.) Eysenck reported that approximately two out of every three people treated with psychotherapy improved markedly. However, he also reported approximately the same two-thirds improvement rate among disturbed people who received no treatment.

Critics questioned the criteria Eysenck used to assess therapy outcomes; they also argued that people in Eysenck's untreated control group differed in important ways from individuals who received treatment. In the late 1970s, researchers reanalyzed Eysenck's clinical data and discovered that his reported spontaneous remission rate of almost 70 percent was actually closer to 40 percent (Bergin & Lambert, 1978). Thus Eysenck's research was eventually discredited.

Clinical researchers then set out to design better studies. More effective criteria of success were developed, including scores on psychological tests, self-ratings, ratings by clinicians not involved in treating subjects, and recidivism rates (such as whether or not additional therapy was sought in a given period of time after initial treatment ended, or what percentage of hospitalized patients were readmitted after discharge). Drawing upon data from these better designed comparison studies, Lester Luborsky and his associates (1975) reported that 80 percent of the studies found significant benefits associated with psychotherapy. In most cases, these improvement rates were markedly better than those for untreated individuals.

Several years later an ambitious evaluation of psychotherapy outcomes was reported by Mary Lee Smith, Gene Glass, and Thomas Miller (1980). These researchers applied a complex statistical procedure called *metaanalysis* to combine and analyze data collectively from 475 psychotherapy outcome studies. Their findings confirmed those of the Luborsky group. On the average, clients treated by psychotherapy were found to score higher on a number of outcome measures than untreated people with similar problems and characteristics. As Figure 16.3 shows, however, there is a considerable overlap in the outcomes reported for the untreated or control samples and the treated groups. The fact that many untreated people do experience improvement with time is testimony to people's capacity for behavioral change perhaps as a result of interactions with others or changes in situations.

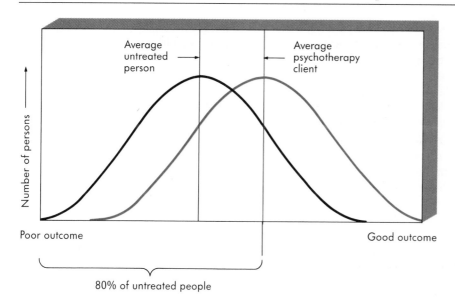

FIGURE 16.3
Normal Distributions Showing Treatment Outcomes for Treated and Untreated Patients

The Smith et al. study discussed in the preceding section also looked at the success rates of different types of therapy. Its finding: No particular type of therapy is *significantly* superior to others. From an overall perspective, only slight differences emerged—for instance, psychoanalytic and person-centered approaches were approximately equal in effectiveness, and both were somewhat less effective than cognitive and behavioral therapies. Furthermore, whether therapy took place in individual or group settings, over the short term or the long term, seemed to have little impact on its effectiveness.

Research also indicates that the most effective psychotherapists are people who genuinely care about their clients and who are able to establish a warm, empathic relationship that helps to foster respect, trust, and the feeling of being cared for (Strupp, 1984; Williams & Chambers, 1990). A clinician who is reserved, aloof, and emotionally detached is not likely to provide the kind of warm, supportive atmosphere that is essential to therapeutic progress.

Efforts to assess the relative success rates of various forms of psychotherapy may diminish in future years, in light of the current trend toward integrating the many diverse theoretical frameworks underlying the practice of American psychotherapy (Goldfried et al., 1990; Jensen et al., 1990). This integrative movement is reflected in a growing tendency among psychotherapists to ignore the ideological barriers dividing schools of psychotherapy and to define what is common among them and what is useful in each of them (Beitman et al., 1989, p. 138). Between one-third and one-half of currently practicing American psychotherapists do not consider themselves to be aligned with one particular type of psychotherapy, preferring instead to view themselves as eclectic in their application of psychotherapy (Beitman et al., 1989; Jayaratne, 1982; Norcross et al., 1988; Prochaska & Norcross, 1983; Watkins et al., 1986). Eclecticism in psychotherapy involves the pragmatic application of clinical techniques from different theoretical systems without necessarily subscribing to the theories from which the techniques are derived. Research indicates that psychotherapists who are eclectic in their clinical practices tend to be older and more experienced. This finding suggests that "with experience comes diversity and flexibility" (Beitman et al., 1989, p. 139). Making evaluation even more difficult is the fact that a

IS ONE TYPE OF PSYCHOTHERAPY MORE EFFECTIVE THAN ANOTHER?

therapist's theoretical orientation (psychoanalytic, humanistic, cognitive, or behavioral) does not necessarily ensure that any significant change in behavior is attributable to the perspective. For instance, just because a psychoanalyst discusses inner conflicts with a patient who later recovers does not necessarily mean that inner conflicts were indeed the cause of the disturbed behavior.

COMMON FEATURES OF PSYCHOTHERAPEUTIC APPROACHES

Certain common features are shared by almost all styles of therapy. Researchers Jerome Frank (1982) and Marvin Goldfield (Goldfield & Padawer, 1982) have analyzed the commonalities of different psychotherapies extensively, and we explore some of their findings.

Combating the Client's Demoralization People who seek the services of a psychotherapist are typically demoralized by anxiety, depression, and a poor self-image, and they often have little hope for escaping from their misery. By inspiring expectations of help, providing new learning experiences, and enhancing people's sense of self-worth and efficiency, psychotherapists may be powerful morale builders. Virtually all effective psychotherapists, regardless of their particular methodology, tend to inspire in their clients a sense of hope and a belief that things will get better. These morale-boosting expectations may well contribute to a reduction in symptoms and an improved sense of well-being (Jacobson, 1968; Prioleau et al., 1983).

Providing a Rationale for Symptoms and Treatment Regardless of their theoretical orientation, virtually all therapists provide their clients with a plausible explanation for their symptoms and a logical scheme for alleviating them. As clients rethink the nature of their problems and possible solutions, they often acquire a new perspective on themselves as well as some fresh ideas about how to respond to their world more effectively. Acquiring a better understanding of oneself and one's problems, along with developing possible solutions, may contribute greatly to the healing process.

Providing a Warm, Supportive Relationship Effective therapists are individuals who are able to establish a caring, trusting, and empathic relationship with their clients. In one study, clients rated their personal relationship and interaction with their therapist as the most important part of their treatment (Sloane et al., 1975). Another study demonstrated that even paraprofessionals (laypeople trained by professionals) who were versed in how to engage in empathic listening were quite effective in helping people overcome behavioral problems (Berman & Norton, 1985). Thus it would seem that the nature of the client–therapist relationship has much to do with the success of the treatment (Henry et al., 1986; Kokotovic & Tracey, 1990). The fact that most therapists attempt to establish a warm, confiding, and empathic relationship with their clients may account, at least in part, for the comparable success rate reported for each method.

Providing a Professional Setting Good therapy does not usually take place over a cup of coffee, in the room of a private home that does double duty as a family room, or over the telephone. Instead, it usually takes place in a dignified, professional setting in a mental health clinic, hospital, or private office. This kind of setting may contribute much to the therapeutic process. An office that is quiet and professional is likely to provide a sense of security and safety that people may not experience in an informal setting, where the possibility of being overheard or interrupted may inhibit spontaneity. In addition, such a setting is likely to enhance the therapist's prestige and, by inference, to heighten the client's expectations for effective treatment.

In view of the widespread and extensive nature of behavioral problems, it is likely that at some point in our lives many of us will think seriously about seeking professional help in the form of psychotherapy. The Health, Psychology and Life discussion, Guidelines for Seeking Professional Help, on page 653 at the end of this chapter offers some suggestions that may facilitate the process of finding a psychotherapist.

BIOLOGICALLY-BASED THERAPIES

We have been dealing exclusively with psychological approaches to treating behavioral disorders. There are also, however, a number of biological or medical therapies. Biomedical approaches to treatment are based on one or both of two assumptions: (1) Many behavioral disorders result from biological abnormalities including altered brain structure and/or altered brain chemistry, and (2) physiological intervention through surgery, electric shock, or drugs will alleviate or reduce significantly the symptoms of behavioral disorders.

Only clinicians with medical degrees may use biomedical treatments. However, psychologists often refer clients to a psychiatrist or other medical practitioner when they feel that biomedical treatment might be helpful. In many cases the treatment of behavioral disorders involves both psychological and biological therapy. This was strongly emphasized by Kurt Salzinger in the "Research Perspectives" segment at the end of Chapter 15. In this section we examine three types of biomedical treatment: psychosurgery, electroconvulsive (shock) therapy, and psychoactive drugs.

PSYCHOSURGERY

In the early decades of this century mental hospitals throughout the Western world overflowed with severely disturbed patients, and there was a shortage of both professional staff and effective treatment strategies. During this time many mental health professionals became frustrated with what they perceived to be a general practice of using mental hospitals as little more than warehouses for severely disordered patients. In the effort to alleviate patient suffering and reduce problems of overcrowding, a number of psychiatrists were motivated to experiment with a variety of often radical biological interventions.

One such person was a Portuguese neuropsychiatrist, Antonio de Egas Moniz. In 1935 Moniz attended a professional conference in London and was impressed by a report describing brain surgery on two chimpanzees in which the prefrontal areas (forwardmost portion of the frontal lobes) of their cerebral cortexes were removed. The effect of this surgery was to abolish the violent outbursts that both animals had been prone to prior to surgery. On the basis of this single instance of chimpanzee brain surgery, Moniz persuaded a colleague, Almeida Lima, to experiment with surgery on the frontal lobes of schizophrenics and other severely disturbed patients. The surgical procedure was to sever the nerve tracts connecting the frontal cortex to lower regions in the brain that mediate emotional responses, most notably the thalamus and hypothalamus. Essentially, the idea was to disconnect thought (mediated by the cortex) from emotion (mediated by lower brain centers). Such a procedure was expected to have a calming effect on patients troubled by severely disruptive emotional patterns.

This operation, known as a **lobotomy,** was originally performed by a very crude surgical procedure in which a hole was drilled through the skull on each side of the head, and a blunt instrument was then inserted and rotated in a vertical arc. The procedure was later refined by the *transorbital lobotomy* technique, in which an icepick-like instrument called a leucotome is inserted into the brain

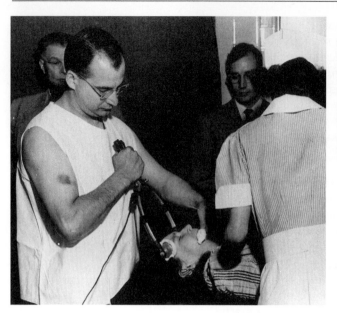
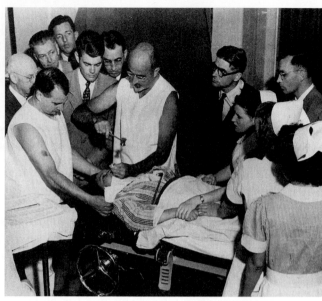

FIGURE 16.4

A Demonstration of a Prefrontal Lobotomy

A patient was often anesthetized by the administration of ECT (electroconvulsive shock) as shown on the left. After ECT the patient undergoes a lobotomy performed by inserting a long, narrow blade through the eye socket.

through an eye socket and rotated back and forth. Figure 16.4 illustrates the lobotomy procedure.

The lobotomy rapidly became popular in Europe as a treatment for a wide variety of disorders including schizophrenia, severe depression, and occasionally anxiety disorders. Moniz claimed enthusiastically that the procedure was very effective in calming severely disturbed psychotics, and that many lobotomized patients were able to leave the hospital. (Strangely, though, his claims were even more widely influential after he was partially paralyzed by a gunshot inflicted by one of his lobotomized patients [Valenstein, 1980].) Neurosurgeons Walter Freeman and James Watts (1950) introduced lobotomy to the United States, where it flourished until the late 1950s. By the time the popularity of lobotomies had begun to wane, over 40,000 people were thought to have been recipients of this surgical intervention (Kalinowsky, 1975).

Lobotomized patients seemed more tranquil or calm after the operation, and thus more manageable. However, some observant clinicians began to raise questions. They suggested that the so-called calming effect was actually more a conversion of emotionally labile patients into lethargic, vegetative patients. In addition, it was noted that very little research evidence had substantiated the effects of this treatment.

Once researchers began to investigate seriously the effects of lobotomies, they found that the claims of pronounced improvements in behavior had been greatly exaggerated. True, lobotomized patients had slightly higher rates of discharge from hospitals than matched controls, but this statistic was counterbalanced by higher rates of recidivism or return to hospitals. Furthermore, these studies provided some profoundly disturbing evidence—that some lobotomized patients had been transformed into lethargic, unmotivated, robotlike personalities that were hollow remnants of the individuals they had once been. This effect was dramatized in Ken Kesey's novel, *One Flew over the Cuckoo's Nest* (1962). Other irreversible side effects were uncovered, including memory loss, inability to plan ahead, seizures, and even death. Furthermore, lobotomies were found to produce no changes in the major manifestations of severe mental illness other than reduction of emotional agitation (Barahal, 1958; Robbin, 1958, 1959).

Such findings prompted several critics to call for a ban on all forms of psychosurgery. Although no formal prohibition was enforced, medical practitioners drastically curtailed their use of this method. (This movement away from psy-

_chosurgery gained momentum with the emergence of calming psychoactive drugs, whose effects, unlike those of lobotomy, are temporary rather than permanent.)

Psychosurgery did not die out completely. In fact, since the early 1970s there has been a growing interest in using surgical techniques to alter behavior when all other reversible treatment methods have failed. Newer surgical techniques produce only a small fraction of the brain damage associated with older procedures. For example, highly refined methods are now available for disconnecting the frontal cortex from lower brain centers, damaging less than 10 percent of the amount of brain tissue destroyed by the transorbital technique (Shevitz, 1976). Other contemporary psychosurgery techniques involve destruction of limited amounts of tissue in precisely located sites within such brain structures as the amygdala, thalamus, and hypothalamus. These refined procedures are often effective in alleviating symptoms of severe depression, uncontrollable rage attacks, extreme anxiety, obsessive–compulsive disorders, schizophrenia, uncontrollable seizures, and severe pain—all of which may have resisted more conventional forms of therapy—with very few serious side effects (Corkin, 1980; Donnelly, 1980; Mirsky & Orzacki, 1980; Kiloh et al., 1988; Sachdev et al., 1990; Valenstein, 1980). Although these newer techniques are clearly an improvement over the lobotomies of the 1940s and 1950s, most contemporary clinicians believe that their use should be limited to patients whose problems are severe, persistent, and resistant to all other treatments.

ELECTROCONVULSIVE THERAPY

Electroconvulsive therapy (ECT) is a procedure in which electrical current is applied to the surface of the head resulting in a convulsive seizure. Students often wonder how such a procedure could have come about to treat behavioral disorders. The story here is an interesting one.

In the early 1930s a Hungarian physician, Lazlo Von Meduna, noticed that hospitalized psychiatric patients often seemed to experience a remission or lessening of their psychotic symptoms after undergoing a spontaneous seizure of the type that occurs in epilepsy. Excited by this discovery, Von Meduna began to experiment with different techniques for artificially inducing convulsions. He first

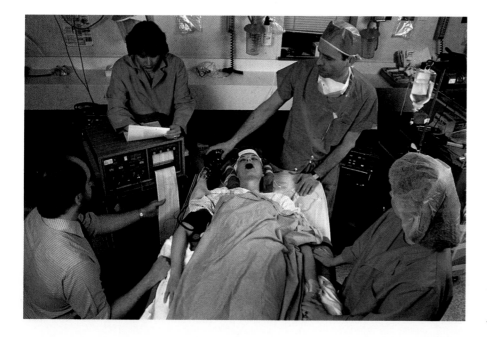

Electroconvulsive therapy (ECT) is used to treat more than 80,000 American patients each year.

used intramuscular injections of camphor oil to elicit seizures. Although several patients were made physically ill by the injections, a number showed remarkable improvement. Von Meduna soon substituted a synthetic camphor, metrazol, which seemed to lessen the side effect of physical illness. The use of *pharmaco-convulsive therapy* (drug-induced seizures) quickly gained a foothold worldwide among psychiatrists desperate for a way to combat severe behavioral disorders.

Unfortunately, pharmacoconvulsive therapy was not without problems. Although the symptoms of behavioral disorders were often reduced, the procedure had other severe side effects, including painful preseizure spasms and uncontrollable convulsions that sometimes resulted in fractures and even death (Weiner, 1985). In the late 1930s two Italian neuropsychiatrists, Ugo Cerletti and Lucino Bini (1938), introduced a safer, better controlled method for inducing seizures using electric shock. By 1940 electroconvulsive therapy had become a major component of psychiatric treatment strategies worldwide.

Early ECT sessions resembled a scene from a horror movie. A wide awake and often terrified patient was strapped to a table, electrodes were attached to each side of the forehead, and a current of roughly 100 volts was then passed between the electrodes for a fraction of a second, producing severe convulsions and a temporary loss of consciousness. Upon regaining consciousness the patient often seemed confused, distressed, and unable to remember events that happened both before and immediately after the procedure. In addition, the seizures induced by the electric current often produced such a rapid and intense contraction of skeletal muscles that bone fractures, bruises, and other injuries sometimes resulted. Altogether, this was not a pretty picture — but one that was repeated countless thousands of times due to compelling evidence that ECT was often amazingly effective in reducing symptoms of severe emotional distress, particularly depression.

Since the early days of the development of ECT, several modifications have been introduced to make this treatment safer and more humane. Today, patients are first put to sleep and administered a powerful muscle relaxant before the shock is delivered. General anesthesia circumvents the terror many patients experienced in the early years of shock therapy. The patient typically wakes up in a half hour or so, with no recollection of the treatment. ECT is now often applied to only one of the cerebral hemispheres, usually the one that is not dominant. This unilateral treatment has significantly reduced the confusion and memory loss associated with ECT.

There is extensive evidence that ECT often produces a rapid and sometimes a dramatic reduction of the symptoms of major depression (Kalinowsky, 1980; Kramer, 1987; Scovern & Kilmann, 1980; Weiner, 1985; Yudofsky, 1982), and the treatment is sometimes effective in counteracting bipolar disorder (Berman & Wolpert, 1987). Research has generally shown ECT to be less effective in treating schizophrenia. The most common application of ECT today is for severely depressed patients who have not responded to antidepressant drugs or who cannot tolerate waiting for the slower acting drugs to take effect (Weiner, 1985). Recently, a review panel commissioned by the National Institutes of Health concluded that while ECT is not without problems, it is nevertheless a relatively effective treatment for severe depression that has not responded to psychotherapy or drug therapy (Kolata, 1985).

Not everyone agrees with this favorable assessment of ECT, however. One outspoken critic is psychiatrist Peter Breggin, who wrote the book *Electroshock: Its Brain-Disabling Effects* (1979). Breggin asserts that the effects of ECT on the brain are often catastrophic. While acknowledging that some depressed patients experience short-term benefits from the procedure, he believes that there is plenty of evidence that extended treatment can lead to complete neurological collapse. Breggin's evidence suggests that psychiatrists who do not use ECT have success rates comparable with those who use ECT extensively. In his opinion, it is reckless and unconscionable to use a treatment that may have devastating effects on the brain when other equally effective and safer strategies are available.

Some of Breggin's concerns have been shared by other researchers. Some have issued warnings about the possibility of permanent memory impairment, which has been observed among some recipients of extensive ECT therapy (Rouche, 1980). Psychiatrist Richard Weiner (1985), an advocate of ECT as a "second-line treatment modality" (a treatment to be used if first-choice measures fail) acknowledges that ECT patients typically have some difficulty in retaining newly learned material following a course of ECT treatments. Controlled studies in his own laboratory have revealed a persistent memory deficit as long as six months after ECT. Furthermore, "there have been a number of complaints by patients and their families of more persistent losses. . . ." (p. 463).

This finding is in line with other research which assessed the proactive (forward-acting) effects of a series of electroconvulsive shocks on the long-term memories of laboratory rats (Crooks, 1972). Here, long-term memory formation was found to be markedly impaired following ECT treatment. Of course, rats are not humans, but more recent evidence of ECT-induced memory deficits should be viewed as an indicator to exercise caution in the use of ECT. The shift to unilateral ECT, which tends to reduce memory deficits and other negative side effects of the treatment, may be viewed as a welcome change in ECT methodology.

One of the most perplexing aspects of electroconvulsive therapy is that no one is sure how the treatment works. We know that ECT alters the electrochemical processes in many central nervous system structures, but we still have not been able to determine which of these changes, if any, are linked with the antidepressant effects of ECT. One popular theory is that ECT increases the availability of the neurotransmitters norepinephrine and serotonin at the synapses in certain brain sites in a fashion similar to the chemical antidepressants (Kety, 1975; Weiner, 1985). A similar explanation for how ECT works suggests that "pathological ratios of brain neurotransmitters are normalized by this mechanism, resulting in therapeutic benefit" (King & Liston, 1990, p. 82). Another hypothesis is that depression is associated with overactivity in selective brain sites, and that the brain becomes less active after ECT treatments in a kind of compensation for the hyperactivity associated with the seizures (Sackheim, 1985). It has even been suggested that the antidepressant effects of ECT can be explained by operant conditioning. According to this interpretation, a patient learns the operant response of not being depressed in order to avoid the aversive stimulus of ECT (Costello, 1976).

The questions and concerns raised by ECT will no doubt continue to be debated, and we can expect that ECT will continue to be used to treat approximately 80,000 Americans per year (Sackheim, 1985; Thompson & Blaine, 1987). Researchers hope eventually to clarify how ECT works and whether or not its potential beneficial effects are outweighed by disruptive or disabling side effects.

PSYCHOACTIVE DRUGS

The use of chemicals to control symptoms of behavioral disorders became a primary strategy of psychiatric practice during the 1950s. Since then, therapy with **psychoactive drugs** has become by far the most common biomedical treatment. The use of psychoactive drugs has contributed both to a decline in the number of people hospitalized for behavioral disorders and to a significant reduction in the average duration of hospitalization. "Now, hospitalization of the mentally ill is seldom measured in terms of years but is more often a matter of months or even weeks" (Avison & Speechley, 1987). Drugs are often so effective in controlling disruptive symptoms that many patients who might previously have required restraints or close observation in locked wards are now able to function reasonably effectively outside of a hospital setting. Even patients who still require hospitalization typically need less supervision than did their counterparts in the days before drugs were introduced. In other cases drug therapy has been successfully used to calm patients so that psychological therapies can be applied.

The four major categories of psychoactive drugs that are used to control or alleviate symptoms of behavioral disorders are *neuroleptics, antidepressants, antimanics,* and *antianxiety drugs.* Table 16.4 lists several commonly used drugs in these categories. The various widely used psychoactive drugs differ considerably in their effects: Some calm, some energize, and some provide an emotional lift. However, they all share one common feature. Generally speaking, all psychoactive drugs merely help to control or manage symptoms rather than cure the disorder. When people cease taking these medications, symptoms tend to recur.

TABLE 16.4 *Major Categories of Psychoactive Drugs*

CATEGORY	USED TO TREAT	CHEMICAL GROUP	GENERIC NAME	TRADE NAME
Antipsychotics	schizophrenic disorders, severe aggressive behavior	phenothiazines	chloropromazine thioridazine trifluoperazine	Thorazine Mellaril Stelazine
		butyrophenones	haloperidol	Haldol
		thioxanthenes	chorprothixine	Taractan
		dihydroindolones	molindone	Moban
		dibenzodiazepine	clozapine	Clorazil
Antidepressants	major depressive disorders, obsessive-compulsive behaviors	tricyclics	doxepin amitriptyline imipramine nortriptyline protriptyline	Sinequan Elavil Trofranil Aventyl Vivactyl
		monoamine oxidase inhibitors	phenelzine tranylcypromine isocarboxazid	Nardil Parnate Marphan
		serotonin reuptake inhibitors	fluoxeline paroxetine	Prozac Paxil
Antimanics	bipolar disorder, mania	inorganic salts	lithium carbonate carbamazepine	Lithane Lithonate Tegretol
Antianxiety	generalized anxiety, phobic anxieties, tension, sleep disorders	propanediols	meprobamate	Miltown Equanil
		benzodiazepines	chlordiazepoxide diazepam alprazolam chlorazepate halazepam lorazepam oxazepam prazepam	Librium Valium Zanax Tranxene Paxipam Ativan Serax Centrax

Besides dramatically enhancing the ability of psychiatrists to treat severely disordered patients, biomedical drug therapy has stimulated an abundance of research, resulting in some important new hypotheses linking many behavioral disorders to neurochemical factors.

ANTIPSYCHOTICS The **antipsychotic drugs,** sometimes called *neuroleptics* or *major tranquilizers,* were first used in the early 1950s to treat schizophrenia. As Table 16.4 shows, there are several varieties of these drugs. The most commonly employed are the *phenothiazine* derivatives. The most widely used drug in this group is chlorpromazine, sold under the name Thorazine. Chlorpromazine has been the number-one medication for treating schizophrenia since it was introduced to American psychiatry in 1952 (Duke & Nowicki, 1986). One effect of this drug and other neuroleptic drugs is to calm and quiet patients, reducing their responsiveness to irrelevant stimuli. However, the antipsychotic effects of these drugs is not merely heavy sedation. In other cases where patients are severely withdrawn or immobile, neuroleptic drugs tend to increase activity and responsiveness. The therapeutic effects of neuroleptics are believed to result from the fact that neuroleptic drugs block dopamine receptor sites in the brain, thus reducing dopamine activity. As we discussed in the previous chapter, schizophrenic symptoms appear to result from excessive dopamine activity or sensitivity in certain regions of the brain (Carlsson et al., 1990; Davison & Neale, 1990; Gershon & Rieder, 1992; Grey et al., 1991; Lipper, 1985).

Unfortunately, a sizable percentage (perhaps as many as 40 percent) of patients who take neuroleptic drugs develop a serious side effect called *tardive dyskinesia (TD)* (Bartzokis et al., 1989; Gureje, 1989; Haley, 1989; Stein, 1989; Yadalam et al., 1990). This neurological disorder, which may occur months to years after drug therapy has commenced or has stopped, is typically manifested as uncontrollable muscular movements of the jaw, lips, and tongue. The severity of the symptoms may range from barely noticeable chewing movements to involuntary biting of the tongue. Some psychiatrists are hopeful that the trend toward using lower dosages of neuroleptic drugs in treating severe behavioral disorders will significantly reduce the problem (Stein, 1989). In countries such as China, where it has been customary to use smaller doses of neuroleptics, the incidence of tardive dyskinesia is lower than in the United States (Ko et al., 1989). Another way to reduce the occurrence of this negative side effect is the targeted strategy (Carpenter & Heinrichs, 1983; Herz et al., 1982). The application of this strategy involves discontinuation of neuroleptics during periods of relative remission and the reinstitution of medication when early signs of relapse appear (Kirkpatrick et al., 1989, p. 52).

In other patients, neuroleptic drugs are not effective and other types of medication are being investigated. For instance, one drug that has shown some promise for treatment-resistant patients is Clozapine (Birmaher et al., 1992; Kane, 1992). Clozapine is not classified as a neuroleptic but is discussed here because of its recent introduction as an antipsychotic. Although Clozapine is considered a useful alternative to neuroleptics, there are several potentially serious side-effects associated with its use as well. The most serious of these is a severe immune deficiency that can be fatal.

ANTIDEPRESSANTS The **antidepressant drugs,** also introduced in the 1950s, consist of three main groups, the *tricyclics,* the *monoamine oxidase (MAO)* inhibitors, and *serotonin reuptake inhibitors* (see Table 16.4). As we saw in Chapter 15, these drugs are used to treat major depressive disorders, and they are often very effective in lifting the spirits of severely depressed patients. While it has been widely believed that these drugs act to increase levels of the neurotransmitters norepinephrine and serotonin in certain areas of the brain (Colasanti, 1982a), it is possible that their antidepressant effects may be related to increased sensitivity of the receptors for those two neurotransmitters. Hopefully, further research will clarify how and why the antidepressants are so effective.

A number of studies comparing tricyclic drugs with other treatments have yielded mixed findings. One study (Murphy et al., 1984) compared improvement rates among four matched groups of depressives who received one of the following treatments: (1) cognitive therapy alone, (2) cognitive therapy plus tricyclics, (3) tricyclics alone, and (4) a placebo drug. All treatments were equally effective —a finding which indicates that expectations of getting better have a lot to do with whether people improve. Another study comparing tricyclics alone to cognitive therapy alone found the psychotherapy to be more effective (Rush et al., 1977). And in two other studies, tricyclics combined with psychotherapy provided the best treatment results (DiMascio et al., 1979; Weissman et al., 1981). More recently, a study of 59 unipolar depressives who were treated with a combination of tricyclics and psychotherapy revealed that the relapse rate among these patients after eight weeks of recovery was only 8.5 percent (Kupfer & Frank, 1987). This figure compares with a relapse rate of approximately 22 percent reported for another group of patients treated solely with drugs (Prien & Kupfer, 1986). Another study compared the recovery rates of hospitalized major depressives who received a standard treatment regimen of antidepressant drugs and brief supportive contacts with hospital staff versus those who were provided cognitive therapy in addition to the standard treatment regimen. The recovery rate of the latter group was over twice as high as that for patients who received only standard treatment (Miller et al., 1989). Considered together, these various findings seem to suggest that a combination of antidepressant drugs and psychotherapy may be the most effective approach to treating major depression (Perry, 1990), although additional research is still needed.

Of the major drugs listed in Table 16.4 to treat depression, the serotonin reuptake inhibitors (Prozac and Paxil) appear to be the most effective (Keegan et al., 1991). The MAO inhibitors have been shown to be generally less effective than the tricyclics, both of which have undergone a marked reduction in use because of their adverse side effects.

ANTIMANICS In 1970 lithium carbonate was approved by the Food and Drug Administration for use as an **antimanic drug.** This medication, a simple inorganic salt, has been found to be the most effective drug for controlling the manic symptoms of bipolar disorder and has even been shown to help reduce depression associated with this disorder (Giannini et al., 1986; Murray, 1990). Lithium therapy appears to be less effective when applied to patients experiencing a state of mixed mania (in which both depressive and manic symptoms occur concurrently) (Schou, 1989). Its greatest benefit, however, seems to be as a prophylactic, reducing the frequency and severity of manic episodes or perhaps preventing them altogether (Lipper, 1985; Prien et al., 1984; Prien & Gelenberg, 1989; Schou, 1989). Lithium is believed to accomplish its antimanic effects by increasing the reuptake of norepinephrine and serotonin, thus reducing the available amount of these neurotransmitters at various synaptic sites in the brain (Colasanti, 1982b).

ANTIANXIETY DRUGS The **antianxiety drugs,** sometimes called minor tranquilizers, are used to reduce symptoms of anxiety and tension in people whose behavioral disturbances are not severe enough to warrant hospitalization. These medications are particularly helpful in reducing the symptoms of generalized anxiety disorders, panic disorders, and some sleep disorders. Like most of the drugs we have discussed in this section, the antianxiety medications were introduced in the 1950s and widely used before their mechanisms of action were understood.

There are two major categories of minor tranquilizers: *propanediols* and *benzodiazepines*. The first to be introduced were the propanediols, the most common of which is meprobamate (Miltown). These drugs accomplish their antianxiety effect by reducing muscular tension; they also have a tendency to produce drowsiness. When people stop taking propanediol medications after a long course of fairly large doses, severe withdrawal can occur, producing such effects as tremors, convulsions, hallucinations, and severe anxiety.

Over the years the propanediols have become gradually less popular, and they have been largely replaced by the more recently developed benzodiazepines. The most widely used of these medications, chlordiazepoxide (Librium) and diazepam (Valium), are among the most frequently prescribed medications in the United States (Duke & Nowicki, 1986).

Like the propanediols, the benzodiazepines also seem to have sedative and muscle-relaxing effects. In addition to these properties, the benzodiazepines are known to facilitate the binding of the neurotransmitter, GABA, to receptor sites. The antianxiety effects of the benzodiazepines are believed to be mediated by the facilitation of GABA (Macdonald et al., 1986).

Throughout this chapter we have reviewed the major psychological and biological approaches to the treatment of behavioral disorders. It is important to remember that there is still considerable disagreement among professionals about causes and appropriate types of treatment for most of the disorders that we have discussed. While the fields of neuroscience and pharmacology have contributed considerably to our understanding and treatment of behavioral disorders, many professionals continue to apply therapy from an eclectic approach rather than focus on a single theoretical perspective. For instance, while drug therapy may be quite effective in alleviating symptoms of a disorder, an eclectic practitioner may augment drug therapy with cognitive or behavioral therapy so medication may be discontinued and a more functional behavior pattern maintained. In the next chapter we shall examine social influences on behavior as well as factors that contribute to our social behavior.

GUIDELINES FOR SEEKING PROFESSIONAL HELP

Many people are reluctant to seek professional help because they incorrectly believe that taking this step is an admission that they are weak and incapable of helping themselves. Quite the contrary, people who seek professional help demonstrate a high level of self-awareness and emotional maturity by recognizing that there are limitations to their ability to help themselves when faced with seriously disruptive psychological problems. If some day you find yourself seeking professional help, give yourself credit for having the wisdom to recognize that a skilled therapist can offer useful information, emotional support, a perspective other than your own, and specific problem-solving techniques, all of which may help you make the desired changes in your life.

As we have seen in this text, however, not all therapists are equally effective in providing successful treatment. How do you go about selecting a therapist? Assuming your symptoms are not so acute that they demand immediate attention, we suggest that you shop carefully for a therapist. Most people, however, do not know where to start in making this kind of decision.

HEALTH PSYCHOLOGY LIFE

A good first step in locating a psychotherapist is to seek referrals from people you know who are likely to be familiar with your community's mental-health resources — your psychology instructor, your health care practitioner, or perhaps your minister, rabbi, or priest. (The clergy often deal with people who have psychological problems, and they are quite familiar with community mental-health resources.) Do not hesitate to talk with friends who have used psychotherapy in the past. Sometimes firsthand recommendations can be especially helpful. You may also want to see if your college or university has a counseling center or clinic for students. Such a service may be free or relatively inexpensive. In addition, city, county, and state psychological associations can provide names of licensed clinical psychologists in your area, and county medical societies have lists of names of psychiatrists.

We recommend that you contact several sources and then pool the information. This process may leave you with several choice options. To narrow down your choices, consider the professional backgrounds of your prospective therapists. Remember that many so-called professional counselors have little or no professional training. Many states now license practicing clinical psychologists, and you may inquire whether or not a therapist is licensed. It is highly appropriate for you to ask about the specific training and credentials or certification of a prospective therapist, and you may also wish to ascertain the number of years a therapist has practiced. These inquiries may be made over the phone. If a prospective therapist is reluctant to provide this information, go elsewhere.

Cost may also be an issue as you seek to narrow your choices. Fees vary considerably, from no charge to $100 or more per 45- to 50-minute session. Psychiatrists are usually on the upper end of the fee scale, psychologists are in the middle, and social workers and counselors are usually on the lower end. A higher fee does not necessarily indicate better therapy skills. Some mental-health agencies and private practitioners offer sliding fee schedules based on the client's income. Many health insurance companies now provide partial to full coverage for psychotherapy services, but note that they may require that you see a licensed psychotherapist.

To help determine if a specific therapist will meet your needs, you may wish to establish the following points at your first meeting:

1. What do you want from therapy? You and your therapist should reach an agreement on goals. This agreement is sometimes referred to as the therapy contract.

2. What is the therapist's approach and what kind of participation is expected of you? You can ask about the general process (what the therapist will do) during therapy sessions. You may also ask how long therapy is expected to last. Behavioral therapists typically recommend fewer sessions than psychoanalytic therapists because their perspectives differ considerably.

3. How do you feel about talking with the therapist? Therapy is not intended to be a light social interaction. It can be difficult. At times it may be quite uncomfortable for you to discuss personal concerns. However, for therapy to be useful, you want to have the sense that the therapist is open and willing to understand you.

While these suggestions may not ensure that you find a therapist who is a perfect fit for your needs, it is likely they will increase the odds that you will select a qualified psychotherapist. If therapy doesn't appear to be progressing discuss this with your therapist. If you feel at all uncomfortable with your sessions or your therapist it may be time to select another.

SUMMARY

PSYCHOANALYSIS

1. Psychoanalysis is based on a number of assumptions; the most fundamental is that disordered behavior results from unconscious conflicts and repressed urges, most of which are rooted in childhood experiences.

2. Major techniques of psychoanalysis include free association, dream analysis, and interpretations of resistance and transference.
3. Freud believed that it is important to break through patients' defenses and to provide them with insight by interpreting the underlying meaning of their experiences, resistances, transferences, and dreams.
4. Psychoanalysis as practiced today tends to be briefer in duration and less focused on restructuring a person's entire personality than was the case in Freud's time.

HUMANISTIC THERAPIES

5. Humanistic therapists, who see their goal as fostering psychological growth, place more responsibility for the success of therapy on the client than on the therapist and tend to focus on the present rather than the past.
6. Rogers' person-centered therapy emphasizes creating a therapeutic environment characterized by three dimensions or characteristics expressed by the therapist: genuineness, unconditional positive regard, and empathic understanding.
7. Gestalt therapy strives to help a person bring together the alienated fragments of the self into an integrated, unified whole.
8. Techniques employed by Gestalt therapists to help people become aware of who they are and what they are feeling include role playing, encouraging people to speak in the first person, and pointing out incongruities or discrepancies between what the client says and does.

COGNITIVE THERAPIES

9. Cognitive therapies are based on the premise that most behavioral disorders result from distortions in a person's cognitions or thoughts.

10. Rational-emotive therapy (RET) is based on the belief that behavioral problems result when people interpret their experiences based on certain self-defeating, irrational beliefs. The goal of therapy is to eliminate these maladaptive cognitions.
11. Like RET, cognitive restructuring therapy also aims to get clients to restructure their thinking, particularly negative self-labels, by arranging certain experiences that will disprove rather than confirm the client's negative self-image.

BEHAVIORAL THERAPIES

12. The central thesis of behavior therapy is that maladaptive behavior has been learned and that it can be unlearned; furthermore, the same principles that govern the learning of normal behavior also determine the acquisition of abnormal behavior.
13. The classical conditioning therapies, which include systematic desensitization and aversive conditioning, apply classical conditioning principles to help people to overcome maladaptive behavior.
14. Systematic desensitization involves training people to relax when confronted with fear-inducing stimuli.
15. In aversive therapy the goal is to associate aversive consequence to an inappropriate or harmful stimulus such as nicotine or alcohol.
16. The operant conditioning therapies, which include positive reinforcement, extinction, and punishment, focus on manipulating consequences of behavior as a way to overcome behavioral problems.
17. In positive reinforcement therapy the therapist first identifies desirable behavior and then provides appropriate reinforcers contingent upon the client voluntarily manifesting the desired behavior.

18. The extinction technique involves eliminating undesired behaviors by eliminating the reinforcers that maintain them.
19. In the punishment technique aversive stimuli are used to punish voluntary maladaptive responses.
20. Behavior change through modeling or observing others can be a helpful therapy technique for extinguishing irrational fears or for establishing new, more adaptive behaviors.

GROUP THERAPY

21. Potential benefits associated with participating in group therapy include a sense of solidarity with others, feedback from other group members as well as the group leader, opportunities to observe how others work out their problems, the satisfaction of helping others, and lower cost.
22. Family therapy with entire family units is based on the premise that an individual's psychological adjustment is profoundly influenced by patterns of social interaction within the family.
23. Today, conjoint or couple therapy (working with two partners together) has become the most common approach for treating relationship problems experienced by a primary couple, married or unmarried.

EVALUATING PSYCHOTHERAPY

24. Research has clearly demonstrated that in most cases improvement rates for people undergoing psychotherapy are markedly better than those for untreated individuals.
25. Research has also shown that no particular type of therapy is significantly superior to others. This may be because even though a therapist approaches behavior problems from a particular perspective it does not necessarily

ensure that behavior change is a result of the particular approach. For instance, a cognitive therapist may be bringing about change in a patient through manipulating reinforcement contingencies, without that intent.
26. All things being equal, experienced psychotherapists in any of the major theoretical frameworks tend to achieve better results than novice therapists.
27. Certain common features shared by almost all styles of therapy include combating the client's demoralization, providing a rationale for the client's symptoms and their treatment, providing a warm, supportive relationship, and providing a professional setting.

BIOLOGICALLY-BASED THERAPIES

28. Lobotomy was originally performed as a very crude surgical procedure designed to improve a patient's mental state by severing the nerve tracts connecting the prefrontal cortex to lower regions in the brain that mediate emotional responses.
29. Lobotomies eventually fell into disrepute when research revealed that they produced no changes in the major manifestations of severe mental illness other than reduction of emotional agitation, and that many lobotomized patients had been transformed into lethargic, unmotivated, robot-like personalities.
30. Newer psychosurgery techniques, which produce only a small fraction of the brain damage associated with the older and more crude lobotomies, have been shown to have some value in alleviating symptoms of severe disorders that have resisted more conventional forms of therapy.
31. There is extensive evidence that electroconvulsive therapy (ECT) often rapidly alleviates the symptoms of major depression. Some

researchers believe that extended ECT treatment may damage the brain and produce severe memory deficits. No one is sure how ECT accomplishes its therapeutic effect.

32. Therapy with psychoactive drugs, by far the most common biomedical treatment, has contributed to both a decline in the number of people hospitalized for behavioral disorders and a significant reduction in the average duration of hospitalization.

33. The four major categories of psychoactive drugs that are used to control or alleviate symptoms of behavioral disorders are antipsychotics, antidepressants, antimanics, and antianxiety drugs.

34. The use of drugs to treat behavioral disorders has provided considerable support to biological theories of disordered behavior.

TERMS AND CONCEPTS

psychotherapy
psychoanalysis
free association
dream analysis
resistance
transference
person-centered therapy
genuineness
unconditional positive regard
empathic understanding
active listening
Gestalt therapy
cognitive therapies
rational-emotive therapy (RET)
cognitive restructuring therapy

behavior therapy
classical conditioning therapies
systematic desensitization
operant conditioning therapies
group therapy
family therapy
couple therapy
lobotomy
electroconvulsive therapy (ECT)
psychoactive drugs
antipsychotic drugs
antidepressant drugs
antimanic drugs
antianxiety drugs

CHAPTER **17**
Social Psychology

PART 6

Social Psychology

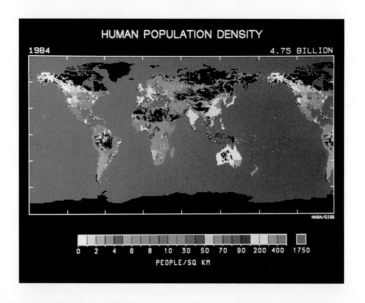

HUMAN POPULATION DENSITY

1984   4.75 BILLION

0 2 4 6 8 10 30 50 70 90 200 400 1750
PEOPLE/SQ KM

C H A P T E R 17

Social Psychology

SOCIAL PERCEPTION

First Impressions
Person Schemas
Implicit Personality Theories

ATTRIBUTION THEORIES

The Correspondent Inference Theory
Covariation Principle
Attribution Errors

ATTITUDES

Acquiring Attitudes
The Function of Attitudes
Do Attitudes Predict Behavior?
Changing Attitudes

PREJUDICE

Outgroups, Ingroups, and the Causes of
  Prejudice
A "Prejudiced Personality"

SOCIAL INFLUENCE ON BEHAVIOR

Comformity
Compliance
Obedience

INTERPERSONAL BEHAVIOR: ATTRACTION AND AGGRESSION

Attraction
Aggression

*I*magine that you have volunteered to participate in a study in which you and several other students will discuss personal problems caused by the pressures of university life. You are told that to avoid embarrassment, you and five other participants (or perhaps two or one, depending on which group you are placed in) will not see one another; instead, you will sit in individual cubicles and talk over an intercom system. Participants' microphones will be activated only when it is their turn to speak, and to preserve anonymity, the experimenters will not listen.

The experiment begins and the first voice you hear is that of a young man. Haltingly, he explains that he is having a great deal of difficulty adjusting to the pressures he is experiencing. He also states, with obvious embarrassment, that he is prone to epileptic-like seizures when he is under stress. You and the other participants talk in turn about your own reactions to stress. Now it is the first young man's turn to speak again. After a very short time, it is apparent that he is in trouble: He seems to fumble for words, then begins choking and pleading for help. He is clearly experiencing a seizure. What do you do?

We have just described an experiment conducted by two social psychologists, John Darley and Bibb Latané (1968). In the actual experimental design, the researchers had prerecorded all participants' voices so that only one subject actually took part in each group discussion, and that subject's reactions were the focus of the study. The results might surprise you. When subjects thought that they were the only ones aware of the emergency, Darley and Latané found that 85 percent offered help. In contrast, only 62 percent of subjects sought help when they thought there were two other bystanders, compared to a mere 31 percent of subjects who thought there were five others in the group.

Social psychologists use the term **diffusion of responsibility** to explain Darley and Latané's findings. Our own sense of responsibility is diminished by the presence of other bystanders. Because we assume that they have as much responsibility to act as we have, we are less likely to intervene to give aid. Diffusion of responsibility helps to explain some other disturbing incidents. One is the widely reported 1964 stabbing murder of a woman named Kitty Genovese as at least 38 residents of a Queens, New York, apartment complex looked on, making no move to intervene or call for help. These bystanders showed signs of extreme anxiety as a result of their experience (as did the subjects of Darley and Latané's experiment), but they still did nothing to help, counting instead on the probability that someone else would intervene.

The wide publicity of the Kitty Genovese incident, the reenactment of a multiple rape in the film *The Accused*, which also took place in the presence of numerous onlookers, as well as other publicized cases does not appear to decrease the tendency for **bystander apathy.** On October 5th, 1992 hundreds of Oregon motorists witnessed the brutal attack of a university student who was assaulted while she waited at a bus stop. After hitting her repeatedly with a tire iron and banging her against parked cars, the assailant threw her into the trunk of his car, from which she later escaped. All of this took place in daylight at the edge of a crowded roadway with motorists continually passing by—no one intervened or called for help (Danks, 1992).

Such incidents illustrate an important fact that we have not yet fully explored in this text: Our actions are greatly influenced by social processes and our perception of our social environments. *Social psychology* is the field of psychology concerned with how social influences affect our behaviors, and it asks a number of questions that we attempt to answer in this chapter. How, for instance, do we form impressions of people, and how do these impressions influence our behavior? How important is physical attractiveness in selecting at potential mate? How likely are we to resist pressures to change our behavior so that they conform with those of other people even when we disagree with their actions or opinions? Is aggressive behavior inevitable for humans and other animals? What factors contribute to aggressive behavior?

The scope of social psychology is far too broad to cover comprehensively in one chapter. Instead of taking a shotgun approach that touches on many topics with little depth, we have limited our discussion to the broadly researched areas of social perceptions, attribution, attitudes, prejudice, social influence, interpersonal attraction, and aggression. We begin with social perception.

At 3:20 A.M. on March 13, 1964, Kitty Genovese drove into the parking lot and parked (1). Noticing a man in the lot, she became nervous and walked in the street toward a police telephone box. The man caught and attacked her with a knife (2). She got away, but the man caught and attacked her again (3) and again (4). During this gruesome murder at least 38 residents in nearby apartments looked on, making no attempt to intervene or call for help.

SOCIAL PERCEPTION

We encounter many people each day, from the clerk at the grocery store to the classmate sitting behind us to the mechanic who is servicing our car. Even if our interactions with these people are very brief, we form impressions or perceptions of them. The term **social perception** describes the ways we perceive, evaluate, categorize, and form judgments about the qualities of people we encounter.

These social perceptions have a critical influence on our interactions. In fact, they are more important in guiding our behaviors than the attitudes and behaviors of the people around us. Thus the subjects in Darley and Latané's diffusion of responsibility experiment did not intervene because they *perceived* that others would probably seek help, not because they observed others helping. Likewise, you may withdraw from a friend because you perceive that she is annoyed with you. Whether she actually is annoyed is not as significant in determining your response as your own perceptions.

Since these readings of other people are so important, it is worthwhile knowing how we form them. Three factors that influence our social perceptions are first impressions, schemas, and implicit personality theories.

FIRST IMPRESSIONS

First impressions are the initial judgments we make about people, and they play an important role in social perceptions. We are more likely to form opinions of others quickly, based on first impressions, than to refrain from forming opinions until we have more information. These first impressions may change as we get to know a person better, but we often tend to hang onto them even in the face of contradictory evidence. Thus initial opinions may have a strong impact on our future interactions with people.

For example, if you first meet a new tenant in your apartment building at a party where he behaves in a loud and egotistical manner, it will probably be hard for you to perceive him as a sensitive, caring person when you later see him comforting a small child who has scraped his knee. The first information we receive about a person often seems to count the most, a phenomenon referred to as the **primacy effect.**

This effect was demonstrated in an experiment in which two lists of traits describing a person were read to two separate groups of subjects (Asch, 1946). In one group, subjects heard a description that began with positive characteristics (such as intelligent and industrious) followed by negative ones (impulsive, stubborn, and so forth). Their overall assessments of this person were positive. Subjects in the other group heard the same list, but in reverse order. The result: Their assessments were far more negative.

Research indicates that negative first impressions are often quickly formed and hard to overcome. In contrast, the opposite tends to be true of positive first impressions, which are often hard to earn but easily lost (Rothbart & Park, 1986). For example, your reticence to conclude that your new dating companion is reliable (positive first impression) may subside only after several encounters in which he or she exhibits this trait. However, one incident of unreliable behavior may cause you to quickly revise your social perception of this person. In contrast, if your companion is a few minutes late for your first date, you may quickly decide that he or she is flaky and unreliable (negative first impression), a characterization that may change only after numerous encounters in which your partner exhibits the trait of reliability.

FIGURE 17.1
What is your first impression of the person in this photograph? Do person schemas contribute to your impression?

PERSON SCHEMAS

What determines whether our first impression of a person is positive or negative? For instance, are you drawn to the person shown in Figure 17.1, or is your impression less favorable? Your answer will depend in to a large extent on the schema you have developed.

Recall from Chapter 8 that schemas are the conceptual frameworks we use to make sense out of our world. The concept of schemas helps explain how we perceive the people we meet. For example, you might have schemas of lawyers as aggressive and verbal, and of professors as studious and somewhat distracted. Social psychologists refer to these generalized assumptions about certain classes of people as **person schemas.**

Person schemas provide a structure for evaluating the people we meet, allowing us to take shortcuts by concentrating on some facts and ignoring others. When we assess a person for the first time, we tend to pick up only the information that fits our existing schemas, ignoring the rest. This process is efficient, but, unfortunately, it is not always the most accurate way of forming impressions (Brigham, 1986). You may have experienced instances where first impressions were quite inaccurate.

Once we fit a person into a schema, we tend to use that schema as a general organizing principle for interpreting further information about the person. For example, if our first impression of a new neighbor is that she is unfriendly, we are likely to evaluate her failure to comment on our shiny new car as further evidence of unfriendliness. If she then acts in a way that does not fit the schema (for example, picking up our garbage after it has been scattered by the wind), we may dismiss that act by concluding that she picked up the mess only because she was worried that it would blow onto her lawn.

IMPLICIT PERSONALITY THEORIES

Just as person schemas guide us in fitting people into preexisting categories, we also make implicit assumptions about personality traits that usually go together. For instance, if we meet a person whom we perceive as intelligent, we may expect that person also to be skillful and imaginative. These assumptions about how traits are related to each other in people's personalities are called **implicit personality theories** (Bruner & Tagiuri, 1954; Cantor & Mischel, 1979). We may not be aware of many of our implicit assumptions. However, since these associations may be firmly rooted, they are likely to be activated when we meet people for the first time. In one study researchers plotted graphically clusters of associations among 60 character traits. The results are shown in Figure 17.2 (Rosenberg et al., 1968).

FIGURE 17.2

A Graphic Portrayal of Associations among 60 Character Traits

SOURCE: (From Rosenberg et al., 1968)

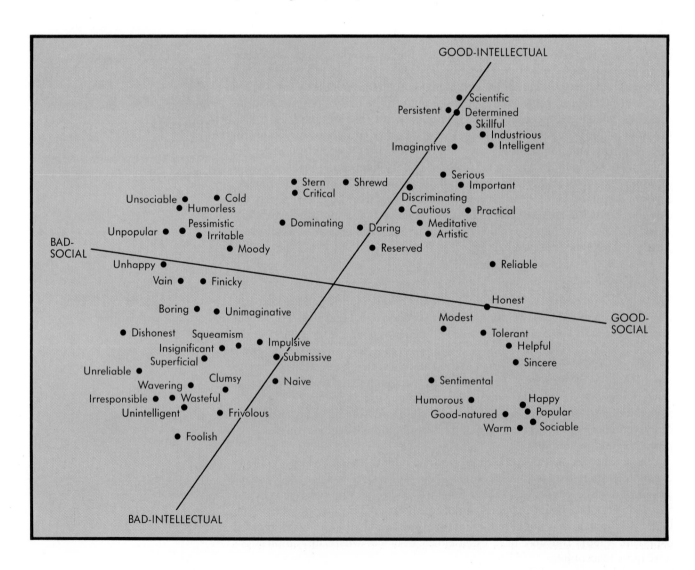

Our implicit personality theories are often organized around **central traits**—traits that we tend to associate with many other characteristics. For example, many people associate the trait of coldness with unsociability, humorlessness, and lack of popularity. Even a single central trait may play an important role in organizing our implicit personality theories about others. In an early study, Solomon Asch (1946) presented two groups of subjects with a list of seven traits, describing a hypothetical person. The list for each group differed on only one central trait dimension—*warm* versus *cold*—yet this difference influenced significantly the subjects' predictions about other traits of the hypothetical person. Thus subjects who had been provided a trait list which included *warm* were more likely to predict that the hypothetical person was generous or had a good sense of humor than subjects whose list contained the word *cold*.

Psychologists use the term **halo effect** to describe our tendency to infer other positive (or negative) traits from our perception of one central trait. The halo effect was demonstrated in a study that involved subjects observing two versions of an interview with a Belgian professor in which he appeared to be either likable or unlikable. Not only did subjects prefer the "likable" person in the interview, they also responded more positively to seemingly unrelated qualities, such as his accent and physical appearance (Nisbett & Wilson, 1977).

ATTRIBUTION THEORIES

An important part of social perceptions are the judgments we make about why people behave as they do. Our responses to other people are strongly influenced by these attributions, and we are constantly attempting to understand the reasons for other people's behavior. Attributions allow us to make sense out of other people's actions, figure out their attitudes and personality traits, and, ultimately, gain some control over subsequent interactions with them through our increased ability to predict their behavior.

According to **attribution theory** (Heider, 1958; Jones, 1979; Kelley, 1971; Ross & Fletcher, 1985), we tend to attribute people's behavior either to *dispositional* (internal) *causes*, such as motivational states or personality traits, or to *situational causes*, such as environmental or external factors. This distinction can have important effects on our relationships with people. For example, suppose you have recently begun dating someone you like very much, and the two of you spend a weekend visiting your date's parents. Much to your dismay, your friend acts like a different person—restrained, impersonal, and physically unresponsive. What has caused the change? If you attribute it to external factors (that your date is ill at ease around his or her parents) you are unlikely to feel that the relationship is seriously threatened. However, if you attribute the change to an internal cause (that your partner no longer feels responsive to you), you may seriously reevaluate the relationship.

Clearly, our attributions of the causes of people's behaviors have an important impact on relationships. How do we make these attributions? Two theories that attempt to explain this process are the correspondent inference theory and the covariation principle.

The **correspondent inference theory** (Jones, 1979; Jones & McGillis, 1976) attempts to explain the attributions we make about people's behaviors by looking at the conditions under which we make those attributions. Theorists Edward E. Jones and his colleagues use the term *correspondent inference* to describe cases in which we attribute a person's behavior to an underlying disposition. For instance, in the earlier example of the new neighbor who behaved raucously at a

THE CORRESPONDENT INFERENCE THEORY

party, you may have inferred that the person had a loud and unpleasant disposition. However, we do not always make dispositional attributions based on the behaviors we observe. If you watch a television game show emcee behaving in a solicitous and charming manner to guest participants, you are unlikely to infer that the host is a genuinely warm and caring person. Why do we make correspondent inferences about people's dispositions in some cases but not in others? Jones and his associates suggest several factors.

One important variable is the *social desirability* or "expectedness" of behaviors we observe. Some common behaviors are so socially acceptable that they reveal virtually nothing about a person. For example, we expect politicians running for office to smile and shake hands with strangers. This expected behavior fits in nicely with our schema of a politician, but it does not tell us very much about the politician's disposition. True, the candidate might actually be a warm and friendly person but it is equally possible that the smiles, handshakes, and baby kissing are due instead to the influence of social norms. Thus we are unlikely to draw correspondent inferences about the politician.

ATTRIBUTIONS AND SOCIALLY UNDESIRABLE BEHAVIOR Do socially undesirable actions have the same impact on our attribution processes as socially acceptable behaviors? For instance, if you observe a tennis pro slam his racket on the court after a bad call, are you more likely to make a correspondent inference about his or her disposition than if you observed polite and controlled behavior? If so, can you explain why unacceptable behavior would be more telling than desirable behavior? Consider this question before reading on.

Several experiments have demonstrated that we are more likely to make correspondent inferences from socially undesirable or norm-deviant behaviors than from socially desirable behaviors (Skowronski & Carlston, 1987). For example, in one study subjects listened to various versions of tapes of a man being interviewed for a job in which the interviewer opened the interaction by specifying the personality traits required for the job—traits such as independence and self-reliance. In one version, the applicant described himself in a way that closely matched the desired attributes, while in another version he described his traits as entirely different from those the interviewer was seeking. Most subjects indicated they were able to make confident judgments about the applicant's true

What correspondent inferences do you make about tennis pro John McEnroe's disposition during a tennis match? Do you think people are more likely to make such inferences when behavior is socially unacceptable?

character only when he had described himself as being the opposite of what the job demanded (Jones et al., 1961).

Such findings are consistent with the correspondent inference theory. Apparently, when a person's behavior fits external social expectations, we tend to discount it as a clue to a person's true nature. It is the unexpected behavior, which deviates from social desirability norms, that influences us to attribute actions to internal dispositions.

A second variable that determines whether we make correspondent inferences about a person's disposition is the degree to which his or her behavior is focused on achieving unique outcomes (or *noncommon effects*) that would be unlikely to occur as a result of some other behavior. For example, suppose a friend of yours, a physics major, signs up for a course in quantum mechanics. Will you be unimpressed, or will your image of your friend change? If you find out that the course is required for a degree in physics, you are likely to attribute your friend's action to external causes, since it accomplishes the unique or noncommon outcome of obtaining a degree, a goal that could not have been achieved in any other way. If, on the other hand, you discover this course is an obscure offering that is neither required nor recommended for a physics major, you are more likely to make a dispositional attribution about your friend's great intellectual curiosity.

A third variable that influences correspondent inferences is whether or not we perceive a person's behavior as resulting from *free choice*. If we know that a person freely chose to behave in a particular manner, we probably assume that these actions reflect underlying dispositions. On the other hand, if that person was pressed to act in a certain way by situational forces, we are more inclined to attribute the behavior to external than internal causes. For example, if one of your friends told you while you were lunching together that she strongly supported a conservative political group, you would probably be more inclined to attribute a conservative political attitude to her than if she were to make the same comments during a dinner hosted by a politically conservative dean at your college.

COVARIATION PRINCIPLE

A second theory of how people make attributions builds on the notion that when we try to figure out the causes and effects of particular events, we generally begin with the premise that cause and effect go together. Thus if a cause is altered, the effect will also be changed so that causes and effects can be said to *covary*. According to Howard Kelley (1967, 1971, 1973), when we make attributions about people's behavior (the effect) we tend to look at three potential causes: the *situation* or context in which the behavior occurs, the *persons involved*, and the *stimuli* or objects toward which the behavior is directed. Kelley's theory is known as the **covariation principle.**

Consider the following illustration of the covariation principle. Suppose you enroll in an art appreciation class. On your first visit to a gallery you observe one member of the class, an intense-looking young man, lingering at each oil painting, staring with apparent rapture. Observing this behavior, you might wonder about this person. Your attribution of causes for this young man's behavior depends on factors inherent in the *situation* or context in which the behavior occurred (the art gallery), the *persons involved* (the intense young man and other classmates), and the *stimuli* or objects toward which the observed behavior is directed (the oil paintings).

Kelley suggests that as we seek additional information to aid our interpretation of the causes of a person's behavior we act like social scientists, carefully analyzing the data, paying particular attention to variations in situation, persons, and stimuli on each of the three following separate dimensions:

1. *Distinctiveness:* The degree to which other stimuli are capable of eliciting the same behavior from the young man. Does he behave in the same way at other

art galleries or museums that your class visits, or does the behavior occur only at this gallery? If it only occurs at this gallery it is highly distinctive. We tend to attribute highly distinctive actions to situational causes.

2. *Consistency:* The degree to which the young man exhibits the same behavior in response to the same stimulus on other occasions. There is high consistence if the person behaves in essentially the same way on other visits to this art gallery? Consistency is important for both dispositional and situational attribution.

3. *Consensus:* The degree to which other people exhibit the same response to the stimulus as the actor. If other people react to the art in this gallery in the same or similar fashion there is a high consensus. We tend to attribute low consensus responses to dispositional causes.

According to Kelley, we take in information about all of these dimensions and use it to determine whether the behavior we have observed is caused by an internal disposition or by the situation. Thus you might create the following checklist concerning the young man:

1. *Distinctiveness: Low.* The young man behaves the same way at other galleries.
2. *Consistency: High.* When you return to the same gallery on another occasion, the young man still displays high interest.
3. *Consensus: Low.* Other visitors do not show the same remarkable interest.

Based on this assessment, you will probably attribute the young man's behavior to the disposition of a genuine interest in art. Had you noted a pattern of high consistency, high consensus, and high distinctiveness, you would probably have attributed the young man's behavior to a situational cause, such as a curiosity about the particular artist displayed at the first gallery.

ATTRIBUTION ERRORS

Both the correspondent inference theory and the covariation principle suggest that we make attributions in a rational, methodical way. Unfortunately, our judgments are not always accurate. We often make errors in the inferences we draw from other people's behavior, and these errors can usually be traced to a few common attribution errors. We look at a few of these errors, including the fundamental attribution error, false consensus error, and the illusion of control.

FUNDAMENTAL ATTRIBUTION ERROR One of the most common attribution errors is a tendency to overestimate dispositional causes and to underestimate situational causes when accounting for the behavior of others. (Interestingly, we tend to do exactly the opposite when accounting for our own behaviors.) This inclination is so pervasive that it has been labeled the **fundamental attribution error** (Baron & Byrne, 1987; Ross, 1977). For example, when a casual acquaintance complains that she has just failed a history exam, do you attribute her poor performance to a tricky test or a lack of adequate preparation time (both situational causes), or are you more inclined to assume she is not very bright (dispositional cause)? If you are like most of us, you probably tend to overestimate the latter cause and discount the former. Had *you* failed the same exam, however, the odds are good that you would look for situational causes.

Some researchers have found that attribution biases depend upon whether one is male or female. For instance, males tend to attribute their failures to situations ("I prepared poorly," or "it was a tricky exam") and their successes to dispositions ("I'm talented," or "smart"). On the other hand many females do just the opposite, they attribute success to situations ("I studied hard," or "I was lucky") and failure to dispositions ("I'm not very smart") (Erkut, 1983).

Do you tend to attribute Bo Jackson's abilities to innate talent or years of hard work?

Consider another example: To what do you attribute the high degree of athletic ability we see in a professional athlete like Bo Jackson? If you are like most people you attribute his ability to a disposition—his innate talent, not years of hard work. In fact, television commentators and sports writers continually comment about innate talent and instinct in athletes when in reality it is years of hard work and training that determine performance.

Research provides evidence of our tendency to make fundamental attribution errors. In one study, for instance, male college students were asked why they had chosen their majors and why they liked their current girlfriend; they were also asked the same questions about their best male friend (Nisbett et al., 1973). Their answers indicated a strong tendency to attribute their best friends' choices to dispositional qualities ("He is the kind of person who likes . . ."), whereas they described their own choices in terms of environmental conditions such as characteristics of their majors or their girlfriends ("Chemistry is a high-paying field"; "She is attractive and intelligent").

Why are we so quick to attribute other people's behavior to their inner dispositions? At least part of the answer lies in the fact that while we know what situational factors affect our own behavior, we have far less information about how such factors affect other people. Thus we take the easiest path and assume that they acted in a particular way because "that is the kind of people they are." It is easier to draw conclusions from the behaviors we can observe than to look for hidden reasons.

Psychologists have investigated a possible link between the fundamental attribution error and the quality of intimate relationships. Couples who share their lives either through marriage or cohabitation routinely make judgments or attributions to explain each other's behavior. For instance, if a man fails to notice that his partner is in need of some affection and nurturance, she might conclude that he is preoccupied with a problem at work (situations) or that he is insensitive and non-nurturing (dispositions). These two kinds of attributions can be expected to have profoundly different implications for the quality of their relationship.

Do you think that couples who experience a considerable amount of relationship conflict would be inclined to explain each other's behavior in ways different from couples who are happy with their relationship? Do distressed couples rely more on internal versus external attributions than happy couples, or is the pattern just the opposite? Think about these questions for a couple of minutes before reading on.

Research suggests that individual partners in distressed relationships are inclined to overestimate the role of internal, dispositional causes when trying to explain what they perceive as their partner's negative behavior, and to attribute positive actions to situational causes. Thus, in such a relationship if one member fails to behave in a nurturing and affectionate manner, the other would likely conclude that he or she is an insensitive and non-nurturing person. In contrast, a kindly act exhibited in a distressed relationship might be attributed to such situational causes as "He wants to impress others that he is a good guy," or "She must want me to do something for her." Patterns among individuals who are happily paired tend to be just the reverse. Thus individual members within a happy marriage tend to attribute their partner's positive behavior to internal, dispositional traits, whereas they are inclined to attribute negative actions to external situations (Bradbury & Fincham, 1988; Fincham et al., 1987).

It is probably not surprising to hear that people who are experiencing unhappy, distressed intimate relationships are inclined to place the blame on each other. What is unclear at this time is whether the attributional biases typical of unhappy partners are the cause or an effect of relationship distress. Hopefully, future research will clarify the nature of this relationship.

FALSE CONSENSUS   Another common attributional error is the assumption that most people share our own attitudes and behaviors (Goethals, 1986). This assumption is known as **false consensus bias,** and it influences us to judge any noteworthy deviations from our own standards as unusual or abnormal.

For example, suppose you note that someone living in your apartment complex never laughs or even cracks a smile while listening to a certain television comedian you find hilarious. Consequently, you make a dispositional attribution: You assume that the other person has no sense of humor. This bias may be so strong that you do not stop to think that there are probably a number of people with good senses of humor who do not enjoy this comedian.

ILLUSION OF CONTROL   Have you ever had a bad experience such as being in an auto accident, and then later lamented that if only you had left at a different time you could have avoided the situation? People often blame themselves or others for events that are beyond their control. This attributional error, called the **illusion of control,** is the belief that we control events in our lives, even those that are actually influenced primarily or solely by external causes. The illusion of control is reflected in the behavior of many gamblers, such as the slot player who thinks he can tell when a machine is ready to get hot by observing its patterns of payoff to other players.

Why do we hold on to the illusion that we are in control of such events? Most of us want to be in control of our own lives, and the feeling of being out of control can be very distressing, even when the uncontrollable event is highly negative. Thus it may actually be less stressful to blame ourselves for losing a job in a round of company layoffs ("I should have seen it coming") than to acknowledge there was nothing we could do.

The illusion-of-control bias was demonstrated in an interesting experiment in which some subjects were given lottery tickets, and others were allowed to pick their own numbers. On the day of the lottery all subjects were urged individually to resell their tickets. Subjects who had not been permitted to choose their own tickets were more inclined to resell them. Furthermore, those subjects who had selected their own tickets and decided to resell them tended to demand higher resale prices than those who had not chosen their lottery numbers (Langer, 1975).

We have been talking about social perceptions and the inferences we make about other people's behavior. These perceptions all contribute to our attitudes about people, groups, and situations. Attitudes have been the subject of more research than any other topic in social psychology in attempts to both predict and explain human behavior. In the following section we explore this topic.

ATTITUDES

The term *attitude* is so commonly used in everyday language that we all have some idea what it means. If you were asked to define what an attitude is, you might reply, "a person's feelings about something." This definition is not far off the mark. One of the pioneers in attitude measurement, L. L. Thurstone, defined an attitude as "the intensity of positive or negative affect for or against a psychological object" (1946, p. 39). Thurstone's interpretation allows us to define people's attitudes as the favorableness or unfavorableness of their affect toward any given object or situation.

Social psychologists Martin Fishbein and Icek Ajzen (1975) built on Thurstone's definition to describe **attitudes** as learned, relatively enduring dispositions to respond in consistently favorable or unfavorable ways to certain people, groups, ideas, or situations. We use this definition because it points out that attitudes are learned, that they may change, and that they may predict behavior.

Many social psychologists, particularly cognitive social psychologists, include cognition in their definition of attitudes. Thus, attitudes may be defined as including affect (physiological arousal), behavior, and cognition (thought). Figure 17.3 portrays this three-component (or *tripartite*) model of attitudes. To illustrate this model, suppose you have a friend who has a strong aversion to dogs. This

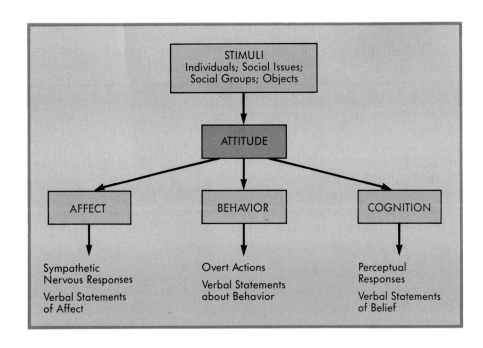

FIGURE 17.3

A Cognitive Model of Attitudes

SOURCE: (From Breckler, 1984)

aversion is based on certain beliefs that dogs are dirty, and that they are also dangerous. These beliefs lead naturally to negative affect or feelings such as disgust and fear, and these *cognitions* and *feelings* induce specific behaviors: If your friend sees a dog while walking in the neighborhood, she changes her route to avoid contact. (Note that this *behavior* could also be explained without reference to attitudes at all by referring to the two-factor theory of avoidance described in Chapter 6.)

ACQUIRING ATTITUDES

How do we develop attitudes? As you might guess, attitudes are shaped by experiences, including our observations of behavior (both other people's and our own); classical and operant conditioning; and direct experiences with the *attitude object* (the people, ideas, or things about which we hold attitudes).

BEHAVIORAL OBSERVATION *Observing Others* As we saw in Chapter 6, we learn some behaviors by observing and imitating influential role models (Bandura, 1986). Attitudes can be learned by the same process. Parents and peers have an especially strong influence on our attitudes. Thus young people whose friends view adult authority figures with mistrust are likely to acquire this attitude, particularly if it serves a social adjustment function for them.

Observing Ourselves Although it is commonly believed that attitudes cause behavior, the reverse may actually be more accurate. That is, our behaviors may determine our attitudes. Social psychologist Daryl Bem (1972) has proposed what he describes as a *self-perception theory* which maintains that when we are not sure how we feel toward a particular attitude object, we sometimes infer our attitudes from our own behavior. An example is a man known by the authors who commented that he could tell when he was really attracted to someone because "My body gets turned on and my tongue freezes!"

Parents have a strong influence on the attitudes of their children. Do you think this child will be more likely to have racist attitudes as an adult?

LEARNING ATTITUDES *Classical Conditioning* Some of our attitudes are acquired through the simple associative process of classical conditioning, described in Chapter 6. Whenever positive or negative experiences (elicited by the unconditioned stimulus, or UCS) are paired with an attitude object (the conditioned stimulus, or CS), new attitudes are likely to be formed. For example, you may have a fairly neutral opinion about dogs: They are often cute, soft, and cuddly and they can keep you company when you're alone. However, if you have a frightening experience with a dog, your attitude (behavior) towards dogs may change. You may find yourself avoiding them or being anxious in their presence.

Advertisers employ classical conditioning techniques in their efforts to sway our attitudes toward a particular product. For example, not too many years ago a manufacturer of a popular brand of men's shirts ran television commercials in which a presumably neutral object (a dress shirt, the CS) was worn by an attractive woman, with the implied suggestion that the shirt was all she was wearing. The expectation was that the women would serve as a UCS, eliciting favorable sexual feelings when men viewed or thought about the shirt. Although the average male viewer may have realized logically that the shirt had nothing to do with attractive women, the association may nevertheless be strong enough to influence his buying habits (the authors remembered it!).

Operant Conditioning We also acquire attitudes by receiving praise, approval, or acceptance for expressing them, and we may be punished for expressing other attitudes. When attitudes produce punishment (or when they fail to elicit social approval), they tend to decrease; when they are reinforced, they tend to increase

Classical conditioning contributes to our attitudes about many of the products we buy.

(Insko & Melson, 1969). For instance, a child who discovers that making derogatory comments about a different racial group will earn approval from her parents is more likely to develop a strong racial prejudice than one whose derogatory comments are met with disapproval. Similarly, groups of friends tend to share similar attitudes because these behaviors are mutually reinforced within the group. We will return to this again when we discuss prejudice.

Direct Experience   Finally, we learn many of our attitudes through direct contact with the attitude object. For instance, you may test-drive a car with a revolutionary new suspension system and as a result of this experience develop a very favorable attitude toward the new design. Attitudes acquired through direct experience are likely to be more deeply ingrained and held more confidently than those learned through observation (Fazio et al., 1983; Fazio & Zanna, 1981; Wu & Shaffer, 1987). Thus trying the new suspension system yourself is likely to influence your attitude much more strongly than watching a television commercial or even hearing about the design from friends who have tried it. Here directly receiving reinforcement is more powerful than the influence of modeling.

THE FUNCTION OF ATTITUDES

Whether we learn them from our own experiences or from observing others, attitudes serve a number of important functions in our lives (Brigham, 1986; DeBono, 1987; Tesser, 1990). One is an *understanding function:* Attitudes provide a frame of reference that helps us structure and make sense out of the world and our experiences. For example, your attitudes about what personal attributes you favor in a date provide you with a frame of reference for evaluating prospective romantic interests. If a person possesses behavioral dispositions you evaluate positively, you are likely to respond favorably to that individual.

Just as we rely on our own attitudes to evaluate unfamiliar situations or objects, we also rely on the attitudes of others. For instance, suppose a friend has just attended the first lecture in a class in which you are considering enrolling. Your first question to her will probably be something like, "Well, how did you like the class and the instructor?" If her attitude is positive, you will be more likely to sign up as well.

FIGURE 17.4

Impression Management

SOURCE: From the Des Moines Register, 1980

SOCIAL ADJUSTMENT AND EXPRESSED ATTITUDES

John Connally, a candidate for the Republican presidential nomination in 1980, glibly revises his position on the Equal Rights Amendment in order to impress a voter. Impression management in action.

The Very Republican Lady from Columbus, Ohio, looked sternly at former Texas Gov. John Connally and asked: "What are your views on the ERA?" "I'm for it," Connally shot back. "I've been for it since 1962."

The Very Republican Lady, obviously no fan of the Equal Rights Amendment, glared. After a short, pained silence, Connally began to revise and extend his remarks. "Actually, I have mixed feelings," he said. "If the amendment would weaken or destroy family life, I'd have to take another look. . . . I wouldn't have voted to extend the time for ratification. That was wrong. . . . So for all practical purposes I guess you could say I'm against it today."

A second function of attitudes is a *social identification function*. The attitudes of others provide us with important information about what they are like, just as the attitudes we express tell others about us. That is why, when you date a person for the first time, you usually exchange information about favorite activities, food preferences, music interests, and so forth. Our overall assessment of other people is often strongly influenced by what we perceive to be their likes and dislikes.

A third function of attitudes is a *social adjustment function*. The attitudes we express sometimes allow us to identify with or gain approval from our peers. For instance, if your very attractive date expresses a deep enthusiasm for great Russian literature, you may also immerse yourself in Tolstoy, Dostoevsky, and Turgenev. Of course, attitudes that serve a social adjustment function in one setting may have quite a different effect in a different environment. For example, if you begin describing your favorite passage from *Crime and Punishment* to some acquaintances during the next Saturday night dance, you might soon find yourself standing alone. This example brings up the concept of **impression management,** which describes our tendency to select carefully what information we reveal about our attitudes (i.e., to obtain reinforcers and avoid punishers), depending on how we think such information will affect the responses of others. Figure 17.4 provides a classic example of impression management (via operant conditioning) in action. In this case the presidential candidate John Connally switches his opinion on an issue as he observes the reaction of a voter.

All of the functions described above provide us with information about the probable consequences of our actions. We experience positive attitudes when we anticipate reinforcing consequences such as acceptance or success. Our attitudes are usually negative when we anticipate failure or rejection.

DO ATTITUDES PREDICT BEHAVIOR?

Whether attitudes serve a positive or negative function, it seems natural to assume that they influence our behavior. If you like jazz, you will be likely to attend a local concert where good jazz is being played, and if you believe strongly that formal religion is important, you will probably participate actively in your church or temple. Do our attitudes, however, always guide our actions? Consider the student who is strongly opposed to cheating but finds at exam time that she is doing so poorly in one course that her chances of acceptance into a graduate program are jeopardized. In this situation, her motive to succeed coupled with her perceived failure may well have a stronger influence on her behavior than her attitude toward cheating.

To what extent do attitudes determine behavior? Social psychologists began investigating the relationship between attitudes and behavior over 50 years ago, with surprising results. One widely known study was conducted by sociologist Richard LaPiere (1934) in the early 1930s, a time when there was considerable prejudice against Chinese people in the United States. LaPiere traveled extensively throughout the West and Midwest with a Chinese couple he described as personable and charming. Considering the prejudices of the time, LaPiere expected to be turned away at many hotels and restaurants. However, his traveling companions were served at all of the 184 restaurants they visited, and were rejected at only one of 67 lodging places. Approximately six months later, LaPiere wrote to each of the places he and the Chinese couple had patronized and asked whether they would accept Chinese people as guests at their establishment. Of those restaurants and hotel proprietors who responded (51 percent of the total), over 90 percent said they would not. Many social scientists interpreted these results as indicating that there is little or no relationship between attitudes and behavior.

In the years following publication of LaPiere's findings, dozens of other studies tested further the relationship between attitudes and actions with similar results. These studies asked people to express their attitudes about a variety of objects such as racial minorities, church attendance, and cheating, then compared their actual behavior in a measurable situation related to those attitudes. The measured relationship between attitudes and behavior in such areas and many others was shown to be so small that one social psychologist concluded that "... it [seems] considerably more likely that attitudes will be unrelated or only slightly related to behavior than that attitudes will closely be related to action" (Wicker, 1969, p. 65).

Intuitively, it seems obvious that attitudes influence behavior, yet the findings of LaPiere and other early researchers point toward just the opposite conclusion. Can you explain this discrepancy? Try to answer this question before reading on, considering how LaPiere obtained support for his conclusions.

LaPiere and other early researchers employed a single instance of behavior (such as the yes or no responses to LaPiere's letter) as an indication of the relationship between attitudes and behavior. In contrast, more recent studies have measured a variety of behaviors relevant to attitudes (Brigham, 1986). The results of these studies have been quite different.

For example, in one study researchers measured people's attitudes toward environmental issues such as pollution control and conservation, and then observed subjects' behaviors over the next two months. Fourteen environmentally relevant behaviors were recorded, including recycling paper, picking up litter, and circulating petitions pertaining to clean environment issues. Considered individually, any one of these behaviors showed only a relatively small or moderate correlation with the subjects' environmental attitudes, but when these actions were treated collectively, attitudes and behaviors were strongly correlated (Weigel & Newman, 1976). A clear implication of this finding is that to make an accurate judgment about someone's attitude toward a particular object, issue, or situation, we should observe as many attitude-reflective behaviors as possible.

As we suspected from the start, studies using multiple behavior indices have suggested that attitudes are strong predictors of behavior. As the earlier example of attitudes toward cheating illustrated, however, our attitudes do not always predict our behaviors. What determines how influential our attitudes will be?

SOCIAL EXPECTATIONS AND BEHAVIOR One important variable is the degree to which other social factors influence our behavior. As long as other influences are minimized, our attitudes are likely to guide our behaviors. One influence that is particularly likely to mask the predictive relationship between attitudes and behavior is social expectations. For example, a teenager who has a negative attitude toward drinking alcoholic beverages will usually say no when offered a drink. But what if he attends a party at the college he plans to attend in the fall, and several college students encourage him to join the party and drink up? In this situation, the need to conform to social expectations is particularly strong, and he may well have a beer despite his attitude toward alcohol consumption.

ATTITUDE SPECIFICITY   Another variable that influences how closely our behaviors reflect our attitudes is the relevance of an attitude to the behavior being considered. People may be less inclined to behave consistently with broad attitudes. For example, you may know people who say they support equality of the sexes but refuse to share equally in household chores. In contrast, when there is a close association between an expressed attitude and a particular situation, the picture is often quite different. For instance, our attitudes about the relative skills of several friends who play tennis is probably a good predictor of whom we would ask to team with us in a doubles tournament.

ATTITUDE RECOGNITION   A third condition that affects how well attitudes can predict behavior is simply whether we recognize our attitudes when we act. We often act without stopping to think about what we are doing. You may believe it is very important to eat a healthy diet, for instance, but if someone passes around a plate of sweet rolls at work, you may pick one up and start eating without even stopping to think. If you are with someone who is also very health conscious when the sweet rolls are passed around, however, that person's abstinence may make you much more aware of your attitude. Then you will be more likely to behave in a way that is consistent with your commitment to health.

A number of studies have shown that attitudes are more strongly related to behavior when subjects recognize the relationship between their attitudes and their behavior (Snyder & Swann, 1976), or when they are made particularly self-conscious (Carver & Scheier, 1978; Diener & Wallbom, 1976). Studies in which subjects have repeatedly reminded themselves of their attitudes (for example, by filling out a series of attitude rating scales) have found that attitudes are more likely to predict behavior (Fazio, 1986; Powell & Fazio, 1984).

DOES OUR BEHAVIOR AFFECT OUR ATTITUDES?   We have seen that our attitudes are often consistent with our behavior, but could this relationship exist because our attitudes are affected by our behavior? Several social psychologists suggest that our behavior may shape our attitudes (Chaiken & Stangor, 1987; Tesser, 1990). For instance, many a college student has looked with amusement or perhaps mild disdain upon those young executive types who dress up in their natty business suits and tuck a *Wall Street Journal* under their arm as they commute to impressive high-rise office buildings. These attitudes often change quickly, however, after the students graduate and join the ranks of the employed.

A classic demonstration of the impact of actions on attitudes was provided by an experiment whose subjects were Duke University women students (Gergen, 1965). Initially, all subjects filled out a questionnaire rating their degree of self-esteem. Some time later, each was interviewed individually. Those in the first group were encouraged to provide honest and accurate self-descriptions; those in the second were urged to present themselves in a very positive light. Some time later, all the women again filled out the self-esteem questionnaire. Of those subjects who had provided presumably inflated descriptions of themselves, most showed a marked enhancement of their self-esteem. In contrast, the self-images of the women in the first group were unchanged. Apparently, even the brief experiences of role playing a positive self-assessment actually boosted these women's attitudes about themselves.

We have just seen that experiences such as taking a job or writing a glowing self-evaluation can produce a change in attitude, but how and why does this attitude change take place? Part of the answer lies in our need for consistency. Just as we attempt to fit new acquaintances into preexisting person schemas in order to minimize the differences between the familiar and the unfamiliar, we also are most secure when our attitudes are consistent both with other attitudes we hold and with our behavior. This is the basic idea behind the *consistency theories*, which see attitude change as "an attempt on the part of the individual to achieve cognitive equilibrium" (Penrod, 1986, p. 257). We consider two noteworthy consistency theories: balance theory and cognitive dissonance theory.

BALANCE THEORY **Balance theory** emerged from the writings of Fritz Heider (1946, 1958), who argued that people are inclined to achieve consistency in their attitudes by balancing their beliefs and feelings about a particular issue, object, event, or situation against their attitudes about other people. According to this theory, the attitudes of other people play a significant role in determining whether we maintain our attitudes or change them. For instance, suppose you are strongly opposed to abortion. Now, suppose a person you know named John also has a strong opinion about abortion. Balance theory predicts that if you like John, and if John also is opposed to abortion, you will feel no need to change your attitude because a balanced cognitive state will exist. Similarly, if you dislike John and John supports abortion, you will still be in a balanced state because your dislike of John will cause you to discount his opinions.

In contrast, you will be in an unbalanced state if you like John and discover that he supports abortion, or if you dislike John and find that he is firmly opposed to abortion, as you are. To restore balance, you might (1) decide that John is not such a good guy after all (which will then allow you to reject his opinions); (2) become a supporter of abortion so that you will not be identified with the viewpoint of someone you dislike; or (3) decide John is not such a bad guy after all.

COGNITIVE DISSONANCE THEORY Like balance theory, **cognitive dissonance theory** is concerned with the ways in which beliefs and attitudes are consistent or inconsistent with one another (Festinger, 1957). The cognitive dissonance model, however, focuses more closely on the internal psychological comfort or discomfort of the individual. According to this theory, a person experiences a state of discomfort, or *dissonance*, whenever two related cognitions (thoughts or perceptions) are in conflict. For example, imagine that you have always considered yourself a supporter of a woman's right to choose abortion, but you find yourself protesting when you discover a close friend is considering an abortion. There is a discrepancy between what you believe and the way you perceive yourself acting, and if you become aware of it (it is quite possible that you will not), you will experience dissonance.

Like hunger, dissonance is an unpleasant state that motivates its own reduction. But while hunger requires a person to interact with the environment to achieve its reduction, dissonance may be reduced merely by realigning the key cognitive elements to restore a state of *consonance*, or psychological comfort. Thus you may reduce your dissonance over the abortion issue by changing your

CHANGING ATTITUDES

attitude to oppose abortion, so that it will be consistent with your behavior. You might also restore consonance by philosophically aligning yourself with the notion that if you believe in something you should support it with your actions even at the risk of personal hardship.

The cognitive dissonance theory has been supported by numerous studies. An example is a study of Princeton University men who had all indicated that they were opposed to banning alcohol from campus (Croyle & Cooper, 1983). These subjects were all asked to write a letter that forcefully argued *in favor of* banning alcohol from campus. Half of these writers were reminded that their participation in this effort was purely voluntary; the other half were authoritatively ordered to register their arguments. At a later point, after the letter-writing process was completed, the researchers again assessed the subjects' attitudes toward the proposed ban.

Based on cognitive dissonance theory, would you predict that subjects in either of these groups demonstrated noteworthy changes in their attitudes toward banning alcohol on campus? Only one group or both? Why? Think about these questions and make your predictions before reading on.

As predicted by the cognitive dissonance theory, writing a letter in favor of a policy they opposed created cognitive dissonance in the Princeton subjects, most of whom reduced this dissonance by changing their attitudes. This shift in attitudes was more pronounced for those subjects who saw their participation as voluntary in nature. Apparently, if we act contrary to our prevailing attitudes, and if we cannot attribute our actions to coercion, we are more likely to see the rationale for what we are doing and to come to believe in it.

This phenomenon is believed to have accounted, at least in part, for the success of certain brainwashing tactics on some American prisoners during the Korean conflict. The captors began by persuading prisoners to make some minor statement, such as "America is certainly not perfect." Next, prisoners might be asked to write down some flaws in the U.S. system of government. Eventually, they might be encouraged to develop a speech denouncing America. The inducement to take these actions might be something quite minor, such as a few extra privileges, more food, and so forth. In the end, the prisoner's awareness that his actions were not induced by coercion and that others were aware of his unpatriotic statements might actually cause him to change his attitude toward his homeland to be consistent with his behavior, thus reducing dissonance (Schein, 1956).

PERSUASION   The balance theory and the cognitive dissonance theory help explain why we change our attitudes. They do not explain how a speaker can persuade members of an audience to change their attitudes, or why a talk with someone we respect can be enough to convert us to supporters of a particular cause.

We know that some persuasive efforts are more effective than others. What makes the difference? Carl Hovland and his colleagues at Yale University tackled this question in the 1950s, and found three elements to be particularly important in persuasive communications: the source of the message, the way in which the message is stated, and the characteristics of the message recipients (the audience) (Houland et al., 1953).

The Communicator   If a close friend you respect and trust becomes involved in a fringe religious movement and tries to persuade you to join, you are more likely to reevaluate your attitude toward such movements than if you were approached by a person you did not like. Research demonstrates that the source or origin of a persuasive communication is a very important determinant of whether or not we change our attitude. The probability that persuasion will succeed is highest when the source of persuasion is seen as possessing any or all of the qualities of credibility, power, and attractiveness.

A communicator with the quality of *credibility* is more likely to succeed in changing our attitude. Two important elements of credibility are perceived expertise and trustworthiness. Our perception of expertise involves our assessment of the communicators' knowledge about a topic and of his or her experience, education, and competence to speak authoritatively about it. For instance, when you watch the Super Bowl on television, you are less likely to dispute the views of a commentator who was once a football pro than those of your roommate, who has no athletic experience.

The second important element of credibility is trustworthiness—our perception of a communicator as being basically honest. Trustworthiness is important because we typically make attributions about why a person is advocating a particular position. As we might predict from the correspondent inference theory discussed earlier, our perception of trustworthiness is enhanced when the communicator seems to be arguing against his or her own best interests, or when the content of the message is not what we expect. For example, one investigation found that university students were more inclined to be persuaded by arguments against pornography if they perceived that the communicator was opposed to censorship than if the communicator favored censorship (Wood & Eagly, 1981). In another study, a convicted felon who argued that police should have fewer legal constraints placed on their efforts to deal with crime produced significantly greater attitude changes than a criminal who argued that police power should be restrained (Walster et al., 1966). In still another study, listeners were more persuaded by a proenvironmental speech if they perceived that the speaker either had a probusiness background or had tailored his or her speech to a probusiness group than if they perceived the opposite to be true (Eagly et al., 1978).

Another factor that influences how persuasive a communicator will be is *power*. At least as it is measured by overt expression, attitude change is particularly likely to occur when these three conditions are met: (1) the communicator has the power to administer reinforcers or punishers to the target; (2) the communicator very much wants his or her message to have the desired effect on the target; and (3) the target knows the communicator will be able to evaluate whether or not she or he conforms to the message (McGuire, 1969; Rosenbaum & Rosenbaum, 1975). In view of these findings, it is not surprising that children often express attitudes similar to those of their parents, and that low-level management people may mirror the attitudes of higher level executives.

A third strong influence on a communicator's effectiveness is attractiveness. A physically attractive communicator is often more effective than one whose appearance is either average or unattractive (Kelman, 1965; Mills & Aronson, 1965). Attractiveness is influenced not only by physical looks, however, but also by likability, pleasantness, and perceived similarity to the audience. A communicator who does not have these qualities is usually less effective in changing people's attitudes than one who does.

The Message Just as the source of a message has a strong influence on whether we are persuaded to change our attitude, the message itself is also a critical factor. Researchers have found that several message characteristics may be particularly important. One factor is the degree of discrepancy between the message and the audience's viewpoint. If the discrepancy is too great, the audience may discount or dismiss the message, especially if the communicator has low credibility. On the other hand, too little discrepancy may result in the audience failing to perceive any difference of opinion or persuasive intent (Hovland et al., 1957; Peterson & Koulack, 1969). Thus attitude change is often greatest at moderate levels of discrepancy.

In some cases, messages will be more effective if they appeal to emotion (particularly the emotion of fear) than if they appeal to logic. However, people who are well informed and personally concerned about a particular issue may be persuaded more effectively by logic than by emotional appeals (Petty & Cacioppo, 1986; Petty et al., 1983). Although appeals to fear are sometimes effective, the relationship between fear and persuasion is very complex and difficult to generalize about.

For example, in one early study researchers used three separate messages to sway attitudes about oral hygiene. Subjects in the high-fear group were shown horrific color slides of rotting teeth and diseased gums, and were told that these terrible conditions were the direct result of poor oral hygiene. Those in the moderate-fear group heard a message about the importance of good oral hygiene illustrated by pictures of mild gum infections and tooth decay. Finally, those in the low-fear group were simply told that failure to brush regularly can lead to tooth decay and gum disease; no pictures were used. The high-fear message was found to be the least effective in changing behavior (and presumably attitudes), whereas the low-fear message produced the greatest change in dental habits (Janis & Feshbach, 1953).

How can this result be explained? Researchers interpreted the results as indicating that fear may promote attitude change only up to a certain point. When tension becomes too great, however, people may attempt to reduce their anxiety by blocking out or discounting the message (McGuire, 1968a). Several later studies have demonstrated that, under some conditions, messages with moderate-fear appeal may be effective in changing attitudes and behavior. If the source had high credibility and if the fear-arousing message contained clear information about what to do to avoid the fearful consequences, people are more likely to be persuaded by the message (Leventhal & Nerenz, 1983; Rogers & Mewborn, 1976).

Novelty is another message characteristic that can make a difference. Generally speaking, messages that are presented in an unusual or novel fashion are more effective than timeworn arguments. People tend to tune out messages they have heard too many times before. Also, the expectation of something new or novel makes a message more attractive (Sears & Freedman, 1965).

Still another quality that helps determine how influential a message will be is whether it presents one or both sides of the issue. Interestingly, the effect of this variable seems to depend on the characteristics of the audience. A one-sided argument seems to be more effective if the audience is poorly educated and or unfamiliar with the issue (Chu, 1967; Hovland et al., 1949), whereas a two-sided presentation works better with a well-educated, well-informed audience (Lumsdaine & Janis, 1953). In fact, well-informed people may react strongly against one-sided arguments in order to protect their sense of free will or as a reaction against feeling coerced into adopting a particular view—a process called *psychological reactance* (Jones & Brehm, 1970).

The Audience   We have just seen that an audience's intelligence and knowledgeability can make a difference in the effectiveness of tactics such as presenting one or both sides of an issue. A variety of other personality factors also seem to influence people's susceptibility to persuasion. For one, the age of an audience seems to make a difference. Researchers have found that teenagers and young adults, whose attitudes and opinions are not yet as well defined as those of older people, are more likely to shift their attitudes in response to a persuasive communication (Sears, 1979).

Another factor that may make a difference is the self-esteem of listeners. Studies conducted in the late 1960s indicated that people with high self-esteem seem generally less likely to yield to persuasion than those with low self-esteem (Cook, 1970; McGuire, 1969). This finding was interpreted as indicating that people with a very positive self-image have confidence in their opinions, which they may view as being more credible than those of the communicator. A more recent investigation, however, reported that people with high self-esteem are just as easily persuaded as those with a low self-image (Baumeister & Covington, 1985). More research is needed to clarify these mixed findings.

The evidence has also been unclear regarding the impact of listeners' intelligence on attitude change. For a persuasive message to be effective, an audience must both comprehend it and be willing to yield to the views of another. High intelligence tends to increase comprehension, but it may also reduce a person's inclination to yield to persuasion. It is difficult, therefore, to draw any definitive conclusion about the relationship between intelligence and persuadability. One researcher, William McGuire (1968b), theorized that attitude change may be greatest among listeners with moderate levels of intelligence, since their likelihood of both understanding a message and yielding to it are relatively strong. Research support for this commonsense interpretation has been mixed (Eagly, 1981; Eagly & Warren, 1976).

When the persuader is able to get the audience to think seriously about the points he or she is making, the chances of attitude change are enhanced (Petty & Cacioppo, 1986). To the extent that the audience members are open to a particular viewpoint, getting them to think about and elaborate on the message in their own minds is likely to increase the probability of attitude change.

PREJUDICE

Consider the following conversation overheard recently by the authors. The speakers are a third-year medical student and a college psychology teacher.

STUDENT: Homosexuals may not be the only people who get AIDS, but they are certainly the major reason why all of us now have to live in fear of this disease.

TEACHER: The vast majority of AIDS cases in Central Africa have occurred among heterosexuals.

STUDENT: Well, if that is true, then it probably just indicates that the Africans will not tolerate promiscuous relationships among homosexuals like what occurs in places like New York and San Francisco.

TEACHER: Many epidemiologists are now predicting that in a few years America will be just like Central Africa, with the majority of AIDS cases reported among heterosexuals.

STUDENT: Well, if this occurs it will be further evidence of what is already clearly obvious, homosexuals are so indiscriminant and promiscuous in their sexual practices that they don't care who they put at risk.

The medical student's point of view is an excellent example of **prejudice,** a negative, unjustifiable, and inflexible attitude toward a group and its members that is based on erroneous information. This definition contains three important elements. First, prejudice is usually characterized by very negative or hostile feelings toward all members of a group, often a minority, without any attention to individual differences among members of that group. Second, prejudice is based on inaccurate or incomplete information. For instance, the medical student in our example assumed incorrectly that AIDS is a disease of homosexuals and that heterosexuals who get AIDS are victims of the promiscuity of homosexual people. Finally, prejudice demonstrates great resistance to change even in the face of compelling contradictory evidence. The medical student was not about to revise his opinion that AIDS is inextricably linked to homosexuality, despite contradictory evidence.

Prejudice is built on **stereotypes,** preconceived and oversimplified beliefs and expectations about the traits of members of a particular group that do not account for individual differences. These stereotyped beliefs, coupled with hostile feelings, often predispose people to act in an abusive and discriminatory fashion toward members of a disliked or hated minority. The widespread incidence of **discrimination** (the behavioral consequence of prejudice in which victims of prejudice are treated differently from other people) throughout the world reveals what a profoundly adverse impact prejudice has on human society. In most every daily newspaper and every evening on the news there are reports of violence between groups fueled by prejudice. The conflicts between Protestants and Catholics in Ireland, between the Serbs and the Bosnians in the former Yugoslavia, the tension between blacks and whites in South Africa are just a few.

To believe that black people are lazy, that women are low in ambition, that men are insensitive, that overweight people are gluttonous, or that homosexuals are promiscuous is to stereotype all members of a group. To devalue or feel contempt for blacks, women, overweight people, or homosexuals is to be prejudiced. To avoid hiring, associating with, renting to, or acknowledging the contributions of such people is to discriminate. How can prejudice be explained? We turn next to that question.

OUTGROUPS, INGROUPS, AND THE CAUSES OF PREJUDICE

Central to any explanation of prejudice is our inclination to define ourselves at least partly according to the particular group to which we belong. We all tend to categorize ourselves according to race, age, education, creed, economic level, and so forth—a process that inevitably leads us to categorize people who do not share the same characteristics as "different." The result is that we divide our world into two groups: "us" and "them" (Baron & Byrne, 1987). The very process of being in the us or **ingroup** category tends to create an **ingroup bias** (a tendency to see one's own group in a favorable light) while at the same time inducing a negative attitude or prejudice against the **outgroup.**

A number of studies have demonstrated that ingroup bias and prejudice toward the outgroup often occur when experimental subjects are separated into we–they groups based on trivial factors that bear no relationship to real-life social categories (Tajfel, 1982; Tajfel & Turner, 1979; Turner, 1984; Wilder, 1981). By perceiving their ingroup as superior to an outgroup, people seem to be attempting to enhance their self-esteem.

COMPETITION BETWEEN GROUPS   If we already tend to view the world in terms of us and them, the addition of another ingredient—competition for jobs, power, or other limited resources—adds to the likelihood that hostility and prejudice will develop. In such circumstances the more dominant group may exploit and discriminate against a less powerful group. This tendency was demonstrated during the development of America, when competition for land between European settlers and Native Americans led to prejudice, mistreatment, and extreme acts of discrimination against the minority Native Americans (Brigham & Weissbach, 1972). Today in the United States, competition for jobs has generated prejudice between whites and Hispanics, Native Americans and German immigrants, Chinese and whites, Cuban immigrants and white Floridians, and whites and blacks (Aronson, 1980). In Germany there is renewed prejudice against immigrants who are competing for limited resources and jobs.

The manner in which intergroup competition can produce hostility, conflict, and prejudice was demonstrated in a classic experiment conducted by Muzafer

Sherif and his colleagues (1961), who set up a summer camp for a group of white, middle-class, bright, well-adjusted boys, ages 11 and 12, near Robbers' Cave, Oklahoma. Initially, the boys lived together in harmony as they worked on a number of cooperative projects, such as building a rope bridge and organizing cookouts. However, the researchers soon divided the boys into two separate groups, the Eagles and the Rattlers. After several days of living, playing, and working in separate groups, both the Eagles and the Rattlers developed strong senses of ingroup solidarity.

The next phase of the experiment was to engage the Eagles and Rattlers in a series of competitions, such as touch football games and a tug-of-war, in which prizes were awarded to the winning teams. As the competition became very intense, so did stereotyping, hostility, and overt conflicts between the groups. Thus the introduction of competition between two clearly defined groups transformed a harmonious atmosphere into one of prejudice and hostility.

FRUSTRATION, SCAPEGOATING, AND PREJUDICE Just as competition can lead to hostility and prejudice under certain conditions, so can frustration. People who are frustrated by their lack of accomplishments or by adverse living conditions often vent their frustration on scapegoats whom they perceive as being less powerful than themselves, such as members of a minority group. An example of how frustration may be tied to prejudice is provided by data relating economic conditions in the South from 1882 to 1930 to violence of whites toward blacks. Research has shown whenever the price of cotton decreased during this period, the lynchings of blacks by whites increased (Hovland & Sears, 1940).

The relationship between frustration and prejudice was demonstrated in an experiment in which researchers first measured subject's attitudes toward a variety of minority groups, then frustrated the subjects by denying them a chance to see a good movie and making them complete a series of difficult tasks instead. The subjects' attitudes toward the same minority groups were measured a second time, after this frustrating experience. This time they demonstrated a marked increase in prejudice not exhibited by control subjects who had not experienced the frustrating condition (Miller & Bugelski, 1948). In related experiments, students who are made to feel like failures have demonstrated an increased tendency to express negative attitudes toward others (Amabile & Glazebrook, 1982; Crocker et al., 1987).

Can you think about cases of prejudice that may be attributed to frustration or scapegoating that are more current? Perhaps the recent increase in violence by blacks against Asians in several large cities in the United States is a result of economic frustration.

SOCIAL LEARNING AND PREJUDICE We have seen that many of our attitudes are acquired by observing and emulating other people, particularly respected role models. Prejudice can also be learned by this process. Racism, sexism, and other negative prejudicial attitudes are often modeled by parents, who thus pass these damaging attitudes on to their impressionable children (Katz, 1976; Stephan & Rosenfield, 1978). For example, research has shown that children's racial attitudes are often closely aligned with those of their parents (Ashmore & Del Boca, 1976). Children may internalize the prejudices they observe in their parents and, in some cases, learning this lesson may earn the reward of approval from their parents or others. Even children whose parents are relatively free of prejudice may acquire prejudicial attitudes from other influential sources such as peers, books, and the television and movie media, which often promote stereotypical beliefs and disparaging assessments of minority group members.

A "PREJUDICED PERSONALITY"

We all have experienced competition and frustration, and most of us have probably observed incidents of prejudice and discrimination. Nevertheless, prejudice is not an attitude that we all adopt. What kinds of qualities predispose a person to develop prejudices? Some research in the late 1940s at the University of California at Berkeley sheds some light on this question. Here, researchers investigated the dynamics of *anti-Semitism* (prejudice against Jewish people) and *ethnocentrism* (general prejudice toward all outgroups). Their findings led them to describe a personality characterized by intolerance, emotional coldness, rigidity, unquestioning submission to higher authority, stereotyped thinking, and identification with power as particularly prone to developing prejudicial attitudes. A person possessing this cluster of characteristics was labeled an **authoritarian personality** (Adorno et al., 1950). These researchers developed a rating scale to detect people with authoritarian personalities, called the *Potentiality for Fascism Scale*, or *F Scale*. Table 17.1 presents some items from the F Scale with which an authoritarian personality would be likely to agree.

How does an authoritarian personality develop? The researchers examined the backgrounds of subjects who scored high on the F Scale and found that such individuals shared certain common features in the manner in which they were reared. Their parents tended to be harsh disciplinarians who used threats, physical punishment, and fear of reprisal to enforce desired behavior. Children were not permitted to express aggressive behaviors themselves, and love was often withheld or made contingent on "being good." As a result, the children were inclined to grow up feeling hostile toward their parents but at the same time dependent on them. They were also fearful of authority figures and generally insecure.

Although research on the so-called authoritarian personality has provided some important insights into the causes of prejudice, we must be cautious in concluding that there is a cause-and-effect relationship between the patterns of child rearing just described and the development of prejudicial attitudes. Parents who raise their children in a harsh, authoritarian fashion may be strongly inclined to be prejudiced themselves, with the result that their children may acquire these same prejudices through social learning.

TABLE 17.1 *Selected Items from the F Scale*

3. America is getting so far from the true American way of life that force may be necessary to restore it.

31. Homosexuality is a particularly rotten form of delinquency and ought to be severely punished.

35. There are some activities so flagrantly un-American that, when responsible officials won't take the proper steps, the wide-awake citizen should take the law into his own hands.

50. Obedience and respect for authority are the most important virtues children should learn.

SOURCE: Adapted from Adorno et al., 1950.

SOCIAL INFLUENCE ON BEHAVIOR

We have seen how our feelings about certain people, groups, ideas, or situations may be changed by the people around us. However, **social influence**—the efforts by others to alter our feelings, beliefs, and behavior—extends beyond merely changing how we feel about something. In this section we examine conformity, compliance, and obedience, all of which are forms of social influence that effect our behavior.

Conformity refers to a tendency to change or modify our own behaviors so that they are consistent with those of other people. Often these shifts in opinion or actions are accompanied, at least to some degree, by a perceived social pressure to conform.

CONFORMITY

Our outward conformity to group standards may or may not mean that we have accepted the group's position. Morton Deutsch and Harold Gerard (1955) suggest that we should make a distinction between **informational social influence,** in which we accept a group's beliefs or behaviors as providing accurate information about reality, and **normative social influence,** in which we conform not because of an actual change in our beliefs, but because we think that we will benefit in some way, such as gaining approval or avoiding rejection. It is helpful to keep in mind this distinction between informational and normative social influence as we explore what we have learned about conformity.

One of the first investigations of social influence explored how norms develop in small groups (Sherif, 1937). During an initial session, each subject was seated alone in a dark room and asked to stare at a tiny pinpoint of light about 15 feet away. The subject was then asked to estimate how far the light moved from its original position. (Actually, the light was stationary, but it appeared to move due to a perceptual illusion.) There was considerable variation in these initial estimates. During a second session, the subject was joined by two other participants; all three repeated the procedure of the first session, voicing their estimates in the presence of each other. This procedure was repeated in two more group sessions. Figure 17.5 shows what happened in the second, third, and fourth sessions. As you can see, the estimates of the three participants progressively converged until by the fourth session they were essentially identical.

In the study just discussed, do you think that the subjects' final estimates reflected a genuine belief that theirs was the correct estimate (informational social

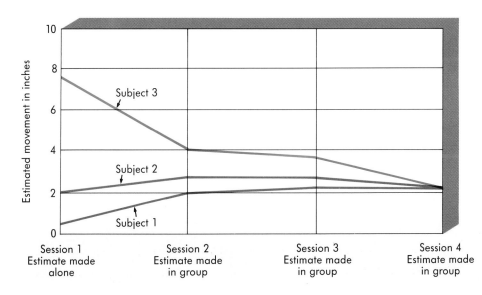

FIGURE 17.5

Results of Conformity Study Judging the Movement of a Light

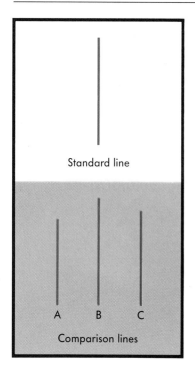

FIGURE 17.6

Line Comparison Task from Asch's Experiment

Which comparison line(s) is/are equal to the standard line?

FIGURE 17.7

Subjects Participating in Asch's Conformity Experiment

The only real subject in the experiment was number 6; the others were confederates of the experimenter.

influence), or do you think they felt pressured to conform even though they privately disagreed with the consensus group estimate (normative social influence)? How would you find out which form of social influence was operative in this case? Give these questions some thought before reading on.

The researchers provided an answer to the question by conducting additional solo sessions after the group norms had been established. In these sessions, subjects' solo estimates continued to reflect the group norm rather than corresponding to their initial estimates in the first individual sessions. The fact that subjects continued to express group estimates clearly demonstrates that they were responding to informational and not normative social influence.

In the study we have been discussing, subjects were faced with an ambiguous situation in which it was difficult to distinguish between reality and imagination. In such a circumstance, it is understandable that they relied on others as sources of information. What about situations, however, in which people clearly know what is correct but still experience pressure to conform to group norms that deviate from the truth? For instance, what if you were asked which of the three comparison lines in Figure 17.6 was equal to the standard one—and although you knew that the answer was B, everyone else answered C? This was the experimental design used by Solomon Asch (1951) in a classic experiment.

THE ASCH EXPERIMENTS   In Asch's experiment, seven men sat around a table and were asked to make a series of 18 line-comparison judgments such as the one just described. Six of the men were confederates of the experimenter; the one subject was unaware that he was being set up. None of the 18 tasks was ambiguous; the correct answer was always readily apparent. The experimental design called for each group member to provide his response in turn as Asch solicited answers sequentially from each man, moving from his left to right around the table. The naive subject was always located so that he was the sixth of the seven subjects to make his judgment (see Figure 17.7). On the first two trials, all seven chose the correct line. On 12 of the remaining 16 trials, however, the confederates unanimously chose the wrong comparison line.

How did the subjects respond? Many showed signs of strain, leaning forward, straining, double-checking, and glancing around at the other group members. Nevertheless, about one in every three subjects adjusted his responses to match the incorrect judgments of the confederates in half or more of the 12 conformity trials. Only 25 percent of the subjects completely resisted group pressure by making the correct response on all 12 trials.

Since the correct answers were so obvious, Asch's experiment seems to clearly illustrate normative social influence. Just to make sure, Asch interviewed the subjects after the experiment was completed. He found that in some cases the answers had been the result of normative social influence: These subjects had gone along with the group consensus against their better judgment because they did not want to appear different from the others. However, some of the conforming subjects stated that they had thought that the majority opinion was probably correct and that their own perceptions were inaccurate. If this explanation is taken at face value, we must conclude that informational social influence occurs even in unambiguous situations where conformity goes clearly contrary to reality. (Of course, it is also possible that subjects who claimed they thought the majority was right might only have been attempting to justify their submission to the influence of the group [Berkowitz, 1986].)

WHEN ARE WE MOST LIKELY TO CONFORM?   In the years since Asch's study, numerous additional experiments have studied conformity. In general this research has found that our tendency to conform will be increased in situations in which some conditions are met. We list these conditions briefly as a conclusion to our discussion of conformity.

1. *Unanimity of the majority group.* We are much more likely to conform if the majority group is unanimous (Allen, 1965; Allen & Levine, 1969); even one dissenter greatly reduces our inclination to conform. Asch found that if one dissident agreed with the subject, the subject was almost 18 percent less likely to conform (Asch, 1951).
2. *Perception that the majority of group members are acting independently.* If we perceive that the other members of a group are acting independently of one another, we are more likely to conform than if we sense some collusion among them (Wilder, 1978).
3. *Majority group size.* The size of the group makes a difference. If there are at least three or four other people in the group, we are more likely to conform. Further increases in group size generally do not increase the likelihood of conformity, and may even decrease it (Gerard et al., 1968; Tanford & Penrod, 1984).
4. *Familiarity with the attitude object.* If we have no preconceived notions about the attitude object, we are more likely to act in a conforming manner than if this is not the case (Berkowitz, 1986).
5. *Low self-esteem.* People whose sense of personal self-worth is low (Santee & Maslach, 1982) or who are especially concerned about social relationships (Mullen, 1983; Thibaut & Strickland, 1956) are more likely to conform than people with higher self-esteem or less regard for social relationships.
6. *Perceptions about other group members.* We are more likely to conform if we consider the other group members to be of higher status than ourselves (Forsyth, 1983; Giordano, 1983), or if we have high regard for the other group members (Berkowitz, 1954, 1986). We are also more likely to conform if we perceive other group members as having power over us (in the sense of being able to administer reinforcers or punishers) (Berkowitz, 1986), or if we know that other group members will be able to observe our actions (Berkowitz, 1954).

COMPLIANCE

Although both conformity and compliance involve yielding to some pressure exerted by others, **compliance** involves an element of coercion as well, in that it takes place in situations where we alter our behavior in response to direct requests from others. Compliance is a very common form of social influence. We all experience a barrage of requests daily—ranging from friends, lovers, or family members asking us to change certain aspects of our behavior to requests by politicians or salespersons for votes or purchase of goods. Social psychologists have noted a number of techniques or forms of pressure that people use to increase the likelihood of compliance with their requests. Two of these methods are the foot-in-the-door technique and the door-in-the-face technique.

FOOT-IN-THE-DOOR TECHNIQUE   Researchers have demonstrated that sometimes the best road to compliance is to begin by getting a person to agree to a relatively minor or trivial request that serves as a setup for a second, more major request (which is the actual goal). This so-called **foot-in-the-door technique** (Freedman & Fraser, 1966) is widely used by salespeople who attempt to produce a favorable attitude toward their product. For example, if a car salesperson can get you to comply with an initial request to "come in the office and we will run some numbers," you are more likely to develop the attitude that "I need that car." It has been suggested that the success of the foot-in-the-door technique is related to the fact that when people comply with a request, they begin to perceive themselves as "the kind of person who does this sort of thing" and thus are inclined to make even greater commitments to a particular line of requests in order to be consistent with their perceived self-image (Eisenberg et al., 1987; Pliner et al., 1974).

DOOR-IN-THE-FACE TECHNIQUE   Suppose you are moving to another apartment and you want your husky neighbor to help you move your piano. Anticipating a likely negative response to your request, you first ask if he would mind spending the afternoon helping you move all your stuff. As expected, he begs off, claiming a heavy study load. Next, you ask if he would have just a few minutes to help with the piano. How can he say no to such a reasonable request after he has already "slammed the door in your face" in response to the larger request? While some people might say no to both requests, research demonstrates that we are often more inclined to comply with a moderate request if we have already refused a larger one than if the smaller request is presented alone (Cialdini, 1985).

This **door-in-the-face technique,** which is essentially the opposite of the foot-in-the-door method, was demonstrated in an interesting study in which college students were asked to serve as unpaid counselors to delinquent youth for two years at the rate of two hours per week. Predictably, none complied with this request. However, when presented with a second, far more moderate request to take the delinquents on a short outing to the zoo, 50 percent complied with this request. In contrast, only 17 percent of a control group of students agreed to this smaller request when it was presented alone (Cialdini et al., 1975).

OBEDIENCE

All of us succumb routinely to social influence by conforming to behavioral standards established by others or by complying with the requests of associates. Less commonly, social influence takes the form of **obedience,** in which we alter our behavior in response to commands or orders from people we may perceive as having power or authority.

MILGRAM'S EXPERIMENTS ON OBEDIENCE TO AUTHORITY   The most dramatic study of obedience was conducted by social psychologist Stanley Milgram (1963). As you may recall from Chapter 2, Milgram sought to determine if subjects would inflict considerable pain on others merely because an authority figure instructed them to do so. His all-male subjects thought they were participating in a study of the effects of punishment on learning. They were told to use an intercom system to present problems to another person (a total stranger who was actually an accomplice of the experimenter) who was strapped in a chair in another room, and to administer a shock each time the "learner" gave the wrong answer to a problem. Labeled switches on the "shock apparatus" ranged from a low of 15 volts to a high of 450 volts; subjects were instructed to increase the voltage with each successive error the learner made.

According to design, the learner made many errors. The result was a progressive escalation of shock intensity that posed a serious dilemma for the subjects, virtually all of whom exhibited high levels of stress and discomfort as they administered the shocks. Should they continue subjecting the learner to pain, or should they refuse to go on? Whenever they hesitated or protested, the experimenter pressured them to continue, using such commands as "It is absolutely essential that you continue," or "You have no other choice, you must go on."

Despite the fact that all subjects were volunteers, paid in advance, and obviously distressed, only a minority failed to exhibit total obedience. In fact, fully 65 percent proceeded to the final 450-volt level! A number of subsequent studies conducted with different research populations reported findings similar to those of Milgram (Kilham & Mann, 1974; Miller, 1986; Shanab & Yahya, 1977).

Why do people succumb to such destructive instances of obedience? This question has been explored and debated by both social scientists and laypersons. Social psychologists Robert Baron and Donn Byrne (1987) have outlined three reasons why people may respond to social influence in the form of destructive obedience. First, many people seem to believe that their personal accountability for their actions is somehow diminished or relieved by those authority figures who issue the commands. In Milgram's research, subjects were told at the outset that the experimenter rather than the participants was responsible for the learner's well-being. Thus we can see how they may have felt less responsible for their own actions. It is disheartening, however, that this same logic has been employed by such people as Nazi war criminal Adolf Eichmann, who committed unimaginable atrocities against the Jewish people during Hitler's reign of terror, and Lieutenant William Calley, who was court-martialed for the 1968 massacre of Vietnamese civilians at My Lai, both of whom justified their acts by claiming, "I was only following orders."

A second factor contributing to obedience is that authority figures often possess highly visible symbols of their power or status that make it difficult to resist their dictates (symbols such as the white coat and title of a researcher, or the uniform and rank of a military officer). The impact of these external trappings of power was demonstrated in one experiment in which people were randomly stopped on the street and ordered to give a dime to a person in need of parking meter change. Subjects were decidedly more inclined to obey this order if it was issued by someone wearing a fire fighter's uniform than if the source of the command was dressed in a business suit or laborer's clothes (Bushman, 1984).

Finally, people often comply with orders, even orders that are potentially destructive in nature, because they are sucked in by a series of graduated demands, beginning with seemingly innocuous or harmless orders that gradually escalate to orders of a more serious or potentially destructive nature. For example, a corporate executive might request that a supposedly loyal employee, who has a friend who works at a competitor company, ask the friend if his or her employer plans to introduce a new product line. Later, such requests might escalate to orders to ask specific questions about the nature of the products on the drawing board, followed by commands to conduct outright industrial espionage. In a sense, this escalation is what occurred with Milgram's subjects, who were first required to deliver only mild shocks followed by progressively more intense punishment. The problem with such a gradual escalation of demand intensity is that a person is often unable to distinguish a definite point at which disobedience is clearly a more appropriate course of action than obedience.

Apparatus used by Milgram to investigate obedience to authority.

INTERPERSONAL BEHAVIOR: ATTRACTION AND AGGRESSION

ATTRACTION

We have been exploring how we form perceptions of people, how we develop attitudes, and how other people influence our behavior. The most influential people in our adult lives are often the people to whom we are closest—our good friends and our partners in long-term intimate relationships. In this section we first analyze why we feel attracted to certain people as friends and lovers, and then we explore some of the causes of aggression.

FACTORS THAT CONTRIBUTE TO INTERPERSONAL ATTRACTION

Have you ever had the experience of meeting a total stranger—at a party, on the first day of school, or in a bookstore—and feeling immediately that you liked one another? If so, you may have wondered what it was that made you feel close to the other person. This question has been the topic of research for over four decades, and the answers that social psychologists have found center on four primary variables: proximity, similarity, reciprocity, and physical attractiveness.

Proximity   Although most people overlook **proximity,** or geographical nearness, in listing factors that attracted them to a particular person, it is one of the most important variables. We often develop close relationships with people whom we see frequently in our neighborhoods, in school, at work, or at church or synagogue.

The classic study of the effect of proximity on attraction was conducted by Leon Festinger and his colleagues (1950), who evaluated friendship patterns among married MIT students living in a housing development consisting of 17 two-story buildings with five apartments per floor. All of the residents were asked to name their three best friends among residents of the housing development. These friends almost invariably lived in the same building, with next-door neighbors being the most likely to be named as a friend and the next most likely living two doors away. When the friendship ratings of all participants were pooled, certain people emerged as being widely liked (that is, included in the lists of many of the residents). The people who were most often listed as friends lived in apartments close to heavily trafficked areas such as mailboxes, stairway entries, and exits. Not coincidentally, people with the fewest friends lived in more out-of-the-way apartments.

The profound impact of proximity on interpersonal attraction has been confirmed by other research (Saegert et al., 1973; Segal, 1974). Why is it such a powerful factor? Social psychologists have offered a number of plausible explanations. One is simply that familiarity breeds liking. Research has shown that when we are repeatedly exposed to novel stimuli—whether they be unfamiliar musical selections, nonsense syllables, works of art, or human faces—our liking for such stimuli increases (Brooks & Watkins, 1989; Moreland & Zajonc, 1982; Nuttin, 1987; Zajonc, 1968, 1970). This phenomenon, called the **mere exposure effect,** explains in part why we are attracted to people in close proximity to us.

The mere exposure effect even seems to influence our view of ourselves. Many of us are seldom satisfied with photographs of ourselves; our faces do not look quite right. One possible reason may be that the face we see in the photo is not the one we see staring back at us in the mirror. Since left and right are reversed in mirror images, the face we see looking back at us is always slightly different from what others see (Figure 17.8). Thus we prefer the mirror image of our faces, whereas others will prefer the natural version. The mere exposure effect

FIGURE 17.8

The Mere Exposure Effect

Which of these photographs of Bill Cosby do you prefer? Most people select the top photo because it is familiar. The bottom photo would most likely be selected by Cosby because it is the mirror image he is familiar with.

was supported by a study in which women subjects were shown two photos of themselves—one a normal photo and the other a mirror-image photo—and asked to indicate which they preferred. A close friend of each subject also indicated photo preferences. The results: While most subjects preferred the mirror-image photographs, most of their friends preferred the normal photos (Mita et al., 1977).

Another likely reason why proximity influences attraction is the fact that the more we see of others, the more familiar we become with their ways and thus the better able we are to predict their behavior. If you have a good idea of how someone is likely to behave in any given situation, you will probably be more comfortable with this person. It is also possible that when we know we will be seeing a lot of a person, we may be more motivated to see his or her good traits and to keep our interactions as positive as possible.

Similarity   A second factor attracting people to one another is **similarity.** Contrary to the old adage that opposites attract, people who are attracted to one another often share common beliefs, values, attitudes, interests, and intellectual ability (Byrne, 1971; Byrne & Griffitt, 1973; Byrne et al., 1966, 1968, 1986; Judd et al., 1983; Moreland & Zajonc, 1982; Wetzel & Insko, 1982). This tendency was demonstrated in one study in which 13 men expressed their attitudes independently on 44 separate issues prior to being housed together for 10 days in the close quarters of a fallout shelter. At intervals of one, five, and nine days of confinement, each subject was asked to list the three men in the group he would like to remain and the three he would most like to see removed from the shelter. The results provided consistent and clear indications that the participants wanted to keep the men who were most like them (judged by the earlier attitude assessments) and to get rid of those who were least like them (Griffitt & Veitch, 1974).

Why do we feel drawn to people who are like us? For one thing, people with similar attitudes and interests are often inclined to enjoy participating in the same kinds of leisure activities. Even more important, however, we are more likely to communicate well with people whose ideas and opinions are similar to ours, and communication is a very important aspect of enduring relationships. It is also reassuring to be with similar people, for they confirm our view of the world, validate our own experiences, and support our opinions and beliefs (Arrowood & Short, 1973; Sanders, 1982). Thus, mutual reinforcement of behavior is important in maintaining close relations with others.

Reciprocity   No doubt all of us have had personal experience (on both the delivery and recipient end) with the old adage "Flattery will get you everything." People tend to react positively to flattery, compliments, and other expressions of liking and affection. In the study of interpersonal attraction, this concept is reflected in the principle of **reciprocity,** which holds that when we are the recipients of expressions of liking and loving, we tend to respond in kind, particularly if our own self-esteem is low (Byrne & Murnen, 1988; Jacobs et al., 1971). Furthermore, when we are provided with indications that someone likes us, we tend to have warm feelings about these people and to respond positively to them—a reaction which often influences them to like us even more (Curtis & Miller, 1988).

The key words in these descriptions of reciprocity are "tend to." We don't *always* like people who appear to like us. In some cases, some of us have experienced the often unsettling realization that we are the love object of someone who engenders only mildly positive feelings in us. Furthermore, when people perceive that expressions of liking directed toward them are merely part of a phony ingratiation strategy rather than genuine reflections of affection, reciprocity of liking and affection is unlikely to occur. These exceptions notwithstanding,

Cross-cultural studies find that there is a strong tendency for men to prefer a young, physically attractive female for a potential mate and for females to prefer an older male with good financial prospects.

undisguised, genuine expressions of liking or loving often serve as important stimulants to interpersonal attraction.

Physical Attractiveness   **Physical attractiveness** may profoundly influence our impressions of the people we meet. In general, research reveals that physically attractive people are more likely to be sought as friends, to impress potential employers favorably, to be treated better, and to be perceived as more likable, interesting, sensitive, poised, happy, sexy, competent, and socially skilled than people of average or unattractive appearance (Baron, 1986; Cash & Janda, 1984; Dion & Berscheid, 1974; Dion & Dion, 1987; Hatfield & Sprechler, 1986; Lerner & Lerner, 1977; Snyder et al., 1977; Solomon, 1987).

But what determines physical attractiveness? Do you think that both sexes are equally influenced by physical attractiveness in forming impressions of people they meet and in selecting a mate?

A recent cross-cultural study of sex differences in human mate preferences provided strong evidence that men worldwide place greater value than women on mates who are both young and physically attractive. In this study, conducted by University of Michigan psychologist David Buss (1989; 1990), over 10,000 subjects from 37 samples drawn from 33 countries on six continents and five islands (African, Asian, European, North and South American, and Oceanian cultures) were asked to rate the importance of a wide range of personal attributes in potential mates. These personal characteristics included such qualities as dependable character, good looks, good financial prospects, intelligence, sociability, and chastity.

In contrast to the apparent widespread male emphasis on youth and beauty, women in these cultures are more inclined to place greater value on potential mates who are somewhat older, have good financial prospects, and are dependable and industrious. This is not to say that physical attractiveness was unimportant in influencing mate selection among the women of these varied cultures. In fact, many of these women rated physical attractiveness as important, albeit less significant than earning potential.

What accounts for the apparent consistency across so many cultures in what males and females find attractive in a potential mate? And why do males rate physical attractiveness and youth as most important while females rate earning potential and dependability most important? According to Buss (1989; 1990) evolution has biased mate preferences in humans as it has other animals. Males are attracted to younger, physically attractive females because these characteristics are good predictors of reproductive value. That is, a younger female has more reproductive years remaining than an older female. Physical attractiveness is important because characteristics such as smooth unblemished skin, good muscle tone, lustrous hair, and full lips are strong cues to reproductive value. On the other hand, females tend to find older established males more attractive because these characteristics are the best predictors of successful rearing of her offspring. That is, females prefer a mate with wealth, a better territory, or a higher rank. Youth and physical attractiveness are less important to females because male fertility is less age-related than it is for females.

Additional evidence that evolution may have biased our perceptions of attractiveness also comes from studies of young infants. A fascinating study conducted by Judith Langlois and her colleagues (1987) at the University of Texas at Austin revealed that infants from two to eight months old demonstrated marked preferences for attractive faces. When they were shown pairs of color slides of the faces of adult women previously rated by other adults for attractiveness, the infants demonstrated a marked inclination to look longer at the most attractive face in the pair. These findings challenge the commonly held assumption that standards of attractiveness are learned through gradual exposure to the current cultural standard of beauty and are merely "in the eye of the beholder" (p. 363).

More recent research by Langlois and her associates (1990) provides additional evidence that infants prefer attractive faces. In one study, 60 12-month-old infants demonstrated positive emotional and play responses when interacting with an adult stranger who wore a professionally constructed, lifelike, and very attractive latex theater mask. In contrast, when the stranger wore a mask portraying an unattractive face, the infants demonstrated more negative emotions and less play involvement. In a second experiment 43 12-month-old infants played significantly longer with attractive dolls than with unattractive dolls. According to the researchers, these results extend and amplify earlier findings showing that young infants exhibit visual preferences for attractive over unattractive faces.

In a related study with college students Langlois et al. (1990) used computer-generated face composites that averaged the features of individual faces. In most cases subjects rated the average composites more attractive than the individual composites. In addition, as the faces became more and more average, by adding additional composites, they were perceived as more attractive. That is, face composites that represent the average characteristics of a population are perceived as more attractive than distinctive characteristics. Langlois interprets this as additional support for an evolutionary bias in what we perceive as attractive.

AGGRESSION

All of us have been victimized by the aggressive behavior of others, whether it be someone who knowingly initiates a false rumor about us, a parent who strikes us in a fit of anger, or a teammate who ridicules our athletic ability. Sometime during our lives, more than a few of us may become victims of violent crimes such as rape, mugging, or assault—a grim prediction substantiated by evidence that roughly six million Americans are victimized annually by violent crimes such as murder, rape, robbery, or aggravated assault (Widom, 1989). A form of interpersonal violence becoming increasingly common on American campuses and throughout our society is addressed in the Health, Psychology and Life discussion, Reducing the Risk of Acquaintance Rape, at the end of the chapter on page 698.

Criminal violence is an extreme form of **interpersonal aggression**—that is, any physical or verbal behavior intended to hurt another person. Many instances of interpersonal aggression may not qualify as criminal acts, but they can nevertheless be very hurtful. Why do people behave aggressively? Explanations have focused on both biological and psychological processes. We look briefly at the evidence for each.

BIOLOGICAL BASES OF AGGRESSION The biological perspective has been approached by a number of researchers and theorists who seek to understand the biological factors that underlie social behaviors in all animal species, including humans. Many of these scientists believe that aggressive behavior, as well as other social behaviors, may be at least partly determined by biological mechanisms. The most intriguing biological approaches to social behavior are the fields of human **ethology** and **sociobiology.** While ethology is defined broadly as the study of the biology of behavior, sociobiology is considered the biology of social behavior. For instance, many ethologists and sociobiologists are interested in how certain behaviors enhanced survival and reproductive fitness of animals including humans. These adaptive behaviors would then be more likely to be retained in the population through successive generations. Among the prominent spokespersons for this viewpoint are Harvard biologists Edward O. Wilson

(1975, 1978), Nobel prizewinner Konrad Lorenz (1974), and the German ethologist Irenaus Eibl-Eibesfeldt (1989).

Lorenz's interpretation is particularly intriguing. He maintained that all animals, humans included, have an "aggressive instinct" directed toward their own kind. Lorenz believed that this aggressive inclination has great survival value and evolutionary significance for the species. For example, when the males of many species fight for mates, the strongest prevail, ensuring that the more fit will reproduce. An innate inhibition prevents most animals from killing members of their own species, but Lorenz believed that humans never developed this inhibition, probably because with neither lethal claws nor sharp teeth, they were unlikely to inflict serious damage on one another. Today, however, our guns and bombs make us the most dangerous of all living creatures. Lorenz suggested that the situation is worsened by social norms that suppress our fighting instincts, thus causing our aggressive urges to build up to the point that they are sometimes released explosively in acts of extreme violence.

Fortunately for us there is no evidence to support Lorenz's argument that aggressive urges build up within us until they reach this critical point. In addition, most contemporary psychologists are not very receptive to the idea that aggression is an instinct. But they do not reject the possibility that biology may contribute to aggression. In fact, there is considerable evidence that aggressive tendencies may be influenced by biological factors (Bell & Hepper, 1987). One study demonstrated that boys and girls who were exposed to high levels of androgens before birth were found to be significantly more aggressive than their same-sexed siblings who had normal hormonal exposure (Reinisch, 1981). Other research has provided convincing evidence that aggressive behavior often results when certain regions within the limbic systems of the brains of humans and other animals are stimulated through implanted electrodes, lesions, or other abnormal physiological processes (Moyer, 1983). For instance, electrical stimulation of certain regions within the hypothalamus and the amygdala can elicit aggressive behavior in animals and surgical procedures to remove part of the amygdala in humans has been shown to greatly reduce aggressive behavior (cf. Groves et al., 1992).

Some researchers have also linked genetic factors with aggression. For example, Finnish psychologist Kirsti Lagerspetz (1979) selected out the most and least aggressive animals from a large sample of mice, and then bred the fighters with one another and the nonaggressive mice with one another. After 25 generations, she had two distinct strains of mice: a vicious, superaggressive strain and a docile, passive strain. Although such experiments suggest that human aggression may have a link with heredity, we must remember that behavioral patterns in nonhuman animals frequently show a stronger influence of nature than of nurture. There is, however, some provocative evidence from twin studies suggesting that human aggressiveness may be genetically influenced (Rushton et al., 1986; Rushton, 1988). These data demonstrate a much higher concordance rate among identical versus fraternal twins for behaviors such as violent tempers and inappropriate aggression.

In another recent study of 31,436 Danish men, researchers compared first-time violent and nonviolent offenders for their likelihood of repeated offenses. These researchers concluded that there was no evidence of heritability of violent behavior, although violent offenders were more likely to have some form of brain damage than nonoffenders (Mednick et al., 1988).

How are we to interpret this apparently conflicting research? Can we conclude that biological factors contribute to aggressive behavior in humans? The answer here is a cautious yes. There is considerable evidence for biological dispositions to aggressive behavior in numerous animal species including humans.

However, aggressive behavior is also heavily influenced by environmental factors. We remind you of the problems addressed in Chapters 13 and 14 regarding parsing out hereditary and environmental influences on behavior. Behavior is the result of continuing interactions between the environment and genes, not additive contributions of each. In the next section we look at some important psychological factors that contribute to aggressive behavior.

PSYCHOLOGICAL BASES OF AGGRESSION   Research on psychological contributions to aggression have focused on three major areas: the frustration-aggression hypothesis, social-learning theory, and the influence of media and film on violence.

The Frustration-Aggression Hypothesis   Over 50 years ago John Dollard and his colleagues (1939) proposed that there is a consistent link between frustration, the emotional state that results when something interferes with obtaining a goal, and aggression. In their widely influential **frustration-aggression hypothesis,** Dollard and his associates asserted that "Aggression is *always* a consequence of frustration" and that "Frustration *always* leads to aggression" (p. 1). According to this theory, we might expect that anytime we are thwarted in our efforts to finish a job, find the proper ingredients for a midnight sandwich, or win in a game of basketball, we become aggressive. This hypothesis does not mean that we always vent our frustration on the object of our frustration (such as our opponents on the basketball court). Rather, Dollard suggested that aggression may be delayed, disguised, or even displaced from its most obvious source to a more acceptable outlet. For instance, we may go home and yell at our dog after losing our basketball game. In spite of these possible modifications in the mode of expression, the frustration-aggression hypothesis maintained that when we are frustrated, some kind of aggressive reaction is inevitable.

This theory is intuitively appealing, and certainly all of us have had the experience of lashing out against something or someone when we are frustrated. Does it seem reasonable to assume, however, that every time we are frustrated we respond with aggressive actions? A number of critics of the frustration-aggression hypothesis did not think so, and psychologist Neal Miller (1941) proposed a revision of the original hypothesis. Miller suggested that frustration can produce a number of possible responses, only one of which is aggression. Other responses to a frustrating situation may include withdrawal, apathy, hopelessness, and even increased efforts to achieve a goal. The response to a frustrating situation may be any behavior acquired through operant conditioning that eliminates or removes one from the aversive situation.

If aggression is only one of several responses to frustrating situations, then what circumstances will cause frustration to produce aggression? Social psychologist Leonard Berkowitz (1978) suggested that two conditions act together to instigate aggression. One is a *readiness* to act aggressively, which is often associated with the emotion of anger. That is, frustrations may induce a readiness or inclination to act aggressively because frustrations are often aversive, arousing negative emotions such as anger (Berkowitz, 1983, 1989). Thus any behavior that reduces the aversive emotion will be maintained by negative reinforcement, as described by two-factor theory in Chapter 6.

The second factor influencing aggression is the presence of *environmental cues,* such as the presence of others who are perceived as accepting aggressive behavior, the availability of weapons, and the presence of an acceptable target for aggression. Thus Berkowitz suggests that while we may respond to frustrating situations with anger, our anger is not likely to lead to aggressive behavior unless suitable environmental cues are present. A number of studies in which subjects experience frustration in either the presence or absence of suitable aggression cues have supported Berkowitz's prediction (Berkowitz & Geen, 1966; Berkowitz & Lepage, 1976; Follingstad et al., 1992; Frodi, 1975; Gustafson, 1989; Leyens & Parke, 1975).

The frustration-aggression hypothesis, as first modified by Miller and later by Berkowitz, provides one important theoretical perspective on the psychological contributions to aggression. That is, aggressive behaviors are learned and maintained by their reinforcing consequences. However, frustration is not the only cause of aggression. What about the grade school student who hits the schoolyard weakling because he has seen another admired classmate do the same thing? Learning theory also helps to explain some other instances of aggressive behavior where frustration may not occur.

Social-Learning Perspectives on Aggression Social psychologists generally agree that human aggressive behavior is learned. We have discussed Albert Bandura's (1986) social-learning theory in several chapters, and this approach also helps us understand aggression. As you recall, Bandura emphasizes the processes of reinforcement and imitation of models. Anyone who has observed a child behaving aggressively to take a desired toy away from another has seen the power of reinforcement in shaping and maintaining aggression. If we learn that aggression will produce reinforcers, it is only natural that such behavior will become part of our repertoire. Even nontangible reinforcers, such as praise for "being tough" or "not taking guff from anybody," may increase a child's inclination to repeat such behaviors.

People may also learn to be aggressive by observing the behavior of others. A child who sees an adult or friend act aggressively may imitate this behavior. As we saw in Chapter 6, Bandura demonstrated this process in a classic experiment in which three, four, and five year olds observed an adult beating a five-foot Bobo doll, then behaved in a similar way when given a chance to play with the doll (see Figure 17.9). Subsequent research revealed that imitation of aggression tends to be most pronounced when the aggressive acts are observed to produce rewards, or at least not to result in punishment (Bandura, 1965; Bandura et al., 1963; Walters & Willows, 1968). Of course, it might be argued that children who observe aggression and then imitate it in a laboratory setting are not necessarily inclined to model such aggressive behavior in the real world.

This argument is countered, however, by extensive evidence that children raised by parents who behave aggressively are strongly inclined to be aggressive themselves, and that children who are victimized by physically abusive parents often tend to behave in the same fashion toward their own children (Bandura, 1960, 1973; Feshbach, 1980; Garbarino & Gilliam, 1980; Kaufman & Zigler, 1987; McCall & Shields, 1986; Straus et al., 1980). This evidence suggests that each generation learns to be violent by being a participant in a violent family (Straus et al., 1980, p. 121).

Parents and other significant role models can help to counteract the social roots of aggression by avoiding modeling aggressive actions such as physically punishing or verbally abusing children or engaging in aggressive or violent encounters with other adults. From very early in life, children can be encouraged to develop socially positive traits such as nurturance, tenderness, sensitivity, cooperation, and empathy. Parents and other adult socializing agents can employ the power of positive reinforcement to strengthen such prosocial qualities in children while at the same time discouraging inappropriate aggression and punishing aggressive behavior consistently but nonphysically (Eron & Huesmann, 1984; Patterson, 1986; Patterson et al., 1982).

The Effects of Violence in the Media and on Film   If children learn to behave aggressively by observing their parents, other adults, and their peers, what effect does viewing violence on film have on behavior? Most children in our society observe thousands upon thousands of murders and other acts of violence on television and on film. The question of whether viewing violence actually increases a person's inclination to act aggressively has been the center of a lively debate. On one side of the issue, some psychologists (particularly psychodynamic psychologists) have argued that observing violence may be cathartic, for when we watch other people behaving violently we vent some of our own frustration and anger vicariously, so that we are less likely to behave aggressively.

Research evidence has not been very supportive of the catharsis hypothesis (Brigham, 1986; Evans, 1974; Lefkowitz et al., 1988; Singer, 1989; Tavris, 1982; Williams, 1986). Most psychologists who are familiar with the extensive research are convinced that exposure to media violence increases the odds that the viewer will behave aggressively (Berkowitz, 1986; Friedrich-Cofer, 1986; Penrod, 1986). In 1982 the National Institute of Mental Health released an extensive analysis of the research literature on the effects of television viewing on behavior, in which they concluded the following:

> The consensus among most of the research community is that violence on television does lead to aggressive behavior by children and teenagers who watch the programs. This conclusion is based on laboratory experiments and on field studies. Not all children become aggressive, of course, but the correlations between violence and aggression are positive. In magnitude, television violence is as strongly correlated with aggressive behavior as any other behavioral variable that has been measured. (p. 6)

More recently Yale University's Dorothy Singer (1989), a recognized authority on the behavioral consequences of television viewing, observed that several excellent longitudinal studies "effectively establish the link between television violence and aggressive behavior in children and adolescents" (p. 445). However, not all psychologists support this interpretation. One dissenter, Jonathan Freedman

FIGURE 17.9

Learning Aggressive Behavior Through Observation

Bandura observed that when an adult model behaved aggressively, children also behaved aggressively. The top row of photos shows the adult model beating the Bobo doll. The bottom rows show children beating and kicking the doll after observing the adult.

(1984), has argued that laboratory studies provide an artificial environment that influences subjects' behavior. Since they have been given permission to act aggressively and because they have no fear of retaliation or punishment, subjects are more likely to imitate aggressive acts they have viewed in experimental studies. Freedman further argues that laboratory studies typically involve isolating subjects and exposing them to a concentrated dose of violence, a situation which is quite different from the real world in which our exposure to violence is tempered by much more extensive exposure to nonviolent human interaction. Furthermore, Freedman suggests that even those studies that have demonstrated a positive relationship between viewing violence and aggressive behavior in a natural setting (Eron et al., 1972; Milavsky et al., 1982) do not necessarily demonstrate a cause-and-effect relationship. He suggests an alternate explanation: Aggressive persons are inclined to select television programs with high violence content.

Freedman's critique should not be dismissed lightly. We must note, however, that while his criticisms of media violence studies may be at least partially accurate, the fact still remains that virtually all of these studies reach the same general conclusion—that filmed violence spawns aggressive behavior. It seems reasonable to conclude that the effect of viewing filmed aggression must be fairly substantial to show consistently across so many diverse research designs. Even if there were a paucity of research supporting a causal relationship between TV violence and aggressive behavior, some experts caution that "violence on television may have other adverse effects such as increasing one's acceptance of aggressive behavior in others, blunting one's sensitivity to violence, and adopting 'mean world' attitudes that are consistent with television's portrayals of aggressive behavior" (Gadnow & Sprafkink, 1989, p. 404).

Throughout this chapter we have examined the powerful influence of social conditions on our behavior. We have seen that our impressions of others, our tendency to conform, our prejudices, and human aggression are all greatly influenced by social circumstances. In addition, we discussed how social behaviors such as mate selection and aggression are influenced biologically as well as by psychological factors. Social psychologists, ethologists and sociobiologists have all had a profound influence on our understanding of social behaviors. And, while some of their theories are still controversial and incomplete they have changed the way we view human social interactions. For instance, the testimony of social psychologists in two recent murder trials in South Africa resulted in the reversal of the death penalty in both cases. Expert psychological testimony argued successfully that group conformity, obedience to authority, and extreme frustration were all contributing factors to the violence that resulted in several deaths (Colman, 1991).

HEALTH
PSYCHOLOGY
&
LIFE

REDUCING THE RISK OF ACQUAINTANCE RAPE

The majority of rapes are committed by someone who is known to the victim, not (as in the popular stereotype) by a stranger lurking in the bushes. A significant number of these acquaintance rapes occur in dating situations, hence the term date rape (Muehlenhard & Linton, 1987). Acquaintance rapes are much less likely to be reported than stranger rapes (Koss et al., 1987; Muehlenhard & Linton, 1987).

In recent years researchers have provided extensive and disheartening evidence regarding the prevalence of sexual coercion in dating and other acquaintance situations. (Although both sexes experience sexual coercion, women are more likely than men to be physically forced into unwanted sexual activity.) A survey of several hundred Cornell University women revealed that 16 percent had been forced to have intercourse against their will (Parrot & Allen, 1984). Thirty-five percent of 930 San Francisco women reported being victims of either attempted or completed acquaintance rape, much of which occurred in dating situations (Russell, 1984); fully 95.3 percent of 275 Arizona State University women reported being coerced into one or more sexual behaviors (Christopher, 1988), and nearly 50 percent of the female college students in another recent study had been victims of physical violence in dating situations (Kiernan and Taylor, 1990). These and countless other studies reveal that acquaintance rape is pervasive in American society.

What motivating factors might cause a man to coerce a female companion to engage in unwanted sexual activity? One factor is a misreading of the situation. Men often misinterpret the actions of women (cuddling, kissing, and so on) as indicating a desire to engage in intercourse (Goodchilds & Zellman, 1984; Muehlenhard, 1988; Muehlenhard & Linton, 1987). If the woman, who just wishes to cuddle, resists the man's advances, he may conclude that she really wants to have intercourse but that she feels the need to offer at least some token resistance so as not to appear too easy (Check & Malamuth, 1983; Muehlenhard & Hollabaugh, 1988; Muehlenhard & Linton, 1987).

Unfortunately, a recent study of 610 female undergraduates revealed that 39.3 percent had engaged in token resistance to sex at least once. Common reasons for saying no when they really meant yes included not wanting to appear promiscuous, uncertainty about partner's feelings, undesirable surroundings, game playing (wanting partners to be more physically aggressive, to beg or talk them into sex, etc.), and wanting to be in control. The authors of this study, Charlene Muehlenhard and Lisa Hollabaugh (1988), maintain that such a double message promotes rape by providing men with a rationale for ignoring sincere refusals. If a man encounters a woman who says no and he ignores her protests and finds that she is indeed willing to engage in sex, his belief that women's refusals are not to be taken seriously will be strengthened (p. 878).

A man who embraces this token-no idea may thus proceed with sexual advances despite further protests from a companion whose resistance is genuine. Such a man may not even define his actions as rape. However, even men who believe their partners when they say no may think it is defensible to use force to obtain sex if they feel they have been led on by such actions as having to pay for all dating expenses, being invited to accompany a date to her apartment, or having the companion accept an invitation to go to his apartment (Goodchilds & Zellman, 1984; Kanin, 1967, 1969; Muehlenhard & Linton, 1987). These findings have important implications for preventing acquaintance rapes. The following list provides suggestions that may be helpful in reducing the risk of being victimized by this form of sexual violence:

1. When dating someone for the first time, seriously consider doing so in a group situation or meeting him at a public place. This arrangement will allow you to assess your date's behavior in a relatively safe environment. If you feel at all uncomfortable with your date arrange for your own transportation home—do not allow him to drive you.

2. Watch for indications that your date is a controlling or dominating person who may try to control your behavior. A man who plans all activities and makes all decisions during a date may also be inclined to be dominant in an intimate setting.

3. If the man drives and pays for all expenses, he may think he is justified in using force to see that he gets what he paid for. If you cover some of the expenses, he may be less inclined to use this rationale to justify acting in a sexually coercive manner. During your first few dates be prepared to pay for any of your expenses including a cab ride home if necessary.

4. Avoid behavior that may be interpreted as teasing. Clearly state to your date what you do and do not wish to do regarding intimate contact. For example, you might say, "I hope you do not misinterpret my inviting you back to my apartment. I definitely do not want to do anything more than relax, listen to some music, and talk." If you become interested in some kind of early intimate contact, you might say, "Tonight I would like to hold you and kiss, but I would not be comfortable with anything else at this point in our relationship." When men are recipients of such direct communication, their inclinations to force unwanted sexual activity or to feel led on are likely to be markedly reduced (Muehlenhard & Andrews, 1985; Muehlenhard et al., 1985). Presenting ambiguous messages (for example, saying you only want to kiss and then allowing petting) may increase the risk of rape in light of men's tendency to believe that no really means yes or that teasing behavior justifies force. By all means, if you do not want to pursue further intimate contact say so. Do not get yourself into the situation of saying no to early advances only to give in. This makes it difficult for your date to know when you really mean no.

5. If, despite direct communication about your intentions, your date behaves in a sexually coercive manner, you may use a strategy of escalating forcefulness—direct refusal, vehement verbal refusal, and, if necessary, physical force (Muehlenhard & Linton, 1987, p. 193). In one study the response rated by men as most likely to get men to stop unwanted advances was the woman vehemently saying, "This is rape, and I'm calling the cops" (Beal & Muehlenhard, 1987). If verbal protests are ineffective, reinforce your refusal with physical force such as pushing, slapping, biting, kicking, or clawing your assailant. Men are more likely to perceive their actions as at least inappropriate, if not rape, when a woman protests not only verbally but also physically (Beal & Muehlenhard, 1987; Muehlenhard & Linton, 1987; Shotland & Goodstein, 1983).

SUMMARY

SOCIAL PERCEPTION

1. The term social perception describes the ways we perceive, evaluate, categorize, and form judgments about the characteristics of people we encounter. Three factors that influence our social perceptions are first impressions, schemas, and implicit personality theories.

2. Our first impressions about a person often seem to count the most, a phenomenon referred to as the primacy effect.

3. Person schemas, which are generalized assumptions about certain classes of people, provide a structure for evaluating the people we meet.

4. Implicit personality theories allow us to draw conclusions about what people are like based on certain implicit assumptions about personality traits that usually go together. Implicit personality theories are often organized around central traits that we tend to associate with other characteristics.

5. The term halo effect is employed to describe our tendency to infer other positive (or negative) traits from our perception of one central trait.

6. Attributions are the judgments we make about why people behave as they do. We tend to attribute people's behavior either to

dispositional (internal) causes, such as motivational states or personality traits, or to situations, such as environmental or situational factors.

7. Two theories attempt to explain the process of making attributions in a rational, methodical manner. The correspondent inference theory suggests that we attribute a person's behavior to an underlying disposition. The covariation principle maintains that we make attributions by analyzing the manner in which causes and effects covary.

8. Biases in attribution processes include the fundamental attribution error (a tendency to overestimate dispositional causes and to underestimate situational causes when accounting for the behavior of others), false consensus bias (the assumption that most people share our own attitudes and behaviors), and the illusion of control (the belief that we control events in our lives).

ATTITUDES

9. Attitudes are learned, relatively enduring predispositions to respond in consistent ways to certain people, groups, ideas, or situations.

10. Attitudes are shaped by experiences, which include our observa-

tions of behavior (both other people's and our own), classical and operant conditioning, and direct experiences with the attitude object (the people, ideas, or things we hold attitudes about).

11. Attitudes serve a number of important functions in our lives, including an understanding function, a social identification function, a social adjustment function, and a value-expressive function.

12. Studies which have measured a variety of behaviors relevant to a given attitude have revealed a strong correlation between attitudes and behavior.

13. Attitudes are particularly strong predictors of behavior when other factors influencing behavior are minimized, when an attitude is highly relevant to the behavior being considered, and when we are quite conscious of our attitudes when we act.

14. Consistency theories suggest that we sometimes change our attitudes in an effort to maintain consistency both among attitudes we hold as well as between our attitudes and behaviors.

15. Two noteworthy consistency theories of attitude change are Heider's balance theory and Festinger's cognitive dissonance theory. Balance theory argues that people are inclined to balance their beliefs and feelings about a particular issue, object, or situation against their attitudes about other people. According to cognitive dissonance theory, people experience an unpleasant state of dissonance whenever they perceive a discrepancy between their actions and their attitudes. In such a situation, attitudes may be changed to be more consistent with behavior, thus resulting in a state of consonance or psychological comfort.

16. Three elements are particularly important in persuasive communications: the source of the message, the way the message is stated, and the characteristics of the message recipients.

17. The probability that persuasion will succeed is highest when the source of persuasion is seen as possessing any or all of the qualities of credibility, power, and attractiveness.

18. Persuasive messages may be most effective when there is a moderate level of discrepancy between the message and the audience's viewpoint. When the message appeals to fear, it may be most effective in inducing attitude change when it elicits moderate fear and when it contains clear information about what to do to avoid the fearful consequence.

19. A message that is presented in an unusual or novel fashion is often more effective than timeworn arguments.

20. A one-sided argument seems to be more effective if the audience is poorly educated and/or unfamiliar with the issue, whereas two-sided arguments tend to work better with a well-educated, well-informed audience.

21. Teenagers and young adults are generally more susceptible than older people to persuasive communication. Research has been unclear about the impact of listeners' self-esteem and intelligence on their inclination to yield to persuasion.

22. Prejudice is a negative, unjustifiable, and inflexible attitude toward a group and its members that is based on erroneous information, often in the form of stereotypes (preconceived and oversimplified beliefs and expectations about the traits of members of a particular group that do not account for individual differences).

23. Prejudice often stems from a marked tendency of people to categorize themselves as belonging to an ingroup (based on race, age, education, creed, economic level, etc.) and to have a negative

attitude against people in outgroups who do not possess those characteristics. By perceiving their ingroup as superior, people seem to be attempting to enhance their self-esteem.

24. People who are frustrated by their lack of accomplishments or by adverse living conditions often vent their frustration in the form of prejudice against members of a minority group that they perceive as being less powerful than themselves.

25. Racism, sexism, and other prejudicial attitudes are often passed directly from parents to children through the social learning mechanisms of observation and emulation.

26. Some evidence suggests that people raised in a harsh, authoritarian fashion may be inclined to develop prejudiced behaviors characterized by intolerance, emotional coldness, rigidity, unquestioning submission to higher authority, stereotyped thinking, and identification with power.

SOCIAL INFLUENCE ON BEHAVIOR

27. The realm of social influence (the effects of others on our behavior) encompasses the related phenomena of conformity, compliance, and obedience.

28. Conformity refers to a tendency to change or modify our own behaviors so that they are consistent with those of other people.

29. Social psychologists make a distinction between conformity that results from informational social influence, in which we accept a group's beliefs or behaviors as providing accurate information about reality, and conformity via normative social influence, in which we conform not because of an actual change in our beliefs but because we think that we will benefit in some way, such as gaining approval or avoiding rejection.

30. Whereas both compliance and conformity involve yielding to pressure exerted by others, compliance involves an element of coercion as well, in that it takes place in situations where we alter our behavior in response to direct requests from others.

31. Two methods employed by people who wish to increase the probability of compliance in others are the foot-in-the-door technique and the door-in-the-face technique.

32. Obedience occurs in situations in which people alter their behavior in response to commands or orders leveled by people they may perceive as having power or authority.

33. Psychologists have suggested three reasons why people may respond to social influence in the form of destructive obedience. First, people may believe that their personal accountability for actions is somehow diminished or relieved by those authority figures who issue the commands. Second, authority figures often possess highly visible symbols of power or status that make it difficult to resist their dictates. Finally, people often comply because they have first been "sucked in" by seemingly harmless commands.

INTERPERSONAL BEHAVIOR: ATTRACTION AND AGGRESSION

34. Factors known to contribute strongly to interpersonal attraction include proximity, similarity, reciprocity, and physical attractiveness. We often develop close relationships with people whom we see frequently, who share similar beliefs, who seem to like us, and whom we perceive as being physically attractive.

35. Cross-cultural studies suggest that physical attractiveness and youth are more important for males selecting a potential mate

than for females, who seek characteristics of wealth, status, and industriousness in potential mates.

36. Explanations for why people engage in interpersonal aggression (that is, any physical or verbal behavior intended to hurt another person) include both biological and psychological influences.

37. The biological perspective, championed by sociobiologists and ethologists, maintains that aggression between members of a species serves to ensure that strong, dominant individuals survive and reproduce.

38. There is considerable evidence that aggressive behavior is at least partially determined by genetics but environmental influences play a significant role.

39. Research has revealed that frustration often precedes aggressive behavior, particularly if suitable cues are present in the environment.

40. Social-learning theorists suggest that aggressive behavior is often learned by receiving reinforcement for aggressive acts and by observing and imitating the aggressive behavior of others.

41. Some psychologists have argued that observing television and film violence may be cathartic, providing a vicarious way to vent our own frustration and anger. However, the evidence has not provided much support for this hypothesis. Most psychologists believe that exposure to violence increases the odds that the viewer will behave aggressively.

TERMS AND CONCEPTS

diffusion of responsibility
bystander apathy
social perception
primacy effect
person schemas
implicit personality theories
central traits
halo effect
attribution theory
correspondent inference theory
covariation principle
fundamental attribution error
false consensus bias
illusion of control
attitudes
impression management
balance theory
cognitive dissonance theory
prejudice
stereotype
discrimination

ingroup
ingroup bias
outgroup
authoritarian personality
social influence
conformity
informational social influence
normative social influence
compliance
foot-in-the-door technique
door-in-the-face technique
obedience
proximity
mere exposure effect
similarity
reciprocity
physical attractiveness
interpersonal aggression
ethology
sociobiology
frustration-aggression hypothesis

Elementary Statistics

Statistics is one of the most commonly used mathematical tools in science. Without statistics it would be virtually impossible to present and interpret the results of scientific experiments. Two particularly useful types of statistics frequently used in psychology are descriptive statistics and inferential statistics. *Descriptive statistics*, as the name implies, are used to describe and summarize the results of research. *Inferential statistics* are used in making decisions about hypotheses and to make generalizations from research samples to larger populations.

DESCRIPTIVE STATISTICS

MEASURES OF CENTRAL TENDENCY

Suppose your psychology instructor gives a sample test to 10 students who attended a study session. How would he or she describe the test results? One way would be to name all students and list their test scores—10 names and 10 scores. That would probably work nicely in a small class. But it would certainly be inefficient and confusing with a class of 500. Moreover, a listing of numbers does not indicate much of anything about the study group as a whole. It also would be helpful to know the average, typical, or most representative score. What is needed is a measure of *central tendency* for the group of scores, a number that represents the average. We shall describe three commonly used measures.

THE MEAN   The **mean** (short for arithmetic mean) is computed by adding up all the scores and dividing by the number of scores. We can express this in mathematical form in the following formula:

$$\overline{X} = \frac{\Sigma X}{N}$$

This formula introduces some elementary statistical symbols. The letter X refers to the independent variable, which can take on many different values. It could be anything—IQ, anxiety, or learning errors. The researcher measures the variable for each subject and assigns a score to each subject to represent the level of the variable for that subject. The capital Greek letter sigma (Σ) in the formula is a shorthand symbol for "add up these scores." We then divide this sum by the number of scores (symbolized by N) to arrive at the mean which is symbolized by $\overline{X}$ (read "X bar").

We have made up a list of 10 test scores from students attending our hypothetical study session and computed their mean in Table A.1. To compute the mean, we add up the 10 scores and divide by 10 ($\overline{X} = 83$). Table A.1 also gives the number of hours each student in our study session studied during the previous week. To keep the variable of study time distinct from test score, we signify study times by Y. So ΣY tells us to add up the study times, which is also done in Table A.1. Dividing this total by the number of scores gives us the mean study time of the students ($\overline{Y} = 8.35$ hours). We can express these steps in a shorthand formula.

$$\overline{Y} = \frac{\Sigma Y}{N}$$

Now if we ask the teacher how the class performed on the test, the teacher could simply report the mean value of 83 points; if we ask how many hours these students studied, the teacher could report the mean from our group, which was 8.35 hours. This method is obviously much simpler than listing all the X and Y

TABLE A.1   *Computation of Mean Test Score and Study Time for 10 Students Enrolled in a Study Session*

STUDENT'S NAME	X (TEST SCORE)	Y (STUDY TIME)
Rita	85	9.2
Charles	78	8.1
Dawn	82	8.4
Bruce	74	7.2
Lauri	89	9.6
Marie	91	9.5
John	87	8.9
Randy	79	6.3
Jeff	81	7.7
Suzan	84	8.6
	$\Sigma X = 830$	$\Sigma Y = 83.5$
	$N = 10$	$N = 10$

The mean of test scores (X) is

$$\overline{X} = \frac{\Sigma X}{N} = \frac{830}{10} = 83.0$$

The mean of study times (Y) is

$$\overline{Y} = \frac{\Sigma Y}{N} = \frac{83.5}{10} = 8.35$$

scores and it gives a better idea of the students' general performance as well as the hours of study time per week that are typical of these students.

THE MEDIAN The **median** is the *middle score* in a list of scores that have been arranged in increasing order. If there is an odd number of scores, then there will be one score exactly in the middle. Thus, if the class had 11 students, the score of the sixth student in order would be the median—there would be five scores higher and five scores lower. With an even number of scores, there is no single middle score; instead, there are two scores that determine the middle (one is above and one is below the theoretical midpoint). In our example of 10 test scores, the middle two scores are the fifth and sixth scores. Table A.2 shows the 10 test scores from Table A.1, but this time we have arranged them in order. The middle point is between the fifth and sixth score (83). We average these two scores to obtain the median.

The mean and the median are typically close, but not usually the same as they are in this case. They will be very close when the distribution of scores is symmetrical or equally balanced around the mean.

Now consider the set of test scores in Table A.3. Here we note that most of the 10 students from a study session didn't do very well with the exception of two students who scored very high. This distribution of scores is asymmetrical and unbalanced. Technically, we call it skewed. The distribution of Table A.3 is skewed to the high end (positively skewed). The mean score is 76 and the median is 72.

THE MODE The **mode** is the *most frequently occurring score*. In a small set of scores as in Tables A.1, A.2, and A.3, there is the possibility that no score will occur more than once and, thus, there is no mode. But suppose a psychologist gives an anxiety test to a group of 200 mental patients. With such a large group, it is convenient to set up a *frequency distribution* showing the various possible scores on the test and, for each possible score, how many people actually got that score. We have set up in Table A.4 such a frequency distribution for the anxiety

TABLE A.2 *Computation of the Median Test Score for 10 Students Enrolled in a Study Session*

NAME	X (TEST SCORE)	
Marie	91	
Lauri	89	
John	87	
Rita	85	
Suzan	84	(The *median* is the average
Dawn	82	of the two middle scores)
Jeff	81	
Randy	79	
Charles	78	
Bruce	74	

The median in this case is the average of the two middle scores (84 and 82).

$$\frac{84+82}{2}=83$$

Note that if we had an odd number of scores, the median would be the middle score.

TABLE A.3   *Comparison of the Mean and the Median for a Set of Test Scores for 10 Students*

NAME	X (TEST SCORE)
Mike	99
Julie	98
Lynn	76
Ryan	74
Bill	72
Lauri	72
Kathy	69
John	68
Sue	68
Bob	64

(The *median* is the average of the two middle scores)

The median test score is $\frac{72 + 72}{2} = 72$

The mean test score is $\overline{X} = \frac{\Sigma X}{N} = \frac{760}{10} = 76$

TABLE A.4   *A Frequency Distribution of the Anxiety Scores of 200 Mental Patients*

SCORE (X)	FREQUENCY (f)
20	10
19	10
18	12
17	15
16	20
15	**27**
14	15
13	21
12	22
11	12
10	10
9	8
8	7
7	5
6	3
5	0
4	2
3	1
2	0
1	0
	$\Sigma f = 200 = N$

The *mode*, the score that occurs most frequently, is equal to 15.

FIGURE A.1

A Frequency Distribution Based on the Data in Table A.4

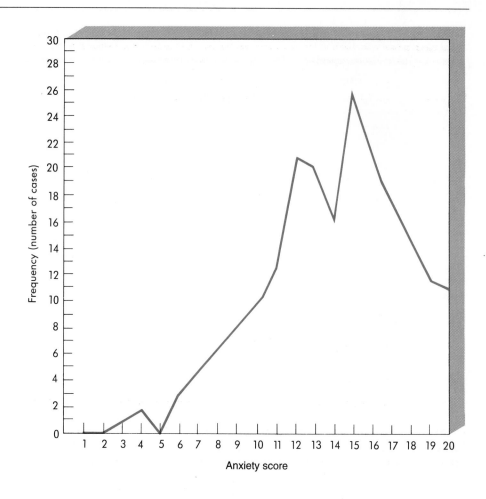

scores from the 200 mental patients. Looking down the frequency column in Table A.4, we see that 27 is the highest frequency. That is, 27 people obtained a score of 15. Therefore, 15 is the *mode* or the *modal score*. Note that the sum of all the frequencies is equal to *N*, the number of people taking the test—in this case, 200.

Frequency distributions can also be represented graphically. Figure A.1 shows a frequency distribution from Table A.4. The horizontal axis of the graph represents the values of the variable *X* (the anxiety score) and the vertical axis represents the frequency of each score.

MEASURES OF VARIABILITY

There are differences among people: Not everyone gets the same score on a test or is the same height; these **individual differences** among people are a fact of life. The variability among people may be large when it comes to anxiety or test scores, but small when it comes to the number of fingers they have. How do we quantify the degree of variability in the scores?

The quickest and least informative measure of the variability in a set of scores is the range. The **range** is defined as the *highest score minus the lowest score*. In Table A.4, we see that the patients' anxiety scores range from a high of 20 to a low of 3, and so the range would be 20 − 3 = 17. Although the range as a measure of variability is easy to compute, it is based on only two scores (the highest and the lowest) and, therefore, tells us little about the variability in the entire distribution. Better measures of variability are the **variance** and **standard deviation,** both of which reflect the degree of spread or fluctuation of scores around the mean.

TABLE A.5 *Two Sets of Scores That Have the Same Mean but Differ in Variability*

SET A	SET B
36	36
22	32
21	28
21	24
20	20
20	20
19	16
19	12
18	8
4	4
$\Sigma X = 200$	$\Sigma X = 200$
$N = 10$	$N = 10$
$\overline{X} = \dfrac{200}{10} = 20$	$\overline{X} = \dfrac{200}{10} = 20$
Range $= 36 - 4 = 32$	Range $= 36 - 4 = 32$

Suppose we have a set of 10 scores with a mean of 20. Two such sets are shown in Table A.5. All but two of the scores in Set A cluster close to the mean. In Set B, we have the same mean, but the variability is higher, with several scores a long way from the mean. If we described both sets with a central tendency measure (such as the mean), the two sets would appear to be similar. If we described the variability of each set using the range, again the two sets would appear to be similar. To reflect the differences between the sets more accurately, we need a measure of variability which takes into account all the scores (not just the highest and lowest).

The **variance** and the **standard deviation** are both measures of variability that are based on all of the scores in the sample. The **variance** is essentially the *average of the squared distances of the scores from the mean.* It is symbolized by: s^2.

To compute the variance, we first subtract the mean from each score as we have done in Table A.6 (on page A-6). These differences are measures of each score's distance from the mean. Now why not just calculate the mean of these distance scores? The reason is that the mean of these distance scores will always be equal to zero, regardless of how variable the scores are. Instead, we square each score before adding them. These squared distance scores are also shown in Table A.6. Now we can add these scores up and divide by the number of scores. These steps are expressed in the following notational form:

$$s^2 = \frac{\Sigma(X - \overline{X})^2}{N} = 52.4$$

The **standard deviation** is simply the *square root of the variance.* This measure is somewhat easier to interpret because it is expressed in the same units as our independent variable, not a squared value like the variance. For this reason the standard deviation is a more preferable measure of variability.

$$s = \sqrt{\frac{\Sigma(X - \overline{X})^2}{N}} = 7.24$$

TABLE A.6 *Computation of the Variance and Standard Deviation for Two Sets of Scores*

	SET A			SET B	
X	*(X − X̄)*	*(X − X̄)²*	*X*	*(X − X̄)*	*(X − X̄)²*
36	16	256	36	16	256
22	2	4	32	12	144
21	1	1	28	8	64
21	1	1	24	4	16
20	0	0	20	0	0
20	0	0	20	0	0
19	−1	1	16	−4	16
19	−1	1	12	−8	64
18	−2	4	8	−12	144
4	−16	256	4	−16	256
Sums	0	524		0	960

SET A

$$s^2 = \text{variance} = \frac{\Sigma(X - \overline{X})^2}{N} = \frac{524}{10} = 52.4$$

$s = \text{standard deviation} = \sqrt{s^2} = \sqrt{52.4} = 7.24$
Range = 36 − 4 − 32

SET B

$$s^2 = \text{variance} = \frac{\Sigma(X - \overline{X})^2}{N} = \frac{960}{10} = 96.0$$

$s = \text{standard deviation} = \sqrt{s^2} = \sqrt{96.0} = 9.80$
Range = 36 − 4 = 32

The standard deviation and the variance are better measures of variability than the range because they take all of the scores into account, not just the highest score and lowest score. If we compare the two data sets in Table A.6, we see that, even though the range is the same in the two sets, both the variance and the standard deviation reflect the smaller average spread of scores in Set A relative to Set B. Unlike Set B, most of the scores in Set A cluster close to the mean of 20. The variance in Set A is 52.4 and in Set B is 96.0. The standard deviation in Set A is 7.24 and in Set B is 9.80. The range is 32 (36 − 4) in both data sets.

NORMAL FREQUENCY DISTRIBUTIONS

Earlier in this appendix, we introduced the *frequency distribution* and showed how it could be represented graphically. Figure A.2 presents the graph of what is called the **normal distribution** (or *normal curve*). This figure is not a graph of an actual data set (as in Figure A.1). Instead, this is a theoretical distribution defined by a mathematical equation. A normal distribution is symmetrical; if you fold it over at the mean, the two halves will overlap each other. Moreover, it is a bell-shaped curve (meaning it looks like a bell); scores near the mean are most common, and the frequency drops off smoothly as we move to the extremes. The normal distribution is very useful because many variables are "normally dis-

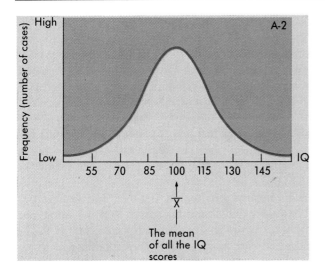

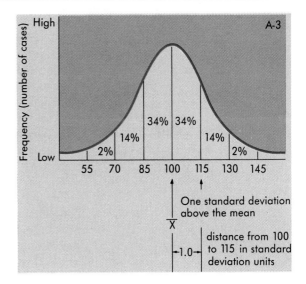

tributed"; that is, the graph of the distribution of the variable would be very similar in shape to the graph in Figure A.2. The variable of IQ is a good example. IQ is normally distributed with a mean of 100 and a standard deviation of 15; if we obtained IQ scores for everybody, the mean IQ would be 100 and the standard deviation would be 15. Furthermore, if we drew a graph representing the frequency of each of the possible IQ scores, it would show the characteristic bell shape of a normal distribution.

If we know that a variable such as IQ is normally distributed and if we know the mean and the standard deviation, we can use the mathematical properties of the normal distribution to deduce more information about the variable. We can do this because, in any normal distribution, the standard deviation can be used to divide the distribution into sections containing fixed percentages of the scores. Figure A.3 shows a normal distribution divided up in this way for the variable of IQ. The fixed percentages are printed in the various sections of the curve. For example, about 34 percent of the IQ scores lie between the mean and a score of 115; that is, 34 percent of the people have IQs between the mean and one standard deviation above the mean. The standard deviation is a distance measure, and the "distance" from 115 to the mean of 100 is one standard deviation unit. An IQ of 130 would be two standard deviation units above the mean; an IQ of 145 would be three standard deviations above the mean. One standard deviation below the mean would be an IQ of 85; two standard deviations below the mean would be an IQ of 70; three standard deviations below the mean would be an IQ of 55. Regardless of the variable being measured, almost all of the scores will fall between three standard deviation units below the mean and three standard deviation units above the mean (for IQ scores, from 55 up to 145). Although it is theoretically possible to obtain scores outside of this range, scores more than three standard deviations from the mean are very rare. It is often convenient to convert the scores into standard deviation scores, called *z* scores, using the following formula:

$$z = \frac{X - \overline{X}}{s}$$

A major advantage of the *z* score is that it can be used as a common yardstick for all tests, allowing us to compare scores on different tests. For example, suppose you receive 80 on your history test, which has a class mean of 70 with a

FIGURE A.2 *(left)*
The Normal Distribution of IQ Scores

FIGURE A.3 *(right)*
The Normal Distribution Divided into Standard Deviation Units

standard deviation of 10. On your psychology test, you got a 90, and the class mean was 85 with a standard deviation of 5. We also know that the distribution of test scores was approximately normal in each class. On which test did you do better? These test scores are not immediately comparable, but if you change each score into a z score using the mean and standard deviation for each test, you will discover that you did equally well on both tests in terms of where you stood in the class distribution (obtaining a z score of + 1.00 on each test). Using the information in Figure A.3, we can infer that your score on each test puts you at approximately the 84th percentile—34 percent of the class scored between your score and the mean and another 50 percent of the class scored below the mean.

Figure A.4 again shows the IQ normal distribution, but this time we have two horizontal axes displayed. The upper one shows IQ scores, and the lower one shows the equivalent z scores. This figure shows that an IQ score of 115 is one standard deviation above the mean, and so the z score corresponding to 115 is + 1.0. If your friend tells you that his z score in IQ is + 2.0, you can see that he has an IQ of 130. If he tells you that his z score is + 3.0 (145), he is either very brilliant or he is pulling your leg.

From Figure A.4, suppose we ask you to figure out what percentage of the people have IQs between 85 and 115, which is the same as asking how many people have z scores between − 1.0 and + 1.0. The answer is 68 percent: 34 percent between 85 and 100, and another 34 percent between 100 and 115. If we know that the scores are distributed normally and we know the mean and standard deviation of the distribution, we can find the percentage of scores between *any* two points by using a simple table (the *Standard Normal table*) that can be found in almost any statistics textbook. An important thing to remember is that these percentages and the z score procedure apply to any normal distribution, not just the IQ distribution. The only difference between the IQ distribution and any other normal distribution of scores is that the other distributions probably have different means and different standard deviations. But if you know that something has a normal distribution and if you know the mean and standard deviation of it, you can set up a figure like the one in Figure A.4.

Suppose, for example, that we told you that waist size in American men is normally distributed with a mean of 34 inches and a standard deviation of 4 inches.

FIGURE A.4 *(left)*
The Normal Distribution and z Scores

FIGURE A.5 *(right)*
The Normal Distribution of Waist Size in American Men (Hypothetical)

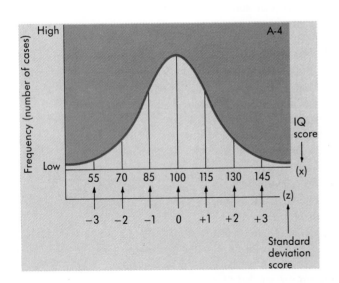

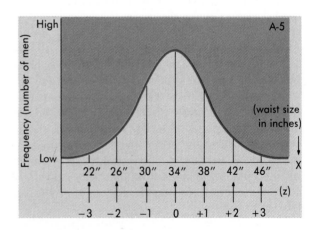

You could now set up a normal frequency distribution as in Figure A.5. Almost all American men have a waist size within the range of 22 inches (z score of -3; 22 is 3 standard deviation units below the mean) to 46 inches (z score of $+3$; 3 units above the mean). Now can you fill in the percentages and answer the following questions?

1. What percentage of men have waist sizes less than 30 inches?
2. What percentage of men have waist sizes greater than 38?
3. If Joe's waist size is 47, is he unusual?
4. If we randomly selected one man from the American population, what is the probability (how likely is it?) that his waist size will be equal to or greater than 38?

This last question brings us to the notion of probability. **Probability** refers to the *proportion of cases that fit a certain description*. In general, the probability of A (the likelihood that a randomly drawn object will be an A object) is equal to the number of A objects divided by the total number of all possible objects. The number of A objects divided by the total number of objects is the *proportion* of objects that are A, and so the probability is just a proportion.

Suppose, as in question 4, we wanted to know the probability that a randomly selected American man will have a waist size equal to or greater than 38. To find the probability of selecting at random such an individual, we have to know what proportion of all men have waist sizes of 38 or greater. In Figure A.5, we can see that 14 percent of the men have waist sizes between 38 and 42 inches and an additional 2 percent are greater than 42, and so we add 14 percent and 2 percent and find that 16 percent of American men have waist sizes of 38 or greater. In proportion terms, this becomes .16 (we move the decimal point two places to the left to translate a percentage into a proportion). In summary, the probability of selecting a man with a waist size equal to or greater than 38 is .16. This means that 16 out of every 100 random selections would yield a man who fits this description.

Suppose that scores on an anxiety scale are normally distributed in the population of all American people with a mean of 50 and a standard deviation of 10. Calculate the probability that a randomly drawn person has an anxiety score that is equal to or less than 40. If you computed it correctly you should have obtained a probability of .16.

CORRELATION

The **correlation coefficient** was introduced in Chapter 2. The correlation coefficient does not describe a single variable as the mean or standard deviation does. Instead, it describes the degree of relationship between two variables. It is basically a measure of the degree to which the two variables vary together, or *covary*. Scores can vary together in one of two ways: (1) a *positive covariation*, in which high scores in one variable tend to go with high scores in the other variable (and low scores go with low scores), or (2) *negative covariation*, in which high scores in one variable tend to go with low scores in the other variable (and low scores go with high scores). When there is a positive covariation, we say that the two variables are *positively correlated*, and when there is a negative covariation, we say they are *negatively correlated*. A common example of positive correlation is the relationship between height and weight—the taller you are, the more you tend to weigh. A common example of negative correlation might be the relationship between the amount of alcohol a person has drunk in an evening and his or her ability to drive an automobile—the more the person has drunk, the lower his or her ability to drive.

Note that we used "tend to go with." Correlations are almost never perfect—not all tall people are particularly heavy, and not all short people are lightweights. In some cases, there may be a *zero correlation* between two variables—that is, no relationship between the variables. We might expect there to be a zero correlation, for example, between your height and your ability to learn psychology. So two variables can be *positively* or *negatively correlated* or *not correlated at all*, and the degree of correlation can be great or small. What we need is a statistic that conveniently measures the degree and the direction (positive or negative) of the correlation between two variables, and this is what the correlation coefficient does.

Table A.7 shows the scores of 10 people on two tests: a test of anxiety and a test of happiness. The possible scores on each test ranged from 1 to 10. Larger scores represent more of the variable being measured. Hence, a high score on the anxiety measure represents a high level of anxiety; a low score represents a low level of anxiety. Intuitively, we would expect a negative correlation between the two variables of anxiety and happiness—the less anxious you are, the more happy you will be, and vice versa.

Table A.7 presents the anxiety and happiness scores for each of the 10 subjects. These data can be more easily visualized in a *scatter plot*, which we have set up in Figure A.6. In this scatter plot, the horizontal axis indicates the anxiety score, and the vertical axis indicates the happiness score. Each person is represented by a point on the graph that locates him or her on the two tests. For example, Clint had an anxiety score of 4 and a happiness score of 7. So we go over (to the right) to 4 on the anxiety scale and then up to 7 on the happiness scale, and we place a dot at that point to represent Clint's scores. The scores from all 10 people are represented in the graph. In this case, the 10 points all fall on a straight line, which means that the correlation is perfect. Further, the line slopes down to the right, which means that the correlation is negative in direction—high anxiety scores go with low happiness scores, and vice versa.

As we have said, however, correlations are almost never perfect. More often, the points are likely to be scattered all over the graph, hence the term "scatter plot." The closer the points are to lying on a straight line, the higher the degree of correlation. If the points seem to cluster about a line that slopes downward to

TABLE A.7 *The Correlation Between Anxiety and Happiness*

NAME	ANXIETY (*X*)*	HAPPINESS (*Y*)
Joan	1	10
Larry	2	9
Ralph	3	8
Clint	4	7
Sue	5	6
Sharon	6	5
Sam	7	4
Bonnie	8	3
Marsha	9	2
Harry	10	1

*Here we have arranged the anxiety scores in order. Note that the happiness scores are in reverse order. When these data are graphed in a scatter plot (see Figure A.6), all the points fall on a straight line, which indicates that the correlation is perfect (in this case, -1.00).

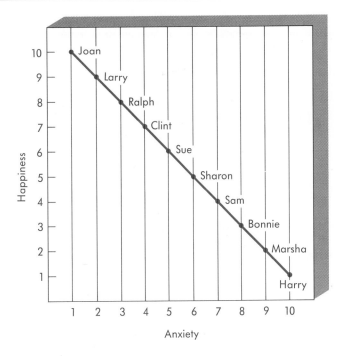

FIGURE A.6

A Scatter Plot of the Data from Table A.7 Relating Anxiety to Happiness

the right, then the correlation will be negative as in Figure A.6. If the points seem to cluster about a line that slopes upward to the right, the correlation will be positive. Figure A.7 shows four scatter plots. In panel A the two variables in question are negatively correlated; the points all seem to cluster about a straight line which slopes downward to the right. In panel B there is a positive correlation; the points again all seem to cluster about a line, but this time the line slopes upward to the right. In panel C there is no correlation; the points are scattered all over, and there is no line that fits them very well. Panel D presents an interesting case. The points do seem to cluster about a line, but it is a curved rather than a straight line. The scatter plot does suggest that there is a relationship between the variables, but it is not a simple relationship. Most correlation coefficients are designed to quantify a simple straight-line relationship and will give misleading results when applied to a complex relationship such as the one in panel D.

FIGURE A.7

Scatter Plots Showing Four Possible Relationships

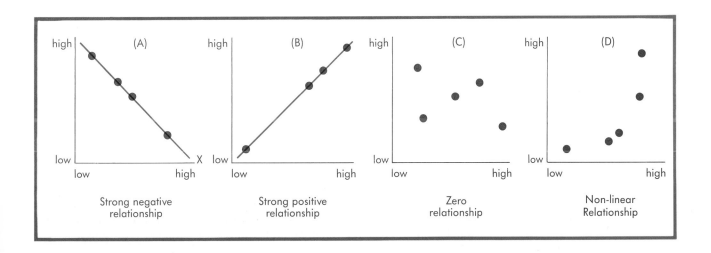

TABLE A.8 *Calculating the Pearson Product-Moment Correlation Coefficient*

NAME	ANXIETY (X)	X^2	HAPPINESS (Y)	Y^2	XY (X TIMES Y)
John	2	4	9	81	18
Ralph	5	25	6	36	30
Mary	9	81	4	16	36
Sue	1	1	3	9	3
Jan	3	9	2	4	6
Harvey	7	49	2	4	14
Jane	8	64	4	16	32
Joanne	6	36	5	25	30
N = 8 people	$\Sigma X = 41$	$\Sigma X^2 = 269$	$\Sigma Y = 35$	$\Sigma Y^2 = 191$	$\Sigma XY = 169$

$$r_{xy} \text{ (the correlation between } X \text{ and } Y) = \frac{N\Sigma XY - (\Sigma X)(\Sigma Y)}{\sqrt{[N\Sigma X^2 - (\Sigma X)^2][N\Sigma Y^2 - (\Sigma Y)^2]}}$$

$$\text{For these data: } r_{\text{ANXIETY} \cdot \text{HAPPINESS}} = \frac{(8)(169) - (41)(35)}{\sqrt{[(8)(269) - (41)^2][(8)(191) - (35)^2]}} = \frac{1352 - 1435}{\sqrt{(2152 - 1681)(1528 - 1225)}}$$

$$= \frac{-83}{\sqrt{(471)(303)}} = \frac{-83}{\sqrt{142713}} = \frac{-83}{377.77} = -.219$$

The **Pearson product-moment correlation coefficient** (symbolized r) is the most often used of several measures of correlation. It can take on any numerical value from -1.0 through 0.0 up to $+1.0$. A perfect negative product-moment correlation, as shown in Figure A.6, is equal to -1.0, and a perfect positive correlation is equal to $+1.0$. Correlations close to zero mean there is little or no relationship between the two variables X and Y. The size of the correlation (ignoring the sign) represents the degree of relationship. The sign of the correlation (positive or negative) tells us the direction of the relationship between the variables, but not the degree of the relationship. Thus a correlation of $-.77$ is just as strong a correlation as a correlation of $+.77$; the only difference is the direction. Table A.8 shows the steps for calculating the Pearson product-moment correlation coefficient in case you want to see exactly how it is done.

In all the examples so far, we have been correlating the scores of a person on two different tests, but we can use correlations in other ways. We might correlate the scores of a person on the same test taken at two different times. If the test measures a variable that should be stable, then the correlation between two administrations of the test would indicate an aspect of the reliability of the test— that is, how consistent are a person's scores on the same test given on two different occasions? A good test should be reliable (see Chapter 13). Another common use of correlation is to determine the test's validity—does the test measure what it is supposed to measure? For example, a test of intelligence should correlate positively with performance in school. If it did, it would help us argue that the test really did measure intelligence. (See Chapter 13 for a discussion of validity.)

LINEAR REGRESSION

One important use of the correlational statistics is in a procedure called **linear regression.** A correlation coefficient tells us the degree to which a person's scores on two tests are related. Suppose, for example, that we try to predict your weight. We have no idea what to guess, because all we know about you is that you are reading this book. If we knew that the average person reading this book weighs 142 pounds, then that would be our best guess, and we would make the same guess for every reader. But if we knew your height, and we also knew the correlation between weight and height, then we could make a much more accurate guess of your weight. For example, if we knew that you were six feet, six inches tall, we would hardly guess 142 pounds. Someone that tall would almost certainly weigh more than 142 pounds. Likewise, if we knew you were four feet, two inches, 142 pounds would also be an inappropriate guess. We would adjust our prediction of your weight according to what we knew about your height. Linear regression is an accurate way of making this adjustment and allowing us to make as accurate a prediction as possible.

The higher the correlation between weight and height, the better we can predict a person's weight from knowing his or her height. If the correlation between the two variables is perfect (either + 1.0 or − 1.0), we can predict perfectly the value of one of the variables if we know the value of the other. But, because correlations are almost never perfect, our predictions are normally close, but usually not exactly correct. The lower the correlation is, the greater will be the average error in prediction.

Linear regression is used in many different settings. Many of you probably took the Scholastic Aptitude Test (SAT). From past research we know there is a positive correlation between scores on the SAT and success in college. Therefore, the SAT can now be given to college applicants and, on the basis of their scores, we can predict approximately how a person will do in college. These predictions are used to help decide whom to admit. Similar procedures are used to process applications for law school, medical school, graduate school, or a job. Using linear regression techniques, the psychologist predicts the applicant's success on the job or in school, and these predictions are used to determine whether or not to hire or admit the applicant. It is a serious business, and the decisions made on this basis are extremely important to the people involved.

Linear regression is based on a mathematical equation for a straight line (hence the term *linear*). What we are looking for is the straight line that comes closest to the most points on a scatter diagram (see Figure A.8). Figure A.8 shows two different hypothetical scatter plots relating scores on the SAT to grade point average in college (GPA). Each point in the diagram represents the SAT score and college GPA for one student. With data on SAT scores and college GPAs, we can proceed to use regression to make predictions for future

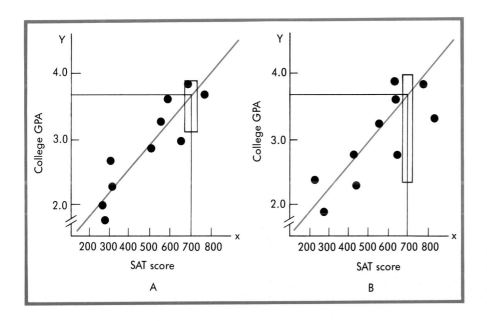

FIGURE A.8

Scatter Plots Showing High (A) and Low (B) Correlations Between SAT Scores and College GPA

students. First, we solve the equation for the best-fitting straight line (known as the *regression line*), a complex procedure we need not describe here. Then we draw the line on the scatter plot. Now we can use the line as a way to predict the GPA given a student's SAT score. For example, consider a student who scores 700 on the SAT; we draw a vertical line up from 700 until it intersects the regression line, and then we draw a horizontal line from this point to the Y axis and read off the predicted GPA. In this case, we come up with a prediction of 3.6 for the student's GPA.

This procedure will not give us perfect predictions. Not all students scoring 700 on their SAT had 3.6 averages in college; some were higher than 3.6 and some lower. As we have said, the main factor in determining the accuracy of the predictions is the degree of correlation between the two variables. If the variables are highly correlated, as depicted in panel A, all the points will cluster closer to the regression line, and none of the predictions is likely to be far off. In fact, if the correlation were perfect, all the points would be right on the line, and there would be no error. (All students with 700 SATs would get 3.6 GPAs.) On the other hand, with low correlations, the points will be widely scattered, and many of them will be a long way from the regression line, as depicted in panel B of Figure A.8. In such a case, the predictions can sometimes be way off. Take a look at the GPAs of the students who scored around 700 on the SAT in the two panels; these points are boxed in on the graphs. In the left panel, which depicts a high correlation, you can see that all the students ended up with high college GPAs, and all were fairly close to 3.6, the average we would predict using the regression line. In contrast, in the right panel, the students with 700 on the SAT varied widely in their GPAs, with some as low as 2.2 and others as high as 3.95. Regression would have predicted 3.6 for all of them, but this prediction would have been way off for some students. *The lower the correlation is between the two variables, the less precise will be our predictions.* In fact, if the correlation drops to zero, a regression equation will not improve our prediction at all—once again, our best guess would be the mean. Given some degree of correlation, however, we can do better using regression than by simply guessing the mean, and the higher the correlation is, the better our predictions will be.

Often there is more than one variable that is correlated with the criterion (the number we are trying to predict). In such cases, a procedure called **multiple regression** can be used to improve and maximize the accuracy of our predictions. For example, in addition to SAT scores, we might also know each student's high school GPA and rank in his or her high school class. Rank, GPA, and SAT scores all could then be combined by using multiple regression to predict college GPA. Multiple regression techniques are also used by stockbrokers to predict the direction and amount of change in the price of a particular stock. As you can imagine, knowledge of an accurate set of predictor variables in this case could be quite valuable.

INFERENTIAL STATISTICS

Inferential statistics are used to make inferences from data, to draw conclusions, and to test hypotheses. Two of the basic concepts in inferential statistics are *estimation* and *hypothesis testing*.

ESTIMATION

One use of inferential statistics is to estimate the actual value of some population characteristic. Suppose, for example, we wanted to know how knowledgeable, on average, American adults are about current events. We could construct a test of current events with carefully worded questions covering as many areas of current news as possible. Since we are interested in the population of all adult Americans, we could test every American age 18 and older (the entire population) and compute a mean score on our test. But it would be handy to have a short-cut method that did not require testing the entire population.

In order to estimate the mean and standard deviation of a variable in a population, we take a *sample* of the population and measure the variable in each member of the sample. We then compute the statistics on the sample scores and use these statistics to estimate what the mean and standard deviation would be if we could test every member of the population. For example, we might sample 200 American adults and use their scores on our current events test to estimate what the whole population of adults is like. Public opinion polls and the TV rating services use this sampling approach and estimation procedure.

It is important that the sample be *representative* of the population, which is usually done by making the sample a random selection from all possible members of the population. A **random sample** is one in which everyone in the specified population has the same chance of being in the sample. For example, it would not be a fair sample for estimating Americans' knowledge of current events if we measured only white female citizens of La Mirada, California. The second factor in sampling is sample size. Generally, the larger the sample, the more accurate the estimates. If you randomly chose one person from the phone book, scheduled him or her for our test of current events, got a score, and then estimated that this score was the mean for all American adults, you would almost certainly be off the mark. A sample larger than a single person is needed. But how many should there be in the sample? The amazing thing about sampling is that the size of the sample necessary to get a fairly accurate idea of the population is much smaller than you might guess. A sample of 200 American adults out of 150 million, if properly drawn, should provide a very accurate estimate of the entire population. There are ways of estimating how big a sample you need for a given level of accuracy. Of course, if the sample is not properly drawn and is not representative, then increasing the sample size will not improve the accuracy of estimation.

HYPOTHESIS TESTING

When we set out to do an experiment in psychology, we always begin with a hypothesis. For our brief discussion, we use the example of a psychologist who wants to know if breathing pure oxygen after strenuous exertion facilitates recovery. The psychologist carefully devises a test of recovery time that gives a consistent score (i.e., it is a reliable measure) and accurately predicts recovery in real life situations (i.e., it is a valid measure). The working hypothesis in the study is that athletes who breathe pure oxygen after exercise will recover more quickly than athletes who breathe normal air. The psychologist gets 30 athletes to volunteer for the experiment and randomly assigns them to one of two groups, 15 per group. The random assignment is designed to create two groups that are approximately equal in average recovery time at the start of the experiment. All of the subjects are then instructed to run 800 meters as quickly as they can. Immediately following each subject's run they are seated and fitted with a breathing mask that delivers either pure oxygen or normal air. Heart rate and respiration rates are measured to determine recovery time.

After all of the subjects are tested the psychologist finds that the mean recovery time for the athletes breathing pure oxygen was 118 seconds and the mean recovery time for athletes breathing normal air was 126 seconds. Can the psychologist conclude that breathing pure oxygen facilitates recovery? Think about your answer before reading on.

If the differences between the recovery times for the two groups was quite large (118 vs. 156 seconds) our psychologist could be confident that breathing pure oxygen does in fact facilitate recovery. Likewise, if the difference in recovery times was very small (118 vs. 119 seconds) we would be fairly confident that breathing pure oxygen had no effect. But what do we conclude about results that fall between these extremes?

There has to be an objective way to decide whether or not the psychologist's hypothesis can be accepted. We cannot leave it up to intuition. Here we can turn to inferential statistics. There are many different kinds of inferential statistics; in this case a *t*-test for comparing two sample means is appropriate.

We want to decide whether the difference between 118 (the mean recovery time for athletes breathing pure oxygen) and 126 seconds (the mean recovery time for the athletes breathing normal air) is a real difference or whether it can be attributed to chance or measurement error. In other words, is it a *statistically significant difference?* A difference is said to be statistically significant if it is very unlikely that it would happen by chance alone. The difference in mean recovery times for the two groups is 8 seconds ($126 - 118 = 8$).

For a moment, let's assume that oxygen has no effect on recovery times. This assumption is called the *null hypothesis.* Note that the null hypothesis predicts no difference, whereas our working hypothesis (that breathing pure oxygen facilitates recovery) does predict a difference. Specifically, the null hypothesis predicts that the variable being manipulated (the independent variable) will have no effect on the behavior being measured (the dependent variable). It is the null hypothesis that is actually tested with inferential statistics. We then draw conclusions about our working hypothesis on the basis of our findings regarding the null hypothesis.

What we need to know is, *if the null hypothesis is true* (that breathing pure oxygen does not effect recovery time), what is the probability that the two samples will differ by eight seconds? If oxygen does not facilitate recovery, then any difference we find between our two groups will be just a chance difference. After all, we would not expect two random groups of 15 people to have exactly the same recovery times. Sample means will differ, and every once in a while there will be a difference of eight seconds by chance alone, with no help from oxygen. The question is, how often will we get a difference this large? Or what is the probability of this difference occurring by chance alone?

In order to answer this question, we must know not only the mean values, but also the standard deviations in the two samples. We have to know how much variability between people there is in recovery times. Look at the three panels in Figure A.9. Each panel shows two frequency distributions, one for the oxygen group and one for the normal air group. Note that in each panel, the mean of the oxygen group is 118 and the mean of the normal air group is 126, but the three panels display quite different pictures in terms of variability in recovery times among people within each group. In the top panel, the variability within each group is very small (all of the recovery times are close to their respective means). In this case it looks as though the eight-second difference is a significant one.

In the middle panel, there is a great deal of variability in recovery times between people within each group. There is a lot of overlap in the two distributions. Many of the subjects breathing normal air recovered more quickly than the mean for the oxygen group. In fact, there is so much overlap in the two distributions that we would probably question whether the difference between 118 and 126 (the two means), which is very small compared to the variability, is just a chance difference. The two distributions look almost identical.

Situations like those depicted in the top panel are very rare indeed. Unfortunately, the middle panel is a more common outcome of an experiment—the means are so close together and there is so much overlap of scores that the groups appear to be indistinguishable on the dependent variable. The bottom panel represents the most common outcome of all. Here, the conclusion is less

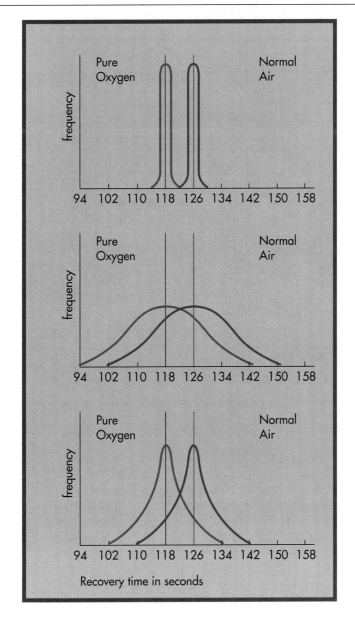

FIGURE A.9

Comparisons of Three Outcomes in Variability

Each figure shows the same means (118 vs. 126) with different amounts of variability.

clear. The two distributions overlap somewhat, much more than in the top panel, but much less than in the middle panel. There is a moderate amount of variability among subjects within each group. Can we conclude whether the 118-to-126–second mean difference is a real one? Stated differently, is there a statistically significant difference between the means?

The *t*-test is designed to answer this question. The *t*-test is a ratio, the ratio of mean difference to an error term. A primary factor in the error term is the variability of scores within each group. In the top panel the difference is eight seconds, but the variability of scores within each group is very small. Therefore, the error term will be small. So if we divide the mean difference by this very small error term, we shall get a large number for the *t* ratio, and we then declare the difference to be significant. In the middle panel, the same eight-second difference will be divided by a very large error term, giving us a very small *t* ratio. We declare the difference insignificant. In the bottom panel, we have the borderline case. We divide the mean difference by a moderate-sized error term, and the *t* value obtained will be moderately large. What do we conclude? Fortunately for

TABLE A.9 *Type I and Type II Errors in Decisions Based on Experimental Data*

EXPERIMENTAL HYPOTHESES

WORKING HYPOTHESIS	NULL HYPOTHESIS
Oxygen Facilitates Recovery	Oxygen Does Not Facilitate Recovery

DECISION ERRORS

TYPE I ERROR: REJECTING THE NULL HYPOTHESIS WHEN IT IS TRUE.

Example: Claiming oxygen facilitates recovery when in fact *oxygen does not facilitate recovery.*

TYPE II ERROR: ACCEPTING THE NULL HYPOTHESIS WHEN IT IS FALSE.

Example: Concluding that oxygen does not facilitate recovery when in fact *oxygen facilitates recovery.*

us, statisticians have prepared tables of the probability of various values of *t* occurring by chance. We compute the *t* ratio and then look it up in the statistical tables to find the chance probability of a *t* as large as the one we found. If the table tells us that the observed *t* ratio is unlikely to happen by chance, we conclude that what we have is not a chance effect but a real difference. Alternatively, most computer solutions to *t*-tests give the exact probability for each computed value of *t*. By convention, we use a cutoff probability of .05. That is, if the probability of obtaining a given *t* value is less than or equal to .05 we conclude that there is a significant difference between the two groups.

The null hypothesis says, "There is no difference in recovery times between groups breathing pure oxygen and those breathing normal air." If we obtain a significant *t* ratio, we conclude that the null hypothesis is wrong. Statistical inference is basically a procedure for drawing conclusions about the null hypothesis. Of course, our inference about the null hypothesis has implications for our working hypothesis. If we reject the null hypothesis and conclude that the observed difference between the groups is significant, then we can further conclude that breathing pure oxygen does facilitate recovery because the athletes in our study who used pure oxygen recovered more quickly than athletes who did not breathe pure oxygen.

We do not discuss the details of actually calculating a *t* ratio. You can find that information in any elementary statistics book. Simply remember that when an experiment is done, the results will usually indicate some differences between the conditions in the study. The *t*-test, as well as many other types of inferential statistics, are used to help the experimenter decide whether the differences are large enough, relative to the variability, to allow rejection of the null hypothesis and support for the working hypothesis.

It is important to realize that statistical decisions are not always perfect; sometimes we make an incorrect decision on the basis of the data even though we have done everything correctly. There is always the chance, for example, that the samples are not truly representative of the populations from which they were drawn. There are two types of errors that can occur when we draw conclusions from experimental data, and these are depicted in Table A.9. A *Type I error* is made when we conclude that the independent variable has an effect on the dependent variable, when the truth of the matter is that it has no effect. A *Type II error* is made when we conclude that the independent variable has no effect on the dependent variable when, in fact, it does. Each type of error has a certain probability of occurring in any given experiment. By tradition, we require strong evidence for an effect of the independent variable on the dependent variable before we accept that such an effect exists. What this means is that we try to minimize the level of Type I error. However, you should note that Type I error and Type II error have an inverse relationship to one another—as one increases, the other decreases. Therefore, minimizing Type I errors will normally result in an increase in Type II errors. The task for the researcher is to balance these two types of errors, which requires a thorough understanding of research design and statistical procedures.

ADVANCED STATISTICAL TECHNIQUES

ANALYSIS OF VARIANCE

The *t*-test is used when testing the difference between the means of two groups. But experiments may have more than two groups, and so the *t*-test is not used in such cases. Instead, a statistical procedure called **analysis of variance** is used. Analysis of variance is conceptually very similar to the *t*-test. The size of the mean difference between groups is compared to an error term which is, in part, a function of the variability within each group. In fact, the analysis of variance procedure and the *t*-test will lead to the same decision in the special case where there are just two groups. The test in analysis of variance is known as the *F*-test, named after the famous English statistician R.A. Fisher. Analysis of variance allows the experimenter to make inferences or draw conclusions about the differences among a set of means. It is a very common statistical procedure and you are likely to encounter the *F*-test if you read psychology journals.

FACTOR ANALYSIS

Factor analysis is a highly sophisticated correlational procedure that is used to identify the basic factors underlying a psychological phenomenon. The technique boils down to finding clusters of tests that correlate with one another. Suppose we administer the following six tests to 100 college students: (1) vocabulary, (2) ability to shoot baskets, (3) ability to write an essay on philosophy, (4) speed at running the 100-yard dash, (5) ability to understand statistics, and (6) speed at swimming 100 meters. Each person takes all six tests, and then we intercorrelate the tests. We correlate test 1 with 2, 1 with 3, 1 with 4, and so on. Suppose we find that tests 1, 3, and 5 correlate highly with one another and that 2, 4, and 6 correlate highly with one another, but that 1, 3, and 5 show little or no correlation with 2, 4, and 6. Why would this result be the case? Look at the tests; tests 1, 3, and 5 all involve thinking or knowledge—they all require "academic ability." On the other hand, tests 2, 4, and 6 all require "physical ability." So probably 1, 3, and 5 all are measuring something in common, which we might call Factor A. Would you guess that Factor A has something to do with intelligence? Tests 2, 4, and 6 also seem to be measuring something in common. We will call it Factor B. Because tests 1, 3, and 5 do not correlate with tests 2, 4, and 6, we conclude that Factor A, which we now have decided to call *intelligence*, is not the same thing as Factor B, which we might label *athletic ability*.

In short, we have isolated two factors that are involved in performance on our six tests; one we call intelligence, and the other we call athletic ability. Factor analysis is basically a correlational technique that allows us to separate performance on a large number of tests into factors, by isolating clusters of tests (even when the clustering is not as obvious as it is in the foregoing example). Correlations between tests are high within a cluster but low among clusters. We assume that the clusters then "represent" and measure psychological factors.

This technique has been used extensively in two areas of psychology, intelligence testing and personality assessment (see Chapters 13 and 14). Intelligence consists of many factors, as does personality. With factor analysis we can identify these factors and hope to learn more about intelligence and personality.

GLOSSARY

Abnormal behavior Behavior that is atypical, maladaptive, socially unacceptable, and produces emotional discomfort.

Absolute threshold Minimum physical intensity of a stimulus that can be perceived by an observer 50 percent of the time.

Accommodation In vision, the focusing process in which the lens adjusts its shape, depending on the distance between the eye and the object viewed, in order to project a clear image consistently onto the retina. In Piaget's theory, the process of adjusting existing knowledge so that new information can fit more readily.

Accumulating damages theory The theory that explains aging as a consequence of the accumulated insults and damages that result from an organism's continued use of its body. Also known as wear-and-tear theory.

Achievement need See *Need for achievement.*

Achievement test Test designed to measure an individual's learning (as opposed to the ability to learn new information).

Acquaintance rape Rape committed by a person who is known to the victim.

Acquired immunodeficiency syndrome (AIDS) A disease, or set of diseases, that appear to result from immunodeficiency. Immunodeficiency may result from drug use, blood transfusions, other diseases, or perhaps the human immunodeficiency virus (HIV).

Acquisition In classical conditioning, the process of learning to associate a conditioned stimulus with an unconditioned stimulus. In operant conditioning, the process of learning to associate responses with a reinforcer or punisher.

Acronym Meaningful arrangement of letters that provides a cue for recalling information; a mnemonic device.

Acrostics Sentences whose first letters serve as cues for recalling specific information; a mnemonic device.

Action potential Electrical signal that flows along the surface of the axon to the terminal buttons, initiating the release of neurotransmitters.

Active listening Technique in which person-centered therapists indicate their acceptance and understanding of what clients say.

Activity theory Theory that the more involved and active older people remain, the more happy and fulfilled they will be.

Adaptation In perception, the decrease in the response of sensory receptors to stimuli when exposed to continual, unchanging stimulation.

Additive color mixing Color mixing that occurs when lights of different wavelengths simultaneously stimulate the retina, so that color perception depends on the adding or combining of these wavelengths. See *Subtractive color mixing.*

Adolescent growth spurt Period of accelerated growth that usually occurs within about two years after the onset of puberty.

Adrenal glands Glands within the endocrine system, located just above the kidneys, that influence emotional state, energy levels, and responses to stress.

Aerial perspective See *Atmospheric perspective.*

Afferent neuron See *Sensory neuron.*

Age regression A phenomenon believed to be associated with hypnosis, in which the hypnotized subject appears to move back in time to reenact events that occurred in earlier years. Age regression seems to be role playing of the subject's current conception of his or her past.

Agoraphobia An anxiety disorder characterized by an intense fear of being in places or situations from which escape might be difficult or in which help might not be available, such as stores, theaters, and trains. Agoraphobia often accompanies panic disorder.

Alcohol Depressant drug that acts to impair motor coordination, reaction time, thinking, and judgment.

Algorithm A problem-solving strategy that involves a systematic exploration of every possible solution; computers and people may use algorithms to find the correct answer.

All-or-none law An action potential will be passed through a neuron's axon as long as the sum of graded potentials reaches a threshold. The strength of an action potential does not vary according to the degree of stimulation.

Altered state of consciousness A non-natural state of consciousness resulting from deliberate efforts to change one's state of consciousness through drugs, meditation, or hypnosis.

Alternate-forms reliability Method of assessing test reliability in which subjects take two different forms of a test that are very similar in content and level of difficulty.

Alzheimer's disease An incurable disease that destroys neural tissue resulting in an impaired capacity to remember, think, relate to others, and care for oneself.

American Psychological Association (APA) The major professional organization of psychologists in the United States.

American Psychological Society (APS) Professional group of academic and research psychologists founded in 1988 as a result of tensions between science and applications-oriented members of APA.

Amniocentesis Method of prenatal screening for fetal abnormalities in which a small sample of amniotic fluid is extracted from the uterus for chromosome analysis.

Amphetamines A group of powerful stimulants, including Benzedrine, Dexedrine, and Methedrine, that dramatically increase alertness and promote feelings of euphoria.

Amygdala A small limbic system structure located next to the hippocampus in the brain that plays an important role in the expression of anger, rage, fear, and aggressive behavior.

Anal stage In Freud's theory of psychosexual development, the period between about 12 months and three years of age, during which the erogenous zone shifts from the mouth to the anal area.

Anandamide A naturally occurring substance that binds to THC receptors in the brain. Marijuana contains THC which also binds to these receptors.

Androgen insensitivity syndrome (AIS) Condition in which the body cells of a chromosomally normal (XY) male fetus are insensitive to the action of androgens, with the result that internal reproductive structures do not develop, external genitals fail to differentiate into a penis and scrotum, and testes do not descend.

Androgens Male sex hormones, the most common of which is testosterone.

Anorexia nervosa Eating disorder characterized by prolonged refusal to eat adequate amounts of food. This condition is most common among young females.

Anterograde amnesia Memory loss for information processed after an individual experiences brain trauma caused by injury or chronic alcoholism.

Antiandrogens Drugs that have the effect of drastically reducing the amount of testosterone circulating in the bloodstream.

Antianxiety drugs Drugs used to reduce symptoms of anxiety and tension in disorders that are not severe enough to warrant hospitalization. Sometimes called minor tranquilizers.

Antidepressant drugs Drugs used to treat major depressive disorder.

Antimanic drugs Drugs used to control the manic symptoms of bipolar disorder.

Antisocial personality disorder Personality disorder characterized by disregard for rights of others, lack of remorse or guilt for antisocial acts, irresponsibility in job or marital roles, failure to learn

from experience, and a profound poverty of deep and lasting emotions.

Anxiety Free-floating fear or apprehension which may occur with or without an easily identifiable source.

Anxiety disorder Any of a number of disorders that produce pervasive feelings of anxiety.

Aptitude test Test designed to predict an individual's ability to learn new information or skills.

Archetypes Powerful, emotionally charged universal images or concepts in Carl Jung's theory of the collective unconscious. *See also Collective unconscious.*

Army Alpha and Beta tests Group IQ tests developed early in this century by the American Psychological Association to assist the army in making job assignments for soldiers.

Arousal A physiological state in which an individual is able to process information effectively and to engage in motivated behavior.

Artificial insemination Procedure in which semen from a male donor is mechanically introduced into a female's vagina or uterus to fertilize an egg.

Artificial intelligence (AI) Field of specialization in which researchers develop computer models to simulate human cognitive processes and to solve problems.

Assessment centers Centers that conduct interviews and tests as well as simulate work situations in order to determine how well suited job candidates are for managerial or executive-level positions.

Assimilation In Piaget's theory, the process by which individuals interpret new information in accordance with existing knowledge or schemas.

Association cortex The largest portion of the cerebral cortex (about 75 percent), involved in integrating sensory and motor messages as well as processing higher functions such as thinking, interpreting, and remembering.

Associative learning Learning by making a connection or association between two events, through either classical conditioning or operant conditioning.

Atmospheric perspective Monocular distance cue based on the fact that distant objects tend to appear more fuzzy and less clear than those close to the viewer due to dust and haze. Also known as aerial perspective.

Attachment Intense emotional tie between two individuals, such as an infant

and a parent. *See also Indiscriminant attachment and Specific attachment.*

Attention Psychological selection mechanism that determines which stimuli an organism responds to or perceives.

Attitude Any learned, relatively enduring predisposition to respond in consistently favorable or unfavorable ways to certain people, groups, ideas, or situations.

Attribution theory Theory that we attempt to make sense out of other people's behavior by attributing it to either dispositional (internal) causes or external (situational) causes.

Auditory cortex Region of the temporal lobe located just below the lateral fissure that is involved in responding to auditory signals, particularly the sound of human speech.

Auditory localization Ability to locate the origins of sounds by differences from ear to ear in variables such as intensity and the time the sound arrives at each ear.

Auditory memory *See Echoic memory.*

Authoritarian Style of parenting in which parents rely on strictly enforced rules, leaving little room for children to discuss alternatives.

Authoritarian personality Personality characterized by intolerance, emotional coldness, rigidity, submission to higher authority, stereotyped thinking, and identification with power.

Authoritative Style of parenting in which parents enforce clear rules and standards but also show respect for children's opinions.

Autonomic nervous system Division of the peripheral nervous system that transmits messages between the central nervous system and the endocrine system as well as the smooth muscles of the heart, lungs, stomach, and other internal organs that operate without intentional control.

Availability heuristic Approach to decision making based on information assessed from memory. It assumes that the probability of an event is related to how frequently it occurred in the past, and that events occurring more frequently are easier to remember.

Aversive conditioning A behavior therapy approach which utilizes aversive stimuli to decrease the occurrence of a specific response. *See Punishment.*

Avoidance conditioning In operant conditioning, the learning of a response to a discriminative stimulus that allows an organism to avoid exposure to an aversive stimulus.

Awareness One's subjective sense of oneself, one's actions, and one's environment.

Axon Extension of a neuron that transmits an impulse from the cell body to the terminal buttons on the tip of the axon.

Backward conditioning In classical conditioning, presenting the unconditioned stimulus prior to the conditioned stimulus. Backwards conditioning results in little or no conditioning.

Balance theory Theory that people are inclined to achieve consistency in their attitudes by balancing their beliefs and feelings about a particular issue, object, event, or situation against their attitudes about other people.

Basal ganglia Neural structures involved in the initiation of motor movement and emotion. Includes the caudate nucleus, putamen, and the substantia nigra.

Basic anxiety In Karen Horney's neo-Freudian theory, the insecurity that results when children perceive their parents as indifferent, harsh, disparaging, or erratic in their responsiveness. *See also Basic hostility.*

Basic hostility In Karen Horney's neo-Freudian theory, a deep resentment associated with basic anxiety which motivates one of three ineffectual patterns of social interaction: moving against others, moving away from others, or moving toward others. *See also Basic anxiety.*

Basic level In a concept hierarchy, the classification that people naturally use when they think about an object (for instance, a yellow-throated warbler is simply a bird).

Basilar membrane Membrane in the cochlea of the inner ear that vibrates in response to pressure waves, causing auditory hair cells on the adjoining organ of Corti to release neurotransmitters that activate neurons of the auditory nerve.

Behavior therapy Therapy based on the assumption that maladaptive behavior has been learned and can therefore be unlearned.

Behavioral geography Application of cognitive map theory based on people's perceptions or internal representations of relationships between geographical locations.

Behavioral medicine Study of how behavior patterns (smoking, drinking, lack of exercise, etc.) and emotions like stress and anxiety can contribute to physical diseases.

Behavioral observation Behavior assessment method that involves observing individuals' behavior as they interact with the environment.

Behavioral toxicology Study of how environmental toxins affect behavior.

Behaviorism Scientific approach to the study of behavior that emphasizes the relationship between environmental events and an organism's behavior.

Belief-bias effect Tendency to accept conclusions that conform to one's beliefs (and reject conclusions that do not conform) regardless of how logical these conclusions are.

Binocular cues Visual cues for depth or distance, such as binocular disparity and convergence, that depend on both eyes working together.

Binocular disparity The difference in the retinal image of an object as seen from each eye, due to the difference in viewing angles, that provides an important binocular cue for depth. Also known as retinal disparity.

Biofeedback Technique providing individuals with information (feedback) about their bodily processes that they can use to modify those processes.

Biological psychology Branch of neuroscience that focuses on the relationship between behavior and physiological events within the brain and the rest of the nervous system. Also known as physiological psychology.

Biologically-based motives Motives such as hunger and thirst that are rooted primarily in body tissue needs; sometimes referred to as drives.

Bipolar (manic-depressive) disorder Mood disorder characterized by intermittent episodes of both depression and mania (highly energized behavior).

Body senses Term used to describe the two interrelated sensory systems of kinesthesis and equilibrium.

Brain stimulation Technique for studying the brain that involves stimulating precise regions with a weak electric current.

Brightness Intensity of light, measured by the number of photons, or particles of electromagnetic radiation, emitted by a light source.

Brightness constancy An element of perceptual constancy: We perceive objects that we see at night or in poor lighting to be the same brightness as they appear during the day.

Broca's area Region of the left frontal lobe that is the primary brain center for controlling speech.

Bulimia Eating disorder characterized by periodic episodes of binge eating followed by deliberate purging using either vomiting or laxatives.

Caffeine Stimulant found in coffee, tea, and chocolate that acts to increase arousal, heart rate, and blood pressure.

California Psychological Inventory Global personality assessment test designed specifically for use with normal populations.

Cannon-Bard theory Theory that emotions occur simultaneously with physiological changes, rather than deriving from body changes as the James-Lange theory suggests.

Cardinal trait In Gordon Allport's trait theory of personality, a powerful, dominating behavioral predisposition that is an organizing principle in a small number of people's lives. *See also Central trait and Secondary trait.*

Case study Method of research that involves in-depth study of one or more subjects who are examined individually using direct observation, testing, experimentation, and other methods.

Catatonic schizophrenia Subtype of schizophrenia characterized by extreme psychomotor disturbances, which may range from stuporous immobility to wild excitement and agitation.

Cell body The largest part of a neuron, containing the nucleus as well as structures that handle metabolic functions.

Central nervous system (CNS) The part of the nervous system that consists of the brain and the spinal cord.

Central trait In Gordon Allport's trait theory of personality, a major characteristic such as honesty or sensitivity. *See also Cardinal trait and Secondary trait.*

Centration Inability to take into account more than one perceptual factor at a time. In Piaget's theory of cognitive development, centration is characteristic of the preoperational stage of development.

Cephalocaudal Pattern of physical and motor development that is normal among humans, in which the head and upper portion of the body develop first and most rapidly.

Cerebellum Brain structure located beneath the overhanging back part of the cerebral hemispheres which functions to coordinate and regulate motor movements.

Cerebral cortex Thin outer layer of the brain's cerebrum (sometimes called the gray matter) that is responsible for movement, perception, thinking, and memory.

Cerebral hemispheres The two sides (right and left) of the cerebrum.

Cerebrum The largest part of the brain, consisting of two cerebral hemispheres.

Chorionic villi sampling (CVS) Method of prenatal screening for fetal abnormalities in which threadlike protrusions on the membrane surrounding the fetus are extracted and cultured for chromosome analysis.

Chunk Meaningful unit of short-term memory. *See also Chunking.*

Chunking Process of grouping items into longer meaningful units to make them easier to remember.

Classical conditioning Learning that takes place when a neutral stimulus (the CS) is paired with a stimulus (UCS) that already produces a response (UCR). After conditioning, the organism responds to the neutral stimulus (CS) in some way. The response to the CS is called a conditioned response (CR).

Climacteric Physiological changes, including menopause, that occur during a woman's transition from fertility to infertility.

Clinical psychology Area of specialization involved in the diagnosis and treatment of behavioral problems.

Closure Perceptual organizing principle that we tend to perceive incomplete figures as complete.

Clustering Mnemonic device involving grouping items into categories.

Cocaine Powerful central nervous system stimulant derived from the leaves of the coca shrub.

Cochlea Coiled, fluid-filled chamber in the inner ear with two flexible surfaces: the oval window and the round window.

Coefficient of correlation Statistic used to describe the degree of relationship between two or more variables. Positive correlations indicate that variables vary together in the same direction; negative correlations indicate the opposite.

Cognitive abilities test (CAT) Group intelligence test widely used in many school systems.

Cognitive dissonance theory Theory that people experience psychological discomfort or dissonance whenever two related cognitions or behaviors are in conflict.

Cognitive learning Learning that involves processes such as thinking and reasoning.

Cognitive learning theory Theoretical perspective that attempts to study the role of thinking and memory processes in learning.

Cognitive map Internal representations of the relationship between events or spatial elements.

Cognitive psychology Approach to psychology focusing on the ways in which organisms process information. Investigates processes such as thinking, memory, language, problem solving, and creativity.

Cognitive restructuring therapy Cognitive therapy aimed at restructuring irrational thinking patterns such as the tendency to use negative self-labels.

Cognitive therapies Approaches to therapy that are based on the premise that most behavioral disorders result from distortions in cognitions or thoughts.

Cohabitation Living together in a sexual relationship without being married.

Collective unconscious In Carl Jung's theory, a kind of universal memory bank that contains all the ancestral memories, images, symbols, and ideas that humans have accumulated throughout their evolvement. *See also Archetypes and Personal unconscious.*

Color constancy An element of perceptual constancy: We perceive objects that we see in the dark to be the same color as they appear during the day even though their retinal images change.

Compensatory model Decision-making model such as the additive model and the utility-probability model in which the desirable potential outcomes of alternative choices are weighed against undesirable potential outcomes. *Compare with Noncompensatory model.*

Complex psychosocial motives Motives that demonstrate little or no relationship to biological needs, but are determined by learning.

Compliance Form of social influence in which people alter their behavior in response to direct requests from others, which usually involve a degree of coercion.

Computerized axial tomography (CAT) A procedure used to locate brain abnormalities that involves rotating an X-ray scanner around the skull to produce an accurate image of a living brain.

Concepts Cognitive categories for grouping events, objects, or processes.

Concordance Degree to which twins share a trait. Expressed as a correlation coefficient.

Concrete operations stage Third stage of cognitive development in Piaget's theory (ages seven through 12), during which children begin to use logical mental operations or rules, mastering the concept of conservation.

Concurrent validity Type of criterion-related validity that involves comparing test performance to other criteria that are currently available. *See also Predictive validity.*

Conditioned reinforcer A stimulus that takes on reinforcing properties after being associated with a primary reinforcer. *See Secondary reinforcer.*

Conditioned response (CR) In classical conditioning, a learned response to a stimulus.

Conditioned stimulus (CS) In classical conditioning, a stimulus that elicits a response only after being associated with an unconditioned stimulus.

Conduction hearing loss Hearing loss caused by the failure of the outer and middle ear to conduct sound energy to the inner ear's receptors, sometimes due to infection or to buildup of ear wax.

Cones Photoreceptor cells distributed across the inner layer of the retina that play an important role in the perception of color.

Confirmation bias In problem solving, the tendency to seek out evidence that confirms a hypothesis and to overlook contradictory evidence.

Conformity Tendency to change or modify behaviors so that they are consistent with those of other people.

Consciousness State of awareness or alertness to processes that are going on inside or outside one's own body.

Conservation The understanding that changing the form of an object does not necessarily change its essential character. Conservation is a key achievement in Piaget's theory of cognitive development. *See also Concrete operations stage.*

Consolidation Process by which information is transferred from short-term electrical activation of neuronal circuits to a longer-term memory coded by physical cell changes in the brain.

Continuous reinforcement schedule In operant conditioning, the presentation of a reinforcer for each occurrence of a specific behavior.

Control group In experimental psychology, a group of subjects who experience all the same conditions as subjects in the experimental group except for the key factor (independent variable) the researcher is evaluating.

Controlled drinking Technique for overcoming alcoholism through teaching skills that allow a person to drink in moderation.

Conventional morality Second level in Lawrence Kohlberg's theory of moral development, consisting of stages 3 and 4, in which the motivating force for moral behavior is the desire either to help others or to gain approval.

Convergence Binocular distance cue based on the fact that the two eyes must converge or rotate toward the inside to perceive objects closer than about 25 feet. The closer the object, the more rotation is necessary and the more muscle tension created.

Convergent thinking Thinking in which an individual responds to information presented in a problem by eliminating possibilities and narrowing his or her responses down to the single best solution.

Conversion disorder Somatoform disorder that is manifested as a sensory or motor system disorder for which there is no known organic cause.

Coronary heart disease (CHD) Any illness that causes a narrowing of the coronary arteries.

Corpus callosum Broad band of nerve fibers that connects the left and right hemispheres of the cerebral cortex.

Correlation coefficient *See Coefficient of correlation.*

Correlational method Research method that uses statistical techniques to determine the degree of relationship between variables.

Correspondent inference theory Theory that the attributions we make about other people's behavior are influenced by a variety of conditions, such as the social desirability of that behavior or whether the behavior results from free choice.

Counseling psychology Area of specialization involved in the diagnosis and treatment of problems of adjustment. Counseling psychologists tend to focus on less serious problems than clinical psychologists; they often work in settings such as schools.

Couple therapy Therapy in which partners meet together with a therapist.

Covariation principle Theory that our attributions about people's behavior are influenced by the situations in which the behavior occurs, the persons involved, and the stimuli or objects toward which the behavior is directed.

Crack Street name for a processed form of cocaine that takes effect more rapidly and is available at a cheaper price than powdered cocaine.

Creativity Ability to produce outcomes that are novel as well as useful or valuable.

Credibility Quality of trustworthiness and perceived expertise that increases the likelihood a communicator will persuade an individual to change his or her attitude.

Criterion-keyed test Assessment test in which each test item is referenced to one of the original criterion groups that were used in developing the test.

Criterion-related validity Method of assessing test validity that involves comparing peoples' test scores with their scores on other measures already known to be good indicators of the skill or trait being assessed.

Critical periods Periods in the developmental sequence during which an organism must experience certain kinds of social or sensory experiences in order for normal development to take place.

Cross-sectional design Research design in which groups of subjects of different ages are assessed and compared at one point in time, so that conclusions may be drawn about behavior differences which may be related to age differences.

Cross-sequential design Research design which combines elements of the cross-sectional and longitudinal designs. Subjects are observed more than once over a period of time.

Crowding Psychological response to a lack of space, characterized by subjective feelings of overstimulation, distress, and discomfort.

Crystallized intelligence Intelligence that results from accumulated knowledge, including knowledge of how to reason, language skills, and understanding of technology. *See also Fluid intelligence.*

Cultural mores Established customs or beliefs in a particular culture.

Cumulative curve A measure of the strength of an operant response; the more frequently an operant response takes place, the steeper the curve.

Dark adaptation Process by which an organism's vision gradually becomes more sensitive to minimal levels of light due to a chemical change in the rods and cones of the retina.

Decentration Ability to evaluate two or more physical dimensions simultaneously. *See also Centration.*

Declarative memory Recall of specific facts, such as information read in a book. *See also Procedural memory, Episodic memory, and Semantic memory.*

Deductive reasoning Reasoning that begins with a general premise which is believed to be true, then draws conclusions about specific instances based on this premise. *See also Inductive reasoning.*

Defense mechanism In Freud's psychoanalytic theory, an unconscious maneuver that shields the ego from anxiety by denying or distorting reality.

Delayed conditioning In classical conditioning, learning that takes place when the conditioned stimulus is presented just before the unconditioned stimulus is presented and continues until the organism begins responding to the unconditioned stimulus.

Delusion An exaggerated and rigidly held belief that has little or no basis in fact.

Dendrite Branchlike extensions from a neuron with the specialized function of receiving messages from surrounding neurons.

Dependent variable In experimental research, the behavior that results from manipulation of an independent variable.

Depressant drugs Psychoactive drugs, including opiates, sedatives, and alcohol, that have the effect of slowing down or depressing central nervous system activity.

Descriptive statistics Mathematical and graphical methods for reducing data to a form that can be readily understood.

Developmental psychology Field of specialization in psychology concerned with factors that influence development and shape behavior throughout the life cycle, from conception through old age.

Dialectic operations Fifth stage of cognitive development (after Piaget's fourth stage of formal operations) proposed by Klaus Riegel, in which an individual realizes and accepts that conflict and contradiction are natural consequences of living.

Difference threshold The minimum difference in intensity that we can distinguish between two stimuli 50 percent of the time. Also known as the just noticeable difference (JND).

Diffusion of responsibility Tendency for an individual to feel a diminished sense of responsibility to assist in an emergency when other bystanders are present.

Discrimination In classical and operant conditioning, the process by which responses are restricted to specific stimuli. In social psychology, the behavioral consequence of prejudice in which one group is treated differently from another group.

Discriminative stimulus In operant conditioning, a stimulus that controls a response by signaling the availability of reinforcement.

Disengagement theory Theory that individuals are more likely to experience happiness in older age if they cut back on the stresses of active life, taking time to relax instead.

Disorganized schizophrenia Subtype of schizophrenia characterized by marked disorganization and regression in thinking and behavioral patterns, accompanied by sudden mood swings and often hallucinations. Also known as hebephrenic schizophrenia.

Displacement Defense mechanism in which a person diverts his or her impulse-driven behavior from a primary target to secondary targets that will arouse less anxiety.

Dissociative disorders Group of disorders, including psychogenic amnesia, psychogenic fugue, and multiple personality, in which the thoughts and feelings that generate anxiety are separated or dissociated from conscious awareness.

Divergent thinking Thinking in which an individual comes up with unusual but appropriate responses to questions, often associated with creativity.

Dizygotic twins *See Fraternal twins.*

DNA (deoxyribonucleic acid) Chemical substance whose molecules, arranged in varying patterns, are the building blocks of genes.

Dominant gene Gene that prevails when paired with a recessive gene, so that it is always expressed in the phenotype.

Door-in-the-face technique Method for encouraging compliance in which an unreasonable request is followed by a more minor, reasonable request (which is the requester's goal in the first place).

Dopamine A neurotransmitter substance released at terminal buttons of dopaminergic neurons in the brain. Dopamine is believed to be involved in movement and emotion. Abnormal levels of dopamine contribute to Parkinson's disease and schizophrenia.

Down syndrome Chromosomal disorder characterized by marked mental retardation as well as distinctive physical traits including short stature, a flattened skull and nose, and an extra fold of skin over the eyelid.

Dream analysis Psychoanalytic technique involving the interpretation of dreams to learn about hidden aspects of personality.

Drive Term commonly used to describe motives that are based on tissue needs, such as hunger and thirst.

Dual-code model of memory Theory that memories may be stored either in sensory codes or in verbal codes.

Echoic memory Auditory sensory memory; fleeting impressions of what we hear. Also known as auditory memory.

Echolalia Speech disturbance characteristic of some forms of schizophrenia in which people repeat virtually every statement they hear uttered.

Educational psychology Field of specialization in psychology concerned with the study and application of learning and teaching methods, focusing on areas such as improving educational curricula and training teachers.

Efferent neuron *See Motor neuron.*

Ego In Freud's psychoanalytic theory, the component of personality that acts as an intermediary between the instinctual demands of the id and the reality of the real world. *See also Id, Superego, and Reality principle.*

Eidetic imagery Also known as photographic memory, the very rare ability to retain large amounts of visual material with great accuracy for several minutes.

Elaborative rehearsal System for remembering that involves using mnemonic devices; it is more effective than maintenance rehearsal.

Electrical recording Technique for studying the brain in which tiny wires implanted in the brain are used to record neural electrical activity.

Electroconvulsive therapy (ECT) Biomedical intervention in which electrical current applied to the brain induces a convulsive seizure. Used to treat depression.

Electroencephalography (EEG) Technique used to measure and record electrical activity of the cortex.

Embryo transfer Procedure in which a female donor is artificially inseminated with sperm, and approximately five days after fertilization the tiny embryo is removed from the woman donor and transferred surgically into the uterus of the mother-to-be, who then carries the pregnancy. Used in cases where a couple wishes to have a child, but the female partner carries a defective gene.

Embryonic stage Second stage of prenatal development, lasting from the beginning of the third week to the end of the eighth week after fertilization, characterized by fast growth and differentiation of the major body systems as well as vital organs.

Emotions An individual's subjective feelings and moods. The term applies to both physiological and behavioral responses to specific stimulus situations.

Empathic understanding Key element of person-centered therapy, referring to therapists' ability to see the world as the client sees it.

Empirical tests Tests in which scientists manipulate conditions or behaviors, for the purposes of testing a hypothesis, and observe the results.

Empiricism The philosophical position that all knowledge is obtained from direct experience.

Encoding In memory, the process of perceiving information, then categorizing or organizing it in a meaningful way so that it can be more easily stored and recalled.

Endocrine system System of ductless glands, including the pituitary, thyroid, parathyroids, adrenals, pancreas, and gonads, that secrete hormones directly into the bloodstream or lymph fluids.

Endogenous opioids Morphine-like substances occurring naturally in the brain that act as neurotransmitters and also act to inhibit the activity of other transmitters. *See Endorphins.*

Endorphins A class of neurotransmitter substances that function to inhibit the transmission pain information. Morphine and other opiates act by facilitating endorphine transmission. *See Endogenous opioids.*

Engineering psychology Field of specialization concerned with creating optimal relationships among people, the machines they operate, and the environments they work in. Sometimes called human factors psychology.

Environmental psychology Field of specialization concerned with assessing the effects on behavior of environmental factors such as noise, pollution, or overcrowding.

Episodic memory Autobiographical memories about one's own experiences.

Equilibrium The sense of balance, localized within the inner ear and comprising two sensory receptors: the semicircular canals and the vestibular sacs.

Escape conditioning In operant conditioning, learning that takes place when an organism performs a response which will terminate an aversive stimulus.

Estrogens Hormones that influence female sexual development.

Excitatory postsynaptic potentials (EPSPs) Effects that occur when excitatory neurotransmitters cause a graded potential to occur on the dendrite or cell body of a receiving neuron.

Exemplar theory Theory that the natural concepts we form in everyday life are structured around prototypes or typical representatives of categories (such as robins and jays as prototypes of the concept bird).

Experimental groups In experimental research, groups of subjects who are exposed to different varieties of independent variables, so that resulting behaviors can be compared.

Experimental psychology Field of specialization in which the primary activity is conducting research.

Experimental research Research conducted in precisely controlled laboratory conditions in which subjects are confronted with specific stimuli and their reactions are carefully measured to discover relationships among variables.

Expert system A computer program designed to solve a particular kind of problem. MYCIN is an expert system to aid physicians in making diagnoses.

Extinction In classical conditioning, the process by which a conditioned response is eliminated through repeated presentation of the conditioned stimulus without the unconditioned stimulus. In operant conditioning, the process of eliminating a response by discontinuing reinforcement for it.

Extroversion Personality trait mani-

fested by sociability, friendliness, and interest in people and events in the external world. *See also Introversion.*

Facial feedback theory Theory that specific facial displays are universally associated with the expression of the emotions of fear, anger, happiness, sadness, surprise, interest, disgust, and shame.

Factor analysis A complex statistical procedure used to categorize or clump a group of related variables. A group of related variables is referred to as a factor.

False consensus bias Attribution bias caused by the assumption that most people share our own attitudes and behaviors.

Family therapy Therapy in which family members meet together with a therapist.

Fear of success Motivation to avoid achievement, especially among women, because of the potential negative consequences of success.

Fetal alcohol syndrome (FAS) Variety of developmental complications including spontaneous abortion, premature birth, infants born addicted to alcohol, and numerous developmental disabilities which are related to the mother's use of alcohol during pregnancy.

Fetal stage Third and final stage of prenatal development, extending from the beginning of the third month to birth, during which bone and muscle tissue form and the organs and body systems continue to develop.

Fetally androgenized female Chromosomally normal (XX) female who, as a result of excessive exposure to androgens during prenatal sex differentiation, develops external genitalia resembling those of a male.

Fetus Term used to describe an unborn infant during the period from the beginning of the third month after fertilization until birth.

Figure In perception, the part of an image on which we focus our attention.

Fixation In Freud's theory of psychosexual development, arrested development that results from exposure to either too little or too much gratification.

Fixed interval (FI) schedule Partial reinforcement schedule in operant conditioning wherein reinforcement is provided for the first response after a specified period of time has elapsed.

Fixed ratio (FR) schedule Partial reinforcement schedule in operant condi-

tioning wherein reinforcement occurs after a fixed number of responses.

Flashbulb memory An apparent vivid recall for an event associated with extreme emotion or uniqueness, such as the assassination of a president or the bombing of Iraq.

Flextime Approach to scheduling work hours in which employees have some flexibility in picking starting and quitting times, as long as they are present during core work hours.

Fluid intelligence Ability to perceive and draw inferences about relationships among patterns of stimuli, to conceptualize abstract information, and to solve problems. *See also Crystallized intelligence.*

Foot-in-the-door technique Technique for encouraging compliance in which a person is first asked to agree to a relatively minor request that serves as a setup for a more major request.

Forensic psychology Field of specialization that works with the legal, court, and correctional systems to develop personality profiles of criminals, make decisions about disposition of convicted offenders, and help law enforcers understand behavioral problems.

Formal concepts Logical, clearly defined concepts with unambiguous rules specifying what features belong to that category.

Formal-operations stage Fourth and final stage in Piaget's theory of cognitive development (ages 12 +), during which individuals acquire the ability to make complex deductions and solve problems by systematically testing hypotheses.

Fovea A small area near the center of the retina containing densely packed cones used for color vision and fine visual acuity.

Fraternal twins Twins produced when two ova are fertilized by two different sperm cells, so that their genetic codes are no more similar than those of any other siblings.

Free association Psychoanalytic technique developed by Sigmund Freud in which patients relax and say whatever comes to their minds.

Frequency theory of pitch discrimination Theory that perception of low tones depends on the frequency with which auditory hair cells in the inner ear's organ of Corti trigger the firing of neurons in the auditory nerve. *See also Volley theory.*

Frontal lobe Largest, foremost lobe in

the cerebral cortex; an important region for movement, emotion, and memory.

Frustration-aggression hypothesis Theory that aggression is always a consequence of frustration, and that frustration leads to aggression.

Functional fixedness Tendency to be so set in our perception of the proper function of a given object that we are unable to think of using it in a novel way to solve a problem.

Functionalism Approach to psychology that emphasized the functional, practical nature of the mind. Influenced by Darwin's theory of natural selection, functionalists attempted to learn how mental processes such as learning, thinking, and perceiving helped people adapt.

Fundamental attribution error Tendency to overestimate dispositional (internal) causes and to underestimate situational (external) causes of behavior.

G-factor One of the two factors in Charles Spearman's conceptualization of intelligence, the g-factor consists of general intelligence, which is largely genetically determined. *See also S-factor.*

Gamete The reproductive cells, or sperm and ovum. Also known as germ cells.

Gate-control theory Theory that neural gates in the spinal cord allow passage of pain signals to the brain; these gates may be closed by the simultaneous firing of nonpain nerve fibers, so that pain is not perceived.

Gender identity An individual's subjective sense of being male or female.

Gender role Set of behaviors that is considered normal and appropriate for each sex in a society.

Genes The chemical blueprints of all living things. Genes are made of DNA molecules, and each chromosome contains thousands of genes.

Gene therapy *See Genetic engineering.*

General adaptation syndrome (GAS) Progressive responses to prolonged stress described by Hans Selye, in which when an organism mobilizes for action and compensates for stress.

Generalization Process by which an organism responds to stimuli that are similar to the conditioned stimulus, without undergoing conditioning for each similar stimulus.

Generalized anxiety disorder

Chronic state of free-floating anxiety that is omnipresent.

Genetic clock theory Theory that aging is built into every organism through a genetic code which preprograms the body cells to stop functioning at a certain point. Also known as programmed theory.

Genetic counseling Counseling that uses information about family histories as well as medical and laboratory investigations to predict the likelihood that a couple will have children with certain disorders.

Genetic engineering Process that uses recombinant DNA techniques to insert a new gene into cells to alter and correct a defective genetic code. Also known as gene therapy.

Genital stage Fifth and final stage in Freud's theory of psychosexual development, beginning with puberty, during which sexual feelings that were dormant during the latency stage reemerge.

Genotype Assortment of genes each individual inherits at conception.

Genuineness Important element of person-centered therapy, referring to therapists' ability to be in touch with his or her own current feelings or attitudes.

Germ cell *See Gamete.*

Germinal stage First of three stages in prenatal development of a fetus, this stage spans the first two weeks after fertilization. Also known as the zygote stage.

Gestalt psychology Approach to psychology which argues that the whole of an experience is different from the sum of its parts. Gestalt psychology is an active force in current investigations of perceptual processes and learning as well as therapy, where it emphasizes the whole person.

Gestalt therapy Therapy approach that attempts to help individuals bring the alienated fragments of their personalities into an integrated, unified whole.

Glia cells Specialized cells that form insulating covers called myelin sheaths around the axons of some neurons, increasing conductivity.

Glycogen A carbohydrate that can be synthesized from glucose for the storage of nutrients. Glycogen can also be converted into glucose for energy.

Glucostatic theory Theory that hunger results when glucoreceptors detect a lack of glucose, either because blood levels of glucose are low or because insulin is not available in sufficient quantity.

Gonadotropins Hormones released by

the pituitary gland that stimulate production of testosterone in men and estrogen in women.

Gonads Glands within the endocrine system (ovaries in females and testes in males) which produce sex hormones that influence development of sexual systems and secondary sex characteristics as well as sexual motivation.

Good continuation Perceptual grouping principle that we are more likely to perceive stimuli as a whole or single group if they flow smoothly into one another than if they are discontinuous.

Graded potential Voltage change in a neuron's dendrites that is produced by receiving an impulse from another neuron or neurons. *See also Excitatory postsynaptic potentials and Inhibitory postsynaptic potentials.*

Ground In perception, the background against which the figure that we focus on stands. *See also Figure.*

Group therapy Therapy in which three or more clients meet simultaneously with a therapist.

Growth hormone Pituitary hormone which controls several metabolic functions including the rate of growth of the bones and soft tissues.

Gustation The sense of taste, which like olfaction is activated by chemical senses in the environment.

H-Y antigen Substance which appears to trigger the transformation of gonads into testes within the first few weeks of prenatal development.

Hallucination False perception that lacks a sensory basis. Can be produced by hallucinogenic drugs, fatigue, or sensory deprivation. Often associated with severe psychotic disorders.

Hallucinogens Class of psychoactive drugs, including LSD and PCP, that alter sensory perceptions, thinking processes, and emotions, often causing delusions, hallucinations, and altered sense of time and space.

Halo effect Tendency to infer other positive or negative traits from our perception of one central trait in another person.

Health psychology Area of specialization concerned with the interaction between behavioral factors and physical health.

Height on a plane Important monocular depth cue based on the fact that objects which are highest on one's plane of view appear to be farthest away.

Hermaphrodite Individual with ambiguous or contradictory sex characteristics resulting from abnormal differentiation of internal and external sex structures.

Heterozygous Genotype that contains different genes for a trait (for instance, both brown-eye and blue-eye genes).

Heuristics Rule-of-thumb (quick-fix) problem-solving strategies such as means-ends analysis and working backward.

Higher order conditioning In classical conditioning, the process by which a conditioned stimulus is used to condition the same response to other stimuli.

Hippocampus Structure in the brain's limbic system that seems to play an important role in memory.

Homosexual Primary erotic, psychological, and social interest in members of the same sex, even though that interest may not be expressed overtly.

Homozygous Genotype that consists of the same genes for a trait (for instance, brown-eye genes inherited from both parents).

Hormones Chemical messengers secreted by the endocrine glands that act to regulate the functioning of specific body organs.

Hospice Facility designed to care for the special needs of the dying, including love and support, pain control, and maintaining a sense of dignity.

Hue The color we perceive, determined partly by the wavelength of light and partly by the complex process by which an organism's visual system mixes wavelengths.

Humanistic psychology Approach to psychology that emphasizes the role of free choice and our ability to make conscious rational decisions about how we live our lives.

Huntington's disease Also known as Huntington's chorea, a genetically transmitted disease that progressively destroys brain cells in adults.

Hypertension Commonly referred to as high blood pressure; a condition of excessive blood flow through the vessels that can result in both hardening and general deterioration of the walls of the vessels.

Hypnosis State of altered consciousness characterized by a deep relaxation and detachment as well as heightened suggestibility to the hypnotist's directives.

Hypochondriasis Somatoform disorder in which the individual is excessively

fearful of contracting a serious illness or of dying.

Hypogonadism State of androgen deprivation resulting from certain diseases of the endocrine system.

Hypothalamus Small structure located below the thalamus in the brain which plays an important role in motivation and emotional expression, as well as controlling the neuroendocrine system and maintaining the body's homeostasis. The hypothalamus is part of the limbic system.

Hypothalamic control theory Theory that the ventromedial hypothalamus and the lateral hypothalamus operate together to maintain a relatively constant state of satiety.

Hypothesis Statement proposing the existence of a relationship between variables, typically as a tentative explanation for cause and effect. Hypotheses are often designed to be tested by research.

Iconic memory Visual sensory memory, including fleeting impressions of what we see. Also known as visual memory.

Id In Freud's psychoanalytic theory, the biological component of personality consisting of life instincts and death instincts. *See also Ego, Superego, Libido, and Pleasure principle.*

Identical twins Twins who share the same genetic code. Also known as one-egg or monozygotic twins.

Illusion False or inaccurate perception that differs from the actual physical state of the perceived object.

Illusion of control Attributional bias caused by the belief that we control events in our own lives which are really beyond our control.

Implicit personality theories Assumptions people make about how traits usually occur together in other people's personalities.

Impression management Tendency of individuals to select carefully what information they reveal about their attitudes, depending on how they think such information will affect their image in the eyes of others.

Imprinting Process by which certain infant animals, such as ducklings, learn to follow or approach the first moving object they see. *See also Critical periods.*

Incentive Any external stimulus that can motivate behavior even when no internal drive state exists.

Independent variable Condition or factor that the experimenter manipulates in an experiment in order to determine whether changes in behavior (the dependent variable) result.

Indiscriminant attachment Attachment typically displayed by human infants during the first few months, when social behaviors are directed to virtually anyone. *See also Specific attachment and Separate attachment.*

Inductive reasoning Reasoning that draws broad conclusions by generalizing from specific instances. *See also Deductive reasoning.*

Industrial/organizational (I/O) psychology Field of specialization concerned with using psychological concepts to make the workplace a more satisfying environment for employees and management.

Inferential statistics Process of using mathematical procedures to draw conclusions about the meaning of research data.

Information processing Emerging approach to understanding psychology that uses computers to help develop models of cognitive processing of information.

Informational social influence One basis of conformity, in which we accept a group's beliefs or behaviors as providing accurate information about reality. *See also Normative social influence.*

Ingroup In social psychology, the group in which people include themselves when they divide the world into "us" and "them."

Ingroup bias Tendency to see one's own group in a favorable light.

Inhibitory postsynaptic potentials (IPSPs) A transitory state of hyperpolarization that occurs when inhibitory neurotransmitters inhibit the postsynaptic membrane of a receiving neuron. *See also Graded potential.*

Insight Sudden recognition of relationships that leads to the solution of a complex problem.

Insomnia Sleep disorder characterized by a consistent inability to get to sleep or by frequent awakenings during sleep.

Instincts Innate patterns of behavior that occur in every normally functioning member of a species under certain set conditions.

Intelligence An operational definition states simply that intelligence is what intelligence tests measure, although intelligence is commonly understood to include the abilities to think rationally and abstractly, act purposefully, and deal effectively with the environment.

Intelligence quotient (IQ) Intelligence measurement derived by dividing an individual's mental age by the chronological age, then multiplying by 100.

Interneurons Neurons of the central nervous system that function as intermediaries between sensory and motor neurons.

Interpersonal aggression Any physical or verbal behavior intended to hurt another person.

Interposition *See Overlap.*

Interview Method used in psychological studies in which an individual is asked questions. Interviews may be informal and unstructured or they may be highly structured.

Introversion Personality trait expressed as shyness, reclusiveness, and preoccupation with the inner world of thoughts, memories, and feelings. *See also Extroversion.*

James-Lange theory Theory that explains emotional states (such as fear) resulting from an organism's awareness of bodily responses to a situation, rather than from cognitions about that situation.

Job description index (JDI) Measure of job satisfaction that assesses five dimensions, including supervision, coworkers, promotions, pay, and the work itself.

Just noticeable difference (JND) *See Difference threshold.*

Karotype Chart in which photographs of an individual's chromosomes are arranged according to size and structure.

Kinesthesis Body sense that provides information about perceptions of the location of various body parts in relation to other parts and about the position of the body in space.

Language acquisition device According to the genetic or nativist view, the prewiring that gives humans the innate ability to learn and understand language.

Latency period Fourth stage of psychosexual development in Freud's theory, extending from about age five to puberty, during which sexual drives remain unexpressed or latent.

Latent content In psychoanalytic theory, the hidden content or true meaning of dreams.

Latent learning Learning that is not demonstrated by an immediately observable change in behavior.

Lateral hypothalamus (LH) One of two areas in the hypothalamus that seem to act as control centers for eating. Destruction of the LH causes dramatic reduction in feeding behavior; stimulation causes overeating. *See also Ventromedial hypothalamus; Hypothalamic control theory.*

Lateralization of function Degree to which a particular function, such as the understanding of speech, is controlled by one rather than both cerebral hemispheres.

Law of effect Theory originally proposed by Edward Thorndike that is the foundation of operant conditioning theory: Behavior followed by reinforcement will be strengthened while behavior followed by punishment will be weakened.

Leaderless group discussion Technique used in some assessment centers that places several job applicants in a group and asks them to solve a business problem while many realistic emergencies and interruptions occur.

Learned helplessness A response produced by exposure to unavoidable aversive stimuli. Characterized by the inability to learn an avoidance response.

Learning Relatively enduring change in potential behavior that results from experience.

Lesion production Technique for studying the brain that involves surgical damage to a precise region of the brain.

Libido In Freud's psychoanalytic theory, the energy that fuels the id and motivates all behavior.

Life review Process by which older people may retrospectively view their past, sorting out their accomplishments from their disappointments.

Light adaptation Process by which an organism's vision adjusts to bright lighting, due to a chemical change within the rods and cones of the retina.

Limbic system Collection of structures located around the central core of the brain that play a critical role in emotional expression as well as motivation, learning, and memory. Key structures of the limbic system include the amygdala, the hippocampus, the septal area, and parts of the hypothalamus.

Linear perspective Important monocular distance cue based on the fact that parallel lines converge when stretched into the distance.

Linguistic-relativity hypothesis Notion that the language of a particular culture determines the content of thoughts among members of that culture, and the way these people perceive and think about their world.

Lipostatic theory Theory that explains long-term eating control as a result of a constant monitoring of levels of body fat, which is used as a barometer to regulate food intake. *See also Set point.*

Lobotomy Surgical procedure which severs the nerve tracts connecting the prefrontal cortex to lower brain areas that mediate emotional responses.

Longitudinal design Research design that evaluates a group of subjects at several points in time, over a number of years, to assess how certain characteristics or behaviors change during the course of development.

Long-term memory (LTM) The third memory system in the three-system model of memory. Information transferred from short-term to long-term memory may be stored for periods of time from minutes to years.

Loudness In hearing, the intensity of a sound as measured by decibels. Loudness is determined by the amplitude of a sound wave.

LSD (Lysergic acid diethylamide) Hallucinogenic drug derived from a fungus that grows on rye grass which produces profound distortions of sensations, feelings, time, and thought.

Lucid dreaming Process of being aware that one is dreaming and of influencing the content of one's own dreams.

Magnetic resonance imaging (MRI) Procedure for studying the brain which uses radio waves to excite hydrogen protons in the brain tissue, creating a magnetic field change.

Maintenance rehearsal System for remembering that involves repeatedly rehearsing information without attempting to find meaning in it. *See also Elaborative rehearsal.*

Major depressive disorder Type of mood disorder characterized by deep and persistent depression.

Manic-depression *See Bipolar disorder.*

Manifest content In psychoanalytic theory, the disguised version of the latent content, or true meaning, of dreams.

Marijuana Drug derived from the hemp

plant Cannabis sativa, containing the chemical THC (delta 9-tetrahydrocannabinol), which is commonly classified as a hallucinogen although it also may have depressant and stimulant effects.

Maturation Orderly unfolding of certain patterns of behavior, such as language acquisition or walking, in accordance with genetic blueprints.

MDMA Common name for 3,4-methylenedioxymethamphetamine (also known as ecstasy); a designer drug chemically related to amphetamines that acts as a central nervous system stimulant.

Mean In descriptive statistics, the arithmetic average obtained by adding scores and dividing by the number of scores.

Means-end analysis Common heuristic problem-solving strategy that involves identifying the difference between an original state and a desired goal, then progressing through a series of subgoals to reach the solution.

Measure of central tendency In descriptive statistics, a value that reflects the middle or central point of a distribution of scores. The three measures of central tendency are the mean, the median, and the mode.

Measure of variability In descriptive statistics, a measure that indicates whether distribution scores are clustered closely around their average or widely spread out. Two measures of variability are the range and the standard deviation.

Median In descriptive statistics, the score that falls in the middle of a distribution of numbers arranged from the lowest to the highest.

Meditation Practice of deliberately altering one's state of consciousness in an effort to achieve a state of deep relaxation. Meditation is characterized by alpha brain waves as well as other physiological measures such as lowered respiration and heart rate.

Medulla Structure low in the brain that controls vital life support functions such as breathing, heartbeat, and blood pressure; it also regulates many reflexive functions such as coughing or sneezing.

Memory (1) Process or processes of storing newly acquired information for later recall; (2) recall for a specific experience, or the total collection of remembered experiences stored in our brains.

Menopause Cessation of menstruation that takes place during the climacteric.

Mental age In IQ testing, the chronological age of children who on the average

receive a test score similar to that of the subject. For instance, a six year old whose composite score is equivalent to that of a nine year old has a mental age of nine.

Mental set In problem solving, a tendency to approach a problem or situation in a predetermined way, regardless of the requirements of the specific problem.

Mere exposure effect Phenomenon by which repeated exposure to novel stimuli tends to increase an individual's preference for such stimuli.

Mnemonic device Memory system, such as clustering or acrostics, that organizes material in a meaningful way to make it easier to remember.

Mode In descriptive statistics, the score that occurs most frequently in a distribution of numbers.

Modeling Learning process wherein an individual acquires a behavior by observing someone else performing that behavior. Also known as observational learning.

Monocular cues Distance cues such as linear perspective and height on a plane that can be used with just one eye.

Monozygotic twins *See Identical twins.*

Mood disorders Class of disorders including major depression and bipolar disorder that are characterized by persistent depression (which in bipolar disorder is accompanied by intermittent episodes of mania).

Morpheme Smallest unit of meaning in a given language.

Motion parallax *See Relative motion.*

Motivation Any condition that might energize and direct an organism's actions.

Motor cortex Region of the cerebral cortex that transmits messages to muscles. The motor cortex controls virtually all intentional body movement.

Motor neuron Neuron that transmits messages from the central nervous system to muscles or glands.

Multifactor motive Motive based on a combination of biological, psychological, and cultural factors.

Multifactorial inheritance Genetic transmission in which several gene pairs interact to produce a trait.

Multiple personality Form of dissociative disorder in which a person alternates between a primary personality and one or more secondary or subordinate personalities.

Mutism Speech disturbance characteristic of schizophrenia in which an individual may not utter a sound for hours or days at a time.

Myelin sheath Insulating cover around some axons that increases a neuron's ability to transmit impulses quickly. Myelin sheaths are made of specialized cells called glia cells.

Narcolepsy Sleep disorder characterized by falling asleep suddenly and uncontrollably.

Narcotics Also known as opiates, a class of depressant drugs that includes opium, morphine, codeine, and heroin.

Natural concepts Concepts that are commonly used in thinking about events and experiences, but that are more ambiguous than formal concepts.

Naturalistic observation Psychological research using the observational method that takes place in a natural setting, such as a subject's home or school environment.

Nature-nurture controversy Controversy over whether individual differences are the result of genetic endowment (nature) or of learning (nurture).

Need for achievement (nAch) Complex psychosocial motive to accomplish difficult goals, attain high standards, surpass the achievements of others, and increase self-regard by succeeding in exercising talent.

Negative afterimage The image that is seen after the retina is exposed to an intense visual image. A negative afterimage may consist of colors that are complements to those of the original image.

Negative reinforcer In operant conditioning, any stimulus that increases the probability of a response through its removal. For example, pounding on the wall (operant behavior) may be maintained by the termination of loud noise (negative reinforcer) in an adjoining room.

Neodissociation theory Ernest Hilgard's explanation of hypnosis as a state in which a subject operates on more than one level of consciousness, so that some behaviors are dissociated from conscious awareness.

Neo-Freudians Psychologists who were in general agreement with Freud's basic interpretation of the structure of personality, his focus on the unconscious, and his emphasis on childhood experience, but dissented regarding other aspects of Freud's theory, such as his emphasis on aggressive impulses and unconscious sexual conflicts.

Neologisms Literally, new words.

Invention of neologisms is characteristic of schizophrenic disorder.

Neural network model A model of the nervous system based on the connections among numerous neurons. Neural network models are believed to simulate real properties of neural connections.

Neuroleptic drugs Class of drugs that have the effect of calming and quieting patients with some psychotic disorders, most notably schizophrenia. Also known as antipsychotic drugs or major tranquilizers.

Neurometrics Technique for electrophysiological measurement of neural functioning. Neurometrics uses computer analysis of EEG patterns and evoked potentials to measure a variety of sensory, perceptual, and cognitive processes mediated by the brain.

Neuron Type of cell that is the basic unit of the nervous system. A neuron typically consists of a cell body, dendrites, and an axon. Neurons transmit messages to other neurons and to glands and muscles throughout the body.

Neurosis Term originally used by Freud to describe anxiety disorders, and widely used until publication of DSM-III to describe a range of disorders that are distressing and often debilitating, but are not characterized by a loss of contact with reality.

Neurotransmitter Chemical messenger that transmits an impulse across the synaptic gap from one neuron to another.

Nicotine Stimulant found in tobacco that acts to increase heart rate, blood pressure, and stomach activity and to constrict blood vessels.

Nightmare Bad dream that occurs during REM sleep.

Node of Ranvier Small gap or exposed portion of the axon of a neuron between the glia cells that form the myelin sheath.

Noncompensatory model Decision-making model, such as the maximax, minimax, and conjunctive strategies, which involves evaluating some rather than all features of the various alternative choices. *Compare with Compensatory model.*

Norm Standard that reflects the normal or average performance of a particular group of people on a measure such as an IQ test.

Normal distribution In descriptive statistics, a distribution in which scores are distributed similarly on both sides of the middle value, so that they have the appearance of a bell-shaped curve when graphed.

Normal state (of consciousness) State of consciousness in which a person is alert and aware of his or her environment, as contrasted to alternative or altered states of consciousness.

Normative social influence Social influence in which we conform not because of an actual change in our beliefs, but because we think we will benefit in some way (such as gaining approval). *See also Informational social influence.*

NREM sleep (Nonrapid eye movement sleep) Stages of sleep during which rapid eye movements typically do not occur. Dreaming occurs far less frequently during NREM sleep than during REM sleep.

Obedience Social influence in which we alter our behavior in response to commands or orders from people perceived as having power or authority.

Obese Condition in which an individual weighs 20 percent or more above the desirable weight for his or her height.

Object permanence Realization that objects continue to exist even when they are not in view. Piaget sees this awareness as a key achievement of the sensorimotor stage of development.

Observational learning *See Modeling.*

Observational method Method of psychological research in which subjects are observed as they go about their usual activities. The observational method provides descriptive information. *See also Naturalistic observation.*

Observer bias Tendency of an observer to read more into a situation than is actually there or to see what he or she expects to see. Observer bias is a potential limitation of the observational method.

Observer effect Tendency of subjects to modify behavior because they are aware of being observed.

Obsessive-compulsive disorder Anxiety disorder characterized by persistent, unwanted, and unshakable thoughts and/or irresistible, habitual repeated actions.

Occipital lobe Region at the rear of the cerebral cortex that consists primarily of the visual cortex.

Oedipus complex In Freud's theory of psychosexual development, the attraction a male child feels toward his mother (and jealousy toward his father) during the phallic stage.

Olfaction The sense of smell, which like taste is activated by chemical substances in the environment.

Olfactory bulb The end of the olfactory nerve that receives input from olfactory receptors.

One-egg twins *See Identical twins.*

Operant conditioning Learning process also known as instrumental conditioning by which an organism learns to associate its own behavior with consequences.

Operant conditioning therapies Behavior modification techniques that attempt to influence behavior by manipulating reinforcers.

Operational definition Definition specifying the operations that are used to measure or observe a variable, such as a definition of obesity specifying a certain weight-height relationship.

Opiates *See Narcotics.*

Opponent-process theory of color vision Theory that explains color vision based on six primary colors which are grouped into three pairs (red-green, blue-yellow, black-white). Receptors in the eye are sensitive to specific pairs, and the presence of one member of a pair inhibits vision of the other. *See also Trichromatic theory.*

Opponent-process theory Theory that when a strong emotional response to a particular stimulus disrupts emotional balance, an opposite emotional response is eventually activated to restore emotional equilibrium.

Optic disk A structure in the retina where the optic nerve exits; sometimes referred to as the blind spot.

Optimum level of arousal Level of arousal at which an individual's performance on a specific task is most efficient.

Oral stage According to Freud, the first stage of psychosexual development spanning birth through 12 to 18 months, during which the lips and mouth are the primary erogenous zone.

Organ of Corti Structure in the inner ear located directly above the basilar membrane, consisting of auditory hair cells, a tectoral membrane, and cilia.

Organ reserve Potential ability of organs such as the heart, lungs, and kidneys to increase their output to a level several times greater than normal under emergency conditions.

Organic amnesia Memory deficits

caused by altered physiology of the brain, which might result from an accident or certain physical illnesses.

Ossicles Set of three tiny linked bones (the malleus, incus, and stapes) in the middle ear that receives a sound stimulus from the tympanic membrane and transfers it to the oval window of the inner ear.

Otis-Lennon School Ability Test (OLSAT) Group IQ test for children of all ages that is widely used in schools.

Outgroup The "them" group when individuals divide the world into "us" and "them."

Overlap Important monocular distance cue based on the fact that objects close to us tend to block out parts of objects that are farther away. Also known as interposition.

Overlearning Technique for memorizing material that involves rehearsing information after it has already been learned.

Panic disorder Anxiety disorder in which an individual experiences numerous panic attacks (four or more in a four-week period) which are characterized by overwhelming terror and often a feeling of unreality or of depersonalization.

Paper-and-pencil questionnaire In personality testing, an objective, self-report inventory designed to measure scientifically the variety of characteristics or traits that makeup personality.

Paranoid schizophrenia Subtype of schizophrenic disorder characterized by the presence of well organized delusional thoughts.

Parasympathetic nervous system Division of the autonomic nervous system that functions to conserve energy, returning the body to normal from emergency responses set in motion by the sympathetic nervous system.

Parietal lobe Region of the cerebral cortex located just behind the central fissure and above the lateral fissure. The parietal lobe contains the somatosensory cortex as well as association areas that process sensory information received by the somatosensory cortex.

Partial reinforcement effect Behaviors that are acquired on partial instead of continuous reinforcement schedules tend to be established more slowly, but are more persistent when no reinforcement is provided.

Partial reinforcement schedule In operant conditioning, schedule which reinforces behavior only part of the time, for example, a ratio or interval schedule.

Participant management Management strategy in which all levels of employees are included in decision making.

Patient-controlled analgesia (PCA) Pain-reduction technique in which the patient uses a computerized program to self-administer analgesic medication through intravenous infusions.

PCP (Phencyclidine hydrochloride) Drug commonly known as "angel dust" that produces sensory distortions and hallucinations as well as having stimulant, depressant, and painkilling properties. Side effects include unpredictable violent behavior.

Pearson product-moment correlation coefficient The most frequently used measure of correlation, ranging from -1.0 to $+1.0$. Correlations close to zero indicate little or no relationship between two variables; correlations close to $+1.0$ or -1.0 indicate more significant positive or negative relationships.

Percentile Numbers from a range of data indicating percentages of scores that lie below them.

Perception Process of interpreting, organizing, and often elaborating on sensations.

Perceptual constancy The fact that objects are normally perceived to be constant in size, color or brightness, and shape despite the fact that their retinal images change according to different conditions.

Perceptual grouping Tendency to organize patterns of stimuli into larger units according to proximity, similarity, and good continuation.

Perceptual organization Process by which we structure elementary sensations (such as the sight of lines, brightness, and points) into the objects we perceive.

Perceptual set Tendency to see, hear, smell, feel, or taste what we expect or what is consistent with our preconceived notions.

Peripheral nervous system (PNS) Portion of the nervous system that transmits messages to and from the central nervous system. Consists of the somatic nervous system and the autonomic nervous system.

Permissive Parenting style in which parents adopt a hands-off policy, making few demands and showing reluctance to punish inappropriate behavior.

Person schemas Generalized assumptions about certain classes of people.

Personal space Invisible boundary or imaginary circle of space with which individuals surround themselves, and into which others are not supposed to enter without invitation.

Personal unconscious In Carl Jung's theory, the part of the unconscious which is akin to Freud's concept of a reservoir of all repressed thoughts and feelings. *Contrast with Collective unconscious.*

Personality Distinctive patterns of behavior, emotions, and thoughts that characterize an individual's adaptations to his or her life.

Personality disorders Diverse class of disorders that is collectively characterized by inflexible and maladaptive personality traits which cause either functional impairment or subjective distress.

Personality psychology Field of specialization that focuses on exploring the uniqueness of the individual, describing the elements that make up human personality, and investigating how personality develops and how it influences people's activities.

Person-centered therapy Therapeutic approach designed to help the client tap his or her own inner resources within a climate of genuineness, unconditional positive regard, and empathic understanding.

PET scan *See Positron emission tomography.*

Phallic stage According to Freud, the third phase of psychosexual development, spanning age three through age five or six, during which the focus of sexual gratification is genital stimulation.

Phenotype Characteristics that result from the expression of various genotypes (for instance, brown eyes or blond hair).

Phenylketonuria (PKU) Disease caused by a recessive gene that results in the absence of an enzyme necessary to metabolize the milk protein phenylalanine.

Pheromones Chemical substances which are secreted by an organism and detected by another organism. Pheromones may function to attract mates, define territories, and facilitate social behavior.

Phobia Any of a number of anxiety disorders which are characterized by a persistent fear of and consequent avoidance of a specific object or situation.

Phonemes Individual sounds (such as those represented by *s* and *sh* in the

English spelling system) that are the basic structural elements of language.

Physiological dependence Addiction to a chemical substance in which withdrawal of that substance results in physiological symptoms such as cramps, nausea, tremors, headaches, or sweating.

Physiological psychology Field of specialization that studies the relationship between physiological processes and behavior. Also known as biological psychology.

Pitch Dimension of hearing that determines how high or low a sound is, measured in hertz. Pitch is determined by the frequency of a sound wave.

Pituitary gland Gland in the endocrine system, located directly below and connected to the hypothalamus. The pituitary gland produces a number of hormones, many of which trigger other endocrine glands to release hormones.

Place theory of pitch discrimination Theory that we discriminate different pitches because sound waves of different frequency displace different regions on the cochlea's basilar membrane.

Pleasure principle According to Freud, the principle guiding the id which seeks immediate gratification of all instinctive drives regardless of reason, logic, or the possible impact of behaviors.

Pons Brain structure located just above the medulla which functions in fine-tuning motor messages, programming species-typical behaviors, processing sensory information, and controlling respiration.

Positive reinforcement therapy Behavior therapy technique which identifies the desired behavior, then uses reinforcers to strengthen the behavior.

Positive reinforcer In operant conditioning, any stimulus presented after a response that increases the probability of the response.

Positron emission tomography (PET scan) Technique for studying the brain that involves injecting a subject with a glucose-like sugar tagged with a radioactive isotope which accumulates in brain cells in direct proportion to their activity level.

Postconventional morality Third and highest level in Lawrence Kohlberg's theory of moral development, in which individuals are guided by values agreed upon by society (stage 5) or by universal ethical principles (stage 6).

Posthypnotic suggestion Suggestion or instruction to a hypnotized person which motivates that person to perform an action or actions after returning to a normal state of consciousness.

Posttraumatic stress disorder (PTSD) Anxiety disorder that typically follows a traumatic event or events, and is characterized by a reliving of that event, avoidance of stimuli associated with the event or numbing of general responsiveness, and increased arousal.

Preconscious Mental state describing thoughts and memories that exist on the fringe of awareness, and that can be readily brought into consciousness.

Preconventional morality Lowest level of moral development in Lawrence Kohlberg's theory, comprising stage 1 and stage 2, in which individuals have not internalized a personal code of morality.

Predictive validity Type of criterion-related validity assessed by determining the accuracy with which tests predict performance in some future situation. *See also Concurrent validity.*

Prejudice Negative, unjustifiable, and inflexible attitude toward a group and its members.

Premenstrual syndrome (PMS) Term used to describe a myriad of physical and psychological symptoms that precede each menstrual period for some women.

Preoperational stage According to Piaget, the second major stage of cognitive development (ages seven to 12). Preoperational children can develop only limited concepts, and they are unable to evaluate simultaneously more than one physical dimension. *See also Centration.*

Primacy effect Term used to describe the phenomenon that the first information we receive about a person often has the greatest influence on our perceptions of that person.

Primary mental abilities In L. L. Thurstone's theory of the structure of intelligence, the separate and measurable attributes (for instance, numerical ability) that make up intelligence.

Primary process thinking According to Freud, wish-fulfilling mental imagery used by the id to discharge tension.

Primary motor cortex The area of the frontal cortex that directly controls motor movement.

Primary reinforcer In operant conditioning, a stimulus that satisfies a biologically based drive or need (such as hunger, thirst, or sleep).

Primary visual cortex The region of the cortex that receives visual information directly from the visual system. *See also Occipital Cortex.*

Proactive interference In memory, the phenomenon that occurs when earlier learning disrupts memory for later learning.

Probability In statistics, the proportion of cases that fit a certain description.

Problem finding Fifth stage of cognitive development (beyond Piaget's fourth stage of formal operations) proposed by P. A. Arlin, in which individuals pose new questions about the world and try to discover novel solutions to old problems.

Procedural memory Recall for how to perform skills such as bicycle riding or swimming. *See also Declarative memory.*

Programmed theory *See Genetic clock theory.*

Projection Defense mechanism in which an individual reduces anxiety created by unacceptable impulses by attributing those impulses to someone else.

Projective tests Personality tests that consist of loosely structured, ambiguous stimuli that require the subject's interpretation.

Prototype Best or most typical representative of a category around which we often structure our concept of that category. *See also Exemplar theory.*

Proximity Perceptual grouping principle whereby, all else being equal, we tend to organize perceptions by grouping elements that are the nearest to each other. In social psychology, the geographical nearness of one person to another, which is an important factor in interpersonal attraction.

Proximodistal Pattern of development normal to humans in which infants gain control over areas that are closest to the center of their bodies (so that, for instance, control is gained over the upper arms before the fingers).

Psychoactive drugs Drugs that have the effect of altering perceptions and behavior by changing conscious awareness.

Psychoanalysis Technique developed by Freud in which an individual's revelations of normally unconscious cognitions are interpreted.

Psychoanalytic approach Approach to psychology developed by Freud which emphasizes the dynamics among the three forces of personality, the id, ego, and superego; the importance of defense mechanisms; and the importance of dreams as the royal road to the unconscious.

Psychoanalytic theory Theory of personality that views people as shaped by ongoing conflicts between primary drives and the social pressures of civilized society.

Psychogenic amnesia Type of dissociative disorder characterized by sudden loss of memory, usually after a particularly stressful or traumatic event.

Psychogenic fugue disorder Type of dissociative disorder characterized by a loss of memory accompanied by a fugue state in which the individual travels from place to place with little social contact with other people.

Psycholinguistics Psychological study of how sounds and symbols are translated to meaning, and of the cognitive processes that are involved in the acquisition and use of language.

Psychological dependence Dependence on a chemical substance in which a person finds the substance so pleasurable or helpful in coping with life that he or she becomes addicted to its use.

Psychology Scientific study of the behavior of humans and other animals.

Psychophysics Study of the relationship between the physical aspects of external stimuli and our own perceptions of these stimuli.

Psychosexual development Stages of development, in Freud's perspective, in which the focus of sexual gratification shifts from one body site to another.

Psychosis Term used until publication of DSM-III in 1980 to describe severe disorders that involve disturbances of thinking, reduced contact with reality, loss of ability to function socially, and often bizarre behaviors.

Psychotherapy Any nonbiological, noninvasive psychological technique or procedure designed to improve a person's adjustment to life.

Puberty Approximately two-year period of rapid physical changes that occur sometime between ages seven and 16 in our society and culminate in sexual maturity.

Punisher Any stimulus whose presentation following a response decreases the strength or frequency of the response. *See also Punishment.*

Punishment A procedure where the presentation of a stimulus following a response leads to a decrease in the strength or frequency of the response. *See also Punisher.*

Quantitative psychology Field of specialization that uses mathematical techniques and computer science to aid in understanding human behavior.

Radical behaviorism A strict approach to the study of behavior which emphasizes operant conditioning principles.

Random sample Sample group of a larger population that is selected by randomization procedures. A random sample differs from a representative sample.

Range In descriptive statistics, a measure of variability that indicates the difference between the highest and lowest scores.

Rational-emotive therapy (RET) Approach to therapy based on the premise that psychological problems result when people interpret their experiences based on self-defeating, irrational beliefs.

Rationalization Defense mechanism in which an individual substitutes self-justifying excuses or explanations for the real reasons for behaviors.

Reaction formation Defense mechanism in which the ego unconsciously replaces unacceptable impulses with their opposites.

Reality principle According to Freud, the tendency to behave in ways that are consistent with reality. The reality principle governs the ego.

Recall In memory tests, a subject's ability to reproduce information that he or she was previously exposed to. Fill-in-the-blank and essay questions test recall.

Receptor Specialized protein molecule on the surface of a dendrite or cell body with which neurotransmitters or certain drugs bind.

Receptor cell Specialized cell that transduces sensory information into neural impulses. Photoreceptors in the retina are receptor cells.

Recessive gene Gene that is expressed in the phenotype only in the absence of a dominant gene, or when it is paired with a similar recessive gene.

Reciprocal determinism According to Albert Bandura, the principle that individual behaviors and thus personalities are shaped by the interaction between cognitive factors and environmental factors.

Recognition In memory tests, a subject's ability to recognize whether he or she has been previously exposed to information. Multiple-choice and true/false questions test recognition.

Recombinant DNA technology Complex technique used by researchers to cut apart and reassemble sections of DNA strands to locate genetic information. Sometimes called gene splicing.

Regression Defense mechanism in which an individual attempts to cope with an anxiety-producing situation by retreating to an earlier stage of development. In statistics, a procedure for predicting the size of one variable based on a knowledge of the size of a correlated variable and the coefficient of correlation between the two variables.

Reflex An automatic response to a specific stimulus. An eye blink to a puff of air is a reflex.

Reinforcement In operant conditioning, any procedure where an event following a specific response increases the probability that the response will occur. *See also Reinforcer.*

Reinforcer In operant conditioning, any response contingent event that leads to an increase in the probability, or strength, of the response.

Relative motion Monocular distance cue based on the fact that moving objects appear to move a greater distance when they are close to the viewer than when they are far away. Also known as motion parallax.

Relative size Monocular distance cue based on the fact that objects of the same size appear to be smaller the farther they are from the viewer.

Relaxation response State of deep relaxation similar to meditation. Often used to reduce a stress response.

Relearning Technique for testing memory that involves measuring how much more quickly a person can relearn material that was learned at some previous time.

Reliability In testing, the dependable consistency of a test.

REM sleep State of sleep characterized by rapid eye movements, and often associated with dreaming.

Replication studies Research conducted for the purpose of verifying previous findings.

Representative heuristic Strategy for categorizing an object or situation based on one's preconceived notion of characteristics that are typical of that category.

Representative sample Sample in which critical subgroups are represented according to their incidence in the larger population that the researcher is studying. *See also Survey.*

Repression In psychoanalytic theory, the defense mechanism by which ideas, feelings, or memories that are too painful to deal with on a conscious level are banished to the unconscious.

Residual schizophrenia Term used to describe the residual phase of schizophrenic disorder, which is a recovery phase during which major symptoms are absent or markedly diminished.

Resistance In psychoanalysis, a patient's unwillingness to describe freely some aspects of his or her life.

Response contingency In operant conditioning, the occurrence of a specific response before a reinforcer is presented.

Resting potential State in which a neuron is not transmitting a nerve impulse. A neuron in this state has a net negative charge relative to its outside environment, and this state of potential energy prepares it to be activated by an impulse from an adjacent neuron.

Reticular activating system (RAS) *See Reticular formation.*

Reticular formation Set of neural circuits extending from the lower brain up to the thalamus that play a critical role in controlling arousal and alertness. Also known as the reticular activating system.

Retina Thin membrane at the back of the eye containing photoreceptors called rods and cones. The retina functions to record images.

Retinal disparity *See Binocular disparity.*

Retrieval Process by which information stored in memory is accessed.

Retroactive interference In memory, the phenomenon that occurs when a later event interferes with the recall of earlier information.

Retrograde amnesia Memory loss for certain details or events that occurred prior to experiencing brain trauma; a form of organic amnesia.

Reuptake The process by which neurotransmitter substance is taken back into the terminal button after its release.

Rodopsin Photopigment contained in the retinal rods.

Rods Photoreceptor cells distributed across the inner layer of the retina that are important in peripheral vision and seeing in dim light.

Rorschach inkblot test Commonly used projective test in which the subject is asked to examine inkblots and say what they look like or bring to mind.

S-factor In Charles Spearman's two-factor theory of the structure of intelligence, s-factors are specific abilities or skills. *See also G-factor.*

Saccadic eye movement Rapid movements of the eyes used to scan a visual scene.

Sample Selected segment of a larger population that is being studied in psychological research. Two kinds of samples are the representative sample and the random sample.

Saturation Proportion of colored or chromatic light to noncolored or nonchromatic light, which determines how colorful light appears.

Schachter-Singer theory Theory that a given body state can be linked to a variety of emotions depending on the context in which the body state occurs.

Schedule of reinforcement The rule that determines the relationship between responses and reinforcement. *See also Fixed ratio, Variable ratio, Fixed interval, and Variable ratio schedules.*

Schemas In reference to memory, conceptual frameworks that individuals use to make sense out of stored information. In Piaget's theory, the mental structures we form to assimilate and organize processed information.

Schizophrenia Class of severe and disabling mental disorders that are characterized by extreme disruptions of perceptions, thoughts, emotions, and behavior. Types identified by DSM-IV include disorganized, catatonic, paranoid, undifferentiated, and residual schizophrenia.

School psychology Field of specialization concerned with evaluating and resolving learning and emotional problems.

Scientific method Careful observation of events in the world, the formation of predictions based on these observations, and the testing of these predictions by manipulation of variables and systematic observation.

Seasonal affective disorder (SAD) Diagnostic category in which major depression or bipolar depression recurrently follows a seasonal pattern.

Secondary reinforcer Stimulus that acts as a reinforcer by virtue of its association with one or more primary reinforcers. Also known as a conditioned reinforcer.

Secondary sex characteristics Physical characteristics typical of mature males or females (such as facial, body, and pubic hair) that develop during puberty as a result of the release of testosterone or estrogen.

Secondary trait In Gordon Allport's trait theory of personality, any of a variety of less generalized and often short-term traits that affect people's behavior in specific circumstances. *See also Cardinal trait and Central trait.*

Secular growth trends Changes in human physical growth patterns (including height, weight, and rates of maturation) measured in sample populations throughout the world.

Sedatives Class of depressant drugs including tranquilizers, barbiturates, and nonbarbiturates that induce relaxation, calmness, and sleep.

Selective attention The process of focusing on one or a few stimuli of particular significance while ignoring others.

Selective perception A form of perceptual set; the tendency to perceive stimuli that are consistent with expectations and to ignore those that are inconsistent.

Self-efficacy Individual's belief that he or she can perform adequately and deal effectively with a particular situation.

Semantic memory General, nonpersonal knowledge about the meaning of facts and concepts.

Semantics Study of meaning in language.

Semicircular canals Three ring-shaped structures in the inner ear that provide information about the body's equilibrium or balance.

Senile dementia Collective term describing a variety of conditions sometimes associated with aging, including memory deficits, forgetfulness, disorientation for time and place, declining ability to think, and so forth.

Sensations Basic, immediate experiences that a stimulus such as a sound elicits in a sense organ such as the ear.

Sensation-seeking motive An explanation for the apparent need for certain levels of stimulation including the need to explore the environment and the need for sensory stimulation.

Sensorimotor stage In Piaget's theory, the period of development between birth and about age two during which infants learn about their worlds primarily through their senses and actions.

Sensorineural hearing loss Hearing loss caused by damage to either the hair cells of the inner ear or the auditory nerve.

Sensory cortex Regions of the cerebral cortex that is involved in receiving sensory messages. *Also see Association cortex.*

Sensory deprivation studies Experimental studies in which subjects lie motionless and are deprived of tactile, visual, and auditory sensations.

Sensory memory First system in the three-system model of memory, in which brief impressions from any of the senses are stored fleetingly, disappearing within a few seconds if they are not transferred to short-term memory. *See also Iconic memory and Echoic memory.*

Sensory neuron Neuron or nerve cell that carries messages to the CNS from receptors in the skin, ears, nose, eyes, and other receptor organs. Also known as afferent neuron.

Separate attachment Attachment typically displayed by infants by about 12 to 18 months, when fear of strangers diminishes and interest in people other than primary caregivers develops. *See also Indiscriminant attachment and Specific attachment.*

Septal area Structure in the brain's limbic system that plays a role in the experiencing of pleasure.

Serial position effect Tendency to remember items at the beginning and end of a list more readily than those in the middle.

Set point Physiologically preferred level of body weight for each individual.

Sex-linked inheritance Genetic transmission involving genes that are carried only on the X chromosome. (Females carry the XX chromosome pair; males carry the XY pair.)

Sexual orientation Sex to which an individual is attracted.

Shape constancy Element of perceptual constancy: We perceive objects as maintaining the same shape even though their retinal images change when we view them from different angles.

Shaping In operant conditioning, a technique where responses that are increasingly similar to the desired behavior are reinforced, step by step, until the desired behavior occurs.

Short-term memory (STM) Immediate recollection of stimuli that have just been perceived; unless it is transferred to long-term memory, information in this memory system is usually retained only momentarily. Also called working memory.

Sign stimulus A stimulus to which all members of a species (occasionally of the same sex) respond to in a similar way. Elaborate rump feathers on some birds serve as a sign stimulus for mating.

Signal detection theory Theory that says our ability to detect a sensory stimulus (signal) depends not only on the intensity of the signal but also on variables such as distractions and motivation.

Similarity In perception, the principle that we tend to group elements that are similar to each other. In social psychology, similarity of beliefs, interests, and values is recognized as a factor attracting people to one another.

Simultaneous conditioning In classical conditioning, learning that takes place when the conditioned stimulus is presented at the same time as the unconditioned stimulus.

Size constancy One form of perceptual constancy: Although the retinal image of an object becomes smaller as it recedes into the distance (or larger as it approaches), the viewer adjusts for this change and perceives the object to be constant in size.

Skewed In descriptive statistics, the term describes an unbalanced distribution of scores.

Sleep Natural, periodically occurring state of rest characterized by reduced activity, lessened responsiveness to stimuli, and distinctive brain wave patterns.

Sleep apnea Sleep disorder characterized by irregular breathing during sleep.

Sleep disorders Class of disorders that interfere with sleep, including insomnia, sleep apnea, sleep terrors, nightmares, and sleepwalking.

Sleep terror Sleep disorder in which a person suddenly awakens from Stage 4 sleep in a panic, typically with no recollection of a bad dream.

Sleepwalking Sleep disorder, also known as somnambulism, characterized by walking in one's sleep during Stage 3 or 4 of NREM sleep.

Social adjustment function One of the most important functions of our attitudes, which is to allow us to identify with or gain approval from our peers.

Social influence Efforts by others to alter our feelings, beliefs, and behavior.

Social-learning theory Theory that emphasizes the role of observation in learning.

Social perception Way in which we perceive, evaluate, categorize, and form judgments about the qualities of other people.

Social phobia Anxiety disorder characterized by a persistent, irrational fear of performing some specific behavior (such as talking or eating) in the presence of other people.

Social psychology Field of specialization concerned with understanding the impact of social environments and social processes on individuals.

Socialization Process by which society conveys behavioral expectations to an individual, through various agents such as parents, peers, and school.

Sociobiology A specialization within biology that seeks to understand the biological factors that underlie social behaviors in all animal species, including humans.

Soma *See Cell body.*

Somatic nervous system Division of the peripheral nervous system that transmits messages to and from major skeletal muscles as well as from sensory organs to the CNS.

Somatization disorder Type of somatoform disorder characterized by multiple and recurrent physical symptoms which have no physical cause.

Somatoform disorder Class of disorders including somatization disorder, hypochondriasis, and conversion disorder that are manifested through somatic or physical symptoms.

Somatosensory cortex Area of the parietal lobe, directly across from the motor cortex in the frontal lobe, which receives sensory information about touch, pressure, pain, temperature, and body position.

Source traits In Raymond Cattell's trait theory of personality, basic, underlying traits that are the center or core of an individual's personality. *See also Surface traits.*

Specific attachment Highly selective attachment often displayed by human infants sometime between six and 18 months, when increased responsiveness is displayed toward primary caregivers and distress may be displayed when separated from parents. *See also Indiscriminant attachment and Separate attachment.*

Specific phobia Anxiety disorder characterized by an irrational fear of specific situations or objects, such as heights, small closed places, or spiders.

Split-half reliability Measure of test reliability in which a subject's performance on a single administration of a test is assessed by comparing performance on half of the test items with performance on the other half of the test items.

Spontaneous recovery In classical conditioning, the spontaneous reappearance of a conditioned response after extinction has taken place.

Stage 1 sleep Light sleep that occurs just after dozing off, characterized by brain waves called theta waves.

Stage 2 sleep Stage of sleep that typically follows Stage 1 sleep, characterized by brief bursts of brain activity called sleep spindles as well as K complex responses to stimuli such as noises.

Stage 3 sleep Stage of sleep that typically follows Stage 2 sleep, characterized by an EEG tracing 20 to 50 percent of which consists of delta waves. There are virtually no eye movements during Stage 3 sleep.

Stage 4 sleep Deepest level of sleep, characterized by an EEG tracing exceeding 50 percent delta waves and virtually no eye movements.

Standard deviation In descriptive statistics, a measure of variability that indicates the average extent to which all the scores in a distribution vary from the mean.

Standard score In descriptive statistics, a measure that indicates how far a score deviates from the average in standard units.

Standardization procedures Uniform and consistent procedures for administering and scoring tests, such as IQ or personality tests.

Stanford-Binet test IQ test developed by Lewis Terman who revised Binet's scale and adapted questions to American students.

State-dependent memory Phenomenon wherein recall of particular events, experiences, or information is aided by the subject being in the same context or physiological state in which the information was first encoded.

Statistical significance Term used to describe research results in which changes in the dependent variable can be attributed with a high level of confidence to the experimental condition (or independent variable) being manipulated by the researcher.

Statistics Mathematical methods for describing and interpreting data. Two kinds of statistics are descriptive and inferential statistics.

Stereotypes Preconceived and oversimplified beliefs and expectations about the traits of members of a particular group that do not account for individual differences.

Stimulants Psychoactive drugs, including caffeine, nicotine, amphetamines, and cocaine, that stimulate the central nervous system by increasing the transmission of neural impulses.

Stimulus contiguity In classical conditioning, the close pairing in time of the conditioned stimulus (CS) and the unconditioned stimulus (UCS). *See also Delayed conditioning.*

Stimulus contingency In classical conditioning, the correlation, or dependency, between a conditioned stimulus (CS) and an unconditioned stimulus (UCS).

Storage Process by which encoded material is retained over time in memory.

Stress Process of appraising events or situations as harmful, threatening, or challenging, of assessing potential responses, and of responding to those events.

Stress-induced analgesia (SIA) Dramatically reduced sensitivity to pain that may occur under highly stressful conditions.

Striving for superiority In Alfred Adler's neo-Freudian theory, a universal urge to achieve self-perfection through successful adaptation to life's circumstances, mastering challenges, and personal growth.

Structuralism Approach to psychology that attempted to break down experience into its basic elements or structures, using a technique called introspection in which subjects provided scientific reports of perceptual experiences.

Sublimation Form of the defense mechanism displacement in which impulse-driven behaviors are channeled toward producing a socially valued accomplishment.

Subtractive color mixing Color mixing process that occurs when pigments are mixed, so that when light falls on the colored object some wavelengths are absorbed (or subtracted) and others are reflected. *See also Additive color mixing.*

Superego According to Freud, the third system of personality which consists of an individual's conscience as well as the ego-ideal (the shoulds of behavior). *See also Id and Ego.*

Surface traits In Raymond Cattell's trait theory of personality, dimensions or traits that are usually obvious (such as integrity or tidiness) and that tend to be grouped in clusters that are related to source traits.

Survey Research method in which a representative sample of people are questioned about their behaviors or attitudes. The survey provides descriptive information. *See also Sample.*

Syllogism Argument consisting of two or more premises, followed by a statement of conclusion that may or may not follow logically from the premises.

Sympathetic nervous system Division of the autonomic nervous system that functions to produce emergency responses such as increased heart rate, pupil dilation, and inhibited digestive activity; the sympathetic nervous system works in tandem with the parasympathetic nervous system.

Synapse Includes the synaptic gap and a portion of the presynaptic and postsynaptic membranes that are involved in transmitting an impulse between neurons. *See also Synaptic gap.*

Synaptic gap Space between transmitting and receiving neurons. *See also Synapse.*

Synaptic vesicle A microscopic sac that contains neurotransmitter substance located in the terminal button of a neuron.

Syntax Set of language rules that govern how words can be combined to form meaningful phrases and sentences; grammar.

Systematic desensitization Behavior therapy using a classical conditioning technique that pairs the slow, systematic exposure to anxiety-inducing situations with relaxation training.

Tachistoscope A device connected to a projector used to control the duration of stimulus presentation.

Tardive dyskinesia A severe movement disorder often associated with long-term use of antipsychotic medication.

Taste bud A specialized receptor cell on the tongue.

Tectorial membrane Membrane located above the basilar membrane in the cochlea of the auditory system.

Temporal contiguity In operant conditioning, the close relation in time between a response and a reinforcer.

Temporal lobe Region of the cerebral cortex located below the lateral fissure that contains the auditory cortex.

Terminal buttons Swollen bulb-like structure on the end of a neuron's axon that releases chemical substances known as neurotransmitters.

Territoriality Tendency to stake out

certain areas with relatively fixed boundaries that others can enter only on invitation.

Testing hypotheses Problem-solving strategy that involves formulating specific hypotheses which generate relatively efficient approaches to solving a problem, then testing these hypotheses in a systematic fashion.

Test-retest reliability Method for evaluating test reliability by giving a subject (or subjects) the same test more than once.

Texture gradients Monocular distance cue based on the fact that textured surfaces (such as a grassy lawn) appear to be smoother, denser, and less textured when they are far from the viewer than when they are close.

Thalamus Structure located beneath the cerebrum in the brain that functions as a relay station, routing incoming sensory information to appropriate areas in the cerebral cortex. Also seems to play a role in regulating sleep cycles.

Thematic Apperception Test (TAT) Projective test for personality assessment in which the subject is shown cards depicting various scenes and is asked to describe what is happening in each scene.

Theories Tentative attempts to organize and fit into a logical explanatory framework all of the relevant data or facts scientists have observed regarding certain phenomena.

Thought Any cognitive processes directed toward problem solving, understanding language, memory retrieval, and perceiving patterns in sensory inputs.

Threshold Minimum level of intensity or strength of a stimulus that is sufficient to activate a sensory process (for instance, the minimum number of molecules that must be present in the air for us to smell a substance).

Thyroid gland Endocrine gland located in the neck which influences metabolism, mood states, and behavior.

Timbre Quality of complex sound that is a product of the combination of fundamental frequency and additional frequency components called overtones.

Trace conditioning In classical conditioning, learning that takes place when presentation of the conditioned stimulus begins and ends before the unconditioned stimulus is presented.

Transduction Process by which sensory organs transform mechanical, chemical, or light energy into the electrochemical energy that is generated by neurons firing.

Transference In psychotherapy, a process in which a patient begins to relate to the therapist in much the same way as to another important person in his or her life (such as a parent).

Trial-and-error Problem-solving strategy that involves trying possible solutions, one by one, to see which one is correct.

Triarchic theory of intelligence Theory that intelligence is a multidimensional trait comprising componential, experiential, and contextual abilities.

Trichromatic theory of color vision Also known as the Young-Helmholtz theory, the postulation that the human eye contains three types of color receptors (for red, green, and blue), which form the basis for our perception of all colors. *See also Opponent-process theory of color vision.*

Two-egg twins *See Fraternal twins.*

Two-factor learning Learning that combines both classical and operant conditioning.

Two-factor theory Influential theory in I/O psychology stating that employees are motivated by two types of needs: extrinsic hygiene needs for job security, adequate pay, and so forth; and intrinsic motivator needs for challenge, autonomy, and recognition.

Tympanic membrane Membrane stretched across the end of the auditory canal that vibrates in response to sound waves. Also known as the eardrum.

Type A Individuals who are hard-driving, ambitious, competitive, easily angered, time conscious, and demanding of both themselves and others, as described by Friedman and Rosenman in their study of coronary heart disease.

Type B Individuals who are relaxed, easygoing, not driven to achieve perfection, happy in their jobs, understanding, and not easily angered, as described by Friedman and Rosenman in their study of coronary heart disease.

Unconditional positive regard In person-centered therapy, the therapist's attitude of unconditional acceptance toward the client.

Unconditioned response (UCR) In classical conditioning, an unlearned response to a stimulus.

Unconditioned stimulus (UCS) In classical conditioning, a stimulus that elicits an unlearned response.

Unconscious Level of mental awareness describing ideas, feelings, and memories that cannot easily be brought into consciousness.

Unconscious mind According to Freud's theory, the vast reservoir of the mind which holds countless memories and feelings that are repressed or submerged because they are anxiety-producing.

Undifferentiated schizophrenia Catchall category assigned to schizophrenics who do not manifest specific symptoms of disorganized, catatonic, or paranoid schizophrenia.

Validity In testing, the ability of a test to measure accurately what it is supposed to measure.

Variable interval (VI) schedule Partial reinforcement schedule in operant conditioning where opportunities for reinforcement occur at variable time intervals.

Variable ratio (VR) schedule Partial reinforcement schedule in operant conditioning where reinforcement is provided after an average of a specific number of responses occur.

Variance In descriptive statistics, a measure of variability that is the average of the squared distances of the scores from the mean.

Ventricle Fluid-filled chambers within the brain.

Ventromedial hypothalamus (VMH) One of two regions of the hypothalamus that seems to act as a control center for eating. Stimulation of the VMH inhibits feeding, and destruction of the VMH may result in extreme overeating. *See also Lateral hypothalamus and Hypothalamic control theory.*

Vestibular sacs Structures at the junction of the semicircular canals and cochlea of the middle ear that provide information about the head's position in space.

Visual cliff Device which produces the illusion of a cliff, allowing researchers to test the ability of animals to perceive and respond to depth cues.

Visual cortex Portion of the occipital lobe that integrates sensory information received from the eyes into electrical patterns that the brain translates into vision.

Visual memory *See Iconic memory.*

Volley theory Related to the frequency theory of pitch discrimination. Postulates that since single auditory neurons cannot fire rapidly enough to enable us to perceive tones in the 1,000 to 4,000 Hz range, pitch perception is made possible by groups of interrelated neurons firing in concert.

Wavelength The distance between adjacent waves. Used to measure electromagnetic energy. Colors of the visual spectrum are associated with different wavelengths.

Wear-and-tear theory *See Accumulating damages theory.*

Weber's fraction Ratio between a just noticeable difference and the intensity of a stimulus. *See also Weber's law.*

Weber's Law One of the major principles of sensation, based on the fact that for various stimulus intensities, the difference threshold tends to be a constant fraction of the stimulus. As the strength of the original stimulus increases, the magnitude of the change must also increase in order for a just noticeable difference to be perceived.

Wechsler Adult Intelligence Scale (WAIS) Intelligence test developed by David Wechsler in the 1930s with subtests grouped by aptitude rather than age level.

Wernicke's aphasia A speech disorder associated with damage to Wernicke's area of the brain. Characterized by the production of meaningless speech and difficulties in speech perception.

Wernicke's area Area of the left temporal lobe that is the brain's primary area for understanding speech.

White matter Areas of the central nervous system that are predominantly axons covered with white myelin sheaths.

Withdrawal symptoms Symptoms associated with the abrupt discontinuation of drug use.

Working backward Common heuristic problem-solving strategy that starts with describing the goal, then defines the step that directly precedes that goal, and works backward in this manner until the steps needed to reach the goal are defined.

Working memory *See Short-term memory.*

Yerkes-Dodson law Principle that the optimum level of arousal for peak performance will vary somewhat depending on the nature of the task.

Young-Helmholtz theory *See Trichromatic theory.*

Zygote Cell produced by the uniting of a sperm cell with an egg cell.

Zygote stage *See Germinal stage.*

BIBLIOGRAPHY

Abel, E. (1984). Opiates and sex. *Journal of Psychoactive Drugs, 16*, 205–216.

Abraham, K. (1911). Notes on the psychoanalytical investigation and treatment of manic-depressive insanity and allied conditions. Originally written in 1911 and later published in E. Jones (Ed.), *Selected Papers of Karl Abraham, M.D.* London: Hogarth Press.

Abroms, K., & Bennett, J. (1981). Changing etiological perspectives in Down's syndrome: Implications for early intervention. *Journal of the Division for Early Childhood, 2*, 109–112.

Abu-Mostafa, Y., & Psaltis, D. (1987). Optical neural computers. *Scientific American, 256*, 88–95.

Adams, J. (1973). *Understanding Adolescence.* Boston: Allyn & Bacon.

Adams, K., & Oswald, I. (1977). Sleep is for tissue restoration. *Journal of the Royal College of Physicians, 11*, 376–388.

Ader, R., & Cohen, N. (1982). Behaviorally conditioned immunosuppression and murine systemic lupus erythematosus. *Science, 215*, 1534–1536.

Adler, A. (1917). *Study of Organ Inferiority and Its Psychical Compensation.* New York: Nervous and Mental Diseases Publishing Co.

Adler, A. (1927). *Practice and Theory of Individual Psychology.* New York: Harcourt, Brace & World.

Adler, A. (1930). Individual Psychology. In C. Murchinson (Ed.), *Psychologies of 1930.* Worcester, MA: Clark University Press.

Adorno, T., Frenkel-Brunswick, E., Levinson, D., & Sanford, R. (1950). *The Authoritarian Personality.* New York: Harper & Row.

Aikawa, J. (1981). *Magnesium: Its Biological Significance.* Boca Raton, FL: CRC Press.

Ainsworth, M. (1963). The development of infant-mother interaction among the Ganda. In B. Foss (Ed.), *Determinants of Infant Behavior* (Vol. 2). New York: Wiley.

Ainsworth, M. (1979). Infant-mother attachment. *American Psychologist, 34*, 932–937.

Ainsworth, M. (1989). Attachments beyond infancy. *American Psychologist, 44*, 709–716.

Alain, M. (1989). Do what I say, not what I do: Children's reactions to parents' behavioral inconsistencies. *Perceptual and Motor Skills, 68*, 99–102.

Aldrich, M., Alessi, A., Beck, R., & Gilman, S. (1987). Cortical blindness: Etiology, diagnosis, and prognosis. *Annals of Neurology, 21*, 149–158.

Alkon, D. (1989). Memory storage and neural systems. *Scientific American,* July, 42–50.

Allen, M. (1976). Twin studies of affective illness. *Archives of General Psychiatry, 33*, 1476–1478.

Allport, G. (1937). *Personality: A Psychological Interpretation.* New York: Holt, Rinehart and Winston.

Allport, G. (1961). *Pattern and Growth in Personality.* New York: Holt, Rinehart and Winston.

Allport, G. (1965). *Letters from Jenny.* New York: Harcourt, Brace & World.

Allport, G. (1966). Traits revisited. *American Psychologist, 21*, 1–10.

Allport, G., & Postman, L. (1947). *The Psychology of Rumor.* New York: Holt, Rinehart and Winston.

Almli, C. (1978). The ontogeny of feeding and drinking behavior: Effects of early brain damage. *Neuroscience and Behavioral Reviews, 2*, 281–300.

Altman, J. (1986). Images in and of the brain. *Nature, 324*, 405.

Altura, B. M., Altura, B. T., Gebrewold, A., Ising, H., & Gunther, T. (1984). Magnesium-deficient diets and microcirculatory changes in situ. *Science, 223*, 1315–1317.

Amabile, T., & Glazebrook, A. (1982). A negativity bias in interpersonal evaluation. *Journal of Experimental Social Psychology, 18*, 1–22.

American Heart Association (1984). *Heart Facts.* Dallas: American Heart Association.

American Psychiatric Association (1987). *Diagnostic and Statistical Manual of Mental Disorders* (3rd ed. rev.). Washington, DC: American Psychiatric Association.

American Psychiatric Association (1993). *DSM-IV Draft Criteria.* Washington, DC: American Psychiatric Association.

American Psychological Association (1988). *1988 APA Membership Register.* Washington, DC: American Psychological Association.

Amice, V., Bercovici, J., Nahoul, K., Hatahet, M., & Amice, J. (1989). Increase in H-Y antigen-positive lymphocytes in hirsute women: Effects of cyproterone acetate and estradiol treatment. *Journal of Clinical Endocrinology and Metabolism, 68*, 58–62.

Amit, Z., & Galina, H. (1986). Stress-induced analgesia: Adaptive pain suppression. *Physiological Reviews, 66*, 1091–1120.

Amkraut, A., & Solomon, G. (1977). From the symbolic stimulus to the pathophysiologic response: Immune mechanisms. In Z. Lipowski, D. Lipsitt, & P. Whybrow (Eds.), *Psychosomatic Medicine: Current Trends and Clinical Applications.* New York: Oxford University Press.

Amoore, J. (1970). *Molecular Basis of Odor.* Springfield, IL: Thomas.

Amoore, J. (1982). Odor theory and odor classification. In E. Theimer (Ed.), *Fragrance Chemistry—The Science of the Sense of Smell.* New York: Academic Press.

Anand, B., & Brobeck, J. (1951). Hypothalamic control of food intake in rats and cats. *Yale Journal of Biological Medicine, 24*, 123–140.

Anastasi, A. (1976). *Psychological Testing* (4th ed.). New York: Macmillan.

Anastasi, A. (1988). *Psychological Testing* (6th ed.). New York: Macmillan.

Anch, A., Browman, C., Mitler, M., & Walsh, J. (1988). *Sleep: A Scientific Perspective.* Englewood Cliffs, NJ: Prentice Hall.

Anderson, J. (1983a). *The Architecture of Cognition.* Cambridge, MA: Harvard University Press.

Anderson, J. (1983b). A spreading activation theory of memory. *Journal of Verbal Learning and Verbal Behavior, 22*, 261–295.

Anderton, B. (1987). Alzheimer's disease: Progress in molecular pathology. *Nature, 325*, 658–659.

Andreasen, N., & Carter, A. (1974). The creative writer: Psychiatric symptoms and family history. *Comprehensive Psychiatry, 15*, 125–131.

Andreasen, N., Ehrhardt, J., Swayze, V., Alliger, R., Yuh, W., Cohen, G., & Ziebell, S. (1990). Magnetic resonance imaging of the brain in schizophrenia. *Archives of General Psychiatry, 47*, 35–44.

Annas, G., & Elias, S. (1990). Legal and ethical implications of fetal diagnosis and gene therapy. *American Journal of Medical Genetics, 35*, 215–218.

Appley, M., & Trumbull, R. (Eds.). (1986). *Dynamics of Stress: Physiological, Psychological, and Social Perspectives.* New York: Plenum Press.

Archer, S. (1982). The lower age boundaries of identity development. *Child Development, 53*, 1551–1556.

Arend, R., Gove, F., & Stroufe, L. (1979). Continuity of individual adaptation from infancy to kindergarten: A predictive study of ego-resiliency and curiosity in preschoolers. *Child Development, 50*, 950–959.

Arlin, P. (1975). Cognitive development in adulthood: A fifth stage? *Developmental Psychology, 11,* 602–606.

Arlin, P. (1977). Piagetian operations in problem finding. *Developmental Psychology, 13,* 297–298.

Arlow, J. (1984). Psychoanalysis. In R. Corsini (Ed.), *Current Psychotherapies.* Ithaca, IL: Peacock.

Armentrout, J., & Burger, G. (1972). Children's reports of parental child-rearing behavior at five grade levels. *Developmental Psychology, 7,* 44–48.

Armstrong, S., Gleitman, L., & Gleitman, H. (1983). What some concepts might not be. *Cognition, 13,* 263–308.

Arnetz, B., Wasserman, J., Petrini, B., Brenner, S., Levi, L., Eneroth, P., Salovaara, H., Hjelm, R., Salovaara, L., Theorell, T., & Petterson, I. (1987). Immune function in unemployed women. *Psychosomatic Medicine, 49,* 3–12.

Aronson, E. (1980). *The Social Animal* (3rd ed.). New York: Freeman.

Aronson, E., & Mills, J. (1959). The effect of severity of initiation on liking for a group. *Journal of Abnormal and Social Psychology, 67,* 31–36.

Arrowood, J., & Short, J. (1973). Agreement, attraction, and self-esteem. *Canadian Journal of Behavioral Science, 5,* 242–252.

Arthur, A. (1987). Stress as a state of anticipatory vigilance. *Perceptual and Motor Skills, 64,* 75–85.

Asch, S. (1946). Forming impressions of personality. *Journal of Abnormal and Social Psychology, 41,* 258–290.

Aserinsky, E., & Kleitman, N. (1953). Regularly occurring periods of eye motility and concomitant phenomena during sleep. *Science, 118,* 273–274.

Ashcraft, M., Fries, B., Nerenz, D., & Falcon, S. (1989). A psychiatric patient classification system: An alternative to diagnosis-related groups. *Medical Care, 27,* 543–557.

Ashmore, R., & Del Boca, F. (1976). Psychological approaches to understanding intergroup conflicts. In P. Katz (Ed.), *Towards the Elimination of Racism,* New York: Pergamon.

Aslin, R., Pisoni, D., & Jusczyk, P. (1983). Auditory development and speech perception in infancy. In M. Harth & J. Campos (Eds.), *Handbook of Child Psychology: Infancy and Developmental Psychobiology* (Vol. 2). New York: Wiley.

Athanasiou, R., Shaver, P., & Tavris, C. (1970). Sex. *Psychology Today,* July, 39–52.

Atkinson, J. (1957). Motivational determinants of risk-taking behavior. *Psychological Review, 64,* 359–372.

Atkinson, J., & Litwin, G. (1960). Achievement motive and test anxiety conceived as motive to approach success and motive to avoid failure. *Journal of Abnormal and Social Psychology, 60,* 52–63.

Atkinson, J., & Raynor, J. (1974). *Motivation and Achievement.* Washington, DC: Winston.

Atkinson, R., & Shiffrin, R. (1968). Human memory: A proposed system and its control processes. In K. Spence & J. Spence (Eds.), *The Psychology of Learning and Motivation: Advances in Research and Theory* (Vol. 2). New York: Academic Press.

Atkinson, R., & Shiffrin, R. (1971). The control of short-term memory. *Scientific American, 234,* 83–89.

Attie, I., & Brooks-Gunn, J. (1989). Development of caring problems in adolescent girls: A longitudinal study. *Developmental Psychology, 25,* 70–79.

Aubert-Tulkens, G., Culee, C., & Rodenstein, D. (1989). Cure of sleep apnea syndrome after long-term nasal continuous positive airway pressure therapy and weight loss. *Sleep, 12,* 216–222.

Austrom, D., & Hanel, K. (1985). Psychological issues of single life in Canada: An exploratory study. *International Journal of Women's Studies, 8,* 12–23.

Avison, W., & Speechley, K. (1987). The discharged psychiatric patient: A review of social, social-psychological, and psychiatric correlates of outcomes. *American Journal of Psychiatry, 144,* 10–18.

Bachrach, A., Erwin, W., & Mohn, J. (1965). The control of eating behavior in an anorexic by operant conditioning techniques. In L. Ullman & L. Krasner (Eds.), *Case Studies in Behavior Modification.* New York: Holt, Rinehart and Winston.

Bahnson, C. (1981). Stress and cancer: The state of the art. *Psychosomatics, 22,* 207–220.

Baillargeon, R. (1987). Object permanence in $3\frac{1}{2}$- and $4\frac{1}{2}$-month-old infants. *Developmental Psychology, 33,* 655–664.

Baker, L., Dearborn, M., Hastings, J., & Hamberger, K. (1984). Type A behavior in women: A review. *Health Psychology, 3,* 477–497.

Baldwin, J., & Baldwin, J. (1988). Factors affecting AIDS-related sexual risk-taking behavior among college students. *Journal of Sex Research, 25,* 181–196.

Bale, J., Bell, W., Dunn, V., Afifi, A., & Menezen, A. (1986). Magnetic resonance imaging of the spine in children. *Archives of Neurology, 43,* 1253–1256.

Balon, R., Jordan, M., Pohl, R., & Yeragani, V. (1989). Family history of anxiety disorders in control subjects with lactate-induced panic attacks. *The American Journal of Psychiatry, 146,* 1304–1306.

Balota, D., & Lorch, R. (1986). Depth of automatic spreading activation: Medicated primary effects in pronunciation but not in lexical decision. *Journal of Experimental Psychology: Learning, Memory, and Cognition, 12,* 336–345.

Baltrusch, H., & Waltz, E. (1985). Cancer from a biobehavioral and social epidemiological perspective. *Social Science and Medicine, 20,* 789–794.

Bancroft, J. (1984). Hormones and sexual behavior. *Journal of Sex and Marital Therapy, 10,* 3–21.

Bandura, A. (1960). *Relationship of Family Patterns to Child Behavior Disorders.* Progress Report, Project M-1734, Stanford University. Stanford, CA: U.S. Public Health Service.

Bandura, A. (1965). Influence of model's reinforcement contingencies on the acquisition of imitative responses. *Journal of Personality and Social Psychology, 1,* 589–595.

Bandura, A. (1969). *Principles of Behavior Modification.* New York: Holt, Rinehart and Winston.

Bandura, A. (1971). *Social Learning Theory.* Morristown, NJ: General Learning Press.

Bandura, A. (1973). *Aggression: A Social Learning Analysis.* Englewood Cliffs, NJ: Prentice-Hall.

Bandura, A. (1977). *Social Learning Theory.* Englewood Cliffs, NJ: Prentice-Hall.

Bandura, A. (1982). Self-efficacy mechanism in human agency. *American Psychologist, 37,* 122–147.

Bandura, A. (1983). Temporal dynamics and decomposition of reciprocal determinism: A reply to Phillips and Orton. *Psychological Review, 90,* 166–170.

Bandura, A. (1986). *Social Foundations of Thought and Action: A Social Cognitive Theory.* Englewood Cliffs, NJ: Prentice-Hall.

Bandura, A., & Mischel, W. (1965). Modification of self-imposed delay of reward through exposure to live and symbolic models. *Journal of Personality and Social Psychology, 2,* 698–705.

Bandura, A., Ross, D., & Ross, S. (1963). Limitation of film-mediated aggressive models. *Journal of Abnormal and Social Psychology, 66,* 3–11.

Bandura, A., & Walters, R. (1959). *Adolescent Aggression.* New York: Ronald Press.

Barahal, H. (1958). 1000 prefrontal lobotomies: Five-to-ten-year follow-up study. *Psychiatric Quarterly, 32,* 653–678.

Barber, T. (1975). Responding to "hypnotic" suggestions: An introspective report. *American Journal of Clinical Hypnosis, 18,* 6–22.

Barber, T., & Wilson, S. (1977). Hypnosis suggestions and altered states of consciousness. Experimental evaluation of a new cognitive-behavioral theory and the traditional trance-state therapy of "hypnosis." *Annals of the New York Academy of Sciences, 296,* 34–47.

Barinaga, M. (1989). Genetic testing for faults raises ethical questions. *The Oregonian,* January 26, C1–C2.

Barinaga, M. (1989). Manic depression gene put in limbo. *Science, 246,* 886–887.

Barnes, D. (1987a). Defect in Alzheimer's is on chromosome 21. *Science, 235,* 846–847.

Barnes, D. (1987b). Biological issues in schizophrenia. *Science, 235,* 430–433.

Barnett, P., & Gottlib, I. (1988). Psychosocial functioning and depression: Distinguishing among antecedents, concomitants, and consequences. *Psychological Bulletin, 104,* 97–126.

Baron, M., Gruen, R., Rainer, J., Kane, J., & Asnis, L. (1985). A family study of schizophrenic and normal control probands: Implications for the spectrum concept of schizophrenia. *The American Journal of Psychiatry, 142,* 447–455.

Baron, M., Risch, N., Hamburger, R., Mandel, B., Kushner, S., Newman, M., Drumer, D., & Belmaker, R. (1987). Genetic linkage between X-chromosome markers and bipolar affective illness. *Nature, 326,* 289–292.

Baron, R. (1986). Self-presentation in job interviews: When there can be "too much of a good thing." *Journal of Applied Social Psychology, 16,* 16–28.

Baron, R., & Byrne, D. (1987). *Social Psychology: Understanding Human Interaction* (5th ed.). Boston: Allyn & Bacon.

Bartlett, F. (1932). *Remembering: A Study in Ex-*

perimental and Social Psychology. Cambridge, England: Cambridge University Press.

Bartrop, R., Lockhurst, E., Lazarus, L., Kiloh, L., & Penny, R. (1977). Depressed lymphocyte function after bereavement. *Lancet, 1,* 834–836.

Bartusiak, M. (1980). Beeper man. *Discover,* November, 57.

Bartzokis, G., Hill, M., Altshuler, L., Cummings, J., Wirshing, W., & May, P. (1989). Tardive dyskinesia in schizophrenic patients: Correlation with negative symptoms. *Psychiatry Research, 28,* 145–151.

Bass, B., & Ryterbrand, E. (1979). *Organizational Psychology* (2nd ed.). Boston: Allyn & Bacon.

Baumeister, R., & Covington, M. (1985). Self-esteem, persuasion, and retrospective distortion of initial attitudes. *Electronic Social Psychology, 1,* 1–22.

Baumrind, D. (1964). Some thoughts on ethics of research after reading Milgram's "Behavioral study of obedience." *American Psychologist, 19,* 421–423.

Baumrind, D. (1971). Current patterns of parental authority. *Developmental Monographs, 4,* 1–103.

Beal, G., & Muehlenhard, C. (1987). Getting sexually aggressive men to stop their advances: Information for rape prevention programs. Paper presented at the Annual Meeting of the Association for Advancement of Behavior Therapy, Boston, November.

Beck, A. (1976). *Cognitive Therapy and Emotional Disorders.* New York: International Universities Press.

Beck, A., Brown, G., Berchick, R., Stewart, B., & Steer, R. (1990). Relationship between hopelessness and ultimate suicide: A replication with psychiatric outpatients. *The American Journal of Psychiatry, 147,* 190–195.

Beck, A., & Ward, C. (1961). Dreams of depressed patients: Characteristic themes in manifest content. *Archives of General Psychiatry, 5,* 462–467.

Beitman, B., Goldfried, M., & Norcross, J. (1989). The movement toward integrating the psychotherapies: An overview. *The American Journal of Psychiatry, 146,* 138–147.

Belec, L., Georges, A., Steenman, G., & Martin, P. (1989). Antibodies to human immunodeficiency virus in the semen of heterosexual men. *Journal of Infectious Diseases, 159,* 324–327.

Belfer, M., Krener, P., & Miller, F. (1988). AIDS in children and adolescents. *Journal of the American Academy of Child and Adolescent Psychiatry, 27,* 147–151.

Belicki, D., & Belicki, K. (1982). Nightmares in a university population. *Sleep Research, 11,* 116–121.

Bell, A., & Weinberg, M. (1978). *Homosexualities: A Study of Diversity Among Men and Women.* New York: Simon & Schuster.

Bell, A., Weinberg, M., & Hammersmith, S. (1981). *Sexual Preference: Its Development in Men and Women.* Bloomington, IN: Indiana University Press.

Bell, R., & Hepper, P. (1987). Catecholamines and aggression in animals. *Behavioral Brain Research, 23,* 1–21.

Belsky, J., & Rovine, M. (1990). Patterns of

marital change across the transition to parenthood: Pregnancy to three years postpartum. *Journal of Marriage and the Family, 52,* 5–19.

Bem, D. (1972). Self-perception theory. In L. Berkowitz (Ed.), *Advances in Experimental Social Psychology* (Vol. 6). New York: Academic Press.

Bem, D. (1983). Further *déjé vu* in the search for cross-situational consistency: A response to Mischel and Peake. *Psychological Review, 90,* 390–393.

Benbow, C., & Stanley, J. (1980). Sex differences in mathematical ability: Fact or artifact? *Science, 210,* 1262–1264.

Bergin, A., & Lambert, M. (1978). The evaluation of therapeutic outcomes. In S. Garfield & A. Bergin (Eds.), *Handbook of Psychotherapy and Behavior Change: An Empirical Analysis* (2nd ed.). New York: Wiley.

Berkowitz, L. (1954). Group standards, cohesiveness, and productivity. *Human Relations, 7,* 509–519.

Berkowitz, L. (1978). Whatever happened to the frustration-aggression hypothesis? *American Behavior Scientist, 21,* 691–708.

Berkowitz, L. (1983). Aversively stimulated aggression: Some parallels and differences in research with animals and humans. *American Psychologist, 38,* 1135–1144.

Berkowitz, L. (1986). *A Survey of Social Psychology* (3rd ed.). New York: Holt, Rinehart and Winston.

Berkowitz, L. (1989). Frustration-aggression hypothesis: Examination and reformulation. *Psychological Bulletin, 106,* 59–73.

Berkowitz, L., & Geen, R. (1966). Film violence and cue properties of available targets. *Journal of Personality and Social Psychology, 3,* 525–530.

Berkowitz, L., & Lepage, A. (1976). Weapons as aggression-eliciting stimuli. *Journal of Personality and Social Psychology, 7,* 202–207.

Berlyne, D. (1970). Novelty, complexity, and hedonic value. *Perception and Psychophysics, 8,* 279–286.

Berlyne, D. (1971). *Aesthetics and Psychobiology.* New York: Appleton, Century, Crofts.

Berman, E., & Wolpert, E. (1987). Intractable manic-depressive psychosis with rapid cycling in an 18-year-old woman successfully treated with electroconvulsive therapy. *The Journal of Nervous and Mental Disease, 175,* 236–239.

Berman, J., & Norton, N. (1985). Does professional training make a therapist more effective? *Psychological Bulletin, 98,* 401–407.

Berndt, T. (1982). The features and effects of friendships in early adolescence. *Child Development, 53,* 1447–1460.

Bernstein, R. (1981). The Y chromosome and primary sexual differentiation. *Journal of the American Medical Association, 245,* 1953–1956.

Berry, D., & Philips, B. (1988). Sleep-disordered breathing in the elderly: Review and methodological comment. *Clinical Psychology Review, 8,* 101–120.

Besson, J., & Chaouch, A. (1987). Peripheral and spinal mechanisms of nociception. *Physiological Reviews, 67,* 67–186.

Best, J. (1992). *Cognitive Psychology* (3rd ed.). St. Paul: West.

Best, J., & Suedfeld, P. (1982). Restricted environmental stimulation therapy and behavioral self-management in smoking cessation. *Journal of Applied Social Psychology, 12,* 408–419.

Bexton, W., Heron, W., & Scott, T. (1954). Effects of decreased variation in the sensory environment. *Canadian Journal of Psychology, 8,* 70–76.

Bick, P., & Kinsbourne, M. (1987). Auditory hallucinations and subvocal speech in schizophrenic patients. *American Journal of Psychiatry, 144,* 222–225.

Binet, A., & Simon, T. (1905). *The Development of Intelligence in Children.* Baltimore: Williams & Wilkins.

Bingol, N., Fuchs, M., Diaz, V., Stone, R., & Gromisch, D. (1987). Teratogenicity of cocaine in humans. *Journal of Pediatrics, 110,* 93–96.

Bird, E., Spokes, E., & Iversen, L. (1979). Brain norepinephrine and dopamine in schizophrenia. *Science, 204,* 93–94.

Birmahr, B., Baker, R., Kapur, S., & Quintana, H. (1992). Clozapine for the treatment of adolescents with schizophrenia. *Journal of the American Academy of Child and Adolescent Psychiatry, 31,* 160–164.

Bischoff, L., (1976). *Adult Psychology* (2nd ed.). New York: Harper & Row.

Bitterman, M. (1975). The comparative analysis of learning. *Science, 188,* 699–709.

Black, B., & Robbins, D. (1990). Panic disorder in children and adolescents. *Journal of the American Academy of Adolescent Psychiatry, 29,* 36–44.

Black, I., Adler, J., Dreyfus, C., Friedman, W., LaGamma, E., & Roach, A. (1987). Biochemistry of information storage in the nervous system. *Science, 236,* 1263–1268.

Blander, A., & Wise, R. (1989). Anatomical mapping of brain stimulation reward sites in the anterior hypothalamic area: Special attention to the stria medullaris. *Brain Research, 483,* 12–16.

Blaney, P. (1986). Affect and memory: A review. *Psychological Bulletin, 99,* 229–246.

Blasi, A. (1980). Bridging moral cognition and moral action: A critical review of the literature. *Psychological Bulletin, 88,* 1–45.

Bleuler, E. (1950). *Dementia Praecox or the Group of Schizophrenias.* New York: International Universities Press.

Bliss, E. (1984). Spontaneous self-hypnosis in multiple personality disorder. *Psychiatric Clinics of North America, 7,* 135–148.

Bloch, S. (1979). Group psychotherapy. In S. Bloch (Ed.), *An Introduction to the Psychotherapies.* Oxford, England: Oxford University Press.

Block, J. (1971). *Lives Through Time.* Berkeley, CA: Bancroft.

Bloch, V., Hennevin, E., & Leconte, P. (1977). Interaction between post-trial reticular stimulation and subsequent paradoxical sleep in memory consolidation processes. In R. Drucker-Colin & J. McGaugh (Eds.), *Neurobiology of Sleep and Memory.* New York: Academic Press.

Bloom, F., Lazerson, A., & Hofstadter, L. (1985). *Brain, Mind, and Behavior.* New York: Freeman.

Bloom, L., & Capatides, J. (1987). Sources of meaning in the acquisition of complex syntax: The sample case of casuality. *Journal of Experimental Child Psychology, 43,* 112–128.

Blum, H. (1986). Psychoanalysis. In I. Kutash & A. Wolf (Eds.), *Psychotherapist's Casebook.* San Francisco: Jossey-Bass.

Blum, K. (1984). *Handbook of Abusable Drugs.* New York: Gardner Press.

Bolles, R. (1979). *Learning Theory* (2nd ed.). New York: Holt, Rinehart and Winston.

Bolter, A., Heminger, A., Martin, G., & Fry, M. (1976). Outpatient clinical experience in a community drug abuse program with phencyclidine abuse. *Clinical Toxicology, 9,* 593–600.

Bonthius, D., & West, J. (1990). Alcohol-induced neuronal loss in developing rats: Increased brain damage with binge exposure. *Alcoholism: Clinical and Experimental Research, 14,* 107–118.

Borke, H. (1975). Piaget's mountains revisited: Changes in the egocentric landscape. *Developmental Psychology, 11,* 240–243.

Borkovec, T. (1970). Autonomic reactivity to sensory stimulation in psychopathic, neurotic, and normal juvenile delinquents. *Journal of Consulting and Clinical Psychology, 35,* 217–222.

Borysenko, M., & Borysenko, J. (1982). Stress, behavior, and immunity: Animal models and mediating mechanisms. *General Hospital Psychiatry, 4,* 59–67.

Bouchard, T. (1984). Twins reared together and apart: What they tell us about human diversity. In S. Fox (Ed.), *Individuality and Determinism.* New York: Plenum.

Bouchard, T., Lykken, D., McGue, M., Segal, N., & Tellegen, A. (1990). Sources of human psychological differences: The Minnesota study of twins reared apart. *Science, 250,* 223–250.

Bouchard, T., & McGue, M. (1981). Familial studies of intelligence: A review. *Science, 212,* 1055–1058.

Bourne, L., Dominowski, R., Loftus, E., & Healy, A. (1986). *Cognitive Processes* (2nd ed.). Englewood Cliffs, NJ: Prentice-Hall.

Bourne, L., Ekstrand, B., & Dominowski, R. (1971). *The Psychology of Thinking.* Englewood Cliffs, NJ: Prentice-Hall.

Bousfield, W. (1953). The occurrence of clustering in the recall of randomly arranged associates. *Journal of General Psychology, 49,* 229–240.

Bower, G. (1970). Analysis of a mnemonic device. *American Scientist, 58,* 496–510.

Bower, G. (1981). Mood and memory. *American Psychologist, 36,* 129–148.

Bower, G., & Clark, M. (1969). Narrative stories as mediators for serial learning. *Psychonomic Science, 14,* 181–182.

Bower, G., & Mayer, J. (1985). Failure to replicate mood-dependent retrieval. *Bulletin of the Psychonomic Society, 23,* 39–42.

Bowlby, J. (1965). *Child Care and Growth of Love* (2nd ed.). Baltimore: Penguin.

Boyce, P., & Parker, G. (1988). Seasonal affective disorder in the southern hemisphere. *The American Journal of Psychiatry, 145,* 96–99.

Boyce, W., Jensen, E., Cassel, J., Collier, A., Smith, A., & Ramey, C. (1977). Influence of life events and family routines on childhood respiratory tract illness. *Pediatrics, 60,* 609–615.

Boyd, J. (1986). Use of mental health services for the treatment of panic disorder. *American Journal of Psychiatry, 143,* 1569–1574.

Boyd, J., & Weissman, M. (1981). Epidemiology of affective disorders. *Archives of General Psychiatry, 38,* 1039–1046.

Boyer, W., & Fieghner, J. (1992). An overview of paroxetine. *Journal of Clinical Psychiatry, 53,* 3–6.

Boyle, C., Berkowitz, G., & Kelsey, J. (1987). Epidemiology of premenstrual symptoms. *American Journal of Public Health, 77,* 349–350.

Bradburn, N., Rips, L., & Shevell, S. (1987). Answering autobiographical questions: The impact of memory and inference on surveys. *Science, 236,* 157–161.

Bradbury, T., & Fincham, F. (1988). Individual difference variables in close relationships: A contextual model of marriage as an integrative framework. *Journal of Personality and Social Psychology, 54,* 713–721.

Brady, J., & Lind, D. (1965). Experimental analysis of hysterical blindness. In L. Ullman and L. Krasner (Eds.), *Case Studies in Behavior Modification.* New York: Holt, Rinehart and Winston.

Braff, D., & Geyer, M. (1990). Sensorimotor gating and schizophrenia. *Archives of General Psychiatry, 47,* 181–188.

Brannon, L., & Feist, J. (1992). *Health Psychology.* Belmont, CA: Wadsworth Publishing Company.

Brandenburg, H., Jahoda, M., Pijpers, L., Reuss, A., Kleyer, W., & Wladimiroff, J. (1990). Fetal loss rate after chorionic villus sampling and subsequent amniocentesis. *American Journal of Medical Genetics, 35,* 178–180.

Brataas, A. (1989). Minnesota normals' go national. *Oregonian,* October 5, A3.

Braungart, J., Fulker, D., & Plomin, R. (1992). Genetic mediation of the home environment during infancy: A sibling adoption study of the HOME. *Developmental Psychology, 28,* 1048–1055.

Breakerfield, X., & Cambi, F. (1987). Molecular genetic insights into neurological diseases. *Annual Review of Neuroscience, 10,* 535–594.

Brecher, R., & Brecher, E. (1966). *An Analysis of Human Sexual Response.* New York: New American Library.

Breckler, S. (1984). Empirical validation of affect, behavior, and cognition as distinct components of attitude. *Journal of Personality and Social Psychology, 47,* 1191–1205.

Breggin, P. (1979). *Electroshock: Its Brain-Disabling Effects.* New York: Springer.

Bremer, J. (1959). *Asexualization.* New York: Macmillan.

Bremer, T., & Wittig, M. (1980). Fear of success: A personality trait or a response to occupational deviance and role overload. *Sex Roles, 6,* 27–46.

Breslau, N., & Davis, G. (1987). Posttraumatic stress disorder: The etiologic specificity of wartime stressors. *The American Journal of Psychiatry, 144,* 578–583.

Brett, J., Brief, A., Burke, M., George, J., & Webster, J. (1990). Negative affectivity and the reporting of stressful life events. *Health Psychology, 9,* 57–68.

Brewer, W., & Nakamura, G. (1984). The nature and functions of schemas. In R. Wyer and T. Srull (Eds.), *Handbook of Social Cognition* (Vol. 3). Hillsdale, NJ: Erlbaum.

Brewster, D. (1854). *North British Review.* Quoted in J. Miller, 1983, *States of Mind.* New York: Pantheon Press.

Briddell, D., & Wilson, G. (1976). Effects of alcohol and expectancy set on male sexual arousal. *Journal of Abnormal Psychology, 85,* 225–234.

Bridgman, P., Malamut, B., Sperling, M., Saykin, A., & O'Connor, M. (1989). Memory during subclinical hippocampal seizures. *Neurology, 39,* 853–856.

Brigham, J. (1986). *Social Psychology.* Boston: Little, Brown.

Brigham, J., & Weissbach, T. (Eds.). (1972). *Racial Attitudes in America: Analyses and Findings of Social Psychology.* New York: Harper & Row.

Brimaher, B., Baker, R., Kapur, S., & Quintana, H. (1992). Clozapine for the treatment of adolescents with schizophrenia. *Journal of the American Academy of Child and Adolescent Psychiatry, 31,* 160–164.

Brittain, C. (1963). Adolescent choices and parent-peer cross-pressures. *American Sociological Review, 28,* 385–391.

Brodbeck, A., & Irwin, O. (1946). The speech behavior of infants without families. *Child Development, 17,* 145–156.

Brody, J. (1986). Federal panel issues warning of obesity peril. *The Oregonian,* February 14, A1.

Broering, J., Moscicki, B., Millstein, S., Policar, M., & Irwin, C. (1989). Sexual practices among adolescents. Paper presented at the annual meeting of the Society for Adolescent Medicine, San Francisco, March.

Brooks, J., & Watkins, M. (1989). Recognition memory and the mere exposure effect. *Journal of Experimental Psychology: Learning, Memory, and Cognition, 15,* 968–976.

Brooks-Gunn, J., & Peterson, A. (1983). *Girls at Puberty: Biological and Psychosocial Perspectives.* New York: Plenum.

Brouillette, R., Fernbach, S., & Hunt, C. (1982). Obstructive sleep apnea in infants and children. *Journal of Pediatrics, 31,* 1–40.

Brown, B., Clasen, D., & Eicher, S. (1986a). Perceptions of peer pressure, peer conformity dispositions, and self-reported behavior among adolescents. *Developmental Psychology, 22,* 521–530.

Brown, B., Lohr, M., & McClenahan, E. (1986b). Early adolescents' perceptions of peer pressure. *Journal of Early Adolescence, 6,* 139–154.

Brown, J. (1958). Some tests of the decay theory of immediate memory. *Quarterly Journal of Experimental Psychology, 10,* 12–21.

Brown, J., & Lawton, M. (1986). Stress and well-being in adolescence: The moderating role of physical exercise. *Journal of Human Stress, 12,* 125–131.

Brown, R. (1973). *A First Language: The Early Stages.* Cambridge, MA: Harvard University Press.

Brown, R., & Kulik, J. (1977). Flashbulb memories. *Cognition, 5,* 73–99.

Bruch, H. (1961). Transformation of oral impulses in eating disorders: A conceptual approach. *Psychiatric Quarterly, 35,* 458–481.

Bruner, J., Goodnow, J., & Austin, G. (1956). *A Study of Thinking.* New York: Wiley.

Bruner, J., & Tagiuri, R. (1954). The perception of people. In G. Lindzey (Ed.), *Handbook of Social Psychology* (Vol. 2). Reading, MA: Addison-Wesley.

Bryden, M., & Saxby, L. (1985). Developmental aspects of cerebral lateralization. In J. Obrzat & G. Hynd (Eds.), *Child Neuropsychology, Vol. 1: Theory and Research.* Orlando, FL: Academic Press.

Buchsbaum, M., Wu, J., DeLisi, L., Holcomb, H., Hazlett, E., Cooper-Langston, K., & Kessler, R. (1987). Positron emission tomography studies of basal ganglia and somatosensory cortex neuroleptic drug effects: Differences between normal controls and schizophrenic patients. *Biological Psychiatry, 22,* 479–494.

Bunney, W., Goodwin, F., & Murphy, D. (1972). The "Switch Process" in manic-depressive illness. *Archives of General Psychiatry, 27,* 312–317.

Bunney, W., Murphy, D., Goodwin, F., & Borge, G. (1970). The switch process from depression to mania: Relationship to drugs which alter brain amines. *Lancet, 1,* 1022.

Bures, J., Buresova, O., & Bolhuis, J. (1987). Processing temporally discontiguous information is neither an exclusive nor the only function of the hippocampus. *Behavioral and Brain Sciences, 10,* 154–156.

Burt, C. (1966). The genetic determination of differences in intelligence: A study of monozygotic twins reared together and apart. *British Journal of Psychology, 57,* 137–153.

Burton, S. (1989). Daytime naps in narcoleptic patients. *Sleep, 12,* 184–185.

Buschke, H. (1977). Two-dimensional recall: Immediate identification of clusters in episodic and semantic memory. *Journal of Verbal Learning and Verbal Behavior, 16,* 201–215.

Bushman, B. (1984). Perceived symbols of authority and their influence in compliance. *Journal of Applied Social Psychology, 14,* 501–508.

Buss, A., & Finn, S. (1987). Classification of personality traits. *Journal of Personality and Social Psychology, 52,* 432–434.

Buss, D. (1989). Sex differences in human mate preferences: Evolutionary hypotheses tested in 37 cultures. *Behavioral and Brain Sciences, 12,* 1–49.

Buss, D., Abbott, M., Angleitner, A., & Asherian, A. (1990). International preferences in selecting mates: A study of 37 cultures. *Journal of Cross Cultural Psychology, 21,* 5–47.

Butler, R. (1961). Re-awakening interests. *Nursing Homes: Journal of American Nursing Home Associations, 10,* 8–19.

Byrne, D. (1971). *The Attraction Paradigm.* New York: Academic Press.

Byrne, D., Clore, G., & Smeaton, G. (1986). The attraction hypothesis: Do similar attitudes affect anything? *Journal of Personality and Social Psychology, 51,* 1167–1170.

Byrne, D., Clore, G., & Worchel, P. (1966). The effect of economic similarity-dissimilarity on interpersonal attraction. *Journal of Personality and Social Psychology, 4,* 220–224.

Byrne, D., & Griffitt, W. (1973). Interpersonal attraction. *Annual Review of Psychology, 24,* 317–336.

Byrne, D., London, O., & Reeves, K. (1968). The effects of physical attractiveness, sex, and attitude similarity on interpersonal attraction. *Journal of Personality, 36,* 259–271.

Byrne, D., & Murnen, S. (1988). Maintaining loving relationships. In R. Sternberg & M. Barnes (Eds.), *The Psychology of Loving.* New Haven, CT: Yale University Press.

Cadoret, R. (1978). Evidence for genetic inheritance of primary affective disorder in adoptees. *American Journal of Psychiatry, 135,* 463–466.

Cadoret, R., Troughton, E., & O'Gorman, T. (1987). Genetic and environmental factors in alcohol abuse and antisocial personality. *Journal of Studies on Alcohol, 48,* 1–8.

Cadwallader, M. (1975). Marriage as a wretched institution. In J. DeLora & J. DeLora (Eds.), *Intimate Lifestyles: Marriage and Its Alternatives.* Pacific Palisades, CA: Goodyear.

Cain, W. (1981). Educating your nose. *Psychology Today,* July, 49–56.

Cain, W. (1988). Olfaction. In R. Atkinson, R. Hernstein, G. Lindzey, & R. Luce (Eds.), *Steven's Handbook of Experimental Psychology, Vol. 1: Perception and Motivation.* New York: Wiley.

Cameron, N. (1947). *The Psychology of Behavior Disorders.* Boston: Houghton Mifflin.

Campbell, A. (1975). The American way of mating: Marriage Si, children only maybe. *Psychology Today,* May, 37–43.

Campbell, C., & Davis, J. (1974). Licking rate of rats is reduced by intraduodenal and intraportal glucose infusion. *Physiology and Behavior, 12,* 357–365.

Campbell, D., & Specht, J. (1985). Altruism: Biology, culture, and religion. *Journal of Social and Clinical Psychology, 3,* 33–42.

Campbell, S. (1976). Double-blind psychometric studies on the effects of natural estrogens on post-menopausal women. In S. Campbell (Ed.), *The Management of the Menopausal and Post-Menopausal Years.* Baltimore: University Park Press.

Campbell, S. (1987). Evolutions of sleep structure following brief intervals of wakefulness. *Electroencephalographic Clinical Neurophysiology, 66,* 175–184.

Campbell, S., & Whitehead, M. (1977). Oestrogen therapy and the menopausal syndrome. *Clinical Obstetrical Gynecology, 42,* 31–47.

Campos, J., Hiatt, S. Ramsay, D., Henderson, C., & Svejda, M. (1978). The emergence of fear on the visual cliff. In M. Lewis & L. Rosenblum (Eds.), *The Development of Affect.* New York: Plenum.

Cannon, W. (1927). The James-Lange theory of emotions: A critical examination and an alternative. *American Journal of Psychology, 39,* 106–124.

Cannon, W., & Washburn, A. (1912). An exploration of hunger. *American Journal of Physiology, 29,* 441–454.

Cantor, N., & Mischel, W. (1979). Prototypes in person perception. In L. Berkowitz (Ed.), *Advances in Experimental Social Psychology* (Vol. 12). New York: Academic Press.

Capron, C., & Duyme, M. (1989). Assessment of effects of socio-economic status on I.Q. in full cross-fostering study. *Nature, 340,* 552–554.

Carboni, E., Imperato, A., Perezzani, L., & DiChiara, G. (1989). Amphetamine, cocaine, phencyclidine and nomifensine increase extracellular dopamine concentrations preferentially in the nucleus accumbens of freely moving rats. *Neuroscience, 28,* 653–661.

Carden, S., & Coons, E. (1989). Diazepam modulates lateral hypothalamic self-stimulation but not stimulation-escape in rats. *Brain Research, 483,* 327–334.

Carelli, M., & Benelli, B. (1986). Linguistic development of twins. *Eta Evolution, 24,* 107–116.

Carey, P., Howards, S., & Vance, M. (1988). Transdermal testosterone treatment of hypogonadal men. *Journal of Urology, 140,* 76–79.

Carlen, P., Penn, R., Fornazzari, L., Bennett, J., Wilkinson, D., Phil, D., & Wortzman, G. (1986). Computerized tomographic scan assessment of alcoholic brain damage and its potential reversibility. *Alcoholism: Clinical and Experimental Research, 10,* 226–232.

Carlson, B., & Goodwin, F. (1973). The stages of mania. *Archives of General Psychiatry, 28,* 221–228.

Carlson, N. (1981). *Physiology of Behavior* (2nd ed.). Boston: Allyn & Bacon.

Carlson, N. (1988). *Foundations of Physiological Psychology.* Boston: Allyn & Bacon.

Carlsson, A. (1977). Does dopamine play a role in schizophrenia? *Psychological Medicine, 7,* 583–595.

Carlsson, M., & Carlsson, A. (1990). Schizophrenia: A subcortical neurotransmitter imbalance syndrome? *Schizophrenia Bulletin, 16,* 425–432.

Carpenter, W., & Heinrichs, D. (1983). Early intervention, time-limited, targeted pharmacotherapy of schizophrenia. *Schizophrenia Bulletin, 9,* 534–542.

Carroll, L. (1988). Concern with AIDS and the sexual behavior of college students. *Journal of Marriage and the Family, 50,* 405–411.

Carson, R. (1989). Personality. *Annual Review of Psychology, 40,* 227–248.

Carson, R., & Butcher, J. (1992). *Abnormal Psychology and Modern Life* (9th ed.). New York: HarperCollins.

Carter, A., Cohen, E., & Shorr, E. (1947). The use of androgens in women. *Vitamins and Hormones, 5,* 317–391.

Cartwright, R. (1978). Happy endings for our dreams. *Psychology Today,* December, 66–77.

Carver, C., & Glass, D. (1978). Coronary-prone behavior pattern and interpersonal aggression. *Journal of Personality and Social Psychology, 36,* 361–366.

Carver, C., & Scheier, M. (1978). Self-focusing effects on dispositional self-consciousness, mirror presence, and audience presence. *Journal of Personality and Social Psychology, 36,* 324–332.

Cash, T., & Janda, L. (1984). The eye of

the beholder. *Psychology Today*, December, 46–52.

Casper, C., Eckert, E., Halmi, K., Goldberg, S., & Davis, J. (1980). Bulimia: Its incidence and clinical importance in patients with anorexia nervosa. *Archives of General Psychiatry, 37*, 1030–1035.

Castillo, M., & Butterworth, G. (1981). Neonatal localization of a sound in visual space. *Perception, 10*, 331–350.

Castro, F., Newcomb, M., McCreary, C., & Baezcondo-Garbanati, L. (1989). Cigarette smokers do more than just smoke cigarettes. *Health Psychology, 8*, 107–129.

Cattell, R. (1950). *A Systematic Theoretical and Factual Study*. New York: McGraw-Hill.

Cattell, R. (1965). *The Scientific Analysis of Personality*. Baltimore: Penguin Books.

Cattell, R. (1973). Personality pinned down. *Psychology Today*, July, 40–46.

Cattell, R. (1982). *The Inheritance of Personality and Ability*. New York: Academic Press.

Ceci, S., Toglia, M., & Ross, D. (1988). On remembering . . . more or less: A trace strength interpretation of developmental differences in suggestibility. *Journal of Experimental Psychology: General, 117*, 201–203.

Centers for Disease Control (1984). Fetal alcohol syndrome: Public awareness week. *Morbidity and Mortality Weekly Report, 33*, 1–2.

Centers for Disease Control (1987). Self-reported changes in sexual behaviors among homosexual and bisexual men from the San Francisco City Clinic cohort. *Morbidity and Mortality Weekly Report, 36*, 187–189.

Centers for Disease Control (1989). Results from the National Adolescent Student Health Survey. *Morbidity and Mortality Weekly Report, 38*, 147–150.

Cerletti, B., & Bini, I. (1938). L'elettroshock. *Archiva Generale Neurologia Psichiatria Psicoanalisis, 19*, 266.

Cesselin, F., Bourgoin, S., Clot, A., Hamon, M., & Le Bars, D. (1989). Segmental release of Metenkephalin-like material from the spinal cord of rats, elicited by noxious thermal stimuli. *Brain Research, 484*, 71–77.

Chadwick, D. (1986). "Grizz"—of men and the great bear. *National Geographic, 169*, 182–213.

Chaiken, S., & Stangor, C. (1987). Attitudes and attitude change. *Annual Review of Psychology, 38*, 575–630.

Chandler, C. (1989). Specific retroactive interference in modified recognition tests: Evidence for an unknown cause of interference. *Journal of Experimental Psychology: Learning, Memory, and Cognition, 15*, 256–265.

Chang, T. (1986). Semantic memory: Facts and models. *Psychological Bulletin, 99*, 199–220.

Channon, S., DeSilva, P., Hemsley, D., & Perkins, R. (1990). A controlled trial of cognitive behavioural and behavioural treatment of anorexia nervosa. *Behavior Research and Therapy, 27*, 529–535.

Charlesworth, E., & Nathan, R. (1982). *Stress Management: A Comprehensive Guide to Wellness*. Houston, TX: Biobehavioral Press.

Charney, D., Heninger, G., & Sternberg, D. (1984). Serotonin function and the mechanism of action of antidepressant treatment. *Archives of General Psychiatry, 41*, 359–365.

Chase, M., & Morales, F. (1990). The atonia and myoclonia of active (REM) sleep. *Annual Review of Psychology, 41*, 557–584.

Chase, M., & Morales, F. (1983). Subthreshold excitatory activity and motor neuron discharge during REM periods of active sleep. *Science, 221*, 1195–1198.

Chase, T., The Troups for (1990). *When Rabbit Howls*. New York: Jove.

Chasnoff, L., Griffith, D., MacGregor, S., Dirkes, K., & Burns, K. (1989). Temporal patterns of cocaine use in pregnancy. *Journal of the American Medical Association, 261*, 1741–1744.

Check, J., & Malamuth, N. (1983). Sex role stereotyping and reactions to depictions of stranger versus acquaintance rape. *Journal of Personality and Social Psychology, 45*, 344–356.

Chesno, F., & Kilman, P. (1975). Effects of stimulation intensity on sociopathic avoidance learning. *Journal of Abnormal Psychology, 84*, 144–151.

Chipuer, H., Rovine, M., & Plomin, R. (1990). LISREL modeling: Genetic and environmental influences on IQ revisited. *Intelligence, 14*, 11–29.

Chitwood, D., & Comerford, M. (1990). Drugs, sex, and AIDS risk. *American Behavioral Scientist, 33*, 465–477.

Chomsky, N. (1965). *Aspects of the Theory of Syntax*. Cambridge, MA: MIT Press.

Chomsky, N. (1968). *Language and Mind*. New York: Harcourt Brace Jovanovich.

Chomsky, N. (1980). The linguistic approach. In M. Piatelli-Palmarini (Ed.), *Language and Learning*. Cambridge, MA: Harvard University Press.

Chorover, S., & Schiller, P. (1965). Short-term retrograde amnesia in rats. *Journal of Comparative and Physiological Psychology, 59*, 73–78.

Choy-Kwong, M., & Lipton, R. (1989). Seizures in hospitalized cocaine users. *Neurology, 39*, 425–427.

Chozick, B. (1986). The behavioral effects of lesions of the amygdala: A review. *International Journal of Neuroscience, 29*, 205–221.

Christenson, S., Abery, B., & Weinberg, R. (1986). An alternative model for the delivery of psychology in the school community. In S. Elliot & J. Witt (Eds.), *The Delivery of Psychological Services in Schools: Concepts, Processes, and Issues*. Hillsdale, NJ: Erlbaum.

Christopher, F. (1988). An initial investigation into a continuum of premarital sexual pressure. *Journal of Sex Research, 25*, 255–266.

Christopher, F., & Cate, R. (1984). Factors involved in premarital decision making. *Journal of Sex Research, 20*, 343–376.

Chu, G. (1967). Prior familiarity, perceived bias, and one-sided versus two-sided communication. *Journal of Experimental Social Psychology, 3*, 243–254.

Chumlea, W. (1982). Physical growth in adolescence. In B. Wolman (Ed.), *Handbook of Developmental Psychology*. Englewood Cliffs, NJ: Prentice-Hall.

Churchland, P., & Churchland, P. (1990). Could a machine think? *Scientific American, 262*, 32–39.

Cialdini, R. (1985). *Influence: Science and Practice*. Glenview, IL: Scott, Foresman.

Cialdini, R., Vincent, J., Lewis, S., Catalan, J., Wheeler, D., & Darby, B. (1975). Reciprocal concessions procedure for inducing compliance: The door-in-the-face technique. *Journal of Personality and Social Psychology, 31*, 206–215.

Ciesielski, K., Beech, H., & Gordon, P. (1981). Some electrophysiological observations in obsessional states. *British Journal of Psychiatry, 138*, 479–484.

Cirignotta, F., Mondini, S., Zucconi, M., Lenzi, P., & Lugaresi, E. (1985). Insomnia: An epidemiological survey. *Clinical Neuropharmacology, 8*, Suppl. 1, 549–554.

Clarizio, H., & Yelon, S. (1974). Learning theory approaches to classroom management: Rationale and intervention techniques. In A. Brown & C. Avery (Eds.), *Modifying Childrens' Behavior: A Book of Readings*. Springfield, IL: Thomas.

Clark, A., Krekoski, C., Parhad, I., Liston, D., Julien, J., & Hoar, D. (1989). Altered expression of genes for amyloid and cytoskeletal proteins in Alzheimer cortex. *Annals of Neurology, 25*, 331–339.

Clark, C., & Geffen, G. (1989). Corpus callosum surgery and recent memory. *Brain, 112*, 165–175.

Clark, D., Salkovskis, P., Gelder, M., Koehler, M., Martin, M., Anastasiades, P., Hackmann, A., Middleton, H., & Jeavons, A. (1988). Tests of a cognitive theory of panic. In I. Hand & H. Wittchen (Eds.), *Panic and Phobias*. Berlin: Springer-Verlag.

Clark, D., & Teasdale, J. (1982). Diurnal variation in clinical depression and accessibility of memories of positive and negative experiences. *Journal of Abnormal Psychology, 91*, 87–95.

Clark, E. (1983). Meanings and concepts. In J. Flavell & E. Markman (Eds.), *Handbook of Child Psychology: Cognitive Development* (Vol. 3). New York: Wiley.

Clarke, A. M., & Clarke, A. D. (1976). *Early Experience: Myth and Evidence*. London: Open Books.

Clarke-Stewart, K. (1977). *Child Care in the Family: A Review of Research and Some Propositions for Policy*. New York: Academic Press.

Clarke-Stewart, K. (1978). And daddy makes three: The father's impact on mother and young child. *Child Development, 49*, 466–478.

Cleckley, H. (1976). *The Mask of Sanity* (5th ed.). St. Louis: Mosby.

Cloninger, C., Martin, R., Clayton, P., & Guze, S. (1981). Blind follow-up and family study of anxiety neuroses. In D. Klein & J. Rabkin (Eds.), *Anxiety: New Research and Changing Concepts*. New York: Raven.

Cochran, S. (1988). Paper presented at the Annual American Psychological Association Convention, Atlanta, August.

Cohen, S. (1980). Aftereffects of stress on human performance and social behavior: A review of research and theory. *Psychological Bulletin, 88*, 82–102.

Cohen, S., & Williamson, G. (1991). Stress and infectious disease in humans. *Psychological Bulletin, 109*, 5–24.

Cohen, S., & Wills, T. (1985). Stress, social support, and the buffering hypothesis. *Psychological Bulletin, 98*, 310–357.

Cohn, J. & Tronick, E. (1987). Mother-infant face-to-face interaction: The sequence of dyadic states at 3, 6, and 9 months. *Developmental Psychology, 23*, 68–77.

Colasanti, B. (1982a). Anti-depressant therapy. In C. Craig & R. Stitzel (Eds.), *Modern Pharmacology*. Boston: Little, Brown.

Colasanti, B. (1982b). Anti-psychotic drugs. In C. Craig & R. Stitzel (Eds.), *Modern Pharmacology*. Boston: Little, Brown.

Colditz, G., Bonita, R., Stamfer, M., Willett, W., Rosner, B., Speizer, F., & Hennekens, C. (1988). Cigarette smoking and risk of stroke in middle-aged women. *New England Journal of Medicine, 318*, 937–941.

Cole, D. (1989). Psychopathology of adolescent suicide: Hopelessness, coping beliefs, and depression. *Journal of Abnormal Psychology, 98*, 248–255.

Coleman, J. (1966). *Equality of Educational Opportunity*. Washington, DC: U.S. Government Printing Office.

Coleman, J., Butcher, J., & Carson, R. (1984). *Abnormal Psychology and Modern Life* (7th ed.). Glenview, IL: Scott, Foresman.

Coles, C., Smith, I., Lancaster, J., & Falek, A. (1987). Persistence over the first month of neurobehavioral differences in infants exposed to alcohol prenatally. *Infant Behavior and Development, 10*, 23–37.

Collins, A., & Loftus, E. (1975). A spreading activation theory of semantic processing. *Psychological Review, 82*, 407–428.

Collins, A., & Quillian, M. (1969). Retrieval time from semantic memory. *Journal of Verbal Learning and Verbal Behavior, 8*, 240–247.

Collins, R. (1983). Head Start: An update on program effects. *Newsletter, Society for Research in Child Development*, Summer, 1–2.

Collins, R. (1984). Head Start: A review of research with implications for practice in early childhood education. Paper presented at the meeting of the American Education Research Association, New Orleans, April.

Colman, A. (1991). Expert psychological testimony in two murder trials in South Africa. *Issues in Criminological and Legal Psychology, 1(17)*, 43–49.

Colwill, R., & Rescorla, R. (1986). Associative structures in instrumental learning. In G. Bower (Ed.), *The Psychology of Learning and Motivation* (Vol. 20). New York: Academic Press.

Commons, M., Richard, F., & Armon, C. (1982). *Beyond Formal Operations: Late Adolescent and Adult Cognitive Development*. New York: Praeger.

Condon, W., & Sander, L. (1974). Neonate movement as synchronized with adult speech: Interactional participation in language acquisition. *Science, 183*, 99–101.

Condry, J., & Dyer, S. (1976). Fear of success: Attribution of cause to the victim. *Journal of Social Issues, 32*, 63–83.

Conrad, R. (1964). Acoustic confusions in immediate memory. *British Journal of Psychology, 55*, 75–84.

Conrad, R. (1972). Short-term memory in the deaf: A test for speech coding. *British Journal of Psychology, 63*, 173–180.

Cook, N. (1986). *The Brain Code: Mechanisms of Information Transfer and the Role of the Corpus Callosum*. New York: Methuen.

Cook, S. (1970). Motives in a conceptual analysis of attitude-related behavior. In W. Arnold and D. Levine (Eds.), *Nebraska Symposium on Motivation, 1969*. Lincoln: University of Nebraska Press.

Coope, J. (1976). Double-blind cross-over study of estrogen replacement. In S. Campbell (Ed.), *The Management of the Menopausal and Post-Menopausal Years*. Baltimore: University Park Press.

Cooper, C., & Marshall, J. (1976). Occupational sources of stress: A review of the literature relating to coronary heart disease and mental ill health. *Journal of Occupational Psychology, 49*, 11–28.

Cooper, J., Bloom, F., and Roth, (1986). *The Biochemical Basis of Neuropharmacology*. Fairlawn, NJ: Oxford University Press.

Cooper, R., & Zubek, J. (1958). Effects of enriched and restricted early environment on the learning abilities of bright and dull rats. *Canadian Journal of Psychology, 12*, 159–164.

Coopersmith, S. (1967). *Antecedents of Self-Esteem*. San Francisco: Freeman.

Coppen, A. (1972). Indoleamines and affective disorders. *Journal of Psychiatric Research, 9*, 163–171.

Coren, S., & Ward, L. (1989). *Sensation and Perception* (3rd ed.). New York: Harcourt Brace Jovanovich.

Corkin, S. (1980). A prospective study of cingulatomy. In E. Valenstein (Ed.), *The Psychosurgery Debate*. San Francisco: Freeman.

Corrigan, R. (1978). Language development as related to stage 6 object permanence development. *Journal of Child Language, 5*, 173–189.

Cortes, R., Gueye, B., Pazos, A., Probst, A., & Palacios, J. (1989). Dopamine receptors in human brain: Autoradiographic distribution of D_1 sites. *Neuroscience, 28*, 263–273.

Coryell, W., Keller, M., Endicott, J., Andreasen, N., Clayton, P., & Hirschfeld, R. (1989). Bipolar II illness: Course and outcome over a five-year period. *Psychological Medicine, 19*, 129–141.

Costello, C. (1976). Electroconvulsive therapy: Is further investigation necessary? *Canadian Psychiatric Association Journal, 21*, 61–67.

Cotman, C., Monaghan, D., & Ganong, A. (1988). Excitatory amino acid neurotransmission: NMDA receptors and Hebb-type synaptic plasticity. *Annual Review of Neuroscience, 11*, 61–80.

Cowart, B. (1981). Development of taste perception in humans: Sensitivity and preference throughout the lifespan. *Psychological Bulletin, 90*, 43–73.

Cox, G., & Merkel, W. (1989). A qualitative review of psychosocial treatments for bulimia. *The Journal of Nervous and Mental Disease, 177*, 77–84.

Cox, J. (1986). Cholecystokinin interacts with prefeeding to impair runway performance. *Behavioral Brain Research, 21*, 29–36.

Cox, V., Kakolewski, J., & Valenstein, E. (1968). Effect of ventromedial hypothalamic damage in hypophysectomized rats. *Journal of Comparative and Physiological Psychology, 65*, 145–148.

Coyne, J. (1976). Toward an interactional description of depression. *Psychiatry, 39*, 28–40.

Craighead, L. (1990). Supervised exercise in behavioral treatment for moderate obesity. *Behavior Therapy, 20*, 49–59.

Craik, F., & McDowd, J. (1987). Age differences in recall and recognition. *Journal of Experimental Psychology: Learning, and Cognition, 13*, 474–479.

Craik, F., & Tulving, E. (1975). Depth of processing and the retention of words in episodic memory. *Journal of Experimental Psychology: General, 104*, 268–294.

Craske, M., & Barlow, D. (1989). Nocturnal panic. *The Journal of Nervous and Mental Disease, 177*, 160–167.

Creekmore, C. (1985). Cities won't drive you crazy. *Psychology Today, 19*, 46–53.

Crick, F. (1982). Do dendritic spines twitch? *Trends in Neuroscience*, February, 44–46.

Crick, F. (1989). The recent excitement about neural networks. *Nature, 337*, 129–132.

Crick, F., & Mitchison, G. (1983). The function of dream sleep. *Nature, 304*, 111–114.

Crocker, J., Thompson, L., McGraw, K., & Ingerman, C. (1987). Downward comparison, prejudice, and evaluations of others: Effects of self-esteem and threat. *Journal of Personality and Social Psychology, 52*, 907–916.

Cronbach, L. (1978). Review of the BITCH test. In O. Buros (Ed.), *The Eighth Mental Measurements Yearbook* (Vol. 1). Highland Park, NJ: Gryphon Press.

Crooks, R. (1969). Alleviation of fear in a dental setting via film-modeling. In American Association of Dental Schools, *Report of Dental Education Summer Internship Program*. Chicago: American Association of Dental Schools.

Crooks, R. (1972). Differential proactive effects of ECS on massed versus spaced-trial learning. Unpublished Ph.D. Dissertation.

Crooks, R., & Baur, K. (1990). *Our Sexuality* (4th ed.). Redwood City, CA: Benjamin/Cummings.

Crowder, R. (1970). The role of one's own voice in immediate memory. *Cognitive Psychology, 1*, 157–158.

Crowder, R. (1976). *Principles of Learning and Memory*. Hillsdale, NJ: Erlbaum.

Crowe, R. (1974). An adoption study of antisocial personality. *Archives of General Psychiatry, 31*, 785–791.

Crowe, R., Noyes, R., Wilson, A., Elston, R., & Ward, L. (1987). A linkage study of panic disorder. *Archives of General Psychiatry, 44*, 933–937.

Croyle, R., & Cooper, J. (1983). Dissonance arousal: Physiological evidence. *Journal of Personality and Social Psychology, 45*, 782–791.

Csikszentmihalyi, M., & Larson, R. (1984). *Being Adolescent: Conflict and Growth in the Teenage Years*. New York: Basic Books.

Cumming, D., Cumming, C., Krausher, R., & Fox, E. (1991). Towards a definition of PMS II: A factor analytic evaluation of premenstrual changes in women with symptomatic premenstrual change. *Journal of Psychosomatic Research, 35*, 713–720.

Cunningham, C. (1986). Use of nuclear magnetic resonance spectroscopy to study the effects of ethanol consumption on liver metabolism and pathology. *Alcoholism: Clinical and Experimental Research, 10,* 246–250.

Cunningham, G., Cordero, E., & Thornby, J. (1989). Testosterone replacement with transdermal therapeutic systems. *Journal of the American Medical Association, 261,* 2525–2531.

Curtis, R., & Miller, K. (1988). Believing another likes or dislikes you: Behavior making the beliefs come true. *Journal of Personality and Social Psychology, 51,* 284–290.

Dale, P. (1976). *Language Development.* New York: Holt, Rinehart and Winston.

Damasio, A. (1992). Aphasia. *New England Journal of Medicine, 326,* 531–539.

Damasio, A., & Damasio, H. (1992). Brain and language. *Scientific American, 267,* 88–95.

Danks, H. (1992). Women never stopped trying to flee attacker. *The Oregonian,* December 4, 1992, A24.

Dare, C., Eisler, I., Russell, G., & Szmukler, G. (1990). The clinical and theoretical impact of a controlled trial of family therapy in anorexia nervosa. *Journal of Marital and Family Therapy, 16,* 39–57.

Darly, J., & Latané, B. (1968). Bystander intervention in emergencies: Diffusion of responsibility. *Journal of Personality and Social Psychology, 8,* 377–383.

Darwin, C. (1872). *The Expression of Emotion in Man and Animals.* New York: Philosophical Library [reprinted in 1955 & 1965 by the University of Chicago Press].

Datan, N., & Thomas, J. (1984). Late adulthood: Love, work and the normal transitions. In D. Offer & M. Sabshin (Eds.), *Normality and the Life Cycle.* New York: Basic Books.

Dattore, P., Shontz, F., & Coyne, L. (1980). Premarital personality differentiation of cancer and noncancer groups: A test of the hypothesis of cancer proneness. *Journal of Consulting and Clinical Psychology, 48,* 388–394.

Davidson, C. (1986). Changing concepts in the pathogenesis of alcoholic liver disease. *Alcoholism: Clinical and Experimental Research, 10,* supplement, 3–4.

Davidson, G. (1984). Hypnotic augmentation of terminal care chemoanalgesia. *Australian Journal of Clinical and Experimental Hypnosis, 12,* 133–134.

Davidson, J. (1984). Response to "Hormones and sexual behavior" by John Bancroft, M.D. *Journal of Sex and Marital Therapy, 10,* 23–27.

Davidson, R. (1984). Affect, cognition, and hemispheric specialization. In C. Izard, J. Kagan, & R. Zajonc (Eds.), *Emotion, Cognition, and Behavior.* Cambridge, England: Cambridge University Press.

Davis, D., Cahan, S., & Bashi, J. (1977). Birth order and intellectual development: The confluence model in the light of cross-cultural evidence. *Science, 196,* 1470–1472.

Davis, H., & Silverman, S. (1960). *Hearing and Deafness.* New York: Holt, Rinehart and Winston.

Davis, J., Wheeler, W., & Willy, E. (1987). Cognitive correlates of obesity in a nonclinical population. *Psychological Reports, 60,* 1151–1156.

Davis, J., & Wirttshafter, D. (1978). Anorexia and body weight loss caused by intraventricular glyceral infusions. *Society for Neuroscience Abstracts, 4,* 173.

Davis, M. (1992). The role of the amygdala in fear and anxiety. *Annual Review of Neuroscience, 15,* 353.

Davis, P., & Schwartz, G. (1987). Repression and the inaccessibility of affective memories. *Journal of Personality and Social Psychology, 52,* 155–162.

Davison, G., & Neale, J. (1986). *Abnormal Psychology* (4th ed.). New York: Wiley.

Davison, G., & Neale, J. (1990). *Abnormal Psychology* (5th ed.). New York: Wiley.

Deater, T., & Tauber, R. (1987). Personal communication, April 20.

DeBono, K. (1987). Investigating the social-adjustive and value-expressive functions of attitudes: Implication for persuasion processes. *Journal of Personality and Social Psychology, 52,* 279–287.

DeCasper, A., & Fifer, W. (1980). Of human bonding: Newborns prefer their mothers' voices. *Science, 208,* 1174–1176.

Deci, E. (1980). *The Psychology of Self-Determination.* Lexington, MA: Lexington Books.

Declerck, A., Ruwe, F., O'Hanlon, J., & Wauquier, A. (1992). Effects of zolpidem and flunitrazepam on nocturnal sleep of women subjectively complaining of insomnia. *Psychopharmacology, 106,* 497–501.

Dehne, N., Mendenhall, C., Roselle, G., & Grossman, C. (1989). Cell-mediated immune responses associated with short term alcohol intake: Time course and dose dependency. *Alcoholism: Clinical and Experimental Research, 13,* 201–295.

DeLaber, J., Goldgaber, D., Lamour, Y., Nicole, A., Huret, J., De Grouchy, J., Brown, P., Gajdusek, D., & Sinet, P. (1987). β amyloid gene duplication in Alzheimer's disease and karyotypically normal Down syndrome. *Science, 235,* 1390–1392

Delamater, J., & MacCorquodale, P. (1979). *Premarital Sexuality: Attitudes, Relationships, Behavior.* Madison: University of Wisconsin Press.

Dembroski, T., MacDougall, J., Shields, J., Petitto, J., & Lushene, R. (1978). Components of the Type A coronary-prone behavior patterns and cardiovascular responses to psychomotor performance challenge. *Journal of Behavioral Medicine, 1,* 159–176.

Dembroski, T., MacDougall, J., Williams, B., & Haney, T. (1985). Components of Type A, hostility, and anger-in: Relationship to angiographic findings. *Psychosomatic Medicine, 47,* 219–233.

Dement, W. (1960). The effects of dream deprivation. *Science, 131,* 1705–1707.

Dement, W. (1972). *Some Must Watch While Some Must Sleep.* Stanford, CA: Stanford Alumni Association.

Dement, W., & Kleitman, N. (1957). Cyclic variations in EEG and their relation to eye movements, bodily motility, and dreaming. *Electroencephalography Clinical Neurophysiology, 9,* 673–690.

Dempster, F. (1985). Proactive interference in sentence recall: Topic-similarity effects and individual differences. *Memory and Cognition, 13,* 81–89.

Denicoff, K., Joffe, R., Lakshmanan, M., Robbins, J., & Rubinow, D. (1990). Neuropsychiatric manifestations of altered thyroid state. *The American Journal of Psychiatry, 147,* 94–99.

Denmark, F., Russo, N., Frieze, I., & Sechzer, J. (1988). Guidelines for avoiding sexism in psychological research. *American Psychologist, 43,* 582–585.

Dennerstein, L., Burrows, G., Wood, C., & Hyman, G. (1980). Hormones and sexuality: The effects of estrogen and progestogen. *Obstetrics and Gynecology, 56,* 316–322.

Denney, N., & Palmer, A. (1981). Adult age differences on traditional and practical problem-solving measures. *Journal of Gerontology, 36,* 323–328.

Depue, R., & Iacono, W. (1989). Neurobehavioral aspects of affective disorders. *Annual Review of Psychology, 40,* 457–492.

Derogatis, L., Abeloff, M., & Melasaratos, N. (1979). Psychological coping mechanisms and survival time in metastatic breast cancer. *Journal of the American Medical Association, 242,* 1504–1508.

Detera-Wadleigh, S., Berrettini, W., Goldin, L., Boorman, D., Anderson, S., & Gershon, E. (1987). Close linkage of c-Harvey-ras-I and the insulin gene to affective disorder is ruled out in three North American pedigrees. *Nature, 325,* 806–807.

Deutsch, J., & Folle, S. (1973). Alcohol and asymmetrical state-dependency: A possible explanation. *Behavioral Biology, 8,* 273–278.

Deutsch, M., & Gerard, H. (1955). A study of normative and informational influence upon individual judgment. *Journal of Abnormal and Social Psychology, 51,* 629–636.

DeValois, R., & DeValois, K. (1975). Neural coding of color. In E. Carterette & M. Friedman (Eds.), *Handbook of Perception* (Vol. 5). New York: Academic Press.

DeValois, R., & DeValois, K. (1980). Spatial vision. *Annual Review of Psychology, 31,* 309–341.

DeValois, R., & Jacobs, G. (1984). Neural mechanisms in color vision. In J. Brookhart & V. Mountcastle (Eds.), *Handbook of Physiology, The Nervous System III.* Bethesda, MD: American Physiological Society.

Devane, W. (1992). Isolation and structure of a brain constituant that binds to the cannabinoid receptor. *Science, 258,* 1946–1949.

de Villiers, P., & de Villiers, J. (1979). *Early Language.* Cambridge, MA: Harvard University Press.

Devlin, M., Walsh, T., Kral, J., Heymsfield, S., PiSunyer, F., & Dantzic, S. (1990). Metabolic abnormalities in bulimia nervosa. *Archives of General Psychiatry, 47,* 144–148.

Devulder, J., De Colvenaer, L., Caemaert, J., Calliauw, L., & Martens, F. (1990). Spinal cord stimulation in chronic pain therapy. *The Clinical Journal of Pain, 6,* 51–56.

Deykin, E., Levy, J., & Wells, V. (1987). Adolescent depression, alcohol and drug abuse. *American Journal of Public Health, 77,* 178–182.

Diamond, M. (1977). Human sexual development: Biological foundations for social development. In F. Beach (Ed.), *Human Sexuality in Four Perspectives.* Baltimore: Johns Hopkins University Press.

Diamond, M. (1979). Sexual identity and sex

roles. In V. Bullough (Ed.), *The Frontiers of Sex Research*. Buffalo, NY: Prometheus Press.

Diamond, M. (1982). Sexual identity, monozygotic twins reared in discordant sex roles and a BBC follow-up. *Archives of Sexual Behavior*, 11, 181–186.

Diamond, M., & Karlen, A. (1980). *Sexual Decisions*. Boston: Little, Brown.

Dickie, J., Ludwig, T., & Blauw, D. (1979). Life satisfaction among institutionalized and non-institutionalized older adults. *Psychological Reports*, 44, 807–810.

Diener, E., & Wallbom, M. (1976). Effects of self-awareness on antinormative behavior. *Journal of Research in Personality*, 10, 107–111.

Dietz, W. (1986). Prevention of childhood obesity. *Pediatric Clinics of North America*, 33, 823–832.

Dilsaver, S. (1989). Panic disorder. *American Family Physician*, 39, 167–173.

DiMascio, A., Weissman, M., Prusoff, B., Neu, C., & Zwilling, M. (1979). Differential symptom reduction by drugs and psychotherapy in acute depression. *Archives of General Psychiatry*, 36, 1450–1456.

Dion, K., & Berscheid, E. (1974). Physical attractiveness and peer perception among children. *Sociometry*, 37, 1–12.

Dion, K., & Dion, K. (1987). Belief in a just world and physical attractiveness stereotyping. *Journal of Personality and Social Psychology*, 52, 775–780.

Dobelle, W. (1977). Current status of research on providing sight to the blind by electrical stimulation of the brain. *Journal of Visual Impairment and Blindness*, 71, 290–297.

Doering, C., Kraemer, H., Brodie, H., & Hamburg, D. (1975). A cycle of plasma testosterone in the human male. *Journal of Clinical Endocrinology and Metabolism*, 40, 492–500.

Dollard, J., Doob, L., Miller, N., Mowrer, O., & Sears, R. (1939). *Frustration and Aggression*. New Haven: CT: Yale University Press.

Domjan, M. (1993). *The Principles of Learning and Behavior*. Pacific Grove, CA: Brooks/Cole Publishing Company.

Donchin, E. (1975). On evoked potentials, cognition, and memory. *Science*, 190, 1004–1005.

Donnelly, J. (1980). In H. Kaplan, A. Freedman, & B. Sadock (Eds.), *Comprehensive Textbook of Psychiatry*. Baltimore: Williams & Wilkins.

Dorfman, R., & Shipley, T. (1956). *Androgens: Biochemistry, Physiology, and Clinical Significance*. New York: Wiley.

Dorpat, T., & Ripley, H. (1967). The relationship between attempted suicide and committed suicide. *Comprehensive Psychiatry*, 8, 74.

Dosher, B. (1984). Discriminating preexperimental (semantic) from learned (episodic) associations: A speed-accuracy study. *Cognitive Psychology*, 16, 519–555.

Douglass, A., Harris, L., & Pazderka, F. (1989). Monozygotic twins concordant for the narcoleptic syndrome. *Neurology*, 39, 140–141.

Douvan, E. (1986). Adolescence. In C. Tavris (Ed.), *Everywoman's Emotional Well-Being*. New York: Doubleday.

Dove, A. (1968). Taking the chitling test. *Newsweek*, July, 32–34.

Doyle, J. (1985). *Sex and Gender*. Dubuque, IA: William C. Brown.

Dressler, W. (1989). Type A behavior and the social production of cardiovascular disease. *The Journal of Nervous and Mental Disease*, 177, 181–190.

Dudley, R. (1991). IQ and heredity. *Science*, 252, 191–192.

Dudycha, G. (1936). An objective study of punctuality in relation to personalities and achievement. *Archives of Psychology*, 204, 1–53.

Duggan, J., & Booth, D. (1986). Obesity, overeating, and rapid gastric emptying in rats with ventromedial hypothalamic lesions. *Science*, 231, 609–611.

Duke, M., & Nowicki, S. (1986). *Abnormal Psychology*. New York: Holt, Rinehart and Winston.

Dunham, R., Kidwell, J., & Wilson, S. (1986). Rites of passage at adolescence: a ritual process paradigm. *Journal of Adolescent Research*, 1, 139–154.

Dusek, D., & Girdano, D. (1980). *Drugs: A Factual Account*. Reading, MA: Addison-Wesley.

Dywan, J., & Bowers, K. (1983). The use of hypnosis to enhance recall. *Science*, 222, 184–185.

Eagly, A. (1981). Recipient characteristics as determinants of responses to persuasion. In R. Petty, T. Ostrom, & T. Brock (Eds.), *Cognitive Responses in Persuasion*. Hillsdale, NJ: Erlbaum.

Eagly, A., & Warren, R. (1976). Intelligence, comprehension, and opinion change. *Journal of Personality*, 44, 226–242.

Eagly, A., Wood, W., & Chaiken, S. (1978). Causal inferences about communication and their effect on opinion change. *Journal of Personality and Social Psychology*, 36, 424–435.

Easterbrooks, M., & Goldberg, W. (1984). Toddler development in the family: Impact of father involvement and parenting characteristics. *Child Development*, 55, 740–752.

Ebbinghaus, H. (1913). *Memory: A Contribution to Experimental Psychology* (translated by H. Ruger and C. Bussenius). New York: Dover. (Originally published in 1885.)

Echterling, L., & Emmerling, D. (1987). Impact of stage hypnosis. *American Journal of Clinical Hypnosis*, 29, 149–154.

Eckholm, E. (1986). Researchers dispute tolling of genetic clock. *The Oregonian*, June 19, F1–F2.

Edlund, M., Swann, A., & Clothier, J. (1987). Patients with panic attack and abnormal EEG results. *The American Journal of Psychiatry*, 144, 508–509.

Egan, J. (1975). *Signal Detection Theory and ROC Analysis*. New York: Academic Press.

Egeland, J., Gerhard, D., Pauls, D., Sussex, J., Kidd, K., Allen, C., Hostetter, A., & Housman, D. (1987). Bipolar affective disorders linked to DNA markers on chromosome 11. *Nature*, 325, 783–787.

Eibl-Eibesfeldt, I. (1991). *Human Ethology*. Hawthorne, NY: Aldine de Gruyter Publishers.

Eich, E., & Metcalfe, J. (1989). Mood dependent memory for internal versus external events. *Journal of Experimental Psychology: Learning, Memory, and Cognition*, 15, 443–455.

Eichorn, D., Hunt, J., & Honzik, M. (1981). Experience, personality, and IQ: Adolescence to middle age. In D. Eichorn, J. Clausen, N. Haan, M. Honzik, & P. Mussen (Eds.), *Present and Past in Middle Age*. New York: Academic Press.

Eimas, P. (1975). Developmental studies of speech perception. In L. Cohen & P. Salapatek (Eds.), *Infant Perception: From Sensation to Perception* (Vol. 7). New York: Academic Press.

Eimas, P. (1985). The perception of speech in early infancy. *Scientific American*, 252, 46–52.

Eisenberg, N., Cialdini, R., McCreath, H., & Shell, R. (1987). Consistency-based compliance: When and why do children become vulnerable? *Journal of Personality and Social Psychology*, 52, 1174–1181.

Ekman, P. (1982). *Emotion and the Human Face* (2nd ed.). New York: Cambridge University Press.

Ekman, P., & Friesen, W. (1984). *Unmasking the Face* (2nd ed.). Palo Alto, CA: Consulting Psychologists Press.

Ekman, P., Levenson, R., & Friesen, W. (1983). Autonomic nervous system activity distinguishes among emotions. *Science*, 221, 1208–1210.

Ellis, A. (1962). *Reason and Emotion in Psychotherapy*. Secaucus, NJ: Lyle Stuart/Citadel Press.

Ellis, A. (1975). *How to Live with a Neurotic*. N. Hollywood, CA: Wilshire Books.

Ellis, A. (1984). Rational-emotive therapy. In R. Corsini (Ed.), *Current Psychotherapies*. Itasca, IL: Peacock.

Ellis, A., & Harper, R. (1975). *A New Guide to Rational Living*. N. Hollywood, CA: Wilshire Books.

Ellis, L., & Ames, M. (1987). Neurohormonal functioning and sexual orientation: A theory of homosexuality-heterosexuality. *Psychological Bulletin*, 101, 233–258.

Ellis, R., & Oscar-Berman, M. (1989). Alcoholism, aging, and functional cerebral asymmetries. *Psychological Bulletin*, 106, 128–147.

Emmerick, H. (1978). The influence of parents and peers on choices made by adolescents. *Journal of Youth and Adolescence*, 7, 175–180.

Ennis, R. (1982). Children's ability to handle Piaget's propositional logic: A conceptual critique. In S. Modgil & C. Modgil (Eds.), *Jean Piaget: Consensus and Controversy*. New York: Praeger.

Epstein, A. (1960). Reciprocal changes in feeding behaviors produced by intrahypothalamic chemical injections. *American Journal of Physiology*, 199, 969–974.

Epstein, A., & Teitelbaum, P. (1967). Specific loss of the hypoglycemic control of feeding in recovered lateral rats. *American Journal of Physiology*, 213, 1159–1167.

Epstein, L., & Wing, R. (1987). Behavioral treatment of childhood obesity. *Psychological Bulletin*, 101, 331–342.

Epstein, L., Wing, R., Koeskie, R., & Valoski, A. (1987). Long-term effects of family-based treatment of childhood obesity. *Journal of Consulting and Clinical Psychology*, 55, 91–95.

Epstein, R., Lanza, R., & Skinner, B. (1980). Symbolic communication between two pigeons. *Science, 220*–221.

Epstein, S. (1983). The stability of behavior across time and situations. In R. Zucker, J. Aronoff, & A. Robin (Eds.), *Personality and the Prediction of Behavior.* San Diego, CA: Academic Press.

Erikson, E. (1963). *Childhood and Society* (2nd ed.). New York: Norton.

Erkut, S. (1983). Exploring sex differences in expectancy, attribution, and academic achievement. *Sex Roles, 9,* 217–331.

Erlenmeyer-Kimling, L., & Jarvik, L. (1963). Genetics and intelligence. *Science, 142,* 1477–1479.

Erlich, S., & Itabashi, H. (1986). Narcolepsy: A neuropathologic study. *Sleep, 9,* 126–132.

Eron, L., & Huesmann, L. (1984). The control of aggressive behaviors by changes in attitudes, values and the conditions of learning. In R. Blanchard and C. Blanchard (Eds.), *Advances in the Study of Aggression* (Vol. 1). Orlando, FL: Academic Press.

Eron, L., Huesmann, L., Lefkovitz, M., & Walder, L. (1972). Does television violence cause aggression? *American Psychologist, 27,* 253–263.

Esquirol, J. (1845). *Mental Maladies: Treatise on Insanity* (translated by E. Hunt). Philadelphia: Lea & Blanchard.

Esterling, B., & Rabin, B. (1987). Stress-induced alteration of T-lymphocyte subsets and humoral immunity in mice. *Behavioral Neuroscience, 101,* 115–119.

Estes, W. (1972). An associative basis for coding and organization in memory. In A. Melton & E. Martin (Eds.), *Coding Process in Human Memory.* Washington, DC: Winston.

Ettinger, R., Thompson, S., & Staddon, J. (1986). Cholecystokinin, diet palatability, and feeding regulation in rats. *Physiology and Behavior, 36,* 801–809.

European Study Group (1989). Risk factors for male to female transmission of HIV. *British Medical Journal, 298,* 411–415.

Evans, F. (1989). Hypnosis and chronic pain. *The Clinical Journal of Pain, 5,* 169–176.

Evans, G. (1980). Environmental cognition. *Psychological Bulletin, 88,* 259–287.

Evans, J., Barston, J., & Pollard, P. (1983). On the conflict between logic and belief in syllogistic reasoning. *Memory and Cognition, 11,* 295–306.

Evans, R. (1974). A conversation with Konrad Lorenz about aggression, homosexuality, pornography, and the need for a new ethic. *Psychology Today,* November, 83ff.

Eveleth, P., & Tanner, J. (1976). *Worldwide Variation in Human Growth.* Cambridge, England: Cambridge University Press.

Everitt, B., Cador, M., & Robbins, T. (1989). Interactions between the amygdala and ventral striatum in stimulus-reward associations: Studies using a second-order schedule of sexual reinforcement. *Neuroscience, 30,* 63–75.

Everly, G. (1989). *A Clinical Guide to the Treatment of the Human Stress Response.* New York: Plenum.

Everson, C., Bergmann, B., & Rechtschaffen, A. (1989). Sleep deprivation in the rat: III. Total sleep deprivation. *Sleep, 12,* 13–21.

Eysenck, H. (1952). The effects of psychotherapy: An evaluation. *Journal of Consulting Psychology, 16,* 319–324.

Eysenck, H. (1990). Genetic and environmental contributions to individual differences: The three major dimensions of personality. *Journal of Personality, 58,* 245–261.

Fackelman, K. (1993). Marijuana and the brain. *Science News, 143,* 88–89.

Fairburn, C., & Beglin, S. (1990). Studies of the epidemiology of bulimia nervosa. *American Journal of Psychiatry, 147,* 401–408.

Falloon, J., Eddy, J., Wiener, L., & Pizzo, P. (1989). Human immunodeficiency virus infection in children. *Journal of Pediatrics, 114,* 1–23.

Fantino, E. (1973). Aversive control. In J. Levin & G. Reynolds (Eds.), *The Study of Behavior: Learning, Motivation, Emotion, and Instinct.* Glenview, IL: Scott, Foresman.

Fantino, E. (1977). Conditioned reinforcement: choice and information. In W. Honig & J. Staddon (Eds.), *Handbook of Operant Behavior.* Englewood Cliffs, NJ: Prentice-Hall.

Fantino, E., & Logan, C. (1979). *The Experimental Analysis of Behavior: A Biological Perspective.* San Francisco: Freeman.

Farley, F. (1986). The big T in personality. *Psychology Today,* May, 44–52.

Farrer, L., O'Sullivan, D., Cupples, A., Growdon, J., & Myers, R. (1989). Assessment of genetic risk for Alzheimer's disease among first degree relatives. *Annals of Neurology, 25,* 485–493.

Faustman, W., & White, P. (1989). Diagnostic and psychopharmacological treatment characteristics of 536 inpatients with posttraumatic stress disorder. *The Journal of Nervous and Mental Disease, 177,* 154–159.

Fava, M., Copeland, P., Schweiger, U., & Herzog, D. (1989). Neurochemical abnormalities of anorexia nervosa and bulimia nervosa. *The American Journal of Psychiatry, 146,* 963–971.

Fava, M., Copeland, P., Schweiger, U., & Herzog, D. (1990). Neurochemical abnormalities of anorexia nervosa and bulimia nervosa. *Annual Progress in Child Psychiatry and Child Development,* 368–386.

Fazio, R. (1986). How do attitudes guide behavior? In R. Sorrentino & E. Higgins (Eds.), *The Handbook of Motivation and Cognition: Foundations of Social Behavior.* New York: Guilford Press.

Fazio, R., Powell, M., & Herr, P. (1983). Toward a process model of the attitude-behavior relation: Assessing one's attitude upon mere observation of the attitude object. *Journal of Personality and Social Psychology, 44,* 723–735.

Fazio, R., & Zanna, M. (1981). Direct experience and attitude-behavior consistency. In L. Berkowitz (Ed.), *Advances in Experimental Social Psychology* (Vol. 14). New York: Academic Press.

Feather, N., & Raphelson, A. (1974). Fear of success in Australian and American student groups: Motive or sex-role stereotype? *Journal of Personality, 42,* 190–201.

Feingold, A. (1988). Cognitive gender differences are disappearing. *American Psychologist, 43,* 95–103.

Fennell, M., & Campbell, E. (1984). The cog-

nitive questionnaire: Specific thinking errors in depression. *British Journal of Clinical Psychology, 23,* 81–92.

Fernald, D. (1984). *The Hans Legacy.* Hillsdale, NJ: Erlbaum.

Ferster, C. (1965). Classification of behavior pathology. In L. Kransner & L. Ullman (Eds.), *Research in Behavior Modification.* New York: Holt, Rinehart and Winston.

Feshbach, N. (1985). Chronic maternal stress and its assessment. In J. Butcher & C. Speilberger (Eds.), *Advances in Personality Assessment* (Vol. 5). Hillsdale, NJ: Erlbaum.

Feshbach, S. (1980). Child abuse and the dynamics of human aggression and violence. In J. Gerbner, C. Ross, & E. Zigler (Eds.), *Child Abuse: An Agenda for Action.* New York: Oxford University Press.

Feshbach, S., & Weiner, B. (1982). *Personality.* Lexington, MA: Heath.

Festinger, L. (1957). *A Theory of Cognitive Dissonance.* Stanford, CA: Stanford University Press.

Festinger, L., Schachter, S., & Back, K. (1950). *Social Pressures in Informal Groups: A Study of Human Factors in Housing.* New York: Harper & Row.

Field, T. (1978). Interaction behaviors of primary versus secondary caretaker fathers. *Developmental Psychology, 14,* 183–184.

Field, T., Vega-Lahr, N., Goldstein, S., & Scafidi, F. (1987). Face-to-face interaction behavior across infancy. *Infant Behavior and Development, 10,* 111–116.

Fincham, F., Beach, S., & Baucom, D. (1987). Attribution processes in distressed and nondistressed couples: Self-partner attribution differences. *Journal of Personality and Social Psychology, 52,* 739–748.

Findlay, J., Place, V., & Snyder, P. (1989). Treatment of primary hypogonadism in men by the transdermal administration of testosterone. *Journal of Clinical Endocrinology and Metabolism, 68,* 369–373.

Fischbach, G. (1992). Mind and brain. *Scientific American, 267,* 48–57.

Fischer, J., Sollie, D., & Morrow, B. (1986). Social networks in male and female adolescents. *Journal of Adolescent Research, 6,* 1–14.

Fishbein, M., & Ajzen, I. (1975). *Belief, Attitude, Intention, and Behavior: An Introduction to Theory and Research.* Reading, MA: Addison-Wesley.

Fisher, C., Daniels, J., Levin, S., Kimzey, S., Cobb, E., & Ritzman, W. (1972). Effects of the spaceflight environment on man's immune system: II. Lymphocyte counts and reactivity. *Aerospace Medicine, 43,* 1122–1125.

Fisher, S., & Greenberg, R. (1977). *Scientific Credibility of Freud's Theories.* New York: Basic Books.

Flavell, J. (1985). *Cognitive Development* (2nd ed.). Englewood Cliffs, NJ: Prentice-Hall.

Fleming, I., Baum, A., & Weiss, L. (1987). Social density and perceived control as mediators of crowding stress in high-density residential neighborhoods. *Journal of Personality and Social Psychology, 52,* 899–906.

Flynn, J. (1987). Massive IQ gains in 14 nations: What IQ tests really measure. *Psychological Bulletin, 101,* 171–191.

Foley, J. (1985). Binocular distance perception:

Egocentric distance tasks. *Journal of Experimental Psychology: Human Perception of Performance, 11,* 133–149.

Foley, V. (1984). Family therapy. In R. Corsini (Ed.), *Current Psychotherapies.* Itasca, IL: Peacock.

Follingstad, D., Kalichman, S., Cafferty, T., & Vormbrock, J. (1992). Aggression levels following frustration of abusing versus nonabusing college males. *Journal of Interpersonal Violence, 7,* 3–18.

Fontaine, R., Breton, G., Dery, R., Fontaine, S., & Elie, R. (1990). Temporal lobe abnormalities in panic disorder: An MRI study. *Biological Psychiatry, 27,* 304–310.

Fontana, A., Kerns, R., Rosenberg, R., & Colonese, K. (1989). Support, stress, and recovery from coronary heart disease: A longitudinal causal model. *Health Psychology, 8,* 175–193.

Ford, C., & Beach, F. (1951). *Patterns of Sexual Behavior.* New York: Harper & Row.

Ford, M. (1985). Two perspectives on the validation of developmental constructs: Psychometric and theoretical limitations in research on egocentrism. *Psychological Bulletin, 97,* 497–501.

Forgays, D., & Belinson, M. (1986). Is floatation isolation a relaxing environment? *Journal of Environmental Psychology, 6(1)PS,* 19–34.

Forrester, W., & King, D. (1971). Effects of semantic and acoustic relatedness on free recall and clustering. *Journal of Experimental Psychology, 88,* 16–19.

Forsyth, D. (1983). *An Introduction to Group Dynamics.* Monterey, CA: Brooks/Cole.

Fortenberry, J., Brown, D., & Shelvin, L. (1986). Analysis of drug involvement in traffic fatalities in Alabama. *American Journal of Drug and Alcohol Abuse, 12,* 257–267.

Fosson, A., Knibbs, J., Bryant-Waugh, R., & Lask, B. (1987). Early onset anorexia nervosa. *Archives of Disease in Children, 62,* 114–118.

Foster, G., & Ysseldyke, J. (1976). Expectancy and halo effects as a result of artificially induced teacher bias. *Contemporary Educational Psychology, 1,* 37–45.

Foulkes, D., & Schmidt, M. (1983). Temporal sequence and unit composition in dream reports from different stages of sleep. *Sleep, 6,* 265–280.

Fox, P., Mintun, M., Raichle, M., Miezin, F., Allman, J., & Van Essen, D. (1986). Mapping human visual cortex with positron emission tomography. *Nature, 323,* 806–809.

Fox, S., Brown, C., Koontz, A., & Kessel, S. (1987). Perceptions of risks of smoking and heavy drinking during pregnancy: 1985 NHIS findings. *Public Health Representative, 102,* 73–79.

Frank, J. (1982). Therapeutic components shared by all psychotherapies. In J. Harvey & M. Parks (Eds.), *The Master Lecture Series, Vol. I: Psychotherapy Research and Behavior Change.* Washington, DC: American Psychological Association.

Frankenhaeuser, M. (1975). Sympathetic-adrenomedullary activity behavior and the psychosocial environment. In P. Venables and M. Christie (Eds.), *Research in Psychophysiology.* New York: Wiley.

Frankish, C. (1985). Modality-specific grouping effects in short-term memory. *Journal of Memory and Language, 24,* 200–209.

Freedman, F. (1984). Effects of television violence on aggression. *Psychological Bulletin, 96,* 227–246.

Freedman, J., & Fraser, S. (1966). Compliance without pressure: The foot-in-the-door technique. *Journal of Personality and Social Psychology, 4,* 195–202.

Freeman, W., & Watts, J. (1950). *Psychosurgery.* Springfield, IL: Thomas.

Freud, S. (1900). *The Interpretation of Dreams.* London: Hogarth Press.

Freud, S. (1905). *Three Essays on the Theory of Sexuality* (J. Strachey, Ed. and Translator). New York: Basic Books (1963: Originally published in 1905).

Freud, S. (1917). Mourning and melancholia. Originally written in 1917 and later published in *Collected Papers* (Vol. 4). London: Hogarth Press.

Freud, S. (1933). *New Introductory Lectures.* In Vol. XXII of The Standard Edition. London: Hogarth Press, 1964.

Freud, S. (1936). *The Problem of Anxiety.* New York: Norton.

Friedman, M., & Rosenman, R. (1974). *Type A Behavior and Your Heart.* New York: Knopf.

Friedman, M., & Ulmer, D. (1984). *Treating Type A Behavior—and Your Heart.* New York: Knopf.

Friedmann, T. (1989). Progress toward human gene therapy. *Science, 244,* 1275–1281.

Friedrich-Cofer, L. (1986). Television violence and aggression: The debate continues. *Psychological Bulletin, 100,* 364–371.

Frodi, A. (1975). The effect of exposure to weapons on aggressive behavior from a cross-cultural perspective. *International Journal of Psychology, 10,* 283–292.

Frumkin, B., & Anisfeld, M. (1977). Semantic and surface codes in the memory of deaf children. *Cognitive Psychology, 9,* 475–493.

Fuhrer, M., & Baer, P. (1965). Differential classical conditioning: Verbalizations of stimulus contingencies. *Science, 150,* 1479–1481.

Fuhriman, A., & Burlingame, G. (1990). Consistency of matter: A comparative analysis of individual and group process variables. *The Counseling Psychologist, 18,* 6–63.

Fukuda, M., Ono, T., Nishino, H., & Nakamura, K. (1986). Neuronal responses in monkey lateral hypothalamus during operant feeding behavior. *Brain Research Bulletin, 17,* 879–884.

Fulker, D., DeFries, J., & Plomin, R. (1988). Genetic influence on general mental ability increases between infancy and middle childhood. *Nature, 336,* 767–769.

Furuhjelm, M., Karlgren, E., & Carstrom, K. (1984). The effect of estrogen therapy on somatic and physical symptoms in postmenopausal women. *Acta Obstetricia et Gynecologica Scandinavica, 63,* 655–661.

Gadnow, K., & Sprafkink J. (1989). Field experiments of television violence: Evidence for an environmental hazard? *Pediatrics, 83,* 399–405.

Gaffney, F., Fenton, B., Lane, L., & Lake, C. (1988). Hemodynamic, ventilatory, and biochemical response of panic patients and normal controls with sodium lactate infusion and spontaneous panic attacks. *Archives of General Psychiatry, 45,* 53–61.

Gage, D., & Safer, M. (1985). Hemisphere differences in the mood state-dependent effect for recognition of emotional faces. *Journal of Experimental Psychology: Learning, Memory, and Cognition, 11,* 752–763.

Gagnon, J. (1977). *Human Sexualities.* Glenview, IL: Scott, Foresman.

Gaito, J. (1974). A biochemical approach to learning and memory: Fourteen years later. In G. Newton and A. Riesen (Eds.), *Advances in Psychobiology* (Vol. 2). New York: Wiley.

Gaitwell, N., Loriaux, D., & Chase, T. (1977). Plasma testosterone in homosexual and heterosexual women. *American Journal of Psychiatry, 134,* 117–119.

Galef, B. (1970). Aggression and timidity responses to novelty in feral Norway rats. *Journal of Comparative and Physiological Psychology, 70,* 370–375.

Gall, C., & Black, P. (1989). Dementia. *American Family Physician, 39,* 241–250.

Gallagher, W. (1988). Sex and hormones. *Atlantic Monthly,* March, 77–82.

Gallatin, J. (1980). Political thinking in adolescence. In J. Adelson (Ed.), *Handbook of Adolescent Psychology.* New York: Wiley.

Gallistel, C. (1986). The role of the dopaminergic projections in MFB self-stimulation. *Behavioural Brain Research, 22,* 97–105.

Garbanino, J., & Gilliam, G. (1980). *Understanding Abusive Families.* Lexington, MA: Lexington Books.

Garber, J., & Seligman, M. (Eds.). (1980). *Human Helplessness: Theory and Application.* New York: Academic Press.

Garcia, J., Kimmeldorf, D., & Hunt, E. (1961). The use of ionizing radiation as a motivatory stimulus. *Psychological Review, 68,* 383–385.

Garcia, J., & Koelling, R. (1966). Relation of cue to consequences in avoidance learning. *Psychonomic Science, 4,* 123–124.

Gardner, H. (1983). *Frames of Mind: The Theory of Multiple Intelligence.* Englewood Cliffs, NJ: Prentice Hall.

Gardner, H. (1990). Interview for program 16, *Discovering Psychology,* a 26-part telecourse from the Annenberg/CPB Project.

Gardner, A., & Gardner, B. (1969). Teaching sign language to a chimpanzee. *Science, 165,* 644–672.

Gardner, A., & Gardner, B. (1975). Early signs of language in child and chimpanzee. *Science, 187,* 752–753.

Garlicki, J., Konturek, P., Majka, J. Kwiecien, N., & Konturek, S. (1990). Cholecystokinin receptors and vagal nerves in control of food intake in rats. *American Journal of Physiology, 258,* E40–E45.

Garvey, M., Wesner, R., & Godes, M. (1988). Comparison of seasonal and nonseasonal affective disorders. *The American Journal of Psychiatry, 145,* 100–102.

Gates, A. (1917). Recitation as a factor in memorizing. *Archives of Psychology,* No. 40.

Gawin, F., & Kleber, H. (1984). Cocaine abuse treatment. *Archives of General Psychiatry, 41,* 903–909.

Gazzaniga, M. (1987). Perceptual and attentional processes following callosal section in humans. *Neuropsychologia, 25,* 119–133.

Gazzaniga, M., & LeDoux, J. (1978). *The Integrated Mind.* New York: Plenum.

Gazzaniga, M., Kutas, M., Van Petten, C., & Fendrich, R. (1989). Human callosal function: MRI-verified neuropsychological functions. *Neurology, 39,* 942–946.

Geary, D. (1989). A model for representing gender differences in the pattern of cognitive abilities. *American Psychologist, 44,* 1155–1156.

Geen, R., Beatty, W., & Arkin, R. (1984). *Human Motivation.* Newton, MA: Allyn & Bacon.

Gehringer, W., & Engel, E. (1986). Effect of ecological viewing conditions on the Ames' distorted room illusion. *Journal of Experimental Psychology: Human Perception and Performance, 12,* 181–185.

Geiselman, R. (1988). Improving eyewitness memory through mental restatement of context. In G. Davies & D. Thomson (Eds.), *Memory in Context: Context in Memory.* Chichester, England: Wiley.

Gelder, M. (1989). Panic disorder: Fact or fiction? *Psychological Medicine, 19,* 277–283.

Gentry, W., Chesney, A., Gary, H., Hall, R., & Harburg, E. (1982). Habitual anger-coping styles: I. Affect on mean blood pressure and risk for essential hypertension. *Psychosomatic Medicine, 44,* 195–202.

George, C., & Main, M. (1979). Social interactions of young abused children: Approach, avoidance, and aggression. *Child Development, 50,* 306–318.

Geracioti, T., & Liddle, R. (1988). Impaired cholecystokinin secretion in bulimia nervosa. *New England Journal of Medicine, 319,* 683–688.

Gerard, H., Wilhelmy, R., & Connolley, R. (1968). Conformity and group size. *Journal of Personality and Social Psychology, 8,* 79–82.

Gergen, K. (1965). The effects of interaction goals and personalistic feedback on the presentation of self. *Journal of Personality and Social Psychology, 1,* 413–424.

Gerrard, M. (1987). Sex, sex guilt, and contraceptive use revisited: The 1980s. *Journal of Personality and Social Psychology, 52,* 975–980.

Gershon, E., Hamovit, J., Guroff, J., & Nurnberger, J. (1987). Birth-cohort changes in manic and depressive disorders in relatives of bipolar and schizoaffective patients. *Archives of General Psychiatry, 44,* 314–319.

Geschwind, N., & Levitsky, W. (1976). Left-right asymmetries in temporal speech region. *Science, 161,* 186–187.

Gesell, A. (1928). *Infancy and Human Growth.* New York: Macmillan.

Getchell, T. (1986). Functional properties of vertebrate olfactory receptor neurons. *Physiological Reviews, 66,* 772–818.

Giannini, A., Pascarzi, G., Losiselle, R., Price, W., & Giannini, M. (1986). Comparison of clonidine and lithium in the treatment of mania. *American Journal of Psychiatry, 143,* 1608–1609.

Gibbs, J., Young, R., & Smith, G. (1973). Cholecystokinin elicits satiety in rats with open gastric fistulas. *Nature, 245,* 323–325.

Gibling, F., & Davies, G. (1988). Reinstatement of context following exposure to post-event

information. *British Journal of Psychology, 79,* 129–141.

Gibson, E., & Spelke, E. (1983). The development of perception. In J. Flavell & E. Markham (Eds.), *Handbook of Child Psychology: Cognitive Development* (Vol. 3). New York: Wiley.

Gibson, E., & Walk, R. (1960). The visual cliff. *Scientific American, 202,* 64–71.

Gibson, J. (1979). *The Ecological Approach to Visual Perception.* Boston: Houghton Mifflin.

Gieringer, D. (1988). Marijuana, driving, and accident safety. *Journal of Psychoactive Drugs, 20,* 93–101.

Giles, D., Jarrett, R., Biggs, M., Guzick, D., & Rush, A. (1989). Clinical predictors of recurrence in depression. *The American Journal of Psychiatry, 146,* 764–767.

Gillam, B. (1980). Geometrical illusions. *Scientific American, 242,* 102–111.

Gillie, O. (1976). Pioneer of IQ faked his research findings. *Sunday Times of London,* October 29, H3.

Giordano, P. (1983). Sanctioning the higher-status deviant: An attributional analysis. *Social Psychology Quarterly, 46,* 329–342.

Glass, D. (1977). *Behavior Patterns, Stress, and Coronary Disease.* Hillsdale, NJ: Erlbaum.

Glass, D., & Singer, J. (1972). *Urban Stress.* New York: Academic Press.

Glass, D., Snyder, M., & Hollis, J. (1974). Time urgency and the Type A coronary-prone behavior pattern. *Journal of Applied Social Psychology, 4,* 125–140.

Gleason, J. (1990). Interview in program 6, *Discovering Psychology,* a 26-part telecourse from the Annenberg/CPB Project.

Gleason, J., & Ratner, N. (1993). *Psycholinguistics.* Fort Worth, TX: Harcourt Brace Jovanovich.

Glick, P. (1989). The family life cycle and social change. *Family Relations, 38,* 123–129.

Glucksberg, S., & Weisberg, R. (1966). Verbal behavior and problem solving: Some effects of labeling upon availability of novel functions. *Journal of Experimental Psychology, 71,* 659–664.

Goethals, G. (1986). Fabricating and ignoring social reality: Self-serving estimates of consensus. In J. Olson, C. Herman, & M. Zanna (Eds.), *Relative Deprivation and Social Comparison: The Ontario Symposium* (Vol. 4). Hillsdale, NJ: Erlbaum.

Gold, P. (1987). Sweet memories. *American Scientist, 75,* 151–155.

Gold, R., Jones, A., Sawchenko, P., & Dapatos, G. (1977). Paraventricular area: Critical focus of a longitudinal neurocircuitry mediating food intake. *Physiology and Behavior, 18,* 1111–1119.

Goldberg, S. (1983). Parent-infant bonding: Another look. *Child Development, 54,* 1355–1382.

Goldberger, L. (1982). Sensory deprivation and overload. In L. Goldberger & S. Bresnitz (Eds.), *Handbook of Stress: Theoretical and Clinical Aspects.* New York: Free Press.

Golden, N., Sokol, R., Kuhnert, B., & Bottoms, S. (1982). Maternal alcohol use and infant development. *Pediatrics, 70,* 931–934.

Goldfarb, W. (1945). Psychological privation in infancy and subsequent adjustment. *American Journal of Orthopsychiatry, 15,* 247–255.

Goldfield, M., & Padawer, W. (1982). Current

status and future directions in psychotherapy. In M. Goldfield (Ed.), *Converging Themes in Psychotherapy: Trends in Psychodynamic, Humanistic, and Behavioral Practice.* New York: Springer.

Goldfried, M., Greenberg, L., & Marmar, C. (1990). Individual psychotherapy: Process and outcome. *Annual Review of Psychology, 41,* 659–688.

Goldgaber, D., Lerman, M., McBride, O., Saffiotti, U., Gajdusek, D. (1987). Characterization and chromosomal localization of a cDNA encoding brain amyloid of Alzheimer's disease. *Science, 235,* 877–880.

Goldgaber, D., & Schmechel, D. (1990). Expression of the amyloid β–protein precursor gene. *Advances in Neurology, 51,* 163–169.

Goldman-Rakic, P. (1992). Working memory and the mind. *Scientific American, 267,* 110–117.

Goldstein, E. (1989). *Sensation and Perception* (3rd ed.). Belmont, CA: Wadsworth.

Goldstein, M., Baker, B., & Jamison, K. (1986). *Abnormal Psychology* (2nd ed.). Boston: Little, Brown.

Goldstein, M., & Palmer, J. (1975). *The Experience of Anxiety: A Casebook* (2nd ed.). New York: Oxford University Press.

Goleman, D. (1987). A reward mechanism for repression. *Psychology Today,* March, 26–30.

Goodchilds, J., & Zellman, G. (1984). Sexual signaling and sexual aggression in adolescent relationships. In N. Malamuth and E. Donnerstein (Eds.), *Pornography and Sexual Aggression.* Orlando: Academic Press.

Goodwin, D., Powell, B., & Brenner, D. (1969). Alcohol and recall: State-dependent effects in man. *Science, 163,* 1358–1360.

Goodwin, F., Cowdry, R., & Webster, M. (1978). Prediction of drug response in the affective disorders. In M. Lipton, A. Dimascio, & K. Killam (Eds.), *Psychopharmacology: A Generation of Progress.* New York: Raven.

Gooren, L. (1988). Hypogonadotropic hypogonadal men respond less well to androgen substitution treatment than hypergonadotropic hypogonal men. *Archives of Sexual Behavior, 17,* 265–270.

Gordon, H. (1986). The cognitive laterality battery: Tests of specialized cognitive functions. *International Journal of Neuroscience, 29,* 223–244.

Gorelick, P., Rodin, M., Langenberg, P., Hier, D., & Costigan, J. (1989). Weekly alcohol consumption, cigarette smoking, and the risk of ischemic stroke. *Neurology, 39,* 339–343.

Gormally, J., Hill, D., Otis, M., & Rainey, L. (1975). A microtraining approach in assertion training. *Journal of Counseling Psychology, 22,* 340–344.

Gorman, J., Liebowitz, M., Fyer, A., & Stein, J. (1989). A neuroanatomical hypothesis for panic disorder. *The American Journal of Psychiatry, 146,* 148–161.

Gormly, A., & Brodzinsky, D. (1989). *Lifespan Human Development* (4th ed.). New York: Holt, Rinehart and Winston.

Gorski, R. (1985). The 13th J.A.F. memorial lecture: Sexual differentiation of the brain: Possible mechanisms and implications. *Canadian Journal of Physiology and Pharmacology, 63,* 577–594.

Gotlib, I., & Robinson, L. (1982). Responses

to depressed individuals: Discrepancies between self-report and observer-rated behavior. *Journal of Abnormal Psychology, 87,* 322–332.

Goto, S., Hirano, A., & Rojas-Corona, R. (1989). An immunohistochemical investigation of the human neostriatum in Huntington's disease. *Annals of Neurology, 25,* 298–304.

Gottesman, I., McGuffin, P., & Farmer, A. (1987). Clinical genetics as clues to the "real" genetics of schizophrenia. *Schizophrenia Bulletin, 13,* 23–47.

Gottesman, I., & Shields, J. (1976). A critical review of recent adoption, twin, and family studies of schizophrenia: Behavior genetics perspective. *Schizophrenia Bulletin, 2,* 360-398.

Gottesman, I., & Shields, J. (1982). *Schizophrenia: The Epigenetic Puzzle.* Cambridge, MA: Cambridge University Press.

Gottfredson, G. (1987). Employment setting, specialization, and patterns of accomplishments among psychologists. *Professional Psychology: Research and Practice, 18,* 452–460.

Gough, H. (1957/1975). *California Psychological Inventory: Manual* (rev. ed., 1975). Palo Alto, CA: Consulting Psychologists Press.

Gould, J., & Marler, P. (1987). Learning by instinct. *Scientific American, 256,* 74–85.

Gould, S. (1981). *The Mismeasure of Man.* New York: Norton.

Gray, C., & Gummerman, K. (1975). The enigmatic eidetic image: A critical examination of methods, data, and theories. *Psychological Bulletin, 82,* 383–407.

Green, B., Lindy, J., Grace, M., & Gleser, G. (1989). Multiple diagnosis in posttraumatic stress disorder: The role of war stressors. *The Journal of Nervous and Mental Disease, 177,* 329–335.

Green, D., & Swets, J. (1974). *Signal Detection Theory and Psychophysics.* New York: Krieger.

Greenberg, M., & Morris, N. (1974). Engrossment: The newborn's impact upon the father. *American Journal of Orthopsychiatry, 44,* 520–531.

Greenberg, R., & Pearlman, C. (1974). Cutting the REM nerve: An approach to the adaptive role of REM sleep. *Perspectives in Biology and Medicine, 17,* 513–521.

Greeno, J. (1980). Psychology of learning 1960–1980: One participant's observations. *American Psychologist, 35,* 713–728.

Greenough, W. (1984). Possible structural substrates of plastic neural phenomena. In G. Lynch, J. McGaugh, & N. Weinberger (Eds.), *Neurobiology of Learning and Memory.* New York: Guilford Press.

Greenough, W., & Green, E. (1981). Experience and the changing brain. In J. McGaugh, J. March, & S. Kiesler (Eds.), *Aging: Biology and Behavior.* New York: Academic Press.

Greenough, W., McDonnald, J., Parnisari, R., & Camel, J. (1986). Environmental conditions modulate degeneration and new dendritic growth in cerebellum on senescent rats. *Brain Research, 380,* 136–143.

Greenwood, S. (1989). Prenatal testing update. *Medical Self Care,* April, 19–20.

Gregory, R. (1978). *Eye and Brain: The Psychology of Seeing* (3rd ed.). New York: McGraw-Hill.

Grey, J., Feldon, J., Rawlins, J., Hemsley, D., & Smith, A. (1991). The neuropsychology of schizophrenia. *Behavioral and Brain Sciences, 14,* 1–84.

Griffiths, P., Merry, J., Browning, M., Eisinger, A., Huntsman, R., Lord, E., Polani, P., Tanner, J., & Whitehouse, R. (1974). Homosexual women: An endocrine and psychological study. *Journal of Endocrinology, 63,* 549, 556.

Griffitt, W., & Veitch, R. (1974). Preacquaintance attitude similarity and attraction revisited: Ten days in a fallout shelter. *Sociometry, 38,* 163–173.

Grillon, C., Courchesne, E., Ameli, R., Geyer, M., & Braff, D. (1990). *Archives of General Psychiatry, 47,* 171–179.

Grilo, C., & Pogue-Geile, M. (1991). The nature of environmental influences on weight and obesity: A behavior genetic analysis. *Psychological Bulletin, 110,* 520–537.

Grochowicz, P., Schedlowski, M., Husband, A., King, M., Hibberd, A., & Bowen, K. (1991). Behavioral conditioning prolongs heart allograft survival in rats. *Brain, Behavior, and Immunity, 5,* 349–356.

Grossman, M., & Stein, I. (1948). Vagotomy and the hunger producing action of insulin in man. *Journal of Applied Physiology, 1,* 263–269.

Groves, P., & Rebec, G. (1992). *Introduction to Biological Psychology,* Dubuque, IA: Wm. C. Brown Publishers.

Guilford, J. (1967). *The Nature of Human Intelligence.* New York: McGraw-Hill.

Guilford, J. (1977). *Way Beyond the I.Q.* Buffalo, NY: Creative Education Foundation and Bearly Unlimited.

Guilford, J. (1982). Cognitive psychology's ambiguities: Some suggested remedies. *Psychological Review, 89,* 48–59.

Guilleminault, C., & Dement, W. (Eds.). (1978). *The Sleep Apnea Syndrome.* New York: Liss.

Gureje, O. (1989). The significance of subtyping tardive dyskinesia: A study of prevalence and associated factors. *Psychological Medicine, 19,* 121–128.

Gurin, J. (1989). Leaner not lighter. *Psychology Today,* June, 32–36.

Gusella, J., Wexler, N., Conneally, P., Naylor, S., Anderson, M., Tanzi, R., Watkins, P., Ottina, K., Wallace, M., Sakaguchi, A., Young, A., Shoulson, I., Bonilla, E., & Martin, J. (1983). A polymorphic DNA marker genetically linked to Huntington's disease. *Nature, 306,* 234–238.

Gustafson, G., & Harris, K. (1990). Women's responses to young infants' cries. *Developmental Psychology, 26,* 144–152.

Gustafson, R. (1989). Frustration and successful vs. unsuccessful aggression: A test of Berkowitz' completion hypothesis. *Aggressive Behavior, 15,* 5–12.

Gustafson, R. (1992). Treating insomnia with a self-administered muscle relaxation training program: A follow-up. *Psychological Reports, 70,* 124–126.

Gwirtsman, H., & Gerner, R. (1981). Neurochemical abnormalities in anorexia nervosa: Similarities to affective disorders. *Biological Psychiatry, 16,* 991–995.

Haber, R. (1969). Eidetic images. *Scientific American, 220,* 36–44.

Halas, E. & Eberhardt, M. (1987). Blocking and appetitive reinforcement. *Bulletin of the Psychonomic Society, 25,* 121–123.

Hales, D. (1980). *The Complete Book of Sleep,* Reading, MA: Addison-Wesley.

Haley, J. (1989). The effect of long-term outcome studies on the therapy of schizophrenia. *Journal of Marital and Family Therapy, 15,* 127–132.

Hall, J. (1986). The cardiopulmonary failure of sleep-disordered breathing. *Journal of the American Medical Association, 255,* 930–933.

Hall, J. (1989). *Learning and Memory* (2nd ed.). Boston: Allyn & Bacon.

Hall, J. (1992). In C. Ezzell, New theory on the origin of twins. *Science News, 142,* 84.

Hall, W. (1987). Developmental psychobiology: Prenatal, perinatal, and early postnatal aspects of behavioral development. *Annual Review of Psychology, 38,* 91–128.

Halpern, D. (1984). *Thought and Knowledge: An Introduction to Critical Thinking.* Hillsdale, NJ: Erlbaum.

Halpern, D. (1986). *Sex Differences in Cognitive Abilities.* Hillsdale, NJ: Erlbaum.

Halpern, D. (1989). The disappearance of cognitive gender differences: What you see depends on where you look. *American Psychologist, 44,* 1156–1158.

Hamamy, H., Al-Hakkak, Z., & Al-Taha, S. (1990). Consanguinity and the genetic control of Down syndrome. *Clinical Genetics, 37,* 24–29.

Hamburg, D., & Takanishi, R. (1989). Preparing for life: The critical transition of adolescence. *American Psychologist, 44,* 825–827.

Hamilton, D., Katz, L., & Leirer, V. (1980). Memory for persons. *Journal of Personality and Social Psychology, 39,* 1050–1063.

Hamilton, E., & Abramson, L. (1983). Cognitive patterns and major depressive disorder: A longitudinal study in a hospital setting. *Journal of Abnormal Psychology, 92,* 173–184.

Hamilton, J. (1943). Demonstrable ability of penile erection in castrate men with markedly low titers of urinary androgen. *Proceedings of the Society of Experimental Biology and Medicine, 54,* 309.

Hamilton, J., Gallant, S., & Lloyd, C. (1989). Evidence for a menstrual-linked artifact in determining rates of depression. *The Journal of Nervous and Mental Disease, 177,* 359–365.

Hammen, C., & Peters, S. (1978). Interpersonal consequences of depression: Responses to men and women enacting a depressed role. *Journal of Abnormal Psychology, 87,* 322–332.

Hampson, J. L., & Hampson, J. G. (1961). The ontogenesis of sexual behavior in man. In W. Young (Ed.), *Sex and Internal Secretions.* Baltimore: Williams & Wilkins.

Haney, C., & Zimbardo, P. (1977). The socialization into criminality: On becoming a prisoner and a guard. In J. Tapp & F. Levine (Eds.), *Law, Justice, and the Individual in Society: Psychological and Legal Issues.* New York: Holt, Rinehart and Winston.

Haney, D. (1983). Girth control. *The Oregonian,* November 21, B1.

Hanna, G. (1988). Gender differences in mathematics achievement among eighth graders: Results from twenty countries. Paper presented at the annual meeting of the

American Association for the Advancement of Science, Boston, February.

Harburg, E., Erfurt, J., Havenstein, L., Chape, C., Schull, W., & Schork, M. (1973). Socioecological stress, suppressed hostility, skin color, and black-white male blood pressure: Detroit. *Psychosomatic Medicine, 35,* 276–296.

Hardy, J., Stolwijk, J., & Hoffman, D. (1968). Pain following step increase in skin temperature. In D. Kenshalo (Ed.), *The Skin Senses.* Springfield, IL: Thomas.

Hare, R. (1970). *Psychopathy: Theory and Research.* New York: Wiley.

Hare, R. (1975). Psychophysiological studies of psychopathy. In D. Fowles (Ed.), *Clinical Applications of Psychophysiology.* New York: Columbia University Press.

Hare, R., Frazelle, J., & Cox, D. (1978). Psychopathy and physiological responses to threat of an aversive stimulus. *Psychophysiology, 15,* 165–172.

Harlow, H., & Harlow, M. (1966). Learning to love. *American Scientist, 54,* 244–272.

Harlow, H., Harlow, M., & Meyer, D. (1950). Learning motivated by a manipulative drive. *Journal of Experimental Psychology, 40,* 228–234.

Harlow, H., Harlow, M., & Suomi, S. (1971). From thought to therapy: Lessons from a primate laboratory. *American Scientist, 59,* 538–549.

Harlow, H., & Zimmerman, R. (1958). The development of affectional responses in infant monkeys. *Proceedings of the American Philosophical Society, 102,* 501–509.

Harrell, J. (1980). Psychological factors and hypertension: A status report. *Psychological Bulletin, 87,* 482–501.

Harris, A., Benedict, R., & Leek, M. (1990). Consideration of pigeon-holing and filtering as dysfunctional attention strategies in schizophrenia. *British Journal of Clinical Psychology, 29,* 23–35.

Harris, E., Noyes, R., Crowe, R., & Chaudhry, D. (1983). Family study of agoraphobia. *Archives of General Psychiatry, 40,* 1061–1069.

Hartmann, E. (1973). *The Functions of Sleep.* New Haven, CT: Yale University Press.

Hartmann, E., Russ, D., Oldfield, M., Sivan, I., & Cooper, S. (1987). Who has nightmares? *Archives of General Psychiatry, 44,* 49–56.

Hartmann, E., Russ, D., van der Kolk, B., Falke, R., & Oldfield, M. (1981). A preliminary study of the personality of the nightmare sufferer: Relationship to schizophrenia and creativity? *American Journal of Psychiatry, 138,* 794–797.

Hartshorne, H., & May, M. (1928). *Studies in the Nature of Character, Vol. I: Studies in Deceit.* New York: Macmillan.

Harvard Medical School (1989). Group therapy—Part I. *The Harvard Medical School Mental Health Letter, 5,* 1–4.

Haseltine, F., & Ohno, S. (1981). Mechanisms of gonadal differentiation. *Science, 21,* 1272–1278.

Hatcher, R., Guest, F., Stewart, F., Stewart, G., Trussell, J., Bowen, S., & Cates, W. (1988). *Contraceptive Technologies 1988–1989* (14th ed.). New York: Irvington.

Hatfield, E., & Sprechler, S. (1986). *Mirror, Mirror . . . The Importance of Looks in Everyday Life.* Albany: State University of New York Press.

Hathaway, S., & McKinley, J. (1942). *Minnesota Multiphasic Personality Inventory.* Minneapolis: University of Minnesota.

Hatton, D., Gilden, E., Edwards, M., Cutler, J., Kron, J., & McAnulty, J. (1989). Psychophysiological factors in ventricular arrhythmias and sudden cardiac death. *Journal of Psychosomatic Research, 33,* 621–631.

Havinghurst, R. (1982). The world of work. In B. Wolman (Ed.), *Handbook of Developmental Psychology.* Englewood Cliffs, NJ: Prentice-Hall.

Hawn, P., & Harris, L. (1983). Laterality in manipulatory and cognitive related activity. In G. Young, S. Segalowitz, C. Corter, & S. Trehub (Eds.), *Manual Specialization and the Developing Brain.* New York: Academic Press.

Hayes, C. (1951). *The Ape in Our House.* New York: Harper & Row.

Hayflick, L. (1974). The strategy of senescence. *The Gerontologist, 14,* 37–45.

Haynes, S., Feinleib, M., & Kannel, W. (1980). The relationships of psychosocial factors to coronary disease in the Framingham study. III. Eight-year incidence of coronary heart disease. *American Journal of Epidemiology, 111,* 37–58.

Hearnshaw, L. (1979). *Cyril Burt: Psychologist.* Ithaca, NY: Cornell University Press.

Hearst, N., & Hulley, S. (1988). Preventing the heterosexual spread of AIDS. *Journal of the American Medical Association, 259,* 2428–2432.

Heath, R. (1972). Pleasure and brain activity in man. *Journal of Nervous and Mental Disease, 154,* 3–18.

Heath, R., McCarron, K., & O'Neil, C. (1989). Antiseptal brain antibody in IgG schizophrenic patients. *Biological Psychiatry, 25,* 725–733.

Hebb, D. (1949). *The Organization of Behavior.* New York: Wiley.

Hebb, D. (1955). Drives and the CNS. *Psychological Review, 62,* 243–254.

Heider, E., & Oliver, D. (1972). The structure of the color space in naming and memory for two languages. *Cognitive Psychology, 3,* 337–354.

Heider, F. (1946). Attitudes and cognitive organization. *Journal of Psychology, 21,* 107–112.

Heider, F. (1958). *The Psychology of Interpersonal Relations.* New York: Wiley.

Heider, K. (1976). Dani sexuality: A low energy system. *Man, 11,* 188–201.

Heim, N. (1981). Sexual behavior of castrated sex offenders. *Archives of Sexual Behavior, 10,* 11–19.

Hein, K. (1989). Commentary on adolescent acquired immunodeficiency syndrome: The next wave of immunodeficiency virus epidemic? *Journal of Pediatrics, 114,* 144–149.

Henderson, A. (1990). Epidemiology of dementia disorders. *Advances in Neurology, 51,* 15–25.

Henderson, N. (1982). Human behavior genetics. *Annual Review of Psychology, 33,* 403–440.

Heninger, G., Charney, D., & Menkies, D. (1983). Receptor sensitivity and the mechanism of action of antidepressant treatment. In P. Clayton & J. Barrett (Eds.), *Treatment of Depression: Old Controversies and New Approaches.* New York: Raven.

Henker, F. (1981). Male climacteric. In J. Howells (Ed.), *Modern Perspectives in the Psychiatry of Middle Age.* New York: Bruner/Mazel.

Henly, A., & Williams, R. (1986). Type A and B subjects' self-reported cognitive/affective/behavioral responses to descriptions of potentially frustrating situations. *Journal of Human Stress, 12,* 168–174.

Henry, W., Schacht, T., & Strupp, H. (1986). Structural analysis of social behavior: Application to a study of interpersonal processes in differential psychotherapeutic outcome. *Journal of Consulting and Clinical Psychology, 54,* 27–31.

Herdt, G., & Davidson, J. (1988). The Sambia "Turnim-man": Sociocultural and clinical aspects of gender formation in male pseudohermaphrodites with 5–alpha-reductase deficiency in Papua, New Guinea. *Archives of Sexual Behavior, 17,* 33–56.

Herman, J., Ellman, S., & Roffwarg, H. (1978). The problem of NREM dream recall re-examined. In A. Arkin, J. Antrobus, & S. Ellman (Eds.), *The Mind in Sleep and Psychophysiology.* Hillsdale, NJ: Erlbaum.

Herman, J., & Roffwarg, H. (1983). Modifying aculomotor activity in awake subjects increases the amplitude of eye movement during REM sleep. *Science, 220,* 1074–1076.

Herz, M., Szymanski, H., & Simon, J. (1982). Intermittent medication for stable schizophrenic outpatients: An alternative to maintenance medication. *The American Journal of Psychiatry, 139,* 918–922.

Herzog, A., Rogers, W., & Woodworth, J. (1982). *Subjective Well-Being Among Different Age Groups.* Ann Arbor: Institute for Social Research, University of Michigan.

Hess, W. (1957). *Functional Organization of the Diencephalon.* New York: Grune & Stratton.

Hesse-Biber, S. (1989). Eating patterns and disorders in a college population: Are college women's eating problems a new phenomenon? *Sex Roles, 20,* 71–84.

Heston, L. (1990). Alzheimer's disease: The end of the beginning? *Psychological Medicine, 20,* 7–10.

Heston, L., & Shields, J. (1968). Homosexuality in twins. *Archives of General Psychiatry, 18,* 149–160.

Hetherington, A., & Ranson, S. (1940). Hypothalamic lesions and adiposity in the rat. *Anatomical Record, 78,* 149–172.

Hicks, R., & Garcia, E. (1987). Levels of stress and sleep duration. *Perceptual and Motor Skills, 64,* 44–46.

Hicks, R., Kilcourse, J., & Sinnot, M. (1983). Type A-B behavior and caffeine use in college students. *Psychological Reports, 52,* 338.

Hicks, R., & Pelligrini, R. (1982). Sleep problems and Type A-B behavior in college students. *Psychological Reports, 51,* 96.

Hilgard, E. (1975). Hypnosis. *Annual Review of Psychology, 26,* 19–44.

Hilgard, E. (1977). *Divided Consciousness: Multiple Controls in Human Thought and Action.* New York: Wiley-Interscience.

Hirsch, J. (1983). In NOVA. Fat chance in a thin world. Boston: WGBH Transcripts.

Hirsch, J., & Knittle, J. (1970). Cellularity of obese and nonobese human adipose tissue. *Federation Proceedings, 29,* 1516–1521.

Hirschhorn, R. (1987). Therapy of genetic disorders. *The New England Journal of Medicine, 316,* 623–624.

Hobfoll, S. (1989). Conservation of resources: A new attempt at conceptualizing stress. *American Psychologist, 44,* 513–534.

Hobson, A. (1989). Dream theory: A new view of the brain-mind. *The Harvard Medical School Mental Health Letter, 5,* 3–5.

Hobson, J., & McCarley, R. (1977). The brain as a dream state generator: An activation-synthesis hypothesis of the dream process. *American Journal of Psychiatry, 134,* 1335–1348.

Hockett, C. (1960). The origin of speech. *Scientific American, 203,* 89–96.

Hodgkin, J. (1988). Everything you always wanted to know about sex. *Nature, 331,* 300–301.

Hodgkins, J. (1962). Influence of age on the speed of reaction and movement in females. *Journal of Gerontology, 17,* 385–389.

Hodgkinson, S., Sherrington, R., Gurling, H., Marchbanks, R., Reeders, S., Mallet, J., McInnin, M., Petersson, H., & Brynjolfsson, J. (1987). Molecular genetic evidence for heterogeneity in manic depression. *Nature, 325,* 805–806.

Hoebel, B., & Teitelbaum, P. (1966). Weight regulation in normal and hypothalamic hyperphagic rats. *Journal of Comparative and Physiological Psychology, 61,* 189–193.

Hofferth, S., Kahn, J., & Baldwin, W. (1987). Premarital sexual activity among U.S. teenage women over the past three decades. *Family Planning Perspectives, 19,* 46–54.

Hoffman, L. (1974). Effects of maternal employment on the child—a review of the research. *Developmental Psychology, 10,* 204–228.

Hoffman, L. (1979). Maternal employment: 1979. *American Psychologist, 34,* 859–865.

Hoffman, L., & Manis, J. (1979). The value of children in the United States: A new approach to the study of fertility. *Journal of Marriage and the Family, 41,* 583–596.

Hohmann, G. (1966). Some effects of spinal cord lesions on experienced emotional feelings. *Psychophysiology, 3,* 143–156.

Holden, C. (1981). Scientist convicted for monkey neglect. *Science, 214,* 1218–1220.

Holen, M., & Oaster, T. (1976). Serial position and isolation effects in a classroom lecture simulation. *Journal of Educational Psychology, 68,* 293–296.

Holiday, H. (1987). X-chromosome reactivation. *Nature, 327,* 661–662.

Holinger, P. (1979). Violent deaths among the young: Recent trends in suicide, homicides, and accidents. *American Journal of Psychiatry, 136,* 1144–1147.

Hollinger, P. (1980). Violent deaths as a leading cause of mortality. *Journal of American Psychiatry, 137,* 472–476.

Hollon, S., DeRubeis, R., & Evans, M. (1987). Causal mediation of change in treatment for depression: Discriminating between nonspecificity and noncausality. *Psychological Bulletin, 102,* 139–149.

Hollon, S., & Garber, J. (1990). Cognitive therapy for depression: A social cognitive perspective. *Personality and Social Psychology Bulletin, 16,* 58–73.

Holmes, D., & Jorgensen, B. (1971). Do personality and social psychologists study men more than women? *Representative Research in Social Psychology, 2,* 71–76.

Holmes, J., & Boon, S. (1990). Developments in the field of close relationships: Creating foundations for intervention strategies. *Personality and Social Psychology Bulletin, 16,* 23–41.

Holmes, T., & Rahe, R. (1967). The social readjustment rating scale. *Journal of Psychosomatic Research, 11,* 213–218.

Holway, A., & Boring, E. (1941). Determinants of apparent visual sight with distant variant. *American Journal of Psychology, 54,* 21–37.

Hooley, J., & Teasdale, J. (1989). Predictors of relapse in unipolar depressives: Expressed emotion, marital distress, and perceived criticism. *Journal of Abnormal Psychology, 98,* 229–235.

Hopkins, B., & Palthe, T. (1987). The development of the crying state during infancy. *Developmental Psychobiology, 20,* 165–175.

Horn, J. (1982). The aging of human abilities. In B. Wolman (Ed.), *Handbook of Developmental Psychology.* Englewood Cliffs, NJ: Prentice-Hall.

Horn, J., & Donaldson, G. (1980). Cognitive development in adulthood. In O. Brim & J. Kagan (Eds.), *Constancy and Change in Human Development.* Cambridge, MA: Harvard University Press.

Horn, J., & Meer, J. (1987). The vintage years. *Psychology Today,* May, 76–90.

Horney, K. (1939). *New Ways in Psychoanalysis.* New York: Norton.

Horney, K. (1945). *Our Inner Conflicts.* New York: Norton.

Horney, K. (1950). *Neurosis and Human Growth.* New York: Norton.

Horton, D., & Mills, C. (1984). Human learning and memory. *Annual Review of Psychology, 33,* 361–394.

Host, L. (1979). The antisocial character. *American Journal of Psychoanalysis, 39,* 235–249.

Houston, J. (1985). *Motivation.* New York: Macmillan.

Houston, J. (1986). *Fundamentals of Learning and Memory* (3rd ed.). New York: Harcourt Brace Jovanovich.

Houston, M., & Hay, I. (1990). Practical management of hyperthyroidism. *American Family Physician, 41,* 909–916.

Hovland, C., & Sears, R. (1960). Minor studies in aggression, VI: Correlations of lynchings with economic indices. *Journal of Personality, 9,* 301–310.

Hovland, C., Harvey, D., & Sherif, M. (1957). Assimilation and contrast effects in reactions to communication and attitude change. *Journal of Abnormal and Social Psychology, 55,* 244–252.

Hovland, C., Janis, I., & Kelley, H. (1953). *Communication and Persuasion.* New Haven, CT: Yale University Press.

Hovland, C., Lumsdaine, A., & Sheffield, F. (1949). *Experiments on Mass Communication.* Princeton, NJ: Princeton University Press.

Howard, A., Pion, G., Gottfredson, G., Flattau, P., Oskamp, S., Pfafflin, S., Bray, D., & Burstein, A. (1986). The changing face of American psychology. *American Psychologist, 41,* 1311–1327.

Howard, A., Pion, G., Sechrest, L., Cordray, D., Kaplan, L., Hall, J., Perloff, R., & Molaison, V. (1987). Membership opinions about reorganizing APA. *American Psychologist, 42,* 763–779.

Hubbard, J. (1975). *The Biological Basis of Mental Activity.* Reading, MA: Addison-Wesley.

Hubbard, T. (1990). Cognitive representation of linear motion: Possible direction and gravity effects in judged displacement. *Memory & Cognition, 18,* 299–309.

Hubel, D., & Wiesel, T. (1979). Brain mechanisms of vision. *Scientific American, 241,* 150–162.

Huggins, G. (1989). Obstetrics and gynecology. *Journal of the American Medical Association, 261,* 2864.

Hughes, J., Gust, S., & Pechacek, T. (1987). Prevalence of tobacco dependence and withdrawal. *American Journal of Psychiatry, 144,* 205–208.

Hull, C. (1920). Quantitative aspects of the evolution of concepts. *Psychological Monographs,* Whole No. 123.

Hull, C. (1943). *Principles of Behavior Theory.* New York: Appleton, Century, Crofts.

Hunt, J. (1982). Toward equalizing the developmental opportunities of infants and preschool children. *Journal of Social Issues, 38,* 163–191.

Hurvich, L. (1978). Two decades of opponent process. In F. Bilmeyer & G. Wyszecki (Eds.), *Color 77.* Bristol, England: Adam Hilger.

Hurvich, L. (1981). *Color Vision.* Sunderland, MA: Sinauer Associates.

Hurvich, L., & Jameson, D. (1957). An opponent process theory of color vision. *Psychological Review, 64,* 384–404.

Hutchings, B., & Mednick, S. (1974). Registered criminality in the adoptive and biological parents of registered male adoptees. In S. Mednick, F. Schulsinger, J. Higgins, & B. Bell (Eds.), *Genetics, Environment, and Psychopathology.* New York: Elsevier.

Hyde, J. (1981). How large are cognitive gender differences? A meta-analysis using W^2 and d. *American Psychologist, 36,* 892–901.

Hyde, J. (1985). *Half the Human Experience: The Psychology of Women.* Lexington, MA: Heath.

Hyde, J., Fennema, E., & Lamon, S. (1990). Gender differences in mathematics performance: A meta-analysis. *Psychological Bulletin, 107,* 139–155.

Imperato-McGinley, J., Peterson, R., Gautier, T., & Sturla, E. (1979). Androgens and the evolution of male-gender identity among male pseudohermaphrodites with 5α-reductase deficiency. *New England Journal of Medicine, 300,* 1233–1237.

Insko, C., & Melson, W. (1969). Verbal reinforcement of attitude in laboratory and nonlaboratory contexts. *Journal of Personality, 37,* 25–40.

Ironson, G., LaPerriere, A., Antoni, M., & O'Hearn, P. (1990). Changes in immune and psychological measures as a function of anticipation and reaction to news of HIV-1 antibody status. *Psychosomatic Medicine, 52,* 247–270.

Irwin, D., & Yeomans, J. (1986). Sensory registration and informational persistence. *Journal of Experimental Psychology: Human Perception and Performance, 12,* 343–360.

Irwin, M., Daniels, M., Bloom, E., Smith, T., & Weiner, H. (1987). Life events, depressive symptoms, and immune function. *American Journal of Psychiatry, 144,* 437–441.

Irwin, M., Patterson, T., Smith, T., Caldwell, C., Brown, S., Gillin, J., & Grant, I. (1990). Reduction of immune function in life stress and depression. *Biological Psychiatry, 27,* 22–30.

Izard, C. (1990). Facial expressions and the regulation of emotions. *Journal of Personality and Social Psychology, 58,* 487–498.

Jabbari, B., Gunderson, C., Wippold, F., Citrin, C., Sherman, J., Bartoszek, D., Daigh, J., & Mitchell, M. (1986). Magnetic resonance imaging in partial complex epilepsy. *Archives of Neurology, 43,* 869–872.

Jacklin, C., Dipietro, J., & Maccoby, E. (1984). Sex-typing behavior and sex-typing pressure in child-parent interaction. *Archives of Sexual Behavior, 13,* 413–425.

Jacobs, G. (1983). Colour vision in animals. *Endeavour, New Series, 7,* 137–140.

Jacobs, L., Berscheid, E., & Walster, E. (1971). Self-esteem and attraction. *Journal of Personality and Social Psychology, 17,* 84–91.

Jacobson, E. (1932). The electrophysiology of mental activities. *American Journal of Psychology, 44,* 677–694.

Jacobson, G. (1968). The briefest psychiatric encounter. *Archives of General Psychiatry, 18,* 718–724.

Jacques, J., & Chason, K. (1979). Cohabitation: Its impact on marital success. *Family Coordinator, 28,* 35–39.

James, F., Large, R., & Beale, I. (1989). Self-hypnosis in chronic pain. *The Clinical Journal of Pain, 5,* 161–168.

James, W. (1884). What is an emotion? *Mind, 9,* 188–205.

James, W. (1890). *Principles of Psychology* (2 vols.). New York: Holt, Rinehart and Winston.

Jamison, K. (1989). Mood disorders and patterns of creativity in British writers and artists. *Psychiatry, 52,* 125–134.

Janet, P. (1929). *The Major Symptoms of Hysteria* (2nd ed.). New York: Macmillan.

Janiger, O., & De Rios, M. (1989). LSD and creativity. *Journal of Psychoactive Drugs, 21,* 129–134.

Janis, I., & Feshbach, S. (1953). Effects of fear-arousing communication. *Journal of Abnormal and Social Psychology, 48,* 78–92.

Janowitz, H., & Grossman, M. (1950). Hunger and appetite: Some definitions and concepts. *Journal of Mount Sinai Hospital, 16,* 231–240.

Janson, P., & Martin, J. (1982). Job satisfaction and age: A test of two views. *Social Forces, 60,* 1089–1102.

Jayaratne, S. (1982). Characteristics and theoretical orientations of clinical social workers: A national survey. *Journal of Social Service Research, 4,* 17–30.

Jemmott, H., & Locke, S. (1984). Psychosocial factors, immunologic mediation, and human susceptibility to infectious diseases: How much do we know? *Psychological Bulletin, 95,* 78–108.

Jemmott, J., Borysenko, J., Borysenko, M., McClelland, D., Chapman, R., Meyer, D., & Benson, H. (1983). Academic stress, power motivation, and decrease in salivary secretory immunoglobulin A secretion rate. *Lancet, 1,* 1400–1402.

Jensen, J., Bergin, A., & Greaves, D. (1990). The meaning of eclecticism: New survey and analysis of components. *Professional Psychology: Research and Practice, 21,* 124–130.

Joe, G., & Simpson, D. (1987). Mortality rates among opioid addicts in a longitudinal study. *American Journal of Public Health, 77,* 347–348.

Johnson, D. (1989). Schizophrenia as a brain disease. *American Psychologist, 44,* 553–555.

Johnson, J., Adinoff, B., Bisserbe, J., Martin, P., Rio, D., Rohrbaugh, J., Zubovic, E., & Eckardt, M. (1986). Assessment of alcoholism-related organic brain syndromes with positron emission tomography. *Alcoholism: Clinical and Experimental Research, 10,* 237–240.

Johnson, M., & Hasher, L. (1987). Human learning and memory. *Annual Review of Psychology, 38,* 631–638.

Johnson, M., & Magaro, P. (1987). Effects of mood and severity on memory processes in depression and mania. *Psychological Bulletin, 101,* 28–40.

Johnson, T. (1986). Paper presented at the Conference on Modern Biological Theories of Aging, Mount Sinai Medical Center, New York, June.

Johnston, W., & Dark, V. (1986). Selective attention. *Annual Review of Psychology, 37,* 43–75.

Johnstone, E., Owens, D., Bydder, G., Colter, N., Crow, T., & Frith, C. (1989). The spectrum of structural brain changes in schizophrenia: Age of onset as a predictor of cognitive and clinical impairments and their cerebral correlates. *Psychological Medicine, 19,* 91–103.

Jones, D., & Reed, R. (1989). G_{olf}: An olfactory neuron specific-G protein involved in odorant signal transduction. *Science, 244,* 790–795.

Jones, E. (1979). The rocky road from acts to dispositions. *American Psychologist, 34,* 107–117.

Jones, E., & McGillis, D. (1976). Correspondent inferences at the attribution cube: A comparative reappraisal. In J. Harvey, W. Ickes, & R. Kidd (Eds.), *New Directions in Attribution Research* (Vol. I). Hillsdale, NJ: Erlbaum.

Jones, E., Davis, K., & Gergen, K. (1961). Role playing variations and their informational value on person perception. *Journal of Abnormal and Social Psychology, 63,* 302–310.

Jones, H., & Conrad, H. (1933). The growth and decline of intelligence: A study of a homogeneous group between the ages of ten and sixty. *Genetic Psychology Monographs, 13,* 223–294.

Jones, M. (1957). The later careers of boys who were early- or late-maturing. *Child Development, 28,* 115–128.

Jones, M. (1958). A study of socialization patterns at the high school level. *Journal of Genetic Psychology, 93,* 87–111.

Jones, M., & Mussen, P. (1958). Self-concep-

tions, motivations, and interpersonal attitudes of early- and late-maturing girls. *Child Development, 29,* 491–501.

Jones, R., & Brehm, J. (1970). Persuasiveness of one- and two-sided communications as a function of awareness: There are two sides. *Journal of Experimental Social Psychology, 6,* 47–56.

Jones, W., & Anderson, J. (1987). Short- and long-term memory retrieval: A comparison of the effects of information load and relatedness. *Journal of Experimental Psychology: General, 116,* 137–153.

Jorgenson, R., & Houston, B. (1981). Family history of hypertension, gender and cardiovascular reactivity and stereotyping during stress. *Journal of Behavioral Medicine, 4,* 175–190.

Judd, C., Kenny, D., & Krosnick, J. (1983). Judging the positions of political candidates: Models of assimilation and contact. *Journal of Personality and Social Psychology, 44,* 952–963.

Julien, R. (1992). *A Primer of Drug Action.* New York: W.H. Freeman and Company.

Jung, C. (1916). *Analytical Psychology.* New York: Moffat.

Jung, C. (1933). *Modern Man in Search of a Soul.* New York: Harcourt, Brace & World.

Jung, C. (1953). *Collected Works.* Princeton, NJ: Princeton University Press.

Kagan, J., Kearsley, R., & Zelazo, P. (1978). *Infancy: Its Place in Human Development.* Cambridge, MA: Harvard University Press.

Kagan, J., & Klein, R. (1973). Cross-cultural perspectives on early development. *American Psychologist, 28,* 947–961.

Kahn, J., Kornfeld, D., Frank, K., Heller, S., & Hoar, P. (1980). Type A behavior and blood pressure during coronary artery bypass surgery. *Psychosomatic Medicine, 42,* 407–414.

Kalat, J. (1992). *Biological Psychology,* (2nd. ed.) Belmont, CA: Wadsworth Publishing Company.

Kales, A., Caldwell, A., Preston, T., Healey, S., & Kales, J. (1976). Personality patterns in insomniacs: Theoretical implications. *Archives of General Psychiatry, 33,* 1128–1134.

Kales, A., Tan, T., Kollar, E., Naitoh, P., Preston, T., & Malmstrom, E. (1970). Sleep patterns following 205 hours of sleep deprivation. *Psychosomatic Medicine, 32,* 189–200.

Kales, J., Kales, A., Bixler, E., Soldatos, C., Cadieux, R., Kashurba, G., & Bela-Bueno, A. (1984). Biopsychobehavioral correlates of insomnia: Clinical characteristics and behavioral correlates. *American Journal of Psychiatry, 141,* 1371–1376.

Kalil, R. (1989). Synapse formation in the developing brain. *Scientific American, 12,* 76–85.

Kalinowsky, L. (1975). Psychosurgery. In A. Freedman, H. Kaplan, & B. Sadock (Eds.), *Comprehensive Textbook of Psychiatry.* Baltimore: Williams & Wilkins.

Kalinowsky, L. (1980). Convulsive therapies. In H. Kaplan, A. Freedman, & B. Sadock (Eds.), *Comprehensive Textbook of Psychiatry.* Baltimore: Williams & Wilkins.

Kallman, F. (1952). Twin and sibship study of overt male homosexuality. *American Journal of Human Genetics, 4,* 136–146.

Kamarck, T., Manuck, S., & Jennings, J. (1990). Social support reduces cardiovascular reactivity to psychological challenge: A laboratory model. *Psychosomatic Medicine, 52,* 42–58.

Kamin, L. (1969). Predictability, surprise, attention, and conditioning. In B. Campbell & R. Church (Eds.), *Punishment and Aversive Behavior.* New York: Appleton, Century, Crofts.

Kamin, L. (1974). *The Science and Politics of IQ.* Potomac, MD: Erlbaum.

Kandel, E. (1983). A cellular mechanism of classical conditioning in Aplysia: Activity dependent amplification of postsynaptic facilitation. *Science, 219,* 400–405.

Kandel, E., & Hawkins, R. (1992). The biological basis of learning and individuality. *Scientific American, 267,* 78–86.

Kane, J. (1992a). New developments in the pharmacological treatment of schizophrenia. *Bulletin of the Menninger Clinic, 56,* 62–75.

Kane, J. (1992b). Clinical efficacy of clozapine in treatment-refractory schizophrenia: An overview. *British Journal of Psychiatry, 160,* 41–45.

Kang, J., Lemaire, H., Unterbeck, A., Salbaum, J., Masters, C., Grzeschik, K., Multhaup, G., Beyreuther, K., & Müller-Hill, B. (1987). The precursor of Alzheimer's disease amyloid A4 protein resembles a cell-surface receptor. *Nature, 325,* 733–736.

Kanin, E. (1967). Reference groups and sex conduct norms. *Sociological Quarterly, 8,* 495–504.

Kanin, E. (1969). Selected aspects of male sex aggression. *Journal of Sex Research, 5,* 12–28.

Kaplan, G., Salonen, J., Cohen, R., Brand, R., Syme, S., & Puska, P. (1988). Social connections and mortality from all causes and from cardiovascular disease: Prospective evidence from eastern Finland. *American Journal of Epidemiology, 128,* 370–380.

Kaplan, M., Lazoff, M., Kelly, K., Lukin, R., & Garver, D. (1990). Enlargement of cerebral third ventricle in psychotic patients with delayed response to neuroleptics. *Biological Psychiatry, 27,* 205–214.

Kaprio, J., Koskenvuo, M., & Rita, H. (1987). Mortality after bereavement: A prospective study of 95,647 widowed persons. *American Journal of Public Health, 77,* 283–287.

Karabenick, S. (1977). Fear of success, achievement and affiliation dispositions, and the performance of men and women under individual and competitive conditions. *Journal of Personality, 45,* 117–149.

Karni, A. (1992). *REM sleep and memory consolidation.* Paper presented at the annual meeting of the Society for Neuroscience, Anaheim, CA.

Karno, M., Hough, R., Burnam, M., Escobar, J., Timbers, D., Santana, F., & Boyd, J. (1987). Lifetime prevalence of specific psychiatric disorders among Mexican Americans and non-Hispanic whites. *Archives of General Psychiatry, 44,* 695–701.

Katschnig, K., & Shepherd, M. (1978). Neurosis: The epidemiological perspective. In H. van Prang (Ed.), *Research in Neurosis.* New York: Spectrum Publications.

Katz, P. (1976). The acquisition of racial attitudes in children. In P. Katz (Ed.), *Towards the Elimination of Racism.* New York: Pergamon.

Katzman, R., Aronson, M., Fuld, P., Kawas, C., Brown, T., Morgenstern, H., Frishman, W., Gidez, L., Eder, H., & Ooi, W. (1989). Development of dementing illnesses in an 80-year-old volunteer cohort. *Annals of Neurology, 25,* 317–324.

Kaufman, J., & Zigler, E. (1987). Do abused children become abusive parents? *American Journal of Orthopsychiatry, 57,* 186–192.

Kaushall, P., Zetin, M., & Squire, L. (1981). A psychological study of chronic, circumscribed amnesia: Detailed report of a noted case. *Journal of Nervous and Mental Disorders, 169,* 383–389.

Kaye, W., Gwirtsman, H., George, D., Jimerson, D., Ebert, M., & Lake, R. (1990). Disturbances of noradrenergic systems in normal weight bulimia: Relationship to diet and menses. *Biological Psychiatry, 27,* 4–21.

Keating, D. (1980). Thinking processes in adolescence. In J. Adelson (Ed.), *Handbook of Adolescent Psychology.* New York: Wiley-Interscience.

Keegan, D., Bowen, R., Blackshaw, S., & Saleh, S. A comparison of fluoxetine and amitriptyline in the treatment of major depression. *International Clinical Psychopharmacology, 6,* 117–124.

Keesey, R., Boyle, P., Kemnitz, J., & Mitchell, J. (1976). The role of the lateral hypothalamus in determining the body weight set point. In D. Novin, W. Wyrwicka, & G. Bray (Eds.), *Hunger: Basic Mechanisms and Clinical Implications.* New York: Raven.

Keesey, R., & Powley, T. (1986). The regulation of body weight. *Annual Review of Psychology, 37,* 109–133.

Keicott-Glaser, J., & Glaser, R. (1988). Psychological influences on immunity. *American Psychologist, 43,* 892–898.

Kelsoe, J., Ginns, E., & Egeland, J. (1989). Reevaluation of the linkage relationship between chromosome 11p loci and the gene for bipolar affective disorder in the Old Order Amish. *Nature, 342,* 238–243.

Kellerman, H. (Ed.) (1987). *The Nightmare: Psychological and Biological Foundations.* New York: Columbia University Press.

Kelley, H. (1967). Attribution theory in social psychology. In D. Levine (Ed.), *Nebraska Symposium on Motivation.* Lincoln: University of Nebraska Press.

Kelley, H. (1971). *Attribution in Social Interaction.* Morristown, NJ: General Learning Press.

Kelley, H. (1973). The process of causal attribution. *American Psychologist, 28,* 107–128.

Kellner, R. (1990). Somatization: Theories and research. *The Journal of Nervous and Mental Disease, 178,* 150–160.

Kellner, R., Abbott, P., Winslow, W., & Pathak, D. (1987). Fears, beliefs, and attitudes in DSM-III hypochondriasis. *The Journal of Nervous and Mental Disease, 175,* 20–25.

Kellogg, W., & Kellogg, L. (1933). *The Ape and the Child.* New York: McGraw-Hill.

Kelman, H. (Ed.) (1965). *International Behavior: A Socio-psychological Analysis.* New York: Holt, Rinehart and Winston.

Kendall, P., & Norton-Ford, J. (1982). *Clinical Psychiatry.* New York: Wiley.

Kendler, K. (1986). Genetics of schizophrenia. In A. Francis & R. Hales (Eds.), *Psychiatry Update: American Psychiatric Association Annual Review* (Vol. 5). Washington, DC: American Psychiatric Press.

Kendler, K., Gruenberg, A., & Tsuang, M. (1985). Psychiatric illness in first-degree relatives of schizophrenics and surgical control patients: A family study using DSM-III criteria. *Archives of General Psychiatry, 42,* 770–779.

Kennedy, J., Giuffra, L., Moises, H., Cavalli-Sforza, L., Pakstis, A., Kidd, J., Castiglione, C., Sjogren, B., Wetterberg, L., & Kidd, K. (1988). Evidence against linkage of schizophrenia to markers on chromosome 5 in a northern Swedish pedigree. *Nature, 336,* 167–170.

Kennedy, K., Fortney, J., & Sokal, D. (1989). Breastfeeding and HIV. *Lancet, 1,* 333.

Keon, T., & McDonald, B. (1982). Job satisfaction and life satisfaction: An empirical evaluation of their interrelationship. *Human Relations, 35,* 167–180.

Kessler, S. (1980). The genetics of schizophrenia: A review. *Schizophrenia Bulletin, 6,* 404–416.

Kety, S. (1975). Biochemistry of the major psychoses. In A. Freedman, H. Kaplan, & B. Sadock (Eds.), *Comprehensive Textbook of Psychiatry.* Baltimore: Williams & Wilkins.

Kety, S., Rosenthal, D., Wender, P., Schulsinger, F., & Jacobsen, B. (1975). Mental illness in the biological and adoptive families of adopted individuals who have become schizophrenic: A preliminary report based upon psychiatric interviews. In R. Fieve, D. Rosenthal, & H. Brill (Eds.), *Genetic Research in Psychiatry.* Baltimore: Johns Hopkins University Press.

Keys, A. (1983). In NOVA. Fat chance in a thin world. Boston: WGBH Transcripts.

Kierkegaard, S. (1844). *The Concept of Anxiety* (2nd ed.). Princeton, NJ: Princeton University Press (revised printing 1980).

Kiernan, J., & Taylor, V. (1990). Coercive sexual behavior among Mexican-American college students. *Journal of Sex and Marital Therapy, 16,* 44–50.

Kilham, W., & Mann, L. (1974). Level of destructive obedience as a function of transmitter and executant roles in the Milgram obedience paradigm. *Journal of Personality and Social Psychology, 29,* 696–702.

Kiloh, L., Smith, J., & Johnson, G. (1988). *Physical Treatments in Psychiatry.* Melbourne: Blackwell Scientific Publications.

Kimble, D. (1988). *Biological Psychology.* New York: Holt, Rinehart and Winston.

Kimble, G. (1989). Psychology from the standpoint of a generalist. *American Psychologist, 44,* 491–499.

Kimura, D. (1992). Sex differences in the brain. *Scientific American, 267,* 118–125.

Kimzey, S. (1975). The effects of extended spaceflight on hematologic and immunologic systems. *Journal of American Medical Women's Association, 30,* 218–232.

King, B., & Liston, E., (1990). Proposals for the mechanism of action of convulsive therapy: A synthesis. *Biological Psychiatry, 27,* 76–94.

King, N., & Montgomery, R. (1980) Biofeedback-induced control of human peripheral temperature: A critical review of the literature. *Psychological Bulletin, 88,* 738–752.

King, T., Schenken, R., Kang, I., Javors, M., & Riehl, R. (1990). Cocaine disrupts estrous cyclicity and alters reproductive neuroendocrine axis in the rat. *Neuroendocrinology, 51,* 15–22.

Kingsbury, S. (1987). Cognitive differences between clinical psychologists and psychiatrists. *American Psychologist, 42,* 152–156.

Kinsey, A., Pomeroy, W., & Martin, C. (1948). *Sexual Behavior in the Human Male.* Philadelphia: Saunders.

Kinsey, A., Pomeroy, W., & Martin, C., and Gebhard, P. (1953). *Sexual Behavior in the Human Female.* Philadelphia: Saunders.

Kirkpatrick, B., Buchanan, R., Waltrip, R., Jauch, D., & Carpenter, W. (1989). Diazepam treatment of early symptoms of schizophrenic relapse. *The Journal of Nervous and Mental Disease, 177,* 52–53.

Klagsbrun, F. (1985). *Married People: Staying Together in the Age of Divorce.* New York: Bantam.

Klaich, D. (1974). *Woman Plus Woman: Attitudes Towards Lesbianism.* New York: Simon & Schuster.

Klaus, M., & Kennell, J. (1982). *Parent-Infant Bonding* (2nd ed.). St. Louis: Mosby.

Klein, D. (1981). Anxiety reconceptualized. In D. Klein & J. Rabkin (Eds.), *Anxiety: New Research and Changing Concepts.* New York: Raven.

Klein, D., & Rabkin, J. (1981). *Anxiety: New Research and Changing Concepts.* New York: Raven.

Kleinhauz, M., & Eli, I. (1987). Potential deleterious effects of hypnosis in the clinical setting. *American Journal of Clinical Hypnosis, 29,* 155–159.

Kleinmuntz, B. (1982). *Personality and Psychological Assessment.* New York: St. Martin's Press.

Klineberg, O. (1935). *Negro Intelligence and Selective Immigration.* New York: Columbia University Press.

Knittle, J., & Hirsch, J. (1968). Effect of early nutrition on the development of rat epididymal fat pads: Cellularity and metabolism. *Journal of Clinical Investigation, 47,* 2001–2098.

Knussmann, R., Christiansen, K., & Couwenbergs, C. (1986). Relations between sex hormone levels and sexual behavior in men. *Archives of Sexual Behavior, 15,* 429–445.

Ko, G., Zhang, L., Yan, W., Zhang, M., Buchner, D., Xia, Z., Wyatt, R., & Jeste, D. (1989). The Shanghai 800: Prevalence of tardive dyskinesia in a Chinese psychiatric hospital. *The American Journal of Psychiatry, 146,* 387–389.

Kohlberg, L. (1964). The development of moral character and moral ideology. In M. Hoffman & L. Hoffman (Eds.), *Reviews of Child Development Research* (Vol. I). New York: Russell Sage Foundation.

Kohlberg, L. (1966). A cognitive-developmental analysis of children's sex-role concepts and attitudes. In E. Maccoby (Ed.), *The Development of Sex Differences.* Stanford, CA: Stanford University Press.

Kohlberg, L. (1968). The child as a moral philosopher. *Psychology Today, 2,* 25–30.

Kohlberg, L. (1969). Stage and sequence: The cognitive-developmental approach to socialization. In D. Goslin (Ed.), *Handbook of Socialization Theory and Research.* Chicago: Rand McNally.

Kohlberg, L. (1981a). *The Philosophy of Moral Development: Essays on Moral Development* (Vol. I). San Francisco: Harper & Row.

Kohlberg, L. (1981b). *The Psychology of Moral Development: Essays on Moral Development* (Vol. II). San Francisco: Harper & Row.

Kohlberg, L., & Candee, D. (1984). The relationship of moral judgement to moral action. In W. Kurtins & L. Gewirtz (Eds.), *Morality, Moral Behavior, and Moral Development.* New York: Wiley.

Kohlberg, L., & Gilligan, C. (1971). The adolescent as a philosopher: The discovery of the self in a postconventional world. *Daedalus,* Fall, 1051–1056.

Kohn, A. (1987). Making the most of marriage. *Psychology Today,* December, 6–8.

Kokotovic, A., & Tracey, T. (1990). Working alliance in the early phase of counseling. *Journal of Counseling Psychology, 37,* 16–21.

Kolata, G. (1985). A guarded endorsement for shock therapy. *Science, 228,* 1510–1511.

Kolata, G. (1986). Maleness pinpointed on Y-chromosome. *Science, 234,* 1076–1077.

Kolata, G. (1987a). Metabolic catch-22 of exercise regimens. *Science, 236,* 146–147.

Kolata, G. (1987b). Manic-depressive gene tied to chromosome 11. *Science, 235,* 1139–1140.

Kolb, B., & Whishaw, I. (1985). *Human Neuropsychology.* New York: Freeman.

Koop, C., & Kaler, S. (1989). Risk in infancy: Origins and implications. *American Psychologist, 44,* 224–230.

Kosnik, A., Carroll, W., Cunningham, A., Modras, R., & Schulte, J. (1977). *Human Sexuality: New Directions in American Catholic Thought.* New York: Paulist Press.

Koss, L., Gidycz, C., & Wisniewski, N. (1987). The scope of rape: Incidence and prevalence of sexual aggression and victimization in a national sample of higher education students. *Journal of Consulting and Clinical Psychology, 55,* 162–170.

Kotelchuck, M. (1976). The infant's relationship to the father: Experimental evidence. In M. Lamb (Ed.), *The Role of the Father in Child Development.* New York: Wiley.

Kraemer, G., & McKinney, W. (1979). Interactions of pharmacological agents which alter biogenic amine metabolism and depression. *Journal of Affective Disorders, 1,* 33–54.

Kraeplin, E. (1918). *Dementia Praecox.* London: Livingstone.

Kramer, B. (1987). Electroconvulsive therapy use in geriatric depression. *The Journal of Nervous and Mental Disease, 175,* 233–235.

Kramer, D. (1983). Post-formal operations? A need for further conceptualization. *Human Development, 26,* 91–105.

Kramer, J., Blusewicz, M., Robertson, L., & Preston, K. (1989). Effects of chronic alcoholism on perception of hierarchical visual stimuli. *Alcoholism: Clinical and Experimental Research, 13,* 240–245.

Krantz, D., & Durel, A. (1983). Psychobiological substrates of the Type A behavior pattern. *Health Psychology, 2,* 393–412.

Krantz, D., Grunberg, N., & Baum, A. (1985). Health psychology. *Annual Review of Psychology, 36,* 349–383.

Krantz, D., & Manuck, S. (1984). Acute psychophysiologic reactivity and risk of cardiovascular disease: A review and methodological critique. *Psychological Bulletin, 96,* 435–464.

Kripke, D., & Simons, R. (1976). Average sleep, insomnia, and sleeping pill use. *Sleep Research, 5,* 110.

Kripke, D., & Sonnenschein, D. (1978). A biologic rhythm in waking fantasy. In K. Pope & J. Singer (Eds.), *The Stream of Consciousness: Scientific Investigations into the Flow of Human Experience.* New York: Plenum.

Kroll, N., & Ogawa, K. (1988). Retrieval of the irretrievable: The effect of sequential information on response bias. In M. Gruneberg, P. Morris, & R. Sykes (Eds.), *Practical Aspects of Memory: Current Research and Issues* (Vol. 1). Chichester, England: Wiley.

Kroll, P., Chamberlain, P., & Halpern, D. (1979). The diagnosis of Briquet's syndrome in a male population. *Journal of Mental Disorders, 34,* 423–428.

Krueger, H., & Bornstein, P. (1987). Depression, sex-roles and family variables: Comparison of bulimics, binge-eaters, and normals. *Psychological Reports, 60,* 1106.

Krupnick, J., & Horowitz, M. (1981). Stress response syndromes. *Archives of General Psychiatry, 38,* 428–435.

Kuehnel, J., & Liberman, R. (1986). Behavior modification. In I. Kutash & A. Wolf (Eds.), *Psychotherapist's Casebook.* San Francisco: Jossey-Bass.

Kukla, A. (1972). Attributional determinants of achievement-related behavior. *Journal of Personality and Social Psychology, 21,* 166–174.

Kulik, J., & Mahler, H. (1989). Social support and recovery from surgery. *Health Psychology, 8,* 221–238.

Kupfer, D., & Frank, E. (1987). Relapse in recurrent unipolar depression. *American Journal of Psychiatry, 144,* 86–88.

Kupperman, H., & Studdiford, W. (1953). Endocrine therapy in gynecologic disorders. *Postgraduate Medicine, 14,* 410–425.

Kurtines, W., & Greif, E. (1974). The development of moral thought: Review and evaluation of Kohlberg's approach. *Psychological Bulletin, 81,* 453–470.

Kushida, C., Bergmann, B., & Rechtschaffen, A. (1989). Sleep deprivation in the rat: IV. Paradoxical sleep deprivation. *Sleep, 12,* 22–30.

Kutash, I., & Wolf, A. (Eds.). (1986). *Psychotherapist's Casebook.* San Francisco: Jossey-Bass.

Labouvie-Vief, G., & Schell, D. (1982). Learning and memory in later life. In B. Wolman (Ed.), *Handbook of Developmental Psychology.* Englewood Cliffs, NJ: Prentice-Hall.

Lacey, J. (1967). Somatic response patterning and stress: Some revisions of activation theory. In M. Appley & R. Trumball (Eds.), *Psychological Stress.* New York: McGraw Hill.

Lagerspetz, K., & Engblom, P. (1979). Immediate reaction to TV violence by Finnish preschool children of different personality types. *Scandinavian Journal of Psychology, 20,* 43–53.

Lamb, M. (1979). Paternal influences and the father's role. *American Psychologist, 34,* 938–943.

Lamb, M. (1981). The development of father-infant relationships. In M. Lamb (Ed.), *The Role of the Father in Child Development* (2nd ed.). New York: Wiley-Interscience.

Lamb, M. (1982). Second thoughts on first touch. *Psychology Today,* April, 9–11.

Lancet, D. (1986). Vertebrate olfactory reception. *Annual Review of Neuroscience, 9,* 329–355.

Landesman, S., Minkoff, H., & Willoughby, A. (1989). HIV disease in reproductive age women: A problem of the present. *Journal of the American Medical Association, 261,* 1326–1327.

Lang, P., Melamed, B. (1969). Case report: Avoidance conditioning therapy of an infant with chronic ruminative vomiting. *Journal of Abnormal Psychology, 74,* 1–8.

Lange, C. (1885). *The Emotions.* Baltimore: Williams & Wilkins, 1922 (originally published in 1885).

Langer, D., Brown, G., & Docherty, J. (1981). Dopamine receptor supersensitivity and schizophrenia: A review. *Schizophrenia Bulletin, 7,* 273–280.

Langer, E. (1975). The illusion of control. *Journal of Personality and Social Psychology, 32,* 311–328.

Langois, J., & Roggman, L. (1990). Attractive faces are only average. *Psychological Science, 1,* 115–121.

Langlois, J., Roggman, L., & Rieser-Danner, L. (1990). Infants' differential social responses to attractive and unattractive faces. *Developmental Psychology, 26,* 153–159.

Langlois, J., Roggman, L., Casey, R., Ritter, J., Rieser-Danner, L., & Jenkins, Y. (1987). Infant preferences for attractive faces: Rudiments of a stereotype? *Developmental Psychology, 23,* 363–369.

Lanzetta, J., Cartwright-Smith, J., & Kleck, R. (1976). Effects of nonverbal dissimulation on emotional experience and autonomic arousal. *Journal of Personality and Social Psychology, 33,* 354–370.

LaPiere, R. (1934). Attitudes vs. action. *Social Forces, 13,* 230–237.

Lashley, K. (1929). *Brain Mechanisms and Intelligence.* Chicago: University of Chicago Press.

Lashley, K. (1950). In search of the engram. *Symposia of the Society for Experimental Biology, 4,* 454–482.

Latané, B., & Darley, J. (1970). *The Unresponsive Bystander: Why Doesn't He Help?* New York: Appleton-Century-Crofts.

Laudenslager, M., Reite, M., & Harbeck, R. (1982). Suppressed immune response in infant monkeys associated with maternal separation. *Behavior and Neural Biology, 36,* 40–48.

Lauer, J., & Lauer, R. (1985). Marriages made to last. *Psychology Today, 19,* 22–26.

Lavie, P. (1987). Ultrashort sleep-wake cycle: Timing of REM sleep. Evidence for sleep-dependent and sleep-independent components of REM cycle. *Sleep, 10,* 62–68.

Lawrence, J., Kelly, J., Hood, H., & Brasfield, T. (1989). Behavioral intervention to reduce AIDS risk activities. *Journal of Consulting and Clinical Psychology, 57,* 60–67.

Lazarus, R. (1981). Little hassles can be hazardous to health. *Psychology Today, 15,* 58–62.

Lazarus, R., & Folkman, S. (1984a). *Stress, Appraisal, and Coping.* New York: Springer.

Lazarus, R., & Folkman, S. (1984b). Coping and adaptation. In W. Gentry (Ed.), *The Handbook of Behavioral Medicine.* New York: Guilford.

Leconte, P., Hennevin, E., & Bloch, V. (1972). Increase in paradoxical sleep following learning in the rat: Correlation with level of conditioning. *Brain Research, 42,* 552–553.

LeDoux, J. (1992). Brain mechanisms of emotion and emotional learning. *Current Opinion in Neurobiology, 2,* 191.

LeDoux, J., Wilson, D., & Gazzaniga, M. (1977). A divided mind: Observations of the conscious properties of the separated hemispheres. *Annals of Neurology, 2,* 417–421.

Lee, E. (1951). Negro intelligence and selective migration: A Philadelphia test of Klineberg's hypothesis. *American Sociological Review, 61,* 227–233.

Lefkowitz, M., Eron, L., & Walder, L. (1988). *Growing Up To Be Violent: A Longitudinal Study of the Development of Aggression.* New York: Pergamon Press.

Leigh, B. (1990). The relationship of substance use during sex to high-risk sexual behavior. *The Journal of Sex Research, 27,* 199–213.

Lemon, B., Bengston, V., & Peterson, J. (1972). An exploration of the activity theory of aging: Activity types and life satisfaction among in-movers to a retirement community. *Journal of Gerontology, 27,* 511–523.

Lenneberg, E. (1967). *Biological Functions of Language.* New York: Wiley.

Leon, B., & Roth, L. (1977). Obesity: Psychological causes, correlations, and speculations. *Psychological Bulletin, 84,* 117–139.

Lerner, R., & Lerner, J. (1977). Effects of age, sex, and physical attractiveness on child-peer relations, academic performance, and elementary school adjustment. *Developmental Psychology, 13,* 585–590.

Lerner, R., & Spanier, G. (1980). *Adolescent Development: A Life-Span Perspective.* New York: McGraw-Hill.

Lester, D. (1989). Suicide among psychologists and a proposal for the American Psychological Association. *Psychological Reports, 64,* 65–66.

Lester, D., & Smith, B. (1989). Applicability of Kübler-Ross's stages of dying to the suicidal individual: A review of the literature. *Psychological Reports, 64,* 609–610.

Levene, J., Newman, F., & Jeffries, J. (1990). Focal family therapy: Theory and practice. *Family Processes, 29,* 73–86.

Leventhal, H., & Nerenz, D. (1983). A model for stress research with some implications for the control of stress disorders. In D. Meichenbaum & M. Jaremko (Eds.), *Stress Reduction and Prevention.* New York: Plenum.

Leventhal, H., & Tomarken, A. (1986). Emotion: Today's problems. *Annual Review of Psychology, 37,* 565–610.

Levy, A., Dixon, K., & Stern, S. (1989). How are depression and bulimia related? *The American Journal of Psychiatry, 146,* 162–169.

Levy, S. (1983). Death and dying: Behavioral and social factors that contribute to the process. In T. Burish & L. Bradley (Eds.), *Coping with Chronic Illness: Research and Application.* New York: Academic Press.

Lewin, J., & Gambosh, D. (1973). Increase in REM time as a function of the need for divergent thinking. In W. Koella & P. Lewin (Eds.), *Sleep: Physiology, Biochemistry, Psychology, Pharmacology, Clinical Implications.* Basel, Switzerland: Karger.

Lewinsohn, P. (1974). A behavioral approach to depression. In R. Friedman & M. Katz (Eds.), *The Psychology of Depression: Contemporary Theory and Research.* Washington, DC: Winston/Wiley.

Lewinsohn, P., & Libet, J. (1972). Pleasant events activity schedules and depression. *Journal of Abnormal Psychology, 79,* 291–295.

Lewis, C. (1981). The effects of parental firm control: A reinterpretation of findings. *Psychological Bulletin, 90,* 547–563.

Lewis, E., Baird, R., Leverenz, E., & Koyama, H. (1982). Inner ear: Dye injection reveals peripheral origins of specific sensitivities. *Science, 215,* 1641–1643.

Lewis, J. (1988). The transition to parenthood: Stability and change in marital structure. *Family Process, 27,* 273–283.

Lewontin, R. (1976). Race and intelligence. In N. Block & G. Dworkin (Eds.), *The IQ controversy.* New York: Pantheon.

Lewy, A., Sack, R., Miller, L., & Hoban, T. (1987). Antidepressant and circadian phase-shifting effects of light. *Science, 235,* 352–354.

Leyens, J., & Parke, R. (1975). Aggressive slides can induce a weapons effect. *European Journal of Social Psychology, 5,* 229–236.

Lieberman, M., & Coplan, A. (1970). Distance from death as a variable in the study of aging. *Developmental Psychology, 2,* 71–84.

Liebert, R., & Spiegler, M. (1982). *Personality: Strategies and Issues.* Homewood, IL: Dorsey Press.

Lieblich, I. (1979). Eidetic imagery: Do not use ghosts to hunt ghosts of the same species. *The Behavioral and Brain Sciences, 2,* 608–609.

Liebowitz, M. (1989). Is there a drug treatment for social phobia? *The Harvard Medical School Mental Health Letter, 5,* 8.

Liebowitz, M., Fyer, A., Gorman, J., Dillon, D., Appleby, I., Levy, G., Anderson, S., Levitt, M., Palij, M., Davies, S., & Klein, D. (1984). Lactate provocation of panic attacks: I. Clinical and behavioral findings. *Archives of General Psychiatry, 41,* 764–770.

Lifson, A., Rutherford, G., & Jaffe, H. (1988). The natural history of human immunodeficiency virus infection. *Journal of Infectious Diseases, 158,* 1360–1366.

Lindgren, H., & Suter, W. (1985). *Educational Psychology in the Classroom* (7th ed.). Monterey, CA: Brooks/Cole.

Linn, M., & Hyde, J. (1989). Paper presented at the annual meeting of the American Association for the Advancement of Science, Washington, DC., April.

Lipper, S. (1985). Clinical psychopharmacology. In J. Walker (Ed.), *Essentials of Clinical Psychiatry.* Philadelphia: Lippincott.

Livson, N., & Peskin, H. (1980). Perspectives on adolescence from longitudinal research. In J. Adelson (Ed.), *Handbook of Adolescent Psychology*. New York: Wiley.

Loehlin, J., Lindzey, G., & Spuhler, J. (1975). *Race Differences in Intelligence*. San Francisco: Freeman.

Loehlin, J., Willerman, L., & Horn, J. (1988). Human behavior genetics. *Annual Review of Psychology, 39,* 101–133.

Loftus, E. (1975). Leading questions and the eyewitness report. *Cognitive Psychology, 7,* 560–572.

Loftus, E., & Burns, T. (1982). Mental shock can produce retrograde amnesia. *Memory and Cognition, 10,* 318–323.

Loftus, E., & Loftus, G. (1980). On the permanence of stored information in the human brain. *American Psychologist, 35,* 409–420.

Loftus, E., Miller, D., & Burns, H. (1978). Semantic integration of verbal information into a visual memory. *Journal of Experimental Psychology, 4,* 19–31.

Loftus, E., & Palmer, J. (1974). Reconstruction of automobile destruction: An example of interaction between language and memory. *Journal of Verbal Learning and Verbal Behavior, 13,* 585–589.

Loomis, A., Harvey, E., & Hobart, G. (1937). Cerebral status during sleep as studied by human brain potentials. *Journal of Experimental Psychology, 21,* 127–144.

Lorenz, K. (1937). The companion in the bird's world. *Auk, 54,* 245–273.

Lorenz, K. (1974). *The Eight Deadly Sins of Civilized Man*. New York: Harcourt Brace Jovanovich.

Lourea, D., Rila, M., & Taylor, C. (1986). Sex in the age of AIDS. Paper presented at the Western Region Annual Conference of the Society for the Scientific Study of Sex, Scottsdale, Arizona, January.

Lovass, O. (1973). *Behavioral Treatment of Autistic Children*. Morristown, NJ: General Learning Press.

Lovass, O. (1987). Behavioral treatment and normal educational and intellectual functioning in young autistic children. *Journal of Consulting and Clinical Psychology, 55,* 3–9.

Luborsky, L., Singer, B., & Luborsky, L. (1975). Comparative studies of psychotherapies. *Archives of General Psychiatry, 32,* 995–1008.

Luce, G. (1965). *Current Research on Sleep and Dreams*. Health Service Publication No. 1389, U.S. Department of Health, Education and Welfare.

Luchins, A., & Luchins, E. (1959). *Rigidity of Behavior*. Eugene, OR: University of Oregon Press.

Luddens, H., Pritchett, D., Kohler, M., Kilisch, I., Kainanen, K., Monyer, H., Sprengel, R., & Seeburg, P. (1990). Cerebellar GABAa receptor selective for a behavioral alcohol antagonist. *Nature, 346,* 648.

Lumsdaine, A., & Janis, I. (1953). Resistance to "counter-propaganda" produced by one-sided and two-sided "propaganda" presentations. *Public Opinion Quarterly, 17,* 311–318.

Lykken, D. (1957). A study of anxiety in the sociopathic personality. *Journal of Abnormal and Social Psychology, 57,* 6–10.

Lynch, G. (1984). A magical memory tour. *Psychology Today,* April, 70–76.

Lynch, G. (1986). *Synapses, Circuits, and the Beginnings of Memory*. Cambridge, MA: MIT Press.

Lynch, G., & Baudry, M. (1984). The biochemistry of memory: A new and specific hypothesis. *Science, 224,* 1057–1063.

Maas, J., Fawcett, J., & Dekirmenjian, W. (1972). Catecholamine metabolism, depressive illness, and drug response. *Archives of General Psychiatry, 26,* 252–262.

Maccoby, E. (1980). *Social Development: Psychological Growth and the Parent-Child Relationship*. New York: Harcourt Brace Jovanovich.

Maccoby, E. (1985). Address presented at a Symposium on Issues in Contemporary Psychology, Reed College, Portland, Oregon, May.

Maccoby, E., & Jacklin, C. (1974). *The Psychology of Sex Differences*. Stanford, CA: Stanford University Press.

Maccoby, E., & Jacklin, C. (1987). Gender segregation in childhood. In H. Reese (Ed.), *Advances in Child Behavior and Development* (Vol. 20). New York: Academic Press.

MacDonald, R., Weddle, M., & Gross, R. (1986). Benzodiazapine, b-carboline, and barbiturate actions on GABA responses. *Advances in Biochemical Psychopharmacology, 41,* 67–78.

MacPhillamy, D., & Lewinsohn, P. (1974). Depression as a function of levels of desired and obtained pleasure. *Journal of Abnormal Psychology, 83,* 651–657.

Maddi, S., Bartone, P., & Puccetti, M. (1987). Stressful events are indeed a factor in physical illness: Reply to Schroeder and Costa (1984). *Journal of Personality and Social Psychology, 52,* 833–843.

Maddison, S. (1977). Intraperitoneal and intracranial cholecystokinin depresses operant responding for food. *Physiology and Behavior, 19,* 819–824.

Mahone, C. (1960). Fear of failure and unrealistic vocational aspiration. *Journal of Abnormal and Social Psychology, 60,* 253–261.

Mahowald, M., & Schenck, M. (1989). REM sleep behavior disorders. In M. Kryger, T. Ruth, & W. Dement (Eds.), *Principles and Practice of Sleep Medicine*. Philadelphia: Saunders.

Maj, J., Papp, M., Skuza, G., Bigajska, K., & Zazula, M. (1989). The influence of repeated treatment with imipramine, (+)- and (−)- oxaprotiline on behavioural effects of dopamine D-1 and D-2 agonists. *Journal of Neural Transmission, 76,* 29–38.

Malmstrom, P., & Silva, M. (1986). Twin talk: Manifestations of twin status in the speech of toddlers. *Journal of Child Language, 13,* 293–304.

Mannion, K. (1981). Psychology and the lesbian: A critical view of the research. In S. Cox (Ed.), *Female Psychology: The Emerging Self* (2nd ed.). New York: St. Martin's Press.

Manson, J., Stampfer, M., Hennekens, C., & Willett, W. (1987). Body weight and longevity. *Journal of the American Medical Association, 257,* 353–358.

Manuck, S., Craft, S., & Gold, K. (1978). Coronary-prone behavior patterns and cardiovascular response. *Psychophysiology, 15,* 403–411.

March, J., Johnston, H., & Greist, J. (1989). Obsessive-compulsive disorder. *American Family Practice, 39,* 175–182.

Markman, E. (1987). How children constrain the possible meanings of words. In U. Neisser (Ed.), *Concepts and Conceptual Development: Ecological and Intellectual Factors in Categorization*. New York: Cambridge University Press.

Marler, P. (1967). Animal communication signals. *Science, 157,* 769–774.

Marmor, J. (Ed.). (1980). *Homosexual Behavior*. New York: Basic Books.

Marshall, D. (1971). Sexual behavior on Mangaia. In D. Marshall & R. Suggs (Eds.), *Human Sexual Behavior: Variations in the Ethnographic Spectrum*. Englewood Cliffs, NJ: Prentice-Hall.

Marshall, G., & Zimbardo, P. (1979). Affective consequences of inadequately explained physiological arousal. *Journal of Personality and Social Psychology, 37,* 970–988.

Martin, D., & Lyon, P. (1972). *Lesbian Women*. New York: Bantam.

Martin, J. (1987). Genetic linkage in neurologic diseases. *The New England Journal of Medicine, 316,* 1018–1019.

Martin, P. (1987). Psychology and the immune system. *New Scientist,* April 9, 46–50.

Martinez, J., Weinberger, S., & Schulteis, G. (1988). Enkephalins and learning and memory: A review of evidence for a site of action outside the blood-brain barrier. *Behavioral and Neural Biology, 49,* 192–221.

Maslow, A. (1965). A philosophy of psychology: The need for a mature science of human behavior. In F. Severin (Ed.), *Humanistic Viewpoints in Psychology*. New York: McGraw-Hill.

Maslow, A. (1968). *Toward a Psychology of Being* (2nd ed.). Princeton, NJ: Van Nostrand Reinhold.

Maslow, A. (1970). *Motivation and Personality* (2nd ed.). New York: Harper & Row.

Maslow, A. (1971). *The Farther Reaches of Human Nature*. New York: Viking.

Mason, J. (1974). Specificity in the organization of neuroendocrine response profiles. In P. Seeman and G. Brawn (Eds.), *Frontiers in Neurology and Neuroscience Research*. Toronto: University of Toronto Press.

Masters, C., & Beyreuther, K. (1990). Protein abnormalities in neurofibrillary tangles: Their relation to the extracellular amyloid deposits of the A4 protein in Alzheimer's disease. *Advances in Neurology, 51,* 151–161.

Masters, W., & Johnson, V. (1966). *Human Sexual Response*. Boston: Little, Brown.

Matas, L., Arend, R., & Sroufe, L. (1978). Continuity of adaptation in the second year: The relationship between quality of attachment and later competence. *Child Development, 49,* 547–556.

Mathews, A. (1981). Treatment of sexual dysfunctions: Psychological and hormonal factors. In J. Boulougouris (Ed.), *Learning Theory Application in Psychiatry*. New York: Wiley.

Matlin, M. (1989). *Cognition* (2nd ed.). Fort Worth, TX: Holt, Rinehart and Winston.

Mattson, M., & Kater, S. (1989). Development

and selective neurodegeneration in cell cultures from different hippocampal regions. *Brain Research, 490,* 110–112.

Mattson, M., Pollack, E., & Cullen, J. (1987). What are the odds that smoking will kill you? *American Journal of Public Health, 77,* 425–431.

Max, L. (1937). An experimental study of the motor theory of consciousness: IV. Action-curved responses in the deaf during awakening, kinaesthetic imagery and abstract thinking. *Journal of Comparative Psychology, 24,* 301–344.

Mayer, J. (1955). Regulation of energy intake and body weight. The glucostatic and the lipostatic hypothesis. *Annals of the New York Academy of Science, 63,* 15–43.

Mayer, J. (1968). *Overweight: Causes and Control.* Englewood Cliffs, NJ: Prentice-Hall.

Mayer, R. (1982). Different problem-solving strategies for algebra word and equation problems. *Journal of Experimental Psychology: Learning, Memory, and Cognition, 8,* 448–462.

Mayer-Gross, W., Slater, E., & Roth, M. (1969). *Clinical Psychiatry* (3rd ed.). Baltimore: Williams & Wilkins.

Mayleas, D. (1980). The impact of tiny feet on love. *Self,* August, 105–110.

Mazziotta, J., Phelps, M., Pahl, J., Huang, S., Baxter, L., Riege, W., Hoffman, J., Kuhn, D., Lanto, A., Wapenski, J., & Markham, C. (1987). Reduced cerebral glucose metabolism in asymptomatic subjects at risk for Huntington's disease. *The New England Journal of Medicine, 316,* 357–363.

McArthur, L., & Resko, B. (1975). The portrayal of men and women in American television commercials. *Journal of Social Psychology, 97,* 209–220.

McCall, G., & Shields, N. (1986). Social and structural factors in family violence. In M. Lystad (Ed.), *Violence in the Home: Interdisciplinary Perspectives.* New York: Brunner/Mazel.

McCarthy, J. (1985). The medical complications of cocaine abuse. In D. Smith & D. Wesson (Eds.), *Treating the Cocaine Abuser.* Center City, MN: Hazelden.

McClelland, D. (1953). *The Achievement Motive.* New York: Appleton, Century, Crofts.

McClelland, D. (1961). *The Achieving Society.* Princeton, NJ: D. Van Nostrand.

McClelland, D. (1985). *Human Motivation.* Glenview, IL: Scott, Foresman.

McClelland, D., Atkinson, J., Clark, R., & Lowell, E. (1976). *The Achievement Motive* (2nd ed.). New York: Irvington.

McClelland, D., & Pilon, D. (1983). Sources of adult motives in patterns of parent behavior in early childhood. *Journal of Personality and Social Psychology, 44,* 564–574.

McCloskey, M., & Zaragoza, M. (1985a). Misleading postevent information and memory for events: Arguments and evidence against memory impairment hypothesis. *Journal of Experimental Psychology: General, 114,* 3–18.

McCloskey, M., & Zaragoza, M. (1985b). Postevent information and memory: Reply to Loftus, Schooler, and Wagenaar. *Journal of Experimental Psychology: General, 114,* 381–387.

McConnell, J. (1962). Memory transfer through cannibalism in planarians. *Journal of Neuropsychiatry, 3,* 542–548.

McConnell, J. (1983). *Understanding Human Behavior.* New York: Holt, Rinehart and Winston.

McCoy, H., McKay, C., Hermanns, L., & Lai, S. (1990). Sexual behavior and risk of HIV infection. *American Behavioral Scientist, 33,* 432–450.

McCrae, R. (1984). Situational determinants of coping responses: Loss, threat, and challenge. *Journal of Personality and Social Psychology, 46,* 919–928.

McDonough, R., Madden, J., Falek, A., Shafer, D., Pline, M., Gordon, D., Bokos, P., Kuehnle, J., & Mendelson, J. (1980). Alteration of T and null lymphocyte frequencies in the peripheral blood of human opiate addicts: In vivo evidence for opiate receptor sites on T lymphocytes. *Journal of Immunology, 125,* 2539–2543.

McFarlane, A., Norman, G., Streiner, D., Roy, R., & Scott, D. (1980). A longitudinal study of the influence of the psychosocial environment on health status: A preliminary report. *Journal of Health and Social Behavior, 21,* 124–133.

McGillivary, B., Bassett, A., Langlois, S., Pantzar, T., & Wood, S. (1990). Familial 5q 11.2→q13.3 segmental duplication cosegregating with multiple anomalies, including schizophrenia. *American Journal of Medical Genetics, 35,* 10–13.

McGinty, D. (1969). Effects of prolonged isolation and subsequent enrichment on sleep patterns in kittens. *Electroencephalography and Clinical Neurophysiology, 26,* 335.

McGrath, M., & Cohen, D. (1978). REM sleep facilitation of adaptive waking behavior: A review of the literature. *Psychological Bulletin, 85,* 24–57.

McGraw, M. (1940). Neural maturation as exemplified in achievement of bladder control. *Journal of Pediatrics, 16,* 580–589.

McGuire, W. (1968a). Theory of the structure of human thought. In R. Abelson, E. Aronson, W. McGuire, T. Newcomb, M. Rosenberg, & P. Tannenbaum (Eds.), *Theories of Cognitive Consistency: A Sourcebook.* Chicago: Rand McNally.

McGuire, W. (1968b). Personality and susceptibility to social influence. In E. Borgatta & W. Lambert (Eds.), *Handbook of Personality Theory and Research.* Chicago: Rand McNally.

McGuire, W. (1969). The nature of attitudes and attitude change. In G. Lindzey and E. Aronson (Eds.), *The Handbook of Social Psychology* (2nd ed.). Reading, MA: Addison-Wesley.

McHugh, M., Koeske, R., & Frieze, I. (1986). Issues to consider in conducting nonsexist psychological research. *American Psychologist, 41,* 879–890.

McIntosh, T., Vink, R., Yamakami, I., & Fadon, A. (1989). Magnesium protects against neurological deficit after brain injury. *Brain Research, 482,* 252–260.

McKey, R., Condelli, L., Ganson, H., Barrett, B., McConkey, C., & Plantz, M. (1985). *The Impact of Head Start on Children, Families, and Communities: Final Report of the Head Start Evaluation, Synthesis and Utilization Project* (NO. OHDS 85-31193). Washington, DC: U.S. Government Printing Office.

McKoon, G., Ratcliff, R., & Dell, G. (1986). A critical evaluation of the semantic-episodic distinction. *Journal of Experimental Psychology: Learning, Memory, and Cognition, 12,* 295–306.

McLeod, P., & Brown, R. (1988). The effects of prenatal stress and postweaning housing conditions on parental and sexual behavior of male Long-Evans rats. *Psychobiology, 16,* 372–380.

McSherry, J., & Ashman, G. (1990). Bulimia and sleep disturbance. *The Journal of Family Practice, 30,* 102–103.

Mead, M. (1963). *Sex and Temperament in Three Primitive Societies.* New York: Morrow.

Meador, B., & Rogers, C. (1984). Person-centered therapy. In R. Corsini (Ed.), *Current Psychotherapies.* Itasca, IL: Peacock.

Meaney, M. (1990). Interview in Program 4, *Discovering Psychology,* a 26-part telecourse from the Annenberg/CPB Project.

Meaney, M., Aitken, D., VanBerkel, C., Bhatnagar, S. (1988). Effect of neonatal handling on age-related impairments associated with the hippocampus. *Science, 239,* 766–768.

Medin, D., & Smith, E. (1984). Concepts and concept formation. *Annual Review of Psychology, 35,* 113–138.

Mednick, S. (1958). A learning theory approach to schizophrenia. *Psychological Bulletin, 55,* 316–327.

Mednick, S., Brennan, P., & Kandel, E. (1988). Predisposition of violence. *Aggressive Behavior, 14,* 25–33.

Mednick, S., Gabrielli, W., & Hutchings, B. (1984). Genetic influences in criminal convictions: Evidence from adoption cohort. *Science, 224,* 891–894.

Mednick, S., Pollock, V., Volavka, J., & Gabrielli, W. (1982). Biology and violence. In M. Wolfgang & N. Weiner (Eds.), *Criminal Violence.* Beverly Hills, CA: Sage.

Mednick, S., Volavka, J., Gabrielli, W., & Itil, T. (1981). EEG as a predictor of antisocial behavior. *Criminology, 19,* 219–231.

Meerwaldt, J., & Van Dongen, H. (1989). Disturbances of spatial perception in children. *Behavioural Brain Research, 31,* 131–134.

Mefford, I., Baker, T., Boehme, R., Foutz, A., Ciaranello, R., Barchas, J., & Dement, W. (1983). Narcolepsy: Biogenic amine deficits in an animal model. *Science, 220,* 629–632.

Megargee, E. (1972). *The California Psychological Inventory Handbook.* San Francisco: Jossey-Bass.

Meichenbaum, D. (1977). *Cognitive-Behavioral Modification: An Integrative Approach.* New York: Plenum.

Meilman, P., Leibrock, L., & Leong, F. (1989). Outcome of implanted spinal cord stimulation in the treatment of chronic pain: Arachnoiditis versus single nerve root injury and mononeuropathy. *The Clinical Journal of Pain, 5,* 189–193.

Mellor, C. (1970). First rank symptoms of schizophrenia. *British Journal of Psychiatry, 117,* 15–23.

Meltzoff, A., & Moore, M. (1983). Newborn infants imitate adult facial gestures. *Child Development, 54,* 702–709.

Melville, J. (1977). *Phobias and Obsessions.* New York: Coward, McCann & Geoghegan.

Melzack, R. (1973). *The Puzzle of Pain.* New York: Basic Books.

Melzack, R. (1980). Psychological aspects of pain. In J. Bonica (Ed.), *Pain.* New York: Raven.

Melzack, R. (1990). The tragedy of needless pain. *Scientific American, 262,* 27–33.

Melzack, R., & Wall, P. (1965). Pain mechanisms: A new theory. *Science, 150,* 971–979.

Melzack, R., & Wall, P. (1983). *The Challenge of Pain.* New York: Basic Books.

Mendelson, J., Teoh, S., Lange, U., Mello, N., Weiss, R., Skupny, A., & Ellingboe, J. (1988). Anterior pituitary, adrenal, and gonadal hormones during cocaine withdrawal. *American Journal of Psychiatry, 145,* 1094–1098.

Mendez, M., Adams, N., & Lewandowski, K. (1989). Neurobehavioral changes associated with caudate lesions. *Neurology, 39,* 349–354.

Mendlewicz, J., Leboyer, M., de-Bruyn, A., & Malafossa, A. (1991). Absence of linkage between chromosome 11p15 markers and manic-depressive illness in a Belgian pedigree. *American Journal of Psychiatry, 148,* 1683–1687.

Mendlewicz, J., & Rainer, J. (1977). Adoption study supporting genetic transmission in manic-depressive illness. *Nature, 268,* 327–329.

Merckelbach, H., Ruiter, C., Van den Hout, M., & Hoekstra, R. (1990). Conditioning experiences and phobias. *Behavior Research and Therapy, 27,* 657–662.

Merikangas, K. (1990). The genetic epidemiology of alcoholism. *Psychological Medicine, 20,* 11–22.

Messenger, J. (1971). Sex and repression in an Irish folk community. In D. Marshall & R. Suggs (Eds.), *Human Sexual Behavior: Variations in the Ethnographic Spectrum.* Englewood Cliffs, NJ: Prentice-Hall.

Meyer, R., & Haggerty, R. (1962). Streptococcal infections in families. *Journal of Pediatrics, 29,* 539–549.

Meyer-Bahlburg, H. (1977). Sex hormones and male homosexuality in comparative perspective. *Archives of Sexual Behavior, 6,* 297–325.

Michel, K. (1987). Suicide risk factors: A comparison of suicide attempters with suicide completers. *British Journal of Psychiatry, 150,* 78–82.

Milavsky, J., Kessler, R., Stipp, H., & Rubens, W. (1982). Television and aggression: Results of a panel study. In D. Pearl, L. Bouthilet & J. Lazer (Eds.), *Television and Behavior: Ten Years of Scientific Progress and Implications for the Eighties* (Vol. II. Technical Reviews). Rockville, MD: National Institute of Mental Health.

Miles, C. (1977). Conditions predisposing to suicide. *Journal of Nervous and Mental Disease, 164,* 231–246.

Milgram, S. (1963). Behavioral study of obedience. *Journal of Abnormal and Social Psychology, 67,* 371–378.

Milgram, S. (1964). Issues in the study of obedience: A reply to Baumrind. *American Psychologist, 19,* 848–852.

Miller, A. (1986). *The Obedience Experiments: A Case Study of Controversy in Social Science.* New York: Praeger.

Miller, G. (1956). The magic number seven plus or minus two: Some limits on our capacity for processing information. *Psychological Review, 63,* 81–97.

Miller, G. (1981). *Language and Speech.* San Francisco: Freeman.

Miller, G., Galanter, E., & Pribram, K. (1960). *Plans and the Structure of Behavior.* New York: Holt, Rinehart and Winston.

Miller, I., Norman, W., & Keitner, G. (1989). Cognitive-behavioral treatment of depressed inpatients: Six- and twelve-month follow-up. *The American Journal of Psychiatry, 146,* 1274–1279.

Miller, J. (1983). Venezuelan connection. *Science News, 124,* 408–411.

Miller, L., & Branconier, R. (1983). Cannabis: Effects on memory and the cholinergic limbic system. *Psychological Bulletin, 93,* 441–456.

Miller, M., & Bowers, K. (1993). Hypnotic analgesia: Dissociated experiences or dissociated control? *Journal of Abnormal Psychology, 102,* 29–38.

Miller, N. (1941). The frustration-aggression hypothesis. *Psychological Review, 48,* 337–342.

Miller, N. (1978). Biofeedback and visceral learning. *Annual Review of Psychology, 29,* 373–404.

Miller, N. (1985). Rx: Biofeedback. *Psychology Today,* February, 54–59.

Miller, N., & Bugelski, R. (1948). Minor studies of aggression, II: The influence of frustrations imposed by the in-group on attitudes expressed toward out-groups. *Journal of Psychology, 25,* 437–452.

Miller, S. (1986). The treatment of sleep apnea. *Journal of the American Medical Association, 256,* 348.

Mills, J., & Aronson, E. (1965). Opinion change as a function of communicator's attractiveness and desire to influence. *Journal of Personality and Social Psychology, 1,* 173–177.

Milner, B. (1966). Amnesia following operation on the temporal lobes. In C. Whitty & O. Zangwill (Eds.), *Amnesia.* London: Butterworth.

Milner, P. (1989). A cell assembly theory of hippocampal amnesia. *Neuropsychologia, 27,* 23–30.

Mirsky, A., & Duncan, C. (1986). Etiology and expression of schizophrenia: Neurological and psychosocial factors. *Annual Review of Psychology, 37,* 291–319.

Mirsky, A., & Orzacki, M. (1980). Two retrospective studies of psychosurgery. In E. Valenstein (Ed.), *The Psychosurgery Debate.* San Francisco: Freeman.

Mischel, W. (1968). *Personality Assessment.* New York: Wiley.

Mischel, W. (1979). On the interface of cognition and personality. *American Psychologist, 34,* 740–754.

Mischel, W. (1984). Convergences and challenges in the search for consistency. *American Psychologist, 39,* 351–364.

Mischel, W. (1986). *Introduction to Personality* (4th ed.). New York: Holt, Rinehart and Winston.

Mischel, W., Shoda, Y., & Rodriquez, M. (1989). Delay of gratification in children. *Science, 44,* 933–938.

Mishkin, M. (1982). A memory system in the monkey. *Philosophical Transactions of the Royal Society of London, 298,* 85–95.

Mishkin, M., Malamut, B., & Backevalier, J. (1984). Memories and habits: Two neural systems. In G. Lynch, J. McGaugh, & N. Weinberger (Eds.), *The Neurobiology of Learning and Memory.* New York: Guilford Press.

Mita, T., Dermer, M., & Knight, J. (1977). Reversed facial images and the mere-exposure hypothesis. *Journal of Personality and Social Psychology, 35,* 597–601.

Moen, P. (1982). The two-provider family: Problems and potentials. In M. Lamb (Ed.), *Nontraditional Families: Parenting and Child Development.* Hillsdale, NJ: Erlbaum.

Moffett, M. (1990). Dance of the electronic bee. *National Geographic, 177,* 134–140.

Mohs, M. (1982). I.Q. *Discover,* September, 18–24.

Molfese, D., & Molfese, V. (1979). Hemisphere and stimulus differences as reflected in the cortical responses of newborn infants to speech stimuli. *Developmental Psychology, 15,* 505–511.

Moller, S. (1991). Carbohydrates, serotonin, and atypical depression. *Nordisk Psykiatrisk Tidsskrift, 45,* 363–366.

Money, J. (1965). Psychosexual differentiation. In J. Money (Ed.), *Sex Research: New Developments.* New York: Holt, Rinehart and Winston.

Money, J. (1968). *Sex Errors of the Body: Dilemmas, Education, Counseling.* Baltimore: Johns Hopkins Press.

Money, J. (1975). Ablatio penis: Normal male infant sex-reassigned as a girl. *Archives of Sexual Behavior, 4,* 65–72.

Money, J. (1988). *Gay, Straight, and In-Between.* New York: Oxford University Press.

Money, J., & Ehrhardt, A. (1972). *Man and Woman, Boy and Girl.* Baltimore: Johns Hopkins University Press.

Money, J., Ehrhardt, A., & Masica, D. (1968). Fetal feminization by androgen insensitivity in the testicular feminizing syndrome: Effect on marriage and maternalism. *Johns Hopkins Medical Journal, 123,* 105–114.

Money, J., Hampson, J., & Hampson, J. (1955). An examination of some basic sexual concepts: The evidence of human hermaphrodism. *Bulletin of Johns Hopkins Hospital, 97,* 301–319.

Monjan, A., & Collecter, M. (1977). Stress-induced modulation of the immune response. *Science, 196,* 307–308.

Monroe, L. (1967). Psychological and physiological differences between good and poor sleepers. *Journal of Abnormal Psychology, 72,* 255–264.

Moore, C., Williams, J., & Gorczynska, A. (1987). View specificity, array specificity, and egocentrism in young children's drawings. *Canadian Journal of Psychology, 41,* 74–79.

Moore, R., & Eichler, V. (1971). Loss of a circadian adrenal corticosterone rhythm following suprachiasmatic lesions in the rat. *Brain Research, 42,* 201–206.

Mora, F., & Ferrer, J. (1986). Neurotransmitters, pathways and circuits as the neural substrates of self-stimulation of the prefrontal cortex: Facts and speculations. *Behavioural Brain Research, 22,* 127–140.

Moran, J., & Desimone, R. (1985). Selective attention gates visual processing in the extrastriate cortex. *Science, 229,* 782–784.

Morden, B., Mitchell, G., and Dement, W. (1967). Selective REM sleep deprivation and compensation phenomena in the rat. *Brain Research, 5,* 339–349.

Moreland, J., & Gebhart, G. (1980). Effect of selective destruction of serotoninergic neurons in nucleus raphe magnus on morphine-induced antinociception. *Life Sciences, 27,* 2627–2632.

Moreland, R., & Zajonc, R. (1982). Exposure effects in person perception: Familiarity, similarity, and attraction. *Journal of Experimental Social Psychology, 18,* 395–415.

Morgan, C., & Morgan, J. (1940). Studies in hunger: The relation of gastric denervation and dietary sugar to the effect of insulin upon food intake in the rat. *Journal of Genetic Psychology, 57,* 153–163.

Mori, E., Yamadori, A., & Furumoto, M. (1989). Left precentral gyrus and Broca's aphasia. *Neurology, 39,* 51–54.

Morris, J. (1969). Propensity for risk taking as a determinant of vocational choice: An extension of the theory of achievement motivation. *Journal of Personality and Social Psychology, 3,* 328–335.

Morris, N., Khan-Dawood, F., & Dawood, M. (1987). Marital sex frequency and midcycle female testosterone. *Archives of Sexual Behavior, 7,* 157–173.

Morris, R., & Willshaw, D. (1989). Must what goes up come down? *Nature, 339,* 175–176.

Morrison, A. (1983). A window on the sleeping brain. *Scientific American, 248,* 94–102.

Moses, N., Banilivy, M., & Lifshitz, F. (1989). Fear of obesity among adolescent girls. *Pediatrics, 83,* 393–398.

Mosher, D., & Tomkins, S. (1988). Scripting the macho man: Hypermasculine socialization and enculturation. *Journal of Sex Research, 25,* 60–84.

Mott, F., & Haurin, R. (1988). Linkages between sexual activity and alcohol and drug use among American adolescents. *Family Planning Perspectives, 20,* 128–137.

Moyer, K. (1983). The physiology of motivation: Aggression as a model. In C. Scheier & A. Rogers (Eds.), *G. Stanley Hall Lecture Series* (Vol. 3). Washington, DC: American Psychological Association.

Muehlenhard, C. (1988). Misinterpreting dating behaviors and the risk of date rape. *Journal of Social and Clinical Psychology, 6,* 20–37.

Muehlenhard, C., & Andrews, S. (1985). Open communication about sex: Will it reduce risk factors related to rape? Paper presented at the Annual Meeting of the Association for Advancement of Behavior Therapy, Houston, November.

Muehlenhard, C., Felts, A., & Andrews, S. (1985). Men's attitudes toward the justifiability of date rape: Intervening variables and possible solutions. Paper presented at the Midcontinent Meeting of the Society for the Scientific Study of Sex, Dallas, June.

Muehlenhard, C., & Hollabaugh, L. (1988). Do women sometimes say no when they mean yes? The prevalence and correlates of women's token resistance to sex. *Journal of Personality and Social Psychology, 54,* 872–879.

Muehlenhard, C., & Linton, M. (1987). Date rape and sexual aggression in dating situations: Incidence and risk factors. *Journal of Consulting Psychology, 34,* 186–196.

Mullen, B. (1983). Operationalizing the effect of the group on the individual: A self-attentive perspective. *Journal of Experimental Social Psychology, 19,* 295–322.

Murdock, B. (1974). *Human Memory: Theory and Data.* New York: Wiley.

Murphy, G., Simons, A., Wetzel, R., & Lustman, P. (1984). Cognitive therapy and pharmacotherapy: Singling out together in the treatment of depression. *Archives of General Psychiatry, 41,* 33–41.

Murray, H. (1938). *Exploration in Personality.* New York: Oxford University Press.

Murray, J. (1990). New applications of lithium therapy. *The Journal of Psychology, 124,* 55–73.

Murray, W. (1985). Hearing: Ears easy prey to onslaughts of noisy world. *The Oregonian,* April 18, C1–C2.

Mussen, P., & Jones, M. (1957). Self-conceptions, motivation, and interpersonal attitudes of late- and early-maturing boys. *Child Development, 28,* 243–256.

Muter, P. (1980). Very rapid forgetting. *Memory and Cognition, 8,* 174–179.

Muuss, R. (1985). Adolescent eating disorder: Anorexia nervosa. *Adolescence, 79,* 525–536.

Mwamwenda, T., & Mwamwenda, B. (1989). Formal operational thought among African and Canadian college students. *Psychological Reports, 64,* 43–46.

Myers, B. (1984). Mother-infant bonding: The status of the critical period hypothesis. *Developmental Review, 4,* 240–274.

Naeser, M., Helm-Estabrooks, N., Haas, G., Auerbach, S., & Srinivasan, M. (1987). Relationship between lesion extent in "Wernicke's area" on computed tomographic scan and predicting recovery of comprehension in Wernicke's aphasia. *Archives of Neurology, 44,* 73–82.

Nakamura, A., Nakashima, M., Sakai, K., Niwam, M., Nozaki, M., & Shiomi, H. (1989). Delta-sleep-inducing peptide (DSIP) stimulates the release of immunoreactive Met-enkephalin from rat lower brainstem slices in vitro. *Brain Research, 481,* 165–168.

Nathan, M., & Guttman, R. (1984). Similarities in test scores and profiles of kibbutz twins and singletons. *Acta Geneticae Medicae et Gemellologiae, 33,* 213–218.

Nathans, J. (1987). Molecular biology of visual pigments. *Annual Review of Physiology, 10,* 163–194.

Nathans, J. (1989). The genes for color vision. *Scientific American,* February, 42–49.

Nathans, J., Davenport, C., Maumenee, I., Lewis, A., Hejtmancik, J., Litt, M., Lovrien, E., Weleber, R., Bachyski, B., Zwas, F., Klingaman, R., & Fishman, G. (1989). Molecular genetics of human blue cone monochromacy. *Science, 245,* 831–835.

Nathans, J., Thomas, D., & Hogness, D. (1986). Molecular genetics of human color vision: The genes encoding blue, green, and red pigments. *Science, 232,* 193–202.

National Institute of Mental Health. (1982). *Television and Behavior: Ten years of Scientific Progress and Implications for the Eighties* (Vol. 1). Washington, DC: U.S. Government Printing Office.

Neely, J., & Durgunoglu, A. (1985). Dissociative episodic and semantic priming effects in episodic recognition and lexical decision tasks. *Journal of Memory and Language, 24,* 466–489.

Neill, J. (1987). "More than medical significance": LSD and American psychiatry 1953 to 1966. *Journal of Psychoactive Drugs, 19,* 39–45.

Neisser, U. (1967). *Cognitive Psychology.* New York: Appleton, Century, Crofts.

Neisser, U. (1982). Memory: What are the important questions? In U. Neisser (Ed.), *Memory Observed.* San Francisco: Freeman.

Nelson, K. (1981). Individual differences in language development: Implications for development and languages. *Developmental Psychology, 17,* 170–187.

Nelson, P., Yu, C., Fields, D., & Neale, E. (1989). Synaptic connections in vitro: Modulation of number and efficacy by electrical stimulation. *Science, 244,* 585–587.

Nemiah, J. (1981). A psychoanalytic view of phobias. *American Journal of Psychoanalysis, 41,* 115–120.

Neugarten, B. (1972). Personality and the aging process. *The Gerontologist, 12,* 9–15.

Neugarten, B., & Hagestad, G. (1976). Age and the life course. In H. Binstock & E. Shanas (Eds.), *Handbook of Aging and the Social Sciences.* New York: Van Nostrand Reinhold.

Neugarten, B., Havighurst, R., & Tobin, S. (1965). Personality and patterns of aging. In B. Neugarten (Ed.), *Middle Age and Aging.* Chicago: University of Chicago Press.

Neugarten, B., & Neugarten, D. (1987). The changing meanings of age. *Psychology Today,* May, 29–33.

Newell, A. (1992). Precis of unified theories of cognition. *Behavioral and Brain Sciences, 15,* 425–492.

Newell, A., & Simon, H. (1972). *Human Problem Solving.* Englewood Cliffs, NJ: Prentice-Hall.

Newman, H., Freeman, F., & Holzinger, K. (1937). *Twins: A Study of Heredity and Environment.* Chicago: University of Chicago Press.

Newman, P. (1982). The peer group. In B. Wolman (Ed.), *Handbook of Developmental Psychology.* Englewood Cliffs, NJ: Prentice-Hall.

Newsom, C., Favell, J., & Rincover, A. (1983). Side effects of punishment. In S. Axelrod & J. Apsche (Eds.), *The Effects of Punishment on Behavior.* New York: Academic Press.

Nicassio, P., Mendlowitz, D., Fussel, J., & Petras, L. (1985). The phenomenology of the pre-sleep state: The development of the pre-sleep arousal scale. *Behavior Research and Therapy, 23,* 263–271.

Nield, T. (1987). Lest you forget. *New Scientist,* May 7, 63.

Niemcryk, S., Jenkins, D., Rose, R., & Hurst, M. (1987). The prospective impact of psychosocial variables on rates of illness and injury in professional employees. *Journal of Occupational Medicine, 29,* 119–125.

Niijima, A. (1982). Glucose-sensitive afferent nerve fibers in the hepatic branch of the vagus nerve in the guinea pig. *Journal of Physiology, 332,* 315–323.

Nisbet, J. (1957). Intelligence and age: Retesting with twenty-four years interval. *British Journal of Educational Psychology, 27,* 190–198.

Nisbett, R., Caputo, C., Legant, P., & Maracek, J. (1973). Behavior as seen by the actor and as seen by the observer. *Journal of Personality and Social Psychology, 27,* 154–164.

Nisbett, R., & Wilson, T. (1977). The halo effect: Evidence for unconscious alteration of judgments. *Journal of Personality and Social Psychology, 35,* 250–256.

Nolen, H., Girgus, J., & Seligman, M. (1991). Sex differences in depression and explanatory style in children. *Journal of Youth and Adolescence, 20,* 233–245.

Nolen-Hoeksema, A. (1987). Sex differences in unipolar depression: Evidence and theory. *Psychological Bulletin, 101,* 259–282.

Norcross, J., Strausser, D., & Faltus, F. (1988). The therapists' therapist. *American Journal of Psychotherapy, 42,* 53–66.

Norman, D., & Bobrow, G. (1975). On data-limited and resource-limited processes. *Cognitive Psychology, 7,* 44–64.

Norman, D., & Rumelhart, D. (1975). *Explorations in Cognition.* San Francisco: Freeman.

Norman, R., Perlman, I., Kolb, H., Jones, J., & Daley, S. (1984). Direct excitatory interactions between cones of different spectral types in the turtle retina. *Science, 224,* 625–627.

Norton, G., Dorward, J., & Cox, B. (1986). Factors associated with panic attack in non-clinical subjects. *Behavior Therapy, 17,* 239–252.

Norton, G., Harrison, B., Hauch, J., & Rhodes, L. (1985). Characteristics of people with infrequent panic attacks. *Journal of Abnormal Psychology, 94,* 216–221.

NOVA. (1983). Fat chance in a thin world. Boston: WGBH Transcripts.

Novak, M., & Harlow, H. (1975). Social recovery of monkeys isolated for the first year of life: I. Rehabilitation and therapy. *Developmental Psychology, 11,* 453–465.

Novick, D., Stenger, R., Gelb, A., Most, J., Yancovitz, S., & Kreek, M. (1986). Chronic liver disease in abusers of alcohol and parenteral drugs: A report of 204 consecutive biopsy-proven cases. *Alcoholism: Clinical and Experimental Research, 10,* 500–505.

Novin, D. (1976). Visceral mechanisms in the control of food intake. In D. Novin, W. Wyrwicka, & G. Bray (Eds.), *Hunger: Basic Mechanisms and Clinical Implications.* New York: Raven.

Novin, D., Robinson, B., Culbreth, L., & Tordoff, M. (1983). Is there a role for the liver in the control of food intake? *American Journal of Clinical Nutrition, 9,* 233–246.

Nurnberger, J., & Gershon, E. (1982). Genetics. In E. Paykel (Ed.), *Handbook of Affective Disorders.* New York: Guilford Press.

Nuttin, J. (1987). Affective consequences of mere ownership: The name letter effect in twelve European languages. *European Journal of Social Psychology, 17,* 381–402.

Obrist, P. (1976). The cardiovascular-behavior interaction—as it appears today. *Psychophysiology, 13,* 95–107.

O'Connell, M., & Rogers, C. (1984). Out-of-wedlock births, premarital pregnancies, and their effect on family formation and dissolution. *Family Planning Perspectives, 16,* 157–170.

O'Connor, R. (1972). Relative efficacy of modeling, shaping, and the combined procedures for notification of social withdrawal. *Journal of Abnormal Psychology, 79,* 327–334.

Oden, G. (1987). Concept, knowledge, and thought. *Annual Review of Psychology, 38,* 203–227.

Offer, D., & Offer, J. (1975). *From Teenage to Young Manhood.* New York: Basic Books.

Ogden, J. (1989). Visuospatial and other "right-hemispheric" functions after long recovery periods in left-hemispherectomized subjects. *Neuropsychologia, 27,* 765–776.

Ohman, A. (1979). Fear relevance, autonomic conditioning, and phobias: A laboratory model. In P. Sjoden, S. Bates, & W. Dockens (Eds.), *Trends in Behavior Therapy.* New York: Academic Press.

Ohtsuka, T. (1985). Relation of spectral types to oil droplets in cones of turtle retina. *Science, 229,* 874–877.

O'Leary, A. (1990). Stress, emotion, and human immune function. *Psychological Bulletin, 108,* 363–382.

Oldbridge, N. (1982). Compliance and exercise in primary and secondary prevention of coronary heart disease: A review. *Preventive Medicine, 11,* 56–70.

Olds, J. (1956). Pleasure centers in the brain. *Scientific American, 193,* 105–116.

Olds, J. (1973). Commentary on positive reinforcement produced by electrical stimulation of septal areas and other regions of rat brain. In E. Valenstein (Ed.), *Brain Stimulation and Motivation: Research and Commentary.* Glenview, IL: Scott, Foresman.

Olds, M., & Forbes, J. (1981). The central basis of motivation: Intracranial self-stimulation studies. *Annual Review of Psychology, 32,* 523–574.

Olson, G., Olson, R., & Kastin, A. (1986). Endogenous opiates: 1985. *Peptides, 7,* 907–933.

Olton, D. (1979). Mazes, maps and memory. *American Psychologist, 34,* 583–596.

O'Neal, J. (1984). First person account: Finding myself and loving it. *Schizophrenia Bulletin, 10,* 109–110.

Oomura, Y. (1976). Significance of glucose insulin and free fatty acid on the hypothalamic feeding and satiety neurons. In D. Novin, W. Wyrwicka, & G. Bray (Eds.), *Hunger: Basic Mechanisms and Clinical Implications.* New York: Raven.

Orlansky, H. (1949). Infant care and personality. *Psychological Bulletin, 46,* 1–48.

Orne, M. (1972). The stimulating subject in hypnosis research. In E. Fromm & R. Shor (Eds.), *Hypnosis, Research Developments, and Perspectives.* Chicago: Aldine.

Orne, M., Dinges, D., & Orne, E. (1984). On the differential diagnosis of multiple personality in the forensic context. *International Journal of Clinical and Experimental Hypnosis, 32,* 118–169.

Orne, M., & Scheibe, K. (1964). The contribution of nondeprivation factors in the production of sensory deprivation effects: The psychology of the panic button. *Journal of Abnormal and Social Psychology, 68,* 3–12.

Ornstein, P., & Naus, M. (1978). Rehearsal processes in children's memory. In P. Ornstein (Ed.), *Memory Development in Children.* Hillsdale, NJ: Erlbaum.

Orth-Gomer, K., & Unden, A. (1990). Type A behavior, social support, and coronary risk: Interaction and significance for mortality in cardiac patients. *Psychosomatic Medicine, 52,* 59–72.

Osborne, R. (1960). Racial differences in mental growth and school achievement: A longitudinal study. *Psychological Reports, 7,* 233–239.

O'Shea, R. (1987). Chronometric analysis supports fusion rather than suppression theory of binocular vision. *Vision Research, 27,* 781–791.

Ostrov, E., Offer, D., Howard, K., Kaufman, B., & Meyer, H. (1985). Adolescent sexual behavior. *Medical Aspects of Human Sexuality, 19,* 28–31, 34–36.

Page, D., Mosher, R., Simpson, E., Fisher, E., Mardon, G., Pollack, J., McGillivray, B., Chapelle, A., & Brown, L. (1987). The sex-determining region of the human Y chromosome encodes a finger protein. *Cell, 51,* 1091–1104.

Pagel, J. (1989). Nightmares. *American Family Physician, 39,* 145–148.

Paige, S., Reid, G., Allen, M., Newton, J. (1990). Psychophysiological correlates of posttraumatic stress disorder in Vietnam veterans. *Biological Psychiatry, 27,* 419–430.

Paivio, A. (1971). *Imagery and Verbal Processes.* New York: Holt, Rinehart, and Winston.

Paivio, A., & Lambert, W. (1981). Dual coding and bilingual memory. *Journal of Verbal Learning and Verbal Behavior, 20,* 532–539.

Palca, J. (1989). Sleep researchers awake to possibilities. *Science, 245,* 351–352.

Palmore, E. (1981). The facts on aging quiz: Part two. *The Gerontologist, 21,* 431–437.

Panksepp, J. (1986). The neurochemistry of behavior. *Annual Review of Psychology, 37,* 77–107.

Pardes, H., Kaufmann, C., Pincus, H., & West, A. (1989). Genetics and psychiatry: Past discoveries, current dilemmas, and future directions. *The American Journal of Psychiatry, 146,* 435–443.

Parke, R. (1969). Effectiveness of punishment as an interaction of intensity, timing, agent nurturance, and cognitive structuring. *Child Development, 40,* 213–235.

Parrot, A., & Allen, S. (1984). Acquaintance rape: Seduction or crime? Paper presented at the Eastern Regional Annual Conference of the Society for the Scientific Study of Sex, Boston, April.

Patterson, G. (1986). Performance models for antisocial boys. *American Psychologist, 41,* 432–444.

Patterson, G., Chamberlain, P., & Reid, J. (1982). A comparative evaluation of parent training procedures. *Behavior Therapy, 13,* 638–650.

Patterson, K., Vargha-Khadem, F., & Polkey, C. (1989). Reading with one hemisphere. *Brain, 112,* 39–63.

Paulsen, K., & Johnson, M. (1983). Sex-role attitudes and mathematical ability in 4th, 8th, and 11th grade students from a high socioeconomic area. *Developmental Psychology, 19,* 210–214.

Peacock, D. (1983). Peacock's crusade. Paper presented at the Forestry Center, Portland, Oregon, January 5.

Peacock, W. (1986). The postnatal development of the brain and its coverings. In A. Raimondi, M. Choux, & C. DiRocco (Eds.), *Head Injuries in the Newborn and Infant.* New York: Springer-Verlag.

Penfield, W., & Perrot, P. (1963). The brain's record of auditory and visual experience. *Brain, 86,* 595–696.

Penrod, S. (1986). *Social Psychology* (2nd ed.). Englewood Cliffs, NJ: Prentice-Hall.

Perley, M., & Guze, S. (1962). Hysteria—the stability and usefulness of clinical criteria. *The New England Journal of Medicine, 266,* 421–426.

Perlman, D. (1985). Scientists unraveling secrets of thing that destroys brains. *San Francisco Chronicle,* April 23, A5.

Perls, F. (1948). Theory and technique of personality integration. *American Journal of Psychotherapy, 2,* 656–686.

Perls, F. (1973). *The Gestalt Approach.* Palo Alto, CA: Science and Behaviour Books.

Permutter, M. (1983). Learning and memory through adulthood. In M. Riley, B. Hess, & K. Bond (Eds.), *Aging in Society: Selective Reviews of Recent Research.* Hillsdale, NJ: Erlbaum.

Perry, S. (1990). Combining antidepressants and psychotherapy: Rationale and strategies. *Journal of Clinical Psychiatry, 51* (Suppl.), 16–20.

Persky, H., Lief, H., Strauss, D., Miller, W., & O'Brien, C. (1978). Plasma testosterone level and sexual behavior of couples. *Archives of Sexual Behavior, 7,* 157–173.

Peskin, H. (1967). Pubertal onset and ego functioning. *Journal of Abnormal Psychology, 72,* 1–15.

Peskin, H. (1973). Influence of the developmental schedule of puberty on learning and ego functioning. *Journal of Youth and Adolescence, 2,* 273–290.

Peterman, T., Cates, W., & Curran, J. (1988). The challenge of human immunodeficiency virus (HIV) and acquired immunodeficiency syndrome (AIDS) in women and children. *Fertility and Sterility, 49,* 571–581.

Peterson, A. (1979). Female pubertal development. In M. Sugar (Ed.), *Female Adolescent Development.* New York: Bruner/Mazel.

Peterson, C., & Seligman, M. (1984). Causal explanations as a risk factor for depression: Theory and evidence. *Psychological Review, 91,* 347–374.

Peterson, L., & Peterson, M. (1959). Short-term retention of individual items. *Journal of Experimental Psychology, 58,* 193–198.

Peterson, P., & Koulack, D. (1969). Attitude change as a function of latitudes of acceptance and rejection. *Journal of Personality and Social Psychology, 11,* 309–311.

Petty, R., & Cacioppo, J. (1986). The elabora-tion likelihood model of persuasion. In L. Berkowitz (Ed.), *Advances in Experimental Social Psychology* (Vol. 19). Orlando, FL: Academic Press.

Petty, R., Cacioppo, J., & Schumann, D. (1983). Central and peripheral routes to advertising effectiveness: The moderating role of involvement. *Journal of Consumer Research, 10,* 135–146.

Phares, E. (1988). *Clinical Psychology: Concepts, Methods, & Profession.* Chicago: Dorsey.

Piaget, J. (1970). Piaget's theory. In P. Mussen (Ed.), *Carmichael's Manual of Child Psychology* (Vol. 1). New York: Wiley.

Piaget, J. (1972). Intellectual evolution from adolescence to adulthood. *Human Development, 15,* 1–12.

Piaget, J. (1977). *The Development of Thought: Equilibrium of Cognitive Structures.* New York: Viking Press.

Piaget, J., & Inhelder, B. (1969). *The Psychology of the Child.* New York: Basic Books.

Pihl, R., & Parkes, M. (1977). Hair element content in learning disabled children. *Science, 198,* 204–206.

Pillemer, D. (1990). Clarifying the flashbulb memory concept: Comment on McCloskey, Wible, and Cohen. *Journal of Experimental Psychology: General, 119,* 92–96.

Pincus, H., Fine, T., Pandes, H., & Goodwin, F. (1986). The animal rights movement: A research perspective. *Americal Journal of Psychiatry, 143,* 1585–1586.

Pitman, R., Orr, S., Forgue, D., Altman, B., & de Jong, J. (1990). Psychophysiological responses to combat imagery of Vietnam veterans with posttraumatic stress disorder versus other anxiety disorders. *Journal of Abnormal Psychology, 99,* 49–54.

Pliner, P., Hart, H., Kohl, J., & Saari, D. (1974). Compliance without pressure: Some further data on the foot-in-the-door technique. *Journal of Experimental Social Psychology, 10,* 17–22.

Plomin, R. and Bergeman, C. (1991). The nature of nurture: Genetic influence on "environmental" measures. *Behavioral and Brain Sciences, 14,* 373–427.

Plomin, R., & Defries, J. (1980). Genetics and intelligence: Recent data. *Intelligence, 4,* 15–24.

Plomin, R., Defries, J., & Fulker, D. (1988). *Nature and Nurture During Infancy and Early Childhood.* New York: Cambridge University Press.

Plomin, R., Pederson, N., McClearn, G., & Nesselroade, J. (1988). EAS temperaments during the last half of the life span: Twins reared apart and twins reared together. *Psychology and Aging, 3,* 43–50.

Plutchik, R. (1980). *Emotion: A Psychoevolutionary Synthesis.* New York: Harper & Row.

Pomerleau, O., & Rodin, J. (1986). Behavioral medicine and health psychology. In S. Garfield & A. Bergin (Eds.), *Handbook of Psychotherapy and Behavior Changes* (3rd ed.). New York: Wiley.

Pomeroy, W. (1965). Why we tolerate lesbians. *Sexology,* May, 652–654.

Posner, M. (1973). *Cognition: An Introduction.* Glenview, IL: Scott, Foresman.

Powell, M., & Fazio, R. (1984). Attitude accessibility as a function of repeated attitudinal expression. *Personality and Social Psychology Bulletin, 10,* 139–148.

Powley, T., & Keesey, R. (1970). Relationship of body weight to the lateral hypothalamic syndrome. *Journal of Comparative and Physiological Psychology, 70,* 25–36.

Prange, A., Wilson, I., & Lynn, C. (1974). L-tryptophan in mania: Contributions to a permissive amine hypothesis of affective disorders. *Archives of General Psychiatry, 30,* 56–62.

Pratt, W., Mosher, W., Bachrach, C., & Horn, M. (1984). Understanding U.S. fertility: Findings from the National Survey of Family Growth, Cycle III. *Population Bulletin, 39,* 3–42.

Premack, D. (1971). Language in chimpanzees. *Science, 172,* 808–822.

Prien, R., & Kupfer, D. (1986). Continuation drug therapy for major depressive episodes: How long should it be maintained? *American Journal of Psychiatry, 143,* 18–23.

Prioleau, L., Murdock, M., & Brody, N. (1983). An analysis of psychotherapy versus placebo studies. *The Behavioral and Brain Sciences, 6,* 275–310.

Prochaska, J., & Norcross, J. (1983). Contemporary psychotherapies: A national survey of characteristics, practices, orientation, and attitudes. *Psychotherapy: Theory, Research and Practice, 20,* 161–173.

Pugeat, M., Lejeune, H., Dechaud, H., Emptoz-Bonneton, A., Fleury, M., Charrie, A., Tourniaire, J., & Forest, M. (1987). Effects of drug administration of gonadotropins, sex steroid hormones, and binding proteins in humans. *Hormone Research, 28,* 261–273.

Pugh, E. (1987). Internal transmitter of transduction. *Annual Review of Physiology, 49,* 715–741.

Pugh, E., & Miller, W. (1987). Special topic: Photo transduction in vertebrates. *Annual Review of Physiology, 49,* 711–714.

Putnam, F., Guroff, J., Silberman, E., Barban, L., & Post, R. (1986). The clinical phenomenology of multiple personality disorder: Review of 100 recent cases. *Journal of Clinical Psychiatry, 47,* 285–293.

Pylyshyn, Z. (1973). What the mind's eye tells the mind's brain: A critique of mental imagery. *Psychological Bulletin, 80,* 1–24.

Pylyshyn, Z. (1984). *Computation and cognitiom: Toward a foundation for cognitive science.* Cambridge, MA: MIT Press.

Qualls, P., & Sheehan, P. (1981). Electromyograph biofeedback as a relaxation technique: A critical appraisal and reassessment. *Psychological Bulletin, 90,* 21–42.

Quinn, R., Staines, G., & McCullough, M. (1974). *Job satisfaction: Is there a trend?* Washington, DC: U.S. Department of Labor, Manpower, & Research Monograph No. 30.

Rachlin, H., Logue, A., Gibbon, J., & Franlel, M. (1986). Cognition and behavior in studies of choice. *Psychological Review, 93,* 33–45.

Radloff, L. (1975). Sex differences in depression. The effects of occupational and marital status. *Sex Roles, 1,* 249–265.

Rahe, R., & Arthur, R. (1978). Life changes and illness reports. In K. Gunderson & R. Rahe (Eds.), *Life Stress and Illness.* Springfield, IL: Thomas.

Rapoport, J. (1989). The biology of obsessions and compulsions. *Scientific American*, March, 83–89.

Rapoport, J. (1991). Recent advances in obsessive-compulsive disorder. *Neuropsychopharmacology*, 5, 1–10.

Ratcliff, R., & McKoon, G. (1986). More on the distinction between episodic and semantic memories. *Journal of Experimental Psychology: Learning, Memory, and Cognition*, 12, 312–313.

Raymond, C. (1986). Popular, yes, but jury still out on apnea surgery. *Journal of the American Medical Association*, 256, 439–441.

Raynor, J. (1970). Relationships between achievement-related motives, future orientation, and academic performance. *Journal of Personality and Social Psychology*, 15, 28–33.

Readhead, C., Popki, B., Takahashi, N., Shine, H., Saavedra, R., Sidman, R., & Hood, L. (1987). Expression of a myelin basic protein gene in transgenic shiverer mice: Correction of the dysmyelinating phenotype. *Cell*, 48, 703–712.

Rechtschaffen, A., Bergmann, B., Everson, C., Kushida, C., & Gilliland, M. (1989). Sleep deprivation in the rat: Integration and discussion of the findings. *Sleep*, 12, 68–87.

Rechtschaffen, A., Gilliland, M., Bergmann, B., & Winter, J. (1983). Physiological correlates of prolonged sleep deprivation in rats. *Science*, 221, 182–184.

Redei, E., Clark, W., & McGivern, R. (1989). Alcohol exposure in utero results in diminished T-cell function and alterations in brain corticotropin-releasing factor and ACTH content. *Alcoholism: Clinical and Experimental Research*, 13, 439–443.

Regier, D., Myers, J., Kramer, M., Robins, L., Blazer, D., Hough, R., Eaton, W., & Locke, B. (1984). The NIMH epidemiologic catchment area program: Historical contact, major objectives, and study population characteristics. *Archives of General Psychiatry*, 41, 934–941.

Register, P., & Kihlstrom, J. (1988). Hypnosis and interrogative suggestibility. *Personality and Individual Differences*, 9, 549–558.

Reichard, S., Livson, F., & Peterson, P. (1962). *Aging and Personality: A Study of 87 Older Men*. New York: Wiley.

Reilly, R., & Lewis, E. (1983). *Educational Psychology: Applications for Classroom Learning and Instruction*. New York: Macmillan.

Reinisch, J. (1981). Prenatal exposure to synthetic progestin increases potential for aggression in humans. *Science*, 211, 1171–1173.

Reinke, B., Holmes, D., & Harris, R. (1985). The timing of psychosocial changes in women's lives: The years 25 to 45. *Journal of Personality and Social Psychology*, 48, 456–471.

Reker, G., Peacock, E., & Wong, P. (1987). Meaning and purpose in life and well-being: A life-span perspective. *Journal of Gerontology*, 42, 44–49.

Relman, A. (1982). Marijuana and health. *The New England Journal of Medicine*, 306, 603–604.

Renneker, R. (1981). Cancer and psychotherapy. In J. Goldberg (Ed.), *Psychotherapeutic Treatment of Cancer Patients*. New York: Free Press.

Rescorla, R. (1967). Pavlovian conditioning and its proper control procedures. *Psychological Review*, 74, 71–80.

Rescorla, R. (1968). Probability of shock in the presence and absence of CS in fear conditioning. *Journal of Comparative and Physiological Psychology*, 66, 1–5.

Rescorla, R. (1987). A Pavlovian analysis of goal-directed behavior. *American Psychologist*, 42, 119–129.

Rescorla, R. (1988a). Pavlovian conditioning: It's not what you think it is. *American Psychologist*, 43, 151–160.

Rescorla, R. (1988b). Behavioral studies of Pavlovian conditioning. *Annual Review of Neuroscience*, 11, 329–352.

Restak, R. (1988). *The mind*. New York: Bantam Books.

Reynolds, D. (1986). *Even in Summer the Ice Doesn't Melt: Japan's Morita Therapy*. New York: Morrow.

Rholes, W., Riskind, J., & Lane, J. (1987). Emotional states and memory biases: Effects of cognitive priming and mood. *Journal of Personality and Social Psychology*, 52, 91–99.

Ribble, M. (1943). *The Rights of Infants: Early Psychological Needs and Their Satisfaction*. New York: Columbia University Press.

Rice, M. (1989). Children's language acquisition. *American Psychologist*, 44, 149–156.

Richards, J., & Rader, N. (1981). Crawling-on-set age predicts visual cliff avoidance in infants. *Journal of Experimental Psychology: Human Perception and Performance*, 7, 382–387.

Richardson, A. (1986). Age trends in eidetikers. *Journal of Genetic Psychology*, 147, 303–308.

Richardson, J. (1983). Mental imagery in thinking and problem solving. In J. Evans (Ed.), *Thinking and Reasoning: Psychological Approaches*. London: Routledge and Kegan-Paul.

Riche, M. (1988). Postmarital society. *American Demographics*, November, 60.

Ridenour, M. (1982). Infant walkers: Developmental tool or inherent danger? *Perceptual and Motor Skills*, 55, 1201–1202.

Riegel, K. (1973). Dialectic operations: The final period of cognitive development. *Human Development*, 16, 346–370.

Ries, W. (1973). Feeding behavior in obesity. *Proceedings of the Nutrition Society*, 32, 187–193.

Rips, L. (1990). Reasoning. *Annual Review of Psychology*, 41, 321–353.

Rips, L., Shoben, E., & Smith, E. (1973). Semantic distance and the verification of semantic relations. *Journal of Verbal Learning and Verbal Behavior*, 12, 1–20.

Riskind, J. (1983). Nonverbal expressions and the accessibility of life experience memories: A congruence hypothesis. *Social Cognition*, 2, 62–86.

Riskind, J., Rholes, W., & Eggers, J. (1982). The Velten Mood Induction Procedure: Effects on mood and memory. *Journal of Consulting and Clinical Psychology*, 50, 146–147.

Ritzer, G. (1977). *Working: Conflict and Change* (2nd ed.). Englewood Cliffs, NJ: Prentice-Hall.

Robbin, A. (1958). A controlled study of the effects of leucotomy. *Journal of Neurology, Neurosurgery, and Psychiatry*, 21, 262–269.

Robbin, A. (1959). The value of leucotomy in relation to diagnosis. *Journal of Neurology, Neurosurgery, and Psychiatry*, 22, 132–136.

Roberts, M. (1987). No language but a cry. *Psychology Today*, June, 57–58.

Robertson, M. (1987). Molecular genetics of the mind. *Nature*, 325, 755.

Robins, L. (1987). The epidemiology of antisocial personality. In J. Cavenar (Ed.), *Psychiatry*. Philadelphia: Lippincott.

Robins, L., Helzer, J., Weissman, M., Orvaschel, H., Gruenberg, E., Burke, J., & Regier, D. (1984). Lifetime prevalence of specific psychiatric disorders in three sites. *Archives of General Psychiatry*, 41, 949–958.

Robinson, L., Berman, J., & Neimeyer, R. (1990). Psychotherapy for the treatment of depression: A comprehensive review of controlled outcome research. *Psychological Bulletin*, 108, 30–49.

Rock, I., & DiVita, J. (1987). A case of viewer-centered object perception. *Cognitive Psychology*, 19, 280–293.

Rodin, J. (1978). The puzzle of obesity. *Human Nature*, February.

Rodin, J., & Salovey, P. (1989). Health psychology. *Annual Review of Psychology*, 40, 533–579.

Rogentine, G., Van Kammen, D., Fox, B., Docherty, J., Rosenblatt, J., Boyd, S., & Bunney, W. (1979). Psychological factors in the prognosis of malignant melanoma: A prospective study. *Psychosomatic Medicine*, 41, 647–655.

Rogers, C. (1961). *Becoming a Person: A Therapist's View of Psychotherapy*. Boston: Houghton Mifflin.

Rogers, C. (1977). *On Personal Power: Inner Strength and Its Revolutionary Impact*. New York: Delacorte.

Rogers, C. (1980). *A Way of Being*. Boston: Houghton Mifflin.

Rogers, C. (1986). Client-centered therapy. In I. Kutash & A. Wolf (Eds.), *Psychotherapist's Casebook*. San Francisco: Jossey-Bass.

Rogers, C. (1987). Sex roles in education. In D. Hargraves & A. Colley (Eds.), *The Psychology of Sex Roles*. New York: Hemisphere.

Rogers, M., Dubey, D., & Reich, P. (1979). The influence of the psyche and the brain on immunity and disease susceptibility: A critical review. *Psychosomatic Medicine*, 41, 147–164.

Rogers, R., & Mewborn, D. (1976). Fear appeals and attitude change: Effects of a threat's noxiousness, probability of occurrence, and the efficacy of coping responses. *Journal of Personality and Social Psychology*, 34, 54–61.

Roggman, L., Langlois, J., & Hubbs-Tait, L. (1987). Mothers, infants, and toys: Social play correlates of attachment. *Infant Behavior and Development*, 10, 233–237.

Rohrbaugh, J. (1979). *Women: Psychology's Puzzle*. New York: Basic Books.

Rollins, B., & Galligan, R. (1978). The developing child and marital satisfaction of parents. In R. Levner & G. Spanier (Eds.), *Child's Influences on Marital and Family Interaction: A Lifespan Perspective*. New York: Academic Press.

Rook, K. (1987). Social support versus companionship: Effects on life stress, loneliness, and evaluations by others. *Journal of Personality and Social Psychology, 52,* 1132–1147.

Rosch, E. (1973). Natural categories. *Cognitive Psychology, 4,* 328–350.

Rosch, E. (1975). Cognitive representations of semantic categories. *Journal of Experimental Psychology: General, 104,* 192–253.

Rosch, E. (1978). Principles of categorization. In E. Rosch & B. Lloyd (Eds.), *Cognition and Categorization.* Hillsdale, NJ: Erlbaum.

Rosch, E., Mervis, C., Gray, W., Johnson, E., & Boyes-Braem, P. (1976). Basic objects in natural categories. *Cognitive Psychology, 8,* 382–439.

Rose, G., & Williams, R. (1961). Metabolic studies of large and small eaters. *British Journal of Nutrition, 15,* 1–9.

Rose, J., Brugge, J., Anderson, D., & Hind, J. (1967). Phase-locked responses to low-frequency tones in single auditory nerve fibers of the squirrel monkey. *Journal of Neurophysiology, 30,* 769–793.

Rose, J., & Fantino, E. (1978). Conditioned reinforcement and discrimination in second-order schedules. *Journal of the Experimental Analysis of Behavior, 29,* 393–418.

Rosenbaum, L., & Rosenbaum, W. (1975). Persuasive impact of a communicator where groups differ in apparent co-orientation. *Journal of Psychology, 89,* 189–194.

Rosenberg, S., Nelson, C., & Vivekananthan, P. (1968). A multidimensional approach to the structure of personality impressions. *Journal of Personality and Social Psychology, 9,* 283–294.

Rosenhan, D. (1973). *Moral Development.* CRM–McGraw-Hill Films.

Rosenthal, D. (1970). *Genetic Theory and Abnormal Behavior.* New York: McGraw-Hill.

Rosenthal, D. (1971). *Genetics of Schizophrenia.* New York: McGraw-Hill.

Rosenthal, D. (1977). Searches for the mode of genetic transmission in schizophrenia: Reflections of loose ends. *Schizophrenia Bulletin, 3,* 268–276.

Rosenthal, D., Wender, P., Kety, S., Welner, J., & Schulsinger, F. (1971). The adopted away offspring of schizophrenics. *American Journal of Psychiatry, 128,* 307–311.

Rosenthal, N., Sack, D., Carpenter, C., Parry, B., Mendelson, W., & Wehr, T. (1985). Antidepressant effects of light in seasonal affective disorder. *The American Journal of Psychiatry, 142,* 163–170.

Rosenzweig, M. (1966). Environmental complexity, cerebral change, and behavior. *American Psychologist, 21,* 321–332.

Rosenzweig, M. (1984). Experience, memory, and the brain. *American Psychologist, 39,* 365–376.

Rosenzweig, M., Bennett, E., & Diamond, M. (1972). Brain changes in response to experience. *Scientific American, 226,* 22–29.

Roses, A., Pericak-Vance, M., Clark, C., Gilbert, J., Yamaoka, L., Yaynes, C., Speer, M., Gaskell, P., Hung, W., Trofatter, J., Earl, N., Lee, J., Alberts, M., Dawson, D., Bartlett, R., Siddique, T., Vance, J., Conneally, P., & Heyman, A. (1990). Linkage studies of late-onset familial Alzheimer's disease. *Advances in Neurology, 51,* 185–196.

Roses, A., Pericak-Vance, M., & Haynes, C. (1987). Linkage analysis in late onset familial Alzheimer's disease. *Cytogenetics and Cell Genetics, 46,* 684.

Ross, A. (1987). *Personality: The Scientific Study of Complex Human Behavior.* New York: Holt, Rinehart and Winston.

Ross, C. (1989). *Multiple Personality Disorder: Diagnosis, Clinical Features, and Treatment.* New York: Wiley.

Ross, H., & Taylor, H. (1989). Do boys prefer daddy or his physical style of play? *Sex Roles, 20,* 23–33.

Ross, L. (1977). The intuitive psychologist and his shortcomings: Distortions in the attribution process. In L. Berkowitz (Ed.), *Advances in Experimental Social Psychology.* New York: Academic Press.

Ross, M., & Fletcher, G. (1985). Attribution and social perception. In G. Lindzey & E. Aronson (Eds.), *Handbook of Social Psychology.* New York: Random House.

Rossi, A., Stratta, P., D'Albenzio, L., DiMichele, V., Serio, A., Giordano, L., Petruzzi, C., & Casacchia, M. (1989). Quantitative computed tomographic study in schizophrenia: Cerebral density and ventricle measures. *Psychological Medicine, 19,* 337–342.

Rossi, A., Stratta, P., D'Albenzio, L., Tartaro, A., Schiazza, G., di Michele, V., Bolino, F., & Casacchia, M. (1990). Reduced temporal lobe areas in schizophrenia: Preliminary evidences from a controlled multiplanar magnetic resonance imaging study. *Biological Psychiatry, 27,* 61–68.

Rossi, A., Stratta, P., Gallucci, M., Passariello, R., & Casacchia, M. (1989). Quantification of corpus callosum and ventricles in schizophrenia with nuclear magnetic resonance imaging: A pilot study. *The American Journal of Psychiatry, 146,* 99–101.

Rothbart, M., & Park, B. (1986). On the confirmability and disconfirmability of trait concepts. *Journal of Personality and Social Psychology, 50,* 131–142.

Rothblum, E. (1988). More on reporting sex differences. *American Psychologist, 43,* 1095.

Rotter, J. (1954). *Social Learning and Clinical Psychology.* Englewood Cliffs, NJ: Prentice-Hall.

Rotter, J. (1966). Generalized expectancies for internal versus external control of reinforcement. *Psychological Monographs, 80,* No. 601.

Rouche, B. (1980). *The Medical Detectives.* New York: Truman Talley Books.

Rousseau, L., Dupont, A., Labrie, F., & Couture, M. (1988). Sexuality changes in prostate cancer patients receiving antihormonal therapy combining the antiandrogen flutamide with medical (LHRH agonist) or surgical castration. *Archives of Sexual Behavior, 17,* 87–90.

Roviario, S., Holmes, D., & Holmsten, R. (1984). Influence of a cardiac rehabilitation program on the cardiovascular, psychological, and social functioning of cardiac patients. *Journal of Behavioral Medicine, 7,* 61–81.

Rowley, H., Lowenstein, D., Rowbotham, M., & Simon, R. (1989). Thalamomesencephalic stroke after cocaine abuse. *Neurology, 39,* 428–430.

Rubin, J., Provenzano, F., & Luria, Z. (1974). The eye of the beholder: Parents' views on sex of newborns. *American Journal of Orthopsychiatry, 44,* 512–519.

Rudel, R., Teuber, H., & Twitchell, T. (1974). Level of impairment of sensorimotor function in children with early brain damage. *Neuropsychologia, 12,* 95–108.

Rumbaugh, D. (1977). *Language Learning by Chimpanzee: The Lana Project.* New York: Academic Press.

Rush, A., Beck, A., Kovacs, M., & Hollon, S. (1977). Comparative efficacy of cognitive therapy and pharmacotherapy in the treatment of depressed outpatients. *Cognitive Therapy and Research, 1,* 17–39.

Rushton, J. (1988). Altruism and aggression. *Aggressive Behavior, 14,* 35–50.

Rushton, J., Fulker, D., Neale, M., Nias, D., & Eysenck, H. (1986). Altruism and aggression: The heritability of individual differences. *Journal of Personality and Social Psychology, 50,* 1192–1198.

Russek, M. (1971). Hepatic receptors and the neurophysiological mechanisms controlling feeding behavior. In S. Ehrenpreis (Ed.), *Neuroscience Research* (Vol. 4). New York: Academic Press.

Russell, D. (1984). *Sexual Exploitation: Rape, Child Sexual Abuse, and Workplace Harassment.* Beverly Hills, CA: Sage.

Rutter, D., & Durkin, K. (1987). Turn-taking mother-infant interaction: An examination of vocalization and gaze. *Developmental Psychology, 23,* 54–61.

Sachdev, P., Smith, J., & Matheson, J. (1990). Is psychosurgery antimanic? *Biological Psychiatry, 27,* 363–371.

Sack, R., Lewy, A., White, D., Singer, C., Fireman, M., & Vandiver, R. (1990). Morning vs. evening light treatment for winter depression. *Archives of General Psychiatry, 47,* 343–351.

Sackheim, J. (1985). The case for ECT. *Psychology Today,* June, 36–40.

Sadker, M., & Sadker, D. (1985). Sexism in the school room of the 80s. *Psychology Today, 19,* 54, 57.

Saegert, S., Snap, W., & Zajonc, R. (1973). Exposure, context, and interpersonal attraction. *Journal of Personality and Social Psychology, 25,* 234–242.

Sager, C. (1986). Couples therapy with marriage contracts. In I. Kutash & A. Wolf (Eds.), *Psychotherapist's Casebook.* San Francisco: Jossey-Bass.

Sanders, G. (1982). Social comparison as a basis for evaluating others. *Journal of Research in Personality, 16,* 21–31.

Sanders, G., & Cairns, K. (1987). Loss of sexual spontaneity. *Medical Aspects of Human Sexuality, 92,* 94–96.

Sano, K. (1962). Sedative neurosurgery. *Neurologia, 4,* 112–142.

Santee, R., & Maslach, C. (1982). To agree or not to agree: Personal dissent amid social pressure to conform. *Journal of Personality and Social Psychology, 42,* 690–700.

Sarason, I., Johnson, J., & Siegel, J. (1978). Assessing the impact of life changes: Development of the Life Experiences Survey. *Journal of Consulting and Clinical Psychology, 46,* 932–946.

Satow, A. (1987). Four properties common among perceptions confirmed by a large sample of subjects: An ecological approach to mechanisms of individual differences in perception: II. *Perceptual and Motor Skills, 64,* 507–520.

Savage-Rumbaugh, E., Pate, J., Lawson, J., Smith, S., & Rosenbaum, S. (1983). Can a chimpanzee make a statement? *Journal of Experimental Psychology: General, 112,* 457–492.

Savage-Rumbaugh, E., Rumbaugh, D., & Boysen, S. (1980). Do apes use language? *American Scientist, 68,* 49–61.

Scarr, S. (1981). Testing for children: Assessment and the many determinants of intellectual competence. *American Psychologist, 36,* 1159–1166.

Scarr, S. (1984). What's a parent to do? *Psychology Today,* May, 58–63.

Scarr, S. (1986). Intelligence: Revisiting. In R. Sternberg & D. Detterman (Eds.), *What Is Intelligence.* Norwood, NJ: Ablex.

Scarr, S., & Carter-Saltzman, L. (1983). Genetic differences in intelligence. In R. Sternberg (Ed.), *Handbook of Intelligence.* Cambridge, MA: Harvard University Press.

Scarr, S., & Weinberg, R. (1976). IQ test performance of black children adopted by white families. *American Psychologist, 31,* 726–739.

Scarr, S., & Weinberg, R. (1978). Attitudes, interests, and IQ. *Human Nature,* April, 29–36.

Schacheve, K. (1990). Attachment between working mothers and their infants: The influence of family processes. *American Journal of Orthopsychiatry, 60,* 19–34.

Schachter, S., & Latané, B. (1964). Crime, cognition, and the autonomic nervous system. In D. Levine (Ed.), *Nebraska Symposium on Motivation* (Vol. 12). Lincoln: University of Nebraska Press.

Schachter, S., & Singer, J. (1962). Cognitive, social, and physiological determinants of emotional state. *Psychological Review, 69,* 379–399.

Schaffer, H., & Emerson, P. (1964). The development of social attachments in infancy. *Monographs of the Society for Research in Child Development, 20,* Whole No. 94.

Schaie, K. (1975). Age changes in intelligence. In D. Woodruff & J. Birren (Eds.), *Aging: Scientific Perspectives and Social Issues.* New York: Van Nostrand.

Schaie, K., & Hertzog, C. (1983). Fourteen-year-cohort-sequential analysis of adult intellectual development. *Developmental Psychology, 19,* 531–543.

Schare, M., Lisman, S., & Spear, N. (1984). The effects of mood variation on state-dependent retention. *Cognitive Therapy and Research, 8,* 387–408.

Schein, E. (1956). The Chinese indoctrination program for prisoners of war: A study of attempted brainwashing. *Psychiatry, 19,* 149–172.

Schiffman, H. (1990). *Sensation and Perception.* New York: John Wiley & Sons.

Schildkraut, J. (1970). *Neuropsychopharmacology of the Affective Disorders.* Boston: Little, Brown.

Schlegel, R., Wellwood, J., Copps, B., Gru-

chow, W., & Sharratt, M. (1980). The relationship between perceived challenge and daily symptom reporting in Type A vs. Type B postinfarct subjects. *Journal of Behavioral Medicine, 3,* 191–204.

Schleifer, S., Keller, S., Camerino, M., Thornton, J., & Stein, M. (1983). Suppression of lymphocyte stimulation following bereavement. *Journal of the American Medical Association, 250,* 374–377.

Schlesier-Carter, B., Hamilton, S., O'Neil, P., Lydiard, B., & Malcolm, R. (1989). *Journal of Abnormal Psychology, 98,* 322–325.

Schmidt, U., & Marks, I. (1989). Exposure plus prevention of bingeing vs. exposure plus prevention of vomiting in bulimia nervosa: A crossover study. *The Journal of Nervous and Mental Disease, 177,* 259–266.

Schmitt, M. (1973). Influences of hepatic portal receptors on hypothalamic feeding and satiety centers. *American Journal of Physiology, 1973, 225,* 1089–1095.

Schneidman, E. (1974). *Deaths of Man.* Baltimore: Penguin Books.

Schneidman, E. (1987). At the point of no return. *Psychology Today,* March, 55–58.

Schneidman, E., Faberow, N., & Litman, R. (Eds.), (1970). *The Psychology of Suicide.* New York: Jason Aronson.

Schou, M. (1989). Lithium prophylaxis: Myths and realities. *The American Journal of Psychiatry, 146,* 573–576.

Schroeder, D., & Costa, P. (1984). Influence of life event stress on physical illness: Substantive effects or methodological flaws? *Journal of Personality and Social Psychology, 46,* 853–863.

Schuele, J., & Wiesenfeld, A. (1983). Autonomic response to self-critical thought. *Cognitive Therapy and Research, 7,* 189–194.

Schulsinger, F. (1972). Psychopathy: Heredity and environment. *International Journal of Mental Health, 1,* 190–206.

Schumacher, M., Coirini, H., & McEwen, B. (1989). Regulation of high-affinity GABA$_A$ receptors in the dorsal hippocampus by estradiol and progesterone. *Brain Research, 487,* 178–183.

Schvaneveldt, R., & Meyer, D. (1973). Retrieval and compassion processes in semantic memory. In S. Kornblum (Ed.), *Attention and Performance IV.* New York: Academic Press.

Schwartz, B. (1984). *Psychology of Learning and Behavior* (2nd ed.). New York: Norton.

Schwartz, G. (1982). Psychophysiological patterning and emotion revisited: A systems perspective. In C. Izard (Ed.), *Measuring Emotions in Infants and Children.* Cambridge, England: Cambridge University Press.

Schwartz, J., & Greenberg, S. (1987). Molecular mechanisms for memory: Second-messenger induced modifications of protein kinases in nerve cells. *Annual Review of Neuroscience, 10,* 459–476.

Schwartz-Bickenbach, D., Schulte-Hobein, B., Abt, S., Plus, C., & Nau, H. (1987). Smoking and passive smoking during pregnancy and early infancy: Effects on birth weight, lactation period, and cotinine concentrations in mother's milk and infant's urine. *Toxicology Letters, 35,* 73–81.

Scovern, A., & Kilmann, P. (1980). Status of

electroconvulsive therapy: Review of the outcome literature. *Psychological Bulletin, 87,* 260–303.

Scribner, S. (1977). Modes of thinking and ways of speaking: Culture and logic reconsidered. In P. Johnson-Laird & P. Wason (Eds.), *Thinking: Readings in Cognitive Science.* New York: Cambridge University Press.

Seagall, M., Campbell, D., & Herskovits, M. (1966). *The Influence of Culture on Visual Perception.* New York: Bobbs-Merrill.

Searle, J. (1990). Is the brain's mind a computer program? *Scientific American, 262,* 26–31.

Sears, D. (1979). Life stage effects upon attitude change, especially among the elderly. Paper presented at the Workshop on the Elderly of the Future, Committee on Aging, National Research Council, Annapolis, Maryland, May.

Sears, D., & Freedman, J. (1965). Effects of expected familiarity of arguments upon opinion change and selective exposure. *Journal of Personality and Social Psychology, 2,* 420–425.

Sears, P., & Barbee, A. (1977). Career and life situations among Terman's gifted women. In J. Stanley, W. George, & C. Solano (Eds.), *The Gifted and the Creative: A Fifty-Year Perspective.* Baltimore: Johns Hopkins University Press.

Sears, R. (1977). Sources of life satisfaction of the Terman gifted men. *American Psychologist, 32,* 119–128.

Sechzer, P. (1968). Objective measurement of pain. *Anesthesiology, 29,* 209–210.

Sedney, M. (1987). Development of androgeny: Parental influences. *Psychology of Women Quarterly, 11,* 311–326.

Segal, M. (1974). Alphabet and attraction: An unobtrusive measure of the effect of propinquity in a field setting. *Journal of Personality and Social Psychology, 30,* 654–657.

Segal, N. (1985). Monozygotic and dizygotic twins: A comparative analysis of mental ability profile. *Child Development, 56,* 1051–1058.

Seiden, R. (1974). Suicide: Preventable death. *Public Affairs Report, 15,* 1–5.

Sekuler, R., & Blake, R. (1985). *Perception.* New York: Knopf.

Seligman, M. (1971). Phobias and preparedness. *Behavior Therapy, 2,* 307–320.

Seligman, M. (1975). *Helplessness: On Depression, Development and Death.* San Francisco: Freeman.

Seligman, M., Abramson, L., & Semmel, A. (1979). Depressive attributional style. *Journal of Abnormal Psychology, 88,* 242–247.

Seligman, M., & Maier, S. (1967). Failure to escape traumatic shock. *Journal of Experimental Psychology, 75,* 1–9.

Selye, H. (1936). A syndrome produced by diverse nocuous agents. *Nature, 138,* 32.

Selye, H. (1956). *The Stress of Life.* New York: McGraw-Hill.

Selye, H. (1974). *Stress Without Distress.* Philadelphia: Lippincott.

Selye, H. (1976). *Stress in Health and Disease.* Woburn, MA: Butterworth.

Sem-Jacobsen, C. (1968). *Depth-Electrographic Stimulation of the Human Brain.* Springfield, IL: Thomas.

Semple, M., & Kitzes, L. (1987). Binaural processing of sound pressure level in the inferior colliculus. *Journal of Neurophysiology, 57,* 1130–1147.

Serbin, L. (1980). Interview in NOVA. The Pinks and the Blues. Boston: WGBH Transcripts.

Seyfarth, R., & Cheney, D. (1992). Meaning and mind in monkeys. *Scientific American, 12,* 122–128.

Shanab, M., & Yahya, K. (1977). A behavioral study of obedience in children. *Journal of Personality and Social Psychology, 35,* 530–536.

Shapiro, C., Bortz, R., Mitchell, D., Bartel, P., & Jooste, P. (1981). Slow-wave sleep: A recovery after exercise. *Science, 214,* 1253–1254.

Shapiro, D., & Goldstein, I. (1982). Biobehavioral perspectives on hypertension. *Journal of Consulting and Clinical Psychology, 50,* 841–858.

Shatz, M., & Gelman, R. (1973). The development of communication skills: Modification in the speech of young children as a function of listener. *Monographs of the Society for Research in Child Development, 38,* Whole No. 5.

Shaw, D., Camps, F., & Eccleston, F. (1967). 5-Hydroxtryptamine in the hindbrain of depressive suicides. *British Journal of Psychiatry, 113,* 1407–1411.

Sheehan, P. (1988). Confidence, memory and hypnosis. In H. Pettinati (Ed.), *Hypnosis and Memory.* New York: Guilford.

Sheffield, F. (1966). A drive induction theory of reinforcement. In R. Haber (Ed.), *Current Research in Motivation.* New York: Holt, Rinehart and Winston.

Sheffield, F., Wulff, J., & Backer, R. (1951). Reward value of copulation without sex drive reduction. *Journal of Comparative and Physiological Psychology, 44,* 3–8.

Shepherd, R., & Cooper, L. (1982). *Mental Images and Their Transformation.* Cambridge, MA: MIT Press.

Shepard, R., & Metzler, J. (1971). Mental rotation of three-dimensional objects. *Science, 171,* 701–703.

Sherif, M. (1937). An experimental approach to the study of attitudes. *Sociometry, 1,* 90–98.

Sherif, M., Harvey, O., White, B., Hood, W., & Sherif, C. (1961). *Intergroup Cooperation and Competition: The Robbers Cave Experience.* Norman, OK: University Book Exchange.

Sherrington, R., Brynjolfsson, J., Petursson, H., Potter, M., Dudleston, K., Barraclough, B., Wasmuth, J., Dobbs, M., & Gurling, H. (1988). Localization of a susceptibility locus for schizophrenia on chromosome 5. *Nature, 336,* 164–167.

Sherwin, B., & Gelfand, M. (1987). Individual differences in mood with menopausal replacement therapy: Possible role of sex hormone-binding globulin. *Journal of Psychosomatic Obstetrics and Gynaecology, 6,* 121–131.

Sherwin, B., Gelfand, M., & Brender, W. (1985). Androgen enhances sexual motivation in females: A prospective crossover study of sex steroid administration in the surgical menopause. *Psychosomatic Medicine, 47,* 339–351.

Shettleworth, S. (1983). Memory in food-hoarding birds. *Scientific American, 248,* 102–110.

Shevitz, S. (1976). Psychosurgery: Some cur-

rent observations. *The American Journal of Psychiatry, 133,* 266–270.

Shields, J. (1962). *Monozygotic Twins Brought Up Apart and Brought Up Together.* London: Oxford University Press.

Shiffrin, R., & Atkinson, R. (1969). Storage and retrieval processes in long-term memory. *Psychological Review, 76,* 179–193.

Shisslak, C., McKeon, R., & Crago, M. (1990). Family dysfunction in normal weight bulimic and bulimic anorexic families. *Journal of Clinical Psychology, 46,* 185–189.

Shotland, R., & Goodstein, L. (1983). Just because she doesn't want to doesn't mean it's rape: An experimentally based causal model of the perception of rape in a dating situation. *Social Psychology Quarterly, 46,* 220–232.

Shoulson, I., Odoroff, C., Oakes, D., Behr, J., Goldblatt, D., Caine, E., Kennedy, J., Miller, C., Bamford, K., Rubin, A., Plumb, S., & Kurlan, R. (1989). A controlled clinical trial of baclofen as protective therapy in early Huntington's disease. *Annals of Neurology, 25,* 252–259.

Shweder, R. (1982). Liberation as destiny. *Contemporary Psychology, 27,* 421–424.

Siegel, D. (1982). Personality development in adolescence. In B. Wolman (Ed.), *Handbook of Developmental Psychology.* Englewood Cliffs, NJ: Prentice-Hall.

Siegel, M. (1987). Are sons and daughters treated more differently by fathers than by mothers? *Developmental Review, 7,* 183–209.

Siegel, S., Hinson, R., & Krank, M. (1978). The role of pre-drug signals in morphine analgesic tolerance: Support for a Pavlovian conditioning model of tolerance. *Journal of Experimental Psychology: Animal Behavior Processes, 4,* 188–196.

Simkin, J., Simkin, A., Brien, L., & Sheldon, C. (1986). Gestalt therapy. In I. Kutash & A. Wolf (Eds.), *Psychotherapist's Casebook.* San Francisco: Jossey-Bass.

Simoni, G., Terzoli, G., & Rossella, F. (1990). Direct chromosome preparation and culture using chorionic villi: An evaluation of the two techniques. *American Journal of Medical Genetics, 35,* 181–183.

Singer, D. (1989). Children, adolescents, and television—1989. *Pediatrics, 83,* 445–446.

Singer, J. (1975). Navigating the stream of consciousness. Research in daydreaming and related inner experience. *American Psychologist, 30,* 727–738.

Singer, J. (1978). Experimental studies of daydreaming and the stream of thought. In K. Pope & J. Singer (Eds.), *The Stream of Consciousness: Scientific Investigations into the Flow of Human Experience.* New York: Plenum.

Singer, J., Lundberg, V., & Frankenhaeuser, M. (1978). Stress on the train: A study of urban commuting. In A. Baum, J. Singer, & S. Valins (Eds.), *Advances in Environmental Psychology* (Vol. I). Hillsdale, NJ: Erlbaum.

Singer, L., Brodzinsky, D., Ramsay, D., Stein, M., & Waters, E. (1985). Mother-infant attachment in adoptive families. *Child Development, 56,* 1543–1551.

Singh, S., Snyder, A., & Pullen, G. (1986). Fetal alcohol syndrome: Glucose and liver metabolism in term rat fetus and neonate.

Alcoholism: Clinical and Experimental Research, 10, 54–58.

Sirvioö, R., Kutvonen, R., Hartikainen, P., & Riekkinen, P. (1989). Cholinesterases in the cerebrospinal fluid, plasma, and erythrocytes of patients with Alzheimer's disease. *Journal of Neural Transmission, 75,* 119–127.

Skeels, H. (1966). Adult status of children with contrasting early life experiences: A follow-up study. *Monographs of the Society for Research in Child Development, 31,* Whole No. 105.

Skinner, B. (1953). *Science of Human Behavior.* New York: Macmillan.

Skinner, B. (1957). *Verbal Behavior.* Englewood Cliffs, NJ: Prentice-Hall.

Skinner, B. (1974). *About behaviorism.* New York: Alfred Knopf.

Skinner, B. (1987). *Upon further reflection.* Englewood Cliffs, NJ: Prentice Hall.

Sklar, L., & Anisman, H. (1981). Stress and cancer. *Psychological Bulletin, 89,* 369–406.

Skowronski, J., & Carlston, D. (1987). Social judgment and social memory: The role of diagnosticity, positivity, and extremity biases. *Journal of Personality and Social Psychology, 52,* 689–699.

Skyrms, B. (1986). *Choice and Chance: An Introduction to Inductive Logic.* Belmont, CA: Dickinson.

Slade, A. (1987). Quality of attachment and early symbolic play. *Developmental Psychology, 23,* 78–85.

Slater, E., & Cowie, V. (1971). *The Genetics of Mental Disorders.* London: Oxford University Press.

Slater, E., & Shields, J. (1969). Genetic aspects of anxiety. In M. Lader (Ed.), *Studies of Anxiety.* Ashford, England: Headley Brothers.

Sloane, R., Staples, F., Cristol, A., Yorkston, N., & Whipple, K. (1975). *Psychotherapy versus Behavior Therapy.* Cambridge, MA: Harvard University Press.

Slocum, W., & Nye, F. (1976). Provider and housekeeper roles. In F. Nye (Ed.), *Role Structure and Analysis of the Family.* Beverly Hills, CA: Sage Foundations.

Smith, D., & Wilson, A. (1973). *The Child with Down's Syndrome.* Philadelphia: Saunders.

Smith, F. (1985). Physicians take a second look at hypnosis. *The Oregonian,* March 7, D1.

Smith, K. (1947). The problem of stimulation deafness. Histological changes in the cochlea as a function of tonal frequency. *Journal of Experimental Psychology, 37,* 304–317.

Smith, M., Glass, G., & Miller, R. (1980). *The Benefits of Psychotherapy.* Baltimore: Johns Hopkins University Press.

Smith, P., & Langoff, G. (1981). The use of Sternberg's memory scanning technique. *Human Factors, 23,* 701–708.

Smith, S., Brown, H., Toman, J., & Goodman, L. (1947). The lack of cerebral effects of I-Tubercurarine. *Anesthesiology, 8,* 1–14.

Snarey, J. (1987). A question of morality. *Psychology Today,* June, 6–8.

Snyder, M. (1983). The influence of individuals on situation: Implications for understanding the links between personality and social behavior. *Journal of Personality, 51,* 497–516.

Snyder, M., & Swann, W. (1976). When actions reflect attitudes: The politics of impression management. *Journal of Personality and Social Psychology, 34,* 1034–1042.

Snyder, M., Tanke, E., & Berscheid, E. (1977). Social perception and interpersonal behavior: On the self-fulfilling nature of social stereotypes. *Journal of Personality and Social Psychology, 35,* 691–712.

Snyder, S. (1984). Drug and neurotransmitter receptors in the brain. *Science, 224,* 22–31.

Snyder, S. (1986). *Drugs and the Brain.* San Francisco: Freeman.

Snyderman, M., & Rothman, S. (1987). Survey of expert opinions on intelligence and aptitude testing. *American Psychologist, 42,* 137–144.

Sohlberg, S., Norring, C., Holmgren, S., & Rosmark, B. (1989). Impulsivity and long-term prognosis of psychiatric patients with anorexia nervosa/bulimia nervosa. *The Journal of Nervous and Mental Disease, 177,* 249–258.

Sokolov, E. (1977). Brain functions: Neuronal mechanisms of learning and memory. *Annual Review of Psychology, 20,* 85–112.

Soloman, Z., Garb, R., Bleich, A., & Grupper, D. (1987). Reactivation of combat-related posttraumatic stress disorder. *American Journal of Psychiatry, 144,* 51–55.

Solomon, R. (1980). The opponent-process theory of acquired motivation: The costs of pleasure and the benefits of pain. *American Psychologist, 35,* 691–712.

Solomon, R. (1982). The opponent-process in acquired motivation. In D. Pfaff (Ed.), *The Physiological Mechanisms of Motivation.* New York: Springer-Verlag.

Solomon, R., & Corbit, J. (1974). An opponent-process theory of motivation. *Psychological Review, 81,* 119–145.

Solso, R. (1991). *Cognitive psychology* (3rd ed.). Boston: Allyn and Bacon.

Sommers-Flanagan, J., & Greenberg, R. (1989). Psychosocial variables and hypertension. *The Journal of Nervous and Mental Disease, 177,* 15–24.

Sontag, S. (1972). The double standard of aging. *Saturday Review,* September 23, 29–38.

Sorenson, R. (1973). *Adolescent Sexuality in Contemporary America.* New York: World.

Spanos, N., Perlini, A., & Robertson, L. (1989). Hypnosis, suggestion, and placebo in the reduction of experimental pain. *Journal of Abnormal Psychology, 98,* 285–293.

Spanos, N., Williams, V., & Gwynn, M. (1990). Effects of hypnotic, placebo, and salicylic acid treatments on wart regression. *Psychosomatic Medicine, 52,* 109–114.

Spearman, C. (1904). General intelligence objectively determined and measured. *American Journal of Psychology, 15,* 201–293.

Speed, N., Engdahl, B., Schwartz, J., & Eberly, R. (1989). Posttraumatic stress disorder as a consequence of the POW experience. *The Journal of Nervous and Mental Disease, 177,* 147–153.

Sperling, G. (1960). The information available in brief visual presentations. *Psychological Monographs, 74,* 1–29.

Sperry, R. (1968). Hemispheric deconnection and the unity of conscious experience. *American Psychologist, 23,* 723–733.

Spielberger, C., Johnson, E., Russell, S., Crane, R., Jacobs, G., & Worden, T. (1985). The experience and expression of anger. In M. Chesney, S. Goldston, & R. Rosenman (Eds.), *Anger and Hostility in Behavioral Medicine.* New York: Hemisphere/McGraw-Hill.

Spielman, A., Saskin, P., & Thorpy, M. (1987). Treatment of chronic insomnia by restriction of time in bed. *Sleep, 10,* 45–56.

Spillman, D., & Everington, C. (1989). Somatotypes revisited: Have the media changed our perception of the female body image? *Psychological Reports, 64,* 887–890.

Spitz, R. (1945). Hospitalism: An inquiry into the genesis of psychiatric conditions in early childhood. *Psychoanalytic Study of the Child, 2,* 313–342.

Spitz, R., & Wolff, K. (1946). Anaclitic depression: An inquiry into the genesis of psychiatric conditions in early childhood: II. In A. Freud (Ed.), *The Psychoanalytic Study of the Child* (Vol. 2). New York: International Universities Press.

Spray, D. (1986). Cutaneous temperature receptors. *Annual Review of Physiology, 48,* 625–638.

Squire, L., & Butters, N. (1984). *Neuropsychology of Memory.* New York: Guilford Press.

Sroufe, L. (1985). Attachment classification from the perspective of infant-caregiver relationships and infant temperament. *Child Development, 56,* 1–14.

Sroufe, L., Fox, N., & Pancake, V. (1983). Attachment and dependency in a developmental perspective. *Child Development, 54,* 1615–1627.

St. George-Hyslop, P., Tanzi, R., Polinsky, R., Haines, J., Nee, L., Watkins, P., Myers, R., Feldman, R., Pollen, D., Drachman, D., Growdon, J., Bruni, A., Foncin, J., Salmon, D., Prommelt, P., Amaducci, L., Sorbi, S., Piacentini, S., Stewart, G., Hobbs, W., Conneally, M., Gusella, J. (1987). The genetic defect causing familial Alzheimer's disease maps on chromosome 21. *Science, 20,* 885–890.

Stanton, P., & Sejnowski, T. (1989). Associative long-term depression in the hippocampus induced by hebbion covariance. *Nature, 339,* 215–218.

Stark, E. (1984). Hypnosis on trial. *Psychology Today,* February, 34–36.

Steiger, H. (1990). An integrated psychotherapy for eating-disorder patients. *American Journal of Psychotherapy, 43,* 229–237.

Stein, J. (1986). Role of the cerebellum in the visual guidance of movement. *Nature, 323,* 217–221.

Stein, L. (1989). The effect of long-term outcome studies on the therapy of schizophrenia: A Critique. *Journal of Marital and Family Therapy, 15,* 133–138.

Stein, L., & Wise, C. (1971). Possible etiology of schizophrenia: Progressive damage to the noradrenergic reward system by 6-hydroxy dopamine. *Science, 171,* 1031–1036.

Stellar, E. (1954). The physiology of motivation. *Psychological Review, 61,* 5–22.

Stephan, W., & Rosenfield, D. (1978). Effects of desegregation on racial attitudes. *Journal of Personality and Social Psychology, 36,* 795–804.

Stern, D. (1986). *The Interpersonal World of the Infant.* New York: Basic Books.

Stern, J., Brown, M., Ulett, G., & Sletten, I. (1977). A comparison of hypnosis, acupuncture, morphine, valium, aspirin, and placebo in the management of experimentally induced pain. *Annals of the New York Academy of Sciences, 296,* 175–193.

Sternberg, R. (1979). The nature of mental abilities. *American Psychologist, 34,* 214–230.

Sternberg, R. (1981). Testing and cognitive psychology. *American Psychologist, 36,* 1181–1189.

Sternberg, R. (1982). Reasoning, problem solving, and intelligence. In R. Sternberg (Ed.), *Handbook of Human Intelligence.* New York: Cambridge University Press.

Sternberg, R. (1984). Testing intelligence without IQ tests. *Phi Delta Kappan, 65,* 694–698.

Sternberg, R. (1985). *Beyond IQ: A Triarchic Theory of Human Intelligence.* New York: Cambridge University Press.

Sternberg, R. (1986). *Intelligence Applied: Understanding and Increasing Your Intellectual Skills.* San Diego, CA: Harcourt Brace Jovanovich.

Sternberg, R., Conway, B., Ketron, J., & Bernstein, M. (1981). People's conceptions of intelligence. *Journal of Personality and Social Psychology, 41,* 37–55.

Sternberg, R., & Salter, W. (1982). Conceptions of intelligence. In R. Sternberg (Ed.), *Handbook of Human Intelligence.* New York: Cambridge University Press.

Stevenson, H. (1983). *Making the Grade: School Achievement in Japan, Taiwan, and the United States.* Stanford, CA: Center for Advanced Study in the Behavioral Sciences, Annual Report.

Stevenson, H. (1992). Learning from Asian schools. *Scientific American, 12,* 70–76.

Stevenson, J., Graham, P., Fredman, G., & McLoughlin, V. (1987). A twin study of genetic influences on reading and spelling ability and disability. *Journal of Child Psychology and Psychiatry, 28,* 229–247.

Stine, E., & Bohannon, J. (1983). Imitation, interactions, and language acquisition. *Journal of Child Language, 10,* 589–603.

Straus, E., & Yalow, R. (1979). Cholecystokinin in the brains of obese and nonobese mice. *Science, 203,* 68–69.

Straus, M., Gelles, R., & Steinmetz, S. (1980). *Behind Closed Doors: Violence in the American Family.* Garden City, NY: Anchor Press.

Striegel-Moore, R., Silberstein, L., & Rodin, J. (1986). Toward an understanding of risk factors for bulimia. *American Psychologist, 41,* 246–263.

Strunin, L., & Hingson, R. (1987). Acquired immunodeficiency syndrome and adolescents: Knowledge, beliefs, attitudes, and behaviors. *Pediatrics, 79,* 825–828.

Strupp, H. (1984). Psychotherapy research: Reflections on my career and the state of the art. *Journal of Social and Clinical Psychology, 2,* 3–24.

Stunkard, A. (1980). *Obesity.* Philadelphia: Saunders.

Stunkard, A. (1983). In NOVA. Fat chance in a thin world. Boston: WGBH Transcripts.

Stunkard, A., Sorensen, T., Hanis, & Teasdale, T. (1986). "An adoption study of human obesity": Reply. *New England Journal of Medicine, 315,* 130.

Stunkard, A., Sorenson, T., Hanis, C., Teasdale, T., Chakraborty, R., Schall, W., & Schulsinger, F. (1986). An adoption study of human obesity. *The New England Journal of Medicine, 314,* 193–198.

Suddath, R., Casanova, M., Goldberg, T., Daniel, D., Kelsoe, J., & Weinberger, D. (1989). Temporal lobe pathology in schizophrenia: A quantitative magnetic resonance imaging study. *The American Journal of Psychiatry, 146,* 464–472.

Suedfeld, P. (1975). The benefits of boredom: Sensory deprivation reconsidered. *American Scientist, 63,* 60–69.

Suedfeld, P. (1980). *Restricted Environmental Stimulation: Research and Clinical Application.* New York: Wiley.

Suedfeld, P., & Kristeller, J. (1982). Stimulus reduction as a technique in health psychology. *Health Psychology, 1,* 337–357.

Suls, J., & Mullen, B. (1981). Life change in psychological distress: The role of perceived control and desirability. *Journal of Applied Social Psychology, 11,* 379–389.

Suomi, S., & Harlow, H. (1972). Social rehabilitation of isolate-reared monkeys. *Developmental Psychology, 6,* 487–496.

Suomi, S., & Harlow H. (1978). Early experience and social development in Rhesus monkeys. In M. Lamb (Ed.), *Social and Personality Development.* New York: Holt, Rinehart and Winston.

Swanson, J., & Kinsbourne, M. (1976). Stimulant-related state-dependent learning in hyperactive children. *Science, 192,* 1354–1357.

Swann, W., Wenzlaff, R., Krull, D., & Pelham, B. (1992). Allure of negative feedback: Self-verification strivings among depressed persons. *Journal of Abnormal Psychology, 101,* 293–306.

Swartz, M., Blazer, D., George, L., & Landerman, R. (1986). Somatization disorder in a community population. *American Journal of Psychiatry, 143,* 1403–1408.

Swedo, S., Rapoport, J., Cheslow, D., Leonard, H., Ayoub, E., Hosier, D., & Wald, E. (1989). High prevalence of obsessive-compulsive symptoms in patients with Sydenham's chorea. *The American Journal of Psychiatry, 146,* 246–249.

Swets, J., Tanner, W., & Birdsall, T. (1961). Decision processes in perception. *Psychological Review, 68,* 301–340.

Syndulko, K. (1978). Electrocortical investigations of sociopathy. In R. Hare & D. Schalling (Eds.), *Psychopathic Behavior: Approaches to Research.* Chichester, England: Wiley.

Tache, J., Selye, H., & Day, S. (1979). *Cancer, Stress, and Death.* New York: Plenum.

Tajfel, H. (1982). *Social Identity and Intergroup Relations.* New York: Cambridge University Press.

Tajfel, H., & Turner, J. (1979). An integrative theory of intergroup conflict. In W. Autin & S. Worchel (Eds.), *The Social Psychology of Intergroup Relations.* Monterey, CA: Brooks/Cole.

Tambs, K., Sundet, J., & Magnus, P. (1984). Heritability analysis of the WAIS subtests: A study of twins. *Intelligence, 8,* 283–293.

Tamminga, C., Foster, N., Fedio, P., Bird, E., & Chase, T. (1987). Alzheimer's disease: Low cerebral somatostatin levels correlate with impaired cognitive function and cortical metabolism. *Neurology, 37,* 161–165.

Tanford, S., & Penrod, S. (1984). Social influence model: A formal integration of research on majority and minority influence processes. *Psychological Bulletin, 95,* 189–225.

Tanzi, R., Gusella, J., Watkins, P., Bruns, G., St. George-Hyslop, P., Van Keuren, M., Patterson, D., Pagan, S., Kurnit, D., & Neve, R. (1987). Amyloid B protein gene: cDNA, mRNA distribution, and genetic linkage near the Alzheimer locus. *Science, 235,* 880–884.

Tartter, V. (1986). *Language Processes.* New York: Holt, Rinehart and Winston.

Tauber, M. (1979). Sex differences in parent-child interaction styles in a free-play session. *Child Development, 50,* 981–988.

Tavris, C. (1982). *Anger: The Misunderstood Emotion.* New York: Simon & Schuster.

Taylor, S. (1986). *Health Psychology.* New York: Random House.

Taylor, S. (1990). Health psychology: The science and the field. *American Psychologist, 45,* 40–50.

Telch, M., Lucas, J., & Nelson, P. (1989). Nonclinical panic in college students: An investigation of prevalence and symptomatology. *Journal of Abnormal Psychology, 98,* 300–306.

Tellegen, A., Lykken, D., Bouchard, T., Wilcox, K., Segal, N., & Rich, S. (1988). Personality similarity in twins reared apart and together. *Journal of Personality and Social Psychology, 54,* 1031–1039.

Terman, L. (1921). In Symposium: Intelligence and its measurement. *Journal of Educational Psychology, 12,* 127–133.

Terman, L. (1925). Mental and physical traits of a thousand gifted children. In L. Terman (Ed.), *Genetic Studies of Genius.* Stanford, CA: Stanford University Press.

Terman, L. (1954). Scientists and nonscientists in a group of 800 gifted men. *Psychological Monographs, 68,* 1–44.

Terman, M. (1988). On the question of mechanism in phototherapy: Considerations of clinical efficacy and epidemiology. *Journal of Biological Rhythms, 3,* 155–172.

Terrace, H. (1979). How Nim Chimsky changed my mind. *Psychology Today,* November, 63–91.

Terrace, H., Petitto, L., Sanders, R., & Bever, T. (1979). Can an ape create a sentence? *Science, 206,* 891–902.

Terry, W. (1989). Birth order and prominence in the history of psychology. *The Psychological Record, 39,* 333–337.

Tesser, A. (1990). Attitudes and attitude change. *Annual Review of Psychology, 41,* 479–523.

Teuting, P., Rosen, S., & Hirschfeld, R. (1981). *Special Report on Depression Research.* Washington, DC: NIMH-DHHS Publication No. 81–1085.

Thatcher, R., Walker, R., & Giudice, S. (1987). Human cerebral hemispheres develop at different rates and ages. *Science, 236,* 1110–1113.

Thelen, M., Farmer, J., Mann, L., & Pruitt, J. (1990). Bulimia and interpersonal relationships: A longitudinal study. *Journal of Counseling Psychology, 37,* 85–90.

Thibaut, J., & Strickland, L. (1956). Psycholog-ical set and social conformity. *Journal of Personality and Social Psychology, 25,* 115–129.

Thigpen, C., & Cleckley, H. (1984). On the incidence of multiple personality disorder. *The International Journal of Clinical and Experimental Hypnosis, 32,* 63–66.

Thoman, E., Liderman, P., & Olsen, J. (1972). Neonate-mother interaction during breast feeding. *Developmental Psychology, 6,* 110–118.

Thomas, A., & Chess, S. (1977). *Temperament and Development.* New York: Bruner/Masel.

Thomas, C., Duszynski, K., & Shaffer, J. (1974). Closeness to parents and the family constellation in a prospective study of five disease states: Suicide, mental illness, malignant tumor, hypertension, and coronary heart disease. *Johns Hopkins Journal, 134,* 251–270.

Thomas, C., Duszynski, K., & Shaffer, J. (1979). Family attitudes reported in youth as potential precursors of cancer. *Psychosomatic Medicine, 41,* 287–302.

Thompson, C., Hamlin, V., & Roenker, D. (1972). A comment on the role of clustering in free recall. *Journal of Experimental Psychology, 94,* 108–109.

Thompson, C., & Isaacs, G. (1988). Seasonal affective disorder—a British sample: Symptomatology in relation to mode of referral and diagnostic subtype. *Journal of Affective Disorders, 14,* 1–11.

Thompson, D., & Campbell, R. (1977). Hunger in humans induced by 2-deoxy-D-glucose: Glucoprivic control of taste preference and food intake. *Science, 198,* 1065–1068.

Thompson, J., & Blaine, J. (1987). Use of ECT in the United States in 1975 and 1980. *American Journal of Psychiatry, 144,* 557–562.

Thompson, J., Jarvie, G., Lahey, B., & Cureton, K. (1982). Exercise and obesity: Etiology, physiology, and intervention. *Psychological Bulletin, 91,* 55–79.

Thompson, R. (1985). *The Brain.* San Francisco: Freeman.

Thompson, R. (1986). The neurobiology of learning and memory. *Science, 233,* 941–947.

Thompson, S. (1981). Will it hurt less if I can control it? A complex answer to a simple question. *Psychological Bulletin, 90,* 89–101.

Thorndike, E. (1911). *Animal Intelligence.* New York: Macmillan.

Thorndyke, P. (1984). Applications of schema theory in cognitive research. In J. Anderson & S. Kosslyn (Eds.), *Essays in Honor of Gordon Bower.* San Francisco: Freeman.

Thorndike, R., Hagen, E., & Sattler, J. (1986). *The Stanford-Binet Intelligence Scale: Fourth Edition.* Chicago, IL: Riverside Publishing Company.

Thurstone, L. (1938). *Primary Mental Abilities.* Chicago: University of Chicago Press.

Thurstone, L. (1946). Comment. *American Journal of Sociology, 52,* 39–40.

Timmerman, M., Wells, L., & Chen, S. (1990). Bulimia nervosa and associated alcohol abuse among secondary school children. *Journal of the American Academy of Child and Adolescent Psychiatry, 29,* 118–122.

Tokunaga, K., Fukushima, M., Kemnitz, J., & Bray, G. (1986). Comparison of ventromedial and paraventricular lesions in rates that become obese. *American Journal of Physiology, 251,* R1221–R1227.

Tolchin, M. (1989). Suicide rate among elderly increases 25% from 1981 to 1986. *The Oregonian,* July 23, A15.

Tolman, E. (1967). *Purposive behavior in animals and man.* New York: Irvington.

Tolman, E., & Honzik, C. (1930). Introduction and removal of reward and maze performance in rats. *University of California Publications in Psychology, 4,* 257–275.

Tolman, E., Ritchie, B., & Kalish, D. (1946). Studies in spatial learning: II. Place learning versus response learning. *American Psychologist, 34,* 583–596.

Tolstedt, B., & Stokes, J. (1983). Relation of verbal, affective, and physical intimacy to marital satisfaction. *Journal of Counseling Psychology, 30,* 573–580.

Tomita, T. (1986). Retrospective review of retinal circuitry. *Vision Research, 26,* 1339–1350.

Tomkins, S. (1962). *Affect, Imagery, and Consciousness: The Positive Effects* (Vol. 1). New York: Springer.

Tomkins, S. (1963). *Affect, Imagery, and Consciousness: The Negative Effects* (Vol. 2). New York: Springer.

Tourney, G. (1980). Hormones and homosexuality. In J. Marmor (Ed.), *Homosexual Behavior.* New York: Basic Books.

Travers, J., Travers, S., & Norgen, R. (1987). Gustatory neural processing in hindbrain. *Annual Review of Neurosciences, 10,* 595–632.

Treisman, A. (1960). Contextual cues in selective listening. *Quarterly Journal of Experimental Psychology, 12,* 242–248.

Treisman, A. (1964). Monitoring and storage of irrelevant messages in selective attention. *Journal of Verbal Learning and Verbal Behavior, 3,* 449–459.

Tresemer, D. (1976). The cumulative record of research on "fear of success." *Sex Roles,* 217–236.

Troll, L. (1975). *Early and Middle Adulthood.* Monterey, CA: Brooks/Cole.

Trujillo, K., Belluzzi, J., & Stein, L. (1989). Effects of opiate antagonists and their quaternary analogues on nucleus accumens self-stimulation. *Behavioural Brain Research, 33,* 181–188.

Tryon, R. (1940). Genetic differences in maze-learning ability in rats. In *39th Yearbook, National Society for the Study of Education.* Chicago: University of Chicago Press.

Tucek, S., Ricny, J., & Dolezal, V. (1990). Advances in the biology of cholinergic neurons. *Advances in Neurology, 51,* 109–114.

Tulving, E. (1972). Episodic and semantic memory. In E. Tulving & W. Donaldson (Eds.), *Organization of Memory.* New York: Academic Press.

Tulving, E. (1977). Cue-dependent forgetting. In I. Janis (Ed.), *Current Trends in Psychology.* Los Altos, CA: Kaufmann.

Tulving, E. (1983). *Elements of Episodic Memory.* New York: Oxford University Press.

Tulving, E. (1986). What kind of a hypothesis is the distinction between episodic and semantic memory? *Journal of Experimental Psychology: Learning, Memory, and Cognition, 12,* 307–311.

Turk, D., Meichenbaum, D., & Berman, W.

(1979). Application of biofeedback for the regulation of pain: A critical review. *Psychological Bulletin, 86,* 1322–1338.

Turk, D., & Rudy, T. (1986). Assessment of cognitive factors in chronic pain: A worthwhile enterprise? *Journal of Consulting and Clinical Psychology, 54,* 760–768.

Turkkan, J. (1989). Classical conditioning: The new hegemony. *Behavioral and Brain Sciences, 12,* 121–179.

Turner, J. (1984). Social identification and psychological group formation. In H. Tajfel (Ed.), *The Social Dimension.* Cambridge, England: Cambridge University Press.

Turner, S., Beidel, D., & Nathan, R. (1985). Biological factors in obsessive-compulsive disorders. *Psychological Bulletin, 97,* 430–450.

Tversky, A., & Kahneman, D. (1973). On the psychology of prediction. *Psychological Review, 80,* 237–251.

Tversky, A., & Kahneman, D. (1981). The framing of decision and the psychology of choice. *Science, 211,* 453–458.

Tversky, B., & Tuchin, M. (1989). A reconciliation of the evidence on eyewitness testimony: Comments on McCloskey and Zaragoza. *Journal of Experimental Psychology: General, 118,* 86–91.

Udry, J., Billy, J., Morris, N., Groff, T., & Raj, M. (1985). Serum androgenic hormones motivate sexual behavior in adolescent boys. *Fertility and Sterility, 43,* 90–94.

Ullman, L., & Krasner, L. (1975). *A Psychological Approach to Abnormal Behavior* (2nd ed.). Englewood Cliffs, NJ: Prentice-Hall.

Underwood, B. (1983). "Conceptual" similarity and accumulated proactive inhibition. *Journal of Experimental Psychology: Learning, Memory, and Cognition, 9,* 456–461.

Urrutia, A., & Gruol, D. (1992). Acute alcohol alters the excitability of cerebellar Purkinje neurons and hippocampal neurons in culture. *Brain Research, 569,* 26–37.

Vaillant, G., & Perry, J. (1985). Personality disorders. In H. Kaplan & B. Sadock (Eds.), *Comprehensive Textbook of Psychiatry* (4th ed.). Baltimore: Williams & Wilkins.

Valenstein, E. (1973). *Brain Control.* Toronto: John Wiley & Sons.

Valenstein, E. (1980). *The Psychosurgery Debate: Scientific, Legal, and Ethical Perspectives.* San Francisco: W. H. Freeman and Co.

Valian, V. (1986). Syntactic categories in the speech of young children. *Developmental Psychology, 22,* 562–579.

Vanderweele, D., & Sanderson, J. (1976). Peripheral glucosensitive satiety in the rabbit and the rat. In D. Novin, W. Wyrcicka, & G. Bray (Eds.), *Hunger: Basic Mechanisms and Clinical Implications.* New York: Raven.

Van Egeren, L., Sniderman, L., & Roggelin, M. (1982). Competitive two-person interaction of Type-A and Type-B individuals. *Journal of Behavioral Medicine, 5,* 55–66.

Van Praag, H. (1981). Management of depression with serotonin precursors. *Biological Psychiatry, 16,* 291–310.

Van Thiel, D., Gavaler, J., Dindzans, V., Gordon, R., Iwatsuki, S., Makowka, L., Todo, S., Tzakis, A., & Starzi, T. (1989). Liver transplantation for alcoholic liver disease: A consideration of reasons for and against. *Al-*

coholism: Clinical and Experimental Research, 13, 181–184.

Vega-Lahr, N., & Field, T. (1986). Type A behavior in preschool children. *Child Development, 57,* 1333–1348.

Veleber, D., & Templer, D. (1984). Effects of caffeine on anxiety and depression. *Journal of Abnormal Psychology, 93,* 120–122.

Velley, L. (1986). The role of intrinsic neurons in lateral hypothalamic self-stimulation. *Behavioural Brain Research, 22,* 141–152.

Venables, P., & Wing, J. (1962). Level of arousal and the subclassification of schizophrenia. *Archives of General Psychiatry, 7,* 114–119.

Veroff, J., Douvan, E., & Kulka, R. (1981). *The Inner American.* New York: Basic Books.

Vinigan, R., Dow-Edwards, D., & Riley, E. (1986). Cerebral metabolic alterations in rats following prenatal alcohol exposure: A deoxyglucose study. *Alcoholism: Clinical and Experimental Research, 10,* 22–26.

Vink, R., McIntosh, T., Demediuk, P., Weiner, M., & Faden, A. (1988). Decline in intracellular free Mg^{2+} is associated with irreversible tissue injury following brain trauma. *Journal of Biological Chemistry, 263,* 757–761.

Vinokur, A., & Selzer, M. (1975). Desirable versus undesirable life events: Their relationship to stress and mental distress. *Journal of Personality and Social Psychology, 32,* 329–337.

Visintainer, M., Seligman, M., & Volpicelli, J. (1983). Helplessness, chronic stress, and tumor development. *Psychosomatic Medicine, 45,* 75–76.

Vogel, G. (1975). A review of REM sleep deprivation. *Archives of General Psychiatry, 32,* 749–761.

von Békésy, G. (1960). *Experiments in Hearing.* New York: McGraw-Hill.

von Frisch, K. (1974). Decoding the language of the bee. *Science, 185,* 663–668.

Wadden, T., & Anderton, C. (1982). The clinical use of hypnosis. *Psychological Bulletin, 91,* 215–243.

Wahba, N., & Bridwell, L. (1976). Maslow reconsidered: A review of research on the need hierarchy theory. *Organization Behavior and Human Performance, 15,* 212–240.

Waldrop, M. (1984). Artificial intelligence in parallel. *Science, 225,* 608–610.

Waldrop, M. (1988). Toward a unified theory of cognition. *Science, 241,* 27–29.

Walduogel, J. (1990). The bird's eye view. *American Scientist, 78,* 342–353.

Wall, H., & Routowicz, A. (1987). Use of self-generated and others' cues in immediate and delayed recall. *Perceptual and Motor Skills, 64,* 1019–1022.

Wallach, M., & Wallach, L. (1983). *Psychology's Sanction for Selfishness: The Error of Egoism in Theory and Therapy.* New York: Freeman.

Wallach, M., & Wallach, L. (1985). How psychology sanctions the cult of the self. *Washington Monthly,* February, 46–56.

Walling, M., Andersen, B., & Johnson, S. (1990). Hormonal replacement therapy for postmenopausal women: A review of sexual outcomes and related gynecologic effects. *Archives of Sexual Behavior, 19,* 119–137.

Wallis, C. (1984). Unlocking pain's secrets. *Time,* June 11, 58–66.

Walster, E., Aronson, E., & Abrahams, D. (1966). On increasing the persuasiveness of a low prestige communicator. *Journal of Experimental Social Psychology, 2,* 375–342.

Walters, J., Apter, M., & Sveback, S. (1982). Color preference, arousal, and the theory of psychological reversals. *Motivation and Emotion, 6,* 193–215.

Walters, R., & Willows, D. (1968). Imitation of behavior of disturbed children following exposure to aggressive and nonaggressive models. *Child Development, 39,* 79–91.

Wang, M., & Freeman, A. (1987). *Neural Function.* Boston: Little, Brown.

Wangensteen, O., & Carlson, A. (1931). Hunger sensation after total gastrectomy. *Proceedings of the Society for Experimental Biology, 28,* 545–547.

Ward, T., & Lewis, S. (1987). The influence of alcohol and loud music on analytic and holistic processing. *Perception and Psychophysics, 41,* 179–186.

Warga, C. (1987). Pain's gatekeeper. *Psychology Today,* August, 51–56.

Warm, J. (Ed.). (1984). *Sustained Attention in Human Performance.* London: Wiley.

Warm, J., & Dember, W. (1986). Awake at the switch. *Psychology Today,* April, 46–53.

Wason, P. (1968). On the failure to eliminate hypothesis—a second look. In P. Wason & P. Johnson-Laird (Eds.), *Thinking and Reasoning.* Baltimore: Penguin.

Waterman, A. (1982). Identity development from adolescence to adulthood: An extension of theory and a review of research. *Developmental Psychology, 18,* 341–358.

Waters, E., Wippman, J., & Sroufe, L. (1979). Attachment, positive affect, and competence in the peer group: Two studies in construct validation. *Child Development, 50,* 821–829.

Waters, H., & Huck, J. (1989). Networking women. *Newsweek,* March 13, 48–54.

Watkins, C., Lopez, F., Campbell, V., & Himmell, C. (1986). *Journal of Counseling Psychology, 33,* 301–309.

Watkins, J. (1984). The Bianchi (L.A. Hillside Strangler) case: Sociopath or multiple personality? *International Journal of Clinical and Experimental Hypnosis, 32,* 67–101.

Watkins, M., Ho, E., & Tulving, E. (1976). Context effects in recognition memory for faces. *Journal of Verbal Learning and Verbal Behavior, 15,* 505–518.

Watson, D., & Pennebaker, J. (1989). Health complaints, stress, and distress: Exploring the central role of negative affectivity. *Psychological Review, 96,* 234–254.

Watson, J. (1925). *Behaviorism.* Chicago: The University of Chicago Press.

Watson, J. (1930). *Behaviorism.* New York: Norton.

Watson, R., & DeMeo, P. (1987). Premarital cohabitation vs. traditional courtship and subsequent marital adjustment: A replication and follow-up. *Family Relations, 36,* 193–197.

Weaver, C. (1980). Job satisfaction in the United States in the 1970's. *Journal of Applied Psychology, 65,* 364–367.

Weaver, C. (1993). Do you need a "flash" to form a flashbulb memory? *Journal of Experimental Psychology: General, 122,* 39–46.

Webb, W. (1975). *Sleep the Gentle Tyrant.* Englewood Cliffs, NJ: Prentice-Hall.

Webb, W., & Bonnet, M. (1979). Sleep and dreams. In M. Meyer (Ed.), *Foundations of Contemporary Psychology.* New York: Oxford University Press.

Webb, W., & Campbell, S. (1983). Relationships in sleep characteristics of identical and fraternal twins. *Archives of General Psychiatry, 40,* 1093–1095.

Wechsler, D. (1944). *The Measurement of Adult Intelligence* (3rd ed.). Baltimore: Williams & Wilkins.

Wehr, T., Giesen, H., & Schulz, P. (1989). Summer depression: Description of the syndrome and comparison with winter depression. In N. Rosenthal & N. Blehar (Eds.), *Seasonal Affective Disorder and Phototherapy.* New York: Guilford Press.

Wehr, T., & Rosenthal, N. (1989). Seasonality and affective illness. *The American Journal of Psychiatry, 146,* 829–839.

Wehr, T., Sack, D., & Rosenthal, N. (1987). Seasonal affective disorder with summer depression and winter hypomania. *The American Journal of Psychiatry, 144,* 1602–1603.

Weigel, R., & Newman, L. (1976). Increasing attitude-behavior correspondence by broadening the scope of the behavioral measure. *Journal of Personality and Social Psychology, 33,* 793–802.

Weilburg, J., Bear, D., & Sachs, G. (1987). Three patients with concomitant panic attacks and seizure disorder: Possible clues to the neurology of anxiety. *The American Journal of Psychiatry, 144,* 1053–1056.

Weinberg, R. (1979). Early childhood education and intervention: Establishing an American tradition. *American Psychologist, 34,* 912–916.

Weinberg, R. (1989). Intelligence and IQ: Landmark issues and great debates. *American Psychologist, 44,* 98–104.

Weiner, R. (1985). Electroconvulsive therapy. In J. Walker (Ed.), *Essentials of Clinical Psychiatry.* Philadelphia: Lippincott.

Weissman, M. (1987). Advances in psychiatric epidemiology: Rates and risks for major depression. *American Journal of Public Health, 77,* 445–451.

Weissman, M., Kidd, K., & Prusoff, B. (1982). Variability in rates of affective disorders in relatives of depressed and normal probands. *Archives of General Psychiatry, 39,* 1397–1403.

Weissman, M., Klerman, G., Markowitz, J., & Quellette, R. (1989). Suicidal ideation and suicide attempts in panic disorder and attacks. *New England Journal of Medicine, 321,* 1209–1214.

Weissman, M., Klerman, G., & Paykel, E. (1971). Clinical evaluation of hostility in depression. *American Journal of Psychiatry, 128,* 261–266.

Weissman, M., Klerman, G., Prusoff, B., Sholomskas, D., & Padian, N. (1981). Depressed outpatients. Results one year after treatment with drugs and/or interpersonal psychotherapy. *Archives of General Psychiatry, 38,* 51–56.

Weissman, M., & Paykel, E. (1974). *The Depressed Woman.* Chicago: University of Chicago Press.

Wender, P., Kety, S., Rosenthal, D., Schulsinger, F., Ortmann, J., & Lunde, I. (1986). Psychiatric disorders in the biological and adoptive families of adopted individuals with affective disorders. *Archives of General Psychiatry, 43,* 923–929.

Wetli, C., & Wright, R. (1979). Death caused by recreational cocaine use. *Journal of the American Medical Association, 241,* 2519–2522.

Wetzel, C., & Insko, C. (1982). The similarity-attraction relationship: Is there an ideal one? *Journal of Experimental Social Psychology, 18,* 253–276.

Wetzler, S. (1985). Mood state-dependent retrieval: A failure to replicate. *Psychological Reports, 56,* 759–765.

Wever, E. (1949). *Theory of Hearing.* New York: Wiley.

Whitam, T. (1977). Coevolution of foraging in *Bombus* and nectar dispensing in *Chilopsis*: A last dreg theory. *Science, 197,* 593–595.

White, L., & Booth, A. (1986). Children and marital happiness. *Journal of Family Issues, 7,* 131–147.

White, P. (1985). The poppy. *National Geographic, 167,* 143–188.

White, W. (1932). *Outlines of Psychiatry* (13th ed.). New York: Nervous and Mental Disease Publishing Company.

Whitman, F., & Diamond, M. (1986). A preliminary report on the sexual orientation of homosexual twins. Paper presented at the Western Region Annual Conference of the Society for the Scientific Study of Sex, Scottsdale, Arizona, January.

Whorf, B. (1956). Science and linguistics. In J. Carroll (Ed.), *Language, Thought, and Reality: Selected Writings of Benjamin Whorf.* Cambridge, MA: MIT Press.

Wickens, C. (1984). *Engineering Psychology and Human Performance.* Columbus, OH: Merrill.

Wicker, A. (1969). Attitudes versus actions: The relationship of verbal and overt behavioral responses to attitude objects. *Journal of Personality and Social Psychology, 33,* 793–802.

Widom, C. (1989). Does violence beget violence? A critical examination of the literature. *Psychological Bulletin, 106,* 3–28.

Wiens, A., & Menustik, C. (1983). Treatment outcome and patient characteristics in an aversion therapy program for alcoholism. *American Psychologist, 38,* 1089–1096.

Wilder, D. (1978). Homogeneity of jurors: The majority's influence depends upon their perceived independence. *Law and Human Behavior, 2,* 363–376.

Wilder, D. (1981). Perceiving persons as a group: Categorization and intergroup relations. In D. Hamilton (Ed.), *Cognitive Processes in Stereotyping and Intergroup Behavior.* Hillsdale, NJ: Erlbaum.

Wilhelm, K., & Parker, G. (1989). Is sex necessarily a risk factor in depression? *Psychological Medicine, 19,* 401–413.

William, K., & Chambers, D. (1990). The relationship between therapist characteristics and outcome of in vivo exposure treatment for agoraphobia. *Behavior Therapy, 21,* 111–116.

Williams, A., Peat, M., Crouch, D., Wells, J., & Finkle, B. (1985). Drugs in fatally injured young male drivers. *Public Health Reports, 100*, 19–25.

Williams, D., Butler, M., & Overmier, J. (1990). Expectancies of reinforcer location and quality as cues for a conditional discrimination in pigeons. *Journal of Experimental Psychology: Animal Behavior Processes, 16*, 3–13.

Williams, P., & Smith, M. (1979). *Interview in The First Question.* London: British Broadcasting System Science and Features Department film.

Williams, R. (1972). *The BITCH Test (Black Intelligence Test of Cultural Homogeneity).* St. Louis: Williams & Associates.

Williams, T. (1986). *The Impact of Television: A Natural Experiment in Three Communities.* New York: Academic Press.

Williamson, P., Csima, A., Galin, M., & Mamelak, M. (1986). Spectral EEG correlates of dream recall. *Biological Psychiatry, 21*, 717–723.

Wilmore, J., & Costill, D. (1988). *Training for Sport and Activity.* Dubuque, IA: Wm. C. Brown Publishers.

Wilson, B., & Lawson, D. (1976). Effects of alcohol on sexual arousal in women. *Journal of Abnormal Psychology, 85*, 489–497.

Wilson, E. (1975). *Sociobiology: The New Synthesis.* Cambridge, MA: Harvard University Press.

Wilson, E. (1978). *On Human Nature.* Cambridge, MA: Harvard University Press.

Wilson, M. (1984). Female homosexuals' need for dominance and endurance. *Psychological Reports, 55*, 79–82.

Wilson, R. (1986). Continuity and change in cognitive ability profile. *Behavioral Genetics, 16*, 45–60.

Winograd, E., & Killinger, W. (1983). Relating age at encoding in early childhood to adult recall: Development of flashbulb memories. *Journal of Experimental Psychology, 12*, 413–422.

Winston, P., & Prendergast, C. (Eds.). (1984). *The AI Business: Commercial Uses of Artificial Intelligence.* Cambridge, MA: MIT Press.

Winterbottom, M. (1958). The relation of need for achievement to learning experiences in independence mastery. In J. Atkinson (Ed.), *Motives in Fantasy, Action and Society.* Princeton, NJ: Van Nostrand.

Wirtshafter, D., & Davis, J. (1977). Body weight: Reduction by long-term glycerol treatment. *Science, 198*, 1271–1274.

Wolfe, J. (1936). Effectiveness of token rewards for chimpanzees. *Comparative Psychological Monographs, 12*, Whole No. 5.

Wolff, G. (1987). Body weight and cancer. *American Journal of Clinical Nutrition, 45*, 168–180.

Wolkin, A., Barouche, F., Wolf, A., Rotrosen, J., Fowler, J., Shiue, C., Cooper, T., & Brodie, J. (1989). Dopamine blockade and clinical response: Evidence for two biological subgroups of schizophrenia. *The American Journal of Psychiatry, 146*, 905–908.

Wolpe, J. (1958). *Psychotherapy by Reciprocal Inhibition.* Stanford, CA: Stanford University Press.

Wolpe, J. (1985). *The Practice of Behavior Therapy* (3rd ed.). New York: Pergamon Press.

Wolpe, J., & Rachman, S. (1960). Psychoana-

lytic "evidence." A critique based on Freud's case of Little Hans. *Journal of Nervous and Mental Disease, 131*, 135–147.

Women on Words and Images (1975). *Channeling Children: Sex Stereotyping on Prime Time TV.* Princeton, NJ: Author.

Wong, D., Wagner, H., Tune, L., Dannals, R., Pealson, G., Links, J., Tamminga, C., Broussolle, E., Ravert, H., Wilson, A., Toung, J., Malat, J., Williams, J., O'Tuama, L., Snyder, S., Kuhar, M., & Gjedde, A. (1986). Positron emission tomography reveals elevated D₂ dopamine receptors in drug-naive schizophrenics. *Science, 234*, 1558–1563.

Wood, J., & Bootzin, R. (1990). The prevalence of nightmares and their independence from anxiety. *Journal of Abnormal Psychology, 99*, 64–68.

Wood, W., & Eagly, A. (1981). Stages in the analysis of persuasive messages: The role of causal attributions and message comprehension. *Journal of Personality and Social Psychology, 40*, 246–259.

Woods, B., Yurgelun-Todd, D., Benes, F., Frankenburg, F., Pope, H., & McSparren, J. (1990). Progressive ventricular enlargement in schizophrenia: Comparison to bipolar affective disorder and correlation with clinical course. *Biological Psychiatry, 27*, 341–352.

Woods, R. (1986). Brain asymmetries in situs inversus. *Archives of Neurology, 43*, 1083–1084.

Woody, C. (1982). *Conditioning Representation of Involved Neural Functions.* New York: Plenum.

Woody, C. (1984). Studies of Pavlovian eyeblink conditioning in awake cats. In G. Lynch, J. McGaugh, & N. Weinberger (Eds.), *Neurobiology of Learning and Memory.* New York: Guilford Press.

Woody, C. (1986). Understanding the cellular basis of memory and learning. *Annual Review of Psychology, 37*, 433–493.

Wooley, S. (1983). In NOVA. Fat chance in a thin world. Boston: WGBH Transcripts.

Wragg, R., & Jeste, D. (1989). Overview of depression and psychosis in Alzheimer's disease. *The American Journal of Psychiatry, 146*, 577–587.

Wright, J., Waterson, E., Barrison, I., Toplis, P., Lewis, I., Gordon, M., MacRae, K., Morris, N., & Murray-Lyon, I. (1983). Alcohol consumption, pregnancy, and low birth weight. *Lancet, 1*, 663–665.

Wu, C., & Shaffer, D. (1987). Susceptibility to persuasive appeals as a function of source credibility and prior experience with the attitude object. *Journal of Personality and Social Psychology, 53*, 677–688.

Wurtman, R. (1982). Nutrients that modify brain function. *Scientific American, 246*, 50–59.

Wurtman, R. (1983). Behavioral effects of nutrients. *Lancet, 1*, 1145–1147.

Wurtman, R., Blusztajn, J., Ulus, I., Coviella, I., Buyukuysal, L., Growdon, J., & Slack, B. (1990). Choline metabolism in cholinergic neurons: Implications for the pathogenesis of neurodegenerative diseases. *Advances in Neurology, 51*, 117–125.

Wurtman, R., & Wurtman, J. (1989). Carbohydrates and depression. *Scientific American,* January, 68–75.

Wyrwicka, W. (1976). The problem of motivation in feeding behavior. In D. Novin, W. Wyrwicka, & G. Bray (Eds.), *Hunger: Basic Mechanisms and Clinical Implications.* New York: Raven.

Yadalam, K., Korn, M., & Simpson, G. (1990). Tardive dystonia: Four case histories. *Journal of Clinical Psychiatry, 51*, 17–20.

Yalom, I. (1975). *The Theory and Practice of Group Psychotherapy* (2nd ed.). New York: Basic Books.

Yarrow, L., Goodwin, M., Manheimer, H., & Milowe, I. (1973). Infancy, experience and cognitive and personality development at ten years. In L. Stone, H. Smith, & L. Murphy (Eds.), *The Competent Infant.* New York: Basic Books.

Yates, A. (1990). Current perspectives on the eating disorders: II. Treatment, outcome, and research directions. *Journal of the American Academy of Child and Adolescent Psychiatry, 29*, 1–9.

Yeomans, J., & Irwin, D. (1985). Stimulus duration and partial report performance. *Perception and Psychophysics, 37*, 163–169.

Yerkes, R., & Dodson, J. (1908). The relation of strength of stimulus to rapidity of habit formation. *Journal of Comparative Neurological Psychology, 18*, 459–482.

Yesavage, J., Leirer, V., Denari, M., & Hollister, L. (1985). Carryover effects of marijuana intoxication on aircraft pilot performance: A preliminary report. *American Journal of Psychiatry, 142*, 1325–1329.

Young, P. (1985). Introduction of gene therapy likely to bring high hopes, ethical fears. *The Oregonian,* May 16, C1.

Youniss, J., & Ketterlinus, R. (1987). Communication and connectedness in mother- and father-adolescent relationships. *Journal of Youth and Adolescence, 16*, 265–280.

Yu, B., Zhang, W., Jing, Q., Peng, R., Zhang, G., and Simon, H. (1985). STM capacity for Chinese and English language materials. *Memory and Cognition, 13*, 202–207.

Yudofsky, S. (1982). Electroconvulsive therapy in the eighties: Techniques and technology. *American Journal of Psychiatry, 36*, 391–398.

Zabin, I., Hirsch, M., Smith, E., & Hardy, J. (1984). Adolescent sexual attitudes and behavior: Are they consistent? *Family Planning Perspectives, 16*, 181–185.

Zajonc, R. (1965). Social facilitation, *Science, 149*, 269–274.

Zajonc, R. (1968). Attitudinal effects of mere exposure. *Journal of Personality and Social Psychology, 9*, Monograph Supplement No. 2, Part 2.

Zajonc, R. (1970). Brainwash: Familiarity breeds comfort. *Psychology Today,* February, 32–35, 60–62.

Zajonc, R., & Markus, G. (1975). Birth order and intellectual development. *Psychological Review, 82*, 74–88.

Zaragoza, M., & Koshmider, J. (1989). Misled subjects may know more than their performance implies. *Journal of Experimental Psychology: Learning, Memory, and Cognition, 15*, 246–255.

Zaragoza, M., & McCloskey, M. (1989). Misleading postevent information and the memory impairment hypothesis: Comment on Beli and reply to Tversky and Tuchin.

Journal of Experimental Psychology: General, 118, 92–99.

Zaragoza, M., McCloskey, M., & Jamis, M. (1987). Misleading postevent information and recall of the original event: Further evidence against the memory impairment hypothesis. *Journal of Experimental Psychology: Learning, Memory, and Cognition, 13*, 36–44.

Zelnick, M., & Kantner, J. (1977). Sexual and contraceptive experiences of young un-married women in the United States, 1976 and 1971. *Family Planning Perspectives, 9*, 55–71.

Zelnick, M., & Kantner, J. (1980). Sexual activity, contraceptive use, and pregnancy among metropolitan-area teenagers: 1971–1979. *Family Planning Perspectives, 12*, 230–237.

Zhang, G., & Simon, H. (1985). STM capacity for Chinese words and idioms: Chunking and acoustical loop hypotheses. *Memory and Cognition, 13*, 193–201.

Ziegler, J. (1984). Scientists ponder drinkers, drunks, differences. *The Oregonian*, July 5, B4–B5.

Zigler, E., & Berman, W. (1983). Discerning the future of early childhood intervention. *American Psychologist, 38*, 894–906.

Zigler, E., & Seitz, V. (1982). Social policy and intelligence. In R. Sternberg (Ed.), *Handbook of Human Intelligence*. Cambridge, England: Cambridge University Press.

Zilbergeld, B. (1983). *The Shrinking of America: Myths of Psychological Change*. Boston: Little, Brown.

Zimbardo, P. (1975). Transforming experimental research into advocacy for social change. In M. Deutsch and H. Hornstein (Eds.), *Applying Social Psychology: Implications for Research, Practice and Training*. Hillsdale, NJ: Erlbaum.

Zimbardo, P., Anderson, S., & Kabat, L. (1981). Induced hearing deficit generates experiment paranoia. *Science, 212*, 1529–1531.

Zimmer, D. (1983). Interaction patterns and communication skills in sexually distressed, maritally distressed, and normal couples: Two experimental studies. *Journal of Sex and Marital Therapy, 9*, 251–265.

Zimmerman, J., Stoyva, J., & Metcalf, D. (1970). Distorted visual feedback and augmented REM sleep. *Psychophysiology, 7*, 298.

Zubenki, G., Moossy, J., & Koop, U. (1990). Neurochemical correlates of major depression in primary dementia. *Archives of Neurology, 47*, 209–214.

Zuckerman, B., Frank, D., Hingson, R., Amaro, H., Levenson, S., Kayne, H., Parker, S., Vinci, R., Aboagye, K., Fried, L., Cabral, H., Timperi, R., & Bauchner, H. (1989). Effects of maternal marijuana and cocaine use on fetal growth. *The New England Journal of Medicine, 320*, 762–768.

Zuckerman, M. (1979). *Sensation Seeking: Beyond the Optimal Level of Arousal*. Hillsdale, NJ: Erlbaum.

Zuger, B. (1989). Homosexuality in families of boys with early effeminate behavior: An epidemiological study. *Archives of Sexual Behavior, 18*, 155–165.

Photo Credits

N A M E   I N D E X

Note that boldface page numbers correspond to photos or photo sources, and italic page numbers correspond to tables.

Abel, E., 99
Abraham, K., 588
Abramson, L., 590
Abroms, K., 414
Abu-Mostafa, Y., 18
Adams, J., 446
Adams, K., 178
Ader, R., 228
Adler, A., 538–539
Adorno, T., 684
Aikawa, J., 105
Ainsworth, M., 432, 434–435, 436
Ajzen, I., 671
Alain, M., 225
Aldrich, M., 86
Alexander, 380
Alkon, D., 261–262
Allen, 687
Allen, M., 590
Allen, S., 699
Allport, G., 252, 524–526, 527
Almli, C., 287
Altman, J., 93
Altura, B. M., 105
Amabile, T., 683
Ames, M., 306
Amice, V., 440
Amit, Z., 145
Amkraut, A., 341
Amoore, J., 142
Anand, B., 284
Anastasi, A., 500, 549
Anch, A., 180, 185
Anderson, J., 247, 248
Anderton, B., 478
Anderton, C., 188
Andreasen, N., 586, 604
Andrews, S., 699
Anisfeld, M., 241
Anisman, H., 341
Annas, G., 416
Appley, M., 332
Apter, M., 294, **295**
Archer, S., 460

Arend, R., 435, 528
Aristotle, 3
Arkes, 368
Arlin, P. A., 468
Arlow, J., 624
Armentrout, J., 446
Armstrong, S., 354
Arnetz, B., 342
Aronson, E., 282, 679, 682
Arrowood, J., 691
Arthur, A., 345
Arthur, R., 337
Asch, S., 663, 665, 686–687
Aserinsky, E., 169
Ashcraft, M., 380
Ashman, G., 292
Ashmore, R., 683
Aslin, R., 377
Athanasiou, R., 42
Atkinson, J., 279
Atkinson, R., 235, 257
Attie, I., 292
Aubert-Tulkens, G., 184
Austrom, D., 469
Avison, W., 649

Bachrach, A., 635
Backer, R., 277
Baer, P., 223
Bahnson, C., 341
Baillargeon, R., 424
Baker, D., 430
Baker, L., 339
Baldwin, J., 464
Bale, J., 93
Balon, R., 576
Balota, D., 248
Baltrusch, H., 341
Bancroft, J., 299
Bandura, A., 218, 224, 278, 375, 544, 545–546, 572, 574, **640**, 672, 696, **697**
Barahal, H., 646
Barbee, A., 408

Barber, T., 190, 191
Bard, P., 320, 321
Barinaga, M., 414, 592
Barlow, D., 567, 568
Barnes, D., 478, 602, 603
Barnett, P., 590
Baron, M., 592, 602
Baron, R., 668, 682, 689, 692
Barrera, 264
Bartlett, F., 251–252
Bartrop, R., 344
Bartusiak, M., 167
Bartzokis, G., 651
Baryshnikov, M., **499**
Bass, B., 473
Baudry, M., 261
Baumeister, R., 681
Baumrind, D., 49, 436
Baur, K., 39, 298, 300, 466
Beach, F., 298, 300, 304
Beal, G., 700
Beck, A., 586, 588, 631, **640**
Beitman, B., 643
Belec, L., 307
Belfer, M., 464
Belicki, D., 185
Belicki, K., 185
Belinson, M., 297
Belko, 309
Bell, A., 304, 305
Bell, R., 694
Belsky, J., 472
Bem, D., 528, 672
Bemis, 291
Benbow, C., 430
Benelli, B., 376
Bennett, J., 414
Benson, 380
Bergin, A., 642
Bergman, C., 502, 504
Berkowitz, L., 687, 695–696, 697
Berlyne, D., 294
Berman, E., 648
Berman, J., 644

Berman, W., 505
Berndt, T., 462
Bernstein, R., 440
Berry, D., 184
Berscheid, E., 692
Besson, J., 144, 145
Best, A., 296
Best, J., 370, 371
Bexton, W., 296
Beyreuther, K., 478
Bianchi, B., 582
Bias, L., 103
Bick, P., 598
Binet, A., 423, 487–489
Bingol, N., 103
Bini, L., 648
Bino, L., **640**
Bird, E., 604
Birmaher, B., 651
Bischoff, L., 465
Black, B., 567
Black, I., 262
Black, P., 478
Blaine, J., 649
Blake, R., 112, 131, 136, 139
Blander, A., 81
Blaney, P., 256
Blasi, A., 460
Bleuler, E., 596
Bliss, E., 581, 582
Bloch, S., 639
Bloch, V., 178
Block, J., 528
Bloom, F., 263, 264, 284, 446
Bloom, L., 379, 393
Blum, H., 622, 623
Blum, K., 102, 103
Bobrow, G., 150
Bodamer, M., 399
Bohannon, J., 375
Bolles, R., 224
Bolter, A., 105
Bonnet, M., 170, 180, 183
Bonthius, D., 100
Boon, S., 641

Boor, 582
Booth, A., 472
Booth, D., 284
Bootzin, R., 185
Boring, E., 156
Borke, H., 426
Borkovec, T., 607
Bornstein, P., 292
Borysenko, J., 342
Borysenko, M., 342
Bouchard, T., 503, 547
Bourne, L., 352, 354, *357*, 367
Bousfield, W., 245
Bower, G., 245, 246, 256
Bowers, K., 188, 190
Bowlby, J., 434
Boyce, P., 587
Boyd, J., 567, 583
Boyle, C., 595
Bradburn, N., 39
Bradbury, T., 670
Brady, J., 579
Braff, D., 598
Branconier, R., 106
Brandenburg, H., 415, 416
Brannon, L., 481
Braungart, J., 547
Breakerfield, X., 413
Brecher, E., 43
Brecher, R., 43
Breckler, S., *671*
Breggin, P., 648–649
Brehm, J., 680
Bremer, J., 298
Bremer, T., 280
Breslau, N., 571
Brett, J., 337
Breuer, 11
Breuer, J., 529
Brewer, W., 252
Brewster, D., 3
Briddell, D., 46
Bridgman, P., 80
Bridwell, L., 278
Brigham, J., 663, 673, 675, 682, 697
Brittain, C., 462
Brobeck, J., 284
Broca, P. P., 85
Brodbeck, A., 375
Brody, J., 288, 475
Brodzinsky, D., 454, 465
Broering, J., 463, 464
Brooks, J., 690
Brooks-Gunn, J., 292, 455
Brouilette, R., 184
Browman, C., 180
Brown, B., 461
Brown, J., 236, 344

Brown, R., 256, 257, 306, 375, 378, 379
Bruch, H., 290
Bruner, J., 354, 664
Bryden, M., 418
Buchsbaum, M., 93
Bugelski, R., 683
Bunney, W., 593
Bures, J., 80
Burger, G., 446
Burlingame, G., 638
Burns, H., 255
Burroughs, W., 99
Burt, C., 503
Burton, S., 184
Buschke, H., 245
Bushman, B., 689
Buss, A., 524
Buss, D., 692
Butcher, J., 628
Butler, R., 480
Butters, N., 262
Butterworth, G., 138
Byrne, D., 668, 682, 689, 691

Cacioppo, J., 680, 681
Cadoret, R., 592, 608
Cadwallader, M., 470
Cain, W., 142
Cairns, K., 472
Calley, W., 689
Cambi, F., 413
Cameron, N., 584
Campbell, A., 472
Campbell, C., 286
Campbell, D., 543
Campbell, E., 590
Campbell, R., 285
Campbell, S., 178, 179, 299
Campos, J., 155
Cannon, W., 283, 320, 321
Cantor, N., 664
Capatides, J., 379
Capron, C., 504
Carboni, E., 97, 101, 103
Carden, S., 81
Carelli, M., 376
Carey, P., 299
Carlen, P., 100
Carlson, A., 283
Carlson, B., 585
Carlson, N., 67, 73, 98, 99, 101, 103, 104
Carlsson, A., 73, 604
Carlsson, M., 73, 651
Carlston, D., 666
Carpenter, W., 651
Carroll, L., 464
Carson, R., 338, 340, 628

Carter, A., 300, 586
Carter-Salzman, L., 504
Cartwright, R., 182
Carver, C., 340, 676
Cash, T., 692
Casper, C., 292
Castillo, M., 138
Castro, F., 101
Catania, A. C., 24–28
Cate, R., 462
Cattell, R., 15, 524, 526–527
Ceci, S., 255
Cerletti, U., **640**, 648
Cesselin, F., 72
Chadwick, D., 197
Chaiken, S., 676
Chambers, D., 643
Chandler, C., 255, 258
Chang, T., 247
Channon, S., 292
Chaouch, A., 144, 145
Charcot, J., 529
Charlesworth, E., 338
Charney, D., 73, 594
Chase, M., 170, 171
Chase, T., 581
Chasnoff, L., 103
Chason, K., 470
Check, J., 699
Cheney, D., 383, 384
Chesno, F., 607
Chess, S., 435
Chitwood, D., 307, 464
Chomsky, N., 375–376
Chorover, S., 264
Choy-Kwong, M., 103
Chozick, B., 80
Christenson, S., 505
Christopher, F., 462, 699
Chu, G., 680
Chumlea, W., 454
Churchland, P. M., 18
Churchland, P. S., 18
Cialdini, R., 688
Ciesielski, K., 574
Cirignotta, F., 183
Clarizio, H., 217
Clark, A., 478
Clark, C., 87
Clark, D., 256, 574
Clark, E., 378
Clark, M., 246
Clarke, A. D., 434
Clarke, A. M., 434
Clarke-Stewart, K., 422, 436
Cleckley, H., 582, 606
Clinton, B., 41
Cloninger, C., 576
Clouser, R., 255
Cochran, S., 308

Cohen, D., 182
Cohen, N., 228
Cohen, S., 332, 345
Cohn, J., 432
Colasanti, B., 73, 652
Colditz, G., 101
Cole, D., *586*
Coleman, J., 510, 565
Coles, C., 100
Collecter, M., 342
Collins, A., 247, 249
Collins, R., 505
Colman, A., 698
Colwill, R., 223
Comerford, M., 307, 464
Commons, M., 468
Condon, W., 377
Condry, J., 280
Connally, J., 674
Conrad, H., 466
Conrad, R., 241
Contrada, 345
Cook, 86, 441
Cook, N., 87
Cook, S., 681
Coons, E., 81
Coope, J., 299
Cooper, C., 336
Cooper, J., 69, 678
Cooper, L., 351
Cooper, R., 507
Coopersmith, S., 436
Coplan, A., 479
Coppen, A., 593
Corbit, J. D., 326
Coren, S., 116, 123, 138
Corkin, S., 647
Corrigan, R., 387
Corsini, R. J., 624, 631
Cortes, R., 73, 604
Coryell, W., 586
Cosby, B., **690**
Costa, P., 337
Costello, C., 649
Costill, D., 465
Cotman, C., 72
Covington, M., 681
Cowart, B., 141
Cowie, V., 602, 608
Cox, G., 292
Cox, J., 286
Cox, V., 284
Coyne, J., 589
Craighead, L., 309
Craik, F., 247, 249
Craske, M., 567, 568
Crick, F., 178, 234, 261
Crisafi, 353
Crocker, J., 683
Cronbach, L., 501

Crooks, R., 39, 298, 300, 301, 466, 637, 649
Crowder, R., 239
Crowe, R., 576, 608
Croyle, R., 678
Csikszentmihalyi, M., *461*, 462
Cumming, D., 595
Cunningham, C., 100
Cunningham, G., 299
Curtis, R., 691

Dahmer, J., 18
Dale, P., 378
Damasio, A., 380, 381
Damasio, H., 381
Danks, H., 661
Dare, C., 292
Dark, V., 115, 149
Darley, J., 5, 661, 662
Darwin, C., 10, 275, 323
Datan, N., 472
Dattore, P., 342
Davidson, C., 100
Davidson, G., 188
Davidson, J., 299, 443
Davidson, R., 320
Davies, G., 255
Da Vinci, L., 534, *565*
Davis, D., 506
Davis, G., 571, 573
Davis, H., 138
Davis, J., 286, 287, 288
Davis, P., 259
Davison, G., 73, 570 , 583, 585, *586*, 588, 651
Deater, T., 210
DeBono, K., 673
DeCasper, A., 377
Deci, E., 278
Declerck, A., 183, 191
Defries, J., 35, *501*
Dehne, N., 100
DeLaber, J., 478
Delamater, J., 463
Del Boca, F., 683
Dember, W., 118
Dembroski, T., 340
Dement, W., 169, 176, 179, 184
DeMeo, P., 470
Dempster, F., 258
Denicoff, K., 95
Denmark, F., 42
Dennerstein, L., 299
Denney, N., 477
Depue, R., 73, 93
DeRios, M., 104
Derogatis, L., 342
Descartes, R. 8
Desimone, R., 149

Detera-Wadleigh, S., 592
Deutsch, M., 256, 685
DeValois, K., 131
DeValois, R., 131
De Villiers, J., 377
De Villiers, P., 377
Devine, W., 105 – 106
Devlin, M., 292
Devulder, J., 145
Deykin, E., 100
Diamond, 86, 441
Diamond, M., 306, 445, 446
Dickens, C., 480
Dickie, J., 479, 480
Diener, E., 676
Dietz, W., 289
Dilsaver, S., 567, 568
DiMascio, A., 652
Dion, K., 692
DiVita, J., 155
Dobelle, W., 126, **127**
Dodson, J., 294
Doering, C., 466
Dollard, J., 695
Domjan, M., 209, 638
Donaldson, G., 467
Donchin, E., 92
Donnelly, J., 647
Dorfman, R., 300
Dorpat, T., *586*
Dosher, B., 244
Douglass, A., 184
Dourish, 286
Douvan, E., 461
Dove, A., **500**
Dow, 299
Doyle, J., 446
Dressler, W., 339, 344
Dudley, R., 502, 504
Dudycha, G., 527
Duggan, J., 284
Duke, M., 568, *586*, 595, 651, 653
Duncan, C., 603
Dunham, R., 453
Durel, A., 340
Durgunoglu, A., 244
Durkin, K., 432
Dusek, D., 101, 104
Duyme, M., 504
Dyer, S., 280
Dywan, J., 188

Eagly, A., 679, 681
Easterbrooks, M., 436
Ebbinghaus, H., 250, 257
Eberhardt, M., 223
Echterling, L., 189
Eckholm, E., 477
Edlund, M., 575

Edwards, 368
Egan, J. 116
Egeland, J., 591 – 592
Ehrhardt, A., 442, 445
Eibl-Eibesfeldt, I., 150, 694
Eich, E., 256
Eichler, V., 169
Eichmann, A., 689
Eichorn, D., 467
Eimas, P., 376, 377
Einstein, A., **495**, 565
Eisenberg, N., 688
Ekman, P., 320, 323, 324, *325*
Eli, I., 189
Elias, S., 416
Ellis, A., 628 – 631, **640**
Ellis, L., 306
Ellis, R., 100
Emerson, P., 432
Emmerick, H., 462
Emmerling, D., 189
Engel, E., 157
Ennis, R., 456
Entwisle, D., 430
Epstein, A., 285
Epstein, L., 289
Epstein, R., 385
Epstein, S., 528
Erikson, E., 404, 431, 437 – 439, 468, 469, 471, 474, 480
Erkut, S., 668
Erlenmeyer-Kimling, L., 35
Erlich, S., 184
Eron, L., 696, 698
Esquirol, J., 587
Esterling, B., 342
Estes, W., 234, 256
Ettinger, R., 286
Evans, F., 188
Evans, J., 368
Evans, R., 697
Eveleth, P., 454
Everington, C., 291
Everitt, B., 80
Everly, G., 575
Everson, C., 176
Eysenck, H., 642

Fackelman, K., 106
Fairburn, C., 292
Falloon, J., 307
Fantino, E., 212, 217, 223
Farley, F., 295
Farrer, L., 478
Faustman, W., 570
Fava, M., 292
Fazio, R., 673, 676
Feather, N., 280
Feingold, A., 431
Feist, J., 481

Fennell, M., 590
Fernald, D., 349
Ferrante, 412
Ferrer, J., 7, 81
Ferster, C., 588
Feshbach, N., 472
Feshbach, S., 549, 680, 696
Festinger, L., 278, 281, 677, 690
Field, T., 339, 432, 436
Fifer, W., 377
Fincham, F., 670
Findlay, J., 299
Finn, S., 524
Fischbach, G., 61, 64
Fischer, J., 461, **602**
Fishbein, M., 671
Fisher, 186
Fisher, C., 344
Fisher, S., 537, 538
Flavell, J., 377, 378
Fleischmann, 35
Fleming, I., 335
Fletcher, G., 665
Flynn, J., 467
Foley, J., 151
Foley, V., 639
Folkman, S., 332, 333
Folle, H., 256
Follingstad, D., 696
Fontaine, R., 575
Fontana, A., 344
Forbes, J., 7, 81
Ford, C., 298, 300, 304
Ford, M., 426
Forgays, D., 297
Forrester, W., 245
Forsyth, D., 687
Fortenberry, J., 106
Fosson, A., 291
Foster, G., 43
Foulkes, D., 170
Fouts, R., 393, 398
Fox, P., 93
Fox, S., 101
Frank, E., 652
Frank, J., 644
Frankenhaeuser, M., 335
Frankish, C., 240
Fraser, S., 688
Freedman, F., 567
Freedman, J., 680, 688, 697 – 698
Freeman, A., 66, 69
Freeman, W., 646
Freud, S., 10 – 11, 15, 182, 259, 305, 524, 528 – 538, 540, 566, 571, 572, 580, 588, 607, 621 – 624, **640**
Friedman, M., 339, 343

Friedman, T., 416
Friedrich-Cofer, L., 697
Friesen, W., 323, *325*
Frodi, A., 696
Frumkin, B., 241
Fuhrer, M., 223
Fuhriman, A., 638
Fukuda, M., 284
Fulker, D., 504
Furuhjelm, M., 299

Gadnow, K., 698
Gaffney, F., 574
Gage, D., 256
Gagnon, J., 446
Gaito, J., 35
Gaitwell, N., 306
Galef, B., 80
Galina, H., 145
Gall, C., 478
Gallagher, W., 300
Gallatin, J., 462
Galligan, R., 472
Gallistel, C., 7, 81
Galton, F., 485, **486**, 487, 488, 506
Gambosh, D., 181
Ganong, A., 72
Garbarino, J., 696
Garber, J., 589, 632
Garcia, E., 34, 183
Garcia, J., 204
Gardner, A., 383
Gardner, B., 383
Gardner, B. T., 393, 396–399
Gardner, H., 496, 498–499, 515, 518–521
Gardner, R. A., 393, 396–399
Garlicki, J., 286
Garvey, M., 587
Gates, A., 266
Gawin, F., 103
Gazzaniga, M., 87
Geary, D., 431
Gebhart, G., 145
Geen, R., 280, 285, 287, 696
Geffen, G., 87
Gehringer, W., 157
Geiselman, R., 255
Geisser, 93
Gelder, M., 568, 574
Gelenberg, 652
Gelfand, M., 300
Gelman, R., 426
Genovese, K., 661, **662**
Gentry, W., 340
George, C., 218
Geracioti, T., 292
Gerard, H., 685, 687
Gergen, K., 676

Gerner, R., 292
Gerrard, M., 463
Gershon, 651
Gershon, E., 584, 591, 592
Gesell, A., 403
Geshwind, N., 87
Getchell, T., 141
Geyer, M., 598
Giannini, A., 652
Gibbs, J., 286
Gibling, F., 255
Gibson, E., 154, 377
Gibson, J., 154
Gieringer, D., 106
Giles, D., 584
Gillam, B., 158
Gilliam, G., 696
Gillie, O., 503
Gilligan, C., 456
Giordano, P., 687
Girdano, D., 101, 104
Glaser, R., 35
Glass, D., 335, 339, 340
Glass, G., 642
Glazebrook, A., 683
Gleason, J. B., 375, *379*
Glick, P., 473
Glucksberg, S., 358
Goate, 478
Goethals, G., 670
Gold, P., 260
Gold, R., 287
Goldberg, S., 406
Goldberg, W., 436
Goldberger, L., 296
Golden, N., 100
Goldfarb, W., 406, 434
Goldfield, M., 644
Goldfried, M., 643
Goldgaber, D., 478
Goldman-Rakic, P., 266
Goldstein, E., 112, 122, 127, 138, 139
Goldstein, I., 340
Goldstein, L., 700
Goldstein, M., 566, 570, 571, 573, *586*, 587, 595
Goleman, D., 532
Goodall, J., **43**
Goodchilds, J., 699
Goodwin, *586*
Goodwin, D., 256
Goodwin, F., 585, 593
Gooren, L., 299
Gordon, H., 87
Gorelick, P., 100, 101
Gormally, J., 637
Gorman, J., 567, 568, 574, 575
Gormly, A., 454, 465
Gorski, R., 441

Gotlib, 472
Gotlib, I., 589, 590
Goto, S., 412
Gottesman, I. I., 602, 612–616
Gottfredson, G., 19
Gough, H., 552
Gould, J., 223, 376
Gould, S. J., 485
Gray, 464
Gray, C., 244
Green, B., 570, 571
Green, D., 116
Green, E., 420
Greenberg, M., 436
Greenberg, R., 180, 340, 537, 538
Greenberg, S., 261
Greeno, J., 224
Greenough, W., 261, 420, 476
Greenwood, S., 416
Gregory, R. L., 158
Grey, J., 73, 603, 604, 651
Grief, E., 460
Griffith, *181*
Griffiths, P., 306
Griffitt, W., 691
Grillon, C., 598
Grilo, C., 289
Grochowicz, P., 228
Grossman, M., 283
Groves, 694
Groves, P., 145, 476
Guilford, J. P., 496
Guilleminault, C., 184
Gummerman, K., 244
Gureje, O., 651
Gurin, J., 287, 309
Gusella, J., 413
Gustafson, G., 378
Gustafson, R., 183, 191, 696
Guthrie, W., 412
Guttman, R., 503
Guze, S., *578*
Gwirtsman, H., 292

Haber, R., 244
Hagestad, G., 465
Haggerty, R., 345
Halas, E., 223
Hales, D., 184
Haley, J., 651
Hall, J., 184, 204, 218, 410
Hall, W., 421
Halpern, D., 366, 429, 430, 431
Hamamy, H., 414
Hamburg, D., 454
Hamilton, D., 253
Hamilton, E., 590
Hamilton, J., 298, 595

Hammen, C., 584, 589
Hammersmith, S., 304
Hammond, 368
Hampson, J. G., 445
Hampson, J. L., 445
Hanel, K., 469
Haney, C., 48
Haney, D., 288, 289
Hanna, G., 431
Harburg, E., 340
Hardy, J., 116, *117*
Hare, R., 607
Harlow, H., 293, 406, 432, 433, 434
Harlow, M., 432
Harper, R., *629*
Harrell, J., 340, 341
Harris, A., 598
Harris, E., 576
Harris, K., 378
Harris, L., 418
Hartmann, E., 178, 182, 185
Hartshorne, H., 527
Harvey, E., 169
Haseltine, F., 440
Hasher, L., 252
Hatcher, R., 595
Hatfield, E., 692
Hathaway, S., 550
Hatton, D., 339
Haurin, R., 463
Havinghurst, R., 473
Hawkins, R., 227
Hawn, P., 418
Hay, I., 95
Hayes, C., 383
Hayflick, L., 477
Haynes, S., 339
Hearnshaw, L., 503
Hearst, N., 307, 308
Heath, R., 7, 80–81, 547
Hebb, D., 260–261, 262, 265, 293, 420
Heider, E., 387
Heider, F., 665, 677
Heider, K., 303
Heim, N., 298
Hein, K., 463
Heinrichs, D., 651
Henderson, A., 478
Henderson, N., 35, *501*
Heninger, G., 73, 594
Henker, F., 466
Henly, A., 339
Hennivan, E., 178
Henry, W., 644
Hepper, P., 694
Herdt, G., 443
Hering, W., 129–130
Herman, J., 170, 181

Hermaphroditus, 441
Herrnstein, R., 31
Hertzog, C., 467
Herz, M., 651
Herzog, A., 479, 480
Hess, W., 284
Hesse-Biber, S., 291
Heston, L., 306, 478
Hetherington, A., 284
Hicks, R., 34, 183, 340
Hilgard, E., 186, 189–190
Hingson, R., 464
Hippocrates, 523
Hirsch, J., 289
Hirschhorn, R., 416
Hitler, A., **525**
Hobart, G., 169
Hobfoll, S., 332
Hobson, A., 180
Hobson, J., 79
Hockett, C., *383*
Hodgkin, J., 440
Hodgkins, J., 465
Hodgkinson, S., 592
Hoebel, B., 287
Hofferth, S., 463
Hoffman, L., 472, 474
Hohmann, G., 318
Holden, C., 50
Holen, M., 259
Holiday, H., 477
Holinger, P., *586*
Hollabaugh, L., 699
Hollon, S., 632
Holmes, D., 41
Holmes, J., 641
Holmes, T., 336, 337
Holway, A. H., 156
Honzik, C., 222, *223*
Hooley, J., 584
Hopkins, B., 377
Horn, J., 467, 474, 475
Horner, M., 280, 281
Horney, K., 538, 539–540
Horowitz, M., 571
Horton, D., 256
Hott, 607
Houston, B., 341
Houston, J., 276, 280, 287,
    293, 294, 350
Houston, M., 95
Hovland, C., 678, 679, 680,
    683
Howard, A., 19, 20
Hubbard, J., 261
Hubbard, T., 6
Hubel, D., 125
Huck, J., 448
Huesmann, L., 696
Huggins, G., 416

Hughes, J., 101
Hull, C., 276, 282, 354
Hulley, S., 307, 308
Hulse, 204
Hunt, J. M., 505
Hurvich, L., 128, 130, 131
Hutchings, B., 608
Hyde, J., 429, 430–431, 446
Hypnos, 186

Iacono, W., 73, 93
Imperato-McGinley, J., 443
Inhelder, B., 387
Insko, C., 673, 691
Ironson, G., 344
Irwin, D., 238
Irwin, M., 342
Irwin, O., 375
Isaacs, G., 587
Itabashi, H., 184
Izard, C., 325

Jabbari, B., 93
Jacklin, C., 429, 446, 447
Jackson, B., **669**
Jacobs, G., 127, 131
Jacobs, L., 691
Jacobson, E., 350
Jacobson, G., 644
Jacques, J., 470
James, F., 188
James, W., 10, 14, 155, 275–
    276, 318, 320, 321, 324
Jameson, D., 130
Jamison, *586*
Jamison, K., 586
Janda, L., 692
Janet, P., 580
Janiger, O., 104
Janis, I., 680
Janowitz, H., 283
Janson, P., 473
Jarvik, L., 35
Jayaratne, S., 643
Jemmott, H., 342, 344, 345
Jensen, A., 508, 509, 510
Jensen, J., 643
Jeste, D., 478
Joe, G., 99
Johnson, D., 604
Johnson, J., 100
Johnson, M., 252, 256, 430
Johnson, T., 477
Johnson, V., 43, 299
Johnston, W., 115, 149
Johnstone, E., 604
Jones, D., 142
Jones, E., 665–666, 667
Jones, H., 466
Jones, M., 455

Jones, R., 680
Jones, W., 248
Jorgensen, B., 41
Jorgensen, R., 341
Judd, C., 691
Julien, R., 101
Jung, C., 538

Kagan, J., 406, 434
Kahn, J., 340
Kahneman, D., 369, 370, 371
Kalat, J., 79
Kaler, S., 412
Kales, A., 176, 183
Kales, J., 34
Kalil, R., 420
Kalinowsky, L., 646, 648
Kallman, F., 306
Kamarck, T., 344
Kamin, L., 223, 503
Kandell, E., 225, 226, 227
Kane, J., 651
Kang, J., 478
Kanin, E., 699
Kantner, J., 463
Kaplan, G., 480
Kaplan, M., 604
Kaprio, J., *586*
Karabenick, S., 280
Karlen, A., 446
Karni, A., 178
Karno, M., 567
Kasparov, G., **19**
Kater, S., 80
Katschnig, K., 576
Katz, P., 683
Katzman, R., 478
Kaufman, J., 696
Kaushall, P., 243
Kaye, W., 292
Keating, D., 456
Keegan, D., 652
Keesey, R., 287, 309
Kellerman, H., 184
Kelley, H., 665, 667–668
Kellner, R., 578, 580
Kellogg, L., 383
Kellogg, W., 383
Kelman, H., 679
Kendall, P., 640
Kendler, K., 602
Kennedy, J., 603
Kennedy, K., 307
Kennell, J., 406
Keon, T., 473
Kesey, K., 646
Kessler, S., 603
Ketterlinus, R., 462
Kety, S., 593, 602, 649
Keys, A., 290

Kiecolt-Glaser, J., 35
Kierkegaard, S., 582, 583
Kiernan, J., 699
Kihlstrom, J., 255
Kilham, W., 689
Killinger, W., 256
Kilman, P., 607
Kilmann, P., 648
Kiloh, L., 647
Kimble, D., 73, 603
Kimble, G., 20, 98
Kimura, D., 86, 431, 441
Kimzey, S., 344
King, B., 649
King, D., 245
King, N., 343
King, T., 103
Kingsbury, S., 16
Kingsley, J., 233
Kinsbourne, M., 256, 598
Kinsey, A., 299, 303, 463
Kirkpatrick, B., 651
Kitzes, L., 138
Klagsbrun, F., 471
Klaich, D., 305
Klaus, M., 406
Kleber, H., 103
Klein, D., 572, 574
Klein, R., 434
Kleinhauz, M., 189
Kleinmuntz, B., 552, 553
Kleitman, N., 169
Klineberg, O., 510
Knittle, J., 289
Knussmann, R., 299
Ko, G., 651
Koelling, R., 204
Koenig, O., 30
Koffka, K., 12, 148
Kohlberg, L., 444, 456, 457–
    460
Köhler, W., 12–13, 148
Kohn, A., 472
Kokotovic, A., 644
Kolata, G., 310, 440, 585, 592,
    648
Kolb, B., 66, 264
Koop, C., 412
Korsakoff, S. S., 264
Koshmider, J., 255
Kosnik, A., 304
Koss, L., 698
Kosslyn, S. M., 25, 28–31
Kotelchuck, M., 436
Koulack, D., 679
Kraemer, G., 594
Kraeplin, E., 596
Kramer, D., 468
Kramer, J., 100
Krantz, D., 337, 340

Krasner, L., 601
Kringlen, **602**
Kripke, D., 167, 183
Kristeller, J., 296
Kroll, N., 255
Kroll, P., 577
Krueger, H., 292
Krupnick, J., 571
Kuehnel, J., 632
Kulik, J., 256, 257, 480
Kulka, A., 279
Kupfer, D., 652
Kupperman, H., 300
Kurtines, W., 460
Kushida, C., 180
Kutash, I., 621, 622, 639

Labouvie-Vief, G., 477
Lacey, J., 574
Lagerspetz, K., 694
Laird, 372
Lamb, M., 406, 436
Lambert, M., 642
Lambert, W., 244
Lancet, D., 141, 142
Landesman, S., 307
Landon, A., 41
Lang, P., 636, *637*
Lange, C., 318, 320, 321, 324
Langer, D., 73
Langer, E., 671
Langlois, J., 692–693
Langolf, G., 34
Lanza, R., 385
Lanzetta, J., 326
LaPiere, R., 675
Larson, R., *461*, 462
Lashley, K., 262
Latané, B., 5, 607, 661, 662
Laudenslager, M., 342
Lauer, J., 471
Lauer, R., 471
Lavie, P., 173
Lawrence, J., 308
Lawson, D., 47
Lawton, M., 344
Lazarus, R., 332, 333, 338
Leconte, P., 178
LeDoux, J., 87, 88, 573
Lee, E., 510
Lefkowitz, M., 697
Leigh, B., 464
Lemon, B., 479
Lenneberg, E., 418
Leon, B., 288
Lepage, A., 696
Lerner, J., 692
Lerner, R., 462, 692
Lester, D., *586*
Levene, J., 639

Levenson, R., *325*
Leventhal, 345
Leventhal, H., 323, 680
Levitsky, W., 87
Levy, A., 292
Levy, S., 342
Lewin, J., 181
Lewinsohn, P., 589
Lewis, C., 437
Lewis, E., 137, 456
Lewis, J., 472
Lewis, S., 99
Lewontin, R., 509
Lewy, A., 587
Leyens, J., 696
Liberman, R., 632
Libet, J., 589
Liddle, R., 292
Lieberman, M., 479
Liebert, R., 543
Lieblich, I., 244
Liebowitz, M., 569, 574
Lifson, A., 307
Lima, A., 645
Lind, D., 579
Lindgren, H., 456
Linn, M., 431, 494
Linton, M., 698, 699, 700
Lipper, S., 73, 603, 651, 652
Lipton, R., 103
Liston, E., 649
Litwin, G., 279
Livson, N., 455
Locke, J., 3, **8**, 403
Locke, S., 342, 345
Loehlin, J., 503, 508, 602, 603
Loftus, E., 42, 247, 253–255, 257
Loftus, G., 257
Logan, C., 223
Loomis, A., 169
Lorch, R., 248
Lorenz, K., **405**, 406, 694
Lougainis, G., **147**
Lourea, D., 308
Lovass, O., 375
Luborsky, L., 642
Luce, G., 176
Luchins, A., *363*
Luchins, E., *363*
Luddens, H., 78
Lumsdaine, A., 680
Lykken, D., 607
Lynch, G., 80, 261
Lyon, P., 303

Maas, J., 593
Maccoby, E., 406, 429, 447
MacCorquodale, P., 463
Macdonald, R., 653

MacPhillamy, D., 589
Maddi, S., 338
Maddison, S., 286
Magaro, P., 256
Mahler, H., 480
Mahone, C., 279
Mahowald, M., 171
Maier, S., 590
Main, M., 218
Maj, J., 73
Malamuth, N., 699
Malmstrom, P., 376
Manis, J., 472
Mann, L., 689
Mannion, K., 304
Manson, J., 288
Manuck, S., 340
March, J., 570, 575
Markman, E., 379
Marks, I., 292
Markus, G., 506
Marler, P., 223, 376, 382
Marmor, J., 305
Marshall, D., 302
Marshall, G., 323
Marshall, J., 336
Martin, D., 303
Martin, J., 413, 473
Martin, P., 342, 345
Maslach, C., 323, 687
Maslow, A., 13–14, 277–278, 540, 541–542, 543
Mason, J., 332
Masters, C., 478
Masters, W., 43, 299
Matas, L., 435
Mathews, A., 300
Matlin, M., 361, 367
Mattson, M., 80, 101
Max, L., 350
May, M., 527
Mayer, J., 256, 285, 288, 290
Mayer, R., 358, 359
Mayer-Gross, W., 602
Mayleas, D., 472
Mazziotta, J., 412
McArthur, L., 447
McBride, 472
McCall, G., 696
McCarley, R., 79, 180
McCarthy, J., 103
McClelland, D., 29, 278, 279, 281
McCloskey, M., 255
McConnell, J., 35, 49
McCoy, H., 307, 464
McCrae, R., 337
McDonald, B., 473

McDonough, R., 99
McDowd, J., 249
McEnroe, J., **666**
McFarlane, A., 336
McGillis, D., 665
McGillivry, B., 603
McGinty, D., 182
McGrath, M., 182
McGraw, M., 422
McGuire, W., 679, 680, 681
McHugh, M., 41
McIntosh, T., 105
McKey, R., 505
McKinley, J., 550
McKinney, W., 594
McKoon, G., 244
McLeod, P., 306
McSherry, J., 292
Mead, M., 444–445
Meador, B., 625
Meany, M., 334–335
Medin, D., 351, 354
Mednick, S., 599, 607, 608, 694
Meer, J., 474, 475
Meerwaldt, J., 418
Mefford, I., 184
Megargee, E., 552
Meichenbaum, D., 344
Meilman, P., 145
Melamed, B., 636, *637*
Mellor, C., 598
Melson, W., 673
Meltzoff, A., 424
Melville, J., 568
Melzack, R., 145
Mendelson, J., 103
Mendez, M., 412
Mendlewicz, J., 592
Menustik, C., 635
Merckelbach, H., 202
Merikangas, K., 100
Merkel, W., 292
Mervis, 353
Messenger, J., 302
Metcalfe, J., 256
Metzler, J., 241
Mewborn, D., 680
Meyer, D., 249
Meyer, R., 345
Meyer-Bahlburg, H., 306
Michel, K., *586*
Milavsky, J., 698
Miles, C., *586*
Milgram, S., 48, 49, 50, 460, 688–689
Miller, A., 184, 689
Miller, G., 240, 246, 373
Miller, I., 102, 103, 652
Miller, J., 413

Miller, K., 691
Miller, L., 106
Miller, M., 190
Miller, N., 343, 683, 695, 696
Miller, T., 642
Miller, W., 123
Mills, C., 256
Mills, J., 282, 679
Milner, P., 33, 260, 263, 265
Mirsky, A., 603, 647
Mischel, W., 523–524, 527, 545, 664
Mishkin, M., 243, 264
Mita, T., 691
Mitchison, G., 178
Mitler, M., 180
Miyago, *181*
Moen, P., 474
Moffett, M., 382
Mohs, M., 510
Molfese, D., 418
Molfese, V., 418
Moller, S., 595
Monaghan, D., 72
Money, J., 306, 440, 442, 445
Moniz, A. de E., **640**, 645–646
Monjan, A., 342
Monroe, L., 182, 183
Montgomery, R., 343
Moore, C., 426
Moore, M., 424
Moore, R., 169
Mora, F., 7, 81
Morales, F., 170, 171
Moran, J., 149
Morden, B., 179
Moreland, R., 690, 691
Morgan, C., 283
Morgan, J., 283
Morhland, J., 145
Mori, E., 85
Morris, J., 279
Morris, N., 300, 436
Morris, R., 261
Morrison, A., 170
Moses, N., 291
Mosher, D., 446
Mott, F., 463
Moyer, K., 694
Muehlenhard, C., 698, 699, 700
Mullen, B., 335, 687
Murdock, B., 234
Murnen, S., 691
Murphy, G., 652
Murray, H., 278–279, 554
Murray, J., 652
Murray, W., 139
Mussen, P., 455
Muter, P., 236

Muuss, R., 292
Mwamwenda, B., 456
Mwamwenda, T., 456
Myers, B., 406

Naeser, M., 86
Nakamura, A., 72
Nakamura, G., 252
Nathan, M., 503
Nathan, R., 338
Nathans, J., 122, 127, 128, 129
Naus, M., 247
Neale, J., 73, 570, 583, 585, *586*, 588, 651
Neely, J., 244
Neill, J., 104
Neisser, U., 236, 238, 251
Nelson, K., 375
Nelson, P., 261
Nemiah, J., 572
Nerenz, D., 680
Neugarten, B., 464, 465, 475, 480
Neugarten, D., 464, 475
Newell, A., 360, 361, 372
Newman, H., 503
Newman, L., 675
Newman, P., 462
Newsom, C., 217
Nicassio, P., 183
Nield, T., 245
Niemcryk, S., 339
Niijima, A., 286
Nisbet, J., 467
Nisbett, R., 665, 669
Nolen-Hoeksema, A., 595
Norcross, J., 643
Norman, D., 150, 247
Norman, R., 131
Norton, G., 567
Norton, N., 644
Norton-Ford, J., 640
Novak, M., 406, 434
Novick, D., 100
Novin, D., 286
Nowicki, S., 568, *586*, 595, 651, 653
Nurnberger, J., 591, 592
Nuttin, J., 690
Nye, F., 474

Oaster, T., 259
Obrist, P., 340
O'Connell, M., 463
O'Connor, R., 225
Oden, G., 350
Offer, D., 462
Offer, J., 462
Ogawa, K., 255
Ogden, J., 86, 87

Ohman, A., 574
Ohno, O., 440
Ohtsuka, T., 129
Olds, *421*
Olds, J., 7, 33, 80
Olds, M., 7, 81
O'Leary, 345
O'Leary, A., 345
Oliver, D., 387
Olson, G., 72
Olton, D., 223
O'Neal, J., 596
Oomura, Y., 285
Orlansky, H., 422
Orne, M., 189, 293, 582
Ornstein, P., 247
Orth-Gomér, K., 344
Orzacki, M., 647
Osborne, R., 510
Oscar-Berman, M., 100
O'Shea, R., 151
Ostrov, E., 463
Oswald, I., 178

Padawer, W., 644
Pagano, B., 255
Page, D., 440
Pagel, J., 184, 185
Paige, S., 570
Paivio, A., 244
Palca, J., 176
Palmer, A., 477
Palmer, J., 254, 570
Palmore, E., 476
Palthe, T., 377
Panksepp, J., 72
Papalia, *421*
Pardes, H., 416, 602
Park, B., 663
Parke, R., 218, 696
Parker, G., 587, 595
Parrott, A., 699
Patterson, G., 696
Patterson, K., 87
Paulsen, K., 430
Pavlov, I., 11, 199–201, 202, **205**, 223
Paykel, E., 588
Peacock, D., 197
Pearlman, C., 180
Pellegrini, R., 340
Pendergast, C., 18
Penfield, W., 112
Pennebaker, J., 333
Penrod, S., 677, 687, 697
Perley, M., *578*
Perlman, D., 478
Perlmutter, M., 477
Perls, F., 624, 626–627, **640**
Perrot, P., 112

Perry, J., 606
Perry, S., 652
Persky, H., 300
Peskin, H., 455
Peterman, T., 307, 308
Peters, S., 584, 589
Peterson, A., 455
Peterson, C., 589, 590
Peterson, L., 236
Peterson, M., 236
Peterson, P., 679
Petty, R., 680, 681
Phares, E., 622
Philips, B., 184
Piaget, J., 387, 404, 423–429, 456
Pillemer, D., 256
Pilon, D., 281
Pincus, H., 7
Pitman, R., 570
Plato, 3
Pleck, 474
Pliner, P., 688
Plomin, R., 35, *501*, 502, 504, 547
Plutchik, R., 316–317
Pogue-Geile, M., 289
Pollin, **602**
Pomerleau, O., 342
Pomeroy, W., 304
Pons, 35
Posner, M., 357
Postman, L., 252
Powell, M., 676
Powley, T., 287, 309
Prange, A., 593
Pratt, W., 463
Premack, D., 384, 393
Prien, R., 652
Prioleau, L., 644
Prochaska, J., 643
Psaltis, D., 18
Pugeat, M., 298
Pugh, E., 123
Putnam, F., 581, 582
Pylyshyn, Z., 351

Qualls, P., 343
Quillian, M., 249
Quinn, R., 473

Rabin, B., 342
Rabkin, J., 572
Rachlin, H., 371
Rachman, S., 572
Rader, N., 155
Radloff, L., 595
Rahe, R., 336, 337
Rainer, J., 592

Ranson, S., 284
Raphelson, A., 280
Rapoport, J., 570, 575
Ratcliffe, R., 244
Ratner, N., *379*
Ray, M., **130**
Raymond, C., 184
Raynor, J., 279
Readhead, C., 416
Rebec, G., 145, 476
Rechtschaffen, A., 176, 177
    180
Redei, E., 100
Reed, R., 142
Regier, D., 567
Register, P., 255
Reichard, S., 480
Reiger, D., 596
Reilly, R., 456
Reinisch, J., 694
Reinke, B., 472
Reker, G., 480
Relman, A., 106
Renneker, R., 341
Rescorla, R., 200, 202–203,
    223
Resko, B., 447
Restak, R. M., *476*
Reynolds, D., 296
Rholes, W., 256
Ribble, M., 434
Rice, M., 375, 378
Richards, J., 155
Richardson, A., 244
Richardson, J., 351
Riche, M., 469, 470
Ridenour, M., 422
Riegel, K., 468
Ries, W., 289
Ripley, H., *586*
Rips, L., 354, 365
Riskind, J., 256
Ritzer, G., 473
Robbin, A., 646
Robbins, D., . 567
Roberts, M., 377
Robertson, M., 585, 592
Robins, L., 568, 570, 577, 606
Robinson, L., 589, 632
Rock, I., 155
Rodin, J., 289, 290, 335, 341,
    342
Roffwarg, H., 181
Rogentine, G., 342
Rogers, C., 13, 447, 463, 540–
    541, 542, 543, 624–626,
    640
Rogers, M., 342
Rogers, R., 680
Roggman, L., 435

Rohrbaugh, J., 41
Rollins, B., 472
Rook, K., 344
Roosevelt, F. D., 41
Rorschach, H., 553–554
Rosch, E., 353, 354–355
Rose, G., 289
Rose, J., 137, 212
Rosenbaum, L., 679
Rosenbaum, W., 679
Rosenberg, S., 664
Rosenbloom, 372
Rosenfield, D., 683
Rosenhan, D., 460
Rosenman, R., 339
Rosenthal, D., 576
Rosenthal, N., 587, 594, 602
Rosenzweig, M., 261, 418–420
Roses, A., 478
Ross, A., 537, 551, 552
Ross, C., 581, 582
Ross, H., 446
Ross, M., 665
Rossi, A., 604
Roth, L., 288
Rothbart, M., 663
Rothblum, E., 41
Rothman, S., 499, 508
Rotter, J., 278
Rouche, B., 649
Rousseau, J., 403
Rousseau, L., 298
Routowicz, A., 245
Roviario, S., 344
Rovine, M., 472
Rowley, H., 103
Rubin, J., 446
Rudel, R., 87
Rudy, T., 145
Rumbaugh, 393
Rumbaugh, D., 384
Rumelhart, D., 29, 247
Rush, A., 652
Rushton, J., 694
Russek, M., 285
Russell, D., 699
Rutherford, E., 137
Rutter, D., 432
Ryterband, E., 473

Sachdev, P., 647
Sack, R., 587
Sackheim, J., 649
Sadker, D., 447
Sadker, M., 447
Saegert, S., 690
Safer, M., 256
Sager, C., 641
Salovey, P., 335, 341
Salter, W., 486

Salzinger, K., 613, 616–619,
    645
Sander, L., 377
Sanders, G., 472, 691
Sanderson, J., 286
Sandhu, 86, 441
Sano, K., 81
Santee, R., 687
Sarason, I., 336
Satow, A., 113
Savage-Rumbaugh, E., 384
Saxby, L., 418
Scarr, S., 504, 505, 510
Schacheve, K., 473
Schachter, S., 321–323, 607
Schaffer, H., 432
Schaie, K., 467
Schare, M., 256
Scheibe, K., 293
Scheier, M., 676
Schein, E., 678
Schell, D., 477
Schellenberg, 478
Schenck, M., 171
Schiffman, H., 115, 144, 154
Schildkraut, J., 593
Schiller, P., 264
Schlegel, R., 339
Schleifer, S., 344
Schlesier-Carter, B., 292
Schmechel, D., 478
Schmidt, M., 170
Schmidt, U., 292
Schmitt, M., 286
Schneidman, E., *586*
Schou, M., 652
Schroeder, D., 337
Schuele, J., 344
Schulsinger, F., 608
Schumacher, M., 80
Schvaneveldt, R., 249
Schwartz, B., 218, 219
Schwartz, G., 259, 320
Schwartz, J., 261
Schwartz-Bickenbach, D., 101
Scovern, A., 648
Scribner, S., 456
Seagall, M., 159
Searle, J., 18
Sears, D., 680
Sears, P., 408
Sears, R., 408, 683
Sedney, M., 444, 446
Segal, M., 690
Segal, N., 503
Seiden, R., *586*
Seitz, V., 505
Sejnowski, T., 261
Sekuler, R., 112, 131, 136, 139
Seligman, M., 589, 590

Selye, H., **328**, 329–332
Selzer, M., 336
Sem-Jacobsen, C., 81
Semple, M., 138
Serbin, L., 447
Seyfarth, R., 383, 384
Shaffer, 341
Shaffer, D., 673
Shanab, M., 689
Shapiro, C., 178
Shapiro, D., 340
Shatz, M., 420, 426
Shaw, D., 593
Sheehan, P., 255, 343
Sheffield, F., 276, 277
Shepard, R., 241
Shepherd, M., 576
Shepherd, R., 351
Sherif, M., 682–683, 685
Sherrington, R., 602
Sherwin, B., 300
Shettleworth, S., 223
Shevitz, S., 647
Shields, J., 306, 503, 576, 602,
    612
Shields, N., 696
Shiffman, 465, 475
Shiffrin, R., 235, 257
Shipley, T., 300
Shisslak, C., 292
Short, J., 691
Shotland, R., 700
Shoulson, I., 412
Shweder, R., 460
Siegel, D., 327, 455
Siegel, M., 446
Siegel, S., 327
Silva, M., 376
Silverman, S., 138
Simkin, J., 626, 627
Simon, H., 240, 360, 361
Simon, T., 487, 488
Simoni, G., 415, 416
Simons, R., 183
Simpson, D., 99
Singer, D., 697
Singer, J., 167, 321–323,
    335
Singer, L., 406
Singh, S., 100
Sirvioö, R., 478
Skeels, H., 406, 504, 505
Skinner, B. F., 12, 25, 207–
    208, 351, 375, 385, 392,
    480, 543–544, 547
Sklar, L., 341
Skowronski, J., 666
Skyrms, B., 365
Slade, A., 435
Slater, E., 576, 602, 608, 613

Sloane, R., 644
Slocum, W., 474
Smith, B., *586*
Smith, D., 414
Smith, E., 351, 354
Smith, F., 188
Smith, G., 286
Smith, K., 139
Smith, M., 445, 642, 643
Smith, P., 34
Smith, S., 351
Snarey, J., 460
Snyder, M., 528, 676, 692
Snyder, S., 97
Snyderman, M., 499, 508
Sohlberg, S., 291, 292
Sokolov, E., 261
Solomon, 692
Solomon, G., 341
Solomon, R., 326
Solomon, Z., 570
Solso, R., 352, 374
Sommers-Flanagan, J., 340
Sonnenschein, D., 167
Sontag, S., 466
Sorenson, R., 463
Spanier, G., 462
Spanos, N., 188
Spearman, C., 495–496
Specht, J., 543
Speechley, K., 649
Speed, N., 571
Spelke, E., 377
Sperling, G., 236, 237
Sperry, R., 87
Spiegel, D., **187**
Spiegler, M., 543
Spielberger, C., 340
Spielman, A., 191
Spillman, D., 291
Spiro, 253
Spitz, R., 434
Sprafkink, J., 698
Spray, D., 144
Sprechler, S., 692
Squire, L., 262
Sroufe, L., 435
Staddon, J., 286
Stampfer, M., 100
Stangor, C., 676
Stanley, J., 430
Stanton, P., 261
Stark, E., 188
Steiger, H., 292
Stein, J., 78
Stein, L., 604, 651
Stellar, E., 284
Stephan, W., 683
Stern, D., 42

Stern, J., 188
Stern, L., 488
Sternberg, R., 486, 496–498, 499, 514–518
Stevenson, H., 510
Stevenson, J., 503
St. George-Hyslop, P., 478
Stine, E., 375
Stokes, J., 471
Straus, E., 286
Straus, M., 696
Strickland, L., 687
Striegel-Moore, R., 292
Stroop, *115*
Strunin, L., 464
Strupp, H., 643
Struss, 380
Studdiford, W., 300
Stunkard, A., 289, 309
Subin, 264
Suddath, R., 604
Suedfeld, P., 296
Suls, J., 335
Suomi, S., 406
Suter, W., 456
Sveback, S., 294, **295**
Swann, W., 589, 676
Swanson, J., 256
Swartz, M., 577
Swedo, S., 570, 575
Swets, J., 116
Syndulko, K., 607

Tache, J., 341
Tagiuri, R., 664
Tago, *181*
Tajfel, H., 682
Takanishi, R., 454
Tambs, K., 503
Tamminga, C., 478
Tanford, S., 687
Tanner, J., 454
Tanzi, R., 478
Tartter, V., 375, 377, 378, 384, 385
Tauber, M., 446
Tauber, R., 210
Tavris, C., 697
Taylor, H., 446
Taylor, S., 18, 329, 332, 335, 340
Taylor, V., 699
Teasdale, J., 256, 584
Teitelbaum, P., 285, 287
Telch, M., 567
Tellegen, A., 503, 547
Templer, D., 101
Terman, L., 407–408, 486, 488, 489
Terrace, H., 385, 392–396

Terry, W., 506
Tesser, A., 673, 676
Teuting, P., 593
Thatcher, R., 429
Thelen, M., 292
Thibaut, J., 687
Thigpen, C., 582
Thoman, E., 446
Thomas, A., 435
Thomas, C., 341
Thomas, J., 472
Thompson, C., 245, 587
Thompson, D., 285
Thompson, G., *130*
Thompson, J., 309, 649
Thompson, R., 78, 262, 263, 440
Thompson, S., 286, 335
Thorndike, E., 11, 207, 208, 509
Thorndyke, P., 252
Thurstone, L. L., 496, 671
Tienari, **602**
Timmerman, M., 292
Tinbergen, 233
Titchener, E., 9
Tokunago, K., 284
Tolchin, M., *586*
Tolman, E., 222, *223*, 278
Tolstedt, B., 471
Tomarken, A., 323
Tomita, T., 123
Tomkins, S., 324, 446
Torgersen, 576
Torrey, E. F., 614
Tourney, G., 306
Townshend, P., 139
Tracey, T., 644
Travers, J., 139
Treisman, A., 238
Tresemer, D., 280
Tripp, P., 176
Troll, L., 465
Tronick, E., 432
Trujillo, K., 81
Trumbull, R., 332
Tryon R., 507
Tucek, S., 478
Tuchin, M., 255
Tulving, E., 243, 244, 247, 257
Turk, D., 145, 343
Turkkan, J., 223
Turner, J., 682
Turner, S., 574
Tversky, A., 369, 370, 371
Tversky, B., 255

Udry, J., 299
Ullman, L., 601
Ulmer, D., 339, 343

Undén, A., 344
Underwood, B., 258
Urrutia, A., 78, 99

Vaillant, G., 606
Valenstein, E., 85, 646, 647
Valian, V., 379
Van Cantfort, T., 399
Vanderweele, D., 286
Van Dongen, H., 418
Van Egeren, L., 339, 340
Van Osten, **349**
Van Praag, H., 593
Van Thiel, D., 100
Vega-Lahr, N., 339
Veitch, R., 691
Veleber, D., 101
Velley, L., 7, 81
Venables, P., 599
Veroff, J., 472
Vinigan, R., 100
Vink, R., 105
Vinokur, A., 336
Visintainer, M., 341
Vogel, G., 180
Von Békésy, Georg, 137
Von Frisch, K., 382
Von Helmholtz, H., 8, 128, 129
Von Meduna, L., 647–648
Von Winterfeldt, 368

Wadden, T., 188
Wahba, N., 278
Waldrop, M., 18
Waldvogel, J., 111
Walk, R., 154
Wall, H., 245
Wall, P., 145
Wallace, 186
Wallach, L., 543
Wallach, M., 543
Wallbom, M., 676
Walling, M., 299, 300
Wallis, C., 144
Walsh, J., 180
Walster, E., 679
Walters, J., 294, **295**
Walters, R., 218, 696
Waltz, E., 341
Wang, M., 66, 69
Wangensteen, O., 283
Ward, C., 588
Ward, L., 116, 123, 138
Ward, T., 99
Warga, C., 145
Warm, J., 118
Warren, R., 681
Washburn, A., 283
Wason, P., 364–365

Waterman, A., 460
Waters, E., 435
Waters, H., 448
Watkins, C., 643
Watkins, J., 582
Watkins, M., 256, 690
Watson, D., 333
Watson, J., 11–12, 350–351, 403
Watson, R., 470
Watts, J., **640**, 646
Weaver, C., 257, 473
Webb, W., 170, 178, 180, 183
Weber, E., 114
Wechsler, D., 486, 489–490
Wehr, T., 583, 587, 594
Weigel, R., 675
Weilburg, J., 575
Weinberg, M., 304
Weinberg, R., 502, 504, 505, 507, 510
Weinberger, 604
Weiner, B., 549
Weiner, R., 648, 649
Weisberg, R., 358
Weiskrantz, 385
Weiss, 295
Weissbach, T., 682
Weissman, M., 568, 583, 588, 592, 652
Wender, P., 592
Wernicke, C., 86
Wertheimer, M., 12, 148
West, J., 100
Wetli, C., 103
Wetzel, C., 691
Wetzler, S., 256

Wever, E., 138
Whishaw, I., 66, 264
Whitam, T., 223
White, L., 472
White, P., 99, 570
White, W., 598
Whitehead, M., 299
Whitman, C., 16
Whitman, F., 306
Whorf, B., 386–387
Wickens, C., 118
Wicker, A., 675
Widom, C., 693
Wiens, A., 635
Wiesel, T., 125
Wiesenfeld, A., 344
Wilder, D., 682, 687
Wilhelm, K., 595
Wilkinson, 380
Williams, A., 106
Williams, D., 223
Williams, K., 643
Williams, P., 445
Williams, R., 289, 339, 500
Williams, T., 697
Williamson, G., 345
Williamson, P., 170
Willows, D., 696
Willshaw, D., 261
Wilmore, J., 465
Wilson, A., 414
Wilson, B., 47
Wilson, E., 693–694
Wilson, G., 46
Wilson, M., 304
Wilson, R., 503
Wilson, S., 191

Wilson, T., 665
Wing, J., 599
Wing, R., 289
Winograd, E., 256
Winston, P., 18
Winterbottom, M., 281
Wirtshafter, D., 287
Wise, C., 604
Wise, R., 81
Wittig, M., 280
Wolf, A., 621, 622, 639
Wolfe, J., 211
Wolff, G., 288
Wolff, K., 434
Wolkin, A., 73, 603
Wolpe, J., 572, 633, **640**
Wolpert, E., 648
Wong, D., 73, 603, 604
Wood, J., 185
Wood, W., 679
Woods, B., 604
Woods, R., 87
Woody, C., 262
Wooley, S., 291, 292
Wragg, R., 478
Wright, J., 100
Wright, R., 103
Wu, C., 673
Wulff, J., 277
Wundt, W., 9
Wurtman, J., 587, 594
Wurtman, R., 175, 290, 478, 587, 594
Wyrwicka, W., 284

Yadalam, K., 651
Yahya, K., 689

Yalom, I., 639
Yalow, R., 286
Yarrow, L., 406
Yates, A., 292
Yelon, S., 217
Yeomans, J., 238
Yerkes, R., 294
Yesavage, J., 106
Young, P., 416
Young, R., 286
Young, T., 128, 129
Youniss, J., 462
Ysseldyke, J., 43
Yu, B., 240
Yudofsky, S., 648

Zabin, I., 463
Zajonc, R., 332, 506, 690, 691
Zanna, M., 673
Zaragoza, M., 255
Zellman, G., 699
Zelnik, M., 463
Zhang, G., 240
Ziegler, J., 99
Zigler, E., 505, 696
Zilbergeld, B., 642
Zimbardo, P., 48, 50, 323, 475
Zimmer, D., 471
Zimmerman, J., 181
Zimmerman, R., 432
Zubek, J., 507
Zubenki, G., 593
Zuckerman, B., 103
Zuckerman, M., 295
Zuger, B., 306

S U B J E C T   I N D E X

Note that boldface page numbers correspond to boldface text entries.

Abnormal behavior, defining, 563–564, **565**
Abnormal prenatal differentiation, 441–443
Absolute threshold, **113**
Accommodation, **122, 423**–424
Accumulating damages theory, **477**
Accused, The, 661
Acetylcholine (ACh), 71–72, 176
Achievement motivation, 278–279
  influencing, 281
Achievement tests, **494**–495
Acoustic coding, 240–241
Acquaintance rape, 698–700
Acquired drives, 276
Acquired immunodeficiency syndrome.
  See AIDS
Acquisition, 205
Acronyms, **246**
Acrostics, **246**
ACTH (adrenocorticotropic hormone),
  96
Action potential, **66**–67
Activation–synthesis hypothesis, 181
Active listening, **625**
Active stage, of schizophrenia, 599
Activity theory, 479
Adapt, 333
Adaptation, **116**
  dark and light, 123–124
Addiction. *See* Drugs
Additive color mixing, 127–**128**
Adenosine deaminase deficiency (ADA),
  416
Adolescence, 453–464
  cognitive development during, 455–456
  moral development in, 456–460
  physical development during, 454–455
  Piaget's formal operations stage, 456
  premarital sex and, 463–464
  psychosocial development in, 460–464
  sexual development and, 462–464
Adolescent growth spurt, **454**
Adoption studies, intelligence and, 504

Adrenal cortex, 96
Adrenal medulla, 97
Adrenals, **96**–97
Adulthood, 464–474
  cognitive development in, 466–468
  physical development in, 465–466
  psychosocial development in, 468–474
Aerial perspective, **153**
Affect, and emotion, 315–316
Affective disorders. *See* Mood disorders
Afferent neurons, **64**
Affiliation, 276
Afterimages, 131
Age
  and job satisfaction, 473–474
  sleep patterns and, 174
Aggression, 693–698
  biological bases of, 693–695
  psychological bases of, 695–698
Aging. *See also* Older years
  double standard of, 466
  neuronal changes in, 476
  theories of, 476–477
Agoraphobia, 568
  biology and, 576
  panic attacks and, 574
AI. *See* Artificial intelligence
AIDS (acquired immunodeficiency syn-
  drome), **307**
  and premarital sex, 463–464
  sexual behavior and, 307–308
  stress and, 342
Alarm, 330
Alcohol, 99–100
  sexual behavior and, 42
Algorithm, **359**–360
All-or-none law, **67**–68
Alternate-forms reliability, **493**
Alzheimer's disease, 71–72, 260,
  478
  memory and, 233
Amacrine cells, 123
Ambiguity, and stress, 335–336
American Psychiatric Association, *Diag-*

nostic and Statistical Manual (DSM),
  566
American Psychological Association
  (APA), **19**–20
  ethics guidelines of, 49–50
American Sign Language (ASL), chim-
  panzee study and, 383
Ames room, 157
Amine theory of mood disorders, 593–
  594
Amnesia, 260
  dissociative, 580
  and electroconvulsive shock therapy,
  264
Amniocentesis, **415**–416
Amniotic fluid, 416
Amphetamines, **101**–102
Amplitude, in beta waves, 171
Amygdala, **80,** 573
Anabolic steroids, 299
Anal stage, **536**
Anandamide, 106
Androgen insensitivity syndrome (AIS),
  442
Androgens, 97, **298,** 299–300
Androgyny, 444
Angel dust (PCP), 104, 105
Animals
  behavior of, 6–7
  dreaming and, 180
  emotional expressions of, 323
  ethics and studies of, 7, 49
  intelligence vs. environmental research
  and, 507
  language studies with, 382–385, 392–
  399
  learning and, 197
Anorexia nervosa, **291**–292
Anterograde amnesia, **260**
Antiandrogens, 298
Antianxiety, 650
Antianxiety drugs, **652**–653
Antidepressant drugs, 73, 650, **651**–652
Antimanic drugs, 650, **652**

Antipsychotic drugs, 650, **651**
Anti-Semitism, 684
Antisocial personality disorder, 605, **606**–608
Anxiety, **532**
  and defense mechanisms, 532–535
  tranquilizers and, 652–653
Anxiety disorders, **567**–577
  theoretical perspectives on, 571–577
Anxiety hierachy, 633
APA. *See* American Psychology Association
Apes, language competence of, 392
Aphasia, 85
  Wernicke's, 380
Aplysia, classical conditioning of, 225–227
Applied research, 34–35
Appraisal, 332–333
Aptitude tests, **494**–495
Aqueous humor, 121
Archetypes, **538**
Army Alpha test, **490**
Army Beta test, **490**
Arousal, **293**
  and emotions, 294–295
  variations in preferences, 295–297
Artificial embryonation, 415
Artificial insemination, **415**
Artificial intelligence (AI), **18, 371**–373
Artificial vision, 126–127
Asch experiments, 686–687
Assimilation, **423**–424
  in memory, 252
Association, networks of, 247–249
Association cortex, **84**
Association fibers, 84
Association theory, 354
Atmospheric perspective, **153**
Atonia, 170
Attachment, 431–436, **432**
  deprivation of, 433–434
Attention, **115**
  selective, 149–150
Attitudes, **671**–681
  acquisition of, 672–673
  changing, 677–681
  function of, 673–674
  as predictors of behavior, 674–675
  recognition of, 676
  specificity of, 676
Attractiveness, and interpersonal behavior, 692–693
Attribution errors, 668–670
Attribution theory, **665**–671
  and socially undesirable behavior, 666–667
Audience, and persuasion, 680–681
Audition, 131–139
  theories of, 137–138

Auditory canal, 134
Auditory localization, **138**
Auditory nerve, 137
Auditory receptors, 136–137
Authoritarian parents, **436**
Authoritarian personality, **684**
Authoritative parents, **436**–437
Authority, conformity, compliance, and obedience to, 687–689
Autonomic lability, 574
Autonomic nervous system (ANS), 63, **74**
Autonomy, 438
Availability heuristic, **369**–370
Aversive conditioning, 634–635
Avoidance conditioning, **210**–211
  two-factory theory of, 221
Avoidant personality disorder, 605
Axon, **65**

Babbling, 378
Backward conditioning, **204**
Balance. *See* Equilibrium
Balance theory, **677**
Barbiturates, 98
Bar graph, 51
Basal ganglia, **82, 575**
Basic anxiety, **539**
Basic hostility, **539**–540
Basic level, **353**
Basilar membrane, **136**
Behavior. *See also* Brain; Central nervous system (CNS); Conditioning
  animal, 6–7
  attitudes as predictors of, 674–675
  biology of, 60–109
  descriptions vs. explanations of, 527–528
  disorganized or catatonic, 599
  human, 5–6
  impact on attitudes, 676–677
  learning and, 197–231
  motivational explanations of, 274–297
  neurotransmitters and, 73
  psychology as study of, 4
  scientific method and, 33–36
  sexual motivation and, 297–308
  social expectations and, 675–676
  social influence on, 685–689
  and stress, 333–335, 344
  thinking as, 350–351
Behavioral disorders, 562–619
  abnormal behavior, 563–564, 565
  anxiety, 567–577
  biological bases of, 612–619
  biologically-based therapies for, 645–653
  classifying, 566–567
  dissociative disorders, 580–582
  mood disorders, 582–595

personality disorders, 604–608
  psychological therapies for, 621–641
  schizophrenia, 595–604
  seeking professional help for, 653–654
  somatoform disorders, 577–580
  treatment of, 620–657
Behavioral observation, **548**–549, 672
Behavioral perspective
  on anxiety disorders, 572–574
  on mood disorders, 588–590
  on schizophrenia, 601–602
Behavioral response, to emotions, 316
Behavioral theories of personality, 524, 543–544
Behavioral therapy, 640
  for behavioral disorders, **632**–638
Behavioral vs. cognitive approaches, 24–31
Behaviorism, **11**–12
Behavior modification, 635
Belief-bias effect, 367–368
Bell-shaped curve, 493
Benzodiazepines, 653
Beta waves, 171–172
Between-group differences, **508**–509
Bias
  ingroup, 682
  in intelligence tests, 499–501
  observer, 43
Binocular cues, **151**–152
Biochemical theory
  of mood disorders, 592–595
  of schizophrenia, 603–604
Biofeedback, 343
Biological bases of learning, 225–228
Biological factors, and homosexuality, 305–307
Biologically-based motives, **282**
Biologically-based therapies, for behavioral disorders, 645–653
Biological needs, 277
Biological perspective
  on behavioral disorders, 612–619
  on mood disorders, 590–595
  on schizophrenia, 602–604
Biological psychology, **15**–16
Biological rhythms, **168**–169
Biology
  and aggression, 693–695
  and anxiety disorders, 574–577
  and forgetting, 260
  and gender identity, 439–444
  of memory, 260–266
  and personality, 547–548
  social learning, gender roles, and, 445–446
Biomedical therapy, 640
Bipolar (manic-depressive) disorder, **583**, 584–587
  antimanic drugs and, 652

Bipolar cells, 123
Birth cohort, 408
Birth-order studies, 506–507
BITCH. *See* Black Intelligence Test of Cultural Homogeneity
Black Intelligence Test of Cultural Homogeneity (BITCH), 500–501
Blind spot, 123
Blocking, 223
Bodily kinesthetic intelligence, 499
Body senses, 111, **146**
Bonding, 406
Borderline personality disorder, 605
Bradykinins, 144
Brain, 63. *See also* Behavioral vs. cognitive approaches; Emotion; Hearing; Memory; Nervous system; Sleep; Vision
  bisected views of, 77
  cortex, 82–84
  development of, 418–420
  language and, 380–382
  left hemisphere of, 381
  lobes in, 84–86
  magnesium treatment for, 105
  mood disorders and, 592–595
  PET scans of, 61
  and schizophrenia, 603–604
  sex differences in, 86
  sex differentiation of, 440–441
  in sleep, 174–176
  split-brain research, 87–90
  stimulation of, 33
  study of, 90–94
Brain stimulation, **91**
Brightness constancy, **156**
Broca's area, **85**, **380**
Bulimia, **292**
Bystander apathy, **661**

Caffeine, 100–101
California Psychological Inventory (CPI), 552
Cancer, and stress, **341**–342
Cancer-prone personality, **341**
Cannabis sativa, 105
Cannon-Bard theory of emotion, 319, **320**–321, 323
Cardinal trait, **525**
Careers, 472
Case studies, 37, **38**–39
Castration, 298
CAT. *See* Computerized axial tomography
Catatonic behavior, 599
Catatonic schizophrenia, **600**–601
Cathartic method, 529
Caudate nucleus, **82**
Cell body, **64**
Cells, glia, 68

Center sulcus, 84
Central nervous system (CNS), **62**–73, 76–79
Central tendency, 52
Central traits, **525**–526, **665**
Centration, **426**
Cephalocaudal growth pattern, **421**
Cerebellum, **78**
Cerebral cortex, **82**–84
Cerebral hemispheres, **76**
Challenge, 333
Chemicals, neurotransmitters, 71–73
Childhood, 418. *See also* Development
Children, parenting and, 471–472. *See also* Development
Choleric people, 253
Chorionic villi sampling (CVS), **416**
Chromosomal disorders. *See* Inheritance, problems in
Chromosomal sex, 439–440
Chromosomes, **408**–409
Chronological age, 488
Chunking, **240**
Cilia, 136–137
Circadian rhythms, **168**–169
Circumannual cycle, 168
Classical conditioning, **198**–199, 672
  acquisition of, 202
  of aplysia, 225–227
  of immune system, 228
  and operant conditioning, 219–221
  stimulus contingency and 202–203
Classical conditioning therapy, **632**–635
Clever Hans, 349, 384
Climacteric, **466**
Climatotherapy, 587
Clinical psychology, **16**
Closure, 148, 149
Clustering, **245**
CNS. *See* Central nervous system
Cocaine, 102–103
Cochlea, **134**–135, 136
Cochlear duct, 136
Codeine, 98
Coding, in short-term memory, 240–242
Coefficient of correlation, **44**
Coexplorer, 626
Cognition, 348–399
  artificial intelligence (AI), 371–373
  gender and, 429–431
  language, 373–385
  and stress, 344
  thinking and, 350–371
Cognitive Abilities Test (CAT), **491**
Cognitive-behavioral therapies. *See* Cognitive therapies
Cognitive development, 404
  in adolescence, 455–456

in adulthood, 466–468
  birth to adolescence, 423–431
  fifth stage of, 467–468
  four stages of (Piaget), 424–428
  in older years, 477–479
Cognitive dissonance, **281**–282
  theory of, 332, **677**–678
Cognitive expectancies, 278, **281**
Cognitive learning, **199**, 221–225
Cognitive map, **222**
Cognitive processes, in emotion, 315
Cognitive psychology, 14, 349. *See also* Cognition
Cognitive restructuring therapy, **631**–632, 640
Cognitive theories of motivation, 278–282
Cognitive therapies, for behavioral disorders, **628**–632
Cognitive vs. behavioral approaches, 24–31
Cohabitation, **469**
Collaterals, 65
Collective unconscious, **538**
Color blindness, 130. *See also* Color vision
  test for, 129
Color constancy, **156**
Color vision, 127–131
  opponent–process theory of, 129–131
  trichromatic theory of, 128–129
  Young-Helmholtz theory of, 128–129
Commissural fibers, 84
Common sense view of emotion, 319
Communication, nonhuman, 382–385. *See also* Language
Communicator, and persuasion, 678–679
Compliance, 687–688
Computerized axial tomography (CAT), **92**, 93
Computers, 18
  simulation, 27–28
Concept formation, 354–355
Concepts, 351–353
Concordance, 289
Concordant, **410**
Concrete operations stage, 425, **426**–427
Concurrent validity, **494**
Condensed speech, 378
Conditioned reinforcers, **211**–212
Conditioned response (CR), **201**–206
Conditioned stimulus (CS), **201**–206, 220
Conditioned taste aversion, **204**
Conditioning
  classical, 199–207, 672, 673
  learning and, 198–199
  and memory, 262

operant, 207–219, 672–673
second-order, 206–207
Conditioning therapy. *See* Classical conditioning therapy
Conduction hearing loss, **139**
Cones, **122**
Confirmation bias, **364**–365
Conformity, **685**–687
conditions for, 687
Connectionism, **18**
Conscience, 531
Consciousness
dreaming, 179–182
hypnosis, 186–191
sleep, 169–179, 183–186
states of, 166–193
Consciousness-altering drugs, opponent-process theory and, 327
Consensus, 668
Conservation, **426**
Consistency, 668
Consolidation, and memory, **261**
Consonance, 677–678
Constructive memory, 251–256
Context, memory and, 256
Contextual intelligence, 498
Continuity, developmental, 404–405
Continuous reinforcement schedule, **212**
Contrast, 150
Control, and stress, 335
Conventional morality, **457**
Convergence, 151, **152**
Conversion disorder, 578–580
Cooing, 378
Cornea, 121
Coronary heart disease (CHD), and stress, 338–340
Corpus callosum, **87**, 88–90
Correlational method, 37, **44**–45
Correspondent inference theory, **665**–666
Cortex
location of functioning, 83, 84–86
memory and, 265
somatosensory, 85
visual, 86
Counseling psychology, **16**
Counterbalanced General Intelligence Test, 500–501
Counterconditioning strategies, 632
Countertransference, 623
Couple therapy, 640–**641**
Covariation principle, **667**–668
Covert behavior, **351**
CPI. *See* California Psychological Inventory
Creativity, 520–521
Cretinism, 96
Criminal investigations, hypnosis and, 188

Criterion, 117–118
Criterion-keyed test, **550**
Criterion-related validity, **494**
Critical periods, **405**–407
Cross-sectional design, **407**
Cross-sequential design, **408**
Crying, 377–378
Crystallized intelligence, **467**
Cues, retrieval, 247
Cultural bias, in intelligence tests, 499–501
Cultural mores, sexuality and, **301**–303
Cumultive record, **209**
Curare, 351
Curves of forgetting, 250
CVS. *See* Chorionic villi sampling
Cycles, 168
sleep, 173–174
Cystic fibrosis, 414

Dani of New Guinea, 303
language and, 386
Dark adaptation, **123**–124
DAT. *See* Differential Aptitude Tests
Daydream, 167
Death, leading causes of, 338
Death instinct, 530
Decentration, **426**
Decibel levels, 133
Decision making, reasoning and, 365–371
Declarative memory, **243**–244
Deductive reasoning, **365**–366
Deep structure, 376
Deep Thought, **372**
Defense mechanisms, 332, **532**–535
Delayed conditioning, **204**
Delirium tremens, 100
Delta waves, 173
Delusions, **585**
schizophrenia and, 597–98
Dementia. *See* Senile dementia; Dementia praecox
Dementia praecox, 596
Dendrites, **64**–65
Dependent personality disorder, 605
Dependent variable, **46**
Depersonalization, 568
Depo-Provera, 298
Depressants, **98**–100
Depression, 73
antidepressant drugs and, 651–652
gender and, 595
summer, 587
Depressive disorder, 583–584
Deprivation
of attachment, 433–434
sensory, 295–297
Depth perception, 151–153
visual cliff experiment, 154–155

Derealization, 568
Descriptive statistics, 51–53, A-0–A-14
Despair, 439
Determinism, 8
reciprocal, 546
Development
adolescence to end of life, 452–483
adulthood and, 464–474
beginning of life and, 408–417
cognitive, birth to adolescence, 423–431
cognitive, during adolescence, 455–456
cognitive, in older years, 477–479
conception through childhood, 402–451
continuous vs. stage, 404–405
critical periods in, 405–407
of gender identity, 439–448
issues in, 403–407
moral, in adolescence, 456–460
motor, 421–422
physical, from birth to adolescence, 418–422
physical, in adolescence, 454–455
physical, in older years, 475–477
prenatal, 417–418
psychosocial, birth to adolescence, 431–439
psychosocial, in adolescence, 460–464
psychosocial, in older years, 479–481
research designs, 407–408
sexual, and adolescence, 462–464
Developmental psychology, **14**
DHT (dihydrotestosterone)-deficient males, 442–443
Diabetes mellitus, 285
Diagnostic and Statistical Manual (DSM I, II, III, III-R, IV), 566
Dialectic operations, **468**
Dieting, 290–291. *See also* Obesity
Difference threshold, **224**
Differential Aptitude Tests (DAT), 431
Differential reinforcement, 209
Differentiation, gender, 441–444
Diffusion of responsibility, **661**
Direct experience, and attitude acquisition, 673
Direct perception, **154**
Discontinuity, developmental, 404–405
Discrete performance anxiety, 569
Discrimination, **206**, **682**
Discriminative stimulus, **209**
Disease
and causes of death, 338
stress and, 331–332, 338–345
Disengagement theory, 479
Disorders. *See* Behavioral disorders
Disorganized schizophrenia, **600**
Displacement, **533**–534

Dissociation theory, **189**–190
Dissociative amnesia, **580**
Dissociative disorders, **580**–582
Dissociative fugue disorder, **581**
Dissociative identity disorder, **581**–582
Dissonance, 677–678
Distance cues, 152–153
Distinctiveness, 667–668
Distributed memory, 262–263
Distributions, normal, 51–52
Dizygotic twins, **410**
DNA (deoxyribonucleic acid), 64, **410**
Dominant gene, **410**–411
Door-in-the-face technique, **688**
Dopamine (DA), 71, 72
    memory and, 266
Dopamine hypothesis, of schizophrenia, 603
Double standard
    of aging, 466
    male–female, 462–463
Down syndrome, **414**
Dream analysis, 529, **622**
Dreaming, 179–182. *See also* Sleep
    and sleep, 170
Drive, **282**
Drive-reduction theory, 276–277
Drugs
    and behavior, 97–106
    depressants, 98–100
    psychoactive, 649–653
DSM. *See Diagnostic and Statistical Manual*
Dual-code model of memory, **244**
Dualism, 8
Duodenum, 286
Dynamics, personality, 532

Ear. *See also* Audition
    anatomy of, 135
    structure and function of, 134–137
Eating
    biological bases of, 282–287
    disorders, 291–292
Echoic (auditory) memory, **238**–239
ECT. *See* Electroconvulsive therapy
Educational psychology, **16**–17
EEG. *See* Electroencephalography
Efferent neurons, **64**
Ego, 182, **530**, 531
Ego-ideal, 531
Ego integrity vs. despair, 439
Eidetic imagery, **244**
Elaborative rehearsal, **247**
Electrical recording, **91**
Electroconvulsive shock therapy (ECT), **264**, 647–649
Electroculogram (EOG), 171
Electroencephalography (EEG), **92**
    and sleep, 169

Electromagnetic spectrum, 119
Electromyograph (EMG), 171
Electroshock: Its Brain-Disabling Effects, 648
Elevation, 152
Embryonic stage, **417**
Embryo transfer, **415**
EMG. *See* Electromyograph
Emotion(s), 315–328. *See also* Limbic system; Stress
    arousal and, 294–295
    components of, 315–316
    heart rate, skin temperature, and, 325
    punishment and, 218
    range of, 316–317
    and stress, 333
    theories of, 317–328
Emotional discomfort, 565
Emotional expression, schizophrenia and, 598–599
Emotional stress, obesity and, 290
Emotion wheel, 316–317
Empathetic understanding, **625**
Empirical tests, 21
Empiricism, 8
Encoding, **234**–235
    of long-term memory, 245–247
Endocrine system, 81, **94**–97
    location of major glands, 95
Endorphin, 71, 72, **145**
Engineering psychology, **17**
Environment
    and brain development, 419
    and depression, 594–595
    heredity and, 403–404, 501–509, 515–521
Environmental enrichment studies, 504, 505–506
EOG. *See* Electroculogram
EPSPs. *See* Excitatory postsynaptic potentials
Equilibrium, **146**
Escape conditioning, **210**
Eskimos, language and, 386
Esteem needs, 277
Estradiol, 441
Estrogens, **299**
Ethics
    in psychological experiments, 48–50
    of studying animals, 7
Ethnocentrism, 684
Ethology, **693**
Etiological perspective, 567
Evaluation, 54–55
Evoked potentials, 92
Excitatory postsynaptic potentials (EPSPs), **70**
Exemplar theory, **354**–355
Exercise, and stress, 343–344
Exhaustion, 331

Expanded language, 379–380
Expectations, 117, 228
Experience
    and attitude acquisition, 673
    and brain development, 418–420
Experiential intelligence, 498
Experimental groups, **46**
Experimental method, 36, 45–48
Experimental psychology, **15**
Experimental research, **45**–48
Experiments, ethics and, 48–50
Expert systems, **372**
Expressive aphasia, 85
External noise, 116
Extinction, **205**, 217–218, 228
    techniques of, 636
Extroversion, **538**
Eye, 119
    structure and function of, 120, 121–127
Eyewitness testimony, and memory, 253–256

Facial feedback theory of emotion, 323–326
Factor analysis, 495–496
Failure, and motivation, 279–280
Fallopian tube, 408
False alarm, 117, 118
False consensus bias, **670**
Families. *See* Family therapy; Parenting
Family therapy, **639**–640
Fathers, child attachment and, 436
Faulty premises, 367
Fear, 199. *See also* Anxiety disorders
    James-Lange theory and, 318
Fear of success, **280**
Feelings. *See* Emotion
Females. *See also* Gender; Women
    double standard in behavior, 462–463
    fetally androgenized, 441–442
    sexuality, hormones and, 299–300
Fertilization, 409
Fetal alcohol syndrome, 100
Fetally androgenized female, **441**–442
Fetal stage, **417**–418
Fetus, **417**
Fight or flight, 330, 333
Figure, **148**
Film
    and gender roles, 447–448
    violence in, 698
First impressions, 663
Fixation, **536**
Fixed interval (FI) schedule, **214**
Fixed ratio (FR) schedule, **213**
Fixed schedule, 212–213
Flashbulb memory, **256**–257
Flotation chambers, 296–297
Fluid intelligence, **467**

Foot-in-the-door technique, **688**
Forensic psychology, **18**
Forgetting, 257–260. *See also* Memory
  motivated, 259
  organic causes of, 260
Formal operations stage, 425, **428**, 456
Framing, 370–371
Fraternal twins, 35, **410**. *See also* Twins
Free association, **529**, **622**
Free will, 8, 12, 13
Frequency, in beta waves, 172
Frequency theory of pitch discrimina-
  tion, **137**
Frontal lobe, **84**–85
Frustration, and prejudice, 683
Frustration–aggression hypothesis,
  695–696
Functional fixedness, 358, 363–**364**
Functionalism, **10**
Fundamental attribution error, **668**–670
Fundamental frequency, 133

GABA. *See* Gamma-amino-butyric acid
Gambler's fallacy, 369
Gametes, **408**
Gamma-amino-butyric acid (GABA), 71,
  72, 98
Ganglion cells, 123
Gate-control theory, **145**
Gender. *See also* Development, begin-
  ning of life and
  and cognitive abilities, 429–431
  and depression, 595
  differentiation of, 441–444
  trends in differences, 431
Gender identity, **439**–448
  biological influences on, 439–444
  social learning influences on, 444–445
Gender-role expectations, 444
Gender roles, 301, **446**
  socialization of, 446–448
  social learning and biological influ-
    ences on, 445–446
Gender-role stereotyping, 280
General adaptation syndrome (GAS),
  328, **329**, 330
Generalization, stimulus, **205**
Generalized anxiety disorder, **571**
Generalized social anxiety, 569
General problem solvers, **372**–373
Generativity vs. stagnation, 439
Genes, 410–411
Gene therapy, **416**–417
Genetic causes of obesity, 289
Genetic clock, **476**–477
Genetic counseling, **414**–416
Genetic engineering, **416**–417
Genetics. *See also* Heredity
  Alzheimer's disease and, 478–479
  anxiety disorders and, 576–577

and intelligence, 502. *See also* Intelli-
  gence
  markers and, 413. *See also* Inheritance
  and mood disorders, 590–592
  and schizophrenia, 602–604
Genetic tests, 413–414
Genital stage, **536**
Genotype, **410**
Genuineness, **625**
Germ cells, **408**
Germinal (zygote) stag, **417**
Gestalt, 148
Gestalt psychology, 12–13, **626**–627,
  640
G-factor, **496**
Gibson's theory of direct perception, **154**
Glands, endocrine, 94–97
Glia cells, **68**
Glucoreceptors, 285
Glucostatic theory of hunger, **285**–286
Glutamate, 71, 72
Gonadotropins, 94, **454**
Gonads, **97**, **440**
Good continuation, **148**
Graded potential, **66**
Grammar (syntax), 374
Graphs, 51–53
Graying of America, 474–475
Ground, **148**
Groups, competition between, 682–683
Group therapy, **638**–641
Growth
  adolescent spurt in, 454
  physical, 420–421
Guilt, 438
Gustation, **139**–141
Gynecology, 299–300

Hallucinations, **103**–106, **585**
  and schizophrenia, 598
Halo effect, **665**
Handedness. *See* Lateralization of func-
  tion
Harm, 333
Head Start, 505
Health psychology, 17–18
Hearing. *See* Audition
Hearing loss, 238–239
Hebb's cell assemblies, **261**, 265
Hebbian synapses, 420
Hedonic value of emotions, 326
Height on a plane, **152**
Hemispheres, 84
  cerebral, 76
Hemophilia, 412
Heredity
  and environment, 403–404, 501–509,
    515–521
  mechanisms of, 410–412
  and obesity, 289

Heritability, **508**
  and personality, **547**–548
Hermaphrodites, **441**
Heroin, 98–99
Hertz (Hz.), 132
Heuristics, **360**–361
  availability, 369–370
  representative, 368–369
Hierarchy of needs, 277–278
Hippocampus, **80**
Histogram, 51
Histrionic personality disorder, 605
HIV (human immunodeficiency virus),
  307
  and stress, 344
Holophrases, 378
Homeostasis, 81
Homosexual, **303**
Homosexuality, 303–307
  attitudes toward, 304
  incidence of, 303–304
  theories of, 304–307
Horizontal cells, 123
Hormonal sex, 440
Hormones, **94**
  climacteric and, 466
  and sexuality, 298–300
  in sleep, 175–176
Human behavior, 5–6
Human immunodeficiency virus (HIV),
  307
Humanistic psychology, 13–14
Humanistic theories of personality, 524,
  540–543
Humanistic therapies, for behavioral dis-
  orders, 624–628
Human sexuality, Freud and, 11
Humors, theory of, 523
Hunger, 283–287
  biological bases of, 282–287
  obesity and, 287–292
Huntington's disease (chorea), **412**–414
H–Y antigen, **440**
Hyperphagia, 285
Hypertension, and stress, **340**–341
Hyperthyroidism, 95
Hypnosis, **186**–191
Hypochondriasis, **578**
Hypogonadism, 299
Hypothalamic control theory of hunger,
  284–285
Hypothalamic–releasing factors, 94
Hypothalamus, **81**
Hypothesis, 34
Hypothesis-testing theory, 354
Hypothyroidism, 95

Iconic (visual) memory, **237**–238
Id, 182, **530**, 531
Ideal self, 541

Identical twins, 35, **410**. *See also* Twins
Identity, gender, 439–448
Identity vs. role confusion, 438
Idiographic approach, 524
Illusion of control, **670**–671
Illusions, visual, **157**
Immune system
  and cancer, 342
  classical conditioning of, 228
  stress and, 342–345
Immunocompetence, 342
Implicit personality theories, **664**–665
Implicit speech, 350
Impression management, **674**
Imprinting, **406**
Incentives, **276**
Incus (anvil), 134
Independent variable, **46**
Indiscriminate attachment, **432**
Inductive reasoning, **365**
Industrial/organizational (I/O) psychology, **17**
Industry vs. inferiority, 438
Infancy, 418. *See also* Children; Development
Inferential statistics, **53**–54, A-14–A-19
Inferiority complex, 539
Informational social influence, **685**
Information processing, 234
  approach, to intelligence, 496–498, 514–518
Ingroup, **682**
Ingroup bias, **682**
Inheritance. *See also* Genetics; Heredity
  gene therapy and, 416–417
  genetic counseling and, 414–416
  multifactorial, 411
  problems in, 412–414
  sex-linked, 411–412
Inhibitory postsynaptic potentials (IPSPs), **70**
Initiative vs. guilt, 438
Inkblot test. *See* Rorschach inkblot test
Insomnia, **183**
  remedies for, 191
Instincts, **275**
  Freud and, 530
Instinct theory, 275–276
Instrumental conditioning, 207
Insulin, 285
Intelligence, 484–521
  in adulthood, 466–467
  and aging, 477
  animal research and, 507
  changes in, 518–520
  defined, 485–487
  Guilford's structure of intellect theory, 496

heredity and environmental influences on, 501–509, 515–521
  measuring, 487–495
  process theories of, 496–499
  racial differences in, 509–511
  Spearman's two-factor theory, 495–496
  theories of, 495–499
  Thurstone's primary mental abilities theory, 496
  triarchic theory of, 498
Intelligence quotient (IQ), **488**
  heredity, environment, and, 501–502
  race and, 509–511
Intelligence (IQ) tests, 487–495, 514–521
  bias in, 499–501. *See also* Intelligence, theories of
  evaluating, 491–495
  group vs. individual, 490–491
Interaction argument, 404
Interactionist language perspective, 377
Interference, and forgetting, 258–259, 268
Internal noise, 116–117
Interneurons, **64**
Interpersonal aggression, **693**
Interpersonal behavior
  acquaintance rape and, 698–700
  attraction and aggression, 690–698
Interpersonal intelligence, 499
Interpretation, psychoanalysis and, 623–624
Interpretation of Dreams (1900), 182
Interval schedule, 212
Interviews, **549**
Intimacy vs. isolation, 438
Intrapersonal intelligence, 499
Introspection, 9
Introversion, **538**, 544
Invariants, **154**
I/O psychology. *See* Industrial/organizational psychology
IPSPs. *See* Inhibitory postsynaptic potentials
IQ. *See* Intelligence quotient
Iris, 121
Isolation, 438

James-Lange theory of emotion, 317–320, **318**
Jobs, 472–473
  age and satisfaction with, 473–474
Just noticeable difference (jnd), **114**–115

Karotype, **414**
K complex, 173
Kinesthesis, 111, **146**–147

Korsakoff's syndrome, **264**
Krause end bulbs, 144

La belle indifference, 580
Language, 373–385. *See also* Eyewitness testimony; Language acquisition theories
  acquisition of, 374–380
  attributes of human, 383
  brain mechanisms for, 380–382
  expanded, 379–380
  nonhuman communication and, 382–385
  structure and rules of, 373–374
  thinking and, 385–387
  vocalizations and, 377–380
Language acquisition device (LAD), **375**–376
Language acquisition theories, 374–380
  interactionist perspective on, 377
  learning perspective and, 375
  nativistic perspective and, 375–376
Latency period, **536**
Latent content, **182**, 622
Latent learning, **222**, 223
Lateral geniculate nucleus, 125
Lateral inhibition, 123
Lateralization of function, 86–**87**
Lateral sulcus, 84
Law of Effect, **207**, 208
Learned helplessness, **589**–590
Learning
  and behavior, 196–231
  biological bases of, 225–228
  classical conditioning and, 199–207
  cognitive influences on, 221–225
  defined, 198
  latent, 222–224
  observational, 224–225
  operant conditioning and, 207–219
Learning, 24
Learning attitudes, 672–673
Learning perspective, on language acquisition, 375
Lesbianism, 305. *See also* Homosexuality
Lesion production, **90**
Leveling, in memory, 252
Libido, 182, **530**
Life, beginning of, 408–417
Life changes, and stress, 335
Life change units, 336–338
Life instincts, 530
Light, 119
  properties of, 120–121
Light adaptation, **124**
Limbic system, **79**–93
Linear perspective, **153**
Linguistic intelligence, 499
Linguistic-relativity hypothesis, **386**
Lipids, 286

Lipostatic theory of hunger, **286**–287
Little Hans case, 572
Lobes, 84–86
Lobotomy, **645**–647
Logical–mathematic intelligence, 499
Longitudinal design, **407**–408
Long-term memory (LTM), **236**, 242–250
  encoding, 245–247
  processing and, 263–265
  retrieval from, 247–249
  testing, 249–250
  types of, 243–244
Loudness, **132**–133
Love and belongingness needs, 277
LSD (lysergic acid diethylamide), **104**
Lymphocytes, 342

Mach bands, 126
Magnesium, treatment with, 105
Magnetic resonance imaging (MRI), **93**
Maintenance rehearsal, **247**
Major depressive disorder, **583**–584
Maladaptive behavior, 565
Males. *See also* Gender
  double standard in behavior of, 462–463
  sexuality, hormones and, 298–299
Malleus (hammer), 134
Mangaians of Polynesia, 301, 302
Mania, 583
Manic-depressive (bipolar) disorder, 583, 584–587
  antimanic drugs and, 652
Manifest content, **182**, 622
Manus of New Guinea, 301
MAO inhibitors. *See* Monoamine oxidase inhibitors
Maps, cognitive, 14, 222
Marijuana, 105–106
Marine animals, classical conditioning and, 225–227
Marriage, 468, 469, 470–471
  cohabitation before, 469–470
Mask of Sanity, The, 606
Maslow's hierarchy of needs, 277–278
Mathematical skills, and gender, 430
Maturation, **404**, 422
  early and late, 454–455
Mean, **52**
Means-end analysis, **360**–361
Measure of central tendency, **52**
Media, violence and aggression in, 697–698
Median, **52**
Medroxyprogesterone acetate (MPA), 298
Medulla, **78**
Melancholic people, 523
Memory, 232–271

  academic, 266–268
  biology of, 260–266
  as constructive process, 251–256
  context and, 256
  defined, 234–235
  distributed, 262–265
  echoic (auditory), 238–239
  flashbulb, 256–257
  iconic (visual), 237–238
  information processing and, 234
  long-term, 242–250
  neural plasticity and, 261–262
  processes of, 234–235
  processing long-term, 263–265
  processing short-term, 265–266
  sensory, 235, 236–237
  short-term (working), 239–242
  state dependency and, 256
  three-system model of, 235–239
Menopause, **466**
Menstruation, 466
Mental abilities, Thurstone's list of, 497
Mental age, **488**
Mental set, **362**–363
Mental structure, Freud's view of, 531
Mere exposure effect, **690**
Message, and persuasion, 679–680
Meta-analysis, 429, 642
Metabolism, and obesity, 289–290
Method of loci, 245
Microvilli, 140
Milgram obedience to authority study, 48
Mind. *See* Behavioral vs. cognitive approaches
Minnesota Multiphasic Personality Inventory (MPPI), 550–552
Mixed mania, 585
MMPI. *See* Minnesota Multiphasic Personality Inventory
Mnemonic devices, **245**
Modality effect, 239
Mode, **52**
Modeling, **216**, 224–225, 637
  punishment and, 218
Molecular neurobiology, 72
Monkeys, stroke simulation in, 49
Monoamine oxidase (MAO), 651
  inhibitors (MAO inhibitors), 592
Monocular cues, **151**, 152–153
Monozygotic twins, **410**
Mood disorders, 582–584, **583**–595
Moon illusion, 159–160
Moral development
  in adolescence, 456–460
  Kohlberg's theory of, 457–460
Mores, 301
Morpheme, **374**
Morphine, 98
Mothers. *See* Attachment

Motion parallax, **153**
Motion sickness, 147
Motivated forgetting, 259
Motivation, 272–313
  and behavior, 274–297
  biological bases of, 282–292
  cognitive theories of, 278–282
  defined, 274
  drive-reduction theory, 276–277
  instinct theory, 275–276
  Maslow's hierarchy of needs, 277–278
  nature of, 273–274
  sensation-seeking, 292–297
  sexual, 297–308
Motor aphasia, 85
Motor conversion, 579
Motor cortex, **84**
  primary brain areas of, 83
Motor development, 421–422
Motor neurons, **64**
Movement, 84–85
MRI. *See* Magnetic resonance imaging
MS. *See* Multiple sclerosis
Multifactorial inheritance, **411**
Multiple intelligences, Gardner's theory of, 498–499
Multiple personality, 581–582
Multiple sclerosis (MS), 68
Muscular dystrophy, 414
Musical intelligence, 499
MYCIN, **372**
Myelin, 65
Myelinated and unmyelinated axons, 65
Myelinated neural fibers, 84
Myelin sheath, **68**
Müller-Lyer illusion, 158–159

Narcissistic personality disorder, 605
Narcolepsy, 184
Narcotics, 98–99
Narrative story memory system, **245**–246
Nasal continuous positive airway pressure (nCPAP), 184
National Adolescent Student Health Survey, cocaine use and, 103
National Institutes of Health (NIH), health psychology and, 17
Nativism, 375
Naturalistic observation, **42**–43
Natural selection, 10
Nature–nurture controversy, **403**–404, 501–509
Need for achievement (nAch), 278–279
Needs, hierarchy of, 277–278
Negative afterimages, 131
Negative correlation, 44–45
Negative-feedback mechanism, 94
Negative reinforcement, **210**
Neo-Freudians, **538**

Nerves, 65
Nervous system
 central, 62–73
 divisions of, 63
 and endocrine system, 94
 peripheral, 62
Networks of association, 247–249
Neural circuits, 119
Neural connections theory, and memory, 260–261
Neural development, 419
Neural plasticity, and memory, **261–262**
Neural processing, of vision, 124–126
Neural transmission, 65. *See also* Neurotransmitters
Neuroendocrine system, 81
Neuroleptics, 651
Neurons, **62–73**
 and aging, 476
 electrical activity, 65–68
Neurosis, **566**
 Freud and, 10–11
Neurotransmitters, 68–73, **69**
 and behavior, 73
 and eating disorders, 292
 hormones and, 94
 mood disorders and, 592
 and pain, 145
 and sleep, 175–176
 substances acting as, 71–73
Newborn language competency, 377
Nicotine, 101
Nightmare, **184–185**
NIH. *See* National Institutes of Health
Node, in association network, 248
Node of Ranvier, **68**
Noise, 116
Nomothetic approach, 524
Nonbarbiturates, 98
Nonexperimental research methods, 38–45
Nonspecific response, 329
Noradrenergic, 78
Norepinephrine (NE), 71, 72, 78
Norepinephrine theory, 593
Normal distributions, **52–53**, 493
Normative social influence, **685**
Norms, in testing, 492–493
Novelty, 1, 50
NREM (nonrapid eye movement) sleep, **169–171**
Nurture argument, 403

Obedience, **688–689**
Obedience to authority study, 48
Obese, **287**
Obesity, 287–292
 overcoming, 309–310
Object permanence, 387, **424**
Observation, and attitudes, 672

Observational learning, 224–225
Observational method, 37, **42–43**
Observer bias, **43**
Observer effect, **43**
Obsessive-compulsive disorder, **569–570**
Obsessive-compulsive personality disorder, 605
Occipital lobe, **86**
Oedipus complex, **536**
Older years, 474–481. *See also* Age; Aging
 cognitive development in, 477–479
 physical development in, 475–477
 psychosocial development in, 479–481
Olfaction, **139–140**, 141–142
Olfactory mucosa, 141
Oligodendrocytes, 68
One Flew Over the Cuckoo's Nest, 646
Operant conditioning, **199**, 207–219, 672–673
 and classical conditioning, 219–221
 punishment and, 217–219
 reinforcement and, 209–217
 in Skinner box, 208–209
Operant conditioning therapies, **635–638**
Operational definition, **54**
Opiates, **98–99**
Opium, 98
Opponent-process theory of color vision, **129–131**
Opponen-process theory of emotion, **326–328**
Optic disk, 123
Optic nerve, 123
Optimum level of arousal, **293–295**
Oral stage, **536**
Organizations, APA, 19
Organ of Corti, **136**
Organ reserve, , **475**
Orphange studies, 504
Ossicles, **134**
Otis-Lennon School Ability Test (OLSAT), 491
Otosclerosis, 139
Outgroup, **682**
Oval window, 136
Overcompensation, 539
Overlap, **152**
Overlearning, **250**, 267
Overtones, 133
Ovulation, 409

Pain, 144–145
 hypnosis and, 188
Pain adaptation, 117
Panic attacks, 574
Panic disorder, **567–568**
Paper-and-pencil questionnaires, **550**

Papillae, 140
Paranoid personality disorder, 605
Paranoid schizophrenia, **601**
Parasympathetic nervous system, 63, **74**, 75
Parent–child relationship, 406
Parenting, 471–472
 styles and social–emotional development, 436–437
Parents
 and gender roles, 446
 role in adolescence, 461–462
Parietal lobe, **85**
Parkinson's disease, 82
Partial reinforcement effect, **212**
Partial reinforcement schedule, **212–215**
Partial report procedure, 237
Pavlovian conditioning, 200–202
Peer group
 and gender roles, 446–447
 role in adolescence, **461–462**
Peer pressure, and sexual liberation, 463
Peg-word memory system, 246
Percentile, 53
Perception, **111–112**, 147–162
 Gestalt psychology and, 12–13
 and schizophrenia, 598
 social, 662–665
 spatial, 150–156
Perceptual constancy, **155**
Perceptual grouping, **148**, 149
Perceptual organization, 147–150
Perceptual set, **161–162**
Performance (verbal) scale, 490
Periaqueductal grey area, **145**
Peripheral nervous system (PNS), 62, 73–74
Permissive parents, 436
Personality, 522–559
Personality. *See also* Disease, stress and
 assessment of, 548–555
 behavioral theories of, 524, 543–544
 biological determinants of, 547–548
 defined, **523–524**
 Freudian theory of development, 528–538
 humanistic theories of, 540–543
 implicit theories of, 664–665
 psychoanalytic theories, 528–540
 social learning theories of, 524, 544–547
 trait theories of, 524–528
Personality disorders, 604–608
Personality psychology, **15**, 524
Personality types, prejudice and, 684
Personal unconscious, **538**
Person-centered therapy, **624–626**, 640
Person schemas, **663–664**
Persuasion, 678–681

PET scans. *See* Positron emission to-mography
Phallic stage, **536**
Pharmaco-convulsive therapy, 648
Phenomenological theories, 540
Phenothiazines, 603, 651
Phenotypes, **410**
Phenylketonuria (PKU), **414**
Pheromones, 142
Phlegmatic people, 523
Phobias, **568**–569
Phonemes, **374**
Phosphene, 126, 127
Photopigments, 123
Photoreceptor cells, 122–123
Phototherapy, 587
Physical attractiveness, **692**–693
Physical development
　in adolescence, 454–455
　in adulthood, 465–466
　infancy to adolescence, 418–422
　in older years, 475–477
Physical growth, 420–421
Physiological arousal, in emotions, 316
Physiological responses to stress, 329–332
Physiology, 8–9. *See also* Biological psy-chology
Pinna, 134
Pitch, **132**, 133
Pituitary gland, 81, **94**–95
PKU. *See* Phenylketonuria
Place theory of pitch discrimination, **137**
Pleasure center of brain, 80–81
Pleasure principle, **530**
Plutchik's emotion wheel, 316–327
PMS. *See* Premenstrual syndrome
PNS. *See* Peripheral nervous system
Poggendorff illusion, 160
Pons, **78**
Pontine reticular formation, 170
Ponzo illusion, 160
Positive reinforcement, **210**, 635–636
Positron emission tomography (PET), **93**
　scans, 61, 575, 604
Postconventional morality, 457–459
Posthypnotic suggestion, **189**
Postive correlation, 44
Post-reinforcement pause, 213
Posttraumatic stress disorder (PTSD), 570–**571**
Potentiality for Fascism Scale (F scale), 684
Practical intelligence, 496–498
Practical problem-solving ability, 486
Pre-conventional morality, **457**
Predictive validity, **494**
Prefrontal cortex, 573
　memory and, 265

Pregnancy, alcohol use during, 100. *See also* Prenatal development
Prejudice, **681**–684
Preliminary Scholastic Aptitude Test/Scholastic Aptitude Test (PSAT/SAT), 431
Premarital sex, 463–464
Premenstrual syndrome (PMS), 595
Premises, 366
　faulty, 367
Prenatal development, 417
Prenatal differentiation, abnormal, 441–443
Preoperational stage, 424–426
Preparedness, 204
Presbycusis, 138
Pressure, 143
Primacy effect, **663**
Primary appraisal, 332–333
Primary drives, 276
Primary gain, 580
Primary mental abilities, **496**
Primary process thinking, **530**
Primary reinforcers, **211**
Primates
　language competence of, 392–399
　language studies with, 383–385
Principles of Psychology, 10
Prisoner study, 48–49
Proactive interference, **258**
Probability, subjective, 368–371
Problem finding, **468**
Problem solving, 356–365
　characteristics of difficult problems, 361–365
　cognitive influence on, 362–365
　stages of, 356–359
　strategies for, 359–361
Procedural memories, **243**
Processing
　of long-term memories, 263–265
　of short-term memories, 265–266
Process theories of intelligence, 496–499
　Gardner's theory of multiple intelli-gences, 498–499
　Sternberg's information-processing ap-proach, 496–498
Prodromal stage, of schizophrenia, 599
Progestational compounds, 97
Programmed theory, **476**–477
Projection, **533**
Projection fibers, 694
Projective tests, **552**–555
Propanediols, 653
Prostaglandins, 144
Proximity, **148**
　and interpersonal attraction, 690–691
Proximodistal growth pattern, **421**
PSAT. *See* Preliminary Scholastic Apti-tude Test

Psilocybin (angel dust), 104, 105
Psychiatry, 16
Psychoactive drugs, 97, **649**–653
　major categories of, 650
Psychoanalysis, 10–11, **621**–624, 640
Psychoanalytic perspective
　and anxiety disorders, 571–572
　on mood disorders, 588
　on schizophrenia, 601
Psychoanalytic theory of personality, 524, 528–540
　Adlerian, 538–539
　Freudian, 528–538
　Horney and, 539–540
　Jungian, 538
Psycholinguistics, **373**
Psychological bases of aggression, 695–698
Psychological reactance, 680
Psychological research. *See* Research
Psychological responses to stress, 332–335
Psychological therapies, for behavioral disorders, 621–641
Psychology, **4**
　areas of specialization in, 14–20
　artificial intelligence (AI) and, 18
　biological, 15–16
　clinical, 16
　cognitive, 14
　connectionism and, 18
　counseling, 16
　defined, 4
　developmental, 14
　educational, 16–17
　engineering, 17
　experimental, 15
　forensic, 18
　goals of, 20–21
　health, 17–18
　history of, 8–14
　humanistic, 13–14
　industrial/organizational (I/O) psy-chology, 17
　methods of, 32–57
　nonhuman animal behavior and, 6–7
　personality, 15
　school, 17
　as science, 4–5
　social, 14
Psychophysics, **112**–118
Psychosexual development, **535**–536
Psychosis, **566**
Psychosocial development, 404
　in adolescence, 460–464
　in adulthood, 468–474
　attachment and, 431–436
　birth to adolescence, 431–439
　Erikson's theory of, 437–439
　in older years, 479–481

Psychosocial factors
  and homosexuality, 305
  and sexuality, 300
Psychosurgery, 645–647
Psychotherapists, seeking, 653–654
Psychotherapy, **621**
  evaluating, 641–645
  common features of approaches, 644–645
Punishment, **211**, 636–637
  and operant behavior, 217–219
Pupil, 121
Putamen, **82**

Qualititative development differences, 404
Questionnaires, 550–552
  survey method and, 39–42

Race, and intelligence, 509–511
Radioactive labeling, **91**–92
Rage center of brain, 80
Random sample, **40**–41
Rape, acquaintance, 698–700
Raphe system, **174**
Rational-emotive therapy (RET), **628**–631, 640
Rationalization, 332, **533**
Ratio schedule, 212
Reaction formation, **535**
Reality principle, **530**–531
Real self, 541
Reasoning, errors in, 366–368
Recall, **249**, 267
Receiver operating characteristic (ROC) curve, 118
Recessive gene, 410–**411**
Reciprocal determinism, **546**
Recitation, 267
Recognition, **249**
Recombinant DNA technology, **413**
Reference memory. *See* Long-term memory
Reflexes, in human infants, 421
Reflexive behaviors, 77
Regression, **535**
Regressive symptoms, and schizophrenia, 601
Rehearsal, and memory, 247
Reinforcement, 209–217
  of initial operant response, 215–217
Reinforcement schedules, 212–215
  applying, 215
Relative motion, **153**
Relative size, **153**
Relaxation training, 343
Relearning, **249**
Religion, and homosexuality, 304
REM (rapid eye movement) sleep, 169–171, 179–180

REM behavior disorder, 171
Repetition, 150
Replication research, 35–36
Representative heuristic, **368**–369
Representative sample, 40
Repression, 259, **532**–533
Research
  applied, 34–35
  basic, 34
  developmental, 407–408
  ethical guidelines for, 49–50
  experimental methods, 45–48
  methods of, 36–37
  nonexperimental methods, 38–45
  purpose of 34–36
  replication, 35–36
  statistical concepts for, 50–55
Research perspectives, 24–31
  cognitive psychology, 24
Residual schizophrenia, 599, **601**
Resistance, 330, **622**–623
Response, 340
Response criterion, 117–118
Resting potential, **66**, 67
Restitutional symptoms, and schizophrenia, 601
Restricted Environmental Stimulation Therapy (REST), 296
Restriction, 296
RET. *See* Rational-emotive therapy
Reticular activating system (RAS), **78**, **174**
Reticular formation **78**–79
Retina, 122–123
Retinal disparity, **151**
Retinal image, 121
Retrieval, **235**
  failure of, 259
Retrieval cues, 247
Retroactive interference, 258
Retrograde amnesia, **260**
RGB monitors, 128
Rods, **122**
Role playing, 626
Roles, confusion in, 438
Rooting reflex, 420, 421
Rorschach inkblot test, **553**–554
Round window, 136
Rubin vase, 148
Ruffini cylinders, 144

SAD. *See* Seasonal affective disorder
Safety needs, 277
Saltatory conduction, 68
Sample, **40**–41
  selection for experiments, 47
Sanguine people, 523
SAT. *See* Scholastic Aptitude Test
Scapegoating, and prejudice, 683
Schacter-Singer theory of emotion, 319

Schemas, **423**
  and memory, 252–253
Schizoid personality disorder, 605
Schizophrenia, 73, 595–604. *See also* Biological perspective, on behavioral disorders
  antipsychotic drugs and, 651
  subtypes of, 599–601
  theoretical perspectives on, 601–604
Schizotypal personality disorder, 605
Scholastic Aptitude Test (SAT), 494
School psychology, **17**
Schools, and gender roles, 447
Science, psychology as, 4–5
Scientific method, **8**
  and behavior, 33–36
SCN. *See* Suprachiasmatic nucleus
Seasonal affective disorder (SAD), **587**–588
Secondary appraisal, 333
Secondary drives, 276
Secondary gain, 580
Secondary sex characteristics, **454**
Secondary traits, **526**
Second-order conditioning, 206–207
Secular growth trends, **454**
Sedatives, **98**
Selective associations, 204
Selective attention, 149–150
Selective perception, **161**
Self, Rogers' concept of, 540–541, 543
Self-actualization, 13, 277
Self-actualization theory, 541–542
Self-efficacy, **546**
Self-perception theory, 672
Semantic coding, 241–242
Semantic memory, **244**
Semantics, 374
  common relations, 379
Semicircular canals, **146**
Senile dementia, 477–479
Sensation, **111**
  principles of, 111–118
Sensation-seeker, 295
Sensation-seeking motives, 292–297
Senses, major, 111
Sensorimotor stage, **424**, 425
Sensorineural hearing loss, **138**–139
Sensory codes, 244
Sensory conversion, 578–579
Sensory cortex, **84**
Sensory deprivation studies, **295**–297
Sensory memory, **235**, 236–237
Sensory neglect, 85–86
Sensory neurons, **64**
Sensory thresholds, 112–118
Separate attachments, **432**
Septal area, **80**–81
Serial position effect 258–259
Serotonin (SE), 71, 72, **145**

Serotonin reuptake inhibitors, 651–652
Set point, **287**
Severe mania, 585
Sex, acquaintance rape and, 698–700
Sex and Temperament in Three Primitive Societies, 444–445
Sex chromosome, 409
Sex differences, in brain, 86
Sex glands, 97
Sex-linked inheritance, **411**
Sexual development, and adolescence, 462–464
Sexual differentiation, 440–**441**
Sexuality, 297–308
    alcohol use and, 42
    biological bases of, 298–303
    and cultural mores, 301–303
    effect of AIDS on behavior, 307–308
    Freud and, 11, 534–536
    homosexuality, 303–307
    in various societies, 302–303
Sexual liberation, 463
Sexual orientation, **303**
S-factors, **496**
Shame and doubt, 438
Shape constancy, **156**
Shaping, **216**
Sharpening, in memory, 252
Short-term (working) memory (STM), **236**, 239–242,
    processing of, 265–266
Sickle-cell anemia, 414
SIDS. *See* Sudden infant death syndrome
Signal detection, 117–118
Signal detection theory, **116**–117
Similarity, **148**
Simultaneous conditioning, **204**
Single living, 468–469
Situation–specific habits, 527
16 Personality Factor Questionnaire (16 PF), 526
Size constancy, 155–156
Skewed distribution, **52**
Skin, 143. *See also* Touch
Skinner box, 208–209
Sleep, **169**–179
    brain mechanisms of, 174–176
    cycle of, 173–174
    disorders of, 183–186
    dreaming and, 170
    functions of, 176–179
    reticular formation and, 79
    stages of, 172–173
    thalamus and, 82
Sleep apnea, 183–184
Sleep deprivation, 176–177
Sleep spindles, 173
Sleeptalking, **185**–186

Sleep terrors, **185**
Sleepwalking, **185**
Smell. *See* Olfaction
SOAR, **372**–373
Social adjustment function, of attitudes, 674
Social and applied psychology, 660–703
Social-cognitive perspective, 544–546
Social competence, 486
Social-emotional development, parenting styles and, 436–437
Social expectations, and behavior, 675–676
Social identification function, of attitudes, 674
Social influence, on behavior, **685**–689
Social isolation, **480**–481
Social learning
    and aggression, 696
    and gender identity, 444–446
    and prejudice, 683
Social learning theories of personality, **224**, 524, 544–547
Socially unacceptable behavior, 565
Socially undesirable behavior, attribution theory and, 666–667
Social perception, **662**–665
Social phobia, **568**–569
Social psychology, **14**, 660–703
    attitudes, 671–681
    attribution theories, 665–671
    interpersonal behavior, 690–698
    prejudice and, 681–684
    social influences on behavior, 685–689
    social perception, 662–665
Social Readjustment Rating Scale (SRRS), 336, 337
Society, and sexual behavior, 300–303
Sociobiology, **693**
Solomon and Corbit's opponent-process theory of emotion, 326–328
Soma, 64
Somatic cells, 416
Somatic nervous system, 63, **74**
Somatization disorder, **577**–578
Somatoform disorders, **577**–580
Somatosensory cortex, **85**
    primary brain areas of, 83
Somniloquy, 185
Sound, 131–132
    properties of waves, 132–133
    stimulus of, 132
Sound waves, 134
Source traits, **526**
Spatial abilities, and gender, 429–430
Spatial intelligence, 499
Spatial perception, 150–156
Specific attachments, **432**
Specific phobias, **569**

Speech disturbances, schizophrenia and, 599
Spinal cord, 63, 76–77
Split-brain research, 87–89
Split-half reliability, **493**–494
Spontaneous recovery, **205**
Spontaneous remission, 642
Sprading activation, 248
S–R. *See* Stimulus-response approach
Stages of sleep, **172**–173
Stage theory, 405
Stagnation, generativity and, 439
Standard deviation, 52–53, 492
Standardization procedures, **492**
Stanford–Binet test, **489**, 494
Stanford University prisoner study, 48–49
Stapes (stirrup), 134
State-dependent memory, **256**
Statistical significance tests, **54**
Statistics, 50–55
    descriptive, 51–53, A-0–A-14
    inferential, 53–54, A-14–A-19
Stereotaxic apparatus, 90, 91
Stereotypes, **682**
    gende-role, 280
Steroids, anabolic, 299
Stimulants, **100**–103
Stimulus, conditioning and, 201–207.
    See also Cognitive learning; Conditioning
Stimulus contingency, 202–203
Stimulus generalization, 572–573
Stimulus intensity, and attention, 150
Stimulus-response (S–R) approach, 1
Stimulus salience, 202
Stimulus thresholds, 114
Stomach, and hunger, 283–284
Storage, **235**
Stress, 328–345. *See also* Emotions; Posttraumatic stress disorder
    adrenal system and, 96–97
    behavioral response to, 333–335
    and disease, 331–332, 338–345
    emotional response to, 333
    and immune system, 342
    life change units and measurement of, 336–338
    managing, 343–344
    nature of, 328–329
    obesity and, 290
    physiological responses to, 329–332
    psychological responses to, 332–335
Stressors, 328, 335–338
Striving for superiority, **539**
Stroke simulation, in monkeys, 49
Stroop effect, 115
Structuralism, **9**–10
Subjective feelings, 316

Sublimation, **534**
Substance P, 144, **145**
Substantia nigra, **82**
Subtractive color mixing, **128**
Subvocal speech, 350
Success
 fear of, 280–281
 and motivation 279–280
Sudden infant death syndrome (SIDS), 184
Suddenness, and stress, 335
Suicide, facts about, 586
Summer depression, 587
Superego, 182, **531–532**
Suppression, 533
Suprachiasmatic nucleus (SCN), **169**
Surface structure, 376
Surface traits, **526**
Survey, 36–37, 39–42
 alcohol and sexual behavior study, 42
 sample selection, 40–41
Syllogism, 364, **366**
 analysis of, 367
Sympathetic nervous system, 63, **74**, 75
Synapse, neurotransmitters and, **68**–69
Synaptic facilitation, **227**
Syntax, **374**
Systematic desensitization, **633**

Tachistiscope, 12
Tardive dyskinesia (TD), 651
Target organs, 94
Taste. *See* Gustation
Taste buds, 140
TAT. *See* Thematic Apperception Test
Tay-Sachs disease, 414
TDF (testis-determining factor), 440
Television
 and gender roles, 447–448
 violence in, 697–698
Temperature, 143–144
Temporal contiguity, 223
Terminal buttons, **65**
Testimony, and memory, 253–256
Testing, personality assessment and, 548–555
Testing hypotheses, **359**
Testosterone, 299
Test–retest reliability, **493**
Tests, of statistical significance, 54. *See also* Intelligence tests; tests by name
Texture gradient, **153**
Thalamus, **81**–82
THC. *See* Marijuana
Thematic Apperception Test (TAT), 279, **554**–555
Theories, 21
Therapists, seeking, 653–654
Therapy

biologically-based, 645–653
 comparative forms, 640
 psychological, 621–645
Thermoreceptors, 144
Thinking, 350–371
 components of, 350–353
 concept formation, 354–355
 and language, 385–387
 problem solving, 356–365
 reasoning and decision making, 365–371
Thought, language and, 386–387. *See also* Thinking
Threat, 333
Three-layer network, 248
Threshold, **112**–118
Thyroid gland, **95**–96
Thyroxine, 95
Timbre, **133**
Tinnitus, **139**
Token economies, 637–638
Tomkins' facial feedback theory, 323–326
Tongue. *See* Gustation
Touch, 142–145
Trace conditioning, **204**
Tracheostomy, 184
Training, 422
Traits
 associations among, 664
 central, 665
Trait theories of personality, 524–528
Tranquilizers, 98
 major, 651
 minor, 652–653
Transformational grammar, 375
Transorbital lobotomy, 645–646
Treatment, of behavior disorders, 620–657
Trial and error, **359**
Triarchic theory of intelligence, **498**
Trichromatic theory of color vision, **128**–129
Tricyclics, 73, 592, 651
Trophic hormones, 94
Trust vs. mistrust stage, 438
Tuneable blueprint, 377
Twins, 35
 affective disorders in, 591
 and anxiety disorders, 576–577
 communication by, 376
 identical and fraternal, 410
 intelligence and, 502–504
 and schizophrenia, 602, 613
2–DG, 92
Two-factor learning, **221**, 572
Two-factory theory of intelligence, 495–496
Tympanic canal, 136

Tympanic membrane, **134**
Type A and B behavior, 339–340

Unconditioned response (UCR), **201**–206, 220
Unconscious mind, 11. *See also* Psychoanalysis
 Freud and, 529–530
 Jung and, 538
Understanding function, of attitudes, 673
Undifferentiated schizophrenia, **601**
United States, aging population of, 474–475
Uterus, 408

Vagus nerve, 286
Validity, **494**
Variability, measures of, 52–53
Variable interval (VI) schedule, **214**–215
Variable ratio (VR) schedule, **213**–214
Variables, 44, 46
Variable schedule, 212
Ventromedial hypothalamus (VMH), **284**–285
Verbal ability, 486
Verbal codes, 244
Verbal scale, 490
Verbal skills, and gender, 429
Vestibular canal, 136
Vestibular sacs, **147**
Violence, media and, 697–698
Vision, 118–131
 artificial, 126–127
 color, 127–131
 neural processing of, 124–126
Visual centers, 119
Visual cliff, **154**–155
Visual coding, 241–242
Visual cortex, **86**
Visual illusions, 157–161
Visual memory, test of, 244
Vitreous humor, 122
Vocalizations, early, 377–380
Volley theory, **138**

WAIS. *See* Wechsler Adult Intelligence Scale
Waking. *See* Sleep
Washoe (chimpanzee), language studies with, 383–384
Weber's law, **114**–115
Wechsler Adult Intelligence Scale (WAIS), **489**–490, 495
Weight regulation, 286, 287. *See also* Hunger
 obesity and, 287–292
Wernicke's aphasia, 380
Wernicke's area, **380**–382
Wet Mind, 30
White light, 127–128

White matter, 84
Whole report procedure, 237
Within-group difference, **508**–509
Women. *See also* Females
    acquaintance rape and, 698–700
    television and, 448

Words, 378
Working backward, **361**
Work world, 472–473

Yerkes-Dodson law, **294**
Yerkes Primate Research Center, 384

Young-Helmholtz theory, **128**–129

Zoophobias, 573
Zulu culture, visual illusion and, 159
Zygote, **408**, 409
Zygote stage, **417**